FOURTH EDITION

Crisis Intervention Strategies

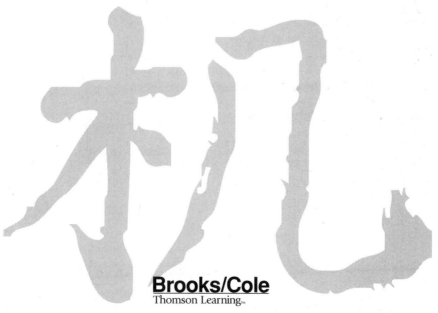

Richard K. James
University of Memphis

Burl E. Gilliland
Distinguished Professor Emeritus,
University of Memphis

Brooks/Cole
Thomson Learning

Australia • Canada • Mexico • Singapore • Spain • United Kingdom • United States

Counseling Editor: *Julie Martinez*
Assistant Editor: *Annie Berterretche*
Editorial Assistant: *Marin Plank*
Marketing Manager: *Caroline Concilla*
Signing Representative: *Kerry Dixon*
Project Editor: *Matt Stevens*
Print Buyer: *April Reynolds*
Permissions Editor: *Bob Kauser*

Production Service: *Scratchgravel Publishing Services*
Text Designer: *Lisa Thompson, Anne Draus*
Copy Editor: *Linda Purrington*
Cover Designer: *Annabelle Ison*
Cover Printer: *Maple-Vail*
Compositor: *Scratchgravel Publishing Services*
Printer: *Maple-Vail*

Printed in the United States of America
2 3 4 5 6 7   04 03 02 01

For permission to use material from this
text, contact us by
Web: http://www.thomsonrights.com
Fax: 1-800-730-2215
Phone: 1-800-730-2214

Library of Congress Cataloging-in-Publication Data
James, Richard K., [date]–
    Crisis intervention strategies / Richard K.
James, Burl E. Gilliland. — 4th ed.
        p.   cm.
    Burl E. Gilliland's name appears first on the
earlier editions.
    Includes bibliographical references and index.
    ISBN 0-534-36641-4 (alk. paper)
    1. Crisis intervention (Mental health
services.   I. Gilliland, Burl E.   II. Title.

RC480.6 .G55   2000
616.89'025—dc21   00-037813

Wadsworth/Thomson Learning
10 Davis Drive
Belmont, CA 94002-3098
USA

For more information about our products,
contact us:
Thomson Learning Academic Resource Center
1-800-423-0563
http://www.wadsworth.com

International Headquarters
Thomson Learning
International Division
290 Harbor Drive, 2nd Floor
Stamford, CT 06902-7477
USA

UK/Europe/Middle East/South Africa
Thomson Learning
Berkshire House
168-173 High Holborn
London WC1V 7AA
United Kingdom

Asia
Thomson Learning
60 Albert Street, #15-01
Albert Complex
Singapore 189969

Canada
Nelson Thomson Learning
1120 Birchmount Road
Toronto, Ontario M1K 5G4
Canada

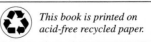
*This book is printed on
acid-free recycled paper.*

We dedicate the fourth edition of this book to the men and women of the Memphis Police Department's Crisis Intervention Team. They are common patrol officers with uncommon skills, who interact every day with the mentally ill on the streets of Memphis. They never cease to amaze us with their ability to deal effectively and safely with some very troubled people. They are the best in the world at what they do; the world is finding that out and is beating a path to their door. Thank you for helping teach the teachers.

We also dedicate this book to the counselors and other crisis workers who deal with the traumatic events that afflict schools and the children within them. They courageously walk into the maelstrom of school crises every day and somehow manage to come back out.

CONTENTS

PART ONE

Crisis Intervention Theory and Application   1

CHAPTER ONE

Approaching Crisis Intervention   3

CHAPTER FIVE

Crisis of Lethality   195

CHAPTER SIX

Sexual Assault   229

CHAPTER SEVEN

Partner Violence   282

PART THREE

Crisis in the Human Services Workplace   469

CHAPTER TEN

Violent Behavior in Institutions   471

PURPOSE OF THE BOOK

The primary purpose of this book is to present applied therapeutic counseling in general, and crisis intervention in particular, in a way that effectively describes actual strategies to alleviate the crisis. In our experience, most clients who enter counseling or psychotherapy do so because of some sort of crisis in their lives. Although "preventive" counseling is the ideal, personal crisis generally provides the impetus that impels real clients into contact with a helping person. We have endeavored to provide a perspective in this book that *puts you into the crisis situation as it is occurring,* enabling you to experience what crisis workers are experiencing as they operate.

RATIONALE

Crisis intervention epitomizes the use of the terms "applied" and "experiential" in the here and now in the helping professions. We are told that in the Chinese language there is no single character that is the equivalent of "crisis" in the English language.

The Primacy of Crisis Intervention

The Chinese characters emblazoned on the front of the book and the beginning of each chapter symbolize both "danger" and "opportunity!" That is the essence of *crisis*—the human dilemma that is common to all cultures. We believe that practically all counseling is initiated as crisis intervention. As much as we would prefer otherwise, people tend either to avoid presenting their problems to a helper until those problems have grown to crisis proportions, or become ensconced in situational dilemmas that wind up in unforeseen crises. Our ideal objective, as human service workers, is to establish primary prevention programs so effective that crisis intervention will seldom be needed. However, it appears that people are not as quick to adopt preventive measures for their psychological health as for their physical health. Therefore, we believe that crisis intervention strategies can be applied in practically all counseling and psychotherapy, not just in crisis situations. From that perspective, we consider this book applicable to the total scope of the helping relationship field.

The Case for an Applied Viewpoint

The materials and techniques we promote in this book come from two sources: First, our own experiences in teaching and counseling in crisis situations; second, interviews with people who are currently in the trenches, successfully performing counseling and crisis intervention. We have obtained input from many different people in the helping professions whose daily and nightly work is dealing directly with human dilemmas, and related their views to the best of current theory and practice from the professional literature. Through many hours of dialogue, these experts have provided the most contemporary strategies and techniques in use in their particular fields. They have also reviewed our rendition of each crisis category and have provided much helpful commentary and critiques on the ecology and etiology, tactics and procedures, terminology, and developmental stages of the specific crises with which they work. Therefore, what you read in the case-handling strategies comes directly from the horse's mouth.

Where controversies exist in regard to treatment modalities, we have attempted to present as many perspectives as possible. If you encounter problems with the tactics and techniques presented, the fault is undoubtedly in our rendition and not in the modalities themselves, which work well for the people who described them to us.

We have endeavored to incorporate, synthesize, and integrate the case-handling strategies of these resource people in a comprehensive, fluid, and dynamic way that will provide crisis workers with a basic set of tenets about effective crisis intervention. This book is not about long-term therapy or theory. Neither is it a volume dealing with crisis from only one theoretical perspective, such as a psychoanalytic approach or a behavioral system. The book incorporates a wide diversity of therapeutic modalities and reflects our eclectic approach to crisis intervention.

Specific crises demand specific interventions that span the whole continuum of therapeutic strategies. The strategies in this book shouldn't be construed as the only ones available for a particular crisis. They are presented as "best bets" based on what current research and practice indicate to be appropriate and applicable. Yet these strategies may not be appropriate for all practitioners with all clients in all situations. Good crisis intervention, as well as good therapy of any other kind, is a serious professional activity that calls for creativity and the ability to adapt to changing conditions of the therapeutic moment. To that extent, crisis intervention at times is more art than science and is not always prescriptive. Therefore, we would caution you that there are no clear-cut prescriptions or simple cause-and-effect answers in this book.

The Case for an Experiential Viewpoint

The fact that no single theory or strategy applies to every crisis situation is particularly problematic for those who seek simple, concrete answers to resolve the client problems they will face. If you are just beginning your career in the human services, we hope that while reading and trying out activities in this book you will suspend your judgment for a while and be open to the experience as you read about crisis workers attempting to implement theory into practice.

Moral Dilemmas.   Another issue that permeates many topics covered in this book is the emotions they generate and the beliefs that pervade them about what is morally "right" and what is morally "wrong." People have been willing to go to prison or die because of the strong beliefs they held about many of these topics. Where such moral issues and beliefs abound, we have tried to deal with them in as even-handed a manner as possible. This book is not about the morality of the issues covered, but rather about what seems to work best for the people who are experiencing the dilemma. We ask you to read it with that view in mind, and for at least a while, suspend your moral view of the situation or problem as you read about crisis workers attempting to grapple with these heart- and gut-wrenching problems.

Finally, because of a virtually unlimited supply of different crises situations, we have had to make tough decisions about what kinds of problems to illustrate in the most *generic and comprehensive way possible* so as to reach the broadest possible audience. We understand and empathize very deeply with readers who may have suffered terrible crises that are not mentioned in this book and are puzzled, chagrined, and angry that we have not given space and time to the particular crisis they have suffered through. We apologize; the space available means that we simply cannot include all situations. However, what we would like you to do is to imagine how the strategies and techniques you are reading about might apply to the particular crisis you have experienced.

Basic Relationship Skills.   The listening and responding skills described in Chapter 2 are critical to everything else the worker does in crisis intervention. Yet on cursory inspection, these techniques and concepts may seem at best simplistic and at worst inane. They do not appear to fix anything, because they are not "fixing" skills. What they do is give the crisis worker a firm basis of operation on which to explore clearly the dilemma the client is facing. Basic listening and responding skills are the prerequisites for all other therapeutic modalities. Our experience has shown us over and over that students and trainees who scoff at and dismiss these basic relationship skills are the ones who invariably have the most trouble meeting the experiential requirements of our courses and workshop training sessions. We feel very strongly about this particular point and thus ask you to read Chapter 2 with an open mind.

Role Play.   If this volume is used as a structured learning experience, the case studies and the exercises at the end of each chapter are a valuable resource for experiential learning. It is essential that you observe effective crisis intervention models at work and then follow up by actually practicing and enacting the procedures you have observed. Intensive and extensive role play is an excellent skill builder. A critical component of training is not just talking about problems but practicing the skills of handling them as well. Talking about a problem is fine, but attempting to handle a live situation gets the trainee involved in the actual business of calming, defusing, managing, controlling, and motivating clients. Role play is one of the best ways of practicing what is preached, and it prepares human services workers for developing creative ways to deal with the variety of contingencies they may face. Role play gives human services workers the chance to find out what works and doesn't work for them in the safety of a training situation and affords their fellow students and trainees an opportunity to give them valuable feedback.

A major problem in role playing is the perception of standing up in a class or workshop and risking making a complete fool of oneself. We want to assure you that in our classes and training sessions we do not expect perfection. If our students and trainees were perfect at crisis intervention, they wouldn't be taking instruction from us in the first place! So put your inhibitions on the shelf for a while and become engaged in the role plays as if the situations were real, live, and happening right now. Furthermore, be willing and able to accept critical comments from your peers, supervisors, or instructors. Your ego may be bruised a bit in the process, but that's far better than waiting until you are confronted with an out-of-control client before you think about what you are going to do. Over and over, our students report that this component of instruction was the most profitable to them and was also the most fun!

Give the exercises in each chapter your best effort, process them with fellow students or trainees, and see what fits best with your own feelings, thoughts, and behaviors. Many times our students and trainees attempt to imitate us. Although it is gratifying to see students or trainees attempting to be "Burl" or "Dick," this is generally an exercise in futility for them. What they need to do is view us critically as we model the procedures and then incorporate their own style and personhood into the procedures. We urge you to do the same.

ORGANIZATION OF THE BOOK
Part One
Crisis Intervention Theory and Application

Part One of the book introduces the basic concepts of crisis intervention. It comprises Chapters 1, 2, and 3.

Chapter 1, Approaching Crisis Intervention. Chapter 1 contains the basic rationale and the theoretical and conceptual information needed for understanding applied crisis intervention.

Chapter 2, Basic Crisis Intervention Skills. Chapter 2 is a conceptual as well as a skill-building model of crisis intervention that applies to all crisis categories. It contains background information and describes relationship skills, strategies, and practical guidelines for initial intervention in all crises. The triage model is introduced for rapidly assessing the severity of the crisis in a multidimensional way.

Chapter 3, Crisis Case Handling. Chapter 3 emphasizes how case handling in crisis intervention is different from long-term therapy. Specific strategies to use with phone, walk-in, and long-term clients are provided along with guidelines for counseling difficult clients.

Part Two
Handling Specific Crises:
Going into the Trenches

Part Two (Chapters 4 through 9) addresses a variety of important types of crises. For each chapter in Part Two, the background and dynamics of the particular crisis type are detailed to provide a basic grasp of the driving forces behind the dilemma. Although some theory is present to highlight the therapeutic modalities used, comprehensive theoretical systems are beyond the scope of this book. For sources of that information, turn to the Reference section at the end of each chapter.

In Part Two we provide scripts from real interventions, highlighted by explanations why the crisis workers did what they did. Throughout this section the emphasis is on live tryout, experiencing, and processing of the cases and issues.

Chapter 4, Posttraumatic Stress Disorder. Posttraumatic stress disorder (PTSD) is the topic of the linchpin chapter in this section. Many of the following chapters discuss problems that may be the precursors of PTSD, or alternately, represent the manifestation of it.

Chapter 5, Crisis of Lethality. Chapter 5 focuses on strategies that crisis workers need in working with people who are manifesting lethal behavior. Suicidal and homicidal ideation flows through many other problems that assail people the human service worker is likely to confront and is a consideration for all providers of crisis intervention services.

Chapter 6, Sexual Assault. Chapter 6 addresses another societal crisis that practical every human services worker will eventually encounter-clients who have either experienced or been affected by sexual assault. Sexually assaulted clientele are a special population because of the negative moral and social connotations associated with the dehumanizing acts perpetrated on them. In addition to examining the immediate aftermath of sexual assault on both children and adults, we also consider adult survivors of sexual/physical abuse they experienced in childhood.

Chapter 7, Partner Violence. Chapter 7 deals with a crisis that many people in a domestic relationship face: being treated violently by their partners. This chapter provides strategies to help people who are suffering abuse in *any kind of domestic relationship*. The chapter also deals with emerging treatment techniques for the batterers themselves.

Chapter 8, Chemical Dependency: The Crisis of Addiction. Chapter 8 deals with one of the most pressing issues of our day, addiction to substances. Because chemical addiction is such a pervasive scourge on our society, no human service worker in the public arena can escape dealing with its effects. Crises of codependency and the long-term effects of substance abuse that create crises in the lives of adult children of addicts are also examined in this chapter.

Chapter 9, Personal Loss: Bereavement and Grief. Chapter 9 presents a type of crisis that every person will sooner or later face: personal loss. Even though the phenomenon of loss has been with us as long as the human species has existed, many people in our contemporary culture are poorly prepared and ill equipped to deal with it. This chapter provides models and strategies for coping with unresolved grief. It uses the ultimate loss—death—to examine a variety of problems associated with termination of relationships, both for the client and the crisis worker.

Part Three
Crisis in the Human Services Workplace

Part Three (Chapters 10 through 13) concentrates on the problems of crisis workers and their employing institutions.

Chapter 10, Violent Behavior in Institutions. Chapter 10 tackles the little publicized, and badly neglected, type of crisis that workers in many institutions face daily: Violent behavior within the walls of the institution. Regardless of the organizational settings where they are employed, workers will find in this chapter useful concepts and practical strategies that they and the institution can put to immediate use with agitated and potentially assaultive clients.

Chapter 11, Crises in Schools. Schools have become a focal point for the violence perpetrated by gangs and disenfranchised and socially isolated children and adolescents.

This chapter will examine systemic efforts to make schools safer from organized gang intrusion. It will also examine what crisis workers need to do in profiling, screening, and working with the potentially violent, individual student who is estranged from the social mainstream of the school. It will also deal with what the crisis worker needs to know in dealing with a problem that has become endemic in youth—suicide. Finally, some of the legal and ethical ramifications of dealing with minors who are contemplating or have engaged in acts of violence will be considered.

Chapter 12, Hostage Crises. Chapter 12 presents another hot topic in our contemporary world. The taking of hostages has become well publicized through terrorism and other acts violence. However, many hostage takings occur within the confines of human service work settings. This chapter provides basic negotiation strategies and survival techniques that may enable a human service worker to contain and survive a hostage situation.

Chapter 13, Human Services Workers in Crisis: Burnout. Chapter 13 is about us: All human service workers who are in the helping professions. No worker is immune to stress, burnout, and the crises that go with human services work. This chapter should prove invaluable for any worker anywhere whose work environment is frenetic and filled with crisis intervention or whose personality tends to generate compulsive behavior, perfectionism, or other stressors that may lead to burnout.

Part Four
New Directions

Part Four focuses on recent developments and the future of the field of crisis intervention.

Chapter 14, Off the Couch and into the Streets. Chapter 14 traces the evolution of crisis intervention into what is rapidly becoming a clinical specialty. It presents the reader with examples of innovative models of proactive and preventive crisis intervention strategies and tactics that encompass both small and large ecological systems.

In summary, we have not been as concerned with intellectualizing, philosophizing, or using theoretical interpretations as with simply focusing on practical matters of how to respond in crisis situations.

ACKNOWLEDGMENTS

In writing a book that covers so many diverse areas of the human condition, it would be extremely presumptuous of us to rely solely on our own expertise and theories of truth, beauty, and goodness to propose crisis intervention techniques as the one true path to dealing with crises. We are not so vain or foolish as to believe we have all the answers to all the problems one may encounter. We decided that the only realistic way to present the most current, reliable, and practical techniques to crisis intervention would be to go straight to the people who do this work day in and day out. They are not "big names," but rather people who go methodically about the business of crisis intervention daily in their respective venues. The number of these workers we have interviewed and talked to through four editions of this book can be counted in the hundreds. They work in such diverse occupational roles as ministers, police officers, psychologists, social workers, psychiatrists, nurses, school counselors, and professional counselors. They work in every kind of agency and institution that deals with people and their dilemmas. They range geographically from across the United States to across the world. They are an encyclopedia of practical knowledge and we are deeply in their debt for the help, advice, time, interviews, and critique they have given us. This book would not be possible without their assistance and we thank them one and all.

We would also like to thank the students in our crisis intervention courses at the University of Memphis, who serve as willing guinea pigs when their sometimes wild-eyed and addle-brained professors come charging into class with a new idea or technique to test out on them. We appreciate you deeply and have stood in awe and admiration in regard to how many of you have gone on to excel in this field.

Finally, we extend our grateful appreciation to the following busy professionals, who were generous enough to serve as reviewers for this edition and help keep us anchored to at least a modicum of reality. They are Alan Cavaiola, Monmouth University; Cary E. Lantz, Liberty University; Karen Neuman, Madonna University; and Susan Witte, Columbia University.

Richard K. James
Burl E. Gilliland

Crisis Intervention Theory and Application

Part One introduces you to the fundamental concepts, theories, strategies, and skills needed to understand and conduct effective crisis intervention. Chapter 1 presents the conceptual and multicultural dimensions of crisis work. Chapter 2 serves as a key to the application of relationship skills, assessment, and counseling strategies to the whole scope of crisis intervention. Chapter 3 explains the major components of effective case management in crisis intervention. Crisis workers will find that the principles, skills, and strategies represented here also apply broadly to *all* human problems, crisis or otherwise.

Crisis Intervention Theory and Application

Part One introduces you to the fundamental concepts, theories, strategies, and skills needed to understand and conduct effective crisis intervention. Chapter 1 presents the conceptual and multicultural dimensions of crisis work. Chapter 2 serves as a key to the application of relationship skills, assessment, and counseling strategies to the whole scope of crisis intervention. Chapter 3 explains the major components of effective case management in crisis intervention. Crisis workers will find that the principles, skills, and strategies represented here also apply broadly to *all* human problems, crisis or otherwise.

CHAPTER ONE

Approaching Crisis Intervention

DEFINITIONS OF CRISIS

There are many definitions of *crisis.* Six are presented here for your thought and study. We believe they collectively represent and define *crisis,* as well as prepare you to consider the theoretical constructs in this chapter. These definitions also set the stage for the remainder of the book.

1. People are in a state of crisis when they face an obstacle to important life goals— an obstacle that is, for a time, insurmountable by the use of customary methods of problem solving. A period of disorganization ensues, a period of upset, during which many abortive attempts at solution are made (Caplan, 1961, p. 18).
2. Crisis results from impediments to life goals that people believe they cannot overcome through customary choices and behaviors (Caplan, 1964, p. 40).
3. Crises are crises because the individual knows no response to deal with a situation (Carkhuff & Berenson, 1977, p. 165).
4. Crises are personal difficulties or situations that immobilize people and prevent them from consciously controlling their lives (Belkin, 1984, p. 424).
5. Crisis is a state of disorganization in which people face frustration of important life goals or profound disruption of their life cycles and methods of coping with stressors. The term *crisis* usually refers to a person's feelings of fear, shock, and distress *about* the disruption, not to the disruption itself (Brammer, 1985, p. 94).
6. Crisis develops in four distinct stages: (a) a critical situation occurs in which a determination is made as to whether a person's normal coping mechanisms will suffice; (b) increased tension and disorganization surrounding the event escalate beyond the person's coping ability; (c) a demand for additional resources (such as counseling) to resolve the event is needed; (d) referral may be required to resolve major personality disorganization (Marino, 1995).

To summarize these definitions, *crisis is a perception or experiencing of an event or situation as an intolerable difficulty that exceeds the person's current resources and coping mechanisms.* Unless the person obtains relief, the crisis has the potential to cause severe affective, behavioral, and cognitive malfunctioning.

CHARACTERISTICS OF CRISIS

The following discussion of characteristics of crisis represents an expanded definition of what *crisis* means.

Presence of Both Danger and Opportunity

Crisis is a *danger* because it can overwhelm the individual to the extent that serious pathology, including homicide and suicide, may result. Crisis is also an *opportunity* because the pain it induces impels the person to seek help (Aguilera & Messick, 1982, p. 1). If the individual takes advantage of the opportunity, the intervention can help plant the seeds of self-growth and self-realization (Brammer, 1985, p. 95).

People can react in any one of three ways to crisis. Under ideal circumstances, many individuals can cope effectively with crisis by themselves and develop strength from the experience. They change and grow in a positive manner and come out of the crisis both stronger and more compassionate. Others appear to survive the crisis but effectively block the hurtful affect from awareness, only to have it haunt them in innumerable ways throughout the rest of their lives. Yet others break down psychologically at the onset of the crisis and clearly demonstrate that they are incapable of going any further with their lives unless given immediate and intensive assistance.

Complicated Symptomology

Crisis is *not* simple; it is complex and difficult to understand, and it defies cause-and-effect description (Brammer, 1985, p. 91; Kliman, 1978, p. xxi). The symptoms that overlie precipitating crisis events become tangled webs that crisscross all environments of an individual. When an event reaches a flashpoint, there may be so many compounding problems that the worker must intervene directly in a variety of areas. Furthermore, the environment of people in crisis strongly affects the ease or difficulty with which the crisis can be handled. Families, individuals, partners, institutions, and employees may all directly affect problem resolution and a return to stability. When large numbers of people are affected at the same time by a crisis, the entire ecological system of a neighborhood, community, geographical region, or country may need intervention.

Seeds of Growth and Change

In the disequilibrium that accompanies crisis, anxiety is always present, and its discomfort provides an impetus for change (Janosik, 1984, p. 39). Often anxiety must reach the boiling point before the person is ready to admit the problem is out of control. One need look no further than the substance abuser for affirmation of this point. By waiting too long, for example, the substance abuser may become so entrenched that one may need a therapeutic jackhammer to break the addiction down into manageable pieces. Even here, however, a threshold point for change may be reached, albeit in last-ditch desperation, where the abuser finally surrenders to the fact that something must be done.

No Panaceas or Quick Fixes

People in crisis are generally amenable to help through a variety of forms of intervention, some of which are described as *brief therapy* (Cormier & Hackney, 1987, p. 240). For problems of long duration, however, quick fixes are rarely available. Many problems of clients in severe crisis stem from the fact that the clients sought quick fixes in the first place, usually through a pill. Such a "fix" may dampen the dreadful responses but does not change the instigating stimulus, so the crisis deepens.

The Necessity of Choice

Life is a process of interrelated crises and challenges that we confront or not, deciding to live or not (Carkhuff & Berenson, 1977, p. 173). In the realm of crisis, *not to choose is a choice,* and this choice usually turns out to be negative and destructive. *Choosing to do something* at least contains the seeds of growth and allows a person the chance to set goals and formulate a plan to begin to overcome the dilemma.

Universality and Idiosyncrasy

Disequilibrium or disorganization accompanies every crisis, whether universal or idiosyncratic (Janosik, 1984, p. 13). Crisis is universal because no one is immune to breakdown, given the right constellation of circumstances. It is idiosyncratic because what one person may successfully overcome, another may not, even though the circumstances are virtually the same. It is foolhardy to maintain a belief that one is immune to psychic assaults, that one can handle any crisis in a stable, poised, and in-command fashion. Thousands of "tough" Vietnam veterans suffering from posttraumatic stress disorder (PTSD) who have turnstiled through VA hospitals and veterans' centers are convincing proof that when a crisis boils over, disorganization, disequilibrium, disorientation, and fragmentation of an individual's coping mechanisms can occur no matter how conditioned against psychological trauma the person may be.

APPLIED CRISIS DOMAINS

Each person and each crisis situation is different. Thus crisis workers must view each person and the events precipitating the crisis as unique. Brammer (1985, pp. 94–95) characterizes applied crisis theory as encompassing three domains: (1) normal *developmental* crises, (2) *situational* crises, and (3) *existential* crises. Given the *ecosystem theory* perspective, we have added a fourth domain, (4) *environmental crises.*

Developmental Crises

Developmental crises are events in the normal flow of human growth and evolvement whereby a dramatic change or shift occurs that produces abnormal responses. For example, developmental crises may occur in response to the birth of a child, graduation from college, midlife career change, or retirement. Developmental crises are considered normal; however, all persons and all developmental crises are unique and must be assessed and handled in unique ways.

Situational Crises

A situational crisis emerges with the occurrence of uncommon and extraordinary events that an individual has no way of forecasting or controlling. Situational crises may follow such events as automobile accidents, kidnappings, rapes, corporate buyouts and loss of jobs, and sudden illness and death. The key to differentiating a situational crisis from other crises is that a situational crisis is random, sudden, shocking, intense, and often catastrophic.

Existential Crises

An "existential crisis" includes the inner conflicts and anxieties that accompany important human issues of purpose, responsibility, independence, freedom, and commitment. An existential crisis might accompany the realization, at age 40, that one will never make a significant and distinct impact on a particular profession or organization; remorse, at age 50, that one chose never to marry or leave one's parents' home, never really made a separate life, and now has lost forever the possibility of being a fully happy and worthwhile person; or a pervasive and persistent feeling, at age 60, that one's life is meaningless—that there is a void that can never be fulfilled in a meaningful way.

Environmental Crises

"Environmental crises" typically occur when some *natural or human caused* disaster overtakes a person or a (large or small) group of people who find themselves, through no fault or action of their own, inundated in the aftermath of an event that may adversely affect virtually every member of the environment in which they live. Such crises may occur in the form of natural phenomena such as hurricanes, floods, tidal waves, earthquakes, volcanic eruptions, tornadoes, blizzards, mud slides, drought or famine, and forest fires. Other instances of environmental crises may be *biologically derived,* such as during a disease epidemic or a huge oil spill; *politically based,* as in war or a refugee crisis associated with war or ethnic cleansing (removal of or destruction of virtually an entire ethnic population of a region); or *severe economic depression,* as opposed to psychological depression.

TRANSCRISIS STATES

Crises are time limited, usually persisting a maximum of six to eight weeks, at the end of which the subjective discomfort diminishes (Janosik, 1984, p. 9). However, what occurs during the immediate aftermath of the crisis event determines whether or not the crisis will become a disease reservoir that will be transformed into a chronic and long-term state. Although the original crisis event may be submerged below awareness and the individual may believe the problem has been resolved, appearance of new stressors may bring the individual to the crisis state again. This emotional roller-coaster may occur frequently and for extended periods of time, ranging from months to years. An adult who has unresolved anger toward a dead parent and transfers that anger to other authority figures, such as supervisors or employers, is in a *transcrisis state.* The adult may have apparently attained functional and normal mental health. However, this appearance is gained at the cost of warding off and repressing the "unfinished business" of making peace with the lost parent. Later, during the stress related to getting along with another authority figure, the person blames that authority figure and has no conscious awareness that the unfinished repressed material (submerged as a transcrisis state) is at the root of the problem. Although the person with the transcrisis state may come to identify the problem as poor relationship skills and enter counseling to improve those skills, this action is also a symptom of the psychological roller-coaster ride that started with the unfinished business. The relationship skills may be temporarily improved, but the source of the transcrisis state may not have been recognized or expunged. It has merely subsided and a temporary state of equilibrium has been achieved, but the original trauma will usually reemerge and instigate a new crisis the moment new stressors are introduced. Dynamically, this pattern is defensive repression. Therapeutically, this transcrisis state calls for crisis intervention techniques.

Transcrisis Differentiated from Posttraumatic Stress Disorder.   Those familiar with posttraumatic stress disorder (PTSD), may ask, "So how is a transcrisis state different from PTSD?" First, PTSD is an identifiable anxiety disorder (American Psychiatric Association, 1994) caused by an extremely traumatic event, and very specific criteria must be present for a diagnosis of PTSD to be made. Although a person who is suffering from PTSD may be in a transcrisis state, not all people who are in a transcrisis state suffer from PTSD. Indeed, it would probably be more appropriate to look at all the different kinds of anxiety and personality disorders found in the fourth edition of the *Diagnostic and Statistical Manual* (DSM-IV) (American Psychiatric Association, 1994) as representative of transcrisis states because of the chronic kinds of thinking, feeling, and acting that keep these individuals constantly in psychological hot, if not boiling, water.

But it is not just anxiety and personality disordered persons who may be in a transcrisis state. A broad range of people, from so-called normal individuals who are constantly fired from jobs because of their uncontrollable tempers, to psychotics who quit taking their medicine because it has unpleasant side effects, are also representative of individuals in transcrisis states. Armsworth and Holaday (1993), in their review of affective, behavioral, cognitive, and physiological-somatic effects of trauma, identified a number of factors that, although not found in PTSD descriptors, would probably be inherent in many transcrisis states. The key differentiating element of a transcrisis state is that whether it is due to trauma, personality traits, substance abuse, psychosis, or chronic environmental stressors, the state is residual and recurrent and always present to some degree. Although people in a transcrisis state are generally capable of functioning at some minimal level, they are always at risk, and any single, small, added stressor may tip the balance and send them into crisis. Therefore, when we assess individuals in crisis, our emphasis is not only on the current clinical/diagnostic state of the individual but also, and as importantly, on the repetitious cycle of problems and the historical precursors that may cause the crisis to arise. A medical analogy would be the person suffering from a chronic sinus condition who continuously takes nasal decongestant and so can function, albeit at less than optimum level. However, if the person is exposed to a virus, the sinus condition may progress into an infection and eventually pneumonia.

Being aware that someone is operating in a transcrisis state also gives us important information regarding the kind and degree of therapeutic intervention to provide, in both the short and the long term. We probably would deal far differently with the salesperson who just turned 45, lost her job with a company she had been with for 20 years, has been unemployed for six months, and is now clinically depressed and suicidal than we would with the salesperson who just turned 45, lost her job for the 20th time, has been unemployed for six months, and is now clinically depressed and suicidal. Although immediate intervention in regard to the suicidal ideation of both women might be very similar, our view as to what caused the depression, how we would treat it, and what transcrisis issues we might expect would be very different.

Transcrisis Points.   A frequent part of *transcrisis states* are transcrisis *points* occurring within the therapeutic intervention. These points are generally marked by the client coming to grips with new developmental stages or other dimensions of the problem.

Transcrisis points do not occur in regular, predictable, linear progression. For example, an abused spouse may go through transcrisis point after transcrisis point talking to a crisis worker over the telephone before making a decision to leave the battering relationship, often calling crisis workers a dozen times in the course of a few days. The abused spouse may then make a decision to leave the battering relationship and go to a spouse abuse shelter only to find that the necessity of making a geographic move or finding a job may instigate a crisis almost as potent as the battering. Human services workers who practice long-term therapy are often shocked, confused, and overwhelmed by the sudden disequilibrium their clients experience. Handling these transcrisis points can be the equivalent of standing in the middle of a Los Angeles freeway and attempting to stop traffic. Behaviorally, such clients may vacillate from a placid to an agitated state so fast that the worker puts out one brush fire only to be confronted by yet another. It is at these transcrisis points that standard therapeutic strategies and techniques are suspended and the therapist must operate in a crisis intervention mode.

Transcrisis points can be seen as benchmarks that are crucial to progressive stages of positive therapeutic growth. These points are characterized by approach-avoidance behavior in seeking help, taking risks, and initiating action steps toward forward movement. Encountering these transcrisis points, a person will experience the same kind of disorganization, disequilibrium, and fragmentation that surrounded the original crisis event.

Leaping one hurdle does not necessarily mean that the entire crisis is successfully overcome. Survivors of a catastrophe may expunge the event from memory and then be faced with repairing gaping wounds in personal relationships that have been torn apart by their long-term pathological behavior. People who have spinal cord injuries may be successfully rehabilitated physically but may retreat into substance addiction or become depressed and/or suicidal as they attempt to begin a new lifestyle from a wheelchair.

Therefore, it is not only the initial crisis with which the worker must contend but also each transcrisis point, as it occurs, if clients are not to slip back into the pathology that assailed them in the first place. Transcrisis points should not be confused with the jumps and starts that go with the working through of typical adjustment problems. Although these points may be forecast with some degree of reliability by workers who are expert in the particular field, their onset is sudden, dramatic, and extremely potent. In that regard, these psychological aftershocks can be just as damaging as the initial tremor and may require extraordinary effort on the part of the human services worker to help the client regain control. This book is also concerned with these transcrisis states and points; the cases portrayed represent both components.

THEORIES OF CRISIS AND CRISIS INTERVENTION

No single theory or school of thought encompasses every view of human crisis or all the models or systems of crisis intervention. We present here a brief overview of theories relevant both to crisis (as a phenomenon) and to crisis intervention (as an inten-

tional helping response). Janosik (1984) conceptualizes crisis theory on three different levels: basic crisis theory, expanded crisis theory, and applied crisis theory. (Applied crisis theory addresses what Brammer [1985] and we call "crisis domains." A brief overview of four domains, rather than "one applied theory" is provided.) The newly emerging ecosystem theory is also briefly explored.

Basic Crisis Intervention

The research, writings, and teachings of Lindemann (1944, 1956) gave professionals and paraprofessionals a new understanding of crisis. Lindemann helped caregivers promote crisis intervention for many sufferers of loss who had no specific pathological diagnosis but who were exhibiting symptoms that appeared pathological. Lindemann's basic crisis theory and work made a substantive contribution to the understanding of behavior in clients whose grief crises were precipitated by loss. He helped professionals and paraprofessionals recognize that behavioral responses to crises associated with grief are normal, temporary, and amenable to alleviation through short-term intervention techniques. These "normal" grief behaviors include (1) preoccupation with the lost one, (2) identification with the lost one, (3) expressions of guilt and hostility, (4) some disorganization in daily routine, and (5) some evidence of somatic complaints (Janosik, 1984, p. 11). Lindemann negated the prevailing perception that clients manifesting crisis responses should necessarily be treated as abnormal or pathological.

Whereas Lindemann focused mainly on immediate resolution of grief after loss, Caplan (1964) expanded Lindemann's constructs to the total field of traumatic events. Caplan viewed crisis as a state resulting from impediments to life goals that cannot be overcome through customary behaviors. These impediments can arise from both developmental and situational events. Both Lindemann and Caplan dealt with crisis intervention following psychological trauma using an equilibrium/disequilibrium paradigm. The stages in Lindemann's paradigm are (1) disturbed equilibrium, (2) brief therapy or grief work, (3) client's working through the problem or grief, and (4) restoration of equilibrium (Janosik, 1984, pp. 10–12). Caplan linked Lindemann's concepts and stages to all developmental and situational events and extended crisis intervention to eliminating the affective, behavioral, and cognitive distortions that precipitated the psychological trauma in the first place.

Differentiating Basic Crisis Theory from Brief Therapy.   The work of both Lindemann and Caplan gave impetus to the use of crisis intervention strategies in counseling and brief therapy with people manifesting universal human reactions to traumatic events. Whereas *brief therapy theory* typically attempts to remediate more or less ongoing emotional problems, *basic crisis theory*, following the lead of Lindemann and Caplan, focuses on helping people in crisis recognize and correct temporary affective, behavioral, and cognitive distortions brought on by traumatic events. Although brief or solution-focused therapy may be the equivalent of crisis intervention (in that it seeks to restore the person to a state of homeostasis or equilibrium), not all brief or solution-focused therapy is related to crisis intervention. Perhaps the following example will clarify the difference between the two.

A student fails one algebra test and concludes that he or she can never pass algebra, therefore cannot become an engineer (as the parents are perceived to expect/demand).

The student progresses to a feeling of helplessness, then to hopelessness, then contemplates suicide. Here, crisis intervention is clearly indicated. The same student fails one algebra test and, feeling uncomfortable, disappointed, and confused, makes an appointment to see the school counselor. Here, the modality becomes a typical brief or solution-focused therapy situation wherein the focus is on how to improve study habits and test-taking skills.

Differentiating between brief or solution-focused therapy and crisis intervention depends on how intensely the client views the problem as intolerable or on how much emotional disequilibrium the client experiences. Severe emotional disequilibrium over the event may escalate the person into crisis and the therapist into a crisis intervention modality.

All people experience psychological trauma at some time during their lives. Neither stress nor the emergency conditions of the trauma in themselves constitute crisis. Only when the traumatic event is subjectively perceived as a threat to need fulfillment, safety, or meaningful existence does an individual enter a state of crisis (Caplan, 1964). A crisis is accompanied by temporary disequilibrium and contains potential for human growth. The resolution of crisis may lead to positive and constructive outcomes such as self-enhancing coping ability and a decrease in negative, self-defeating, dysfunctional behavior (Janosik, 1984, pp. 3–21).

Expanded Crisis Theory

Expanded crisis theory was developed because basic theory, which depended on a psychoanalytic approach alone, did not adequately address the social, environmental, and situational factors that make an event a crisis. As crisis theory and intervention have expanded, it has become clear that an approach that identifies predisposing factors as the main or only causal agent falls short of the mark. A prime example of this restrictive view was the erroneous diagnosis, by practitioners who first encountered PTSD victims, that pathology preceding the crisis event was the real cause of the trauma. As crisis theory and intervention have grown it has become apparent that given the right combination of developmental, sociological, psychological, environmental, and situational determinants, anyone can fall victim to transient pathological symptoms. Therefore, expanded crisis theory draws not only from psychoanalytic but also from general systems, adaptational, interpersonal theory (Janosik, 1984) and chaos theory (Butz, 1997; Gleick, 1987). The following are synopses of the major theoretical components of an expanded view.

Psychoanalytic Theory.   Psychoanalytic theory (Fine, 1973), applied to expanded crisis theory, is based on the view that the disequilibrium that accompanies a person's crisis can be understood through gaining access to the individual's unconscious thoughts and past emotional experiences. Psychoanalytic theory presupposes that some early childhood fixation is the primary explanation of why an event becomes a crisis. This theory may be used to help clients develop insight into the dynamics and causes of their behavior as the crisis situation acts on them.

Systems Theory.   Systems theory (Haley, 1973, 1976) is based not so much on what happens within an individual in crisis as on the interrelationships and interdependence among people and between people and events. The fundamental concept of systems theory is analogous "to ecological systems in which all elements are interrelated, and in which change at any level of those interrelated parts will lead to alteration of the total system" (Cormier & Hackney, 1987, p. 217). Belkin (1984) adds that this theory "refers to an emotional system, a system of communications, and a system of need fulfillment and request" in which all members within an intergenerational relationship bring something to bear on the others and each derives something from the others (pp. 350–351).

Systems theory represents a turning away from traditional approaches, which focus only on what is going on within the client, and adopts an interpersonal systems way of thinking. There is great value in looking at crises in their total social and environmental settings—not simply as one individual being affected in a linear progression of cause-and-effect events.

Adaptational Theory.   Adaptational theory, as we use the term, depicts a person's crisis as being sustained through maladaptive behaviors, negative thoughts, and destructive defense mechanisms. Adaptational crisis theory is based on the premise that the person's crisis will recede when these maladaptive coping behaviors are changed to adaptive behaviors.

Breaking the chain of maladjusted functioning means changing to adaptive behavior, promoting positive thoughts, and constructing defense mechanisms that will help the person overcome the immobility created by the crisis and move to a positive mode of functioning. As maladaptive behaviors are learned, so may adaptive behaviors be learned. Aided by the interventionist, the client may be taught to replace old, debilitating behaviors with new, self-enhancing ones. Such new behaviors may be applied directly to the context of the crisis and ultimately result in either success or reinforcement for the client in overcoming it (Cormier & Cormier, 1985, p. 148).

Interpersonal Theory.   Interpersonal theory (Rogers, 1977) is built on many of the dimensions Cormier and Hackney (1987) describe as enhancing personal self-esteem: openness, trust, sharing, safety, unconditional positive regard, accurate empathy, and genuineness (pp. 35–64). The essence of interpersonal theory is that people cannot sustain a personal state of crisis for very long if they believe in themselves and in others and have confidence that they can become self-actualized and overcome the crisis.

When people confer their locus of self-evaluation on others, they become dependent on others for validation of their being. Therefore, as long as a person maintains an external locus of control the crisis will persist. The outcome goal, in interpersonal theory, is returning the power of self-evaluation to the person. Doing so enables the person once again to control his or her own destiny and regain the ability to take whatever action is needed to cope with the crisis situation.

Chaos Theory.   Chaos theory, frequently referred to as "chaos and complexity theory," derives from the principle of nonlinear dynamics (Gleick, 1987). Early conceptualizations of chaos theory by scientists in fields such as biology, chemistry, mathematics, and physics viewed the theory as referring to systems or events that appeared random, but at a closer look revealed an underlying global order. Butz (1997, pp. 7–9, 122–123) provides linkages from the physical sciences to the social and psychological sciences for chaos and complexity theory: (1) regarding human behavior, in the state of chaos predictability is lost; (2) systems whose complexity and dynamics appear chaotic at the local level, when observed on a global level may show an underlying order; (3) equating chaos with a state of overwhelming anxiety, defined as an acute sense of apprehension and fear, usually marked by physiological signs, chaos is considered to offer potential for intrapsychic growth or change.

Chaos theory is really sort of a theory of evolution when applied to human functioning such as crisis intervention. It is evolutionary in that it is essentially an open-ended, ever-changing, "self-organizing system" whereby a new system may emerge out of the crisis. A chaotic (crisis) situation—which Postrel (1998, p. xv) calls "emergent complex messiness"—evolves into a "self-organizing" mode whenever a critical mass of people come to perceive that they have no way to identify patterns or preplan options to solve the dilemma at hand. Because the chaotic situation falls outside of known alternative solutions, human services workers necessarily resort to spontaneous, trial-and-error experimentation to try to cope with the crisis. The "messiness" of the crisis lies not in disorder but in an order that is unknown, unpredictable and spontaneous, an ever-shifting pattern driven by millions of uncoordinated, independent factors that necessitate experimentation yet may finally result in a global clarification of the crisis. Such experimentation may lead to false starts, temporary failure, dead ends, spontaneous innovation, creativity, improvisation, brainstorming, cooperative enterprise, and other "evolutionary" attempts to make sense of and cope with the crisis.

Experimentation by a critical mass of people (or even by a single individual) can also provide the impetus to reframe and refine the crisis in terms of new and divergent ways of viewing the dilemma and generation of new and different options for coping with the crisis. An example of chaos theory at work occurred while Francine Shapiro was struggling with a difficult problem. She went to lunch, sat on a park bench, and looked up in the sky. She noticed her eyes moving back and forth watching the birds and also noticed that she suddenly became unusually relaxed and the problem seemed to have diminished. She wondered about that change, and thought her eye movement back and forth watching the birds might have had something to do with it. Shapiro thus practically stumbled on the fact that the eye movement had something to do with her transformation, and her further examination of the event led to the discovery of the essential principles of Eye Movement Desensitization/reprocessing, later known as EDMR for short. Later, she was able to apply EDMR strategies to many of the intractable cases of PTSD that had been plaguing her in her professional work. This real-life scenario illustrates the nonlinear, spontaneous, random, unfolding, non–cause-and-effect quality that chaos theory appears to explain. Out of what was a seemingly chaotic situation, Shapiro appeared to stumble onto a new "organizing" theme. But it was not a "stumble" because she possessed the "self-organizing" background to "reorganize" the chaos through her "aha!" experience and, in essence, to convert or reframe her disequilibrium (disorganization) into equilibrium (a new organization of thought patterns).

In chaos theory, the term "self-organizing" really refers to people coming to view the situation or a crisis globally and thus pragmatically discovering an underlying order within what was previously perceived as fundamentally chaotic disorder. Postrel (1998, pp. xiv–xviii, 39–40) characterizes chaos theory as seeming to seek order randomly, without design or control. Thus, "chaos" may denote systems that are self-organizing, but such systems do not simply "self-organize" around nothing. They evolve to the most fundamental principles and continuously self-organize around those principles.

Hence comes the theme, in crisis theory terms, of danger and opportunity. Even though a crisis may appear to epitomize an insoluble and chaotic impasse, careful examination of such chaos may actually reveal the key to understanding an important, profound, and hitherto unrecognized global message. The recognition of such a global message can provide both the impetus and the motivation needed to initiate positive or purposeful action toward alleviating the dilemma (Butz, 1993, 1995, 1997; Chamberlain, 1993, 1994; Gilliland & James, 1998; Postrel, 1998).

ECOSYSTEM THEORY

We believe that a new theory of crisis intervention is rapidly evolving, one we choose to call an *ecosystem theory.* The three major components that we envision playing a part in the evolution of this theory are electronic media impact, systemic interdependency, and a macrosystemic approach.

Electronic Media Impact

First, extensive and extended electronic media coverage—bringing disasters and traumatic events such as Hurricane Andrew, the bombing of the federal building in Oklahoma City, massive shootings and murders such as those that occurred in Columbine High School in Littleton, Colorado, shooting of children in a Jewish Community Center in Los Angeles, multiple homicides and suicide by a gunman in brokerage firms of Atlanta, hostage taking in schools, post offices, and other public buildings, E-mail solicitation by pedophiles, the random strikes of the "Unibomber," and the murder trial of O. J. Simpson into our living room—has ripple effects that spread far beyond the immediate victims of those terrible events. These traumatic events morbidly hold our attention and give rise to a belief that trouble and terror are all around us. We have become a global community through technology, and because crises make big news, we are given a nightly serving of "instacam" tragedies that—even though half a world away—give us pause to wonder if the next crisis will not come right into our living rooms. It is small wonder that we have not become more stressed, more isolated, and more prone to paranoia and victimization as we grudgingly realize that we are becoming more connected to the world through the electronic media than, perhaps, to our neighbors.

However, on the positive side of the technology revolution, we are now able to better predict the course of natural disasters such as hurricanes, volcanic eruptions, earthquakes, and forest fires and prepare for them. We also have at our fingertips access to a variety of information systems that can help us respond quickly and effectively to those disasters and in many instances avert or mitigate the widespread effects such disasters have on the total ecology. Through the World Wide Web, human services workers can gain immediate access to vast data and reference banks that can provide up-to-date information and techniques on how to handle any crisis they may encounter. Further, linkage to the Internet gives us the ability to talk to crisis workers in Montreal, Canada; Brisbane, Australia; or Littleton, Colorado, and exchange ideas and information with them in real time. The expertise of thousands of other therapists is as close as our computer keyboard.

Systemic Interdependency

Second, we are slowly coming to understand that John Donne's famous lines "Do not ask for whom the bell tolls. / It tolls for thee" indeed refer to us all and that we are all part of the ecological mainstream of the world. Disasters such as the *Exxon Valdez* oil spill affect not just Alaskan sea otters and shorebirds but also everyone who uses fossil fuels. The rampant upsurge in drug use, violence, and urban decay affect not only the people who live in New York, Manila, and London but also those in Carmi, Illinois; Thunder Bay, Ontario; and Pristina, Kosovo. However much we might wish to isolate ourselves from those problems and put off paying the psychological, social, financial, and environmental costs, we cannot. If we postpone payment, those costs will invariably grow exponentially larger the longer we procrastinate, and they will set the stage for even greater crises in the future.

A Macrosystemic Approach

Third, with the emergence of crisis intervention as a therapeutic specialty and expanded research into what happens in the immediate aftermath of a crisis, we have come to understand that unresolved crises play havoc not only with the client's personal, social, financial, and environmental resources but also with the total ecological system within which that person resides. As a result, institutions that range from individual school buildings to national service organizations to the federal government have and are developing approaches to confront crises throughout the total ecosystem within which they operate. Because we all ultimately share in the cost, crisis intervention becomes everyone's business.

An ecosystem theory of crisis intervention is based on viewing the total ecology within which the crisis resides and espouses the notion that major catastrophic events impact and alter the total ecological framework within which the individual operates. Subsequently, ecosystem theory proposes that it is not enough to deal only with the emotional trauma that resides within the survivors of these disasters. Rather, because there is great negative potential for the total ecosystem to be permanently damaged and altered as a result of such disasters, large teams of people with expertise in a variety of human and environmental specialties must be trained as rapid reaction teams to attempt to restore stability and equilibrium to the environment. This macrosystemic and proactive intervention approach is discussed at length in the last chapter of this book.

CRISIS INTERVENTION MODELS

Three basic crisis intervention models discussed by both Leitner (1974) and Belkin (1984) are the *equilibrium* model, the *cognitive* model, and the *psychosocial transition* model. These three models provide the groundwork for many different crisis intervention strategies and methodologies. All crisis intervention models are based on theory. Nowhere is this fact better exemplified than in the work of Strickler and Bonnefil (1974, p. 38), who link crisis theory with a psychosocial approach to psychotherapy through the following points:

1. Treatment goals are structured to enhance the client's competency in coping with difficulties by using problem-solving skills.

2. The treatment targets specific and pertinent problem areas that involve the client's interpersonal conflicts and role dysfunction.
3. The client's attention is kept on the specific problem area through active focusing techniques.
4. The treatment is geared primarily to the level of the client's conscious and near-conscious emotional conflicts. These conflicts are handled by searching out their situational references and by keeping a focus within them.
5. Precipitating events are recognized as very important to the dynamics of the problem situation.
6. The modification of the client's character traits or personality patterns is not a fundamental objective of the treatment.
7. The phenomenon of client transference to the interventionist is normally not considered important to the therapeutic process unless such transference presents an impediment to treatment.
8. Treatment is based on background information derived from a knowledge of personality, ego functioning, and sociocultural functioning.

These important principles provide the bridge between crisis theory and intervention. They clearly demonstrate that the principles of crisis psychology provide the foundation for clinical practice (Belkin, 1984, p. 427). They also set the stage for a brief examination of the equilibrium, cognitive, and psychosocial transition models of crisis intervention.

The Equilibrium Model

The equilibrium model is really an equilibrium/disequilibrium model. People in crisis are in a state of psychological or emotional disequilibrium in which their usual coping mechanisms and problem-solving methods fail to meet their needs. The goal of the equilibrium model is to help people recover a state of precrisis equilibrium (Caplan, 1961).

The equilibrium model seems most appropriate for early intervention, when the person is out of control, disoriented, and unable to make appropriate choices. Until the person has regained some coping abilities, the main focus is on stabilizing the individual. Up to the time the person has reacquired some definite measure of stability, little else can or should be done. For example, it does little good to dig into the underlying factors that cause suicidal ideation until the person can be stabilized to the point of agreeing that life is worth living for at least another week. This is probably the purest model of crisis intervention and is most likely to be used at the onset of the crisis (Caplan, 1961; Leitner, 1974; Lindemann, 1944).

The Cognitive Model

The cognitive model of crisis intervention is based on the premise that crises are rooted in faulty thinking about the events or situations that surround the crisis—not in the events themselves or the facts about the events or situations (Ellis, 1962). The goal of this model is to help people become aware of and to change their views and beliefs about the crisis events or situations. The basic tenet of the cognitive model is that people can gain control of crises in their lives by changing their thinking, especially by recognizing and disputing the irrational and self-defeating parts of their cognitions, and by retaining and focusing on the rational and self-enhancing elements of their thinking.

The messages that people in crisis send themselves become very negative and twisted, in contrast to the reality of the situation. Dilemmas that are constant and grinding wear people out, pushing their internal state of perception more and more toward negative self-talk until their cognitive sets are so negative that no amount of preaching can convince them anything positive will ever come from the situation. Their behavior soon follows this negative self-talk and begets a self-fulfilling prophecy that the situation is hopeless. At this juncture, crisis intervention becomes a job of rewiring the individual's thoughts to more positive feedback loops by practicing and rehearsing new self-statements about the situation until the old, negative, debilitating ones are expunged. The cognitive model seems most appropriate after the client has been stabilized and returned to an approximate state of precrisis equilibrium. Basic components of this approach are found in the rational-emotive work of Ellis (1982), the cognitive-behavioral approach of Meichenbaum (1977), and the cognitive system of Beck (1976) and Beck and associates (1987).

The Psychosocial Transition Model

The psychosocial transition model assumes that people are products of their genes plus the learning they have absorbed from their particular social environments. Because people are continually changing, developing, and growing, and their social environments and social influence (Dorn, 1986) are continuously evolving, crises may be related to internal or external (psychological, social, or environmental) difficulties. The goal of crisis intervention is both to collaborate with clients in assessing the internal and external difficulties contributing to the crisis and to help them choose workable alternatives to their current behaviors, attitudes, and use of environmental resources. Clients may need to incorporate adequate internal coping mechanisms, social supports, and environmental resources in order to get autonomous (noncrisis) control over their lives.

The psychosocial model does not perceive crisis as simply an internal state of affairs that resides totally within the individual. It reaches outside the individual and asks what systems need to be changed. Peers, family, occupation, religion, and community are but a few of the external dimensions that promote or hinder psychological adaptiveness. With certain kinds of crisis problems, few lasting gains will be made unless the social systems that affect the individual are also changed or the individual comes to terms with and understands the dynamics of those systems and how they affect adaptation to the crisis. Like the cognitive model, the psychosocial transition model seems to be most appropriate after the client has been stabilized. Theorists who have contributed to the psychosocial transition model include Adler (Ansbacher & Ansbacher, 1956), Erikson (1963), and Minuchin (1974).

ECLECTIC CRISIS INTERVENTION THEORY

Eclectic crisis intervention involves intentionally and systematically selecting and integrating valid concepts and strategies from all available approaches to helping clients. Eclecticism is a hybrid of all available approaches. It operates from a task orientation, as opposed to concepts. Its major tasks (Gilliland & James, 1998, p. 367; Thorne, 1973, p. 451) are (1) to identify valid elements in all systems and to integrate them into an internally consistent whole that does justice to the behavioral data to be explained; (2) to consider all pertinent theories, methods, and standards for evaluating and manipulating clinical data according to the most advanced knowledge of time and place; and (3) to identify with no specific theory, keep an open mind, and continuously experiment with those formulations and strategies that produce successful results.

Throughout this book, the reader will find an eclectic approach integrated into interventions presented. Distinctive threads of the equilibrium/disequilibrium model, the cognitive model, and the psychosocial transition model are woven into the fabric of crisis intervention strategies for each type of crisis explored. The eclectic theory fuses two pervasive themes: (1) all people and all crises are unique and distinctive, and (2) all people and all crises are similar. We do not see these themes as mutually exclusive.

All people and all crises are similar in that there are global elements to specific crisis types. The dynamics of bereavement are generic and provide us with general guidelines for intervention. However, treating individual cases of bereavement is anything but generic. How a family perceives the impact of the death of a member depends on a number of factors: the deceased member's place in the family, what each member of the family does in response to the death, and how the changed family system now operates. Treatment of surviving family members who have lost a child after rearing five others, as opposed to those who have lost their only child, born late in the parents' life, who had become the focus of existence for the couple, may call for far different intervention strategies even if bereavement is the generic issue.

An eclectic approach does not mean taking a therapeutic shotgun and aimlessly blasting away at the crisis. Using an eclectic approach means not being bound by and locked into any one theoretical approach in a dogmatic fashion. Rather, it means being well versed in a number of approaches and theories and being able to assess the client's needs so that appropriate techniques can be planned and fitted to them. Many human services workers avow an eclectic approach but in actuality use the word to rationalize not being able to do anything very well. Being a true eclectic means doing lots of hard work, reading, studying, experiencing, and being supervised and critiqued by other professionals. It also means taking risks and having a willingness to abandon an approach that on first inspection might seem reasonable and proper but, once entered, proves fruitless for the particular situation.

Eclecticism performed well is equal parts skill and intuition. Paying attention to your feeling as much as to your cognition about the situation is crucial. Changing to a more effective intervention is often based on nothing more scientific than a feeling that something is amiss. Although having a feeling is little justification, in the scientific sense, for doing something, it can nevertheless be a sound basis for action. We know of no formula for deciding when to move from a nondirective to a highly directive stance with a client in crisis, nor is there an equation that tells a therapist that mental imagery may be more effective than confrontation as an intervention technique. We unabashedly believe that in an eclectic approach the performing art of crisis intervention clearly reaches its zenith.

CHARACTERISTICS OF EFFECTIVE CRISIS WORKERS

Almost everyone can be taught the techniques in this book, and with practice can employ them with some degree of skill. However, the crisis worker who can take intervention to the performing art level is more than the sum of techniques read about and skills mastered. A master of this art is going to have some combination of the two, and a good deal of the following experiences.

Life Experiences

The worker handles a crisis or not to the extent that he or she is a whole person or not (Carkhuff & Berenson, 1977, pp. 162–163). A whole person has a rich and varied background of life experiences. These life experiences serve as a resource for emotional maturity that, combined with training, enables workers to be stable, consistent, and well integrated not only within the crisis situation but also in their daily lives.

However, life experiences alone are not sufficient to qualify one to be a crisis worker, and can be debilitating if they continue to influence the worker in negative ways. This issue is central to crisis intervention because many people who work as volunteers, support personnel, and professionals are products of their own crisis environments. They have chosen to work with people experiencing the same kind of crisis they themselves have suffered, and they use their experiential background as a resource in working with others. For example, recovering addicts may work in alcohol and drug units, battered women work in spouse abuse centers, and PTSD victims counsel in veterans' centers. These professionals have had firsthand experience with the trauma their clients have experienced. Does this background give them an edge over other workers who have not suffered the same pain?

The answer is a qualified yes: qualified in that the person who carries emotional baggage into the helping relationship may be even less effective than the person who has had few if any life experiences. We see examples of emotional carryover into the intervention process in the proselytizing alcoholic who vilifies others to assuage his own insecurities and fears about "falling off the wagon" and in the child abuse worker, herself a former victim of sexual abuse, who castigates mothers for their failure to confront abusing fathers. Such human services workers may have tremendous difficulties because they mingle many of their own problems with those of their clients. The workers alternate among feeling states characterized by sympathy, anger, disappointment, and cynicism, which are detrimental both to themselves and to their clients.

We do not believe crisis workers must have "lived in the crisis" to be able to understand and deal with it effectively. We do believe that interventionists who have successfully overcome some of life's problems and have put those problems into perspective will have assets of maturity, optimism, tenacity, and tough-mindedness that will help them marshal their psychological resources to assist their clients.

We are not proposing that people lacking a variety of life experiences should actively pursue trauma as a means of becoming seasoned enough to be effective interventionists. We would also caution that on-the-job training in this business is a very arduous way to win one's spurs, particularly for a worker who has spent a sheltered, constricted life and decides through misguided idealism to become a Florence Nightingale and fix the problems of the world. This rose-colored view does little for clients in general and may do much harm to workers as their good intentions pave the road to burnout. We hasten to add that chronological age has very little to do with having or not having self-enhancing life experiences and a broader, more resilient viewpoint. We know people ranging in age from 21 to 65 who are emotional adolescents. They are threatened by face-to-face encounters with the real world and may be characterized by rigidity, insularity, and insecurity.

The ideal crisis worker we envision is one who has experienced life, has learned and grown from those experiences, and supports those experiences in his or her work by thorough training, knowledge, and supervision. This individual constantly seeks to integrate all these aspects into his or her therapeutic intervention in particular and into living in general.

Professional Skills

Professionally, we seek to inculcate in our students the following helping skills:

Attentiveness
Accurate listening and responding
Congruence between thinking, feeling, and acting therapeutically
Reassuring and supporting skills
Rudimentary ability to analyze, synthesize, and diagnose
Basic assessment and referral skills
Ability to explore alternatives and solve problems

This list is not all-inclusive, but provides a flavor of the outcome we expect of people who go through our crisis intervention courses at the University of Memphis.

Although these skills would be the hallmark of those who perform any human services work, the difference in crisis intervention is that these skills must be used when problem onset is sudden and dramatic, emotions are highly volatile, and background information may be sketchy at best.

Poise

The nature of crisis intervention is that the worker is often confronted with shocking and threatening material from clients who are completely out of control. Probably the most significant help the interventionist can provide at this juncture is to remain calm, poised, and in control (Belkin, 1984, p. 427). Creating a stable and rational atmosphere provides a model for the client that is conducive to restoring equilibrium to the situation. Practicing relaxation techniques is one way to keep calm in such highly charged situations, but more important is the worker's faith that the client can be pulled through the crisis. In our teaching we can model patience and understanding with troubled clients. What we cannot model is faith and belief in the client's ability to overcome the situation. This trait is one that must abide deep within the interventionist; we know of no easy way to teach it.

Creativity and Flexibility

Creativity and flexibility are major assets to those confronted with perplexing and seemingly unsolvable problems (Aguilera & Messick, 1982, p. 24). It is one thing to teach a person a repertoire of skills. It is quite another thing to teach the use of those skills in ways that are adaptable to clients' needs. Most training programs known to us pay scant attention to creative therapeutic functioning. In our own courses and training workshops, students and trainees have difficulty when confronted with conducting role plays with peers because they have no formula for getting the "right" answer. Although practice in tough role-play situations builds confidence, how creative individuals are in difficult situations depends to a large measure on how well they have nurtured their own creativity over the course of their lives by taking risks and practicing divergent thinking.

Energy

Functioning in the unknown areas that are characteristic of crisis intervention requires energy, organization, direction, and systematic action (Carkhuff & Berenson, 1977, p. 194). Professional training can provide organizational guidelines and principles for systematic acting. What it cannot do is provide the energy requisite to perform this work. The chapter on burnout in this book (Chapter 13) speaks to many of the maladies that workers suffer and suggests ways to bolster morale, but being energized is still largely incumbent on the worker. Feeling good enough about oneself to tackle perplexing problems day after day calls for not only an initial desire to do the work but also the ability to take care of one's physical and psychological needs so that energy levels remain high.

Quick Mental Reflexes

Crisis work differs from typical therapeutic intervention in that time is a critical factor. Crisis intervention requires more activity and directiveness than ordinary therapeutic endeavors usually do. Time to reflect and mull over problems is a rare commodity in crisis intervention. The worker must have fast mental reflexes to deal with the constantly emerging and changing issues that occur in the crisis. We know of no videotape or spa that provides fitness activities in these areas. The worker who cannot think fast and accurately is going to find the business very frustrating indeed.

Other Characteristics

The following chapters describe attributes that effective crisis interventionists have found of utmost importance to themselves and their clients. These attributes are tenacity, the ability to delay gratification, courage, optimism, a reality orientation, calmness under duress, objectivity, a strong and positive self-concept, and abiding faith that human beings are strong, resilient, and capable of overcoming seemingly insurmountable odds. Poll yourself: Do you have these traits?

We also want you to understand that admission into the inner circle of the profession is not reserved solely for a few supermen and superwomen. Most interventionists we know, including ourselves, are at times perplexed, frustrated, angry, afraid, threatened, incompetent, foolish, vain, troubled, and otherwise unequal to the task. We allow ourselves and our students and trainees at least one mistake per day and go on from there. We would like you to remember that cognitive billboard and place it squarely in the forefront of your mind.

CRISES AND THE PERSONHOOD
OF CRISIS WORKERS

Each crisis encapsulates a process leading to the potential for constructive change, not only for the client but also for the helper (Carkhuff & Berenson, 1977, pp. 162–163). The crisis helping relationship is reciprocal and is greater than the sum of its parts. The helper changes as a result of every contact with a client. Successful resolution of the crisis results in two products: (1) helping the client overcome the crisis and (2) effecting positive change in the helper as a result of the encounter.

Rewarding Work.   Positive change is not merely summed up in so many cases successfully handled or so many techniques effectively employed. Successfully helping a client negotiate a crisis enables us to incorporate the experience into our own life and become more holistic, enabling, and competent in all our endeavors. Standing up to the intense heat of the crisis situation to help people through seemingly unsolvable problems is some of the most gratifying and positively reinforcing work we know. The intense personal rewards that accrue to crisis workers lead us to believe that this work would be high on Glasser's (1976) list of positive addicting behaviors.

To Do or Not to Do Crisis Work.   For those who may decide that human services work (and particularly crisis intervention) is not their calling, this book also has applicability. Consider, for a moment, yourself as a client. Everyone is at times subject to the whims of a randomly cruel universe, and the kinds of crises that are dealt with in this book are apt to be visited on us all. Understanding how to navigate through these constellations of problems is a valuable resource. How well we live depends on our ability to handle the problems that confront us when we least expect them. As you read through the material, you may find yourself "living into" some of these problems and asking yourself, "I wonder how I'd fare if I were a client?" We believe that this too is a worthwhile perspective if you can look beyond the dilemmas to the coping techniques and bank them for future reference and use.

MULTICULTURAL PERSPECTIVES
IN CRISIS INTERVENTION

We are living in a pluralistic world. In the United States, whether we realize it or not, we are living in a pluralistic culture. Kiselica (1998, p. 6) identifies four attributes that are widely accepted as components needed in crisis workers and other helping professionals who intervene with clients in the multicultural world in which we work: (1) *self-knowledge,* particularly an awareness of one's own cultural biases; (2) *knowledge* about the status and cultures of different cultural groups; (3) *skills* to effect culturally appropriate interventions, including a readiness to use alternative strategies that better match the cultures of crisis clients than do traditional strategies; and (4) *actual experience* in counseling and crisis intervention with culturally different clients. Derald Wing Sue (1992, p. 12, 1999a, 1999b) reminds us that failure to understand the worldview of clients may lead human services workers to make erroneous interpretations, judgments, and conclusions that result in doing serious harm to clients, especially the culturally different. This reality alone makes it mandatory for individuals concerned with the personal and professional development of crisis workers to ensure that the recruitment, training, and assessment of those workers take into account a multicultural perspective (Ridley, Li, & Hill, 1998). Pedersen (1987) informs us that Western cultural biases in our conventional thinking pertain less to geography than to social, economic, political, and ethnocentric values. A vast majority of the world's population lives by a non-Western perspective. Despite the fact that the world is culturally pluralistic, many of our books, professional teachings, research findings, and implicit theories and assumptions in the field of counseling are specific to North American and European culture. Such theories and assumptions are usually so ingrained in our thinking that they are taken for granted and seldom challenged even by our most broad-minded leaders and professionals (Ponterotto & Pedersen, 1993).

Awareness of Cultural Values.   Unintentional and unexamined cultural and racial assumptions can impair the functioning of counselors and crisis workers (Arredondo, 1999; Ridley, 1995; Thompson & Neville, 1999). It is of the utmost importance that the recruitment, screening, orientation, training, evaluation, and retention of workers deal with the realities of a multicultural clientele (Ponterotto & Pedersen, 1993; Sue, 1999a). A multicultural perspective in the thought processes, emotional attitudes, and behaviors of crisis workers can go a long way toward eliminating the negative effects of institutionalized racism, ethnocentrism, ageism, religionism, homophobia, able-bodied–ism, sexism, and other forms of cultural and personal bias that clients may encounter in some crisis agencies (Heppner, 1998; Pedersen, 1987, p. 18, 1998; Ponterotto & Pedersen, 1993; Robinson & Ginter, 1999; Thompson & Neville, 1999). Sue (1999a), Ivey (1987), and Arredondo (1999) emphasize that counseling and therapy should begin with counselors' awareness of their own assumptions, values, and biases regarding racial, cultural, and group differences before considering individual variations on those themes. Ivey (1987) states that "only by placing multicultural counseling at the core of counseling curricula can we as counselors truly serve and be with those whom we would help" (p. 169).

In summary, crisis workers must not operate within a framework of what Paniagua (1994) calls cultural encapsulation and self-reference. That means that in working with clients, in addition to considering ethnographic variables (nationality, ethnicity, language, race, religion), workers will also consider demographic variables (such as social, economic, educational, political, familial) and affiliation variables (formal as well as informal). This broad view of crisis work from a multicultural context expands the perspective of workers as they respond to all clients in an increasingly pluralistic society.

Culturally Biased Assumptions

Pedersen (1987) discusses 10 frequent culturally biased assumptions that crisis agency directors might consider in their preservice and in-service training programs. These assumptions are listed here for identification purposes.

1. The assumption that people all share a common measure of "normal" behavior (the presumption that problems, emotional responses, behaviors, and percep-

tions of crises are more or less universal across social, cultural, economic, or political backgrounds) (p. 17).

2. The assumption that individuals are the basic building blocks of all societies (the presumption that crisis intervention and counseling are directed primarily toward the individual rather than units of individuals or groups such as the family, organizations, political groups, or society) (p. 18).

3. The assumption that the definition of problems can be limited by academic discipline boundaries (the presumption that the identity of the crisis worker or counselor is separate from the identity of the theologian, medical doctor, sociologist, anthropologist, attorney, or representative from some other discipline) (p. 19).

4. The assumption that Western culture depends on abstract words (the presumption of crisis workers and counselors in the United States that others will understand these abstractions in the same way as workers intend them) (pp. 19–20).

5. The assumption that independence is valuable and dependencies are undesirable (the presumption of Western individualism that people should not be dependent on others or allow others to be dependent on them) (p. 20).

6. The assumption that formal counseling is more important than natural support systems surrounding a client (the presumption that clients prefer the support offered by counselors over the support of family, peers, and other support groups) (pp. 20–21).

7. The assumption that everyone depends on linear thinking (the presumption by counselors and crisis workers that each cause has an effect, and each effect is tied to a cause—to explain how the world works—and that everything can be measured and described in terms of good or bad, appropriate or inappropriate, and/or other common dichotomies) (pp. 21–22).

8. The assumption that counselors need to change individuals to fit the system (the presumption that the system does not need to change to fit the individual) (p. 22).

9. The assumption that the client's past (history) has little relevance to contemporary events (the presumption that crises are mostly related to here-and-now situations and that crisis workers and counselors should pay little attention to the client's background connections) (pp. 22–23).

10. The assumption that counselors and crisis workers already know all their assumptions (the presumption that if counselors and crisis workers were prone toward reacting in closed, biased, and culturally encapsulated ways that promote domination by an elitist group, they would be aware of it) (p. 23).

All 10 assumptions are, of course, flawed and untenable in a pluralistic world. Cormier and Hackney (1987) warn that human services workers who do not understand their own cultural biases and the cultural differences and values of others may misinterpret the behaviors and attitudes of clients from other cultures. Such workers may incorrectly label some client behavior as resistant and uncooperative. They may expect to see certain client behaviors (such as self-disclosure) that are contrary to the basic values of some cultural groups. The culturally insensitive counselor or crisis worker may also stereotype, label, or use unimodal or ineffective counseling approaches in an attempt to help clients from other cultures (pp. 256–258).

Culturally Effective Helping

Sue (1992) states that multicultural helping is enhanced when the human services worker "uses methods and strategies and defines goals consistent with the life experiences and culture values of the client" (p. 13). Belkin (1984) points out that cross-cultural counseling need not be negative; that it may effectively resolve client problems as well as provide a unique learning experience for both client and helper; and that the main "barrier to effective cross-cultural counseling is the traditional counseling role itself, which is not applicable to many cross-cultural interactions" (p. 527). Belkin further states that the principal cross-cultural impediments are (1) language differences, (2) class-bound values, and (3) culture-bound values (p. 534). Belkin also identifies both *barriers* to and *benefits* of intracultural counseling. The *barriers* cited are (1) unjustified assumption of shared feelings, (2) client transference (the shifting of emotions related to a person, such as a parent, from an earlier period in life to current feelings toward the counselor), and (3) counselor countertransference (shifting of the counselor's unresolved feelings for significant others to current emotions felt toward the client). The *benefits* given are (1) shared experience, which may enhance rapport, (2) client willingness to self-disclose some materials, and (3) common mode of communication, which may enhance the counseling process (p. 542). Belkin concludes that perhaps the most positive discovery and/or belief of the effective cross-cultural counselor is that humans everywhere are more alike than they are different (p. 543).

Cormier and Hackney (1987) cite several strategies that culturally effective helpers use. For instance, such helpers (1) examine and understand the world from the *client's* viewpoint, (2) search for alternative roles that may be more appealing and adaptive to clients from different backgrounds, and (3) help clients from other cultures make contact with and elicit help from indigenous support systems (p. 259).

Cormier and Hackney (1987) also specify that to be culturally effective, helpers should *not* (1) impose their values and expectations on clients from different backgrounds, (2) stereotype or label clients, client behaviors, or cultures, and (3) try to force unimodal counseling approaches upon clients (pp. 258–259). Sue (1992) cites an example of such unimodal expectations: traditional helpers may tend to emphasize the need for clients to verbalize their emotions. He points out that some clients (such as traditional Japanese) may have been taught as children not to speak until addressed; that many cultures highly value restraint in expressing strong feelings; that patterns of communication, contrary to ours in the United States, may "tend to be vertical, flowing from those of higher prestige and status to those of lower prestige and status" (p. 12). The unenlightened worker seeking to help such a client may perceive that person to be inarticulate, unintelligent, lacking in spontaneity, or repressed (p. 13).

Figure 1.1 is a diagram of the effects of ecology on client–counselor interactions. Notice that the "crisis" triangle has a component at each corner: the crisis worker, the client, and their ecological backgrounds. The two-way arrows between the three corners indicate the mutual and dynamic interaction that constantly occurs among all the possible ecological factors that impact both crisis worker and client: family, race, religion, locale, physical ability, sex, economic class, vocation, physical needs, social affiliations, and so on. No therapy is done in a sterile vacuum, free from the multiple effects of the ecological background. That statement is even more true in the highly charged emotional context of crisis intervention. The wise crisis interventionist under-

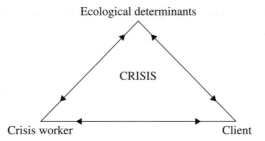

FIGURE 1.1   The dynamic effects of ecology on client–counselor interactions

stands this complexity and, when faced with an out-of-control client whose ecological background may be extremely different from his or her own, goes slowly and carefully. The wise worker is highly sensitive to and asks questions about the person's preferred mode of receiving assistance.

The worker should also understand that his or her own cultural biases have an even higher potential for surfacing when faced with oppositional, defiant clients who may not think, talk, act, look, or even smell like the worker. Thus ecological dynamics are a two-way street. Being aware of the impact that the ecology exerts on both participants and the interactive effect it has on each is crucial if the relationship is going to progress and the crisis is to be resolved.

A recurrent comment we are often confronted with in our classes commonly comes from an apparent belief that "to counsel one, you gotta be one!" We take the view that this stance is neither true nor workable. Particularly in crisis intervention, we seldom have the freedom of choice to choose which clients we will get or take; and we generally do not have time to make referrals simply because that client's ecological background does not fit nicely into our own. What we can do and must do is be acutely sensitive to the emerging needs of the individual and, in Carl Rogers's terms (Raskin & Rogers, 1995), prize that person in regard to his or her distinctive individuality in the context of the crisis situation. Above all else, research on the outcomes of therapy tells us that establishing a relationship built on trust and credibility is far and away the most important condition to a successful outcome of any kind of therapeutic endeavor (Capuzzi & Gross, 1995, pp. 12–25).

Multicultural Issues in Outreach

Understanding the cultural milieu in which he or she operates is of critical importance to the crisis worker who performs field work or outreach services. Cultural differences are particularly problematic when the worker is transported to and works on the "turf" of the client and has little time to become attuned to the cultural and ecological framework within which the client operates. We are not simply talking about "foreigners," either. The midwestern farmer faced with rebuilding after a disastrous flood, or transient street people in dire need of social and mental health services, may have views about what constitutes helpful intervention that are very different from the crisis worker's. Such individuals may take umbrage at the crisis worker's attempts to intrude into their world (Hopper, Johnston, & Brinkhoff, 1988).

Although it may be difficult enough in crisis to work with people from the same generic cultural background and who speak English as a first language, the manifestation and communication of first-generation Americans' or immigrants' personal problems may be very different from what the crisis worker is used to handling. As a result, assessment and intervention become more complex and difficult. Confidentiality issues are also problematic. People in the United States who have "green cards" or student visas run the risk of having information about their mental health status given to government agencies, who may then make negative evaluations about their immigrant status. This issue is further compounded by language problems that make communicating clients' needs and crisis workers' attempts to communicate their services subject to misinterpretation. Particularly for foreign students, having to leave school because of "mental problems" may cause tremendous loss of face in their families and in their home countries. If not handled sensitively, the worker's attempts to provide help may exacerbate rather than mollify the crisis (Oropeza, Clark, Fitzgibbon, & Baron, 1991).

Shelby and Tredinnick (1995) spent considerable space reporting on the cultural differences they encountered doing disaster relief work in the aftermath of Hurricane Andrew. The large Caribbean and Latin American populations they dealt with had punitive religious interpretations of the disaster and punitive child-rearing practices, particularly under stress, that differed greatly from what the crisis workers had previously encountered. The workers had to be very sensitive in not challenging these deeply held beliefs instead of allowing survivors to process feelings of guilt and responsibility in line with their religious interpretation of the event. Furthermore, educating parents with ethnically different views of child rearing about the ways children generically respond after a trauma, along with the normal developmental issues they face, may indeed be a tall order given the brevity of crisis intervention. Such interventions, although needed, may be something the crisis worker wishes to consider carefully. Shelby and Tredinnick also found that African American and Hispanic populations tended to rely on extended support systems much more heavily than did Caucasians. Therefore, the workers' efforts needed to focus more on systemic approaches that dealt with extended family networks as opposed to individuals.

While working with families in the Philippines after a disastrous volcanic eruption, one of the authors found that many of the young adults relied on their parents and grandparents rather than on human services workers for guidance and counseling relative not only to issues concerning the crisis at hand but also for personal and career decisions. Whereas the typical young adult in European or Western cultures may accept human services from outside the family as a matter of course, many of their Filipino counterparts would not even think about making important decisions, crisis or otherwise, without first considering their parents' wishes. This finding is congruent with Helms and Cook's (1999) emphasis on the importance of helping professionals acquiring knowledge and developing skill in interventions that cut across race and culture. In summary, although crisis work is never easy, cultural insensitivity may make it even more difficult.

SUMMARY

We consider all six definitions of crisis to be valid and useful. Our composite definition of *crisis,* derived from all six sources, is *a perception or experiencing of an event or situation as an intolerable difficulty that exceeds the person's current resources and coping mechanisms.* This general definition is enhanced by considering several important principles and characteristics of crisis:

1. Crisis embodies both danger and opportunity for the person experiencing the crisis.
2. Crisis is usually time limited but may develop into a series of recurring transcrisis points.
3. Crisis is often complex and difficult to resolve.
4. The life experiences of crisis and other human services workers may greatly enhance their effectiveness in crisis intervention.
5. Crisis contains the seeds of growth and impetus for change.
6. Panaceas or quick fixes may not be applicable to many crisis situations.
7. Crisis confronts people with choices.
8. Emotional disequilibrium and disorganization accompany crisis.
9. The resolution of crisis and the personhood of crisis workers interrelate.

Workers will find understanding these principles and characteristics of crisis to be of enormous value in their role as helpers.

Understanding transcrisis states and transcrisis points help in understanding many crises that workers encounter. Clients experiencing crises rooted in their transcrisis states or transcrisis points show recurring traumalike symptoms derived from earlier traumatic events. Transcrisis states and points have parallels with and differences from PTSD.

Several theoretical thrusts are basic, expanded, and ecosystem crisis intervention theory, plus applied crisis domains. *Basic crisis theory,* founded in the works of Lindemann (1944, 1956) and Caplan (1964), helps us view crisis as situational or developmental rather than pathological in nature. *Expanded crisis theory* adds to and enhances basic theory by incorporating and adapting components from general systems, psychoanalytic, adaptational, interpersonal, and chaos theory. *Applied crisis domains* integrates the concepts of developmental, situational, existential, and environmental crises into a holistic theoretical structure containing basic, expanded, and ecosystem crisis theory concepts. *Ecosystem theory* is an emerging system that incorporates the total ecology within which the crisis situation occurs. The person(s), events, environment, and total ecology are inextricably related. Therefore, an ecosystem crisis may encompass all the people, the culture, the communications technology, and the collective environmental composition of a locale, region, or even nation.

Three fundamental crisis intervention models are equilibrium, cognitive, and psychosocial transition. The *equilibrium model,* probably the most widely known model of the three, defines equilibrium as an emotional state in which the person is stable, in control, or psychologically mobile. It also defines disequilibrium as an emotional state that accompanies instability, loss of control, and psychological immobility. The *cognitive model* views the crisis state as resulting from faulty thinking and belief about life's dilemmas and traumas. The *psychosocial transition model* assumes that people are products of both hereditary endowment and environmental learning and that crisis may be caused by psychological, social, or environmental factors. The psychosocial transition model therefore instructs us to look for intervention strategies in all three realms: psychological, social, and environmental.

An eclectic theoretical position incorporates and integrates all valid concepts of crisis intervention. The strength of eclectic crisis intervention theory is that it encourages workers to select, integrate, and apply useful concepts and strategies from all available approaches to helping clients.

Effective crisis workers share a number of characteristics. Effective workers demonstrate competency in their professional skills. They maintain poise while confronting the difficult issues of clients from different cultures. They are both creative and flexible in their dealing with client problems. They possess a great deal of energy and know how to organize and direct their energy toward systematic action. They can think and react quickly. Finally, effective crisis workers are positive in their outlook, work, philosophy, and approach to helping clients.

Multicultural perspectives in crisis intervention are a crucial component of the crisis worker's repertoire of both attitudes and skills in helping people in crisis. Unintentional and unexamined cultural and racial assumptions have unexcused and destructive effects on worker–client relationships.

REFERENCES

Aguilera, D. C., & Messick, J. M. (1982). *Crisis intervention: Theory and methodology* (4th ed.). St. Louis: C. V. Mosby.

American Psychiatric Association. (1994). *Diagnostic and statistical manual of mental disorders* (4th ed.). Washington, DC: Author.

Ansbacher, H. L., & Ansbacher, R. R. (1956). *The individual psychology of Alfred Adler.* New York: Greenberg.

Armsworth, M. W., & Holaday, M. (1993). The effects of psychological trauma on children and adolescents. *Journal of Counseling and Development, 72*(1), 49–56.

Arredondo, P. (1999). Multicultural counseling competencies as tools to address oppression and racism. *Journal of Counseling and Development, 77*(1), 102–108.

Beck, A. T. (1976). *Cognitive therapy and the emotional disorders.* New York: International Universities Press.

Beck, A. T., Rush, A. J., Shaw, B. F., & Emery, G. (1987). *Cognitive therapy of depression.* New York: Guilford Press.

Belkin, G. S. (1984). *Introduction to counseling* (2nd ed.). Dubuque, IA: William C. Brown.

Brammer, L. M. (1985). *The helping relationship: Process and skills* (3rd ed.). Upper Saddle River, NJ: Prentice Hall.

Butz, M. R. (1993, August). *Chaos theory and familial dynamics: What does it look like?* Paper presented at the annual convention of the American Psychological Association, Toronto, Canada.

Butz, M. R. (1995). Chaos theory, philosophically old, scientifically new. *Counseling and Values, 39,* 84–98.

Butz, M. R. (1997). *Chaos and complexity: Implications for psychological theory and practice.* Washington, DC: Taylor & Francis.

Caplan, G. (1961). *An approach to community mental health.* New York: Grune & Stratton.

Caplan, G. (1964). *Principles of preventive psychiatry.* New York: Basic Books.

Capuzzi, D., & Gross, D. R. (Eds.). (1995). *Counseling and psychotherapy: Theories and interventions.* Upper Saddle River, NJ: Prentice Hall.

Carkhuff, R. R., & Berenson, B. G. (1977). *Beyond counseling and therapy* (2nd ed.). New York: Holt, Rinehart & Winston.

Chamberlain, L. (1993, August). *Strange attractors in patterns of family interactions.* Paper presented at the Annual Convention of the American Psychological Association, Toronto, Canada.

Chamberlain, L. (1994, August). *Is there a chaotician in the house? Chaos and family therapy.* Paper presented at the Annual Convention of the American Psychological Association, Los Angeles.

Cormier, L. S., & Hackney, H. (1987). *The professional counselor: A process guide to helping.* Upper Saddle River, NJ: Prentice Hall.

Cormier, W. H., & Cormier, L. S. (1985). *Interviewing strategies for helpers: Fundamental skills and cognitive behavioral in-*

terventions (2nd ed.). Pacific Grove, CA: Brooks/Cole.

Dorn, F. J. (Ed.). (1986). *The social influence process in counseling and psychotherapy.* Springfield, IL: Charles C Thomas.

Ellis, A. E. (1962). *Reason and emotion in psychotherapy.* New York: Lyle Stuart.

Ellis, A. E. (1982). Major systems. *Personnel and Guidance Journal, 61,* 6–7.

Erikson, E. (1963). *Childhood and society* (2nd ed.). New York: Norton.

Fine, R. (1973). Psychoanalysis. In R. J. Corsini (Ed.), *Current psychotherapies* (pp. 1–33). Itasca, IL: F. E. Peacock.

Gilliland, B. E., & James, R. K. (1998). *Theories and strategies in counseling and psychotherapy* (4th ed.). Boston: Allyn and Bacon.

Glasser, W. (1976). *Positive addiction.* New York: Harper & Row.

Gleick, J. (1987). *Chaos: Making a new science.* New York: Penguin Books.

Haley, J. (1973). *Uncommon therapy.* New York: Norton.

Haley, J. (1976). *Problem-solving therapy.* New York: McGraw-Hill.

Helms, J. E., & Cook, D. A. (1999). *Using race and culture in counseling and psychotherapy: Theory and process.* Boston: Allyn and Bacon.

Heppner, P. P. (Ed.). (1998). Lesbian, gay, and bisexual affirmative training. (Special issue). *The Counseling Psychologist, 26*(5).

Hopper, M. J., Johnston, J., & Brinkhoff, J. (1988). Creating a career hotline for rural residents. *Journal of Counseling and Development, 66,* 340–341.

Ivey, A. E. (1987). Cultural intentionality: The core of effective helping. *Counselor Education and Supervision, 26,* 168–172.

Janosik, E. H. (1984). *Crisis counseling: A contemporary approach.* Monterey, CA: Wadsworth Health Sciences Division.

Kiselica, M. S. (1998). Preparing Anglos for the challenges and joys of multiculturalism. *The Counseling Psychologist, 26,* 5–21.

Kliman, A. S. (1978). *Crisis: Psychological first aid for recovery and growth.* New York: Holt, Rinehart & Winston.

Leitner, L. A. (1974). Crisis counseling may save a life. *Journal of Rehabilitation, 40,* 19–20.

Lindemann, E. (1944). Symptomatology and management of acute grief. *American Journal of Psychiatry, 101,* 141–148.

Lindemann, E. (1956). The meaning of crisis in individual and family. *Teachers College Record, 57,* 310.

Marino, T. W. (1995). Crisis counseling: Helping normal people cope with abnormal situations. *Counseling Today, 38*(3), 25, 40, 46, 53.

Meichenbaum, D. H. (1977). *Cognitive–behavior modification: An integrative approach.* New York: Plenum.

Minuchin, S. (1974). *Families and family therapy.* Cambridge, MA: Harvard University Press.

Oropeza, B. A., Clark, F., Fitzgibbon, M., & Baron, A. (1991). Managing mental health crises of foreign college students. *Journal of Counseling and Development, 69,* 280–283.

Paniagua, F. A. (1994). *Assessing and treating culturally diverse clients: A practical guide.* Newbury Park, CA: Sage.

Pedersen, P. (1987). Ten frequent assumptions of cultural bias in counseling. *Journal of Multicultural Counseling and Development, 15,* 16–24.

Pedersen, P. (Ed.). (1998). *Multiculturalism as a fourth force.* New York: Brunner/Mazel.

Ponterotto, J. G., & Pedersen, P. B. (1993). *Preventing prejudice: A guide for counselors and educators.* Newbury Park, CA: Sage.

Postrel, V. (1998). *The future and its enemies: The growing conflict over creativity, enterprise, and progress.* New York: Free Press.

Raskin, N. J., & Rogers, C. R. (1995). Person-centered therapy. In R. J. Corsini & D. Wedding (Eds.), *Current psychotherapies* (5th ed.). Itasca, IL: F. E. Peacock.

Ridley, C. R. (1995). *Overcoming unintentional racism in counseling and therapy: A practitioner's guide to intentional intervention.* Newbury Park, CA: Sage.

Ridley, C. R., Li, L. C., & Hill, C. L. (1998). Multicultural assessment: Reexamination, reconceptualization, and practical applications. *The Counseling Psychologist, 26*(6), 827–910.

Robinson, T. L., & Ginter, E. J. (Eds.). (1999). Racism: Healing its effects. (Special issue). *Journal of Counseling and Development, 77*(1), 3–108.

Rogers, C. R. (1977). *Carl Rogers on personal power: Inner strength and its revolutionary impact.* New York: Delacorte.

Shelby, J. S., & Tredinnick, M. G. (1995). Crisis intervention with survivors of natural disaster: Lessons from Hurricane Andrew. *Journal of Counseling and Development, 73,* 491–497.

Strickler, M., & Bonnefil, M. (1974). Crisis intervention and social casework: Similarities and differences in problem solving. *Clinical Social Work Journal, 2,* 36–44.

Sue, D. W. (1992, Winter). The challenge of multiculturalism: The road less traveled. *American Counselor, 1,* 6–14.

Sue, D. W. (1999a, August). *Multicultural competencies in the profession of psychology.* Symposium address delivered at the 107th Annual Convention of the American Psychological Association, Boston.

Sue, D. W. (1999b, August). *Surviving monoculturalism and racism: A personal journey.* Division 45 Presidential Address delivered at the 107th Annual Convention of the American Psychological Association, Boston.

Thompson, C. E., & Neville, H. A. (1999). Racism, mental health, and mental health practice. *The Counseling Psychologist, 27,* 155–223.

Thorne, F. C. (1973). Eclectic psychotherapy. In R. Corsini (Ed.), *Current psychotherapies* (pp. 445–486). Itasca, IL: F. E. Peacock.

Basic Crisis Intervention Skills

INTRODUCTION

The purpose of this chapter is to provide a general overview of crisis intervention from a practitioner's standpoint. To that end we present and fully describe an applied crisis intervention model. We present the Triage Assessment System as a rapid but systematic technique for the crisis worker's use in adjudicating the severity of a client's presenting crisis situation and gaining some sense of direction in helping the client cope with the dilemma. We augment the model by discussing fundamental skills and intervention concepts. We illustrate many of the skills and concepts with dialogues between client and worker. Finally, we share some thoughts on using referrals, give some suggestions regarding counseling difficult clients, and provide a laboratory exercise.

This chapter is a prerequisite for succeeding chapters, and we urge you to consider this foundation material carefully. Read, think, and react. Examine the examples of the techniques carefully. Discuss our responses and formulate your own. Practice the laboratory exercises. To obtain the necessary skills to become a successful crisis worker, you will need to learn some new practices in how you make assessments and deal with people in volatile situations. What we propose in this chapter will not make you perfect, but it will give you, with practice, some proven methods and abilities as a starting point. We have never—repeat, never—seen a consistently successful crisis interventionist who did not practice what we are about to preach to you. If you can learn the techniques in this chapter, you should find them adaptable to any crisis situation.

THE SIX-STEP MODEL OF CRISIS INTERVENTION

Even though human crises are never simple, we have found that it is desirable for the crisis worker to have a relatively straightforward and efficient model of intervention. The six steps described here and summarized in Figure 2.1 (Gilliland, 1982) can be used as such a model. This six-step model is the hub around which the crisis intervention strategies in this book revolve, and the steps are designed to operate as an integrated problem-solving process. The six steps of our model have been used by both professional counselors and lay workers in helping clients with many different kinds of crises.

ASSESSING:

Overarching, continuous, and dynamically ongoing throughout the crisis; evaluating the client's present and past situational crises in terms of the client's ability to cope, personal threat, mobility or immobility, and making a judgment regarding type of action needed by the crisis worker. (See crisis worker's action continuum, below.)

Listening →

Acting →

LISTENING: Attending, observing, understanding, and responding with empathy, genuineness, respect, acceptance, nonjudgment, and caring.

1. *Define the problem.* Explore and define the problem from the client's point of view. Use active listening, including open-ended questions. Attend to both verbal and nonverbal messages of the client.

2. *Ensure client safety.* Assess lethality, criticality, immobility, or seriousness of threat to the client's physical and psychological safety. Assess both the client's internal events and the situation surrounding the client, and, if necessary, ensure that the client is made aware of alternatives to impulsive, self-destructive actions.

3. *Provide support. Communicate* to the client that the crisis worker is a valid support person. Demonstrate (by words, voice, and body language) a caring, positive, nonpossessive, nonjudgmental, acceptant, personal involvement with the client.

ACTING: Becoming involved in the intervention at a nondirective, collaborative, or directive level, according to the assessed needs of the client and the availability of environmental supports.

4. *Examine alternatives.* Assist client in exploring the choices he or she has available to him or her now. Facilitate a search for immediate situational supports, coping mechanisms, and positive thinking.

5. *Make plans.* Assist client in developing a realistic short-term plan that identifies additional resources and provides coping mechanisms—definite action steps that the client can own and comprehend.

6. *Obtain commitment.* Help client commit himself or herself to definite, positive action steps that the client can own and realistically accomplish or accept.

Crisis Worker's Action Continuum

Crisis worker is nondirective   Crisis worker is collaborative   Crisis worker is directive

(Threshold varies from client to client)   (Threshold varies from client to client)

Client is mobile   Client is partially mobile   Client is immobile

The crisis worker's level of action/involvement may be anywhere on the continuum according to a valid and realistic assessment of the client's level of mobility/immobility.

FIGURE 2.1 The Six-Step Model of Crisis Intervention

ASSESSING

Assessing is a pervasive strategy throughout crisis intervention. This action-oriented, situation-based method of crisis intervention is our preferred method for systematically applying several worker-initiated skills. The process of applying these skills is fluid rather than mechanistic. The entire six-step process is carried out under an umbrella of assessment by the crisis worker. The first three steps of (1) defining the problem, (2) ensuring client safety, and (3) providing support are more listening activities than they are actions. The final three steps of (4) examining alternatives, (5) making plans, and (6) obtaining commitment to positive action are largely action behaviors on the part of the worker, even though listening is always present along with assessment as an overarching theme.

LISTENING

Steps 1, 2, and 3 are essentially listening activities.

Step 1: Defining the Problem

The first step in crisis intervention is to define and understand the problem from the client's point of view. Unless the worker perceives the crisis situation as the client perceives it, all the intervention strategies and procedures the helper might use may miss the mark and be of no value to the client. Throughout the crisis intervention process, workers direct their listening and acting skills according to the dictates of the definition. As an aid to defining crisis problems, we recommend that intervention sessions begin with crisis workers practicing what we call the *core listening skills:* empathy, genuineness, and acceptance or positive regard (Cormier & Cormier, 1991, pp. 21–39). These skills and the exercises described later in this chapter should greatly enhance your competency in this first step of crisis intervention.

Step 2: Ensuring Client Safety

It is imperative that crisis workers continually keep client safety at the forefront of all crisis intervention procedures. We define client safety simply as minimizing the physical and psychological danger to self and others. Although we position client safety in the second step, we apply this step in a fluid way, meaning that safety is a primary consideration throughout crisis intervention. The dimension of safety receives equal consideration in the worker's assessing, listening, and acting strategies. In this book and pervading our teaching and practice of crisis intervention, client safety is present, whether we overtly state it or not. We encourage students and crisis workers to make the safety step a natural part of their thinking and behaving.

Step 3: Providing Support

The third step in crisis intervention emphasizes communicating to the client that the worker is a person who cares about the client. Workers cannot assume that a client experiences feeling valued, prized, or cared for. The support step provides an opportunity for the worker to assure the client that "here is one person who really cares about you."

In Step 3, the person providing the support is the worker. This means that workers must be able to accept, in an unconditional and positive way, all their clients, whether the clients can reciprocate or not. The worker who can truly provide support for clients in crisis is able to accept and value the person no one else is willing to accept and to prize the client no one else prizes.

ACTING

Steps 4, 5, and 6 essentially involve acting strategies.

Step 4: Examining Alternatives

Step 4 in crisis intervention addresses an area that both clients and workers often neglect—exploring a wide array of appropriate choices available to the client. In their immobile state, clients often do not adequately examine their best options. Some clients in crisis actually believe there are no options.

In the fourth step, effective workers help clients recognize that many alternatives are available and that some choices are better than others. It may help for workers to realize that there are different ways to think about alternatives: (1) *situational supports,* which may represent excellent sources of help, are people known to the client in the present or past who might care about what happens to the client; (2) *coping mechanisms* are actions, behaviors, or environmental resources the client might use to help get through the present crisis; and (3) *positive and constructive thinking patterns* on the part of the client are ways of thinking that might substantially alter the client's view of the problem and lessen the client's level of stress and anxiety. Crisis workers who can objectively examine a number of alternatives from these three perspectives can be of great assistance to clients who are feeling hopelessly stuck and lacking in choices.

The effective crisis worker may think about an infinite number of alternatives pertaining to the client's crisis but discuss only a few of them with the client. Clients experiencing crisis do not need a lot of choices; they need appropriate choices that are realistic for their situation.

Step 5: Making Plans

The fifth step in crisis intervention, making plans, flows logically and directly from Step 4. Much of the material throughout this book focuses either directly or indirectly on the crisis worker's involvement with clients in planning action steps that have a good chance of restoring the clients' emotional equilibrium. A plan should (1) identify additional persons, groups, and other referral resources that can be contacted for immediate support, and (2) provide coping mechanisms—something concrete and positive for the client to do now, definite action steps that the client can own and comprehend. The plan should focus on systematic problem solving for the client and be realistic in terms of the client's coping ability. It may include collaboration between the client and crisis worker—for example, facilitation of relaxation techniques.

It is important that planning be done in collaboration with clients so that clients feel a sense of ownership of the plan. We have seen too many instances where helpers decided for clients what they should do. The critical element in developing a plan is that clients do not feel robbed of their power, independence, and self-respect. Some clients may not object when a helper decides for them what they should do. At the moment, such clients may be so engrossed in their crisis that it really does not matter to them. They may even believe that a plan imposed on them is what they should have. It is often easy to manipulate emotionally distraught clients to accept a plan benevolently imposed on them. The central issues in planning are clients' *control* and *autonomy*. The reasons for clients to carry out plans are to restore their sense of control and to ensure that they do not become dependent on support persons such as the worker.

Step 6: Obtaining Commitment

The sixth step, obtaining commitment, flows directly from Step 5, and the issues of control and autonomy apply equally to the process of obtaining an appropriate commitment. If the planning step is effectively done, the commitment step is apt to be easy. Many times the commitment step is brief and simple, consisting of asking the client to verbally summarize the plan: "Now that we have gone over what you plan to do next time you start to get angry with her, summarize for me what actions you will take to ensure that you do not lose your temper and what you will do to make sure you keep it from escalating into another crisis." During this step, the crisis worker demonstrates responsibility in carrying out his or her part of the plan if a collaboration has been agreed on. The objective in Step 6 is to enable the client to commit to taking one or more definite, positive, intentional action steps designed to move that person toward restoring precrisis equilibrium.

During the sixth step the crisis worker does not forget about all the other helping steps and skills such as assessing, ensuring safety, and providing support. The worker is careful to obtain an honest, direct, and appropriate commitment from the client before terminating the crisis intervention session. Later, the worker follows up on the client's progress and makes necessary and appropriate reports. Such follow-up and reporting are performed in an empathic, ethical, and supportive manner. The core listening skills are as important to the commitment step as they are to the problem definition or any other step.

ASSESSMENT IN CRISIS INTERVENTION
Assessing Client Functioning

Because many of the assessments in crisis situations occur spontaneously, subjectively, and interactively in the heat of the moment, we are not dealing here with formal techniques such as *DSM-IV* diagnostic criteria or the use of assessment instruments that are typically used in ongoing clinical evaluations. Our six-step model of crisis intervention emphasizes an immediacy mode of actively, assertively, intentionally, and continuously assessing, listening, and acting to systematically help the client regain as much of the precrisis equilibrium, mobility, and autonomy as possible. Two of those terms, *equilibrium* and *mobility,* and their antonyms, *disequilibrium* and *immobility,* are commonly used by crisis workers to identify client states of being and coping. Because we will be using these terms often, we would like to define them first by their dictionary meaning and then give a common analogy so their meaning becomes thoroughly understood.

Equilibrium. A state of mental or emotional stability, balance, or poise in the organism.

Disequilibrium. Lack or destruction of emotional stability, balance, or poise in the organism.

Mobility. A state of physical being whereby the person can autonomously change or cope in response to different moods, feelings, emotions, needs, conditions, influences; being flexible or adaptable to the physical and social world.

Immobility. A state of physical being whereby the person is not immediately capable of autonomously changing or coping in response to different moods, feelings, emotions, needs, conditions, influences; unable to adapt to the immediate physical and social world.

A healthy person is in a state of approximate equilibrium, like a motorist driving, with some starts and stops, down the road of life—in both the short and the long haul. The person may hit some potholes but does not break any axles. Aside from needing an occasional tune-up, the person remains more or less equal to the task of making the drive. In contrast, the person in crisis, whether it be acute or chronic, is experiencing serious difficulty in steering and successfully navigating life's highway. The individual is at least temporarily out of control, unable to command personal resources or those of others in order to stay on safe psychological pavement.

A healthy person is capable of negotiating hills, curves, ice, fog, stray animals, wrecks, and most other obstacles that impede progress. No matter what roadblocks may appear, such a person adapts to changing conditions, applying brakes, putting on fog lights, and estimating passing time. This person may have fender-benders from time to time but avoids head-on collisions. The person in a dysfunctional state of equilibrium and mobility has failed to pass inspection. Careening down hills and around dangerous curves, knowing the brakes have failed, the person is frozen with panic and despair and has little hope of handling the perilous situation. The result is that the person has become a victim of the situation, has forgotten all about emergency brakes, downshifting, or even easing the car into guard railings. He or she flies headlong into catastrophe and watches transfixed as it happens.

Our analogy of equilibrium and mobility applies to most crisis situations. Thus, it becomes every crisis worker's job to figuratively get the client back into the driver's seat of the psychological vehicle. As we shall demonstrate, sometimes this means the client must leave the driving to us, sometimes sitting alongside and pointing out the rules of the road, and sometimes just pretty much going along for the ride!

Assessing in Crisis Intervention

Overarching the six-step model is assessment. Such assessment is not a formal procedure such as that employed in long-term clinical work. Rather, it is a pervasive, intentional, and continuous activity of the crisis worker. Assessment is critically important because it enables the worker to determine (1) the severity of the crisis; (2) the client's current emotional status—the client's level of emotional mobility or immobility; (3) the alternatives, coping mechanisms, support systems, and other resources available to the client; and (4) the client's level of lethality (danger to self and others).

Assessing the Severity of Crisis

It is important for the crisis worker to evaluate the crisis severity as quickly as possible during the initial contact with the client. Crisis workers generally do not have time to perform complete diagnostic work-ups or obtain in-depth client histories. Therefore, we recommend a rapid assessment procedure, the Triage Assessment System (Myer et al., 1991), as a quick and efficient way of obtaining information relevant to the specific crisis situation. The triage system enables the worker to gauge the severity of the client's current functioning across affective, behavioral, and cognitive domains. The degree of severity of the crisis may affect the client's mobility, which in turn gives the worker a basis for judging how directive to be. The length of time the client has been in the present crisis will determine how much time the worker has in which to safely defuse the crisis. Crisis is time limited; that is, most acute crises persist only a matter of days before some change—for better or worse—occurs. The severity of the crisis is assessed from the client's subjective viewpoint and from the worker's objective viewpoint. Objective assessment is based on an appraisal of the client's functioning in three areas that we refer to as the ABCs of assessment: *affective* (feeling or emotional tone), *behavioral* (action or psychomotor activity) and *cognitive* (thinking patterns).

Affective State.   The crisis worker who is sensitive to the client's emotional tone can mentally record affective reactions to assess the seriousness of the crisis as well as discern ways to help the client. Abnormal or impaired affect is often the first sign that the client is in a state of disequilibrium. The client may be overemotional and out of control or severely withdrawn and detached. Often the worker can assist the client to regain control and mobility by helping that person express feelings in appropriate and realistic ways. Some questions the worker may address are, Do the client's affective responses indicate that the client is denying the situation or attempting to avoid involvement in it? Is the emotional response normal or congruent with the situational crisis? To what extent, if any, is the client's emotional state driven, exacerbated, impacted, or otherwise influenced by other people? Do people typically show this kind of affect in situations such as this? Certainly, to ignore an unusual or unhealthy display of affect would be a mistake on the part of the worker.

Behavioral Functioning.   The crisis worker focuses much attention on *doing, acting out, taking active steps, behaving,* or any number of other psychomotor activities. In crisis intervention we believe that the quickest (and often the best) way to get the client to become mobile is to facilitate positive actions that the client can take at once. People who successfully cope with crisis and later evaluate their experiences report that the most helpful alternative during a crisis is to engage in some concrete and immediate activity. However, it is important for the worker to remember that it may be very difficult for immobilized people to take independent and autonomous action even though that is what they need to do most. These are appropriate questions that the worker might ask the client to get the client to take constructive action: "In cases like this in the past, what actions did you take that helped you get back in control? What would you have to do now to get back on top of the situation? Is there anyone who, if you contacted them right now, would be supportive to you in this crisis?" The fundamental problem in immobility is loss of control. Once the client becomes involved in doing something concrete, which is a step in a positive direction, an element of control is restored, a degree of mobility is provided, and the climate for forward movement is established.

Cognitive State.   The worker's assessment of the client's thinking patterns may provide answers to several important questions: How realistic and consistent is the client's thinking about the crisis? To what extent, if any, does the client appear to be rationalizing, exaggerating, or believing part-truths, to exacerbate the crisis? How long has the client been engaged in crisis thinking? How open does the client seem to be toward changing beliefs about the crisis situation? The answers to these and other questions about the client's thought patterns may provide some directions for crisis intervention. The worker may use such cognitive assessment to determine how to help the client refute irrational or confused thinking and develop more positive and productive thought patterns about the crisis and about workable alternatives.

THE TRIAGE ASSESSMENT SYSTEM

Because rapid and adequate assessment of a client in crisis is one of the most critical components of intervention (Hersh, 1985), we have given assessment a preeminent place in our crisis intervention model, as an overarching and ongoing process. Constant and rapid assessment of the client's state of equilibrium dictates what the interventionist will do in the next seconds and minutes as the crisis unfolds (Aguilera, 1997). Unhappily, many assessment devices that can give the human services worker an adequate perspective on the client's problem are unwieldy and time consuming, and mandate that the client be enough in control to complete the assessment process or be physically present while undergoing evaluation. Although we might gain a great deal of helpful information with an extensive intake form, a background interview, or an in-depth personality test, events often occur so quickly that these are unaffordable and unrealistic luxuries.

The Value of Speed, Simplicity, Efficiency, Reliability, and Validity.   What the interventionist needs in a crisis situation is a fast, efficient way of obtaining a real-time estimate of what is occurring with a client. Such a tool should also be simple enough that a worker who may have only rudimentary assessment skills can use the device in a reliable and valid manner. Myer, Williams, Ottens, and Schmidt (1991, 1992) formulated a three-dimensional crisis assessment model (see Figure 2.2) and rating scale (see Figure 2.3), the Triage Assessment Form (TAF), an instrument we believe holds great promise in performing rapid and valid assessment of a client in crisis. For our own use as interventionists, the TAF meets the five composite criteria cited earlier better than anything else we have found. A successful triage assessment instrument in crisis intervention should be able to be performed rapidly by a broad cross-section of crisis workers who have had little if any training in standardized testing or assessment procedures.

To determine if the TAF was a reliable instrument that would meet the foregoing criteria, Watters (1997) conducted a two-hour training session on understanding and use of the TAF, with five different groups comprised of police officer trainees, school counselors, agency workers, mental health workers, and counselors-in-training. Before training none of the groups had any familiarity with the TAF. She compared triage ratings of

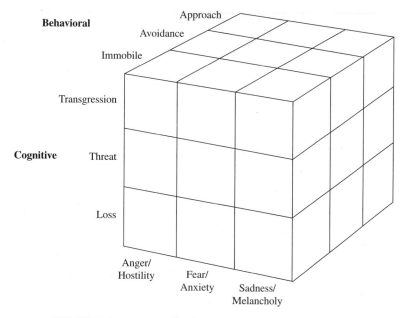

FIGURE 2.2   Three-Dimensional Crisis Assessment Model

SOURCE: R. A. Myer, R. C. Williams, A. J. Ottens, and A. E. Schmidt, 1991, *Three-Dimensional Crisis Assessment Model* (DeKalb, IL: Northern Illinois University).

these groups on three crisis scenarios (Minimal Impairment, Moderate Impairment, and
Severe Impairment) with expert ratings. She found that police officer trainees tended to
overrate and label the Moderate Impairment scenario as Severe Impairment, while mental health workers underrated Moderate Impairment (probably because they were more
seasoned and would have had to see and hear far more problematic behavior before rating it Moderate). Also mental health workers believed that the Moderate scenario could
be handled easily. Overall, however, the ratings of all groups were reliable and comparable with the ratings of the experts, and were particularly so in the Minimal Impairment and Severe Impairment range. Watters concluded that the TAF was indeed a reliable instrument for fast and efficient assessment in regard to the amount of affective,
behavioral, and cognitive dysfunction a client was experiencing.

Although simple to use, the TAF is also elegant in that it cuts across affective, behavioral, and cognitive dimensions of the client, compartmentalizes each dimension as to its
typical response mode, and assigns numeric values to these modes that allow the worker
to determine the client's current level of functioning. These three severity scales represent mechanisms for operationally assigning numeric values to the crisis worker's action
continuum in Figure 2.1. The numeric ratings provide an efficient and tangible guide to
both the degree and the kind of intervention the worker needs to make in most crisis situations. The rationale and examples for each of the scales are as follows.

The Affective Severity Scale.   No crisis situation that we know of has positive emotions attached to it. Crow (1977) metaphorically names the usual emotional qualities
found in a crisis as yellow (anxiety), red (anger), or black (depression). Invariably, these

TRIAGE ASSESSMENT FORM: CRISIS INTERVENTION

©R.A. Myer, R.C. Williams, A.J. Ottens, & A.E. Schmidt

CRISIS EVENT:

Identify and describe briefly the crisis situation: _____

_____

_____

AFFECTIVE DOMAIN

Identify and describe briefly the affect that is present. (If more than one affect is experienced, rate with #1 being primary, #2 secondary, #3 tertiary.)

ANGER/HOSTILITY: _____

_____

ANXIETY/FEAR: _____

_____

SADNESS/MELANCHOLY: _____

_____

Affective Severity Scale

Circle the number that most closely corresponds with client's reaction to crisis.

1	2	3	4	5	6	7	8	9	10
No Impairment	Minimal Impairment		Low Impairment		Moderate Impairment		Marked Impairment		Severe Impairment
Stable mood with normal variation or affect appropriate to daily functioning.	Affect appropriate to situation. Brief periods during which negative mood is experienced slightly more intensely than situation warrants. Emotions are substantially under client control.		Affect appropriate to situation but increasingly longer periods during which negative mood is experienced slightly more intensely than situation warrants. Client perceives emotions as being substantially under control.		Affect may be incongruent with situation. Extended periods of intense negative moods. Mood is experienced noticeably more intensely than situation warrants. Lability of affect my be present. Effort required to control emotions.		Negative affect experienced at markedly higher level than situation warrants. Affects my be obviously incongruent with situation. Mood swings, if occurring, are pronounced. Onset of negative moods are perceived by client as not being under volitional control.		Decompensation or depersonalization evident.

FIGURE 2.3   Triage Assessment Form: Crisis Intervention

SOURCE: R. A. Myer, R. C. Williams, A. J. Ottens, and A. E. Schmidt, 1991, unpublished manuscript (Northern Illinois University, DeKalb, Illinois).

negative emotions appear singularly or in combination with each other when a crisis is present. In their model, Myer and associates have replaced the term *depression*, because of its diagnostic implications, with *sadness/melancholy*. When any of these core negative emotions become all pervasive such that the client is consumed by them, the potential for these emotions to motivate destructive behavior becomes extremely high.

The Behavioral Severity Scale.   Although we depict a client in crisis as more or less behaviorally immobile, immobility can take three different forms. Crow (1977) proposes that behavior in a crisis approaches, avoids, or is paralyzed in the client's attempts to act. Although Crow's proposal may seem contradictory to our own on first inspection, it is

BEHAVIORAL DOMAIN

Identify and describe briefly which behavior is currently being used. (If more than one behavior is utilized, rate with #1 being primary, #2 secondary, #3 tertiary.)

APPROACH: _____

_____

_____

AVOIDANCE: _____

_____

_____

IMMOBILITY: _____

_____

_____

Behavioral Severity Scale

Circle the number that most closely corresponds with client's reaction to crisis.

1	2	3	4	5	6	7	8	9	10
No Impairment	Minimal Impairment		Low Impairment		Moderate Impairment		Marked Impairment		Severe Impairment
Coping behavior appropriate to crisis event. Client performs those tasks necessary for daily functioning.	Occasional utilization of ineffective coping behaviors. Client performs those tasks necessary for daily functioning, but does so with noticeable effort.		Occasional utilization of ineffective coping behaviors. Client neglects some tasks necessary for daily functioning, performs others with decreasing effectiveness.		Client displays coping behaviors that may be ineffective and maladaptive. Ability to perform tasks necessary for daily functioning is noticeably compromised.		Client displays coping behaviors that are likely to exacerbate crisis situation. Ability to perform tasks necessary for daily functioning is markedly absent.		Behavior is erratic, unpredictable. Client's behaviors are harmful to self and/or others.

(continued on next page)

FIGURE 2.3   Triage Assessment Form: Crisis Intervention *(continued)*

not. A client may seem highly motivated, but is either acting out maladaptively toward a specific target or in a random, non–goal-directed manner with no specific target discernible. Oppositionally, the client may attempt to flee the noxious event by the fastest means possible even though the immediate threat to the client's well-being is gone. Although in many instances taking stock of the situation before acting is an excellent plan, clients transfixed in the face of immediate danger need to flee or fight. Although a great deal of energy may be expended and the client may look focused, once the crisis goes beyond the client's capacity to cope in a meaningful and purposeful manner, we would propose that the client is immobilized, stuck in the particular approach, avoidance, or static behavior in a continuous loop no matter how proactive he or she may seem to be. At the severe impairment end of the continuum, maladaptive behavior often takes on a lethal aspect either in regard to the client or others.

The Cognitive Severity Scale.   Ellis has written at length about the part that thinking plays in emotions and behavior (Ellis, 1971; Ellis & Abrahms, 1978; Ellis & Grieger, 1977; Ellis & Harper, 1979). In a crisis situation, the client's cognitive processes typically perceive the event in terms of transgression, threat, loss, or any combination of the three. These "hot" cognitions, as Dryden (1984) calls them, can take on catastrophic dimensions at the extreme end of the continuum. Such highly focused irrational thinking can cause the client to obsess on the crisis to the extent that little, if

COGNITIVE DOMAIN

Identify if a transgression, threat, or loss has occurred in the following areas and describe briefly. (If more than one cognitive response occurs, rate with #1 being primary, #2 secondary, #3 tertiary.)

PHYSICAL (food, water, safety, shelter, etc.):
TRANSGRESSION ____ THREAT ____ LOSS ____

_____
_____
_____

PSYCHOLOGICAL (self-concept, emotional well being, identity, etc.):
TRANSGRESSION ____ THREAT ____ LOSS ____

_____
_____
_____

SOCIAL RELATIONSHIPS (family, friends, co-workers, etc.):
TRANSGRESSION ____ THREAT ____ LOSS ____

_____
_____
_____

MORAL/SPIRITUAL (personal integrity, values, belief system, etc.):
TRANSGRESSION ____ THREAT ____ LOSS ____

_____
_____
_____

Cognitive Severity Scale

Circle the number that most closely corresponds with client's reaction to crisis.

1	2	3	4	5	6	7	8	9	10
No Impairment	Minimal Impairment		Low Impairment		Moderate Impairment		Marked Impairment		Severe Impairment
Concentration intact, Client displays normal problem-solving and decision-making abilities. Client's perception and interpretation of crisis event match with reality of situation.	Client's thought may drift to crisis event but focus of thoughts is under volitional control. Client's problem-solving and decision-making abilities minimally affected. Client's perception and interpretation of crisis event substantially match with reality of situation.		Occasional disturbance of concentration. Client perceives diminished control over thoughts of crisis event. Client experiences recurrent difficulties with problem-solving and decision-making abilities. Client's perception and interpretation of crisis event may differ in some respects with reality of situation.		Frequent disturbance of concentration. Intrusive thoughts of crisis event with limited control. Problem solving and decision-making abilities adversely affect by obsessiveness, self-doubt, confusion. Client's perception and interpretation of crisis event may differ noticeably with reality of situation.		Client plagued by intrusiveness of thought regarding crisis event. The appropriateness of client's problem-solving and decision-making abilities likely adversely affected by obsessiveness, self-doubt, confusion. Client's perception and interpretation of crisis event may differ substantially with reality of situation.		Gross inability to concentrate on anything except crisis event. Client so afflicted by obsessiveness, self-doubt, confusion that problem-solving and decision-making abilities have "shut down." Client's perception and interpretation of crisis event may differ so substantially from reality of situation as to constitute threat to client's welfare.

DOMAIN SEVERITY SCALE SUMMARY

Affective ____

Cognitive ____

Behavioral ____

Total ____

FIGURE 2.3 Triage Assessment Form: Crisis Intervention *(continued)*

g can occur within or beyond the boundaries of the crisis event. The sumes all the client's psychic energy as the client attempts to integrate it belief system. The client may generate maladaptive cognitions about nterpersonal, or environmental stimuli. Transgression, threat, or loss may be perceived in relation to physical needs such as food, shelter, and safety; psychological needs such as self-concept, emotional stability, and identity; relationship needs such as family, friends, co-workers, and community support; and moral and spiritual needs such as integrity and values. To differentiate between transgression, threat, and loss, think of these dimensions in terms of time. *Transgression* is the cognition that something bad is happening in the present moment, *threat* is the cognition that something bad will occur, and *loss* is the cognition that something bad has occurred. When cognitions of the crisis move to the severe impairment end of the continuum, the perception of the event may be so severe as to put the client or others at physical risk. Sometimes the client's thinking moves from "It's a pain in the neck that this is happening, but I'll get over it" to "It's absolutely intolerable, I will not stand for this, and I'll never get over it." This kind of shift, from cool to hot cognitions (Dryden, 1984) is setting the client up to make some bad decisions. Such decisions most probably will result in even worse behavioral consequences for the client and others.

Comparison with Precrisis Functioning.   Although it may not always be possible, the worker should seek to assess the client's precrisis functioning in the same manner. Comparing precrisis ratings with current ratings lets the worker gauge the degree of deviation from the client's typical affective, behavioral, and cognitive operating levels. The worker can then tell how atypical the client's functioning is, whether there has been a radical shift in that functioning, and whether that functioning is transitory or chronic. For example, a very different counseling approach would be used with a chronic schizophrenic suffering auditory hallucinations as compared to an individual experiencing similar hallucinations from prescription medicine. Such an assessment can be made in one or two questions without having to ferret out a great deal of background information. In summary, the TAF provides infinite three-dimensional combinations of assessment as to degree of impairment the crisis is causing, targets specific areas of functioning, and lets the crisis worker evaluate the client quickly and then construct specific interventions aimed directly at areas of greatest immediate concern. The TAF is quick, efficient, easy to learn, and from our own initial research with beginning crisis workers, highly reliable.

PSYCHOBIOLOGICAL ASSESSMENT

Although psychobiological assessment for psychopathology is beyond the scope of this book and most crisis situations both in terms of immediacy of assessment and the assessment skills required of most human services workers, mounting evidence indicates that the neurotransmitters play an exceedingly important role in the affective, behavioral, and cognitive functioning of individuals (Armsworth & Holaday, 1993; Kolb & Whishaw, 1990; van der Kolk, 1996a).

For at least three reasons, human psychobiology can be an important consideration in crisis intervention. First, evidence exists that when people are involved in traumatic events, dramatic changes occur in discharge of neurotransmitters, such as endorphins, and in the central and peripheral sympathetic nervous systems and the hypothalamic-pituitary-adrenocortical axis. These neurological changes may become residual and long-term and have subtle and degrading effects on emotions, acting, and thinking (Burgess-Watson, Hoffman, & Wilson, 1988; van der Kolk, 1996b).

Second, research indicates that abnormal changes in neurotransmitters such as dopamine, norepinephrine, and serotonin are involved in mental disorders that range from schizophrenia (Crow & Johnstone, 1987) to depression (Healy, 1987). Psychotropic drugs are routinely used for a host of mental disorders to counteract such neurological changes. A common problem faced by human services workers is the deranged or violent client who has gone off medication because of its unpleasant side effects or inability to remember when to take it (Ammar & Burdin, 1991).

Third, both legal and illegal drugs have a major effect on mental health. Although the way illegal drugs change brain chemistry and behavior has gained wide attention, legal drugs may promote adverse psychological side effects in just as dramatic a manner. In particular, combinations of nonpsychotropic drugs are routinely given to combat several degenerative diseases in the elderly. At times, these drugs may have interactive effects that generate unanticipated psychological disturbances. One has to read no further than the over-the-counter books on prescribed drugs to obtain a rather frightening understanding of the psychological side effects prescription drugs can cause.

Therefore, the human services worker should attempt to assess prior trauma, psychopathology, and use, misuse, or abuse of legal and illegal drugs in an effort to determine whether they correlate with the current problem. "Talking" therapies do little good when neurobiological substrates are involved. If the human services worker has reason to suspect any of the foregoing problems, an immediate referral should be made for a neurological/drug evaluation.

ASSESSING THE CLIENT'S CURRENT EMOTIONAL FUNCTIONING

Two major factors in assessing the client's emotional stability are the *duration* of the crisis and the *degree* of emotional stamina or coping at the client's disposal at the moment. The duration factor concerns the time frame of the crisis. Is it a one-time crisis? Is it recurring? Has it been plaguing the client for a long time? A one-time, relatively short-duration crisis is what we call *acute* or *situational.* We would label a long-term pattern of recurring crisis as *chronic, long-term,* or *transcrisis.* The degree factor concerns the client's current reservoir of emotional coping stamina. Whereas during normal periods of the client's life the coping reservoir is relatively full, during crisis the client's reservoir is relatively empty. Assessing the degree factor, then, involves the crisis worker's determination of how much emotional coping strength is left in the client's reservoir. Has the client run out of gas, or can the client make it over a small hill?

Client's Current Acute or Chronic State

In assessing the crisis client's emotional functioning, it is important that the crisis worker determine whether the client is a normal person who is in a *one-time* situational crisis or a person with a *chronic,* crisis-oriented life history. The one-time crisis is assessed and treated quite differently from the chronic crisis. The one-time crisis client usually requires direct intervention to facilitate getting over the one event or situation that precipitated the crisis. Having reached a state of precrisis equilibrium, the client can usually draw on normal coping mechanisms and support people and manage independently. The chronic crisis client usually requires a greater length of time in counseling. That individual typically needs the help of a crisis worker in examining adequate coping mechanisms, finding support people, rediscovering strategies that worked during previous crises, generating new coping strategies, and gaining affirmation and encouragement from the worker and others as sources of strength by which to move beyond the present crisis. The chronic case frequently requires referral for long-term professional help.

Client's Reservoir of Emotional Strength

The client who totally lacks emotional strength needs more direct response from the crisis worker than the client who retains a good deal of emotional strength. In order to formulate an objective judgment, the worker must be very sensitive to the client's emotional functioning. A feeling of hopelessness or helplessness is a clue to a low reservoir of emotional strength. In some cases, the assessment can be enhanced by asking open-ended questions for the specific purpose of measuring that reservoir. Typically, if the reservoir is low, the client will have a distorted view of the past and present and will not be able to envision a future. Such questions can reveal the *degree* of emotional stamina remaining: "Picture yourself after the current crisis has been solved. Tell me what you're seeing yourself doing and how you're feeling. How do you wish you were feeling? How were you feeling about this before the crisis got so bad? Where do you see yourself headed with this problem?" The answers may be of great value to the worker in establishing the degree of emotional control retained by the client. In general, the lower the reservoir of emotional strength, the less the client can get hold of the future. The client with an empty reservoir might respond with a blank stare or by saying something like "There are no choices" or "No, I can't see anything. The future is blank. I can see no future." The worker's assessment of the client's current degree of emotional strength will have definite implications for the strategies and level of action the worker will employ during the remainder of the counseling.

Strategies for Assessing Emotional Status

The crisis worker who assesses the client's total emotional status may look at a wide array of factors that affect both the duration (chronic versus acute) and the degree (reservoir of strength) of emotional stability. Some factors to be considered are the client's age, educational level, family situation, marital status, vocational maturity and job stability, financial stability and obligations, drug and/or alcohol use, legal history (arrests, convictions, probations), social background, level of intelligence, lifestyle, religious orientation, ability to sustain close personal relationships, tolerance for ambiguity, physical health, medical history, and past history of dealing with crises. A candid look at such factors helps the crisis worker decide whether the client will require quick referral (for medical treatment or examination), brief counseling, long-term therapy, or referral to a specific agency.

Every client's profile of emotional stability can be expected to be different. Ordinarily, no one factor alone can be used to conclude that the client's reservoir of emotional coping ability is empty. However, some patterns often can be pieced together to form a general picture. A person in middle age who has experienced many disappointments related to undereducation would be viewed differently from a young person who has experienced a first career disappointment. A person who has experienced many serious medical problems and hospital stays would feel differently from a person who is having a first encounter with a medical problem.

Carefully phrased open-ended questions are a valuable assessment tool for judging the client's emotional background and status and for involving the client in the ongoing assessment in a way that is facilitative for the client. For example, the worker might ask, "How is your current treatment different from the treatments you've received in the past?" "How has your increased level of drinking affected your feelings toward your wife and children?" "What could you do to make yourself feel better?" Open-ended questions can be worded in an infinite number of ways. (See the section on open-ended questions in the latter part of this chapter.)

What we have been talking about is the facilitative assessment of the individual. By "facilitative assessment," we mean that data gleaned about the client are used as a part of the ongoing helping process, not simply filed away or kept in the worker's head. The key to facilitative assessment is to focus on the client's inner emotional world—not the worker's analysis of that world.

ASSESSING ALTERNATIVES, COPING MECHANISMS, AND SUPPORT SYSTEMS

Throughout the helping process the crisis worker keeps in mind and builds a repertory of options, evaluating their appropriateness for the client. In assessing alternatives available to the client, the worker must first consider the client's viewpoint, mobility, and capability of taking advantage of the alternatives. The worker's own objective view of available alternatives is an additional dimension. Alternatives include a repository of appropriate referral resources available to the client. Even though the client may be looking for only one or two concrete action steps or options, the worker brainstorms, in collaboration with the client, to develop a list of possibilities that can be evaluated. Most will be discarded before the client can own and commit to a definite course of action. The word *own* has a special connotation in planning and committing to a course of action. "Owning" means that options are not imposed on the client by the worker. The important thing for clients is that they feel a deep and genuine commitment to their choices and that they do not depend on or merely agree to choices they believe workers have discovered for them.

The worker ponders questions such as, What actions or choices does the client have now that would restore the person to a precrisis state of autonomy? What realistic actions (coping mechanisms) can the client take? What institutional, social, vocational, or personal (people) strengths or supports are available? [Note that "support systems" refers to people!] Who would care about and be open to assisting the client? What are the financial, social, vocational, and personal impediments to client progress?

ASSESSING FOR SUICIDE/HOMICIDE POTENTIAL

Not every crisis involves the client's contemplating suicide or homicide. However, in dealing with crisis clients, workers must always explore the possibility of harm to self and others, because destructive behavior takes many forms and wears many masks. The rash of indiscriminate shootings during the late 1990s, in which people were gunned down in public places by people who were suicidal, homicidal, or both, attests to the need for crisis workers to be both wary of and competent in their appraisal of potential suicidal and homicidal clients. What may appear to the crisis worker as the main problem may camouflage the real issue: the intent of the client to take his or her life as well as someone else's life. Contrary to popular belief, most suicidal and homicidal clients emit definite clues and believe they are calling out for help or signaling warnings. However, even the client's closest friends may ignore those clues and do nothing about them. For that reason, we believe that every crisis problem should be assessed as to its potential for suicide and homicide. The most important aspect of suicidal/homicidal evaluation is the crisis evaluator's realization that suicide and homicide are always possible in all types of clients. A more detailed coverage of assessing for suicide/homicide potential can be found in Chapter 5.

SUMMARY OF ASSESSMENT

A major difference between crisis intervention and other human services endeavors such as counseling, social work, and psychotherapy is that the crisis worker generally does not have time to gather or analyze all the background and other assessment data that might normally be available under less stressful conditions. A key component of a highly functioning crisis worker is the ability to take the data available and make some meaningful sense out of it. This may be somewhat unsettling to those human services workers who are accustomed to having complete social and psychological workups available to them before they proceed with intervention. However, the ability to quickly evaluate the degree of client disequilibrium and immobility—and to be flexible enough to change your evaluation as changing conditions warrant—is a priority skill that students should seek to cultivate.

From onset to resolution of crisis, assessment is a central, continuous process. The crisis worker must not assume that because the crisis appears on the surface to have been resolved, assessment is no longer needed. The balance sheet of assessing the client's crisis in terms of severity, current emotional status, alternatives, situational supports, coping mechanisms, resources, and level of lethality is never complete until the client has achieved his or her precrisis level of mobility, equilibrium, and autonomy. Only then are the psychological debts of the client reconciled.

The resumption of precrisis equilibrium does not imply that the client needs no developmental or long-term therapy or medical treatment. It does mean that the worker's job is done, and the acute phase of the crisis is over.

LISTENING IN CRISIS INTERVENTION

Crisis intervention is a pragmatic system of counseling and assisting individuals that abbreviates the therapeutic schedule and condenses strategies. Crisis intervention is not a long, drawn-out procedure that deals with either restorative or developmental issues. This compression of time and strategies often requires the crisis worker to be more proactive and assertive than the long-term counselor or therapist. It is a procedure that may be used by both professionals and laypeople with some training. We believe that accurate and well-honed listening skills are a necessary and, indeed, sometimes sufficient, skill that all helpers must have.

For that reason, listening skills are a major component of our six-step intervention model. Our preferred conceptual model for effective listening comes from person-centered counseling (Egan, 1982, 1990; Rogers, 1977). We will present brief descriptions of selected techniques that are applicable to many kinds of helping relationships, crisis or otherwise. Excerpts from real-life clients we will call Rita, Jake, and Jean are scattered throughout the rest of this chapter to illustrate helpful as well as unhelpful strategies.

Open-Ended Questions

Often workers are frustrated by a client's lack of response and enthusiasm. Workers may make statements such as "All my clients ever do is grunt or shake their heads indicating yes or no." We can do something about getting fuller, more meaningful responses if we ask questions that are not dead ends.

Open-ended questions usually start with *what* or *how* or ask for more clarification or details. Open-ended questions encourage clients to respond with full statements and at deeper levels of meaning. Remember that open-ended questions are used to elicit from clients something about their feelings, thoughts, and behaviors. Here are some guidelines for forming open-ended questions.

1. *Request description:* "Please tell me . . . ," "Tell me about . . . ," "Show me . . . ," "In what ways does . . . ?"
2. *Focus on plans:* "What will you do . . . ?" "How will you make it happen?" "How will that help you to . . . ?"
3. *Stay away from "why" questions:* Beginners in the crisis intervention business invariably are intrigued and puzzled by the odd and bizarre things people in crisis think, feel, and do. As a result, beginners feel compelled to find out why a person thinks, feels, or does those "really crazy" things. It is our contention that "why" questions are generally poor choices for obtaining more information. Even though they may provide the client with an opening to talk more, they also make the client defend his or her actions. Notice the response of Jake, the husband of Rita, whom you will meet later in this chapter, as the crisis worker queries him about the reasons for his behavior.

   CW: Why do you continue to beat your wife?
   Jake: Hey! If she'd be a little more affectionate, I wouldn't have to beat her up! It's her fault!

As the example demonstrates, what generally happens is that clients become defensive and attempt to intellectualize about the problem or externalize it to somebody or something else without taking responsibility or ownership of the problem.

Closed-Ended Questions

Closed-ended questions seek specific, concrete information from the client. They are designed to elicit specific behavioral data and yes or no responses. Closed questions usually begin with verbs such as *do, did, does, can, have, had, will, are, is,* and *was.* Contrary to what typically occurs in long-term therapy, closed-ended questions are often used early on in crisis intervention to obtain specific information that will help the crisis worker make a fast assessment of what is occurring. Also, whereas in long-term therapy the formulation of a plan of attack on the problem might be weeks or months in the making, crisis intervention often calls for instigating plans of action immediately. Closed-ended questions are particularly suited to obtaining commitments to take action. Here are some guidelines for forming closed-ended questions.

1. *Request specific information:* "When was the first time this happened?" "Where are you going to go?" "Are you thinking of hurting her?" "Have you gone back there?" "Does this mean you are going to kill yourself?"
2. *Obtain a commitment:* "Are you willing to make an appointment to…?" "Will you confront him about this?" "Do you agree to . . . ?" "When will you do this?"
3. *Negative interrogatives:* A negative interrogative is a closed question often used as a subtle way to coerce the listener into agreeing with the speaker. *Don't, doesn't, isn't, aren't,* and *wouldn't* all tend to seek or imply agreement. The negative interrogative statement "Don't you believe that's true?" really is a camouflaged exclamatory statement saying, "I believe that's true, and if you have an ounce of sense you'll agree with me!" Such statements generally have little place in a crisis interventionist's repertoire of verbal skills. A far better way of asking for compliance is with an assertive owning statement.

CW: Jake, I understand how difficult it is for you, but, for the sake of both you and Rita, I'd really like you to continue to build on last week's success by agreeing to the "stay away from her" contract again this week.

Owning Feelings

Owning means communicating possession: "That's mine." Often in conversation we avoid specific issues by "disowning" statements with phrases such as these: "They say . . . ," "I heard the other day that you . . . ," "It's not right for you to . . . ," and "Don't you think you ought to . . . ?" Whether intentional or not, such verbal manipulation functions to avoid ownership of responsibility for what's being said or to avoid awareness of one's own position on thoughts and feelings concerning an issue.

Owning or "I" statements are probably more important in crisis intervention than in other kinds of therapy because of the directive stance the crisis worker often has to take with clients who are immobile and in disequilibrium. Therefore, we have illustrated a number of different types of owning statements the crisis worker may find useful for particular problems that occur during intervention. Although used more often in crisis intervention than in normal therapeutic settings, owning statements should be employed sparingly, from the standpoint that the crisis worker's main job is to focus on the client and not on him- or herself. Given that admonition, when working with clients in crisis it is very important to own your feelings, thoughts, and behaviors because many clients are using you as a model. So if you imply "We think this way" (meaning I and the director of the clinic, the school principal, the population of North America, the world, or God), then the client does not have much of a chance against that awesome cast and is liable to become dependently compliant or defensively hostile.

CW: (*Authoritatively.*) You know that the Family Trouble Center is a branch of the police department, and we can have you arrested, don't you?
Jake: (*Defiantly.*) Yeah, well, so what. I might as well be in jail anyway.

Disowned Statements.   Many of us chronically disown many human qualities that indicate we are less than perfect! Beginning crisis workers are particularly vulnerable to this fallacy because they do not want to be seen as inadequate, insecure, or otherwise unequal to the task. Small wonder that clients learn to distrust or become dependent on such all-knowing, well-integrated individuals. Let us take, for example, my feeling of confusion. If I pretend I understand when in fact I am confused, the client who is listening to me is going to be doubly confused. Being willing to own my confusion or frustration and to attempt to eliminate it is a trust-reinforcing event for two reasons: (1) both client and worker can reduce the need to pretend or fake understanding of one another and begin to see more clearly where communications are getting crossed; and (2) the client can begin to become actively involved with the worker in an attempt to work together.

CW: Right now I don't know what to think. You say you love her, yet your actions do everything to drive her away.

Jake: I know 'cause it confused me too! Well, it's like I want her to love me and then I get jealous and paranoid, and like a switch gets flipped and then I lose it. It frustrates me. I'm my own worst enemy and I hate myself for it.

Conveying Understanding.   Clients in crisis often feel that no one understands what they are going through. The "I understand" statement is an owning statement that clearly conveys to the client that you do understand what is happening. This statement may have to be combined with what is commonly called a "broken record" response because the individual may be so agitated or out of touch with reality he or she does not hear what is being said the first time.

CW: OK, Jake, I do understand it's frustrating when she gives you the cold shoulder, and all the ways you try to win her affection don't work.

Jake: (*Pounding his fist on the table and yelling.*) Every damn thing I do anymore is wrong!

CW: I understand right now that it's so frustrating the only thing that seems to work is lashing out at her physically.

Value Judgments.   At times the crisis worker has to make judgment calls about the client's behavior, particularly when the client is in danger of doing something hurtful to him- or herself or to others. Owning statements specifically speak to the worker's judgment about the situation and what he or she will do about it.

Jake: (*Making threatening gestures and with a trembling voice.*) I . . . I . . . just caaann't taaake much more . . . of this. I'll huuurt her . . . huuurt her real bad.

CW: (*Making a judgment.*) The way you say that really concerns me. I believe that would not be in your best interests and wouldn't get you what you want, which is back with Rita. I'd have to call the police to see that you are both kept safe.

However, using owning statements does not generally mean making value judgments about the client's character, because such judgments are put-downs and do nothing to change behavior.

CW: (*Sarcastically.*) Yeah, you're a really big man to have to punch your wife out because you aren't as smart as she is. That really shows me a lot. I think maybe a stint out on the county work farm might take some of that energy out of you.

Positive Reinforcement.   To be genuine in crisis work is to say what we feel at times. When a client has done well and I'm happy and feel good about it, I say so. However, such positively reinforcing statements should always be used in regard to a behavior, as opposed to some personal characteristic.

CW: Jake, I know this is about the last place you'd like to be and I think it took a lot of guts to come in here and admit to me you've got some problems.

However, the use of positive reinforcement is also a double-edged sword. Many times in crisis intervention, reinforcing a client for a behavior may breed dependency or be seen as anything but reinforcing by the client.

Jake: (*Sneeringly.*) Guts my ass! If it weren't for the cops, I sure as hell wouldn't be in this stinkhole with a jerk like you.

Personal Integrity.   Similarly, when a client starts to browbeat, control, or otherwise put us on the hot seat, it does little good to try to hide our anger, disappointment, or hurt feelings.

Jake: (*Sneeringly.*) What do you know, you're nothing but a snot-nosed girl! I don't have to take this crap!
CW: (*Calmly.*) I don't appreciate the demeaning comments, the language, or your attitude toward me. I'd like an apology, and I'd also like you to be civil. If you can't, I'll assume you'd rather explain your problems to your probation officer.

Assertion Statements.   Finally, because crisis intervention often calls for the crisis worker to take control of the situation, requests for compliance in the form of owning statements are often very directive and point specific. These owning statements, also known as *assertion statements,* clearly and specifically ask for a specific action from the client.

CW: I want you to commit to me and yourself that you'll stay away from her for the next week. I want you to sign this contract that you'll do that for your own safety and hers as well.
Jake: (*Wistfully wringing his hands.*) I dunno, that's a long time. I really miss her right now.
CW: I understand it's hard, particularly when you'd like to do something, but I need for you to sign this paper so I can be sure you're committed to doing this.

Climate of Human Growth

According to Rogers (1977), the most effective helper is one who can provide three necessary and sufficient conditions for client growth. These conditions he named *empathy, genuineness,* and *acceptance* (pp. 9–12). To create a climate of empathy means that the crisis worker accurately senses the inner feelings and meanings the client is experiencing and directly communicates to the client that the worker understands how it feels to be the client. The condition of genuineness (also called *realness, transparency,* or *congruency)* means that the worker is being completely open in the relationship: nothing is hidden, there are no facades, and there are no professional fronts. If the worker is clearly open and willing to be fully him- or herself in the relationship, the client is encouraged to reciprocate. The term *acceptance* (also referred to as *caring* or *prizing*) means that the crisis worker feels an unconditional positive regard for the client. It is an attitude of accepting and caring for the client without the client's necessarily reciprocating. The condition of acceptance is provided for no other reason than that the client is a human being in need. If these conditions of empathy, genuineness, and acceptance can be provided for the client, then the probability that the client will experience positive emotional movement is increased.

Communicating Empathy

In describing the use of empathy to help clients, we will focus on four important techniques: (1) attending, (2) verbally communicating empathic understanding, (3) nonverbally communicating empathic understanding, and (4) silence as a way of communicating empathic understanding (Cormier & Cormier, 1991; Gilliland & James, 1998, pp. 116–118).

Attending.   The first step in listening has little to do with words and a lot to do with looking, acting, and being attentive. In most initial counseling and therapy sessions, the client enters with some anxiety related to the therapy itself in addition to the stress brought on by the crisis. In crisis situations, such anxiety is increased exponentially. Shame, guilt, rage, and sorrow are but a few of the feelings that may be manifested. Such feelings may be blatant and rampant or subtle and disguised. Whatever shape or form such feelings take, the inattentive crisis worker can miss the message the client is attempting to convey. Worse, an inattentive attitude implies lack of interest on the part of the worker and does little to establish a trusting relationship.

The effective crisis worker focuses fully on the client both in facial expression and in body posture. By nodding, keeping eye contact, smiling, showing appropriate seriousness of expression, leaning forward, keeping an open stance, and sitting or standing close to the client without invading the client's space, the crisis worker conveys a sense of involvement, concern, commitment, and trust.

Vocal tone, diction, pitch, modulation, and smoothness of delivery also tell clients a great deal about the attentiveness of crisis workers. By attending closely to clients' verbal and nonverbal responses, crisis workers can quickly tell whether they are establishing an empathic relationship or exacerbating the clients' feelings of distrust, fear, and uncertainty about becoming involved in the relationship.

Attentiveness, then, is both an attitude and a skill. It is an attitude in that the worker focuses fully on the client right here and now. In such moments the crisis worker's own concerns are put on hold. It is a skill in that conveying attending takes practice. It is just as inappropriate for the crisis worker to look too concerned and be too close in proximity as it is to lean back with arms folded and legs crossed, giving a cold stare. An example of an appropriate blend of both verbal and nonverbal skill in attending to a client may help to clarify what we mean. (Clients Rita, Jake, and Jean are presented to demonstrate basic techniques of listening and responding. The case history of Rita is recounted at the end of this chapter.)

Rita: (Enters room, sits down in far corner, warily looks about the room, crosses her legs and fidgets with her purse, and avoids direct eye contact, manifesting the appearance of a distraught woman who is barely holding together.)

CW: (*Rises behind desk. Observing the behavior and physical appearance of the client, moves to a chair a comfortable distance and a slight angle from Rita's, sits down, leans forward in an open stance, and with an appearance of concern and inquisitiveness looks directly at Rita.*) I'd like to be of help. Where would you like to start?

The crisis worker sees the apprehension in the client and immediately becomes proactive. The crisis worker moves close to the client but does not sit directly in front of her in what could be construed as a confronting stance. The worker inclines forward to focus attention—eyes, ears, brain, and whole body—into the client's world. The whole posture of the crisis worker is congruent with the verbal message of offering immediate acceptance and willingness to help. In summary, effective attending is unobtrusive, natural, and without pretense. It is a necessary condition for effective listening.

Verbally Communicating Empathic Understanding.

When you can accurately hear and understand the core emotional feelings inside the client and accurately and caringly communicate that understanding to the client, you are demonstrating effective listening. The deeper your level of listening (understanding), the more helpful you will be to your clients. For instance, reflecting a client's message at the interchangeable level is helpful.

Rita: I'm thinking about just walking in and telling Jake I want a divorce—regardless of what Sam is ready to do. I don't think I can go on much longer. My ulcer is beginning to act up, I'm an emotional wreck, and everyone is expecting more of me than I can give.

CW: You're feeling a sense of urgency because it's adversely affecting your physical and emotional being.

A deeper level of listening and communicating empathic understanding to Rita might be expressed thus:

CW: Rita, your sense of urgency is getting to the point where you're about ready to take a big risk with both Jake and Sam. I sense that your physical and emotional stresses have about reached their limits and you're realizing that no one else is going to act to give you relief—that you are the one who is going to have to decide and act.

The second response is more helpful because it confirms to Rita a deeper understanding than the first response. Both responses are helpful because they are accurate and neither add to nor detract from the client's verbal, nonverbal, or emotional messages. Whereas the first response is considered minimally helpful, the second response is more facilitative because it lets the client know the worker heard a deeper personal meaning (risk) and a personal ownership of possible action. A word of caution to the worker, however: beware of reading into the client's statements more than the client is saying, and take care to keep your response as brief as possible.

Effective communication of empathic understanding to the client means focusing on the client's expressed affective and cognitive messages. The worker deals *directly* with the client's concerns and does not veer off into talking *about* the client's concerns or some tangential person or event. That distinction is important.

Rita: I'm afraid Jake might attack me even worse if I tell him I want a divorce.

CW: He did beat you pretty badly. Sam would probably go bananas at that. Jake, your husband, has such a violent temper. (*Talking about the situation and tangentially focusing on Jake.*)

CW: You're feeling some reservations about telling Jake because you really don't want to be beaten up again. (*Dealing with Rita's current feelings and concerns.*)

The latter response is preferred because it stays on target with Rita's feelings and concerns in the here-and-now and because it avoids getting off onto Jake, Sam, or any other third party or issue. The central issue in empathic understanding is to hone in on the client's current core of feelings and concerns and communicate to the client (in the worker's own words) the gist of what the client is experiencing.

Nonverbal Communication. Empathic understanding means accurately picking up and reflecting more than verbal messages. It involves accurately sensing and reflecting all the unspoken cues, messages, and behaviors the client emits. Nonverbal messages may be transmitted in many ways. Body posture, body movement, gestures, grimaces, vocal pitch, movement of eyes, movement of arms and legs, and other body indicators should be carefully observed by the worker. Clients may transmit emotions such as anger, fear, puzzlement, doubt, rejection, emotional stress, and hopelessness by different body messages. Crisis workers should be keenly aware of whether nonverbal messages are consistent with the client's verbal messages. A part of empathic understanding is the communication of such inconsistency to the client who may not be consciously aware of the difference. For example:

CW: (*Observing the way Rita's face lights up whenever she speaks or thinks about Sam.*) Rita, I notice you are talking about all the trouble it is for you to keep seeing Sam on the sly. But your body tells me that those are the moments you live for— that right now your only ecstasy is when you're with Sam.

It is important that the crisis worker avoid reading more into body language than it warrants. Communicating empathy in the nonverbal realm is no place for fishing expeditions or long-shot hunches.

The crisis worker's main concern with nonverbal communication, however, involves the worker's own messages. All the dynamics of the client's body language apply to the worker as well. Your nonverbal messages must be consistent with your verbal messages. It would not be empathic or helpful if your words were saying to the client, "I understand precisely what you're feeling and desiring," but your body were saying, "I don't care," or "I'm bored," or "My mind isn't fully focused on what you're saying." Your voice, facial expression, posture—even the office arrangement and environment— must say to the client: "I'm fully tuned in to your world while you're with me. I want to give my total mental and emotional energy to understanding your concerns while you're here. I will not be distracted." If your body can communicate such messages so that they are unmistakably understood by the client, then you will have effectively communicated empathy to the client nonverbally, and you will stand a better chance of being helpful.

Silence. Silence is golden. Beginning crisis workers often feel compelled to initiate talk to fill any void or lapse in the dialogue because they believe they would not be doing their job otherwise. Nothing could be further from the truth. Clients need time to think. To throw up a barrage of questions or engage in a monologue says more about the crisis worker's insecurity in the situation than it does about resolving the crisis. Silence gives the client thinking time—and the crisis worker too.

Indeed, at such times, verbiage from the crisis worker may be intrusive and even unwelcome. Remaining silent but attending closely to the client can convey deep, empathic understanding. Nonverbally, the message comes across: "I understand your struggle trying to put those feelings into words and it's OK. I know it's tough, but I believe you can handle it. However, I'm right here if you need me."

Rita: The last beating . . . I was so ashamed, yet I couldn't seem to do anything except go back to him.

CW: It hurts you not only to get beaten but also that others might find out—which seems even worse. As a result, you don't see any alternatives.

Rita: (*Thinks hard, eyes focused into the distance for more than a minute.*) Yes and no! I see alternatives, but I guess until now I haven't had the guts to do anything. I rationalized that something must be wrong with me or that the situation would get better, but it hasn't for five years. It has gotten worse.

CW: (*Silence. Looks at Rita for some 30 seconds while collecting thoughts.*) A couple of things strike me about what you said. First, you've decided to quit blaming yourself. Second, by the fact that you're here now, you've chosen at least one alternative to that five-year merry-go-round of abuse.

In this scene, silence is allowed to work for both the client and the worker. The client needs time to work through her response to the worker and she is unconditionally allowed to do this. The same is true of the crisis worker. The client's comment is synthesized and processed for its full meaning. By reacting immediately, the crisis worker might make less than a potent response. Taking time to digest both the content and the affect of the client enables the worker to formulate a response that is more likely to be on target and helpful.

Communicating Genuineness

Contrary to the thinking of most beginning human services workers, as evidenced by their behavior, being fully oneself and not some pseudotherapist or mimic of a particular therapist one has heard or seen is an absolutely necessary condition, particularly in crisis intervention. Rogers (1969, p. 228) says it in clear, simple, and succinct terms:

> When I can accept the fact that I have many deficiencies, many faults, make a lot of mistakes, am often ignorant where I should be knowledgeable, often prejudiced when I should be open-minded, often have feelings which are not justified by the circumstances, then I can be much more real.

Rogers's statement means putting on no false fronts but rather being oneself in the relationship and communicating what "oneself" is to the client. In short, it is being honest. The advice to be honest is not simply a platitude. To be honest is to be congruent; it means that the crisis worker's awareness of self, feelings, and experience is freely and unconditionally available and communicable, when appropriate during intervention in a crisis.

Egan (1975, 1982, 1986, 1990) has listed essential components of genuineness that would serve the beginning crisis worker well.

1. *Being role free.* The crisis worker is genuine in life as well as in the therapeutic relationship and is congruent both in experiencing and communicating feelings (Egan, 1975, p. 91).
2. *Being spontaneous.* The crisis worker communicates freely, with tact and without constantly gauging what to say, because such helpers behave freely without being impulsive or inhibited and are not rule bound or technique bound. Worker behavior is based on a feeling of self-confidence (p. 92).
3. *Being nondefensive.* Crisis workers who behave nondefensively have an excellent understanding of their strengths and weaknesses. Thus, they can be open to negative, even hostile, client expressions without feeling attacked or defensive. The crisis worker who is genuine understands such negative expressions as saying more about the client than the worker and tries to facilitate exploration of such comments rather than defend against them (pp. 92–93).
4. *Being consistent.* People who are genuine have few discrepancies between what they think, feel, and say and their actual behavior. Crisis workers who are consistent do not think one thing and tell a client another or engage in behavior that is contrary to their values (pp. 93–94).
5. *Being a sharer of self.* When it is appropriate to the situation, people who are genuine engage in self-disclosure, allowing others to know them through open verbal and nonverbal expression of their feelings (p. 94).

The following dialogue between the crisis worker and Rita demonstrates comprehensively the points both Rogers and Egan make.

Rita: Just what the hell gives? Here I am going crazy and you put it back on my shoulders. You're supposed to help get me out of this mess!

CW: I can see that you're really mad at me because I don't behave the way you think I ought to.

Rita: Well, how can you be such a caring person if you let me hang out there, pushing me to take such risky chances? I could lose everything.

CW: You see me as being a real hypocrite because I'm pushing you to take some action rather than sympathizing with you.

Rita: God knows I could use some . . . and when you act so callously (*Cries.*) . . . you're like every other damn man!

CW: What would I be doing if I were acting in the most helpful way I possibly could, in your opinion, right now?

Rita: Well, I know you can't solve this for me, but I'd sure as hell like for you to point the way or help me solve this.

CW: So, what you're really wanting is to be able to solve this dilemma on your own, and what you're wanting from me is to help you find your own inner choices that are best for you. What I want to do is to help you find those choices. Let's look at your current options right now.

The dialogue aptly depicts the crisis worker owning feelings, using "I" statements, and focusing on the client's emergent concerns rather than allowing the focus to shift to tangential matters or defensive responses of the worker. Such statements allow the crisis worker to retain integrity, squarely face client hostility without becoming hostile in turn, and model a safe and trusting atmosphere in which clients see that it is all right for them to demonstrate angry feelings and still be accepted by the crisis worker. At the same time, the crisis worker stands by and is consistent with a therapeutic approach without being intimidated by or defensive with the client. The crisis worker above all has the self-confidence and congruence to make such statements in a way that is facilitative for the client.

Communicating Acceptance

The crisis worker who interacts with complete acceptance of clients exudes an unconditional positive regard for clients that transcends clients' personal qualities, beliefs, problems, situations, or crises. The worker is able to prize, care for, and fully accept clients even if they are doing things, saying things, and experiencing situations that are contrary to the worker's personal beliefs and values. The worker is able to put aside personal needs, values, and desires and does not require clients to make specific responses as a condition of full acceptance.

Rita: I hate to bother you with all my problems. I know you're married and have never been divorced. You must think I'm a terribly screwed-up mess.

CW: I hear your concern, and I want you to know that what has happened to you and what you choose to do have nothing to do with my regard for you. What I'm really hoping we can do is to help you arrive at those choices that will best help you get through this crisis and successfully get back in total control of your life.

Rita: I appreciate that very much. But sometimes I wonder whether my running around with Sam doesn't strike you as unwise and immature.

CW: I hope I'm not giving off negative vibes to give you that impression, because your personal preferences have nothing to do with my caring for you. It seems like you really have a concern about my feelings about how you should act.

Rita: Not really. It's just something inside me—that if I were you, I'd be wondering.

CW: So, a source of concern inside you is whether I may evaluate you negatively. What I want you to know is that my esteem for you is not based on what you do.

Even when clients persist in projecting onto the crisis worker negative evaluations or notions such as those expressed by Rita, the worker doesn't have to buy into such notions. If the worker can truly feel an unconditional positive regard for the client, there will be no need for denial, defensiveness, or diversion from the reality of the worker's true feelings. If the worker demonstrates caring and prizing of the client, regardless of the client's situation or status, the client will be more likely to accept and prize him- or herself. That is the essence of acceptance in crisis intervention.

Facilitative Listening

Listening is the first imperative in crisis intervention. When we use the word *listening,* we are applying the term broadly to several important behavioral and communications skills discussed in this chapter. To function in a facilitative way, workers must give full attention to the client by

1. Focusing their total mental power into the client's world
2. Attending to the client's verbal and nonverbal messages (what the client does not say is sometimes more important than what is actually spoken)
3. Picking up on the client's current readiness to enter into emotional and/or physical contact with others, especially with the worker
4. Emitting attending behavior by both verbal and nonverbal actions, thereby strengthening the relationship and predisposing the client to trust the crisis intervention process.

One important aspect of listening is for the worker to make initial owning statements that express exactly what he or she is going to do.

CW: Rita, I can see you're really hurting. So that I can fully understand what's going on and what needs to be done, I'm going to focus as hard as I can on what you're saying and how you're saying it. As well as listening to what you do say, I'm going to be listening for those things that aren't said because they may have some bearing on your problems too. So if I seem to be really concentrating on you, it's because I want to fully comprehend in as helpful and objective a way as possible what the situation is and your readiness to do something about it.

The second important aspect of listening is to respond in ways that let the client know that the crisis worker is accurately hearing both the facts and the emotional state from which the client's message comes. Here we are searching for both the affective and content dimensions of the problem. The crisis worker combines the dilemma and feelings by using restatement and reflection.

CW: As you lay the problem out—the abuse by your husband, the job pressures, the wonderful yet guilt-ridden times with Sam—I get the feeling of an emotional switchboard with all the lines plugged in and even crossed over, and you're a beginning operator who might be able to handle one or two incoming calls, but now you're just sitting paralyzed wishing you'd never taken the job, wondering how you can get out, wanting answers, but having so many problems that you don't even know the right questions to ask.

The third facet in effective listening is facilitative responding. It provides positive impetus for clients to gain a clearer understanding of their feelings, inner motives, and choices. Facilitative responses enable clients to feel hopeful and to sense an inclination to begin to move forward, toward resolution and away from the central core of the crisis. Clients begin to be able to view the crisis from a standpoint of more reality or rationality, which immediately gives them a sense of control. Here the crisis worker targets an action.

CW: So, given all the wires running into the switchboard, which ones do you want to pull and which ones do you want to keep plugged in? You've given me all kinds of information about how well you've handled the business up to this crisis point. Look back on how you handled that particular phone line. What worked then that might work now? Using that as an example, can we sort each one of these out and get the circuits plugged in or just say that particular call isn't important right now and unplug the line?

The fourth dimension of effective listening is evidenced by the worker's helping clients to understand the full impact of the crisis situation. Such an understanding allows clients to become more like objective, external observers of the crisis and to refocus it in rational ways rather than remaining stuck in their own internal frame of reference and emotional bias.

Rita: I feel like the whole world is caving in on me. I wonder if I'll ever be able to get out from under all the mess I'm in now.

CW: You're sounding emotionally frozen by what is happening. I'm wondering what would happen if we could step back for a moment and look at it as if we were third-party observers to your situation—as if you were someone else in a soap opera. What would you say to that person?

Rita: Well . . . (*Moment of thought.*) I'd say she's not the first or only one to experience lots of trouble—that things may look horrible now, but that eventually things get worked out—especially if she's lucky and can bear up long enough.

CW: Then looking at it from outside yourself does give you an additional view.

Helping clients refocus is not a solution in itself. It is an extension of the art of listening that may facilitate forward movement when clients are emotionally stuck.

These four aspects of listening don't operate in a fragmented or mechanical way. Such listening requires skill, practice, an emotionally secure listener, and both physical and emotional stamina on the part of the listener. The following dialogue gives a brief but comprehensive demonstration of how effective listening is combined in its many dimensions. The client now is Jean, Rita's daughter. Don't be perplexed at our shift in clients. One person in crisis may well put a significant other into a crisis situation also. In this instance, Rita's problems have boiled over into her 13-year-old daughter's life.

Jean: I feel put down and ignored by my mother. Every time anything is mentioned about Sam—that's her secret boyfriend—she gets mad and leaves the room. Everything has changed. It's like I'm no longer important to her. I don't know what's happening or what to do.

CW: You're feeling hurt and disappointed, and you're also bewildered by her responses to you.

Jean: (*Crying and very upset.*) I . . . I feel like I no longer count. I'm feeling like I'm in the way. Like I'm suddenly no good . . . I feel like now I'm the problem.

CW: You're blaming yourself even though you're trying to understand what has happened and what you should do.

Jean: (*Crying is slowing down.*) By Sunday night I felt like killing myself. I planned to do it that night. I was feeling abandoned, alone, and hopeless. I just wanted to find some way to end the hurting. I didn't think I could go on another day. I felt like I was no longer her daughter—like she had either disowned me or had been living a lie. I don't know if I can go on.

CW: Even though you were feeling you were at the brink of death, you somehow managed to pull out of it. What did you do and what are you doing now to keep from killing yourself?

Jean: (*Not crying—pondering the crisis worker's last response.*) Well, Marlene and her parents came by. I spent the night with them. That really helped. It was lucky for me that they came by and invited me. They were so kind and understanding. I had a bad night. Worrying about all that stuff. But they, especially Marlene, helped me so much.

CW: Let's see if you can tell me what you have learned from that experience that can help you the next time you feel like killing yourself.

Jean: (Pause, as if studying the crisis worker's response.) To get away . . . with someone who cares and understands.

CW: Tell me someone you can contact whenever you feel hopeless and lonely and suicidal so that next time you won't have to depend on luck.

Jean: Well, I'd call Marlene again . . . or my uncle and aunt. They'd be quick to invite me over . . . and there are several friends at school I could call. *(Dialogue continues.)*

This segment of dialogue contains several of the elements of listening that we have described. It contains accurate reflective listening, open-ended questions, and attention to the client's safety (without asking closed questions, giving advice, or encroaching on the client's prerogatives and autonomy). Also, the crisis worker keeps the focus right on the central core of the client's current concerns, paving the way for the client's forward movement from the immediate crisis toward safer and more adjustive actions. The worker's selective responses are geared toward enabling the client to become aware of and pursue immediate short-term goals. The worker does not digress into external events, past events, the mother, the secret boyfriend, gathering background information, or conducting long-term therapy.

ACTING IN CRISIS INTERVENTION

As shown in Figure 2.1, the crisis worker's level of action and involvement in the client's world, based on a valid and realistic assessment of the client's level of mobility/immobility, may be anywhere on a continuum ranging from nondirective through collaborative to directive. The appropriateness of alternative coping mechanisms hinges on the client's degree of mobility. Thus assessment of client mobility is a key concept governing the degree of the crisis worker's involvement.

One of the first things the worker must determine is what event precipitated the crisis. What brought on the disequilibrium? The answer may not be very clear in the client's complex and rambling story. So the worker may have to ask, early in the interview, "What *one event* brought you to seek counseling today?" When you discover the major precipitating event that took away the client's autonomous coping ability, it will likely signal your primary focus with the client. During the worker's *acting* mode (helping clients examine alternatives, plan action steps, and make a commitment), the worker may function mainly in one of three ways: nondirective, collaborative, or directive.

Collaborative Counseling

The collaborative approach enables the crisis worker to forge a real partnership with the client in evaluating the problem, generating acceptable alternatives, and implementing realistic action steps. When the assessment indicates that the client cannot function successfully in a nondirective mode but has enough mobility to be a partner in the crisis intervention process, the worker is collaborative to that degree. Collaborative counseling is a "we" approach, whereas nondirective counseling is a "you" approach. Consider some typical worker statements in the collaborative mode: "You have asked me where you might find a safe place to spend the night. Let's consider the places we know of around here." "You've come up with a lot of good ideas, but you sound a little confused about which one to act on. Could we put our heads together and make a priority list of alternatives?" Usually the collaborative client's crisis is more severe than that of the fully mobile client. But the collaborative client is a full partner in identifying the precipitating problem, examining realistic alternatives, planning action steps, and making a commitment to carrying out a realistic plan. The collaborative client is not as self-reliant and autonomous as the fully mobile client but does have enough ego strength and mobility to participate in resolving the problem. The worker is needed to serve as a temporary catalyst, consultant, facilitator, and support person. The concept of collaborative counseling is based on the precept that the worker serves as a catalyst to help the client map out immediate action steps in order to get started. The client can then take over, having once achieved a state of precrisis equilibrium. Here is an example of a collaborative response to a client:

Rita: I've thought about going to my mother's or going to the battered women's shelter or even calling my school counselor friend for a place to stay tonight.

CW: Let's examine these three choices and maybe some others available to you that I know of to see which one will best meet your requirements for tonight.

Nondirective Counseling

The nondirective approach is desirable whenever clients are able to initiate and carry out their own action steps. As a general rule, the less severe the crisis, the less directive the crisis worker has to be. The worker uses a great amount of active listening and many open-ended questions to help clients clarify what they really want to do and examine what outcomes various choices might produce. These are some possible questions: "What do you wish to have happen?" "What will occur if you choose to do that?" "What persons are available now who could and would assist you in this?" "Picture yourself doing that—vividly see yourself choosing that route. Now, how does that image fit with what you're really trying to accomplish?" "What activities did you do in the past that helped you in situations similar to this?" These are only a few of the possible open-ended questions the crisis worker may pose. Nondirective questions are geared to a sensitive and accurate identification of the client's current inner feelings, needs, and goals.

In nondirective counseling the worker focuses on the client's inner world, determines that the client has the capability, energy, mobility, and autonomy to make reasonable choices, and facilitates realistic forward movement of the client. The worker does not manage, manipulate, prescribe, dominate, or control. It is the client who owns the problem, the coping mechanisms, the plan, the action, the commitment, and the outcomes. The worker is a support person who may listen, encourage, reflect, reinforce, self-disclose, and suggest. Nondirective counseling assists clients in mobilizing what already is inside them—the capacity, ability, and coping strength to solve their own problems in ways that are pretty well known to them already but that are temporarily out of reach. Here is an example of a nondirective response.

Rita: This is it. I've had the last beating I'm going to take from that jerk! I'm simply going to get myself out of this hell!

CW: You've made a decision to choose a different life for yourself, and you've decided that you are the one who is going to start it.

Directive Counseling

The directive approach is necessary when the client is assessed as being too immobile to cope with the current crisis. The crisis worker is the principal definer of the problem, searcher for alternatives, and developer of an adequate plan, and instructs, leads, or guides the client in the action. Directive counseling is an "I" approach. This is an example of a worker-directed statement: "I want you to try something right now. I want you to draw a deep breath, and while you are doing it, I want you to just focus on your breathing. Don't let any other thoughts enter your mind. Just relax and notice how your tensions begin to subside." By using a very directive stance, the worker takes temporary control, authority, and responsibility for the situation.

Rita: I don't know which way to turn. My whole world has caved in. I don't know what I'll do tonight. It's all so hopeless. I'm scared to even think about tonight. (*Rita appears stunned and in a state of panic.*) I don't know what to do.

CW: I don't want you to go home in the state you're in now. I'm going to call Domestic Abuse Services, and if they have room for you at their shelter, I want you to consider spending at least one night there. Domestic Abuse Services has offices and a counseling service at one location and a shelter at a different address, which is unlisted. I don't want you to worry. We have a van that can take you to the shelter. In the morning you can leave the shelter and go talk with the Domestic Abuse Services counselors, or you can come back and talk with me; but right now my main concern is that you are safe for today and tonight.

There are many kinds of immobile clients: (1) clients who need immediate hospitalization due to chemical use or organic dysfunction, (2) clients who are suffering from such severe depression that they cannot function, (3) clients who are experiencing a severe psychotic episode, (4) clients who are suffering from severe shock, bereavement, or loss, (5) clients whose anxiety level is temporarily so high that they cannot function until the anxiety subsides, (6) clients who, for any reason, are out of touch with reality, and (7) clients who are currently a danger to themselves or others.

In the real world of crisis intervention, every crisis worker must deal with some clients who need directive counseling and whose lethality level should be assessed early in the interview. These clients are more apt to be suicidal or homicidal than are clients who are ready to respond to collaborative or to nondirective counseling. The worker must be able to make a fairly accurate and objective assessment of the client's level of mobility. However, if the worker makes an error of judgment (believing a client to be immobile who in fact is not), no harm is usually done because the client may simply respond by refusing to accept the worker's direction. In most cases of this sort, the worker can then shift into a collaborative mode and continue the helping session. Many times a worker will begin in a directive mode and then shift into a collaborative mode during the session. For example, with a highly anxious client the worker may begin by directing the client in relaxation exercises, which may lower the client's anxiety level to the point where the worker can make a natural shift into a collaborative mode to continue the counseling.

Action Strategies for Crisis Workers

Crisis workers who use the six-step model we have described may begin each session with a nondirective approach and shift to a more directive approach as the ongoing assessment indicates. A number of action strategies and considerations may enhance the worker's effectiveness in dealing with clients in crisis.

Recognize Individual Differences.   View and respond to each client and each crisis situation as unique. Even for experienced workers, staying attuned to the uniqueness of each person is difficult. Under the pressures of time and exhaustion, and misled by overconfidence in their own expertise, workers find it all too easy to lump problems and clients together and provide pat answers and solutions. Treating clients generically is likely to cost the worker and the client a great deal more in the long run than it saves in time and effort in the short run. Stereotyping, labeling, and taking for granted any aspect of crisis intervention are definite pitfalls.

Assess Yourself.   Ongoing self-analysis on the part of the worker is mandatory. At all times, workers must be fully and realistically aware of their own values, limitations, physical and emotional status, and personal readiness to deal objectively with the client and the crisis at hand. Crisis workers need to run continuous perceptual checks to ascertain if they have gotten in over their heads. (See Chapter 13 for a complete description of this phenomenon called "burnout.") If for any reason the worker is not ready for or capable of dealing with the crisis or the client, the worker must immediately make an appropriate referral.

Show Regard for Client's Safety.   The worker's style, choices, and strategies must reflect a continuous consideration of the client's physical and psychological safety as well as the safety of others involved. The safety consideration includes the safety of the worker as well as the ethical, legal, and professional requirements mandated in counseling practice. The greatest intervention strategies and tactics are absolutely useless if clients leave the crisis worker and go out and harm themselves or others. The golden rule is "When in doubt about client safety, get help." The safety requirement may mean appropriate referral interventions, including immediate hospitalization.

Provide Client Support.   The crisis worker should be available as a support person during the crisis period. Clients may need assistance in developing a list of possible support people, but if no appropriate support person emerges in the examination of alternatives, the worker can serve as a primary support person until the present crisis is over. A warm, empathic, and assertive counseling strategy should be used with clients who are extremely lonely and devoid of supports. For example, "I want you to know that I am very concerned about your safety during this stressful time, and that I'm available to help. I want you to keep this card with you until you're through this crisis, and call me if you feel yourself sliding back into that hopeless feeling again. If you call either of these numbers and don't get an answer or get a busy signal, keep trying until you get me. You *must* make contact with *me*. I will be very disturbed if you are in a seriously threatening situation again without letting me become involved with you. I really want to impress on you my genuine concern for you and the importance of making an agreement or contract to call me whenever your safety is threatened. Will you give me that assurance?"

Define the Problem Clearly.   Many clients have complicated and multiple problems. Make sure that each problem is clearly and accurately defined from a practical, problem-solving viewpoint. Many clients define the crisis as someone else's problem or as some external event or situation that has happened. Attempting to solve the crisis of some third party (who isn't present) is counterproductive. Pinpoint the client's own problem with the event or situation and keep the focus on the client's central core of concern. Also, attempt to distill multiple problems down into an immediate, workable problem and to concentrate on that problem first. We cannot overemphasize the tenacity with which the worker must avoid being drawn off on tangents by some highly emotional or defensive clients with difficult problems. Consider these exchanges with Rita's husband Jake:

Jake: You don't seem to like me much.
CW: Right now, that's not the issue of importance. What I'm trying to do is help you identify the main source of your problem.

Another example:

Jake: Haven't you ever hit your wife too?
CW: No, but that's not what we're working on now. I'm trying to help us figure out a way for you to avoid fighting with her whenever you first get home each evening.

In both instances the worker stays focused on the client and does not get caught up on side issues such as worker competency, beliefs, and attitudes.

Consider Alternatives.   In most problem situations, the alternatives are infinite. But crisis clients (and sometimes workers) have a limited view of the many options available. By using open-ended questions, elicit the maximum number of choices from the client. Then add your own list of possible alternatives to the client's list. For example, "I get the feeling that it might help if you could get in contact with a counselor at the Credit Counseling Bureau. How would you feel about our adding that to our list?" Examining, analyzing, and listing alternatives to consider should be as collaborative as possible. The best alternatives are ones that the client truly *owns*. Take care to avoid imposing your alternatives on the client. The alternatives on the list should be workable and realistic. They should represent the right amount of action for the client to undertake now—not too much, not too little. The client will generally express ownership of an option by words such as "I would really like to call him today." Worker-imposed options are usually signaled by the worker's words, such as "*You need to* go to his office and do that right away." Beware of the latter! An important part of the quest for appropriate alternatives is to explore with the client what options worked before in situations like the present one. Often the client can come up with the best choices, derived from coping mechanisms that have worked well in the past. But the stresses created by the immediate crisis may keep clients from identifying the most obvious and appropriate alternatives for them. Here the crisis worker facilitates the client's examination of alternatives:

CW: Rita, you say you're feeling frightened and trapped right now and you don't know where to turn. But it sounds like you'd take a step in a positive direction if you could get some of your old zip back. What are some actions you took or some people you sought out in previous situations when you felt frightened or stuck?
Rita: Oh, I don't know that I've been in a mess quite this bad before.
CW: Well, that may be true. But what steps have you taken or what persons have you contacted before in a mess like this, even if it wasn't this bad?

Rita: Hmm . . . Well, a time or two I did go talk to Mr. Jackson, one of my auto mechanics instructors when I was at the Area Vo-Tech School. He's very understanding and helpful. He always seemed to understand me and believe in me.

CW: How would you feel about reestablishing contact with him whenever you're down again?

Plan Action Steps.   In crisis intervention the worker endeavors to assist the client to develop a short-term plan that will help the client get through the immediate crisis, as well as make the transition to long-term coping. The plan should include the client's internal coping mechanisms, as well as sources of help in the environment. The coping mechanisms are usually brought to bear on some concrete, positive, constructive action that clients can take to regain better control of their lives. Actions that initially involve some physical movement are preferred. The plan should be realistic in terms of the client's current emotional readiness and environmental supports. It may involve collaboration with the worker until the client can function independently. The effective crisis worker is sensitive to the need of the client to function autonomously as soon as feasible.

Rita: Right now I'd like to just be free of the whole mess for a few days . . . just get off this dizzy merry-go-round long enough to collect my thoughts.

CW: It sounds to me like you really mean that. Let's see if together we can examine some options that might really get you the freedom and breathing space you need to pull the pieces back together.

Rita: I can't really let go. Too many people depending on me. That's just wishful thinking. But it would be wonderful to get some relief.

CW: Even though you don't see any way to get it, what you're wanting is some space for yourself right now—away from work, kids, Jake, Sam, and the whole dilemma.

Rita: The only way that would happen is for my doctor to order it—to prescribe it, medically.

CW: How realistic is that? How would that help you?

Rita: It would call a halt to some of the pressures. The treadmill would have to stop, at least temporarily. Yes, I guess that kind of medical reason wouldn't be so bad.

CW: Sounds like consulting your doctor and laying at least part of your cards on the table might be one step toward getting medical help in carving out some breathing space for yourself.

Rita: I think so. Yeah, that's it! That's one thing I could do.

CW: Let's together map out a possible action plan—for contacting your doctor and requesting assistance in temporarily letting go. Let's look at *when* you want to contact your doctor, *what* you're going to say, and *how* you're going to say it—to make sure you get the results you must have right now.

The crisis worker is attempting to work collaboratively with Rita and to facilitate Rita's real ownership of her plan. The worker also implies a view of Rita as competent and responsible.

Use the Client's Coping Strengths.   In crisis intervention it is important not to overlook the client's own strengths and coping mechanisms. Often the crisis events temporarily immobilize the individual's usual strengths and coping strategies. If they can be identified, explored, and reinstated, they may make an enormous contribution toward restoring the client's equilibrium and reassuring the client. For example, one woman had previously relieved stress by playing her piano. She told the worker that she was no longer able to play the piano because her piano had been repossessed. The crisis worker was able to explore with her several possible places where she could avail herself of a piano in times of stress.

Attend to Client's Immediate Needs.   It is important for crisis clients to know that their immediate needs are understood and attended to by the crisis worker. If a client is extremely lonely, attempt to arrange for the client to be with someone. The client may need to make contact with relatives, friends, former associates, or former friends. The client may need follow-up appointments with the crisis worker or referral to another worker, counselor, or agency. The client may simply need to be heard—to ventilate about a loss, a disappointment, or a specific hurtful event.

Use Referral Resources.   An integral aspect of crisis intervention is the use of referral resources. A ready list of names, phone numbers, and contact people is a necessity. It is also important for the crisis worker to develop skill in making referrals as well as in working with a wide variety of referral agencies. Many clients need to be referred early to make contact with sources of help regarding financial matters, assistance from social agencies, legal assistance, long-term individual therapy, family therapy, substance abuse, severe depression, or other personal matters. A worker might use referral resources for such purposes as to obtain emergency eyeglasses for a junior high school student whose family cannot buy them, to get dental care for a child who is suffering excruciating pain and whose family cannot pay, to prevail on a parole officer to mandate that a specific parolee cease abusing his wife and children, and to ensure that a client disabled by an automobile accident receives help for his vocational rehabilitation as well as for his depressed mental state. We have compiled a list of suggestions and cautions we have found to be useful in working with a variety of agencies. Generally, we find that a breakdown in our communication with agencies follows our having overlooked a few obvious and simple cautions.

1. Keep a handy, up-to-date list of frequently used agencies. Keep up with personnel changes.
2. In communities that publish a directory of human services, have available the most recent edition.
3. Cultivate a working relationship with key people in agencies you frequently use.
4. Identify yourself, your agency, and your purpose when telephoning.
5. Know secretaries and receptionists by name; use their names when you call. Treat them with dignity, respect, and equality.
6. Follow up on referrals you make.
7. Don't assume that all clients have the skill to get the services they need. Be prepared to assist, to avoid runaround and bureaucratic red tape.
8. Whenever necessary, without engendering dependency, go with clients to the referral agencies to assist and to ensure that effective communication takes place.
9. Be sensitive to the client's needs for transportation and child care.
10. Write thank-you messages (with copies to their bosses) to persons who are particularly helpful to you and your clients.

11. Don't criticize fellow professionals or the agencies they represent, and don't carry tales about either workers or agencies.
12. Keep accurate records of referral activities.
13. Remember that police and fire departments are referral resources also.
14. Know frequently used agencies' hours, basic services, mode of operation, limitations, and, if possible, policies such as insurance, sliding scale fees, and so forth.
15. Be aware of any agency services the client is already using.
16. Use courtesy and good human relations skills when dealing with agency personnel. Put yourself in their shoes and treat them as you would like to be treated.
17. Give agencies feedback on how they did; obtain feedback from them, too.
18. Avoid expecting perfection of other agencies.
19. Be aware of sensory impairment in clients, especially in older adults, and make those impairments known in referrals.
20. If the client can do so, it is a good idea for the client to make the call (this creates a personal link between the client and the referral agency).
21. If the agency has an orientation session, seek to attend and to participate in it.
22. Practice honesty in communicating to referral agencies regarding the status or needs of clients. (Honest and ethical portrayal of the client's needs will build credibility with other agencies.)
23. Obtain permission of the client before attempting to refer.
24. Observe rules of confidentiality and rights of privacy in regard to all clients and fellow workers.

Develop and Use Networks.   Closely allied with referral is a function we call *networking* (Haywood & Leuthe, 1980). Networking, for us, is having and using personal contacts within a variety of agencies that directly affect our ability to serve clients effectively and efficiently. Although each person in our network is a referral resource, it is the relationship we have with that individual that defines it as a network. Effective crisis workers can't sit behind a desk and wait for assistance to come to them. They must get out into the community and get to know personally the key individuals who can provide the kinds of services their clients require. A personal relationship based on understanding and trust between the worker and vital network people is invaluable in helping the worker cut through bureaucratic red tape, expedite emergency assistance, and personalize many services that might otherwise not be available to clients.

As crisis workers, we do not operate alone in the world. We are interdependent. Networking permits us to spread the responsibilities among other helping professionals. We mean "helping professionals" in the broadest possible context: lawyers, judges, parole officers, ministers, school counselors, federal, state, and local human services workers, directors and key people in crisis agencies, business and civic leaders, medical doctors, dentists, police, and political leaders may play important roles in the networking process. The development and use of effective networking is an indispensable function of the successful worker.

Get a Commitment.   A vital part of crisis intervention is getting a commitment from the client to follow through on the action or actions planned. The crisis worker should ask the client to summarize verbally the steps to be taken. This verbal summary helps the worker understand the client's perception of both the plan and the commit-ment, and gives the worker an opportunity to clear up any distortions. It also provides the worker an opportunity to establish a follow-up checkpoint with the client. The com-mitment step can serve both as a motivational reminder to the client and to encourage and predispose the client to believe that the action steps will succeed. Without a definite and positive commitment on the part of the client, the best of plans may fall short of the objectives that have been worked out by the worker and the client.

Step 6, the commitment step, does not stand alone. It would be worth little without the foundation of the five preceding steps. The actions that a client in crisis owns and to which the client commits are derived from solid planning (Step 5), which is, in turn, based on systematic examination of alternatives (Step 4). The three acting steps (Steps 4, 5, and 6) are based on effective listening in Steps 1, 2, and 3. All six steps are carried out under the umbrella of assessing. Commitment is individually tailored to the specific client crisis situation. The following segment is one example of a crisis worker func-tioning during the commitment step.

CW: So, Rita, it seems to me that what you've decided to do is to reinitiate some kind of meaningful contact with Mr. Jackson. That seems to be one thing you've de-cided that might really help right now. So that we're both very clear on what you've committed yourself to doing, would you please summarize how and when you're going to proceed?

Rita: I'm going straight to my office today and phone him at school. I'll either talk to him or leave a message for him to call me. As soon as I talk to him, I'll set up a definite day and time to meet with him.

CW: And when you've set up . . .

Rita: Oh, yes! And when I've set up my appointment with him I'm going to phone you and let you know how it went.

CW: Good. And in the meantime, you have my number on the card if you need me—especially if the safety of either you or your children becomes jeopardized.

Rita: That's right, and I'll call if I lose my nerve with Sam. I've got to get some space for myself there—at least some temporary space.

Experienced crisis workers are generally able to sense how far and how fast the cli-ent is able to act. Usually the client is encouraged to commit to as much action as fea-sible. If we cannot get her or him to make a giant leap forward, we'll accept one small step in a positive direction. The main idea is to facilitate some commitment that will re-sult in movement of the client in a constructive direction.

SUMMARY

Crisis intervention from a practitioner's standpoint incorporates fundamental counsel-ing skills into a six-step model of systematic helping. The model focuses on facilitative listening and acting within an overarching framework of assessing. The six-step model is an organized and fluid process of applying crisis intervention skills to the emerging feelings, concerns, and situations that clients having most types of trauma might present.

The six steps in crisis intervention serve to organize and simplify the work of the crisis worker. Step 1 explores and defines the problem from the client's point of view.

Step 2 ensures the client's physical and psychological safety. Step 3 provides supports for the person in crisis. Step 4 examines alternatives available to the client. Step 5 assists the client in developing a plan of action. Finally, Step 6 helps the client to make a commitment to carry out a definite and positive action plan and also provides for worker follow-up.

Assessment of the person and the crisis situation is the keystone for initiating intervention. Assessment techniques include evaluating the severity of the crisis; appraising clients' feeling or emoting, behaving, and thinking patterns; assessing the chronic nature and lethality of the crisis; looking into the client's background for contributing factors; and evaluating the client's resources, coping mechanisms, and support systems. The Triage Assessment System is a unique, swift, efficient, and utilitarian strategy for evaluating the severity of a crisis on the three fundamental (ABC) dimensions of the client's affect, behavior, and cognition. The triage system can provide for rapid and valuable information for crisis workers to use while involved with an ongoing crisis situation. Also, psychobiological assessment is essential.

Listening is a fundamental for all successful counseling, including crisis intervention. Essential components of effective listening and communication include effective attending, empathy, genuineness, and acceptance. Action skills include nondirective, collaborative, and directive worker strategies, showing consideration for individual differences and client safety, examining alternatives with clients experiencing crises, helping clients plan for and commit themselves to appropriate choices, and wise use of referral resources.

Essential relationship skills include attending, listening, communicating, showing empathy and acceptance, exhibiting genuine responses, and ensuring client safety.

CLASSROOM EXERCISES

The Case of Rita

The case of Rita, based on a real situation in our counseling practice, is presented here for you to consider because it clearly demonstrates and emphasizes the six steps in crisis intervention. We suggest that you make notes as you read and reread it. Suppose you were the crisis worker to whom Rita had come for help (in person, not on the telephone). As an exercise to discover how well you have learned the six-step crisis intervention model, write a personal narrative description of how you might use the six-step model to help Rita during the initial session you have scheduled with her. (We have also written our description. Please write your description before reading ours, found at the end of this case; then compare your crisis intervention strategies with the narrative we have prepared. Remember, in crisis intervention, there is no one best way. Yours may be as effective as ours or more so. We hope the exercise will prove instructive for you.)

Rita is a 35-year-old businesswoman. She is a graduate of high school and a post–high school vocational-technical institute. She holds a certificate in auto mechanics. She has never been to a counselor before. She has come to the crisis worker at the suggestion of a close friend who is a school counselor. Rita owns and operates an automobile tune-up and service shop. She employs and supervises a crew of mechanics, tune-up specialists, and helpers. She works very hard and keeps long hours but maintains some flexibility by employing a manager. Rita's husband Jake is a college-educated accountant. They have two children: a daughter, 13, and a son, 8. The family rarely attends church, and they don't consider themselves religious. But they are church members. Their close friends are neither from their church nor from their work.

Rita's presenting problem is complex. She constantly feels depressed and unfulfilled. She craves attention but has difficulty getting it in appropriate ways. For diversion, she participates in a dance group that practices three nights a week and performs on many Friday and Saturday evenings. Rita, Jake, and their children spend most of their Sundays at their lake cottage, which is an hour's drive from their home. Their circle of friends is mainly their neighbors at the lake.

Rita's marriage has been going downhill for several years. She has become sexually involved with Sam, a wealthy wholesaler of used automobiles. She met him through a business deal whereby she contracted to do the tune-up and service work on a large number of cars for Sam's company. Sam's contracts enable Rita's business to be very successful. Rita states that the "chemistry" between her and Sam is unique and electrifying. She says she and Sam are "head over heels in love with each other." She lives with Jake but no longer feels any love for him.

According to Rita, Sam is unhappily married too, and Sam and his current wife have two small children. Rita states that she and Sam want to get married, but she doesn't want to subject her two children to a divorce right now and she's very fearful of her own mother's wrath if she files for a divorce. Sam fears his wife will "take him to the cleaners" if he leaves her for Rita right now. Lately, Sam has been providing Rita with expensive automobiles, clothing, jewelry, and trips out of town. Also, Sam has been greatly overpaying Rita's service contracts, making her business flourish. Jake doesn't know the details of Rita's business dealings with Sam, but he is puzzled, jealous, frustrated, impulsive, and violent. Jake used to slap Rita occasionally. Recently, however, he has become more frustrated, impulsive, and violent. Jake has beaten Rita several times in recent months. Last night he beat her worse than ever. Rita has no broken bones, but she has several bruises on her body, legs, and arms. The bruises do not show as long as she wears pantsuits.

Rita has told her problems only to her school counselor friend. She fears that her boyfriend would kill her husband if he found out about the beatings. Rita is frustrated because she cannot participate with the dance group until her bruises go away. Rita is feeling very guilty and depressed. She is not especially suicidal, however. She is feeling a great deal of anger and hatred toward Jake, and she suffers from very low self-esteem. She is feeling stress and pressure from her children, from her mother, from Jake, and even from Sam, who wants to spend more and more time with Rita. Recently, Rita and Sam have been taking more and more risks in their meetings. Rita's depression is getting to the point where she doesn't care. She has come to the crisis worker in a state of lethargy—almost in a state of emotional immobility. But Rita has decided to share her entire story with the worker because she feels she is at her "wit's end," and she wouldn't dare talk with her minister, her physician, or other acquaintances. Rita has never met the crisis worker, and she feels this is the best approach, even though she is uncomfortable in sharing all this with a stranger.

I. A Crisis Worker's Narrative

Write your own narrative describing how you would use the six-step model of crisis intervention with Rita. If you are participating in a class, workshop, or other study group, get together with others (preferably in small groups of five to seven people) to share descriptions of your particular method of crisis intervention.

Following is an example of one narrative description of how to intervene in the case of Rita. Read this narrative only after you have written your own and met in small groups to discuss your own and others' narratives.

Narrative of Rita's Case

First, I would explore and define Rita's problem from her point of view. I would use active listening techniques. I would avoid closed questions. Apparently Rita is feeling trapped because of several situational conditions: her marriage, her relationship with Sam, her own web of unfulfilling activity, and the beatings by her husband, Jake. I would try to identify the one area that precipitated the crisis and immediately focus on that. After Rita's whole story had been fully examined, I might say, "Rita, what one thing caused you to come to see me today?" I would start with that one event or stressor. Active listening would bring us to that point.

Second, I would take whatever steps I deemed necessary to ensure Rita's safety. From the case data, I assume that Jake does not physically abuse the children, but he might do so. If my assessment indicated that Rita was in imminent danger, I would refer her to Domestic Abuse Services and inform her of their shelter options. Other safe places could be explored with Rita to ensure the safety of both herself and her children.

Third, I would offer myself as an immediate support person. I would also attempt during the session to develop other viable support people to whom Rita could turn, especially in an emergency. I would assume that Rita's school counselor friend is a positive support person, and I would encourage Rita to maintain that relationship as well as explore others.

Fourth, I would encourage Rita to examine the various alternatives available to her. I would give special attention to the options that Rita could own and do for herself that would contribute directly to restoring her precrisis level of equilibrium.

Fifth, I would try to help Rita develop a plan of action that she could own and that would represent a positive action step toward her precrisis level of equilibrium. The plan would be concrete, positive, realistic, and clearly oriented toward alleviating her crisis. If her stress level were high, I might immediately use relaxation techniques to help her through the current stressful and anxious state. This could be one method by which Rita might begin to learn to deal with future stresses as she encountered them.

Sixth, before the end of the session with Rita, I would try to get a commitment from her to carry out some action that would be positive and that would help her restore her equilibrium or make a step toward it. I would ask her to summarize the commitment as a means of helping to solidify it in her mind as an immediate objective and to motivate her toward attainment of the stated goal. I would assure Rita of my support and encouragement and make arrangements for the two of us to check back with each other to follow up on her progress.

In terms of problem solving, I would covertly brainstorm two important components while I listened and responded to Rita: (1) I would make a mental list of adequate situational supports; and (2) I would make a mental list of adequate coping mechanisms. I would not disclose all these to Rita. The mental options would be available to me to effect referrals or to ask appropriate open-ended questions in helping her to discover the alternatives available to her. I would take care not to impose my own solutions, alternatives, or plans on Rita.

Throughout the crisis intervention session, I would be engaged in assessing Rita's situation using a variety of criteria described earlier in this chapter, including the Triage Assessment Form (TAF). Given the information in the case description, I would judge her scores on the Affective Severity Scale to be in the 7-to-8 range (she is angry, depressed, and lethargic); her Behavioral Severity Scale scores to be in the 4-to-5 range (she is behaviorally mobile enough to present herself for intervention and to describe her situation in candid detail); and her Cognitive Severity Scale scores to be in the 2-to-4 range (her thinking is pretty clear and is in sync with reality). Rita's overall TAF Severity Scale score is therefore estimated to be in the 13-to-16 range, which places her in the low-to-moderate domain.

During the listening, safety, and support phases of the session, I would be active with Rita. My degree of action would depend on my assessment of Rita's mobility or immobility. If Rita were assessed as immobile, I would be quite directive; if she were partially mobile, I would be collaborative. If she were totally mobile, I would be nondirective. From the case data and the TAF estimate, I assume that Rita is mobile enough for me to function in a collaborative mode. Depending on my own ongoing assessment, I would move toward either directive or nondirective, but I believe I would function largely in the collaborative mode most of the time.

I would certainly avoid asking closed questions. By continuing to focus on Rita's situation with open-ended questions, I would try to get her to concentrate on what she wants to do; that is, I would focus on alternatives. I would hope to get her to consider as many realistic alternatives as possible. I would assist her in brainstorming to identify these alternatives. From a repertory of choices, I would hope that her plan, mentioned in Step 5, would be a sound one that would move her toward attainment and success. The optimum plan would be simple and realistic. I would not be trying to get her to solve all her situational problems. My first goal would be to help her get the present crisis under control and then work toward having the mobility to independently take charge of her life.

In problem-solving Rita's case with her, I would start with a list of support people gleaned from the case data. In crisis intervention, a support person is someone whom the client trusts and who is always available. That person or persons could be an acquaintance, a friend, relative, co-worker—anyone who could be called on to provide temporary comfort, encouragement, or support. In Rita's case, the most obvious support people would be the crisis worker (myself), her school counselor friend, her own children, other dancers in her dance group, her "lake" friends, her shop manager and shop employees, and her former vocational-technical instructors. Other possible supports include her mother, her physician, other members of her family, and even former classmates from school. These are the kinds of people who would be identified and remembered by the crisis worker as possible appropriate supports for Rita to consider. Normally, we recommend using only one or two support persons at a time, not a whole host of people. I would encourage Rita to choose and contact one or two appropriate support people.

Adequate coping mechanisms stored in the crisis worker's mental repertory for possible assistance to Rita could be: leaving Jake the next time he beats her; breaking off the relationship with Sam; setting priorities on the amount of time she is spending on various activities; devising better or different ways to obtain positive attention when she needs it; calling a support person on the phone; calling the Crisis Center or Domestic Violence Services; calling me (the crisis worker); consulting an attorney for legal advice; consulting her physician for a complete physical examination, diagnosis, and advice; initiating marriage counseling with Jake, if he agrees; initiating couples' counseling with Sam, if he agrees; planning ways to spend time with and engage in activities with her school counselor friend; entering individual counseling on a continuing basis; doing something that is recreational or relaxing for herself, such as working on cars or developing a new dance routine; enrolling in an assertiveness training course to enhance her self-esteem and improve her coping behaviors; wearing tights or colored hose to her dance rehearsals until the bruises heal; and thinking of something innovative and creative that she would enjoy to get away from the turmoil.

In helping Rita (using the six-step crisis intervention model), I would seek to involve Rita in prioritizing any of the alternatives, plans, support persons, or coping mechanisms she might wish to pursue. If chosen action steps could truly represent Rita's own priorities, the chances of success would be greatly increased. Finally, and most important, I would reemphasize getting Rita to commit herself to one or more of the actions that we collaboratively developed as her plan. I would ask her to summarize her plan so that she and I could agree on what she was committing herself to. I would try to respond to her during the commitment phase in a way in which she would feel supported by me but not dependent on me. I would certainly want her to be motivated and predisposed toward success.

II. Assessing a Crisis

Adequate assessment is an absolute necessity in effective crisis intervention. In the rapidly changing scene of an active crisis, assessment is difficult, puzzling, and frustrating for beginners. Making a valid assessment during an ongoing crisis is perhaps more an art than a science and comes with practice, making mistakes, obtaining feedback, and plunging in again. This exercise is designed to allow you to try out your assessing skills in the safety of the classroom. It will further allow you to upgrade your skills as you move through the course. Finally, it will provide you with a way to compare the skills you had at the start of the course to your skills at the end.

Divide into groups of seven. Each person chooses one of the following roles: (1) a suicidal client, (2) a battered client, (3) a violent client, (4) a posttraumatic client, (5) a substance-abusing client, (6) a sexual assault victim, (7) a grieving client. Each person will assume the role of one of the foregoing clients for the next class meeting. It is helpful to quickly read the chapter containing the material on the particular client before the next class meeting so you can adequately depict the typical dynamics of the crisis.

At the next class meeting, each person is to role-play the client assigned for approximately five minutes. One other person in the group acts as the crisis worker. The crisis worker's role is to elicit enough information so that a domain severity assessment can be made. While the crisis worker and the client are working with one another, other group members monitor the dialogues and use the Triage Assessment Form in this chapter to assess the severity of the problem in regard to its affective, behavioral, and cognitive components. Write down your thoughts as you systematically go through the form. After each person has completed the role assignment, discuss your respective ratings. Pay particular attention to why you gave the ratings you did and what those ratings imply for any subsequent intervention you might use. Don't worry about trying to be perfect or about any lack of knowledge you may have about the problem. Just go ahead and do it! Clearly, there are no wrong answers at this point in your education.

After you have finished, save your notes and ratings. As you move through subsequent chapters, reassemble your group and replay the crisis appropriate to that chapter. The "client" should attempt to replay the role as closely as possible to the initial rendition. Group members will repeat their triage assessment of the client. You will then pull out your initial ratings and compare them with your current ratings. Group discussion should identify changes that occurred and why members may have rated the person differently from the first time. By reassessing these role plays, you should start to feel more comfortable about making educated guesses in crisis situations.

III. Crisis Intervention Role Play

Class members form pairs. You will practice two roles: (1) being a crisis worker and (2) reliving a real crisis from your past experience. All sessions must be tape-recorded; to begin each tape, the person serving as crisis worker obtains the client's spoken permission to record the session. The crisis worker practices accurate listening skills: attending, observing, understanding, and responding with empathy, genuineness, respect, acceptance, nonjudgment, and caring. The client relates the past crisis to his or her partner as if the crisis event were being reexperienced in the present moment. When each partner has had an opportunity to play the roles of both crisis worker and client, the class regroups for discussion. Some of the possible discussion questions are:

1. To you as a client, what aspects of the process were most helpful? What aspects would you like to see improved?
2. To you as a client, what was the most threatening part of the exercise?
3. For you as a worker, what did you perceive to be your strongest and most positive intervention technique?
4. For you as a worker, what did the exercise bring out that you wish to improve upon?
5. What additional skills or learnings do you need to make your next session more successful?

Take the taped session home, listen to it, and in your role as the crisis worker, write a six-step plan for intervention. At the next class meeting, share that plan with the client and obtain verbal feedback from that person.

IV. Restatement and Reflection

Most of us would like to improve the odds that we really do accurately interpret clients' messages when they talk to us. There are many hints to aid us in listening to clients. We will deal with two methods in these exercises.

1. *Restatement of ideas.* Make a simple statement in your own words telling the client what you heard him or her say. This helps to be sure that you and the client are talking about the same thing. *Example:*

Client: I don't think I can go back home tonight—just too many heavy problems for me to handle.
Worker: You don't think you can face what's at home.

2. *Reflection of feelings.* Reflecting feelings means sending the client the message that confirms your understanding of what the client must be feeling. In that way you let the client know you heard him or her and give the client a chance to correct or clarify (you may have received half the message but not all of it). Reflective listening also helps the client see the basis for his or her behavior. *Example:*

> *Client:* My boss really chewed me out in front of my friends last night.
> *Worker:* Sounds like it really embarrassed you.

To help you learn to make appropriate responses that contain both restatement and reflection, we have prepared a practice sheet (Worksheet 2.1). Do the exercise as directed on the sheet without consulting anyone else. Then obtain feedback from others as the directions indicate.

V. Open-Ended Questions

Asking open-ended questions does not guarantee that every client will respond with full statements. The purpose of this exercise is to help you become aware of how you state your questions so that you can get fuller, deeper levels of response. Decide whether the following counselor questions are closed- or open-ended.

1. Do you have a girlfriend?
2. Tell me about your family.
3. How old are you?
4. How did that happen?
5. When will you go?
6. Tell me about school.
7. What happened next?
8. Isn't that a silly choice?

Change the following closed-ended questions to open-ended questions.

1. How long have you been out of work?
2. Can I help?
3. Did you like that story?
4. Are you angry with me?
5. Do you have to hit Sally every time you get drunk?

VI. Owning Feelings

Worksheet 2.2 is designed to let you try out owning your own feelings and expressing them in responses that indicate that you are owning them. We call such messages *"I" messages.* When we disown a feeling, we usually give someone else the responsibility for it and begin statements with words that refer outside ourselves, such as *they, you, people,* and *all people.*

VII. Worker–Client Communications

Communication is often not a simple matter. Words come so fast and easily at times that we have our responses formulated in our heads before we hear the full message of the client who is speaking.

WORKSHEET 2.1 Restatement and Reflection

DIRECTIONS: In your own words, write a restatement and a reflection of the client's statement. In small groups, give one another feedback, making checkmarks under Yes or No to indicate whether others find your responses appropriate.

Client's Statement	Worker's Restatement	Worker's Reflection	Yes	No
1. When he says those hateful things to me, I wish I could die.				
2. I don't need her, and I frankly don't think I need counseling. She's the one with problems.				
3. You're so wonderful. Nobody else understands me, but you do. I think I love you.				
4. Life is like a roller-coaster, up and down. Isn't that kind of the way it is with you?				

WORKSHEET 2.2 Owned Message Practice

DIRECTIONS: Read the situation in the first column. Examine the disowned message in the second column. Then write in the third column an "I" message that indicates you take responsibility for your feelings. The purpose is *not* to resolve the problem but rather to communicate that you are aware of your feelings and are being honest about them at this moment. In small groups, give each other feedback, making checkmarks under Yes or No to indicate whether the message indicates owning one's own feelings. If, after you have shared your responses, others feel that most of your responses are not "I" messages, please elicit help in restating your message.

Situation	Disowned Message	Owned Message	Yes	No
1. Client has been sulking and acting sad all session.	Come on, now. Stop moping around. Life isn't that bad.	I'm really puzzled. You say things are OK! Yet your behavior doesn't fit with OK.		
2. Macho man brags about beating wife. Has just responded, "Women need to be kept in control."	Well, I wonder if you'd do that to the Raider linebackers.			
3. People complain about client's body odor. (It's bothering you, too.)	James, you really should bathe more frequently.			
4. Cynthia has a reputation for being promiscuous and has talked at some length about it.	We workers feel that talk only leads to acting out behavior.			
5. John is extremely overweight. Wants to lose weight but doesn't seem to be able to stick to a plan.	Face it, John. You're fat. I'm sorry, but that's it. No wonder you can't get dates. Why not try jogging?			

WORKSHEET 2.3 Total Listening Practice

DIRECTIONS: Read the client's statement in the first column. Then write a restatement of the message, a reflection of the message, an "I" message that owns your feelings but communicates acceptance, and an open-ended question that elicits more information. Break into dyads (pairs) and role-play the client and the worker in dialogue beyond initial responses to one of the statements.

Client's Statement	Restatement	Reflection	Owning "I" Statement	Open-Ended Question
1. I used to like him as a boss. But he chewed me out today. I hate his guts.				
2. He beat the daylights out of me last night.				
3. Well, I really wonder what life's all about—love, too, for that matter.				
4. You're just like all the rest. You don't really care about me. I think I'll kill myself.				

Worksheet 2.3 is designed to help you practice (1) attentive listening and (2) formulating responses that communicate acceptance of the feeling behind the message as well as awareness of the message's content. An accepting response combines (1) restatement, (2) reflection, (3) owning one's feelings, and (4) an open-ended question designed to get to the fuller meaning. Thus Worksheet 2.3 is a culmination of the communications skills you've been practicing.

REFERENCES

Aguilera, D. C. (1997). *Crisis intervention: Theory and methodology* (8th ed.). St. Louis: Mosby.

Ammar, A., & Burdin, S. (1991, April). *Psychoactive medication: An introduction and overview.* Paper presented at the Fifteenth Annual Convening of Crisis Intervention Personnel, Chicago.

Armsworth, M. W., & Holaday, M. (1993). The effects of psychological trauma on children and adolescents. *Journal of Counseling and Development, 72*(1), 49–56.

Burgess-Watson, I. P., Hoffman, L., & Wilson, G. V. (1988). The neuropsychiatry of posttraumatic stress disorder. *British Journal of Psychiatry, 152,* 164–173.

Cormier, W. H., & Cormier, L. S. (1991). *Interviewing strategies for helpers: Fundamental skills and cognitive behavioral interventions* (3rd ed.). Pacific Grove, CA: Brooks/Cole.

Crow, G. A. (1977). *Crisis intervention: A social interaction approach.* New York: Association Press.

Crow, T. J., & Johnstone, E. C. (1987). Schizophrenia: Nature of the disease process and its biological correlates. *Handbook of Physiology,* vol. 5. Bethesda, MD: American Physiology Society.

Dryden, W. (1984). *Rational emotive therapy: Fundamentals and innovations.* London: Croom Helm.

Egan, G. (1975). *The skilled helper: A model for systematic helping and interpersonal relating.* Pacific Grove, CA: Brooks/Cole.

Egan, G. (1982). *The skilled helper: Model, skills, and methods for effective helping* (2nd ed.). Pacific Grove, CA: Brooks/Cole.

Egan, G. (1986). *The skilled helper: A systematic approach to effective helping* (3rd ed.). Pacific Grove, CA: Brooks/Cole.

Egan, G. (1990). *The skilled helper: Model, skills, and methods for effective helping* (4th ed.). Pacific Grove, CA: Brooks/Cole.

Ellis, A. (1971). *Growth through reason.* Palo Alto, CA: Science and Behavior Books; Hollywood, CA: Wilshire Books.

Ellis, A., & Abrahms, E. (1978). *Brief psychotherapy in medical and health practice.* New York: Springer.

Ellis A., & Grieger, R. (1977). *Handbook of rational-emotive therapy.* New York: Springer.

Ellis, A., & Harper, R. A. (1979). *A new guide to rational living* (rev. ed.). Upper Saddle River, NJ: Prentice Hall; Hollywood, CA: Wilshire Books.

Gilliland, B. E. (1982). *Steps in crisis counseling.* Memphis: Memphis State University, Department of Counseling and Personnel Services. (Mimeographed handout for crisis intervention courses and workshops on crisis intervention.)

Gilliland, B. E., & James, R. K. (1998). *Theories and strategies in counseling and psychotherapy* (4th ed.). Boston: Allyn and Bacon.

Haywood, C., & Leuthe, J. (1980, September). *Crisis intervention in the 1980s: From networking to social influence.* Paper presented at the annual convention of the American Psychological Association, Montreal, Canada.

Healy, D. (1987). Rhythm and blues: Neurochemical, neuropharmacological, and neuropsychological implications of a hypothesis of circadian rhythm dysfunction in the affective disorders. *Psychopharmacology, 93,* 271–285.

Hersh, J. B. (1985). Interviewing college students in crisis. *Journal of Counseling and Development, 63,* 286–289.

Kolb, B., & Whishaw, I. Q. (1990). *Fundamentals of human neuropsychology* (3rd ed.). New York: W. H. Freeman.

Myer, R. A., Williams, R. C., Ottens, A. J., & Schmidt, A. E. (1991). *Three-dimensional crisis assessment model.* Unpublished manuscript, Northern Illinois University, Department of Educational Psychology,

Counseling, and Special Education, DeKalb, Illinois.

Myer, R. A., Williams, R. C., Ottens, A. J., & Schmidt, A. E. (1992). A three-dimensional model for triage. *Journal of Mental Health Counseling, 14,* 137–148.

Rogers, C. R. (1969). *Freedom to learn: A view of what education might become.* Columbus, OH: Merrill.

Rogers, C. R. (1977). *Carl Rogers on personal power: Inner strength and its revolutionary impact.* New York: Delacorte.

van der Kolk, B. A. (1996a). The body keeps the score: Approaches to the psychobiology of posttraumatic stress disorder. In B. A. van der Kolk, A. C. McFarlane, and L. Weisaeth (Eds.), *Traumatic stress* (pp. 214–241). New York: Guilford Press.

van der Kolk, B. A. (1996b). Trauma and memory. In B. A. van der Kolk, A. C. McFarlane, and L. Weisaeth (Eds.), *Traumatic stress* (pp. 279–297). New York: Guilford Press.

Watters, D. (1997). A study of the reliability of the Triage Severity Scale. Doctoral dissertation, The University of Memphis. *Dissertation Abstracts International, 58-08A,* 3028.

CHAPTER THREE

Crisis Case Handling

HANDLING CRISIS CASES VERSUS LONG-TERM CASES

To understand crisis case handling, we must first clearly differentiate between crisis intervention and long-term counseling and psychotherapy. We can distinguish between what crisis interventionists and long-term therapists do, the principles that underlie the two modes, their objectives, client functioning, and assessment procedures.

Comparing What Crisis Workers and Long-Term Therapists Do

On first glance, typical models for long-term therapy do not look radically different from a crisis intervention model. Our own long-term six-step systematic counseling model (Gilliland & James, 1997, pp. 393–396) incorporates defining problems, examining alternatives, planning courses of action, and obtaining client commitment in much the same operational format as crisis intervention.

What is radically different is that in long-term therapy, defining problems, identifying alternatives, and planning are much broader in scope, more methodological, and rely on continuous feedback loops to check effectiveness of intervention. A typical counseling session with a long-term client reviews progress since the previous session, collaboratively refines the plan of action if needed, processes the content of the session and the client's feelings about it, and then proposes a new homework assignment to be tried out before the next meeting. Crisis intervention models do not operate on such liberal time dimensions nor problem scopes. In crisis intervention, exploring the problems, identifying alternatives, planning, and committing to a plan are all much more compressed in time and scope. What in long-term therapy may occur in a rather leisurely fashion over a period of weekly sessions may in crisis intervention commonly occur in one-half to two hours.

Whereas in long-term therapy a great deal of background exploration may provide the therapist a panoramic view of client dynamics, the crisis worker's exploration typically is narrow and starts and stops with the specific presenting crisis. The long-term therapist's view of alternatives and planning a course of action commonly incorporate psychoeducational processes that seek to change residual, repressive, and chronic client modes of thinking, feeling, and acting. In contrast, the crisis worker seeks to quickly determine previous coping skills and environmental resources available to the client and use them in the present situation as a stopgap measure to gain time and provide a modicum of stability in an out-of-control situation. Whereas the long-term therapist would view comprehensive personality change as a necessary part of the therapeutic plan, the crisis worker would endeavor to change personality only to the degree necessary for restoring precrisis functioning.

A long-term therapist would look toward a methodological manipulation of treatment variables, assess those variables on a variety of dimensions, and process the outcomes with the client. A crisis worker often uses a "best guess" based on previous experience with what works and does not work with a particular problem. Whereas protocols for treatment in long-term therapy may be quite flexible and induce many tryouts of different procedures, crisis intervention is a good deal more rigid and may typically involve set procedures for moving the client from an immobile to a mobilized state.

Finally, assessment and feedback of outcome measures in long-term therapy typically involve a great deal of processing between client and therapist as to the efficacy of treatment. If treatment outcomes are not as expected, a feedback loop is integrated into the model that will allow a return to any of the previous steps. Feedback and assessment in crisis intervention typically occur on a here-and-now basis, with emphasis on what changes have occurred in the previous minutes and what the client will do in the next few hours.

Comparison of Principles, Objectives, Client Functioning, and Assessment

There are many approaches to long-term therapy. Although Thorne's (1968, pp. 11–13) approach is dated and somewhat psychoanalytic, it is one of the most comprehensive and eclectic systems we have found. To provide a clear delineation between crisis intervention and long-term therapy, we have contrasted our own model of crisis intervention with Thorne's *principles, objectives, client functioning,* and *assessment* of case handling. Tables 3.1, 3.2, 3.3, and 3.4 contain and illustrate that comparison.

TABLE 3.1   Principles Compared Between Long-Term Therapy and Crisis Intervention

Long-Term Therapy Mode	*Crisis Case-Handling Mode*
1. *Diagnosis:* Complete diagnostic evaluation	1. *Diagnosis:* Rapid triage crisis assessment
2. *Treatment:* Focus on basic underlying causes; on the whole person	2. *Treatment:* Focus on the immediate traumatized component of the person
3. *Plan:* Personalized comprehensive prescription directed toward fulfilling long-term needs	3. *Plan:* Individual problem-specific prescription focused on immediate needs to alleviate the crisis symptoms
4. *Methods:* Knowledge of techniques to systematically effect a wide array of short-term, intermediate-term, and long-term therapeutic gains	4. *Methods:* Knowledge of time-limited brief therapy techniques used for immediate control and containment of the crisis trauma
5. *Evaluation of results:* Behavioral validation of therapeutic outcomes in terms of the client's total functioning	5. *Evaluation of results:* Behavioral validation by client's return to precrisis level of equilibrium

TABLE 3.2   Objectives Compared Between Long-Term Therapy and Crisis Intervention

Long-Term Therapy Mode (listed in no particular order, but global in scope)	*Crisis Case-Handling Mode (listed in linear order with a crisis-specific focus)*
1. *Prevent problems:* More basic than cure. Use preventive procedures whenever possible.	1. *Define problem:* Clarify in concrete terms the issues that precipitated the crisis.
2. *Correct etiological factors:* Involves comprehensive treatment of broad-based psychological and environmental factors in both the past and present.	2. *Ensure client safety:* Assess client lethality and provide for the physical and psychological safety of the client and significant others.
3. *Provide systematic support:* Comprehensive measures directed toward improvement of the state of health of the individual.	3. *Provide support:* Establish conditions, either by the crisis worker or significant others, whereby the client feels secure and free of threat or abandonment.
4. *Facilitate growth:* Treatment should ideally facilitate rather than interfere with natural environmental and developmental processes.	4. *Examine alternatives:* Provide options for alleviating the immediate situational threat in relation to the crisis.
5. *Reeducate:* Treatment seeks to reeducate and teach new models of adjustment for lifelong coping.	5. *Develop a plan:* Formulate a stepwise procedure using client coping skills, crisis worker expertise, and systemic measures to energize the client to take action.
6. *Express and clarify emotional attitudes:* Major emphasis is on methods of securing emotional release and expression in a permissive and accepting environment.	6. *Obtain commitment:* Obtain agreement as to specific time, duration, and number of activities required to stabilize the client and/or crisis situation.
7. *Resolve conflict and inconsistencies:* Viewed from a psychoanalytic standpoint, therapy aims to help the client achieve *insight* into the causation and dynamic roots of the behavior.	
8. *Accept reality:* Help the client to *accept* what cannot be changed.	
9. *Reorganize attitudes:* Move the person toward exhibiting a more positive view of life.	
10. *Maximize intellectual resources:* Improve the functions of sensing, perceiving, remembering, communicating, thinking, and self-control.	

TABLE 3.3   Client Functioning Compared Between Long-Term Therapy and Crisis Intervention

Long-Term Therapy Mode	*Crisis Case-Handling Mode*
1. Client shows sufficient *affect;* manifests some basis for experiencing and understanding his or her emotional state.	1. *Affectively,* the client is impaired to the extent that there is little understanding of his or her emotional state.
2. Client shows some ability to *cognitively* understand the connection between behavior and consequences—between what is rational and irrational.	2. *Cognitively,* the client shows inability to think linearly and logically.
3. There is some modicum of *behavioral* control.	3. *Behaviorally,* the client is out of control.

TABLE 3.4 Assessment Compared Between Long-Term Therapy and Crisis Intervention

Long-Term Therapy Mode	*Crisis Case-Handling Mode*
1. *Intake data:* Client is stable enough to provide in-depth background regarding the problem; lengthy intake form may contain details of the client's total history: family, medical history, drug use, education, therapy background, social history.	1. *Intake data:* Client may not be able to fill out an intake form because of instability or time constraints; a verbal and/or visual evaluation of current maladaptive state may be the only data available.
2. *Safety:* Client safety is not the primary focus unless there are clues pointing toward imminent danger to self and others.	2. *Safety:* Crisis worker's first concern is client and others' safety; determining whether client is suicidal, homicidal, or otherwise a danger or threat to someone.
3. *Time:* The therapist has time to procure a variety of assessment data to confirm or contraindicate the hypothesized problem; total case diagnosis and workups are gathered before the treatment plan is developed; personality assessment indexes are generally gathered to compare client functioning against norm groups on standard pathology measures.	3. *Time:* Crisis worker has no time for administering formal instruments. Worker must rely on immediate verbal and nonverbal cues emitted by the client to make assessment of degree of pathology.
4. *Reality testing:* The therapist assumes the client is in touch with reality unless assessment data or other clues indicate otherwise.	4. *Reality testing:* Using simple questioning procedures, the crisis worker must determine whether the person is in touch with reality and how effectively the person is functioning.
5. *Referrals:* Referral resources have implications for long-term development. Examples of referrals might be to family services, mental health centers, vocational/educational assistance, and job placement services.	5. *Referrals:* Referral resources have implications of immediacy in terms of getting the client to safety and some degree of stability. Examples of referrals might be to the police, emergency rooms of hospitals, psychiatric or medical evaluation, immediate support people.
6. *Consultation:* Consultants and other backup resources are available as needed. Collaboration is normally initiated after consultation with the client and/or the therapist's supervisor.	6. *Consultation:* Professional consultants who are trained in the diagnosis of pathology are on call for backup purposes.
7. *Drug use:* The therapist relies on data from the intake material and on information developed in the normal course of the therapy to ascertain the level and type of prescription medication or illicit drug or alcohol use.	7. *Drug use:* The crisis worker relies on verbal and visual responses to ascertain the level and type of prescription medication or illicit drug or alcohol use.

We are now ready to turn our attention exclusively to crisis case handling on telephone crisis lines, at walk-in facilities, and in long-term therapy settings. ·

CASE HANDLING ON TELEPHONE CRISIS LINES

The telephone has long played an integral role in crisis work. We present here a rationale for using the telephone as a crisis tool, followed by several useful and appropriate telephone counseling strategies.

The Telephone as a Crisis Tool

"Reach out and touch someone" is a slogan that is particularly appropriate to crisis counseling. The first telephone crisis hotline was established in 1906 by the National Save-a-Life League to prevent suicide (Bloom, 1984). The tremendous growth of "hotlines," in number, types of assistance, kinds of problems handled, and geographical coverage attests to the fact that people in crisis avail themselves of telephones to solve a wide variety of personal problems (Haywood & Leuthe, 1980; Waters & Finn, 1995). Picking up the daily newspaper or the telephone directory in any medium-sized city or major metropolitan area, you can quickly find a list of emergency numbers to call for a variety of human services assistance programs. These services may range from generic crisis hotlines to a variety of specialized services such as local "warm" lines for latch key children (Waters & Finn, 1995) to the National Center for Disease Control AIDS hotline (Saffran & Waller, 1996). There is even a line for a pet loss support group (Turner, 1997). Typically, generic crisis phone lines are open 24 hours a day, 365 days a year, whereas other specialized services may operate during regular business hours. There are several reasons for the upsurge in use of the telephone to solve psychological problems:

Convenience.   Telephones have become such an easy way of communicating that calling for psychological assistance is a natural extension of "taking care of business." Certainly one major factor in the increased use of hotlines is that over 97 percent of households in the United States now have telephones (Kleespies & Blackburn, 1998). As in the case of battering, most crises do not occur during normal business hours. When help is needed in a crisis, it is needed immediately.

Anonymity.   Guilt, embarrassment, shame, self-blame, and other debilitating emotions make face-to-face encounters with strangers very difficult, particularly in the immediate aftermath of a traumatic event. Telephone counselors understand that clients have such feelings and are generally not concerned about identifying a client unless a life-threatening emergency is involved. Conversations are usually on a first-name-only basis for both the worker and the client. Thus, a victim of date rape may call a rape hotline and freely discuss her emotions without having to muster the courage to face what may be perceived as a judgmental human services worker.

Control.   A great deal of fear, anxiety, and uncertainty occur when a client's life is ruptured by a crisis. The concept of secondary victimization by institutions (Ochberg, 1988) is well known to victims of a crisis who have sought assistance from a social agency and then have been victimized by its bureaucratic callousness. In telephone counseling, the client decides when and if assistance is to be sought. At any time during a dialogue on a crisis line, the client may terminate the conversation without fear of recrimination.

Immediacy of Access.   Most institutions and clinics and many private practitioners use pagers. At our own university, a harried residence hall supervisor who is trying to deal with a distraught student who is suffering from severe homesickness and academic failure can call campus security. The security staff will page a member of the staff of the student counseling center who is the after-hours "beeper keeper." The psychologist will immediately respond to the request for assistance by checking with the residence hall supervisor on the current mental status of the student and will then come to the dorm, talk to the student over the phone, or request additional help from security to transport the student to the city crisis stabilization unit.

Cost Effectiveness.   Crisis lines are inexpensive—both for the client and the community. Clients who cannot pay for private therapy or afford transportation can usually avail themselves of a phone. Most community agency hotlines are staffed by volunteers. Although the idea of obtaining counseling from a volunteer may seem no better or worse than talking to a bartender or hairdresser, volunteers typically go through a good deal of training in initial point-of-contact mental health counseling. Volunteers have few pretensions about their "professional role" and are often seen by callers as having more credibility than a paid professional because they "do it out of the goodness of their hearts."

Access to Support Systems.   Support groups make extensive use of telephone networks. From Alcoholics Anonymous to support groups for relatives of military personnel in a war zone, telephone support networks have provided constant links to group members between organized meetings.

Avoidance of Dependency Issues.   A user of telephone crisis lines can't become dependent on a particular human services worker, who may not be readily available. Standard practice in most crisis lines discourages workers from forming lasting relationships with clients so that dependency issues do not arise.

Availability of Others for Consultation.   Crisis lines are seldom staffed by one person. When someone encounters a difficult client, other staff at the agency are available for consultation. Furthermore, at least one phone line is reserved for calling support agencies when emergency services are needed.

Availability of an Array of Services.   A vast array of information, guidance, and social services is quickly available via telephone linkages. The specialized services of different agencies and the expertise they offer can provide on-the-spot guidance for emotionally volatile situations. Many an angry mother or father has received "five-minute parenting sessions" from the staff of a metropolitan "parenting line" that thus short-circuited potential child abuse. Any crisis hotline should have readily available a list of phone numbers of specialized agencies to which they can refer callers.

Service to Large and Isolated Geographical Areas.   Many rural areas that have no after-hours mental health facilities or staff are tied into 800-number crisis lines that cover huge geographical areas. These crisis lines in turn are tied into emergency service staff such as police, paramedics, and hospital emergency rooms that serve those rural areas and can respond to a crisis line call for assistance that may be 150 miles away.

Agency Proactivity.   Although hotlines have been mainly reactive to clientele, as agency philosophy has changed, so has the use of telephones. A family trouble center in one city is closely allied with the police department. On a typical Monday morning, an average of 250 domestic violence reports from the previous week will be delivered by a police officer to the center. Volunteers will immediately start making phone calls to check on the complainants and apprise them of their rights, offer brief phone counseling, invite them in to discuss their problems, or broker services for them with other community agencies (Winter, 1991). In other agencies, where the identity of the client is known, the staff may make periodic calls back to ascertain if the client is still stable or in need of further assistance.

Telephone Counseling Strategies

Conducting crisis intervention over the telephone is a double-edged sword. Although phone counseling offers the advantages just listed, for generating responses the crisis worker is entirely dependent on the content, voice tone, pitch, speed, and emotional content of the client. For many human services workers, it is unsettling to deal with ambiguous client responses and not be able to link body language to verbal content. Furthermore, the worker depends entirely on his or her own verbal ability to stabilize the client and has little physical control over the situation. It takes only one experience of having a suicidal client hang up on a worker to understand how frustrating and emotionally draining crisis intervention over the telephone can be. Consequently, a great deal of care and effort needs to be taken in responding to clients. In the following paragraphs we outline an effective telephone counseling strategy.

Making Psychological Contact.   First, psychological contact needs to be made, and this endeavor takes precedence over anything else the phone worker does. By psychological contact we mean that the worker attempts to establish as quickly as possible a nonjudgmental, caring, accepting, and empathic relationship with the client that will give the worker credibility and elicit the client's trust. Therefore, Step 3, *provide support,* in the six-step model in Chapter 2 becomes the first order of business. It is safe to assume that people who use crisis lines have exhausted or are separated from their support systems. If the client feels no trust in the relationship and hangs up the phone, the crisis worker cannot make an astute dynamic analysis, synthesize material, diagnose the problem, and prescribe a solution! In establishing psychological contact on the phone, providing support is a first priority and is highly integrated with defining the problem through active listening and responding skills.

CW: (Two A.M. on Monday morning. Phone rings.) Metro crisis line. This is Chris. Can I help you?

Telephone caller (TC): (Silence with soft muffled sobs.)

CW: (Waits patiently.) I understand it's pretty hard to talk sometimes, especially when things seem so overwhelming, but if you could, just take a deep breath and then let it out. I wonder if you could just do that?

TC: (Takes a deep breath and exhales. Sobs less frequently.)

CW: (In a soft, modulated, soothing tone.) That's good! Just do that a few more times. Just relax. I'll stay right on the line until you feel like talking. We've got plenty of time.

The phone worker must be able to react in a calm and collected manner. Thus the worker's voice must be well modulated, steady, low keyed with an adequate decibel level, but not high pitched. Neither should the content of the worker's response be deprecating, cynical, cajoling, or demeaning. Although the foregoing criteria may seem obvious, few people realize how their voice sounds or are aware of what happens to their voice level and pitch when they are caught up in a rapidly escalating and evolving emotional event. Furthermore, when the person on the other end of the line is acting out, angry, intoxicated, or otherwise demanding of the worker to "fix things right now," the worker needs a great deal of self-discipline and emotional security to refrain from becoming caustic, judgmental, and demanding.

Defining the Problem.   Once psychological contact is established, the worker attempts to define the problem by gaining an understanding of the events that led to the crisis and by assessing the client's coping mechanisms. Open-ended questions on the *what, how, when, where, who* continuum usually let the worker get a clear picture of the event itself. However, for assessing the coping mechanisms of the client over the phone, it may be hard to get a clear picture of the client's affect. Thus it behooves the worker to become more sensitive to the underlying emotional content and to try to reflect the implied feeling content more than might be required in a face-to-face encounter. Reflecting feelings is a tough job for most beginning mental health workers and is even more difficult on the phone. Yet the worker absolutely must try to reflect feelings, because there is no way to visually assess the client.

One real plus of phone counseling is that the beginning crisis worker can have supportive aids readily at hand without detracting from the counseling session. One useful tactic is to have a reference list of feeling words that cover the gamut of emotions. A second tactic is to have at hand a list of standard questions the counselor can check off to be sure that all areas typically pertinent to the problem are covered. A third tactic is to keep handy a notepad on which the worker can jot down the salient aspects of the events and coping mechanisms the client has used and make a rapid assessment on the triage scale.

TC: *(Timorously.)* O . . . O . . . O . . . K. I just don't know where to start, it's just an avalanche. I've got no place to turn so I thought this was my only chance so I called.

CW: I'm glad you did call. Sounds like right now you're really overwhelmed so perhaps you could just take it from where you felt like things fell apart and tell me about that. And I want you to take your time. Take plenty of time and tell me what's going on, we've got all the time in the world and I'm here to listen until you say everything you need to and we get a real clear picture of what's going on and what you need to do. It'd help if you could give me your first name, please.

TC: It's Cicily. (*Client explains she has just moved to town from out of state in an attempt to reconcile with her estranged husband. The husband indicated that he wanted nothing more to do with the marriage and was filing for divorce. She indicates that she was pretty much in denial about the failed marriage and had taken a last chance on getting it back together. The denial has now been given a rude reality check. The job that was supposedly waiting for her has also fallen through. She is currently at a friend's house, with her 4-year-old son, with less than $200 and a car on its last legs. She has no relatives or support system besides her friend from college days.*)

CW: (Crisis worker listens intently to client's story. Makes interruptions only to clarify and summarize what's going on with the client. Chris deeply reflects the feelings of aloneness, hopelessness, and helplessness that wash over the client. The crisis worker allows the client to grieve and ventilate over her failed marriage. When the client's emotional behavior starts to escalate, the crisis worker uses calming techniques such as asking the client to take a deep breath or reinforces the concept that they have plenty of time to work through this problem.)

As Chris listens to her he is rapidly jotting notes down and making an assessment on the triage scale. Her predominant emotion is anxiety, which is free-floating out into all areas of her life. She is having a lot of difficulty controlling her emotions. Her score on the Affective Severity scale is 7. She indicates that she has been essentially frozen in time for the last four days after her meeting with her estranged husband. Her friend has been taking care of her son while Cicily has sat either paralyzed staring aimlessly at TV or has been hysterically sobbing in bed. Finally, at the urging of her friend she called the crisis line. Her score on the Behavioral Severity scale equals 7 because clearly her daily functioning is impaired. She is immobilized and frozen. As she relates her problems, her thinking seems fairly linear and she is able to put her story together logically. However, she has been perseverating on the crisis to the exclusion of anything else. There is a lot of wishing and hoping for things to get better and that somehow her husband will have a change of heart. She is filled with self-doubt and cannot make a decision about what to do. Her score on the Cognitive Severity scale equals 8. Overall her triage scale score is 22. This woman is clearly in crisis and may need more help than the crisis line can provide over the phone. Chris's immediate concern is with her statement about "This was my only chance."

Ensuring Safety and Providing Support.   During problem definition, the phone worker must be very specific in determining the client's lethality level. If the worker detects the potential for physical injury, then closed-ended questions that obtain information specific to the safety of the client should be asked, not only without hesitation but also with empathic understanding that clearly depicts the worker's overriding concern for and valuing of the client. These questions typically start with *do, have,* and *are,* and in phone dialogues they should be put directly and assertively to the client. (For example, one might ask, "Do you have the pills there with you now?" Or "Are you alone, or is someone there who might help you before you do it?") The phone counselor should check what support systems are available to ensure the client's safety. For many phone clients there will be no support system—the phone counselor is the immediate and sole support system.

CW: I can really hear the hurt and fright in your voice. It's scary being all alone, seeming to have nobody to lean on. I'm concerned about your saying this was "Your last chance." Do you mean by that you're thinking of suicide?

TC: (Somewhat emphatically.) I had, but I just couldn't bear to see that bastard and his new girlfriend get custody of Jimmy.

CW: OK. That's good! I needed to check that out. Now you said you were staying with an old college friend and she asked you to call. Is that where you are now?

TC: Yes, but I hate putting her out like this. But I don't have any other place to go. *(Starts sobbing heavily again.)*

CW: But she's OK with you staying there?

TC: Yesssss. But I hate being a burden on her.

CW: But that's what friends are for. Would you do the same for her if things were reversed?

TC: Well, sure, no question.

CW: So for the time being you've got a roof over your head, have something to eat, and are safe?

TC: Yes, I guess so, but I don't know how long this can go on.

CW: What we're going to do is see if we can get some stuff done that will allow you to get back on your own. OK? Are you willing to do that? (*Cicily acknowledges she'll try.*) Good! Although I can't get your husband back, and I know that really left you feeling hopeless and all alone, I can find out about the job problem and perhaps see if we can't do something about that. So let's start with that if it's OK with you. We've got a number of referral sources here that might be able to match your skills, education, and abilities with a job. Would you be willing to tell me a little bit about yourself in that area—education—employment background—desirable kind of work? I could pass that on to some of our referral sources and see what we could do. (*Chris listens while Cicily goes through her background, education, and other pieces of pertinent information, reinforcing her for staying on task, mobilizing her thoughts, and keeping her terrifying emotions in control.*)

Looking at Alternatives and Making Plans. Creating alternatives and formulating a plan are integral to one another in any crisis situation but are even more closely tied together in phone counseling. To alleviate the immediate situational threat, the phone counselor needs to jointly explore alternatives that are simple and clear-cut. Without the benefit of an eyewitness view or an in-depth background of the client, the worker needs to be cautious about proposing alternatives that may be difficult to carry out because of logistical or tactical problems of which the worker is unaware. Alternatives need to be explored in a slow, stepwise manner with checks by the worker that the client can do the physical and psychological work necessary to complete the task. Role play, verbal rehearsal, and having the client recapitulate objectives are vital ingredients of a functional plan. No plan should be accepted until the client can reassure the worker that he or she thoroughly understands the plan and has the means and ability to put it into action.

CW: OK! I've got that information and I'll pass it along to the day shift, and they'll pass it along to the JOBS Council and a couple of employment agencies that work with us. I want you to call back to our number about 1 P.M. tomorrow and we'll have some information for you. Can you do that?

TC: Well yes, I can do that. (*Cicily has calmed down and is only occasionally sniffling and lamenting her outcast state. Her triage scale score has moved down to about 15. Chris now approaches other areas of her crisis.*)

CW: I wonder what you did when you got into predicaments beforehand? Maybe there was nothing quite like this, but I'm guessing there were other times when you were overwhelmed.

TC: Well nothing like this, but I did take care of my mother before she died, kept a job with a printing company, and worked on my degree. Sometimes that was pretty overwhelming.

CW: So what did you do to take care of being overwhelmed?

TC: I'd make a list and set down my goals of what I was going to do and what I had to do. Like Alcoholics Anonymous, one day at a time, you know. It worked pretty well, but I just have got so many things now, I don't know if I can get it all lined out.

CW: But that worked before, and I understand there are lots of things going on like never before, but if it worked then, how's about giving it a try now? (*Chris immediately seizes on her past coping technique and attempts to put it to work. He acknowledges her belief that this is indeed different than before and doesn't discount the fact that it may be tough. He methodically helps her develop a game plan for tomorrow, not the rest of her life.*) So we've got day care for Jimmy taken care of, and you don't really need the car for a while, you can get a MATA bus or streetcar and go anywhere you need to. Even though you've only got 200 bucks cash, you could cash in that $3000 worth of U.S. savings bonds your mother gave to Jimmy if you had to, until you got back on your feet. You could then repurchase them so you won't feel like you're robbing your son of his inheritance. So you've written those things down that you can do tomorrow right? So we're just managing this, like you say, one day at a time, not worrying much beyond that and doing what can be done. Do you feel like we're making progress?

TC: I guess I do. I can do those things.

Obtaining Commitment.   Commitment to a plan of action generated over the phone should be simple, specific, and time limited. If at all possible, the worker should try to obtain the client's phone number and call the client back at a preset time to check on the plan or, if the agency accepts walk-in clients, the worker should try to have the person schedule an appointment as soon as possible. If the worker is linking with other agencies, then a phone call should be made to the referral agent to check whether the client has completed the task. Although it is preferable to have the client take the initiative in contacting other agencies so that dependence on the worker is not created, conditions may block the client from doing so. In that case, the worker should have no hesitation in offering to make the call.

CW: So there are three things you're going to do tomorrow. First you're going to call the day care number I gave you and get Jimmy in there. Second, you're going to go to the bank and open an account and cash in the bonds. Third, you're going to call back here at 1 P.M. and ask for the information on the job hunt. Those places I told you about will probably want you to come down, so you'll call them and make an appointment. Will you call back tomorrow night and ask for me? I come on at 11 P.M. I know this has been a pretty upsetting deal, so could you kinda repeat that to me and write down that stuff?

TC: Yes. I've got it, and I'll call back. Thanks a lot, you're a real lifesaver.

CW: You're welcome, now get a good night's sleep. It's a fresh day tomorrow, and you'll get through it fine with that attitude. (*Chris judges Cicily now to be at a total triage rating of about 8. Affectively she is in control of her emotions. She is thinking clearly enough to help establish a plan in a collaborative manner with the crisis worker, and has committed to act on it the next day. Chris judges her to be mobilized enough that he can let her go off the line.*)

The call has taken over an hour and a half, but in that time a woman who is in a severe developmental and situational crisis has been able to grieve away some of the lost relationship with her husband, work through her terror of being all alone and jobless in a strange city, and start to make specific plans on how she'll get out of the dilemma. She still has many issues and a long road ahead of her, but she has returned to being a functional human again. By any criterion of therapy, the crisis worker has done a good night's work!

Regular, Severely Disturbed, and Abusive Callers

The foregoing dialogue is a textbook example of how things ought to go in telephone crisis line work. The problem is that the real world seldom functions in such neat and tidy ways. Many callers use the crisis line for reasons other than its intended use. When this happens, the overriding questions telephone workers must pose to themselves are, What is the person getting out of using the crisis line at this time, and is it helpful to the person? How is this person's use of the crisis line at this time affecting its operation? (McCaskie, Ward, & Rasor, 1990). Crisis lines should not cater to a caller's every whim, fantasy, deviant behavior, or self-indulgence.

Regular or chronic callers can be a plague to crisis lines and devour time and energy of staff, which legitimate callers may desperately need (Peterson & Schoeller, 1991). Chronic callers can also be very frustrating to telephone workers because they do not improve (McCaskie, Ward, & Rasor, 1990). These callers can pose a serious morale problem for the volunteers and staff who receive such calls, particularly when the calls become sexually explicit and the deviant fantasies of callers are directed at the crisis worker (Knudson, 1991; Tuttle, 1991). A counterpoint to this negative view is the approach of the staff at the Lawrence, Kansas, Headquarters Crisis Center, who believe that *chronic* is a negative term and implies these callers will never improve (Epstein & Carter, 1991). All behavior is purposive. If seen in that light, no matter how aberrant or weird the content of the call, it is important to remember that those who regularly use the crisis line do so for a reason—it helps them make it through the day. For these clients, it becomes part of their lifestyle and method of coping.

One misconception about crisis line counseling is that most calls are from occasional callers who need to get "cooled off, fixed, and sent on their way." It is mistaken to believe that patching up these situational crises is all that the crisis line does or should do (McCaskie, Ward, & Rasor, 1990). Even though regular callers are not easily handled, they represent a major component of what crisis lines deal with and need to be handled in specific ways that do not end with telephone workers becoming frustrated and clients acting out in order to get their needs met. Therefore, although the term *chronic* is often used in telephone crisis work, we believe it to be somewhat pejorative and agree with the staff at the Headquarters Crisis Center that *regular* better captures the essence of this clientele.

Understand the Regular Caller's Agenda. Helping people in crisis is different from being nice to them. The agenda of regular callers places the crisis worker in a dilemma. Although the worker may feel ethically bound to respond to the caller and the agency's protocol dictates that all calls must be taken, that does not mean that workers need to suffer the abuse and invective leveled at them by such callers. A very real difference exists between what callers may want and what they may need, and helping a caller is generally predicated much more on needs than on wants. Often what these regulars want is a reaffirmation that their problems are unsolvable. Thus they become dependent on the telephone worker to sustain their problem. The worker therefore needs to recognize such patterns and not support them when this blocks progress (McCaskie, Ward, & Rasor, 1990). Telephone workers do themselves and their callers a service when they show that they are not willing to be manipulated or abused and that they value their own needs as highly as they value those of the caller. Generally, if a telephone worker spends more than 15 to 20 minutes with a caller, the client's crisis becomes the worker's crisis (Knudson, 1991).

Given the foregoing admonition, the telephone worker needs to remember that the sameness of the material and the dependency these clients demonstrate day in and day out make it easy to forecast their repetitious behavior and treat them as bothersome, inept, boring, and unimportant clients. Many of these are "Yes, but . . ." callers. Although they seem highly receptive to the suggestions and plans that crisis workers make with them, in the end they find all kinds of excuses and explanations to not follow through on what they promised to do—which makes them extremely exasperating (Waters & Finn, 1995, p. 269).

Regular callers may tend to be placed in a stereotypical catchall category because they represent an aggravation to the crisis line. However, the reasons these people call are diverse. Identifying specific types is at least as important as identifying the specific caller (Peterson & Schoeller, 1991). From that standpoint, McCaskie, Ward, and Rasor (1990) have constructed brief descriptions of some of the more typical personality disorders of regular callers, their outward behavior, inner dynamics, and strategies for counseling them.

Paranoid. Paranoids are guarded, secretive, and can be pathologically jealous. They live in logic-tight compartments and it is difficult if not impossible to shake their persecutory beliefs. They see themselves as victims and expect deceit and trickery from everyone. The counseling focus is to stress their safety needs.

Schizoid. Schizoids have extremely restricted emotional expression and experience. They have few social relationships and feel anxious, shy, and self-conscious in social settings. They are guarded, tactless, and often alienate others. The counseling focus is to build a good sense of self-esteem through acceptance, optimism, and support.

Schizotypal. Schizoid types have feelings of inadequacy and insecurity. They have strange ideas, behaviors, and appearances. The focus of counseling is to give them reality checks and to promote self-awareness and more socially acceptable behavior in a slow-paced, supportive manner.

Antisocial. Antisocials use others, cannot relate to the needs of society or its rules and regulations, and behave in relation to their own self-gratification with little if any thought of the welfare of others. These clients call only when they are in serious personal trouble. The focus of counseling is to get them to assume responsibility for their behavior and the very real and personal consequences their behavior will undoubtedly incur.

Narcissistic. Narcissists are grandiose, extremely self-centered, and believe they have unique problems that others cannot possibly comprehend. They see themselves as victimized by others and always need to be right. The focus of counseling is to get them to see how their behavior is seen and felt by others, while not engaging in a "no win" debate or argument with them.

Histrionic. Histrionics move from crisis to crisis. They have shallow depth of character and are extremely ego involved. They crave excitement and become quickly bored with routine and mundane tasks and events. They may behave in self-destructive ways and can be demanding and manipulative. The focus of counseling is to stress their ability to survive using resources that have been helpful to them in the past.

Obsessive-compulsive. Obsessive-compulsives are preoccupied by and fixate on tasks. They expend and waste vast amounts of time and energy on these endeavors. They often do not hear counselors due to futile attempts to obtain self-control over their obsessions. The focus of counseling is to establish the ability to trust others and the use of thought stopping and behavior modification to diminish obsessive thinking and compulsive behavior.

Manic depressive. The violent mood swings of these callers range from "superman/superwoman" ideation when in a manic phase to 'born loser" ideation in a depressive stage. If they feel thwarted in their grand plans, they may become very aggressive to those that would stop them. At the other end of the continuum, their depressive "doom, despair, and agony on me" outlook puts them at risk for suicidal behavior. Slowing down and pacing these callers in the manic phase is difficult, but needs to be done to put a psychological governor on their runaway behavior. Confrontation about their grandiose plans only alienates them. In the depressive stage, suicide intervention is a primary priority.

Dependent. Dependents have trouble making decisions and seek to have others do so—often inappropriately. Feelings of worthlessness, insecurity, and fear of abandonment predominate. They are particularly prone to become involved and stay in self-destructive relationships. The focus of counseling is to reinforce strengths and act as a support for their concerns without becoming critical of them or accepting responsibility for their lives.

Self-defeating. Self-defeating types choose people and situations that lead to disappointment, failure, and mistreatment by others. They reject attempts to help them and make sure that such attempts will not succeed. The focus of counseling is stressing talents and the behavioral consequences of sabotaging themselves.

Avoidant. Avoidant types are loners who have little ability to establish or maintain social relationships. Their fear of rejection paralyzes their attempts to risk involvement in social relationships. The focus of counseling is encouragement of successive approximations to meaningful relationships through social skills and assertion training.

Passive-aggressive. Passive-aggressives cannot risk rejection by displaying anger in an overt manner. Rather, they engage in covert attempts to manipulate others and believe that control is more important than self-improvement. The focus of counseling is to promote more open, assertive behavior.

Borderline. The borderline personality is so named because such people are chameleonlike and at any given time, may resemble any of the foregoing mental disorders. Also, they are always on the "borderline" of being functional and dysfunctional. They are one of the most problematic of callers and are dealt with at length later in this chapter.

Handling the Severely Disturbed Caller

"The behavior of the severely disturbed is primitive, disorganized, disoriented, and disabling. These people are likely to elicit discomfort, anxiety, and outright fear in the observer. These are strange people. These are different people. These are people we lock away in mental institutions, pumping them full of strong drugs that turn the mania into docileness" (Greenwald, 1985b). This stereotypical public view of the mentally disturbed, quoted in the University of Illinois at Chicago's Counseling Center hotline training manual, introduces hotline workers to the mentally disturbed. These are many of the people who call crisis hotlines. On the neophyte phone counselor's first meeting with the disorganized and disjunctive thought processes of the mentally disturbed, all the training the crisis worker has ever received is likely to fall by the wayside.

These callers represent a cornucopia of mental illnesses. They may be delusional and hallucinatory; be unable to remotely test what they are doing, believing, or thinking against reality; be emotionally volcanic or conversely demonstrate the emotionality of a stone; lack insight or judgment about their problems and be unable to relate any linear or logical history of these problems; be so suspicious in their paranoid ideation that they believe even the phone worker is out to get them; be manipulative, resistant, and openly hostile and noncompliant to the simplest requests; not have the slightest idea of appropriate interpersonal boundaries with significant others or the crisis worker; demonstrate obsessive behavior and compulsive thoughts that they continually harp on to the exclusion of any effective functioning; have no meaningful interpersonal relationships with the possible exception of crisis line workers; impulsively place themselves in problematic and dangerous situations over and over; and present themselves in childlike or even infantile ways (Grunsted, Cisneros, & Belen, 1991). Whether these behaviors are biochemically or psychologically based makes little difference. These people are so distanced from our own reality and so threatening that the beginning phone counselor's immediate reaction is to get off the line!

However, if the worker pictures the disturbed client as a person whose developmental processes have gone terribly awry, then the call may take on structure and sense and become less intimidating. No matter how bizarre the call may be, these primary axioms apply to the caller's behavior (Greenwald, 1985a, p. 1):

1. Behavior is always purposeful and serves motives that may be either conscious or unconscious.
2. Behavior is comprehensible and has meaning even though the language used may not.
3. Behavior is characteristic and consistent with personality even though it is exaggerated.
4. Behavior is used to keep a person safe and free of anxiety.

The following rules for dealing with disturbed callers are abstracted from a number of crisis hotlines (Epstein & Carter, 1991; Greenwald, 1985a, 1985b; Knudson, 1991; Tuttle, 1991).

Slow Emotions Down. Although disturbed callers have many feelings that have been submerged from awareness, it is not the best strategy to attempt to uncover these feelings. The caller is being besieged by too many feelings and needs to find a way to get them in control. Focusing on here-and-now issues that are concrete and reality oriented is the preferred mode of operation. Do not elicit more feelings with open-ended questions such as "Can you tell me more about that?" Instead, use calming interventions that force the person to order thinking in small, realistic bits of detail.

CW: I understand how scary those thoughts are that keep creeping into your mind and the "things" you think are in the room. What I want you to do right now is look around the room and tell me what is there. Then tell me what happened to start this thinking.

The idea is to slow emotions down. Although the worker may acknowledge the feelings, they are not the focus of attention. By breaking up freewheeling ideation into discrete, manageable pieces, the telephone worker gives the caller a sense of regaining control. The worker may also bring the caller back to reality from a flashback by asking the client what he or she is doing:

CW: You say you're in that alley and he's assaulting you. Were you smoking a cigarette then? I know you just lit a cigarette a minute ago. I want you to slowly inhale, smell that smoke, and tell me where you are. Now blow the smoke out and see where it goes around the room.

Refuse to Share Hallucinations and Delusions. If a caller is hallucinating or delusional, the telephone worker should never side with the psychotic ideation.

Caller: Do you see, hear, smell, feel those things?
CW: No! I'm sorry, I don't. I understand right now you do and that's terrifying, but what I want to do is get you some help. So stay with me. What is your [doctor's, sister's, friend's] phone number so we can get some support for you?

Little if any good ever comes of participating in such thinking, and as the delusion increases, it becomes difficult to extricate oneself from it. Yet grandiose thinking, no matter how bizarre, should not be denied.

CW: (*Inappropriate and sarcastic.*) Come on, now. The CIA isn't really listening to an auto mechanic by electronic eavesdropping. Certainly they've got better things to do than that. Why do you believe that?
CW: (*Appropriate and empathic.*) It's pretty clear that you really believe the CIA is listening to you. When did this start?

The worker affirms the paranoid delusion is real without agreeing to its veracity. By asking a *when* question, the worker can start eliciting information that will allow assessment of the scope and extent of the paranoia. A *why* question is never appropriate because of the defensive reaction it may elicit in any caller, especially in a paranoid.

Determine Medication Usage. If at all possible, the worker should elicit information as to use of any medication, amount and time of dosage, and particularly, stopping medication without consulting the attending physician. Changing, forgetting, or disregarding medication is one of the most common reasons that people become actively psychotic (Ammar & Burdin, 1991). Furthermore, having this information will give the worker a better idea of the type of mental disturbance the caller is being treated for. Regardless of the reasons or excuses clients give for not taking medicine, the worker should endeavor to get them to their prescribing physician so medication can be adjusted or reinstituted.

CW: Lemuel, I want you to call up your doctor as soon as we get off the phone. I understand that the medicine gives you a bad taste in your mouth and makes you feel queasy. However, your doctor needs to know that, and you need to let her know you're not on your meds.

Becoming familiar with the major tranquilizers, antidepressants, and antipsychotic drugs is important for this work (Pope, 1991). However, given all the different kinds of drugs and their numerous generic and trade names, keeping track of them all is extremely difficult. The *Physician's Desk Reference* (*PDR*) provides information on what these drugs do, how much is generally given, and what the side effects are. No crisis line office should be without a current edition.

Keep Expectations Realistic.   The telephone worker should keep expectations realistic. The caller did not become disturbed overnight. No crisis worker is going to change chronic psychotic behavior during one phone call. The crisis worker is buying time for the caller in a period of high anxiety and attempting to restore a minimum amount of control and contact with reality. If the caller is trying to "milk" the worker through an interminable conversation, confronting the problem in a direct manner will generally determine whether the caller is lonely or is in need of immediate assistance.

CW: It seems as if this can't be solved, and you say you can't wait until tomorrow to go to the clinic. I'm concerned enough that I think we ought to make arrangements to transport you to the hospital right now.

Maintain Professional Distance.   Calls from severely disturbed individuals may evoke all kinds of threatening feelings in phone workers, leaving them feeling inadequate, confused, and in crisis themselves! Maintaining professional distance when exceedingly painful and tragic stories are related is difficult for the most experienced phone worker. When these feelings begin to emerge, it is of utmost importance for workers to make owning statements about their own feelings and get supervision immediately. Passing the line to another worker in no way indicates inadequacy.

CW: Frankly, I'm a bit confused as to what to do. I've done everything I know, and I'm tapped out. I'd like to connect you with Irma, who may have some other ideas, while I talk to our director.

As confused and disoriented as disturbed callers may be, they seem to have a sixth sense about sensitive areas in others. Countertransference (the attributing to clients of the therapist's own problems) is not uncommon, and disturbed callers can sometimes unearth the worker's own hidden agendas and insecurities. A worker's strong reactions, either positive or negative, to these callers should alert the hotline worker that processing and feedback with a co-worker or supervisor is needed.

TC: (Paranoid.) I know who you are, when you work on the hotline, and where you live.

CW: (Inappropriately responding to the threat in a shaky voice.) What have I ever done to you? I'm trying to help you, and you get bent out of shape. I've got a good mind to hang this phone up right now or even call the police. We can trace these calls, you know!

CW: (Appropriately responding to the implication in a clear, firm, but empathic voice.) Jacques, those things are not important to what's going on with you right now. What is important is making you feel safe enough to go back to your apartment to-night and go to the doctor in the morning. I understand why you might get upset over my suggesting you see the doctor, but I also want you to clearly understand it's your safety I'm concerned about. So what's making you angry with me?

By deflecting the caller's paranoia and refocusing the dialogue back on the client's is-sues, the telephone worker directively forces the caller, in an empathic manner, to re-spond to his own emotional state.

Avoid Placating.   Placating and sympathizing do little to bolster the caller's confi-dence or to help move the client toward action.

Caller: (Depressed.) I'm just not any good to anybody, much less myself.

CW: (Inappropriately sympathetic.) From all you've told me, you've had a really rocky road. Nobody should have to suffer what you have, but things can only look up.

Rather, by empathically responding and exploring past feelings and coping skills when life was better, the telephone worker not only acknowledges the dilemma but also fo-cuses on the client's strengths.

CW: You do sound pretty hopeless right now, but I wonder how you were feeling when things weren't this way, and what you were doing then that you aren't doing now.

Assess Lethality. Many clients who call crisis lines have active suicidal or homicidal ideation. It may seem puzzling that such people would call a crisis line when they seem so bent on harming themselves or others. What these callers are doing is trying to put distance between their thoughts and the actions that might result from those lethal thoughts. As much as the callers may avow intentions of lethality, they are still in enough control of themselves to attempt to place a buffer (the telephone worker) be-tween thinking and acting.

Caller: If I can't have him, she sure as hell won't. I'll kill them both, and you, the po-lice, or nobody else can stop me.

CW: Yet you called here, for which I'm glad. Something is holding you back, and I'd like to know what that something is.

Caller: Well, I'm a Christian, but their sins go beyond redemption.

CW: So as a Christian, you probably think the commandment "Thou shalt not kill" is pretty important. What you're saying is you're about to commit sin, just as they did. How will that help you and how will it look in the eyes of God?

Although it may be construed that the telephone worker is manipulating the spiritual philosophy of the caller to achieve an end, the major goal of the crisis worker is to disrupt the irrational chain of thinking that is propelling the client toward violence. In that regard, when dealing with the disturbed caller, the overriding thesis is "Save the body before the mind" (Grunsted, Cisneros, & Belen, 1991). Crisis intervention over the telephone with the severely disturbed is clearly not meant to be curative. It is a stopgap measure designed to be palliative enough to keep action in abeyance until help arrives. Whether that help is in the form of getting the police or a mobile intervention team to the site, setting up an appointment for a therapy session the next morning, obtaining a support person, or helping a lonely, depressed person get through the night, the idea is to psychologically hold the disturbed caller's hand until help arrives.

Although no crisis line staff members that we know of would ever instruct their workers to give out their full names or home phone numbers, at times callers can be very seductive in their attempt to extract personal information from crisis line workers. Rookies on the crisis line may be very taken with the heartbreaking stories they hear or feel very gratified by the strokes that dependent callers can give them. Under no circumstances should a crisis line worker ever give out his or her full name or other personal information, nor should the worker ever agree to meet the caller for social or professional reasons. The crisis line's credibility is built on anonymity, and that works both ways. In addition, serious ethical problems may arise when that anonymity is breached. Finally, crisis line workers who do not observe the foregoing run the risk of putting themselves in physical harm's way.

Given the preceding severely disturbed callers, our admonition is still to treat these clients not as types, but as individuals with their own idiosyncratic problems. However, the severely disturbed are not the only regular or problem callers

Other Problem Callers

Telephone crisis workers must sometimes deal with "rappers," pranksters, manipulators, sexually explicit callers, or even callers presenting legitimate sexual problems. It must be remembered and accepted that every call is an attempt by the caller to fulfill some need or purpose. We have prepared several suggestions that should help workers to understand and cope with such callers.

Rappers. Some callers may just wish to "rap" or "talk." The question becomes whether time should be spent just listening to someone who only wants to "rap" with no seemingly pressing issues. However, if "lonely" is tacked onto the description of the person, this may change the telephone worker's perception of the productivity of the call. It may also be that the caller is having trouble bringing issues into the open and is testing the waters to muster enough courage to get to the real dilemma. By allowing some leeway in approaching issues but at the same time gently confronting the caller's loneliness or reluctance to get down to business, the worker sets reasonable limits on the conversation and still provides a supportive forum (McCaskie, Ward, & Rasor, 1990).

Pranksters. Teenagers who are bored at an overnight party may call the line just to bedevil the workers. If the prank call is treated seriously they will probably hang up and not call back. If they are hung up on, they will continue to call (Waters & Finn, 1995, p. 270).

Manipulators. A variety of callers achieve their unmet needs by playing games with telephone workers. Questioning the worker's ability, role reversal where the worker is tricked into sharing details of his or her personal life, and harassment are typical manipulative games. Redirecting the manipulative ploy and focusing on the unmet needs of manipulators forces them to look at the reasons for their manipulative behavior (Waters & Finn, 1995, p. 269).

Sexually explicit callers. "Call 1-900-LUST. Cindy's lonely and wants to talk to you!" The proliferation of these ads on late-night television, the Internet, and in porn magazines is a sad testimony to the existence of thousands of men whose insecurities, aberrances, and deviance make "sex talk" a multibillion-dollar business. An even sadder testimony is given by those individuals who use crisis lines for the same purpose. It should not be too amazing that Wark's (1984) interviews with a number of sexually explicit callers found them to be characterized by having low self-esteem, feelings of isolation, lack of trust, a sense of being sexually unfulfilled, and little insight into their behavior. The sexually explicit caller is a particular millstone hung on the crisis line because many female volunteers resign from frustration with frequent sex calls (Baird, Bossett, & Smith, 1994; Fenelon, 1990). Switches to opposite-sex workers and reframing the call in a context suggesting that the caller needs help put a severe damper on such callers.

Legitimate sexual problems. However, many callers who have serious sexual or sexually related problems call crisis lines because of the anonymity it allows to frankly discuss their most private issues. These calls may embarrass workers who are not psychologically prepared for such intimate details, feel shocked at what they hear because of the criminal, exploitative nature, or do not have the technical expertise to handle them. Telephone workers must have education in dealing with sexual concerns and training in legal and ethical knowledge about what to do with them if the caller is a danger to a third party (Horton, 1995, p. 292). The very nature of calls dealing with sexual matters places crisis workers in a potentially value-laden, belief-centered moral and religious arena where the worker's own opinions come into play. Although in most instances the major role of the worker is to *not* let his or her opinions hold sway and influence clients, avoiding these hot areas may also mean denying the caller much-needed information (Horton, 1995, p. 307). Providing options and information about "responsible" sex is a viable approach, although we note that a very fine line runs between the worker's own biases and providing balanced information and must be monitored carefully. We absolutely agree with Horton (1995) that telephone workers or, for that matter, any other crisis workers should not

1. regard their own opinion as being "common sense" and the only rational alternative,
2. approach the listener or the inquiry with a closed mind,
3. confuse options with facts,
4. stereotype and judge the caller's sexual actions. (p. 308)

Even though the preceding types of callers are striving to fulfill their needs, they often pose problems for telephone workers. Following are some techniques to help prepare crisis workers to deal with this sometimes difficult clientele.

Pose Open-Ended Questions.   Appropriate use of open-ended questions can help defuse the problems generated by chronic or regular callers (Epstein & Carter, 1991).

TC: You people don't know anything. Everything you've told me is a bunch of crap.
CW: What did you expect to gain from this call, then?
TC: Just to tell you what I think of your lousy service.
CW: If you were me, what would you be doing or saying right now?

These questions refocus the problem back to the caller and force movement toward problem solving rather than keeping the worker subjected to condemnatory statements.

Set Time Limits.   When it is apparent that attempts to refocus the problem to the caller are futile, then a time limit should be set (Knudson, 1991).

TC: You ought to be congratulating me on getting my act together, no thanks to you.
CW: I'm glad you've done something positive since you last called. Now we can talk about your current situation for five minutes. Then I'll have to take another call.

Terminate Abuse.   When the caller's behavior escalates to what the worker perceives as abusiveness, the call should be terminated in a clear and firm manner (McCaskie, Ward, & Rasor, 1990).

TC: You bitch! Don't you dare hang up this goddamned phone!
CW: (*Assertively.*) I'm sorry, but that is language we do not tolerate, so I'm going to another caller now.

Switch Workers.   Particularly with a sexually explicit caller, switching the call to another worker, preferably a male, takes the stimulus thrill out of the situation and makes it very difficult for the caller to bring masturbation to orgasm, which is usually the end goal of such a call (Knudson, 1991).

TC: I'd love to cover you with honey and lick you all over.
CW (Female): (*Calmly and coolly.*) Given your specific problem, I'm going to switch you to Ralph. (*Signals to Ralph.*)
CW (Ralph): (*Assertively.*) I understand you have a problem. How can I help you?

If a male is not available, the call should be shifted to a supervisor and terminated. The caller should be told that the worker will hang up and that action should be taken immediately (McCaskie, Ward, & Rasor, 1990).

CW (Supervisor): (*Authoritatively and firmly.*) We are *not* here to answer demeaning remarks. I am going to hang up, and we will continue to do so until your behavior changes.

To bait a telephone worker and hold her on the line, sexually explicit callers often externalize their fantasies by reporting some hypothetical significant other's problem in florid detail. When the first hint of this ploy occurs, the worker should interpret the behavior as the caller's own and make the switch (Knudson, 1991).

TC: I'm really worried about my uncle and his 10-year-old daughter. She's a little doll, and he's always giving her these massages in her bedroom and I . . .
CW: (*Interrupts.*) That's out of my area of expertise; please hold the line and let me switch you to our child abuse expert, Ralph.

Covert Modeling. Covert modeling or conditioning (Cautela, 1976; Kazdin, 1975) has been used by Baird, Bossett, and Smith (1994) to extinguish repeated calls by sexually explicit clients. In covert modeling, the client is asked to use mental imagery to picture either reinforcing or extinguishing a particular behavior. The following worker response is abridged from their technique.

CW: As you're talking, I'm wondering if you recognize your real problem and want help with it. I know this would be pretty difficult to give up. But sometime soon, I'm not sure exactly when, but as you reach for the phone you'll think to call a therapist instead. And this notion that you'll call a therapist and get help will get stronger every day as you think of it. You'll also start to feel better as you realize the crisis line isn't fulfilling your needs as therapy will. I'm going to hang up now and let you think about getting help with your real problem.

By suggesting that the need to call the therapist will grow, the worker plants the seed for anxiety about the caller's present behavior to grow along with the need to change. Both negative and positive reinforcers are used in the image: the need to seek help and the good feeling that will come from doing so. The worker also speaks of seeking help for the "real problem." This unspecified problem allows the worker to respond emphatically without accusing the caller of terrible, deviant behavior but still clearly states that the caller needs help. The worker does not continue in a dialogue with the client but instead hangs up to let the seed start to grow.

Formulate Administrative Rules. Administratively, crisis lines need to set specific rules to extinguish abusive behavior by doing the following (Knudson, 1991; McCaskie, Ward, & Rasor, 1990):

1. Limiting number and duration of calls from any single caller
2. Limiting the topics that will be discussed
3. Requiring that only specific workers versed in handling abusive callers take such calls
4. Using speaker phones for on-the-spot consultation
5. Requiring the caller to establish a face-to-face relationship with an outside worker and allow communication between the therapist and crisis line personnel
6. Allowing the staff to prohibit calls for a day, a week, or more, if physical threats are made

The Headquarters Crisis Center of Lawrence, Kansas, uses a tracking log for regular callers that lists their name, phone number, address, style of interaction, major and tangential issues, effective and ineffective response modes, their physician/therapist, medications, support groups, and lethality levels. The log is kept current and available to staff, saving them a great deal of time and energy. This center also has an internal messages notebook labeled "Client Concerns." It contains information about regular callers that workers can quickly read to become updated on the caller's circumstances. It is an effective method to keep staff current and can be used to offer feedback and suggestions to clients (Epstein & Carter, 1991). Staff should be brought together on a regular basis to discuss these callers, plan strategy for them, and make suggestions and voice personal concerns (McCaskie, Ward, & Rasor, 1990).

Finally, it is our own recommendation that supervisors be acutely aware of the impact that such callers can have on personnel. Crisis center administrators should be ready, willing, and able to process debilitating emotions that such calls often evoke in workers in a caring, empathic, and supportive manner through regularly planned supervision and emergency debriefing sessions when necessary. Crisis intervention over the telephone is tough, grueling work, particularly when clients such as the foregoing emerge. Crisis calls are frequently one-time events with very little opportunity for positive feedback. Particularly because crisis lines are run chiefly by volunteers, they need to be aware that not everyone can be helped (Waters & Finn, 1995, p. 271).

CASE HANDLING AT WALK-IN CRISIS FACILITIES

Unlike contact with the faceless and anonymous telephone client, crisis worker contact with walk-in clients is close up and personal. We'll describe the types of presenting crises generally seen at walk-in facilities. Then we'll examine how cases are handled at a typical community mental health clinic.

Types of Presenting Crises

Clients who present themselves for crisis counseling at walk-in facilities generally fall within one of four categories—those who are experiencing:

1. Chronic mental illness
2. Interpersonal problems in their social environment
3. Intrapersonal problems in their own development
4. A combination of the three foregoing categories

Chronic Crisis.   Since the enactment of the federal Community Mental Health Centers Act of 1963, the major responsibility for treatment of the mentally ill has fallen on community mental health centers. Although in theory the act was designed to deinstitutionalize patients and return those who are able to functional living, in fact the act has placed many people in chronic crisis.

In addition, the Vietnam War, increased drug abuse, a rise in crime, fragmentation of families, and a host of other societal ills have caused a tremendous upsurge in the need for mental health services. Originally focused on reintegrating the long-term hospital patient into the community, mental health centers have tended to assign chronic cases a less-than-priority status. The unspoken reason is that these clients are extremely frustrating to mental health providers because they show little progress and are a constant financial and emotional drain on the resources of the agencies that come in contact with them. Many community mental health centers have deemphasized this role and moved more toward dealing with developmental problems of "normal," more highly functioning people (Slaikeu, 1990, p. 284). Perhaps more ominously, funding cutbacks have forced community mental health centers to look more closely at a client's ability to pay as a precondition for treatment, which means that people who may most need service may be relegated to a waiting list. Furthermore, because of legal ramifications and funding problems, severely disturbed people who are committed to state hospitals typically have very brief stays and are turnstiled back onto the streets.

The result is that a host of chronically mentally ill people who are poorly functioning, impoverished, homeless, victims or perpetrators of crime, and without support systems of any kind are left to fend for themselves. These people often have multiple problems besides a primary diagnosis of psychopathology. They may be noncompliant with treatment, disregard their medication, abuse alcohol and drugs, have other severe physical problems, and be victimized financially, physically, and psychologically by others (Bender, 1986; Nurius, 1984; Pope, 1991). It is easy to see why such people often wind up in crisis when understaffed and underfunded mental health clinics (Roberts, 1991, p. 31) and other social services agencies cannot care for them. The chronically mentally ill are often on a first-name basis with local police and personnel in emergency rooms, mental health clinics, and social services agencies.

Social/Environmental Crisis.   Chronics are not the only people who avail themselves of, or are brought to, walk-in facilities. Runaways, addicts, battered women, crime victims, survivors of violent events, the sexually abused, the terminally ill, divorcées, the unemployed, and relatives of the chronically physically and mentally ill are some of the many participants in a drama of social crisis that is played out every day and night in mental health clinics, emergency rooms, student counseling centers, social services agencies, and police stations across the country. Many precipitating events may be unexpected and sudden and may have an impact far beyond the individual on families and communities, leaving these systems disorganized and out of control. Crises that are generated in the social environment are some of the most potent for mental health workers because of their ramifications across systems and the heightened emotionality and immediacy that accompany them for both clientele and workers.

Developmental Crisis.   It used to be thought that development was fixed by the end of adolescence. In this view, when a person became physically mature, somehow other aspects of the person were set in concrete and one lived out one's life according to a set script determined by genetic and environmental factors. However, starting with Havinghurst's (1952) and Erikson's (1963) theories of general developmental tasks through the life span and with Roe's (1956) and Super's (1957) theories of career development, theory and research have continued to flesh out a series of stages that extend from infancy to old age.

Perhaps two works—one that deals with adult men, *The Seasons of a Man's Life* (Levinson, 1978), and the other with adult women, *Passages* (Sheehy, 1976)—have done more than any others to popularize the notion that people are constantly faced with challenges and tasks as they move through life. Choosing a college, dealing with an unwanted pregnancy, raising children, selecting an occupation, purchasing a first home, coping with job loss and mobility, maintaining a marriage or relationship, confronting physical decline, preparing for retirement, caring for one's parents, and experiencing chronic illness and hospitalization are typical tasks that people face as they move from adolescence to old age. Whether people can successfully transit through these developmental tasks has a great deal to do with how well they face the next stage of living and its tasks. If they are not successful and remain stuck in a particular stage, they become excellent candidates for crisis (Levinson, 1978). In reality, passage through one stage to another invariably involves some degree of crisis and makes growth possible. However, when lack of skills and knowledge, inability to take risks, absence of support systems, or lack of material resources combine with chance factors and pile up, the individual's coping skills become unequal to the task and a developmental crisis results. Although these crises may lack the duration and severity of crises among the chronically mentally ill or victims and survivors of social/environmental trauma, their sheer numbers impact mental health delivery systems and provide a fertile field for the crisis interventionist.

Combination of Types.   The foregoing crisis types rarely occur as discrete categories. Overlapping among types and problems that face crisis workers is the rule rather than the exception. Attempting to stabilize a chronic schizophrenic without providing food and shelter, treating a trauma survivor without first working on a drug addiction, or considering vocational exploration without handling the depression of a middle-aged executive who has just lost her job is a waste of valuable time. Crisis workers must be able to assess and set priorities on problems according to their immediacy, react swiftly to rapidly changing conditions, understand and move adroitly through social services bureaucracies, and still maintain an empathic and caring attitude toward their clientele without suffering burnout (Intrater, 1991).

Case Handling at a Community Mental Health Clinic

We have chosen Midtown Mental Health Clinic in our hometown of Memphis, Tennessee, as a generic representation of how clients are taken care of who walk into or are brought to a community mental health facility. This clinic's catchment area includes a number of housing projects, the downtown area, the University of Tennessee medical facility, the city hospital, private hospitals that have inpatient psychiatric facilities, the Memphis Veterans Administration Hospital, the Memphis Mental Health Institute (a state psychiatric hospital), the county jail, several halfway shelters for drug addicts and the homeless, and a variety of other social services agencies. Furthermore, its catchment area has the highest crime rate and incidence of domestic violence in the city, a high percentage of school dropouts, and some of the most impoverished areas of the city.

Entry.   Clients may come to the mental health clinic on their own, be brought by relatives or social services agencies, or be taken into custody by the police. At the moment of entry, disposition of the case begins. A person in crisis who walks in or is brought to Midtown may range across the triage scale score from mildly to severely disturbed. If the person is severely disturbed, a senior clinician is summoned. An attempt is made to remove the client to an isolated office to reduce environmental stimuli and calm the client so that an assessment can proceed. The clinician tries to obtain a case history. If this is not possible, the clinician makes a visual and verbal assessment in regard to information-processing problems, tangential thinking, hallucinations, disassociation, threats to oneself or others, or severe drug abuse. If any of these symptoms is present, then a psychiatrist is called to evaluate the client and decide whether hospitalization is warranted.

Commitment.   If the client is so mentally fragmented as to be clearly out of touch with reality or deemed an imminent danger to self or others, he or she is committed to an inpatient mental health facility. The person is asked to voluntarily commit to hospitalization. If he or she is unwilling to do so, a physician may write an involuntary commitment order. An officer of the Crisis Intervention Team, a special unit of the Memphis Police Department trained to deal with the mentally ill, is then called to transport the patient. Under no circumstances do mental health workers become involved in transportation, because of safety concerns and the possibility of stigmatizing themselves as punitive agents in the patient's eyes. If patients are financially able, they may be transported to a private psychiatric facility. If they are indigent, they are taken to the city hospital psychiatric emergency unit for evaluation and subsequent placement at the Memphis Mental Health Institute state hospital.

Intake Interview.   If the individual is coherent enough to provide verbal and written information, an intake interview is started. Following closely the six-step model in Chapter 2, the intake worker first attempts to define the problem, assess for client safety, and apprise clients of their rights. In a patient and methodical manner, the intake worker goes through a standard intake interview sheet. Through open-ended questions and active listening, the worker tries to obtain as comprehensive a picture of the client as possible. The worker also attempts to determine the precipitating problem that brought the client to the clinic. The intake worker must be nonjudgmental, empathic, and caring and must also obtain concrete and specific information from a client who may not be able or willing to reciprocate.

Two critical components are always appraised in this initial assessment: degree of client lethality and drug use. It is a given that crisis situations either involve or have the possibility of acting-out behavior. Therefore the intake worker evaluates clients in relation to their plans or intent to do harm to themselves or others. Because of the widespread use of prescription and illicit drugs, the worker checks to determine if drugs are involved in the presenting problem. Drug involvement may take a variety of forms:

1. The client may be having negative psychological side effects from drugs prescribed for an unrelated physical problem.
2. The client may have stopped taking prescribed antianxiety or antipsychotic drugs because of their extremely unpleasant physical side effects.
3. Drugs and/or alcohol may have been abused by the client to anesthetize him- or herself against terrifying psychological problems.
4. The client may be addicted to illegal drugs, prescription drugs, or alcohol.

Thus, intake workers need to have a thorough understanding of the *Physician's Desk Reference (PDR)*. The intake worker must also have a working knowledge of the side effects of "street drugs" because of the high incidence of their use in the Midtown area.

Disposition.   After the intake has been completed, the worker constructs and writes a proposed diagnosis and treatment recommendations. The intake worker discusses the treatment recommendations and possible services with the client. It is then the client's decision to accept or reject services. If services are accepted, the intake worker introduces the client to the therapist who will most likely be in charge of the case. A full clinical team meeting is held to confirm or alter the initial diagnosis and treatment recommendations. At that time a primary therapist is designated and assumes responsibility for the case.

Anchoring.   On their initial visit, clients are never left alone. From their intake interview to disposition to a primary therapist, workers help clients feel a personal interest is being taken in them and their problems. The worker takes and hands over the client to the therapist who will be in charge of the case. The therapist gives the client a verbal orientation about what is going to occur. The idea behind this methodical orientation is to demystify the world of mental health, familiarize clients with what their treatment will be, and provide them with a psychological anchor in the form of a real person who will act as their advocate, support, and contact person. Quickly establishing rapport with the primary therapist is helpful in forestalling future crisis and is extremely important to unstable clients given the threatening implications of entering a mental health facility, possible loss of freedom, and the bureaucratic maze of the mental health system. It is also designed to immediately empower clients and make them feel they have taken a step in the right direction.

Once basic needs have been met, the client is given a card with an appointment time and day on it. In many instances, a compeer volunteer is assigned to the client. Compeers are trained volunteers who act as support and socializing agents for clients who do not have friends or relatives to assist and encourage them.

Short-Term Disposition.   Many crises relate to the basic physical necessities of living. If that is the case, the intake worker makes short-term provisions for food, clothing, shelter, and other necessities while setting in motion the wheels of other social services agencies to provide long-term subsistence services. If clients are unable to care for themselves, the Tennessee Department of Family Services is appointed as a conservator to handle their money and look after their basic needs. Thus it is very important that the intake worker and other staff thoroughly understand and can access the local social services network.

Long-Term Disposition.   An interdisciplinary team reviews and evaluates the intake worker's diagnosis and recommendations. If the team considers it necessary, a psychiatrist and a pharmacist conduct a psychiatric or pharmacological evaluation of the client. If a psychological evaluation is required, a psychometrist evaluates the person on standardized personality and intellectual measures. Depending on the client's needs, team members from various specialty units join the team. Once the team is complete, it formulates objectives and goals and a therapeutic plan is put into operation. The team reviews this plan on a regular basis, and changes it if necessary.

Twenty-Four-Hour Service.   Midtown operates 24 hours a day. After regular working hours, telephone relays are linked into the crisis hotline. Telephone workers there evaluate the call and make a decision on whom should handle it.

Mobile Crisis Teams.   For certain clients, particularly geriatric cases, it may be necessary to make home visits. At other times, when a client is out of control and unwilling or unable to go to the clinic, crisis workers go wherever the client is. With the advent of the police department's Crisis Intervention Team, this need has diminished a good deal in Memphis. However, in many other cities these mobile teams are on call and often follow up after local police departments have contained the situation.

Telephone Follow-Up.   The telephone can serve long-term clients who are at transcrisis points in their therapy. Such clients may avail themselves of their therapist by phone for perceptual checks and support. As clients move through developmental stages of therapy, they often face new and terrifying aspects of their growth toward mental health. Phone calls to their therapist help dissipate the ambiguity and rapidly oscillating emotions as clients test what are for them risky new behaviors.

TRANSCRISIS HANDLING IN LONG-TERM THERAPY

Clients in long-term therapy are not immune from crisis. Therapy tends to move in developmental stages with psychological troughs, crests, and plateaus. Even though clients have success in meeting therapeutic goals, each new stage brings with it what are seen in many instances to be even more formidable obstacles. The beginning therapist who has seen a client make excellent progress is often in for a rude awakening when the client's progress comes completely undone and behavior regresses to pretherapeutic functioning. We'll discuss here a number of crisis situations that might arise in the course of long-term therapy. The six-step model of crisis intervention is an appropriate guide to action in these situations.

Anxiety Reactions

A puzzling aspect of therapy occurs when clients are highly successful in achieving tremendously difficult goals and then are completely undone by a task that to the objective observer does not seem all that difficult. Although it seems cognitively irrational, the fear of failure to achieve this minor goal becomes a self-fulfilling prophecy. The client fears that others will see through her or his sham of competence and irrationally thinks that any real progress is a delusion. At such times, clients engage in various types of flight behavior. Severe anxiety is one way of escaping the threatening situation. Consider Melanie's present dilemma. Melanie has escaped from an alcoholic marriage and subsequently completed two years of secretarial science at a community college, but she has fallen apart when faced with an interview for a job she desperately wants.

Melanie: (Extremely anxious and agitated. Calling her therapist at 1 A.M.) I hated to call you, but I'm so scared. I've thrown up twice and I've got the shakes. This hasn't happened since I walked out on Bill over three years ago. God, I can't get a grip and I need to do my best tomorrow. I know I'll just blow it. I can't think straight, and I can't remember a thing about interviewing. Everything's just running together.

The therapist puts Melanie at a 5 on the triage scale for cognitive threat and a 6 for affective anxiety/fear. If the therapist does not help diminish the anxiety, the potential is that Melanie may move upward to 8–9 on these scales by the time she goes for her job interview the next day.

TH: Just do this for a minute, Melanie. Take a deep breath and let it out slo-o-owly. That's right! Now take another! OK, again. *(Continues in a patient, calm voice for about two minutes, taking Melanie through a brief deep-breathing exercise to calm her anxiety attack.)*

After the deep breathing exercise, when Melanie has regained some semblance of control, the therapist paces with her through the role play they had conducted the previous session, has her write down her blunders and strong points, discusses those with her, determines that her attack is receding, and assesses her now as being between a 2 and a 3 on the subscales. A quick review of the client's other successes reinforces and further buttresses the positive change in current functioning.

TH: Now notice the change in your voice. I'll bet you've also calmed down to where you aren't shaking. Did you notice how much more you're in control now? Remember what you're there for. Although a lot depends on this for you, you've also done even bigger, more threatening and scary things in your life like getting the hell out of that malignant marriage. Remember! You've become very good in secretarial science. They need you as much or more than you need them. I want you to put that up as a big signboard in your head, in dayglow pink: THEY NEED YOU JUST AS MUCH AS YOU NEED THEM!

By role-playing the scene, the therapist puts Melanie back on familiar ground and puts the problem back into context—getting a job as opposed to having a free-floating anxiety attack. By marshaling the client's resources and very specifically and objectively reminding her of what her strengths are, the therapist concretizes the vague dread she feels at having to face the interview. The therapist's exhortation about who needs whom is not placating here. It is realistic. Melanie's ego needs to be reminded of these facts so that she will have a positive mental set both toward her personhood and her skills as she enters the interview. Finally, the therapist offers her the opportunity to have a safety net.

TH: Melanie, I think you're ready to get some sleep and go knock their socks off tomorrow. However, if you wake up tomorrow morning and really have some questions or think you need to role-play that interview once more, give me a call. I've got some free time before your interview and we can go over it once more. Now go to bed, get some sleep, and dream about that Day-Glo pink billboard.

By leaving her with a positive injunction and making time for her the next day, the therapist continues to provide a support system and a security net for Melanie.

Regression

The risk of taking the next step in therapeutic development may become too overwhelming even though clients have been highly successful in attaining prior goals. When clients are overwhelmed, they may regress in their behavior, retreating to maladaptive but familiar ways of behaving, feeling, and thinking.

Melanie: (*Somewhat embarrassed and mumbling in a childlike voice.*) I know what you're going to say, but I was thinking I really couldn't cut this, and Bill made that offer even after I got him arrested that he still loved me and was getting help, and I know he doesn't drink much anymore.

TH: (*Interpreting the dynamics.*) What you're really saying is the prospect of that interview is scaring the hell out of you, and it's so scary that you'd give up three years of hard work and sacrifice to go back to a really lousy, not to mention dangerous, way of living, when you're about to get the gold ring. I'm wondering why you've decided to sabotage yourself now.

By interpreting the dependency needs of the client, the therapist welds regressive thinking to the current threat of becoming independent as manifested in the job interview. Although the client's behavior and affect are not blatant, she is moving insidiously higher on the triage cognitive loss subscale. Left alone, that negative self-talk could convince the client to give up her new self-identity and go back to the long-dead and dangerous marriage.

Melanie: Oh, I just knew you'd say that, but I'm not sure I can do this. I mean a big outfit like United Techtronic.

TH: (*In a cool, clear, no-nonsense, but not condemning, voice.*) Big or small, United Techtronic is not the question. The question is, Are you going to choose to blow this, before you even see if you can cut it? That's one way of never finding out if you're good enough. You can make that choice, although you've now been making a different one for three years. I'd hope you wouldn't do that—I believe you are good enough—but then, it's your choice.

This reality-based approach directly confronts the client with the underlying and unwarranted irrational decision she is about to make and vividly points out how she is attempting to delude herself into buying back into a dependent status and revictimizing herself.

Problems of Termination

When clients have met their goals for therapy, are fully functioning, and are ready to get back to the business of living their own lives, they may suddenly produce terrible problems that only their therapist can solve. Whatever these problems are, it is an excellent bet that they have been told that it's time to terminate or they have figured out that termination is about to happen. At such times it is a common occurrence for dependency issues to arise. These problems generally can be resolved by successively approximating the client to termination. For example, instead of every week, the therapist schedules the client every two weeks, then once a month, and then for a six-month follow-up. The other option is to clearly discuss the possibility that this issue will arise.

TH: Melanie, I think it's time we discussed your spreading your wings and flying away from here. You landed that job and . . .

Melanie: (*Interrupts.*) But I couldn't have done that without you. You give me the courage to try those things. You've been so wonderful, I just couldn't have done any of this without you. And there's still the problem with the kids and . . .

TH: (*Gently interrupting.*) I appreciate those compliments. They mean a lot to me. Yet although we've worked together on those things, it's been you who's done it, not I. What I want to talk about with you now is some of those fears and really being on your own, like what you just said. That's pretty normal to have those feelings, lots of people do. Sort of like when you left home the first time. I want you to know I'll be here if you need me, but I want you also to know that I think it's time for you to be on your own. I'd like to discuss this with you in today's session.

Crisis in the Therapy Session

One of the scariest times for a therapist occurs when a technique has done its job exceedingly well and the client gains insight or release from a deeply buried traumatic experience—and then completely loses control. This unexpected turn of events can unsettle the most experienced therapist. As this wellspring of affect emerges, it may go far beyond cathartic insight and leave the client in a severe state of disequilibrium.

At this point it is absolutely mandatory to stay in control of the situation and take a firm and directive stance, no matter how frightening the client's actions or how personally repulsive the uncovered material may be. Our own admonition to our students is "You may feel physically sick, start to break out in a sweat, and wish to be anyplace else but in that room. However, you are the therapist, and after the session is over you can have a world-class anxiety attack if you wish—you probably deserve it—but right now you are going to stick with the client." By demonstrating cool levelheadedness to the client, the therapist is modeling behavior that the client can emulate.

TH: I'm just wondering if the reason you ever got in that abusive marriage is that sometimes your father might have abused your mother and that's what was modeled as the way a marriage ought to be.

Melanie: (Recoils in a shocked state.) He never did have intercourse with me.

TH: (Taken aback.) I'm not quite sure what you said—"intercourse"?

Melanie: (Breaking down and sobbing.) For 12 years that bastard would mess with me and my sister, and Momma knew, she knew and wouldn't do anything about it. *(Completely breaks down.)* I . . . God . . . he beat us if we didn't do . . . he'd make us masturbate him . . . oh Lord . . . how could he . . . I've kept this secret . . . I can't handle this. I should have done something . . . killed him . . . *(Uncontrolled and wracked sobbing and shaking.)*

TH: (Recomposing herself and gently touching Melanie's arm and quietly talking in a consoling and affirming voice.) I am truly sorry for uncovering that old wound, but you *can* handle it. You've finally got it out. You lived with that hell as a child and another hell as an adult. You are a survivor.

Psychotic Breaks

Staying calm and cool is even more important when a person is having a psychotic break with reality. No matter how delusional or disassociative the client becomes, the central thesis is that the client can maintain contact with reality and take constructive action.

Manuel: (Walks into the therapist's office unannounced and unknown.) I need help, and they recommend you. But no telephones, they listen to me through the telephone. *(Picks up the telephone in a threatening manner.)*

TH: (In a slow, even voice.) I need for you to put that telephone down before we go any further. I will help you, but I want you to put the telephone back on the stand. We've never had the pleasure of meeting. What is your name?

Manuel: It's Manuel. *(Hesitates.)* I'm just coming apart, they won't leave me alone.

TH: I understand that, but I need you to put the phone down and keep it together so you can tell me who's after you. Go ahead and sit down and tell me what's bothering you.

Manuel: It's my supervisor. He wants to fire me and catch me stealing so he listens in on my phone conversations, he's in league with Satan and he's probably in this room. I can smell the brimstone. *(Starts to become agitated and mumble about Hell.)*

TH: (Calmly but in an assertive voice.) OK! You're having trouble with your supervisor. Now we're getting somewhere. That's good, but stay with me, I personally guarantee Satan is not here. I want to know about your supervisor and how long this has been going on. I also want to get you to a safe place where nobody can hurt you, but to do that I need your help, and I need you to stay in contact so I can help you.

Manuel: OK. *(Sits down and starts to talk about his supervisor.)*

The therapist immediately seeks to establish contact by obtaining the client's name while at the same time establishing ground rules for conduct in the therapist's office. When the young man starts to dissociate and talk incoherently, the therapist directively seeks to keep Manuel in contact with reality by focusing discussion on his grievance with his supervisor. The only acknowledgment he gives to evil spirits is his concern for the client's safety. The therapist reinforces the client for staying in contact with him and repeats his request to put the telephone down. Because psychotic clients may have difficulty hearing others because of the intrusive hallucinations assailing them, the therapist slowly and clearly repeats his requests for compliance. By staying in control, the therapist turns a potentially violent situation with an unknown client into a satisfactory resolution.

Manipulative Clients

Most clients try to manipulate their therapists during the course of therapy, for a variety of reasons. These reasons may range from avoiding engagement in new behaviors to testing the therapist's credibility. Clients with personality disorders are the ultimate test of the therapist's ability to handle manipulative behavior, and can create severe crises for themselves and the therapist if not dealt with in very specific ways (Kocmur & Zavasnik, 1993). The borderline personality type in therapy is an open Pandora's box of crises, as graphically described by Beck and Freeman (1990) and Chatham (1989).

Presenting Problems.   Manipulative clients have problems like no other client has. They include the following:

1. A wide variety of presenting problems that may shift from day to day and week to week
2. Unusual combinations of symptoms ranging across a wide array of neurotic to subpsychotic behaviors
3. Continuous self-destructive and self-punitive behavior
4. Impulsive and poorly planned behavior that shifts through infantile, narcissistic, or antisocial behavior
5. Intense emotional reactions out of all proportion to the situation
6. Confusion regarding goals, priorities, feelings, sexual orientation, and so on
7. A constant feeling of emptiness with chronic free-floating anxiety

Therapeutic Relationship.   Manipulators do everything in their power to turn the therapuetic relationship upside down. They have

1. Frequent crises such as suicide threats, abuse of drugs, sexual acting out, financial irresponsibility, and problems with the law

2. Extreme or frequent misinterpretations of the therapist's statements, intentions, or feelings
3. Unusually strong, negative, acting-out reactions to changes in appointment time, room changes, vacations, fees, or termination in therapy
4. Low tolerance for direct eye contact, physical contact, or close proximity in therapy
5. Unusually strong ambivalence on issues
6. Fear of and resistance to change
7. Frequent phone calls to, spying on, and demands for special attention and treatment from the therapist

Borderline Patients

Borderlines vacillate between autonomy and dependence, view the world in black-and-white terms, are ever-vigilant for perceived danger, have chronic tension and anxiety, are guarded in their interpersonal relationships, and are uncomfortable with emotions (Beck & Freeman, 1990, pp. 186–187). Because of these personality traits, they are apt to continuously test the therapeutic relationship to affirm that the therapist, like everybody else, is untrustworthy and not capable of living up to their expectations, while at the same time they are desperately craving attention, love, and respect (McHenry, 1994; Yeomans, 1993).

From that standpoint, it is important to set clear limits for borderline personalities, structure specific therapeutic goals, provide empathic support, caringly confront manipulative and maladaptive behavior, and rigorously stick with these guiding principles (Chatham, 1989). This is easier said than done because of the dramatic kinds of problems and emotions borderlines display. The following dialogue with Tommy, a college student, depicts such problematic behavior.

Tommy: (*Calling the therapist at 2 A.M.*) I can't take this any longer. Nobody cares about me. I think I'm going crazy again—all these weird voices keep coming into my mind. It'd just be easier if I got a gun and blew myself away.

TH: If that's the case, then I'm concerned enough about your welfare to call 911 and get the police there immediately to take you to the hospital. (*Wise in the ways of borderlines, the therapist immediately confronts Tommy's statement.*) If things are that serious, a phone conversation won't get the job done.

Tommy: Well, I didn't say I was going to kill myself right now! You always jump to conclusions. I just couldn't sleep or study because of all these voices and I really need to talk about them.

TH: I'm willing to talk for 15 minutes, but if I don't see you calmed down and functional by that time, I'll feel warranted in calling 911.

By voicing legitimate concerns about the client's safety and setting a specific time limit on the conversations, the therapist reaffirms therapeutic control and does not become engaged in a rambling dialogue. The latter would serve nothing other than to reinforce maladaptive client behavior and cause a sleepless therapist to be angry and irritable the next day! No special considerations other than those normally given to any other clients should be given to the borderline.

Tommy: But Dr. James, I really need to change the appointment and see you tomorrow. I've got this research presentation and my group's meeting during our appointment time. Can't you move somebody else around?

TH: I have an appointment with another client at that time, Tommy. As I told you, to reschedule I need to know 48 hours in advance. It wouldn't be fair to him anymore than it would be fair to you if I did that to your regular time.

Tommy: (*Sarcastically.*) You just really don't give a damn about me, do you?

TH: The fact is, I do give a damn, and that's why I'm not going to cave in and change the appointment time. We're not talking about rejection here, we're talking about a reasonable policy that I use on everybody. I know lots of times it would be easy for you to believe I'm blowing you off. At times you certainly aren't the easiest client to deal with, but I knew that going in, and I committed to see this through with you. I'll expect you at our regular Thursday time.

The therapist owns both his positive and his negative feelings about the client and directly interprets and confronts the client's underlying fear of rejection (Chatham, 1989). Finally, by reminding the client of his regular appointment, the therapist targets behavior rather than affect. Focusing on behavior is far less problematic than dealing with relational issues either inside or outside therapy, because of the client's low tolerance for intimacy (Beck & Freeman, 1990, p. 196).

Treatment noncompliance is par for the course with borderlines.

TH: So how did your assignment go in thought stopping and not arbitrarily categorizing women as saints or prostitutes?

Tommy: Well, I was real busy this week. Besides which, you didn't really make that thought stopping stuff very clear. And then the rubber band reminder on my wrist broke.

TH: (*Frustrated and becoming agitated.*) This is the sixth week I've gone through this with you. You continuously put women in those one-up or one-down positions. Yet you continuously complain that no females are interested in you. How do you ever expect to have an equitable relationship unless you change your thinking?

Tommy: (*Flushed and shouting.*) Oh yeah? You're so perfect? I'll bet your supervisor would like to know the way you verbally harass your clients. Screw you! Who needs therapy or bitches, anyway? They're all sluts anyway. (*Storms out of the room and slams the door.*)

The therapist's frustration may turn to anger if the therapist ascribes malicious intentions to the client's nonperformance, particularly when trying to change the client's black-and-white thinking. Overt frustration often results in reciprocal acting out by the client. The borderline's passive noncompliance is a balancing act between fear of change and fear of offending the therapist through outright refusal to comply with therapeutic requests. When noncompliance is consistently the normative response, the therapist needs to step back from the situation, seek outside consultation, confront these issues openly, and acknowledge freely the client's right to refuse an assignment rather than doggedly proceeding (Beck & Freeman, 1990).

TH: Tommy, I feel really frustrated right now. We've been going at this one assignment for six sessions. Maybe I'm the problem—pushing too fast. On the other hand, I feel you maybe don't want to make me disappointed so you go through the motions. You've always got the right to say no to an assignment, and we can certainly discuss the pros and cons of that. What do you want to do about this assignment?

A favorite ploy of the borderline and other dependent types of clients is to externalize and project their problems onto others. They then attempt to get the therapist to intercede for them by acting as an intermediary or otherwise "fixing" the problem.

Tommy: If you could just write my econ professor a note telling him I'm under your care. I've only missed five classes, and he's threatening to flunk me.

TH: School and therapy are separate, and I won't get into that.

Tommy: *(Whining and pleading.)* But you know how bad off I've been.

TH: If you are sick enough to miss class, perhaps you should consider an academic withdrawal for medical reasons.

Tommy: Well, I'm not that bad off that I need to quit school.

TH: How has getting others to make excuses for you helped in the past?

In refusing to be used by the client, the therapist avoids a pitfall that would invariably lead to more dependent behavior and the continuation of cyclical self-reinforcing dependent and manipulative behavior.

Finally, the watchword with borderlines and other clients who consciously or unconsciously seek to manipulate the therapist is: Remain calm throughout therapy, and do not respond to each new crisis as an emergency. The key question therapists must ask themselves is, Who's doing the majority of work here? If the answer is, Not the client! Then there is a good chance the therapist is getting manipulated.

The preceding examples are a representative variety of problems that may confront therapists as they engage in long-term therapy with clients in crisis. Although these examples have not included all the crises a therapist is likely to encounter with these trying individuals, they have illustrated typical responses following the six-step model when crisis intervention is needed in long-term therapy. In summary, the following eight points encapsulate the therapist's role when a crisis erupts:

1. Listen closely to client concerns.
2. Assess for safety needs.
3. Make clear owning and assertive statements about the therapist's role in the current dilemma.
4. Interpret defense mechanisms in light of current problems.
5. Concretely and objectively deal with current functioning to the exclusion of other, tangential issues.
6. Speak forthrightly and clearly to the problem in the here-and-now.
7. Take direct, immediate action to restore mobility and equilibrium.
8. Provide an immediate, temporary support system during the crisis.

No matter what one's theoretical orientation, when the potential for crisis arises, most experienced therapists move quickly to help clients control their behavior until equilibrium can be reestablished. When therapy goes awry and leads to crisis situations, a major reason is that the therapist has chosen to disregard the warning signs of impending problems, remain passive, and not be proactive in confronting issues in a caring, supportive manner. Yet to approach therapy in an action-oriented manner requires therapists to have a clear notion of client dynamics and an even clearer notion of their own dynamics, particularly in taking well-gauged risks and being able to live with those risks without self-reproach, guilt, or anxiety over being wrong. To do otherwise jeopardizes the therapist's own mobility and equilibrium and puts both the client and the therapist in harm's way.

COUNSELING DIFFICULT CLIENTS

Crisis workers must be prepared to deal with many different types of clients, some of whom are "difficult." To assist in coping with such clients, we have prepared a brief overview that includes examples of appropriate ground rules as well as suggestions for confronting difficult clients.

Ground Rules for Counseling Difficult Clients

Crisis workers, counselors-in-training, counselors in community agencies, and volunteer workers frequently ask us for suggestions for dealing with "difficult" clients. People in agencies that do a lot of crisis intervention as well as general counseling sometimes have to deal with clients who are angry, uncooperative, or less articulate than we would choose them to be. Generally, we are asked to provide specific strategies that a crisis worker may use to help difficult clients effectively, both individually and in small groups (such as mediating with couples or a family in crisis).

Before the start of the counseling session, the worker can obtain an understanding and a commitment from clients who are known to be difficult. At the time the appointment is made, the worker can set a tone of positive expectancy. A set of ground rules can be agreed on at the outset. The ground rules can be structured to help avoid defensive, uncommunicative, defiant, and other problem behaviors before such behaviors actually have a chance to occur in the session.

The ground rules may vary according to the particular situation. We offer the following typical set of ground rules for dealing with difficult clients. Workers who must deal with difficult clients regularly may wish to print a set of ground rules to place in the hands of selected client groups at the initial session or before the first meeting.

1. We start on time and quit on time; if couples are involved, both parties must be present; we will not meet unless both parties are present.
2. There will be no physical violence or threats of violence.
3. Everyone speaks for him- or herself.
4. Everyone has a chance to be fully heard.
5. We deal mainly with the here-and-now; we try to steer clear of getting bogged down in the past and in blaming others.
6. Everyone faces all the issues brought up—nobody gets up and leaves just because the topic is uncomfortable, and everyone stays for the entire session.
7. Everyone gets an opportunity to define the current problems, suggest realistic solutions, and make at least one commitment to do something positive; at least *one positive action step* is desired from each person present.
8. Everyone belongs, because he or she is a human being and because he or she is here.
9. The crisis worker will not take sides.

10. There will be no retribution, retaliation, or grudges over what is said in the session; whatever is said in the session belongs and stays in the session.
11. The time we spend together is for working on the concerns of people in the group—not for playing games, making personal points, diversion, ulterior purposes, or carrying tales or gossip outside the session.
12. When we know things are a certain way, we will not pretend they are another way—we will confront and deal with each other as honestly and objectively as we possibly can.
13. We will not ignore the nonverbal or body messages that are emitted—we will deal with them openly if they occur.
14. If words or messages need to be expressed to clear the air, we will say them either directly or with role playing; we will not put them off until later.
15. We will not expect each other to be perfect.
16. In the event the ground rules are broken, the consequences will be discussed in the group. People who comply with the rules will not be denied services because one person disobeys the rules.

The crisis worker may go over the ground rules, in person or over the phone, before the first session. If this is not possible, a brief orientation that includes the ground rules is advisable at the start of the first meeting.

Confronting Difficult Clients

In dealing with difficult clients (such as the highly emotional or defensive, people who deny any involvement in either the problem or the solution, and the belligerent) the worker may have to *confront* such behavior directly. We can confront clients with what they are doing by paying particular attention to *nonverbal behavior* and giving immediate feedback: "You're saying one thing but seem to be doing another; look how you're turning away and frowning whenever she says she wants the marriage to last." It is also essential to use good, focused, *open-ended questions* with difficult clients. If the worker is helping a couple, one of whom is uncooperative, the worker must remain neutral. Regardless of how difficult a client is, the worker must not take sides, exhibit frustration, or show preference for one or the other.

There is a possibility that a client may be so difficult that the session may have to be terminated. (This should happen very, very infrequently.) In such a rare case, the worker would openly admit, "We're getting nowhere, so let's adjourn and see if we can figure out a way to try again." The worker might then reword the ground rules. The individuals may have to be seen separately for a while before they are ready to meet as a couple or in the group again. Consultation with a professional colleague for suggestions would be one of the first steps the group leader would take after such an adjournment. Also, we must recognize that we cannot succeed with every client. Sometimes all we can do is let some of the clients ventilate, admit that we cannot help the situation, and perhaps refer the clients to a different worker, counselor, or agency.

The worker must be prepared to deal with various kinds of difficult clients: the nonverbal (nontalking) person, clients sent by court order, clients from a particular ethnic or social group who are uncomfortable when talking with or facing a crisis worker, and clients who are "forced" or coerced into coming. The worker uses the utmost empathy when needed. We must also be sensitive to the need for confrontation, assertion, and directive tactics and ready to use them ("I will not permit you to violate our ground rules by attacking her that way"). Role playing may be needed to model appropriate assertion among group members.

In confronting a client who is belligerent and shows the potential for violence, the crisis worker should be sensitive to the possibility of imminent danger. The worker should focus on defusing the client's anger as well as ensuring the safety of the crisis worker and others. The potentially violent client is addressed extensively in Chapter 10.

The worker has the option of "staffing," or seeking the expert professional help of other highly trained, experienced, and skilled professionals. Consulting assistance from a competent professional colleague often provides a key to a specific difficult case. Knowing when to seek professional help and supervision ourselves is an important strategy in the referral, networking, and counseling process. We cannot afford to burn ourselves out by taking our clients' problems home with us, so we must try to solve them at work, with colleagues.

CONFIDENTIALITY IN CASE HANDLING

One benchmark of crisis is the dramatic onset of potentially violent behavior. Although we deal extensively with the control and containment of such behavior in Chapter 10, a particular admonition to the crisis interventionist is appropriate here in discussing case handling. That admonition involves the issues of confidentiality and privileged communication. Confidentiality indicates an explicit promise to reveal nothing about an individual except under conditions agreed to by the source or the subject (Siegel, 1979). The category of privileged communication is designed to protect confidential information from disclosure in legal proceedings (Dekraii & Sales, 1982). The limits of confidentiality and privileged communication come under scrutiny when a case involves the potential for violent behavior.

Principles Bearing on Confidentiality

Three important principles have a bearing on this issue. Those principles involve the legal, ethical, and moral codes of the helping professions.

Legal Principles.   Legally, the clients of certain professionals have the right of confidentiality through privileged communication. Such professionals include pastors, lawyers, medical doctors, and to a lesser extent licensed psychologists, social workers, and counselors. Depending on the type of setting and the geographic locale in which they practice, human services workers have varying degrees of privileged communication in the eyes of the law. Emphatically, volunteers, no matter what agency they work for, do not have such legal protection unless specifically provided by law.

Ethical Principles.   Ethical standards do not have the weight of law. Although they may closely parallel the law (Thompson, 1983, p. xv), ethical standards are general guiding codes of conduct for a particular profession. Violation of ethical standards may result in censure or loss of license mandated by the profession's ethics board, but it does not necessarily expose the professional to legal problems. Ethics are general guiding principles of conduct for the particular profession, and only that. Professional asso-ciations such as the American Psychological Association, the National Association of Social Workers, and the American Counseling Association have specific standards that speak to confidentiality. Certainly, standard professional conduct and reasonable level of care dictate that what is said in confidence remains so; otherwise, the human services worker quickly loses credibility with the clientele.

Moral Principles.   In the early days of psychotherapy, it was believed that the thera-pist could remain value free and suspend moral judgment (Thompson, 1983, p. 1). This view has been vigorously attacked by London (1964), who maintains that no one in the mental health field can define terms such as *health, illness,* and *morality* without refer-ence to morals, nor can they define a proper method of treatment without involving their own moral commitment (p. 5). Although critics may wrangle over the degree to which therapist morals enter into the therapeutic endeavor, they do agree that there is no value-free brand of therapy and thus no morally neutral therapist (Thompson, 1983, p. 3). Although moral precepts may vary widely, when one shares problems of a deeply personal nature, common decency dictates that the recipient should keep the confidence of the individual who shares such information.

The Intent to Harm and the Duty to Warn

Given the legal, ethical, and moral principles that uphold a client's right to confidenti-ality, it's nevertheless true that when the client provides information about the intent to do harm to himself or herself or another person, rules of confidentiality take on an en-tirely different perspective. The professional is then essentially faced with making a de-cision about whether to inform the authorities, significant others, or a potential victim of such threats and taking action to ensure the client does not carry them out. It is al-most a sure bet, because of the often emotional and highly volatile world of the crisis worker, that a client will eventually appear with such potentially lethal behavior that the crisis worker will have to make a decision about telling someone in order to keep the client or another person safe.

The Tarasoff case (*Tarasoff* v. *Board of Regents of the University of California,* 1976) is the premier example of a therapist, a supervisory staff, and an institution not adequately dealing with a client threat, and it has reconceptualized professional think-ing in regard to confidentiality and the duty to warn a potential victim. The Tarasoff case resulted when a a male client told his therapist on a university campus that he in-tended to murder a young woman. Although the intended victim was not specifically identified, the therapist figured out who she was but took no steps to warn her of the client's threats. The therapist wrote a letter to the campus police about the client's ho-micidal ideation, and the client was immediately taken into custody for observation. Af-ter evaluation, the client was found rational and, having promised to stay away from the woman, was released. The therapist's supervisor requested the police return the letter and directed that all copies of it and subsequent notes related to the incident be de-stroyed. Two months later the client killed the woman (Thompson, 1983, p. 167).

The parents of the woman sued the university, and on appeal to the State Supreme Court of California, the court found for the plaintiff. In this precedent-setting case, the court held that when a psychotherapist ascertains that a threat is neither remote nor idle in its content, the public good demands that disclosure of the threat to a third party outweighs the benefits of preserving confidentiality (Cohen, 1978).

As far as we can ascertain, this finding holds true whether it involves phone counseling, a private therapy session, or working with someone in crisis on a street corner. Based on the foregoing case, the following points are paramount in guiding the human services worker's actions where a client makes a clear threat of violent behavior toward another person or the client's self.

1. It is a good practice to convey very clearly what you can and cannot hold in confidence and to apprise the client of this before intervention is started (Wilson, 1981). As ridiculous as it may seem, prior to starting a counseling group at a correctional facility, we always warn the participants that we cannot preserve their anonymity if they threaten themselves or others, reveal plans to escape, or attempt to smuggle contraband into or out of the facility. It is noteworthy that we have had to act on this statement more than once!

2. Planning ahead through consultation with supervisors, fellow professionals, the police, attorneys, and others who are expert and have experience with danger and violence will be invaluable to you when you may have to make split-second decisions. Similarly, developing contingency plans for what you would do, how you would do it, and what you might do given a variety of client reactions is exceedingly important in the fast and furious world of crisis intervention (Costa & Altekruse, 1994).

3. If you are unclear about the implications of a client's threats or unsure about what to do, the cardinal rule is to consult with another professional or an immediate supervisor and keep notes of the consultation (Wilson, 1981). If you are still not sure what to do, consult with another professional. All call-in or walk-in agencies should have a supervisor well versed in dealing with this problem and readily available. Consultation is always advisable (Thompson, 1983, p. 170) and is substantiating protection from legal and ethical problems that may arise, particularly when the threat is not clear. If for some reason another professional is not available, the general rule for determining a clear and present danger is that such a danger is present if a client specifies victim identity ("my husband"), motive ("revenge"), means ("gun"), and plan ("I'll wait for him after work") (Thompson, 1983, p. 83). Danger is also present if the client is unable to understand what he or she is contemplating, is incapable of exercising self-control, and is incapable of collaborating with the worker. Corey, Corey, and Callanan (1988) believe if at least two of the foregoing elements are present, the therapist has a duty to warn.

4. If the client does concretely state a threat, then you are bound morally, legally, and ethically to take action. It is your duty to warn the victim if you know who it is (Wilson, 1981), unless state statute clearly indicates otherwise. Patiently and emphatically explain your concerns to the client and attempt to get the client calmed enough to get him or her to a place of safety. Tell the client what you are doing and why. Inform the client that you are prepared to hospitalize him or her. Committing a client to a hospital is generally accepted by everyone as far less disruptive and protects the client as well as potential victims. The client is also far less likely to perceive the therapist as another "enemy" and place the therapist on a "hit list" (Thompson, 1983, p. 169). If the client is vehement or acting out, avoid a confrontation. This has now become a matter for the police or security. If neither is immediately available, then get another co-worker as a support person to help contain and calm the client until help arrives. In a crisis intervention setting, no

worker should ever be alone; cases such as this graphically demonstrate the necessity for having more than one person on duty at the same time.

5. When a client indicates clear intent to harm, feeling guilty about breaking confidence has little merit. Your principal duty is to the client, not the relationship, your ethical dilemma, or any other pangs of conscience or second-guessing that may immobilize you from keeping a potential victim out of harm's way (Wilson, 1981). Apprise clients in a supportive and empathic manner of your responsibility to protect them, and invite the clients to participate in the process if possible and surrender any weapons they may have. Inform those who need to know, such as your supervisor, the institution's attorney, the police, psychiatric hospital, and so on, and the intended victim (Costa & Altekruse, 1994).

6. Threats of legal reprisal by the client should not dissuade the crisis worker from reporting threats against others (Wilson, 1981). There is no legitimacy in threats of reprisal, given the law in most states. However, to be safe, document in writing that you noted potential danger signs, discussed relevant suicidal and violent issues, and were professional and empathic (Costa & Altekruse, 1994). It is also a good bet to obtain professional liability insurance!

Tarasoff has mandated three conditions that are necessary and sufficient for a duty to warn to occur: (1) there must be a special relationship, such as therapist to client; (2) there must be a reasonable prediction of conduct that constitutes a danger; (3) there must be a foreseeable victim. But what if there is no malice aforethought or history of violence or any other life-threatening issues except that the client has a fatal and communicable disease? Crisis intervention with an AIDS client is a classic example of the knotty ethical dilemmas that crisis workers are likely to face. Stanard and Hazler's (1995) discussion of the pros and cons of the *Tarasoff* decision as it applies to clients who are HIV-positive and who either refuse or are unwilling to tell their partners they are infected, raises several questions for the crisis worker.

Although on first blush the crisis worker's response would be, "Of course the partner must be told!" the issue is far more complex. What if the partner or partners are anonymous? What if the client had a much more socially acceptable but still potentially lethal disease, such as tuberculosis? Certainly consenting adult partners of HIV-positive individuals would be aware of the high-risk behavior in which they were engaging. They should also be able to say no to a partner, which isn't the case for the victim of a stalker or a child abuser. Other complicating factors include the unreliability of diagnostic tests, exactly what behaviors put an individual at risk, and whether contraceptives are used. Furthermore, to threaten to disclose the client's illness might drive the person away and quite possibly lead to a further spread of the disease by the client. It could be argued that a far more appropriate course of action would be to hold the knowledge of the disease in confidence and counsel the individual regarding abstinence from sexual contact (Stanard & Hazler, 1995).

Cohen (1990) developed a model rule concerning the limits of confidentiality in AIDS cases. The rule states that the counselor has an obligation to disclose if, and only if, there is medical evidence that the person is HIV-positive, the person is in a high-risk relationship, and there is little likelihood of disclosure by the client. Although this rule seems to ease the Solomon-like decision a crisis worker might have to make in warning another, Stanard and Hazler (1995) enjoin the therapist to consider other core issues as well, such as (1) the client's autonomy to choose whom and when to tell, (2) the counselor's doing no harm to the client, (3) the counselor's doing what is beneficial for the client, and (4) the counselor's being just to the client. Breaching confidentiality would undoubtedly do much harm to all those ethical principles and destroy the relationship between the worker and the client.

Clearly, disclosure issues should be dealt with early on by any worker who routinely works with clients who may be HIV-positive by very specifically stating under what circumstances workers might have a duty to warn others. The AIDS client, although representing a particularly thorny ethical problem, is but one among many the crisis worker will face.

No particular formula applies in any threatening situation as to what to say, when to say it, and what degree of action is warranted. In any case involving a severe lack of control, the crisis intervention should be handled with empathy, concern, positive regard, and concreteness. Clients may make many threats in the heat of the moment and have every intention of carrying them out. However, handled in a sensitive and timely manner by the crisis worker, both client and potential victim can be kept from personal harm.

It is from that standpoint that we urge all workers to learn by rote memory their profession's ethical standards, and if they do not have membership in a profession, to learn the set of ethical standards by which their institution operates. Before signing on as a volunteer or in any professional capacity, find out what the agency's policy is in regard to confidentiality, legal rights, ethical standards, and liability insurance. Finally, state law on confidentiality is variable; it is the therapist's responsibility to know what it is.

Legal, Ethical, and Moral Issues of Telephone Counseling

The technological advances of caller identification, call blocking, and call tracing pose some complex legal and ethical dilemmas for the telephone hotline. Although these features can allow hotlines to identify suicidal callers and get help to them or identify where abused children or battered women may live, it could also let them trace pedophiles who had admitted to a crime or identify people with communicable diseases. It could prevent regular callers from tying up the hotline for more severe emergency cases that might not otherwise be handled or give workers time to prepare themselves for known, difficult callers (Horton, 1995, p. 287).

These technologies pose a moral and ethical dilemma to the hotline. Given the ability to screen and identify calls, is it right to deny services to problematic clients? Furthermore, given the expectation and the safety callers feel due to the anonymity of call-in services, using these technologies could easily put confidentiality on a collision course with duty to warn. Could other agencies demand the logs of such hotlines when involved in legal proceedings? Would the hotline workers be held civilly or criminally liable for their actions, given knowledge of whom they were working with and what they might have said? Because most telephone hotline workers are volunteers, they receive minimal training and the agencies they work for are not bound by state or federal supervision or legislation (Seely, 1997a, 1997b). These issues further compound the problems of how to ethically use these new technologies. We have no answer to these dilemmas at present, but believe they are issues that need to be addressed at every level of government and most certainly within the agencies that provide such hotline services.

SUMMARY

Case handling in crisis intervention differs from long-term therapy. Although crisis intervention deals with many of the same components as long-term therapy, crisis work can be differentiated by its emphasis on expediency and efficiency in attempting to stabilize maladaptive client functioning, as opposed to fundamental restructuring of the client's personality. Case handling in crisis intervention emphasizes concern for client safety, brevity in assessment, rapid intervention, compressed treatment time, and termination or referral once equilibrium has been restored.

Case handling in crisis intervention involves three different settings: (1) telephone crisis lines, (2) walk-in facilities, and (3) long-term therapy settings. Telephone crisis lines are efficient, readily available, and inexpensive; they preserve anonymity and provide support systems and information services. Crisis lines provide immediate access to help and use a vast number of trained volunteers and paraprofessionals as crisis interventionists who would not otherwise be available to clients.

Since the Community Mental Health Act of 1963, the major responsibility for treating the mentally ill has fallen on community mental health centers. Such centers, along with a wide variety of other community social services agencies, are on the front lines in dealing with crises of chronic mental illness, severe developmental problems, and social and environmental issues that afflict individuals. Because of the wide variety of clientele seeking services, walk-in facilities must have close linkages with other social services agencies, the legal system, and both short-term and long-term mental health facilities. Mental health workers who staff such facilities must have a broad background in dealing with a wide variety of psychological problems and be ready and able to deal with whatever crisis walks in the door.

Clients in long-term therapy may also experience crises as they move through the therapeutic process. These crises may be instigated by situational events in the client's environment; by attempts to engage in new, more adaptive behaviors; or by past traumatic material that is uncovered in the therapy session. When such crises occur, therapy may degenerate to the point that clients undergo severe traumatic stress and revert to pretherapeutic functioning levels. At these points in therapy, long-term work must be suspended and the therapist must concentrate on the emergent crisis until the client has achieved success in overcoming the current stumbling block.

In all crisis work, as indeed in all therapy, client confidentiality is a moral, ethical, and sometimes legal requirement. In many instances, crisis workers are faced with the possibility of violent behavior and the need to ensure the safety of clients and significant others. Therefore, when clients disclose an intent to do harm either to themselves or others, the crisis worker has a moral, ethical, and legal duty to take action, break confidence, and warn intended victims, significant others, or legal authorities.

C L A S S R O O M   E X E R C I S E

This exercise will take about forty minutes. Each student will play the role of a telephone crisis worker for about twenty minutes. Tape-recording your role as the telephone worker will be helpful. For this exercise, bring a telephone to the classroom (it will be used as a prop only). Divide into pairs and put your back to the other person so that you cannot see them. One person will play the hotline worker and the other will play one of the difficult or disturbed clients detailed in this chapter. The instructor will assign you your roles. The caller can say anything but cannot hang up, nor can the hotline worker. Hint to the caller: Attempt to manipulate the hotline worker as much as you can or be as crazy as you want, but if the hotline worker does his or her job well, you need to shape up! The telephone worker's task is to move through the six-step model and attempt to get the caller to some reasonable level of equilibrium and commitment to do something positive. Safety is always a consideration particularly with these call-in clients. After you are done, switch roles and proceed with the role play again. Here are some questions for discussion:

1. Listen to your tape and make a triage assessment of the client. What's the difference from start to finish on your triage rating?
2. What's the difference for you personally between being able to see a client and only being able to listen to the client?
3. How did you feel after dealing with such a difficult caller? Still want to be in this business, or does long-haul trucking sound like a viable career option?
4. If you could instant-replay your session, what would you do differently? What were you most proud of?

REFERENCES

Ammar, A., & Burdin, S. (1991, April). *Psychoactive medication: An introduction and overview.* Paper presented at the Fifteenth Annual Convening of Crisis Intervention Personnel, Chicago.

Baird, B. N., Bossett, S. B., & Smith, B. J. (1994). A new technique for handling sexually abusive calls to telephone crisis lines. *Community Mental Health Journal, 30,* 55–60.

Beck, A., & Freeman, A. (1990). Cognitive therapy of personality disorders. New York: Guilford Press.

Bender, M. G. (1986). Young adult chronic patients: Visibility and style of interaction in treatment. *Hospital and Community Psychiatry, 37,* 265–268.

Bloom, B. L. (1984). *Community mental health: A general introduction* (2nd ed.). Pacific Grove, CA: Brooks/Cole.

Cautela, J. R. (1976). The present status of covert modeling. *Journal of Behavior Therapy and Experimental Psychiatry, 6,* 323–326.

Chatham, P. M. (1989). *Treatment of the borderline personality.* Northvale, NJ: Aronson.

Cohen, E. (1990). Confidentiality, counseling and clients who have AIDS: Ethical foundations of a modern rule. *Journal of Counseling and Development, 66,* 282–286.

Cohen, R. N. (1978). *Tarasoff* vs. *Regents of the University of California.* The duty to warn: Common law and statutory problems for California psychotherapists. *California Western Law Review, 14,* 153–182.

Corey, G., Corey, M. S., & Callanan, P. (1988). *Issues and ethics in the helping professions* (3rd ed.). Pacific Grove, CA: Brooks/Cole.

Costa, L., & Altekruse, M. (1994). Duty-to-warn guidelines for mental health counselors. *Journal of Counseling and Development, 72,* 346–350.

Dekraii, M. B., & Sales, B. C. (1982). Privileged communication of psychologists. *Professional Psychology, 13,* 372–388.

Epstein, M., & Carter, L. (1991). *Headquarters training manual.* Lawrence, KS: Headquarters Crisis Center.

Erikson, E. H. (1963). *Childhood and society.* New York: Norton.

Fenelon, D. A. (1990, April). *Recognizing and dealing with the bogus sex caller.* Paper presented at the Fourteenth Annual Convening of Crisis Intervention Personnel, Chicago.

Gilliland, B. E., & James, R. K. (1997). *Theories and strategies in counseling and psychotherapy* (4th ed.). Upper Saddle River, NJ: Prentice Hall.

Greenwald, B. (1985a). *In-Touch Hotline training materials: Coping.* Chicago:

University of Illinois at Chicago Circle Campus, Counseling Center.

Greenwald, B. (1985b). *In-Touch Hotline training materials: The disturbed caller.* Chicago: University of Illinois at Chicago Circle Campus, Counseling Center.

Grunsted, V. L., Cisneros, M. X., & Belen, D. V. (1991, April). *Working with the disturbed hotline caller.* Paper presented at the Fifteenth Annual Convening of Crisis Intervention Personnel, Chicago.

Havinghurst, R. J. (1952). *Developmental tasks and education.* New York: Longmans, Green.

Haywood, C., & Leuthe, J. (1980, September). *Crisis intervention in the 1980s: From networking to social influence.* Paper presented at the annual convention of the American Psychological Association, Montreal, Canada.

Horton, A. L. (1995). Sex-related hotline calls. In A. R. Roberts (Ed.), *Crisis intervention and time related cognitive treatment* (pp. 292–312). Thousand Oaks, CA: Sage.

Intrater, L. C. (1991, April). *The effective crisis therapist.* Paper presented at the Fifteenth Annual Convening of Crisis Intervention Personnel, Chicago.

Kazdin, A. E. (1975). Covert modeling, imagery assessment, and assertive behavior. *Journal of Consulting and Clinical Psychology, 43,* 716–724.

Kleespies, P. M., & Blackburn, E. J. (1998). The emergency telephone call. In P. M. Kleespies (Ed.), *Emergencies in mental health practices: Evaluation and management* (pp. 174–195). New York: Guilford Press.

Knudson, M. (1991, April). *Chronic and abusive callers: Appropriate responses and interventions.* Paper presented at the Fifteenth Annual Convening of Crisis Intervention Personnel, Chicago.

Kocmur, M., & Zavasnik, A. (1993). Problems with borderline patients in a crisis intervention unit: A case history. *Crisis, 14,* 71–75, 89.

Levinson, D. J. (1978). *The seasons of a man's life.* New York: Knopf.

London, P. (1964). *The modes and morals of psychotherapy.* New York: Holt, Rinehart & Winston.

McCaskie, M., Ward, S., & Rasor, L. (1990, April). *Short-term crisis counseling and the regular caller.* Paper presented at the Fourteenth Annual Convening of Crisis Intervention Personnel, Chicago.

McHenry, S. S. (1994). When the therapist needs therapy: Characterological countertransference issues and failures in the treatment of the borderline personality disorder. *Psychotherapy, 31,* 557–570.

Nurius, P. S. (1984). Stress: A pervasive dilemma in psychiatric emergency care. *Comprehensive Psychiatry, 25,* 345–354.

Ochberg, F. M. (Ed.). (1988). *Post-traumatic therapy and victims of violence.* New York: Brunner/Mazel.

Peterson, B., & Schoeller, B. (1991, April). *Identifying and responding to problem and repeat callers.* Paper presented at the Fifteenth Annual Convening of Crisis Intervention Personnel, Chicago.

Pope, R. (Speaker). (1991). *Crisis counseling of the walk-in.* (Videotape Recording No. 6611-91B). Memphis, TN: Memphis State University, Department of Counseling and Personnel Services.

Roberts, A. R. (1991). Crisis intervention units and centers in the United States. In A. R. Roberts (Ed.), *Contemporary perspectives on crisis intervention and prevention* (pp. 18–31). Upper Saddle River, NJ: Prentice Hall.

Roe, A. (1956). *The psychology of occupations.* New York: Wiley.

Saffran, M., & Waller, R. (1996). Mental health related calls to the CDC National AIDS hotline. *AIDS Education and Prevention, 8*(1), 37–43.

Seely, M. F. (1997a). The discrete role of the hotline. *Crisis, 18*(2), 53–54.

Seely, M. F. (1997b). The role of hotlines in the prevention of suicide. In R. M. Maris and M. M. Silverman (Eds.), *Review of suicidology,* (pp. 251-270). New York: The Guilford Press.

Sheehy, G. (1976). *Passages.* New York: Dutton.

Siegel, M. (1979). Privacy, ethics, and confidentiality. *Professional Psychology, 10,* 249–258.

Slaikeu, K. A. (Ed.). (1990). *Crisis intervention: A handbook for practice and research.* Boston: Allyn and Bacon.

Stanard, R., & Hazler, R. (1995). Legal and ethical implications of HIV and duty-to-warn for counselors: Does *Tarasoff* apply? *Journal of Counseling and Development, 73,* 397–400.

Super, D. (1957). *The psychology of careers.* New York: Harper.

Tarasoff v. *Board of Regents of the University of California,* 551 P.2d 334 (1976).

Thompson, A. (1983). *Ethical concerns in psychotherapy and their legal ramification.* Lanham, MD: University Press of America.

Thorne, F. C. (Ed.). (1968). *Psychological case handling; Vol. 1: Establishing the conditions necessary for counseling and psychotherapy.* Brandon, VT: Clinical Psychology Publishing.

Turner, W. (1997). Evaluation of a pet loss support hotline. *Anthrozooes, 10*(4), 225–230.

Tuttle, A. (1991). *Advantages and strategies of telephone crisis counseling* (audio tape). Memphis, TN: The Crisis Center.

Wark, V. (1984). *The sex caller and the telephone counseling center.* Springfield, IL: Charles C Thomas.

Waters, J., & Finn, E. (1995). Handling crisis effectively on the telephone. In A. R. Roberts (Ed.), *Crisis intervention and time limited cognitive treatment* (pp. 251–289). Thousand Oaks, CA: Sage.

Wilson, L. (1981). Thoughts on Tarasoff. *Clinical Psychologist, 34,* 37.

Winter, B. E. (1991, April). *The Family Trouble Center: A pilot program for domestic violence intervention.* Paper presented at the Fifteenth Annual Convening of Crisis Intervention Personnel, Chicago.

Yeomans, F. (1993). When a therapist overindulges a demanding borderline patient. *Hospital and Community Psychiatry, 44,* 334–336.

Handling Specific Crises: Going into the Trenches

Part Two focuses on applying intervention strategies to several of the currently most prevalent types of crises in the human experience. The purpose of Part Two is to provide crisis workers with information about the background, dynamics, and intervention methodologies needed to effectively help individuals or groups in crisis.

Part Two contains a wide array of crisis case illustrations to enhance our descriptions of not only the usual and accepted intervention practices but also many innovative strategies for intervention. It examines posttraumatic stress disorder, suicide, sexual assault, domestic violence, substance addiction, and personal loss. Three central themes pervade these chapters:

1. Some crises are *time limited* and some are *transcrisis,* in that the person in crisis may progressively experience severe problems, either deal with or suppress them, and then experience and exhibit repeated responses and symptoms of the same crisis over a period of many years.

2. No one set of theories, assumptions, strategies, or procedures is appropriate for intervening in *all* crisis situations; rather, a systematic and eclectic approach is recommended and demonstrated as the preferred mode of helping in a broad assortment of crisis problems and settings. The techniques employed in these chapters are "best bets" for the particular kind of client in the particular environment. They are, however, not the only "bets." They are meant to give you a variety of approaches and situations that will start to help you form your own "Gestalt" of an effective crisis worker.

3. Crisis intervention is hallmarked by elastic, fluid situations that change in seconds and minutes and may move from a very benign to volatile situation in that time. Many of the case illustrations model such dynamics to give you a flavor of what the crisis worker must do to respond quickly and effectively.

CHAPTER FOUR

Posttraumatic Stress Disorder

Our discussion and treatment of the more common types of crises that you, as a mental health worker or consumer of mental health care, are likely to encounter opens with posttraumatic stress disorder (PTSD). The reason we begin here is that many other crises we review in this book may be rooted in PTSD. For example, suicide (Chu, 1999; Kramer, Lindy, Green, & Grace, 1994) and substance abuse (Brown, Recupero, & Stout, 1995; Ruzek, Polusny, & Abueg, 1998) may be the end products of attempting to cope with trauma. In contrast, rape, sexual abuse, battering, loss, violence, and hostage situations may precipitate the disorder (Ackerman et al., 1998; Bigot & Ferrand, 1998; Darves-Bornoz et al., 1998; Foa & Zoellner, 1998).

To understand the impact PTSD has had on our view of mental health in general and of crisis intervention in particular, it is worth noting the sheer volume of articles on PTSD found in *Psychological Abstracts*. From 1974 to 1989, 698 articles were listed. From 1990 to 1995, 1,400 articles on PTSD were listed, and from 1996 to mid-1999 there were 1,702! That dramatic upward shift has much to say about how important PTSD is in the world of mental health professionals. Although we will speak to immediate intervention with acute distress in other parts of this book, we concern ourselves in this chapter with the long-term residual effects of trauma on survivors.

BACKGROUND

Psychic trauma is a process initiated by an event that confronts an individual with an acute, overwhelming threat (Freud, 1917/1963). When the event occurs, the inner agency of the mind loses its ability to control the disorganizing effects of the experience, and disequilibrium occurs. The trauma tears up the individual's psychological anchors, which are fixed in a secure sense of what has been in the past and what should be in the present (Erikson, 1968). When a traumatic event occurs that represents nothing like the security of past events, and the individual's mind is unable to effectively answer basic questions of how and why it occurred and what it means, a crisis ensues. The event propels the individual into a traumatic state that lasts as long as the mind needs to reorganize, classify, and make sense of the traumatic event. Then and only then does psychic equilibrium return (Furst, 1978).

If the person can effectively integrate the trauma into conscious awareness and organize it as a part of the past (as unpleasant as the event may be), then homeostasis returns, the problem is coped with, and the individual continues to travel life's rocky road. If the event is not effectively integrated and is submerged from awareness, then the probability is high that the initiating stressor will reemerge in a variety of symptomatic forms months or years after the event. When such crisis events are caused by the reemergence of the original unresolved stressor, they fall into the category of delayed or posttraumatic stress disorder (PTSD).

PTSD is a newborn compared with the other crises we will examine, at least in regard to achieving official designation as such. In 1980, PTSD found its way into the third edition of the *Diagnostic and Statistical Manual of Mental Disorders (DSM-III)*, by the American Psychiatric Association, as a classifiable and valid mental disorder. The antecedents of what has been designated as PTSD first came to the attention of the medical establishment in the late 19th and early 20th centuries. Two events serve as benchmarks.

First, with the advent of rail transportation and subsequent train wrecks, physicians and early psychiatrists began to encounter in accident victims trauma with no identifiable physical basis. Railway accident victims of this type became so numerous that a medical term, *railway spine,* became an accepted diagnosis. In psychological parlance, the synonymous term *compensation neurosis* came into existence for invalidism suffered and compensation from insurers as a result of such accidents (Trimble, 1985, pp. 7–10).

Concomitantly, Sigmund Freud formulated the concept of *hysterical neurosis* to describe trauma cases of young Victorian women with whom he was working. He documented symptoms of warded-off ideas, denial, repression, emotional avoidance, compulsive repetition of trauma-related behavior, and recurrent attacks of trauma-related emotional sensations (Breuer & Freud, 1895/1955). However, what Freud found and reported on the pervasive childhood sexual abuse of these women as the traumatic root of their hysteria was anathema to a puritanical, staid Victorian society and he was forced to disavow and then reject his findings (Herman, 1997, pp. 13–17).

Second, the advent of modern warfare in World Wars I and II, with powerful artillery and aerial bombardment, generated terms such as *shell shock* and *combat fatigue* to attempt to explain the condition of traumatized soldiers who had no apparent physical wounds. Various hypotheses were proposed to account for such strange maladies (Trimble, 1985, p. 8), but Freud (1919/1959) believed that the term *war neurosis* more aptly characterized what was an emotional disorder that had nothing to do with the prevailing medical notion of neurology-based shell shock.

The U.S. Medical Service Corps came to recognize combat fatigue in World War II and the Korean War as a treatable psychological disturbance. The treatment approach was that combat fatigue was invariably acute and that treatment was best conducted as quickly and as close to the battle lines as possible. The idea was to facilitate a quick return to active duty. The prevailing thought was that time heals all wounds and that little concern needed to be given to long-term effects of traumatic stress. Such has not been the case (Archibald, Long, Miller, & Tuddenham, 1962). Indeed, a notable proponent of establishing the Vietnam Veterans Centers, Arthur Blank, ruefully commented that when he was an army psychiatrist in Vietnam, he felt there would be no long-term difficulties for veterans (MacPherson, 1984, p. 237).

Because societies attempt to erase the horrific memories of war as quickly as possible and further believe that soldiers who suffer from "shell shock and combat fatigue" may be cowardly malingerers, the belief that there might be long-term effects of trauma held little interest after the World Wars—both for society and mental health practitioners. Returning soldiers were expected to go on with the business of living with little regard to what the war might have done to their mental health (Herman, 1997, p. 26).

Although PTSD can and does occur in response to the entire range of natural and human-made catastrophes, it was the debacle of Vietnam that clearly brought PTSD to the awareness of both the human services professions and the public. Through a combination of events and circumstances unparalleled in the military history of the United States, veterans who returned from that conflict began to develop a variety of mental health problems that had little basis for analysis and treatment in the prevailing psychological literature. This combination of events and circumstances had insidious and long-term consequences that were not readily apparent either to the victims or to human services professionals who attempted to treat them. Misdiagnosed, mistreated, and misunderstood, military service personnel became known to a variety of social services agencies that included the police, mental health facilities, and unemployment offices (MacPherson, 1984, pp. 207–330, pp. 651–690).

As the war continued to grind on, more and more veterans started having psychological problems. Rebuffed by the Veterans Administration, these veterans formed self-help groups to try to come to terms with their psychological issues. These "rap" groups rapidly coalesced and became a political force that pushed the federal government to come to grips with their problems. One major result of their lobbying efforts was the establishment of the Vietnam Veterans Centers, where alienated veterans could seek help for a variety of readjustment problems. An informal network of mental health professionals became interested in the veterans and started to classify their symptoms and compare them to the work Kardiner (1941) had done on war neurosis. Their review of clinical records led them to generate 27 of the most common symptoms of the Vietnam veterans' "traumatic neurosis" (van der Kolk, Weisaeth, & van der Hart, 1996, p. 61).

At the same time, researchers in the growing women's movement were looking at psychological problems after domestic violence, rape, and child abuse. What they were finding in the victims who had suffered from these civilian assaults closely paralleled the problems that Vietnam veterans were experiencing. Their research rediscovered what Freud had found 80 years beforehand and had dismissed, that victims of physical and sexual assault suffered long-term effects of the psychological trauma (Herman, 1997, p. 32). These different research avenues culminated in combining the "Vietnam veterans syndrome," the "rape trauma syndrome," the "abused child syndrome," and the "battered woman syndrome" into one diagnostic category—Posttraumatic Stress Disorder—in the third edition of the American Psychiatric Association's *Diagnostic and Statistical Manual* in 1980 (van der Kolk, Weisaeth, & van der Hart, 1996, p. 61).

Although the Vietnam War may be no more to you than a reference in a high school history book, the wall memorial in Washington, D.C., or your "crazy old Uncle Harold" who continues to wear combat fatigues and a headband with a ponytail, the war's effects are a crucial history lesson in mental health provision (or the lack thereof) that any aspiring mental health worker should learn. For that reason, the psychological lessons learned from the Vietnam War continue to play a major role in our discussion of PTSD in the fourth edition of this book.

It should be clearly understood that, even thirty years after the fact, the events that caused the trauma in many of these approximately one million veterans who suffered and suffer from PTSD are as alive for them today as they were then (Bryant, 1998; Keane, 1998; Kukla et al., 1990; Vietnam Veterans: Thirty Years After, 1995). What perhaps is even more ominous in regard to the Vietnam veterans is their "graying."

Mounting evidence indicates that World War I and II veterans have manifested delayed onset or worsening of posttraumatic complaints as they have grown older. Aging, with its subsequent loss of social supports through death, increased health problems, declining physical and mental capabilities, and economic hardship appears to put older veterans at increased risk (Aarts & op den Velde, 1996, pp. 359–374; Hamilton & Workman, 1998). Thus, it would appear that as this population ages, the mental health professions are a long way from being done with the legacy of Vietnam.

DYNAMICS OF PTSD
Diagnostic Categorization

PTSD is a complex and diagnostically troublesome disorder. To be identified as having PTSD, a person must meet the following conditions and symptoms as specified in the *DSM-IV* (American Psychiatric Association, 1994, pp. 427–429). First, the person must have been exposed to a traumatic event in which he or she was confronted with an event that involved actual or threatened death or serious injury, or a threat to self or others' physical well-being. Examples include but are certainly not limited to military combat, physical or sexual assault, kidnapping, being held hostage, severe vehicle accidents, earthquakes and tornadoes, being a refugee from a war zone, concentration camp detention, and life-threatening illness. The person's response to the trauma was intense fear, helplessness, or horror. As a result, he or she has persistent symptoms of anxiety or arousal that were not evident before the traumatic event.

Second, the person persistently reexperiences the traumatic event in at least one of the following ways:

1. Recurrent and intrusive distressing recollections of the event
2. Recurrent nightmares of the event
3. Flashback episodes that may include all types of sensory hallucinations or illusions that cause the individual to dissociate from the present reality and act or feel as if the event were recurring
4. Intense psychological distress on exposure to internal or external cues that symbolize or resemble an aspect of the traumatic event
5. Physiologic reactivity on exposure to events that symbolize or resemble some aspect of the trauma, such as a person who was in a tornado starting to shake violently at every approaching storm

Third, the person persistently avoids such stimuli in at least three of the following ways:

1. Attempts to avoid thoughts, dialogues, or feelings associated with the trauma
2. Tries to avoid activities, people, or situations that arouse recollections of the trauma
3. Has an inability to recall important aspects of the trauma
4. Has markedly diminished interest in significant activities
5. Feels detached and removed emotionally and socially from others
6. Has a restricted range of affect by numbing feelings
7. Has a sense of a foreshortened future such as no career, marriage, children, or normal life span

Fourth, the person has persistent symptoms of increased nervous system arousal that were not present before the trauma, as indicated by at least two of the following problems:

1. Difficulty falling or staying asleep
2. Irritability or outbursts of anger
3. Difficulty concentrating on tasks
4. Constantly being on watch for real or imagined threats that have no basis in reality (hypervigilance)
5. Exaggerated startle reactions to minimal or nonthreatening stimuli

Fifth, the disturbance causes clinically significant distress or impairment in social, occupational, or other critical areas of living. Examples include not being able to keep a job, having a failed marriage, or becoming a substance abuser.

PTSD is not confined to adults. Children also experience PTSD and manifest symptoms that closely parallel those of adults, with the following notable differences. Children usually do not have a sense they are reliving the past, but rather relive the trauma through repetitive play. Their nightmares of the traumatic event may change to more generalized nightmares of monsters or of rescuing others. A foreshortened future for a child generally involves a belief that they will never reach adulthood. Children may believe they can see into the future and can forecast ominous events. Physical symptoms may appear that include headaches and stomachaches that were not present before the event (American Psychiatric Association, 1994, pp. 424–428).

For a diagnosis of PTSD, the foregoing symptoms must be experienced for at least one month. Delayed onset is specified if the start of symptoms is at least six months after the trauma (American Psychiatric Association, 1994, pp. 424–429).

Finally, the dramatic personality changes that may occur with long-term, intensive trauma have led critics to call for a diagnostic category of "complex PTSD" or "disorders of extreme stress not otherwise specified" (DESNOS) (Herman, 1997, p. 121; van der Kolk, 1996b, pp. 202–204). The DESNOS classification opens a Pandora's box of psychological evils that include the inability to regulate feelings, suicidal and other self-destructive behaviors, impulsive and dangerous risk-taking behaviors, anger management problems, amnesia and dissociation from reality, somatic complaints that take a variety of physical forms, chronic character changes that range from consuming guilt to permanent ineffectiveness in coping with life, adopting distorted and idealized views of perpetrators of the trauma, an inability to trust others, a tendency to victimize or be revictimized, and despair and hopelessness that previously held beliefs about a "fair and just" world are no longer valid. It should be readily apparent that PTSD is an extremely serious condition and that the *DSM-IV* criteria do not begin to depict all the consequences and effects of the disorder that assail the individual and ripple out to significant others in the victim's life.

Conflicting Diagnoses

Given the wide variety of maladaptive behaviors that characterize the disorder, it is not uncommon for those who suffer from PTSD to have companion diagnoses of anxiety, depressive, organic mental, and substance use disorders (American Psychiatric Association, 1994, p. 427). Further, because of presenting symptoms, PTSD may be confused with adjustment, paranoid, somatoform, and personality disorders (Herman, 1997, pp. 116–117; Zanarini et al., 1998; Zlotnick et al., 1999). One of the hallmarks of PTSD is that it is often comorbid. That is, the person will have other preliminary mental illness diagnosed in the course of treatment. There are few "pure" cases, and few symptoms are unique to the disorder (Atkinson, Sparr, & Sheff, 1984).

Thus *it is our opinion that, no matter what the diagnosis, assessment in crisis intervention should always attempt to determine if there has been exposure to prior trauma,* particularly when the crisis seems to have occurred spontaneously, with no clear, immediate, precipitating stimulus.

Because of their symptoms, Vietnam veterans with PTSD could be and in most instances were viewed by human services professionals as having inadequate personalities or long-term character disorders. These same views also have held sway in the broad arena of domestic violence and sexual assault victims (Herman, 1997). Diagnosis of the problem is confounded even more because the time of onset after the stimulating trauma is so variable. Both human services workers and people closely related to victims may find the disorder hard to understand, particularly the delay of onset (Scurfield, 1985, pp. 221–226).

The Question of Preexisting Psychopathology

Historically, for a variety of political and social reasons, society does not perceive being a victim of war, domestic violence, or other types of human cruelty as the equivalent of being mentally ill. Vietnam veterans who early on sought help from Veterans Administration (VA) hospitals were misdiagnosed or thought to have some preexisting psychopathology or character disorder. As a result, they were revictimized by a bureaucratic and rigidly conservative mental health system that added psychic insult to psychic injury (Ochberg, 1988, p. 4). Victims of domestic violence fared no better and were often seen to have a "masochistic" personality that subconsciously enjoyed physical assaults (Herman, 1997, p. 117). Such revictimization and discounting by supposedly "caring" professionals exacerbate the trauma survivor's problems exponentially.

Many mental health professionals and members of the victims' support system continue to believe that victims of PTSD might actually be suffering from some other inherent or preexisting malady that is "the real cause of their problems." Although undoubtedly some people, because of a previous psychiatric history, are more predisposed to breaking down under stress than are others (Martini, Ryan, Nakayama, & Ramenofsky, 1990; Ullman & Siegel, 1994), there is little evidence to suggest that PTSD is activated primarily because of some preexisting pathology (Wilson, Smith, & Johnson, 1985, pp. 142–172).

Furthermore, the magnitude of the trauma, both in amount and degree, will predict higher potential for PTSD (Shalev, 1996, p. 86). Exposure to multiple rape, being held in a concentration camp, extended child abuse, or prolonged front-line combat typically puts the individual at far greater risk for PTSD than a one-time physical assault by a parent or an auto accident where no one was killed.

However, no absolute factors guarantee that one person as opposed to another will develop PTSD. Given the right conditions, though, it appears *anyone can be a candidate.* Several years ago the collapse of a concrete walkway in a crowded hotel gave us a prime example of how one event may suddenly produce PTSD symptoms. Biographical data gathered following the Kansas City Hyatt Regency skywalk disaster revealed that few survivors had character disorders before the event. Yet six months after the event itself many were suffering from a variety of presenting symptoms (Wilkinson, 1983). White (1989) found the same result in a study of burn victims suffering PTSD symptoms. The overwhelming majority of the victims had no past psychiatric history.

Probably the best summing statement about who will and who will not manifest PTSD was made by Grinker and Spiegel (1945) in their study of World War II veterans. They concluded that no matter how strong, normal, or stable a person might be, if the stress were sufficient to cross that particular individual's threshold, a "war neurosis" would develop. In summary, susceptibility to PTSD is a function of several factors: genetic predisposition, ecological factors, constitution, personality makeup, past life experiences, state of mind, cultural artifacts, phase of maturational development at onset, spiritual beliefs, social support system before and after the trauma, and content and intensity of the event (Boman, 1986; DeVries, 1996; Furst, 1967; Green & Berlin, 1987; Kelman, 1945; Martini et al., 1990; Moses, 1978; Shalev, 1996, pp. 77–95).

Physiological Responses

In the last ten years a tremendous number of psychobiological studies have conclusively demonstrated that trauma affects the individual in a variety of physical ways. Researchers have discovered that neurotransmitters, hormones, cortical areas of the brain, and the nervous system play a much greater role in PTSD than was previously suspected (Berga & Girton, 1989; Blanchard et al., 1994; Bremner et al., 1995; Gerardi et al., 1994; Mason et al., 1988; Ross et al., 1994; van der Kolk, 1983, 1984, 1988, 1996a). The underlying thesis is that the brain is much more like a "wet" hormonal gland than a "dry" cybernetic computer (Berglund, 1985). When a person is exposed to severe stress, neurotransmitters, neuromodulators, hormones, endogenous opioids, and specific cortical functions designed to deal with the emergency are activated (Bremner et al., 1995; Grinker & Speigel, 1945; Selye, 1976; Siegel, 1995; van der Kolk, 1996a, pp. 215–234). Although cessation of the traumatic event may remove the person from danger and no longer require the body's system to function on an emergency basis, if the stress is prolonged, the nervous system may continue to function in an elevated and energized state as if the emergency were still continuing (Burgess-Watson, Hoffman, & Wilson, 1988; van der Kolk, 1996a, pp. 214–234).

Furthermore, there is evidence that intense and continuous stress can cause permanent physical changes to occur in the brain. These changed physiological states are important because they not only cause individuals extreme physical and psychological duress long after the traumatic event but also imply why people do not "get over" PTSD. In their study and review of the neuroanatomical correlates of the effects of stress on memory, Bremner and associates (1995) and Gurvitz, Shenton, and Pittman (1995) found significant decreases in the hippocampal area of the brain (combat veterans) where explicit memory encoding and memory consolidation take place as did Stein and associates (1994) (women suffering from severe child sexual abuse). Indeed, there is a great deal of psychophysiological assessment evidence that indicates that stimulus presentation of sights, sounds, and smells associated with the long-past traumatic event to

PTSD sufferers will immediately send the neuroendocrine system into overdrive and cause physiological responses such as increased heart rate, blood pressure, triglyceride and cholesterol levels as well as decreased blood flow to the skin and gastrointestinal and renal areas. These psychophysiological responses are not evinced in control subjects who are presented with the same stimuli (Lating & Everly, 1995).

Affective-State-Dependent Retention

Changed physiological functioning due to traumatic stimuli is important as a building block in Bower's (1981) hypothesis of *affective-state-dependent retention*. Bower has proposed that because the traumatic event was stored in memory under completely different physiological (increased heart rate, higher adrenal output) and psychological (extreme fright, shock) circumstances, different mood states markedly interfere with recollecting specific cues of the event. Therefore, the important elements of the memory that need exposure in order to reduce anxiety are not accessible in the unaroused state (Keane et al., 1985, p. 266) and can be remembered only when that approximate state of arousal is reintroduced by cues in the environment (Keane, 1976; Weingartner, Miller, & Murphy, 1977). Indeed, there is evidence that release of neuromodulators such as norepinephrine when an individual is in a stressful situation leads to pathological response to recall of previous traumatic events for which the individual has no previous memory (Bremner et al., 1995). To the contrary, the classic dissociative, numbing response, and "forgetting" of the traumatic event may be caused by excessive endogenous opioids secreted during prolonged stress (van der Kolk, 1996a, p. 227). Thus the notion that a victim of PTSD can "just forget" or adopt a "better, more positive attitude" does little to effect change in the victim (Keane et al., 1985, p. 266). This proposal has important implications for treatment, particularly with respect to returning the person to as close an approximation of the event as possible.

INCIDENCE, IMPACT, AND TRAUMA TYPE
Incidence

If PTSD has been with us for so long, what made it finally surface with such profound impact? Epidemiological studies indicate that a lifetime rate of 0.5 to 1.3 percent can be expected in the general civilian population of the United States (McFarlane & de Girolamo, 1996, pp. 140–141). Other countries with different lifestyles, philosophies, and cultural traditions may be much lower (Chen et al., 1993; Lindal & Stefansson, 1993). So, in the common course of events, the chances of "catching" PTSD are small. However, when studies target particular at-risk groups such as adolescents and young adults, hazardous occupations, severe burn cases, refugees, and psychiatric cases, the incidence of PTSD in these populations is seen to be much greater (McFarlane & de Girolamo, 1996, pp. 129–154).

Quoted in MacPherson (1984, p. 224), Blank states, "Long term presence of stress reactions is not unique. They isolated that with World War II veterans. What is unique, however, about Vietnam veterans and stress is the long term persistence in large numbers." The numbers of returning Vietnam veterans that were having some kind of personality disorder far exceeded what statistics would predict. Although a definite number can't be given, it is estimated that 26 percent or 960,000 Vietnam veterans have had episodes of PTSD (Kukla et al., 1990). This massive number of veterans in severe psychological trouble was simply too large to ignore.

Residual Impact

People's basic assumptions about their belief in the world as a meaningful and comprehensible place, their own personal invulnerability, and their view of themselves in a positive light account to a great extent for their individual manifestations of PTSD (Figley, 1985b, pp. 401–402). Even in the most well-integrated people, who have excellent coping abilities, good rational and cognitive behavior patterns, and positive social support systems, residual effects of traumatizing events linger.

An outstanding example of such residual effects is the experience of a retired Marine captain who had seen extensive field duty as a combat infantryman in Vietnam in 1968. The anecdote he relates typifies the residual effects in an individual who is psychologically well integrated, is securely employed in a professional job, has a tightly knit, extended family support system, and on the whole enjoys life and has a positive outlook on it.

Chris: I had just gotten home from work late one summer evening. The kids had decided to camp out in the woods down by the creek. A thunderstorm was rolling in and I decided I'd better go down and check on them to see if they were packed in for the night. It had started to rain pretty heavily and there was a lot of thunder and lightning. I pulled on a poncho and got a flashlight, crossed the road, and went into the woods. I don't suppose it was 200 yards to where the kids were camped. Now, I'd grown up running those woods, so I knew it like the back of my hand. However, once I got into the woods things kinda went haywire. I immediately thought, "Get off the trail or you'll get the whole platoon zapped." I slipped off the path and became a part of the scenery. Every sense in my body went up to full alert. I was back in Nam again operating with my platoon and I was on a natural, adrenaline high. Time and place kinda went into suspended animation and I eased through the woods, kinda like standing off and watching myself do this, knowing it was me, but yet not me too. The last thing I remember before walking into the clearing where the kids had their tent set up was that we could have ambushed the hell out of that place. I don't harp and brood on Nam, put it behind me after I got out of the Corps, but that night sure put me in a different place than central Indiana, July 1984. I just couldn't believe that would ever happen. It's a bit unnerving.

Importance of Trauma Type

Catastrophes, when viewed by the public, tend to fall into one category: bad. However, one of the interesting phenomena around PTSD is that there is a marked distinction between natural and human-made catastrophes. Acts of God create far fewer victims of PTSD than do human-made ones. Human-made acts of trauma create even more victims of PTSD when the trauma directly affects the social support system of the family. Holocaust survivors, hostages, raped women, children of murdered parents, and victims of incest are all strong potential candidates for PTSD. Survivors of uncommissioned human-made disasters such as the breaking of the Buffalo Creek dam and commissioned trauma such as the Chowchilla bus kidnapping clearly carry high potential for PTSD. (The Buffalo Creek disaster occurred when a coal company retainer dam broke during a series of heavy rainstorms. The resulting flood wiped out the residents of the Buffalo Creek valley in West Virginia. The bus kidnapping occurred in the late 1970s when a Chowchilla, California, school bus carrying elementary and secondary school children was hijacked at gunpoint. The children were taken from the bus, and forced into a truck buried underground. Finally they were able to tunnel out.) What makes these events so particularly terrible is that they would seem to be tragedies that should not have happened, responsibility for them can be quickly placed, and they clearly violate accepted standards of moral conduct (Figley, 1985a, pp. 400–401). Thus, there exists in any human-made catastrophe the likelihood of more severe posttraumatic psychological problems as compared to those wrought by "God."

Vietnam: The Archetype

In a comparative analysis of PTSD among various trauma survivor groups, Wilson, Smith, and Johnson (1985) isolated a number of variables that were hypothesized as predisposing to PTSD: degree of life threat; degree of bereavement; speed of onset; duration of the trauma; degree of displacement in home continuity; potential for recurrence; degree of exposure to death, dying, and destruction; degree of moral conflict inherent in the situation; role of the person in the trauma; and the proportion of the community affected. They compared these variables in a variety of trauma survivor groups: Vietnam combat veterans as well as victims of rape, auto accident, armed robbery, natural disasters, divorces, life-threatening illness of a loved one, family trauma, death of a significant other, multiple trauma, and a control group. Veterans were significantly affected in seven of the ten dimensions, with rape victims a distant second in terms of number of predisposing variables present. When the data were transformed to fit precise PTSD criteria, all trauma groups were significantly different from the control group (pp. 142–172). In plain words, the data suggest that one could not experience a catastrophic event more likely to produce "complex" PTSD than Vietnam.

Why was this? Although any war could be construed to produce many PTSD symptoms, the rules of war got changed in Vietnam. First, the average age of the soldier in Vietnam was 19.2, as opposed to 26.0 in World War II (Brende & Parson, 1985, p. 19). A psychologically immature 19-year-old soldier was not mentally prepared for the psychic trauma that awaited him in Vietnam (MacPherson, 1984, pp. 62–63).

Hypervigilance.   In Vietnam, there was no front line and no relief from constant vigilance. A 365-day combat tour was exactly that. In comparison to World War II troops, who might be in acute combat situations for a few days or weeks and then be pulled off the line, Vietnam "grunts" spent extended periods of time in the field, and even when they were in a base camp, they had to be alert for rocket attacks and combat assaults on their position. Hypervigilance became an iron-clad rule of survival. Listen to Billie Mac, a composite character of many combat veterans we have interviewed.

Billie Mac: I was 18 when the plane set down at Da Nang. The crew chief told us to hit the ground running because Da Nang was under a rocket attack. I was scared stiff.

Well, Da Nang was heaven, rockets and all, to what later happened. It got a lot, lot worse than that.

Lack of Goals.   No territory was ever "won," so there was no concrete feeling of accomplishment. Combat troops felt betrayed by U.S. politics, over a war for which there were no fixed goals for winning and a command structure that was waging a war of attrition, with "body counts" being the primary way of judging whether a mission was successful (Lifton, 1974; MacPherson, 1984, p. 58).

Billie Mac: We swept that one village at least a half dozen times. Sometimes we'd dig in and dare the NVA to hit us, and they did. We lost a half dozen guys in that pesthole. For what? For nothin'. We gave it up and they moved right back in.

Victim/Victimizer.   It further compounded the virulent psychological milieu of Vietnam that veterans, unlike most individuals who suffer from PTSD, played two roles— that of victim and that of victimizer. Because both enemies and allies were Vietnamese, a soldier could not distinguish friend from foe, nor could vigilance be relaxed around women or children because of their potential lethality. Because the enemy was Asian and had extremely different cultural values from Americans, it was relatively simple to dehumanize the killing or the maiming of them, particularly when troops saw such things done to their comrades. The nasty way guerrilla war is fought brought out brutality on both sides (Lifton, 1974). Shifts of role from victim to aggressor could occur in seconds (Brende & Parson, 1985, p. 96).

Billie Mac: I couldn't imagine killing a kid or woman. That was true until our medic tried to take care of a kid covered with blood. We all thought he was wounded. When John went over to the dink, he opened up his arms and had a grenade. Blew him and the medic away. Kill them after that? You bet!

Bonding, Debriefing, and Guilt.   The way the armed services filled units had much to do with lack of a support system within the service itself. Personnel replacements were parceled piecemeal into units. Although this method put rookies with veterans, it was not the best way to bond a unit together. The rotation system also took its psychological toll. Each person did a 365-day tour. The stress of being "short" caused men to become very self-preservative and immobilized. Units as a whole were never moved out of combat, and a man who entered combat singly returned singly without benefit of debriefing time. The war was essentially fought in patrol and platoon actions. It was a loner's war, and the soldier who fought alone went home alone (MacPherson, 1984, pp. 64–65). One day a man might be sweating out an ambush in the jungle and two days later be sitting on his front porch back home.

It is no great surprise that returning soldiers who had no transition period from Vietnam to the United States were viewed as "different" and "changed" by their relatives (Brende & Parson, 1985, pp. 48–49). Such rapid transitions out of life-threatening situations left many with survivor's guilt (Spiegel, 1981). They were glad to be out of Vietnam, but felt guilty of betrayal for leaving comrades behind; or they took responsibility when they were away from their units and friends were hurt or killed (MacPherson, 1984, p. 237).

Billie Mac: It was inside of a week from jungle to home. My folks thought it was pretty weird because I put my fatigues on and slept in the woods. I just couldn't take being confined in that house. I kept thinking about the guy who took my place as squad leader, Johnson. I knew he was gonna get somebody wasted. I needed to be there, but I sure didn't want to be. I immediately got drunk and stayed that way for a long time.

Civilian Adjustment.   The rapid change from intense alertness in order to preserve one's life to trying to readjust to a humdrum society made many question where the "real world" was. Furthermore, the returnee's basic belief system would be quickly jarred when, on his arrival home, he would be greeted with insensitivity and hostility for having risked his life for his country (Brende & Parson, 1985, p. 72). Veterans would quickly find that for all the ability they showed in making command decisions of life-or-death importance and the authority they had over expensive equipment in Vietnam, the onus of having been there relegated them to civilian jobs far below their capabilities (MacPherson, 1984, p. 65).

Billie Mac: Any job I could get stunk. They were all menial and they acted like they were doing me a favor. Hell! I'd made a lot bigger and smarter decisions than anybody I ever had as a boss.

Substance Abuse.   The ease with which soldiers could obtain alcohol and drugs to numb themselves and escape mentally from the reality of Vietnam had severe consequences, both in addiction on return and in the public's growing misconception that veterans were all "drug-crazed baby killers" and were to be shunned because they were too erratic and undependable (Brende & Parson, 1985, p. 72; MacPherson, 1984, pp. 64–65, 221–222).

Billie Mac: Yeah, I drank. Yeah, I shot kids. I drank mainly to try to forget about shooting kids. Anybody who hadn't been there could never understand.

Attitude.   The time period during which a vet served in Vietnam seems to be highly correlated with PTSD. Historically the war can be divided into trimesters. Anyone serving in Vietnam during the last two trimesters, from the time of the Tet offensive to the wind-down in the war, would have, from a psychological standpoint, a much greater reason to question the purpose of being there than those who had served early on. The prevailing attitude of "Nobody can win, so just concentrate on surviving" cynicism was in direct opposition to the "Save a democracy from the perils of communism" idealism of the first trimester (Laufer, Yager, & Grey-Wouters, 1981).

Antiwar Sentiment.   The impact of the antiwar sentiment that veterans met on their return home cannot be minimized. It is unique to the Vietnam War and found its focal point in returnees. Veterans were spurned immediately on their arrival in the United States, suffered prejudice on college campuses as they came back to school, were left out of jobs because of antiwar sentiments, and were disenfranchised from government programs through meager G.I. Bill benefits and government disavowal of physical problems associated with exposure to the chemical defoliant, Agent Orange.

Perhaps worst of all were the comparisons their fathers made—men who had fought the "honorable" fight of World War II and could not understand the problems their sons suffered in a war that was not black or white but was a dirty shade of gray (MacPherson, 1984, pp. 54–58). It is interesting to note that Vietnam combat veterans diagnosed with PTSD who had fathers who were also combat veterans are likely to have more severe problems than those Vietnam veterans whose fathers had not seen combat (Rosenheck & Fontana, 1998).

Billie Mac: I tried to talk to my old man about it. He'd been in World War II on Okinawa. Hell, he might as well have been in the Revolutionary War for all he could understand about Nam. He finally got so mad that he told me I was nuts and no damn good. He didn't mean that, but I'll never forget it.

All these factors came together in a sort of witch's brew for veterans trying to make meaning out of a situation that was life-threatening and generally considered pointless (Williams, 1983). To survive such a situation called for imposing psychological defense mechanisms that made a fertile breeding ground for PTSD. When these psychological defense mechanisms go awry, symptoms are typically seen in the three major PTSD diagnostic categories of intrusive thoughts, avoidance, and increased nervous system arousal.

Intrusive-Repetitive Ideation

Intrusive-repetitive thoughts become so problematic for the individual that these thoughts begin to dominate existence. Intrusive thoughts generally take the form of visual images that are sparked by sights, sounds, smells, or tactile reminders that bring the repressed images to awareness (Donaldson & Gardner, 1985, pp. 371–372).

Billie Mac: That day at the village when Al got it keeps coming back. I don't go fishing in the bayou anymore. It smells and looks like Nam, and every time I'd go I'd start thinking about that village and I'd get the shakes.

Over time, triggers for intrusive thoughts may become associated with subtle, and more generalized stimuli that are seemingly irrelevant to the trauma (van der Kolk & McFarlane, 1996, p. 10). These thoughts not only occur in conscious contact with reality, but also in the form of flashbacks and nightmares.

Billie Mac: The reason that got me to the vets center is real simple. I was having these awful nightmares about being in a firefight while on a long-range reconnaissance patrol near Laos. The next thing I know, I'm dug into a bunker watching an enemy truck convoy's headlights come down the Ho Chi Minh Trail with my rifle aimed at them. The only problem was that it was on the banks of the Wolf River in Memphis, Tennessee, and it was headlights on I-40. It was also not 1970 but 1988. I knew if I didn't get help I was going to kill somebody.

Denial/Numbing

Accompanying emotions of guilt, sadness, anger, and rage occur as the thoughts continue to intrude into awareness. To keep these disturbing thoughts out of awareness, the individual may resort to self-medication in the form of alcohol or drugs. Use of alcohol and drugs may temporarily relieve depressive, hostile, anxious, and fearful mood states (Horowitz & Solomon, 1975), but what usually occurs is a vicious cycle that alternates between being anesthetized to reality by the narcotic and experiencing elevated intrusion of the trauma with every return to sobriety. The ultimate outcome is increased dependence on the addictive substance as a method of keeping the intrusive thoughts submerged (LaCoursiere, Bodfrey, & Ruby, 1980).

Billie Mac: The drinkin' is no damn good. I know that, but try going without sleep for a week and knowing every time you nod off, that horrible nightmare's gonna come. Then it starts popping up in the daytime and you drink more to keep it pushed back.

As people attempt to cope with catastrophes, they become passive (immobile and paralyzed) or active (able to cope with the situation). Individual reactions fall into three major groupings: momentary freezing, flight reaction, and denial/numbing. In the prolonged stress of a combat situation, denial/numbing is the most common response and allows the soldier to cope and live with the experience in three ways: by believing he is invulnerable to harm, by becoming fatalistic, or by taking matters into his own hands and becoming extremely aggressive. Any of these proactive stances allows the victim to get through the trauma and cope with it without losing complete control (Figley, 1985a, pp. 406–408). Typically, survivors of trauma will let down these defense barriers and will have acute stress disorders immediately after the trauma, but will recover. For those who do not, continued emotional numbing and repression can have severe consequences.

Billie Mac: Looking back on it, I can't believe how callous I have become. SOP (standard operating procedure) was "It don't mean nothin', screw it, drive on." This would be right after a B-40 round had blown your buddy's brains all over you. You had to put it behind you to survive. A guy fell off the construction site I was working on last fall and splattered himself all over the pavement. I sat on a steel beam about thirty feet above the guy and just kept eating my lunch. No big deal!

Submerging emotions out of conscious awareness does not mean that they are summarily discarded. The price is that emotional numbing left in place and not relieved can generalize to other aspects of one's life and result in later psychological difficulties (Wilkinson, 1983). Shunted into the unconscious for a long time, trigger events in the form of everyday stressors can pile up and cause emotional blowouts when the individual is least prepared for them (Figley, 1985a, p. 408).

Increased Nervous Symptom Arousal

Autonomic hyperarousal in people with PTSD causes them to be nondiscriminating to stimuli that may hold no threat to them at all. Acoustic startle response is a cardinal feature of the trauma response (van der Kolk, 1996a, p. 221)

Billie Mac: I can't stand the sound of a chopper. Every time I hear one, I want to run. I get the feeling that every time I hear the 5 o'clock traffic chopper, it's gonna circle in, pick me up, and take me to a hot LZ (landing zone). One came over the building I was working on. I didn't hear it at first. When I did hear it, I jumped and fell ten feet and broke my arm.

In the same vein, hypervigilance, when there is no immediate threat, is constantly with the person and causes concentration and attention problems. As these problems distort information processing, the resulting inability of the person to decode messages from the central nervous system causes them to react to the environment in either exaggerated or inhibited ways (van der Kolk & McFarlane, 1996, pp. 14–15).

Billie Mac: This may sound kinda weird, but I don't ever sit with my back to a door. Matter of fact, I really don't like sitting anywhere where my back might be to somebody else! I get real jumpy.

Dissociation

Dissociation at the moment of trauma is perhaps the most important long-term predictive variable for PTSD and is invariably connected to "complex" PTSD (Herman, 1997, pp. 118–129; Marmar et al., 1991). Dissociation can be a last-resort adaptive way of coping with the trauma while it is going on, but the lack of integration of traumatic memories and derealization of the event seems to be a leading cause of why PTSD develops. If dissociation continues, it can severely interfere with daily living and breed disconnectedness and isolation (van der Kolk, 1996b, p. 286). At its penultimate, dissociation can become dissociative identity disorder (formerly multiple personality disorder).

Billie Mac: It's like a lot of times I'm looking at me doing something sorta through a videocamera, maybe. Like I'm smaller than real life and I sorta know it's me but it's not like I'm really there. The first time I did that was when we were in that village and my buddy Al got it.

What the person needs most is to bring these thoughts and behaviors into conscious awareness and come to grips with them so they can be resolved. Yet rather than confronting the intrusive and threatening material, the person is more likely to deny its existence and use a variety of avoidance responses to escape from the situation (Horowitz, Wilner, Kaltreider, & Alvarez, 1980). This issue is particularly problematic in therapy and is why those who suffer from PTSD may be particularly resistant and noncompliant to approaches that reexpose them to the feared trauma (Bernstein, 1986).

Family Responses

Natural disasters leave so few emotional scars because such disasters often strike intact social support systems simultaneously (Figley, 1988). In natural disasters that affect the whole community, everyone becomes a survivor. Family members help each other through the horror of the disaster, and there is no blaming the victim (Figley, 1985a, p. 409). One of the keystones for bridging the gap between traumatic events and a return to adequate and wholesome functioning is a strong support system that is most generally based within the family. But when the trauma is intrafamilial and takes the form of child and spouse abuse, those who are most traumatized are most generally the ones who are denied the most social support within the family. Those who should provide the most comfort are the ones who are inflicting the most pain (Figley, 1985a, p. 411).

Further exacerbating family relationships is the ingrained tendency in trauma victims to "not feel." Whereas the individual would like to be able to demonstrate feelings of caring and love, experience has taught the victim that exposure of feelings is foolhardy because it invariably makes the victim vulnerable to further pain. These concepts strike at the very heart of what sustains family life—trust. The response of family members is to feel misunderstood, unloved, fearful, and angry. The response is reciprocal and plunges all members deeper into a vortex of family discordance.

From a family system perspective, if children, parents, or spouses attempt to regulate the continuing warfare in which the victim is engaging, they will be worn down and out by the effort. The victim may also become so dependent on the stabilizing person (usually the spouse) that the victim's needs breed resentment in anyone else who demands time and effort (usually children). The outcome of this spiral is what the victim may fear most from the support system—rejection. Feelings of guilt, numbing, anger, and loss plague the victim, and the spiral continues ever downward into more inappropriate behavior patterns and ultimate disintegration of the family.

Family members who cannot deal with the trauma may paradoxically turn on the victim. Sadly, this is too often the occurrence in the case of mothers who deny their spouses' abuse of the children, finally are confronted with the issue by children and family services, and then blame the children for the trouble they have caused! The same is true for rape victims who, if children, may have parents who are psychologically unable to provide support for them and indeed, revictimize them for having done something that led to the assault in the first place. If adults, rape victims may have a spouse who is unable to respond in supportive ways or who blames the victim for "promiscuous or seductive" behavior that invited the rape or "didn't resist enough" (Notman & Nadelson, 1976).

In attempting to deal with a family member who has suffered a traumatic experience, other members may experience the stress to the degree that they become "infected" by it (Figley, 1988). Indeed, if other family members have inadequate coping skills, their own problems may escalate to crisis proportions as the victim's reactions to the trauma create stress within the family. Or, if other members of the family have a hidden agenda of keeping the family in pathological homeostasis, they may engage in enabling the victim's disorder, much as an alcoholic's family may sabotage attempts at recovery. In summary, it should be clear that treating trauma victims also means treating the family.

MALADAPTIVE PATTERNS CHARACTERISTIC OF PTSD

Summed dynamically, PTSD involves five common patterns: death imprint, survivor's guilt, desensitization, estrangement, and emotional enmeshment.

Death Imprint.   The traumatic experience provides a clear vision of one's own death in concrete biological terms (Ochberg, 1988, p. 12). Particularly in young victims, the sense of invulnerability is vanquished and is replaced by rage and anger at one's newfound mortality (Lifton, 1975). For veterans in particular, there is a continuing identity with death. The normal boundary between living and dying is suspended. It is not unusual for veterans to describe themselves as already dead. The only way they have of testing the boundary between life and death is to seek sensation, even if it means danger and physical pain (Brende & Parson, 1985, p. 100). Combined with rage reactions, sensation-seeking behaviors put victims squarely on a collision path with law enforcement agencies, employers, and families.

Billie Mac: After every law officer in Mississippi started chasing me, I ditched the car and ran into a woods. They even had bloodhounds after me. I slipped through them like they were a sieve. It was crazy, but for one of the few times since I've been back I really felt alive. I'd done that a hundred times on patrol.

Survivor's Guilt.   A second pattern is guilt. Guilt comes in a variety of forms: guilt over surviving when others did not, guilt over not preventing the death of another, guilt over not having somehow been braver under the circumstances, guilt over complaining when others have suffered more, and guilt that the trauma is partly the victim's fault (Frederick, 1980). Most commonly, guilt takes the form of intrusive thoughts such as "I could have done more, and if I had he/she'd still be here," or "If I had just done this or that, it (the trauma) wouldn't have happened." Dynamically, the basis of these thoughts may be relief that the other person was the one to die or the victim was lucky to get off so lightly (Egendorf, 1975).

Billie Mac: I was the only one in my outfit to get out of Tet without a scratch. I wonder why. Why me out of all those people? I've screwed my life up since then. Why did I deserve to get out clean when all those other good men didn't? Going to the wall in D.C. last year tore me to pieces. I cried and cried when I saw the names of my buddies up there. Things really got screwed up after that.

For other types of trauma victims, bereavement is closely allied to survivor's guilt. Facilitating grief includes the expression of affect, reconciliation of the loss of a loved one or a missed part of one's life, the ambivalence of not having shared the same fate as others, and moving on to new and meaningful relationships (Ochberg, 1988, p. 10). Because numbing of affect is a major dynamic response to PTSD, it is extremely difficult for survivors to let loose their emotions and grieve.

Desensitization. A third pattern is desensitizing oneself to totally unacceptable events and then trying to return to a semblance of normalcy in a peaceful world. Feelings of guilt and fear may arise over pleasurable responses to physical violence against others. These feelings may become so acute that the victim conceals firearms for protection against imagined enemies but is simultaneously terrified of the guns and what might happen, because of the violence that continuously seethes below the victim's own calm outer appearance. These strong bipolar emotional currents that flow back and forth within the individual lead to hostile, defensive, anxious, depressive, and fearful mood states that find little relief (Horowitz & Solomon, 1975).

Billie Mac: I don't hunt anymore. I hate it. Yet this one guy who was my boss didn't know how close he came to getting killed. I was within one inch of taking him out, I was so hot. It would have been a pleasure, the guy was such an ass.

Estrangement.   A fourth pattern is the feeling that any future relationships will be counterfeit, that they mean little or nothing in the great scheme of things. As the person tries to ward off reminders of the experience, severe interpersonal difficulties occur. Because of the vastly different experiences they have undergone, PTSD victims become estranged from their peers and truncate social relationships with them because "they don't understand"—and indeed "they" do not. Victimization may also be part of estrangement. From being victimized in the original trauma, to possible secondary victimization by social services, hospitals, and mental health providers, to revictimization by significant others, the survivor is crushed under the weight of dealing with these initial and secondary assaults (Ochberg, 1988). The result is that the person becomes more isolated from social support systems and develops secondary symptoms that range across diagnostic categories of psychopathology (Horowitz & Solomon, 1975).

Billie Mac: I was sitting at my dad's watching TV when Saigon fell. I went nuts and trashed the house. What the hell was it all for? That really cooked it with my old man. I moved out after that and haven't said anything to him since.

Particularly for victims of sexual abuse, estrangement may take the form of negative intimacy. Invasion of one's personal space and being cause feelings of filthiness and degradation that make reestablishing old relationships or engendering new relationships an extremely difficult ordeal (Ochberg, 1988, pp. 12–13).

Emotional Enmeshment.   A fifth pattern is a continuous struggle to move forward in a postholocaust existence but with an inability to find any significance in life (Lifton, 1973, pp. 191–216; Lifton, 1975). Emotional fixation, particularly for veterans, has disastrous effects on family life. Sent to Vietnam as adolescents and exposed to prolonged trauma that the majority of the population will never experience, these victims cannot bring themselves to engage in equitable relationships with their families and friends, nor can their families begin to understand their aberrant behavior (Brende & Parson, 1985, pp. 116–117).

Billie Mac: I can't believe what I've done to my kids. I love them more than anything in the world. At times, I'm the greatest dad in the world, coach the Little League team, take them everywhere. The next minute I'm all over them. I've knocked them around in a rage and that scares the hell out of me. I'm some kind of Jekyll and Hyde, and my kids are afraid of me.

TREATMENT OF ADULTS

Given the foregoing constellation of problems that afflict the person with PTSD, treatment is complex, and the human service worker may expect numerous transcrisis events and crisis points to occur during treatment. Assessment is particularly important in PTSD because it is camouflaged by so many other symptoms and problems.

Assessment

Assessment of PTSD should consider at least three goals: First, are there symptoms of PTSD present? Although their presence may seem to be a given, duration of time from onset may mean that different symptoms are more pronounced at different times. Second, diagnoses of presenting problems such as drug abuse or a variety of personality disorders may mask PTSD unless care is taken to assess for prior trauma. It is highly probable that people in crisis will present with comorbid problems and PTSD will generally not be identified as the undergirding problem unless care is taken in assessing for traumatic incidents. Third, because of contextual differences in terms of physical, temporal, social, and political climate, these variables may have a great deal to do with how the event is interpreted (Newman, Kaloupkek, & Keane, 1996, pp. 242–245).

The following examples indicate just how important contextual variables are. A Vietnam veteran with PTSD in the 1970s would be perceived as a crazed baby killer as opposed to a Vietnam veteran in the 1990s, who would be viewed with compassion because of the dramatic change in the political climate and the social view of men and women who fought in that war. Likewise, domestic violence, which was formerly seen as a private matter between husband and wife, is now viewed as a societal ill to the extent that the label "battered woman syndrome" has been attached to it. The self-reliant and tightly knit farm community of Iowa with an extended support system that has been devastated by a tornado may react to that disaster far differently from insular and emotionally distant apartment dwellers in New York City who have been blown out of their apartments by a natural gas explosion. Thus the potential to acquire PTSD or manifest it should always take into consideration a thorough background assessment that includes gender, race, socioeconomic class, culture, race, religion, time components, geographical area, number of incidents of prior exposures to trauma, strength of interpersonal relationships, occupational risk, sociopolitical attitudes, and a host of other contextual variables that may have unforeseen impact on the resiliency of the individual to withstand or fall victim to PTSD.

Assessment of PTSD falls into two main categories, structured or semistructured interviews and empirically derived measures. A comprehensive assessment of PTSD should include information about the person's life context, symptoms, beliefs, coping repertoire, and various strengths and weaknesses. If time permits, any assessment of PTSD should be multimodal. At present no single device can be said to definitively indicate PTSD across the entire range of PTSD client populations (Newman, Kaloupkek, & Keane, 1996, p. 245).

Structured Interview.   If time is available, the structured interview probably remains the best diagnostic device for determining whether a person has PTSD. Several structured interview guides such as the Diagnostic Interview Schedule module for PTSD, the Structured Clinical Interview PTSD module for *DSM-III-R* (Spitzer, Williams, Gibbon, & First, 1990), the Anxiety Disorders Interview-Revised (DiNardo & Barlow, 1988), the Structured Interview for PTSD (Davidson, Kudler, & Smith, 1990), the PTSD Interview (Watson et al. 1991), and the PTSD Symptom Scale Interview (Foa, Riggs, Dancu, & Rothbaum, 1993) are used to assess PTSD.

We believe one of the best structured interviews is the Clinician Administered PTSD Scale (CAPS-1) (Blake et al., 1990). It assesses all the symptoms outlined in the *DSM-IV*, as well as eight associated symptoms that include guilt over acts committed or omitted, survivor guilt, homicidality, disillusionment with authority, feelings of hopelessness, memory impairment, sadness and depression, and feelings of being overwhelmed. It also examines the impact of symptoms on social and occupational functioning, improvement in PTSD symptoms since a previous CAPS-1 assessment, overall response validity, and overall PTSD severity. Current status for all symptoms is assessed first, and if criteria for PTSD are not met, the questions are asked again for a "worst case," one-month period since traumatic onset. The items also have a "QV" code for question validity, when the interviewer has doubts about the truthfulness of the response. The CAPS-1 also pays very careful attention to the assessment of lifetime

PTSD. Its major drawbacks are the length of time required for administration and its lack of validation with nonveterans (Newman, Kaloupek, & Keane, 1996, p. 253).

Self-Reports.   Self-reports are useful for their efficiency in time, cost, and ease of administration. Because crisis intervention often allows only the most rudimentary assessment, if time is of the essence we prefer Figley's (1990) Traumagram Questionnaire, a graphically represented client self-report. It can be self-constructed on the spot. The questionnaire elicits the number, length of time, and self-reported degrees of stress of all previous traumatic experiences and can be easily incorporated into a standard interview format. By plotting the number of events across their length of time on an x-axis and then plotting the degree of stress on the y-axis on a scale of 1 (minimum) to 10 (maximum), the interviewer can quickly gain a graphic representation of the total number, type, and duration of traumas and the degree of stress the client has experienced. It gives the interviewer a good picture of what the client feels are the relative degree of the power of significant events and also gives the interviewer an opportunity to explore the dimensions of each of these events. It also allows the crisis worker to examine one of the "best bet" indicators for PTSD. That is, the repeated exposure of the subject to traumatic events. Its major weakness is the subjective bias of the victim.

Empirically Derived Scales.   A variety of empirically derived PTSD instruments have been generated. Of them, the following seem to have reasonable utility in determining if PTSD is present and are reasonably efficient in terms of time and cost to administer. The Mississippi Scale for Combat Related PTSD (Keane, Caddell, & Taylor, 1988) is widely used and has a number of versions for different client populations. The Impact of Events Scale (Horowitz, Wilner, & Alvarez, 1979) is one of the most widely used instruments for detecting PTSD and has been employed with a variety of trauma-related populations. The scale only assesses the extent of avoidance/numbing rather than the full scope of PTSD symptoms that are covered by the other tests mentioned here. The Keane *PK* scale of the MMPI/MMPI-2 has been formulated for the specific purpose of diagnosing PTSD (Keane, Malloy, & Fairbank, 1984). Because it is embedded in the MMPI/MMPI-2, its score can be compared to the validity scales of the total instrument to determine whether faking or malingering is occurring. Note that some people, such as insurance claimants, malingerers, or incarcerates, may have less than honorable motives in claiming they have PTSD and their reports may not be valid.

Overview of Assessment.   Their affiliative responses show a clear distinction between individuals with character disorders and those suffering from PTSD. In general, victims of PTSD avoid interpersonal relationships, as opposed the ingratiating gregariousness of a sociopath. PTSD victims have few close friends, prefer being alone, and discuss few intimate details of their lives. Unexpected contact with other people or stimuli reminiscent of the traumatic event may make victims extremely "jumpy" and "edgy" (Keane et al., 1985, p. 270).

The human services worker should never dismiss a report, no matter how trivial it may seem, of involvement in a catastrophic situation or a major loss (Scurfield, 1985, pp. 238–239). Because PTSD victims may be very reluctant to talk about the trauma they have been through, human services workers should try to get background information from relatives, co-workers, and any other people who have personal knowledge of the victim. The personal history is particularly important when substance abuse is involved, because if PTSD is not identified, all the efforts of the worker will not ameliorate the substance abuse problem.

Our own clinical experience with depressed clients has uncovered many who have suffered sexual abuse as children. We are coming more and more to believe that until ruled out, PTSD should be suspected as a causative agent. However, getting at it may prove extremely difficult, particularly given the severe social taboos associated with talking about incestuous and abusive relationships. Therefore, in an initial assessment, even though the interviewer may have a strong hunch that repression of a traumatic event is causing the problem, the causative agent should never be exposed, interpreted, or even guessed at until a high degree of trust has been built (Scurfield, 1985, pp. 238–239).

Finally, assessment in treatment of PTSD must be ongoing and overarching, particularly during the course of therapy. The changes that occur in the client vacillate dramatically—sometimes daily or even hourly. Because of the intrusive nature of much of the therapy, it is common to see upsurges in symptoms and problem behaviors.

Assessment for Billie Mac.   In the case of Billie Mac, a CAPS-1 interview showed little if any evidence of traumatic experience prior to Vietnam besides the death of a grandfather, to whom he was quite close. In Vietnam, he was in major battle after major battle, interspersed with patrols and sweeps. He was the only man out of his original company to walk away physically unscathed after the Tet offensive.

After Vietnam, the traumatic wake continued. Violent episodes with his father, his wife, and his children, scrapes with the law, drunken binges, barroom brawls, prolonged bouts of depression interspersed with manic acting out, alcohol addiction treatment, job loss due to nonperformance, suicidal ideation, plus the standard symptoms of PTSD marked his years since Vietnam with almost continuous crises. There were very few months in the 25 years since his return that he would not rank extremely high on the Triage Assessment Scale. Affectively, he goes far beyond what the situation warrants, with large mood swings that cycle through anger, fear, and sadness. He rarely ranks lower than 6 on the Affective Severity scale, and his average is 7.

In the cognitive domain he has suffered physical, psychological, social, and spiritual transgression, threat, and loss. His problem-solving abilities are characterized by self-doubt, confusion, and excessive rumination on Vietnam and his abortive attempts to reacclimatize to the civilian world. His severity rating is consistently an 8 to 9, in the Marked Impairment range.

Billie Mac's behavior invariably makes the situation worse. He either approaches the situation in a hostile-aggressive manner or avoids it for fear of acting out against others. He is immobilized between these two extremes, and significant others report that they feel he is erratic, unpredictable, and dangerous. A most conservative estimate places him at a minimum of 8 on the Behavioral Severity scale. His total scale score is 24, which places him in the lower range of the Marked Impairment category. As he presents for treatment, he is in serious trouble, and at times of stress his triage rating scale score spikes into the lethal Severe Impairment range. His CAPS-1 interview ratings indicate very high frequency and intensity of PTSD symptoms, and the MMPI-2 PK scale confirms his PTSD surely falls into the more complex variety.

Phases of Recovery

Brende and Parson (1985, pp. 185–186) have compiled the work of Wilson (1980), Figley (1978), and Horowitz (1976) to construct five phases of recovery in the PTSD victim. These phases directly parallel treatment approaches, and each has its own crisis stage.

1. *The emergency or outcry phase.* The victim experiences heightened "fight/flight" reactions to the life-threatening situation. This phase lasts as long as the survivor believes it to last. Pulse, blood pressure, respiration, and muscle activity are all increased. Concomitant feelings of fear and helplessness predominate. Termination of the event itself is followed by relief and confusion. Questions about why the event happened and what its consequences are dominate the victim's thoughts.

2. *The emotional numbing and denial phase.* The survivor protects psychic well-being by burying the experience in subconscious memory. By avoiding the experience, the victim temporarily reduces anxiety and stress symptoms. Many victims remain forever at this stage unless they receive professional intervention.

3. *The intrusive-repetitive phase.* The survivor has nightmares, volatile mood swings, intrusive images, and startle responses. Other pathological and antisocial defense mechanisms may be put into place in a futile attempt to rebury the trauma. At this point the delayed stress becomes so overwhelming that the victim is propelled to seek help or becomes so mired in the pathology of the situation that outside intervention is mandated.

4. *The reflective-transition phase.* The survivor develops a larger personal perspective on the traumatic events and becomes positive and constructive, with a forward- rather than backward-looking perspective. The victim comes to grips with the trauma and confronts the problem.

5. *The integration phase.* The survivor successfully integrates the trauma with all other past experiences and restores a sense of continuity to life. The trauma is successfully placed fully in the past.

Neat and orderly progression for the PTSD victim through these stages is the exception rather than the rule. More likely is a precipitating crisis far removed in chronological time from the event itself and then a continuing series of crises that escalate until the victim voluntarily seeks help or is forced to seek it. Once intervention occurs, a cyclic pattern of avoidance, recall, recovery, and more avoidance continues until the core issues that gave birth to PTSD are resolved (Figley, 1985a, pp. 402–404). The human services worker can expect a series of transcrisis events as this process unfolds.

Initiating Intervention

As disequilibrium from the trauma subsides, some form of reorganization takes place. The reorganized state is either adaptive or maladaptive, and it is important to intervene before maladaptive reorganization occurs (Scurfield, 1985, p. 239), or treatment may become much more difficult (Horowitz, 1976, p. 123). Generally, victims of trauma refuse early intervention because they either see the event as too difficult to deal with or believe that people of good character ought to be able to cope with such events on their own without outside intervention. These two faulty assumptions get victims into the delayed part of the disorder, where most of the treatment population will emerge.

Importance of Acceptance

Given the variety of negative and conflicting emotional baggage the victim brings to the session, it is of paramount importance that the human services worker provide an accepting atmosphere so that the victim can start to recount and encounter the trauma. Disclosure of the trauma is difficult for the PTSD victim, because recounting what has happened may be horrifying and socially unacceptable. Also, open-minded acceptance of the client's story may be extremely difficult for and repugnant to the human services worker; but if therapeutic progress is to be made, nothing less will do (Brende & Parson, 1985, p. 178).

Billie Mac: (*Thinking to himself.*) If I tell about killing that kid, what will the counselor think? A baby killer, that's what! Yet, it's bugging the hell out of me. (*Slowly tells the counselor about the incident.*)

HSW: (*Stating personal feelings.*) I know how hard it was for you to talk about that. A part of me wonders how you or anybody could ever kill a child. However, I understand how scared you were, wondering whether he had a grenade, what a moral quandary that put you in, and the guilt and anguish you feel as you recall the incident.

Therapy with veterans either individually or in groups is ideally conducted with veterans as leaders because of the defensiveness and hostility with which most veterans view professionals who have not undergone the experience of combat. One could easily extrapolate this notion to group work with other kinds of trauma victims. The problem is that professionals who have also experienced the trauma or the setting within which it occurs are often not readily available. Therefore, the Veterans Center of Memphis has published a list of 12 "rules of the road" for establishing the credibility of nonveterans who work therapeutically with veterans (Memphis Vietnam Veterans Center, 1985). These rules should be adapted to any intact group such as police officers, emergency medical technicians, and others whose common bond is more than the incidence of PTSD.

1. The client has the experiential knowledge you don't have; you have the clinical and technical knowledge he or she doesn't have. Together you can forge a working alliance.
2. Make your desire to understand come across so that considerable experiential gaps are bridged.
3. Realize that the client wants you to help him or her help you understand. In the process, he or she recreates and reexperiences the sources of the problems and you, by providing the therapeutic climate, gain an in-depth understanding of the traumatic experience.
4. An opposite-sex therapist serves as a role model, that is, in the case of a male veteran, a woman who can understand and accept the victim for what he is and has done without prejudging him.
5. Clinical experience and expertise is built over time—as your understanding and technical expertise grow, you will be accepted by the individual or the group despite your lack of direct experience.
6. As a nonmember of the "exclusive" group, you can challenge the defense of exclusivity, that one who wasn't there can't understand, thus serving to break through his or her feelings of isolation and "contamination."

7. Your technical naivete often helps the individual to explore and express him- or herself. In his or her effort to help you understand the technical aspects of combat, emergency medical service, or police tactical procedures, he or she uncovers unknown areas of conflict.

8. At the same time, because of your naivete, you must guard against becoming too involved in problems and memories, thereby "triggering" situational stress that may need immediate attention and treatment.

9. Realize that moral conflicts will probably be raised for you personally as stories unfold; guard against any display of emotional revulsion to a client who describes atrocities. Be nonjudgmental and objective.

10. Guard against overidentification or hero worship, or you will blunt your problem-solving ability.

11. Expect to need controls and to have to clearly enforce them for your sake and the client's—don't try to do therapy with a client who is drunk or "stoned," refuse to be a party to long tirades on the phone, bar all weapons and mean it.

12. Heed the signs of burnout: thinking or talking too much about your clients to others, finding yourself having client-specific symptoms such as nightmares, and so on. Step back and evaluate whether you may be too immersed in trying to do too much for too many.

These rules are adaptable to any kind of trauma survivors and the people who work with them *and apply particularly to those who work with adult survivors of childhood sexual abuse.* One further admonition is necessary for any human services worker who would work with trauma victims. Frick and Bogart (1982) identified one of the stages that veterans go through as "rage at their counselor." This transference stage (attributing to the human services worker qualities and attributes of significant others in the client's life) is important in coming to terms with the traumatic experience. Human services workers may well become the focal point of all the frustration, grief, fear, lost opportunity, confusion, lack of progress, attempts at reconciliation with society, family, and friends that mark the trauma survivor's attempt to reintegrate into the social mainstream. Human services workers need to deal with such anger by owning their mistakes in being insensitive to issues, accepting and reflecting the victim's anger while at the same time not being defensive, containing impulsive responses after being attacked, owning their own anger, and not becoming discouraged and giving up.

Risks of Treatment

It is also incumbent on the human services worker to state clearly the risks inherent in treatment. It may be hard to make such statements and to propose a poor prognosis, but probably the victim will have pondered many of the same questions. After the initial crisis has passed and the victim is back to a state of at least semiequilibrium, the human services worker should convey clearly the following risks, as outlined by Brende and Parson (1985, pp. 168–174):

1. There may be only partial recovery; there are no magical cures for this tenacious and pernicious problem.

2. Because of the continuing nature of the crisis, either long bouts with hospitals or weekly trips to the therapist are required that will play havoc with keeping a job.

3. As catharsis of the event occurs, it is inevitable that the victim gets worse before getting better. Fear of a psychotic breakdown may occur as the victim learns more about the disorder.

4. As the struggle to find oneself goes forward, personality change may put heavy burdens on interpersonal relationships as significant others see a very different person emerge from the therapeutic experience.

5. Psychic pain may become almost intolerable as the victim reexperiences disturbing memories and emotions that, as they are voiced, may cause rejection by friends and professionals alike.

6. Because of the numerous self-constraints placed on volatile emotions, the victim may fear that giving vent to those emotions will lead to uncontrolled anger and result in physical harm to others. Because of the hurt suffered, it will also be very difficult for the victim to give up the idea of revenge on both real and imagined perpetrators of the traumatic event.

7. Because of the compartmentalized and constricted lifestyle that follows the trauma, the victim will safeguard against change and may have extreme difficulty following directions and doing what others may suggest, no matter how reasonable and proper. Giving up such maladaptive self-reliance will put the victim at the mercy of others, a seemingly intolerable situation.

8. A great deal of pain will result from coming to accept the world as it is with all its frailties and injustices. In attempting to gain reentry into such an imperfect world, the victim is in danger of losing patience with it and falling back into the vortex of PTSD.

9. Correlative with accepting the frailties of the world is also the acceptance of one's own set of infirmities; bad memories may return; relationships may not always be excellent; others may obtain better jobs for no legitimate reason. Acceptance of oneself, including the guilt, sorrow, and regret that goes with it, is the sine qua non of getting through PTSD, but it may be an extremely difficult and fearsome task that will call for far more courage than surviving the catastrophe itself.

Individual Intervention

Multiphasic/Multimodal Treatment.   Individual treatment goes hand in hand with group work. From crisis stage to crisis stage, a multimodal therapeutic approach is used with heavy reliance on various combinations of behavioral and cognitive-behavioral therapy (Fairbank & Brown, 1987; Scurfield, 1985, p. 250). Although cognitive behavioral approaches have been the generic therapeutic modality with the most successful outcome data to date (International Society for Traumatic Stress Studies, 1997; Rothbaum & Foa, 1996, pp. 491–509), various combinations of specific treatment techniques within the realm of cognitive behavior therapy have been tailored to deal with specific components of PTSD. Further, because of the idiosyncratic nature of the course of PTSD, various other techniques that employ psychodynamic (Lindy, 1996, pp. 525–536) and humanistic approaches (Turner, McFarlane, & van der Kolk, 1996, pp. 537–558) may be appropriate. Although this may sound like a shotgun approach that aimlessly blasts away at the problem, such is not the case. The complexity of this malady calls for some of the very best in eclectic therapy and eclectic treatment planning. We further believe that an important component to any psychotherapeutic approach in the treatment of PTSD is the use of psychotropic medication.

Psychotropic Medication.   Pharmacotherapy for PTSD is predicated on substantial findings that a number of psychobiological systems are dysregulated in people with the disorder (International Society for Traumatic Stress Studies, 1997; Ratna & Barbenel, 1997). From what is presently known about the biology of PTSD, drugs that regulate neurotransmitters and neuromodulators ought to be helpful in providing at least some palliative relief from the psychophysiological responses that occur with the disorder.

Because so many different psychobiological abnormalities may predominate in various PTSD cases, almost every class of psychotropic medication has been prescribed for PTSD clients. There is as yet no fixed pharmaceutical regimen for PTSD. The effects of medications for PTSD seem to be so narrow for individuals and specific groups that they are often not generalizable to other populations (Davidson & van der Kolk, 1996, p. 511).

An excellent example is the antidepressant fluoxetine (Prozac), which has been given the highest level of research evidence rating for effectiveness by the International Society for Traumatic Stress Studies in its *Practice Guidelines* (1997). Van der Kolk and his associates (1994) found that fluoxetine did indeed reduce numbing and arousal responses in a clinical treatment group but *did not* in a group of veterans. Further compounding the problem is that one of the side effects of fluoxetine is that while it may reduce numbing and arousal responses, it can also *increase* startle responses (Davidson & van der Kolk, 1996, p. 512).

Davidson and van der Kolk (1996, p. 521) propose that at early onset of PTSD, drugs such as the benzodiazepines or clonidine that decrease autonomic arousal are the best choice. If PTSD is in place, then antidepressants should be introduced, along with a willingness to use a second drug such as a mood stabilizer, anticonvulsant, or benzodiazepine as adjunctive treatment if the primary drug does not ameliorate symptoms (Davidson & van der Kolk, 1996; International Society for Traumatic Stress Studies, 1997). Because presenting symptoms can seriously interfere with treatment, we believe that careful prescription and monitoring of psychotropic medication is critical in allowing PTSD therapy to proceed successfully.

Emergency/Outcry

In the first phase of recovery, the emergency or outcry phase, the major problem is to get the victim stabilized; this means reducing the anxiety and physical responses associated with the trauma (Meadows & Foa, 1999). Meditation, relaxation, and biofeedback may be used (Kolb & Mutalipassi, 1982).

Anxiety Reduction.   In relaxation training and meditation, the human services worker teaches the victim how to relax body muscle groups systematically and to focus calmly on mental images that produce psychic relief of body tensions and stress (Benson, 1976; Wolpe, 1958). Victims learn how to exercise self-control over many of their stresses and anxieties and dampen debilitating physiological responses.

HSW: OK, Billie Mac. Just imagine that you are lying on the beach with that soft warm sand, the calm breeze blowing gently over you, the gentle lapping of the cool, crystal-clear water, and just easily focus your attention on that scene. Now just notice the difference in your body too. Notice the difference between how your muscles feel when they are tense and relaxed. Starting with your legs, just tense them up, feel how your muscles tighten up. Now relax them, and just feel that tightness drop away. Notice the difference and the really pleasant feelings that occur when your muscles are just hanging loose and flaccid. Continue to picture the scene on the beach as you work your way up your body, alternating between tensing and relaxing your muscles. Notice as you continue to do this how you can change the way your body feels and what you can focus on in your mind's eye.

Relaxation alone is helpful in alleviating current symptoms and enabling the victim to regain a measure of emotional and behavioral control, and it is also a preliminary step in tackling the cluster of problems so characteristic of PTSD. Through deep relaxation or hypnosis, the client may be moved imaginally back in time to the traumatic event. Regressing the client in this manner is necessary to elevate bad memories of the traumatic event, and the intrusive images that accompany them, to conscious awareness (Brom, Kleber, & Defares, 1989; Kingsbury, 1988; Spiegel, 1989).

Extinguishing Intrusive Images

Given the previously discussed neuropsychological foundations of PTSD, Ochberg (1988) has concluded that PTSD should be viewed first in terms of autonomic nervous system (ANS) arousal and any treatment should take into consideration the physiological aspects of the disorder. Thus a standing hypothesis for PTSD treatment has evolved that proposes a return of the client to the original state of elevated psychophysiological arousal in order to affect current maladaptive response sets (Malloy, Fairbank, & Keane, 1983). Once the victim has learned how to relax, other therapeutic strategies such as systematic desensitization, flooding, implosion, and Gestalt techniques may be employed to create ANS arousal (Black & Keane, 1982; Crump, 1984; Fairbank & Keane, 1982; Grisby, 1987; Keane & Kaloupek, 1982; Marafiote, 1980; Parson, 1984; Scurfield, 1985; Stutman & Bliss, 1985).

The human services worker continues to work slowly through the relaxation exercises and the mental imagery, continuously reinforcing the client for being able to shift to calm, relaxed scenes and away from the intrusive, anxiety-producing images. Practice for the victim in this and the other techniques to be covered in individual therapy is important. We recommend that sessions be audiotaped so that the victim can practice the procedures at home on a daily basis.

Numbing/Denial

Once the victim has learned how to relax, the second phase of intervention occurs, coincident with the victim's emotional numbing and denial phase of recovery. This phase is concerned with bringing to conscious awareness the traumatic event and the hidden facts and emotions about it that the victim denies (Brende & Parson, 1985, pp. 191–192). In a gentle but forceful way, the human services worker guides the victim, in the here-and-now of the therapeutic moment, to reexperience in the fullest possible detail what occurred in the traumatic experience so that submerged feelings are uncovered and ultimately expunged (Scurfield, 1985, p. 245). While deeply relaxed, the victim is asked to reexperience the terrible events of the trauma, with the injunction that at any time the memories can be switched off and the victim can return to the pleasant image of the beach.

HSW: Now go back to the village and tell me what is happening.

Billie Mac: (*Lying down, relaxed, eyes closed.*) The point man all of a sudden comes under fire and gets popped. I see him get hit. He's lying in the open across a ditch about 100 meters from the tree line. It's really getting hot, a lot of fire from concealed bunkers. They're using him as bait. This goes on for about five minutes, I guess. All of a sudden I decide to go and get him. Me and some other guys just get up and run across the open field to the ditch. We're getting all kinds of fire and out of five of us, only me and Al make it to the ditch without getting dinged. The point man is only about five meters from me, but I can't get at him. (*Billie Mac breaks into a sweat with slight tremors.*) I finally spot where the concealed bunker is that's making it so hot for us. I've got a LAW [light antitank weapon] and I get a bead on the bunker and zap it. At about the same time there's an explosion right next to me, a B-40 grenade, I guess, and that's all I remember until I wake up on the medivac chopper. (*Breaks into profuse sweating and major tremors.*)

HSW: All right, just shift out of that scene and back to the beach and just relax. Notice the cool water, the warm sand, the gentle breeze, and just let your muscles relax. (*Billie Mac noticeably relaxes and, with continued directives from the human services worker, returns to a calm, relaxed state.*)

Although the account of the combat situation is fearsome in its intensity, the human services worker suspects that it alone is not responsible for the traumatic reaction. Billie Mac was in many such situations, but this village is the focal point of his nightmares and intrusive thoughts. The human services worker suspects that there is more here than what Billie Mac is revealing, and seeks to slowly peel away the psychological walls that defend the trauma from awareness. The human services worker believes that the recounting of the combat situation, despite having psychological value as a defense mechanism, is probably not historically accurate. The victim has left out certain traumatic parts of the story, and the human services worker's job becomes one of trying to fill in the gaps (Horowitz, 1976, pp. 117–118). Having built a very strong rapport and mutual trust with the victim (Keane et al., 1985, p. 291), the human services worker probes into the situation and actively seeks to interpret and clarify the content of the client's story with respect to its potentially overwhelming effect (Scurfield, 1985, p. 245).

HSW: Go back to the village and the ditch right before you take out the bunker. What do you see?

Billie Mac: I see the point man, he's alive, but bad off.

HSW: What are you thinking?

Billie Mac: I've got to get him, but I can't, the fire's too heavy.

HSW: What do you feel?

Billie Mac: Scared, I um . . . I can't seem to do anything . . . the rounds are really coming . . .

HSW: What's happening around you?

Billie Mac: Al keeps yelling, "Take the bunker out with the LAW!"

HSW: Then what?

Billie Mac: I . . . can't . . . do it . . . it . . . I'm terrified. (*Starts to shake uncontrollably.*)

HSW: Stay right with that, Billie. I'm right here.

Billie Mac: Al grabs the LAW, stands up and fires it and—Oh, my God! Get down! Oh, Jesus, the B-40 got Al. He's gone. His blood's all over me . . . I killed him. It was my job and I couldn't do it and I killed Al. (*Breaks into uncontrollable sobbing and shaking.*)

HSW: It's OK! Just erase that scene from your mind and slide back to that warm, quiet beach. Just put yourself out of the firefight and back to that beach and relax, just focusing that soft sand in your mind.

As the victim breaks through the defenses that have let him numb and shield the actual events from awareness, the full force of the reality of the incident floods over him, along with the overwhelming feelings of fear, guilt, remorse, and terror that accompany the event. As these thoughts come into awareness, they give the human services worker a much clearer picture of the how and why of Billie Mac's phase 2 (denial and numbing) and those of phase 3 (intrusive-repetitive thoughts). The human services worker, using tolerable doses of reminiscence about the event, seeks to push forward into full awareness what the true scene at the event was and not what the victim's mind has fantasized it to be.

HSW: Now shift out of the scene at the beach and go back to the village. The B-40 has just gone off and Al is gone. What happens next?

Billie Mac: I can't remember . . . I don't know . . . I passed out.

HSW: (*Gently.*) Yes, you can. Just think a moment and picture the scene.

Billie Mac: Oh, God! You've got to get the point man now. You've got to go get him. I'm up and running, the fire is terrible, it's only 20 feet to him but it's like a mile, I'm so damned scared. (*Breath coming in rapid, ragged gasps.*) I've got him and am dragging him back to the ditch. Bullets are kicking up all around me, I'll be cut in two. He weighs a ton. I get to the ditch and roll him and me into it. I turn him over and . . . Oh, Mother of Mary! He's dead. Why, oh why, didn't I get there sooner? I could have saved him. You puke-faced coward. (*Starts uncontrolled sobbing.*)

HSW: (*Very calmly.*) You are OK. Just shift out of that scene and back to the beach. Just take all the time you need to relax and erase that scene from your mind. Just let the cool breeze blow over you, smell the clean salt air, and enjoy that feeling of being completely relaxed. (*Time passes, and Billie Mac becomes noticeably more relaxed.*) Now I'm going to count up from 1 to 10 and when I reach 10 you'll be fully alert and refreshed.

The human services worker does this and brings Billie Mac back to present time. The worker then processes the events of the imagery session with Billie Mac.

Interpretation.   At this point, the worker uses a more psychodynamic approach, actively intervening in the situation by clarifying and interpreting what the client says. By dynamically integrating the there-and-then of the trauma with the client's maladaptive attempts to cope and atone in the here-and-now of the therapeutic moment, the therapist hopes that the client can build a comprehensible picture that will make sense of the memory (Lindy, 1996, p. 534).

HSW: So it's not just that terrible fight at the village, but more what you didn't do. You feel as if you were a coward there, and that cowardice cost the life of your friend. It's almost as if all these years you'd been trying to atone for that in the only way you know how. That is, by doing things that would almost guarantee that you die too. The brushes with the law, the uncontrollable rage that winds up in knock-down, drag-out fights, the DWIs, and the suicide attempt.

Billie Mac: I don't know. (*Sobbing.*) I feel so terrible about it. How could I have frozen? It would have been better if I had got killed rather than live with this.

HSW: Yet you did act. You went after the man, and you couldn't know whether a minute or two would have saved his life. It seems as if that minute or two of indecision has caused 30 years of terrible retribution that you can never pay off. I'd like to suggest that it has been paid with interest, and now the time has come to pay the balance. Are you willing to do that?

Billie Mac: (*Shakily.*) I guess . . . although I don't know how much more I can take. You bitch! How could you do this! This really hurts!

HSW: I understand how rough you feel this is and how callous and uncaring I must seem. Remember! We've made it this far. Trust me and yourself. Together we can pull through this.

Even if the human services worker is right on target with her interpretation, getting Billie Mac to integrate the material and also allowing him to reconcile himself to the event are much more difficult. Breaking through the subconscious defenses of the client is not a one-shot deal, and denial is more often the rule than insight and acceptance. Billie Mac's negative reaction to the worker is typical of the client's transference of his or her ills to the worker as the hurtful affect is brought into awareness. At this point it is the worker's primary task to remain as empathic as possible to what is going on with the client (Lindy, 1996, p. 536).

Reflection and Transition

Although it can be extremely traumatic for the client, the human services worker will encourage the client to experience the full range of emotional responses he or she felt at the time of the event, as well as how he or she tried to make sense of it (Donaldson & Gardner, 1985, p. 370). This marks the fourth phase of the crisis, the reflective-transition phase (Brende & Parson, 1985, p. 192). The human services worker will help the client by combining behavioral techniques of flooding and thought stopping.

Flooding. Flooding is one of the most effective, if not controversial, techniques for getting rid of the bad memories of PTSD (Cooper & Clum, 1989; Keane, Fairbank, Caddell, & Zimmering, 1989; Lyons & Keane, 1989). In flooding (Stampfl & Levis, 1967), the fear-evoking stimuli are presented continuously. The rationale is that if the victim is literally flooded with anxiety-provoking stimuli, the client will discover that there is no basis for fear. Continuously flooding the client causes the stimuli that are generating the anxiety to diminish; that is, repeating the response without reinforcement diminishes the tendency to perform that response. As the victim reenacts the trauma, the human services worker puts in the missing pieces of the puzzle and ferrets out all conditioned stimuli buried in memory. The result is that no noxious components of memory are left to recondition debilitating responses (Keane et al., 1985, p. 265). This technique is a very serious therapeutic endeavor and should not be undertaken by neophytes until they have received supervised training.

Thought Stopping.   Thought stopping is a simple but powerful device that enables the victim, with help from the human services worker, to change debilitating, intrusive thoughts to self-enhancing ones. The human services worker initially sets the scene and builds the images until the fear-evoking stimuli are at maximum arousal, and then shouts "Stop!" and replaces them with positive, self-enhancing thoughts (Williams & Long, 1979, p. 285). The human services worker tells the victim that at the point when the intrusive scene is most terrifying, the human services worker will slam a book sharply on the table and state in a firm voice, "Stop! Shift back to the beach!" The victim will be passive throughout the procedure, with the human services worker setting and enhancing the scene. An audiotape of the session is made, and the client is given the assignment of listening to the tape and then using the procedure whenever the intrusive images occur.

HSW: Now erase the beach scene and come back to the village. You're in the ditch. Smell the stench of that ditch, feel death all around you. You can almost see the grim reaper there. You'd like to run away, but there's nowhere to run. Oh, what a fool you were to ever make the dash out here in no-man's-land. Look back and see your squad members shot up, contorted in pain, with the blood and dirt covering them. Peek over the ditch and see the point man, he's in terrible pain, screaming for help, but there's a blizzard of fire coming from the bunker. It's certain death to stick your head above the dike.

Feel the conflict. You want to do something, you know you've got to take the bunker out, but you are paralyzed. You can smell the fear in you, sweating out of your pores. Look at Al, he expects you to do something, you're the squad leader, but you can't. Feel Al's stare. Listen to him yelling, "Take the bunker now, man." Your fingers are glued to the LAW. Feel Al grab the LAW. Watch him as he stands up in that dreadful hail of death and fires the LAW into the bunker, and in the next instant see the explosion and the dirt fly as the B-40 round hits and Al disappears in the flame and smoke. Smell the smoke of cordite and the sheared copper odor of blood. Enhance those images—hear, smell, feel, see, taste that terrible moment. It's all there now as it really was. (*Billie Mac is writhing in the reclining chair.*) NOW STOP! (*Slams book down on desk.*) Shift away.

Billie Mac: (*Screaming.*) I can't do it!

HSW: (*In a soft but commanding voice.*) Yes, you can! Just slide out of that and into that soft warm sand. Stay with that beach scene, smell the salt air, the cool breeze, and know that you can do that any time you want. Notice the difference in how your body feels, what goes through your mind. Just enjoy that feeling of knowing you can move into that scene.

This sequence is repeated over and over until the victim is able to switch volitionally from the intrusive image to the relaxing one with ease.

Journaling.   For PTSD clients, speaking of what has happened to them is extremely difficult. Journaling is an excellent method of opening up affect and allowing nonverbal catharsis to occur. By putting down their thoughts in their own words and then hearing them, victims place the terrible memories at a safe enough psychological distance that they and the human services worker can analyze them (Cienfuegos & Monelli, 1983). Journal writing gives the human services worker a catalyst for encouraging the kind of free association necessary to open the crystallized defenses of the victim who might otherwise never explore the traumatic event (Progoff, 1975). Billie Mac wrote a description in one of those endless nights when no sleep will come or worse, the terror that comes with sleep.

Where Did B.M. Go?
What happened to B.M.—the boy from Mississippi—happy-go-lucky, not a care in the world, who loved life, sports, the sunshine, the rain . . . and everything in the used-to-be-beautiful world. Everyone told B.M., "Go to school. Play sports. Go to college." But B.M. decided to do for his country. B.M. wanted to go to war and fight to win . . . to serve his country . . . to make everyone proud of him. B.M. went to war, B.M. killed, massacred, mutilated, burnt, hated—a hate that was like a drunk hate—tore his own heart out a little at a time, time after time.

B.M. fought and survived a war that 127 warriors that went with B.M. didn't. B.M. looked at everyone around him and wondered why the people hated him. Why they were scared of him . . . why they feared the warrior from Vietnam who went to a fight they were scared to fight.

B.M. wanted to love . . . to be loved. It seemed like the world was completely different from him and didn't have the same ideals about life and love.

B.M. became a drunk. He drank to forget the war, the brave warriors who had given their lives in Vietnam, to forget the people that he was living around. To these people B.M. was a cold-blooded murdering S.O.B.—a baby-killing M.F.

B.M. had been taught all his life, "Thou shalt not kill, love thine enemy." B.M. lost his morals. B.M. killed his enemies. B.M. cut the heads and ears off some of his enemies. B.M. lost his soul. B.M. is lost to God and can't be forgiven. People can say, "Ask God to forgive you, B.M." But B.M. can't forgive himself and can't ask for forgiveness. B.M. has accepted that feeling like someone took his heart out and stomped it into the ground. There is not a day in his life that he doesn't feel hurt or hurts the ones he loves.

B.M. just wants to be loved . . . to love himself again; to get rid of that hard feeling deep down inside of his heart. B.M. wants to have peace of mind. Is it too much for him to ask, to seek, to search for? Is death what it will take for B.M. to finally find peace within himself?

Why can't B.M. get out of all these depressing moods he stays in . . . and cries about nothing when he is driving down the road.

Sometimes B.M. thinks he is a crazy S.O.B. Maybe the people are right. Why can't B.M. keep a job? Because B.M. was a fuckup after he got back from Vietnam. His vengeance and his screwed-up attitude keep him in trouble. B.M. would get so much on his mind and B.M. would keep putting it back inside. The more he put it back, the worse his depression would get until it would erupt in a rage of vengeance, which would always wind up hurting himself or the people he loved. Even the government deceived B.M. They told B.M., "Don't worry, B.M. You go and fight this war for your country and if anything happens we will take care of you." B.M.'s response to this is, "Fine! I will do all I can for my government and my country." But give me my heart and soul back. Make me sleep at night. Make me quit crying. Take this depression away. Help me find a job and help me feel alive again. Give me back what you took from me. B.M. is what you took and I want myself back.

I wish I could give back the lives I have taken from the world, but I know that I can't. I would if I could, and I am the one that will have to live with that in my heart throughout eternity.

B.M. vividly and dramatically illustrates the anguish of PTSD in his writing: Anguish from both an intrapersonal and interpersonal standpoint, of guilt he feels within himself for his moral transgressions and rage at the transgressions visited on him by an impersonal government and an uncaring society; anguish over what he was and is and how he is now attempting to resolve and reintegrate these two vastly different people that were and are B.M. Billie Mac continuously uses his initials, pointing over and over to himself, but in the third person. Only in the last paragraph does his plea change clearly to subjective, first-person, owning statements. Even these statements are couched in terms of magical thinking—wish fulfillment. The use of Billie Mac's initials as an identifier of what he really perceives himself to be is not happenstance. The initials "B.M." also stand for bowel movement. Indeed, Billie Mac's self-assessment is that he is mostly worthless "shit" to himself and others. This is typical of the kind of self-condemnation that an individual who is both victim and victimizer experiences.

This excruciating piece of writing is an initiating step in the long process that moves from self-condemnation to what Lifton (1973) calls *animated guilt*. Animated guilt enables the victim to start taking responsibility for past actions and start to experience new degrees of personal liberation. This rather dramatic example of journal writing was done voluntarily, but when clients in a crisis situation will not talk about their experiences, sometimes suggesting that they write down their feelings can be a way of breaking the impasse (Gilliland & James, 1998). Keeping a journal not only can be an extremely effective way of dealing with unbidden feelings and thoughts as they surface, but also can provide the worker and the client with an assessment of how therapy is progressing (Pearsons, 1965).

Integration

Gestalt Techniques.   The Gestalt technique of reaching into the victim's past and bringing to conscious awareness what Gestalt practitioners call "unfinished business" is particularly helpful in draining the pustulant affect that infects the event (Scurfield, 1985, p. 246). For Billie Mac this technique will take a different twist and will be the last part of the crisis, that of making atonement, penance, and restitution (Horowitz & Solomon, 1975).

HSW: The empty chairs in front of you represent various people. Al, the point man, other members of your squad that got hit on that day in the village. I want you to tell them what you felt about what you did. I may move to one of the chairs or have you take their place. Right now I want you to imagine Al in that chair over there. What are you going to say to him?

Billie Mac: I'm . . . so sorry. I froze. I shouldn't have done that. I killed you, and I can't ever forget that.

HSW: (Takes Al's chair.) Hey, man, what about that time at Chu Lai, and the A Shau valley? You didn't freeze then. You saved my bacon then. Remember how I froze? You didn't say squat. You think you're perfect?

Billie Mac: You were my best friend and I let that happen. *(Sobs.)*

HSW: (*As Al.*) You think you got a corner on the market? Everybody was scared. I just did it. You gave me back my life a half dozen times. I'll never forget that. You did well by me, buddy. I got no regrets.

Billie Mac: Jesus, I miss you, I loved you so damn much.

HSW: (*As Al.*) Then remember the good times we had. That R & R in Bangkok, when we took the town apart. Those are the parts I remember. I love you too, buddy, but it's time we were done with that village. It's time for you to say goodbye to me.

(*The HSW gets up and goes over and takes Billie Mac into his arms and hugs him. Billie Mac weeps, releasing a flood of emotion.*)

For each man in the squad, the scene is replayed. Sometimes Billie Mac takes the role of the other man, and sometimes the human services worker does. Each piece of unfinished business is slowly and patiently worked through until Billie Mac has reconciled accounts with each person who was there on that terrible day. Clearly, Billie Mac goes through a painful but necessary grieving process that must take place if he is to put the event behind him (Brende & Parson, 1985, p. 105). As Billie Mac makes atonement for that day long past, and the trauma is expunged, the human services worker seeks to pull him to the present time and help him move forward with his life. Intensive intervention slacks off and the victim may then go through a series of booster sessions on an "as needed" basis, with a minimum of a booster session once a month for three to four months (Balson & Dempster, 1980). This point marks the fifth, or integration, phase of the crisis.

GROUP TREATMENT

There are two types of treatment groups for people who have been exposed to trauma. The first type is preventive, short term, and typically used for those suffering acute distress. These are generally known as *debriefing groups* and are composed of members who have just survived a common traumatic experience (Mitchell, 1983). Debriefing for acute traumatic stress is discussed in detail in the last chapter of this book. The second type is longer term and is typically composed of class-specific members who have been exposed to the same type of trauma but at different times and under different circumstances. Commonly called a *support group,* this group deals with a variety of transcrisis issues and is the focal point of this chapter's discussion of group work with clients who suffer from PTSD.

Support Groups.   Rap groups were started for veterans in 1970 by Robert Lifton and Chaim Shatan in New York City. Lifton and Shatan were human services professionals who had become disaffected with the Veterans Administration's constant refusal to acknowledge that many Vietnam veterans were suffering from combat-induced psychological problems. The outcome of this dilemma was that professionals finally came to recognize the success of rap groups and to integrate them into more traditional formats (Walker, 1983).

Emotional attachment and social involvement is one of the basic and most important ingredients in armor-plating the individual against PTSD. For most of those who suffer from PTSD, social isolation and emotional estrangement is the norm. Thus group work is helpful because of the shared experience, mutual support, sense of community, reduction of stigma, and restoration of self-pride it fosters. The primary task of any group therapy is to help people regain a sense of safety and of mastery because of the shared sense of having gone through the trauma (van der Kolk, McFarlane, & van der Hart, 1996, p. 433). Further, confrontation by peers is more acceptable than confrontation by professionals because it is reality-oriented (Scurfield, 1985, pp. 247–248).

Groups also serve an educative function. The terrifying nature of PTSD calls for clearly delineating what is happening and why. Answers to victims' questions—such as "What are common PTSD symptoms?" "Why do victims use drugs?" "How long will it take to get better?" "Am I crazy?" "What do I do in this situation?" "Will I ever be as I was before this happened?"—help build a cognitive anchor for the victim (Brewi, 1986).

We now switch our client emphasis to a more contemporary scene, the men and women who work in police, fire, emergency and disaster services and who, because of their repeated exposure to trauma, are excellent candidates for PTSD (Bierens-de-Haan, 1998; Corneil et al., 1999; Epstein, Fullerton, & Ursano, 1998; Tucker et al., 1999; Ursano et al., 1999; Wagner, Heinrichs, & Ehlert, 1998; Wilson, Poole, & Trew, 1997). We will follow one individual in this group as a generic example of emergency service workers who become at risk for PTSD because of their constant exposure to traumatic events.

The Case of Ryan.   Ryan Sanchez is a 35-year-old who has been a patrolman for seven years with the police department. In that time he has received numerous commendations and citations for his work. Approximately one month ago he was referred to the police psychologist for a rather dramatic deterioration in job performance. He was caught sleeping on the job, had missed several days of work, and was insubordinate to his field commander when confronted with his inadequate performance at a crime scene. That episode culminated in his being hauled away bodily by other patrol officers after he attempted to punch his field supervisor. He was referred for clinical evaluation by his watch commander.

An MMPI-2 administered by the police psychologist indicated a high potential for faking good—presenting a better picture of one's personality than one actually feels about it. The PK scale also indicated a good possibility of PTSD. The police psychologist believed that Ryan's initial interview and his MMPI-2 scores were an attempt by Ryan to present a better picture of his mental health than he was actually experiencing. The psychologist then conducted a CAPS-1 interview and found a variety of problems that reached into both Ryan's job and family.

Prior to Ryan's career with the police department, he served as an emergency medical technician (EMT) for eight years. He decided to leave EMT work because of its stress, but still wanted to work in an "exciting and meaningful" job. He then joined the police department. He has a college degree in biology and a certificate in emergency medical technology. He has been married for 15 years to Mary, a nurse, and has two daughters, Katrina, 12, and Stacey, 8. He has been separated from his wife for five months, is currently living with his parents, and sees his daughters on his off-duty days. He reports that his wife had become progressively more paranoid over other women, accused him of having affairs with them, constantly checked to see if he has perfume or lipstick marks on him after work, and finally attempted to run down, in a mall parking lot, an off-duty female police officer whom she suspected of having an affair with Ryan. That incident resulted in her temporary arrest, but charges were later dropped after she apologized to the female officer.

Ryan reports that at about this time he started suffering a bad case of "nerves." Specifically, he started to experience flashbacks to a series of traumatic events he experienced both as an EMT and a police officer. He reports a series of instances as an EMT where he was powerless to save lives of terminal auto accident victims—a number of which were children or adolescents. He reports having become very protective of his daughters as a result and says he wishes, "I could put them in a castle with high walls and a moat around it and keep them locked up so nothing could hurt them." His protective view of his children severely strained his relationship with them, and they do not want to go and visit him because of his anger when they are not under his close supervision

He was also an EMT respondent to a natural disaster 11 years ago when a propane truck overturned and blew up, killing over thirty people. They were charred and burned so badly that rigor had set in, but were still alive. He was relegated to being the mayor's aide de camp and spent most of his time passing information to the mayor about rescue efforts. He felt completely helpless and out of control and was enraged over his assignment. He very much wanted to be in on the rescue efforts although he paradoxically reports that it was the most horrific scene he had ever witnessed. He reports having had nightmares about it for a number of months after the event. In the last six months those nightmares have returned with increasing frequency. He also reports that within the last six months he becomes severely agitated to the point of a panic attack whenever he is near a propane truck, and will go out of his way to avoid them or bulk plants and tank farms where petroleum products are stored.

One other traumatic event is reported as remarkable. This event involved a missing person report while Ryan was a police officer. He and two detectives met the father of a young woman reported missing, at her abandoned apartment. Because they did not have a search warrant, they could not conduct a thorough search of the apartment. Ryan had a hunch that the woman's body was in the apartment buried under a huge mound of bags in a closet, but he was admonished by the detectives that there was nothing they could do. Because it was below freezing in the apartment, there was no foul odor to indicate the presence of a body. Two weeks later he again met the father at the apartment. The father had come in a rental truck and had begun to haul his daughter's belongings out of the apartment when he noticed a foul odor. On his arrival, Ryan immediately knew the odor was that of a dead body. On entering the apartment he immediately found the woman under the bags of clothing. He reports an indelible picture of the father sitting in the yellow rental truck with a glazed stare that he cannot get out of his mind. He also reported that his uniform smelled like death and repeated washings would not get rid of it. He finally threw his whole uniform out, but lately he believes that somehow his new uniforms have soaked up the smell from his leather uniform jacket. He has never undergone formal debriefings for any of these traumatic events and said that although they bothered him some at the time they happened, he moved on past them—or so he thought.

He does not use alcohol, and that fact is confirmed by his watch commander. He reports he has been taking "tranquilizers" and "sleeping medication" since his separation from his wife. He also reports that things are so bad both on the job and at home that he has recently contemplated killing himself, but he has not formulated a plan because he doesn't want his daughters to be labeled because their dad "was another nutso who blew his brains out." He admits to the psychologist that he clearly has lost control of his life and wonders if he indeed, does not have PTSD or is suffering a "breakdown" of some kind.

Ryan's symptoms fit a clear diagnosis for PTSD. He has recurrent, intrusive thoughts and dreams about the traumatic events and experiences severe psychological distress to external cues of the events. He now avoids stimuli that remind him of at least two of the events. He has increased arousal symptoms, hypervigilance over his daughters' safety, difficulty concentrating on his job, and problems falling asleep. The psychologist's diagnosis is posttraumatic stress disorder, with delayed onset. Although delayed onset is relatively uncommon (McFarlane & Yehuda, 1996, p. 159), it is not uncommon for a domino effect to occur in emergency medical workers where one event triggers other supposedly long-forgotten ones (van der Kolk & McFarlane, 1996, p. 9). As his social support system has given way at home, Ryan has become increasingly at risk, and the precipitating event of his wife's vehicular assault on a fellow police officer and his subsequent separation from his family has activated the traumatic memories. Ryan is referred to a behavioral health maintenance organization for individual treatment and is also referred to an independent support group that is co-sponsored by the police, fire, and emergency workers unions and the city and county governments. The police psychologist also makes an antisuicide contract with Ryan and contacts the human services worker who will be attending Ryan, to tell the worker about Ryan's suicidal ideation.

Triage Assessment.   Affectively, Ryan is experiencing extended periods of intense, negative moods that are markedly higher than the situation warrants. Although he has no clear intent or plan for committing suicide, he is agitated and depressed enough to consider it. At times he perceives his negative mood states as not being very controllable. His affective rating is 7 to 8. Cognitively, Ryan's thinking is generally equal to the task of moving forward in day-to-day living. However, his ability to control intrusive thoughts and images about the traumatic events is limited and his perception of events, particularly his obsessiveness about his daughters' safety, differs noticeably from the reality of the situation. His cognitive rating is 6 to 7. Behaviorally, Ryan's inability to function at work is noticeably affecting his job performance. His behavioral rating is 6 to 7. Ryan's full-scale triage ranges between 19 and 22. He is in crisis and in need of immediate therapeutic assistance.

Ryan's initial meeting with the human services worker involves carrying forward the antisuicide contract, obtaining a referral to a psychiatrist to review his medication, explaining what individual therapy will entail, and an invitation to join a support group.

HSW: We've got some men and women that meet on Wednesday night to talk about many of the problems you're trying to deal with now. I think you've got a lot in common with them and believe it might be helpful for you to meet them. They've all been or are in the police, fire, or emergency departments and are trying to come to terms with their experiences there. You don't have to talk if you don't want to, that's up to you. You'll probably feel a lot of different emotions, and some of those aren't going to be too pleasant. However, all of the people you'll meet have been feeling a lot of the same kinds of things even though they may have different kinds of problems that brought them into the center. From that standpoint they all know what you're going through, and while it may get tough, they'll support you and not pass judgment. I'd really like to see you come in. You don't have to, but we know that social support is one of the most important ingredients to getting better, and right now it sounds like you could use some of that.

The group meets for an hour and a half each week. The first item is that individuals are asked to introduce themselves by name and unit. This structured event is not just for the purpose of getting into "war stories"; it serves to move men and women psychologically back in time and place to the starting point of their trauma and to cement the "we-ness" of the group. After introductions, anything on anybody's mind is fair game for conversation.

The group will be composed of "veterans" who have been through many such sessions and "greenhorns" who are at their first meeting. Command officers are separated from rank-and-file members so there are no possibilities of recriminations by command staff. Everything said in the group is confidential, and members indicate their willingness to abide by that rule by signing a statement to that effect. The groups are run by independent contractors who are not answerable to the city or county government about personnel decisions or any other matters that could put their clients' jobs at risk. Topics range from problems of day-to-day living, the institutions they work for, issues and questions about PTSD and trauma, replays of how and what they did during traumatic events, family and job issues, and how all these problems affect them.

The leaders of the group are two psychologists who have extensive experience with the police, firefighters, and EMTs. Although they have never served in any of those occupations, they have credibility because of their previous work with these groups, and that is critically important. Distrust and suspicion are strong in the early stage of such groups, and human services workers can be expected to be tested over and over again until they have proved themselves to be congruent and trustworthy (Gressard, 1986).

The leaders are not group therapists in the truest sense of the word. They are more like participatory members who have been endowed with the task of keeping the group within loose guidelines concerning time, monopolizing the group, facilitating support and responses from the other members, and, in a few extreme instances, acting as empathic but firm sergeants-at-arms. As leaders they must be willing to keep a low profile while group members interact. Their leadership role is subtle rather than directive and requires an infinite supply of patience as the group struggles toward resolution of its problems. If therapy in a classical sense of the word is to occur, it happens much later in the game. A clear distinction between the rap/support group and a long-term therapy group is that trauma and the expiation of associated guilt are the main focus, not life adjustment. Life adjustment problems represent another stage in the crisis of this malady and are handled later. The typical support group starts something like this:

HSW: Hi, everybody. We've got some new people here and because they don't know everybody I'd like you all to introduce yourself and your unit. I'm Theo Ewing, a psychologist. I work with the Crisis Intervention Team on the city police department.

Jane: Jane Shore, patrol officer, delta shift, west precinct, city. Age 21. (Rookie on the force, training officer shot in a liquor store holdup. Robbers got away. Feels responsible, nightmares, startle reactions, hypervigilance, some paranoid ideation about abilities.)

Leann: Leann Sung: EMT, RN, county hospital. Age 50. (Twenty years emergency room and ambulance duty, attendant at multiple disasters, catastrophes. Burned out, suicide attempt after caught stealing amphetamines from ER pharmacy, peptic ulcer, numbing of affect.)

Alonzo: Alonzo Brown, sheriff's deputy, Able shift, north sector, county. Age 42. (Shot and killed carjacker after carjacker killed hostage by cutting her throat. First shooting, first violent deaths witnessed, nightmares, intrusive images, high blood pressure, alcohol abuse problem.)

Lamont: Lamont Evans, Paramedic, Life flight. Age 29. (Life flight helicopter crashed and burned. He and other paramedic thrown clear. Everybody else died—including two auto accident victims being lifted to hospital. Survivor's guilt, hypervigilance, startle reactions, nightmares, wife has left, phobic reaction to helicopters since accident.)

Rachelle: Rachelle Johnson, driver, Engine House 47, county fire department. Age 36. (Saw wall collapse on two members of her engine company during warehouse fire. Helped pull both dead firefighters from rubble. One was her best friend. Nightmares, survivor's guilt, somatic and general anxiety reactions, eating disorder.)

Ryan: Ryan Sanchez, patrol officer, Charlie shift, center precinct, city. *(Personal data previously given.) (Introductions continue around the group and group welcomes Ryan.)*

HSW: Has anybody got anything that's hot?

Lamont: Well, two things, I haven't had any more helicopters crashing nightmares since last time, I guess that's something. And the wife said she might come back. *(General congratulations from the group.)*

Rachelle: Man! that's something. I wish I could get rid of the damn things, none of those drugs are doing any good. I can't eat. I can't sleep. I don't know how much longer I can take it.

Jane: Ditto that! I can't get by it, and it seems to get worse.

Lamont: *(Gently.)* We've all been there and know how tough it is; you knew it'd get worse before it got better, we all told y'all that. It's hell. Y'all been talkin' to your counselors?

Because of the mutual support and resources within the group, lots of suggestions are given about how Rachelle and Jane can grapple with their emotional turmoil. Survivor's guilt is a common thread that runs through emergency, fire, and police personnel. The expectation is that these people are supposed to lay their lives on the line, and when others die or are injured there are always second-guessing and fears of being seen as letting their comrades down. Lamont's comments are therapeutic in that they are accepting and understanding of the guilt both women feel.

Rachelle: Yeah, I been talkin' to her. But it just seems like the more stuff comes up, the worse I feel. Why did they die and not me?

HSW: So it still boils down to the survivor's guilt stuff we've talked about. Lamont, Rachelle, and Jane have both talked about the same issues. *(The group leader takes a few minutes to speak to the typical behavioral dynamics of someone who has survived a trauma when others did not, which is typical of the psychoeducational function that is also a part of support groups.)* Any thoughts?

Jane: I've always wanted to be a cop, and I really thought I'd make a good one, but it's tough being a rookie and a woman at that. I've replayed that robbery a thousand times. I don't know what I could have done different and Loren, my training officer, told me I did fine. I'm glad he's gonna be all right, but I still think I screwed up somehow. Maybe I'm paranoid, but I'm not so sure the other cops on my shift trust me. Hell! I'm not so sure I trust myself.

Ryan: Well, I'm new here so I don't know much, but I heard about that and it sounded OK to me. What did you think you did wrong?

Jane: Well, that's what's driving me nuts. I don't think I did, but I think the others think I did.

Ryan: Well, if it's because you're a woman, lose that thought. I've got a female for a partner, and she's tops.

HSW: Jane, did you hear what Ryan said?

Jane: Yeah! And thanks.

The leader immediately breaks in so that two people get reinforcement. The newer member of the group for talking and Jane, who can use the affirmation from a male officer who is a veteran.

Alonzo: So what's happened to cause the change in you, Lamont?

Lamont: I'm not blaming myself as much. I still feel bad about the others that died, but I'm getting reconciled to it. I'm really lucky to be alive, and I've got to start working on putting my life back together. And I'm finally realizing that engine failure had nothing to do with Lamont. My counselor calls it *reframing,* kinda lookin' at it from a different viewpoint. I mean both of you were doing what you were supposed to be doing when those things went down. You can't ask more than that.

Alonzo: I wish I could "reframe" my problems that easy. I mean this crackhead carjacks this woman, practically cuts her head off in front of me. I've got no clear shot until he drops her, then I shoot him. Then the shoot team gives me a clouded report. Should have acted sooner, should have had more patience. How the hell do you do both of those at once? I did it all by the book. What that's all about? Then I get a wrongful death suit laid on me by both the victim and the murderer's families. It's not enough I feel bad about both of them, but now I'm the culprit. I'll never get rid of that image. And no damn support from the department. I've been a cop for 19 years, and if I can make it for one more year without having a stroke with this sky-high blood pressure, they can all kiss my ass goodbye. Why shouldn't I drink?

Leann: Yeah well, that's what they do, is use you up. Twenty years at county ER. I've seen it all. When I got caught swiping the speed, I'd been on for four straight shifts through four gun assaults and two knifings, three multiple-injury car accidents, and burn cases of five kids in an apartment fire. I was about to collapse. And I've done that over and over for all these years. And you know what, the ER supervisor who caught me said he could forget it if I could take just the one more shift, said he "knew I needed a pick-me-up." When I said no to that SOB, he turned me in. That's the sum total of my life, no family, a speed freak, a burned-out ER nurse with an ulcer, and a system that uses you up and then dumps you. So tell me why suicide doesn't look like a good career option. (*Starts to weep silently.*)

HSW: Are you still contemplating killing yourself, Leann?

In no uncertain terms, the leader immediately checks out Leann's comment. As she is a past attempter, such comments are never seen as offhand statements.

Leann: No, not really, it just makes me so angry that they'd do that. I told them about that jerk, but they still put me on disciplinary sick leave and didn't do a thing to that blackmailing twirp.

HSW: So it's also the system that you feel betrayed by. It's like after all these years of doing your very best, the system turns its back on you. Not only does it make you madder than hell, but at a deeper level it really hurts to think that somehow, an institution that you've given most of your life to, would not stick up for you when the chips were down or would even try and blackmail you. *(Leann and Alonzo both nod their heads vigorously in agreement.)*

Although it may appear that the support group has dissolved into a gripe session about uncaring bureaucracies, the stresses put on individuals by notoriously understaffed human services institutions and departments add a great deal to the recipe for posttraumatic stress disorder when emergency situations occur (see Chapter 13, on burnout). The group leader reflects these feelings and gives the member a chance at catharsis, but also poses a problem-solving question.

HSW: I wonder what you might do about changing some of that institutional behavior?

Rachelle: I know one thing, if it hadn't of been for the unions pushing for this kind of support and now the new debriefing program, we wouldn't be here now. There's got to be more safeguards for people who work in the high-stress jobs we do, and the only way I see that happening is through the union's collective membership. I think I'll talk to my rep about some of that stuff.

Alonzo: That's right! At least they can get all the certifiables in one place and keep an eye on us. *(Group laughs.)* I know how much that hurts Leann, 'cause I feel the same way. But you gotta think of all you've done and all the lives you saved and the people you've helped. I'm pretty cynical right now, like you, but I had a person stop me the other day and thank me for something I did a long time ago, that he said kept him out of jail. I couldn't really even remember the incident it's been so long ago, but he sure did. It made me feel good. How many people out there do you suppose you've been involved with who wouldn't be alive now if you hadn't of been there?

Alonzo, who has been vitriolic in ventilating his feelings, switches roles and becomes a support person to Leann. In mutual help groups such as this, such role shifts are common and the need to become a helper rather than a beneficiary is extremely important (Silverman, 1986). Theo, the leader of the group, recognizes this shift and wisely lets Alonzo carry the dialogue.

Alonzo: Eh, ah, Ryan. What's happening with you, man?

Ryan: *(Details his problems.)* I mean, I like you guys and all, but I don't know that this group stuff will help much. I mean you can't fix my marriage, and all this other crazy PTSD stuff, I guess the shrink will sort that out. I just don't know.

Rachelle: I understand, Ryan, I haven't been here that long myself, but I'll tell you this much, these people understand what I'm going through. Maybe we can't save your marriage, but we can sure be here for you, 'cause these other folks sure been here for me.

Rachelle's comment encapsulates the essence of why it is called a *support group*. As the group session closes, each member is given the floor to speak on what has occurred for him or her personally during the meeting. No one else is allowed to respond to his or her comments. Summing statements include both reflections about the impact of the discussion on oneself and reinforcing comments to others. Finally, the group rises, joins hands, and has a silent moment of meditation. The emotionally positive high voltage that flows through the locked hands of some very tough men and women is both touching and powerful, and it conveys far better than words the caring and support each man and woman feel for their comrades.

Evidence suggests that victims who have suffered other types of catastrophic intrusion into their lives can profit from support groups. Donaldson and Gardner (1985) report that incest victims quickly gain an intense sense of relief in coming together with other victims in mutual support groups. A typical comment is "No one else understands, but I can come out of the closet here." Defining these groups at a deeper level is Foulkes's (1948) comment that participants in such support groups can reinforce each other's normal reactions and break down each other's pathological reactions because they collectively constitute the very norm from which the individuals deviate. As such, members of a veterans' rap group we work with have what one member called very good "crap detectors": "We can smell it immediately when somebody isn't coming clean with us."

The Life Adjustment Group

PTSD may be seen as a two-generation treatment approach. In the first generation, treatment focuses on accessing and working through the trauma and its symptoms. Although this will be difficult, the second generation of treatment may be even more so. In the second generation, treatment moves to the client's attempts to readjust to contemporary society, which will generally not be an easy task (Johnson, Feldman, & Southwick, 1994). As the guilt and horror of the situation are resolved, clients are moved into the life adjustment group, and another crisis ensues. It is not enough to bring to light hidden traumatic experiences. The key is to integrate past experiences, to find meaning and new ways of coping, to make atonement not only for oneself but for others, and to find new directions in life (Brende & Parson, 1985, pp. 199–201). The group at this point will diminish and absences will increase. The reason is twofold. First, threatening material will again be covered. Second, action and behavioral change now become mandatory. Moving from the insight gained about what happened in the past to taking that insight and applying it to present time is a giant step, and one that is guaranteed to be rife with crisis. What is now called for is to get on with the business of living. At this juncture, intervention will take many forms, depending on what the particular problems are that the individual faces. Such problems range from maintaining sobriety to salvaging careers.

However, one thread will usually run through the circumstances of all clients at this stage. That thread is of vital importance and must be rewoven into the fabric of their lives. It is their family. Any comprehensive PTSD treatment program should take into consideration the need to reestablish the basic support system of the family, which is of critical importance in helping the survivor move forward in his or her posttraumatic world.

Family Treatment

If the trauma is unresolved and chronic, its residue will eventually become enmeshed in the victim's interpersonal network (Figley, 1988, p. 91). As reluctant as the victim of trauma may be to seek help, often the family is even more unwilling to participate in the recovery process (Solomon, 1986). Even though family members may be suffering terribly because of the victim's actions toward them and their respondent actions toward the victim and each other, they offer much resistance to change the status quo, even though they adamantly maintain that change is needed. As strange as it may seem, although families may be stressed to the limit in adapting to the PTSD victim, they do try to adapt, at times in pathological ways. As the victim changes, the family may be in for a rude awakening and may not be able to make parallel changes.

Therefore, one of the crisis worker's major tasks is assessing the family's willingness to engage in treatment. The family's ability to resolve the crisis is a function of the nature of the event, the family's definition of the event, the resources they can bring to bear on it, the buildup of stressors that led to the event, and the effectiveness of their past and current coping skills (McCubbin et al., 1980).

Treatment objectives are to develop and implement an intervention program to deal with both the stress disorder of the victim and assorted family dysfunctions that were in place prior to the event or have developed after the event. Learning about the disorder, dealing with the boundary distortions of intimacy and separation caused by it, alleviating psychosomatic results of rage and grief, urging recapitulation of the trauma, facilitating resolution of the trauma-inducing family conflicts, clarifying insights and correcting distortions by placing blame and credit more objectively, offering new and more positive and accurate perspectives on the trauma, establishing and maintaining new skills and rules of family communication, and initiating new coping and adapting skills as family dynamics change are some of the many tasks the worker will have to tackle (Figley, 1988, pp. 86–88; Rosenthal, Sadler, & Edwards, 1987).

The foregoing list of tasks is a major order and is best dealt with by referral to a therapist who is a specialist in families and conjoint therapy. However, it is practically a must if the family has any hope of survival as a healthy system, and the crisis worker should understand that at an early point in the therapeutic process, the family members need to be apprised of their role in the trauma and urged to become proactive in its solution. Finally, for the victims, relearning how to be effective members of their families and society calls for the same kind of courage that propelled them into treatment in the first place. However, this time it may be much more difficult, because they will be working with the people they need the most and probably have hurt the most.

EYE MOVEMENT DESENSITIZATION AND REPROCESSING (EMDR)

Eye movement desensitization (EMD) is a relative new treatment technique for PTSD. Developed by Francine Shapiro (1989a, 1989b) at the Mental Research Institute in Palo Alto, California. Shapiro (1991) later added the "R" to the acronym to indicate a reprocessing of information, along with changing to more positive cognitions and desensitization of the traumatic memory.

The procedure is, to say the least, controversial. EMDR is so simplistic and is extolled as so fast and effective in comparison to combinatorial approaches using cognitive behavior techniques that it has been viewed with skepticism—particularly because the intractableness of PTSD is such that there are as many failures as successes in treating the disorder. However, a number of replicating studies have been done (Carlson et al., 1998; Cocco & Sharpe, 1993; Forbes, Creamer, & Rycroft, 1994; Montgomery & Ayllon, 1994; Scheck, Schaeffer, & Gillette, 1998; Shapiro, 1999; Silver, Brooks, & Obenchain, 1995;

Thomas & Gafner, 1993; Vaughan, Armstrong, Gold, & O'Connor, 1994; Vaughan, Wiese, Gold, & Tarrier, 1994) that do show significant results for EMDR when compared with other treatment modalities. On the contrary, other studies (Cahill, Carrigan, & Frueh, 1999; Cusack & Spates, 1999; Devilly & Spence, 1999; Devilly, Spence, & Rapee, 1998; Jensen, 1994; Oswalt, Anderson, Hagstrom, & Berkowitz, 1993; Renfrey & Spates, 1994) have not found such stunning results, and reviews of the research on the theory and efficacy of EMDR have been extremely critical (Lee, Gavriel & Richards, 1996; Muris & Merckelbach, 1999a, 1999b; Rosen, 1999).

At this point it appears EMDR may be at least as effective in treatment of simple PTSD as the cognitive behavior approaches, but may run into problems with more complex PTSD. From that viewpoint, we present EMDR here as a possible intervention alternative to the more intrusive treatment approach we have already described.

According to Shapiro (1995, pp. 55–73), there are eight basic treatment components to EMDR: history taking and treatment planning, preparation, assessment, desensitization, installation, body scan, closure, and reevaluation.

History and Treatment Planning. Initially, clients are evaluated for their ability to handle the high levels of disturbance that may occur with treatment. A comprehensive clinical picture of the client is obtained and a determination is made of the specific targets to be reprocessed, these targets include past events, current stimuli that trigger symptoms, and positive attitudes and behaviors needed for the future (Shapiro, 1995, p. 68).

HSW: (To Ryan.) It appears that at least three events from your past are predominate. The propane truck, the dead body of the missing girl, and the young woman in the auto accident who died in your arms. It also seems that the reemergence of all these traumatic work events occurred closely after your wife, in a fit of jealous rage, attempted to run down the female officer. The constant theme that emerges from all of these events is that you feel powerless, frustrated, and angry, but were and are paralyzed to do much about these events because of a variety of social and job prohibitions and your own moral stand. It appears that at least three triggers that set these flashbacks and anxiety attacks off are propane trucks, yellow rental trucks, and verbal battles with your wife— particularly over custody and safety of your daughters.

Preparation. Preparation for therapy entails explaining to the client what is going to happen, the effects that can be expected, and safety procedures. Shapiro also makes a point of discussing secondary gain issues. That is, if the therapy is successful and the pathology is reduced, what will the client have to give up (Shapiro, 1995, p. 69)? Although this may seem strange, a veteran may not want to lose his or her disability payments or "wounded warrior" status if the PTSD is eradicated.

Assessment. Shapiro (1989a, 1989b, 1995) proposes that EMDR treats traumatic memory by requiring that the client maintain in awareness one or more of the following:

1. an image of the memory
2. a negative self-statement or assessment of the trauma
3. the physical anxiety response

Once the memory is identified, the client is asked to choose the image that best fits it along with a negative cognition and the chief physical response that goes with it. Although Shapiro (1989a, 1989b, 1995) proposes that it is optimal when all three conditions are held at the same time, she maintains that the presence of any one is sufficient for desensitization to occur. Anxiety level is assessed by Wolpe's (1982) Subjective Units of Discomfort (SUDs) scale (0 = no anxiety; 10 = highest anxiety possible). Because negative self-cognitions are also part of the disorder, shifts in the client's cognitive view of the traumatic event are also assessed by a Validity of Cognition (VOC) scale that Shapiro (1989a) developed (1 = the cognition is completely untrue to 7 = the cognition is completely true).

Ryan: (*Generating images.*) I'm standing on the freeway overpass looking down on a scene from Dante's Inferno. It looks like a war zone. There are burning wrecks everywhere. I can see blackened bodies. Some are still alive. There are paramedics and firemen and other rescue workers all covered with soot. I can smell burned rubber and flesh. I can hear lots of moans and cries for help and shouting. I can feel the heat coming up out of the freeway on my face and arms. Sometimes when I come upon a propane truck, it all comes back like that. That's why I avoid them if at all possible. (*Generating negative self-statements.*) I'm powerless. I need to be down there, but I'm not sure I can take it. I've never seen anything like this. I'm a coward. I hate myself for feeling that way. (*Generating physical anxiety response.*) My skin feels like its been sandpapered. Every nerve in my body is on fire. I want to run, down there or away, but do something. I can't stand just watching it all.

Clients are then asked to rate themselves on the SUDs and VOC and indicate the physical location of the symptoms (Shapiro, 1989a, 1989b, 1995, p. 70).

Ryan: The SUDs is way beyond 10. The VOC is 7.

Clients are next asked how they would like to feel and are told to generate a new positive self-statement that reflects the desired feeling (Shapiro, 1989a, 1989b, 1995).

Ryan: Like I'm in control. I'm not a coward. Not necessarily a hero.

Clients are then asked to judge how true that new statement is (Shapiro, 1989a, 1989b).

Ryan: A generous VOC for that would be 2.

Desensitization.   Shapiro (1989b) then gives the client a standard set of instructions designed to diminish performance anxiety and performance demands. She indicates that this step is important because clients may also have difficulty accepting the initial changes they feel in themselves. Her instructions are as follows:

> What we will be doing is often a physiology check. I need to know from you exactly what is going on, with as clear feedback as possible. Sometimes things will change and sometimes they won't. I may ask you if the picture changes—sometimes it will and sometimes it won't. I may ask if something else comes up—sometimes it will and sometimes it won't. There are no "supposed to's" in this process. So just give as accurate feedback as you can as to what is happening, without judging whether it should be happening or not. Just let whatever happens, happen. (p. 213)

Clients are then told to generate the scene, the negative statements, and their noxious feelings and visually track the human services worker's finger. The therapist's finger is moved rapidly and rhythmically back and forth, about one foot from the client's face, at approximately two back-and-forth movements per second with a sweep of about 12 inches across the client's field of vision. For clients who may have trouble with this approach, Shapiro uses slightly different formats, where the therapist's fingers are to the side of the client's vision field and are alternately moved up and down. The movement is repeated 12 to 24 times for one set. (This is called a *saccade,* which means a sort of a pulling or pressing movement.) After each set of saccades, clients are asked to erase the scene from their minds and take a deep breath. They are then asked to bring up the noxious image again and ascribe a SUDs level to it. If the image has not changed after two sets of saccades, the client is asked if the picture has changed or if anything new has come into the image. If so, the new image is desensitized before returning to the old image. Periodically, clients are asked to assess the image, cognition, and memory. Their answers are used to determine new insights, perceptions, or alterations.

Ryan: (*After two saccades.*) I dunno. It's not as strong now or something. Maybe an 8. It's like it's moving, or I'm moving. I'm not frozen.

HSW: OK. See yourself moving and put that "I'm not helpless, I'm moving and taking control" billboard under that picture. Can you think of that?

Ryan: Yeah. It's also like I'm frustrated or angry too now.

HSW: That's OK! New images and thoughts come into this. That's normal. We'll work those through too.

The therapist continues to attack the client's image, but this time has him insert the "I'm a coward" billboard into the scene until it too is diminished and changed to a more positive self-statement. The therapist continues eye movements and processes with Ryan until he reports a SUDs of 1.

Installation.   The idea of the installation phase is to install a new, positive cognition of the event. The installation phase starts once the client's SUDs rating has dropped to a 1 or 0. Ryan has changed his image, and the therapist will continue to pursue this until there are no longer additions to the emotional meaning of the image or there is no longer additional positive input.

Ryan: OK! I'm equal to this. I could handle it down there, but my job is up here coordinating things. I'm where I can do my best.

Note that the cognition is not kept in a negative sense, "I'm not a coward," but is put positively and proactively. While the client focuses on the target image and the new positive cognitions, the eye movements are continued until the client can report a VOC for the new positive thoughts at a level of 6 or 7. If the cognition fails to change after two sets of eye movements, there may be a mismatch between the cognition and the image, or vice versa. In each case, both image and cognition must be congruent with one another. If they are not, then one or the other needs to be replaced (Shapiro, 1989a, 1989b, 1995, p. 71).

Body Scan.   After the positive cognition has been fully installed, clients are instructed to think of a physical location of anxiety in their body if the SUDs level remains high. They are asked to concentrate on the body sensation while new saccades are given. When the focal point of physical discomfort subsides, clients are asked to return to the original picture of the trauma and the standard EMDR procedure is resumed (Shapiro, 1989a, 1989b). Shapiro believes there is a physical resonance between the body and dysfunctional material. She believes this phase is important because it can uncover new areas of unprocessed or unthought-of material (Shapiro, 1995, p. 730).

Ryan: I wish I could jump out of my skin I'm so anxious. It feels like it's burning from the inside out.

HSW: OK, I want you to focus in on your skin. Feel the burning sensation. (*Starts and finishes another saccade.*)

Ryan: (*After two more saccades.*) Huh. It's kinda gone now. That's really weird!

Closure.   When no new events or negative cognitions are elicited, the EMDR procedure is terminated. The client is never left in a state of emotional disequilibrium whether reprocessing for the event is done or not. The client is debriefed, and reminded that additional intrusive images that may arise after the session are a positive sign of additional processing. Shapiro (1995, p. 73) also recommends that clients keep a journal of their thoughts, situations, dreams, and other information that may come to mind about the memory. This information can be used to target new images at the next session.

Reevaluation.   At each new session an assessment is made of the previous targets. The client is asked to reaccess previous reprocessed targets, and the client's journal is examined for any intrusion of the previously examined material.

Ryan: It's weird. That image of the propane truck explosion is just kinda vague or misty or something. I decided to drive by a bulk plant that I always avoid. It's right on my way to my folks' house. Well, I decided to hell with it, let's see. Usually I'd think I was going to have a panic attack the last couple of months if I went near it. But I drove by it and it was just a bulk plant. Nothing more! Didn't feel a thing! Fancy that!

In subsequent sessions the therapist may successively move through images of the propane truck, the body in the closet, the father of the murdered girl in the rental truck, and the scenes with Ryan's estranged wife. However, if the target and the triggers are well worked out, generalization of effect can occur and positive benefits accrue in other areas of the client's life (Shapiro, 1989a, 1989b, 1995, p. 74). Shapiro (1989b) reports that a success rate of 60 to 70% removal of symptoms can occur in one session through the treatment of one to three distinct memories! She also indicates that specialized and intensive training is needed with more difficult cases. We support her admonition and urge that any human services worker who aspires to treat PTSD on an individual basis obtain specific and intense training for any of the techniques we report in this chapter.

CHILDREN AND PTSD

Childhood trauma is important not only for what it does to children, but also for after-effects that carry into adulthood. Terr (1995, p. 302) likens childhood trauma to rheumatic fever. Although rheumatic fever is a serious disease of childhood, the damage it causes can later be lethal in adults in a variety of ways. Childhood trauma operates in the same way and can lead to character problems, anxiety disorders, psychotic thinking, dissociation, eating disorders, increased risk of violence by others and by oneself, suicidal ideation and behavior, drug abuse, self-mutilation, and disastrous interpersonal relationships in adulthood (Pynoos, Steinberg, & Goenjian, 1996, pp. 331–352; Terr, 1995).

Terr (1995, p. 303) proposes a division of childhood trauma into two categories: Type I, which is one sudden, distinct traumatic experience, and Type II, which is longstanding and comes from repeated traumatic ordeals. Lack of full cognitive and moral development causes distinctive differences in how children react to trauma. It appears that even infants have the capacity to remember traumatic experiences (Hopkins & King, 1994).

Children who suffer from Type I traumas appear to exhibit certain symptoms and signs that differentiate their condition from those that result from more complicated Type II traumas. Type I events are characterized by fully detailed, etched-in memories, omens such as retrospective rumination, cognitive reappraisals, reasons, misperceptions, and mistiming of the event (Terr, 1995, p. 309). In contrast, Type II traumas result in the psyche's developing defensive and coping strategies to ward off the repeated assaults on its integrity. Massive denial, psychic numbing, repression, dissociation, self-anesthesia, self-hypnosis, identification with the aggressor, and aggression turned against self are prominent. Emotions generated from Type II traumas are an absence of feeling and a sense of rage and/or unremitting sadness. These symptoms may be diagnosed in childhood as conduct disorders, attention-span deficit disorders, depressive disorders, or dissociative disorders (Terr, 1995, pp. 311–312).

Terr's (1983) in-depth, four-year follow-up on children who were victims of the Chowchilla, California, bus kidnapping is the benchmark study in childhood PTSD. The victims of this trauma were a group of 26 elementary and high school children who were kidnapped together with their school bus, were carried about in vans for 11 hours by their kidnappers, and were buried alive in a truck trailer for eighteen hours before they dug their way out—a horrific Type I trauma.

Etched Memories.   Terr (1983) found that the children still had specific feelings of traumatic anxiety over the event after four years. When asked to speak about it, children generalized their anxiety from the event to statements like "I'm afraid of the feeling of being afraid." Unlike combat veterans, who might boast about harrowing experiences, the children were profoundly embarrassed by their experience, were unwilling to talk about the event, and shied away from any publicity. They generally voiced feelings of being humiliated and mortified when asked about their experience. Whereas 8 of 15 children had overcome their fear of vehicles such as vans and buses, they still reported occasional panic attacks triggered by unexpected sudden confrontation with stimuli such as seeing a van parked across the street from their house and vaguely wondering if some of the kidnappers' friends had not come back for them.

Eighteen of the children were found to employ suppression or conscious avoidance of the trauma. Parents often aided them in this endeavor, although the two children whose parents encouraged them to talk about the experience were still not spared its residual effects. Their typical response was that they hated the feeling of helplessness they experienced and needed to feel in control of the situation. All the children could remember almost every second and minute of the contents of the event. However, they were able to remember few, if any, of the emotions or behaviors they experienced during the ordeal. This remarkable retrieval of full, precise verbal memories of almost all Type I traumas indicates that these memories are indelibly etched into the psyche, no matter how the child tries to suppress them, and are carried forward into adulthood (Terr, 1995, p. 309).

Developmental Issues.   Trauma may have severe repercussions on developmental expectations and acquisition of developmental competencies in children (Pynoos, Steinberg, & Goenjian, 1996). Eth and Pynoos (1985, p. 44) believe that continuous intrusion of a traumatic event, evolution of a cognitive style of forgetting, and interference of depressed affect with mental processes very definitely influence school achievement. Children who experience trauma are likely to have problems with "narrative coherence," the ability to organize material into a beginning, middle, and an end. This inability to organize a linear story has direct repercussions on reading, writing and communicative ability (Pynoos, Steinberg, Goenjian, 1996, p. 342).

Trauma may cause anxious attachment to caretakers and separation anxiety. Developmentally, the child regresses socially, which can result in poor affiliation with peers, social isolation, and avoidance of school. Parents may exacerbate this behavior because of their own unresolved fears of the traumatic event, and may become overprotective of the child. Conversely, memories where the primary caretaker was either unable or unwilling to provide help and succor during the traumatic event does severe harm to the developmental expectation that the caregiver is capable of providing nurturance and security (Pynoos, Steinberg, & Goenjian, 1996, pp. 340–345).

Sense of a Foreshortened Future.   Terr (1983) found that intrusive thoughts did not repeatedly enter the children's conscious thoughts; however, sleep brought very different problems. Whereas a few reported daydreams, the children had nightmares through which ran many repetitious themes of death. The children believed these dreams to be highly predictive of the future and made comments such as "I'm 11 now, but I don't think I'll live very long, maybe 12, 'cause somebody will come along and shoot me." Adolescents in particular are brought face to face with their own vulnerability and, in the case of those who have experienced the murder of a parent, report that they will never marry or have children because they fear history will be repeated (Eth & Pynoos, 1985, p. 48; Terr, 1995, p. 308).

Reenactment.   In an attempt to gain mastery over a Type I trauma, children replay the event and develop a reason or purpose for it. Once the reason is found, children often feel intensely guilty about it. "I should have listened to what Mom said and come home right after school!" In Type I traumas the question is "How could I have avoided that?" as opposed to the question of Type II traumas, "How will I avoid it the next time?" (Terr, 1995, p. 310).

The play of children with PTSD is very distinctive because of its thematic quality, longevity, dangerousness, intensity, contagiousness for siblings, and unconscious linkage to the traumatic event (Bergen, 1958; Maclean, 1977; Terr, 1981). The clearly prevalent dynamic is a continuing reenactment of the children's plight during the trauma (Eth & Pynoos, 1985, p. 42). This thematic play can be characterized as burdened, constricted, and joyless (Wallerstein & Kelly, 1975). Traumatic play is also problematic because it replaces normal developmental play that is a vital component in childhood maturation (Parker & Gottman, 1989). For adolescents, reenactment may take the form of delinquent behavior (Eth & Pynoos, 1985, p. 47) ranging from truancy, sexual activity, and theft to reckless driving, drug abuse, and obtaining weapons (Newman, 1976).

Physical Responses.   Physiologically, approximately half the children in the Chowchilla kidnapping manifested physical problems that could be construed to be related to the trauma of being held prisoner without food, water, or bathroom access (Terr, 1983). In young children suffering from PTSD, regression may occur and previously learned skills such as toilet training may have to be retaught (Bloch, Silber, & Perry, 1956). Sleep disturbances and severe startle responses can cause a variety of educational and social problems in school (Pynoos, Steinberg, & Goenjian, 1996, p. 350).

Displacement.   In the Chowchilla survivors, a great deal of displacement of affect occurred, with emotions about the event being shifted to a related time, an associated idea, or another person—particularly the interviewing psychiatrist. Prior to the follow-up interviews, children displayed a variety of displaced behaviors, including the belief by one of the children that the psychiatrist had placed notes posing questions about the kidnapping in her school locker (Terr, 1983).

Transposition.   Misperceptions, visual hallucinations, and peculiar time distortions often occur in children who have experienced Type I traumas—as opposed to Type II traumas, in which the perpetrators and events have a long history with the children and are rarely misperceived once the events are brought to awareness (Terr, 1995, p. 311). In the Chowchilla survivors, one of the most profound changes occurred in transposition of events surrounding the trauma. Events that happened after the trauma were remembered as having happened before the trauma (Terr, 1983). Also, there was a general belief that the traumatic events were predictive of what was about to happen to them. Ayalon (1983), in a study of victims of terrorism, found a similar effect in children. Children attempted to resolve their vulnerability and lack of control by saying they should have listened to the omens and "shouldn't have stepped in the bad luck square." Thus, in PTSD, such distortions of time become part of the child's developing personality and are attempts to take personal responsibility and even feel guilty for events over which they had no control.

Terr's (1983) study indicates that whereas children behave differently from adults in their attempt to resolve the traumatic event, they are no more flexible or adaptable than adults after a trauma, and it would be erroneous to assume that they "just grow out of the event." Furthermore, these children did not become toughened by their experience, but simply narrowed their sphere of influence in very restrictive ways to control their environment better.

Type II Traumas.   Children who have suffered continued physical and sexual abuse and refugee children from war-torn countries are typical victims of Type II traumas. Massive denial and psychic numbing are primarily associated with Type II traumas. These children avoid talking about themselves, go years without talking about their ordeals, and try to look as normal as they can. If they do tell their stories, they may later deny they did. This aspect is quite different from Type I children, who tell their stories over and over again. Denial may become so complete that Type II children will forget whole spans of childhood (Terr, 1995, p. 312). Type II children are indifferent to pain, lack empathy, fail to define or acknowledge feelings, and absolutely avoid psychological intimacy. In adulthood, this massive denial cuts across narcissistic, antisocial, borderline, and avoidant personality disorders (Terr, 1995, p. 313). Although self-hypnosis and dissociation in Type II children may take the form of dissociation identity disorders (formerly multiple personality disorder) in adulthood, such children most often develop anesthesias to pain and to sex and emotionally distance themselves in the extreme (Terr, 1995, p. 314).

That does not mean the rage at what happened to them is not there. Rage includes anger turned inward against the self and outward toward others and can range from self-mutilation to murder. Reenactments of anger occur so frequently in Type II traumas that habitual patterns of aggression are formed, and the seething anger is probably as debilitating as the chronic numbing. Paradoxically, defenses may be formed, whereby the child becomes completely passive or identifies with the aggressor (Terr, 1995, p. 315).

At times crossover changes from Type I to Type II traumas may occur, wherein a single event such as an accident that requires long-term hospitalization and many painful operations turns into a Type II trauma. Children who come out of Type I traumas with permanent physical handicaps, disfigurement, long-term pain, or loss of significant others may be forced into adaptational techniques of Type II traumas but still retain clear and vivid memories of the event. Children who are physically injured or disfigured and suffer psychic trauma tend to perpetually mourn their old selves and may employ regression, denial, guilt, shame, and rage over their disabilities (Terr, 1995, p. 316). Thus when traumatic shock interferes with the normal course of bereavement, unresolved grief continues and the child becomes a candidate for a major depressive disorder (Terr, 1995, pp. 316–317).

Secondary Stressors.   A variety of problems that have to do with how a traumatized child looks, acts, feels, and thinks may promote secondary stressors in his or her social milieu (Pynoos, Steinberg, & Goenjian, 1996, p. 341). Communicable disease, altered physical appearance, social distancing, memory impairment, decreased intellectual functioning, guilt, and shame are a few of the problems that can follow in the wake of a trauma. All these problems may present a very different before-and-after picture of the child and alter perceptions by family, peers, and teachers to the detriment of the child. These negative response patterns are then additive to the initial trauma and present additional psychological burdens to adaptation.

Intervention Strategies

Intervention in cases of PTSD, like intervention in other types of crises, begins with assessment. For children, the methods of assessment and therapy used are different from those used for adults. Early assessment is critical in determining the potential for trauma (Terr, 1979, 1981, 1983) and should happen as soon as possible after the event (Mowbray, 1988, p. 206).

Interviewing.   There is some evidence that allowing children to talk about their experience in an interview format also helps in reducing long-term symptoms of PTSD (Nader, 1997, p. 293). However, parent resistance may be severe, and interviewers should carefully explain to both the parents and the child what the purpose for the interview is and how it is going to be done. Interviewing should involve determining the degree and severity of exposure to trauma and assessing the child's response as it relates to the degree of exposure (Pynoos & Nader, 1988).

Pynoos, Steinberg, and Goenjian (1996, pp. 336–337) suggest that more precise, rather than general features of the traumatic experience be elicited, such as hearing unanswered screams for assistance, smelling bad odors, closeness to the threat, being trapped, witnessing atrocities, degree of brutality and other specific traumatic conditions. Given the targeting of what will probably be very traumatizing material, the crisis worker needs to proceed in as patient, caring, and empathic way as possible.

Instruments.   Because of the need to systematically measure the response of children to trauma, a number of instruments have been developed in the last ten years (Nader, 1997, pp. 307–338). The Clinician Administered PTSD Scale for Children (CAPS-C) (Nader et al., 1994) is a comprehensive children's version of the adult CAPS. It measures standard PTSD symptoms plus additional symptoms of childhood PTSD. It further determines social and scholastic functioning, along with how well the child is coping with the event. The Diagnostic Interview for Children and Adolescents–Revised (DICA-R) (Reich, Shayka, & Taibleson, 1991) is a widely used semistructured interview to assess common psychiatric diagnoses and includes a PTSD subscale. It has separate questionnaires for children ages 6–12 and adolescents ages 13-17. These and other interview schedules typically use variations of Likert scales (least to most numeric ratings) to measure the amount of trauma experienced or currently present. Caution should be used in administering any of the childhood PTSD scales because there is generally a shortage of reliability and validity studies that have been done on them.

Projective Techniques.   Because children submerge their affect and parents are loath to deal with the trauma until it causes severe repercussions in their lives, children are rarely brought in for counseling until behavior has reached crisis proportions (Mowbray, 1988, p. 206). Triage assessment at this time may not reveal that trauma is the underlying agent. In that regard, the crisis worker who works with children should have a good knowledge of both projective and question-and-answer personality inventories that will ferret out the trauma. A classic example is the art work of sexually and physically abused children whose drawings are replete with exaggerated genitalia or action scenes depicting physical assault (D. Bottoms, Assistant Director, Carl Perkins Child Abuse Center, personal communication, January 28, 1999).

Legal Ramifications.   Criminal or other legal ramifications are often involved with children who are victims of trauma. If that is the case, the child should be referred to a professional well versed in taking legal testimony, such as a police officer or child welfare worker. Because of the worker's own liability and possible witness status, interviews where legal ramifications are suspected should be taped and comprehensive summaries written. Children should be asked specific and concrete *what, when, who, where,* and *how* questions about their experience. They should be allowed to proceed at their own pace, assured that they were not to blame, and should *always be believed* (Mowbray, 1988, p. 206).

This last point is extremely important. Because of adult fear of false accusations, reports by children are often construed as fantasies or distortions of what really happened. In the overwhelming majority of cases, particularly those involving sexual abuse or assault, this is categorically not true (Salter, 1988). Saywitz, Goodman, Nicholas, and Moan (1991) conducted a study that found that children were highly resistant to misleading questions regarding physical exams involving their genitals, and the researchers suggested that childhood events surrounding abuse are not very open to distortions, insertions, deletions, or other types of suggestions.

Therapy

Treatment of PTSD for children falls into two main categories, cognitive behavior and play therapy.

Cognitive Behavior Therapy.   The International Society for Traumatic Stress Studies (1999) proposes cognitive behavior therapy as the treatment of choice for children. Although Saigh (1987) has reported success using flooding techniques (a very emotionally invasive technique that seeks to extinguish intrusive feelings, thoughts, and images by subjecting the client to vivid imagery of the feared event) with school-age children, we want to emphatically emphasize that this is a *hazardous* procedure for children and may exacerbate symptoms. Any cognitive behavior therapy should give the child a sense of empowerment and control. Relaxation techniques, cognitive restructuring, stress inoculation, anger management, desensitization and any other behavioral or cognitive behavioral techniques should all be paced *at the child's speed*. A good deal of discussion with the child and the caretakers about what is going to occur, how the child has the power and control over what will be included, and adequate time for processing, debriefing, and follow-up should all be a part of the therapeutic regimen (Deblinger & Heflin, 1996).

Play Therapy.   Regrettably, few controlled studies have been done on the efficacy of play therapy. Nevertheless, we believe play therapy has considerable merit and can be efficacious. However, nondirective play therapy may be ill advised, because restitutive play becomes increasingly destructive and serves only to increase anxieties (Terr, 1979).

A safer approach to reenacting the trauma is to use guided imagery (Sluckin, Weller, & Highton, 1989) or a variety of play therapy techniques (Landreth, 1987) that include puppets (Carter, 1987; James & Myer, 1987), sand play (Allan & Berry, 1987; Vinturella & James, 1987), poetry (Gladding, 1987), writing (Brand, 1987), music (Bowman, 1987), computer art (Johnson, 1987), and drama (Irwin, 1987), as well as drawing the traumatic event and telling a story about it (Eth & Pynoos, 1985, p. 37). All these techniques may be controlled and paced by the therapist in consideration of the psychological safety of the child. Play therapy would seem efficacious because it enables the therapist to enter the trauma on the child's cognitive terms, reduce the threat of the trauma, establish trust, and determine the child's current means of coping and ways of defending against the trauma (Gumaer, 1984). Furthermore, as thematic trauma-related play subsides and more socially appropriate play reappears, we believe this is an excellent assessment device for determining how well treatment is proceeding.

EMDR.   Shapiro (1995, pp. 276-281) indicates a number of special considerations for using EMDR, especially with young children. First, the worker must pay special consideration to safety concerns. Although Shapiro does not believe parents should be seen with the child, she does believe parents should brief the worker with the child present. Then the parent should leave and allow the child to present his or her version. This two-step sequence allows the parents' authority to be transferred to the worker and also gives the child a sense of being special when the worker's attention is focused exclusively on him or her. For children, average EMDR sessions should be no longer than 45 minutes, with eye movements interspersed with other activities. Because children do not have the cognitive ability to conceptualize SUDs units, more concrete representations of the degree of discomfort need to be made. Holding a hand close to the floor can represent a "little" hurt, while holding a hand at shoulder height can represent a much "bigger" hurt. Because most children are familiar with the workings of a body thermometer, we have used pictorial representations of a thermometer to let children indicate how much discomfort they are feeling. Because play is such an integral part of a child's world, eye exercises can be accomplished more easily by drawing puppets on the worker's fingers or using finger puppets to perform the saccades. Creativity in helping the child "bring up the picture" is important, so sound effects such as starting an engine or "blowing up the picture" with a loud explosion can involve the child at their experiential level. Installing new, positive cognitions needs to be simplified. "I'm fine" or "I'm safe" may be highly appropriate because of their simplicity and straightforwardness for young children. Art work may also be effective in helping concretize the memory. Drawing the event and then holding the picture in his or her mind while eye exercises are conducted allows the child a concrete way of visualizing the memory. Shapiro reports that (much as in Gumaer's [1984] method of serial drawing to determine if treatment is effective) when the child is asked to redraw the event after successive eye movements, the intensity of the event as depicted in the drawings is likely to diminish.

Moving Beyond the Trauma

One way survivors move from the tightly wrapped intrapersonal world of agony they have lived in to a more self-actualized and healthy interpersonal focus is to use their experience to help other victims (Lifton, 1973, pp. 99–133). Listen to two Vietnam veterans, one a volunteer and one a professional in the human services field.

Jim: I'm in the group not because of what happened in Nam. I'm pretty much through that. A year's worth of the VA and some excellent help from other people got me over being nuts. I'm here because I owe those folks and maybe, I'm not sure how, to pay some back for what I got.

George: Why did I become a social worker at the vet center? Because I'd been in Nam, hassled with my own stuff, and thought I knew something about it and could help other people. Frankly, I think I've done about all I can here, and I believe I'm ready to start something else professionally. I'm going back to school and would like to concentrate on working with kids.

For both these men, the ghosts of PTSD have been exorcised. They have integrated all aspects of the traumatic experience, both the positive and the negative. They know pretty clearly who they were before, during, and after the event. They have accepted responsibility for their own actions, as imperfect as those actions may have been at the time, and have made atonement for any guilt they carried (Scurfield, 1985, p. 246). They epitomize the full meaning of the Chinese characters for *crisis* that represent both danger and opportunity.

SUMMARY

Posttraumatic stress disorder (PTSD) has probably been in existence as long as humankind has been rational enough to personalize the disasters that assail us. However, it was the debacle of the Vietnam War that brought PTSD enough publicity to become a classifiable malady. The psychologically virulent milieu that was the Vietnam War became a breeding ground for trauma, which found its way back to the United States in an estimated 960,000 service personnel who have PTSD or related disorders.

PTSD has multiple symptoms and for that reason is often confused with a variety of other disorders. Its basis is maladaptive adjustment to a traumatic event. The disorder is both acute and chronic. In its chronic form it is insidious and may take months or years to appear. Its symptoms include, but are not limited to, anxiety, depression, substance abuse, hypervigilance, eating disorders, intrusive-repetitive thoughts, sleep disturbance, somatic problems, poor social relationships, suicidal ideation, and denial and affective numbing of the traumatic event. Both natural and human-made disasters may be responsible for PTSD, but it is far more likely to occur in victims who have been exposed to some human-made disaster that should have been prevented and is beyond accepted moral and societal bonds.

Slow to recognize the disorder, human services professionals did little to ameliorate problems returning Vietnam veterans suffered. Self-help groups were started by veterans when they had no other place to turn. Through lobbying efforts by such men, Vietnam Veterans Centers were set up throughout the United States. Along with other mental health professionals who had been grappling with the problems of veterans and other victims of trauma, staffers at the centers began doing research and developing treatment approaches for PTSD. Those research and treatment approaches have spread out to civilian areas of trauma so that much common ground is being found between war-related and civilian-related traumatic events. Recent research on the psychobiological aspects of PTSD is uncovering a great deal of the intricate interplay between traumatic events and the brain's physiological responses to the trauma. Contemporary treatment includes both group and individual intervention that is multimodal in nature and considers psychological, biological, and social bases as equally important. Children are also not immune to PTSD, and they do not just "grow out of it."

If PTSD has taught the human services one thing, it is that no traumatic experience should ever be dismissed in a cursory manner and that any initial assessment of a crisis client should investigate the possibility of a traumatic event buried somewhere in the client's past. Assessment and intervention are particularly difficult when the traumatic event is of a familial or sexual nature. A great deal of finesse and skill is necessary to uncover and treat such problems because of clients' reluctance to talk about socially taboo subjects or the feeling that a person should have the intestinal fortitude to bear up under the trauma. From what we now know, the latter assumption is patently false; under the right circumstances, anyone can fall victim to PTSD.

CLASSROOM EXERCISES

Experiencing Your Own Trauma Responses

A.

Do not deal with a real personal trauma of yours or anyone else's in this exercise! If you have read this chapter carefully, you should understand why.

Take a moment to think of a "near miss" with a traumatic experience you may have had. You may have been close to a tornado or an earthquake. Perhaps you may have had a nonlethal collision or had to swerve violently to avoid a deer in the road. Maybe you have been walking down a dark street late at night in a strange neighborhood and had the feeling you were being followed or stalked. As you think about the event, let your mind go back to focus as accurately as it can on it. You may want to shut your eyes as you do this. What does that scene look like? Who else is in it? Are there any smells or sounds associated with it? Can you feel (tactile) anything? Now write those descriptions down. Now again go back to the scene. What are your feelings as you experience it? What are you thinking? How are you acting? Now write down your feelings, the one major thought that went through your mind, and the actions you took. Now look at the Triage Assessment Form in Chapter 2. Rate yourself on the event as if it had just happened. Now look at the EMDR section of this chapter and give yourself a SUDs and a VOC rating as if it had just happened. Set this information aside.

B.

Now think about the event again, but this time think of it in present time as a historical anecdote in your life. Proceed to redo the instructions in Part A of the exercise but do them as they relate to you in the present moment. Now answer these questions:

1. How much difference do you find between the two?
2. Why do you think that is?
3. What do you suppose would be the difference if your "near miss" had turned into a full-blown traumatic event?

C.

Now find a partner. Relate to your partner your "near miss" as it occurred in Part A. As your partner listens, he or she should perform a triage assessment. Compare your triage with that of your partner's. If there are major differences in your ratings, why do you think that is so? Discuss with your partner your outcomes and the answers to your questions in Part B.

D.

Reassemble in your group or class, and discuss these questions.

1. How do you feel right now after having gone through Parts A and B?
2. Given all the information you have read in this chapter, it's still unclear from re-

search why some people get PTSD and others don't under practically the same circumstances. Why do you think that's so?

3. The history of psychotherapy is full of gurus and panaceas that promise techniques and systems that will cure everything from a lousy love life to Alzheimer's disease. EMDR has its rabid supporters and equally rabid opponents. If it really does work, as yet nobody really knows for sure why it does. But then nobody really knows for sure why aspirin works, but it does! So what do you think? Given the choice and with no other alternative, would you choose a tried and tested treatment such as the cognitive behavior approaches (which might be much like massive chemotherapy for cancer in its noxious side effects) or would you opt for the newer, less proven (but probably much less painful) EMDR? (Sorry! You can't have both.)

4. Finally, and your instructor is not to be held accountable in this, why do you think there is so much resistance to acceptance of new techniques in the field of psychotherapy? (You will have to take our word of 75 years collective experience in the field on this last statement that there is.)

RESOURCES

Interest in both cause and cure of PTSD has initiated a tremendous upsurge in research in the past few years. For any human services worker who would like more firsthand information from practitioners, the veterans centers and veterans hospitals scattered throughout the United States are an excellent resource. Three web sites have what we believe are pertinent and reliable information about PTSD. They are:

1. International Society for Traumatic Stress Studies: http://www.istss.org/quick/tgdoc.html. The society publishes treatment guidelines and other pertinent information on PTSD.

2. National Center for PTSD: http://www.dartmouth.edu/dms/ptsd/. Sponsored by the U.S. Department of Veterans Affairs, this site covers a broad array of research, training, and public information,

3. The Sidran Foundation: http://www.sidran.org/about.html. Sidran is a nonprofit foundation devoted to education, advocacy, and research to benefit people who are suffering from traumatic stress.

REFERENCES

Aarts, P. G., & op den Velde, W. (1996). Prior traumatization and the process of aging. In B. A. van der Kolk, A. C. McFarlane, and L. Weisaeth (Eds.), *Traumatic stress* (pp. 359–377). New York: Guilford Press.

Ackerman, P., Newton, J., McPherson, B., Jones, J., & Dykman, R. (1998). Prevalence of posttraumatic stress disorder and other psychiatric diagnoses in three groups of abused children (sexual, physical, and both). *Child Abuse and Neglect, 22*(8), 759–774.

Allan, J., & Berry, P. (1987). Sandplay. *Elementary School Guidance & Counseling, 21,* 300–306.

American Psychiatric Association. (1980). *Diagnostic and statistical manual of mental disorders* (3rd ed.). Washington, DC: Author.

American Psychiatric Association. (1994). *Diagnostic and statistical manual of mental disorders* (4th ed.). Washington, DC: Author.

Archibald, H. C., Long, D. M., Miller, C., &

Tuddenham, R. D. (1962). Gross stress reaction in combat—a 15 year follow-up. *American Journal of Psychiatry, 119,* 317–322.

Atkinson, R. M., Sparr, L. F., & Sheff, A. G. (1984). Diagnosis of posttraumatic stress disorder in Viet Nam veterans: Preliminary findings. *American Journal of Psychiatry, 141,* 694–696.

Ayalon, O. (1983). Coping with terrorism. In D. Meichenbaum and M. Jaremko (Eds.), *Stress reduction and prevention.* New York: Plenum.

Balson, P., & Dempster, C. (1980). Treatment of war neurosis from Vietnam. *Comprehensive Psychiatry, 21,* 167–176.

Benson, H. (1976). *The relaxation response.* New York: Avon.

Berga, S. L., & Girton, L. G. (1989). The psychoneuroendocrinology of functional hypothalamic amenorrhea. *Psychiatric Clinics of North America, 12,* 105–116.

Bergen, M. (1958). Effect of severe trauma on a four-year-old child. *Psychoanalytic Study of the Child, 13,* 407–429.

Berglund, R. (1985). *The fabric of the mind.* Victoria: Penguin Books Australia.

Bernstein, A. (1986). The treatment of non-compliance in patients with posttraumatic stress disorder. *Psychosomatic medicine, 27,* 37–40.

Bierens-de-Haan, B. (1998). Le debriefing emotionnel collectif des intervenants humanitaires: L'experience du CICR. *Schweizer Archiv für Neurologie und Psychiatrie, 149*(5), 218–228.

Bigot, T., & Ferrand, I. (1998). Victimologie de la priese d'otage: Etude aupres de 29 victimes. *Annales Medico Psychologiques, 156*(1), 22–27.

Black, J. L., & Keane, T. M. (1982). Implosive therapy in the treatment of combat related fears in a World War II veteran. *Journal of Behavior Therapy and Experimental Psychiatry, 13,* 139–165.

Blake, D. D., Weathers, F., Nagy, L. M., Kaloupek, D. G., Klauminzer, G., Charney, D. S., & Keane, T. M. (1990). A clinician rating scale for assessing current and lifetime PTSD: The CAPS-1. *The Behavior Therapist, 13,* 187–188.

Blanchard, E. B., Hickling, E. J., Taylor, D. E., & Loos, W. R. (1994). The psychophysiology of motor vehicle accidents related to PTSD. *Behavior Therapy, 25,* 453–467.

Bloch, D. A., Silber, E., & Perry, S. E. (1956). Some factors in the emotional reaction of children to disaster. *American Journal of Psychiatry, 113,* 416–422.

Boman, B. (1986). Early experiential environment, maternal bonding and the susceptibility to post-traumatic stress disorder. *Military Medicine, 151,* 528–531.

Bower, G. H. (1981). Mood and memory. *American Psychologist, 36,* 129–148.

Bowman, R. P. (1987). Approaches for counseling children through music. *Elementary School Guidance & Counseling, 21,* 284–291.

Brand, A. G. (1987). Writing as counseling. *Elementary School Guidance & Counseling, 21,* 266–275.

Bremner, J. D., Krystal, J. H., Southwick, S. M., & Charney, D. S. (1995). Functional neuroanatomical correlates of the effects of stress on memory. *Journal of Traumatic Stress, 8,* 527–550.

Brende, J. O., & Parson, E. R. (1985). *Vietnam veterans: The road to recovery.* New York: Plenum.

Breuer, J., & Freud, S. (1955). Studies on hysteria. In J. Strachey (Ed. and Trans.), *The standard edition of the complete psychological works of Sigmund Freud* (Vol. 2, pp. 1–10). London: Hogarth Press. (Original work published 1895.)

Brewi, B. (Speaker) (1986). *Crisis intervention with the Vietnam veteran* (Cassette recording No. 9). Memphis: Department of Counseling and Personnel Services, Memphis State University.

Brom, D., Kleber, R. J., & Defares, P. B. (1989). Brief psychotherapy for posttraumatic stress disorders. *Journal of Consulting and Clinical Psychology, 57,* 607–612.

Brown, P. J., Recupero, P. R., & Stout, R. (1995). PTSD substance abuse, comorbidity, and treatment utilization. *Addictive Behaviors, 20,* 251–254.

Bryant, R. (1998). An analysis of calls to a Vietnam veterans' telephone counseling service. *Journal of Traumatic Stress, 11*(3), 589–596.

Burgess-Watson, I. P., Hoffman, L., & Wilson, G. V. (1988). The neuropsychiatry of post-traumatic stress disorder. *British Journal of Psychiatry, 152,* 164–173.

Cahill, S., Carrigan, M., & Frueh, C. (1999). Does EMDR work? and if so, why? *Journal of Anxiety Disorders, 13*(1–2), 5–33.

Carlson, J., Chemtob, C., Rusnak, K., Hedlund, L., & Muraoka, M. (1998). Eye movement desensitization and reprocessing (EMDR) treatment for combat-related posttraumatic stress disorder. *Journal of Traumatic Stress, 11*(1), 3–24.

Carter, S. R. (1987). Use of puppets to treat traumatic grief. *Elementary School Guidance & Counseling, 21,* 210–215.

Chen, C., Wong, J., Lee, N., Chan, H., Mun-Wan, C. Tak-Fai Lau, J., & Fung, M. (1993). The Shatin community mental health survey in Hong Kong II. Major findings. *Archives of General Psychiatry, 50*(2), 125–133.

Chu, J. (1999). Trauma and suicide. In D.G. Jacobs (Ed.), *the Harvard Medical School guide to suicide assessment and intervention* (pp. 332–354). San Francisco: Jossey-Bass.

Cienfuegos, A. J., & Monelli, O. (1983). The testimony of political repression as a therapeutic instrument. *American Journal of Orthopsychiatry, 53,* 43-51.

Cocco, N., & Sharpe, L. (1993). An auditory variant of eye movement desensitization in a case of childhood PTSD. *Journal of Behavior Therapy and Experimental Psychiatry, 24,* 373–377.

Cooper, N., & Clum, G. A. (1989). Imaginal flooding as a supplementary treatment for PTSD in combat veterans. A controlled study. *Behavior Therapy, 20,* 381–391.

Corneil, W., Beaton, R., Murphy, S., Johnson, C., & Pike, K. (1999). Exposure to traumatic incidents and prevalence of posttraumatic stress symptomatology in urban firefighters in two countries. *Journal of Occupational Health Psychology, 4*(2), 131–141.

Crump, L. D. (1984). Gestalt therapy in the treatment of Vietnam veterans experiencing PTSD symptomatology. *Journal of Contemporary Psychotherapy, 14,* 90–98.

Cusack, K., & Spates, R. (1999). The cognitive dismantling of eye movement desensitization and reprocessing (EMDR) treatment of posttraumatic stress disorder. *Journal of Anxiety Disorders, 13*(1–2), 87–99.Darves-Bornoz, J. M., Lepine, J. P., Choquet, M. Berger, C., Degiovanni, A., & Gailliard, P. (1998). Predictive factors of chronic PTSD in rape victims. *European Psychiatry, 13,* 281-287.

Davidson, J. R., & van der Kolk, B. A. (1996). The psychopharmacological treatment of posttraumatic stress disorder. In B. A. van der Kolk, A. C. McFarlane, and L. Weisaeth (Eds.), *Traumatic stress* (pp. 510–524). New York: Guilford Press.

Davidson, J., Kudler, H., & Smith, R. (1990). *The Structured Interview for PTSD (ST-PTSD).* Unpublished measure available from authors at Dept. of Psychiatry, Box 3812, Duke University Medical Center, Durham, NC.

Deblinger, E., & Heflin, A. H. (1996). *Cognitive behavioral interventions for treating sexually abused children.* Thousand Oaks, CA: Sage.

Devilly, G., & Spence, S. (1999). The relative efficacy and treatment distress of EMDR and a cognitive-behavior trauma treatment protocol in the amelioration of posttraumatic stress disorder. *Journal of Anxiety Disorders, 13*(1–2), 131–157.

Devilly, G., Spence, S., & Rapee, R. (1998). Statistical and reliable change with eye movement desensitization and reprocessing: Treating trauma in a veteran population. *Behavior Therapy, 29*(3), 435–455.

DeVries, M. (1996). Trauma in cultural perspective. In B. A. van der Kolk, A. C. McFarlane, and L. Weisaeth (Eds.), *Traumatic stress* (pp. 398–413). New York: Guilford Press.

DiNardo, P. A., & Barlow, D. H. (1988). *Anxiety disorders interview scale revised.* Albany, NY: Center for Phobia and Anxiety Disorders.

Donaldson, M. A., & Gardner, R., Jr. (1985). Diagnosis and treatment of traumatic stress among women after childhood incest. In C. R. Figley (Ed.), *Trauma and its wake: The study of post-trauma stress disorder* (pp. 356–377). New York: Brunner/Mazel.

Egendorf, A. (1975). A Vietnam veteran rap group and themes of post-war life. *Journal of Social Issues, 31,* 111–124.

Epstein, R., Fullerton, C., & Ursano, R. (1998). Posttraumatic stress disorder following an air disaster: A prospective study. *American Journal of Psychiatry, 155*(7), 934–938.

Erikson, E. (1968). *Identity, youth, and crisis.* New York: Norton.

Eth, S., & Pynoos, R. S. (1985). Developmental perspective on psychic trauma in childhood. In C. R. Figley (Ed.), *Trauma and its wake: The study of post-trauma stress disorder* (pp. 36–52). New York: Brunner/Mazel.

Fairbank, J. A., & Brown, T. A. (1987). Current behavioral approaches to the treatment of posttraumatic stress disorder. *Behavior Therapist, 10,* 57–64.

Fairbank, J. A., & Keane, T. M. (1982). Flooding for combat-related stress disorders: Assessment of anxiety reduction across traumatic memories. *Behavior Therapy, 13,* 499–510.

Figley, C. R., (Ed.). (1978). *Stress disorder among Vietnam veterans.* New York: Brunner/Mazel.

Figley, C. R. (1985a). From victim to survivor: Social responsibility in the wake of catastrophe. In C. R. Figley (Ed.), *Trauma and its wake: The study of post-trauma stress disorder* (pp. 398–416). New York: Brunner/Mazel.

Figley, C. R. (Ed.). (1985b). *Trauma and its wake: The study of post-trauma stress disorder.* New York: Brunner/Mazel.

Figley, C. R. (1988). Post-traumatic family therapy. In F. M. Ochberg (Ed.), *Post-traumatic therapy and victims of violence* (pp. 83–113). New York: Brunner/Mazel.

Figley, C. R. (Speaker). (1990). *Posttraumatic stress disorder: Managing bad memories in individuals and family systems.* (National teleconference). Tallahassee: Florida State University, School of Social Work.

Foa, E. B., & Zoellner, L. (1998). Posttraumatic stress disorder in female victims of assault: theory and treatment. In E. Sanavio (Ed.), *Behavior and cognitive therapy today: Essays in honor of Hans J. Eysenck (*pp. 87–101). Oxford, England: Anonima Romana.

Foa, E. B., Riggs, D. S., Dancu, C. V., & Rothbaum, B. O. (1993). Reliability and validity of a brief instrument for assessing Post-traumatic Stress Disorder. *Journal of Traumatic Stress, 6,* 459–473.

Forbes, D., Creamer, M., & Rycroft, P. (1994). Eye movement desensitization and reprocessing in posttraumatic stress disorder. *Journal of Behavior Therapy and Experimental Psychiatry, 25,* 113–120.

Foulkes, S. H. (1948). *Introduction to group analytic psychotherapy.* London: Heineman.

Frederick, C. (1980). Effects of natural vs. human-induced violence: Evaluation and change. *Services for Survivors* (pp. 71–75). Minneapolis Medical Research Foundation/NIMH, Mental Health Services Development Branch.

Freud, S. (1959). Introduction to psychoanalysis and the war neurosis. In J. Strachey (Ed. and Trans.), *The standard edition of the complete psychological works of Sigmund Freud* (Vol. 5). London: Hogarth Press. (Original work published 1919.)

Freud, S. (1963). Introductory lectures on psychoanalysis XVII. In J. Strachey (Ed. and Trans.), *The standard edition of the complete psychological works of Sigmund Freud* (Vol. 16). London: Hogarth Press. (Original work published 1917.)

Frick, R., & Bogart, M. L. (1982). Transference and countertransference in group therapy with Vietnam veterans. *Bulletin of the Menninger Clinic, 46,* 429–444.

Furst, S. S. (1967). A survey. In S. S. Furst (Ed.), *Psychic trauma.* New York: Basic Books.

Furst, S. S. (1978). The stimulus barrier and the pathogenicity of trauma. *International Journal of Psychoanalysis, 59,* 345–352.

Gerardi, R. J., Keane, T. M., Cahoon, B. J., & Klauminzer, G. W. (1994). An in vivo assessment of physiological arousal in PTSD. *Journal of Abnormal Psychology, 103,* 825–827.

Gilliland, B. E., & James, R. K. (1998). *Theories and strategies in counseling and psychotherapy* (4th ed.). Boston, MA: Allyn and Bacon.

Gladding, S. T. (1987). Poetic expressions: A counseling art in elementary schools. *Elementary School Guidance & Counseling, 21,* 307–311.

Green, M. A., & Berlin, M. A. (1987). Five psychosocial variables related to the existence of Post-Traumatic Stress Disorder symptoms. *Journal of Clinical Psychology, 43,* 643–649.

Gressard, C. F. (1986). Self-help groups for Vietnam veterans experiencing post-traumatic stress disorder. *Journal for Specialists in Group Work, 11,* 74–79.

Grinker, R. R., & Spiegel, J. P. (1945). *Men under stress.* Philadelphia: Blakiston.

Grisby, J. P. (1987). The use of imagery in the treatment of posttraumatic stress disorder. *Journal of Nervous and Mental Disease, 175,* 55–59.

Gumaer, J. (1984). *Counseling and therapy for children.* New York: Free Press.

Gurvitz, T. V., Shenton, M. E., & Pittman, R. K. (1995). *Reduced hippocampal volume on magnetic resonance imagining in chronic post-traumatic stress disorder.* Paper presented at the International Society for Traumatic Stress Studies, Miami.

Hamilton, J., & Workman, R. (1998). Persistence of combat-related posttraumatic stress symptoms for 75 years. *Journal of Traumatic Stress, 11*(4), 763–768.

Herman, J. L. (1997). *Trauma and recovery.* New York: Basic Books.

Hopkins, O., & King, N. (1994). PTSD in children and adolescents. *Behavior Change, 11,* 110–120.

Horowitz, M. J. (1976). *Stress response syndromes.* New York: Aronson.

Horowitz, M. J., & Solomon, G. F. (1975). A prediction of delayed stress response syndromes in Vietnam veterans. *Journal of Social Issues, 31,* 67–80.

Horowitz, M. J., Wilner, N., & Alvarez, W. (1979). Impact of Events Scale: A measure of subjective stress. *Psychosomatic Medicine, 41,* 209–218.

Horowitz, M. J., Wilner, N., Kaltreider, N., & Alvarez, W. (1980). Signs and symptoms of post-trauma stress disorders. *Archives of General Psychiatry, 37,* 85–92.

International Society for Traumatic Stress Studies. (1997). *Practice guidelines for the treatment of posttraumatic stress disorder.* http://www.istss.org/quick/tg.doc. html

Irwin, E. C. (1987). Drama: The play's the thing. *Elementary School Guidance & Counseling, 21,* 276–283.

James, R. K., & Myer, R. (1987). Puppets: The elementary counselor's right or left arm. *Elementary School Guidance & Counseling, 21,* 292–299.

Jensen, T. (1994). An investigation of EMD/R as a treatment for PTSD symptoms of Vietnam combat veterans. *Behavior Therapy, 25,* 311–325.

Johnson, D. R., Feldman, S. C., & Southwick, S. M. (1994). The concept of the second-generation program in the treatment of PTSD among Vietnam veterans. *Journal of Traumatic Stress, 7,* 217–235.

Johnson, R. G. (1987). Using computer art in counseling children. *Elementary School Guidance & Counseling, 21,* 262–265.

Kardiner, A. (1941). *The traumatic neurosis of war.* New York: Hoeber.

Keane, T. M. (1976). *State dependent retention and its relationship to psychopathology.* Unpublished manuscript, State University of New York at Binghamton.

Keane, T. M. (1998). Psychological effects of combat. In B. Dohrenwend (Ed.), *Adversity, stress, and psychopathology* (pp. 52–65). New York: Oxford University Press.

Keane, T. M., Caddell, J., & Taylor, K. (1988). Mississippi Scale for Combat-Related Posttraumatic Stress Disorder. Three studies in reliability and validity. *Journal of Consulting and Clinical Psychology, 56,* 85–90.

Keane, T. M., Fairbank, J. A., Caddell, J. M., & Zimmering, R. T. (1989). Implosive (flooding) therapy reduces symptoms of PTSD in Vietnam veterans. *Behavior Therapy, 20,* 245–260.

Keane, T. M., Fairbank, J. A., Caddell, J. M., Zimmering, R. T., & Bender, M. E. (1985). A behavioral approach to assessing and treating post-trauma stress disorder in Vietnam veterans. In C. R. Figley (Ed.), *Trauma and its wake: The study of post-traumatic stress disorder.* (pp. 257–294). New York: Brunner/Mazel.

Keane, T. M., & Kaloupek, D. G. (1982). Imaginal flooding in the treatment of post traumatic stress disorder. *Journal of Consulting and Clinical Psychology, 50,* 138–140.

Keane, T. M., Malloy, P. F., & Fairbank, J. A. (1984). Empirical development of an MMPI subscale for the assessment of combat-related posttraumatic stress disorder. *Journal of Consulting and Clinical Psychology, 52,* 888–891.

Kelman, H. (1945). Character and the traumatic syndrome. *Journal of Nervous and Mental Disease, 102,* 121–153.

Kingsbury, S. J. (1988). Hypnosis in the treatment of posttraumatic stress disorder. An isomorphic intervention. *American Journal of Clinical Hypnosis, 31,* 81–90.

Kolb, L. C., & Mutalipassi, L. R. (1982). The conditioned emotional response: A subclass of the chronic and delayed stress disorder. *Psychiatric Annals, 12,* 969–987.

Kramer, T., Lindy, J., Green, B., & Grace, M. (1994). The comorbidity of post-traumatic stress disorder and suicidality in Vietnam veterans. *Suicide and Life Threatening Behavior, 24,* 58–67.

Kukla, R. A., Schlenger, W. E., Fairbank, J. A., Hough, R. L., Jordan, B. K., & Marmar, C. R. (1990). *Trauma and the Vietnam War generation: report of findings from the National Vietnam Veterans' Readjustment Study.* New York: Brunner/Mazel. Research Triangle Park, NC: Research Triangle Institute.

LaCoursiere, R. B., Bodfrey, K. E., & Ruby, L. M. (1980). Traumatic neurosis in the etiology of alcoholism: Vietnam and other trauma. *American Journal of Psychiatry, 137,* 966–968.

Landreth, G. L. (1987). Play therapy: Facilitative use of child's play in elementary school counseling. *Elementary School Guidance & Counseling, 21,* 253–261.

Lating, J. M., & Everly, G. S. (1995). Psychophysiological assessment of PTSD. In G. S. Everly, Jr., & J. M. Lating (Eds.), *Psychotraumatology* (pp. 129–146). New York: Plenum.

Laufer, R., Yager, T., & Grey-Wouters, E. (1981). Post-war trauma: Social and psychological problems of Vietnam veterans in the aftermath of the Vietnam War. In A. Egendorf, C. Kadushin, & R. S. Laufer (Eds.), *Legacies of Vietnam* (Vol. 1). Washington, DC: U.S. Government Printing Office.

Lee, C., Gavriel, H., & Richards, J. (1996). Eye movement desensitization: Complexities, and future direction. *Australian Psychologist, 31 (3),* 168–173.

Lifton, R. J. (1973). *Home from the war: Vietnam veterans—neither victims nor executioners.* New York: Simon & Schuster.

Lifton, R. J. (1974). "Death imprints" on youth in Vietnam. *Journal of Clinical Child Psychology, 3,* 47–49.

Lifton, R. J. (1975). The postwar war. *Journal of Social Issues, 31,* 181–195.

Lindal, E., & Stefansson, J. (1993). The lifetime prevalence of anxiety disorder in Iceland as estimated by the US National Institute of Mental Health Diagnostic Interview Schedule. *Acta Psychiatrica Scandinavica, 88,* 29–34.

Lindy, J. D. (1996). Psychoanalytic psychotherapy of postraumatic stress disorder: the nature of the therapeutic relationship. In B. A. van der Kolk, A. C. McFarlane, and L. Weisaeth (Eds.), *Traumatic stress* (pp. 525–536). New York: Guilford Press.

Lyons, J. A., & Keane, T. M. (1989). Implosive therapy for the treatment of combat-related PTSD. *Journal of Traumatic Stress, 2,* 137–152.

Maclean, G. (1977). Psychic trauma and traumatic neurosis: Play therapy with a four-year-old boy. *Canadian Psychiatric Association Journal, 22,* 71–76.

MacPherson, M. (1984). *Long time passing: Vietnam and the haunted generation.* New York: Doubleday.

Malloy, P. F., Fairbank, J. A., & Keane, T. M. (1983). Validation of a multimodal assessment of posttraumatic stress disorders in Vietnam veterans. *Journal of Consulting and Clinical Psychology, 51,* 488–494.

Marafiote, R. (1980). Behavioral strategies in group treatment of Vietnam veterans. In T. Williams (Ed.), *Post-traumatic stress disorders of the Vietnam veteran* (pp. 49–70). Cincinnati: Disabled American Veterans.

Marmar, C. R. Weiss, D. S., Schlenger, W. E., Fairbank, J. A., Jordan, K., Kulka, R. A., & Hough, R. L. (1991). Peritraumatic dissociation and posttraumatic stress in male Vietnam theater veterans. *American Journal of Psychiatry, 151,* 902–907.

Martini, R. D., Ryan, C., Nakayama, D., & Ramenofsky, M. (1990). Psychiatric sequelae after traumatic injury: The Pittsburg regatta accident. *Journal of the American Academy of Child and Adolescent Psychiatry, 29,* 70–75.

Mason, J. W., Giller, E. L., Kosten, T. R., & Harkness, L. (1988). Elevation of urinary norepinephrine/cortisol ratio in posttraumatic stress disorder. *Journal of Nervous and Mental Disease, 176,* 498–502.

McCubbin, H., Joy, C., Cauble, E., Comeau, J., Patterson, J., & Needle, R. (1980). Family stress and coping: A decade review. *Journal of Marriage and Family, 43,* 855–872.

McFarlane, A. C., & de Girolamo, G. (1996). The nature of traumatic stressors and the epidemiology of posttraumatic reactions. In B. A. van der Kolk, A. C. McFarlane, and L. Weisaeth (Eds.), *Traumatic stress* (pp. 129–148). New York: The Guilford Press.

McFarlane, A. C., & Yehuda, R. (1996). Resiliency, vulnerability, and the course of posttraumatic reactions. In B. A. van der Kolk, A. C. McFarlane, and L. Weisaeth (Eds.), *Traumatic stress* (pp. 155–181). New York: Guilford Press.

Meadows, E. A., & Foa, E. B. (1999). Cognitive behavioral treatment for traumatized adults. In P. A. Saigh & J. D. Bremmer (Eds.), *Posttraumatic stress disorder: A comprehensive text.* Boston: Allyn and Bacon.

Memphis Vietnam Veterans Center. (1985). *The nonveteran helper.* Unpublished pamphlet of the Memphis Vietnam Veterans Center.

Mitchell, J. (1983). When disaster strikes: The critical incident stress debriefing process.

Journal of Emergency Medical Services, 8, 36–39.

Montgomery, R. A., & Ayllon, T. (1994). Experimental desensitization across subjects: Subjective and physiological measures of treatment efficacy. *Journal of Behavior Therapy and Experimental Psychiatry, 25,* 217–230.

Moses, R. (1978). Adult psychic trauma: The question of early predisposition and some detailed mechanisms. *International Journal of Psychoanalysis, 59,* 353–363.

Mowbray, C. T. (1988). Post-traumatic therapy for children who are victims of violence. In F. M. Ochberg (Ed.), *Post-traumatic therapy and victims of violence* (pp. 196–212). New York: Brunner/Mazel.

Muris, P., & Merckelbach, H. (1999a). Eye movement desensitization and reprocessing. *Journal of the American Academy of Child and Adolescent Psychiatry, 38*(1), 7–8.

Muris, P., & Merckelbach, H. (1999b). Traumatic memories, eye movement, phobia, and panic: A critical note on the proliferation of EMDR. *Journal of Anxiety Disorders, 13*(1–2), 209–223.

Nader, K. O. (1997). Assessing traumatic experiences in children. In J. P. Wilson & T. M. Keane (Eds.), *Assessing psychological trauma and PTSD* (pp. 291–348). New York: Guilford Press.

Nader, K. O., Kreigler, J. A., Blake, D. D., & Pynoos, R. S. (1994). *Clinician Administered PTSD Scale, Child and Adolescent Version (CAPS-C).* White River Junction, VT: National Center for PTSD.

Newman, C. J. (1976). Children of disaster: Clinical observations at Buffalo creek. *American Journal of Psychiatry, 133,* 306–312.

Newman, E., Kaloupkek, D. G., & Keane, T. M. (1996). Assessment of posttraumatic stress disorder in clinical and research settings. In B. A. van der Kolk, A. C. McFarlane, and L. Weisaeth (Eds.), *Traumatic stress* (pp. 242–273). New York: Guilford Press.

Notman, M., & Nadelson, C. (1976). The rape victim: Psychodynamic considerations. *American Journal of Psychiatry, 133,* 408–412.

Ochberg, F. M. (Ed.). (1988). *Post-traumatic therapy and victims of violence.* New York: Brunner/Mazel.

Oswalt, R., Anderson, M., Hagstrom, K., & Berkowitz, B. (1993). Evaluation of the one-session eye movement desensitiza-tion reprocessing procedure for eliminating traumatic memories. *Psychological Reports, 73,* 99–104.

Parker, J. G. & Gottman, H. J. M. (1989). Social and emotional development in a relational context. In T. J. Berndt & G. W. Ladd (Eds.), *Peer relationships in child development* (pp. 95–131). New York: Wiley.

Parson, E. R. (1984). The reparation of the self: Clinical and theoretical dimensions in the treatment of Vietnam veterans. *Journal of Contemporary Psychotherapy, 14,* 4–56.

Pearsons, L. (1965). *The use of written communications in psychotherapy.* Springfield, IL: Charles C Thomas.

Progoff, I. (1975). *At a journal workshop.* New York: Dialogue House Library.

Pynoos, R. S., & Nader, K. (1988). Psychological first aid and treatment approach to children exposed to community violence: Research implications. *Journal of Traumatic Stress, 1,* 445–473.

Pynoos, R. S., Steinberg, A. M., & Goenjian, A. (1996). Traumatic stress in childhood and adolescence: Recent developments and current controversies. In B. A. van der Kolk, A. C. McFarlane, and L. Weisaeth (Eds.), *Traumatic stress* (pp. 331–358). New York: Guilford Press.

Ratna, L., & Barbenel, D. (1997). The pharmacology of post traumatic stress disorder. A literature review and case report of treatment with nefazodone. *International Journal of Psychiatry in Clinical Practice, 1*(3), 169–177.

Reich, W., Shayka, J. J., & Taibleson, C. (1991). *Diagnostic Interview for Children and Adolescents (DICA).* St Louis: Washington University.

Renfrey, G., & Spates, C. R. (1994). Eye movement desensitization: A partial dismantling study. *Journal of Behavior Therapy and Experimental Psychiatry, 25,* 231–239.

Rosen, G. (1999). Treatment fidelity and research on eye movement desensitization and reprocessing (EMDR). *Journal of Anxiety Disorders, 13*(1–2), 173–184.

Rosenheck, R., & Fontana, A. (1998). Warrior fathers and warrior sons: Intergenerational aspects of trauma. In Y. Danieli (Ed.), *International handbook of multigenerational legacies of trauma* (pp. 225–242). New York: Plenum Press.

Rosenthal, D., Sadler, A. G., & Edwards, W. (1987). Families and posttraumatic stress disorder. *Family Therapy Collections, 22,* 81–95.

Ross, R. J., Ball, W. A., Dinges, D. F., & Kribbs, N. B. (1994). Motor vehicle dysfunction during sleep in posttraumatic stress disorder. *Sleep, 17,* 723–732.

Rothbaum, B., & Foa, E. (1996). Cognitive behavior therapy for posttraumatic disorder. In B. A. van der Kolk, A. C. McFarlane, and L. Weisaeth (Eds.), *Traumatic stress* (pp. 491–509). New York: Guilford Press.

Ruzek, J., Polusny, M., & Abueg, F. (1998). Assessment and treatment of concurrent posttraumatic stress disorder and substance abuse. In V. Follette & J. Ruzek (Eds.), *Cognitive behavioral therapies for trauma* (pp. 226–255). New York: Guilford Press.

Saigh, P. A. (1987). In vitro flooding of childhood posttraumatic stress disorders: A systematic replication. *Professional School Psychology, 2,* 135–146.

Salter, A. C. (1988). *Treating child sex offenders and victims.* Newbury Park, CA: Sage.

Saywitz, K. J., Goodman, G. S., Nicholas, E., & Moan, S. F. (1991). Children's memories of a physical examination involving genital touch: Implications for reports of child sexual abuse. *Journal of Consulting and Clinical Psychology, 59,* 682–691.

Scheck, M., Schaeffer, J., & Gillette, C. (1998). Brief psychological intervention with traumatized young women: The efficacy of eye movement desensitization and reprocessing. *Journal of Traumatic Stress, 11*(1), 25–44.

Scurfield, R. M. (1985). Post-trauma stress assessment and treatment: Overview and formulations. In C. R. Figley (Ed.), *Trauma and its wake: The study of posttrauma stress disorder* (pp. 219–256). New York: Brunner/Mazel.

Selye, H. (1976). *The stress of life.* New York: McGraw-Hill.

Shalev, A. Y. (1996). Stress versus traumatic stress; From acute homeostatic reactions to chronic psychopathology. In B. A. van der Kolk, A. C. McFarlane, and L. Weisaeth (Eds.), *Traumatic stress* (pp. 77–101). New York: Guilford Press.

Shapiro, F. (1989a). Efficacy of the eye movement desensitization procedure in the treatment of traumatic memories. *Journal of Traumatic Stress, 2,* 199–223.

Shapiro, F. (1989b). Eye movement desensitization: A new treatment for post-

traumatic stress disorder. *Journal of Behavior Therapy and Experimental Psychiatry, 20,* 211–217.

Shapiro, F. (1991). Eye movement desensitization and reprocessing procedure: From EMD to EMD/R—A new treatment model for anxiety and related traumata. *Behavior Therapist, 14,* 128, 133–135.

Shapiro, F. (1995). *Eye movement desensitization and reprocessing: Basic principles, protocols, and procedures.* New York: Guilford Press.

Shapiro, F. (1999). Eye movement desensitization and reprocessing (EMDR) and the anxiety disorders: Clinical and research implications of an integrated psychotherapy treatment. *Journal of Anxiety Disorders 13*(1–2), 53–67.

Shatan, C. (1978). The emotional content of combat continues. In C. R. Figley (Ed.), *Stress disorders among Vietnam veterans* (pp. 43–52). New York: Brunner/Mazel.

Siegel, D. J. (1995). Memory, trauma, and psychotherapy: A cognitive science view. *Journal of Psychotherapy Practice and Research, 4,* 93–122.

Silver, S. M., Brooks, A., & Obenchain, J. (1995). Treatment of Vietnam War veterans with PTSD: A comparison of eye movement desensitization and reprocessing, biofeedback, and relaxation training. *Journal of Traumatic Stress, 8,* 337–341.

Silverman, P. R. (1986). The perils of borrowing: Role of the professional in mutual help groups. *Journal of Specialists in Group Work, 11,* 68–73.

Sluckin, A., Weller, A., & Highton, J. (1989). Recovering from trauma: Gestalt therapy with an abused child. *Maladjustment and Therapeutic Education, 7,* 147–157.

Solomon, Z. (1986). The effect of combat-related stress disorder on the family. *Psychiatry, 51,* 323–329.

Spiegel, D. (1981). Vietnam grief work under hypnosis. *American Journal of Clinical Hypnosis, 24,* 33–40.

Spiegel, D. (1989). Hypnosis in the treatment of victims of sexual abuse. *Psychiatric Clinics of North America, 12,* 295–305.

Spitzer, R. L., Williams, J. B., Gibbon, M., & First, M. B. (1990). *Structural clinical interview for DSM-III-R-patient edition (with psychotic screen)-SCID-P.* Washington, DC: American Psychiatric Press.

Stampfl, T. G., & Levis, D. J. (1967). Essentials of implosive therapy: A learning-theory-based psychodynamic behavioral therapy. *Journal of Abnormal Psychology, 72,* 496–503.

Stein, M. B., Hannah, C., Koverola, C. Yehuda, R., Torchia, M., & McClarty, B. (1994, December). *Neuroanatomical and neuroendocrine correlates in adulthood of severe sexual abuse in childhood.* Paper presented at the 33rd annual meeting of the American College of Neuropsychopharmacology, San Juan, Puerto Rico.

Stutman, R. K., & Bliss, E. L. (1985). Posttraumatic stress disorder, hypnotizability, and imagery. *American Journal of Psychiatry, 142,* 741–743.

Terr, L. C. (1979). Children of Chowchilla: Study of psychic trauma. *Psychoanalytic Study of the Child, 34,* 547–623.

Terr, L. C. (1981). "Forbidden games": Posttraumatic child's play. *Journal of the American Academy of Child Psychiatry, 22,* 221–230.

Terr, L. C. (1983). Chowchilla revisited: The effects of psychic trauma four years after a school-bus kidnapping. *American Journal of Psychiatry, 140,* 1543–1550.

Terr, L. C. (1995). Childhood traumas: An outline and overview. In G. S. Everly, Jr., & J. M. Lating (Eds.), *Psychotraumatology* (pp. 301–320). New York: Plenum.

Thomas, R., & Gafner, G. (1993). PTSD in an elderly male: Treatment of EMD/R. *Clinical Gerontologist, 14,* 57–59.

Trimble, M. R. (1985). Post-traumatic stress disorder. History of a concept. In C. R. Figley (Ed.), *Trauma and its wake: The study of post-trauma stress disorder* (pp. 5–14). New York: Brunner/Mazel.

Tucker, P., Pfefferbaum, B., Nixon, S., & Foy, D. (1999). Trauma and recovery among adults highly exposed to a community disaster. *Psychiatric Annals, 29*(2), 78–83.

Turner, S. W., McFarlane, A. C., & van der Kolk, B. A. (1996). The therapeutic environment and new explorations in the treatment of posttraumatic stress disorder. In B. A. van der Kolk, A. C. McFarlane, and L. Weisaeth (Eds.), *Traumatic stress* (pp. 537–558). New York: Guilford Press.

Ullman, S. E., & Siegel, J. M. (1994). Predictors of exposure to traumatic events and posttraumatic stress sequelae. *Journal of Community Psychology, 22,* 328–338.

Ursano, R., Fullerton, C., Vance, K., & Kao, T. (1999). Posttraumatic stress disorder and identification in disaster workers. *American Journal of Psychiatry. 156*(3), 353–359.

van der Kolk, B. A. (1983). Psychopharmacological issues in posttraumatic stress disorder. *Hospital and Community Psychiatry, 34,* 683–691.

van der Kolk, B. A. (Ed.). (1984). *Posttraumatic stress disorder: Psychological and biological sequelas.* Washington, DC: American Psychiatric Press.

van der Kolk, B. A. (1988). The biological response to psychic trauma. In F. M. Ochberg (Ed.), *Post-traumatic therapy and victims of violence* (pp. 25–38). New York: Brunner/Mazel.

van der Kolk, B. A. (1996a). The body keeps the score : Approaches to the psychobiology of postraumatic stress disorder. In B. A. van der Kolk, A. C. McFarlane, and L. Weisaeth (Eds.), *Traumatic stress* (pp. 214–241). New York: Guilford Press.

van der Kolk, B. A. (1996b). Trauma and memory. In B. A. van der Kolk, A. C. McFarlane, and L. Weisaeth (Eds.), *Traumatic stress* (pp. 279–297). New York: Guilford Press.

van der Kolk, B. A., Dreyfuss, D., Michaels, M., Shera, D., Berkowitz, B., Fisler, R. & Saxe, G. (1994). Fluoxetine in posttraumatic stress disorder. *Journal of Clinical Psychiatry, 55*(12), 517–522.

van der Kolk, B. A., & McFarlane, A. C. (1996). The black hole of trauma. In B. A. van der Kolk, A. C. McFarlane, and L. Weisaeth (Eds.), *Traumatic stress* (pp. 3–23). New York: Guilford Press.

van der Kolk, B. A., McFarlane, A. C., & van der Hart, O. (1996). A general approach to treatment of posttraumatic stress disorder. In B. A. van der Kolk, A. C. McFarlane, and L. Weisaeth (Eds.), *Traumatic stress* (pp. 417–440). New York: Guilford Press.

van der Kolk, B. A., Weisaeth, L., & van der Hart, O. (1996). History of trauma in psychiatry. In B. A. van der Kolk, A. C. McFarlane, and L. Weisaeth (Eds.), *Traumatic stress* (pp. 47–74). New York: Guilford Press.

Vaughan, K., Armstrong, M. S., Gold, R., & O'Connor, N. (1994). A trial of eye movement desensitization compared to image habituation training and applied muscle relaxation in post-traumatic stress disorder. *Journal of Behavior Therapy and Experimental Psychiatry, 25,* 283–291.

Vaughan, K., Wiese, M., Gold, R., & Tarrier, N. (1994). EMD: Symptom change in PTSD. *British Journal of Psychiatry, 154,* 533–541.

Vietnam Veterans: Thirty Years After. (1995, December 10). *All things considered.* New York and Washington, DC: National Public Radio (NPR).

Vinturella, L., & James, R. K. (1987). Sand play: A therapeutic medium with children. *Elementary School Guidance & Counseling, 21,* 229–238.

Wagner, D., Heinrichs, M., & Ehlert, U. (1998). Prevalence of symptoms of posttraumatic stress disorder in German professional firefighters. *American Journal of Psychiatry, 155*(12), 1727–1732.

Walker, J. I. (1983). Comparison of "rap" groups with traditional group therapy in the treatment of Vietnam combat veterans. *Group, 7,* 48–57.

Wallerstein, J. S., & Kelly, J. B. (1975). The effects of parental divorce: Experiences of the preschool child. *Journal of the American Academy of Child Psychiatry, 14,* 600–616.

Watson, C. G., Juba, M. P., Manifold, V., Kucala, T., & Anderson, P. E. (1991). The PTSD Interview: Rationale, description, reliability, and concurrent validity of a DSM-III based technique. *Journal of Clinical Psychology, 47,* 179–188.

Weingartner, H., Miller, H., & Murphy, D. L. (1977). Mood-state-dependent retrieval of verbal associations. *Journal of Abnormal Psychology, 86,* 276–284.

White, A. C. (1989). Post-traumatic stress. *British Journal of Psychiatry, 154,* 886–887.

Wilkinson, C. B. (1983). Aftermath of a disaster: The collapse of the Hyatt Regency steel skywalk. *American Journal of Psychiatry, 140,* 1134–1139.

Williams, C. C. (1983). The mental foxhole: The Vietnam veteran's search for meaning. *American Journal of Orthopsychiatry, 53,* 4–17.

Williams, R. L., & Long, J. D. (1979). *Toward a self-managed life style* (2nd ed.). Boston: Houghton Mifflin.

Wilson, F., Poole, A., & Trew, K. (1997). Psychological distress in police officers following critical incidents. *Irish Journal of Psychology, 18*(3), 321–340.

Wilson, J. P. (1980). Conflict, stress, and growth: Effects of the war on psychosocial development. In C. R. Figley & S. Leventman (Eds.), *Strangers at home.* New York: Praeger.

Wilson, J. P., Smith, W. K., & Johnson, S. (1985). A comparative analysis of PTSD among various survivor groups. In C. R. Figley (Ed.), *Trauma and its wake: The study of post-trauma stress disorder* (pp. 142–172). New York: Brunner/Mazel.

Wolpe, J. (1958). *Psychotherapy by reciprocal inhibition.* Stanford, CA: Stanford University Press.

Wolpe, J. (1982). *The practice of behavior therapy.* New York: Pergamon Press.

Zanarini, M., Frankenburg, F., Dubo, E., Sickel, A., Trikha, A., Levin, A., & Reynolds, V. (1998). Axis I comorbidity of borderline personality disorder. *American Journal of Psychiatry, 155*(12), 1733–1739.

Zlotnick, C., Warshaw, M., Shea, M., Allsworth, J., Pearlstein, T., & Keller, M. (1999). Chronicity in posttraumatic stress disorder (PTSD) and predictors of course of comorbid PTSD in patients with anxiety disorders. *Journal of Traumatic Stress, 12*(1), 89–100.

CHAPTER FIVE

Crisis of Lethality

In crisis work the possibility of dealing with suicidal and/or homicidal clients is always present. Thus, in Chapter 2 we emphasized the importance of the crisis worker's continuous awareness and assessment of risk level for all clients in crisis. In this chapter we present strategies to help crisis workers strengthen their skills in assessing, counseling for, intervening in, and preventing lethal behavior, with the major emphasis on suicide. The strategies addressed in this chapter are solidly based on the concepts, including the six steps in crisis intervention, found in Chapter 2. We present the examples and cases assuming that workers will use these fundamental crisis intervention concepts in dealing with suicidal and/or homicidal clients as well as with clients in any other category of crisis. In this chapter, we take the position that it is the appropriate role of the crisis worker to intervene and attempt to prevent all suicides and homicides that he or she possibly can, despite highly controversial viewpoints about suicide sometimes suggesting (Roleff, 1997; Stone, 1999, pp. 69–93) that a person has a justified right, under certain circumstances, to choose to end his or her own life.

BACKGROUND
The Many Faces of Lethality

Although in this chapter the focus on lethal behavior is mainly concerned with the intent to harm oneself, we have also included harm and intent to harm others. As we have seen in recent years, sometimes a lethal individual who is suicidal either may target a specific victim or may shoot (or bomb) at random at close range into a crowd. Whenever this happens, we are confronted with a serious crisis of lethality! We are not talking here about the act of the criminal who murders a shopkeeper in a holdup, although that criminal is indeed lethal. Nor are we referring to an *instrumental* act of homicide that occurs for some financial or other concrete gain, such as killing a person for insurance or to be able to marry another person. Rather, we are speaking about a suicidal/homicidal person who is engaged in an *expressive* act designed to reduce psychological pain. Such suicidal/homicidal people are likely to be emotionally distraught and may feel gravely wronged, depressed, helpless, disempowered, and hopeless, and may attempt to solve their own dilemmas through harm to others and then to themselves.

Although crisis workers may not be able to identify every client having a high suicidal or homicidal risk and may not succeed in preventing such clients from harming themselves and others, it is possible to provide the kinds of support, intervention, and prevention that have proved to be helpful to self-destructive and/or lethal people (Berman & Jobes, 1994, 1996; Dunne, McIntosh, & Dunne-Maxim, 1987; Fujimura, Weis, & Cochran, 1985; Shneidman, 1996, pp. 139–156).

The Scope of the Suicide Crisis

Suicide can strike any family, and it is an alarming societal concern (Dixon, Heppner, & Rudd, 1994). On a worldwide basis, about 2,000 people kill themselves each day. Stone (1999, pp. 9–10) reports that this number is about 80 per hour, or three-quarters of a million people per year. According to Peters, Kochanek, and Murphy (1998), in the United States, there are 84.4 reported deaths from suicide each day, amounting to 30,903 every year. Stone (1999, p. 1) reports that between 300,000 and 600,000 U.S. citizens a year survive a suicide attempt and that about 19,000 of those survivors are permanently disabled because of the debilitating effects of the attempted suicide. Most official reports indicate that the real numbers of suicide attempts as well as injury caused by suicide attempts are grossly underreported. Ross (1999) reports that experts claim that upward of 60,000 Americans die annually by suicide.

Suicide is the eighth leading cause of death in the United States. About 1.4 percent of the people in the United States die by suicide. Young people between the ages of 15 and 24 constitute the largest increase in suicides during the past 30 years. Men kill themselves at approximately four times the rate for women (Peters, Kochanek, & Murphy, 1998; Stone, 1999, p. 10).

The highest-risk group for many years has been Caucasian men over 35, but the suicide rate among teenagers and young black males has been dramatically increasing since the middle 1900s (Fujimura et al., 1985). Even though the elderly make up roughly 10 percent of the total population, 25 percent of all suicides occur in the over-65 population. Women over age 65 have a suicide rate twice that of the total population, and men over age 65 kill themselves at a rate four times the national norm (Janosik, 1984, p. 153).

The suicide rate among children and adolescents tripled between 1950 and 1985, and suicide is now the second (behind accidents) leading cause of death among children and teens (American Association for Counseling and Development, 1985; Malley, Kush, & Bogo, 1994). Garland and Zigler (1993) reported that between 1982 and 1989 there was an alarming escalation trend of suicide among adolescents, increasing by more than 200 percent compared with a general population suicide rate increase of 17 percent. Malley, Kush, and Bogo (1994), citing Peach and Reddick (1991), stated that between 1961 and 1991, adolescent suicide increased by 300 percent. Roberts (1991, p. 219) reviewed research on the prevalence of suicide attempts among all adolescents and estimated that between 10 and 15 percent of adolescents had attempted suicide. Other data reported by Shaffer, Vieland, and Garland (1990, p. 3154), based on written self-report surveys, estimated that between 9 and 10 percent of all ninth and tenth graders (mean age, 14 years) had attempted suicide.

Assisted Suicide and Euthanasia in Terminal Illness

During the latter half of the twentieth century, much attention was paid to *assisted suicide* and *euthanasia* in both the literature and the popular media. The two terms are not synonymous. Stone (1999, p. 78) differentiates between the two by pointing out that, in *assisted suicide*, someone else provides the means (lethal agent) but the person who is dying administers it. In *euthanasia,* someone else administers it. Whether people with terminal illness should be able to die with dignity in the time, place, circumstance, and method of their choice is both controversial and complex and is fraught with diverse ethical, moral, emotional, and legal dimensions beyond the scope of this chapter. In speaking of assisted suicide, Belkin (1993) points out that there is no simple assisted suicide. Stone (1999, pp. 76–89) discusses the many ramifications of both assisted suicide and euthanasia in the terminally ill. He cites four major polls (Gallup, Harris, Roper, and General Social Surveys) that show that since the mid-1930s both medical and non-medical opinion have gradually shifted in the direction of accepting assisted suicide. He states that the impetus for this shift has not come from the legal, medical, or political establishment, but that the pressure for change in public attitude has been the result of the experiences of millions of the slowly dying, their families, and increasing numbers of their physicians (p. 89). Further information about assisted suicide and euthanasia may be obtained by contacting the Hemlock Society or Choice in Dying—The National Council for the Right to Die, both of which are listed near the end of Chapter 9.

THE DYNAMICS OF SUICIDE

According to Fujimura and associates (1985), two different approaches have been advanced to explain suicidal behaviors: Freud's psychodynamic approach (Allen, 1977) and Durkheim's (1951) sociological approach. In the psychodynamic view, suicide is triggered by an intrapsychic conflict that emerges when a person experiences great psychological stress. Sometimes such stress emerges either as regression to a more primitive ego state or as inhibition of one's hostility toward other people or toward society so that one's aggressive feelings are turned inward toward the self. In extreme cases, self-destruction or self-punishment is chosen over urges to lash out at others.

In Durkheim's approach, societal pressures and influences are major determinants of suicidal behavior. Durkheim (1951) identified three types of suicide: egoistic, anomic, and altruistic (pp. 152–176). *Egoistic* suicide is related to one's lack of integration or identification with a group. *Anomic* suicide arises from a perceived or real breakdown in the norms of society. *Altruistic* suicide is related to perceived or real social solidarity, such as the traditional Japanese *hara-kiri* or, to put it in a current context, the episodes of suicidal attacks by Middle East extremist groups. A fourth type of suicide, identified by Fujimura and associates (1985) and Stone (1999, pp. 76–93), is *dying with dignity*. This type of suicide is typified by a person's choosing death in the face of a painful and incurable illness.

Characteristics of People Who Commit Suicide

What about a person's inner dynamics may make suicide or homicide seem sensible? Shneidman (1985) made a substantial contribution toward clarifying suicide when he formulated 10 common characteristics present in an individual when the act is accomplished.

Shneidman's (1985, 1987) 10 common characteristics are grouped under six aspects of suicide (1985, pp. 121–149):

Situational characteristics: (1) "The common *stimulus* in suicide is unendurable psychological pain" (p. 124) and (2) "The common *stressor* in suicide is frustrated psychological needs" (p. 126).

Conative characteristics: (1) "The common *purpose* of suicide is to seek solution" (p. 129) and (2) "The common *goal* of suicide is cessation of consciousness" (p. 129).

Affective characteristics: (1) "The common *emotion* in suicide is hopelessness-helplessness" (p. 131) and (2) "The common *internal attitude* toward suicide is ambivalence" (p. 135).

Cognitive characteristic: "The common *cognitive state* in suicide is constriction" (one's thinking patterns are so restricted that alternative thoughts cannot emerge) (p. 138).

Relational characteristics: (1) "The common *interpersonal act* in suicide is communication of intention" (letting another person know that one's decision makes sense) (p. 143) and (2) "The common *action* in suicide is egression" (the right to exit or go out as one wishes, or the right to autonomously find a way out of one's pain) (p. 144).

Serial characteristic: "The common *consistency* in suicide is with lifelong coping patterns" (the decision to complete the suicide is logical and in harmony with one's lifestyle and lifelong coping strategies) (p. 147).

This list of characteristics points us toward what makes sense to the individual about to embark on suicide. It is not meant to suggest that all suicides are alike. In using the word *common,* Shneidman is careful to note that suicides, taken together, do reflect similarities. However, he also reminds us that each suicide is idiosyncratic and that there are no absolutes or universals (1985, pp. 121–122). Sometimes such idiosyncratic characteristics become clearer when we examine the suicide notes, audiotapes, or videotapes left behind by people who completed suicide.

Similarities Between Suicide and Homicide

Often the person who is suicidal is also homicidal. The frequency with which we witness murder/suicide in American society emphasizes the similarities of motive, sense of hopelessness, opportunity, means, and lethality of method. The 1999 mass murder and suicide witnessed at Columbine High School in Littleton, Colorado, represent a prime example of the parallels of suicide/homicide. We emphasize here that not all suicides or suicidal persons are homicidal. However, whenever suicide and murder are concomitant acts, the similarities call for attention by human services workers, law enforcement personnel, the medical professions, clergy, the media, and all society as well.

Analyzing Suicide/Homicide Notes for Commonalities Between Suicide and Homicide

Perhaps an examination of the following suicide/homicide notes will help to clarify our position that there are many parallels between suicide and homicide.

Specimen Suicide/Homicide Notes.   On Tuesday, July 27, 1999, a man by the name of Mark O. Barton beat his second wife to death in their apartment in Stockbridge, Georgia ("Gunman Kills," 1999). The following day he beat his two children to death in the same apartment. Then on Thursday, July 29, he went on a shooting spree in two different securities brokerage firms in Atlanta, killing 9 people there and critically wounding 13 others before taking his own life while being pursued by police. Including the murder of 3 members of his own family, Barton killed 12 people in three days, and he was a prime suspect in the murder six years earlier of his first wife and her mother in Alabama. Investigation following the murders and suicide produced four suicide notes found in Barton's apartment along with the bodies of his wife, son, and daughter. The first note, found in the living room, was generated on Barton's personal computer and the other three notes were found on each of the three bodies. The text of all four notes ("Georgia Killing Spree," 1999) were released by the Henry County, Georgia, police and were published in the nationwide media (TV, newspapers, and radio) and are here quoted verbatim for instructional purposes only.

First Suicide/Homicide Note
July 29, 1999, 6:38 A.M. To Whom it May Concern: Leigh Ann is in the master bedroom closet under a blanket. I killed Matthew and Mychelle Wednesday night. There may be similarities between these deaths and the death of my first wife and her mother. However, I deny killing her and her mother. There's no reason for me to lie now. It just seemed like a quiet way to kill and a relatively painless way to die.

There was little pain. All of them were dead in less than five minutes. I hit them with a hammer in their sleep and then put them face down in a bathtub to make sure they were dead. I am so sorry. I wish I didn't. Words cannot tell the agony. Why did I?

I have been dying since October 1. I wake up at night so afraid, so terrified that I couldn't be that afraid while awake. It has taken its toll. I have come to hate this life and this system of things. I have come to have no hope.

I killed the children to exchange them for five minutes of pain for a lifetime of pain. I forced myself to do it to keep them from suffering so much later. No mother, no father, no relatives. The fears of the father are transferred to the son. He already had it and now to be left alone. I had to take him with me.

I killed Leigh Ann because she was one of the main reasons for my demise as I planned to kill the others. I really wish I hadn't killed her now. She really couldn't help it and I love her so much anyway.

I know that Jehovah will take care of all of them in the next life. I'm sure the details don't matter. There is no excuse, no good reason. I am sure no one would understand. If they could, I wouldn't want them to. I just write these things to say why.

Please know that I love Leigh Ann, Matthew, and Mychelle with all my heart. If Jehovah is willing, I would like to see them again in the resurrection, to have a second chance. I don't plan to live very much longer, just long enough to kill as many people that greedily sought my destruction.

You should kill me if you can. Mark O. Barton.

Second Note [Left on the body of Leigh Ann.]
I give you my wife, Leigh Ann Vandiver Barton. My honey, my precious love. Please take care of her. I will love her forever.

Third Note [Left on the body of Matthew.]
I give you Matthew David Barton. My son, my buddy, my life. Please take care of him.

Fourth Note [Left on the body of Mychelle.]
I give you Mychelle Elizabeth Barton. My daughter, my sweetheart, my life. Please take care of her.

Suicide Notes as a Source of Knowledge Regarding Suicides and Homicides.
As disturbing as the contents of suicide messages often are, they may convey information that is needed to inform and sensitize survivors and caregivers and to help prevent future suicides. Crisis intervention components such as risk factors, suicide clues, cries for help, prevention, postvention (follow-up procedures), and suicide research may benefit from careful analysis of the material contained in the suicide/homicide completer's messages.

Analysis of the Barton Notes Using Shneidman's Characteristics.
In the case of Mark O. Barton, his sense of despair and hopelessness is made rather clear. His confusion, contrition, anger, depression, ambivalence, paranoia, sorrow, and remorse are there to be recognized. If society can pick up on such factors as the cues, cries for help, and hopelessness, expressed in such suicide/homicide messages, people with suicidal or homicidal ideations may be identified and helped before suicides and homicides are actually completed. Even so, *there are no sure methods of prevention.* Barton's (after the fact) suicide/homicide notes appear to give voice to all of Shneidman's (1985) characteristics cited previously. Inferred in the notes one can find Barton's perceived (1) *situational characteristics*—unendurable psychological pain and frustrated psychological needs; (2) *conative characteristics*—motivation toward seeking both a solution to his problems and cessation of consciousness; (3) *affective characteristics*—hopelessness, helplessness, and ambivalence; (4) *cognitive characteristics*—constricted thinking, that is, unable to engage in alternative thought patterns or optional behaviors; (5) *relational characteristics*—communication of intention, that is, letting others know why the suicide/homicide makes sense, and egression, that is, the right to choose to go out this way; and (6) *serial characteristic*—difficulty with lifelong coping patterns, that is, in harmony with lifelong pathological patterns of coping or solving problems, probably unconscious (on purpose to oneself—hidden from awareness, not known, realized, or intended). Given that Barton's own faulty thinking (in evidence throughout his first suicide/homicide note quoted earlier) contributed to the horrible pain, suffering, and grief that his acts caused in society, in his own family, and in his victims' families, it is highly regrettable that these debilitating psychological characteristics could not have been identified and help provided to Barton before these multiple tragedies occurred. The message for crisis workers: listen, attend to, and act on people's messages that contain self-destructive cues, threats to harm others, ascriptions of unmitigated blame on others, cries for help, helplessness, or hopelessness.

MYTHS ABOUT SUICIDE

There are a good many commonly held myths about suicide that the crisis worker should know and take into account while assessing potentially suicidal clients (Fujimura et al., 1985; Kirk, 1993, pp. 1–4; Shneidman, Farberow, & Litman, 1976, p. 130; Stone, 1999, pp. 51–63; Webb & Griffiths, 1998–1999, p. B42). Some of the myths are as follows:

1. *Discussing suicide will cause the client to move toward doing it.* The opposite is generally true. Discussing it with an empathic person will more likely provide the client with a sense of relief and a desire to buy time to regain control.
2. *Clients who threaten suicide don't do it.* A large percentage of people who kill themselves have previously threatened it or disclosed their intent to others.
3. *Suicide is an irrational act.* Nearly all suicides and suicide attempts make *perfect sense* when viewed from the perspective of the people doing them.
4. *People who commit suicide are insane.* Only a small percentage of people attempting or committing suicide are psychotic or crazy. Most of them appear to be normal people who are severely depressed, lonely, hopeless, helpless, newly aggrieved, shocked, deeply disappointed, jilted, or otherwise overcome by some emotionally charged situation.
5. *Suicide runs in families—it is an inherited tendency.* Sometimes more than one member of a family does commit suicide. But suicide is not inherited. Self-destructive tendencies may be learned, situational, or linked to depression or other conditions.
6. *Once suicidal, always suicidal.* A large proportion of people contemplate suicide at some time during their existence. Most of them recover from the immediate threat, learn appropriate responses and controls, and live long, productive lives, free of the threat of self-inflicted harm.
7. *When a person has attempted suicide and pulls out of it, the danger is over.* Probably the greatest period of danger is during the upswing period, when the suicidal person becomes energized following a period of severe depression. One danger signal is a period of euphoria following a depressed or suicidal episode.
8. *A suicidal person who begins to show generosity and share personal possessions is showing signs of renewal and recovery.* Many suicidal people begin to dispose of their most prized possessions once they experience enough upswing in energy to make a definite plan. Such disposal of personal effects is sometimes tantamount to acting out the last will and testament.
9. *Suicide is always an impulsive act.* There are several types of suicide. Some involve impulsive actions; some are very deliberately planned and carried out.

ASSESSMENT AREAS

Workers who deal with suicidal/homicidal clients should assess the presence of warning signs in three areas: risk factors, suicidal/homicidal clues, and cries for help. The reason we urge crisis workers to focus attention on these areas is that most suicidal and many homicidal clients will manifest signs in a number of them.

Risk Factors

The American Association of Suicidology (1997), Battle (1991), Battle, Battle, and Tolley (1993), Bernard and Bernard (1985), Gilliland (1985), Hazell and Lewin (1993), Hersh (1985), Kirk (1993, p. 7), Stone (1999, pp. 57–60), and Webb and Griffiths (1998–1999, pp. A44–45) have identified numerous risk factors that may help the crisis worker in assessing suicide potential. We recommend that the following list be used as a risk-assessment checklist. Whenever a person manifests four or five of these risk factors, that should be an immediate signal for the crisis worker to treat the person as a high risk in terms of suicide potential.

1. Client exhibits presence of suicide or homicide impulses and serious intent.
2. Client has a family history of suicide, threats of harm, and abuse of others.
3. Client has a history of previous attempts.
4. Client has formulated a specific plan.
5. Client has experienced recent loss of a loved one through death, divorce, or separation.
6. Client's family is destabilized as a result of loss, personal abuse, violence, and/ or because the client has been sexually abused.
7. Client is preoccupied with the anniversary of a particularly traumatic loss.
8. Client is psychotic (and may have discontinued taking prescribed medications).
9. Client has a history of drug and/or alcohol abuse.
10. Client has had recent physical and/or psychological trauma.
11. Client has a history of unsuccessful medical treatment.
12. Client is living alone and is cut off from contact with others.
13. Client is depressed, is recovering from depression, or has recently been hospitalized for depression.
14. Client is giving away prized possessions or putting personal affairs in order.
15. Client displays *radical shifts* in characteristic behaviors or moods, such as apathy, withdrawal, isolation, irritability, panic, or anxiety or changed social, sleeping, eating, study, or work habits.
16. Client is experiencing a pervasive feeling of hopelessness/helplessness.
17. Client is preoccupied and troubled by earlier episodes of experienced physical, emotional, or sexual abuse.
18. Client exhibits *profound degree of one or more emotions*—such as anger, aggression, loneliness, guilt, hostility, grief, or disappointment—that are uncharacteristic of the individual's normal emotional behavior.
19. Client faces threatened financial loss.
20. Client exhibits ideas of persecution.
21. Client has difficulty in dealing with sexual orientation.
22. Client has an unplanned pregnancy.
23. Client has a history of running away or of incarceration.
24. Client manifests ideas and themes of depression, death, and suicide in conversation, written essays, reading selections, art work, and drawings.
25. Client makes statements or suggestions that he or she would not be missed if they were gone.
26. Client experiences chronic or acute stressors (representing important issues, especially in young people such as adolescents).

The crisis worker must realize that assessing suicide or homicidal risk is no simple matter. There are no direct "if–then" connections. Some risk factors are more lethal than others and must be given more weight or attention. Some crisis centers, researchers, and practitioners have developed weighted scales for crisis workers to use in assessing clients' suicide lethality. There are many such scales in existence. One such instrument, the Scale for Assessment of Suicidal Potentiality (Battle, 1985), is a checklist containing 121 weighted items in the nine risk categories of (1) demographics, (2) symptoms of behavior, (3) stress, (4) resources outside of self, (5) personal and social history, (6) suicide plan, (7) prior suicidal behavior, (8) suicidal communication, and (9) personality features and other clinical signs. Instruments such as the Battle scale are not meant to be highly precise, but they are quite helpful to crisis workers in evaluating and considering all the factors relevant to a client's total risk level.

Another instrument, the Boston Assessment of Suicide Ideation Correlates (BASIC) is designed to assess manifestations of clinical suicide ideation and empirical factors that have been previously identified as being related to risk for suicide attempt (Knight & Kleespies, 1999). This scale is predicated on the equilibrium model that assumes stability of intent to live when positive and negative stressors are in balance. The BASIC accumulates data on relevant demographic, diagnostic, emotional, cognitive, behavioral, historical, and situational variables currently identified in the suicide literature as significant predictors of suicide attempts. It assembles in one scale the relevant factors associated with suicide risk. Although the BASIC is somewhat lengthy, it possesses good content validity, and clients report that the content accurately relates to their problems.

Suicide Clues

Most suicidal clients, feeling high levels of ambivalence or inner conflict, either emit some clues or hints about their serious trouble or call for help in some way (Shneidman et al., 1976, pp. 429–440). The clues may be verbal, behavioral, situational, or syndromatic. *Verbal clues* are spoken or written statements, which may be either direct ("I'm going to do it this time—kill myself") or indirect ("I'm of no use to anyone anymore"). *Behavioral clues* may range from purchasing a grave marker for oneself to slashing one's wrist as a "practice run" or suicidal gesture. Even so, such behavioral clues are more often interpreted as "cries for help" than as genuine wishes to die (Shneidman et al., 1976, pp. 129, 432). *Situational clues* might include concerns over a wide array of conditions such as the death of a spouse, divorce, a painful physical injury or terminal illness, sudden bankruptcy, preoccupation with the anniversary of a loved one's death, or other drastic changes in one's life situation. *Syndromatic clues* include such constellations of suicidal symptoms as severe depression, loneliness, hopelessness, dependence, and dissatisfaction with life (Shneidman et al., 1976, pp. 431–434).

Cries for Help

Fortunately for the crisis worker, nearly all suicidal people reveal some kind of clues or cries for help. According to Shneidman and associates (1976), no one is 100 percent suicidal. People with the strongest death wishes are invariably ambivalent, confused, and grasping for life (p. 128).

Assessment of warning signs can be translated into life-saving actions by crisis workers or anyone else in the physical or emotional proximity of suicidal persons (Moldeven, 1988). However, if the risk factors, clues, or cries for help go unnoticed or unrecognized, the chances for effective intervention are greatly reduced.

Using the Triage Assessment Form in Addressing Lethality

Crisis workers intervening with clients in acute crises should not omit an assessment for suicide lethality. The triage assessment system (Myer, Williams, Otten, & Schmidt, 1992) described in Chapter 2 provides a rapid and efficient basis for the worker to assess lethality. The worker must not hesitate to ask questions such as "Are you thinking about killing yourself?" ". . . about killing someone else?" "How?" "When?" "Where?" The triage assessment of the client in acute crisis provides for immediate revision of the worker's estimate of crisis severity based on the client's response to these important and necessary questions or rapidly elevated TAF ratings. A client triage profile that may have looked safe before such answers may look quite different a few moments later, as noted in the following examples. If the client is seriously thinking of killing or harming some specific other person, the worker will need to consider the duty to warn implications dictated by case law developed in the *Tarasoff* case described in Chapter 3.

Before the questions, the client's presenting problem to a career counselor is job loss due to a plant closing. The counselor identifies the client's depression and frustration over failure to find a suitable replacement job, but the estimated TAF *affect* value of 3 or 4, *cognition* score of 6 or 7, and *behavior* score of 4 or 5 (total TAF of 13 to 16) yields a "low to moderate" severity summary. Such a total score shows no urgent or immediate concern for the client's severity/lethality status. Nevertheless, the career counselor senses that something is not quite right: the client's voice reveals a hint of verbal euphoria, while the body language seems to contradict the verbal behavior with a slight hint of hopelessness. As a result of the emerging hints and cues (as an example, the client makes a nonchalant side remark inferring that he or she will not be around much longer), the counselor probes directly into the client's inner world by asking, "What does that mean?" "How?" "When?" and "Where?" and then rethinks and reframes the TAF assessment, as shown next, to ensure the client's safety.

After the questions, the client's somewhat guarded and vague responses (for example, the client, obviously stressed and depressed, states, "for me, there is no future"), elicited by the counselor's probing questioning, raises in the counselor's mind a hunch that the client may not be as safe as the first assessment indicated. Thus, a second TAF assessment of 9 or 10 on *affect,* 8 or 9 on *cognition,* and 8 or 9 on *behavior* (total, 25 to 28), amounts to a dramatic escalation and prompts the counselor to attend specifically to the client's safety by asking directly, "I'm starting to wonder whether you're feeling so trapped, helpless, and hopeless that you're thinking of suicide. Is this true?"

This example of using the TAF as a rapid assessment tool shows how quickly the emotional tone may change in a crisis intervention case; and it clearly demonstrates that whenever a crisis worker begins to suspect a higher level of severity or lethality than at first is revealed, the worker should not hesitate to directly ask the question and probe deeply into the emotionally charged world of the client. Always err on the side of safety.

The second example of lethality assessment would trigger an intervention strategy of immediate hospitalization to ensure the client's safety. A similar rapid increase in the worker's assessment of lethality is also applicable in cases of homicidal intent or any other situation involving threats of harm to self or others.

COUNSELING SUICIDAL CLIENTS

We know enough about suicide/homicide to help people who are at risk if we can be aware of their crisis and can be in contact with them at the time of their greatest need. According to Fujimura and associates (1985), people in the emotional vicinity of suicidal/homicidal individuals are in key positions for preventing loss of life. The important thing is that those support people (family members, crisis workers, counselors, teachers, and friends) learn to recognize, evaluate, and intervene whenever suicidal persons give clues and cries for help (p. 613).

Developmental Crisis Counseling: Adult Age-Specific Examples

In this chapter we address crisis counseling and crisis intervention with lethal adult clients. We address crisis work with lethal children in Chapter 11, "Crisis in the Schools." Therefore, we have generally omitted discussion of children's crises in this chapter.

This section contains examples of general counseling strategies to use with adults of different ages. Whereas "crisis intervention" technically refers to the interruption of the immediate traumatic phase of a person's crisis (such as suicide or a state of hopelessness), we use the term "crisis counseling" to denote the systematic strategies crisis workers employ to assist clients to progress toward a state of precrisis equilibrium or functioning. Case examples, emphasizing appropriate responses to cries for help, are used to illustrate work with adults.

Ruby, Age 21.   Ruby was a senior at a large university. She had achieved average grades throughout college, except during her freshman year. During her freshman year at a small liberal arts college, she had experienced an emotional and suicidal breakdown as the anniversary date of her older sister's suicide approached. She had left the small college, returned home, and undergone psychiatric treatment. Ruby had later enrolled in the university in her home town, where she lived in a residence hall. She went home frequently but managed to succeed fairly well in her studies and social life. Ruby was referred to the crisis worker by her mother following a weekend mother–daughter discussion during which Ruby disclosed some recurring suicidal ideations to her mother. The mother expressed concern that the fifth anniversary of her sister's suicide seemed to be looming in Ruby's mind and asked the crisis worker to call Ruby in for a conference. During the first interview with Ruby, the worker established that Ruby did not have a specific, highly lethal plan, but that she did have a lot of suicidal ruminations.

Ruby: I think Mother thinks I'm crazy. Sometimes I wonder if she's right. (*Long pause.*) It's weird, you calling me in this way. Do you think I may be going crazy?

CW: No, I certainly don't. What I'm hearing is a lot of confusion and unsettled emotion. I'm glad you feel comfortable enough to ask me. I'm wondering what's happening in you to bring up the question.

Ruby: Well, as I told you before, I've just been sitting in my room by myself, staring at the wall. Not sleeping, not eating, not going out. And I've had this strange sensation—of both wanting to run and scream, and just giving up. And I've thought about my sister's death constantly. More than at any time since I was a freshman.

It's like I'm destined to go the way she went. Sometimes I think I can't stand it any longer. Then I catch myself and wonder if I *am* crazy.

Ruby's mother "cried out" for help. As a result, Ruby received the treatment she needed. She got over the fifth anniversary of her sister's suicide, thanks to an alert and sensitive mother and a team of competent professional workers in her university and community.

Deborah, Age 27.   Deborah had been in therapy, off and on, for 11 years—since she was 16. Deborah (1) had a history of suicide attempts, some of them serious, some of them gestures; (2) had used a wide variety of drugs in her college years—in fact, she had dropped out of college after two years because of drug use and resulting poor academic performance; (3) had had a history of episodes of severe depression, loneliness, hopelessness, and helplessness followed by mood swings to euphoric and deep religious activity and commitment; (4) had been hospitalized numerous times for psychiatric care; (5) had experienced a great sense of loss and grief at the divorce of her parents when she was 16 years old; (6) had recently gone into self-imposed isolation and remorse—cutting herself off from friends, family, and co-workers; (7) was feeling a new sense of meaninglessness related to her career—she had been seeking something that she really chose to do (as opposed to working for her father). Deborah, in tears, was trembling and in a state of acute anxiety.

The crisis worker (a Crisis Intervention Team police officer, described in CIT officer training in Chapter 14) found Deborah preparing to jump from a bridge spanning the Mississippi River. Police and highway patrol officers had stopped all traffic and people were out of their cars, watching. The scene was tense and it appeared that at any moment Deborah would jump.

CW: (*In a clearly audible but confident, soft, caring, and empathic voice.*) My name is Mark. Tell me your name.

Deborah: My name is Deborah. What do you want?

CW: I want to help you, if I can, Deborah. I can see that you are under some kind of terrible pressure. I'd like to talk to you and see if there is any way I can be of help to you.

Deborah: I don't know that anybody can help me.

CW: Deborah, I'm concerned about your safety and about what's bothering you right now. With the wind blowing and all the commotion around here, I'm having a difficult time hearing you. I need for you to come down off that railing, and come over here to the curb and sit down so we can talk.

Deborah: I'm not sure talking will do any good. Just go away and leave me alone. I don't need you here.

CW: Deborah, do you remember my name? My name is Mark. Let's take some time to talk. We've got time, plenty of time to just sit down together and talk. You do remember my name, don't you?

The crisis worker makes a point to try to establish a first-name mutual communication with Deborah. Whenever a person such as Deborah is emotionally overwhelmed and immobile, one effective way to break through that immobility is to *personalize* the interaction. A good way to personalize a relationship with a client in crisis is to establish a first-name communication as early as possible.

Deborah: I know. Your name is Mark. How do I know I can trust you? I don't see how you can make my life any better. I've about had it with this life, with this great big lump of hurt deep inside me that won't go away. I'm really tired of this depression and lack of meaning in this life.

CW: Deborah, what I want to do right now is to get a chance to talk about your troubles with you. I can't do that unless I can get you to just take some time to talk to me over here, where we'll have a little more quiet. I just want us to take plenty of time to talk about that big lump of hurt and that depression that has robbed you of life's meaning. Won't you just give me some of your time? I can take all the time we need to hear what you have to tell me. Maybe I *can* help. I sure want to try.

The crisis worker is employing another simple but effective technique that has proved over and over to be nonthreatening and reassuring to clients in emotional crisis: that "We have time"; "Let's take some time."

Deborah: How do I know you won't just put me in jail?

CW: (*In a calm, low key, confident, reassuring, caring voice tone.*) Deborah, what I want to do is to understand what's bothering you so I can get you some help. Right now, all I'm asking you to do for me is just to come over here to the curb, so you and I can take plenty of time to talk, so I can clearly understand just how upset and depressed you are feeling. Maybe there *is* some way I can help. I'd like to find out what it is if you can help me. I'm certainly *not* here to put you in jail. What I want to do is to try to find out what part of you is hurting inside so that I can get you to some place of safety and get the help that you deserve. I don't want to see you get hurt. Won't you help me to understand? I'd really like to help you if I can.

In this case, the crisis worker was able, in a few minutes' time, to validate himself to Deborah. Deborah complied with the crisis worker's request and was later taken to the emergency room of a public hospital, where she received medical and psychological evaluations. She received the emergency treatment necessary to get her over her suicidal intention that had precipitated the acute crisis and was referred for appropriate long-term treatment to deal with her chronic condition.

The case of Deborah provides a brief example of how some simple verbal techniques, delivered with compassion, caring, and genuineness, can make a dramatic difference in the compliance and survival of many clients who are in acute disequilibrium. Contrasted with verbal techniques that connote threat, demand, fear, judgment, or a punitive attitude, the crisis worker's demeanor clearly demonstrates a safer, more humane, respectful, effective, and efficient way of conversing with and obtaining compliance from a person who is emotionally upset, volatile, and immobile.

Simone, Age 36.   Simone was the director of a rape crisis center in a large metropolitan area. She had established a reputation as an effective leader, public relations person, fund raiser, recruiter, and trainer of volunteer workers for the center. Simone was also charismatic, energetic, enthusiastic, and knowledgeable about the technical, medical, emotional, and legal aspects of rape and sexual assault. She was tireless, dedicated, popular, and widely known as the leader of one of the best organized and most effective crisis agencies in the community. In her role as director, Simone's ability to communicate via the media and various venues of public appearances and her compulsive and perfectionist work habits had paid off by providing excellent service to the clientele and earning for herself several awards that recognized her for outstanding contributions and achievement. Now, after six years as director of the center, Simone was approaching burnout. Several factors, fully explored in Chapter 13, impacted both her professional and personal life. Simone was astute enough to finally recognize that she was on the verge of some kind of breakdown, so she sought counseling from a professionally trained worker at her agency's employee assistance program (EAP) clinic. Specimen dialog excerpts from Simone's second session with the worker at the EAP clinic are shown for illustrative purposes.

CW: So, Simone, from what I can glean from your intake material and from what you told me a few days ago in your initial interview, I sense that *you* are fully aware of your vulnerability right now, but you doubt that your co-workers or your clients are aware of the pressures you are feeling.

Simone: That's right. And there's no use in my problems interfering with the work at the center. That's the most important thing. Even so, my issues are affecting me, at least. And, right now, I'm really feeling trapped; no good to them or myself either.

CW: What's the most pressing issue in your entrapment?

Simone: Well, part of the problem is at home. I've been all torn up lately because my live-in, Renee, my significant other for over six years, has taken off. It happened right under my nose. She has come under the influence of another lover and has managed to leave me high and dry with little money, with all the bills, and with house and everything and lots of loose ends that put me under lots of pressure. Also, she moved out, taking most of our furniture, much of which I bought myself. And she took both our cats, too! This all happened just when we were getting ready for our one big fund-raising event of the year at the center and just as we were preparing for the accreditation site team to visit the center in a few weeks. I'm feeling so hurt, so humiliated, and so betrayed that I am overwhelmed with anger, disappointment, and depression. I have scarcely slept for over a week. I thought our relationship was for keeps. Now I don't know what to do. I still care about her so much! I want her back! I'd do about anything to have her back. I shouldn't feel this way, but I think that if she came crawling back right now, I'd take her back with open arms. I'm such a nebbish! I'm feeling so worthless and undesirable and tired of this nightmare that sometimes I just wish I'd sleep forever.

CW: What you've just said worries me. Now I'm concerned about your safety. Are you feeling so depressed, worthless, tired, and angry that you might consider suicide?

Simone: I don't know how I feel any more. I guess I wouldn't go that far. Suicide, that is. I want her back more than anything. But I've even thought to myself, "If I can't have her, then nobody can." But I know that's not realistic either.

CW: I'm also concerned about that too, Simone. Does that mean that you might consider doing harm to Renee or even to her new lover?

Simone: When it came right down to it, I wouldn't. But I'd certainly feel like it sometimes. No, I'm just distraught and mad as hell right now. I'm really harmless, I guess. I don't know what I need. Some space, maybe. Another job, maybe. I don't know.

The case of Simone provides one glimpse of a crisis worker inquiring both about the client's suicidal and homicidal potential. Simone's affective, behavioral, and cognitive (ABC) functioning provided the EAP worker with an opportunity to make a rapid assessment (estimate) of her lethality level using the Triage Assessment Form (TAF, described at length in Chapter 2). The worker determined that Simone's possible threat to self and others was in the low-to-moderate range on all dimensions of the TAF. Therefore, the primary interventions in the case of Simone would focus on the "burnout" issue. The worker proceeded to focus on several strategies (which are fully described in Chapter 13) to help Simone distance herself from her personal loss, reframe her professional stress and burnout symptoms, and find appropriate ways to attain renewal and revitalization.

Gertrude, Age 51. Gertrude was an eminent and successful primary school principal who had devoted her life to children and the teaching profession. She was exceptionally capable, hardworking, conscientious, and efficient. She was also compulsive and perfectionist in her work and personal habits. At age 51, Gertrude faced some life and career decisions that she regarded as catastrophic: (1) she had been cured of TB only to discover she had cancer, and she could not bear to think about her physician's recommendation to accept early retirement (even though her physician had told her that about half of cancer patients can now be cured); (2) she felt trapped between the two perceived unacceptable choices of continuing to hold the principalship in her debilitating physical condition, or becoming the ex-principal who had been forced into early retirement; and (3) she was totally unprepared to alter her whole identity, which had included serving the students, faculty, parents, community, school, and the teaching profession. Gertrude had no family. She had never married because she had devoted all her energies and talents to education. She came to the crisis worker in desperation. The following dialogue took place some 10 minutes into the initial interview.

Gertrude: (*In tears.*) It is so hopeless. Why me? Why has God forsaken me? What have I done to cause me to come to this? I don't think I can bear it. (*Sobs. Pause.*) It's so unfair. I have no choice. (*Sobs.*)

CW: You're feeling hurt, hopeless, and vulnerable—and you're looking for better answers and choices than you've been able to find so far.

Gertrude: (*Still in tears.*) I guess I'm just getting too old and cranky to do this job.

CW: Well, Gertrude, I want you to know that I'm glad you have the courage to discuss it. And I don't view you as old and cranky. What scares me is the desperation and danger you're feeling. You're feeling that, right now, there are no acceptable choices, but what you'd like to find are some choices other than pain and oblivion in your future.

Gertrude: (*Still in tears; nonverbal clues show that she is experiencing acute fear, anxiety, and hopelessness, and has almost given up.*) None. None at all. There is no future.

CW: Gertrude, it sounds to me like you've considered suicide. I feel a need to know your thinking on this subject.

Gertrude: (*Still in tears.*) Oh God! I've thought about that a lot. Toyed with it a lot. And I'll have to admit that it becomes more appealing all the time.

The crisis worker did not suddenly jump to the conclusion that Gertrude was suicidal. As the crisis interview progressed, more and more of her background and verbal and nonverbal clues pointed toward suicide. When Gertrude said, "There is no future," the worker immediately judged that her words and her nonverbal signs of desperation must not be ignored or pushed aside. The alertness and forthright response of the crisis worker provided the pivotal point from which to help start Gertrude on her way out of her desperate course toward oblivion. Crisis counseling was followed by medical and psychiatric referrals. Long-term therapy was required to bring Gertrude from the brink of self-destruction to the point where she could come to accept the unacceptable— medical retirement.

Roy, Age 65.   Roy had been a farmer all his life. At age 63 he went into semiretirement, turning his land, equipment, buildings, and livestock over to his two sons, who also were career farmers. One year after he began his semiretirement, his wife died. About a year later, he was despondent and could find no purpose in life, even though he was in excellent health and had the good fortune of financial independence. The foreman of the farm, Juan, came on Roy standing on a tractor in the hall of the barn. Roy held a rope with a hangman's noose in it and he was attaching the rope to an overhead cross beam. Roy, thinking he was completely alone, was surprised at Juan's appearance.

Juan: What on earth are you doing there, man?

Roy: Where the hell did you come from? What are you doing here?

Juan: I'll tell you what I'm gonna do right now! I'm taking that rope away from you this minute! You're going to get in my pickup truck this minute. I'm driving you straight to the mental health center. That's where we're going. And I'll tell them boys of yours what you've tried to do, too! Don't you know that it'd just kill them boys if you finished what you were planning to do? What the hell did you think you were doing, anyways?

His chance rescue brought Roy to the mental health center for crisis intervention counseling, medical evaluation, and psychotherapy. Juan's alert and decisive actions clearly show that one does not have to be a trained human services worker to contain and control a situation where human life is at risk. Any person who has the experience, empathy, ethics, strength, willingness, and ability to recognize a potential suicide can intervene to prevent another person's harm to self and others. Even though the trained crisis worker at the mental health center knew nothing about Roy's problems, he recognized, as soon as Juan brought Roy in, that a person of Roy's age, gender, life circumstance, style, and sense of private independence would rarely, if ever, present himself for counseling. Thus, chance discovery or mandatory commitment were about the only ways Roy would ever have been stopped from killing himself, once he had decided to do so.

In assessing Roy's responses, the worker quickly concluded that he definitely exhibited six of the lethality characteristics that Fujimura and associates (1985) defined as high-risk factors: (1) the plan was definite and readily accessible, (2) the method was irreversible, (3) there was indication of sleep disruption, (4) support people would not be around, (5) rescue would be improbable, and (6) the most valued possessions had been disposed of. Also, the crisis worker knew that among men Roy's age there are very few suicide gestures or attempts. Older men are more likely to accomplish the act than to merely attempt it (Shneidman et al., 1976; Stone, 1999).

Dennis, Age 78.   Dennis had a long, productive, and successful career as a carpenter. He and his wife had reared seven children. Dennis had worked until he was 65 and had remained physically alert and healthy until he was 74, at which time he had a stroke that paralyzed the right half of his body from head to toe. Following his partial recovery and release from the hospital, he had gradually regained a small percentage of the psychomotor control of the impaired right half of his body. His hearing, which had been getting progressively worse over a number of years, had declined to the point where he had a serious hearing deficit. It had become increasingly difficult for him to communicate. He had become feeble and slow at walking, but he refused to use a cane or a walker. Because his seven children were involved in plying their own careers and rearing their own families, Dennis had become totally dependent on his wife, Millie, age 75. Although his wife was in relatively good health and of sound mental status, the situation had become quite serious. Maintaining the household and providing total care for her husband quickly had become a greater responsibility than she was able to assume.

Dennis became more and more withdrawn. He refused to exercise; he refused to go out of the house except to go to the doctor; he became self-conscious about his unsteady pattern of walking; and he soon began to make statements such as "I'm no good to anyone now," "I should have just passed on instead of being left like I am," "People would be better off without me around," and "Someday I may just take that rifle and end it all." At first his wife, children, and grandchildren attempted to refute him and discount such statements. Finally, Dennis was taken to the family physician, who prescribed medication to deal with his suicidal symptoms. Nothing was done to provide psychiatric, psychotherapeutic, or physical therapy treatment. Dennis became even more withdrawn, he slept most of the time, and he lost interest in much of the family activity.

Following one of his verbal expressions of a wish to die, the crisis worker was summoned for a home visit. The worker was sensitive to Dennis's hearing loss and also judged by Dennis's body language that Dennis would respond to the crisis worker's sitting close and physically touching him. The worker sat very close to Dennis, took him by the hand, and gently stroked the back side of the impaired but sensitive right hand and arm as they talked. The worker used a very loud, clear, calm, and even voice to talk with Dennis. The worker sought to provide clear, nonthreatening, caring messages combined with the gentle physical stroking. Dennis responded positively. The worker provided long periods of time for Dennis to formulate ideas and speak them. (Family members had rarely waited for Dennis to respond. They would ask him a question and, before he was able to respond, would go on to something else. Dennis felt that they ignored him and that he was being treated like a retarded child.) The worker was able to establish good rapport with Dennis.

CW: (*Loudly, while gently stroking Dennis's arm.*) So you are feeling like you aren't being listened to lately, and you really do miss talking to people.

Dennis: (*Long pause; eyes and facial expression show him formulating a response.*) Yeah. They . . . won't . . . wait . . . for . . . me to finish. Some . . . won't wait . . . for me to start.

CW: What you'd like is for someone to let you talk at your own speed. It bothers you for them to "run off and leave you."

Dennis: (*Long pause; tears in his eyes.*) I . . . guess it's hard . . . for them to . . . to talk to me. I . . . have to have time . . . to get it . . . out.

CW: (*Still gently stroking, looking him in the eyes, and waiting for his responses.*) It makes you feel sad, not to be understood. You really want people to take time to hear what you have to say.

Dennis: (*Tears in his eyes; long pause.*) I guess they . . . don't think . . . I . . . have . . . anything . . . worth saying. I'm . . . so . . . old and stove up . . . guess I'm no-account now.

CW: Being, as you say, "stove up" doesn't mean you're worth any less. They tell me you've built lots of this town with your own hands. You've accomplished lots of things in your life, which you must be proud of. Tell me something you've done, which really makes you proud you did.

Dennis: (*Long pause; thoughtful; no tears; smiles.*) I've . . . raised . . . helped raise . . . a bunch of fine children. . . . I've been a good dad . . . a good provider.

CW: (*Still gently stroking.*) That's true, I'm sure. I want you to think back to raising those kids. Think back to the happiest times you had with your growing kids, and just imagine you're back there now. Just take your mind back. Tell me exactly what you're doing with them that makes you feel good—a good daddy.

Dennis: (*Long pause; smile; look of intensity and reminiscence.*) We'd all go down to the . . . swimming hole . . . on Sunday afternoons . . . We took a basket of . . . of sandwiches . . . and melons . . . and a great big ball. We . . . we played games . . . their mother . . . Millie and I . . . we'd play all kinds of games . . . big ones . . . little ones. . . . All the children . . . running, playing, squealing. . . . Yeah . . . (*Laughs.*) . . . all sorts of games. . . . We had a time! . . . Millie and I . . . we had some good times with those children . . . had a real good time . . . a good life.

The worker continued using what are called *reminiscence techniques* (Ebersole, 1976a, 1976b). Many interesting facets of Dennis's past were highlighted, remembered, and relished: family, carpentry, social life, travel, hardships. His whole life was reviewed and appreciated. These reminiscence techniques (American Association of Retired People, 1986) have been used quite effectively with many elderly people—to strengthen their sense of valuing how their life has been lived. The worker went back to see Dennis several times and used the reminiscence technique during a part of each visit. The worker was able to facilitate several productive strategies to help Dennis: The family hired a part-time worker to help with Dennis's daily care; the family physician prescribed physical therapy to enhance Dennis's muscular functioning; a counselor provided communications skills that the family members could learn, including verbal and nonverbal skills, delayed responding, and touching; and the crisis worker called in a gerontologist, who taught Dennis's children how to use the reminiscence technique with their father. The crisis worker did not ignore the suicide threats that Dennis voiced. Along with reminiscence, Dennis was encouraged to talk about his self-destructive feelings. Finally, the family counselor held a group session concerning the suicide issue, after which Dennis never mentioned it again.

Assessing and responding to suicidal ideation in elderly people is a difficult and delicate task. Work with elderly clients must invariably take into account their age, mental and physical impairments; vast storehouse of experiences; and unique gerontological needs. Although each is unique, they are usually reachable, responsive, and appreciative. The crisis worker who visited Dennis made a statement that is typical of those who develop closeness and rapport with elderly clients: "I can truly say that I received much more from Dennis than I gave. I was blessed and enriched by the experience. I think I learned more than he did."

INTERVENTION STRATEGIES

Suicide intervention strategies involve "interrupting a suicide attempt that is imminent or in the process of occurring" (Fujimura et al., 1985, p. 612). Because each person and each problem situation is unique, each suicide situation is also unique. There are no clear, simple strategies recommended for every case, but, as Kirk (1993, p. 53) points out, one of the most essential qualities the crisis interventionist can possess is a commitment to life. In the previous section on counseling, we purposely showed such commitment in the crisis worker who moved from assessing to acting. That is the way crisis intervention works—in a fluid, ongoing, caring, emerging process. We now present some additional strategies that crisis workers might use in continuing to intervene with the representative clients we have described.

Adults

The following discussion provides both attitudinal and behavioral guidelines for crisis workers who are involved in suicide/homicide work with adult clients. Most of these guidelines may also apply to younger populations, but they are particularly applicable to intervening with adults. We have incorporated a number of guidance tips from our own repertoire, along with those of several other contributors (Bernard & Bernard, 1985; Hersh, 1985; Hipple, 1985; Hipple & Cimbolic, 1979; Hipple & Hipple, 1983; Kirk, 1993; Reinecke, 1999; Stone, 1999).

Guidelines for Crisis Workers.   At the beginning of the interview, the crisis worker must establish a sense of rapport and trust right away in order to create a working relationship and provide clients with an anchor to life. It is also important to begin to re-establish in clients a sense of hope and to diminish their sense of helplessness—to take immediate steps to speak and act on the clients' current pain. The worker will want to look for the hidden messages behind the suicidal/homicidal behavior, trying to discover what the behavior in its simplest form is saying and to whom. In many instances it is necessary to establish stay-alive or no-harm contracts that provide clients with some concrete and immediate structure. Courtois (1991) cautions that suicidal lethality contracts must not be imposed on clients. Rather, such stay-alive contracts must be mutually agreed on by both client and crisis worker. That caution applies also to no-harm homicidal contracts.

Ambivalence.   Another area of importance is to help clients discover their ambivalence; part of them may be oriented toward self-destruction, and part toward living. The worker can help clients clarify and understand their inner conflicts and gain a new perspective regarding the horns of the dilemmas on which they are stuck. Reinecke (1999) identified the inner conflicts in some adult suicidal/homicidal clients as having roots in their early childhood, that is, the development of an insecure attachment style. Such attachment behavior may be conceptualized as a retreat from the world and its disappointments related to a desperate attempt to maintain relatedness to a vital attachment figure. Reinecke suggests that, in addition to interventions focused on alleviating dysphoria and anxiety, reducing hopelessness, eliminating immediate stressors, and enhancing rational problem solving, crisis workers may wish to examine, with the client, the functional role of the suicidal behavior in reestablishing secure relationships.

Safety First.   Always, client safety is primary. Even though confidentiality of the suicidal/homicidal person's communication is important, confidentiality must be reconsidered if a life or harm to others is at risk. The crisis worker must consider whether important others need to be contacted to gather information, rally community support, or establish a network of support people interested in and committed to keeping the client alive, protecting targeted individuals from homicide, or both.

Vigilance.   The crisis worker can use history taking to evaluate the client's developmental background and show how the current suicidal crisis evolved. The worker can also determine whether the crisis is situational or systemic; that is, do the roots go deep into the client's personal history? For instance, Boudewyn and Liem (1995) found a strong relationship between childhood sexual abuse and suicidal behaviors in adulthood. One point to remember is to follow up on missed appointments. The suicidal/homicidal person must not be ignored. During the crisis interview itself, the crisis worker must be acutely sensitive to the client's verbal or behavioral cries for help. Ignoring these cries may be interpreted by the client as confirmation of a feeling of worthlessness.

Complexity.   The crisis worker should realize that suicidal/homicidal behavior is a symptom of complex interactions of biological, psychological, and sociological factors. Such clients typically believe that their situation is hopeless. Part of the crisis worker's task is to help clients reframe their thinking so they recognize they have options. Control is a central issue. Most suicidal/homicidal clients believe they have lost control of their lives. The worker can use the six steps of crisis intervention to help clients to get in touch with the fact that they can control their thoughts, feelings, and behaviors and to recognize that those external situations, events, and people cannot really make choices for them.

Euthanasia and Assisted Suicide.   Adult suicidal ideation and behavior sometimes raises complex moral, legal, ethical, and philosophical questions for the crisis interventionist (Belkin, 1993; Stone, 1999, pp. 69–75; Zinner, 1985, p. 75). For example, do terminally ill cancer or Lou Gehrig's disease patients have a right to die with dignity through an act of suicide (euthanasia) or assisted suicide to avoid prolonged pain, suffering, and/or astronomical financial burdens? Some people, who agree with Dr. Kevorkian, apparently feel so strongly that individuals should have a right to choose to die with dignity in their own way and time, that they are willing to go to jail to demonstrate their strong belief in that right to choose. We are living in a time characterized by what Stone calls "prolonged dying." In the early 1900s, when the average age at death was 47, people typically died fairly quickly at home, as a result of infectious diseases or injury. Today, 70 to 80 percent of adults will die in an institution such as a hospital or nursing home, probably die as a result of degenerative diseases such as heart disease, diabetes, stroke, or cancer. Our deaths may be prolonged, painful, and financially draining for ourselves, our families, and society. Do we have a right to refuse medical treatment; to refuse heroic or artificial interventions to keep us alive when there is no hope of getting better or even of survival? These questions must be examined by every facet of our society as we embark on the changing human conditions and health care problems that confront our society in a new millennium (Belkin, 1993; Stone, 1999, pp. 76–82).

Referrals.　Crisis workers must be prepared to provide simple, clear-cut, and appropriate referral sources. Clients may need access to a central telephone number for crisis referral or a safe place to stay where overnight observation is available. Thus, a repertory of referral resources is a necessity if the crisis worker is to be effective with suicidal clients.

Guidelines for Family, Friends, and Associates.　The family, friends, and associates of the suicidal/homicidal person can do many things to contribute to prevention, as well as coping with completed acts of suicide or homicide. They can focus on prevention by correcting the alienated lifestyle that cuts off the at-risk person's connectedness with others. Crisis workers can serve an important educational role by helping families, friends, and associates learn about and become attuned to the risk factors, cues, and cries for help that suicidal/homicidal people generally display in some way.

　　Family, friends, and associates can provide the suicidal/homicidal person with permission to live, let live, and accept himself or herself: the person may need to hear directly that he or she has value and deserves to live. They can also help the person gain permission to be human—to accept his or her own fallibility and to give up perfectionism. This may mean that people around the suicidal/homicidal person must learn to deal with the person's perception of loss and despair without encouraging helplessness or dependency.

　　Family, friends, and associates who attend to the many cues we have described can help the suicidal/homicidal person by genuinely and assertively confronting the lethal issues. For instance, they can watch for the lethal person's preoccupation with an anniversary date of a significant loss, such as the death of a loved one, and intervene in a directive manner if needed. Finally, significant others can help the survivors cope with suicide/homicide after it happens. When bereaved groups cannot get past the shock of the death and/or exhibit excessive blame or guilt, crisis workers can meet with them and help them deal with their grief.

Some "Don'ts."　Hipple (1985) and Kirk (1993) have identified some "don'ts" of suicide management that also serve to supplement the intervention considerations we have listed, and these "don'ts" apply to almost anyone we work with who is suicidal:

1. Don't lecture, blame, or preach to clients.
2. Don't criticize clients or their choices or behaviors.
3. Don't debate the pros and cons of suicide.
4. Don't be misled by the client's telling you the crisis is past.
5. Don't deny the client's suicidal ideas.
6. Don't try to challenge for shock effects.
7. Don't leave the client isolated, unobserved, and disconnected.
8. Don't diagnose and analyze behavior or confront the client with interpretations during the acute phase.
9. Don't be passive.
10. Don't overreact. Keep calm.

11. Don't keep the client's suicidal risk a secret (be trapped in the confidentiality issue).
12. Don't get sidetracked on extraneous or external issues or persons.
13. Don't glamorize, martyrize, glorify, heroize, or deify suicidal behavior in others, past or present.
14. Don't fail to make yourself available and accessible.
15. Don't terminate the intervention without obtaining some level of positive commitment.
16. Don't forget to follow up.
17. Don't forget to document and report.

Older Adults

All the strategies for helping suicidal/homicidal clients, from children through adults, are useful for helping older adults, such as Gertrude, age 51, Roy, age 65, and Dennis, age 78. The crisis worker must keep in mind what research into the age factor among suicidal clients has shown: "In general, for both sexes, the intensity of the wish to kill and the wish to be killed decreases with advancing age, while the intensity of the wish to die increases with age" (Shneidman et al., 1976, p. 165). Research indicates that the percentage of failed attempted suicides decreases with age and the percentage of completed suicides increases with age (Stone, 1999, pp. 45–50). It seems that workers may have fewer second chances at helping people above 60 than they would normally expect among youths and younger adults.

In intervening with older adults, workers should pay particular attention to all forms of verbal and behavioral clues to suicidal risk. The worker's own silent assessment during the interview helps bring to the forefront a special consideration for dealing with older people. An excerpt from an interview with Roy, age 65 (showing parenthetical worker self-talk), is one example.

Roy: Well, now there's really nothing else to live for. A man's got to have some purpose. I've got nothing to go to—nothing to get up for in the morning. I just don't know what's gonna happen. I'd have been a goner for sure if that foreman, that guy Juan, hadn't showed up when he did.

CW: (*Thinking to herself/himself: "Wow! He's not fooling! What a lucky and admirable rescue that foreman accomplished! With all this intake information pointing toward suicide lethality, I don't need any more assessment data right now. I'm remembering his age, his male image, his having disposed of all his property, his wife's death—these are potent indicators—and this morning, an aborted self-hanging! It's a wonder he's even here!"*) Roy, what happened this morning is scary, indeed. I'm certainly thankful that Juan found you and brought you in. What I want us to do right now is to make sure you are safe. I'm setting up a complete medical evaluation for you today. As soon as that's done, I want you and me to begin exploring options—other than your killing yourself. I believe that together you and I can find some definite reasons for you to live and that we can find ways to help you reduce your loneliness and sleepless nights and other problems that have been posing a risk to your life. I'm thankful that you are here alive, and I want you to know that I am available to you and will help in any way I can. After you are stabilized and safe, I want to make a referral for you to attend some group meetings that I think you will find very helpful and even enjoyable.

Roy's situation was unique, but it contained similarities to problems experienced by many other older people. The worker's knowledge of risks associated with Roy's age group and sensitivity to Roy's present emotional functioning were key assessment factors in the helping process. The worker's clear and accurate inner self-talk enhanced and facilitated the intervention and referral.

PREVENTION

The need for suicide prevention has been recognized as a problem in local communities as well as nationally. A resolution in the U.S. House of Representatives ("Recognizing Suicide as a National Problem," 1998) emphasized the importance of comprehensive prevention strategies and encouraged initiatives to (1) prevent suicide; (2) respond to people at risk for suicide and people who have attempted suicide; (3) promote safe and effective treatment for people at risk for suicidal behavior; (4) support people who have lost someone to suicide; and (5) develop an effective national strategy for prevention of suicide. The resolution stated, in part, that

> While no single prevention program would be appropriate for all populations and communities, the point of this resolution is to create a climate for suicide prevention, to recognize as a Nation that we must become aware of the problem, that we are to address it and eventually solve it. (p. 1)

It's Everyone's Concern

Shneidman (1996, p. viii) stated that "the keys to understanding suicide are made of plain language; that the proper language of suicidology is *lingua franca*—the ordinary everyday words that are found in the verbatim reports of beleaguered suicidal minds." Suicidal people often provide clues about their frustrated psychological needs and the words they use constitute the essential vocabulary of suicide. This vocabulary becomes our cue for attending to people's psychological pain, and, in Shneidman's words (p. viii), "Suicide prevention can be everybody's business." Tierney (1994) has shown that organized, proactive, and comprehensive training significantly increases crisis worker competency in attending to suicidal cues, and effecting suicide intervention and prevention, and that it is not really possible or desirable to separate and compartmentalize intervention and prevention. For example, most of the treatment considerations listed in the sections entitled "Counseling Suicidal Clients" and "Intervention Strategies" in this chapter are indeed preventive in thrust. The intent of this section is to augment what we have already emphasized in the name of counseling and intervention.

Crisis workers who help suicidal/homicidal clients are also primary prevention workers. Effective suicide prevention involves comprehensive educational and communications programs designed to touch, influence, sensitize, and educate every segment of society. Because every segment of society is affected by suicides and homicides, effective and pervasive prevention must also involve every segment of society. This means taking suicide out of the closet and publicly dealing with all its dimensions in an honest, realistic, and responsible manner.

Educating for Prevention

All our institutions, as well as individuals, can contribute to suicide prevention (Morgan, 1981; Pretzel, 1972; Shneidman et al., 1976; Wekstein, 1979). The techniques, strategies, and attitudes reflected throughout this chapter can be used in educational institutions, business and industry, the print media, television, radio, churches and religious organizations, governmental and community agencies, and professional offices to help alleviate the pain and loss of life accompanying the phenomenon of suicide ("Horror of Suicide," 1985). As in all other plagues to human existence, prevention is the preferred mode of responding to suicidal people (Crow & Crow, 1987; Morgan, 1981). The most effective means of suicide prevention appears to be educating the general public, mental health professionals, and agency personnel regarding the characteristic thinking and behavior of suicidal people (Schneidman et al., 1976).

Four Methods of Prevention

Shneidman and associates (1976) have identified four methods to effect a reduction in the suicide rate in this country (pp. 145–146):

1. Increase the acumen for recognition of potential suicide among all potential rescuers.
2. Facilitate the ease with which each citizen can utter a cry for help.
3. Provide resources for responding to the suicidal crisis.
4. Disseminate the facts about suicide.

When Prevention Fails

Hipple (1985), Shneidman (1985, 1987), and others recommend postintervention programs in the case of clients who commit suicide, to help survivors cope, grieve, understand, and become instruments for preventing future suicides. Ross (1999) uses the term *postvention* to denote the use of education, counseling, and support groups to aid survivors with healing experiences and insights, thereby making it another form of prevention.

Psychological Autopsy: A Postvention Technique

Postvention techniques are procedures or initiatives carried out following traumatic crisis episodes (for example, suicides, murders, sudden deaths, or disastrous events) to help survivors cope with the aftermath of such events. Postvention techniques are generally accomplished after the precipitating crisis event has been contained. Such techniques may serve to help survivors or the public at large to move toward emotional healing, reconciliation, restoration, or prevention of such crises in the future. One such postvention technique is the *psychological autopsy*. Shneidman (1987) developed the technique for the purpose of compiling detailed postmortem mental histories following suicides. Psychological autopsies provide some of the most valuable data we have for suicide prevention. On the basis of nearly 40 years of study, treatment, and prevention work with people who have manifested suicidal tendencies, Shneidman states that suicide "is not a bizarre and incomprehensible act of self-destruction. Rather, suicidal people use a particular logic, a style of thinking that brings them to the conclusion that death is the only solution to their problems. This style can be readily seen, and there are steps we can take to stop suicide, if we know where to look" (p. 56).

Based on the proposition that most suicides make perfect sense at the moment to the people who complete them, the psychological autopsy (Shneidman, 1987) may not only provide information that helps prevent future suicides but may also represent a postvention method of helping survivors either gain a better understanding of why it happened or feel less guilt and responsibility for the deceased's demise (Roberts, 1995). Survivors of suicidal people generally receive less sympathy and encounter more social isolation, negative responses, and stigmatization than do other bereaved individuals (Moore & Freeman, 1995). Structured group counseling in which other survivors provide support is suggested as a postvention strategy to meet the special needs of people bereaved by suicide. A brief example of one type of psychological autopsy illustrates the point.

Jearlene, age 27, killed herself by carbon monoxide poisoning. She had had a chaotic and turbulent life, punctuated by a destabilized family, drug and alcohol addiction, and numerous suicide attempts. Despite all her problems, she had been a friendly, energetic, charismatic person who worked in an office supply business. She left behind several friends and co-workers who admired her and were surprised at her suicide, even though some of them were aware of her dilemmas and her occasional suicidal ideations. Several days after Jearlene's funeral, her co-workers were still in acute grief. Some of them were emotionally stuck, asking themselves and each other, "Why?" Some of them were feeling guilty because they did not pick up on the cues and do something to save Jearlene. A psychological autopsy was convened by a crisis interventionist, who met with the group of bereaved co-workers and led them through the following steps:

1. *Constructing the "why."* The crisis worker helped the group piece together the cues, clues, and signs (pooled from the knowledge contained within the group) that made Jearlene's suicide more understandable (from Jearlene's point of view).
2. *Commemorating the positive traits and accomplishments.* The group made a list of Jearlene's attributes and achievements that they particularly wanted to highlight and remember.
3. *Saying good-bye.* Each group member took turns saying a verbal goodbye to Jearlene using the "empty chair" strategy. Some members expressed anger as well as love. This was a very emotional experience for everyone.
4. *Turning loose.* The crisis worker summarized the material from the preceding three steps and led the group in brainstorming and making another list, gleaned from Jearlene's case, that may help prevent future suicides.
5. *Absolving guilt.* The crisis worker obtained a commitment from a member of the group to edit and distribute the psychological autopsy lists to every member of the group. Last, the crisis worker made a statement that essentially (a) expressed appreciation for the group's participation, (b) assured the members that they were not responsible for Jearlene's death, and (c) gave the group permission to end the acute grieving phase and enter the long-term period of grief (by never forgetting Jearlene and what she had meant to each of them, but going on with their work and lives), using the "Jearlene experience" as a means to appreciate each day of life and to be attuned to other people's dilemmas and needs.

The psychological autopsy may take many forms. In a hospital setting, the medical staff may analyze medical and psychological data, and the steps taken would look quite unlike the ones shown in the case of Jearlene. In a nursing home, the staff, family, and friends may participate in a format vastly different from the five steps just described. In a school, the strategies vary according to the circumstance, the developmental level of the children involved, and the needs of the school community, including children, teachers, and parents (Roberts, 1995). Suffice it to say that, whatever the setting, the psychological autopsy serves the purposes of understanding the suicide, gaining data for prevention, and reframing the tragedy into a postvention context.

WHEN CRISIS INTERVENTION FAILS

Crisis intervention does not always work. Sometimes even the most skilled professionals and crisis workers cannot succeed. We must remember that if people really intend to kill themselves, despite our best efforts to intervene, they can manage to accomplish the dreaded deed. The following suggestions have been provided to help workers cope with the loss of clients.

Worker Stress and Grief After Losing a Client

Guided debriefings by experts are necessary for workers who have lost a client. *Having a client commit suicide or homicide is one of the most stressful events that can occur in the experience of a crisis worker.* The guilt, recrimination, rumination, and perseveration may lead to constant second-guessing. The "What ifs," "shoulds," "oughts," and "might have beens" all lead to feelings of owning responsibility. If a client commits suicide or homicide, a *psychological autopsy,* or *debriefing* (see Chapter 12, on hostage crises, the section on debriefing), and *supervision* should be mandatory for the worker. Indeed, the impact of having failed to save a person that was a client or a victim of the client's can be overwhelming and can cause the crisis worker to experience what is called *vicarious traumatization* (see Chapter 13, on burnout, the section on vicarious traumatization). Such cases call for the utmost of professional expertise to provide intentional and intensive debriefing of the traumatized workers. It is absolutely essential that such workers realistically examine (under the guidance of outside consultants) what happened, learn from the event, and absolve themselves from guilt and responsibility for the regrettable loss.

Initiating the Healing of Emotional Wounds.   We cannot overemphasize the vital importance of worker debriefings. Workers often are devastated and vulnerable to permanent emotional wounds whenever they wrongly believe that they could or should have prevented the suicide or homicide. Generally, only an outside consultant's objective view and processing of the event with workers can lead them to discover that there was nothing they could have done to prevent the death(s) and that the workers must find ways to turn the guilt loose, reframe the negative aspects of the event, and begin the healing process. The recent increase in random violence and shootings in schools and public places entails a concomitant necessity for the care and nurture of crisis workers, many of whom deal with grief after losing clients. Debriefing or psychological autopsy procedures offer the best hope we know of to counter guilt, grief, and loss and to help workers begin to heal and return to their own previous level of equilibrium and normalcy.

Workers Must Survive.   When crisis workers fail to save a suicidal person, they must first avail themselves of the help we have described earlier; then we encourage them to go home; continue the renewal and reframing that the debriefing process started; be kind to themselves, their families, friends, and associates; get some rest and sleep; and awaken with vigor, sensitivity, and resolve. Never forgetting the suicide or homicide victims, workers must go forward, ready to meet, understand, and help future clients. Even though crisis workers try as much as they can, we cannot be successful 100 percent of the time. We are not perfect. We are 100 percent human. But we survivors can and must find ways to handle our grief and healing. And when we do this, we can emerge capable of continuing to provide excellent crisis intervention work and service to society.

The Unique Nature of Grief over Suicide

Helping Clients Who Are Vulnerable Survivors.   Whenever suicide/homicide has been threatened, attempted, or completed, many clients, friends, and family members who are survivors often feel disbelief and betrayal or robbed of the chance to say goodbye or repair relationships. Ross (1999) describes how anger, guilt, sadness, puzzlement, understanding, denial, and blame (of self, victim, or others) blend into one scrambled monstrous emotion. Most of us have lost loved ones and been to funerals; we know the routine. Suicide survivors have no such formal guidelines. Other people may focus more on the suicide than do the survivors. Survivors frequently sense that they are the objects of gossip and criticism, and they may be right. They may search for one or more years for answers that are never found. But that search is absolutely necessary for healing because it facilitates the restoration of self-worth to both the bereaved and the deceased. Survivors are haunted by memories and may experience posttraumatic stress; they may "feel the pain" of the deceased and fantasize their own suicide, thereby perpetuating the legacy of being destined for suicide. Healing and grief work are therefore important activities for survivors.

Healing Grief Work After a Suicide/Homicide.   Ross (1999) recommends a variety of strategies for survivors to use, beginning right after the suicide or homicide of a loved one. Some of these strategies are formal, some are simple and informal.

One strategy is spending time alone with the body, putting notes in the casket, and setting up an appreciation table; leaving funeral attendees with the sense that this was a special person, not "just a suicide." Another strategy is giving oneself and others, including children, permission to express grief and emotions; seeking support groups or counseling early; talking with people who are empathic and trustworthy and inviting them to contribute as support people. It also helps to listen to one's own body and reserve one's stamina and energy. Grief hurts; healing works. Sometimes the healing process is enhanced by such unusual activities as kicking a box, stomping on the grave, or intentionally going out and working with survivors. One can expect the process of healing to be scary, confusing, and fatiguing. Sometimes the person who is grieving experiences forgetfulness, shortness of temper, and other moods that are uncharacteristic.

Some survivors have put together memory books and other commemorative projects as healing strategies and have even generated rituals for death day anniversaries and special holidays. Ross (1999) also cites screaming, "cussing," crying, and humor as acceptable options for healing. Suicide is not funny, but sometimes laughter may provide the same sort of release as tears. Seeking spiritual understanding for strength and solace is also important. Forgiving the suicide victim, oneself, and others can nurture freedom from the burden of unforgivingness—perhaps the greatest gift one can give oneself.

SUMMARY

The phenomenon of suicide is democratic in that it affects every segment of society and it is everybody's business. Suicide and homicide have many similarities and parallels in terms of motive, risk, and assessment of lethality. Suicide is a serious problem that is on the rise among all groups, especially youth, but the highest risk group is, and has remained for many years, Caucasian males over 65. Researchers find few common denominators in their quest to identify suicide/homicide risk types and to predict and prevent suicide/homicide.

Crisis workers can strengthen their knowledge and competency in dealing with suicidal clients by becoming familiar with the dynamics of suicide, counseling techniques, intervention strategies, and prevention considerations. Background information, concepts, and applications are helpful in building skills. Finally, workers should be familiar with the parallels and similarities between suicide and homicide.

The dynamics of suicide are important because crisis workers who deal with suicidal clients need to know that there are several different types and characteristics of suicide. There are many reasons why people kill or attempt to kill themselves (for example, to alleviate psychological stress or to avoid protracted pain associated with terminal illness), and there are differing points of view about suicide among various social, ethnic, and age groups. A thorough knowledge of the dynamics of suicide can sensitize workers to the causes and signs of suicide. A good many myths about suicide complicate the assessment, counseling, intervention, and prevention that workers attempt to provide. Among these myths there are two that are particularly salient in impeding crisis work: (1) discussing suicide will cause a person to think about doing it or to act upon it, and (2) people who threaten suicide don't do it. Since neither myth has substantive evidence of empirical support, crisis workers are advised to directly question clients who display any suicidal or homicidal ideations. Despite the difficulties, however, we now know enough about suicide to be of great help to suicidal people. A great number of risk factors have been identified that serve as danger signals and help to determine levels of lethality. For example, some of the highest risks are the presence of serious intent, a history of prior attempts, and evidence of a specific and lethal plan. These risk factors are important criteria for both assessing and acting in the realm of suicide intervention. Workers who are sensitized to the dynamics find that suicidal people often send out subtle but definite clues and/or cries for help.

Intervention strategies show how crisis workers can be appropriately assertive, directive, and forceful. In work with suicidal clients, workers should not be passive. Researchers have gathered a list of do's and don'ts that pertain exclusively to intervention with suicidal clients. (For example, don't lecture, blame or preach; don't criticize clients or their choices or behaviors; and don't debate the pros and cons of suicide.) A number of special considerations affect coping with the act of suicide and with suicidal people. In suicide intervention, workers must consider many environmental and social factors in addition to attending to client safety. (For example, age, gender, social status, availability of supports from family and friends, and community attitudes surrounding the person at risk.)

Counseling around the issue of suicide/homicide also involves suicide prevention and facilitating the grief and healing of clients who are survivors as well as the care and debriefing of crisis workers who experience the loss of clients to suicide or homicide. The most effective means of keeping people from killing themselves is education. Making the general public aware of the dynamics, dangers, cues, myths, and rudimentary techniques for counseling and intervention is the primary goal of prevention.

C L A S S R O O M   E X E R C I S E S

The Case of Tom

Tom, his wife, Sheila, and his daughter Renee (age 7) live in a small town surrounded by a large agricultural area. Tom is employed as a heavy equipment operator. He likes the outdoors, particularly hunting, and he prides himself on being "macho." He was an excellent high school athlete and could have gone to a small college on a football scholarship. But he took a job working for his father and an uncle, married Sheila (who had been his classmate and the high school homecoming queen), and obligated himself with a large mortgage on a home next door to his parents. Tom began to drink heavily, drive fast cars, frequently take risks on the highways, get into fights at taverns, come home late at night, and neglect his physical health. He felt remorseful, guilty, depressed, and suicidal following each fling at a tavern. Sheila and her supervisor at work repeatedly attempted to persuade Tom to see a therapist. Sheila finally prevailed on Tom to call the tricounty crisis line after she walked into their bedroom at 7:30 P.M. Saturday and discovered him preparing to shoot himself in the head with his deer rifle. The volunteer crisis worker received the call from Tom later that evening.

Tom: (*In a fearful, tense, and anxious voice.*) I wouldn't have called, but my wife insisted. She caught me trying to shoot myself tonight. Now I'm scared as hell. She sort of demanded that I get help.

CW: Tom, I'm glad you called. You did the right thing when you called, because you can be helped, and I want us to start right now. I can hear the tenseness in your voice. What I want to do first is for you to stay on the line, sit down, and tell me what's happening in your life right now—in the past day or so—that's brought you so close to killing yourself. That's what I want to know first.

Tom: Well, everything. All these pressures. Everybody expecting big things from me, and I'm not really worth a shit! My wife and kid would be better off if I was out of the way, and I would be too. I ain't the happy-go-lucky guy I look like on the surface.

CW: So Tom, you're really down; you've had a very close call, and you're frightened. What happened to cause the stress at this time?

Tom: Well, it's a buildup of lots of things. I'm getting nowhere on a treadmill. And yesterday—it just hit me—I realized I'm a nothing. A dependent kid in a man's clothing. One of my friends I went to high school with has his MBA. Another one owns a car dealership. I'm still working for my daddy—can't get away from Mamma. I'm a dud—a nobody. And I'm stuck. A nobody, going nowhere.

CW: So you're trying yourself, sentencing yourself, and you've nearly executed yourself because you're stuck—and you're realizing that what you're really wanting is to be in a successful career, independent from your folks. And it really hurts when you face it head on. You're feeling powerless right now.

Tom: That's it. And Sheila deserves a better man than that! I'm stuck, so she's stuck with me, and I ain't much to look at.

I. Simulated Telephone Interview

Generate a role play to carry the interview forward, with one volunteer taking the role of Tom and another volunteer taking the role of the crisis worker. Place two chairs back to back in the middle of the room to simulate the telephone interview. Make an audio-tape recording of the interview. To make it realistic, Tom and the crisis worker must not be able to see each other. Continue the simulated telephone call with the objective of taking Tom through the six-step crisis counseling model described in Chapter 2. If possible, get a realistic commitment from Tom not to kill himself without first meeting with the crisis worker, going to a hospital, or going directly to a therapist. If the person taking the role of the crisis worker gets stuck, have someone else take over and continue the telephone counseling. When the simulated telephone session has been completed, convene the whole group for discussion and suggestions. Role players should take time to disassociate themselves from the characters they have portrayed during the role play. Here are some questions to facilitate discussion:

1. What were the advantages and drawbacks of the lack of visual contact between the crisis worker and Tom?
2. If this client–worker simulation were repeated, what could you do to improve on the first session?
3. What other strategies could the worker use?
4. What other alternatives might the worker help Tom explore?
5. What feelings (frustration, stress, and so on) were experienced by members of the group who were observers?
6. What are the implications and suggestions from the group with respect to helping suicidal clients who call on crisis hot lines?

II. Interview, Take Two

Listen to the recording of the simulated telephone interview. Two new volunteers will now repeat the exercise, with the group again considering all six questions. Compare the tape recording of the two sessions.

III. Postintervention Meeting: The Psychological Autopsy

Suppose that the entire group were the tricounty crisis center staff and volunteer workers in a meeting called a week after the telephone interview. The purpose of the meeting is to deal with the death of Tom, who shot himself the following Friday, despite the best efforts of the center, support people, and other intervention and referral resources.

Make a list of the points that need to be addressed and discuss the issues that need to be brought before the combined group. All participants should have opportunities to express their feelings and concerns. Make a list of actions the center might want to take as a result of the experience with Tom.

RESOURCES

For readers who wish to access additional information regarding the crisis of lethality, the following organizations are sources well worth consideration. The *Encyclopedia of Associations* (Maurer & Sheets, 1999) contains exhaustive listings in addition to the ones we present here.

Suicide and Prevention
American Association of Suicidology (AAS)
4201 Connecticut Avenue, NW, Suite 310
Washington, DC 20008
Phone: (202) 237-2280 Fax: (202) 237-2282
Web site: http://www.cyberpsych.org
Encourages the study of suicide prevention and related phenomena of self-destruction. Promotes education and disseminates information through programs and publications designed to further societal understanding of suicide and suicide prevention. Cooperates with other organizations that are involved in the study of suicidology. Affiliated with the International Association for Suicide Prevention.

American Suicide Foundation (ASF)
120 Wall Street, FL 22
New York, NY 10005-4001
Phone: (212) 410-1111 Fax: (212) 410-0532 Toll Free: (800) 278-4042
Supports research and provides substantial grants for professionals who wish to investigate the causes and prevention of suicide. Educates professionals in the treatment of suicidal individuals. Disseminates vital information on suicide and suicide prevention.

Homicide: Murdered Children or Adults
Parents of Murdered Children (POMC)
100 East 8th Street, B-41
Cincinnati, OH 45202
Phone: (513) 721-5683 Fax: (513) 345-4489
E-mail: natlpomc@aol.com
Web site: http://www.pomc.com
Provides self-help for anyone who has a child, friend, or family member murdered. Offers support and friendship to people who have experienced violent death of a loved one. Fosters physical and emotional health for survivors. Works to heighten society's awareness of the problems faced by those who survive a homicide victim. Provides information about the grieving process and the criminal justice system as it pertains to survivors of homicide victims. Establishes self-help and support groups. Distributes literature and provides guest speakers and prevention programs to stop/prevent violence.

REFERENCES

Allen, N. (1977). History and background of suicidology. In C. L. Hatton, S. M. Valente, & A. Rink (Eds.), *Suicide assessment and intervention* (pp. 1–19). New York: Appleton-Century-Crofts.

American Association for Counseling and Development. (AACD). (1985, September 5). Congress eyes youth suicide; AACD to testify. *Guidepost,* pp. 1, 5.

American Association of Retired People. (AARP). (1986). Reminiscence: Thanks for the memory. *News Bulletin, 27*(8), p. 2.

American Association of Suicidology. (1997). *Youth suicide fact sheet* (revised). Washington, DC: Author.

Battle, A. O. (1985, November). *Outpatient management of the suicidal adolescent* (paper, presentation, and assessment instrument). Symposium on Suicide in Teenagers and Young Adults, University of Tennessee, College of Medicine, Department of Psychiatry, Memphis.

Battle, A. O. (1991, January 19). *Factors in assessing suidical lethality.* Paper presented at Crisis Center Preservice Volunteer Training, University of Tennessee, College of Medicine, Department of Psychiatry, Memphis.

Battle, A. O., Battle, M. V., & Tolley, E. A. (1993). Potential for suicide and aggression in delinquents at juvenile court in a southern city. *Suicide and Life Threatening Behavior, 23*(3), 230–243.

Belkin, L. (1993). There's no simple suicide. *The New York Times Magazine*, November 14, 1993, pp. 48, 50–55, 63, 74–75.

Berman, A. L., & Jobes, D. A. (1994). Treatment of the suicidal adolescent. (Special Issue: Suicide assessment and intervention.) *Death Studies, 18,* 375–389.

Berman, A. L., & Jobes, D. A. (1996). *Adolescent suicide: Assessment and intervention.* Washington, DC: American Psychological Association (Paperback).

Bernard, J. L., & Bernard, M. L. (1985). Suicide on campus: Response to the problem. In E. S. Zinner (Ed.), *Coping with death on campus* (pp. 69–83). San Francisco: Jossey-Bass.

Boudewyn, A. C., & Liem, J. H. (1995). Childhood sexual abuse as a precursor to depression and self-destructive behavior in adulthood. *Journal of Traumatic Stress, 8,* 445–459.

Courtois, C. A. (1991, August 16). *The self-destructive person and the suicidal bind.* Paper presented at the 99th annual convention of the American Psychological Association, San Francisco.

Crow, G. A., & Crow, L. I. (1987). *Crisis intervention and suicide prevention: Working with children and adolescents.* Springfield, IL: Charles C Thomas.

Dixon, A. W., Heppner, P. P., & Rudd, D. (1994). Problem-solving appraisal, hopelessness, and suicide ideation: Evidence for a mediation model. *Journal of Counseling Psychology, 41*(1), 91–98.

Dunne, E. J., McIntosh, J. L., & Dunne-Maxim, K. (Eds.). (1987). *Suicide and its aftermath: Understanding and counseling the survivors.* New York: Norton.

Durkheim, E. (1951). *Suicide.* New York: Free Press.

Ebersole, P. (1976a, August). Reminiscing. *American Journal of Nursing, 76,* 1304–1305.

Ebersole, P. (1976b, November–December). Problems of group reminiscing with institutional aged. *Journal of Gerontological Nursing, 2,* 23–27.

Fujimura, L. E., Weis, D. M., & Cochran, J. R. (1985). Suicide: Dynamics and implications for counseling. *Journal of Counseling and Development, 63,* 612–615.

Garland, A. F., & Zigler, E. (1993). Adolescent suicide prevention. *American Psychologist, 42*(2), 169–182.

Georgia killing spree: Notes left behind. (1999, July 31). *Pensacola News Journal,* p. 2A.

Gilliland, B. E. (1985, November). *Surviving college: Teaching college students to cope* (paper and presentation). Symposium on Suicide in Teenagers and Young Adults, University of Tennessee, College of Medicine, Department of Psychiatry, Memphis.

Gunman kills 12, self in Atlanta (1999, July 30). *Pensacola News Journal,* p. 1A.

Hazell, P., & Lewin, T. (1993). An evaluation of postvention following adolescent suicide. *Suicide and Life Threatening Behavior, 23*(2), 101–109.

Hersh, J. B. (1985, January). Interviewing college students in crisis. *Journal of Counseling and Development, 63,* 286–289.

Hipple, J. (1985). Suicide: The preventable tragedy (mimeographed monograph, 25 pp.). Denton: North Texas State University.

Hipple, J., & Cimbolic, P. (1979). *The counselor and suicidal crisis*. Springfield, IL: Charles C Thomas.

Hipple, J., & Hipple, L. (1983). *Diagnosis and management of psychological emergencies; A manual for hospitalization*. Springfield, IL: Charles C Thomas.

Horror of suicide: Young people have a right to know. (1985, September 24). *The Commercial Appeal,* Memphis, Section A, p. 4 (editorial).

Janosik, E. H. (1984). *Crisis counseling: A contemporary approach*. Belmont, CA: Wadsworth.

Kirk, W. G. (1993). *Adolescent suicide: A school-based approach to assessment and intervention*. Champaign, IL: Research Press.

Knight, J. A., & Kleespies, P. M. (1999, August 22). *The Boston assessment of suicide ideation correlates (BASIC): Development of a suicide risk assessment for veterans*. Paper presented at the 107th annual convention of the American Psychological Association, Boston.

Malley, P. B., Kush, F., & Bogo, R. J. (1994). School-based adolescent suicide prevention and intervention programs. *The School Counselor, 42,* 130–136.

Maurer, C. M., & Sheets, T. E. (Eds.). (1999). *Encyclopedia of Associations* (34th ed.) (Vol. 1, Parts 1, 2, and 3). Farmington Hills, MI: Gale Research.

Moldeven, M. (1988). *Suicide prevention programs in the Department of Defense: A planning aid for mental health, crisis intervention, and human resources administrators in the public and private sectors*. Del Mar, CA: Author.

Moore, M. M., & Freeman, S. J. (1995). Counseling survivors of suicide: Implications for group postvention. *Journal for Specialists in Group Work, 20*(1), 40–47.

Morgan, L. B. (1981). The counselor's role in suicide prevention, *Personnel and Guidance Journal, 59,* 284–286.

Myer, R. A., Williams, R. C., Ottens, A. J., & Schmidt, A. E. (1992). A three-dimensional model for triage. *Journal of Mental Health Counseling, 14,* 137–148.

Peach, L., & Reddick, T. L. (1991). Counselors can make a difference in preventing adolescent suicide. *The School Counselor, 39,* 107–110.

Peters, K. D., Kochanek, K. D., & Murphy, S. L. (1998). Deaths: Final data for 1996. *National Vital Statistics Report, 47*(9). Hyattsville, MD: National Center for Health Statistics. DHHS Publication No. (PHS) 99-1120. (Data to be published in the 1996 annual volume of *Vital Statistics of the United States.*)

Pretzel, P. (1972). *Understanding and counseling the suicidal person*. Nashville: Abingdon Press.

Recognizing suicide as a national problem, 105th Cong., 2nd Sess. 1 (1998, October 9). *Congressional Record, 144*(141), 1.

Reinecke, M. A. (1999, April). *Suicide as an attachment behavior*. Paper presented at the Twenty-Third Annual Convening of Crisis Intervention Personnel, Chicago.

Roberts, A. R. (Ed.). (1991). *Contemporary perspectives on crisis intervention*. Upper Saddle River, NJ: Prentice Hall.

Roberts, W. B., Jr. (1995). Postvention and psychological autopsy in the suicide of a 14-year-old public school student. *The School Counselor, 42,* 322–330.

Roleff, T. L. (Ed.). (1997). *Suicide: opposing viewpoints*. San Diego, CA: Greenhaven.

Ross, E. B. (1999, April). *After suicide: A ray of hope*. Paper presented at the Twenty-Third Annual Convening of Crisis Intervention Personnel, Chicago.

Shaffer, D., Vieland, V., & Garland, A. (1990). Adolescent suicide attempters: Response to suicide-prevention programs. *Journal of the American Medical Association, 264,* 3151–3155.

Shneidman, E. S. (1985). *Definition of suicide*. New York: Wiley.

Shneidman, E. S. (1987, March). At the point of no return: Suicidal thinking follows a predictable path. *Psychology Today,* pp. 54–58.

Shneidman, E. S. (1996). *The suicidal mind*. New York: Oxford University Press.

Shneidman, E. S., Farberow, N. L., & Litman, R. E. (1976). *The psychology of suicide*. New York: Aronson.

Stone, G. (1999). *Suicide and attempted suicide: Methods and consequences*. New York: Carroll & Graf.

Tierney, R. J. (1994). Suicide intervention training evaluation: A preliminary report. *Crisis, 15,* 69–76.

Webb, S. B., & Griffiths, F. (1998–1999). *Young people at risk of suicide: Part A, School facilitators' Handbook; Part B., Supplementary resources.* New Zealand: College of Education, Massey University.

Wekstein, L. (1979). *Handbook of suicidology.* New York: Brunner/Mazel.

Zinner, E. S. (Ed.). (1985). *Coping with death on campus.* San Francisco: Jossey-Bass.

CHAPTER SIX

Sexual Assault

BACKGROUND

Sexual assault is a uniquely serious crime that threatens people of all ages and stations of life. Survivors of rape and sexual assault/abuse often experience prolonged trauma symptoms that are difficult for them to transcend and are challenging for caregivers who seek to help them. The scope of the problem and pervasiveness of the crime are of particularly grave concern to crisis workers.

Rape, Sexual Abuse, and Assault: The Scope of the Problem

The findings of two comprehensive funded research studies by D. Kilpatrick and C. Edmunds ("Two Rape Surveys," 1992), sponsored by the National Institute on Drug Abuse, found that 683,000 American women were raped in 1990 and that 12.1 million women had been raped at least once during their lives. Heppner and associates (1995) reported that FBI estimates show that one in four women will be raped during their lifetime. Also, according to Eisler (1995, pp. 19–20) the FBI estimates that a woman is raped every six minutes, with a recent U.S. Bureau of Statistics study indicating that in some states more than half the survivors of sexual abuse are girls under age 18. An estimated 250,000 U.S. children, most of them girls, are sexually molested in their homes every year—usually by members of their families. A report by Ratna and Mukergee (1998) indicated that 1 in 6 women and 1 in 10 men experienced sexual abuse during childhood. Statistics in other nations in Asia, Africa, and Latin America are equally grim.

The Unique Situation of Sexual Abuse Survivors

Abundant evidence suggests that crises resulting from sexual abuse differ in nature, intensity, and extent from other forms of crisis (Burgess & Holmstrom, 1985; Finkelhor, 1979, 1984, 1987; Hartman & Burgess, 1988; Kelly, 1988; Williams & Holmes, 1981). Many survivors experience long-term residual effects, which Hartman and Burgess (1988) have delineated as *rape trauma* or *sexual trauma*. Some clinicians (Daniluk & Haverkamp, 1993, p. 16) have used the term *sexual abuse survivors syndrome* to describe the posttraumatic-stress-like symptoms that often follow in the aftermath of childhood sexual abuses. Frazier and Borgida (1985) report that many psychologists classify rape trauma as a particular example of posttraumatic stress disorder, because the emotional trauma resultant from such assault frequently emerges, as debilitating transcrises, during ensuing developmental stages of survivors' lives.

Sexual Assault: A Pervasive Crime

Any person at one time or another may be the victim of sexual abuse (Molmen, 1982, p. 12). Although the majority of assaults are perpetrated on children and females under age 30 (Amir, 1971; Bass & Thornton, 1983), sexual assault survivors have been identified among males and females from every segment of the population—children, adolescents, adults, and older adults (Williams & Holmes, 1981).

DEFINING RAPE

There are many definitions of rape. Some are based on legal constructs; some are derived from other sources. We prefer to use Benedict's (1985) definition of rape as "any sexual act that is forced on you" (p. 1). Brownmiller (1975) distinguishes between most legal definitions and what she refers to as a woman's definition of rape. She sees the legal definition of rape as "the forcible perpetration of an act of sexual intercourse on the body of a woman not one's wife" (p. 380) as much too narrow and protective of male supremacy. Brownmiller's preferred definition from a woman's perspective is that rape is "a sexual invasion of the body by force, an incursion into the private, personal inner space without consent—in short, an internal assault from one of several avenues and by one of several methods [that] constitutes a deliberate violation of emotional, physical, and rational integrity and is a hostile, degrading act of violence" (p. 376). That definition appears to encompass the whole scope of rape, as well as other forms of sexual abuse/misuse. Although we prefer, in applied situations, the simplicity of the Benedict definition, the more thorough and comprehensive definition of Brownmiller is probably a better definition for both technical and conceptual use.

FUNDAMENTAL ASSUMPTIONS REGARDING RAPE AND SEXUAL ABUSE

From the literature, we have derived nine assumptions about rape and sexual abuse that undergird the basic concepts and interventions found in this chapter:

1. *Rape is not sex.* Rape, incest, sodomy, digital or object penetration of the vagina or anus, forced oral sex, forced fondling, forced masturbation, and other forms of sexual abuse or misuse are acts of aggression, violence, force, or the willful exercise of power, dominance, or control over other persons, rather than expressions of sexuality (Benedict, 1985, pp. 5–12; Burgess, 1985; Carnes, 1983; Chaplin, Rice, & Harris, 1995). Walker (1989) identifies pornography as one aspect of sexual abuse, and husband–wife sexual assault as rape—a criminal act (p. 124).

2. *Rape is an uninvited act.* There is overwhelming evidence that survivors seldom invite or provoke sexual assault. People do not ask for or deserve the various negative feelings or emotions that result from rape and other forms of sexual abuse/misuse. These emotional responses may include a feeling of fear of death or serious injury,

panic, terror, degradation, humiliation, helplessness, violation, being overwhelmed, shame, guilt, anger, denial, blame, betrayal, disbelief, loss of control, rage, loss of self-esteem, and immediate or delayed trauma (Benedict, 1985; Brownmiller, 1975).

3. *Rape can happen to anyone.* Contrary to common opinion, survivors of rape and other forms of sexual abuse/misuse include persons of all ages, races, cultural backgrounds, social groups, and sexes and sexual orientations (although most rapes are committed on females)—from young children through older adults. Most of the recorded rapes of men have occurred in penal institutions, although such assaults may occur anywhere. Men are more reluctant to report rapes than are women (Bass & Thornton, 1983; Benedict, 1985; Burgess, 1985; Colao & Hosansky, 1983, p. 17; Patchett, 1995; Williams & Holmes, 1981). Recently, date and acquaintance rape (Harrison, Downes, & Williams, 1990), husband–wife rape, and partner–partner rape (Walker, 1989, p. 124) have been reported with growing frequency.

4. *Rapists come from every segment of society.* People who rape and commit other forms of sexual abuse/misuse have been identified in every stratum of society—from judges to messenger boys, from weaklings to muscular types, from vagrants to corporate executives, from husbands and fathers to strangers, from partners, known friends, and relatives to unknown intruders (Benedict, 1985, pp. 9–10; Burgess, Groth, Holmstrom, & Sgroi, 1978; Burgess & Holmstrom, 1979; Greer & Stuart, 1983; Groth & Birnbaum, 1979; Hursch, 1977; Kempe, 1984; Medea & Thompson, 1974, pp. 29–36; Minard, 1993, p. 10).

5. *The incidence of sexual assault has been underreported.* The literature describes rape and other types of sexual offense as being a widespread social problem of epidemic proportions. That statement is based on *reported* levels of assault. What is more disturbing is that the literature consistently estimates that "fifty to ninety percent of all rapes or attempted rapes go unreported" (Sussman & Bordwell, 1981, p. 15). Most instances of incest and molestation are never reported. The vast majority of crime survey reports do not report sexual abuse of children under the age of 12 (Bass & Thornton, 1983; Benedict, 1985, pp. 186–192; Brownmiller, 1975, p. 175; Geiser, 1979, pp. 9–10; James & DeVaney, 1994; Medea & Thompson, 1974; Minard, 1993, p. 9; Sussman & Bordwell, 1981, p. 15; Townley, 1985, p. 24).

6. *Nearly all reported perpetrators of sexual abuse/misuse are men; most survivors are women and children.* Reported sexual assault and abuse/misuse in all their many forms are predominately male crimes (Chaplin, Rice, & Harris, 1995; Minard, 1993). Most research indicates that males between the ages of 18 and 35 inflict 99 percent of the reported sexual assaults in the United States (Medea & Thompson, 1974; Plummer, 1984, p. v; Townley, 1985, p. 162). However, Holmes, Holmes, and Unholz (1993) state that female pedophilia is underreported and that female offenders are typically mothers or other caregivers who abuse young boys.

7. *The recovery of survivors of sexual assault/abuse/misuse is enhanced by the empathic help and understanding of the people close to them.* Whether the survivor's support people are family, friends, associates, medical or legal personnel, crisis workers, or long-term therapists, the important ingredients in the helping relationship are acceptance, genuineness, empathy, caring, and nonjudgmental understanding (Baker, 1995; Benedict, 1985; Patchett, 1995; Remer & Ferguson, 1995; Sadowski & Loesch, 1993).

8. *Rape predisposes the victim to a variety of psychological and behavioral posttraumatic issues.* The intensity and duration of the postrape syndrome is influenced by

a variety of factors internal to the survivor (for example, emotional health/stability prior to the trauma, use of drugs and alcohol, depression, self-esteem problems, debilitating thoughts and negative self-talk, attributions of causality of the assault, and vocational impairment) and also external to the survivor (family support, law enforcement, legal and court system, and social stigma) (McDuffie, 1999; Regehr, Cadell, & Jansen, 1999; Shipherd & Beck, 1999).

9. *Some rapists are sexually aroused by force and aggressive resistance of victims.* A counterpoint to number 1 (that rape is not sex) is that some research indicates that certain types of rapists are aroused by the use of force and violence against victims and such arousal may be heightened by aggressive resistance of victims (Balyk, 1997; Brown & Forth, 1997; Butz & Spaccarelli, 1999; Drieschner & Lange, 1999; Knight, 1999). Moreover, a woman victim must deal with the possibility of sexually transmitted disease or pregnancy as biological and health consequences of the unwanted sexual assault.

The Dynamics of Rape

The etiology of rape has roots deeply embedded in the psychosocial and cultural fabric of the particular society in which it occurs (Baron & Straus, 1989; Brownmiller, 1975; Eisler, 1987–1995; Ullman, 1996a, 1996b). According to Brownmiller (1975) and Eisler (1987–1995), the cultural mechanism of male dominance constitutes the driving force in rape in all cultures. The psychosocial, cultural, and personal attitudes and responses of both males and females are important dynamics in consideration of the phenomenon of rape (Amir, 1971; Benedict, 1985; Williams & Holmes, 1981). An understanding of how these dynamics affect both individuals and society can enhance the effectiveness of crisis workers who must provide help for both victims of rape and perpetrators (Benedict, 1985; Eisler, 1995).

Psychosocial and Cultural Dynamics.   Rape is a complex phenomenon. Sussman and Bordwell (1981) interviewed convicted rapists and have vividly demonstrated that each rapist's reasons for assault are individual. Yet the vast majority of rapes have to do with the power relationships between men and women (p. 12). Somehow the contemporary sociocultural milieu produces some males who feel such absence of power and control in their lives that they develop a need to "take it" (control). These males come to believe that it is their "right" (p. 5) and proceed to rationalize and justify their behavior, even though they have invaded and taken by force another person's life and body. The rapist's justification for committing this ultimate act of humiliation and degradation comes down to forcing the person to submit. Because most survivors are females and children, rape is largely an act based on adult male supremacy, even though adult males are themselves sometimes raped. The notion of male supremacy has its roots deep in our cultural history, which has always equated the property rights of men with access to and control of the bodies of women, children, and others who are perceived as dependents (Brownmiller, 1975). Indeed, Eisler (1987–1995, pp. 153–154) describes rape and sexual assault as one of several threats widely used to ensure the continued domination and control of women.

Social Factors.   Baron and Straus (1989) characterize rape as a social phenomenon and theorize four different causes: gender inequality, pornography, social disorganization, and legitimization of violence. *Gender inequality* relates economic, political, and legal status of women in comparison to men. *Pornography* reduces women to sex objects, promotes male dominance, and encourages or condones sexual violence against women. *Social disorganization* erodes social control and constraints and undermines freedom of individual behavior and self-determination. *Legitimization of violence* is the support the culture gives to violence, as portrayed in the mass media (such as television programming), laws permitting corporal punishment in schools, violent sports, excessive military exploits, and video games.

In the Western world, aggression, exercise of power, and domination are portrayed as accepted male characteristics, whereas peacefulness, compliance, and submission are deemed appropriate for females. These attitudes and values are woven into our social fabric. Brownmiller (1975) and others have documented a part of the history of rape as a psychosocial means by which the victors in wars reward themselves and humiliate their vanquished foes. The wholesale rape and killing of helpless women and children represents the ultimate vulnerability and defeat of a people. It likewise represents the ultimate humiliation and subjugation of a person. Whether it is inflicted on hundreds, as reported in war, or on one person, the purpose is quite similar—the use of unrestrained power to force the vanquished into total submission.

Societal attitudes about rape have long impeded survivor advocacy. In recent years, improved communications, wider reporting, and better research information have tended to improve the lot of the survivor. However, several negative dimensions have been noted, such as the complicating effect of the automobile (increased mobility), the accelerated maturation rate of children and adolescents, population concentration in urban centers, emergence and acceptance of violence in the visual media, greater amounts of personal leisure time, more discretionary money to spend (Amir, 1971; Brownmiller, 1975), and the emergence of shame and dissociation as factors in the revictimization of childhood sexual abuse survivors (Kessler & Bieschke, 1999).

Cultural Factors. Our cultural heritage has apparently lagged behind our technological and social patterns. Despite factors such as industrialization, population mobility, birth control, the feminist movement, employment of women outside the household, smaller families, higher divorce rates, single-parent families, blended families, relaxed moral codes, and higher economic standards of living, our attitudes about sex, sexuality, and sexual assault have been slow to change (Williams & Holmes, 1981). One example of this cultural lag is the persistent belief that rape is a crime committed for sex (Benedict, 1985; Brownmiller, 1975). In a global perspective, Eisler (1995, pp. 237–239) characterizes rape as an expression of the linkage between sex and violence: a cultural mechanism that the dominant society uses to control and exercise power over women, minorities, and the powerless.

Personal and Psychological Factors.   Personal and psychological factors unique to men who perpetuate sexual abuse affect both their decision to assault and the way the assault is carried out (Amir, 1971; Groth & Birnbaum, 1979; Williams & Holmes, 1981). Factors unique to women tend to affect their responses to rape and their recovery process (Amir, 1971; Benedict, 1985; Williams & Holmes, 1981). The male offender

1. Acts in a hostile, aggressive, condescending, and domineering manner, even though he often feels weak, anxious, inadequate, threatened, and dependent

2. Believes he should act strong, courageous, and manly
3. Lacks the skills to make his point in society
4. May be *angry*—the angry rapist is likely to use more violence and force than is needed to compel the victim to submit and is likely to threaten, beat, and revile the person
5. May need to exercise *power*—the power rapist is likely to use the assault situation to prove to himself and to the victim that he is powerful, omnipotent, and in total control
6. May show *sadistic* patterns—the sadistic rapist frequently uses extreme violence and often mutilates or murders the victim in order to attain a feeling of total triumph over the victim

The female who is assaulted

1. Fears for her life
2. May respond by exhibiting no emotions—appearing unaffected
3. Feels humiliated, demeaned, and degraded
4. May suffer immediate physical and psychological injury as well as long-term trauma
5. May experience impaired sexual functioning
6. May blame herself and feel guilty
7. May experience difficulty relating to and trusting others—especially men
8. May experience fantasies, daydreams, and nightmares—vividly reliving the assault or additional encounters with the assailant—or may have mental images of scenes of revenge
9. May feel intense anger or hatred toward the assailant
10. Will never be the same, even though most survivors, over time, develop ways to recover, cope, and go on with their lives
11. May be fearful of going to the police or a rape crisis center
12. May be reluctant to discuss the assault with members of her family, friends, and others because of the risk of rejection and embarrassment.

The prevalence of rape is one of society's most shameful phenomena. How we come to prevent the specter of rape and improve the lot of survivors of the crime depends on many factors: for example, using the positive capabilities of a variety of media to educate the public and finding ways to stop perpetrators from raping people (Amir, 1971; Eisler, 1995).

Myths About Rape

One of the most difficult obstacles that human services workers face in dealing with all forms and aspects of rape and sexual abuse is the abundance of debilitating myths that abound in society (Benedict, 1985; Ganas et al., 1999). Although here we focus on only a few of the main ones, there are many more myths in society that complicate the lives of survivors and impede the work of human services workers.

Principal Myths. Social and cultural myths about rape have received much attention in the literature on sexual abuse (Benedict, 1985, pp. 5–12). Six categories of society's most prevalent and harmful myths have been identified and refuted, as follows:

1. *Rape is sex.* The notion that rape equals sex is perhaps the most destructive myth of all. If we believe that rape is sex, then it follows that rape doesn't hurt (physically or psychologically) any more than sex does. We can even believe that the survivor enjoys and is erotically stimulated by it. The fact is that rape is no joke. Rape is violence, torture, and a life-threatening event. It is utterly humiliating. It is robbery of another person's essence by personal assault. Rape is *wrong, inexcusable,* and a *horrifying* crime (Sussman & Bordwell, 1981). However, rape cannot be entirely separated from sex because it partakes of the psychosocial context of sex (Eisler, 1995) and we cannot escape the fact that rape can result in both pregnancy and sexually transmitted diseases.

2. *Women "cry" rape to gain revenge.* Ganas and associates (1999) hypothesize that this myth permeates our society because such myths (1) provide comfort for our social structure (people don't want to believe that rape really occurred), (2) serve to focus the blame for sexual violence on victims rather than perpetrators, and (3) are easier to believe than the reality of knowing that rape can happen to anyone. Although "revenge" reports are sometimes heard, in the vast majority of instances when women report having been raped, the crime did happen.

3. *Rape is motivated by lust.* Eisler (1995) and Groth and Birnbaum (1979) believe that the motivation for rape is most likely to be domination, power, anger, revenge, control, frustration, or sadism. Benedict (1985, p. 8) and Eisler (1995, pp. 237–239) report that some men may come to associate sex with violence, thereby viewing women not as human beings but as objects of prey and/or domination and viewing sex as an act of power, control, and triumph. However, one counterpoint view, based on studies of the evolutionary theories of rape by Thornhill and Palmer (2000), suggests that the motives of rapists are primarily sexual, that the exercise of power is said to be mostly a means to an end.

4. *Rapists are weird loners.* No such contention can be supported by the research. Rapists come from every walk of life (Amir, 1971; Medea & Thompson, 1974, pp. 29–36). The rapist could be the man next door, a charming businessman, a laborer, a relative, a transient, or anyone else.

5. *Victims or survivors of rape provoked the rape or wanted to be raped.* Ganas and associates (1999) and Sussman and Bordwell (1981) have clearly shown that what the survivor does before the rape has little, if anything, to do with the rapist's decision to assault. Although most rapists deny that they are rapists, rationalize that women provoke or want it, or deny that the sexual assaults are rape, there are virtually no documented cases in which women have lured men into raping them. It is true that many women are unlucky enough to be in the wrong place at the time of the assault or are otherwise out of reach of assistance. However, being scantily dressed or otherwise vulnerable is never a cause, invitation, or a reason to be raped.

6. *Only bad women are raped.* This myth is one of the most blatant examples of a "blame the victim" attitude (Brownmiller, 1975). This myth is taken to mean that, if the woman has a "bad" reputation, the rape is justified. Brownmiller's point is that a person's alleged reputation has nothing to do with whether she deserves to be raped. Rape is rape! Whether the person is a professional hooker or a minister should make no difference. Neither deserves to be assaulted, and both are entitled to equal protection and treatment.

Who Believes Rape Myths?   It is not easy or simple to eradicate or even to refute the preceding myths in society at large (Ganas et al., 1999). Heppner and associates (1995) found that college students believed many myths about rape, and they discovered numerous differences in how men and women construed rape prevention messages. That study identified many sex differences in the ways men and women experienced rape perceptions and changed during and after a session on rape prevention intervention consisting of didactic, video, and question-and-answer discussion. Initially both men's and women's attitudes showed decreased belief in rape myths; at a two-month follow-up, however, men had regained more of their former beliefs than women had. The research implies a need for altering attitudes about rape through long-term preventive psycho-educational interventions (versus one-time interventions) that provide programming that is relevant and unique for both men and women.

The research of Varelas and Foley (1998) indicated that both black and white college students who strongly believed rape myths were more tolerant of rapists and less tolerant of victims than were those having weaker beliefs. Women with strong beliefs in the myths were less likely to report sexual assaults and to assist in legal actions against rapists. These studies point to the critical need for society at large as well as caregivers, families, and survivors, to receive informational and educational programs to expunge rape myths.

LONG-TERM CONSEQUENCES OF SEXUAL ABUSE OF CHILDREN

The sexual abuse of children wreaks lasting damage in the lives of victims. The protracted psychological trauma and resultant abnormal conditions inflicted on such victims are matters of great concern to society (Briere & Runtz, 1987, 1988, 1993; Kessler & Bieschke, 1999).

Psychological Trauma and Sequelae

Survivors of child sexual abuse are highly vulnerable to episodes of long-term intermittent revictimization. If survivors are left untreated they may experience recurring episodes of revictimization and exhibit debilitating symptoms (transcrisis points) for many years (Briere & Runtz, 1993; Kessler & Bieschke, 1999; Schetky, 1990).

Effects on Children of All Ages and Genders. Sexual abuse during childhood has received increased attention during the past several decades (Kessler & Bieschke, 1999). A good many researchers have explored and reported on the psychological trauma and sequelae (negative and damaging conditions that follow) that resulted from sexual abuse of female and male children of all ages. Some of the noteworthy findings of this research are that (1) histories of adult survivors of childhood sexual abuse show that adult survivor symptoms are significantly correlated with depression, anxiety, shame, and humiliation (Briere & Conte, 1993; Briere & Runtz, 1988; Kessler & Bieschke, 1999); (2) posttraumatic stress disorder is associated with childhood sexual abuse (Briere & Runtz, 1993); (3) survivors of childhood sexual abuse demonstrate a propensity to be victimized again later in adulthood (Kessler & Bieschke, 1999; Runtz, 1987; Russell, 1986); (4) revictimization or repetition of the sexual abuse tends to recur through the survivor's reenactment of the physical, sexual, or emotional abuse that was experienced during childhood (Schetky, 1990); (5) although girls are sexually assaulted more frequently than boys, the incidence of assaults on males age 19 and younger is alarming. (Child sexual abuse statistics vary among several researchers. Salter [1988] reporting on the incidence of child sexual abuse in nonclinical population studies, estimated that up to 38 percent of females and 11 percent of males had been sexually abused.) And studies indicate that the impact of resultant increased negative risk of clinical sequelae such as PTSD, aggressive behavior, and sexually related problems following sexual assault are greater for boys than for girls (Holmes & Slap, 1998); and (6) sexually abused children are at high risk for PTSD and symptoms of posttraumatic stress, anxiety, and depression in the immediate period after disclosure and termination of the abuse (McLeer et al., 1998).

Survivors of childhood sexual abuse do not usually experience repetition of their victimization on the conscious level; that is, they do not intentionally precipitate abuse. However, researchers have found in these survivors a tendency to experience revictimization such as rape, battering, assault, and other forms of abuse during adulthood (DeYoung, 1983; Donaldson & Gardner, 1985; Fromuth, 1983, 1986; Kessler & Bieschke, 1999; Kluft, 1990; Runtz, 1987; Russell, 1986).

Consequences of Sexual Assault on Adolescent Males.   Even when rape and sexual assault on children and adolescents does not later result in full-blown PTSD, the emotional and behavioral fallout is far reaching and destructive. In a survey of a nonclinical sample of 1385 adolescent Mexican American and White non-Hispanic males, 54 males who reported being sexually assaulted one or more times were compared with 1331 males who reported no history of sexual assault (Kuhn, Charleanea, & Chavez, 1998). Sexually assaulted male survivors were more emotionally distressed, socially isolated, deviant (for example, lying and stealing), likely to affiliate with deviant peers, and to come from homes in which there was parental substance use, than males who did not report sexual assault. Significant differences were not found between Mexican American and White non-Hispanic assault survivors.

Social Change Influences. According to Finkelhor (1984), several factors have contributed to the emergence of child sexual abuse as a problem for society. Resolution of the problem has been championed by the women's movement, the children's protection movement, and a coalition of groups with successful experience in promoting social issues (p. 3). It has been established that the sexual abuse of children is a worldwide problem and not one confined to the United States (pp. 5–6). The rate of abuse has grown with the advent of widespread divorce, remarriage, and easy conjugal pairings and dissolutions (increasing the amount of exposure of children to stepfathers, boyfriends, and lovers of children's mothers) (p. 7). Rapid change in sexual norms has accompanied an erosion of traditional, externalized sexual controls, aided and abetted by popular pornography, portraying children as sex objects (p. 8). The sexualization of life, which pervades the media, has led to new, increased, and heightened expectations. Such expectations, faced by many men who are locked into situations in which they feel a sense of sexual deprivation and lack of power and control, have contributed to the abuse of children by men seeking alternatives for their sexual gratification and other personal needs (p. 9). An additional factor, proposed by Finkelhor (1984), is that women have become less willing to accept subservient, passive, compliant, childlike roles. Some men, threatened by the assertiveness of women, have turned to children as compliant sex partners (p. 9).

Finkelhor (1979) reports that sexual deviance and victimization are more likely to emerge in families characterized by a high degree of social isolation. Such deviance has been observed in isolated Appalachian families as well as in some cities and suburbs. In fairly self-contained communities, the tolerance of sexual deviance, such as incest, may be passed on from generation to generation (pp. 25–26). Finkelhor also identifies role confusion and fear of abandonment as sources for the sociopathology of child abuse (pp. 26–27). He concurrently reports a positive correlation between the isolated circumstances of those in extreme poverty and the incidence of incest and child sexual abuse.

Perspectives on Long-Term Child Sexual Abuse.   Clearly, the toll that child sexual abuse extracts from society is devastating. Pedophiles—adults who have an abnormal sexual desire for children—and abusers are able to carry on their activities because children are largely powerless and vulnerable and because families and society have been reluctant to face and deal with the realities of the abuse.

There is abundant research to confirm the fact that adult survivors of childhood sexual abuse often experience enduring problems such as posttraumatic stress disorder (Christo, 1997) and psychological distress phenomena such as depression, alienation, inhibitions, social introversion, and interpersonal hypersensitivity (Lundberg-Love et al., 1992). Such survivors have also been found to manifest long-term physical health deficits (Moeller, Bachmann, & Moeller, 1993; Stevenson, 1999). Compared with nonabused populations, Moeller and associates (1993) found that survivors experienced more hospitalizations for illnesses, a greater number of physical and psychological problems, and overall poorer health. Kessler and Bieschke (1999) also found that survivors showed more symptoms of shame, dissociation, and further victimization during adulthood than did nonabused subjects. Clearly, the long-term consequences of child sexual abuse are not only excessive and debilitative dysfunctioning during childhood, but such consequences are also likely to manifest themselves during adulthood (Christo, 1997; Kessler & Bieschke, 1999; Lundberg-Love et al., 1992).

Criminal Justice System Initiatives.   We shall enumerate and discuss a number of initiatives that typify actions society might take to improve the criminal justice system's response to child sexual abuse.

1. *Law enforcement training.* According to Prior, Glaser, and Lynch (1997), an important initiative is to focus on training of police, who work with child abuse cases, to ensure that law enforcement personnel working with abused children are well versed in procedures needed to engender positive trust of the police by victims.

2. *The courts.* Another important example, described by Park and Renner (1998), is to educate members of the judicial system (the courts) to make improvements in taking child sexual abuse testimony. An example of such improvement is to sensitize courts and the criminal justice system in acknowledging the differing developmental capabilities between child and adult witnesses. In child abuse testimony, the aim is to ensure that questions asked to children would neither exceed their cognitive threshold of comprehension nor fail to respect the fact that children are not responsible for their sexuality by definition of being a child. The purpose of the latter is to absolve the child from blame and guilt.

3. *System interventions.* An initiative, described in empirical social work studies by Henry (1997), is aimed at ameliorating the level of trauma experienced in child victims,

following disclosure of sexual abuse, through improving the methods of social system investigative interviews and interventions. Such improved methods require that the interviews be done by persons who are competent in engendering trust and who possess the personal qualities and training to effectively assist child victims. The improved social system interventions are described by Henry (1997) as intervening in ways that the majority of children feel positive support in dealing with issues such as their stress, personal loss at being removed from the home, and trauma caused by dealing with the legal system.

4. *Factors related to prosecution.* A key element in the successful prosecution of perpetrators is the accurate and timely investigative reporting and recording in cases of child sexual abuse. Brewer, Rowe, and Brewer (1997), studying cases involving recently disclosed abuse, found that offenders who were charged with abusing multiple child victims were significantly more likely to be successfully prosecuted than were offenders in cases involving less recently reported abuse and offenders charged with abusing only one victim. On a more global view, Finkelhor's (1994) investigations found that, in the criminal justice processing of child sexual abusers, compared with other violent criminals, slightly fewer child sexual abusers are prosecuted. But of those prosecuted, slightly more are convicted.

In cases where families decline to prosecute offenders, Cross, Martell, McDonald, and Ahl (1999) found that 41 percent of the sexually abused children were placed outside the home since the first interview, as compared to 19 percent of children in cases where families accepted prosecution. Cross and associates further found that children were significantly more likely to be placed outside the home when the alleged abuse lasted more than one month, when families were found to be more dysfunctional, when maternal support was lacking, and when cases were declined for prosecution. The implication is that families should opt for prosecution and generally resist efforts to convince families to decline prosecution.

5. *Monitoring of offenders on probation.* Studies reveal that most offenders are sentenced to probation with a condition of inpatient or outpatient treatment (Lurigio, Jones, & Smith, 1995). In such cases, close monitoring of offenders and coordination between therapists and probation officers becomes imperative. Criminal justice investigations reported by Weeks and Widom (1998) indicated that, among incarcerated adult male sex offenders, perpetrators reported higher rates of their own childhood sexual abuse than other criminal offenders. That finding suggests that close monitoring is necessary in managing probationary treatment of child sexual offenders.

6. *Specialized police.* More and more police are becoming specially skilled and educated regarding child sexual abuse. Maguire (1993) recommends that police expertise be more fully used by practitioners, the media, the public, and criminal justice personnel in child sexual abuse work. Maguire suggests that scholarly efforts (research studies) focus on improving delivery of specialized police services to incorporate police expertise within the child protection team that already includes medical, law, social work, and mental health professionals.

These six areas we have discussed represent a sample of the large body of research concerning the criminal justice system's response to child sexual abuse. Caregivers who are involved in cases of child sexual abuse should become familiar with key personnel and procedures of the criminal justice system in their locale, keep abreast of current research and literature on child abuse, and become involved in advocacy and initiatives to stem the tide of abuse. One example of current research and writing that human services professionals may find invaluable is the book by Seth C. Kalichman titled *Mandated Reporting of Suspected Child Abuse: Ethics, Law, and Policy* (second edition, 1999).

Phases of Child Sexual Abuse

According to Murphy (1985), who was reporting on the dynamics of sexual abuse developed by Sgroi (1982), the behavior of the abuser may be traced through five phases: (1) engagement, (2) sexual interaction, (3) secrecy, (4) disclosure, and (5) suppression. These phases apply to both intra- and extrafamilial abuse.

Engagement Phase.   The abuser's objective in the engagement phase is to get the child involved in sexual activity with the abuser. Both access to the child and opportunity (privacy) are needed if the abuser is to be successful. Therefore, if one were looking for possible instances of unreported abuse, one would identify times and situations when the potential abuser and the child were alone together. One must also look for different strategies that two different types of abusers (child molesters and child rapists) may employ (Murphy, 1985, p. 1).

Molesters tend to use enticement and entrapment to get the child engaged in sexual activity. *Enticement* may include deceit, trickery, rewards, or the use of adult authority to tell the child in a matter-of-fact way that the child is expected to participate. *Entrapment* is used to manipulate the child into feeling obligated to participate through traps, blackmail, and so forth. Molesters may make pornographic pictures or videotapes and convince the child that there is no choice other than going along with the secret activity, and may also seek to impose guilt by making the child feel responsible for the abuse (Murphy, 1985, p. 1).

Child rapists use *threat* (particularly the threat of harm) or the imposition of superior physical *force* to engage the child in the abusive activity. Typically, the rapist will threaten to kill or injure the child or someone dear to the child or threaten to commit suicide himself, convincing the child that he or she will be blamed for the rapist's death if the child resists or reports the rape. In using superior force, the rapist may simply overpower the child, restrain the child by tying him or her, give the child drugs or alcohol, or physically brutalize the child into submission (Murphy, 1985, p. 1).

The vast majority (about 80 percent) of abusers use the first two strategies—enticement and entrapment. Abusers tend to repeat their engagement patterns and show little tendency to move from nonviolent to violent strategies. Molesters are apt to consistently entice or trap children, whereas child rapists tend to use threat or force almost exclusively. The strategy used by the abuser is an important issue in treatment, because survivors typically wonder throughout their lives why they permitted it to occur (Murphy, 1985, p. 1).

Sexual Interaction Phase.   Types of abuse may include (blatant or surreptitious) masturbation (the abuser may masturbate prior to making physical contact with the child), fondling, digital penetration, oral or anal penetration, dry intercourse, intercourse, forcing or coercing the child into touching the abuser's genitals, forced prostitution, and pornography. Children may be coaxed into cooperating, though not consenting, because abusers—as adult authority figures—often command, engage, or enlist cooperation from the child. Children lack the maturity, experience, and age to be able to consent, but they may cooperate because of their subservient status (Murphy, 1985, p. 2; Plummer, 1984, p. 145).

Secrecy Phase.   Abusers communicate to children that others must not discover the sexual activity. The objective of abusers is to continue the activity. This necessitates avoiding detection and maintaining access to the child while continuing the abuse. The techniques for maintaining the secrecy may involve incorporating "rules" or "games," implicating the child in the activity, and setting the child up to be responsible for keeping the secret (Bass & Thornton, 1983; Murphy, 1985, p. 2).

Disclosure Phase.   Sometimes the abuser is discovered accidentally. Other times the abuse is disclosed intentionally by the child or someone else. Intentional disclosure is usually made by the child. Intentional disclosure often enormously complicates the abuse because parents and others refuse to face it or believe it. Accidental discovery may come as a result of such consequences as pregnancy, STDs, sexual acting out, promiscuity, and physical trauma. The way the abuse is disclosed can affect the child's self-esteem and reaction to treatment. For instance, disbelieving adults sometimes respond by blaming and punishing the child—and allow the sexual abuse to continue (Molmen, 1982, pp. 35–36; Murphy, 1985, p. 2).

Suppression Phase.   The suppression phase may begin as soon as disclosure takes place. Suppression may be attempted by the abuser, the child, the parents, other family members, professionals, the community, or an institution. There are many reasons for suppression: fear of publicity; fear of reprisal; to protect the reputation of a family, an abuser, or an institution; to avoid prosecution; to avoid responsibility; to protect the child; to avoid embarrassment; to avoid the kinds of confrontation and intervention required to deal effectively with the difficult and sensitive situation; and fear of getting involved.

Survival Phase.   On the basis of our own experience and the reports of a number of other writers (Besharov, 1990; Kendrick, 1991), we have added a sixth phase, the survival phase. It is during this phase that we recommend implementing strategies for helping the child and the family respond to and recover from the abuse as much as possible. Phase 6 includes stopping the abuse, providing needed medical and psychological treatment for the child, and helping the significant others close to the child to overcome the trauma, fear, anger, betrayal, and despair caused by the abuse (Benedict, 1985; Grossman & Sutherland, 1983). It also involves preventing further abuse (Bass & Thornton, 1983; Colao & Hosansky, 1983; Plummer, 1984; Townley, 1985) and prosecuting and/or getting counseling for the abuser (Benedict, 1985).

Pervasiveness, Blame, and Prediction in Survivors of Childhood Sexual Abuse

Information regarding the extent to which children are sexually abused varies from study to study. So also does the attribution of blame and the degree to which child abuse contributes to the development of PTSD. These issues are herewith briefly discussed.

Widespread Abuse.   With the passing of the Vietnam era, we might erroneously conclude that PTSD has seen its heyday—given that the same terrible errors in national
judgment are not repeated. However, the discovery of PTSD as an identifiable malady
has led investigators to examine other traumatized populations aside from veterans. Although the occasional headline sensationalizes a mother throwing her newborn, or even
a baby up to 1 year old, into a dumpster, the untold story of child abuse involves the
adult survivors of childhood physical and, more particularly, sexual abuse. The incidence of child sexual abuse reported in nonclinical population studies varies. Morrow
and Smith (1995) reported that such abuse ranges from 20 to 45 percent of women in the
United States and Canada. Both Moody (1994) and Ratna and Mukergee (1998) reported that 10 percent of all men in the United States were sexually abused during childhood. Moody (1994) estimated that between 19 and 64 percent of women in the United
States experienced sexual abuse prior to the age of 18 and Ratna and Mukergee (1998)
estimated that one in six women were sexually abused as children. One random survey
found that more than one in four women and one in six men were sexually molested at
least once during their childhood (p. 251). A very conservative estimate by Wyatt and
Powell (1988) put the number of reported child sexual abuse cases at 200,000 a year.

Attribution of Blame.   Different ways of ascribing blame has been shown to affect
how survivors of child sexual abuse cope with the effects of the earlier trauma. Arata
(1999) studied the role of child sexual assault, attributions of blame, and coping on adjustment to rape. Undergraduate females were assessed for child sexual abuse history,
adult victimization history, attributions of blame for the adult assault, coping strategies
for the adult rape, and trauma symptoms. Rape survivors with a history of child sexual
abuse were found to have higher levels of trauma symptoms, made greater use of nervous
and cognitive coping strategies, and were more likely to blame themselves or society.

Child Abuse as Predictor of PTSD.   Child sexual abuse has been shown to be predictive of the development of PTSD in later life (Darves-Bornoz et al., 1998; Kessler &
Bieschke, 1999; Pfefferbaum, 1997; Regehr, Cadell, & Jansen, 1999). In a comparison
of the prevalence of PTSD and other diagnoses in three groups of abused children,
Ackerman and associates (1998) studied three groups of abused children: sexual abuse
(SA) only, physical abuse (PA) only, and both (BOTH). Children in the BOTH group
had more diagnoses overall. PTSD was significantly comorbid (disorder or trauma
caused by two variables) with most affective disorders. On the Child Behavior Checklist,
caregivers rated girls less disturbed than boys and the SA group less disturbed than the
other groups. Teachers rated the boys more adversely than girls but did not report differences by abuse group. A younger age of onset of SA and coercion to maintain secrecy
predicted a higher number of total diagnoses. Also, children had more diagnoses when
PA had come from males rather than from females. The research of Darves-Bornoz and
associates (1998) indicated that added physical violence such as physical assault during
rape of children was predictive of chronic PTSD and early psychological and behavioral
attitudes, low self-esteem, permanent feelings of emptiness and running away, and early
emotional disorders such as agoraphobia and depressive disorders.

Dynamics in Adulthood.   The aftermath of childhood sexual abuse cuts a wide traumatic and astounding swath for adult survivors (Kessler & Bieschke, 1999; Kreidler &
England, 1990). A long list of studies have found that a significant number of females

(institutionalized, outpatient, psychiatric patients, and clients in clinics) were sexually abused as children (Briere & Runtz, 1987; Consentino et al., 1995; Coons, Bowman, Pellow, & Schneider, 1989; Craine, Henson, Colliver, & MacLean, 1988; Everill & Waller, 1995; Finkelhor, 1993; Hunter, 1995; Kessler & Bieschke, 1999; Lindberg & Distad, 1985; Mennen & Meadow, 1995; Morrow & Smith, 1995; Ratna & Mukergee, 1998; Salter, 1995). Adult women survivors consistently demonstrate the symptoms similar to Vietnam veterans, in addition to compulsive sexual behavior, sadomasochistic sexual fantasy, sexual identity issues, and loss of sexual interest (Briere & Runtz, 1987; Craine et al., 1988). Survivors also experience an increase in rape, battery, sexual abuse, and other forms of physical and emotional abuse in adulthood (Coons et al., 1989; Kessler & Bieschke, 1999; Schetky, 1990), and, like veterans, are prone to use alcohol and drugs to submerge bad memories from awareness, as well as to engage in suicidal ideation and attempts (Kovach, 1986; Rew, 1989). Male survivors of childhood sexual abuse fare no better and report essentially the same symptoms with concomitant sexual orientation ambiguity, mistrust of adult males, homophobia, and body image disturbances (Myers, 1986). Some research indicates that early sexual abuse may be one precursor of vulnerability to date and acquaintance rape in women.

DATE AND ACQUAINTANCE RAPE

Much of the research reported on date and acquaintance rape deals with sexual assaults occurring on college and university campuses. Mills and Granoff (1992) found that 28 percent of college women surveyed acknowledged that they had been victims of rape or attempted rape. Few told anyone, although those reporting attempted rape were more likely to tell someone than were those who had actually been raped. A number of male respondents admitted to committing what is legally defined as rape and admitted to continuing to make sexual advances even when their dates had told them "No!"

Dominant Perspectives on Date and Acquaintance Rape

Humphreys and Herold (1996) identified three main theoretical perspectives that drive and inform date and acquaintance rape: socialization, psychopathology, and feminist theories. *Socialization theories* of date rape emphasize gender socialization processes that promote a rape-supportive culture (attitudes and beliefs) wherein sexual coercion is seen as normal and acceptable behavior (Truman, Tokar, & Fischer, 1996). *Psychopathology theories* imply that rapists are psychologically maladjusted people who represent a small segment of the population. The focus of psychopathological theories emphasizes that behavior is derived from within the individual, and not from social pressures or interactions. *Feminist-based theories* have emphasized the patriarchal culture and the unequal power distribution between women and men as causes of date and acquaintance rape (Humphreys & Herold, 1996). Most of the current research reports and writings draw on at least one of these perspectives.

Date Rape Risk

Date rape survivors in college have been found to be more likely to have experienced stress and maltreatment, and negative home environment/neglect during childhood than were women who reported no date rape experience (Sanders & Moore, 1999). Date rape participants in the Sanders and Moore study were also more likely to have experienced sexual abuse during childhood. But the relationship between date rape and other negative childhood experiences remained significant after the sexual abuse variable was teased out. Thus forms of maltreatment that were not specifically sexual were also associated with an increased likelihood of sexual victimization and the consequences of trauma later in life. Such maltreatment was significantly associated with dissociation, depression, and other psychological symptoms of trauma.

Shapiro and Chwarz (1997), investigating the relationship between date rape and sexual self-esteem in women, found that women who had been raped reported significantly more trauma symptoms and lower sexual self-esteem in the areas of moral judgment, adaptiveness, and control than did women who had never been raped. Results suggest that date rape has significant consequences for women, with implications for clinical treatment of women who have been date raped. Himelein and associates (1994) suggested "that child sexual abuse is an underlying risk factor for both heightened sexual activity and sexual victimization in dating"—that is, child sexual abuse sequelae. It is further suggested that precocious knowledge of sex, confusion about sexual norms, isolation, and neediness might predispose a young abuse survivor to early and frequent sexual activity, which may in turn increase the risk of dating victimization (p. 414). Alcohol consumption as a risk factor has also been linked to date and acquaintance rape (Norris & Cubbins, 1992). A study by Abbey, McAuslan, and Ross (1998) found that college men's mutual effects of beliefs and experiences with regard to dating, sexuality, and alcohol consumption increased the likelihood that a male would misperceive a female companion's sexual intentions, and that this *misperception* may lead to sexual assault. It is noted that the use of a *date rape drug* (gamma hydroxy butyrate or GHB) in contrast, in the commission of a sexual assault, constitutes a premeditated and *deliberate* assault. Whether sexual assault is associated with either alcohol or date rape drug consumption, it is still of serious concern (Boyd, 2000).

Regarding alcohol use and date and acquaintance rape, researchers Schwartz and Leggett (1999) found that women raped while intoxicated were not less emotionally affected and did not blame themselves any more than women who were raped by force while not intoxicated. It is interesting to note that most of these women did not classify their experiences as rape, although all were victims under criminal law. Norris and Cubbins (1992) found that three-fourths of acquaintance rapes involved drinking behavior, and that if both members of a dating couple had been consuming alcohol, the rape was not judged as severely as when only the woman had been drinking. In the latter case, the man was likely viewed as taking advantage of a vulnerable woman. The implication was that if a woman reported that she had been raped after drinking with her date, her report may not have been taken as seriously and the impact of psychological trauma may have been underestimated.

Preventing Date, Acquaintance, and Other Forms of Rape

Mills and Granoff (1992) and Dunn, Vail-Smith, and Knight (1999) suggest that continuing educational and support services (for both men and women) are critically needed to address, in a culturally unbiased manner, the causes and prevention of date and acquaintance rape. Educational programs, especially at the secondary school level, have been recommended as preventive measures in reducing date and acquaintance sexual assaults (Page, 1997). Tang (1998) views collective and social actions on the part of women's groups and education as important tools to counter sexual assault in society. Tang cites several pressing problems that need to be addressed through such educational programs: underreporting of sexual assault; low founding (lack of establishing evidence), charging, and conviction rates; the status of rape shield rules; and the defense of honest but mistaken belief consent. Such programs teach students to avoid potentially dangerous situations and how to respond in the event of perpetration.

Ullman, Karabatsos, and Koss (1999) found that both victim and offender use of alcohol prior to attack were directly associated with more severe victimization of women and that alcohol use played both direct and indirect roles in the outcomes of sexual assaults. Ullman and associates recommended that rape and alcohol abuse prevention efforts can benefit from incorporating information about alcohol's role in different sexual assault contexts. We recommend that such prevention initiatives also address strategies to avoid assaults connected with the use of date rape drugs. Frazier, Valtinson, and Candell (1994) demonstrated that coeducational and interactive rape prevention programs can succeed in the short run. Their preventive interventions, presented to members of fraternities and sororities, showed that participants endorsed significantly fewer rape-supportive attitudes immediately following the interventions than did control group members. But, like Heppner and colleagues' (1995) participants, experimental and control group members no longer differed after one month. Clearly, the research indicates that rape prevention programs should be comprehensive and ongoing, rather than programmed as one-time interventions.

In evaluating date rape prevention programs for college students, Lanier and Elliot (1997) found that males manifested more rape-tolerant attitudes than females. That finding appears to indicate that rape prevention programs should focus heavily on male responsibility for prevention of date and acquaintance rape. The value and effect of profoundly verbalizing no in situations where women are vulnerable to rape cannot be underestimated. Sawyer, Pinciaro, and Jessell's (1998) studies of the effects of coercion and verbal consent, on university students' perception of date rape, concluded that in the absence of a verbalized "no," university students' perceptions of rape are not consistent with current legal definitions. In other words, even though an act is legally defined as rape, male students are generally more prone to deny that a rape occurred unless an assertive or aggressive no is verbalized by the victim. Another prevention strategy, reported by Lanier and associates (1998) used a theatrical production based on social learning. Results showed that both male and female subjects, who viewed the intervention play, demonstrated evidence of a modest improvement in attitudes toward date rape compared with control subjects. The researchers concluded that social learning theory can be used to design effective interventions (such as plays, psychodrama, videos, skits, and role play) for use in date rape prevention.

DYNAMICS OF SEXUAL ABUSE IN CHILDHOOD

Manifestations of PTSD do not just spring forth full blown in adulthood (McLeer, Deblinger, Henry, & Orvaschel, 1992). Sexually abused children have significantly more specific PTSD symptoms than do physically abused and other psychiatrically hospitalized children (Deblinger, McLeer, Atkins, & Ralphe, 1989; McLeer et al., 1992; Wolfe, Gentile, & Wolfe, 1989). In addition, these children have a wide variety of other problems that include concentration difficulties, aggressive behavior, social withdrawing, somatic complaints, overcompliance, depression, antisocial tendencies, behavioral regression, poor body image/self-esteem, hyperactivity, suicidal ideation, and extreme, generalized fears (Conte & Schuerman, 1988; Justice & Justice, 1979; Sgroi, Porter, & Blick, 1982). Abused children typically either internalize the trauma and become withdrawn and depressed or externalize the trauma and become aggressive and angry. Although the foregoing symptoms may be indicative of many disorders of childhood, the following are not and are rarely ever found with any stressor other than sexual abuse (McLeer et al., 1992; Salter, 1988, pp. 230–235).

Sexually abused children come early to school and stay late and are rarely, if ever, absent. They barricade themselves in their rooms or otherwise hide and attempt to seal themselves off from their assailants. They engage in inappropriate and persistent sexual play with peers. They have a detailed and age-inappropriate understanding of sexual behavior and may have physical and somatic symptoms with overlying sexual content. They may engage in excessive, compulsive, and even public masturbation and may even approach other adults sexually. Small children may act out sexually with real or stuffed animals. Teenagers may run away and engage in prostitution. These behaviors provide a template with which varying patterns of psychopathology seen in adult survivors are drawn (Goodwin, 1988).

DYNAMICS OF SEXUAL ABUSE IN FAMILIES

The incestuous family may operate much like an alcoholic or battered family does in developing a series of messages or rules that pivot around denial, duplicity, deceit, role confusion, violence, and social isolation (Courtois, 1988, p. 45). Children receive messages such as

1. Do not show feelings, especially anger.
2. Be in control at all times; do not ask for help.
3. Deny what is happening, and do not believe your own senses/perceptions.
4. No one is trustworthy.
5. Keep the secret because no one will believe you anyway.
6. Be ashamed of yourself; you are to blame for everything.

Intergenerational Transmission of Sexual Abuse

Typically, there is intergenerational transmission of sexual abuse and other severe maladjustment in the family, such as battering or alcoholism. Incestuous fathers display inordinate amounts of jealousy and paranoia over their daughters' dating and relationships with other males and attempt to rigidly control behavior through threats and intimidation (Salter, 1988, p. 237). Abusive fathers are controlling tyrants who erect a facade of respectability in the community and often try to isolate their children and spouses or partners by forbidding them to socialize outside the home and refusing to let them have close friends. However, because of their sensitivity to power, they become meek and contrite when confronted with their abuse (Herman, 1981, p. 178).

Mothers are often oppressed and economically dependent, abused by their mates, and products of incestuous families themselves (Courtois, 1988, pp. 54–55; Herman, 1981, pp. 178–179). Mothers may be physically or mentally disabled, causing the eldest daughter to take on the role of "little mother," which extends to fulfilling the father's sexual demands (Herman, 1981, p. 179). Although some mothers may confront the abuse once they discover it, many others engage in denial and helplessness, and when confronted with the reality of the situation may revictimize the child by physical or verbal abuse (Salter, 1988, p. 209).

MEMORIES OF CHILDHOOD SEXUAL ABUSE

The term "false memories" has recently come to be used to identify instances when people mentally falsify events that occurred in the past, especially traumatic events. Many people are not conscious of such falsifications. Workers in the helping professions should be conversant with and prepared to deal with survivors and offenders who manifest false memories.

False Memories

The "false memory" concept applied both to work with adults who were abused as children and to perpetrators of abuse has raised concern and controversy among human services workers (Rubin, 1996). Enns, McNeilly, Corkery, and Gilbert (1995) presented a detailed review of the historical, theoretical, empirical, and ethical issues, as well as implications for psychotherapy, research, and societal changes needed. The research findings indicate that psychotherapy with and advocacy of survivors should be done by workers who are highly trained and skilled in dealing with the trauma, the repressed and dissociated memory issues, the risks, and the needs of survivors of child sexual abuse. Similarly, professionals who deal with perpetrators' memories should have a thorough understanding of the complex forms of abuser memory and forgetting that are frequently encountered. The discrepancies, emotions, dissociations, memory blackouts, and discomfort with traumatic memories may affect the way both survivors and perpetrators perceive the past abusive events (Rubin, 1996).

Doubts and Controversy

The studies of lost and distorted memories of childhood traumas by Bremner (1998) have raised doubts about the degree to which traumatic memories are susceptible to distortion due to misleading and suggestive statements (as may occur during psychotherapy). The findings also suggest that stress as well as the adult's neuroanatomical conditions can lead to modifications in memory traces. Even so, at some unconscious memory level the person almost never forgets the essential details of the source of the trauma. Conversely, from the results of Feigon and de Rivera's (1998) "recovered memory" survey of 154 psychiatrists, it was concluded that the numbers of false accusations of childhood sexual abuse, appearing to emerge from the psychotherapy of adults, constitute a real problem requiring public acknowledgment as such by the mental health professions. Their study indicates that the specific content of false memories extracted from client interviews depends on the particular interviewer, the way questions are asked, the context in which the interview takes place, and the emotional state of the interviewee. Thus survivors need helpers who can deal appropriately with their healing and recovery. Perpetrators need workers who can help them deal with the many problems associated with their acts, memories, forgetting, fears, and repression of the sexual abuse they carried out on others.

INTERVENTION STRATEGIES WITH CHILDREN

Programs, centers, and agencies for helping survivors of sexual abuse have been established in most cities. Telephone hotlines and rape crisis centers are now within reach of the majority of the population. Listings of resources and agencies to assist survivors throughout the country have been compiled by a number of researchers, such as Bass and Thornton (1983), Benedict (1985), Grossman and Sutherland (1983), and Townley (1985). Survivors can also acquire information and assistance through crisis hotlines, community mental health centers, or emergency line 911. In most cities, people needing help can look in the telephone directory under "Rape" or call the local number of the Department of Human Services. Almost any practicing nurse, psychologist, social worker, certified counselor, or other human services worker can refer survivors and their families to appropriate sources of assistance. Rape and other forms of sexual assault cover a broad spectrum of abuse and require a wide variety of crisis intervention strategies. The conceptual basis for the intervention strategies is the six-step model discussed in Chapter 2. We will present three more-or-less representative cases to illustrate various kinds and stages of crisis work.

Individual Therapy for Children

Assessment includes thorough documentation of the abusive events for possible legal use. Using anatomically correct dolls helps confirm what actually occurred in the abuse. No specific measures currently exist for measuring the effects of psychological abuse in young children, although a complete psychological evaluation may be useful in gauging the child's overall level of functioning (McLeer et al., 1992; Wheeler & Berliner, 1988, p. 235). The previously mentioned behavioral indicators of childhood sexual abuse and PTSD criteria for children are currently the best indicators that sexual abuse has occurred.

Play Therapy Preferred.   Play therapy is the recommended treatment of choice for abused children (White & Allers, 1994, pp. 390–391). Farrell and associates (1998) and Weaver and associates (1998) found that selected cognitive behavioral interventions (skills learned through procedures such as relaxation training, positive self-talk, cognitive restructuring, stress inoculation, and emotive imagery) may effectively decrease the anxiety and depression levels in sexually abused children (aged 8–10) who exhibit PTSD symptoms. Concerning play therapy with abused children, White and Allers (1994) identified characteristic behaviors that maltreated children may manifest during play as developmental immaturity, opposition and aggression, withdrawal and passivity, self-deprecation and self-destruction, hypervigilance, inappropriate sexuality, and dissociation. They advocate play therapy for alleviating the effects of these behaviors and the traumas that caused such behaviors.

Developmental immaturity is evidenced through delayed play age (cognitive and language delays) as compared with the play age of nonabused children. Abused children may show either a loss of recently acquired play skills or a failure to learn skills appropriate to their age. *Opposition* and *aggression* are present when abused children exhibit impaired and aggressive play behaviors, such as hostility and physically or sexually abusive acts toward other children during play. *Withdrawal* and *passivity* are used by abused children to exhibit behaviors such as avoidance, fearfulness, isolation, passiveness, inattentiveness, and noncooperation. *Self-deprecating* and *self-destructive* children often show low self-esteem; describe themselves as bad, incapable, or ugly; and are more likely to use a toy truck to hit or jab themselves as a self-destructive gesture, versus swinging the toy at another child. *Hypervigilance,* through heightened awareness, often signals abused children's expectations of being punished, and such children scan the surroundings for cues of external danger. *Inappropriate sexual behavior* may be seen when sexually abused children exhibit socially unacceptable sexual activities such as open masturbation, excessive sexual curiosity, and exposure of the genitals. Such children may assume that any relationship with an adult will include sexual contact, and they may invite the adult to be involved with them sexually and/or grab the adult's breast or genitalia. *Dissociation* is a mechanism used by abused children to deny and avoid the painfulness of their traumatic experience. Abused children may be oblivious to the presence of others or be absorbed and seemingly hypnotized in their own dreamlike state. Play therapy with these children should be conducted only by people who are specially trained in the process and in the use of materials that are known to be safe, appropriate, and therapeutic when used with abused and neglected children.

Affirmation and Safety Needed

Initial intervention techniques call for intentionally and positively managing the crisis of disclosure and the resulting fear and anxiety. Affirmation and validation are crucial in regard to what has happened, what is happening, and what will happen to the child, the offender, and significant others. Our admonition in the PTSD chapter on *not* using flooding techniques with children holds even more firmly with sexual abuse. Because small children are not fully developed, most instrumental and operant behavioral techniques that may be used with adult survivors are also not efficacious. Yet anxiety about and fear of the abusive events and the abuser need to be reduced, and this calls for reexposure to the trauma. This work is best accomplished by use of play therapy, where the child is given puppets, dolls, and drawing materials to safely distance him- or herself from the trauma. By gently and directively encouraging reenactment and discussion through the safety of the play material, the therapist may enable the child to gradually extinguish fear and anxiety feelings and develop skills in communicating healthy inner feelings and experiences without revictimizing the child (Baker, 1995; Gil & Johnson, 1993; Merrick, Allen, & Crase, 1994; Oates, O'Toole, Lynch, Stern, & Cooney, 1994; Sadowski & Loesch, 1993).

Regaining a Sense of Control

Anger and grief are emotional by-products for children of sexual abuse. Venting of these feelings should be encouraged, particularly if most adults are not comfortable with them and may attempt to repress such feelings when children exhibit them (Wheeler & Berliner, 1988, p. 237). Drawing, painting, modeling clay, sand play, writing, and learning to verbalize emotions are all therapeutic vehicles to ventilate angry feelings and loss. Play techniques can also give the child a renewed sense of empowerment by allowing play figures to be acted on, thus reducing long-standing feelings of helplessness (Sadowski & Loesch, 1993). Punching out a Bobo doll or picking up a play telephone and calling the police can give children a sense of control in a situation where they have little (Salter, 1988, p. 215). Along with relaxation and other stress reduction measures, play techniques can be used to teach the child to control anger when the child constantly acts out with peers or significant others.

Education

Education about adult sex offenders and sex itself are important for children because they will have little if any knowledge of why or what has happened to them. Children need to know that it is the adult and not the child who made the mistake. Where physical injuries resulted, children need to have these explained and need to be told that their bodies will be OK. Many children believe that others will be able to tell what happened by looking at them. Children need to know that although they may feel different, sexual abuse does not make them look different.

Cognitively, children usually have little understanding of sexual functions. Typically they will not initiate questions about sex, but when workers initiate education about sex through slides or books, children will respond with their own questions. Every child who has been sexually assaulted needs some type of sex education and information on what the assault means (Baker, 1995; Gil & Johnson, 1993; McLeer et al., 1992; Merrick, Allen, & Crase, 1994; Oates et al., 1994; Salter, 1988, pp. 217–218).

Providing appropriate learning experiences for young children is quite different from educating people in other age and developmental groups. In addition to the play therapy catalysts (such as drawing, painting, modeling, and sand play mentioned earlier), a highly effective means of teaching important social and survival lessons to children is through professionally developed puppetry programs. One example is the Kids on the Block (1995) system, which uses the unique and dynamic medium of puppetry to educate children and their adult caregivers on how to think about and respond to important and emotionally charged issues that impact children's lives. Trained volunteers perform with puppet characters designed to realistically represent children and the dilemmas they may face. Through carefully researched and scripted dialogues, these puppets ("children") talk about important issues and then engage in interactive question-and-answer periods with children in the audience, who converse directly with the puppets. In 1996, more than 1700 Kids on the Block puppet troupes were located in all 50 states and in more than 28 different countries (D. Degnan, personal communication, January 22, 1996). This form of puppetry has proved to be an effective strategy for expunging children's myths and misconceptions about physical and sexual abuse and replacing them with facts and sensitivity (Sullivan & Robinson, 1994).

Assertiveness training may be seen as more a preventive measure to keep children out of harm's way than a remedial measure for sexually abused children. Yet sexually abused children have learned to be compliant to deviant requests and clearly need to learn how to "Just say NO!" (Salter, 1988, p. 219). Because abused children are at greater risk for revictimization, teaching them cues and warning signs is important so that they can avoid future abuse (Wheeler & Berliner, 1988, p. 242).

Prevention

Preventive approaches in schools and families can probably do much to reduce child sexual abuse by equipping children and caregivers to deal effectively with it before it happens (Cashwell, Bloss, & McFarland, 1995; Cole, 1995). Minard (1993, p. 14) recommends that preventive programs be implemented in the primary grades and continued throughout the school years. Indications are that rape prevention efforts are more effective when they are delivered through well-organized, systematic, interactive, long-term, and dynamic educational interventions. The use of puppetry, such as the Kids on the Block (1995) system, is one example of a primary prevention and educational program that works.

INTERVENTION STRATEGIES FOR RAPE AND BATTERY: THE CASE OF JEANETTE

Jeanette is a 50-year-old teacher. She has been living alone in a small house since the younger of her two children went away to college two months ago. Jeanette was divorced seven years ago. When she returned home from the store at 9:30 P.M. last evening and emerged from her car in her driveway, she was met by a gunman in his middle 20s. She dropped a small bag of groceries and some items from her purse as she was abducted at gunpoint and forced into the gunman's car, which was parked on the street. Jeanette was beaten, driven away to an isolated area several miles from her home, raped, beaten again, robbed, and abandoned, bleeding and bruised, with her clothing in shreds. She was weak and dazed, but found the strength and courage to find her way to the nearest house, where she called for help. Now Jeanette is experiencing physical and emotional trauma. She is amazed at herself for being alive, because she believes the attacker meant to kill her. (Jeanette's case is stranger rape—most rape will come from someone who is known.)

Immediate Aftermath

In some situations the most helpful and appropriate immediate response from a crisis worker is empathy and assurance that the survivor is still alive. Jeanette's rape is a case in point.

Jeanette: I spent most of the night in the emergency room. It was horrible—the rape. I don't know how I came out alive and without any broken bones. He intended to kill me. Part of the time I was in a daze. I don't know what came over me. I must have blacked out. He may have thought I was dead. I don't know how long I lay out there alone after he left me. I certainly didn't fight back or protest.

CW: Jeanette, I'm so proud of you for the way you handled it. You did whatever it took to stay alive. You saved yourself, and that took courage. Whatever you did, whether it was blacking out or offering no protests, was right, because it preserved your life, and that's the important thing right now.

Jeanette: Well, that's probably a good way to look at it. Right now, I'm tired—exhausted. I thank the Lord I'm here. I feel like I'm in a sort of twilight zone. Maybe part of me did die. I'm feeling so alone and vulnerable.

CW: So you're needing rest and comfort now. After what you've been through, I can see how you would be feeling like you're in a twilight zone. My concern for you right now is that you'll be able to get some rest in a safe and comfortable place. Where would you feel safe in resting the remainder of today and tonight?

Jeanette: I don't know. Home, I guess, but . . . (*Pause, with apprehensive look.*)

CW: But you'd like someone there with you whom you really trust and feel comfortable with. Who might that be in this locale?

Jeanette: Well, my sister. I'd want her there with me. She's the only one I can think of. I don't think I can go into that driveway by myself today. There's no way I'd go there after dark by myself.

The crisis worker's intuition is right when she guesses that the place of safety and comfort for Jeanette would be her own home but that the frightening part would be getting past the place in her driveway where she was abducted. The crisis worker is also correct in reassuring Jeanette for her actions, which brought her out alive.

An important issue for rape survivors is control. Jeanette has experienced an emotionally draining loss of control to the attacker, and she needs to be reassured that that loss of control is neither total nor permanent. She did what she had to do to survive, and that took courage. It is important to her for others to recognize her and give her credit. Whatever small amount of control she has, she can build on as a basis for beginning her long journey toward recovery. Also, the crisis worker does not impose on Jeanette a place for resting or an accompanying person of trust and understanding. These immediate choices are both derived from Jeanette and are undoubtedly more appropriate than any choices the crisis worker might have generated or insisted that Jeanette take.

The Following Three Months

Critical Needs.   During the three months following a sexual assault, a survivor such as Jeanette

1. May need continuing medical consultation, advice, or treatment; she may experience soreness, pain, itching, nausea, sleeplessness, loss of appetite, and such
2. May have difficulty resuming work; the added stress of the sexual assault may create too much stress in the workplace
3. Needs to have people reach out to her, listen to her, and verbally assure her—not shun her or fear continuing to relate to her
4. Needs the acceptance and support of family and friends
5. May have difficulty resuming sexual relations and needs understanding without pressure
6. May exhibit unusual mood swings and emotional outbursts, which others will need to understand and allow

7. May experience nightmares, flashbacks, phobias, denial, disbelief, and other unusual effects
8. May go into depression, which may be accompanied by suicidal ideation

Critical Supports.   Support people can be of great help during this phase of recovery. They may assist survivors of sexual assault by

1. Understanding and accepting the survivor's changed moods, tantrums, and so on, and allowing her the freedom to act them out
2. Supporting and being available, but not intruding—while supporting the survivor through encouraging her to regain control and to recover her life
3. Ensuring that she doesn't have to go home alone (without overprotecting her)
4. Realizing that recovery takes a long time and lots of hard work
5. Allowing her to make her own decisions about reporting the rape and prosecuting the assailant
6. Leaving it up to her to decide whether she wants to change jobs or places of residence
7. Responding to her in positive ways, so that she does not sense that the crisis worker blames her for "letting it happen" or that the crisis worker feels she is not capable of taking care of herself
8. Allowing her to talk about the assault to whomever she wishes, whenever she wishes, but not disclosing the assault to anyone without her prior consent
9. Showing empathy, concern, and understanding without dominating her
10. Recognizing that she will likely suffer from low self-esteem (ways should be found to show her that she is genuinely valued and respected)
11. Recognizing that her hurt will not end when the physical scratches and bruises are gone—that her emotional healing will require a long time
12. Finding ways to help her trust men again—assisting male associates (friends, co-workers, brothers, and her father) to show tolerance, understanding, and confidence. It is detrimental to her for male support persons to exhibit and express myths about rape. Typically, men have more difficulty understanding rape than women.
13. Encouraging female co-workers, friends, sisters, and her mother to believe in her and not avoid her or avoid talking with her openly about the rape
14. Including her children, if she has children, in many of the considerations concerning help toward emotional recovery
15. Referring her to sexual assault support groups for survivors and family members. Support groups can be of enormous help. Many YWCA Rape Crisis Centers and National Organization for Women (NOW) chapters have support groups.
16. Recognizing that her husband, partner, or lover may develop symptoms similar to those of the survivor (nightmares, phobias, rage, guilt, self-blame, self-hate, and such) and may need help similar to that needed by the survivor herself.
17. Encouraging the survivor's husband or lover to give her time to recover, free from pressure, before resuming sexual activity and to let her know he/she is still interested in her, still desires her, but that former patterns of sex life will be resumed at the survivor's own pace. It is important for a husband or lover to talk this out openly with her, to clear the air for both parties.

INTERVENTION STRATEGIES FOR CHILD SEXUAL ABUSE: THE CASE OF SUSIE

Perpetrators of child sexual assault do not discriminate as to sex or age. Both boys and girls at any age may become victims. We present here the case of a young girl, but it should be clearly understood that boys can also be victimized, and although the behavioral outcomes are different for them, they are no less catastrophic.

Susie, age 8, is the middle child in the family. She, her brother, age 11, and a 5-year-old sister live with her mother and stepfather, whom her mother married nearly two years ago. Susie's mother, Allene, and father divorced when the youngest child was about 1 year old. Susie's stepfather started off by fondling her. This went on for several weeks. Although Susie was bewildered, scared, and intimidated, no one else knew about the abusive activity. Recently, while everyone else was out of the house, her stepfather raped her. He threatened to kill Susie, Allene, and her sister if she told anyone. The following morning Susie confided in her brother, who in turn, told Allene what had happened. Incredulous over this discovery and paralyzed as to what to do, Allene called the child abuse hotline that she remembered seeing advertised on TV and in the local newspaper. The following dialogue and discussion is representative of what an absolutely outstanding child advocacy agency, the Exchange Club–Carl Perkins Child Abuse Center of Jackson, Tennessee, does.

Disclosure

Allene: (*Calling the child advocacy hotline. Angry, crying uncontrollably, barely in control.*) Hello. Hello! I want to report a (choke, sob) rape. He . . . that bastard . . . he raped my baby. That sonofabitch raped my daughter. Oh, how could I have not seen . . . How could I have let this happen? (*Continues ranting and raving in hysterics, beseeching the hotline worker for help and railing at her husband.*)

CW: Okay, I understand you're extremely upset and have every right to be, but I need for you to be in control right now. My name's Delaine. I need to know your name, where you live and whether you're safe from who did this to your daughter.

Allene: (*Regaining a bit of control and giving her name and address.*) It was my . . . It was . . . my husband . . . Chester. Her asshole stepfather . . . I found her underwear. It was all bloody . . . Oh my god! My baby . . . My poor baby. He's gone in his truck . . . He's headed for Chicago on a run . . . I'll kill him . . . By God! I will kill him if it's the last thing I ever do!

CW: So you are safe, and he's not in the house. How badly hurt is your daughter? Does she need an ambulance and medical attention?

Allene: I don't know. She's kinda in a daze. Just walking around holding on to her teddy bear. Oh that bastard. I'll castrate that bastard before I kill him.

CW: Allene, I hear how angry and shocked you are, but I need for you to follow me very closely. This is extremely important. I want you not to do anything with Susie. Don't wash her up or change her clothes. I want you to take her to Madison County General Hospital and bring her underwear with you in a plastic baggie. Do you have a way to get to the hospital? Are you OK enough to get to the hospital? (*Gets acknowledgment from the mother that she can get to the hospital.*) There are going to be people at the hospital who are going to want to talk to you and Susie, and we're going to need to do a medical exam of her. This is not going to be easy, but we know how to do this. You did the right thing. I'll meet you at the hospital, and I'll help you get through this. We will get through this! Do you understand? Now tell me what you're going to do and when you'll get to the hospital. (*Allene restates what the crisis worker has told her and assures the worker she can do those things.*)

The initial shock that accompanies discovery and disclosure are invariably highly dramatic and volatile for parents who have been blind to the perpetrator's intent. Because rape is a violent crime, the primary consideration of the crisis worker is to determine if people are now safe from the perpetrator and if they need medical attention. The initiating crisis is multifold. The crisis worker needs to make sure that there is no physical injury to the child and that the out-of-control parent is sufficiently functional to take care of the child and do the things necessary to preserve evidence. She will also need to restore the mother to equilibrium. Exacting revenge by assaulting the perpetrator would put both mother and daughter in jeopardy. The scene at the hospital can be extremely threatening, and the crisis worker does all she can to indicate that the mother has done the right thing and that, as difficult as it may be, the crisis worker will be there with her to the conclusion. The crisis worker's initial job will be to do crisis intervention with the mother by making sure everyone is safe and helping her to get back in control of her emotions and actions (Bottoms, 1999).

Immediate Aftermath

In cases where there is physical injury, the survivor will need immediate medical evaluation and care. The crisis worker, after determining the mother can get herself and her daughter to the hospital, immediately makes other phone calls to the Department of Human Services, and the police department. She also calls the hospital and informs them that a child sexual assault victim is on her way and that a sexual assault team needs to be assembled. After these phone calls are made, she immediately leaves for the hospital.

Allene: (*At the hospital, in a room with the crisis worker.*) All I can think about is that no-good lying creep. He's lucky he's on the road, or he'd be dead now. I'd shoot the asshole's balls right off of him. I've got a 9mm S&W and by God . . . as God is my witness . . . I will do it. What's happening to my daughter? They took her away. Is she going to be all right? I've read some stuff on this. It's not just him raping her now, but she'll be scarred for life! How could it happen? How could I be so stupid? What in the hell is wrong with me? He was so nice to her, to all of us! How, oh how could I have been so stupid? (*Starts uncontrolled sobbing and pacing, slamming her purse down again and again.*)

CW: You've certainly been through a lot in the last few hours. And you've done a remarkable job of taking care of Susie. Your concerns about her physical injuries now and her psychological injuries later are certainly justified. I'm not going to sugar-coat this. You're obviously a very good mother who has suddenly been thrust into this—nothing you or Susie did caused it. It was perpetrated on her and you. We are here to assist you in any way we can. We want to provide someone to be with you and Susie during these critical hours, as well as providing aftercare and follow-up counseling. But right now, even though your husband is away, I'm concerned about your anger. It's certainly justifiable, but what Susie needs is for you to be the best mother you can be right now. If you shoot your husband, how will you be able to support your daughter when she needs you most? You won't! You will be in jail. That's where your husband deserves to be, not you. Let the police handle your husband. What we need to do is handle this and care about Susie. Can you do this? That's really what you want isn't it, to help your daughter get through this?

Allene: I . . . I . . . I guess so. I appreciate it. Everything happened so fast! I don't know how I managed without falling apart. It's like a wild, awful dream—an ugly nightmare. I don't know how I'll handle it when the dust settles. I'm so mad—I could kill him! I feel like I've been raped too. There's so much on me right now. I don't know if I'm capable of bearing up under all that's got to be done. Damn, damn, damn that man! Excuse me, I shouldn't blow up like that.

CW: That's all right. You have a perfect right to be angry and to say it. It's good that you care enough to be upset, and it's good to see you direct your anger at him—the real cause of Susie's hurt and your anger. Both of you deserve better treatment than he gave you, and no child asks to be raped.

Allene: That's right. I trusted him! And he took advantage of her. She was helpless—a helpless child. I've got to show her where I stand on this. First, I'm going to take good care of her, and then I'm going to send that rotten louse to jail for good!

CW: Allene, I know things are really crazy right now, and you don't know what's happening. I want to take care of that by telling you what's going to happen and how things are going to be done so you know what's going on and don't feel so out of control. I'll go through each step of what is going to happen today and what we can do to ensure that Susie goes through this in good shape. I'm going to explain what will happen very carefully to you. If you have any questions, stop me. There are no stupid questions about this. I want you to fully understand what's happening so you can start to get back in control.

Allene, the important thing is that you gain control. Right now, I'm being very directive, and will be doing so until you get past this emergency and back on top of things. You have choices, and if, at any time, you feel like making any of the choices yourself, please feel free to do so. You can stop me at any time, and that will be OK. (*The crisis worker patiently goes through all the details of what is going to happen, stopping whenever Allene has questions, and checking to see that she understands what she's being told.*)

Allene shows a variety of legitimate concerns. The crisis worker permits her to express her anger, isn't threatened by Allene's outburst, encourages her to keep owning and expressing her feelings, and lets her know that neither she nor Susie was to blame for the assault. That strategy is important in letting Allene know that she can be in control and that the worker believes in her, without the worker's jumping in and expressing the anger for her. This is no place for the human services worker who is not calm, cool and detached in her or his professional demeanor. Our admonition early on in this book, that the worker must be solid as the rock of Gibraltar during a crisis, is never more needed than here. There is probably nothing more heart wrenching and sickening than the aftermath of a severe sexual or physical assault on a child. Intervention here clearly calls for a strong constitution. But more importantly, if the worker manifests her or his own anger directly at the parent or the perpetrator, then that anger may be misinterpreted as directed toward the victim.

At times, when the perpetrator is still an immediate threat, the worker must take on the trappings of a crisis worker who deals with battering victims. The family may need to be moved to a safe place until the perpetrator is apprehended. The crisis worker continuously reinforces the mother for doing the right thing and for caring about her daughter. This is an extremely important strategy, because adult caretakers may engage in severe guilt and recrimination because they believe they should have been vigilant. The crisis worker also must make sure that the mother will not exact revenge on the perpetrator and put herself in jeopardy with the law. It will indeed, do Susie little good if her mother is facing a charge of assault with intent to commit murder.

Finally, the crisis worker patiently educates the parent on what is going to happen. Education about the aftermath of a child assault is critical in giving parents back the sense of control they feel they have lost. Two components of education are important. First, detailing what the legal proceedings are and what the mother and child need to prepare for allows them to know what is ahead of them and not be blind sided by all the legal, social, and psychological ramifications of a child sexual assault. Second, giving the parent information on how to deal with the child in the immediate aftermath of the discovery is critical in ensuring that child is not revictimized and the parent does not feel guilty for doing or saying the wrong thing (Bottoms, 1999).

An even more shocking revelation may occur during the initial disclosure and interview. That is, it is not uncommon for the parent to disclose that she was also sexually abused as a child and swore this would never happen to any of her own children.

Allene: (*Head in her hands, slumped over.*) It's my fault. I let this happen. God knows I should have known. Uncle Ralph did the same thing to me when I was 14. I tried to tell Mom, but she just blew it off cause Uncle Ralph helped us out when Mom went through her divorce. And now my own daughter . . . I couldn't even protect her. I'm no better than my mother.

CW: (*Coolly reacting, letting Allene talk through her own sexual assault.*) There's a big difference. As I hear you say it, your mother didn't follow up because she was afraid and dependent on your uncle. You weren't afraid, and when you found out you took immediate action. See the difference? A big difference! Right now you are being the best mother in the world. Do you see that difference?

The worker, although taken aback, immediately discriminates between what Allene's mother didn't do and what Allene did do. She underscores and reinforces Allene for taking action and reaffirms her as a fit parent.

Interviewing the Child

Whenever a child is sexually assaulted, there are two primary concerns. First is taking care of the child and seeing she or he is safe. Second is obtaining evidence to prosecute the perpetrator. If the child has not been injured or if the discovery is made a good while after the assault, then an interview needs to be conducted that will allow the necessary evidence to be obtained. In the past, report of a child assault would entail numerous interviews with medical staff, police, and social services. The intimidating circumstances and the necessity to repeat the story over and over has a high potential for making the child feel terrorized, guilty, confused, and unequal to the task of meeting the demands of a variety of strange and threatening adults. The potential for re-victimizing the child and the parent while going through this procedure is extremely high if not handled appropriately (Bottoms, 1999).

To stop this from happening, the Carl Perkins Center employs an interview proce-dure that many other child advocacy agencies around the country employ. This ap-proach is a good model for dealing with cases of sexual or severe physical assault on children and is now starting to be instituted across the country. One trained forensic in-terviewer with a listening device in her or his ear will conduct the interview and tape-record it. Other agencies' staff will be behind a one-way mirror. If they need more in-formation on a particular part of the assault, they will transmit that information to the worker in the room via a "bug" in the worker's ear. Note here the emphasis on "trained." Because this is a criminal matter, the worker needs to be able to obtain infor-mation without biasing the testimony of the child. In other words, the typical mental health worker will not have the expertise to do this. However, the psychological well-being of the child is critical in the aftermath of disclosure, so the typical police interro-gation will likely put the child under severe threat. Therefore, whoever does the inter-view should be skillful not only in obtaining evidence, but also in making the child feel safe while the interview occurs. At Carl Perkins the interview is conducted in a pleas-ant, child-friendly room by a very caring child-centered forensic worker at the center, not in the stark confines of a police interrogation room (Bottoms, 1999).

If there is no knowledge of abuse and the child discloses an assault in a spontane-ous manner, then the crisis worker needs to be cool-headed, listen to the child, and be prepared to make an immediate referral. Often the workers at the Carl Perkins Center have put on a Kids-on-the-Block puppet show at a local school. After the presentation on prevention, they will invite children who may have been victimized to come down and talk to them about their experience. At times they have been flooded by children! In that case, the worker needs to write down pertinent information in a calm manner and make an immediate referral to Children and Family Services (Bottoms, 1999).

After the examination, the crisis worker needs to affirm to children that she or he is OK physically and that some part of her or his body is not "broken," or that they do not now have AIDS or that they will not die, or in the case of a girl, that she is not pregnant (Bottoms, 1999).

CW: *(Very empathic, sits down beside Susie and takes her hand.)* Susie, I'm Delaine from the Carl Perkins Center for Children. I'm guessing some pretty scary things have happened and you're probably having some pretty scary feelings right now. I want to talk to you about some of those scary things. It's OK to be scared, because it was a pretty scary deal. But you're safe now and your mom and we are going to make sure you stay safe. So if you'd like, I'll try to answer any questions you have about what happened and what's going to happen.

Susie: *(After the examination and the initial interview by a forensic expert.)* When Chet did this to me and he stuck his thingie in me, it really hurt. Am I gonna die, 'cause I started bleeding? Will I get pregnant?

CW: No, you're not going to die. It's normal to feel sore after all that and to bleed some. But the doctors said you were OK and Dr. Ann will be back to see you and tell you you're OK. I checked with the doctor, and you're not old enough to get pregnant yet. Dr. Ann will tell you about all this, so don't worry about that.

It is extremely important for young children who have little information about how their bodies function to immediately allay fears of what may happen to their body as a result of the assault. A somewhat controversial issue is whether the initial examination should be done at the child advocacy center, as opposed to a hospital. Many times the child-friendly atmosphere of the center is much more conducive than a hospital for examining victims. The counterargument is that examinations should not be done at the center because the child might associate that frightening procedure with the center's physical environment and generalize it to subsequent attempts to work there with the child (Bottoms, 1999).

Preparing the Child for Testimony

Sexual assault is a criminal matter, and at some point the child may have to testify in a courtroom. That appearance may be terrifying to a small child who will have to give testimony against a caretaker who may have either been very nice to the child or made threats against the child and his or her family. Depending on the age of the child, the Carl Perkins Center uses puppets, books, and videos to educate the child on what testimony in a courtroom entails. Immediately before the child's appearance in court, a staff member from the center will take the child to the courtroom to acclimate him or her to what may be perceived as a frightening experience. The staff explains about everybody's role and how things will happen. He or she will role-play traffic court so the child gets an idea of how courts operate. Children can explore the courtroom, ask questions, and sit in the judge's and witness chair so that they become familiarized with a courtroom and are not terror stricken when they are asked to engage in the real situation.

Another problematic area is time of court appearance. Courts are notorious for not starting on time. Sitting all day on a bench outside a court waiting for it to convene while the perpetrator is seated on an adjacent bench is clearly not conducive to the child or the family's good mental health. As a result, the Carl Perkins staff keeps the child and the family at the center until a call is received from the courthouse that court is about to convene. Only then is the child and family transported to the courthouse. After the court appearance, children are then brought back to the center and debriefed. Questions such as "How did that feel?" and "What was that like for you?" are posed to alleviate the residual fears of having confronted their perpetrators at close range (Bottoms, 1999).

There are many transcrisis points from disclosure and discovery of the assault to court appearance. The span of time covered may be up to a year from disclosure and discovery to court appearance, and there will be lots of transcrisis points as time seems to drag on interminably. It is important that each one of these crisis points be met head on by crisis workers. Thus the Carl Perkins Center staff immediately swings into action in dealing with the child and the family and stays with them in support and therapeutic roles for at least a year after the initial contact is made (Bottoms, 1999).

Aftermath

We agree with the Carl Perkins Center staff that any child who has been sexually abused needs counseling. Discovery of an incestuous relationship throws the entire family into crisis. The father, and possibly the mother, faces loss of what has become an addictive behavior, possible criminal sanctions, loss of his or her family, and social stigmatization.

The nonoffending parent finds her- or himself torn between her or his partner and the assaulted child. The child may find her- or himself discredited, shamed, punished, and still unprotected (Herman, 1981, p. 183). The worker will also face a crisis in deciding what to do and whether or not to believe the child's story. However, discovery of child sex abuse is no different from discovery of any other physical abuse, and state laws mandate that it must be reported (Sandberg, Crabbs, & Crabbs, 1988). It is a criminal activity and should be dealt with in that manner. For those workers who are unsure of themselves, it may be reassuring to know that fewer than 5 percent of complaints of child sexual abuse are false. Conversely, it is not uncommon for children to retract their complaints under pressure from the family (Goodwin, 1982). Therefore, until clearly proved otherwise, the child's allegations should be accepted as valid, and the worker's primary consideration should be reporting the abuse to Child Protective Services and obtaining safety for the child (Sandberg, Crabbs, & Crabbs, 1988).

Because the behavior is both criminal and addictive, treating the problem via family therapy is fruitless. What is called for is immediately referring the problem to and cooperating with family services and law enforcement agencies that do not subscribe to a family reunification policy (Sandberg, Crabbs, & Crabbs, 1988). It then becomes much more possible to remove the father from the home through a court order. Removing the child from the home has negative ramifications because it may be construed as banishment and may also serve to strengthen parent bonds against the child. The child needs assurance that she is not to blame for the incest; she should be praised for her courage and clearly told that she is helping, not hurting, her family and will not be abandoned even if she retracts her story (Herman, 1981, pp. 184–185).

Counseling

The Carl Perkins Center uses a variety of approaches to deal with the traumatic wake of childhood sexual abuse. Individual and group counseling for children and home intervention with parents are all part of the comprehensive postvention package of a one-year follow-up (Bottoms, 1999).

Group counseling is used to normalize the assault. Children meet in group twice a month for a year. Children who are involved in groups find out that they are not alone and that other children are having the same kinds of thoughts, feelings, and behaviors. Universal characteristics such as lying, stealing, and promiscuity are typical aftermath behaviors that will assail children who have been sexually victimized. The center attempts to deal with these issues before they become behavioral problems, through play therapy, therapeutic games, and role plays that deal with the inappropriate behavior. These issues are not sugar coated. Group leaders discuss these problems in a straightforward manner and teach children how to deal appropriately with the feelings, behaviors, and thoughts that are likely to confront children as they work through the trauma they have experienced. The idea is that if these problems are talked about openly and honestly, then survivors will not be further victimized and will be empowered to start taking control of their lives back (Bottoms, 1999).

The assaulted child may have been told, not only by the perpetrator, but also by other family members that the child itself is the cause of the family's breakup. Constant reinforcement is used to convey to children that the assault wasn't their fault. Workers who are not versed in dealing with sexually abused clients will not understand the importance of driving this point home. The fact is, that many, many sexually abused clients will believe it is their fault and that they, and they alone, as a result of their disclosure, have caused all the problems that have occurred for the family.

Groups are set up in age ranges of two to three years. Groups are not run for 3- to 5- year-olds, because of their short attention span and lack of mature cognitive development. The 3- to 5-year-olds receive only individual counseling. Because of the curriculum and techniques used, groups are also divided into readers and nonreaders. Individual counseling is concurrently provided for the group. Individual counseling runs twice a month on alternate weeks that groups meet. Different children manifest different problems as they work through the trauma of the abuse. When a child starts to manifest a particular characteristic, such as stealing, then individual counseling is tailored to fit that child's specific needs (Bottoms, 1999).

Aftercare is critically important if a host of maladies are not to appear in later childhood and carry on into adulthood. Boys will typically perpetrate sexual assaults on other children, bully other kids, vandalize property, and generally direct their anger outwardly. Girls typically turn their anger inward and engage in alcohol and drug abuse, eating disorders, and promiscuity.

Boundary Issues

Boundary issues are endemic to this population. The positive feedback and attention these children receive from engaging in sexual activities from long-term perpetrators transfers over to and generalizes to a variety of other situations and people. Thus one of the primary thrusts of counseling at Carl Perkins is to reestablish appropriate personal and interpersonal boundaries. Sexual assault turns understanding of normal boundaries upside down. An example of the lack of understanding sexually assaulted children have of interpersonal boundaries is related by the Assistant Director of the Carl Perkins Center:

Assistant Director: I was on a home visit working with the mother of a young girl who had been sexually abused. My purpose for the visit was to work with the mother in teaching her parenting techniques to use with the daughter. I really wasn't there to deal with the young girl, but she incessantly demanded attention from both myself and the mother. Providing her with alternative activities such as coloring books and dolls didn't satisfy her demand for us to attend to her. The little girl left the room and then reappeared with a negligee on and tried to get me to look at her. When that didn't work, the girl got up and sat as close to me as she could. When I still continued to attend to the mother, she climbed in my lap. When I still did not attend to her, she started kissing me, and finally attempted to stick her tongue in my mouth. In her attempt to get my attention and affection, she knew no interpersonal boundaries. It doesn't take a rocket scientist to figure out how that had come to be. Love, attention, and sex are all rolled into one as far as these kids are concerned. I can't tell you the number of times we have discovered these 6-, 7-, and 8-year-olds having sex with other kids when they should be playing with dolls and trucks with those kids. So a lot of time is spent on talking about what appropriate boundaries are.

Home Visits

The Carl Perkins staff meet with the nonoffending parent twice a month for a year. After they've been discovered, these children behave differently. Without knowledge and training, parents are likely to be shocked by these previously unseen behaviors as the child acts out. Thus home visits and parent training to educate and normalize the behavioral changes that are likely to occur are critically important. If such training does not occur, then warfare between the parent and child will create another crisis. Forewarned is forearmed, and if parents start seeing these behaviors, the center staff immediately start tackling these issues with the child. Therefore, center staff keep close contact with the home to catch and stop inappropriate behavior before it gets started (Bottoms, 1999).

A classic example is stealing or shoplifting. The immediate knee-jerk reaction of many parents is to use shame as a way of modifying the behavior. Yet using shame to extinguish behavior compounds all kinds of shame-based issues the child may already have. Another example is sexual acting out. Parents who have started to date again after removal of the perpetrator will be horrified when their child attempts to become intimate with their date. Due to the vacuum left by the removal of the perpetrator, the child's need for love and affection, and her or his confusion over boundaries, make the new boyfriend or girlfriend of the parent a target for the child's commingled notions of how love and sex are intertwined and how she or he obtain that love through sexual gratification (Bottoms, 1999).

Home intervention also includes many case management activities. These activities range across many support activities. Getting ready for court, obtaining an attorney, looking for alternative living arrangements and transportation, applying for victims compensation and other state support mechanisms for families are but a few of the many activities that occur in helping the family restabilize (Bottoms, 1999).

Preventing Revictimization

Perhaps most tragic of all the issues that assail a family is revictimization of the child by the nonoffending parent. Often a role reversal occurs whereby the child is not only the sexual object of the perpetrating parent, but also becomes the chief confidant and comfort provider for the nonoffending parent. She or he takes on the role of being the real partner of the nonoffending parent and usurps the nonoffender parent's role. This role reversal may be completed by the nonoffending parent psychologically taking over the child role. Thus, crisis workers spend a good deal of time with nonoffending parents, teaching them to reassume the role as head of household and to stand their ground when the child attempts to reassume her or his pseudo-adult role. Finally, time is spent on talking about the nonoffending parent not falling into another relationship that has the same outcome, as the parent may be highly likely to do (Bottoms, 1999).

What the Carl Perkins Center does with families who have been involved with sexual abuse is not short-term, brief therapy. The multiple crises that erupt after disclosure should make it readily apparent that there are no quick fixes to this horrific problem. At least a year of continuing crises may be expected as the family attempts to restabilize and reinvent itself, and to be successful it will need help every step of the way. For those interested in knowing how to establish a center like Carl Perkins, the National Network of Children's Advocacy Centers' Board has produced a manual, *Best*

Practices, that gives step-by-step details on how to start a center (O'Leary, 1994). The address of the National Network of Children's Advocacy Center is 1319 F Street NW, #10001, Washington, DC, 20004-1106.

Treatment of Offenders

Although it may be extremely difficult for human services workers who are enraged and repulsed by incest and pedophilia to accept the idea that offenders should be given any consideration other than removal from the family and jail time, treatment should be made available. The offender is engaged in addictive behavior, and for many offenders, the problem is treatable (Pithers, Kashima, Cumming, & Beal, 1988). Offenders rarely seek treatment voluntarily, however. Treatment mandated by court order and revocation of probation for termination of treatment or relapse are legal sanctions that increase the likelihood of compliance (Herman, 1981, p. 186). Whether treatment is voluntary or mandated, sex offender treatment programs are demonstrating increased success. Chaplin and associates (1995) suggest that child molesters lack empathy, have higher sexual deviancy scores than do nonmolesters, and are more likely than nonmolesters to justify their abuse. The researchers' findings "support the development of treatments that effectively reduce deviant arousal, and that alter child molesters' cognitions and attitudes about child molesting, and enhance victim empathy" (p. 255). Although treatment of child sex offenders and various crises they experience is a very specialized therapeutic modality that is beyond the scope of this book, Salter's (1988) *Treating Child Sex Offenders and Victims* is an excellent and comprehensive work on the subject, and we recommend it for those who are interested in issues of offender treatment.

SUPPORT AND THERAPY GROUPS FOR ADULT SURVIVORS

Offenders, mothers, and older victims alike can profit from support and therapy groups composed of their peers. Support and therapy groups are extremely important because participants find they have and can discuss mutual problems, are less stigmatized and isolated, and have the opportunity to see that other members are successfully moving past the addiction and trauma (Herman, 1981, p. 186; Salter, 1988).

For offenders, the group breaks down cognitive distortions, isolation, secrecy, and denial and promotes treatment compliance (Salter, 1988, p. 112). For mothers, the notion of entering a support/therapy group may be very threatening. However, it is quite possibly the only way they will be able to get their families back together. Mothers should be told that fact in plain and simple terms and should be highly encouraged to join such groups. Groups for spouses enable members to come to terms with doubts of their own womanhood, regain a sense of control and empowerment in themselves and their families, reduce blame and guilt in themselves, and restore mother–daughter bonds (Brittain & Merriam, 1988; Salter, 1988, p. 211).

For victims, groups provide a number of potential positive outcomes and help them to move from victim to survivor. Victims may be reluctant to participate, but they should be encouraged to do so, although not all victims may be ready or immediately able to participate in groups. Education as to what the group is about, who the members are, confidentiality issues, what kinds of problems members are working on, and the safety and support of the group format are critical components in assessing, selecting, motivating, and committing survivors to group work (Courtois, 1988, pp. 253–262). Courtois (1988, pp. 245–249) lists the following benefits of group treatment for survivors of childhood sexual abuse:

1. The individual's sense of shame, stigmatization, and negative self-image is reduced by meeting other survivors who appear "normal."
2. Commonality of experience raises members' consciousness about incest wherein the experience becomes more normalized and may be seen from an interpersonal and sociocultural perspective rather than an "only me" perspective.
3. The group serves as a new "surrogate" family where new behaviors and methods of communicating, interacting, and problem solving can be practiced in a safe, accepting, and nurturing environment.
4. The group allows for safe exploration and ventilation of feelings and beliefs that have been denied and submerged from awareness.
5. Childhood messages and rules that were generated within the abusive environment can be challenged and dissected to determine how they still influence the survivor's maladaptive behavior patterns. The case of Pearl provides an example of how support groups may constitute an integral component in the therapeutic regimen of adult survivors of child sexual abuse.

INTERVENTION STRATEGIES FOR ADULT SURVIVORS: THE CASE OF PEARL

Pearl was sexually abused by her stepfather regularly from ages 8 through 15. For 20 years she suppressed all memories and emotions related to the abuse, which had included fondling, digital penetration, and intercourse. Now, at age 35, she has regained her memory of the abuse and is experiencing severe symptoms of delayed rape trauma syndrome. Her marriage is breaking up; her career is in shambles; her communications and relationship with her three children are adversely affected by her personal turmoil; her rage toward her stepfather and her anger toward her mother have robbed her of her self-respect and her affection toward her parents, who live across town from her. Her only daughter, the middle child, has recently reached her eighth birthday, and Pearl is deeply obsessed with her daughter's safety. Pearl feels a great deal of guilt, shame, remorse, and loss of self-esteem. For several years she has been experiencing suicidal ideations, and since the recovery of her memory of the abuse, these ideations have seriously intensified.

Interventions with Pearl included both individual counseling and support group work in which she willingly participated. In support group meetings, Pearl received the encouragement, validation, and information she needed to absolve herself from guilt, shame, and remorse. She also acquired essential advice from support group members on implementing safety measures she could take to ensure that her 8-year-old daughter would not fall prey to the kinds of sexual abuse she herself had suffered. That advice allayed her fears and concerns about her daughter' vulnerability. Often the affirmation and informational resources obtained in support groups are key elements in the emotional healing, fear reduction, enhancement of self-esteem, and rehabilitation of adult survivors of child sexual abuse. It was certainly so with Pearl.

Assessment

Particularly among older women who suffered childhood sexual abuse under severe societal and family strictures of secrecy and denial, the abuse will be disguised and repressed. Often they may have been under the care of mental health professionals and been diagnosed with a variety of mental illnesses ranging from schizophrenia to depression and borderline personality. Presenting problems are typically depression, anxiety, dissociation, and compulsive disorders (Courtois, 1988). Although the client may present as competent, responsible, mature, and otherwise capable, these characteristics are a facade for underlying emotional problems. Affectively, behaviorally, and cognitively, abuse victims may present themselves in a bipolar manner, rigidly adhering to one end or the other of the continuum—"I'm great" or "I'm terrible"—or rapidly oscillating between the two (Courtois, 1988).

Triage assessment of these people can be problematic, to say the least. At one moment they present as affectively calm and controlled, perhaps to the point of rigidity. At the next moment, because of some real or imagined slight, particularly in interpersonal relationships, they may become extremely labile with angry tirades or uncontrolled crying and then offer profuse, guilt-ridden apologies for their behavior. Cognitively, they may present themselves as competent and perceptive thinkers and then, when faced with a stimulus that causes a flashback or intrusive image, completely dissociate themselves from present reality and respond in a confused, disjointed manner. Behaviorally, such individuals may run the gamut of *DSM-IV* (American Psychiatric Association, 1994) diagnostic categories—and then appear perfectly appropriate! If there is any key to making an accurate assessment of adult survivors of childhood sexual abuse, it is their consistent inconsistency across triage dimensions. The astute crisis worker who is struggling to make an assessment where such inconsistency is displayed should consider childhood sexual abuse as a working hypothesis.

A crisis invariably initiates therapy; as in other forms of PTSD, the crisis may not seem related to a past traumatic event. During the intake interview, if some of the common symptoms of PTSD are revealed, then childhood sexual abuse should be suspected as a causative agent and further assessment should target it as a possibility. The crisis worker who suspects PTSD due to childhood sexual abuse in an adult should immediately make plans to refer the client for a comprehensive psychiatric assessment after the initiating crisis is contained.

Pearl initially presented at a community mental health center with suicidal thoughts and actions. At intake she showed the counselor cuts she had inflicted on herself with a box cutter. She was dissociative and saw herself "out of her body" as she drew the knife up and down her arms. She had also cut off her parakeet's head, although she was extremely remorseful about its death and could not imagine why she would have done such a terrible thing. She was currently depressed and saw no reason for living. The counselor rated her overall on the Triage Assessment Form (Myer, Williams, Ottens, & Schmidt, 1991, 1992) at 27, set up a stay-alive contract with her, and referred her to a psychiatrist for evaluation and medication (refer to the Triage Assessment Form, described in Chapter 2). After several false starts and stops at counseling, Pearl finally admitted the real issue, that she had been abused sexually and physically as a child by her stepfather and that the abuse had been denied by her mother.

Treatment of Adults

Basically, crisis intervention with survivors of sexual abuse incorporates the principles of the six steps discussed in Chapter 2. A major component of therapy is to use a post-traumatic stress treatment model like the one described in Chapter 4. In that regard, assessment for PTSD has been underused with incest victims (Courtois, 1988, p. 150). However, Finkelhor (1987) proposes that the trauma of childhood sexual abuse goes beyond other causal agents of PTSD because of the unique dynamics of traumatic sexualization, social stigmatization, betrayal of trust by loved ones, and powerlessness of children.

Frazier and Burnett (1994) found that rape trauma nurses and rape victims' sisters provided the most supportive and appropriate environment for survivors' recovery. Male friends and boyfriends were found to be least supportive. Survivors endorsed the following positive mechanisms: taking precautions; controlling self-thoughts by thinking positively, imagining oneself feeling positive emotions, and covertly telling oneself to behave and mentally imaging oneself behaving in positive and constructive ways; talking about the event (suppressing negative thoughts about the event); gaining a support system; going to counseling; and keeping busy. In contrast, survivors associated higher negative symptoms with staying at home and becoming isolated from social contact and support. Strategies focused on emotions rather than problems and on approach rather than avoidance appeared to be most helpful.

Pearson (1994) found that a variety of techniques may be appropriately used in individual therapy to address the unique needs of sexually abused survivors: relationship-building strategies, questioning, family-of-origin techniques, writing techniques, gestalt work, role playing and psychodrama, transactional analysis and inner-child work, hypnotherapy and guided imagery, cognitive strategies, and behavioral and life skills training were cited as appropriate. Pearson stated that there is little evidence to suggest which of the these techniques are most effective for treating individually unique issues. Draucker (1999) identified three psychotherapeutic needs of women who have been sexually assaulted: (1) focusing on feelings and problem solving while relying on survivors' own strengths and resources to make decisions, (2) making current treatment goals and plans to live in a violence-free environment rather than to leave any battering relationships they are in, and (3) exploring issues in depth. Survivors expressed a need for quality therapeutic relationships that facilitate their own healing powers.

Discovery and Admission

For survivors of childhood sexual abuse, particular problems arise in the therapeutic process that do not arise with victims of other traumatic experiences. If the client is otherwise in crisis and childhood sexual abuse is suspected, do not explore incest material immediately because of the likelihood of compounding the present crisis through decompensation, regression, or dissociation. Client safety is paramount and should always be a primary or conjoint consideration with exploration of the incest (Courtois, 1988, p. 173). At the time the client chooses to own the trauma of incest, the potential for crisis rises exponentially. The worker needs to be very sensitive to the client's admission, gently encouraging the client to disclose the incest and directively and positively affirming the client for doing so.

Pearl: (*Apprehensively.*) I don't know what you'll think about this. But I guess I can trust you. I just can't live with this anymore. (*Pauses.*)

CW: (*Suspecting from previous indicators what is coming.*) Whatever it is, I can see how deeply troubling it is and how difficult it must be. I am here to listen and try to understand. Whatever it is, I want you to know that you will still be the same Pearl, and that person is not going to be any different in my eyes. I hope what I've just said makes it easier to get it out for you.

Pearl: (*Starts sobbing.*) This is really bad.

CW: (*Softly touching her arm and speaking gently.*) I'm guessing this is about something that somebody did to you or that happened to you, and it's OK, really OK to talk about it.

Pearl: I had sex with my stepfather. (*Relates a long history of sexual and physical torment by her stepfather and real mother, with the counselor listening and empathically responding.*)

Pearl: (*Gently weeping.*) I know you're a counselor and all, but you must think I'm horrible.

CW: I understand how terribly difficult that was. I also want you to know that I believe what you said. I don't think you're horrible at all. What I think is that you were a victim and that you are a survivor of those terrible things that shouldn't have happened and did. I want to correct one thing you said. You did not have sex with your stepfather. You were 12 years old and had no choice. He had and forced sex on you. That's a big difference. Now I want to give you an idea of what is happening to you, why these bad memories keep coming back, and what they do to disrupt your life.

Psychoeducation

Psychoeducation about the role that PTSD plays in incest trauma is important at this point because it can help allay clients' fears that they are "different," "dirty," or "mentally ill," and it assures them that PTSD is responsive to treatment. Education about PTSD also removes the mystique, confusion, and "craziness," anchoring present maladaptive behavior as purposive and reasonable given the survivor's traumatic history. It also allows the client to believe that something can be done through treatment (Courtois, 1988, p. 173).

CW: (*After an explanation and showing Pearl the* DSM-IV *PTSD classification.*) So you are not "nuts." Those are the reasons these things are currently happening. We can treat this. It is a long road, and at times it is going to seem as if things are getting worse instead of better. We will have to go back and dig into those memories, and they are going to be painful. I want you to think about this because it is not an easy task. It is something you will need to choose. If you choose to do so, I want you to know that we'll go through this together. (*The counselor then explains what the treatment procedures will be and answers questions the client has about different components of the treatment.*)

Validation

As the client starts through the process of therapy, numerous transcrisis points will occur as long-buried trauma is brought back to awareness. In an active, directive, continuous, and reinforcing manner, the human services worker (Courtois, 1988, pp. 167–170):

1. Validates that the incest did happen, despite denial of this fact by significant others; the client is not to blame, it is safe to talk about it, and the worker does not loathe the client for having been a participant
2. Acts as an advocate who is openly, warmly interested in what happened to the survivor as a child and makes owning statements to that effect
3. Reinforces the resourcefulness of the victim to become a survivor
4. Provides a mentor/reparenting role model to help with childhood developmental tasks that were missed.

Extinguishing Trauma

When we speak of extinguishing trauma, we are referring to effecting a psychological extinction—that is, facilitating the reduction or loss of a conditioned response as a result of the absence or withdrawal of reinforcement. In practical terms, this means the reduction or loss of both Pearl's negative beliefs about herself and her debilitating behaviors that were responses to her childhood sexual abuse. The crisis worker sought to extinguish Pearl's negative beliefs and behaviors by systematically leading her to mentally refute her erroneous perceptions that she was responsible, culpable, or guilty and had her reframe her previous beliefs to help her gain a new insight that she was an innocent victim and can now view herself more realistically as a guilt-free survivor. The crisis worker's procedures and dialogue with Pearl in the preceding sections on discovery and admission and on psychoeducation are examples of strategies to extinguish trauma such as Pearl experienced.

When working through traumatic events, the client will experience a dramatic increase in affective and autonomic arousal (Ochberg, 1988). The human services worker must be very careful to provide palatable doses of the traumatic material that do not exceed the client's coping abilities (Courtois, 1988, p. 174) and promote a crisis within the therapy session. Careful processing with the client before and after each session of extinguishing and reframing traumatic memories is important in preventing such crises.

CW: Let's take a look at what we did today.

Pearl: I'm pretty scared. I didn't remember a lot of that stuff until we dug that memory up.

CW: That's pretty typical. Any reasonable person would bury that stuff. If you really start to feel like you're losing it, I want you to call me.

Pearl: (*Later that evening, calling.*) I really hate to disturb you, but I've really got this urge to start cutting myself. I'm also having thoughts about killing my other pet bird. They're starting to get pretty real.

CW: (*Very directively.*) Do you feel like you're losing it enough that you need to be hospitalized?

Pearl: I don't know. Maybe if I just talk this through.

CW: OK. Remember what I said about this being rough. What you went through today brought back a lot of old memories and some ugly fresh ones. That's normal. It's nasty, but it is normal. Now I want you to think of how we changed that scene, how you told yourself all those negative things about yourself being dirty and no good, and what the reality of that scene is. (*A dialogue ensues that recaps the day's events. Pearl is able to regain control, and after a 20-minute dialogue is able to feel secure enough to relax and go to bed.*)

The worker should be aware that extinguishing one traumatic event does not lessen the fear and trepidation of moving on to other events. This is particularly true in the case of adult survivors of childhood sexual abuse, who may experience increased intrusive behavioral symptoms and regress to former maladaptive behaviors even though they are making good progress in erasing bad memories (Cogdal & James, 1991). Clients may appear to be getting worse instead of better—which is threatening and scary for both client and worker.

The worker should be prepared for this contingency, tell the client of its likelihood, and affirm that it is totally acceptable for the client to check in with the worker if these symptoms and behaviors reemerge between sessions. The worker's role when this happens is to be understanding, affirming, and calming. Constant validation is important because many clients will be discouraged at the length of treatment, afraid and angry over revictimization and extension of the traumatic experience's "life," and flee from therapy (Courtois, 1988, p. 177).

Cognitive Restructuring

Reframing the client's negative and distorted beliefs about him- or herself is critical in allowing the client to separate the fact and fiction of an abusive childhood (Courtois, 1988, p. 181). While imaginally flooding an abusive childhood scene, clients paste mental billboards under the scene (Cogdal & James, 1991). These billboards typically deliver all the myths and distorted messages that the abuser gave in addition to the client's own childhood negative self-talk.

CW: (*With the client deeply relaxed, eyes closed.*) Picture that videotape, the bedroom, the "game," him making you get on him and suck his "peter," almost strangling as you do so. Feel the pain and the disgust. But he makes you keep doing it until he gets off, and the semen is running all over, sticky and wet. Notice the messages underneath that scene. "This is what fathers do to educate their daughters to become women." "You aren't a good daughter if you don't do this." "I'll kill you if you don't keep our secret." Feel the confusion, the fear, and the repulsion as you do this. Put those messages in big block letters underneath that scene. Do you see them?

Pearl: (*Eyes closed and body twisting.*) Yes!

CW: Freeze that scene and the billboards. Take a snapshot of it. Let it develop. Hold it in your hands.

The client is then asked to destroy the image along with the negative parental injunctions and her own negative self-injunctions (Cogdal & James, 1991).

CW: Now I want you to get rid of that scene. It is in your past and it is gone, so now get rid of it from your memory also. Do that now, and tell me what is happening.

Pearl: I set a match to it. It is burning, it's a huge fire now with yellow, sick-smelling smoke.

CW: Let it burn.

Pearl: It's just a crisp cinder now, all gone.

CW: All gone? Is there anything else you want to do with it?

Pearl: CRUSH IT!

CW: Do it! What's happening?

Pearl: I'm grinding it up with my boot heel. It's nothing, he's nothing.

CW: Fine. Now relax and slip back into that soft, cool mountain glade. Just relax and feel the tranquillity, calmness, and peacefulness.

The client then replays the scene, but this time substitutes positive, self-enhancing counterinjunctions based on the facts and not on the fictional messages of the event. The worker guides the image and reframes the father in a truer psychological image (Cogdal & James, 1991).

CW: Go back to the bedroom with him now. Picture the scene, but change it. See him as small, very small, weak. He is a small, selfish, pouting boy, dressed up in a man's pajamas. He looks ridiculous. Put these billboards under the scene. "The only people he has power over are little girls." "It is his fault this is happening." "It is WRONG!" "It is criminal!" "I should have felt confused, fearful." "I had the right to feel that way!" "I also have the right to be *angry* about it." "*No*body has the right to do that. *No*body!" Now freeze that picture and snapshot it. Let it develop. Look at it. What are you feeling and thinking?

Pearl: (*Yelling.*) You asshole! You bastard! You are gone from my life, you puke! You lied to me, you scared me to death and kept at it. You used me because you were afraid of everybody else. I was the only one you could use, you scumbag. You've got no power over me now, you pissant, or my memories. You are history!

CW: I want you to save that picture. Put it someplace else, safe in your memory, and every time that image starts to come back, pull out the picture and look at it. See that scene for what it really is, and see those billboards, flashing. Have you got it?

Pearl: Yes. I've got it.

CW: How do you feel?

Pearl: Better, relaxed, relieved maybe.

Catharsis

Like Vietnam veterans, survivors of childhood sexual abuse have developed excellent coping skills to deny and numb feelings. Recognizing and labeling feelings is of utmost importance in helping clients give voice to shunted emotions and warded-off feelings. Pearl's bitter and angry emotions are not unlike those of Vietnam veterans as they relive and extinguish bad memories. Developmentally, clients have to literally relearn and identify their emotional states. In our own work with survivors, we use a sheet of faces with different emotions and feeling words attached to them to help clients relabel their emotions. Far from seeing this exercise as childish, clients report that they pull out and use these sheets on a daily basis to validate their present emotional state.

Grief Resolution

Beginning to recognize past, buried feelings is to start on the road to acknowledging feelings of anger and rage, as Pearl does in the preceding dialogue. These feelings will ultimately end in sadness and grieving for the loss of a happy childhood, her loss of who she might have been without the trauma, and the loss of a psychologically healthy family instead of the malevolent one she grew up in (Courtois, 1988, p. 181). It is likely to be one of the most painful stages as the client comes to grips with the reality that there is no retrieving the past or changing it and that attempts to do so are fruitless. Only the future holds promise for her, and she can control only that (Courtois, 1988, p. 181; Hays, 1985).

Grieving and resolution, particularly with perpetrators of the abuse, is another transcrisis point in therapy.

Pearl: I had a call from my mother last night. I wanted to be assertive with her and tell her how I felt, like I had worked out in group. But when it came down to it I just couldn't. I haven't got the guts. (*Starts crying.*) I'll never get rid of this. Why couldn't she have been different? Why does she still try that stuff of browbeating me? Wasn't what she did enough?

CW: You have every right to feel sad that she wasn't or still isn't what you'd hope a mother might be. I wish she could change, but I have my doubts. So if she won't, what will you do?

Pearl: I guess she won't. I guess I'll just kiss her off.

CW: You survived with her battering you, and you've survived for ten years without her. Perhaps it's time you did say goodbye. (*Patiently lets Pearl silently weep.*)

Changing Behavior Through Skill Building

Although coming to terms with past trauma and stopping maladaptive present behavior are critical to the adult survivor, changing behavior to more self-determining choices is the major end goal of therapy. The vacuum left by the removal of bad memories and the psychic energy previously expended to maintain control of those memories is not easily filled. Pearson (1994) recommends using several categories of techniques for skill building, which have already been listed in the section on treatment of adults. Reeducation is necessary for survivor skill building, and the worker may assume a teaching role in transmitting basic life skills such as communication, decision making, conflict resolution, cognitive restructuring, and boundary setting (Courtois, 1988, pp. 181–182). From that standpoint, the crisis worker should not be unsettled by the emergence of some rather unusual and personal questions.

Pearl: Er, ah, I was just wondering, Dr. James, how you treat your kids. I mean, if they act up do you ground them, or what? What do you talk about at dinner? And do you and your wife ever argue?

Although such questions may be construed as intruding on the private life of the worker or attempts by the client to shift focus from her problems, it is important to answer these questions as honestly and succinctly as possible, without shifting the focus away from the client's personal concerns. The client is testing her perceptions against the most valid and stable validity check she currently has—her therapist. For that reason, it is important to urge survivors to join therapy or support groups so that new behaviors can be tested out and discussed with peers.

SUMMARY

Benedict (1985, p. 1) defined rape as "any sexual act that is forced on you." We accepted and prefer that definition for use in applied work settings. Another definition that is perhaps more relevant in theoretical and conceptual work is preferred by

Brownmiller (1975, p. 376). She defined rape as "a sexual invasion of the body by force, an incursion into the private, personal inner space without consent—in short, an internal assault from one of several avenues and by one of several methods [that] constitutes a deliberate violation of emotional, physical, and rational integrity and is a hostile, degrading act of violence."

The sexual assault research consistently finds that the incidence of sexual assault is greatly underreported. The majority of reported rapists and other sexual abusers are males, and they come from all walks of life. Most abusers appear to perceive those they attack as objects of prey rather than as people. Abusers display a variety of pathologies. They usually assault not out of lust or desire for sexual gratification but out of a perceived need to control, exert power over, punish, vanquish, defeat, hurt, destroy, degrade, or humiliate others. Typically, abusers deny, minimize, and/or rationalize their behavior to the extent that they themselves rarely define their attacks as abuse. Instead, they usually claim that the survivor asked for, deserved, seduced, wanted, needed the experience in order to grow up, or somehow caused the abusive activity to occur.

Rape is a complex phenomenon that encompasses and affects the psychosocial, cultural, and personal aspects of society. There are no cause and effect formulas that explain why one person sexually assaults another. Consequently, many erroneous assumptions, beliefs, and myths about rape are held by different people, and women and men often differ in their perceptions about rape. But there is virtually unanimous agreement that the rampant specter of sexual assault must be confronted by society. Recently, the human services professions have directed a great deal of attention to rape and sexual assault on children. Substantive work has been done in the areas of crisis work, counseling, legal, social, and psychological interventions to help children and to prevent child sexual abuse. Such intervention and prevention has been made even more urgent in light of recent findings that child sexual abuse extends debilitating traumas far into adulthood of survivors. An enormous amount of research has shown that adult survivors of child sexual abuse often suffer a wide diversity of emotional, physical, psychological, and social pathologies that manifest themselves in various degrees of transcrisis and PTSD symptoms later in adulthood. These findings have produced a greater degree of urgency than ever before to help victims of sexual abuse and to stop offenders from assaulting.

Date and acquaintance rape, especially on college campuses, has become a pressing problem. The problem is exacerbated by the use of drugs and/or alcohol that are usually found to be associated with date rape. A great deal of research, training, and information dissemination is being undertaken to help stop date and acquaintance rape and especially to educate teenagers and college-age people about the dangers, vulnerabilities, and prevention strategies regarding such sexual assaults. One impediment to preventing date and acquaintance rape is the differential perceptions between men and women. The research consistently reveals that men are more tolerant of rape than are women. Changing those differing perceptions or belief systems in men is a major task worthy of the best efforts of all of society and human services professionals who seek to provide interventions in the area of date and acquaintance rape.

Crisis intervention and other human services work in the area of rape and sexual assault of children require unique and specialized knowledge and strategies. Children are vulnerable to many kinds of pressures and perpetrators of child sexual abuse know all the angles needed to ensnare child victims. Society is becoming more aware of the abuse and the legal, medical, social, mental health, law enforcement, court systems, and human services professions are becoming increasingly involved in attempting to stop the abuse and to work with abused children and their families. It has recently become more widely recognized and accepted than before that children are not responsible for sexual assault and that strategies employed in counseling, crisis intervention, legal proceedings, and prosecution of offenders should demonstrate the recognition that children's physical, cognitive, and maturational development must be treated vastly different from those of adults.

An important issue in crisis intervention with survivors of sexual assault is control. The cases depicted in this chapter demonstrated that crisis workers sought to assist survivors to regain control of their lives and to return to a precrisis state of equilibrium as soon as feasible. In cases when survivors were emotionally immobile, crisis workers demonstrated directive techniques. When survivors were partially mobile, workers were collaborative. And when survivors were mobile, workers were nondirective. Workers sought to attain the nondirective mode as soon as possible so that clients could take charge of their own lives and make their own choices and that crisis workers could function with a minimum of intrusion.

In recent years the public has become increasingly aware of the phenomenon of rape and other forms of sexual abuse, and that new awareness appears to have ushered in a greater sensitivity to and advocacy for the rights and needs of survivors. The helping professions have provided many additional programs for assisting survivors: crisis intervention, research, counseling, medical services, long-term mental health care, new laws and legal advocacy, more vigorous efforts to prosecute offenders, and more sympathetic and proactive news media. However, much remains to be done in the arena of sexual assault. There remains a pressing need for caregivers and society at large to better understand the dynamics of sexual abuse and the needs of survivors and their families. There is a great need for society to overcome a number of long-standing myths about rape and other forms of sexual abuse. There is a need for better reporting and improved police and legal responding. There is a need for survivors to accept counseling and not to blame themselves. And there is a need for survivors' families, friends, and co-workers to be willing and able to respond to survivors with openness, genuineness, acceptance, understanding, and respect, all of which are key attitudes or conditions for nurturing recovery from the debilitating trauma and effects of sexual assault.

CLASSROOM EXERCISE

Counseling Simulations in Small Groups

The instructor constructs one-page scenarios of one or more sex-abuse survivor situations. The cases in this chapter may be used as models for developing the scenarios. A realistic source is recent newspaper accounts of rapes and sexual assaults. Divide the class randomly into task groups, which will conduct their own crisis intervention sessions simultaneously, rather than before the whole class. One person enacts the role of survivor and one the role of crisis worker, and the remaining persons are observer/evaluators. Only the survivor in each group is given a copy of a sexual assault scenario. The survivor will need a few minutes to read and get into the mood to enact the role. Then the survivor and crisis worker enact a crisis intervention session.

For a specified length of time, the survivors are interviewed by the crisis workers in the groups, with the observer/evaluators taking notes. The instructor will circulate around the room, briefly looking in on each group as it engages in its crisis intervention session. The crisis worker in each group is instructed to be as helpful as possible, incorporating the strategies suggested in this chapter into the six-step crisis counseling model learned in Chapter 2.

Whenever the instructor calls "time" to conclude the crisis intervention sessions, a few moments should be reserved for observer/evaluators to provide constructive feedback to their respective groups. Some suggested guidelines for observer/evaluators are provided by these questions:

1. What verbal responses and nonverbal behaviors did the crisis worker exhibit that appeared most helpful to the survivor?
2. What verbal responses and nonverbal behaviors (if any) appeared the least helpful or to elicit negative responses from the survivor?

After each observer/evaluator has had an opportunity to provide constructive feedback in the respective groups, each task group is allowed a brief period of discussion and a period for the survivor to disassociate from the role. The survivor can "derole" by taking a moment to completely disassociate from the role taken by telling other members of the task group, "This is the reason I am not the person I portrayed in that scenario," or make a similar statement of disengagement from the role played. The exercise should be concluded by providing an opportunity for one observer/evaluator from each group to share a one-minute summary statement (of that particular group's experience) with the entire class.

RESOURCES

For readers who wish to access additional and more comprehensive information regarding rape and sexual assault, we have listed here organizations that specialize in providing current data, coping strategies, and suggestions for prevention regarding crises described in this chapter. The *Encyclopedia of Associations* (Maurer & Sheets, 1999) also contains exhaustive lists of organizations from which to choose.

Rape and Sexual Abuse
National Coalition Against Sexual Assault (NCASA)
125 N. Enola Drive
Enola, PA 17025
Phone: (717) 728-9764 Fax: (717) 732-1575
E-mail: ncasa@redrose.net
Seeks to end sexual violence through advocacy, education, and public policy initiatives. Disseminates information about sexual violence, prevention, and support of victims and survivors.

National Clearinghouse on Marital and Date Rape (MCMDR)
2325 Oak Street
Berkeley, CA 94708
Phone: (510) 524-1582 or (510) 524-7770
Website: http://members.aol.com/ncmdr/index.html

Seeks to stop marital, cohabitant, and date rape and to assist victims and survivors of such sexual assault. Provides educational supports to the public and resources to battered women's shelters, crisis centers, district attorneys and legislators through media appearances, lectures, training workshops, telephone consultations and a speakers' bureau.

Giarretto Institute (formerly Adults Molested as Children) (AMACU)
232 East Gish Road, First Floor
San Jose, CA 95112
Phone: (408) 453-7611 Fax: (408) 453-9064
E-mail: giarretto@earthlink.net
Website: http://www.giaretto.org
Provides therapy and guided self-help to sexually abused children and their families and to men and women who are unable to cope with the trauma of having been sexually abused as children. Offers information and training on child sexual abuse. Advocates and uses multidisciplinary approaches to alleviate the devastating effects of trauma in sexual abuse victims and survivors.

REFERENCES

Abbey, A., McAuslan, P., & Ross, L. T. (1998). Sexual assault perpetration by college men: The role of alcohol, misperception of sexual intent, and sexual beliefs and experiences. *Journal of Social & Clinical Psychology, 17,* 167–195.

Ackerman, P. T., Newton, J. E. O., McPherson, W. B., Jones, J. G., & Dykman, R. A. (1998). Prevalence of post traumatic stress disorder and other psychiatric diagnoses in three groups of abused children (sexual, physical, and both). *Child Abuse and Neglect, 22,* 759–774.

American Psychiatric Association. (1994). *Diagnostic and statistical manual of mental disorders* (4th ed.). Washington, DC: Author.

Amir, M. (1971). *Patterns in forcible rape.* Chicago: University of Chicago Press.

Arata, C. M. (1999). Coping with rape: The roles of prior sexual abuse and attributions of blame. *Journal of Interpersonal Violence, 14,* 62–78.

Baker, D. A. (1995, June). *Talking with young people who have experienced sexual abuse.* Paper presented at the American School Counselor Association Conference and Exposition, New Orleans.

Balyk, E. D. (1997). Paraphilias as a sub-type of obsessive-compulsive disorder: A hypothetical bio-social model. *Journal of Orthomolecular Medicine, 12*(1), 29–42.

Baron, L., & Straus, M. A. (1989). *Four theories of rape in American society.* New Haven: Yale University Press.

Bass, E., & Thornton, L. (Eds.). (1983). *I never told anyone: Writings by women survivors of child sexual abuse.* New York: Harper & Row.

Benedict, H. (1985). *Recovery: How to survive sexual assault—for women, men, teenagers, their friends and families.* Garden City, NY: Doubleday.

Besharov, D. J. (1990). *Recognizing child abuse: A guide for the concerned.* New York: Free Press.

Bottoms, D. (Speaker). (1999, September). The role of the Exchange Club Carl Perkins Child Advocacy Center in treating child sexual abuse. Department of Counseling, Educational Psychology and Research, University of Memphis, cassette recording #7411-99.

Boyd, T. (2000, April 7). Date-rape drug: GBH means socializing in a new way—even with friends. *Pensacola News Journal,* pp. B1, B3. (From Tracy Boyd, journalist for *The Detroit News*)

Bremner, J. D. (1998). Traumatic memories lost and found: Can memories of abuse be found in the brain? In L. M. Williams & V. L. Banyard (Eds.), *Trauma and memory* (pp. 217–227). Thousand Oaks, CA: Sage.

Brewer, K. D., Rowe, D. M., & Brewer, D. D. (1997). Factors related to prosecution of child sexual abuse cases. *Journal of Child Sexual Abuse, 6*(1), 91–111.

Briere, J., & Conte, J. (1993). Self-reported amnesia for abuse in adults molested as children. *Journal of Traumatic Stress, 6,* 21–31.

Briere, J., & Runtz, M. (1987). Post sexual abuse trauma: Data and implications for clinical practice. *Journal of Interpersonal Violence, 2,* 367–379.

Briere, J., & Runtz, M. (1988). Symptomatology associated with childhood sexual victimization in a nonclinical adult sample. *Child Abuse and Neglect, 12,* 51–59.

Briere, J., & Runtz, M. (1993). Childhood sexual abuse: Long-term sequelae and implications for psychological assessment. *Journal of Interpersonal Violence, 8,* 312–330.

Brittain, D. E., & Merriam, K. (1988). Groups for significant others of survivors of child sexual abuse: A report of methods and findings. *Journal of Interpersonal Violence, 3,* 90–101.

Brown, S. L., & Forth, A. E. (1997). Psychopathy and sexual assault: Static risk subtypes. *Journal of Consulting & Clinical Psychology, 65*(5), 848–857.

Brownmiller, S. (1975). *Against our will: Men, women, and rape.* New York: Simon & Schuster.

Burgess, A. W. (Ed.). (1985). *Rape and sexual assault: A research handbook.* New York: Garland.

Burgess, A. W., Groth, A. N., Holmstrom, L. L., & Sgroi, S. M. (1978). *Sexual assault of children and adolescents.* Lexington, MA: Lexington Books.

Burgess, A. W., & Holmstrom, L. L. (1979). *Rape: Crisis and recovery.* Bowie, MD: Robert J. Brady.

Burgess, A. W., & Holmstrom, L. L. (1985). Rape trauma syndrome and post traumatic stress response. In A. W. Burgess (Ed.), *Rape and sexual assault: A research handbook* (pp. 56–60). New York: Garland.

Butz, C., & Spaccarelli, S. (1999). Use of force as an offense characteristic in subtyping juvenile sex offenders. *Sexual Abuse: Journal of Research and Treatment, 11*(3), 217–232.

Carnes, P. (1983). *The sexual addiction.* Minneapolis, MN: CompCare.

Cashwell, C. S., Bloss, K. K., & McFarland, J. E. (1995). From victim to client: Preventing the cycle of sexual reactivity. *The School Counselor, 42,* 233–238.

Chaplin, T. C., Rice, M. E., & Harris, G. T. (1995). Salient victim suffering and the sexual responses of child molesters. *Journal of Consulting and Clinical Psychology, 63,* 249–255.

Christo, G. (1997). Child sexual abuse: Psychological consequences. *Psychologist, 10*(5), 205–209.

Cogdal, P. A., & James, R. K. (1991, August). *Combinatorial technique to treatment of adult incest survivors.* Paper presented at the American Psychological Association convention, San Francisco, CA.

Colao, F., & Hosansky, T. (1983). *Your children should know. Teach your children the strategies that will keep them safe from assault and crime.* New York: Berkeley Books.

Cole, C. V. (1995). Sexual abuse of middle school children. *The School Counselor, 42,* 239–245.

Consentino, C. E., Meyer-Bahlburg, H. F. L., Rer-Nat, D., Alpert, J., Weinberg, S. L., & Gaines, R. (1995). Sexual behavior problems and psychopathology symptoms in sexually abused girls. *Journal of the American Academy of Child and Adolescent Psychiatry, 34,* 1033–1042.

Conte, J. R., & Schuerman, J. R. (1988). Research with child victims. In G. E. Wyatt & G. J. Powell (Eds.), *Lasting effects of child sexual abuse* (pp. 157–170). Newbury Park, CA: Sage.

Coons, P. M., Bowman, E. E., Pellow, T. A., & Schneider, P. (1989). Posttraumatic aspects of the treatment of victims of sexual abuse and incest. *Psychiatric Clinics of North America, 12,* 325–335.

Courtois, C. A. (1988). *Healing the incest wound. Adult survivors in therapy.* New York: Norton.

Craine, L. S., Henson, C. E., Colliver, J. A., & MacLean, D. G. (1988). Prevalence of a history of sexual abuse among female psychiatric patients in a state hospital. *Hospital and Community Psychiatry, 39,* 300–304.

Cross, T. P., Martell, D., McDonald, E., & Ahl, M. (1999). The criminal justice system and child placement in child sexual abuse cases. *Child Maltreatment: Journal of the*

American Professional Society on the Abuse of Children, 4(1), 32–44.

Daniluk, J. C., & Haverkamp, B. E. (1993). Ethical issues in counseling adult survivors of incest. *Journal of Counseling and Development, 72,* 16–22.

Darves-Bornoz, J. M., Lepine, J. P., Choquet, M., Berger, C., Degiovanni, A., & Gaillard, P. (1998). Predictive factors of chronic post-traumatic stress disorder in rape victims. *European Psychiatry, 13,* 281–287.

De Young, M. (1983). Case reports: The sexual exploitation of victims by helping professionals. *Victimology, 6,* 92–98.

Deblinger, E., McLeer, S. V., Atkins, M. S., & Ralphe, D. (1989). Posttraumatic stress in sexually abused, physically abused, and nonabused children. *Child Abuse and Neglect, 13,* 403–408.

Donaldson, M. A., & Gardner, R. (1985). Diagnosis and treatment of traumatic stress among women after childhood incest. In C. R. Figley (Ed.), *Trauma and its wake: The study and treatment of post-traumatic stress disorder* (pp. 356–377). New York: Brunner/Mazel.

Draucker, C. B. (1999). The psychotherapeutic needs of women who have been sexually assaulted. *Perspectives in Psychiatric Care, 35,* 18–28.

Drieschner, K., & Lange, A. (1999). A review of cognitive factors in the etiology of rape: Theories, empirical studies, and implications. *Clinical Psychology Review, 19*(1), 57–77.

Dunn, P. C., Vail-Smith, K., & Knight, S. M. (1999). What date/acquaintance rape victims tell others: A study of college student recipients of disclosure. *Journal of American College Health, 47,* 213–219.

Eisler, R. (1987–1995). *The chalice and the blade: Our history, our future.* San Francisco: Harper-Collins.

Eisler, R. (1995). *Sacred pleasure: Sex, myth, and the politics of the body.* San Francisco: Harper-Collins.

Enns, C. Z., McNeilly, C. L., Corkery, J. M., & Gilbert, M. S. (1995). The debate about delayed memories of child sexual abuse: A feminist perspective. *The Counseling Psychologist, 23,* 181–279.

Everill, J., & Waller, G. (1995). Disclosure of sexual abuse and psychological adjustments in female undergraduates. *Child Abuse and Neglect, 19,* 93–100.

Farrell, S. P., Hains, A. A., & Davies, W. H. (1998). Cognitive behavioral interventions for sexually abused children exhibiting PTSD symptomology. *Behavior Therapy, 29,* 241–255.

Feigon, E. A., & de Rivera, J. (1998). "Recovered memory" therapy: Profession at a turning point. *Comprehensive Psychiatry, 39,* 338–344.

Finkelhor, D. (1979). *Sexually victimized children.* New York: Free Press.

Finkelhor, D. (1984). *Child sexual abuse: New theory and research.* New York: Free Press.

Finkelhor, D. (1987). The trauma of child sexual abuse: Two models. *Journal of Interpersonal Violence, 2,* 348–366.

Finkelhor, D. (1993). Epidemiological factors in the clinical identification of child sexual abuse. *Child Abuse and Neglect, 17,* 67–70.

Finkelhor, D. (1994). Current information on the scope and nature of child sexual abuse. *Future of Children, 4*(2), 31–53.

Frazier, P., & Borgida, E. (1985). Rape trauma syndrome evidence in court. *American Psychologist, 40,* 984–993.

Frazier, P. A., & Burnett, J. W. (1994). Immediate coping strategies among rape victims. *Journal of Counseling and Development, 72,* 633–639.

Frazier, P. A., Valtinson, G., & Candell, S. (1994). Evaluation of a coeducational interactive rape prevention program. *Journal of Counseling and Development, 73,* 153–158.

Fromuth, M. E. (1983). *The long term psychological impact of childhood sexual abuse.* Unpublished doctoral dissertation, Auburn University, Alabama.

Fromuth, M. E. (1986). The relationship of childhood sexual abuse with later psychological and sexual adjustment in a sample of college women. *Child Abuse and Neglect, 10,* 5–15.

Ganas, K., Sampson, G., Cozzi, C., & Stewart, T. (1999, April). *Exposing our biases: Dealing with a rape survivor in a nonjudgmental manner.* Paper presented at the Twenty-Third Annual Convening of Crisis Intervention Personnel, Chicago.

Geiser, R. L. (1979). *Hidden victims: The sexual abuse of children.* Boston: Beacon Press.

Gil, E., & Johnson, T. C. (1993). *Sexualized children: Assessment and treatment of sexualized children and children who molest.* Rockville, MD: Launch Press.

Goodwin, J. (1982). *Sexual abuse: Incest victims and their families.* Boston: John Wright.

Goodwin, J. (1988). Post-traumatic symptoms in abused children. *Journal of Traumatic Stress, 1,* 475–488.

Greer, J. G., & Stuart, I. R. (Eds.). (1983). *The sexual aggressor: Current perspectives on treatment.* New York: Van Nostrand Reinhold.

Grossman, R., & Sutherland, J. (1983). *Surviving sexual assault.* New York: Congdon & Weed.

Groth, A. N., & Birnbaum, H. J. (1979). *Men who rape: The psychology of the offender.* New York: Plenum.

Harrison, P., Downes, M., & Williams, D. (1990). Date and acquaintance rape: Perceptions and attitude change strategies. *Journal of College Student Development, 32,* 131–139.

Hartman, C. R., & Burgess, A. W. (1988). Rape trauma and treatment of the victim. In F. M. Ochberg (Ed.), *Post-traumatic therapy and victims of violence* (pp. 152–174). New York: Brunner/Mazel.

Hays, K. F. (1985). Electra in mourning: Grief work and the adult incest survivor. *Psychotherapy Patient, 2,* 45–58.

Henry, J. (1997). System intervention trauma to child sexual abuse victims following disclosure. *Journal of Interpersonal Violence, 12*(4), 499–512.

Heppner, M. J., Good, G. E., Hillenbrand-Gunn, T. L., Hawkins, A. K., Hacquard, L. L., Nichols, R. K., DeBord, K. A., & Brock, K. J. (1995). Examining sex difference in altering attitudes about rape: A test of the elaboration likelihood model. *Journal of Counseling and Development, 73,* 640–647.

Herman, J. (1981). *Father–daughter incest.* Cambridge, MA: Harvard University Press.

Himelein, M. J., Vogel, R. E., & Wachowiak, D. G. (1994). Nonconsensual sexual experiences in precollege women: Prevalence and risk factors. *Journal of Counseling and Development, 72,* 411–415.

Holmes, R. M., Holmes, A. T., & Unholz, J. (1993). Female pedophilia: A hidden abuse. *Law and Order, 41*(8) 77–79.

Holmes, W. C., & Slap, G. B. (1998). Sexual abuse of boys: Definition, prevalence, correlates, sequelae, and management.

Journal of the American Medical Association, 280, 1855–1862.

Humphreys, T. P., & Herold, E. (1996). Date Rape: A comparative analysis and integration of theory. *Canadian Journal of Human Sexuality, 5,* 69–82.

Hunter, M. (Ed.). (1995). *Adult survivors of sexual abuse: Treatment innovations.* Thousand Oaks, CA: Sage.

Hursch, C. J. (1977). *The trouble with rape.* Chicago: Nelson-Hall.

James, S. H., & DeVaney, S. B. (1994). Reporting suspected sexual abuse: A study of counselor and counselor trainee responses. *Elementary School Guidance and Counseling, 28,* 257–263.

Justice, B., & Justice, R. (1979). *The broken taboo.* New York: Human Services.

Kalichman, S. C. (1999). *Mandated reporting of suspected child abuse: Ethics, Law, and Policy* (2nd ed.). Washington, DC: American Psychological Association.

Kelly, L. (1988). *Surviving sexual violence.* Minneapolis: University of Minnesota Press.

Kempe, R. S. (1984). *The common secret: Sexual abuse of children and adolescents.* New York: W. H. Freeman.

Kendrick, J. M. (1991). Crisis intervention in child abuse: A family treatment approach. In A. R. Roberts (Ed.), *Contemporary perspectives on crisis intervention* (pp. 34–52). Upper Saddle River, NJ: Prentice Hall.

Kessler, B. L., & Bieschke, K. J. (1999). A retrospective analysis of shame, dissociation, and adult victimization in survivors of childhood sexual abuse. *Journal of Counseling Psychology, 46,* 335–341.

Kids on the Block (1995). *Keeping up with the kids.* Columbia, MD: The Kids on the Block, Inc.

Kluft, R. P. (1990). Incest and subsequent revictimization: The case of therapist–patient sexual exploitation, with a description of the sitting duck syndrome. In R. P. Kluft (Ed.), *Incest-related syndromes of adult psychopathology* (pp. 263–288). Washington, DC: American Psychiatric Association Press.

Knight, R. A. (1999). Validation of a typology for rapists. *Journal of Interpersonal Violence, 14*(3), 303–330.

Kovach, J. (1986). Incest as a treatment issue for alcoholic women. *Alcoholism Treatment Quarterly, 3,* 1–15.

Kreidler, M. C., & England, D. B. (1990). Empowerment through group support: Adult women who are survivors of incest. *Journal of Family Violence, 5,* 35–41.

Kuhn, J. A., Charleanea, M., & Chavez, E. L. (1998). Correlates of sexual assault in Mexican-American and White non-Hispanic adolescent males. *Violence and Victims, 13*(1), 11–20.

Lanier, C. A., & Elliott, M. N. (1997). A new instrument for the evaluation of a date rape prevention program. *Journal of College Student Development, 38,* 673–676.

Lanier, C. A., Elliott, M. N., Martin, D. W., & Kapadia, A. (1998). Evaluation of an intervention to change attitudes toward date rape. *Journal of American College Health, 46,* 177–180.

Lindberg, F. H., & Distad, L. J. (1985). Post-traumatic stress disorders in women who experienced childhood incest. *Child Abuse and Neglect, 9,* 329–334.

Lundberg-Love, P. K., Marmion, S., Ford, K., & Geffner, R. (1992). The long-term consequences of childhood incestuous victimization upon adult women's psychological symptomatology. *Journal of Child Sexual Abuse, 1*(1), 81–102.

Lurigio, A. J., Jones, M., & Smith, B. E. (1995). Child sexual abuse: Its causes, consequences, and implications for probation practice. *Federal Probation, 59*(3), 69–76.

Maguire, E. R. (1993). The professionalization of police in child sexual abuse cases. *Journal of Child Sexual Abuse, 2*(3), 107–116.

Maurer, C. M., & Sheets, T. E. (Eds.). (1999). *Encyclopedia of associations* (34th ed.) (Vol. 1, Parts 1, 2, and 3). Farmington, MI: Gale Research.

McDuffie, L. (1999, April). *Syndrome of rape.* Paper and program presented at the Twenty-Third Annual Convening of Crisis Intervention Personnel, Chicago.

McLeer, S. V., Deblinger, E., Henry, D., & Orvaschel, H. (1992). Sexually abused children at high risk for post-traumatic stress disorder. *Journal of the American Academy of Child and Adolescent Psychiatry, 31*(5), 875–978.

McLeer, S. V., Dixon, J. F., Henry, D., Ruggiero, K., Escovitz, K., Niedda, T., & Scholle, R. (1998). Psychopathology in non-clinically referred sexually abused children. *Journal of the American Academy of Child and Adolescent Psychiatry, 37,* 1326–1333.

Medea, A., & Thompson, K. (1974). *Against rape. A survival manual for women: How to avoid entrapment and how to cope with rape physically and emotionally.* New York: Farrar, Straus & Giroux.

Mennen, F. E., & Meadow, D. (1995). The relationship of abuse characteristics to symptoms in sexually abused girls. *Journal of Interpersonal Violence, 10,* 259–274.

Merrick, M. V., Allen, B. M., & Crase, S. J. (1994). Variables associated with positive treatment outcomes for children surviving sexual abuse. *Journal of Child Sexual Abuse, 3*(2), 67–87.

Mills, C. S., & Granoff, B. J. (1992). Date and acquaintance rape among a sample of college students. *Social Work, 37*(6), 504–509.

Minard, S. M. (1993). The school counselor's role in confronting child sexual abuse. *The School Counselor, 41,* 9–15.

Moeller, T. P., Bachmann, G. A., & Moeller, J. R. (1993). The combined effects of physical, sexual, and emotional abuse during childhood: Long-term health consequences for women. *Child Abuse and Neglect, 17*(5), 623–640.

Molmen, M. E. M. (1982). *Avoiding rape: Without putting yourself in protective custody.* Grand Forks, ND: Athena Press.

Moody, E. E., Jr. (1994). Current trends and issues in childhood sexual abuse prevention programs. *Elementary School Guidance and Counseling, 28,* 251–256.

Morrow, S. L., & Smith, M. L. (1995). Constructions of survival and coping by women who have survived childhood sexual abuse. *Journal of Counseling Psychology, 42,* 24–33.

Murphy, W. D. (1985, October). The dynamics and phases of sexual abuse (Mimeographed, 3 pages). Sexual Abuse Treatment Project, Department of Human Services, University of Tennessee, Memphis.

Myer, R. A., Williams, R. C., Ottens, A. J., & Schmidt, A. E. (1991). *Three-dimensional crisis assessment model.* Unpublished manuscript, Northern Illinois University, Department of Educational Psychology, Counseling, and Special Education, DeKalb, IL.

Myer, R. A., Williams, R. C., Ottens, A. J., & Schmidt, A. E. (1992). A three-dimensional model for triage. *Journal of Mental Health Counseling, 14,* 137–148.

Myers, M. F. (1986). Men sexually assaulted as adults and sexually molested as boys.

Archives of Sexual Behavior, 18, 203–215.

Norris, J., & Cubbins, L. A. (1992). Dating, drinking, and rape. *Psychology of Women Quarterly, 16,* 179–191.

Oates, R. K., O'Toole, B. I., Lynch, D. L., Stern, A., & Cooney, G. (1994). Stability and change in outcomes for sexually abused children. *Journal of the American Academy of Child and Adolescent Psychiatry, 33,* 945–953.

Ochberg, F. M. (Ed.). (1988). *Post-trauma therapy and victims of violence.* New York: Brunner/Mazel.

O'Leary, N. (Ed). (1994). *Best practices: A guidebook to establishing a children's advocacy center program.* Washington, DC: National Network of Children's Advocacy Centers.

Page, R. M. (1997). Helping adolescents avoid date rape: The role of secondary education. *High School Journal, 80,* 75–80.

Park, L., & Renner, K. E. (1998). The failure to acknowledge differences in developmental capabilities leads to unjust outcomes for child witnesses in sexual abuse cases. *Canadian Journal of Community Mental Health, 17*(1), 5–19.

Patchett, A. (1995, October). The comfort of strangers: Getting raped can be just the beginning of a nightmare. *Vogue,* pp. 90, 94, 102, 104.

Pearson, Q. M. (1994). Treatment techniques for adult female survivors of childhood sexual abuse. *Journal of Counseling and Development, 73,* 32–37.

Pfefferbaum, B. (1997). Posttraumatic stress disorder in children: A review of the past 10 years. *Journal of the American Academy of Child & Adolescent Psychiatry, 36,* 1503–1511.

Pithers, W. D., Kashima, K. M., Cumming, G. P., & Beal, L. S. (1988). Relapse prevention: A method of enhancing maintenance of change in sex offenders. In A. C. Salter (Ed.), *Treating child sex offenders and victims* (pp. 131–170). Newbury Park, CA: Sage.

Plummer, C. A. (1984). *Preventing sexual abuse: Activities and strategies for working with children and adolescents.* Holmes Beach, FL: Learning Publications.

Prior, V., Glaser, D., & Lynch, M. A. (1997). Responding to child sexual abuse: The criminal justice system. *Child Abuse Review, 6*(2), 128–140.

Ratna, L., & Mukergee, S. (1998). The long term effects of childhood sexual abuse: Rationale for and experience of pharmacotherapy with nefazodone. *International Journal of Psychiatry in Clinical Practice, 2,* 83–95.

Regehr, C., Cadell, S., & Jansen, K. (1999). Perceptions of control and long-term recovery from rape. *American Journal of Orthopsychiatry, 69,* 110–115.

Remer, R., & Ferguson, R. A. (1995). Becoming a secondary survivor of sexual assault. *Journal of Counseling and Development, 73,* 407–413.

Rew, L. (1989). Long-term effects of childhood sexual exploitation. *Issues in Mental Health Nursing, 10,* 229–244.

Rubin, L. J. (1996). Childhood sexual abuse: Whose memories are faulty? *The Counseling Psychologist, 24,* 140–143.

Runtz, M. (1987, June). *The sexual victimization of women: The link between child abuse and revictimization.* Paper presented at the meeting of the Canadian Psychological Association, Vancouver, British Columbia, Canada.

Russell, D. E. H. (1986). *The secret trauma: Incest in the lives of girls and women.* New York: Basic Books.

Sadowski, P. M., & Loesch, L. C. (1993). Using children's drawings to detect potential child sexual abuse. *Elementary School Guidance and Counseling, 28,* 115–123.

Salter, A. (1995). *Transforming trauma: A guide to understanding and treating adult survivors of child sexual abuse.* Newbury Park, CA: Sage.

Salter, A. C. (1988). *Treating child sex offenders and victims: A practical guide.* Newbury Park, CA: Sage.

Sandberg, D. N., Crabbs, S. K., & Crabbs, M. A. (1988). Legal issues in child abuse: Questions and answers for counselors. *Elementary School Guidance and Counseling, 22,* 268–274.

Sanders, B., & Moore, D. L. (1999). Childhood maltreatment and date rape. *Journal of Interpersonal Violence, 14,* 115–124.

Sawyer, R. G., Pinciaro, P. J., & Jessell, J. K. (1998). Effects of coercion and verbal consent on university students' perception of date rape. *American Journal of Health Behavior, 22,* 46–53.

Schetky, D. H. (1990). A review of the literature on the long-term effects of childhood sexual abuse. In R. P. Kluft (Ed.), *Incest-related syndromes of adult psychopathol-*

ogy (pp. 35–54). Washington, DC: American Psychiatric Press.

Schwartz, M. D., & Leggett, M. S. (1999). Bad dates or emotional trauma? The aftermath of campus sexual assault. *Violence Against Women, 5,* 251–271.

Sgroi, S. M. (1982). *Handbook of clinical intervention in child sexual abuse.* Lexington, MA: Lexington Books.

Sgroi, S. M., Porter, F. S., & Blick, L. C. (1982). Validation of child sexual abuse. In S. M. Sgroi (Ed.), *Handbook of clinical intervention in child sexual abuse* (pp. 39–79). Lexington, MA: Lexington Books.

Shapiro, B. L., & Chwarz, J. C. (1997). Date Rape: Its relationship to trauma symptoms and sexual self-esteem. *Journal of Interpersonal Violence, 12,* 407–419.

Shipherd, J. C., & Beck, J. G. (1999). The effects of suppressing trauma-related thoughts on women with rape-related posttraumatic stress disorder. *Behavior Research and Therapy, 37,* 99–112.

Stevenson, J. (1999). The treatment of long-term sequelae of child abuse. *Journal of Child Psychology & Psychiatry & Allied Disciplines, 40*(1), 89–111.

Sullivan, L. A., & Robinson, S. L. (1994, April). *An evaluation of a preschool child abuse and neglect prevention program: The Kids on the Block go to preschool.* Research report from the University of Alabama at Birmingham, presented at the Conference on Human Development.

Sussman, L., & Bordwell, S. (1981). *The rapist file: Interviews with convicted rapists.* New York: Chelsea House.

Tang, K. (1998). Rape law in Canada: The success and limits of legislation. *International Journal of Offender & Comparative Criminology, 42,* 258–270.

Thornhill, R., & Palmer, C. T. (2000). *A natural history of rape: Biological bases of sexual coercion.* Cambridge, MA: MIT Press.

Townley, R. (1985). *Safe and sound: A parent's guide to child protection.* New York: Simon & Schuster.

Truman, D. M., Tokar, D. M., & Fischer, A. R. (1996). Dimensions of masculinity: Relations to date rape supportive attitudes and sexual aggression in dating situations. *Journal of Counseling & Development, 74,* 555–562.

Two Rape Surveys Contrast (1992, April 24). *The Commercial Appeal* (Memphis, TN), p. A4.

Ullman, S. E. (1996a). Correlates and consequences of adult sexual assault disclosure. *Journal of Interpersonal Violence, 11,* 554–571.

Ullman, S. E. (1996b). Social reactions, coping strategies, and self-blame attributions in adjustment to sexual assault. *Psychology of Women Quarterly, 20,* 505–526.

Ullman, S. E., Karabatsos, G., & Koss, M. P. (1999). Alcohol and sexual assault in a national sample of college women. *Journal of Interpersonal Violence, 14,* 603–625.

Varelas, N., & Foley, L. A. (1998). Blacks' and Whites' perceptions of interracial and intraracial date rape. *Journal of Social Psychology, 138,* 392–400.

Walker, L. E. (1989). *Terrifying love: Why women kill and how society responds.* New York: Harper & Row.

Weaver, T. L., Chard, K. M., & Resick, P. A. (1998). Issues in treating rape and sexual assault. In N. Tarrier & A. Wells (Eds.), *Treating complex cases: The cognitive behavioral approach,* (pp. 377–398). Series in Clinical Psychology. Chichester, England, UK: Wiley.

Weeks, R., & Widom, C. S. (1998). Self-reports of early childhood victimization among incarcerated adult male felons. *Journal of Interpersonal Violence, 13*(3), 346–361.

Wheeler, J. R., & Berliner, L. (1988). Treating the effects of sexual abuse on children. In G. E. Wyatt & G. J. Powell (Eds.), *Lasting effects of child sexual abuse* (pp. 227–247). Newbury Park, CA: Sage.

White, J., & Allers, C. T. (1994). Play therapy with abused children: A review of the literature. *Journal of Counseling and Development, 72,* 390–394.

Williams, J. E., & Holmes, K. A. (1981). *The assault: Rape and public attitudes.* Westport, CT: Greenwood Press.

Wolfe, V. V., Gentile, C., & Wolfe, D. A. (1989). The impact of sexual abuse on children: A PTSD formulation. *Behavior Therapy, 20,* 215–228.

Wyatt, G. E., & Powell, G. J. (Eds.). (1988). *Lasting effects of child abuse.* Newbury Park, CA: Sage.

CHAPTER SEVEN

Partner Violence

To anyone who watched television in 1994–1995 and saw the O. J. Simpson trial, the full impact of partner violence came full force into the homes of America. Perhaps even more astounding, his major defense lawyer, Johnnie Cochran, has had his own *physical abuse* of his ex-wife detailed in a book written by her (Cochran Berry, 1995). But O. J. Simpson and Johnnie Cochran, for all their notoriety, are only two grains of sand on a very large beach of domestic violence. The pervasiveness of domestic violence is so great that it cuts across social, ethnic, sexual orientation, economic, cultural, religious, race, and geographical boundaries (Angless, Maconachie, & Van Zyl, 1998; Browne & Herbert, 1997; Hotaling & Sugarman, 1986, 1990; Levinson, 1989; Merrill, 1996; Sev'er, 1997; Shaloub-Kevorkian, 1997; Wessel & Campbell, 1997; West, 1998a, 1998b; West, Kaufman Kantor, & Jasinski, 1998).

Certainly, physical abuse in domestic situations is not limited to husband-and-wife relationships. Indeed, single, separated, and divorced women are actually at greater risk for battering than are married women (Stark & Flitcraft, 1987). Furthermore, battering is not confined to heterosexual relationships: lesbians, gays, and bisexuals are not immune to battering one another (Coleman, 1994; Lobel, 1986; Renzetti & Miley, 1996; West 1998a). Men are also assaulted by women (Langhinrichsen-Roling, Neidig, & Thorn, 1995; Stets & Straus, 1990; Straus & Gelles, 1990). There are "granny bashers" who batter their parents (Aitken & Griffin, 1996; Quinn & Tomita, 1997). Finally, child abuse, both physical and sexual, is endemic to society (Browne & Herbert, 1997; Chalk & King, 1998).

Therefore it should be clearly understood that the concepts discussed in this chapter apply to *all partners* or people involved in any established current or former cohabiting relationship. It is with these cohabiting relationships that this chapter is most concerned about, because the violence that people in these relationships experience cause ripple effects to flow out into the rest of the family, the community, and society. Because women form the major target group of severe domestic violence, this chapter focuses on crisis intervention with women who are involved in domestic violence and the men who batter them.

The terms *battering, abuse,* and *assault* are often used interchangeably in the literature. In this chapter, *battering* indicates any form of physical violence perpetrated by one person on another and typically includes a life-threatening history of injuries and psychosocial problems that entrap a person in a relationship. *Abuse* is a more general term that indicates that physical violence is only one weapon in an armory of coercive weapons. *Abuse* denotes the unequal power relationship within which the assault occurs and further suggests that a presumption of trust has been violated. *Assaultive behavior* can include not only harmful acts against a person but also both verbal and behavioral threats to significant others, pets, or property. *Domestic violence* subsumes any act of assault by a social partner or relative, regardless of marital status (Stark & Flitcraft, 1988).

THE INCIDENCE OF DOMESTIC VIOLENCE

The history of spouse beating in Western society goes as far back as the patriarchal system does. Whereas an assault on or rape of another man's wife caused and still causes immediate and severe legal punishment and moral outrage, abuse by a man of his own wife is quite another story (Pleck, 1987). Common law in the United States early acknowledged the right of a man to chastise his wife for misbehavior without being prosecuted for doing so (*Bradley* v. *State of Mississippi,* 1824). Indeed, the law's attitude toward wife beating to the current day is aptly summarized in the case of the *State of North Carolina* v. *Oliver* in 1874. The court ruled that "if no permanent injury has been inflicted, it is better to draw the curtains, shut out the public eye, and leave the parties to forgive and forget." The implications of such "blind" justice are ominous.

There is no more anxiety-provoking call for a police officer than a domestic disturbance call. More police die as a result of intervening in domestic violence calls than in any other type of crime (Resnik, 1976, p. 9). Furthermore, domestic disturbance calls far outnumber other types of police calls in which the possibility of violence exists (Benjamin & Walz, 1983, p. 63). Domestic violence injures more women than automobile accidents, muggings, and rapes combined (American Medical Association, 1991). Every 15 seconds in the United States a woman is beaten (Bureau of Justice Statistics, 1991). The National Crime Survey found that once a woman is victimized, her chances of revictimization in the next 6 months is 32 percent. It also found that only about 48 percent of women who are assaulted report the assault to the police (Bureau of Justice Statistics, 1995).

Straus and Gelles (1986) reported in their 10-year survey from 1975 to 1985 that a best estimate is that about 4 million women are abused every year in the United States. In a later report, Van Hasselt and associates (1988) estimated that there are about 1.8 million domestic assaults on women annually. Current estimates put the figure at about 2 million a year. Whichever figure one chooses to believe, the bottom line is that those statistics translate into criminal assault, criminal offenses against the family, and murder. These figures probably underestimate the magnitude of the problem: Cultural norms tolerate and in some instances condone family violence, confidentiality keeps violence a family secret, poor and non-English-speaking women are underreported, women who were institutionalized or hospitalized are not included, gay and lesbian incidents of violence are not reported, and gender roles based on power differentials that are still sanctioned keep a number of domestic violence cases out of the legal system (Brasseur, 1994; Carden, 1994).

One of the major reasons much domestic violence is not reported is that the medical system fails to do so. Kurz and Stark (1987) reported that whereas 75 percent of the battered women they studied volunteered information that they had been abused, the problem was acknowledged by clinicians in only 5 percent of the cases. Using a trauma screen to determine how the physical injury has occurred, they found that the single most common cause of a female injury brought to medical attention was abuse. In emergency room settings, an estimated 20 to 35 percent of female patients seek treatment for domestic violence; in family practices, between 25 and 40 percent of women report abuse; internal medicine clinics report that 17 percent of women claim ongoing abuse; and 11 percent of obstetric patients are abused during pregnancy. However, only 2 to 10 percent of battered women are commonly identified as such by physicians (Hamberger, 1994). Both nurses and physicians have been criticized and found wanting in regard to being aware of and skillful enough in their questioning of patients to make a diagnosis of battering. The failure of health care professionals to adequately detect partner violence stems from a fear of offending patients, lack of training and knowledge, inability to cure the problem, lack of time, and lack of insurance coverage (Tilden et al., 1994). This failing should not be too surprising, because little emphasis on domestic violence has been given in medical schools or nurses' training (Bokunewicz & Copel, 1992; Matthews, 1993; Sampselle, 1991; Sassetti, 1993; Taylor & Campbell, 1992). Compounding the problem are state reporting laws that are not nearly as stringent as child abuse laws in requiring health care professionals to report injuries from suspected partner violence (Chalk & King, 1998, p. 173).

In response to these grim findings, the Board of Trustees of the American Medical Association launched a campaign in 1991 against domestic violence, describing the problem as an epidemic of staggering proportions (American Medical Association, 1991). Although the medical profession has started to take notice of domestic violence and respond by raising the consciousness level of practitioners in interviewing and diagnostic methods (Brasseur, 1994; Hamberger, 1994), the medical profession's consciousness level is still far from perfect.

Another culprit in the helping professions is the clergy. Many clerics who deal with family violence have a great deal of difficulty with the issue, and a number were found to place the blame on the woman (Wood & McHugh, 1994). However, other human services workers should not feel smug. Research indicates that they, too, may have biases against and stereotypes about abused women that interfere with and hinder treatment (Ross & Glesson, 1991). Noteworthy is the fact that although crisis workers are not contacted as often by abused women as other professionals are, they were reported to be the most helpful (Hamilton & Coates, 1993).

EMERGING APPROACHES TO PARTNER VIOLENCE

Despite the long and current history of partner abuse, only since 1974 has there been a consistent and planned systematic approach to the problem. Erin Pizzey's book *Scream Quietly or the Neighbors Will Hear* (1974) was responsible for the start of the first women's shelter in England. Subsequently, in the United States, the National Organization for Women, along with grassroots organizations such as the Massachusetts Coalition of Battered Women Service Groups, has come to the forefront in developing funding sources, shelters, support groups, organizing and training manuals, and legislation for battered women.

Media attention about the severity of the problem has raised public consciousness. Television documentaries, newspaper articles, and media coverage has attracted attention, changed public perspective, and removed some of the cloak of secrecy from domestic violence.

Such increased public awareness and the efforts of feminist and other citizens' groups resulted in the formation of the National Coalition Against Domestic Violence to promote a national power base for battered women (Capps, 1982). This group has exerted a good deal of social and legislative pressure to combat the problem of domestic violence. One outcome has been a shift in police procedures, increased law enforcement of partner violence, and enhanced legal protection through tougher protective orders and warrantless arrest. In many cities and states, a police call to a domestic dispute where battering is involved now results in a mandatory arrest; and if convicted, the batterer is mandated by the court to either participate in counseling and anger management programs or go to jail (Shupe, Stacey, & Hazlewood, 1987). Domestic violence units have been formed in police departments, probation and parole offices, states attorney's offices, and domestic violence courts, which all coordinate efforts to reduce domestic violence (Chalk & King, 1998, p. 172).

A growing number of women have entered academia in the past 20 years, particularly in the social sciences. Their research on family violence, gender roles, and male dominance has resulted in social activism that has debunked the "safe haven" notion of the family (Jasinski & Williams, 1998, pp. vi–vii).

Stories such as those of Francine Hughes (subject of *The Burning Bed),* who suffered prolonged and severe beatings by her husband and who finally killed him by pouring kerosene around his bed and setting it on fire, have had an impact on the courts by challenging legal precedents and assumptions about homicide and self-defense (Edwards, 1989). Indeed, psychologist Lenore Walker's (1989) book *Terrifying Love* is a chilling and eye-opening account of her experiences as an expert witness in murder trials of battering victims who have killed their assailants. The result has been that recognition of a history of abuse and threat is a valid part of a legal defense for battered women who kill their husbands (Chalk & King, 1998, pp. 171–172).

In their 10-year follow-up study of family violence in 1985, Straus and Gelles (1986) found an overall decline in husband-to-wife violence of 6.6 percent and severe husband-to-wife violence (battering) decreased by 26.6 percent. However, what is perplexing is that wife-to-husband violence had increased to a rate higher than that of husband-to-wife violence. Other studies support this increase into the 1990s, particularly when courtship is involved (Bland & Orne, 1986; Bookwala, Frieze, Smith, & Ryan, 1992; Carrado et al., 1996; Caulfield & Riggs, 1992, Fiebert & Gonzales, 1997; Makepeace, 1986; Morse, 1995).

Clearly, a great deal of violence by women against men is retaliatory or in self-defense. Also, when women are the victims of assault, that usually means more serious injury than when the opposite occurs. Furthermore, no research places men in the same systematic victimization status of women who are literally terrorized into attempting to escape the relationship (Kaufman Kantor & Jasinski, 1998, pp. 9–10). The apparent statistical decrease in women reporting domestic violence is puzzling given that the number of shelters for abused women has grown from zero in 1975 to over two thousand today (Pleck, 1987), and those shelters are constantly full of battered women. Shelters across the country are continuously full beyond capacity and must turn people away. The bottom line is that with an estimate of 1.5 to 2 million domestic assaults a year on women and an untold number on men, the market for crisis counseling for battering victims and those who assault them has not dried up!

DYNAMICS OF PARTNER VIOLENCE
Psychosocial and Cultural Dynamics

The overarching dynamic that has held sway over the battering of women is the belief in male supremacy. This belief is the natural result of a long-term sexist, paternalistic social order that rewards aggressive behavior in men, but expects women to be passive and submissive (Benjamin & Walz, 1983, p. 65). Clashing with the emergent status of women outside the home, this tradition has produced a volatile mix of personality dynamics. The flash point of such a mix occurs when the man who lives the traditional male image of chief breadwinner and director of the family perceives himself as losing power in the conjugal relationship.

The question of power is the fuse that ignites this explosive mixture. In this view, the woman's position is to obey, conciliate, perform traditional domestic duties, and, in general, be subservient. Any attempt to establish herself in her own right is likely to be met with punishment for overstepping her bounds (Benjamin & Walz, 1983, pp. 74–77). Violence, though, is not something that develops only in families. It involves a complex interplay of social, cultural, and psychological factors, and to say that a patriarchal system alone is responsible for battering would seem to fall far short of the mark (Dutton, 1995, pp. 27–62).

The fact is that a great many men who have patriarchal attitudes go through their entire married lives without assaulting their wives and the sociopolitical beliefs of abusers don't discriminate them from nonabusers (Hotaling & Sugarman, 1986; Straus & Gelles, 1986). So is there one true theory of the abusive/assaultive personality that leads to partner violence? At least 20 distinct theories on battering of women have been identified (Okun, 1986). The following 11 theories encapsulate past and present thinking about the causes of battering.

Attachment Theory.   Disruptions of attachment in early life arouse intense anger, grief, sorrow, and anxiety in the child and diminish the child's ability to form mutual and trusting relationships as an adult. High correlations appear among spousal violence and the number of separation-and-loss events abusers and their families of origin experienced and the erratic care-giving patterns of batterers' parents. Thus, men whose parents were unreliable, abusive, needy, or otherwise unequal to the task of child rearing may be very sensitive to fears of abandonment and enmeshment. As a result, they may use verbal and physical abuse as a way to distance themselves from an intimate relationship that they believe will hurt them in some way (Bowlby, 1980).

Coercive Control.   Morgan (1982) used the term *conjugal terrorism* to describe a tactic akin to brainwashing and political terrorism, whereby violence or the threat of violence is used to break the victim's resistance and bend her to the will of the terrorist (batterer). Typical brainwashing and terrorist tools such as social and physical isolation, torture, sleep deprivation, malnourishment, dictating the use of the victim's time, bondage, false confessions, and denouncing and belittling the victim to significant others are all standard operating procedures of abusers to enhance the victim's dependency on them. Johnson (1995) identifies this type of batterer as indeed a terrorist, representative of the type that women who seek out shelters describe. This pathological male is a great deal different from the general population of batterers and is extremely dangerous (Kaufman Kantor & Jasinski, 1998, p. 1).

Cultural Reinforcement.   Sociological theories cover a wide gamut of specific theories that are psychosocially and culturally bound. These theories range from finding the roots of violence in the culture at large down to the family unit. Societal attitudes about the legitimate use of violence to achieve personal ends have their roots in a tradition of perceived "national interest." As a nation, we promote and glorify the controlled use of aggression for protection, law and order, self-defense, and national interest (Benjamin & Walz, 1983, pp. 64–66). Force is a major resource in maintaining the existing social structure and projecting national presence. This notion has been extended to the family by at least implicit permission of the state. For the state, the family is the basic disciplinary agent—family over individual, male over female, adult over child. Control is direct, continuous, personalized, and an efficient way of keeping intact the past social order of the state (Capps, 1982). When males are incapable of demonstrating their supposed superior status through other skills or abilities, they still have the resource of physical force to maintain their dominant position.

Exchange Theory.   Exchange theory (Gelles & Cornell, 1985) is a variant of a learning theory approach. It proposes that batterers hit people because they can (Carden, 1994). As long as the costs for being violent do not outweigh the rewards, violence will invariably be used as a method of control. Particularly when social control agents such as the police, criminal charges, imprisonment, loss of status, and loss of income are not used as negative sanctions that increase the cost of the behavior, batterers will continue to batter. Sexual inequality in regard to size, financial resources, and social status allows batterers to become violent without fear of retribution. Although there may be loss of status in the larger society for being a child or wife beater, there are certain subcultures where aggressive and violent behavior are proof of being a "real man." Finally, exacting "costs" from a partner to pay for her or his supposed "sins and transgressions" is in and of itself satisfying to the batterer (Gelles & Cornell, 1985, pp. 120–125).

Feminist Theory.   Feminist theory views social phenomena as determined by the sexist, patriarchal structure of our society and battering as merely one outcome of a structure that allows rape, incest, prostitution, foot binding, and a host of other sexist restrictions to keep women in servile positions (Schechter, 1982; Stark & Flitcraft, 1988). Feminists believe that women have not achieved the political, economic, and social independence that would empower them to leave abusive relationships (Bograd, 1992; Dobash & Dobash, 1992; Pagelow, 1992). They do not believe that a woman has any culpability in promoting or maintaining a violent relationship because the perpetrator alone commits the act; he alone is morally and legally responsible for it and should be the one to suffer the consequences (Avis, 1992; Bograd, 1992). A strict feminist view categorically separates woman battering from other forms of intrafamily violence or at the most sees the other forms of family violence as a by-product of how women are brutalized (Okun, 1986; Pleck, 1987). The feminist view also holds that until women are seen as other than subservient, compliant victims, little will change. Feminists criticize the mass media for romanticizing violence, male dominance, and female submissiveness (Dines, 1992; Jarvie, 1991). Feminist theory calls for a complete restructuring of society to eradicate the power differential that males enjoy that allows them to batter.

Intraindividual Theory.   There is evidence that psychopathology and neurophysiological disorders may play a greater part in some perpetrators of battering than was previously thought. Personality disorders, attention deficit disorder, psychosis, internal head trauma and substance abuse have been identified as possible contributing factors that lead to aggression and rage reactions (Browne & Herbert, 1997, p. 61; Dutton, 1994, 1995, pp. 26–29; Jasinski & Williams, 1998, p. 42).

Learning Theory.   Learning theory approaches operate on the principle that both perpetration and acceptance of physical and psychological abuse is conditioned and learned behavior. A great deal of research indicates a strong relationship between being abused by parents and/or witnessing interparental violence as a child and being violent toward a partner as an adult (Astin, Ogland-Hand, Coleman, & Foy, 1995; Barnett & Hamberger, 1992; Beasley & Stoltenberg, 1992; Jouriles & Norwood, 1995). Foremost among these theories is Lenore Walker's (1984, 1989) theory of learned helplessness, which she adapted from animal studies conducted on random, noncontingent punishment. Applied to battering in particular, the theory proposes that battered women stay in abusive relationships because they have been conditioned to believe they cannot predict their own safety and that nothing they or anyone else does will alter their terrible circumstances.

Walker (1984, 1989) proposed a number of factors in childhood and adulthood that are building blocks for learned helplessness. Childhood factors include witnessing or experiencing battering, sexual abuse or molestation, health problems or chronic illness, stereotypical sex roles, and rigid tradition. Such experiences teach the child that external, autocratic, and often whimsical forces dictate outcomes. In adulthood, factors that are instigated by the batterer include an emergent pattern of violence, sexual abuse, jealousy, over possessiveness, intrusiveness and isolation, threat of harm, observed violence toward others, animals, or things, and alcohol or drug abuse. Given these conditions, the victim cannot escape the noncontingent punishment.

The term *helplessness* has caused a great deal of furor from feminists because they see this pejorative term as casting women in a victim role with few resources or little empowerment. However, according to Walker (1989), women are not helpless in the standard sense of the term. What learned helplessness does mean is that battered women choose behavioral responses that have the highest predictability of causing them the least harm in the known situation (pp. 50–52). Because of the extreme and often lethal violence that occurs when these women attempt to leave and the lack of social support in making any attempt, it is understandable that a "Better the devil I know!" philosophy predominates for many abused women.

Masochism.   Psychoanalytic theory, which has held masochism to be the primary motivating factor in abusive relationships, is now mostly obsolete in the scientific community. There is no empirical research to substantiate the notion that erotic enjoyment of pain through battering is a trait found in abused women (Moss, 1991; Okun, 1986; Stark & Flitcraft, 1988). From a feminist point of view, this theory held sway for a long time because the male-dominated field of psychiatry found it a convenient pigeonhole for a troublesome problem. Until interest in the problem was generated in the 1970s, little research was presented to refute the idea.

Nested Ecological Theory.   Dutton (1985, 1995) proposed an ecological theory that integrates many of the foregoing theories. Four layers of variables operate within the ecosystem. First is a core of individual experience composed of intrapersonal psychological factors such as shame, denial, and hostility. Second is a family system layer, in which the individual experiences such negative actions as abandonment, neglect, and abuse. Third is a community/peer layer, which inculcates fundamental religious training, alcohol and drug use, and rigid gender role socialization. Finally, in a larger societal context, the individual is exposed to sociopolitical gender inequities, media portrayal of subjugation and violence against women, and racial/ethnic prejudices.

Sociobiology.   Sociobiology proposes that evolutionary adaptation requires aggression for survival. Thus, there is the inherited tendency to aggress against someone who threatens the chances of survival and, deductively, procreation of the species. If the foregoing is true, then it would be reasonable to expect that males would aggress against other real or imagined males who were trying to take away the female. The question then arises, Why would the male assault the object he wishes to possess instead of other intruding males? The sociobiologists have no clear answer for this question (Dutton, 1995, pp. 29–34).

System Theory.   System theory posits that battering is not attributable to the standard victim–abuser dichotomy. Rather, *conjugal violence* and *battering relationship* are more appropriate terms to depict battering as part of a violence-prone system. The violence is a maladaptive but efficient way to keep the system in homeostasis. Through learning history and rigidly polarized roles for both parties, the system is able to maintain itself (Wiehe, 1998, pp. 87–90).

Although each of the preceding theoretical stances has merit, to this point none has proven itself to completely explain the phenomenon of battering. Certainly, there is much to be said for a feminist perspective couched in paternalistic sociocultural terms. If it had not been for the feminist movement's willingness to take on battering as a social issue, it would probably still be "behind drawn shades." There is also clear evidence that at least one factor contributing to our bulging prison population is that certain people will attempt to get away with anything they can with little regard to the expense of others, as long as they believe they can escape the consequences of their actions. Similarly, evidence exists that legions of people with personality disorders would think nothing of manipulating anyone in any manner to satisfy their insatiable narcissistic or dependency needs. There is also clear evidence from a national perspective that Teddy Roosevelt's admonition "Speak softly and carry a big stick!" is extremely effective and has trickled down to the family unit. It doesn't take a doctorate in sociology to figure out that ecological and cultural variations may have profound affects on the kind and incidence of partner violence. Finally, it is hard to argue against the contention that the founding fathers' belief that "a man's home is his castle" has much to do with society's refusal to intervene in the sacrosanct realm of the home.

Psychological Factors

Psychologically, both parties to a battering situation have certain identifiable characteristics. Men in a battering relationship may

1. Demonstrate excessive dependency and possessiveness toward their women—although they deny it
2. Be unable to express any emotion except anger and generally have poor communication skills where emotional issues are concerned
3. Have unrealistic expectations of their spouses and idealize marriage or the relationship far beyond what realistically may be expected
4. Have a lack of self-control and, paradoxically, set up rigid family boundaries for everyone else
5. Be alcohol or drug abusers
6. Were abused as children or saw their mothers abused
7. Deny and minimize problems, particularly battering, that they generate in families
8. Emotionally cycle from hostility, aggressiveness, and cruelty when they do not get their way, to charm, manipulation, and seductiveness when they do
9. Be characterized as jealous, denying, impulsive, self-deprecating, depressive, demanding, aggressive, and violent
10. Feel a lack of comparative power to the woman in economic status, decision making, and communication skills

(This list was derived from Babcock, Jacobson, Gottman, & Waltz, 1993; Barnett, Pittman, Ragan, & Salus, 1980; Finkelhor, Gelles, Hotaling, & Straus, 1983; Gelles & Cornell, 1985; Okun, 1986; Shupe et al., 1987; Walker, 1984, 1989.)

Women in a battering relationship may

1. Have a lack of self-esteem as a result of being told over and over that they are stupid, incompetent, and otherwise inadequate
2. Experience a lack of control and little confidence in their ability to take any meaningful steps to improve their marriage
3. Have experienced a history of abuse that leads them to accept their role as victim, or saw their mothers abused and accepted it as their lot
4. Be so ashamed that they hide their physical and emotional wounds and become socially and emotionally isolated
5. Lack personal, physical, educational, and financial resources that would allow them to get out of the battering situation
6. Be extremely dependent and are willing to suffer grievous insult and injury to have their needs met
7. Have an idealized view of what a relationship should be and somehow feel they can "fix or change" the man
8. Do not have good communication skills, particularly in regard to asserting their rights and feelings

9. Learn stereotyped sex roles and thus feel guilty if they do not adhere to a rigid patriarchal system
10. Be unable to differentiate between sex and love and believe that love is manifested through intense sexual relationships

(This list was derived from Benjamin & Walz, 1983; Finkelhor et al., 1983; Gelles & Cornell, 1985; Ibrahim & Herr, 1987; Okun, 1986; Walker, 1984, 1989).

In one way or another, all the concepts we've just enumerated have to do with power. Partner battering all points back to this basic encultured dynamic. If men acted on impulse or some other drive, they would beat up their bosses, secretaries, friends, or neighbors as often as they do their mates and children. Although some sociopaths might fit this category of indiscriminate violence, they are in the minority (Gondolf, 1985; Hastings & Hamburger, 1988; Holtzworth-Munroe & Stuart, 1994). Only in a conjugal relationship do many men generally believe in and exercise their ability to coerce, abuse, and beat women and children (Hart, 1980).

Stressors

If power is the fuse, then stress is the match that lights the fuse. As the idealized image of the relationship breaks down and environmental stresses build up, couples become engaged in an ever-upward spiral of violent interaction (Barnett et al., 1980). Although they are not generic to all battering, a list of factors that seem to appear over and over in domestic violence has been compiled by Barnett and associates (1980, pp. 7–9), Benjamin and Walz (1983), Finkelhor and associates (1983), Gelles and Cornell (1985), Jasinski and Williams (1998), Okun (1986), Parker and associates (1993), and Walker (1984, p. 51). These factors may be introduced by the batterer to control the situation, may occur as a product of the relationship itself, or may be environmentally introduced from outside the relationship.

1. *Geographic isolation.* Because of geographic location, the victim has no friends near who can provide a support system. A farm woman who cannot drive is an example of the worst case—literally being marooned and held captive by an abusive husband.
2. *Social isolation.* Because of extreme emotional dependence, the woman expects all needs to be met by her partner and has no significant others to turn to when she is assaulted.
3. *Economic stress.* When a woman is unemployed or underemployed, has inadequate housing, is pressured by creditors, and cannot feed and clothe her children by herself, she becomes human chattel to her abusive partner.
4. *Medical problems.* Long-term, chronic medical problems for either spouse or children exact tremendous financial and emotional cost.
5. *Inadequate parenting skills.* A lack of knowledge of parenting skills and conflict over parental roles can lead to situations that start as minor disciplinary problems and escalate into violence in the family.
6. *Pregnancy.* Ranging from heralding an unwanted child through creating anxiety over providing for the new baby to arousing jealousy over a wife's attention to a newborn, pregnancy is an especially acute crisis point for potential abuse.

7. *Family dysfunction.* A veritable kaleidoscope of problems causes dysfunction in the family. Some of these problems are related to age and number of children, presence of stepchildren, loyalty conflicts, death, desertion, and career change.

8. *Alcohol and drug abuse.* Chemical dependence serious enough to cause economic chaos and severe emotional disturbance characterizes addictive families and has spin-offs that commonly include spouse abuse. The insidious problem with alcohol and drugs is that they are often used as an excuse for behavior (battering) that is normally prohibited by societal norms and standards.

9. *Educational and/or vocational disparity.* When a female in a relationship has higher educational attainment or higher vocational status than the male, this may raise questions of adequacy and responsibility with both parties. Furthermore, if the man is unemployed and the woman is employed, the man has a great deal of time to brood on his inability to function as the head of household, which males already suffering from feelings of inadequacy may find extremely demeaning.

10. *Age.* One of the most consistent risk factors of battering is age range. Approximately 20 percent of men in the age range of 18 to 25 and 17 percent of men in the age range of 26 to 35 committed at least one act of violence in the past year.

Myths About Battering

The following myths encapsulate numerous arguments used by those who would submerge, camouflage, and diminish battering (Gelles & Cornell, 1985; Massachusetts Coalition of Battered Women Service Groups, 1981; Okun, 1986; Stark & Flitcraft, 1988; Straus et al., 1980).

1. *"Battered women overstate the case."* Any person who has contusions, lacerations, and broken bones is not overstating anything. In any other instance such outcomes are referred to as *assault and battery.*

2. *"Battered women provoke the beating."* Although some women may be classified as the stereotypical "nag," there can certainly be many significant others in a man's life who fit into the "nag" category.

3. *"Battered women are masochists."* If such women did have masochistic tendencies, they would find a variety of ways to suffer pain, not just an abusive mate.

4. *"Battering is a private, family matter."* When beaten women are disenfranchised from their homes and the children of battering relationships learn the pathological roles a battering father models, battering transcends the home and becomes society's problem.

5. *"Alcohol abuse is the prime reason for wife abuse."* Although alcohol plays a part in many cases of abuse, it may be only an excuse for, and not the cause of, violent behavior.

6. *"Battering occurs only in problem families."* The dynamic representation of stress factors that assail families shows that any family at any given point may be classified as "problem."

7. *"Only low-income and working-class families experience violence."* Members of those socioeconomic classes do come to the attention of the police and welfare

agencies to a much greater degree than middle- or upper-class members, but statistics from wife abuse shelters indicate that battering has no class boundaries.

8. *"The battering cannot be that bad or she would not stay."* The host of personal factors that tie the women to the relationship militate heavily against simply picking up and leaving.

9. *"A husband has patriarchal rights."* What a man does in his own family is not his own business when the emotional overflow of what he does spills over into the community. No amount or kind of justification from the Bible or any other authority—be it person, institution, or book—can excuse spouse abuse.

10. *"The beaten spouse exaggerates the problem to exact revenge."* Reporting a beating—whether committed by a total stranger or one's spouse—is no exaggeration. If revenge were the motive, there would be a host of ways of going about it that would be far less traumatic than calling or showing up at an abuse shelter.

11. *"Women are too sensitive, especially when they are pregnant."* If a person is too sensitive who objects to being kicked in the stomach or vagina, thrown down a flight of stairs, or hit in the face with a lamp, then we would suppose that everyone is overly sensitive.

12. *"Battering is rare."* The statistics reported in this chapter clearly indicate otherwise. Family violence is endemic in society.

13. *"Battering is confined to mentally disturbed or sick people."* It appears that less than 10 percent of family violence is caused by mental illness. Although continued physical and psychological abuse may cause many victims to suffer serious emotional distress and posttraumatic stress disorder, they did not enter the relationship "sick." Furthermore, most perpetrators are not mentally ill by any *DSM-IV* definition.

14. *"Violence and love cannot coexist."* Strange as it may seem, members of violent families may still love one another. This paradoxical aspect is most problematic because children in such families grow up believing you hit the people you love.

Profiling the Batterer

Researchers have examined multiple personality and behavioral typologies of batterers. Dutton (1995), Gondolf (1985), Hastings and Hamberger (1988), Holtzworth-Munroe and Stuart (1994), and Saunders (1992) have all developed typologies of batterers based on clusters of demographic, personality, and abuse variables.

Holtzworth-Munroe and Stuart (1994) have compiled three major groupings of: family only, dysphoric (anxious)/borderline, and generally violent/antisocial. Characteristics of the family-only batterer include high dependency, impulsivity, poor communication skills, and family-of-origin violence. The dysphoric/borderline has a history of parental rejection and child abuse, delinquent acts, poor communication and social skills, violence-as-a-solution ideation, extreme fears of abandonment, and low remorse. The generally violent/antisocial batterer has all the foregoing characteristics, but to a much more profound degree and probably falls into what Jasinski and Williams (1998, p. 1) call the *terroristic* batterer. Such people are extremely aggressive, impulsive, and view violence as appropriate to any provocation both inside and outside the home. The family-only batterers are the largest group, and their behavior is consistent with Walker's (1979) cycle of violence. Its members are likely to be contrite and apologetic after battering incidents. Gondolf (1985) reports this group type to be most prevalent, with a 52 percent occurrence rate. The dysphoric/borderline and antisocial types are typical of how women who flee to shelters describe their batterers. They are the most dangerous, and according to Gondolf comprise about 41 percent and 7 percent of batterers.

The Cycle of Violence

Barnett and associates (1980) schematically represented the phases leading to the explosion of violence in the family. Walker's (1984) cycle theory of violence: (1) tension building, (2) battering and abuse, (3) contrition and loving respite closely parallels these phases and her research supports the theory (p. 95).

Phase I. Tranquillity prevails. The relationship may have been characterized as calm to this point, with no previous violent incidents, or a period of calm may follow an earlier violent episode.

Phase II. Tension starts to build. A variety of stresses impinge on the relationship. They may come in combination or singly from the common group we have already mentioned. However, there is no reduction of tension and the situation grows more strained.

Phase III. A violent episode occurs. The episode may range from harsh words to a severe beating. At this phase, communication has broken down and the situation is out of control.

Phase IV. The relationship takes on crisis proportions. A variety of options becomes available.

   A. The abuser becomes remorseful and asks forgiveness. Sooner or later the victim forgives the abuser and calm is restored.
   B. The abuser is not remorseful and feels his control over the situation has been established. The victim gives in and relinquishes control, and calm is restored.
   C. The victim takes new action. Within this option are two possibilities: the abuser negotiates the situation, and, given that the negotiation is agreeable to the victim, calm is restored; or the abuser rejects the new action and a crisis state continues.

It is at this last point, in which no possibility of resolution exists, that the victim is most likely to seek help by referring herself to an abuse center. If effective assessment and intervention do not occur when the violence emerges (Phase II), the likelihood that the violence will recur and will be of greater intensity is dramatically increased (Barnett et al., 1980, p. 34). Dutton (1995, pp. 126–139) has demonstrated that this cycle closely fits that of the borderline personality disorder type of abuser.

Not all battering relationships fit the cycle of violence. Battering between partners may be a once-in-a-lifetime affair. But many women have reported being constantly terrorized and assaulted with no intermittent periods of relief (Dutton, 1993). These are most probably the victims of the antisocial type of batterer, who sees little need for contrition or remorse in his dealing with a partner or anybody else for that matter.

Realities for Abused Women

Why, then, do women stay in an abusing relationship? For those who have no experience with violence in a relationship, it is an easy thing to say, "Throw the bum out!" or "I wouldn't tolerate that, I'd call the cops and have you arrested!" or "Forget you, nobody does that to me, I'm leaving!" In actuality, most women who are in battering relationships do leave, and this in itself is a courageous act because it is one of the most dangerous things a woman can do. The batterer tends to do poorly on his own and would often rather kill or die than be separated from the woman, because he is more terrified of abandonment than violence or punishment (Walker, 1989, p. 65). It is remarkable that a number of women do leave given their clear understanding that lives hang in the balance—their own, those of their children, and even the batterer's.

Most women leave a battering relationship an average of three to six times, but do so with varying degrees of permanency (Dobash & Dobash, 1979; Walker, 1979). The following reasons for staying in the relationship have been gleaned from a number of researchers (Benjamin & Walz, 1983; Okun, 1986; Pagelow, 1981; Walker, 1979, 1984, 1989), and these realities have nothing to do with the myths we've previously stated.

1. The woman has a fear of reprisal or of aggravating the attacks even more.
2. Even though the situation may be intolerable for the woman, her children do have food, clothing, and shelter.
3. The woman would suffer shame, embarrassment, humiliation, and even ridicule if her secret got out.
4. Her self-concept is so strongly dependent on the relationship and perceived social approval that leaving would be very destructive to her.
5. Early affection and prior love in the relationship persist and, by staying, the woman hopes to salvage them.
6. If financially well off, the woman is unable to forego a reduction in her financial freedom.
7. In the cyclic nature of abuse, her mate may not be terrible 24 hours a day, seven days a week. The victim may tend to forget the batterings and remember only the good times.
8. Early role models of an abusive parent may lead her to believe that relationships exist in no other way.
9. The woman may hold religious values that strongly militate against separation, divorce, or anything less than filial subjugation to the man's wishes.
10. The woman may be undereducated, have small children to raise, and have no job skills.
11. She may be kept so socially, physically, geographically, and financially isolated that she has no resources of any kind to help her get out.
12. She may be so badly injured that she is unable physically to leave.
13. She may believe the man's promise to reform.
14. She may be concerned for children who are still at home.
15. Love or sorrow at the mate's professed inability to exist without her may impel her to stay.

Secondary victimization may result by labeling battered women as hysterical, depressed, schizophrenic, alcoholic, or child neglecters and abusers. Such labeling may provide professionals with "reasons" to do things to battered women ranging from overmedication with psychotropic drugs to sending them to jail and removing their children from the home. Any one of the revictimizations by well-meaning or not-so-well-meaning institutions undermines assertiveness and reinforces submissiveness and compliance, which in turn increases vulnerability to abuse (Stark & Flitcraft, 1988; Walker, 1989). It is little wonder that a woman making her first call to an abuse center may be taking only an initial step in a series that sometimes goes on for years before she can make a complete break from the battering relationship.

INTERVENTION STRATEGIES

In the last 25 years the raising of consciousness that domestic violence is epidemic and that it extracts tremendous financial and emotional cost from society has caused an exponential rise in attempts at intervention. To that end, intervention strategies for battering are different from other types of crises we explore, because they target both victim and victimizer.

Assessment

Assessment in battering and domestic violence is complex, and is subject to controversy and many unanswered questions in regard to its precursors, onset, and outcomes both for victims and victimizers. Assessment is also problematic because of the transcrisis nature of battering. Both batterers and those who are battered do not present themselves in a "steady state" that is amenable to stable and consistent measurement.

Personality Measures.   Assessment of battered women by personality measures is somewhat confounding and contradictory to what one might logically expect. One never really knows whether the personality factors found in battered women were present before they were battered or are the result of the victimization (Gelles & Cornell, 1985, p. 71). However, Walker (1989, p. 105) reports that as the battering progressively becomes worse, Minnesota Multiphasic Personality Inventory (MMPI) profiles change notably. Using the MMPI, Rosewater (1982) found that the profiles of battered women appear similar to those of other emotionally disturbed individuals. However, investigation of subscale inconsistencies indicated that battered women differ from others who have serious mental illness. This is an important distinction that debunks the notion that most battered women are unstable. For example, battered women may have real reasons to be fearful about their safety, and such fears are not indicative of paranoid ideation (Walker, 1984, p. 75).

The question arises, Are there particular attributes, traits, or psychological profiles that will indicate those women who are potential victims of batterers? In an extensive review of characteristics of battered women, Hotaling and Sugarman (1986) found only one characteristic—having witnessed or been a victim of personal violence as a child—as a consistent characteristic. When they reviewed the responses of 699 women who participated in the first National Violence Study, the researchers could not find even that characteristic (Hotaling & Sugarman, 1990). Thus, there appears to be little empirical evidence that there are any consistent predisposing factors that predict who will and who will not become a victim of abuse.

The Battered Woman Scale (Schwartz & Mattley, 1993) is used to measure traits that arise as a result of experiences in battering relationships. Overall, battered women present many of the symptoms of posttraumatic stress disorder and can be placed for diagnostic purposes within the PTSD category of the *DSM-IV* (American Psychiatric Association, 1994; Astin, Lawrence, & Foy, 1993). Weaver (1998) found in her study of women who had been either sexually or physically abused as children, raped as adults or battered, only battering was a common marker for PTSD. Thompson and associates (1999) found that suicide, PTSD symptomology, and physical partner abuse go hand in hand. Women incarcerated for killing or seriously assaulting their partners also show increased levels of PTSD symptomology (Hattendorf, Ottens, & Lomax, 1999; O'Keefe, 1998). Indeed, Walker (1989, pp. 48–49) proposes the battered woman syndrome as a subcategory of PTSD. Therefore, if PTSD symptoms are present, then partner violence should always be suspected.

Clinical Interview.   Probably the best assessment device for partner abuse is a clinical interview. Any family history taking should include questions about hitting, threats, controlling, destruction of property or pets, forced sex, alcohol and drug use, and the partner's hypervigilance and paranoia about the client's actions (Jasinski & Williams, 1998, p. 37).

Walker (1984, p. 122) also has one major rule of assessment that supersedes all others and to which we strongly subscribe: *When a woman calls or comes in to report a battering, believe her and start intervention immediately.* It is a safe bet that whenever a battered woman seeks help, she is not carrying out the act as some impetuous, hysterical, spur-of-the-moment way to get back at her mate. Battered women refer themselves only after their problems have become exceedingly serious. Walker (1984, p. 26) found that only 14 percent of battered women surveyed would seek help after a first incident, 22 percent would seek help after a second incident, and 49 percent would seek help only after a series of incidents had taken place.

Given the length of time that passes and the degree of severity of the crisis that is typically reached before help is sought, triage assessment of the battered woman should look first and foremost to her safety and the safety of significant others, such as her children. We can assume that a battered woman making an initial call to a crisis line will be at the extremely high end of the assessment scale. She will be behaviorally out of control because of the beating she has just had. She will be affectively out of control because of the trauma she has just suffered and the threat of more to come. Cognitively, she may be just holding together and may not be far from dissociating from the terrible reality of her situation.

Sadly, many in the helping professions still confuse the effects of domestic abuse with symptoms of other diagnoses. It is extremely important to be aware of these masking symptoms. Compared to women who are not abused, they are 5 times more likely to attempt suicide, 15 times more likely to abuse alcohol, 9 times more likely to abuse drugs, 6 times more likely to report child abuse, and 3 times more likely to be diagnosed as psychotic or depressed. It is little wonder that these women experience low self-esteem (Aguilar & Nightingale, 1994).

Crisis workers typically encounter battering victims in the following four settings: in hospital emergency rooms and other medical care settings, on telephone crisis lines, in police follow-up operations on domestic violence calls at crisis centers, and at shelters (discussed later in this chapter).

Medical Settings.   Many of these women will not acknowledge abuse no matter how empathic and supportive the medical worker is. Therefore, when physical abuse is suspected, the worker should state that this is just a routine part of any medical examination and that the supportive service information the woman is about to get is also routinely provided. In that way, the woman is given control of the situation, is given support by the worker, and her autonomy is respected (Hamberger, 1994).

No one else should be present in the interview for the sake of the patient's safety. The worker needs to ask specific and direct questions while walking a tightrope of not being confrontive or antagonistic. The following questions are abridged from Snyder's (1994) and Hamberger's (1994) protocols for hospital emergency room staff.

CW: Lots of times people get into arguments, and they get physical with one another. I'm wondering if some of your bruises occurred that way? When you and your husband or boyfriend argue, does he get angry? Do you feel afraid? I'm wondering if he ever loses his temper with the children, and when you step in he loses it with you and maybe winds up hitting you. How does he act with you if he's been drinking or using drugs? Sometimes when people get jealous they overreact and get physical. Did this happen with him? Have you ever been with someone who tried to really control you by hitting you or threatening to hurt you? Are you in one of those relationships now?

By raising the issue of arguing, the worker normalizes the situation and opens the door for the client to talk about the reasons that brought her to the medical facility. By asking about her fears, the worker validates her affective and cognitive bases regarding the situation. These and other questions move from general relationship issues to what Hamberger (1994) calls "funneling" to more behavioral specifics about the abuse, such as number and severity of incidents, types of weapons used, and who did the battering.

Juanita: Well . . . I sorta got hit with a broom handle.
CW: (*Empathically but assertively.*) A broom handle has to be attached to somebody's hand. Whose hand was it? Is he the man who brought you here?

Specific information about what she can do and what the hospital can do should be given if the patient admits she has been physically abused. Medical staff should be well acquainted with local and state laws governing abuse so they can know what legal obligations they have and what can be done to keep the woman safe. Very specific step-by-step protocols should be formulated and made available to all staff, along with in-service education on domestic violence and its signs. Brasseur (1994) abstracted a typical protocol from Chicago's Rush–Presbyterian–St. Luke's Medical Center to be followed once a battered woman has been identified:

1. Assign a primary nurse.
2. Notify appropriate support services within the hospital.
3. Give a complete physical exam, along with a neurological exam and X rays.
4. Document statements about who caused the injuries.
5. Make a body map of old and new injuries.
6. Depending on the jurisdiction, make a call to the police, identify the assailant, and have him arrested, if possible.
7. Take photographs of the victim's injuries.
8. Inform the patient of her right to access her medical files and how to do it.

9. Discuss with the woman a posthospital plan that will include shelter or other re-ferral, safety plans if she is not leaving the abusive situation, and community support services.

When a protocol such as the foregoing is followed, identification rates of victims of partner violence go up (McLeer & Anwar, 1989; Olson et al., 1996; Tilden & Shepard, 1987).

Crisis Lines.   Of all the dilemmas a crisis telephone worker faces, battering is one of the worst. Although the threat of further injury or death to the woman may be extremely high, unless the crisis worker feels danger is imminent and can get the woman to give her name and address so that a 911 call can be made, the best the crisis worker can do is offer short-term assistance to help ease physical pain and calm the emotional state of the client. Even then the crisis worker may have raging internal debates about what to do. If the client is helped to a safe place, will that only enrage her mate even more? Is the woman really ready to make such a move? What assets does the battered woman have so that she can leave? What are her debits? That is why the worker should carefully go over each area, making sure that all pertinent information and all possibilities of available action have been carefully considered. No other type of crisis we commonly deal with presents as critical a need for comprehensive yet fast assessment.

It is also worth remembering that if the worker calls back a week later, the client may be going through a "honeymoon phase" and may seem not to have a care in the world, only to turn around later at the next battering and beseech the crisis worker to help her. These situations that oscillate from extreme need one day, to little if any need the next, can make workers cynical and uncaring if they do not carefully manage their stress levels. Yet such ambivalence is more typical than not as clients slowly come to grips with the risks and realities of leaving the situation or quite possibly facing death there.

Components of Intervention

As a call comes in to the abuse center and the crisis worker picks up the phone, the assessment process begins with active listening. The crisis worker immediately has to be concerned with a variety of roles. The worker must not only be a good listener but also supportive, facilitative, and concerned with the caller's safety and must act as an advocate (Barnett et al., 1980, p. 44).

Listening.   Facilitative listening and responding are crucial. The victim must know that the crisis worker understands and accepts her present situation in a nonjudgmental, non-value-laden way. Only then will the battered woman be able to open up and share her feelings about her predicament (Heppner, 1978). The crisis worker also immediately reflects that she understands the difficulty and urgency of the situation by positively reinforcing the battered woman for calling and taking a first step toward resolving her problem.

CW: You did the right thing by calling. No matter how bad it seems and what terrible things have happened, you've made a big step on the road to straightening it out. We're here to help, and we'll stick with it as long as it takes.

Juanita: I . . . I . . . don't know. It's gone on so long. I feel so ashamed. I don't know what to do! It's so confusing.

CW: I understand how you feel and how difficult it was to make this call. The hurt, the fear, the uncertainty of it all. So start anywhere you want. We won't do anything unless *you* decide it's best for you. Right now, I want to listen to what you have to say. I'll listen for as long as it takes, so take your time and tell me what's happened.

Supporting. The caller is given both explicit and implicit permission to ventilate. The free flow of the victim's anger, hurt, fear, guilt, and other debilitating feelings may take from a few minutes to two hours to an extended period of months. Supportiveness means empathizing but not sympathizing with the victim. A sense of lack of social support is one of the major factors for battered women (Perrin, Van Hasselt, Basilio, & Hersen, 1996) and this lack may be particularly severe for immigrants with different cultural backgrounds (Sev'er, 1997, pp. 3–5). Many victims are only partially mobile and any action steps they take may be months away from happening. Thus supporting a victim does not mean intervention on a one-shot basis. The crisis worker may have to exert an excruciating amount of patience over a long period of time as the victim slowly moves toward making a decision to take action. No matter how bad the victim's situation looks to the worker, only the victim herself can decide when she is ready to take action to alleviate her traumatic situation (Dagastino, 1984).

CW: OK! I understand it's a hard decision to make—getting out. Your marriage has had some good times and you'd really like to hang onto that part of it, even though the beatings are happening more often. You say you want some time to think about it. That's OK! It's your decision, and we'll help whenever you need us.

Breaking away from a battering relationship is a slow developmental process. The crisis worker cannot move the victim any faster than she is willing to go. The crisis worker must be acutely aware of being manipulated into becoming sympathetic to the victim's needs and attempting to "fix" things for her. Many times the victim will project anger onto the police, a minister, or other significant persons. At some point the victim needs to see that displacement and shifting of responsibility to others is not going to solve the problem. The crisis worker must be aware of this possibility and not get trapped into proposing external remedies.

The victim is actually demonstrating what Heppner (1978) calls the "wishing and hoping syndrome." The victim wishes the situation would change, that her spouse would treat her the way he used to, and hopes the crisis worker can effect a change in her husband. However, cessation of battering by the abuser rarely happens without legal or therapeutic intervention (Dagastino, 1984). Under no circumstances should the crisis worker attempt to rescue the victim by talking to the batterer. It is dangerous and takes responsibility and autonomy away from the victim. Instead, the conversation should be redirected away from what can be done to "fix" the batterer and toward what the victim is now able to do.

CW: Although I hear you wanting me to come and straighten your husband out and make things the way they were, I can't do that. I wish I could, but I'm not a marriage counselor. If you think marriage counseling would work, I can give you some names of people who do that. What I can do is help you make some decisions about what you want to do right now.

A typical response to the crisis worker's refusal to fix the problem is anger.

Juanita: You're no damn help at all. You're just as bad as the rest. You're a horrible counselor. I'm gonna have to go back to him, and he'll kill me, just because you wouldn't do anything.

Because abuse workers do not want to lose clients, such ploys often rub a raw nerve in the workers and propel them to do something they may later regret. The crisis worker should realize that when a victim doubts the worker's ability, she is also doubting her own ability. She is probably looking for a way to resume the relationship and may be displacing her own incompetence to make changes by blaming the worker (Dagastino, 1984). The best response the crisis worker can make is not to be confrontive but to be empathic, realizing that right now the woman is looking for a way to go back to her mate.

CW: I'm sorry you're angry with me because I won't talk to your husband. I realize the frustration you feel. Yet I'm also not like the others who'll tell you how to act and what to do. I want you to know I'd be happy to work on a plan of action you want to take.

The excerpt typifies the response of a crisis worker who is being supportive yet not taking over for the victim. Usually abuse victims have not been independent to any degree and quickly fall back into a dependent state. If the crisis worker keeps foremost in mind that the woman he or she is now talking to is ultimately going to have to be her own defender and protector, then the crisis worker is not likely to fall into a sympathy trap. The crisis worker who becomes angry or engages in denouncing or criticizing the husband is making a fundamental mistake. The worker may provoke the victim to defend the violent batterer and to attack the crisis worker (Dagastino, 1984).

Facilitating. To facilitate the movement of a victim to action takes a great deal of tenacity and patience. Typically the crisis worker will have to deal with feelings of dependency, ambivalence, and depression, which are all clear-cut signs of the client's immobility. Overarching these immobilizing feelings is the learned helplessness we referred to earlier. To generate movement in the victim, the crisis worker strongly reinforces the victim's attempts at rational decision making, self-control, and statements of personal power (Heppner, 1978).

CW: You said that you couldn't do anything, but that's not true. You called here, didn't you? When you first started talking, you were crying uncontrollably, and now you're speaking in a rather level, controlled voice. I also notice a lot of "I" statements, which say to me you're starting to take responsibility. Maybe you don't know it, but those are all signs that you're starting to feel some personal power for the first time in a long while, and I think that's great!

Ambivalence about the situation is predominant in most women who seek help from abuse centers. Ambivalence is particularly strong with regard to the man who, after beating the woman, apologizes, showers her with gifts, and tells her what she wants to hear and what society leads her to believe (Conroy, 1982). To deal with this ambivalent state, the crisis worker cycles between asking open-ended questions and reflecting and clarifying the victim's feelings as an effective means of helping the victim to begin to examine previously denied feelings and thoughts.

CW: What were you thinking and feeling while he was beating you?

Juanita: It was like I was standing off to the side watching a movie of this. It was like this can't really be happening, especially to me.

CW: So that's how you cope with it. Kind of separating yourself from the beating, as if it's happening to someone else.

Juanita: Yes, I guess I've done it that way for a long time. I'd go crazy otherwise.

CW: What is your understanding of why you're being battered?

Juanita: I don't know. I guess I'm just not a good wife.

CW: You're not living up to his expectations, then. How about your own?

Juanita: I'm not sure. I mean, I've never thought of that. It's always been what he wants.

CW: How do you cope with the beating other than just kind of separating yourself from the situation when it happens?

Juanita: I try to do what he wants, but when it starts to build—the tension—I just try to stay out of his way and be nice, although I know sooner or later I'm gonna get it. I dread the waiting. Actually sometimes I push the issue just to get it over with. I know he'll always apologize afterward and treat me nice.

CW: So you do what he wishes even though you know the bottom line is a beating. Yet because of the anxiety you may even push things to get it over with. Seems like you're willing to pay a steep price to get his love back.

Juanita: When you say that, I can't believe I'm letting this happen to me. What a fool . . . a stupid fool!

CW: Then you feel foolish about paying that price. What's keeping you in the relationship?

Juanita: God! I don't know. Love! Honor! Obey! The kids. The good times. Martyrdom. I don't have a job, and I'm pregnant again. I've got to get out. He'll wind up killing me.

Using open-ended questions, restatement, and reflection, the crisis worker relentlessly hammers at the victim's faulty and illogical perception of the abusive situation. Only by looking and listening through the victim's eyes and ears can the crisis worker form an accurate perception of what steps to take and how the crisis worker will operate on the nondirective-to-directive continuum of intervention.

Women who have been abused also have in common the feeling of depression. Invariably, once a victim has related the details of the assault, her affect becomes flat. Depression has taken over. Beneath the depression is a volcano of residual anger that is trying to find an outlet. The crisis worker's job is to help move the victim out of her depressed state and let the angry feelings out (Dagastino, 1984). This is the first step toward taking action.

CW: As you relate the details, it sounds like you're reporting it but not living it. I wonder if that's a typical way you hold it in . . . control it.

Juanita: I guess . . . if I really thought about it, I'd kill the SOB. How could the bastard do this to me?

CW: How does it feel to let some of those angry feelings out?

Juanita: Scary! I'm really scared I would kill him if I got the chance.

CW: That is a legitimate feeling after what you've been through, but that won't get you where you want to go. Let's take a look at some of the alternatives between killing and being killed.

In summarizing the facilitation of the victim's movement from an immobile to a mobile state, the Massachusetts Coalition of Battered Women Service Groups (1981, pp. 25, 67) has made the following points. We agree with them totally.

1. *Be real.* Don't hide behind a role. You are what you are. To pretend to be something else makes the crisis worker false and discredited in the eyes of the victim.
2. *Set limits.* The crisis worker is not Superman or Superwoman. Owning feelings of puzzlement, anger, stupidity, tiredness, and so forth allows the crisis worker to stay on top of the game. If the worker is tired, is taking on a lot of anger, and cannot work it through with the victim, the worker should own the feelings, ask for time out, and get out of the situation until the problem can be gone over with a fellow professional and a fresh start can be made.
3. *Give the victim space and time to "freak out."* Remember that the victim is experiencing a flood of emotions that have been building over a long period of time. Knowing that anger is one step on the way to becoming her own person can be reassuring and empowering to the victim. Give her time to ventilate before settling down to a plan of action.
4. *Allow the victim to go through the pain, but stay with her.* A crisis worker's first response may be to become a psychological crutch because the victim is so fragile that she cannot hold together. The crisis worker who remembers that the victim has been down a long road of pain and is just now beginning to experience that pain will realize that the victim possesses a lot of staying power. Belief in the victim's ability to get out of the mess she is in is of overriding importance.
5. *Maintain eye and ear contact.* Both nonverbal and verbal responses of the victim are important; they tell the crisis worker whether what the victim is saying is congruent with what she is doing. Reading nonverbal responses may be difficult over the phone, but the worker needs to be aware of intonations, pauses, and sighs. How something is said may be as important as what is said. Also, what is not said may be as important as what is said.
6. *Be respectful and nonjudgmental.* The victim's actions must be carefully separated from the victim herself. What the victim does may be asinine; that does not mean the victim is an ass.
7. *Restate and reflect the victim's thoughts and feelings.* Simple as this sounds, it is often extremely difficult. There is no greater therapeutic help than manifesting these skills.
8. *Set priorities together.* Two heads are better than one. This is why the crisis worker is there. If the victim could handle the problem alone, she would. Likewise, the abuse worker is not in business to run the victim's life for her.
9. *Look at options.* Brainstorming can uncover a variety of previously hidden ideas and actions.
10. *Stay away from why's.* Asking *why* a person does something like staying in a battering relationship is an open invitation to philosophizing, rationalizing, and intellectualizing. Furthermore, a *why* question often leads the victim, rightly or wrongly, to assume she is being judged. When a victim feels she is being judged, she is apt to respond in defensive ways that do little to help her or her situation.
11. *Give the victim time to experience catharsis, but do not let her get stuck in self-pity.* The client needs to accomplish movement, and the crisis worker needs to

move gently from nurturing emotional release to helping the client start to make plans, however small, concerning her own predicament.

12. *Get back to the victim.* Even if the battered woman says, "I guess I can make it now," get her phone number and call a few days later to make sure she is getting along all right. Many abused women are so embarrassed by their plight and their own self-assessed stupidity that they cannot bring themselves to make another call and admit they have failed again. Note: It is important to determine when the abuser will *not* be home. Furthermore, it is important to determine if the phone has caller I.D. or call-back features so the victim's safety will not be compromised.

13. *Peer supervision and feedback are essential for domestic abuse workers.* The intensity of wife abuse is such that few, if any, crisis workers can remain totally objective all the time. Cross-supervision by trusted coprofessionals keeps the worker on track, reduces personal stress, and helps avoid burnout.

Ensuring Safety.   The crisis worker's first job is to determine how critical the situation is (Walker, 1984, p. 122). All the listening and responding skills known to humanity are of little use if the victim has multiple fractures or if her significant other has threatened to come back and kill her. The crisis worker calmly and cautiously makes an assessment of how bad the situation is. Does the victim need and want medical attention, shelter, a place to send her children, a way out of the house if her husband returns? All these questions are posed in a measured, deliberate way to avoid adding to the panic the victim already feels. Although the situation may be critical and the best alternative may be for the victim to come directly to the shelter, the crisis worker has to remember that the woman cannot be forced into making that choice. This does not mean, however, that the worker cannot make such a recommendation.

CW: From what you've said, it sounds like the situation is pretty bad. Bad enough that you might consider leaving and coming to the shelter.

Because of a fear of the unknown, the victim may balk at this alternative (Dagastino, 1984). Patiently, the crisis worker explains the role and function of the shelter, answers any questions the victim has, and tries to allay her fears. If, after all this, the victim is still unwilling to make a decision, the worker does not push the issue.

In initially reporting the battering, victims often appear to feel that it is an isolated incident and not abuse. They refuse to see it on an ever-escalating continuum. They delude themselves with the belief that "He really does love me, and if I'm a better person, it'll never happen again." As the crisis worker intervenes, he or she should be aware that such incidents are not isolated. Indeed, there is a consistent pattern leading up to the climax of battering (Walker, 1984, p. 24). The crisis worker endeavors to lay that pattern out so that the victim sees it not as isolated but as continuous and predictable. Seeing the pattern is particularly important when the victim is not sure whether to leave or stay.

CW: As you tell me about it, I hear a sort of pattern. For about a week he gets surly, starts criticizing the way the house looks, the way you look, the food you cook, and your control over the kids. Those criticisms start out mild, but become more severe until you finally have had enough and say something to the effect that he ought to take more responsibility if he doesn't like things. That winds up with your getting beat up. I wonder if you can look back and see how the situation has repeated itself.

Juanita: Well, I don't know. I really think it was different this time. I mean this was the first time I needed emergency treatment. He was really sorry afterward.

CW: OK. Granted the beating was more severe, but I believe from what you're saying that there's a very definite pattern to it. What's different is that the pattern seems to be repeating itself more frequently and it's getting more intense.

Often the client may be very immobile and may not even hear the question, so the worker may need to pose it again (Dagastino, 1984).

CW: When did he say he'd be back, and what'd he say he'd do?

Juanita: I just don't know whether to take it anymore. I love him, but I'm really scared.

CW: OK, I understand you are afraid, but I need to know how much time we've got and what threats he made.

By gently guiding the victim back to immediate and pressing issues, the crisis worker keeps the session on track but does not deny the emotional hurt and confusion the victim is experiencing.

By the time the battered woman becomes desperate enough to make the call for help, she does not have time to be analyzed. What she needs is some behavioral action-oriented techniques she can use on a short-term basis (Walker, 1979, pp. 75–77). Just knowing and having a plan, lets the victim regain some composure and feel she has obtained some control over the situation. The whole focus of the conversation is to prepare her to get through that one day. At this time, the worker does not worry about tomorrow or any other time. Tomorrow, the worker may call the victim and talk about the next day. If the worker attempts to deal with future events that extend beyond a week, the victim gets lost (Dagastino, 1984).

Because of the flood of critical needs the victim faces, the worker must realistically judge which needs may require immediate action and which ones can be deferred. To help make sense of the heavy flow of information, the crisis worker writes down what the victim tells her so that she can quickly identify and set priorities on the very practical concerns that are pressing at the victim. Issues such as getting enough money for the children's lunch the next day may be just as important as taking care of a broken nose, and the worker will need to remember this. By calmly, clearly, and concisely feeding back to the victim her written summary, the crisis worker takes the victim step by step through a review of her most critical needs. By dissecting the crisis in this manner, the worker assures the victim that her problems can be broken down and managed (Dagastino, 1984).

CW: Here are all the things I hear happening to you right now. No wonder you're feeling paralyzed; anyone in that situation would feel the same. You've said you have no job, the children don't want to leave, and that he might kill you. Let's take them one at a time and sort through each problem and put them back together.

A careful examination of the woman's fears about these problems, what priorities need to be set on them, and the options she has in dealing with them are extremely important. Until the abused woman can confront such fears openly, she cannot begin developing strategies to deal with her problems (Heppner, 1978).

CW: You're afraid to leave because you feel sure he will come after you when he comes back, and you're not sure what he might do, so that causes tension to build.

Yet I really believe if we make a plan right now you'll feel better, even if you don't have to use it.

If the victim states that she does not know what to do, the crisis worker immediately looks at the two basic alternatives—staying and leaving. A key ingredient is determining the level of danger at home. Is the abuser really going to act out, or is the fear of his acting out propelling the woman into making the call? To learn what has happened before, the crisis worker asks questions such as "When he's gone out and gotten drunk before, what has he done?" From the answers, the crisis worker gains a realistic assessment of the danger level of the situation. If the victim is unwilling to leave the house, then the crisis worker role-plays the scene of the drunken abuser returning home. Assuming the role of the abuser, the worker goes through, in a systematic way, each situation of potential confrontation and then discusses the potential positive and negative outcomes of the victim's attempt to handle the confrontation (Dagastino, 1984).

CW: (*In role.*) Hey, honey, come in the bedroom, I need you real bad.
Juanita: (*Typical response.*) I can't stand having sex with you when you are drunk.
CW: (*As self.*) Now, look at how you responded to that. When you shut him off like that, he gets angry, right? What could you do or say differently? How could you change things? How about turning the tables so he had no desire for you at all? What'd happen if you had a facial on and your hair up in curlers, and had on a frowzy housecoat? Although that might not make you very alluring, would that turn him off?

By looking at options and posing alternative ways of behaving, the worker attempts to provide coping techniques that may defuse the crisis. By the time the worker is done, the victim is feeding back a plan, point by point, either for staying in the house or for moving out. Having an escape plan is critical (Walker, 1984, p. 122).

CW: All right! You've figured out how to get out of the house. You'll keep the back door open. You've given the kids a note to go over to the neighbors. You've got our number, and you know you can get to your car, parked out back, and get to a phone booth and call us.

In summary, both short- and long-term safety depends on helping abused women take action steps rather than remaining immobilized. Wife abuse crises are different from other types of crises in this respect. For many victims, it may not be a question of returning to a precrisis equilibrium. The equilibrium was never there in the first place. Therefore, for many women, taking first, tentative steps toward action is likely to be extremely frightening, confusing, and full of trepidation.

The following points seem worthwhile for crisis workers to know and understand in helping abused women make such decisions and take action (Massachusetts Coalition of Battered Women Service Groups, 1981, pp. 25, 67).

1. Help women think and act on their situation by providing legitimate reinforcement for their efforts.
2. Help women figure out what they want by providing a sounding board for examining ideas and alternatives.
3. Help women identify feelings that prevent them from making decisions.
4. Be honest. The worker cannot tell a person what to do but can clearly state from her own life how the situation would affect her.

5. Help women to do things for themselves, but do not let them become dependent on the worker.
6. Know and offer resources from which battered women can get specific kinds of assistance: Spell out *who, what, where, when,* and *how.*
7. Help women gain a sense of self-confidence and ability to take care of themselves.
8. Be challenging. Support women, but do not be afraid to push them toward a decision-making point.
9. Be open to choices. Each woman has control over her life; the crisis worker must not attempt to assume control for clients.
10. Hear and understand what women have to say, particularly if it does not run parallel to the worker's own beliefs, attitudes, and outlooks.
11. Build on the commonalities that women, particularly battered women, share, but recognize the worth of the individual differences of each person.
12. Assess lethality. "I'm fed up and whipped" may really mean "I'm ready to commit suicide."

The following crisis worker's response to a battered woman, who after two hours of talking on the telephone still could not make up her mind about what to do, aptly illustrates the application of the 12 points just made.

CW: I understand your mixed feelings of wanting to stay and wanting to leave; also the constant fear you live with while waiting for the next time, maybe even wishing it would happen quickly so the tension will ease off. But my guess is that tension reduction only occurs for a short period and then starts to build all over again. I also understand that you feel like you're locked into this, but there are some alternatives, which we have gone over. I want you to pick at least one of those, whichever seems best for you, and do it. I won't take no for an answer. Do something that will make you feel better right now. Go take a hot bath if that'll help, and don't spare the bath oil. I think it would be safer for you to come to the shelter right now, but if you don't really feel you can do that, I understand. However, if you feel the tension start to rise and feel like you just can't take it anymore, I want you to promise to call back here. I won't take no for an answer. I'll call you tomorrow afternoon to see how things are going. What would be a good time?

Advocacy.   Because battered women have been isolated for much of their lives, they generally have little knowledge of alternatives open to them. This is especially true with respect to their rights and options with both legal and welfare systems. Understanding the laws and how to weave through bureaucratic obstacles and how to cut through the red tape that is often put in the way of someone seeking help from the system is of paramount importance. The wife abuse worker who excels has an excellent networking system to tap into and get immediate help for a variety of problems.

Transcrisis Perspective.   All the preceding intervention procedures cannot be accomplished in a 20-minute phone call. Even minor crises may require two or three calls to get the client stabilized, in touch with her feelings, and into some semblance of preabuse equilibrium. The crisis worker is not providing a short-term elixir that merely calms the victim and then blithely sends her on her way. What is being provided is a blend that not only deals with the immediate crisis but also has a long-term application.

Many battered women need to go through a complete reeducation process about who they are and what they can do. This process should not be hurried even if it takes a year to accomplish this goal.

Indeed, the transcrisis of the battered woman does not end when she gets off the phone and decides to come to the center or go to the shelter. The initiating interview or hotline call is only the first part of the crisis resolution. Other crises will continue to plague the victim.

Ibrahim and Herr's (1987) work with battered women who were involved in a group counseling format that concentrated on vocational exploration and economic independence is an excellent example of a transcrisis point. When these women reached the stage of vocational implementation, ready actually to go out into the world of work and test their skills, they experienced all kinds of threatening and anxious feelings and became immobile and paralyzed. The women needed 15 two-hour sessions of intensive support by the group leaders to work through this stage!

SHELTERS

A center and a shelter are generally two different entities within a domestic abuse program. The center deals with telephone and on-site, short-term crisis intervention and counseling. The shelter is a longer-term facility where women and their families can stay for short or extended periods of time. A comprehensive program will have both a center and a shelter and will be staffed around the clock with a 24-hour hotline and an open-door policy for walk-ins (Barnett et al., 1980). There will be tie-ins to other social services agencies: police, free or sliding-scale legal services, hospitals, medical staff and mental health facilities, mobile crisis teams that provide transportation for abuse victims, and direct links to emergency housing facilities with follow-up services (Benjamin & Walz, 1983, p. 83).

The typical shelter is linked to the abuse center and is well publicized, but for security reasons its location may not be made public. For the same reason, it will be well patrolled by the police and will be secure. Staffed by both professionals and volunteers, it will have adequate cooking, sleeping, bath, child and infant care facilities for a number of families, and funds for clothing, food, and transportation (Langley & Levy, 1977). It should also provide a variety of counseling services to help women ventilate feelings, explore alternatives, and make immediate plans for what they will do next (Benjamin & Walz, 1983, p. 84). This ideal shelter is a rarity due to lack of funds.

Counseling Women at Shelters

Women who enter the shelter fit into two categories: those who are unsure about leaving the battering relationship and those who have made a definite commitment to leave it (Dagastino, 1984). Women who fall into the first category need to be monitored on an hour-by-hour basis and are the more critical of the two categories. The crisis worker maintains constant contact with these women and reinforces them for having had the courage to come to the shelter.

CW: I'm glad you made it. I know it took a lot of courage.
CW: (*10 minutes later.*) Getting settled in? Come on with me, there's some other women I would like you to meet.

CW: (*2 hours later.*) How are things going? Got the kids settled in? They're great-looking children. Want to have a cup of coffee and talk?

Vacillation between going back and staying is characteristic of these women. The longer the women stay at the shelter, the greater is the probability that they will not return to their mates (Hilbert & Hilbert, 1984). However, until women can recover their self-esteem and come to understand that they are not the cause, they are at risk to leave and go back (Schutte, Bouleige, Fix, & Malouff, 1986). The worker does not try to force women to stay at the shelter but does try to get them to take some psychological "time out" to review their situation in a more objective way (Dagastino, 1984).

Juanita: I'm all mixed up. I don't know if I'm wrong or not. I'm Catholic, and I'm Hispanic. Women in my family just don't walk out of a marriage. The church and my family both say we just need to work things out, but I really think he'll kill me.

CW: Let's assume you're taking a one-day vacation so you can get some rest before you go back and deal with it. It's fine if you want to go back home, but do this much for me—just take it easy for a while. I can see that you're physically all right and not hurt, and I'm relieved. This is a great time to talk about what you can do if you do or don't go back.

The shelter worker checks repeatedly with the new arrival and reinforces her decision to come. She conveys her concern for the victim and with the help of other women in the shelter, sees that the victim and her family are settled. The focus is on the here-and-now. During the first few hours of the victim's separation from her abuser, the worker will probably have to be very directive. Few women at this time have the ego strength to stand on their own, and most need an abundance of support and help. The objective is to keep the victim moving, thinking, and acting so that she is preoccupied and does not have time to let fear, guilt, or any other debilitating and anxiety-ridden emotions overcome her. Domestic chores such as cleaning and cooking seem to be particularly helpful in this regard. In all instances, the worker should be carefully attuned to the victim's needs. Some may find help sitting, talking, or crying with a worker or a group of other women. Others may be so exhausted that they need to go to bed and sleep. Whatever the victim needs, the worker should be adaptable to those needs and flexible enough to change as circumstances demand (Dagastino, 1984).

Shelter Dynamics.   A variety of positive dynamics occur at shelters. There is substantial support from other women who have experienced the same kind of trauma. This support enables victims to begin gaining the courage to face people, recovering their lost self-esteem, and learning that the beatings were not their fault (Schechter, 1982, pp. 55–60).

Wife abuse shelters are not vacation spas where one's every whim is catered to. Although an abundance of caring and sharing occurs, women who live in shelters are encouraged to start trusting themselves to make decisions. Part of the decision-making process includes determining what is best for the shelter. This is not an easy task. Limits have to be set with respect to pets, children, cooking, and so on (Schechter, 1982, pp. 63–64). Women get bored, boss each other around, miss their men, miss sex (pp. 55–60), and have problems relating to people from different ethnic and racial backgrounds and sociocultural milieus (Massachusetts Coalition of Battered Women Service Groups, 1981, p. 28).

Victim: Getting used to a shelter is overwhelming. You like it, but you don't want to be there, 'cause it isn't home. You've got to put together all your psychological know-how in getting along with different types of people. Wondering if you're going to make it, especially when you see all the pain and confusion and don't know whether it's yours or theirs or what, and hoping nobody finds out you're here. Trying to be understood and feeling like you are a blabbermouth here when you couldn't talk at home. Trying to look forward and all the time wanting to forget . . . wanting to forget . . . wanting to forget. (Schechter, 1982, pp. 59–60)

At a shelter, everything is not always as it seems. Many women who come to the shelter are extremely dependent and exceptionally adept at manipulating the workers there (Walker, 1984, p. 126). A statement like "You really understand—you've made my whole life better" is reinforcing to the worker but may actually be manipulation. The woman is using the house and the worker as a security blanket and is not making any progress toward getting out on her own (Dagastino, 1984). The wise shelter worker comes to see the manipulation for what it is, a refusal to take responsibility for oneself and a shift from dependency on an abusive partner to dependency on a caring shelter worker (Weincourt, 1985). Gently but firmly, the worker extinguishes such behavior.

CW: I appreciate what you said, and I appreciate your wanting to cook my dinner and all other things you want to do for me. Yet I believe your time and mine could be better spent working on getting you set up in an apartment and looking for a job.

Grief.   Besides being dependent, many abused women go through a grief process. Sorrow and depression, guilt and self-blame, and decision-making difficulty are all hallmarks of the grieving process. What would be viewed as normal in a woman who suffered the death of a spouse may be viewed as pathological in an abused woman. However, these responses are just as legitimate for an abused woman who is trying to come to terms with the loss of a significant relationship, shared parental responsibilities, and a clearly defined role as a wife (Campbell, 1989).

There are a lot of *yes, buts* as workers start to confront abused women with making a new future. As victims shift from a depersonalized view of their situation to depression over it, the process can be extremely frightening to a shelter worker unless she knows that this, too, is another step in the transcrisis that battered women go through (Dagastino, 1984). The woman's grief often puzzles those trying to help her. Many human services workers may be threatened by these feelings and deny the woman's need to mourn by concentrating on dealing with concrete aspects of the woman's dilemma, such as providing food, clothing, and housing. Her grief can be understood, however, if one asks the question "For what is she mourning?" In most cases, she has defined herself in terms of her relationship with the batterer, and if that relationship ends, she feels as if she has lost everything—including her sense of self (Turner & Shapiro, 1986). She clings quite tightly to the dreams she has for the relationship—including the expectations with which she entered into it. When the relationship ends, she must come to terms with the fact that these dreams will never materialize. Therefore, she is not grieving so much for what was, but for what she hoped could have been (Spanno, 1990). A crisis worker can and should validate that the woman's loss is very real and that she has a legitimate right to mourn and experience the feelings she has over the loss (Russell & Uhlemann, 1994). At this point, the counseling process is little different from what we discuss in the chapter on personal loss (Chapter 9).

Juanita: I wanted this to work so much. We could have had it so good, but I couldn't take him beating on me and the kids too. What went wrong with that good-looking, happy couple in this picture? He was so handsome and so good to me in the beginning. Then it just slowly went to hell and now this. (*Weeps while slowly turning over in her hands a wedding picture that she brought with her to the shelter.*)

CW: It's really hard to say goodbye to all those things that were and might have been. It must hurt even more than the beatings to know that all those hopes and dreams won't come to pass.

Juanita: It tears my heart out, but I know I did the right thing. Sooner or later he would have killed me or the kids in one of his rages. It's so weird! I still love that SOB.

CW: The grief you're feeling is as real as if a close friend or a relative had died. Perhaps even more tragic because when this relationship died, a part of you died with it, Juanita. The part of you who struggled out of the barrio, went to college, got an education, made a success out of herself, married the perfect man, and then with all those expectations dashed because of the way he treated you and the children.

Juanita: I can't let that stop me. Nothing else did. I made the right decision coming here. I also made the right decision getting a warrant on him. Maybe that last act of love will get him the help he needs or the jolt he needs to wake him up so he doesn't do it to somebody else.

CW: As you say that, I see so much determination coming through the tears. I also see a new, different, stronger person as you say those farewells, as tough as they are.

A woman who has been involved in an abusive relationship needs to grieve and to have her grief validated. The crisis worker does this although reinforcing that although there is now an altered future, it has potential to be a good one. It is through this process that the battered woman can come to see the relationship for what it really was—abusive. The crisis worker will make a very bad therapeutic mistake if she expects the woman to rejoice. If she is expected to be happy for leaving and is discouraged from feeling her sense of loss and expressing it, she may never confront the truth about the relationship. The end result may well be a return to the partner or one just like him (Spanno, 1990).

Depression. Depression comes in many guises. Many women who come into the shelter sleep much of the time. On first appearance, they may seem to be lazy. Actually, they may be going through a stage of trying to regroup their psychic energy. The worker's task becomes one of trying to help them move past their inactivity, but not by pressuring them or taking them on a guilt trip (Massachusetts Coalition of Battered Women Service Groups, 1981, p. 27).

CW: I've noticed you pretty much sticking to your room and sleeping a lot. I was a little concerned and was wondering how you were feeling. I wonder if you've had a chance to talk to anyone about how you feel since you got here.

Juanita: I feel so guilty. It seems like I have slept ever since I've gotten here and the other women have been so good to take care of the kids. I'm not really like this, I just don't seem to have any get-up-and-go. I'm really sorry to be so much trouble.

CW: What you are doing is exactly what you should be doing, getting your energy back. You burned up a tremendous amount of it making the decision to get out and get here. The other women have felt the same way so they understand. In a few days you'll do the same for somebody else. If you want to talk, we're here. If you want to rest, that's just fine too. The main thing is you're safe and that's what's important right now.

Terror.   For many women, a stress-related syndrome similar to agoraphobia arises after they have been in the shelter for a while (Massachusetts Coalition of Battered Women Service Groups, 1981, p. 27). They may have extreme and unexplainable attacks of terror that are touched off by seemingly innocuous incidents. These incidents greatly restrict their activities and new freedom. Fear of their mates, fear of their predicament, fear of their separation from a definable past, and fear of an undefinable future can all cause the onset of terror. Under no circumstances should the shelter worker allow it to continue. Victims must be encouraged and helped step by step to pull themselves away from the security blanket of the shelter and out into the real world. Such progress may take place in very small, slow steps, but the steps must be taken. As women take these steps, they receive very specific, positive reinforcement for what they have accomplished, enabling them not to fall back into learned helplessness but instead to take responsibility for their behavior (Weincourt, 1985). Invariably, victims will not be able to see that they have done much of anything, or they tend to diminish their successes.

CW: I know you're still scared to death to go down and talk to them at Federal Express about that job. It's a big step, but a week ago you couldn't walk down to the grocery store and now you're doing that fine. So let's take it a step at a time. Look at what you overcame. We can go through the job interview, play it a step at a time, talk about those steps right here where it's safe, and give you a chance to really become confident about going down there.

Those Who Have Decided to Leave.   The second category of women who come to the shelter are in for a long haul and are not going back to the battering situation. For women who are in for the duration, the crisis worker deals with immediate specifics such as finding a place to live, financial aid, and child care. Emotional support has a low priority because these women are so busy that all they want and need is very practical advice and help. These women are very different from those experiencing acute crisis because they are highly motivated to change their lives. They are much easier to work with, because they have made a decision to get out of their domestic pressure cooker (Dagastino, 1984).

Follow-Up

Once women leave the shelter, they should be provided with follow-up. As immediate demands are relieved, the emotional impact of their decision should be dealt with over the long term. These women are urged to go for counseling with the idea that no one can be beaten even once without suffering some psychological damage. It is not uncommon for a woman to be so busy getting her act together that her emotional reactions are delayed. The victim may be out on her own, well established, and watching television at the time that she experiences a sudden emotional breakdown. The crisis worker apprises the victim of what to expect in the way of emotional aftershocks. Such residual psychological trauma seems to be particularly characteristic of women who initially appear to be very much in control (Dagastino, 1984).

CW: Even though you feel like you've made the break from your husband, don't be surprised if later on you get depressed and really feel like you need and miss your husband. That's to be expected. We know that, and we're here to help then too!

Indeed, in the worst of scenarios, the victim may become lonely, forget about the terrible abuse she suffered in the past, invite her ex-mate over for dinner, and get beaten up again. Therefore, in following up with the victim, the crisis worker should understand that there may be relapses and that the victim may fall into old ways of behaving. Thus, crisis workers not only may have to check up on their clients but also they may have to be indirect about it so the women do not become dependent on them (Dagastino, 1984).

CW: Hello, Juanita. Just called to see if you've been able to make that appointment for counseling at the Human Services Clinic. I know it's hard to get in there at times and thought if you hadn't, I could call the clinic and we'd have one of the people here drive you down and help you get started.

The crisis worker continues to be a support system until the victim is well connected to a long-term support source, and only then does the crisis worker fade from the victim's life.

Long-term support is particularly critical for abused women. Research indicates that women who leave the shelter and strike out on their own continue to undergo emotional changes for at least six months after leaving. Therefore, support and advocacy are critical during this time frame. Those who have a support group and advocates who help them access services do significantly better in reaching their goals than do those women who lack such services (Sullivan et al., 1994). Support services also build self-esteem, increase locus of control, reduce stress, and enhance feelings of belongingness and support (Tutty, Bidgood, & Rothery, 1993). Follow-up and support is particularly important for women who have little education, few job skills, and minimal financial support (Webersinn, Hollinger, & Delamatre, 1991).

Do the shelter experience and its follow-up services significantly alter a woman's chance of not becoming involved in an abusive relationship again? The data are not clear on this issue. Research indicates that the greater the number of times a woman leaves an abusive relationship, the more likely she is to leave permanently (Schutte, Malouff, & Doyle, 1988). Going to a shelter without benefit of follow-up and other support services may actually *increase* violence (Berk, Newton, & Berk, 1986). Finally, because shelters tend to be based on Western forms of feminism, ethnic minorities with different cultural backgrounds report difficulties in adapting to a shelter environment (Hamby, 1998, p. 238). Clearly, entering a shelter is a major step and not one to be taken lightly.

INTERVENTION WITH CHILDREN

There has been a tendency in the battered women's movement to look at children as "secondary" victims (Peled, 1997). They are not. Children are often lost in the shuffle of domestic violence; but that violence has direct impact on their lives both in the present and in the future (Wolak & Finkelhor, 1998, pp. 73–111). In that light, crisis workers need to be as concerned for children as they are for the women who are immersed in battering relationships. Of primary concern is the safety of the children, so a lethality assessment should be conducted to determine where the children should reside and who will supervise them during visitation and other events where the perpetrator may be present. For children who are old enough to take action on their own, a safety plan should entail how to determine whether the situation is becoming lethal, how to get away from the perpetrator, and where they can go to be safe. If they are in a shelter, they need to know how to keep the location a secret from not only the perpetrator but other relatives and acquaintances. If there is evidence of abuse toward the children, which is highly likely in partner violence, then the crisis worker is mandated to refer the case to a state welfare agency (Wolak & Finkelhor, 1998, pp. 100–101).

Children who have witnessed partner violence or have just fled or been removed from a home can benefit from immediate crisis counseling to stave off typical PTSD symptomology. (See Chapter 4, on PTSD, and Chapter 6, on sexual assault, the sections on children for complete assessment and intervention strategies.) Specific immediate intervention with a trained crisis worker should allow the child to recount the events and their feelings about them, correct negative misattributions about self-blame, and work through overwhelming negative feelings (Wolak & Finkelhor, 1998, p. 101).

There is probably no age too early to start therapy for children who come from abusive home settings. Douglas (1991) used conjoint therapy with mother and child and used attachment theory to help toddlers age 15 to 36 months work through traumatic battering events they had witnessed. Hughes's (1982) brief intervention strategy includes intervention with children, mothers, schools, and shelter staff members. Her model is comprehensive in that it provides individual counseling; initiates group meetings for peers, siblings, and family; teaches parenting skills to mothers; establishes a liaison with school personnel; and trains shelter staff members in child advocacy and child development issues.

COURTSHIP VIOLENCE

To believe that only women who are partners in a conjugal relationship are victims of violence is to be badly mistaken. Studies on courtship violence estimate that it occurs in anywhere from 22 to 67 percent of courtship relationships and cuts across college, high school, and nonschool dating populations (Burcky, Reuterman, & Kopsky, 1988; Henton et al., 1983; Makepeace, 1983). A conservative estimate is that violence occurs in approximately 25 percent of courtship relationships.

As simplistic as the following may sound as a predictor of violence, Bergman (1992) found that number of dating partners and dating frequency had the highest positive correlation and that grade point average had the highest negative correlation. Even more ominous, in a study of high school students by Burcky and associates (1988), dating violence affected girls as young as 12. These researchers also found that assaultive behavior was not just shoving and pushing. Among those experiencing dating violence, 37.5 percent reported that the minimum assaultive behavior was being punched, and approximately 9 percent reported having been assaulted with a gun or knife! It is noteworthy and may presage the future of these relationships that the percentage of violence found closely parallels that found in samples of married couples and that this violence is reciprocal in nature (Jasinski & Williams, 1998, p. 30; Straus et al., 1980; Straus & Gelles, 1986).

What is astounding is that Henton and colleagues (1983) found that 25 percent of victims and 30 percent of offenders interviewed interpreted violence in courtship as a sign of love! Although we are not encouraging everyone to go off to be monks, nuns, or "nerdy" scholars, we do urge young women and men reading this book to take very seriously dating behavior that increasingly turns from verbal arguments into physical confrontation. Research study after research study indicates that violence invariably escalates the longer people are in an abusive relationship. To think that people will give up violent behavior for "love" or any other reason is to think wrong. Worse, to think that one has the power to get a partner to give up an addictive behavior such as battering is patently false!

Although Burcky and associates (1988) offer specific recommendations to counselors for education and intervention, there is little indication that high school counselors or college student development personnel are highly aware of or know what to do about the problem (Bogal-Allbritten & Allbritten, 1985). In that regard, the best directive we can offer to anyone who is physically assaulted even once in a dating relationship is, no matter how great the love, how great the good times, how great the sex, how many flowers, apologies, and promises to change are given after an initial assault, *get out of the relationship now!* No battered woman we have met set out with the intention to go with or marry someone who would beat her. However, by letting such behavior occur early in courtship, many battered women unwittingly set the stage for some terrible consequences of their early tolerance.

And if *you* have assaulted someone in a dating relationship, *get help now!* By assaulted, we don't necessarily mean that you put the person in the hospital. It may have been a series of hard shakes, a shove or two, or a slap in the heat of an argument or a moment of jealousy. Although you can easily rationalize this behavior away, the chances are good that this behavior will increase in the future. Besides the harm you do to someone you profess to love, the changes in the law and increased judicial sensitivity to battering mean that you will probably spend some time in jail if you are convicted of an assault on your girlfriend or boyfriend. If your school counselor doesn't know anger management techniques, there are therapists who do. The section on treating batterers will give you an idea of what you need to look for in a therapist, and the final section of this chapter provides references to books on anger management.

GAY AND LESBIAN VIOLENCE

Because there has been little research on gay and lesbian partner violence, and practically none among bisexual and transgendered persons, we are limiting the focus in this section mostly to violence in gay and lesbian relationships. The reasons for this lack of research are multifold. First, the law limits what may be considered a partner relationship. As a result, any police report that involves a gay or lesbian couple will be booked as a simple assault and not as domestic violence. Second, although statistics indicate that same-gendered sexual orientation is prevalent in about 10 percent of the people in the United States (Gebhard, 1997; Janus & Janus, 1993), the attitude of the general public is highly negative, scornful, and often openly hostile to gays and lesbians. This prevailing attitude keeps many same-sex relationships under wraps, so when violence occurs, no report is made. There is also reluctance on the part of same-sex partners to report violence because of the added stigma attached to an already stigmatized perception that gay and lesbian relationships are unhealthy (Elliot, 1996). Finally, unless they, themselves are gay or lesbian, few service providers or researchers have the inclination, resources, or education about same-sex relationships to provide meaningful help (Island & Letellier, 1991; Renzetti, 1996).

Prevalence of Violence.   The sparse statistics on gay and lesbian relations indicate that same-sex relationships are no more immune from partner violence than heterosexual ones. In lesbian relationships, a benchmark percentage for physical, sexual, and psychological abuse ranges between 33 and 50 percent (Lie & Gentlewarrier, 1991; Lockhart, White, Causby, & Isaac, 1994). When all former relationships were considered, the figure moved up to 64 percent (Bologna, Waterman, & Dawson, 1987). In gay relationships, the data are even more sparse. Estimates are that about 10 to 20 percent of males in gay relationships are assaulted each year (Island & Letellier, 1991). When all previous gay relationships are taken into consideration the figure moves up to 44 percent (Bologna, Waterman, & Dawson, 1987). The bottom line is that it appears that a great deal of violence occurs in such relationships (Bartholomew, 1999; Gillis, 1999; Ristock, 1999; Stanley, 1999). From our own experience of crisis intervention with women and men of same-sex orientations, their presenting problems usually revolve around "outing" (the telling of others such as parents and employers of the victim's same-sex orientation), jealousy and mistrust, unwanted breakups, and feelings of loss, grief, and betrayal over dissolved relationships—all of which have the potential for violent confrontations.

Complicating Factors.   Although many of the same coercive controls used by heterosexual batterers are employed in the homosexual community, there are differences. Positive HIV status can be used as a coercive control. Failing health or threat of infection may be used to make the partner feel afraid or guilty. If the victim is infected, the coercive partner may refuse to provide support or get medical care for the victim, or double "out" (tell people she or he is both homosexual and HIV positive) the partner (West, 1998a, p. 170). Indeed, the coercive partner often uses "homophobic" control by threatening to "out" the partner and by constantly reminding the partner that no one in a homophobic world will believe her or him or will dismiss the violence (particularly the police) as inconsequential or what the person may "deserve" (Hart, 1986). A further complicating factor is that battering may be seen as "mutual." That is, in a same-sex relation there is no clear "identifiable" assailant and victim. Thus, the assaulter can discount the victim's accusations by claiming that both were equally responsible for the violence. The foregoing is particularly true of gays who may be made to feel inadequate for "not taking it like a man" (West, 1998a, pp. 169–170).

To date, what research there is seems to indicate that many of the factors that influence violence in heterosexual partners are contributors to violence among same-sex partners. Intergenerational transmission of violence, alcohol abuse dependency and autonomy issues, and power imbalances seem to contribute to same-sex partner abuse.

Crisis Intervention Involving Gay and Lesbian Violence

Worker Competency.   First and foremost, crisis workers have an ethical obligation to help gays and lesbians as much as they would heterosexuals involved in partner violence (Buhrke & Douce, 1991, p. 231). This means that heterosexual workers must acquire knowledge and skills for work with this clientele and not allow their own homophobia to harm clients (Morrow, 1999) by obtaining training in counseling gays and lesbians (Fassinger, 1991; Gilliland & Crisp, 1995; Matthews & Lease, 1999).

Sensitivity. Our own experience indicates a number of issues that make crisis intervention difficult and sensitive with same-sex partners who have engaged in violent acts. First is the person's reluctance to talk about the problem because of trust issues with the crisis worker and the fear that the client will be held in low esteem for his or her sexual orientation. The worker must show a great deal of sensitivity and unconditional positive regard for the client to establish safe ground for the client to talk about such traumatic personal issues.

Specific Issues. Second, any exploratory assessment should deal with issues specific to same-sex couples. That is, threats of "outing" the other person's sexual orientation or his or her HIV-positive status, exploration of internalized homophobia, degree of closeting (hiding same-sex orientation from others), and acceptance of sexual orientation are all components that adversely affect gays and lesbians and may be used for coercion. It should never be assumed that one person is the victim and the other the perpetrator. Marrujo and Kreger (1996) found that a third of the lesbian battering relationships they investigated fell into what they call a "participant" category. Although they didn't initiate the aggression, participants did fight back, and once engaged, gave as good as they got. The worker can sort out who did what by the partners' responses. Aggressors may paradoxically propose that they are the real victims, participants may see themselves as righteously justified in retaliating, and victims may express a desire to end the conflict and be safe.

Severity. Third, by the time a gay or lesbian is likely to seek therapeutic help with a relationship that involves battering, a triage rating will put them in the highly impaired range. Interestingly, the person who may seek out therapy in a violent same-sex relationship may be the *batterer*. He or she may have typical feelings of conjugal paranoia that involve jealousy, betrayal, and fears of abandonment over some new or old partner. These feelings may rapidly oscillate to guilt, contrition, self-doubt, and self-disparagement as the client attempts to repair the damage to the relationship. The person may be dominated by an "all or none," "If I can't have him/her, nobody will," cognitive set, and be constantly attempting to keep the relationship intact and out of the arms of some other real or imagined threat (Bartholomew, 1999).

Safety and Support. Fourth, a major concern is establishing a safety net and a support system because the client will believe that support people or resources are not available to him or her (and in fact may have few, if any). Locating a support system or a safe place may be very difficult for gay or lesbian clients because a majority report they would not use support groups or go to a shelter (Lie & Gentlewarrier, 1991).

Lethality. Fifth is a question of lethality. Gays or lesbians at the end game stage of domestic violence are so caught up in the emotionality of the event that their functioning is highly erratic and potentially lethal to themselves or others. At this stage, the worker should consider the threat of suicide and/or homicide and make a threat assessment (see

Chapter 5, regarding suicide/homicide assessment). If that threat assessment is high in regard to means, motive, opportunity, and plan, keeping the client safe from self and others becomes an immediate and overriding concern.

Precipitating Factors.   Sixth, dependency versus autonomy, jealousy, and the perceived balance of power are major precipitating factors in battering in same-sex relationships (Renzetti, 1992). Balancing closeness and attachment with one's partner with independence and autonomy is difficult in any relationship, regardless of sexual orientation. In same-sex relationships, an absence of support outside the relationship may cause couples to turn more intensely to one another. Such dependency on one another may cause major stressors when one partner perceives the other as having become too autonomous, and fears abandonment. Jealousy is certainly not exclusive to same-sex relationships. However, it may be more pronounced in same-sex relationships because another person of the same sex may pay attention to one partner and not to the other. As a result, such envy and jealousy may promote possessiveness and attempts to restrict and control the freedom of the other person, much as in a heterosexual relationship. Distrust in same-sex relationships also tends to be much more pronounced than in heterosexual ones (Wiehe, 1998, p. 79). This is true because it is not uncommon for former lovers to still be in the support system of same-sex couples (all the same-sex people in a community may constitute each other's support system), whereas it is much easier to terminate those relationships in a heterosexual world (Kurdek, 1994). Finally, the term *balance of power* refers to the ability of the person to influence and get others to do what he or she wants. Although heterosexual couples may have a division of labor in regard to household chores divided along stereotypical male–female lines, same-sex couples may have terrible conflicts over such domestic duties because they may perceive an inequity of power in doing these chores (Wiehe, 1998, p. 80).

Treatment Issues.   Complex issues revolve around treatment delivery. Group therapy may be helpful for victims because it reduces feelings of isolation and provides a safe place to work through their issues with empathic others. It may also be helpful for perpetrators, for the same isolation issues, and it may also offer a place where the peer group can confront the batterer. The problem is that mixing homosexuals with heterosexuals in groups is not recommended (Margolies & Leeder, 1995), and it may be very difficult to generate an intact gay or lesbian group. Couples therapy, mediation, conflict resolution, or any other approach that brings the two warring parties together is debatable from the standpoint of safety.

TREATING BATTERERS

With the unveiling of battering as a major societal problem, class action suits have been brought in New York City and Oakland, California, to give battered women equal protection under the law. During the early 1980s, the Coalition for Justice for Battered Women in San Francisco was instrumental in getting police to redefine how they handle domestic disputes and how the district attorney prosecutes domestic assault cases (Sonkin, Martin, & Walker, 1985, p. 25). Police do not mediate but arrest, and district attorneys do not dismiss but prosecute. In short, batterers need to realize that domestic violence is a punishable crime (Sonkin et al., 1985, p. 41), and in more and more cities and states it is becoming exactly that.

Although arrest may deter battering (Gondolf, 1984; Sherman & Berk, 1984), many communities have adopted a diversion program modeled along the lines of the program the Coalition for Justice for Battered Women in San Francisco helped create to treat adjudicated batterers. In our own community of Memphis, an adjudicated batterer is given a thorough assessment and diagnostic interview after adjudication. Although specific treatment recommendations such as parent training, drug abuse treatment, and individual mental health counseling are generated for each person, the vast majority will be recommended for anger management and given a choice: Come to anger management group for 24 weekly two-hour sessions, or go "11-29" (11 months and 29 days in the county penal farm). Approximately 75 percent of the batterers grudgingly opt for the anger management program; about 25 percent hope they won't be found by the police after an arrest warrant is issued for failure to appear at an anger management program. Certainly, most batterers, particularly those so adjudicated, do not willingly come to a treatment program, nor are they willing to admit that they have problems. People who enter counseling for abuse often manifest outright denial, minimization, or justification and projection of blame to escape owning their abusive behavior (Shupe et al., 1987, pp. 26–28).

Denying batterer: I never touched her. Sure, I'd been drinking a little, and we had an argument. She must have fallen, because she was pretty drunk too! (*The complainant had three broken teeth, a fractured jaw, and two broken ribs, plus numerous contusions, cuts, and abrasions.*)

Minimizing batterer: Well, I might have pushed her when we were arguing at the top of the stairs, but I'd never hit her. (*The complainant had a broken nose, a bruised kidney, and two black eyes from the "push."*)

Projecting batterer: Listen, she ain't no rose. She gives as good as she gets. Besides, I got some rights, like dinner when I get home from work, instead of a drunk sittin' in front of the TV suckin' on a drink. She deserved a lesson! She always gets the kids to stick up for her. (*Both the woman and her two children were treated at an emergency room for contusions and lacerations from being whipped with a power cord.*)

Although individual counseling, partner counseling, and partner counseling in groups have been attempted (Shupe et al., 1987, pp. 26–27; Tolman & Bennett, 1990), the prevalent mode of counseling for batterers is mainly court-ordered group counseling. Generally, couples counseling is not recommended until the batterer has made a great deal of progress on anger management and other personality issues (Hamberger, 1994; Kaufman, 1992). Groups provide opportunities for social learning and retraining that would be nearly impossible in individual or couple therapy (Adams & McCormick, 1982). The group also provides a support system for what are typically emotionally isolated individuals and enables these men and women to start to learn how to depend on others in times of stress.

Treatment Goals

Group treatment formats, however they are configured, have four major purposes: (1) ensure the safety of the victimized partner, (2) alter the batterer's attitudes toward violence, (3) increase the batterer's sense of personal responsibility, and (4) learn nonviolent alternatives to past behaviors (Edleson & Tolman, 1992). Groups typically use either the Duluth model, which operates with a power and control focus, or an anger management model, which seeks to understand and control anger (Hamby, 1998, pp. 223–225). We believe there is merit in both approaches.

To accomplish these goals, most groups have a combination of anger management, stress reduction, communication skills, and sex role resocialization components (Dutton, 1995; Gondolf, 1985; Hamby, 1998; Sonkin et al., 1985; Tolman & Bennett, 1990). Therapeutically, most programs use some form of cognitive-behavioral approach that deals with batterers' irrational thinking and also provides techniques to restructure maladaptive cognitions, overreaction to violent urges, self-sabotage, setting oneself up for violence, and selective forgetting; offers assertiveness training and teaches problem solving; and handles premature "cures" (Dutton, 1995; Faulkner, Stoltenberg, Cogen, & Nolen, 1992; Hamby, 1998; Jennings, 1990; Kriner & Waldron, 1988; Tolman & Bennett, 1990). Programs typically are psychoeducational structured learning experiences with some time reserved for role play, discussion, and processing concepts and ideas (Edleson & Syers, 1990; Scales & Winter, 1991). Coleaders are generally used so that they can model together the types of behaviors the batterers need to learn, and any interactions between one leader and a member can be facilitated by the other group leader (Sonkin et al., 1985, p. 98). Groups typically meet once a week for two hours and range from 8 to 32 sessions (Tolman & Bennett, 1990). Before a batterer is inducted into a group, an assessment and intake interview should be conducted to obtain a profile of the battering behavior, incidence of other psychological problems, and motivation to participate in counseling.

Assessment

The Conflict Tactics Scale (Straus, 1979) has been the only instrument used on any wide scale to measure intrafamilial conflict. The scale looks mainly at physical means used to resolve conflicts, does not adequately account for verbal abuse, and entirely ignores the emotional, social, sexual, and economic forms of abuse. It also does not look at power differential—one of the key ingredients in domestic violence (Poynter, 1989). It certainly was not meant to—nor does it—predict who will be violent or who, after being arrested or completing counseling, will recidivate. Instruments have been developed that measure the more subtle nuances of coercion, control, and power that may be used instead of physical battering (Marshall, 1992; Rodenburg & Fantuzzo, 1993; Shepard & Campbell, 1992; Tolman, 1989).

One test that should always be given is an alcohol-screening test such as the Michigan Alcohol Screening Test (Selzer, 1971) or Substance Abuse Subtle Screening Inventory (Miller, 1983) with follow-up interview questions. Determining alcohol abuse is important for two reasons. First, numerous studies have shown *chronic* alcohol abuse to be a strong predictor of more violent behavior (Blount, Silverman, Sellers, & Seese, 1994; Heyman, Jouriles, & O'Leary, 1995; Tolman & Bennett, 1990; Wesner, Patel, & Allen, 1991). Second, any individual who is under the influence of a mind-altering substance needs to get dried out first. In the program at the Memphis Family Trouble Center (FTC), anybody appearing intoxicated or under the influence of a mind-altering substance is asked to leave and obtain help for the drug problem or have their probation revoked (Winter, 1991).

Probably the worst "bets" for success in anger management and those most likely to recidivate are those individuals who fall into personality disorder categories. Therefore, tests like the Millon Clinical Multiaxial Inventory (Millon, 1987) may be used to determine borderline, narcissistic, depressive, somatoform, antisocial, and other pathological types. If elevated scores on the Millon indicate psychopathology, these individuals may be served better in individual therapy that targets their pathology rather than in a generic anger management group. Dutton (Dutton, 1994, 1995; Dutton & Starzomski, 1993, 1994) has extensively examined borderline personality disorder (BPD) as a unifying personality construct in domestic violence. Dutton's research seems to indicate that the individual who batters looks much more like a full-blown BPD than a normal individual who does not batter. His research presents a strong argument that there are at least some batterers whose major problem is intimacy anxiety and fear of abandonment, hallmarks of the borderline personality, as opposed to the more universal and feminist notion of domestic violence as being an attempt to reinforce male dominance and preserve a patriarchal order (Dutton, 1995, p. 138). This "either/or" view has much to say about how treatment for batterers should be conducted and has bred a great deal of controversy in regard to treatment approaches.

The Intake Interview

The worker should provide a comprehensive intake interview to assess the batterer's psychological status and motivation and provide information on what may be expected from a counseling group (Sonkin et al., 1985; Tolman & Bennett, 1990). First, the worker should assess lethality, both for suicidal and homicidal ideation and/or behavior. As paradoxical as it may seem, many batterers are so dependent on their partners that the thought of being without them is worse than death, so suicide and murder may seem viable and realistic options. There are apparent relationships between lethality and a number of factors common in battering relationships, such as frequency of violent incidents, severity of injuries, threats to kill, suicide threats by the woman, length and incidence of the batterer's drug use, frequency of intoxication, and forced or threatened sexual acts (Sonkin et al., 1985, p. 73).

A fast assessment of the history of the violent relationship would seek details on the first, last, worst, and typical episode to provide a comprehensive profile of the kind, degree, and length of abuse. Assaults and violence on other family members, previous criminal activity, violence outside the home, increased social proximity of victim, attitudes toward violence, life stresses, general mental functioning, physical health, and physical and emotional isolation provide important background information on the potential for future violent behavior. The more these indicators appear, the more likely the client is to engage in lethal behavior (Sonkin et al., 1985, pp. 75–83).

It should be remembered that these men and women are in crisis, and appropriate measures should be taken to ensure everyone's safety. Bodnarchuk and associates (1995) estimate that based on the National Family Violence Surveys, their domestic violence clients fell into the most dangerous 1 percent of the U.S. population. During intake interviews, such people should be given clear messages about expectations inside and outside the group and what the consequences of inappropriate behavior will be. For instance, at the FTC threats of violence or intimidation against group members or leaders are not tolerated and are grounds for expulsion. Although no police officer ever attends an anger management group at the FTC, a police substation is immediately adjacent to the center, and an emergency alarm will summon help immediately. All participants are aware of this. Finally, there is evidence that clients who are apprised of the procedures, purpose, and goals of the group are less likely to drop out and less likely to recidivate (Tolman & Bennett, 1990).

Motivation

Motivation depends on a number of variables. Men who are younger, less educated, have lower incomes, were abused as children, and are minorities drop out at a significantly higher rate (Tolman & Bennett, 1990) than do those who are older, have no arrest record, are better educated, employed, have more children, and were more likely to have witnessed abuse but not been abused themselves as children (Demaris, 1989; Grusznski & Carrillo, 1988). Most people who come to the kinds of counseling programs that crisis workers operate do so because of external pressure, either through the court system or in an attempt to gain back their partner. Introduction to the program should indicate that there are clear consequences for not attending. The FTC introduces court-ordered participants to its program by specifically detailing its scoring system—which awards points for being on time, discussion, and homework—and how many of these points it will take to graduate. Counselors also apprise clients of what behaviors will not be tolerated and what will happen as a consequence if participants choose to violate the rules. Tolman and Bennett (1990) report that structured groups tend to be more effective, and it appears from the FTC's low attrition rate (10 percent) that the threat of having probation revoked and spending up to a year in jail is a strong external motivator for obtaining the points necessary to complete the program.

A Typical 24-Session Anger Management Group

The following is an abbreviated version of a typical 24-session group counseling format for batterers. The content of the course is taken from the Memphis Police Department's Family Trouble Center (FTC) anger management program. The counselor dialogue is abstracted from Betty Winter (1991), director of the program and facilitator of numerous anger management groups.

It would be an error to think that only men go through treatment for perpetrating domestic violence. Although better than 90 percent of those who go through the FTC program are men, the percentage of women adjudicated for anger management is increasing. Therefore we will use the generic terms "clients, "members," and "participants" in describing the FTC anger management program.

Sessions 1–2.   A great deal of anger is ventilated over being arrested and adjudicated to the program. They are mad and hostile about being there. The crisis worker starts the group by sitting in the middle of it and letting the group interview her. She responds to any professional and personal questions she deems appropriate.

CW: *(After giving qualifications.)* One of my major credentials is that I get angry a lot, but I've never been arrested for it. Now that I've given you my credentials, I'd like you to give me your credentials, the ones that got you here. I'd like you all to pair off, and I'd like for each pair to share with one another what caused you to get here. Then I'd like each pair to report back to the group.

By putting herself at risk with this group and letting them interview her, the crisis worker turns the tables on these angry clients. It is very difficult for these "macho" clients not to own up to what brought them here when a woman can face up to their angry and caustic interrogation of her and her credentials.

The rules of attendance and conduct are reviewed, and positive and negative consequences of appropriate and inappropriate behavior are explained. For many of these individuals, it will be the first structure they have experienced since high school, so they will need to know very clearly what is expected of them. The major purpose of this counseling is corrective and remedial. It is counseling within the criminal justice system. If psychological growth occurs, that is beneficial, but it is also clearly an *added* dividend. The hoped-for result of counseling is that these clients will not batter again and will not come to the attention of the justice system. As a result, initially trust is not high, and in these early sessions the therapist meets the issue head on.

CW: I don't expect you to share everything in this group. Take some time to see how safe you feel in here. Although what you say will be held in confidence within the bounds of the legal and ethical standards I've talked about, you're undoubtedly feeling pretty victimized by the system right now. Nobody will force you to say anything you don't want to.

Paradoxically, the admonition to not trust probably does much to establish trust and breaks down some barriers and paranoia about the group. The group is given an explanation of what taking an anger time-out is and is given a homework assignment of taking practice time-outs at home. Finally, the concept of choices is introduced.

CW: You'll think this is crazy, but you did have a choice in coming here. If you don't like what we're about, you can leave. (*Gets up, walks to the door, and opens it.*) Of course, you will have chosen to violate your probation terms and will probably go to jail.
Batterer: That's no damn choice.
CW: Granted, it's not a good choice, but it is a choice, just like what got you here. Battering was a bad choice, but it was one you made. During the course of the time we're here, we'll be looking at a lot of those choices you make.

Most of the clients do not realize that when they do something, they are making choices. Furthermore they don't realize the variety of choices open to them. The concept of decision making and choosing wisely will be woven throughout the 24 sessions. Another key component of the group is instituted in these first sessions: dyadic interaction—"that pairing crap," as participants call it. Clients are immediately paired off and start working with one another in pairs. Pairing off starts to generate closeness and bonding in the group. It also conveys early on that there is interest in hearing their story.

Open-ended questions and reflective responses are standard counseling techniques to obtain information and establish trust. However, these facilitative techniques assume an open and honest relationship, and the client's desire to change. They are not conducive to facilitating the start-up phase of a group of hostile and anxious batterers. Therefore, a combination of both open-ended and closed-ended questions and supportive and confrontive statements is needed to break through defense systems, reflect threatening feelings, and reframe irrational thinking (Sonkin et al., 1985, pp. 64–65).

CW: (*Indirectly confrontive.*) How did you come to be here?

Batterer: I sorta hit my wife.

CW: (*Directly confronting the minimization with a semiopen question.*) I don't understand "sorta"! What do you mean?

Batterer: (*Projecting and blaming.*) I mean she made me mad. She was running her mouth, so I had to hit her.

CW: (*Confronting all-or-none thinking.*) You say "had" as if there were no options other than to smack her.

Batterer: Not really—she was really being a bitch!

CW: (*Proposing consequences and obtaining facts.*) So your choice for stopping her bitching was breaking her jaw. That choice also got you arrested. What happened?

Batterer: She swore out a warrant, and I got sent to jail.

CW: (*Confrontive closed question.*) Had you ever been in jail before?

Batterer: Lord no!

CW: (*Empathically reflecting feeling.*) I'm betting that was a scary experience.

Batterer: You better believe it. There were some bad dudes in there. I didn't know if I was gonna get out of there in one piece.

CW: (*Reflecting feeling and exploring affect.*) So you were feeling pretty alone and helpless. I'm wondering how you're feeling right now?

Batterer: Madder than hell that I got to be here.

CW: (*Closed question that seeks to elicit defensive responding.*) Do you understand why you're here?

Batterer: (*Projecting.*) 'Cause she swore out a warrant on me.

CW: (*Confronting projection by making client own behavior.*) No! You are here because you put your wife in the hospital by beating her. That's criminal assault. The judge gave you a choice, and you are still free to exercise it. You may come here to 24 group sessions for people who have battered. You have the opportunity to learn some things here that may help you with future relationships and that may also keep you out of harm's way in the future. Or you may walk out of here right now.

Batterer: That's not much of a choice.

CW: (*Confronting batterer with consequences of his behavior.*) Maybe not, but it's more of a choice than you gave your partner.

The responses are typical of a batterer's way of defending himself with denial, externalization of blame, and black-and-white kinds of statements that give little consideration to behavioral options and long-term consequences of behavior. The crisis worker gently but firmly wades into the client's defense system while at the same time attempting to establish rapport. This is not an easy job.

Sessions 3–4. The time-out assignment is discussed. Participants start looking for physical anger cues, and are asked to write down the signs as a homework assignment. Their lists are used to construct a group list of warning signals. The difference between anger as an emotion and violence as an action is discussed. Basic stress management skills and relaxation techniques are taught and practiced. The worker gives a homework assignment that combines recognizing physical cues of anger with the use of relaxation techniques.

The prevailing pragmatic philosophy of the FTC program is that it will be extremely difficult if not impossible to change ideology. Rather, the notion is that the batterer's sex role expectations may differ from his or her partner's and that he or she can be taught how to negotiate those differences. That notion is much more palatable and makes much more sense within clients' social and work environment than attempting to reindoctrinate them into a more feminist view of role expectations.

Sessions 5–6.   Physical anger cues are discussed. The leader presents Walker's (1979) cycle of violence and asks members to determine where they are on the continuum. The idea is to make them aware of this cycle and its commonality to all relationships, both at home or in the workplace, and to help them gain some dynamic insight into their own behavior and that of their partners as they go around in this destructive cycle. Clients are apprised of the difficulty of getting out of the cycle because of how long it has happened and its familiarity. Anger diaries are started. Anger diaries help to identify instigators of anger and the physical and cognitive responses to it. They also help batters start to identify feelings that support anger, such as guilt, shame, and depression. The diaries start to condition responsibility, because the person must constantly attend to diaries as he or she monitors anger.

Homework involves adding up the financial cost of battering. Members are to write down all the real and hidden monetary costs incurred from their violence.

Sessions 7–8.   These sessions cover the financial consequences of battering. Few batterers have stopped to think of its cost. Costs vary, but it is not uncommon for a group to average a minimum of $10,000 per person in financing his or her anger.

CW: Add up all the money you've spent on lawyers, work time lost, furniture broken, hospital bills, bail, fines, motel rooms, not to mention divorce proceedings and alimony as a direct or indirect result of violence. What could it have bought you? Wouldn't it be great to never have to spend another dime on your anger? You see, learning to control your anger will make you money. How many of you would be against that?

Time is also spent on the characteristics and dynamics of victims. These factors paradoxically start to describe some of the background of batterers because they have also become victims, albeit of their own behavior. Indeed, once they can start to see themselves as victims, they gain insight into how their victims feel. This is the start of empathic understanding for these clients.

CW: Add up all the emotional costs: the guilty, angry, hurt, depressed, dependent, hopeless, helpless feelings. Wouldn't it be great to never have another lousy feeling like that? How does that fit with your partner's notions of being your victim? Is there any difference between how your partner may feel about you after a beating and how you feel about the court system?

The recurring theme of choices is the basis for the next homework assignment. Members are asked to write down three bad choices and three good choices they have made in their relationships. Anger diaries are used to help the batterers identify the emotional cost that their choice of anger and violence takes on them.

Sessions 9–10.   The leader discusses good and bad choice making. He or she introduces the topics of irrational thinking and the maladaptive behavior resulting from it.

Cognitive-behavioral techniques from Albert Ellis's (1990) *Anger: How to Live With It and Without It* are illustrated. Specific emphasis is placed on absolutist thinking and *should, must,* and *ought* statements. Discussion focuses on how these statements get constructed, what environmental cues set up "*must*urbatory" thinking ("I must have my self-gratification or it will be absolutely intolerable") and how irrational, self-defeating thoughts and subsequent maladaptive behavior are tied together.

A violence and abuse assessment is made of the family of origin. Leaders ask members to respond to such questions as "Did your father hit your mother, or vice versa?" "How were disagreements handled?" "How did you feel about your parents?" "How were you disciplined as a child?" "How do all those events that you learned from early childhood carry over into your present family?" "How do you feel about that?" "How do those irrational beliefs spoken to earlier in the session operate in conjunction with the behavior that was modeled for you and you learned as a child?"

Members are given didactic instruction on how transgenerational violence occurs. Processing the following discussion questions generally results in a shocking and nasty insight, because the very thing the batterers hated most about their own parents they may now be perpetrating on their children. This will be the first time that many of the batterers have ever talked about their childhood experiences with domestic violence, and it is usually a very emotional experience.

CW: What was your feeling as a child in regard to the abuse you saw? How do you suppose your kids are affected by your violent behavior? Do they feel any different from the way you did? Guess at their feelings and what they might be thinking about you and why they might feel and think that way.

The homework assignment is to start changing members' ways of responding to stressful situations by

1. Watching out for environmental cues that start *must*urbatory thinking
2. Using cooler cognitions, such as "It'd be nice, convenient if XYZ happened, but it doesn't *have* to happen"

Sessions 11–12.   These next two sessions focus on feelings. Homework discussion centers on any different responses the members saw in their family as they tried to use cooler, more positive approaches and how members felt about those responses. Many of the members will be incredulous and confused by the changes they see. Participants are asked to list several positive and negative feelings they have. Usually most of them will have a great deal of difficulty with this task, because they have never had to identify any feelings they have. Feelings generally get lumped into two categories, angry and happy. A lecture is given on how males, in particular, are taught at a very early age to "stuff" their feelings and not acknowledge them as real. The anger diaries are used to expand their ability to label and identify the many feelings that support anger.

Outcomes from denying feelings are discussed. Examples are given from Stoop and Arterburn's (1991) *The Angry Man: "Why Does He Act That Way?"* This session is very difficult, because members will be asked to share feelings—a very threatening experience for most of them. Leader statements such as the following are designed to minimize the threat.

CW: Although there are risks, when you tell someone how you feel you become vulnerable and you also become a lot more real. You become much more lovable and find it easier to love when you tell someone how you feel. You need to be prepared for them to do the same and understand that there is the possibility of feeling some pain and hurt from what is said. You don't tell someone your feelings just to get their sympathy. You share your feelings with significant others as a way of taking care of yourself, so you don't have to stuff feelings anymore until they finally boil over and get you in trouble or hurt you.

Outcomes may be very dramatic as clients start to talk about their feelings, relive their experiences as children, and grapple with feelings of guilt, helplessness, dependency, and insecurity that they have had since childhood. It is not uncommon for some highly charged emotional catharsis to occur at this point and, as these feelings emerge, for some strong bonds to form as clients start, for the first time, to share deeply but closely held feelings with another person. The homework assignment involves the construction and use at home of three sentences using positive feelings and three sentences using negative feelings.

Sessions 13–14.   The attempt to convey verbally both positive and negative feelings is discussed and leads into issues of power and control. Power and control are the focus of the session, discussed in relation to faulty belief systems. The stereotypical concept of power in batterers' issues develops out of a mistaken concept of independence: "I've got it, so you don't!" A new way of looking at power is interdependence: "The two of us together are more powerful than any one person!" They are posed questions about how they can form a team with their partner to reduce those powerless feelings. It is interesting that many of these clients who are physically strong may feel extremely powerless and frustrated when they are dealing verbally with others and when they are being "outtalked" in a relationship and may regress to their only way of regaining power and control—violence.

CW: When you allow someone else to push your button, who is in control? How do you use anger as a control tool? Abuse is a last-ditch effort to gain control back in a relationship. Why is that so? Do you believe that you try to get power and control only when you feel you don't have any? If power and control are the bottom line, do abuse, anger, and battering get the job done for you? If they really do get the job done, then why do you still have to rely on them?

Closely allied with different ways of obtaining power and control are the concepts of aggressiveness and assertiveness. Because of their inability to use words in powerful ways, most of the participants have difficulty making clear assertions about what their wants and needs are. Furthermore, they have an overriding fear that they will be rejected if they ask for something, and their insecurity does not handle rejection well at all. As a result, they use aggression to meet their needs. The group is taught how to construct assertion statements and given an assignment of using them at home.

Sessions 15–16.   The most difficult part of an assertion statement for the group is the "I" or owning part. On the board, the leader puts up "I" or assertion statements and "you" or aggression statements so members know what they sound like, how they differ, and what can happen when each is used. Each member is asked to formulate a problem in terms of "I" and "you" statements and practice with a partner. Using a describe, express, specify, and consequences script (Bower & Bower, 1976), members are asked to identify what behaviors in others bother them, to express how those behaviors make them feel, to specify what new behaviors they want, and to be able to positively reinforce others if those behaviors happen. Careful construction of these clear, precise, and owned assertive statements is made with role plays to try them out.

Because jealousy is so common to most of the stories that brought members here, time is devoted to members retelling their original story using the skills they have learned in their sixteen sessions. As these stories are reprocessed, other feelings undergirding the jealousy begin to surface. Hurt, betrayal, insecurity, lack of trust, dependency are all threatening feelings that are denied and replaced by jealousy, which allows placement of blame on the partner for "transgressions" and thus allows batterers a face-saving way of not having to deal with their own problems.

Batterer: I hate to admit it, but all that stuff makes sense. Still and all, I don't believe I can trust her.

CW: Maybe you know she can't trust you, so you don't trust her. Could you use some of those "I" statements and discuss it with her, and no matter what she said, not use "you" statements?

The homework is to name a time in their lives when jealousy turned to violence. The members are also asked to mentally substitute a new feeling every time they start to feel jealous and to report back on their experience.

Sessions 17–18.   Jealousy assignments are processed in these sessions. Because alcohol and drugs play a predominant role in the vast majority of battering incidents, members are educated about how the problem applies to battering: specifically, that alcoholism and drug abuse is not necessarily the cause of battering but does release inhibitions enough that batterers can give themselves permission to become violent.

Results of the Michigan Alcohol Screening Test (Selzer, 1971) or the Substance Abuse Subtle Screening Inventory (Miller, 1983) are given to each participant. Participants are shown how alcohol or drugs can be a trigger for violent behavior and an excuse for making violent behavior acceptable.

Sessions 19–20.   Sex is an overriding concern because of all the myths that surround it. Much of the need of the batterer to feel superior, confident, and capable is tied to sex, and, particularly for men, their concept of manhood. Many times, particularly with young female leaders, members will say things and use language designed to shock and embarrass the leaders. Although X-rated language just for the sake of X-rated language is not tolerated, some leeway is given for the street vernacular that is commonly used. The ability of group leaders, particularly young women, to weather the language goes a long way toward establishing their credentials with these men.

Batterer: So she wouldn't give me a blow job so I smacked her. That's part of earning her keep, to blow my pipes, man!

CW: (Young female graduate student.) So forcing oral sex on her keeps you in control. I wonder if the way you said that isn't designed to shock and embarrass me and kinda control me through verbal sex like you control her physically through sex.

Batterer: Hey, I thought we was supposed to be talking about the real stuff in here.

CW: (Very calmly, with eyes leveled at the batterer, avoiding the taunt.) I'm wondering how you'd like it if Harold (*240-pound ironworker in the group*) were to request oral sex of you, and if you didn't comply, start pounding on you, particularly in your groin. Do you start to get some of the feelings your partner would get? (*The group members nod their heads in agreement.*) I wonder if you can respond to that?

The many myths that hold men up to impossible Hollywood "stud" or women to "love goddess" standards are discussed and debunked. For many of the clients, this will be the first valid information they have ever received about sexual behavior. They will typically experience relief after being told that no man or woman could live up to some of the performance expectations they have self-propagandized for themselves. Homework assignments focus on irrational and negative thoughts clients generate for themselves in their sexual relations. They are asked to watch for and write down some of their unrealistic expectations of themselves. They are also asked to attempt to use assertion statements when asking for sex. Coming to understand that making requests for sex ("I'd like to make love to you") rather than demanding sex ("You get in here and do it") may not only get them sex, but better sex is a revelation. Finally, the leader asks each member to pick one of the subjects already covered in the group and be prepared to teach a review on it next session.

Sessions 21–22. Each group member picks one of the major topics from the foregoing sessions and teaches it. Discussion centers on a review of the issue from the standpoint of the effect it has had on the member. Many members may have stage fright at being responsible for "teaching." The crisis worker is extremely supportive and reinforcing of their efforts. Taking responsibility for teaching the concepts is important in validating that the participants have learned and can transmit that knowledge to others. The homework assignment is to put everything they have learned into operation and return next time to finalize their game plan for not recidivating (backsliding into criminal violence).

Sessions 23–24. Individuals are asked to conduct assessments of what their affective, behavioral, or cognitive "hot spots" are and how they will be sure to cue themselves to recognize when they are approaching a "hot spot" and what they now know they can do about that. The leader gives postassessments and gives points for participation, homework, and attendance. Reflections and feelings are given about the group. The leader gives a "Good, Bad, and Ugly" exercise.

CW: If you had to tell the judge anything about this program, what would it be? What did you like best and least? What would you like to see changed? What techniques seemed to work for you, and what didn't?

Members then discuss how they are putting their comprehensive anger management plans into action. They also indicate the strengths they now see in themselves and positively reinforce one another for their efforts. Depending on how cohesive the group has become, it is not uncommon for the clients to bring food, exchange phone numbers, and have a graduation party for one another at the last session.

Program Success

Do anger management programs work? The result are equivocal. Overall, batterers report that such programs help them gain control of their anger, enable them to communicate better with their partners, and reduce their violence. Shupe and associates (1987) found that battered women in approximately 7 out of 10 cases reported that physical and sexual violence stopped after their partners went through an anger management program. When violence did recur after the men graduated from these programs, it was almost always remarkably reduced. Relationships were also improved, and many women who had not attended indicated that they had picked up pointers that their partners brought home from the sessions (pp. 113–117).

Research indicates that batterers must attend at least 75 percent or more of the sessions in anger management groups to have a chance of avoiding recidivism (Chen, Bersani, Myers, & Denton, 1989). At the FTC in Memphis, batterers must attend all the sessions or make them up before their satisfactory completion is recorded and forwarded to the court system. The FTC program works closely with the court system and the district attorney's office to ensure compliance. As a result, perpetrators are tracked fairly well. The latest two-year follow-up indicates that 70 percent of those who completed the program did not recidivate. For noncompleters, only 23 percent did not recidivate (Memphis Police Department, 1999). What is clear is that arrest alone will not change much of anything in a domestic violence situation without concomitant treatment for the batterer (Gelles, 1993; Hirschel, Hutchison, & Dean, 1992).

Although most clients come to counseling angry and hostile because they are pressured or required to be there, the majority report that they learn from and even come to enjoy the camaraderie of the group (Scales & Winter, 1991). The majority of outcome studies of battering groups have found positive outcomes. Increases in self-esteem (Kriner & Waldron, 1988) and assertiveness (Douglas & Perrin, 1987); decreases in depression and anger (Hamberger & Hastings, 1986), in jealousy and negative attitudes toward women (Saunders & Hanusa, 1986), and in overall decrease of psychological symptoms (Hawkins & Beauvais, 1985); reduction in both self-reported and corroborated physical and psychological abuse on postcounseling follow-up (Edleson & Syers, 1990; Poynter, 1989); and more cohesive, expressive, and less conflict-ridden family life (Poynter, 1989) have all been found in a variety of studies involving battering groups with different cultural, racial, and socioeconomic backgrounds.

Other researchers have found little evidence to indicate that rates of violence of perpetrators who obtain and complete treatment are very different from those who do not (Rosenfeld, 1992; Tolman & Bennett, 1990). There are several problems with determining the efficacy of treatment programs. First, there is no standard model of treatment. There are probably as many different programs and different styles of intervention as there are programs! Also, the expertise of individuals providing the treatment may vary a great deal. A critical prerequisite for batterers not recidivating is that some severe consequences are needed for not completing the program or for battering again. Such consequences are not always enforced. Tracking batterers is difficult. Many of these people are very transient and move from jurisdiction to jurisdiction. There is no good way to determine if they have recidivated when they are halfway across the country. Frankly, because of the severity of their pathology, we believe some people do not or cannot profit from group programs. We know of very few severe borderlines or sociopaths who would gain much from two hours a week in such a program, no matter how good it was or how good the facilitator was.

Whether the programs truly change their participants or whether they work in other ways, as graphically described in the following excerpt, we believe that clients who complete an anger management program are not reported to the police nearly as often as those who have nothing happen to them.

> *Batterer:* Man, I ain't never gonna beat up on a woman again. Nothing will ever make me go through this shit twice! (Shupe et al., 1987, p. 103)

IF YOU ARE IN AN ABUSIVE RELATIONSHIP

We finish this chapter by offering some advice to any women or men who may be involved in an abusive relationship. If you are being victimized in an abusive relationship, the following points summarizing Bowker's (1986) advice from 1,000 battered women in her book *Ending the Violence: A Guidebook Based on the Experiences of 1000 Battered Wives* (p. 110) may be of help:

1. Obtain a divorce or separate and see a lawyer.
2. Get counseling for yourself and/or the batterer.
3. Secure help immediately; don't let the pattern become established.
4. Be independent and raise your self-esteem.
5. Tell others about the violence; keep no secrets.
6. Be firm with the batterer.
7. Call the police to arrest the batterer, file charges, and follow through on the prosecution.
8. Ask friends and neighbors for help.
9. Go to a battered women's shelter.
10. Go to women's groups and women's therapists.

If you are physically and mentally abusive and believe you have a problem with your anger, we suggest seeking out an anger management group. Although Edleson and Syers (1990) found self-help much less effective than groups in reducing violence, we understand it may be a very big step to commit to such a group when you are not forced to do so. It may also be that no group is available in your area. Although self-help may not be as effective, we recommend two books on anger management: *Dr. Weisinger's Anger Management Work Out Book* by Hendrie Weisinger (1985) and *Learning to Live Without Violence* by Daniel Sonkin and Michael Durphy (1982).

Conclusion.   Although research indicates that witnessing battering as a child is a primary modeling factor for both the abused and the abuser, as innocuous an event as one's favorite professional football team winning a game may have an impact on battering (White, Katz, & Scarborough, 1992). Carden (1994) states that "Seventeen years after the founding of the first program designed to eliminate wife abuse by working with the wife abuser, we have only the most primitive notions about what works, why and how it works, or even whether in the long run, it does work" (p. 573).

SUMMARY

Battering has deep roots in the psychological, sociological, and cultural makeup of the United States and in many other countries that go back to the beginnings of their patriarchal systems. Battering is pervasive through all socioeconomic levels of society and knows no ethnic, racial, or religious boundaries. Same-sex relationships are also not immune from domestic violence. Dynamically, battering may be seen as having much to do with the concept of power. A number of stressors that insinuate themselves into a relationship can escalate relational problems to violence.

A variety of theories have been proposed to explain why battering occurs. However, it is still unclear as to what propels people into battering relations, why people batter, and what will keep them from battering again.

Domestic violence is sequential, developmental, and dynamic. The situation of the battered client is unlike many other crises in that it is almost always transcrisis in nature; that is, it is cyclic, reaching many peak levels over extended periods of time. For a variety of reasons, it is the rare person who leaves a violent relationship for good after the first battering. Continued and increased violence over a period of years is the typical pattern of battering relationships.

In the last decade, crisis lines, shelters, and programs for battered women and their children have grown exponentially across the United States. Courts and law enforcement agencies have become much more proactive in protecting the rights of these women. However, the number of battered women still far exceeds the capacity of human services to effectively deal with them in comprehensive ways.

One of the most frustrating components of intervention with clients who are victims of domestic violence is their seeming inability to extract themselves from the terrible situations they face. Providing counseling in such trying circumstances calls for a great deal of empathic understanding. The worker's job is to help keep the client as safe as possible, provide options and, working patiently with the victim, help her or him explore alternatives and choose a plan of action.

Recently, the focus on domestic violence has shifted to include treatment of the batterer. Anger management groups for batterers are starting to appear throughout the country. Typically sent to such groups by court order, batterers learn to understand the factors that lead them to violence, learn to recognize and communicate their feelings, and learn to avoid or stop confrontations that lead them to act out their feelings in violent ways.

CLASSROOM EXERCISES

The Case of Joyce

The following is a typical case of an abused wife. Joyce is a 34-year-old woman who has been married 10 years. She has three children, all under 10 years old: Sheena, age 9; Jack, age 6; and Beth, age 2. Her husband is a prominent attorney. The family presents an ideal picture of an upper-middle-class family. They live in a fashionable suburb. The husband has been successful to the extent that he has been made a full partner in a large law firm. The family is very active in church, the country club, and various other social organizations. Joyce is an active member of several charitable, civic, and social groups. Joyce's initial call to the abuse center was vague and guarded. She expressed an interest in inquiring for "another woman" in regard to the purpose of the center. After she had received information and an invitation to call back, a number of weeks elapsed. Joyce's second call occurred after receiving a severe beating from her husband. This is a segment of that conversation.

CW: (*Answering phone.*) Abuse center. May I help you?

Joyce: I feel terrible calling you so many times, but I've gotta have help right away. (*Sobbing.*)

CW: OK! Tell me what's happened that you need help now.

Joyce: Well, last night he beat me worse than ever. I thought he was really going to kill me this time. It had been building up for the past few weeks. His fuse was getting shorter and shorter, both with me and the kids. It's his work, I guess. Finally he came home late last night. Dinner was cold. We were supposed to go out, and I guess it was my fault . . . I complained about his being late, and he blew up. Started yelling that he was gonna teach me a lesson. He started hitting me with his fists . . . knocked me down . . . and then started kicking me. I got up and ran into the bathroom. The kids were yelling for him to stop and he cuffed Sheena . . . God, it was horrible! (*Wracked with sobs for more than a minute. CW waits.*) I'm sorry, I just can't seem to keep control.

I. Simulated Telephone Interview

In small groups of five or six, one person takes the role of Joyce and one person takes the role of the crisis worker. The remaining group members are observers. The crisis worker picks up where the telephone dialogue left off, following the six-step model discussed in Chapter 2. Pursue the crisis intervention session through to gaining a commitment, if possible, from Joyce. At the conclusion of the intervention, the observers will provide feedback to both crisis worker and client. These are typical discussion questions:

1. Did the crisis worker *really* hear what the victim was saying, both verbally and nonverbally?
2. What did the crisis worker do to attend to the client's safety and security needs?
3. What evidence indicates that the client understood and owned realistic options?
4. What typical dynamics did you see occurring—denial, guilt, fear, rationalization, withdrawal, and so on—in the victim? How did the crisis worker handle them?
5. Did the crisis worker attempt to impose solutions or alternatives on Joyce?

After these questions have been discussed, all those who played the role of Joyce should have the opportunity to disassociate themselves from the simulated role. They each make a statement to members of the group, explaining why they are *not* Joyce and noting ways in which they are personally different from that person. Typically we say, "Word your statement in such a way that all of us who observed will never again associate you with that role." Then we call for a round of applause from the group for the people doing the role play.

II. Simulated Support Group

Five or six female volunteers from the group take the roles of abused women who are now in residence at the wife abuse shelter. Either the instructor or a volunteer crisis worker from the group conducts a short session of a support group for abused women. Use a "fishbowl" arrangement—that is, the support group players are seated in the center of the room. Role players should draw on their own experience and reading of this chapter to make the exercise as realistic as possible. During the process the crisis worker will want to focus on these issues:

1. The effects of being transplanted from one's home to crowded conditions of living in a socioeconomically and ethnically diverse group of women
2. The desire to reestablish contact with the husband even though the consequences may be extremely negative (particularly note any dependency needs)
3. Bringing to the surface and dealing with the dynamic responses of victims, including disbelief, denial, fear, anger, negotiation, pride, striving for independence, and resolution
4. Typical problems such as employment, finances, child care, transportation, legal aid, food, clothing, permanent shelter, schooling for children, and vocational skills
5. What each abuse victim wants to do over the long term.

After the role-playing session, discuss questions like these: How does the crisis worker act as facilitator of solutions to these problems? Does the worker let group members take responsibility, or is the worker responsible for them? How does the worker resolve conflict? How does the worker respond to group members who exhibit overt helplessness and dependency? Again, after the discussion the role players should disassociate themselves from their roles and receive a round of applause.

RESOURCES

There are a variety of domestic violence web sites that provide information and support services.

The National Domestic Violence Hotline
Although states, counties, and municipalities have done much to deter domestic violence, many rural areas of the United States are without any kind of support services. To help remedy this problem, in February 1996 President Clinton established a toll-free national hotline for victims of domestic violence. That number is 1-800-799-SAFE or for hearing impaired TDD 1-800-787-3224. This hotline receives about 11,000 calls a month, has translators available for a host of foreign languages, and covers all fifty states, the District of Columbia, Puerto Rico, and the Virgin Islands. It provides crisis intervention and links callers to local domestic violence programs. The World Wide Web also provides a great deal of information and assistance to people dealing with domestic violence. Use the search words "domestic violence" or "domestic violence hotline" to access this information.

REFERENCES

Adams, D., & McCormick, A. (1982). Men unlearning violence: A group approach based on the collective model. In M. Roy (Ed.), *The abusive partner* (pp. 170–197). New York: Van Nostrand Reinhold.

Aguilar, R. J., & Nightingale, N. N. (1994). The impact of specific battering experiences on the self-esteem of abused women. *Journal of Family Violence, 9,* 35–45.

Aitken, L., & Griffin, G. (1996). *Gender issues in elder abuse.* Newbury Park, CA: Sage.

American Medical Association. (1991, June). *Report of the Council on Scientific Affairs: Violence against women,* Proceedings of the House of Delegates. Chicago: Author.

American Psychiatric Association. (1994). *Diagnostic and statistical manual of mental disorders* (4th ed.). Washington, DC: Author.

Angless, T., Maconachie, M., & Van Zyl, M. (1998). Battered women seeking solutions: A South African study. *Violence Against Women 4*(6), 637–658.

Astin, M. C., Lawrence, K. J., & Foy, D. W. (1993). Posttraumatic stress disorder among battered women: Risk and resiliency factors. *Violence and Victims, 8,* 17–28.

Astin, M. C., Ogland-Hand, S. M., Coleman, E. M., & Foy, D. W. (1995). Posttraumatic stress disorder and childhood abuse in battered women: Comparisons with maritally distressed women. *Journal of Consulting and Clinical Psychology, 63,* 308–312.

Avis, J. M. (1992). Where are all the family therapists? Abuse and violence within families and family therapy's response. *Journal of Marital and Family Therapy, 18,* 225–232.

Babcock, J. C., Jacobson, N. S., Gottman, J. M., & Waltz, J. (1993). Power and violence: The relationship between communication patterns, power discrepancies, and domestic violence. *Journal of Counseling and Clinical Psychology, 61,* 40–50.

Barnett, O. W., & Hamberger, L. K. (1992). The assessment of maritally violent men on the California Personality Inventory. *Violence and Victims, 7,* 15–28.

Barnett, E. R., Pittman, C. R., Ragan, C., & Salus, M. K. (1980). *Family violence: Intervention strategies* (DHHS Publication No. OHD 580-30258). Washington, DC: U.S. Government Printing Office.

Bartholomew, K. (1999, August). *Violence in male same-sex relationships: Prevalence, incidence, and injury.* Paper presented at the 107th Annual Convention of the American Psychological Association, Symposium on Outing Same-Sex Partner Abuse-Defining the Issues, Boston.

Beasley, R., & Stoltenberg, C. D. (1992). Personality characteristics of male spouse abusers. *Professional Psychology, 23,* 310–317.

Benjamin, L., & Walz, G. R. (1983). *Violence in the family: Child and spouse abuse* (Report No. EDN00001). Washington, DC: National Institute of Education. (ERIC Document Reproduction Service No. ED 226-309).

Bergman, L. (1992). Dating violence among high school students. *Social Work, 37,* 17–21.

Berk, R. A., Newton, P. J., & Berk, S. (1986). What a difference a day makes: An empirical study of the impact of shelters for battered women. *Journal of Marriage and the Family, 48,* 481–490.

Bland, R., & Orne, H. (1986). Family violence and psychiatric disorder. *Canadian Journal of Psychiatry, 31,* 129–137.

Blount, R. W., Silverman, I. J., Sellers, C. S., & Seese, R. A. (1994). Alcohol and drug use among abused women who kill, abused women who don't, and their abusers. *Journal of Drug Issues, 24,* 165–177.

Bodnarchuk, M., Kropp, R., Ogloff, J., Hart, S., & Dutton, D. (1995). *Predicting cessation of intimate assaultiveness after group treatment* (No. 4887-10-91-106) Ottawa: Health Canada, Family Violence Prevention Division.

Bogal-Allbritten, R. B., & Allbritten, W. L. (1985). The hidden victims: Courtship violence among college students. *Journal of College Student Personnel, 26,* 201–204.

Bograd, M. (1992). Values in conflict: Challenges to family therapists' thinking. *Journal of Marital and Family Therapy, 18,* 245–256.

Bokunewicz, B., & Copel, L. C. (1992). Attitudes of emergency nurses before and after a 60-minute educational presentation on partner abuse. *Journal of Emergency Nursing, 18,* 24–27.

Bologna, M. J., Waterman, C. K., & Dawson, L. J. (1987). *Violence in gay male and lesbian relationships: Implications for practitioners and policy makers.* Paper presented at the Third National Conference for Family Violence Researchers, Durham, NH.

Bookwala, J., Frieze, I., Smith, C., & Ryan, K. (1992). Predictors of dating violence: A multivariante analysis. *Violence and Victims, 7,* 297–311.

Bower, S. A., & Bower, G. H. (1976). *Asserting yourself: A practical guide for positive change.* Reading, MA: Addison-Wesley.

Bowker, L. H. (1986) *Ending the violence: A guidebook based on the experiences of 1000 battered wives.* Holmes Beach, FL: Learning Publications.

Bowlby, J. (1980). *Attachment and loss: Vol. 3. Loss.* New York: Basic Books.

Bradley v. *State of Mississippi,* 1 Miss. 156 (1824).

Brasseur, J. W. (1994, October). The battered woman: Identification and intervention. *Clinical Reviews, 4,* 45–74.

Browne, K., & Herbert, M. (1997). *Preventing family violence.* Chichester, England: Wiley.

Burcky, W., Reuterman, N., & Kopsky, S. (1988). Dating violence among high school students. *The School Counselor, 35,* 353–358.

Bureau of Justice Statistics. (1991). U.S. Department of Justice. *Female victims of violence.* Washington, DC: U.S. Department of Justice.

Bureau of Justice Statistics. (1995). U.S. Department of Justice. *Violence against women: Estimates from the redesigned survey.* Washington, DC: U.S. Department of Justice.

Buhrke, R. A., & Douce, L. A. (1991). Training issues for counseling psychologists working with lesbians and gay men. *The Counseling Psychologist, 19,* 248–252.

Campbell, J. C. (1989). A test of two explanatory models of women's responses to battering. *Nursing Research, 38,* 18–24.

Capps, M. (1982, April). *The co-optive and repressive state versus the battered women's movement.* Paper presented at annual meeting of Southern Sociological Society, Memphis, TN.

Carden, A. D. (1994). Wife abuse and the wife abuser: Review and recommendations. *The Counseling Psychologist, 22,* 539–582.

Carrado, M., George, M., Loxam, E, Jones, L., & Templar, D. (1996). Aggression in British hetrosexual relationships: A descriptive analysis. *Aggressive Behavior, 22,* 401–415.

Caulfield M., & Riggs, D. (1992). Dating violence: The primacy of previous experience. *Journal of Social and Personal Relationships, 3,* 457–471.

Chalk, R., & King, P. A. (Eds). (1998). *Violence in families: Assessing prevention and treatment programs.* Washington, DC: National Academy Press.

Chen, H., Bersani, C., Myers, S. C., & Denton, R. (1989). Evaluating the effectiveness of a court-sponsored abuser treatment program. *Journal of Family Violence, 4,* 309–322.

Cochran Berry, B. (1995). *Life after Johnnie Cochran: Why I left the sweetest talking lawyer in L.A.* New York: Basic Books.

Coleman, V. E. (1994). Lesbian battering: The relationship between personality and the perpetuation of violence. *Violence and Victims, 9,* 139–152.

Conroy, K. (1982). Long-term treatment issues with battered women. In J. P. Flanger (Ed.), *The many faces of violence.* Springfield, IL: Charles C Thomas.

Dagastino, A. (Speaker). (1984). *Crisis intervention series: Helping abused women in abuse centers and shelters* (Cassette Recording No. 4-1). Memphis: Memphis State University Department of Counseling and Personnel Services.

Demaris, A. (1989). Attrition in batterers' counseling: The role of social and demographic factors. *Social Service Review, 63,* 142–154.

Dines, G. (1992). Pornography and the media: Cultural representations of violence against women. *Family Violence and Sexual Assault Bulletin, 8,* 17–20.

Dobash, R. E., & Dobash, R. (1979). *Violence against wives.* New York: Free Press.

Dobash, R. E., & Dobash, R. P. (1992). *Women, violence, and change.* London: Routledge.

Douglas, D. (1991). Intervention with male toddlers who have witnessed parental violence. *Journal of Contemporary Human Services, 72,* 515–523.

Douglas, M. A., & Perrin, A. (1987, July). *Recidivism and accuracy of self-reported violence and arrest.* Paper presented at the Third National Conference for Family Violence Researchers, University of New Hampshire, Durham.

Dutton, D. G. (1985). An ecologically nested theory of male violence towards intimates. *International Journal of Women's Studies, 8,* 404–413.

Dutton, D. G. (1994). The origin and structure of the abusive personality. *Journal of Personality Disorders 8*(3), 181–191.

Dutton, D. G. (1995). *The domestic assault of women.* Vancouver, BC: University of British Columbia Press.

Dutton, D. G., & Starzomski, A. (1993). Borderline personality organization in perpetrators of psychological and physical abuse. *Violence and Victims, 8*(4), 327–338.

Dutton, D. G., & Starzomski, A. (1994). Psychological differences between court-referred and self-referred wife assaulters. *Criminal Justice and Behavior: An International Journal, 21*(2), 203–222.

Dutton, M. A. (1993). Understanding women's responses to domestic violence: A redefinition of battered woman syndrome. *Hofstra Law Review, 21,* 1191–1242.

Edleson, J. L., & Syers, M. (1990). Relative effectiveness of group treatments for men who batter. *Social Work Research and Abstracts, 26,* 10–17.

Edleson, J. L., & Tolman, R. M. (1992). *Intervention for men who batter.* Newbury Park, CA: Sage.

Edwards, S. M. (1989). *Policing domestic violence: Women, the law, and the state.* London: Sage.

Ellis, A. (1990). *Anger: How to live with it and without it.* New York: Carroll.

Elliot, P. (1996). Shattered illusions: Same-sex domestic violence. In C. M. Renzetti (Ed.), *Violence in gay and lesbian domestic relationships* (pp. 1–8). Binghampton, NY: Haworth.

Fassinger, R. E. (1991). The hidden minority: Issues and challenges in working with lesbian women and gay men. *The Counseling Psychologist, 19,* 157–176.

Faulkner, K., Stoltenberg, C. D., Cogen, R., & Nolen, M. (1992) Cognitive behavioral group treatment for male spouse abusers. *Journal of Family Violence, 7,* 37–55.

Fiebert, M., & Gonzalez, D. (1997). Women who initiate assaults: The reasons offered for such behavior. *Psychological Reports, 80,* 583–590.

Finkelhor, D., Gelles, R. J., Hotaling, G. T., & Straus, A. A. (Eds.). (1983). *The dark side of families.* Newbury Park, CA: Sage.

Gebhard, P. H. (1997). *Memorandum on the incidence of homosexuals in the United State.* Bloomington: Indiana University, Center for Sex Research.

Gelles, R. (1993). Constraints against family violence: Do they work? *American Behavioral Scientist, 36,* 575–586.

Gelles, R. J., & Cornell, C. P. (1985). *Intimate violence in families.* Newbury Park, CA: Sage.

Gilliland, B. E., & Crisp, D. (1995, August). *Homophobia: assessing and changing attitudes of counselors-in-training.* Paper presented at the 103rd Annual Convention of the American Psychological Association, New York.

Gillis, J. R. (1999, August). *Community education and services for same-sex partner abuse.* Paper presented at the 107th Annual Convention of the American Psychological Association, Symposium on Outing Same-Sex Partner Abuse-Defining the Issues, Boston.

Gondolf, E. (1984). *Men who batter: Why they abuse women and how they stop their abuse.* Indiana, PA: Domestic Violence Study Center, Indiana University of Pennsylvania.

Gondolf, E. (1985). Fighting for control: A clinical assessment of men who batter. *Social Casework, 65,* 48–54.

Grusznski, R. J., & Carrillo, T. P. (1988). Who completes batterers' treatment groups? An empirical investigation. *Journal of Family Violence, 3,* 141–150.

Hamberger, L. K. (1994). The battered woman: Identification and intervention. *The Female Patient, 19,* 29–30, 32–33.

Hamberger, L. K., & Hastings, J. E. (1986, August). *Skills training for treatment of spouse abusers: An outcome study.* Paper presented at the meeting of the American Psychological Association, Washington, DC.

Hamby, S. L. (1998). Partner violence: Prevention and intervention. In J. L. Jasinski & L. M. Williams (Eds.), *Partner violence: A comprehensive review of 20 years of research* (pp. 210–258). Newbury Park, CA: Sage.

Hamilton, B., & Coates, J. (1993). Perceived helpfulness and use of professional services by abused women. *Journal of Family Violence, 8,* 313–321.

Hart, B. (1980, June). Testimony at a hearing before the U.S. Commission on Civil Rights, Harrisburg, PA.

Hart, B. (1986). Lesbian battering: An examination. In K. Lobel (Ed.), *Naming the violence: Speaking out about lesbian battering* (pp. 173–189). Seattle, WA: Seal.

Hastings, J. E., & Hamberger, L. K. (1988). Personality characteristics of spouse abusers: A controlled comparison. *Violence and Victims, 3,* 31–47.

Hattendorf, J., Ottens, A., & Lomax, R. (1999). Type and severity of abuse and posttraumatic stress disorder symptoms reported by women who killed abusive partners. *Violence Against Women, 5*(3), 292–312.

Hawkins, R., & Beauvais, C. (1985, August). *Evaluation of group therapy with abusive men: The police record.* Paper presented at the meeting of the American Psychological Association, Los Angeles.

Henton, J., Cate, R., Koval, J., Lloyd, S., & Christoper, S. (1983). Romance and violence in dating relationships. *Journal of Family Issues, 4,* 467–482.

Heppner, M. J. (1978). Counseling the battered wife: Myths, facts, and decisions. *Personnel and Guidance Journal, 56,* 522–525.

Heyman, R. E., Jouriles, E. N., & O'Leary, K. D. (1995). Alcohol and aggressive personality styles: Potentiator of serious aggression against wives? *Journal of Family Psychology, 9,* 44–57.

Hilbert, J. C., & Hilbert, H. C. (1984). Battered women leaving the shelter: Which way do they go? A discriminate function analysis. *Journal of Applied Social Sciences, 8,* 291–297.

Hirschel, J. D., Hutchison, I. W., & Dean, C. W. (1992). The failure of arrest to deter spouse abuse. *Journal of Research in Crime and Delinquency, 29,* 7–33.

Holtzworth-Munroe, A., & Stuart, G. L. (1994). Typologies of male batterers: Three subtypes and the differences among them. *Psychological Bulletin, 116*(3), 476–497.

Hotaling, G. T., & Sugarman, D. B. (1986). An analysis of risk markers in husband to wife violence: The current state of knowledge. *Violence and Victims, 1,* 101–124.

Hotaling, G. T., & Sugarman, D. B. (1990). A risk-marker analysis of assaulted wives. *Journal of Family Violence, 5,* 1–13.

Hughes, H. M. (1982). Brief interventions with children in a battered women's shelter: A model preventive program. *Family Relations Journal of Applied Family and Child Studies, 31,* 495–502.

Ibrahim, F. A., & Herr, E. L. (1987). Battered women: A developmental life-career counseling perspective. *Journal of Counseling and Development, 65,* 244–248.

Island, D., & Letellier, P. (1991). *Men who beat the men who love them: Battered gay men and domestic violence.* New York: Harrington Park.

Janus, S. S., & Janus, C. L. (1993). *The Janus Report on sexual behavior.* New York: Wiley.

Jarvie, I. (1991). Pornography and/as degradation. *International Journal of Law and Psychiatry, 14,* 13–27.

Jasinski, J. L., & Williams, L. M. (Eds.). (1998). *Partner violence: A comprehensive review of twenty years of research.* Newbury Park, CA: Sage.

Jennings, J. L. (1990). Preventing relapse versus "stopping" domestic violence: Do we expect too much too soon from battering men? *Journal of Family Violence, 5,* 43–60.

Johnson, M. (1995). Patriarchal terrorism and common couple violence: Two forms of violence against women. *Journal of Marriage and Family, 57,* 283–294.

Jouriles, E. M., & Norwood, W. D. (1995). Physical aggression toward boys and girls in families characterized by the battering of women. *Journal of Family Psychology, 9,* 69–78.

Kaufman, G. (1992). The mysterious disappearance of battered women in family therapists' office: Male privilege colluding with male violence. *Journal of Marital and Family Therapy, 18,* 233–243.

Kaufman Kantor, G., & Jasinski, J. L. (1998). Dynamics and risk factors in partner violence. In J. L. Jasinski & L. M. Williams (Eds.), *Partner violence: A comprehensive view of twenty years of research* (pp. 1–44). Newbury Park, CA: Sage.

Kriner, L., & Waldron, B. (1988). Group counseling: A treatment modality for batterers. *Journal of Specialists in Group Work, 13,* 110–116.

Kurz, D., & Stark, E. (1987). Health education and feminist strategy. In K. Yllo & M. Bograd (Eds.), *Feminist perspectives on wife abuse.* Newbury Park, CA: Sage.

Kurdek, L. (1994). Areas of conflict for gay, lesbian, and heterosexual couples: What couples argue about influences relationship satisfaction. *Journal of Marriage and the Family, 56,* 923–934.

Langhinrichsen-Roling, J., Neidig, P., & Thorn, G. (1995). Violent marriages: Gender difference in levels of current violence and past abuse. *Journal of Family Violence, 10*(2), 159–176.

Langley, R., & Levy, R. C. (1977). *Wife beating: The silent crisis.* New York: Dutton.

Levinson, D. (1989). *Family violence in cross-cultural perspective.* Newbury Park, CA: Sage.

Lie, G. Y., & Gentlewarrier, S. (1991). Intimate violence in lesbian relationships: Discussion of survey findings and practice implication. *Journal of Social Service Research, 15*(1/2), 41–59.

Lobel, K. (1986). *Naming the violence: Speaking out about lesbian battering.* Seattle, WA: Seal.

Lockhart, L. L., White, B. W., Causby, V., & Isaac, A. (1994). Letting out the secret: Violence in lesbian relationships. *Journal of Interpersonal Violence, 9*(4), 469–492.

Makepeace, J. (1983). Life-events stress and courtship violence. *Family Relations, 32,* 101–109.

Makepeace, J. (1986). Gender difference in courtship violence victimization. *Family Relations, 35,* 383–388.

Margolies, L., & Leeder, E. (1995). Violence at the door: Treatment of lesbian batterers. *Violence Against Women, 1*(2), 129–157.

Marrujo, B., & Kreger, M. (1996). Definition of roles in abusive relationships. *Journal of Gay & Lesbian Social Services, 4*(1), 22–32.

Marshall, L. L. (1992). Development of the severity of violence against women scales. *Journal of Family Violence, 7,* 103–121.

Massachusetts Coalition of Battered Women Service Groups. (1981). *For shelter and beyond: An educational manual for working with women who are battered.* Boston, MA: Red Sun Press.

Matthews, C., & Lease, S. H. (1999, August). *Lesbian, gay, and bisexual family.* Paper presented at the 107th Annual Convention of the American Psychological Association, Symposium on Research, and Practice with Lesbian, Gay and Bisexual Clients, Boston.

Matthews, M. K. (1993). Survivors of abuse. *Primary Care, 20,* 391–402.

McLeer, S., & Anwar, R. (1989). A study of women presenting in an emergency medical department. *American Journal of Public health 79*(1), 65–66.

Memphis Police Department. (1999). *Recidivism rates for completers and non-completers of anger management programs in Shelby County 1997–1999.* Memphis, TN: Author.

Merrill, G. S. (1996). Ruling the exceptions: Same sex battering and domestic violence theory. In C. M. Renzetti and C. H. Miley (Eds.), *Violence in gay and lesbian domestic partnerships* (pp. 9–21). New York: Harrington Park Press/Haworth Press.

Miller, G. (1983). *SASSI: Substance Abuse Subtle Screening Inventory.* Bloomington, IN: SASSI Institute.

Millon, T. (1987). *Manual for the Millon Clinical Multiaxial Inventory* (2nd ed.). Minneapolis, MN: National Computer Systems.

Morgan, S. M. (1982). *Conjugal terrorism: A psychological and community treatment model of wife abuse.* Palo Alto, CA: R & E Research Associates.

Morrow, S. L. (1999, August). *First to do no harm: Therapist working with lesbian, gay, and bisexual clients.* Paper presented at the 107th Annual Convention of the American Psychological Association, Symposium on Research and Practice with Lesbian, Gay, and Bisexual clients, Boston.

Morse, B. (1995). Beyond the Conflict Tactics Scale: Assessing gender difference in partner violence. *Violence and Victims, 10*(4), 251–272.

Moss, V. A. (1991). Battered women and the myth of masochism. *Journal of Psychosocial Nursing, 29,* 19–23.

O'Keefe, M. (1998). Posttraumatic stress disorder among incarcerated battered women: A comparison of battered women who kill their abusers and those incarcerated for other offenses. *Journal of Traumatic Stress, 11*(1), 71–85.

Okun, L. (1986). *Woman abuse: Facts replacing myths.* Albany: State University of New York Press.

Olson, L., Anctil, C., Fullerton, L., Brillman, J., Arbuckle, J., & Sklar, D. (1996). Increasing emergency room physician recognition of domestic violence. *Annals of Emergency Medicine 27*(6), 741–746.

Pagelow, M. D. (1981). *Woman battering: Victims and their experiences.* Newbury Park, CA: Sage.

Pagelow, M. D. (1992). Adult victims of domestic violence: Battered women. *Journal of Interpersonal Violence, 7,* 87–120.

Parker, B., McFarlane, J., Soeken, K., Torres, T., & Campbell, D. (1993). Physical and emotional abuse in pregnancy: A comparison of adult and teenage women. *Nursing Research, 42,* 173–177.

Peled, E. (1997). The battered women's movement response to children: A critical analysis. *Violence Against Women, 3*(4), 424–446.

Perrin, S., Van Hasselt, V., Basilio, I., & Hersen, M. (1996). Assessing the effects of violence on women in battering relationships with the Keane MMPI-PTSD Scale. *Journal of Traumatic Stress, 9*(4), 805–816.

Pizzey, E. (1974). *Scream quietly or the neighbors will hear.* London: Penguin Books.

Pleck, E. (1987). *The making of societal policy against family violence from colonial times to the present.* New York: Oxford University Press.

Poynter, T. L. (1989). An evaluation of a group programme for male perpetrators of domestic violence. *Australian Journal of Sex, Marriage, and Family, 10,* 133–142.

Quinn, M. J., & Tomita, S. K. (1997). *Elder abuse and neglect* (2nd ed.). New York: Springer.

Renzetti, C. (1992). *Violent betrayal: Partner abuse in lesbian relationships*. Newbury Park, CA: Sage.

Renzetti, C. (1996). The poverty of services for battered lesbians. In C. M. Renzetti & C. H. Miley (Eds.), *Violence in gay and lesbian domestic partnerships* (pp. 61–68). Binghampton, NY: Haworth Press.

Renzetti, C., & Miley, C. (1996). Violence in gay and lesbian partnerships. *Journal of Gay and Lesian Social Services, 14*(1), 1–116.

Resnik, M. (1976). *Wife beating: Counselor training manual*. Ann Arbor, MI: NOW Domestic Violence Project.

Ristock, J. L. (1999, August). *Exploring dynamics in abusive lesbian relationships*. Paper presented at the 107th Annual Convention of the American Psychological Association, Symposium on Outing Same-Sex Partner Abuse, Boston.

Rodenburg, F. A., & Fantuzzo, J. W. (1993). The measure of wife abuse: Steps toward the development of a comprehensive assessment technique. *Journal of Family Violence, 8*, 203–228.

Rosenfeld, B. (1992). Court-ordered treatment of spousal abuse. *Clinical Psychology Review, 12*(2), 205–226.

Rosewater, L. B. (1982). *An MMPI profile for battered women*. Unpublished doctoral dissertation, Union Graduate School, Ann Arbor, MI.

Ross, M., & Glesson, C. (1991). Bias in social work intervention with battered women. *Journal of Social Services Research, 14*, 79–105.

Russell, B., & Uhlemann, M. R. (1994). Women surviving an abusive relationship: Grief and the process of change. *Journal of Counseling and Development, 72*, 362–367.

Sampselle, C. M. (1991). The role of nursing in preventing violence against women. *Journal of Obstetric, Gynecologic, and Neonatal Nursing, 20*, 481–487.

Sassetti, M. R. (1993). Domestic violence. *Primary Care, 20*, 289–303.

Saunders, D. G. (1992). A typology of men who batter: Three types derived from cluster analysis. *American Journal of Orthopsychiatry, 62*, 264–275.

Saunders, D. G., & Hanusa, D. (1986). Cognitive-behavioral treatment of men who batter: The short-term effects of group therapy. *Journal of Family Violence, 1*, 357–372.

Scales, K., & Winter, B. (1991, April). *Anger management for spouse abusers: The interpersonal transaction group*. Paper presented at Crisis Convening XV, Chicago.

Schechter, S. (1982). *Women and male violence*. Boston: South End Press.

Schutte, N. S., Bouleige, L., Fix, J. L., & Malouff, J. M. (1986). Returning to partner after leaving a crisis shelter: A decision faced by battered women. *Journal of Social Behavior and Personality, 1*, 295–298.

Schutte, N. S., Malouff, J. M., & Doyle, J. S. (1988). The relationship between characteristics of the victim, persuasive techniques of the batterer, and returning to a battering relationship. *The Journal of Social Psychology, 128*, 605–610.

Schwartz, M. D., & Mattley, C. (1993) The battered woman scale and gender identities. *Journal of Family Violence, 8*, 277–287.

Selzer, M. L. (1971). Michigan Alcohol Screening Test: The quest for a new diagnostic instrument. *American Journal of Psychiatry, 127*, 1653–1658.

Sev'er, A. (1997). *Across-cultural exploration of wife abuse*. Lewiston, NY: The Edwin Mellen Press.

Shalhoub-Kevorkian, N. (1997). Tolerating battering; Invisible methods of social control. *International Review of Victimology, 5*(1), 1–21.

Shepard, M. F., & Campbell, J. A. (1992). The abusive behavior inventory: A measure of psychological and physical abuse. *Journal of Interpersonal Violence, 7*, 291–305.

Sherman, L. W., & Berk, R. A. (1984). The specific deterrent effects of arrest for domestic assaults. *American Sociological Review, 49*, 1261–1272.

Shupe, A., Stacey, W. A., & Hazlewood, L. R. (1987). *Violent men, violent couples*. Lexington, MA: Lexington Books.

Snyder, J. A. (1994). How we do it: Emergency department protocols for domestic violence. *Journal of Emergency Nursing, 20*, 64–68.

Sonkin, D., & Durphy, M. (1982). *Learning to live without violence*. San Francisco: Volcano Press.

Sonkin, D. J., Martin, D., & Walker, L. E. (1985). *The male batterer: A treatment approach*. New York: Springer.

Spanno, T. K. (1990, April). *Eclipse of the self: The grief of the battered women*. Paper presented at Crisis Convening XIV, Chicago.

Stanley, J. (1999, August). *Exploration of partner violence in male same-sex relationships* Paper presented at the 107th Annual Convention of the American Psychological Association, Symposium on Outing Same-Sex Partner Abuse, Defining the Issues. Boston.

Stark, E., & Flitcraft, A. (1987). Violence among intimates: An epidemiological review. In V. B. Van Hasselt, R. L. Morrison, A. S. Bellack, & M. Hersen (Eds.), *Handbook of family violence.* New York: Plenum.

Stark, E., & Flitcraft, A. (1988). Personal power and institutional victimization: Treating the dual trauma of women battering. In F. M. Ochberg (Ed.), *Posttrauma therapy and victims of violence* (pp. 115–151). New York: Brunner/Mazel.

State of North Carolina v. *Oliver,* 70 N. C. 60, 61–62 (1874).

Stets, J. E., & Straus, M. A. (1990). Gender differences in reporting of marital violence and its medical and psychological consequences. In M. A. Strauss & R. J. Gelles (eds.) *Physical violence in American families: risk factors and adaptations to violence in 8,145 families* (pp. 151–165). New Brunswick, NJ: Transaction.

Stoop, D., & Arterburn, S. (1991). *The angry man: "Why does he act that way?"* Dallas, TX: Word Publishing.

Straus, M. A. (1979). Measuring intra-family conflict and violence: The C.T. Scale. *Journal of Marriage and Family, 41,* 75–88.

Straus, M. A., & Gelles, R. J. (1990). *Physical violence in American families: Risk factors and adaptations to violence in 8,145 families.* New Brunswick, NJ : Transaction

Straus, M. A., & Gelles, R. J. (1986). Societal change and change in family violence from 1975 to 1985 as revealed by two national surveys. *Journal of Marriage and Family, 48,* 465–479.

Straus, M. A., Gelles, R. J., & Steinmetz, S. (1980). *Behind closed doors: Violence in the American family.* Garden City, NY: Anchor/Doubleday.

Sullivan, C. M., Campbell, R., Angelique, H., Eby, K. K., & Davidson, W. S. (1994). An advocacy intervention program for women with abusive partners: Six-month follow-up. *American Journal of Community Psychology, 22,* 101–120.

Taylor, W. K., & Campbell, J. C. (1992). Treatment protocols for battered women. *Response to the Victimization of Women and Children, 14,* 16–21.

Thompson, M., Kaslow, N., Kingree, J., Puett, R., Thompson, N., & Meadows, L. (1999). Partner abuse in posttraumatic stress disorder as risk factors for suicide attempts in a sample of low-income, inner-city women. *Journal of Traumatic Stress, 12*(1), 59–72.

Tilden, V. P., Schmidt, T. A., Limandri, B. J., Chiodo, G. T., Garland, M. J., & Loveless, P. A. (1994). Factors that influence clinicians' assessment and management of family violence. *American Journal of Public Health, 84*(4), 628–633.

Tilden, V. P., & Shepard, P. (1987). Increasing the rate identification of battered women in an emergency department: Use of a nursing protocol. *Research in Nursing and Health, 10,* 209–215.

Tolman, R. M. (1989). The development of a measure of psychological maltreatment of women by their male partners. *Violence and Victims, 4,* 159–177.

Tolman, R. M., & Bennett, L. W. (1990). A review of quantitative research on men who batter. *Journal of Interpersonal Violence, 5,* 87–118.

Turner, S. F., & Shapiro, C. H. (1986). Battered women: Mourning the death of a relationship. *Social Work, 31,* 372–376.

Tutty, L. M., Bidgood, B. A., & Rothery, M. A. (1993). Support groups for battered women: Research on their efficacy. *Journal of Family Violence, 8,* 325–343.

Van Hasselt, V. B., Morrison, R. L., Bellack, A. S., & Hersen, M. (1988). *Handbook of family violence.* New York: Plenum.

Walker, L. E. (1979). How battering happens and how to stop it. In D. Moore (Ed.), *Battered women* (pp. 59–78). Newbury Park, CA: Sage.

Walker, L. E. (1984). *The battered woman syndrome.* New York: Springer.

Walker, L. E. (1989). *Terrifying love: Why battered women kill and how society responds.* New York: Harper & Row.

Weaver, T. L. (1998). Method variance and sensitivity of screening for traumatic stressors. *Journal of Traumatic Stress 11*(1), 181–185.

Webersinn, A. L., Hollinger, C. L., & Delamatre, J. E. (1991). Breaking the cycle of violence: An examination of factors relevant to treatment follow-through. *Psychological Reports, 68,* 231–239.

Weincourt, R. (1985). Never to be alone: Existential therapy for battered women. *Journal of Psychosocial Nursing, 23,* 24–29.

Weisinger, H. (1985). *Dr. Weisinger's anger management work out book.* New York: Quill.

Wesner, D., Patel, C., & Allen, J. (1991). A study of explosive rage in male spouses counseled in an Appalachian mental health clinic. *Journal of Counseling and Development, 70,* 235–241.

Wessel, L. & Campbell, J. (1997). Providing sanctuary for battered women: Nicaragua's Casas de la mujer. *Issues in Mental Health Nursing, 18*(5), 455–476.

West, C. M. (1998a). Leaving a second closet: Outing partner violence in same-sex couples. In J. L. Jasinski and L. M. Williams (Eds.), *Partner violence: A comprehensive review of 20 years of research* (pp. 163–183). Newbury Park, CA: Sage.

West, C. M. (1998b). Lifting the "Political Gag Order." In J. L. Jasinski and L. M. Williams (Eds.), *Partner violence: A comprehensive review of 20 years of research.* (pp. 184–209). Newbury Park, CA: Sage.

West, C. M., Kaufman Kantor, G., & Jasinski, J. L. (1998). Sociodemographic predictors and cultural barriers to help-seeking behavior by Latina and Anglo-American battered women. *Violence and Victims, 13*(4), 361–375.

White, G. F., Katz, J., & Scarborough, K. E. (1992). The impact of professional football games on violent assaults on women. *Violence and Victims, 7,* 157–171.

Wiehe, V. R. (1998). *Understanding family violence.* Newbury Park, CA: Sage.

Winter, B. (Speaker). (1991). The Family Trouble Center anger management program (Videocassette recording #6781-A-91). Memphis, TN: Memphis State University Department of Counseling and Personnel Services.

Wolak, J., & Finkelhor, D. (1998). Children exposed to partner violence. In J. L. Jasinski and L. M. Williams (Eds.), *Partner violence: A comprehensive review of twenty years of research* (pp. 73–112). Newbury Park, CA: Sage.

Wood, A. D., & McHugh, M. C. (1994). Woman battering: The response of the clergy. *Pastoral Psychology, 42,* 185–196.

CHAPTER EIGHT

Chemical Dependency: The Crisis of Addiction

"Wine is a mocker, strong drink is raging" (Proverbs 20:1). "At the last it biteth like a serpent, and stingeth like an adder" (Proverbs 23:32). These biblical verses depict the continuing saga of drugs and addiction with which humankind has struggled over the ages. Efforts to treat the problem of substance abuse go back at least to the Romans, who attempted aversive conditioning of drunkards by placing spiders in the bottom of wine cups (J. W. Smith, 1982, p. 875).

Whole economies have been founded on drug use. The United States has been no shirker in this regard. The discovery that an acre of corn could be made much more salable by turning it into alcohol played a dominant role in developing the economies of colonial New England and the early American frontier.

In 1785, nearly everyone in the United States would have thought the idea of abstinence to be ludicrous, but by 1835 a temperance movement "demonizing" alcohol was in full swing (Levine, 1984). The effort to "keep a devil out of the mouth of America" culminated in the Volstead Act and ratification of the Eighteenth Amendment to the Constitution, which brought prohibition to the country in 1920 (Asbury, 1950; Edwards, 1985). This "Noble Experiment" allowed the rampant growth of organized crime, which provided a thirsty public with bathtub gin, Canadian whiskey, and moonshine. The Twenty-First Amendment repealing prohibition in 1933 is a large legislative memorial to the futility of trying to prohibit a drug, and in a social perspective it has much to say about what a society believes to be good or evil.

The cost of buying illegal drugs in the United States ranges in estimates from 50 to 150 billion dollars a year (Bugliosi, 1996; Collier, 1989). Legal drugs are also big business. For the past two decades the total retail amount spent yearly on alcoholic beverages in the United States has remained fairly constant at the rate of about $67 billion, or approximately $270 per person (U.S. Bureau of the Census, 1995). But the real monetary cost far exceeds mere payment for drugs. If drug-related medical care, lost productivity, fractured families, insurance, crime, law enforcement, and treatment are added up, the citizenry of the United States spends between $240 billion to $0.5 trillion each year for the pleasure of putting addictive substances in their bodies (Doweiko, 1999, pp. 8–9).

Although alcohol consumption has declined over the past two decades by about 15 percent, the important percentage is this: Ten percent of those who drink consume 50 percent of the alcohol used in the United States (Kaplan, Sadock, & Grebb, 1994). That 10 percent translates into between 6 million to approximately 20 million people abusing or addicted to alcohol, depending on the degree of abuse (Kotz & Covington, 1995;

Lieber, 1995). That figure *excludes* from 1 to 3 million children and adolescents who are thought to be abusing or addicted to alcohol (Ellis, McInerney, DiGiuseppe, & Yeager, 1988; Turbo, 1989).

To the foregoing numbers, toss in the following very conservative figures. There are about 9 million regular users of marijuana (Angell & Kassifer, 1994, p. 537), between 600,000 and 800,000 known heroin addicts (Witkin & Griffin, 1994), between 800,000 and 1.6 million cocaine users (Angell & Kassifer, 1994; Cornish, McNicholas, & O'Brien, 1995), another 800,000 regular amphetamine users (Nash & Park, 1997), about 10 to 20 percent of children and adolescents who have "huffed" inhalants, an unknown amount of prescription drug abusers, and about 50 million tobacco users (Brownlee et al., 1994).

Perhaps one of the most telling statistics is found in the National Comorbidity Study (Anthony, Warner, & Kessler, 1997), which is an excellent statistical model of the drug-abusing behavior of men and women in the 15- to 54-year-old population of the United States. About 1 in 13 people at some time in their life will have such a problem with a controlled substance they are dependent on it. About 1 in 6 will have a problem with alcohol such that they are dependent on it. These figures are probably conservative, because the study had no way to consider potential respondents who already died from the abusive agents they ingested.

SOCIOCULTURAL DETERMINANTS OF SUBSTANCE ABUSE

Drug abuse is especially important in the social context of what various special-interest groups think should be done about it. Big business, law enforcement, the judiciary, religious organizations, human services providers of all types, the medical establishment, legislatures, journalists, educators, family members of alcoholics, and survivors of drunk drivers, to name but a few, all have a vested interest in either providing, controlling, or eradicating intoxicants. Whereas every one of these principals may agree that abuse is a problem, reaching a unified decision on how to handle the problem is about as likely as winning the grand prize in a state lottery.

Given all the lip service and fanfare that drug abuse and addiction get, it is somewhat paradoxical in regard to what the medical establishment *does not do or know* about it. Even though an alcohol-using patient's treatment may be initiated because of an injury in an automobile accident, a perforated ulcer, a partner battering, mental illness, or a host of other stated physical or emotional causes, the underlying disease of addiction occurs more often than any other etiology. The problem is enormously complicated by the fact that among all these presenting problems, medical and mental health professionals frequently do not recognize, diagnose, or report that chemical addiction is connected to the presenting malady (Doweiko, 1999, pp. 2–3; Saitz, Mulvey, Plough, & Samet, 1997). An interesting footnote is that less than 1 percent of typical medical school curriculums are devoted to addressing drug abuse (Selwyn, 1993). Yet the *DSM-IV* (American Psychiatric Association, 1994, pp. 175–272) has devoted 97 pages to diagnosing substance abuse disorders alone.

The society and the cultural background of an individual seem to have a great deal to do with what kinds of pharmacological and extrapharmacological effects will occur with use of addictive substances. Using alcohol as an example, at a 0.40 percent blood alcohol content (BAC) most people pass out, and that is generally construed to be the LD-50 level—the level of intoxication at which about half of the people die from an overdose (Goode, 1984, p. 62). Physiological outcomes are much the same for everyone having that BAC. However, psychological outcomes are very different as the user progresses to a 0.40 percent BAC level. Whereas one person with a BAC of 0.10 percent may want to fight a whole motorcycle gang, another may be the caricature of the garrulous, happy drunk, and another may sit stone-faced and bother no one.

It is a chemical fallacy that a specific dose of drug Z will invariably cause effect A in a user. What does seem to be true is that set and setting have a great effect on the behavior of the drug user. *Set* can be defined as the mental and emotional state of the user, including expectations, intelligence, personality, feelings, and so on. *Setting* is the social and physical environment of the user at the time of use. It can be defined as immediate surroundings, such as a living room as opposed to a bar or, in a broader context, can be the legal and religious perspective of the country (Goode, 1984, p. 35).

Set and setting define which situations are considered appropriate for drug use and which are not. Nowhere is this clearer than in the fallacious belief that alcohol automatically releases inhibitions. In a comprehensive study of a number of tribes in southern Africa who have very different beliefs about what is appropriate and inappropriate behavior, MacAndrew and Edgerton (1969) found that people would not automatically lose their inhibitions and violate norms due to ingestion of alcohol unless the particular culture permitted it. Furthermore, when a member of one culture was placed in a different cultural setting, that person might act in extraordinary ways when drinking that were very different from his or her own societal norms (Heath, 1985, p. 470).

ALCOHOL: NUMBER ONE ABUSED SUBSTANCE

The choice of potential abusive agents available today is much like a cafeteria menu. However, we believe that alcohol is still the best drug to illustrate what happens in the crisis of addiction. There are several reasons for our choice:

1. *Duration.* No other drug has the longevity, legacy, and legislative attempts to control or promote it. From the Whiskey Rebellion of George Washington's era to Carrie Nation and the Women's Christian Temperance Union to Alcoholics Anonymous to the founding of the National Institute of Alcohol Abuse and Alcoholism (NIAAA), alcohol continues to play a great role in how the United States attempts to deal with drug abuse.

2. *Legality.* There are only limited conditions under which one can go to jail for possession or use. Even with stiffer penalties for drunk driving and juvenile possession, social acceptability plays an important part in determining punishment. Some of the worst punishment for DUI (driving under the influence) vehicular homicide barely equals the mandatory time a person might serve when caught with a small amount of crack cocaine.

3. *Widespread use.* Although other drugs receive a great deal of publicity, they are "peanuts" in sheer numbers of users compared to the 50 to 65 million people in the United States alone who are directly and indirectly affected by alcoholism (Beasley, 1987).

4. *Indirect financial cost.* Indirect costs due to job absenteeism and firings; family violence and divorce; hospital care; and law enforcement, judicial, and correctional

activities related to alcoholism are most likely greater than any other public health issue and range upward to $130 billion (Angell & Kassifer, 1994; Costello, 1982, p. 1197).

5. *Psychological cost.* If one believes only part of the literature on the malignancy of codependency and enabling, the bankruptcy of family systems, the physical and sexual assaults on others (Gelles & Straus, 1988), and the legacy that adult children of alcoholics inherit (Brabant & Martof, 1993; Hardwick, Hansen, & Bairnsfather, 1995), the mental health costs are truly astounding.

6. *Physical cost.* Although not as shocking in immediate behavior or nearly as sudden in onset as crack, PCP, LSD, and other mind-altering central nervous system stimulants, the pernicious effects of alcoholism cut a wide physiological path through its victims. The American Medical Association (1993) estimates that 25 to 40 percent of hospitalization in the United States is directly or indirectly related to alcohol. Liver and pancreatic disease, Korsakoff's syndrome, reproductive and sexual dysfunction, cancer, heart disease, bone loss, gastrointestinal problems, reduced immunity, malnutrition, and particularly the insidious effects of fetal alcohol syndrome exact a tremendous physical toll on alcohol abusers (Backover, 1991; Doweiko, 1996, p. 66; Pattison & Kaufman, 1982a). Piled on top of these long-term effects are the short-term effects of alcohol overdose that consistently earn it between 15 to 20 percent of all emergency room admissions and about the same percentage of emergency room deaths (Beasley, 1987; Drug Abuse Warning Network, 1983). Between 15 and 30 percent of all nursing home beds are filled with people with chronic alcohol abuse problems (Schuckit, 1986).

7. *Links to crime.* A great deal of publicity is given to "speed freaks" and "crackheads" and the violent crimes they commit, or to the cocaine and heroin addicts who need a "fix" and steal everything they can get their hands on or prostitute themselves for their drug of choice, but alcohol abuse contributes to a majority of the assaults and murders related to drug use in the United States and has done so for a long time (MacDonald, 1961; National Foundation for Brain Research, 1992; Pernanen, 1976; Shupe, 1953).

8. *Implication in accidents.* The Mothers Against Drunk Driving (MADD) group has good reason to be in existence. About 40 to 50 percent of all highway deaths are alcohol-related (Blondell, Frierson, & Lippmann, 1996; McGinnis & Foege, 1993). Death on the highway gets a lot of notoriety, but drunk boating, drunk home repair, drunk walking into traffic, drunk falling down stairs, drunk hunting, drunk smoking in bed, and drunk swimming are a few of the many ways that a high percentage of people succeed in killing themselves and others by ingesting alcohol.

9. *Suicide.* The lifetime risk of suicide among alcoholics is approximately 15 percent (Schuckit, 1986).

10. *Alcohol is a drug.* Because alcohol can be legally purchased, people forget that it is a drug (Doweiko, 1996, p. 14). There is no biochemical aspect of alcohol use that is different from what most would consider drug use. The important distinction is the arbitrary view of the culture, which generally does not identify a person who drinks one beer as a drug user, whereas a person who smokes one marijuana cigarette is.

11. *Polyuse.* As we turn the corner into a new century, very few pure alcoholics, like the stereotypical street bum or party lush of yore, exist. Far more characteristic is the polyabuser (Doweiko, 1996, p. 6), who lubricates other drugs with alcohol for the cheap, compounding effects they can deliver.

12. *Embroilment in controversy.* Controversy surrounds the issues of both the etiology and treatment of alcoholism. Is it a biological disease or the "dis-ease" with one's ability to cope? Beliefs are so embedded in the culture and so strongly held that they influence and color funding, research, legislation, theory, and treatment. As a result, a number of models have emerged to explain alcoholism and how it should be treated.

MODELS OF ADDICTION

Currently there is no single, clear-cut model or treatment approach based on theory or research that holds sway over another. The debate over the efficacy of these models continues and serves to define competing schools of thought, rather than facilitating agreement among proponents. Doweiko (1990) uses the term *final common pathway* to advise that each of the theories of drug addiction contains an element of truth and efficacy (pp. 160–161). We take an eclectic approach and hold that at present *no one model is better and each has usefulness in treatment.* The following brief summary lists each of the major models alphabetically.

Behavioral Learning Model.   Drinking is caused and maintained by the association of alcohol intake with positive rewarding experiences, according to the behavioral learning model. Habituation is progressively strengthened by repetitive use of alcohol to combat anxiety and alleviate stress (Pattison & Kaufman, 1982b, p. 12).

Biopsychosocial Models.   As the term implies, addiction has multiple determinants (Marlatt, 1997, pp. xii–xiii). This is an eclectic model that subsumes many of the other more specific models in this list. It does give equal relevance to biological, social, and psychological aspects of addiction. It would appear as more and more research starts to identify the biological underpinnings of addiction that this model will have greater significance.

Cognitive Models.   A basic cognitive model operates on the assumption that thoughts or beliefs are the primary causative factors in substance abuse. A negative event such as a serious social, financial, or medical problem does not cause the person to start substance abusing; rather, the core attribution ("I can't stand the nightmares of that automobile wreck and the pain of all that physical rehabilitation") leads to an emotional response ("I feel lousy and depressed") and propels one into addictive beliefs ("Drugs will give me courage and take the pain away") that result in addictive behavior ("I'll go to a bar and stay drunk") (Beck, Wright, Newman, & Liese, 1993).

Disease Model.   In the disease model of addiction, drug use is seen as an aberrant condition afflicting otherwise healthy people, and exposure to the drug is seen as leading to physiological addiction. Through a sequence of internal events, alcoholics lose control of their drinking behavior (Jellinek, 1946, 1952, 1960). With increased use, more and more alcohol is needed to meet physiological needs. When use ceases or is reduced, the drug reaches too low a level for the tolerance that has been created, the person goes into withdrawal, and physiological craving leads to continued use (Oetting & Beauvais, 1986). The World Health Organization's (1952) and the American Medical

Association's (1956) acceptance of a diagnostic framework for alcohol abuse as a disease has lent much credibility to the disease model.

Gateway Model.   The gateway model proposes an orderly progression from one drug to another and particularly applies to young people as they move into heavier and heavier drug use (Dupont, 1984; Hamburg, Kraemer, & Jahnke, 1975). The research of Kandel, Yamaguchi, and Chen (1992) lends a great deal of credence to the progression from alcohol and cigarettes to marijuana and inhalants and then on to "hard" drugs.

Genetic Predisposition Model.   The genetic model proposes an inherited and transmitted predisposition to become a substance abuser (Cadoret & Gaith, 1978; Cotton, 1979; Goodwin, 1979; Schuckit & Rayses, 1979; Vaillant, 1983; Vaillant & Milofsky, 1982). It is closely allied to and supports the disease model. Research studies found that adopted children of an alcoholic parent, monozygotic twins of an alcoholic parent, and children from multiproblem families with an alcoholic parent were four to five times as likely to become alcoholics as were children from comparable groups who had no alcoholic parents. Gene (Blum et al., 1990; Noble et al., 1991) and neurotransmitter research (Kranzler & Anton, 1994) have isolated what appear to be distinct biological differences in how alcoholics and nonalcoholics process alcohol.

Lifestyle Model.   In the view of this model, the rewards of living in an altered state of consciousness outweigh all other costs of a destructive, drug-dependent lifestyle. For the people described by the lifestyle model, a drug-free existence is no existence at all (Pattison & Kaufman, 1982b, p. 12).

Parental Influence Model.   Besides the preponderance of alcohol use by parents, the rise of illicit drug use by parents sets models for children and makes "Do as I say, not as I do!" hypocritical in the extreme. "If my parents use it, why can't I?" is the cynical response seen in national television commercials on the war against drugs.

Peer-Cluster Model.   This model links drug use to small groups of people, including pairs such as best friends or boyfriend–girlfriend, who share beliefs, attitudes, values, and a rationale for drug use. Drug use plays an important role in group membership and identification (Oetting & Beauvais, 1986).

Prescriptive Model.   The prescriptive model suggests that alcoholism begins in self-prescription and physician prescription of alcohol and other drugs as tranquilizing agents to relieve acute or chronic pain symptoms (Blume, 1973; Pattison & Kaufman, 1982b, p. 11).

Problem Behavior Model.   The more problematic the behavior of the individual, the more likely the individual is to come into contact with people, places, and instances where drugs are available (Jessor & Jessor, 1977).

Psychoanalytic Model.   This model posits that certain pathological personality traits established early in childhood predispose the individual to alcoholism (Barry, 1974; Zwerling, 1959). Spotts and Shontz (1980) traced the obsession with a particular drug to specific flaws in early development and demonstrated how the action of that drug meshed with the resulting personality.

Psychosocial Model.   The psychosocial model proposes that a constellation of factors involving an individual's personality, environment, and behavior are interrelated and organized so as to develop a dynamic state designated as *problem-behavior proneness.* These variables define both the personal problems and the social environments that may underlie involvement with drugs—the greater the level of drug use, the greater the level of deviance (Jessor, Chase, & Donovan, 1980; Jessor & Jessor, 1977).

Sanctioned-Use Model.   The rampant use of Ritalin to diminish the hyperactivity associated with attention-span deficit disorder has become a double-edged sword (Guffey, 1992; Safer, 1994). The sanctioned and prescribed use of Ritalin by a generation of schoolchildren to keep them calm sends a clear message that it is not only OK to take drugs, it is beneficial. If Ritalin and other prescribed drugs are OK, then why is anything else that makes one feel good, considered bad? Amphetamine use to keep airmen awake during World War II and as late as the Gulf War was profligate, as was its use for depression and weight loss by physicians in the 1960s and 1970s (Emonson & Vanderbeek, 1995; Kaplan & Sadock, 1990). The overprescription and resulting abuse of Valium when it first came on the market is legendary. Given the foregoing, "Just say 'No!' to drugs!" would seem at a minimum, hypocritical, and at the maximum, ludicrous.

Sociocultural Models.   Sociocultural models examine factors external to the individual. The environment is seen as a chief contributing factor and is inclusive of demographic and ethnographic variables such as race, age, socioeconomic status, employment, education, social norms, religion, crime rates, belief systems, consumption rates, drinking behavior, and so on. In its emphasis on environmental factors, this approach empirically challenges the disease model (Heath, 1978; Lukoff, 1980).

Stress-Coping Model.   The use of drugs is seen as a substitute for effective behavioral and cognitive coping skills when the individual is placed under stress. The less effective the coping skills of the individual, the higher the likelihood of drug use as a palliative remedy (Wills & Shiffman, 1985)

The Model Controversy

The major division of thought about models of alcoholism segregates the disease-genetic-biological models from all the other models, which propose chemical dependency as something other than biologically based. At the center of this controversy have been the treatment principles of AA, therapist credentials, research funding, and third-party payments by health insurance companies.

Alcoholics Anonymous (AA).   AA bases its approach to alcoholism on the disease model. One of AA's abiding principles has been the insistence that there is a permanent change in the alcoholic's biochemistry and that willpower and insight are useless as essential forces for change. The disease model communicates hope and implies that only one part of the alcoholic is disabled. It is psychologically efficacious because it reduces the guilt, confusion, and self-doubt about moral worth and lack of willpower that might otherwise plague the alcoholic (Stuckey & Harrison, 1982, p. 871).

For AA, the disease basis of alcoholism may be compared with diabetes. Certainly diabetes is a permanent condition, but by watching their diet, diabetics can contain their level of blood sugar within normal limits. The analogy is clear that if the alcoholic remains abstinent, then his or her body will not be affected. Just as there is no such thing as an ex-diabetic, there is also no such thing as an ex-alcoholic. Thus, in the disease concept, the alcoholic is always "recovering" (Bissell, 1982, p. 811). This concept has been systematized in AA's 12-step program to recovery (Stuckey & Harrison, 1982, p. 866). Although a variety of other treatments have sprung up to compete with AA, Weisner, Greenfield, and Room (1995) found that across the United States, AA was still the program of choice for the bulk of the alcohol-abusing population.

The AA Model's Shortcomings.   Alcoholism as a disease or an illness is not well defined in the health professions (Chrisman, 1985, p. 15); and 50 years after Jellinek's first proposal that specific types of alcoholism fit a disease model, what that disease is remains vague and uncertain (Ames, 1985, p. 24). A true disease model must also reject the influence of situational factors on alcohol consumption (Peele, 1986). Finally, people who abstain from drinking for a number of years are no less likely to relapse into alcoholism than are people who have been chemically dependent and then drink moderately for a number of years. It seems that both abstinence and nonproblem drinking can be maintained over long periods of time, and neither precludes the possibility of relapse (Sobell & Sobell, 1978, pp. 19–20).

AA Credentials.   The fact remains that the AA approach works for many, many recovering alcoholics. One key to its success may be that it consists of recovering alcoholics helping recovering alcoholics. Many recovering addicts view with suspicion therapists who have not suffered from alcoholism. Although this parochial thinking is akin to saying that to be effective, medical doctors must suffer from the diseases they treat, it's true that many traditionally trained therapists from universities and medical schools have had little course work or practical experience in addictions and automatically debunk AA treatment approaches and philosophy with little basis other than "It's not scientific!" Historically, traditional techniques that professionals have used in addiction treatment have had a dismal record of enabling patients to beat addiction in comparison to AA and its participants. Many clients, particularly those who have suffered relapses, are not overly impressed by therapeutic credentials (Schaef, 1986, pp. 7–9).

One reason for the number of conflicting views of what alcoholism is and how to treat it may have to do with competition for funding. Since the advent of the National Institute for Alcohol Abuse and Alcoholism (NIAAA) and the National Institute of Drug Abuse (NIDA) and the provision of money for research, education, and treatment, the field of drug abuse treatment has grown exponentially. Because AA had been the principal actor until the NIAAA and NIDA arrived on the scene, it would prove little for others to attempt entrance into the abuse field singing the same theory song and playing the same treatment tune as AA. Therefore, to obtain recognition, other theoreticians proposed alternate approaches to the disease model. No research evidence exists to support this cynical view; nevertheless, our subjective opinion, based on numerous dialogues with experts in the field, is that there is some truth to this controversial viewpoint.

A related point about the controversy over models is that until the time that treatment of substance abuse became a paying proposition, few professionals cared to be bothered with it. The field was left largely to the volunteer efforts of AA. However, with the advent of payments from insurance companies to health care providers for the treatment of drug addiction, hospitals and health care professionals became very interested in the problem, as evidenced by a dramatic increase in the number of drug dependence treatment units throughout the country. We hope that movement toward rapprochement, which now appears to be well under way between more moderate elements in the field, will continue and will result in a systematic, eclectic paradigm of theory and treatment that uses the best of all models and discards the worst. It is from this complex, conflicted, commingled, and convoluted perspective that we present this chapter.

DEFINITIONS OF COMMONLY USED TERMS

Many definitions are coined in an attempt to adequately describe those who get into trouble with drugs. To facilitate the reading of this chapter, we list the following commonly used terms in alphabetical order. As with all the other controversial aspects of chemical dependency, these are not the only definitions for these terms. Rather, they represent *general* definitions. A number of chemical dependency theorists and treatment specialists might disagree with these definitions or even argue the existence of some of the constructs!

Abuse. The chronic, recurrent misuse of chemicals (Lawson, Ellis, & Rivers, 1984, p. 37). Abuse is when one or more of the following occur in a maladaptive pattern during a 12-month period: failure to fulfill major role obligations, such as work and school; physical impairment that creates a hazard, such as operating machinery; recurrent legal problems; recurrent social problems, such as physical fights (American Psychiatric Association, 1994, p. 183).

Addiction. A cellular change that occurs with the increased use of most depressant drugs. The primary clinical features are the development of tolerance and the development of withdrawal symptoms on the removal of the drug (Lawson et al., 1984, p. 37). Addiction is progressive, potentially fatal, and marked by preoccupation with chemical use and distortion of one's worldview to support continued use, even in the face of its many negative consequences (Doweiko, 1996, p. 4).

Addictive behavior. Currently a more preferred term, at least by many psychologists, to indicate abuse, dependency, and so forth because it focuses on behavior rather than fixed categories. It implies that addiction is a behavior and if that is so, behavior can be changed while addiction as a chronic, progressive disease cannot. The addition of "behavior" also allows addiction to be broadened beyond substance abuse and include behaviors such as gambling and sex (Marlatt, 1997, pp. xiii–xiv).

Alcoholism. A highly complex condition characterized by preoccupation with alcohol and loss of control over its consumption so that intoxication results if drinking is begun, by chronicity, by progression, and by a tendency to relapse.

It is associated with physical disability and impaired emotional, occupational, and/or social adjustment as a result of persistent use (Shearer, 1968, p. 6).

Chemical dependent. Any person who has a dependence on drugs such that the substance governs his or her life to the extent that it severely impairs the ability to function psychologically and/or physically (Lawson et al., 1984, p. 37). Currently the "in" term for a person receiving treatment for a drug problem.

Codependent/codependency. Reciprocal and complementary in nature, dependency is based on the chemical dependent's need for care to survive and the caretaker's need to control the addict's behavior (O'Brien & Gaborit, 1992). A codependent is any significant person in the chemical dependent's life, such as spouse, parent, lover, or child, who is enmeshed in the chemical dependency (Maxwell, 1986, p. 7); codependency is characterized by extreme preoccupation with and dependence (emotional, social, and sometimes physical) on a person or object. Eventually this dependence on another person becomes a pathological condition that affects the codependent in all other relationships (Wegscheider-Cruse, 1985, p. 2).

Dependence. As defined by *DSM-IV,* dependence is a cluster of cognitive, behavioral, and physiological symptoms indicating that the individual continues use of the substance despite significant substance-related problems. There is a pattern of repeated self-administration that usually results in tolerance, withdrawal, and compulsive drug-taking behavior (American Psychiatric Association, 1994, p. 176). However, the *DSM-IV* definition does not give what we believe is adequate justice to both physical and *psychological* dependence. Psychological dependence occurs in users who have a strong urge to alter their state of consciousness through the use of a chemical. This mental state may be the only factor involved, even in cases of the most intense craving and perpetuation of compulsive abuse. These two types of dependence may occur independently or in combination with one another (Lawson et al., 1984, p. 37).

Drug. A psychoactive substance that has a direct and significant impact on the processes of the mind with respect to thinking, feeling, and acting. The term *drug* is a cultural artifact and a social fabrication because it denotes something that has been arbitrarily defined by certain segments of society as a drug (Goode, 1984, p. 15).

Enabler/enabling. Any person who knowingly practices specific behaviors that allow the chemical dependent to continue the abuse/addiction and not be subjected to the full negative consequences of his or her behavior. The enabler may or may not be a family member and may have an overlapping relationship with codependency (Doweiko, 1996, p. 292). Where overlapping, maintenance of the relationship is more important than the problem of chemical dependency (Maxwell, 1986, p. 103).

Habituation. The degree to which one is accustomed to taking a certain drug. A habituated user can and will take more of a drug than a first-time experimenter (Goode, 1984, p. 33).

Misuse. Use of a chemical with some adverse physical, psychological, social, or legal consequence (Lawson et al., 1984, p. 37).

Tolerance. The biological ability of the body to transform and excrete the chemical from the body and the increasing insensitivity of its effects on the central nervous system. More of the drug must be used to achieve the desired effect (Doweiko, 1996, p. 4).

Use. The intake of a chemical substance into the body with the goal of somehow altering one's state of consciousness (Lawson et al., 1984, p. 37).

Withdrawal. The production of physical and psychological symptoms by the body on cessation or reduction in use of the drug. Symptoms are variable, depending on length and amount of use, and indicate that tolerance to the chemical has developed (Doweiko, 1996, p. 4).

These definitions do not nearly convey the power that chemical dependence holds over people. The comments of two chemical dependents we know paint a striking picture of what being addicted and chemically dependent really means.

Federal correctional incarcerate (polyuser): Think of the best sex you ever had, man! Think how great that feeling was. I mean the best and greatest. Well, that ain't nothin' compared to shovin' that spike in your arm and getting that first rush. That's why I do it.

University professor (recovering alcoholic): When you get stressed out, there may be a number of things you do to get over it. You may go out and jog, pray, meditate, have a fight with your wife, chop wood, and so on. The problem with that is the payoff is variable. It may or may not work. When I get stressed out, I drink. My way works *all* the time and *every* time. It's invariable. I know what will happen before I do it. Beat that!

THE DYNAMICS OF ADDICTION

The dynamics of chemical dependency are complex and sophisticated, and extend beyond the addict into the systems with which he or she interacts.

Defense Mechanisms

Drug abusers offer examples of all the defense mechanisms one might find in a text on abnormal psychology. Gordon, a recovering alcoholic we will follow throughout the rest of this chapter, is a composite, displaying the following maladaptive defense mechanisms.

Denial.   Alcoholism is often called the "disease of denial" (Lawson et al., 1984, p. 36). Denial is a normal adaptive process for self-protection, but within the alcoholic it becomes rigid and maladaptive. It stops help-seeking behavior, contributes to treatment failure, and sets up relapse (Kearney, 1996). Denial is the emotional refusal to acknowledge a person, situation, condition, or event the way it actually is (Perez, 1985, p. 5).

Gordon: Real men handle their problems. I'll handle mine. I've had a lot of problems lately. Sure I like a drink. Do a lot of business that way. Most of my friends drink. I get loaded every once in a while, but so would you if you had the pressures I do right now.

Displacement.   Displacement is the venting of hostility on a person or object, neither of which deserves it (Perez, 1985, p. 6).

Gordon: Yell at my wife? You betcha. Always griping at me for not being at home. Hey! I provided a great living, then when I really needed her support because of the pressure at work, she'd just whine more.

Fantasy.   Alcoholics use fantasy to escape from a variety of threatening circumstances and emotions. They escape boredom with the job, anxiety in coping with relationships, and frustration over career progress by retreating to a drug-induced euphoria. That euphoric state is far more rewarding than the real world and one to which the alcoholic feels compelled to return again and again (Perez, 1985, p. 6).

Gordon: Having a drink takes the edge off. I mean, you can just relax and put it out of your mind for a while—the job, the old lady, everything. I can really get it together and plan the next big project.

Projection.   Alcoholics often attribute motives within themselves to significant others. Sensitivity, suspiciousness, and hostility toward others are outward manifestations of the distancing, estrangement, and lack of communication that characterize the alcoholic (Perez, 1985, p. 6).

Gordon: Amy never did love me. Oh, she loved the house, the club, and the private schools for the kids, and all that. I finally figured that out and told her that straight to her face!

Rationalization.   Alcoholics make all kinds of excuses to support their addiction and their felt inadequacies of acting and behaving (Perez, 1985, p. 6).

Gordon: By God! I had severe back problems from doing the engineering on that sorting machine. Hell! Even the doctor gave me a prescription for the pain. That machine had to get finished. What's wrong with taking a couple of pops at midnight? It made my back quit aching.

Intellectualization.   Alcoholics speak in generalizations or theoretical terms in an impersonal manner and thereby remove themselves from hurtful feelings (Maxwell, 1986, p. 65).

Gordon: They say I drink too much. Well, I've done some extensive reading on the subject and I certainly don't fit the category of a drunken bum. What do they know, anyway? They're not doctors.

Minimizing.   Alcoholics play down the seriousness of the situation (Maxwell, 1986, p. 64).

Gordon: This is just temporary. I got a little out of line. No problem. I'll just have to watch things a little closer.

Reaction Formation.   Reaction formation occurs as a defense against perceived threat and is one of the most harmful defense mechanisms because it distances dependents from their true feelings. Addicts constantly fear rejection and go out of their way to find it—even if it is not there (Perez, 1985, p. 11).

Gordon: Those kids of mine, too. The little ingrates. Gave them everything. Lisa just stares at me. Mark even said I didn't love him because I missed a lousy soccer game. He sure didn't miss his personal computer I got him. No time for the old man 'cause he was too busy himself. That kid never loved me. Always took up for his mom.

Regression.   Alcoholics are often immature and narcissistic, with resulting behavior similar to that of emotional prepubescence. The behavior is intended to manipulate, control, and get one's way. Temper tantrums, sulking, and pouting are all common forms of regression (Perez, 1985, p. 6).

Gordon: There was no use talking to her, so I just clammed up. Wouldn't support me in the business. Me apologize? She's the one who ought to apologize! I'm not saying one word to her until she does.

Repression.   Alcoholics deal with threatening and hurtful events by burying them in unconscious memory (Perez, 1985, p. 7). When sober, alcoholics repress the dependency needs and angry feelings that accompany them, and they remember nothing of the personality and behavior changes that occur when they are intoxicated (Zimberg, 1982, p. 1002).

Gordon: Warnings about my job performance? No way! They just dropped it on me one day. Things were fine up to that point! The same with the family. No warning! No nothing! They just up and leave. I never touched a hair on their head!

These defense mechanisms are far different from those of the average person. They may be extremely intrusive into others' lives: grossly inconvenient, inexcusable, objectionable, and socially undesirable. The chemical dependent's defenses are primitive and regressive and much like those of an infant. They may personify the alcoholic as a self-centered and dependent person. The two major components of a sociopathic personality—having no conscience and being excessively egocentric—can dominate in the chemical dependent (Perez, 1985, p. 9).

Also enmeshed in the hostile and angry feelings of the alcoholic is depression (Hoffman, 1970; Kristianson, 1970; Spiegel, Hadley, & Hadley, 1970). When floods of guilt come pouring through the walls of drug abusers' defenses, they are overwhelmed by an inability to take any kind of reasonable control over their lives and undo the damage they have done to themselves and significant others. The cyclical battering alcoholics take between having no conscience and having an overpowering one is draining and leaves little psychic energy for anything but depression when they start sobering up.

The defense mechanisms of most chemical dependents serve one goal and one goal only: to support, nurture, and help feed the one god in the addict's life, the drug. Nothing else matters. No service is given to anything else until its needs are fulfilled. Feeble attempts to control it are marked by guilt and remorse, but those feelings are niggardly in comparison with the urge to get "fixed" (Stuckey & Harrison, 1982, p. 868).

Gordon: I can't understand how things got this way. We used to have a great family. Yeah! I hate thinking about it. When I get to thinking about it, I feel rotten. Well, you can't function on the job with that kind of cloud hanging over you, so I'd have a drink and I'd feel better. Four or five and you can forget it all. But what else was I to do under all that?

Enabling and Codependency

The concepts of enabling and codependency are also fraught with controversy. Little empirical research exists to assess the basic assumptions of the concepts (Hands & Dear, 1994). Because alcoholism is typically a male disease (Doweiko, 1996, p. 14), these concepts may be seen as disempowering women, who struggle against terrific odds to keep a family together for a variety of economic, religious, cultural, and safety reasons (Haaken, 1993; Inclan & Hernandez, 1992; Uhle, 1994). Furthermore, many of the personality traits attributed to the codependent could be found in a stereotypical negative personality profile of most women (Cowan & Warren, 1994). In that regard, as may be seen from the chapter on partner violence, a woman in an alcoholic relationship is not altogether different from a woman who is in a battering relationship. Indeed, alcohol abuse and battering tend to go hand in hand, so it should not be surprising if many of the same dynamics prevail, along with the criticisms that go with them.

Critics also argue that codependents tend to be judged not on their own merits but by the addict's inability to get off drugs. Codependency dictates that the person has some as yet unsubstantiated "disease," "addiction," or "syndrome" of codependency that probably originated in and was "caught" from a dysfunctional family of origin (Myer, Peterson, & Stoffel-Rosales, 1991; Trois, 1995). Perhaps most insidious is the notion that once "caught," codependents must admit to their low self-esteem, their enmeshment and powerlessness in a pathological relationship, their inability to withstand rejection, and their avoidance of issues. If individuals are not willing to admit to this prescriptive and pejorative model, then they are clearly in "denial" (Doweiko, 1996, pp. 299–302).

However, enablers are not just spouses. A person who gives a street bum money and knows full well it will be spent on cheap wine is an enabler. Employers and employees may be just as culpable. Either out of fear of retribution by a union or threat of legal action, an employer may back off confronting an employee about substance abuse. When it is the supervisor who is abusing, any confrontation by employees may wind up getting them fired. As crazy as it sounds, chemical dependents are so good at manipulation they can make enablers feel like they are doing them a favor by

1. Doing the individual's work
2. "Covering" for poor work performance
3. Accepting excuses or making special arrangements
4. Overlooking frequent absenteeism or tardiness
5. Overlooking evidence of chemical abuse (Doweiko, 1999, p. 323)

The foregoing cautions are of paramount importance to a crisis interventionist who works with the significant others of a chemical dependent. Although some constellations of behaviors and personality traits support the concepts (Carson & Baker, 1994; Fischer, Spann, & Crawford, 1991; Hinkin & Kahn, 1995; Lyon & Greenberg, 1991; Walfish, Stenmark, Shealy, & Krone, 1992; Wright & Wright, 1990), a thorough analysis of the bases and reasons for that codependency should be made before labeling the individual.

With that qualifier, we now present the concept of the enabling codependent. First, though, it should be understood that codependency and enabling are not necessarily synonymous. Enabling has to do with one's *behavior* toward a chemical dependent. Codependency has to do with one's *relationship* to the chemical dependent (Doweiko, 1999, p. 325). One may be an enabler without being codependent, as in the case of the passerby who gives the street bum a handout. The bum is enabled to buy the wine, but there is no more than a passing relationship.

When a family is enmeshed in addiction, the crisis is compounded, and a strange phenomenon can occur. In an attempt to keep the family in equilibrium, members will first reject and then begin to tolerate the addict. To keep the family in homeostasis, various members unconsciously assume roles that not only keep the system on an even keel but also enable the addict to fall further into the addiction (Ford, 1987, pp. 16–17; Perez, 1985, p. 19).

The marital relationship becomes highly competitive, with the alcoholic's dependency needs counterbalanced by the spouse. Being forceful, blunt, active, and domineering are ways that the spouse seeks to retake control of the situation. However, neither alcoholic nor spouse gains dominance, and this continuous warfare results in each blaming the other for the family's problems (Kaufman & Pattison, 1982a, p. 667). By attempting to maintain the system, even though it is extremely pathological, family members become codependents. They also manifest many of the *maladaptive* and *unconscious* defense mechanisms their addicted counterparts have. We have used the responses of Amy, Gordon's wife, to illustrate these defenses, which immobilize the family system.

Suppression.   Codependents may suppress the problems the addict brings to the family by maintaining a "stiff upper lip" and not allowing their emotions to surface (Maxwell, 1986, pp. 78–79). This is a defense of quiet desperation and is based on the hope that some miraculous change will occur in the dependent.

Amy: I made a commitment when I got married that it was for keeps. He was probably an alcoholic when we got married, but a contract is a contract. In sickness and health and all that.

Dissociation.   For those who dissociate themselves from the problem and repress it, their perception of events is drastically altered by putting the problem aside. Dissociation means distancing the problem emotionally, and sometimes geographically (Maxwell, 1986, p. 80).

Amy: When it got really bad I'd make sure the kids were busy doing something and then I'd throw myself into the club work. That kept my mind off his problem. The best two weeks of my life every year would be going back home to my parents. I'd take the kids and we could get away.

Repression.   Repression of events takes dissociation a step further. By burying hurtful events in unconscious memory, codependents avoid having to grapple with the terrible feelings that accompany those events (Maxwell, 1986, p. 82).

Amy: I mean he's horrible all the time when he's bombed, but what he actually says I'm not real sure. He's real nasty, but I can't quite put my finger on what he actually does.

Escape to Therapy. Seeking therapeutic assistance may be another form of escape for codependents. A lot of catharsis may occur in therapy, but little real change is considered because it would also mean that the codependents would have to face reality and make some serious changes away from the maladaptive coping patterns that they have established (Maxwell, 1986, p. 82).

Amy: If somehow he could just change. I don't know, maybe you could talk him into coming here. I know that I at least get a little peace of mind from coming to these sessions.

Intellectualization. Codependents use intellectualization to keep themselves distanced from the hurtful affect. In attempting to keep the system in balance, they are obsessive-compulsive in planning and attending to details. By compulsively paying attention to the many details of these events, intellectualizers order their outward world but do nothing about their inner turmoil (Maxwell, 1986, pp. 83–84).

Amy: It's exhausting, but I've figured out when he's really going on a bender. So I plan activities down to the last detail to keep everybody busy and out of his way. By putting together a stepwise plan, I can keep it down to a dull roar.

Displacement. By displacement, a codependent moves feelings off the focal point of the problem, the addict's behavior, and moves it to less frightening and hurtful subject matter (Maxwell, 1986, p. 86).

Amy: I've been reading about this new vitamin therapy, and I'm really concerned Gordon's going to get sick because he's so run down. I've been giving him all kinds of good information on this and even got him an appointment with this M.D. who practices holistic medicine.

Reaction Formation. As the alcoholic becomes more and more irresponsible, a typical reaction for the codependent is to become more and more responsible. In actuality, this assumed responsibility for the family is focused directly on the alcoholic. Taking over for the alcoholic, codependents "save" the marriage and the family by behaving in ways exactly opposite to their internal feelings about the situation (Maxwell, 1986, pp. 88–90).

Amy: The family has to keep going. That's why I'd take those plans for him when he couldn't make the plane and call in sick for him. I know he said some terrible things to me and the kids, but he really didn't mean them. He wouldn't act that way when he was sober.

Reaction formation overextends the codependent in every conceivable way and can lead to physical or emotional breakdown. In the latter stages of alcoholism, codependents may resort to the very immature defenses of passive aggression and hypochondriasis (Maxwell, 1986, pp. 88–90).

Passive Aggression. By being late, forgetting, starting arguments and then leaving, overspending, and implying the threat of suicide the codependent keeps everyone in a state of uproar.

Amy: I don't know what's come over me. I've watched the money so carefully over the years. Gordon's still getting a paycheck, but I just can't seem to get bills paid and we're getting duns from creditors.

Hypochondriasis.   The defense of hypochondriasis converts anger into physical complaints. This is an extremely effective punishment of others because no matter how much consolation they receive, codependents obtain attention by this defense mechanism, and they don't give it up without a struggle (Maxwell, 1986, pp. 94–95).

Amy: (*Weeping.*) I'm sorry for breaking down like this. It's just with everything else I keep getting these terrible migraines. They knock me flat for a day at a time, and then I get behind and can't handle all the other stuff and wind up bawling.

The typical response to the chemically dependent person is first to reject and then to tolerate the objectionable behavior. This marks a person as an enabler (Maxwell, 1986, p. 103). In the early phases of enabling, there is denial and rationalization that the behavior will improve, and the enabler takes responsibility and assumes guilt for the alcoholic. In the middle phases, the enabler becomes hostile, disgusted, and pitying and becomes preoccupied with protecting and shielding the alcoholic. In advanced phases, the enabler's feelings of extreme hostility, withdrawal, and suspicion become generalized to the total environment. In the final phases, responsibility for and quarreling with the alcoholic become all encompassing. Outside interests and maintenance of self are disregarded in all-consuming and obsessive attempts to keep the system and the alcoholic stabilized (Kaufman & Pattison, 1982b, 1022–1024).

In the final phase of enabling, all the foregoing defense mechanisms are evidenced as variations on the following three enabler roles characterized by Ellis, McInerney, DiGiuseppe, and Yeager (1988), and may be immediately recognized by the crisis worker and called to account: (1) the *silent sufferer* achieves pathological satisfaction by being a martyr to the cause of maintaining the relationship; (2) the *messiah* condemns the drug use and appears to fight the addiction vigorously to save the addict, but never pushes the issue enough so the addict will have to face the consequences of his or her actions; and (3) the *joiner* subsidizes and attempts to control the chemical dependent by doing drugs with the chemical dependent or doling out money for drugs.

Each of the phases of codependency is for naught. Chemically dependent people listen to nothing. They respect only action, and only when that action threatens to interrupt their dependency in some way. Only when enablers decide to stop rescuing dependents and let them start to suffer the natural consequences of their actions will there be any change in the dependents' behavior (Stuckey & Harrison, 1982, p. 870).

CHILDREN IN ALCOHOLIC FAMILIES

Children raised in homes where open communication is practiced and consistency of lifestyles is the norm usually have the ability to adopt a variety of roles dependent on the situation. Children growing up in alcoholic homes seldom learn the combinations of roles that mold healthy personalities. They become locked into roles based on their perception of what they need to do to survive and bring some stability to their lives in a chaotic family (Black, 1981, p. 14). The following generic roles of children who live in alcoholic families have been profiled by Black (1981) and Wegscheider-Cruse (1989). Although these roles are stereotypical and no child can be so neatly categorized, they do represent common themes of personality patterns in such families.

The Scapegoat.   The scapegoat is the stereotypical troubled child of an alcoholic family. This acting-out child is the one who comes to the attention of school administrators, police, and social services. These children have extremely poor self-images and attempt to enhance themselves by rebellious, attention-seeking behavior. Acting-out children use unacceptable forms of behavior to say, "Care about me" or "I can't cope." Socially, these children generally gravitate toward peers who have equally low self-esteem and are prone to engage in delinquent behavior. They fill correctional facilities, mental health institutions, and chemical dependency units in hospitals. Termed "scapegoats" by Wegscheider-Cruse (1989), they enable the addiction by becoming another stressor that can serve as an excuse for substance abuse and by focusing the family's anger and energy away from the addict and onto themselves (Black, 1981, pp. 25–27).

The Hero.   The oldest child is most likely to be a very sophisticated child or family hero (Wegscheider-Cruse, 1989). This is the little adult who takes care of the alcoholic, the spouse, and the other children. In attempting to care for the family, the responsible child enables the alcoholic by giving her or him more time to drink. Not only are such children highly responsible to the family, they are also highly responsible in their academic and extracurricular endeavors. Outwardly, they appear as stalwart and outstanding young men and women who are successful in much that they do. Heroes learn to completely rely on themselves, because adults neither can be depended on nor are astute or sensitive enough to provide direction (Black, 1981, pp. 17–20).

The Lost Child.   This is usually the middle or younger child. Called "the lost child" by Wegscheider-Cruse (1989), this child follows directions, handles whatever has to be handled, and adjusts to the circumstances, however dysfunctional they may be. The lost child outwardly appears to be more flexible, spontaneous, and somewhat more selfish than others in the home. These children don't feel, question, get upset, or act in any way to draw attention to themselves. They enable the alcoholic by not being a "bother." Typically, the lost child is academically average in school. Socially, this child doesn't take leadership roles and is generally a loner (Black, 1981, pp. 21–23).

The Family Mascot.   The family mascot is usually the youngest child, who placates and comforts everybody in the family and makes them feel better (Wegscheider-Cruse, 1989). This child thinks that by making family members feel better, he or she can divert attention from the problem and it will subside or go away. This placating child may operate in three distinctive patterns.

First, the mascot may act the clown and distract the family through humorous antics. Socially these people may be the life of the party but have few close friends because they discount everybody's feelings as a stress reduction mechanism. Academically, if mascots defuse stress by humor, such antics may land them in trouble with their teachers (George, 1990, pp. 72–76).

The mascot may also assume a role of sympathetic counselor to the rest of the family. Highly sensitive to the needs of others, this child may be the apologist for the

family's behavior and attempt to apply psychological balm to the emotional wounds other members of the family suffer. Such sensitive characteristics are well rewarded at school, where such children are praised for their compliant, helpful, and sharing qualities. The mascot abets the alcoholic by distracting the family from being forced to come to grips with the constant conflicts they are engaged in (Black, 1981, pp. 23–25).

The mascot may also assume the "sick" role in the family by manifesting continuous and sometimes severe psychosomatic illnesses. This overprotected child becomes the illness focal point for the family, and enables the chemical dependency by deflecting the family focus on sickness away from the addict (George, 1990, p. 76).

To keep the foregoing dysfunctional family roles operational, ironclad family rules must be followed, as discussed in the next section.

Family Rules in Alcoholic Families

There is a clear method to the madness of the foregoing roles, and to survive, members of addictive families learn unspoken rules very quickly. In the parlance of substance abuse programs, families of addicts have a metaphorical pink elephant sitting in the living room that everybody sees, that everybody walks around, and that nobody acknowledges. The presence of this elephant makes children think there is something wrong with them, because nobody else seems to be much concerned with the elephant (the addictive behavior) or at least isn't acknowledging it. What is even more disconcerting is that these children tend to believe that everyone else lives in an idyllic Cleaver or Huxtable family. Yet this is certainly not the Bill Cosby show, and to make things livable in the grim reality of addictive families, children have to adopt the following rules to survive (McGowan, 1991).

Don't Talk/Don't Have Problems.   Because of the denial of alcoholism in an alcoholic family, seldom are any of the children's problems recognized and the family problem—alcoholism—is never discussed. In the alcoholic family, parents make clear injunctions, "We don't have that problem here, and you better not talk about it" (Doweiko, 1999, p. 337). If one does talk about it, then bad things happen (Black, 1981, pp. 33–37).

Lisa: Early on, Dad would be throwing up in the sink in the morning. Mom would just say he was sick. It scared me 'cause I thought he had, like, cancer or something, and he was gonna die. Every time I'd ask a question about it, she'd just blow me off or get mad at me.

Don't Trust.   The single most important ingredient in a nurturing relationship is honesty. No child can trust or be expected to trust unless those around him or her are also open and honest about their own feelings. One should never trust that parents will be there emotionally, psychologically, or even physically for a member of an addictive family (Doweiko, 1999, pp. 338–339). Children not only cannot depend on the alcoholic, but they also may not be able to depend on the other enabling parent because he or she is so busy trying to meet the alcoholic's needs and will minimize, rationalize, or blatantly deny that certain events are taking place (Black, 1981, pp. 39–45).

Mark: Even though it's a long way to the ballpark, I always plan on riding my bike. Dad says he'll take me but he works late a lot and can't get home on time.

Sometimes Mom has to take care of him when he's sick, or she doesn't feel well herself. So I just always plan on getting myself there for practice and the games.

Don't Feel. Members of addictive families have a well-developed denial system in regard to feelings—particularly one's own feelings. Members quickly learn that vocalizing feelings of fear, guilt, anger, sadness, embarrassment, and other hurtful feelings just brings more pain to the family. Although these feelings are shunted aside and submerged in the maladaptive roles family members assume, they are experienced over and over in addictive families and do not go away when one gains adulthood and leaves the addictive family of origin (Black, 1981, pp. 45–49).

Mark: I really wish Dad and Mom could have been there to see me get most valuable player, but Lisa was, and my coach told me how proud he was of me, and then the whole team went to his house for ice cream. Well, it wasn't that big a thing anyway . . . just a Little League championship.

Don't Behave Differently. Any attempt to shift roles within the family is not allowed because this would turn the system topsy-turvy. If role vacancies do occur, they must be quickly filled by other members of the family (George, 1990, p. 79).

Lisa: Oh yeah! I tried to be Little Miss Goody Two-Shoes, the perfect kid. Got good grades in school, went out for the volleyball team, dated "nice" guys and was a "nice" girl. But I got yelled at anyway so forget that. I might as well get yelled at for having fun.

Don't Blame Chemical Dependency. Assigning blame to people, things, and situations outside the family is typical of the denial of personal responsibility for one's actions that pervades a chemically dependent family. Although the addict may receive some severe judgment by the rest of the family, family members believe that it is fate that keeps an iron grip on the family's misery.

Amy: I know he can be such an SOB, but it's been the lot of the O'Leary women to marry that kind of guy for three generations now. I swear my younger sister married a clone of Gordon. It just runs in the family, I guess.

Do Behave as I Want. The family must behave as the alcoholic wants so the drinking behavior can continue. For those who don't comply, various sanctions and threats are applied. They include "I won't love you"; "I won't support you with money or my presence"; "I'll go out and get drunk"; or "I'll abuse you physically" (Doweiko, 1996, p. 304).

Gordon: (*Shouting.*) All I'm good for is to bring home a paycheck. We haven't got the money to go to Disney World! The only time you little parasites love me is when I'm giving you money. If you don't shut up, I'll shut you up with the back of my hand. (*Takes another long drink from his highball and stares sullenly at the TV.*)

Do Be Better and More Responsible. No matter what the family attempts to do to compensate for the alcoholic, it will never be good enough. As all the defense mechanisms of the alcoholic so clearly indicate, blame is projected onto significant others to compensate for the alcoholic's slide into failure (Doweiko, 1996, pp. 306–307).

Mark: Here's my report card. I made the honor roll!

Gordon: (Blearily staring at Mark's report card.) Yeah, well thoze AAAsss er OK, but whash that goddamn C in mashmaticks? Yule nevr getinna collash tha waye. Wy the hell didn you get the yard cutnraked like I tole ya? Now, get your tail out there 'n get on it!

Don't Have Fun.   "Fun" is drinking. Broken promises because of hangovers and benders in regard to vacations, recital attendance, going to ball games, and so on, and angry recriminations keep "fun" out of the family. Not inviting friends overnight or for birthday parties because of the unpredictability of the alcoholic's temper keep "fun" out of such households. Finally, family members are so busy working to keep the system in some semblance of equilibrium, they are too tired to have fun (Doweiko, 1996, pp. 306–307).

Mark: Hey, Lisa. Are you going to invite all your cool girlfriends over for a slumber party on your birthday?

Lisa: (With eyes downcast and a look of disappointment.) Well, I wanted to, and asked Mom, but she said Dad wouldn't like it. And you know how he gets.

Mark: (Angrily and kicking the wastebasket with his foot.) Yeah. I know.

Certainly, the trauma experienced by children who live and survive in chemically dependent families would seem bitter enough. However, the trauma and the crises of childhood in a chemically dependent family do not end with an escape from home or maturation into adulthood. The traumatic wake of being reared in a chemically dependent family often ripples into adulthood in the form of a variety of transcrisis events that might seem on first glance to have little reason for being and no discernible links to one's family of origin.

Adult Children of Alcoholics

In the 1980s a new phenomenon gained a great deal of publicity and attention in therapeutic settings and became a darling of the media talk shows. In the past, the primary focus of treatment of alcoholism was on the addicted person. Rarely were family members seen as the primary recipients of treatment for their own codependent and personal problems arising from the addiction (Schaef, 1986, p. 6). Given a best-guess estimate, there are about 28 million children of alcoholics in the United States (Collette, 1990; Mathew, Wilson, Blazer, & George, 1993), so it is not difficult to understand why a treatment approach that focuses on codependents themselves would quickly gain a great deal of notoriety and credibility.

The zealotry that sometimes assails the chemical dependency field is not missing here. As reported by Schaef (1986) in her review of the codependency literature, Wegscheider-Cruse (1984) believes that 96 percent of the population of the United States is codependent, and Larsen's (1983) predictions indicate a potential number of codependents larger than the current population of the United States! In the popular self-help literature, almost every problem of identity development or impulse control has been associated with codependency (Hogg & Frank, 1992).

The whole concept of the ACOA movement is based on a "damaged goods" model (Wolin & Wolin, 1995) that sees people as essentially passive and victims of their environment with few compensatory resources. Such "victim" status may give people who come into treatment lots of excuses for not doing what they need to do to move on with their lives. Research studies indicate that this victim status is simply not universally true (D'Andrea, Fisher, & Harrison, 1994; Senchak, Leonard, Greene, & Carroll, 1995), because numerous ACOAs have had the resilience to have lived in an alcoholic family and then do as well with their adult lives as anybody else (Giunta & Compas, 1994; Lyon & Seefeldt, 1995; Tweed & Ryff, 1991).

Many of the characteristics attributed to adult children of alcoholics (ACOAs) are not necessarily unique to them. Assessment devices such as the Children of Alcoholics Screening Test (CAST), the Adult Children of Alcoholics Tool (ACAT), and the Family of Origin Scales (FOS) all seem to have a fair amount of reliability and validity (Capps, Searight, Russo, & Temple, 1993; Hawkins & Hawkins, 1995; Lease & Yanico, 1995; Martin, 1995; Sheridan, 1995) in differentiating ACOAs from adults who come out of healthy families. However, when ACOAs are compared to adults who come out of severely dysfunctional homes where no alcoholism was present, there is little difference in the two groups (Dodd & Roberts, 1994; Fisher, Jenkins, Harrison, & Jesch, 1993; Hall, Bolen, & Webster, 1994; Hardwick, Hansen, & Bairnsfather, 1995; Harvey, Boswell, & Romans, 1995).

Finally, Doweiko (1999, p. 345) points out that the ACOA movement is essentially a white, middle-class invention. Virtually nothing is known about minority children who live in poverty and whose parents do other kinds of drugs. What they may or may not become as adults is virtually anybody's guess. It is with these qualifiers that we introduce the ACOA, who is proceeding out of the transcrisis of the family of origin's alcoholism into his or her own crisis.

Facts. There is clear evidence that the following three facts relate to ACOAs (Black, 1981, p. 105; Kerr & Hill, 1992; Mathew et al., 1993; Neff, 1994; Rodney, 1994; Schafer, 1989; Sher, Walitzer, Wood, & Brent, 1991; Woititz, 1983, p. 103):

1. Alcoholism runs in families. Rarely is a case seen in isolation. There may be generational skips, but alcoholism is invariably found in the extended family of the alcoholic.
2. Children of alcoholics run a higher risk of developing alcoholism than do children in the mainstream of the population. Males are four times as likely and females are three times as likely as their peers from nonalcoholic families to become alcoholic.
3. Children of alcoholics tend to marry alcoholics. Rarely do they go into the marriage with that knowledge, but the phenomenon occurs over and over.

Much like sufferers of PTSD and submerged trauma, ACOAs may present themselves in transcrisis with problems that bear little resemblance to the instigating issues of familial alcoholism. Thus, the astute crisis worker would do well to assess the client's family of origin for amount and duration of drug use before making a triage assessment decision.

Feelings.   On reaching adulthood, the majority of children of alcoholics continue to experience problems related to trust, dependency, control, identification, and expression of feelings. They have difficulty saying no and may be manipulated by others and extend themselves beyond any reasonable human capacity (Brabant & Martof, 1993; George, 1990, p. 85; Sheridan & Green, 1993).

ACOAs often experience an overwhelming sense of fear. In particular, the fear of abandonment is predominant and intensifies after childhood. These fears are episodic in that extreme high and low mood swings are experienced and are manifested either by clinging behavior or an inability to form meaningful relationships. Because they have learned to stifle feelings so well as children, ACOAs have a fear of confrontation and seldom argue or fight, even when their emotions are boiling over. Fear results in a tendency for ACOAs to discount their own perceptions and not have the courage to check out other people's perceptions (Black, 1981, p. 116; George, 1990, p. 86).

Anger is seldom acknowledged by the ACOA. Because the ACOA as a child was seldom if ever allowed to acknowledge or display anger, it is a feeling that is often repressed, twisted, and distorted in the ACOA. This feeling is invariably denied, yet it manifests itself in a variety of mental and physical health problems that include psychosomatic illnesses, phobias, depression, narcissism, anxiety, panic, and eating disorders (Hibbard, 1993; Mathew et al., 1993). Behaviorally, anger is most often manifested as passive-aggressive behavior toward others. Particularly for females, anger seldom comes out in confrontive ways but rather continuously seethes in a chronic state. Attachment and individuation problems cause ACOA females to be highly sensitive to real or implied criticism. In contrast, ACOA males tend to have higher rates of state anger, and when they lose control, they lose it in a hurry. However, for both sexes, anger's bedfellow is guilt (Black, 1981, p. 115; George, 1990, p. 86; Potter-Efron & Potter-Efron, 1991).

Guilt is a tenacious feeling that ACOAs may hold on to for 10, 30, or even 60 years. The guilt may be over a range of things, from wishing parents would die to not doing enough for the family to running away from the problem. If no resolution with or confrontation of a parent occurs before the parent's death, the guilt may lead to more severe disturbances (Black, 1981, p. 120; George, 1990, p. 86).

Effects of Childhood Roles.   Dynamically, the adaptive roles ACOAs take on in childhood may follow them into adulthood. Heroes become extremely responsible adults who are scared to death of losing control. Heroic ACOAs had little fun as children, and they have little ability to enjoy life as adults. Heroes have to be in charge, stay in one-up positions, and allow no room for equal relationships. For the responsible ACOA, alcohol can remove the stress and anxiety of always retaining rigid control (Black, 1981, p. 123; George, 1990, p. 89).

For the ACOA lost child, life is a perpetual roller-coaster. These adults perceive themselves as having few alternatives because, when forced to make commitments based on logical and linear thinking, they have few mental resources to call on. They have never learned that choices are available to them, because they have never had to make a decision; they have merely adjusted to changing conditions. They find mates who are chaotic representatives of their former childhood experiences. The problem is that these relationships are insubstantial because no one takes responsibility for making decisions. The result is a person who is lonely, depressed, and isolated socially. Alcohol can give these people a false sense of power and control (Black, 1981, p. 85; George, 1990, p. 89).

Placaters or family mascots are experienced by others as nice people because of their attempts to please others. They are adept at diverting attention from themselves; otherwise they'd have to deal with their own pain (Black, 1981, pp. 23–25). These ACOAs have always been so responsible for others that they have lost the ability to take care of themselves and their own needs. Chemical dependents are perfect marriage partners for these individuals because they can continue their loving and supportive role that they perfected in their alcoholic family of origin. The comic placater as an adult is the life of every party but of no use in an emotional maelstrom. The psychosomatic version of the placater draws sympathy and attention but never focuses on any issues of change that would allow for a more fulfilling and productive life. Finally, the placater who is always sensitive to and supportive of others actually does little to help others confront the dilemmas they face. As a result, placaters make excellent enablers (Black, 1981, pp. 59–61; George, 1990, p. 90).

Finally, acting-out children may experience life as adults in two operating modes. First, they may continue to rebel, but in more sophisticated and dramatic ways. Their rebellion extends out from the family into society. They lack education and job skills, have anger control problems, marry early, and produce illegitimate children. In law enforcement terms, they graduate from misdemeanors to felonies. They are prime candidates for having severe addiction problems and also suffer from mental health problems. They are the stereotypical bad apples that live on the edge of society or are outcast from it (Black, 1981, pp. 62–63; George, 1990, p. 89).

If the acting-out child assumes the scapegoat role, as ACOAs they become everyone's doormat because they are incapable of standing up for themselves. They allow themselves to be used and abused by others. Indeed, they become excellent candidates to marry into or work in abusive relationships. Their low self-concept makes them prime candidates for chemical dependency because of the false sense of well-being it provides (George, 1990, p. 89). The bottom line is that ACOAs comprise approximately 60 percent of all patients in chemical dependency programs (Liepman, White, & Nirenberg, 1986, p. 39).

Potential Problems. Many ACOAs are seen as valuable members of both their families and society, and indeed they are. Yet in adulthood these ways of surviving often lead to unhealthy and extreme patterns of coping that draw them into problems with substance abuse, marrying someone who becomes an abuser, or having an unusual number of personal problems in their adult years (Black, 1981, pp. 16–17). Woititz (1983) compiled a chilling summary of potential problems ACOAs are likely to face. ACOAs

1. Guess at what "normal" is
2. Are procrastinators supreme
3. Lie when it would be as easy to tell the truth
4. Judge themselves without mercy
5. Take themselves too seriously and have little fun
6. Have difficulty with intimate relationships
7. Overreact to changes over which they have no control

8. Constantly seek approval and affirmation
9. Feel they are different from other people
10. Are super responsible or irresponsible
11. Are loyal even when the loyalty is undeserved
12. Are impulsive

Whether one believes that ACOAs are doomed to suffer the sins of the fathers being revisited on them, or that they merely use their ACOA status to rationalize less-than-adequate coping skills as a adults, one thing is sure: There are a lot of them out there!

MULTIVARIATE DIAGNOSIS

Matching Treatment to Client.   Although we agree with Maxwell (1986, p. 33) that treatment approaches to drug abuse should be based on dealing with the abusive chemical first, we also believe that treatment should be geared toward the individual and his or her particular circumstances. A great deal of work has been done in the last decade in attempting to match specific treatment with the individual. Research outcomes have varied (National Institute on Alcohol Abuse and Alcoholism, 1998; Project Match Research Group, 1998; Soyka, 1999), but it appears that tailoring intervention to specific client needs has a better chance of success as far as program completion and relapse is concerned (Longabraugh et al., 1997; McLellan, Grisson, Zanis, & Randall, 1997; Nielsen, Nielsen, & Wraae, 1998).

A therapeutic approach for a 45-year-old housewife who anesthetizes herself in front of the soap operas with a pitcher of martinis every afternoon may be quite different from one for the 16-year-old who has been doing street drugs with his peer group (Lawson et al., 1984, p. ix). Not only do setting events contribute to how treatment is carried out, but also the particular personality constellation, demographics, learning history, ethnicity, social support systems, term of abuse, sex, age, and drinking systems determine the behaviors of the alcoholic and dictate specific treatment (McCrady, 1982, p. 682).

Dual Diagnosis.   It has only been in the past decade that human services professionals have come to understand that many chemically dependent clients also may have underlying mental health problems (Doweiko, 1996, pp. 259–267). Estimates vary, but it appears that up to 50 percent of all alcohol and substance abuse problems mask other psychiatric problems (Brown et al., 1989; Carey, 1989; Gorski, 1994; Graubart, 1991). One classical example of this problem has been the attempt to treat PTSD sufferers for their chemical dependency problems only. They may be dried out for a while, but the nightmares and sleeplessness that PTSD causes will invariably drive them back to self-medicating to get some sleep.

The concurrent issues of a mental illness and drug and alcohol abuse pose a big problem. It has been found that drug abuse is seven times and alcohol abuse is 10 times as prevalent in the mentally ill as in the general population (Kivlahan et al., 1991). The major issue with concurrent drug or alcohol abuse with a mental disorder is that, contrary to the individual's self-medication plan to ease the pain of the disorder or desire to experience the drug's effects, research shows that such drug use almost invariably *aggravates* the disorder, because the mentally ill seem to be especially sensitive to the drugs' effects.

The crisis worker should be acutely aware of these people because they are disproportionately high users of emergency medical and mental health services (Doweiko, 1996, pp. 270–275). They compose a high percentage of the potentially violent mentally ill that our own Memphis Police Department Crisis Intervention Team officers deal with on our city streets, and reports from other police jurisdictions tend to support that high percentage. They go off their medication for the mental illness; start abusing drugs for their enjoyment or sense of expanded control; become psychotic, violent, or physically ill; and wind up in emergency rooms or confrontations with authorities over and over again. Therefore, crisis workers on emergency call or admission should always consider a dual diagnosis as a distinct possibility when a drug-abusing client calls or shows up.

Our own theoretical approach, backed by a great deal of reported research (Beck et al., 1993; Pattison & Kaufman, 1982b), is that alcoholism is a multivariate construct and implies the following:

1. Multiple patterns of use, misuse, and abuse may be denoted as a pattern of alcoholism.
2. Multiple interactive etiological variables may combine to produce a pattern of alcoholism.
3. All persons are vulnerable to the development of some type of alcoholism problem.
4. Treatment interventions must be multimodal to correspond to a specific person's particular pattern of alcoholism.
5. Treatment outcomes will vary in accordance with specific alcoholism patterns, persons, social contexts, treatment processes, posttreatment adjustment patterns, and the interaction of all these factors.
6. Preventive interventions must be multiple and diverse in order to address diverse etiologic factors.
7. Treatment of other life problems can improve outcomes in people with alcohol problems.
8. Therapist characteristics are partial determinants of outcomes.
9. People treated for alcohol problems will fall on a continuum with respect to drinking behaviors, alcohol problems, and courses of outcome.
10. Those who significantly reduce or abstain from alcohol consumption usually enjoy improvement in other life areas as the period of reduced consumption becomes more extended.

INTERVENTION STRATEGIES

Crisis in a substance abuser's life rarely manifests itself as a one-time occurrence. The abuser's life is characterized by both a transcrisis state and transcrisis points. A transcrisis state is related to the whole process of addiction with all the economic, social, physical, and psychological problems that chemical dependency entails. *Transcrisis points* are related to the recurrent crises in the chemical dependent's everyday life that seem to erupt in spontaneous ways whenever the person encounters stressors and that are rarely identified as being rooted in the greater underlying transcrisis of addiction. These transcrisis points continue through the course of withdrawal, therapy, and follow-up.

Assessment

Assessing chemical dependency is a complex task, and is critical for formulating differential diagnoses, specific outcome goals, and valid treatment modalities (Kaufman & Pattison, 1982b, p. 1091). Although a biochemical test is a fairly reliable and valid indicator of the presence or amount of drugs in a person's system—breathalyzers being one familiar assessment device—it will not tell us whether a person is an occasional user, an abuser, or a full-blown addict. Let us turn then to the old standby of assessment techniques, the paper-and-pencil test.

Personality Inventories.   A wide variety of personality tests have been used in attempts to characterize an alcoholic personality (Knox, 1976). A prototype is the MacAndrew Alcoholism Scale, from the Minnesota Multiphasic Personality Inventory (MMPI). The MacAndrew has been fairly successful in predicting alcoholism and a general tendency toward addiction (Greene, 1980; Knox, 1980). However, the MacAndrew scale appears to have a cultural bias (African Americans tend to score higher than Caucasians) and categorizes clients who suffer blackouts for *any* reasons, who are exhibitionistic or extroverted, who are assertive, or who enjoy risk taking as chemically dependent when they may not be (Doweiko, 1999, p. 350; Isenhart & Silversmith, 1997).

Another self-report inventory that specifically targets substance abuse but is camouflaged as to its purpose is the Substance Abuse Subtle Screening Inventory (SASSI). It has subscales that allow the examiner to use a series of decision rules to determine whether the individual is a chemical abuser (Miller, 1983).

A major problem with these and other personality tests, though, is that they are unstable over time. The alcoholic may have very different scores and configurations prior to and after detoxification (Knox, 1976) and even the MMPI is subject to subterfuge by addicts who may be straightforward, defensive, or exaggerate their drinking (Doweiko, 1999, p. 350; McDermott et al., 1997, p. 351). These and other tests have general use in determining personality types of abusers, which may be important in determining other psychological disorders, but no absolute pattern of personality has yet been found that covers all types of alcoholism (Mendelson & Mello, 1979).

Direct Measures.   Direct psychometric methods are related to alcoholic behavior and use. Prototypical are the Michigan Alcohol Screening Test (MAST), which asks questions about alcohol consumption and drinking behavior; the Alcadd Test, which measures drinking in terms of regularity, preference over other activities, loss of control, rationalization of use, and emotionality (Ornstein, 1976); and the CAGE, which is a simple four-item questionnaire about one's drinking history. A major problem with these self-report questionnaires is that deception is easy, and what drug abusers have to say about their chemical dependency should be always highly suspect (Knox, 1980, p. 58).

The Addiction Severity Index provides a severity rating based on the impressions of the person who administers the test and is one of the most widely used instruments to detect substance abuse problems. It examines client functioning in the areas of medical, employment, alcohol, drugs, legal, family-social, and psychiatric problems (Doweiko, 1999, p. 351; McDermott et al., 1997).

Triage Assessment.   In any assessment of chemical dependents, the crisis worker should follow two rules that Doweiko (1990, p. 214) proposed and we believe should be chiseled in granite. First, always seek collateral information. A spouse's or an employer's response to a MAST may be very different from the alcoholic's. Second, until proven otherwise, always assume deception. For example, alcoholics will invariably attempt to minimize their use, whereas cocaine and opiate addicts may exaggerate their use to impress others. Given the foregoing warning, the crisis worker should attempt to obtain information from as many different sources as possible before attempting to make a valid assessment of a chemical dependent (Doweiko, 1990, p. 215).

Until chemical dependents have hit rock bottom, they will cover their figurative and literal drug tracks affectively, behaviorally, and cognitively in self-defeating efforts to deny to themselves and to others the control that the drug exercises over them. Although Doweiko (1999, p. 354) reports that most alcoholics will report truthfully the amount they consume if they are not facing legal, employment, or other kinds of trouble, therein lies the problem. Most of the chemical dependents we deal with *are* in trouble and have every reason to lie about what they drink. A standard measure that many of our co-workers in chemical dependent treatment programs use in interviews about consumption of alcohol should give a vivid illustration of what we are talking about. Whatever an alcoholic reports as the amount consumed should be doubled to arrive at a very conservative estimate of the real amount used!

Diagnostic Intake.   In a tailor-made treatment program that will probably be done on an outpatient basis, it is absolutely critical to obtain as comprehensive and complete a clinical assessment of the individual as possible. Combined with a complete medical workup and psychometric measures, the profile should provide circumstances for referral, drug and alcohol use patterns, legal history, military record, educational and vocational history, developmental and family history, psychiatric and medical records, sexual health, motivation, social-recreational-community involvement, and previous treatment history (Doweiko, 1996, pp. 320–324; Poley, Lea, & Vibe, 1979). The Continuous Data Questionnaire (CDQ) is such an intake format (Poley et al., 1979).

The CDQ accomplishes a number of important tasks. First, it monitors a client at many points in the treatment process. Second, it is not concerned with drug issues to the exclusion of other problems. Its comprehensiveness allows the worker to obtain information on a variety of areas that may need remediation. Third, the CDQ gives a historical perspective to make an excellent analysis of what treatment goals need to be established and how those goals are being met.

Assessment by the Worker.   An initiating interview to determine drug abuse is unlike many other exploratory interviews because the defense mechanisms of the chemical-dependent person will be granite hard, and the worker must be aware that these defenses will do all they can to safeguard the abuser's secret. Analysis starts by monitoring the verbal defenses of the client. Hedging, minimizing, seduction, changing the subject, projecting onto significant others, and refusal to speak directly about oneself in the here-and-now are defenses all clients may manifest. However, these are extremely pronounced in the alcoholic. For example, ruminating on past drinking episodes and drinking friends should not be viewed as innocent, idle nostalgia; rather, it suggests that the person has not learned to fill the social void in his or her life left by giving up the abusing agent and that physically detoxified is not psychologically detoxified (Perez, 1985, pp. 34–37).

Doweiko (1996, p. 325) believes that redundancy is important in the interview. Doweiko proposes that the purpose of asking the same question is not to trap the client, but to reframe the question so that the same piece of information can be explored from different perspectives.

CW: (*Early in the interview.*) How much would you say that you spend on drinking in a normal week?

CW: (*Later in the interview.*) What do you estimate would be the cost of a normal night on the town?

Behavioral assessment includes such simple procedures as noticing whether there is alcohol on the client's breath. Chewing peppermint or gum and heavy use of cologne or perfume may be attempts to mask alcoholic odors. Physical appearance of an alcoholic may include facial puffiness, a red nose, sudden weight gain, a glazed look or a hunted, fearful aspect, shaking, rigid attending and listening, or a very casual, laid-back approach (Perez, 1985, pp. 34–37). Having conducted the intake assessment, the worker should write a summary in narrative form that includes all the points we have discussed in the CDQ.

Assessment of Spirituality.   A major component of triage assessment for chemical dependency is a careful analysis of the individual's spiritual resources. This analysis has little to do with religion: It does not mean the number of times the individual attended church, the amount of money put in the collection plate, or pages of the Bible read per day. This part of assessment should focus on the narcissistic desire to change life from what it is to "how I want it and how it must be." The assessment should also focus on the despair and hopelessness addicts feel and the emptiness in their lives that they attempt to fill through their addiction. Therefore, we believe that the spirituality of the chemically addicted should be given a good deal of emphasis in triage assessment, and diagnosis and treatment goals should routinely incorporate spirituality in program planning.

An Example: Intake Analysis and Summary of Gordon Brand.   Gordon Brand was seen after initial admission for polydrug overdose. Stage of treatment is initial assessment. The client is a 42-year-old male Caucasian who was brought to St. Polycarp by the paramedics for treatment of a drug overdose. BAC was 0.37 percent on admission, with evidence of Xanax ingestion. Gordon was semicomatose on entry and was in intensive care for 24 hours.

Chemical use. Preferential drug is alcohol. Over the past three months, Gordon reports consuming a bit less than a pint of whiskey per day, although this quantity is subject to scrutiny because of client's defensive responses. Drinking is continuous, and Gordon does not remember when he was last abstinent. Drinking has been with peers from work and alone at home. Lately drinking has been mostly by himself. Xanax was prescribed by Gordon's family physician for "stress" and Gordon has used it rather extensively for a number of years, especially when he was trying to "cut down" alcohol use.

Educational and vocational background. Gordon is a college graduate with a degree in mechanical engineering and a master's in business administration. He is employed as director of internal operations by United Tectonics. His income is approximately $120,000 a year, with numerous perquisites. He reports no absences from work due to alcohol- or drug-related problems but does report he has missed approximately 20 days of work in the last two months due to "intestinal problems" and generally feeling "unwell." His best estimate of being late to work is 10 times during the last month. He indicates he is moderately satisfied with his job, but says he would be extremely satisfied if the company president "would get off his back and leave him alone." He rates his job performance as quite good and says it would be excellent if he were not currently ill. He is not sure how much money he owes at present because "that was always his wife's job." Cost of drinking is "peanuts." He vaguely remembers his wife saying something about bills being overdue.

Family status. Gordon currently resides with his wife and children in an upper-middle-class subdivision and has lived there for the past eight years. He relates that he used to love his wife a great deal, but now gets along poorly with her. He maintains that he gets along moderately well with his children, Lisa and Mark, although "They side with their mother on most things." Prior to the last two months he often (several times a week) did things with his family. He believes his family is very important to him but is extremely angry that his wife is not more supportive. He also feels he is extremely important to his family but states this in economic terms: "All I'm good for is to bring home a paycheck." He does not handle arguments with his wife well and "clams up" after initial exchanges. His dealings with his children are much the same, and he reports, "They don't listen to me and are rebellious."

Social involvement. He reports having many business acquaintances, but no real friends. Gordon has been involved with a number of charitable and service organizations in the community, until the last couple of years, when he got so involved in work that he could not do those things anymore. He enjoyed service activities, particularly with the Boys' Club. His recreational pursuits are "tinkering" in his shop at home, fishing and hunting, and reading military history.

Judicial involvement. Aside from being found by the police passed out in his car, he has no prior arrest record. He reported one domestic disturbance call when he and his wife were arguing, but smoothed that over with the officer who responded to the call.

Health. His physical and mental health have been average to poor. He last saw a doctor about six months ago and was told that he had the beginning of major health problems, "something to do with my guts and stress." He has been taking antacid for the problem. He has "fallen down" on his eating habits because of both stress and a nervous stomach and only occasionally eats regular, well-balanced meals. He averages about five or six hours' sleep a night and uses alcohol and Xanax to help him get to sleep, particularly when he is under stress. He has never been in the hospital for other than minor medical problems. He has never considered suicide, but states it is not the worst thing in the world. His sexual health is poor. He has not had or cared to have sex in a long time.

Gordon presents the appearance of a man coming out from addiction. After he was stabilized for his overdose, he slept for almost 24 hours. His withdrawal symptoms were severe enough that he was given benzodiazopines to ease the pain of withdrawal.

His appearance is sallow and wan. He is overweight and his muscle tone is poor, with his flesh sagging over his body. He has a hunted look to his eyes and is constantly wringing his hands. His agitation is further demonstrated by pitched-up and accelerated speech patterns.

Personality profile. His personality and emotional development are rated moderately low in responsibility to self and others, very low in self-worth and general feeling of well-being, and high on anxiety and depression. He is more tense than relaxed, more critical than tolerant, more depressed than happy, more nervous than calm, more un-friendly than friendly, more unforgiving than forgiving, and much more sickly than healthy. The MMPI supports this self-analysis and also indicates he is depressed. His validity scale scores indicate he is attempting to present a better picture of himself than what he is. The MAST and CAGE scores confirm he is a heavy alcohol abuser.

Motivation. He is ambivalent about changing. Although he can articulate goals, they are generally nonspecific, such as "straightening things out at home and work." His rating of present attempts to accomplish these tasks is that they are very unsuccessful, and he rates as moderately important a goal to stop abusing alcohol "for a while." His most de-sirable use of alcohol would be to drink socially, "because drinking alone really isn't all that good and probably helped get me here in the first place." He believes no one is in-terested in his problems "except to get on my back."

Corroboration. Follow-up includes checking with Gordon's employer, wife, and doctor. Their story is a good deal different from what Gordon reports. Mr. Fredricks, the presi-dent of United, indicates that Gordon was one of his best employees until about three years ago, when his drinking got steadily worse and his performance declined. At first, Mr. Fredricks said nothing about the drinking, because Gordon still had a performance rating that was superior to those of most other members of the staff—drunk or sober. Later, Mr. Fredricks gave him some fatherly advice about his problem, which Gordon ignored. Three months ago, the advice turned into a warning about absences and poor performance. Mr. Fredricks now feels that unless Gordon dries out and takes care of his problem, termination is imminent. Mr. Fredricks also agreed that Gordon had been such a valuable employee that the company would pick up any cost for treatment that insur-ance did not cover. The employer agreed to support and coordinate efforts with the hos-pital. Analysis of employer cooperation in regard to chemical dependency treatment is excellent.

Gordon's wife, Amy, supports his employer's analysis of the problem. His drinking has steadily escalated to the point that the family has become completely dysfunctional. She and the children are terrified of Gordon when he is drunk, which is most of the time. He has become an isolate from his family and only relates to them when he wants something. Any mention of his drinking causes severe arguments and then a period of sullen hostility. Amy also reports serious financial problems, saying that they are be-hind on the house and car notes and owe credit card accounts of $17,000. Two months ago Gordon got drunk, became violent, and threatened her. The police intervened in the situation and Gordon left the house. She threatened to obtain a restraining order on Gordon but relented after he promised to remain sober and be the husband and father he used to be. He kept his vow for two weeks, then he started drinking even more heavily.

She states that she is near a nervous breakdown and has a number of physical complaints that are probably due to the stress of trying to deal with Gordon for so many years. She is "sick" of it and is thinking of filing for divorce. She did agree to come to the hospital for an interview if Gordon agreed to treatment. General analysis of the home situation is that it is extremely poor and may not be redeemable.

Gordon's doctor indicated that he had given Gordon a severe upbraiding six months ago about his drinking and stated that he would no longer give him prescriptions for Xanax. He had recommended at that time that Gordon seek immediate treatment for severe alcohol abuse. He also told Gordon that he was having liver, pancreas, and intestinal problems due to alcohol and that if he kept drinking he was going to be in critical trouble in short order. Gordon became hostile and told his family doctor of 15 years that he wasn't much good if he couldn't give him some tranquilizers for the stress he was experiencing.

Spirituality. Gordon was reared in a strict fundamentalist church, but left it during college because they were "real bluenoses who never had any fun." He later tried a more liberal church, attending fairly regularly with his wife in the early years of their marriage, but quit attending that church because they were "pretentious asses." Aside from his nonattendance of any organized religious services, Gordon is spiritually bankrupt with the exception of the spirits he drinks. Any relationship that presently exists between him and a higher power is in name only: "Well, sure, I believe in God." He is alone, helpless, and hopeless in a hostile world.

Conclusions. General analysis of interviews with Gordon, his boss, his wife, and his doctor is that Gordon shows clear signs of chemical dependency (alcohol) across physical, psychological, and social components of his life. He denies that he has a problem with alcohol and has put in place strong defense mechanisms to shield him from the reality of the situation. He is in extreme peril of losing his job, his family, and quite possibly his life. He is in need of immediate treatment. Recommendations after case staffing with the chemical dependency unit were that

1. He be apprised of the seriousness of his physical condition
2. He be apprised of the likelihood of keeping his job
3. He be apprised of the perilous state of his marriage
4. He fully experience the crisis he is in and that workers gain his agreement to undergo treatment first in the chemical dependency unit and later on an outpatient basis
5. If Gordon agreed to undergo treatment, his family be contacted with the proposal that they also undergo treatment as codependents
6. If he agreed to treatment, particular goals be established for a comprehensive rehabilitation plan
7. Controlled drinking is not an option due to the seriousness of his physical problems and the failure of his previous self-managed attempts to quit

Total Triage Assessment.   The total triage assessment of Gordon is 28. He is in the lethal range and needs to be in a place where he can be safe. Affectively his rating is 9. He is angry and depressed, with many of the standard defensive affective responses characteristic of full-blown addiction. Behaviorally he is out of control in regard to his chemical dependency. His BAC level was approaching LD-50 on admission. Overlaid with tranquilizers, he is lucky to be alive. He obtains a 10 without even considering how he acts in regard to his work or family. Cognitively he is deeply rooted in denial about his addiction and has paranoid ideation about his family and his employer. His perception of the events leading up to his admission to the emergency room is radically different from the view of others who know him. His periods of memory loss and obsessive-compulsive thoughts about drinking mark him at a 9.

Crisis Points in Chemical Dependency Treatment

Clients who are addicted will have used drugs to shield themselves from all kinds of hurtful feelings, thoughts, and behaviors. Once this shield is taken away, all the problems will tend to converge like an accordion, and clients will be assailed from all sides at once. The very reasons that the alcoholic drank in the first place will return in condensed, magnified, and more powerful ways. Each instance will present a crisis point for clients. As a result, the whole therapeutic inpatient treatment program may be seen as transcrisis in nature. Successfully jumping one hurdle generally means getting ready immediately for the next one and the next one after that.

The first crisis to be dealt with is getting the client motivated to dry out. Working with a "wet" person is impossible, because all the person is interested in is getting "fixed" (Parker, 1986). To get the person to detoxify means creating enough of a crisis that the person voluntarily agrees to stay. The best way to do this is by attacking the client's vulnerable points. For Gordon, there are two: his job and his health.

The Counselors.   Gordon is about to meet two chemical dependency counselors, Carolyn and Ray. They can be loosely described as the good-guy/bad-guy team. Carolyn is a recovering alcoholic who is direct, assertive, and confrontive. At times she uses self-disclosure about her own dependency so that the client can't get away with saying, "Nobody knows the trouble I've seen." She has a high degree of credibility. She is also a good model. The alcoholic can look at her as a peer and say, "Here is a tough, competent person who has been where I am, and if that's true, then there's hope for me" (Graham, 1986).

Ray is more nondirective and unconditionally accepting. His stock in trade are the basic skills of empathic listening and responding. His job is to build a healthy, trusting relationship and focus on the client's positive attributes, to promote faith in the client, and to help the client come to his or her own self-realizations about the problem. Ray is also a model in that he is a professional who is not an alcoholic. Clients cannot reject treatment on the basis that "they're just a bunch of burned-out boozers here."

Another reason that Carolyn and Ray operate as a team is that drug users are the most manipulative group of clients we know. Clients may con one person, but they will have a much more difficult time conning two people. Teaming is also a support mechanism for the workers. Working with drug addicts is one of the toughest jobs in therapy (Parker, 1986). They are going to do their best to make Gordon aware of the serious trouble he is in with drugs.

Carolyn: Hello, Gordon. I'm Carolyn and this is Ray. We're from the chemical dependency unit, and we'd like to talk with you.

Gordon: Well, that's fine, but I don't know why you're talking to me. I made a dumb mistake, and took some pills I shouldn't have, but that won't ever happen again.

Carolyn: Maybe not. But from your intake interview and the problem that got you here, we think you very seriously need to consider coming into treatment.

Gordon: I really need to get out of here and get back to my job. It's hanging by a thread as it is.

Ray: We understand how concerned you are about your job. We've talked to your employer, Mr. Fredricks, and he understands the situation. He's willing to support you if you go into treatment.

Gordon: (*Angrily.*) I'll bet! That SOB used to be my best friend. He'll use me being a drunk to give me the axe. That's all the excuse he'd need.

Carolyn: He may be the biggest SOB in the state. But he cares about you and has offered you a choice. He believes that if you don't seek help from us, then you're not going to have a job at all. He also said you'll have your same job when you finish treatment. I have him outside, and I want you to hear it with your own ears. (*After a lengthy conversation, Mr. Fredricks leaves.*)

Gordon: He really means it. My God! No job. What'll I do?

Ray: Look at it this way. You know you've got some pretty severe physical problems. What difference will a few days make? You meet your commitment to your boss, and you're also someplace where your physical problems can be monitored. It's a no-lose deal.

Gordon: I'm no drunken bum!

Ray: We understand that, but I'm wondering if this statement rings true: that drinking at times produces results you dislike.

Gordon: Yes, I could say that.

Ray: Seems like it would be worth your time to find out a bit more about that. What's a few days' difference one way or the other?

Gordon: But going into a dry-out ward. It's like I can't handle my problems.

Ray: I'd guess that going into treatment would seem like a sign of weakness, but I'd like to point out that if anything else was wrong with you it would be a sign of mature and healthy thinking to get it taken care of, wouldn't it? You have a serious illness here that needs help.

Carolyn: If you had cancer, would you try to do surgery on yourself? You do want to get better in regard to your health problems, don't you? The doctor told you how serious your physical problems are, didn't he? That you have liver, pancreas, and severe intestinal problems and that if they're not taken care of, you will most likely die. Do you believe he's putting you on, or is that what you want? Notice your hands right now. They're shaking so hard you couldn't hold a pencil and write your name.

Gordon: I can too.

Carolyn: Go ahead and do it then. (*Hands Gordon the pencil and paper.*)

Gordon: (*Attempts to write down his name and produces an illegible scrawl that wobbles across the page.*)

Carolyn: In all honesty, is that your typical signature?

Gordon: (*Voice breaks.*) I . . . no, it isn't. I'm . . . I'm sick.

Carolyn: Yes, you are! That's why we're concerned about you and want you to come into the program.

Gordon: (*Downcast but still defiant.*) OK. I'll give it a try, but I'm not promising anything. If I don't like it, I'll leave.

Ray: That's all we ask. Now let us tell you in general what your treatment is going to be. We want you to know what's going to happen so you can help us plan what'll be most effective for you.

Creating a Crisis for Gordon.   The human services workers are creating a crisis for Gordon. They are not above putting the client in a corner to get him to stay and will do all they can to motivate him to do so. Very few clients are self-motivated to change their abusing behavior (Lawson et al., 1984, p. 67). Outside motivation must often be used. In this case it is Gordon's job and his health. For most male alcoholics, their job is critical, and it is the last part of their environment to suffer. There are two major reasons for this. First, a job is at the core of one's self-esteem, and to lose that is to admit that the chemical dependent has hit rock bottom. Second, without a job, there is no money to keep up one's supply of the addictive substance (Parker, 1986; Trice & Beyer, 1982, pp. 955–956).

For a long time, confrontation was held to be the technique of choice in the chemical dependency treatment approach because of the need to crack through the client's denial system. However, the main ingredient that has been found to be effective with chemical dependents is no different from most other client problems: the ability to enter the client's world as empathically as possible with the highest level of interpersonal skills possible (Miller, Genefield, & Tonigan, 1993). Carolyn's confrontations are not based on some personal agenda, nor are they directed at the client's global attributes. Rather, they are targeted at specific behaviors, thoughts, and affects the client uses to deny the problem or to support a return to drinking. Empathic understanding of a chemical dependent does not mean being permissive, does not mean shielding the client from the natural consequences of his or her actions, and does not mean avoiding appropriate confrontation when chemical dependents seek to lie and delude themselves and others.

Balancing confrontation about poor job performance is an empathic and genuine concern for Gordon's health that specifically tells him that someone now cares what happens to him. The confrontation is firm but not blaming (Huberty & Brandon, 1982, p. 1082). The information reported is factual but not judgmental. By alternating between the two approaches, the workers seek to set the stage for Gordon through a combination of fear for his life and hope through treatment. While creating the crisis, the workers avoid directly confronting or accusing Gordon of being an alcoholic. Early attempts to make clients confess to their addiction will likely lead to very defensive behavior. Although the word *manipulate* has an ugly connotation, in a sense all therapists manipulate their clients to positively increase the chances of successful therapy (Lawson et al., 1984, p. 77). The first few days of treatment are going to be the most difficult, and throughout this time, one of the workers' major tasks will be to keep Gordon from leaving against medical advice (Parker, 1986).

Using Family Intervention to Create a Crisis.   Whereas Gordon's case is clearly one of "hitting bottom" in addiction parlance, for those chemical dependents who have not "bottomed out" Vernon Johnson (1980, 1986) and the Johnson Institute (1972) have developed a family intervention model that involves carefully coaching family and friends in a supportive group confrontation of the chemical dependent in language he or she clearly understands. This creates a severe crisis for the chemical dependent and the family. It is not something that is done on the spur of the moment, out of frustration, or with malice and intent to punish the chemical dependent's transgressions (Doweiko, 1996, p. 331).

The ingredients for creating such a crisis must be planned and rehearsed beforehand with a professional in the chemical dependence field who is well versed in such an intervention. As many family members and significant others as possible should be present to combat the denial, bargaining, and promises to change that are sure to be a part of the addict's defense system. At a very minimum, at least two or more caring people—four or more would be ideal—who are willing to be honest about what they see in the addict's behavior should be present. Significant others such as a boss, a minister, co-workers, and close friends should be involved to support the family with their factual presentations. Each of the interveners should be willing to undergo formal training and education about the illness of addiction. They should also be willing to accumulate and write down specific data about the self-destructive behavior of the addict, rehearse what facts they will report and how they will report these facts with a professional, and then commit to caringly confront the addict with these facts (Johnson, 1986).

Individual confrontation with addicts is futile because of their superior ability to deny, threaten, cajole, plead, and otherwise subvert attempts to interfere with pursuit of their addiction. Therefore, support and corroboration of accounts is important in pinning the addict down. Very clear consequences of separation and detachment from the addict are detailed and followed through on if the offered treatment is refused. This is neither an attempt to bluff the addict into treatment nor an empty threat that may have been used before. Logical consequences of actions and the commitment to follow through on those actions should be calmly and specifically detailed (Johnson, 1986).

The human services worker's role in this endeavor is to first provide support and educate family members about how the crisis setting is created. The worker then helps the family assemble the most powerful and influential people in the addict's life and teaches them how to collect facts of the addict's behavior and how to confront the addict with those facts in a caring manner. During the intervention, the worker acts as a facilitator by coordinating each person's intervention, gently confronting the addict with his or her attempts to defend himself or herself, provides a point-by-point listing of the symptoms of addiction that the intervention has detailed, and then confronts the addict with the choice of undergoing treatment or of having the family and friends detached from the addict. If the addict agrees, then the worker indicates what the treatment options are, that the addict's bags are packed, and that a car is waiting to take him or her to the treatment center. If the foregoing is not done in a coordinated and united manner, the prospects for successful intervention are minimal (Doweiko, 1990, pp. 233–234; Johnson, 1986; Wegscheider-Cruse, 1985). In no instance do we believe that a family should attempt this intervention without first consulting a professional substance abuse worker.

Detoxification

Detoxification is a very serious medical process, depending on how badly addicted the alcoholic is. Although the procedure may seem to run counter to the goal of detoxification, Gordon is given benzodiazepines (tranquilizers) to allow him to control the tremors, hyperactivity, convulsions, and anxiety attacks that accompany alcohol withdrawal (Schuckit, 1995, p. 105). Gordon's detoxification is monitored very closely because alcohol and barbiturate withdrawal can be lethal. During the process, Gordon is allowed to sleep as much as possible, eat a well-balanced diet, and watch television. If he is up to it, other clients who have gone through detoxification will come in and talk with him. The others do not come to proselytize but to let him know that, as tough as it is, they made it through this preliminary crisis stage and so will he (Parker, 1986).

Henry (another patient): Hi! My name's Henry Schultz. I'm another patient here. Ray thought you might be up for some company.

Gordon: Man, I'm glad to talk to somebody. This is tough, I guess I was strung out.

Henry: It *is* tough! I went through it three weeks ago. I guess you could use a drink, huh?

Gordon: Brother, could I!

Henry: Yeah, I know. That's not gonna get easier for a while, either. They make you come face up to it here. It's no piece of cake, but they really care about you. I just wanted to tell you I'm here if you want to talk. I'm getting into AA in a big way, and it's really helping.

Gordon: I don't know about that, spilling your guts and all. I don't think I could do that.

Henry: I thought the same thing. Lay my soul bare in front of a bunch of drunks, no way! But it's easier than you think. Especially when you meet the people. Hell! There's all kinds of people in it, some big shots, little shots, but all of us are not-so-hot shots when it comes to drinking. (*The conversation continues for a good bit, with Gordon asking all kinds of questions about treatment and about Henry's drinking problems, and guardedly discussing himself.*)

This initial dialogue with one of the other clients is important because it safely lets Gordon consider what the possibilities for recovery are, provides a peer as a resource, gives him a role model, and establishes at least one relationship within the therapeutic community (Parker, 1986).

PRINCIPLES OF TREATMENT
Evolving Treatment Approaches

The Minnesota Model.   The Minnesota model has long been the most widely used treatment format for chemical dependents. It has two major components. The first is its comprehensive treatment team that uses experts from a wide variety of disciplines to evaluate and implement treatment procedures in whatever parts of the client's life are needed. The second is the inpatient, 28-day treatment regimen, which became an industry standard. Unfortunately, there is little evidence to support the efficacy of the 28-day program over any other program as far as rehabilitation is concerned. Furthermore, the model tends to "cookie-cutter" all clients through the same daily regimen, and there is ample evidence to indicate that chemical dependents are far less likely to relapse when programs are individually tailored (Beutler, Patterson, Jacob, & Shoham, 1993; DiClemente, Carroll, Connors, & Kadden, 1994; Donovan, Kadden, DiClemente, & Carroll, 1994; Donovan & Mattson, 1994; Mattson & Donovan, 1994; McKay & Maistro, 1993).

What is also clear is that the 28-day inpatient program is a lot more expensive than an outpatient treatment program. As a result, health care providers have balked at the expense and the model's inability to show that its inpatient time line does any better than any other inpatient time line or outpatient approach (Doweiko, 1996, pp. 341–343). Thus there has been a rapid movement away from the time frame of the model to either very brief stays in the hospital or no admission at all (Knack & Murray, 1996).

The Outpatient Treatment Controversy.   A great deal of criticism has been leveled at outpatient programs mandated by many health care providers. The two main criticisms have been that many patients are just too sick to be on an outpatient basis and should be treated in a hospital setting until they can be stabilized and the more cynical, criticism that health care providers can "get by on the cheap." Whether these criticisms are warranted remains unclear because of the newness of alternatives to the Minnesota model time frame.

On the positive side, outpatient treatment is not financially ruinous, clients can continue to stay in their home environment and assume more responsibility for their recovery, the treatment can be extended over a much longer time period, and noncompliance can be easily monitored by random urine checks (Doweiko, 1996, pp. 349–350).

Inpatient or Outpatient?   When a decision has to be made for inpatient versus outpatient status, monetary cost is (one hopes) not the only consideration. For Gordon, the decision ideally is based on the following five criteria (Group for the Advancement of Psychiatry, 1990).

1. *Is the client's condition associated with significant medical or mental health problems?* Gordon comes to the hospital in bad shape physically and has been warned by his doctor of the physical effects alcohol is having on him.
2. *Is the client's withdrawal going to be severe?* Although Gordon isn't quite to the delirium tremens stage, he is going to go through a tough time withdrawing and will need medical supervision to do it.
3. *What is the severity of the client's addiction and polyuse?* Gordon has a long history of alcohol abuse and a shorter history of polyuse with Xanax. From his physical symptoms and medical problems, he is severely addicted to alcohol.
4. *Have there been multiple failed attempts at outpatient treatment?* Gordon has never had any kind of treatment for chemical dependence.
5. *How are the client's support systems?* Gordon's support systems are questionable. His wife and children are fed up with his behavior. Whether they would willingly participate in treatment or sabotage it is open to question. The support of his boss is highly favorable.

Given the mixed bag of responses to the foregoing questions, Gordon will receive a combination of both inpatient and outpatient treatment, which is the least restrictive treatment necessary for his present condition.

Contemporary Model.   Knack and Murray (1996) describe a principles-of-treatment approach that is different from traditional Minnesota model of treating chemically dependent patients. The fundamental principles are contained in the following statements:

1. There is a trend toward simultaneous treatment of addictions and psychiatric disorders so that patients can talk about the voices they hear or about their urges to drink, all in the same context, without having to hide part of their problems.

2. Case management styles have moved away from the 28-day model of treatments toward a longer continuum of holistic and total care based on the assessed needs and circumstances of each patient. Each patient is admitted to a level of treatment appropriate for that particular person.

3. Weekly reviews of each patient's progress enable treatment managers to assign and rapidly move patients from one level of a treatment continuum to other levels as appropriate. Both evening and day treatment outpatient schedules provide the flexibility to accommodate the many different levels of individual treatment needed to serve large numbers of patients.

4. Computer-based quantitative admissions assessment protocol and follow-ups provide treatment managers with the information and flexibility needed to move patients among different levels of treatment and least restrictive environments and to validate patient progress and program outcomes.

5. Outpatient aftercare programs in the evening provide for group supports, including family therapy. Aftercare programs include levels of intensity on a continuum of assessed individual patient needs and family/social circumstances.

6. Patient autonomy and responsibility are the main driving forces governing treatment decisions. Individual patient progress, ability to assume responsibility, momentum, autonomy, and adequate functioning are the factors that govern evidence of treatment outcomes. Success is viewed as a succession of progressive, incremental, and intentional levels of functioning.

7. Maintenance of sobriety is the responsibility of the patient. Failure to maintain sobriety, for example, may result in the patient being reassigned to a different level or intensity of treatment, but not be kicked out of the program.

8. Professional family therapy is provided as an important treatment component. It is a key component of treatment for those patients who have significant family connections.

9. Scientific evidence indicates that chemical dependency has a biological basis. With this new understanding, treatment regimens clearly must take into account that genetics and biological background are important factors to be considered.

10. A viable treatment program must be holistic. Patients are evaluated and treated in a comprehensive way, including their psychiatric, addiction, medical, family, housing, and other needs. The variety of professionals who may participate in a coordinated way to provide such holistic treatment includes counselors, social workers, staff psychologists, addiction therapists, psychiatrists, internal medicine physicians, nurses, physicians' assistants, occupational therapists, recreation therapists, educational therapists, and physical therapists.

11. Being in a hospital bed and being in drug treatment are no longer synonymous. Some patients need to be in hospital beds while they are in certain levels of treatment, but that is based strictly on medical needs alone.

12. Gender issues are an important factor in chemical dependency treatment. Women and men have different biological and emotional needs and responses to treatment strategies.

13. Multicultural issues are essential in the educational component of chemical dependency treatment programs. The world represents a pluralistic environment and patients need to develop understanding and tolerance of diversity in order to function adequately in the social environment as well as the workplace.

Treatment Goals

After Gordon's assessment and detoxification, but prior to going into treatment, Carolyn and Ray carefully go over treatment goals with Gordon. His treatment plan contains a comprehensive set of goals. Each was developed from his assessment plan, which identifies a specific debilitating condition, a goal to alleviate that condition, and a set of specific objectives for attaining the goal. Here are two sample goals.

1. *Gordon's drinking goal.*
   Condition: Excessive consumption of alcohol. Gordon has difficulty meeting the demands of his work and social responsibilities without drinking.
   Goal: Eliminate the consumption of alcohol.
   Objectives: Gordon will
   a. Eliminate the intake of alcohol both during working hours and after working hours every day, including the weekend
   b. Express his feelings and choose positive coping behaviors, which he will employ to deal with stress-producing persons, events, or situations
   c. Demonstrate, for the appropriate length of treatment time called for in Gordon's assessment protocol, positive responses to his individualized treatment regimen; also, demonstrate in individually tailored aftercare that he is able to cope successfully with people, events, and situations at work and at home that trigger anxiety and avoid the use of alcohol to reduce that anxiety.
   d. Use the group and St. Polycarp's staff as a source of support and strength in attaining the goal of eliminating alcohol consumption by actively participating in group, helping other people attain their goals, and committing himself to accepting help and support from others in working on his own goals.

2. *Gordon's emotional and social goal.*
   Condition: Gordon either withdraws from interaction or inappropriately acts out with others, including his own family, when he is stressed.
   Goal: Emit appropriate emotional and social responses while in the presence of others who may produce stress, including his own family.
   Objectives: Gordon will
   a. Engage in nondrug conversation with a staff member at least twice each day and with a peer at least three times each day during inpatient treatment
   b. Carry on at least one nonargumentative discussion with each family member (Amy, Mark, Lisa) during each visit during inpatient treatment
   c. During aftercare, carry on at least two nonargumentative discussions per day with Amy and at least one such discussion per day with both Mark and Lisa
   d. Engage in a minimum of one social activity (game room, gym, horseshoe pit, lake area, dancing, or such) during inpatient treatment
   e. Engage in a minimum of two social activities (in absence of alcohol) with his family during six months of aftercare—activities to be planned by family as a group.

Formulating comprehensive treatment goals reflects a multimodal approach that recognizes and addresses biological, psychological, and social aspects of addiction (Frances, 1988). The major advantage of the multimodal approach is that the variety of needs that the chemically dependent present can be better accommodated.

Multimodal treatment at St. Polycarp is based on the therapeutic community model, which emphasizes both abstaining from alcohol and addressing emotional factors of drug use. The therapeutic community perspective views drug abuse as a disorder of the whole person reflecting problems in conduct, attitudes, values, moods, and emotional management (De Leon, 1989). At the center of the therapeutic community is involvement with one's peer group. Through involvement with each other, chemical dependents learn how to manage emotional issues effectively; practice new, more adaptable behaviors; confront and support each other appropriately; and take responsibility for themselves (Polcin, 1992).

Treatment Protocol

Gordon's crisis treatment schedule contains a systematic and integrated set of components tailored to fit his needs. His inpatient status lasts only long enough to get him through detoxification and stabilization to the point where he can be a responsible participant in his treatment. After that, the bulk of his treatment will be on an outpatient basis. Gordon's outpatient treatment components will consist of (1) individual therapy, (2) group counseling and group education, (3) family counseling, and (4) participation in an AA group. All these treatment components will be closely monitored by the St. Polycarp staff, and changes in level of intensity of treatment, medications, therapy, and counseling formats may be adjusted any time his program evaluations indicate such changes are needed.

Gordon's protocol is monitored via computerized tracking. At each individual therapy session, both Gordon and the therapist examine via the computer screen his assessed progress, medical and psychological status, goals, and projected need of and change in level and intensity of treatment. There are no secrets. Gordon is in a collaborative and participative role in his own therapy.

Individual Therapy

The individualized therapy for Gordon will include both inpatient and outpatient formats. We emphasize here that we are dealing only with those aspects of treatment that impact the *crisis* stage of his progress toward recovery. His inpatient treatment will be as brief as feasible to provide for him the least restrictive environment. Yet it will also keep him connected to the appropriate levels of treatment to ensure that he progresses from a crisis state of chemical dependency to the point where he can assume sufficient responsibility to benefit from noncrisis modes of treatment. Gordon's ultimate goal will be reaching a state of autonomy and equilibrium in handling his own drug-free functioning. Except for transcrisis points that might emerge during times of unusual stress in his life, the crisis mode of treatment will be over. After detoxification and stabilization on an inpatient basis, Gordon will meet with Carolyn regularly, on an outpatient basis, and concurrently meet with his AA group in the evenings and with his family counseling group in the late afternoons.

Carolyn: (*Sitting with Gordon in front of the computer screen in the private counseling room.*) I've edited the contract you made yesterday. Take a look at it and tell me if we've left anything out. Also, tell me if you think the behavioral components are within your capacity to attain and if you're ready to make a firm commitment to accomplish these stated incremental goals.

Gordon: (*Scanning the screen.*) Yeah. That looks OK. I wonder if I can get a copy of this to take to group this afternoon?

Carolyn: Sure. That's fine. Now, let's do a little more work on where we left off yesterday on those processes we called "stress inoculation" and "emotive imagery." You remember that, to get the most benefit out of this procedure, we do it in a very relaxed manner.

Gordon: Yeah. That was pretty good. I never thought I could be that relaxed, but it worked really well. I've thought about it and practiced it since we did it yesterday. I believe it really helps, though I don't understand why.

Carolyn: The important thing is that you know it works for you, because this kind of technique gives you the power and control to do it without me or anyone else, and that's the ultimate goal.

Carolyn proceeds to carry Gordon through the steps of stress inoculation. She uses relaxation techniques and emotive imagery to empower Gordon to attain the ability to retrieve those vivid and powerful internal images and messages and to give himself the appropriate inoculative self-talk to get him over the rough shoals and reefs that will invariably beset him as he embarks on a new and chemical-free existence. Emotive imagery pairs specific emotions with the vividly described and verbalized images that, during the process of stress inoculation (Cormier & Cormier, 1991), Carolyn asks Gordon to visualize in his mind's eye.

Carolyn: (*During the middle of an individual session, while Gordon is relaxed with his eyes closed.*) As vividly as you can, just see and feel the stresses at the office today. You've had it! In your mind's eye, you can see the inviting and familiar neon sign as you approach the Olde English Inn. In your mind's nose, you can whiff the aroma of the beverages being served up in the Inn. In your mind's ears, you can hear the low and familiar drone around the pub. As you perceive these images, noises, and aromas, notice that, because of your commitments to stay off the stuff, you are both drawn toward and scared of the conflicting feelings you're having right now. (*Silence and a time of processing what has been presented ensues.*) Now, vividly perceive yourself as you fortify yourself, ahead of time, against any similar conflict. Perhaps you're saying to yourself, "I know that a drink might relax me, but I know that the consequences would rob me of the progress I've made. I can see the neon sign and pass it by and still feel relaxed, comfortable, empowered, centered, and in control. I am the master of me! My urges are not my captors! And I feel energized knowing that my future, my family, my job, and my reputation are more important than caving in to that Inn. My own strength is my comfort and my knowledge is my guide. I can take a deep breath and relax and enjoy a sense of triumph and accomplishment. I can even feel transcendent and avoid surely being robbed of my autonomy by caving in to the seductive imagery of the pub." Just relish and appreciate the power of that moment when you feel triumphant and in complete control of the situation. (*Long pause.*)

Gordon: (*After a long period of thoughtful and thoroughly relaxed silence.*) I can feel the conflict. It isn't easy. But I *can* see myself doing those things. I *can* smell the booze! I *can* hear the sounds. And I *can* feel the urge to go into that Inn. But I can also feel and enjoy the power and control that is building within me. I won't lie about it. The smell of that pub is inviting. But, right now, the feeling of power and control and even the joy of winning this battle is important to me. I can cherish and savor the feeling that I get when I prove to myself that I can overcome and subdue this demon that can destroy my life—if I let it. I am in control of me!

Here, Carolyn and Gordon have shown only one thumbnail sketch of how stress inoculation may be enhanced when used with relaxation therapy and emotive imagery. Other cognitive-behavioral techniques (Beck et al., 1993) are appropriately used to further enhance Gordon's progress toward overcoming the crisis, and they are demonstrated in the section on the treatment group.

The Treatment Group

There are a number of reasons groups are effective in treating addiction. First and foremost, the relationship skills of chemical dependents are typically wretched. Chemical dependents desperately need positive social interaction to replace isolated self-involvement with their chemical seducer (Lawson et al., 1984, p. 122). Belonging, acceptance, affection, social interaction, nonuniqueness, equality, and development of a new self-concept are all relationship needs that can best be met by the treatment group (Dinkmeyer & Muro, 1979). The group format offers opportunities for peers to successfully confront clients in ways that the individual therapist can rarely, if ever, do that are as helpful as the power and objectivity of the group. Specific outcomes of the treatment group (George & Dustin, 1988; Knack & Murray, 1996; Ohlsen, 1970) include

1. Learning more effective social skills through feedback from others
2. Gaining support for new behaviors by reality testing in a safe environment
3. Encouragement of experimentation and risk taking through modeling by others
4. Re-creation of the world outside, with all its diversity and problems
5. Providing opportunity for honest feedback by peers rather than "know-it-all" professionals
6. Learning through emotional closeness of others
7. Having a safe environment to self-disclose about threatening issues and being accepted by others while doing so
8. Productive tension that propels and promotes change
9. Increased focus on here-and-now events rather than past activities
10. Emotional investment not only in oneself but also in other members
11. Imparting facts and information about chemical dependence and salient aspects of its effects
12. Regaining a sense of humor
13. Instilling hope
14. Gaining an inner spiritual strength as a basic foundation for recovery and permanent psychological sustenance.

Crisis treatment at St. Polycarp consists of several kinds of group work: group therapy, group education, multiple-family therapy, and AA group meetings. Usually there are from 6 to 10 members in the group, who represent a heterogeneous mix of sex, age, and race. This mix occurs by design because the staff wants the unique problems of each member to surface. Addicts have severe blind spots for their own defenses but not necessarily for each other's. Thus the members' diversity should allow them to be able to see through their peers' defense mechanisms, confront these blind spots, and help their peers accomplish treatment goals (Ohlsen, 1970, pp. 109–110). For brevity's sake, we will introduce four representative members of Gordon's group.

Alice is a 55-year-old Caucasian housewife who had been finishing off her afternoon in an alcoholic haze of martinis. Her children have left, and she is now an "empty nester." Her husband and children had denied her drinking until she was involved in an auto accident, left the scene, and was picked up driving while intoxicated. She was remanded to St. Polycarp by a judge.

Liz is a 35-year-old African American nurse. She was in charge of an intensive care unit. She burned out on the job and was caught raiding the pharmaceutical cabinet. She yo-yos between depressants (alcohol and pills) to take the pain of the job away and amphetamines to get her "up" for her job. She is on suspension and in danger of losing her job and her license.

Manuel is a 24-year-old suspended bank guard whose father died an alcoholic when Manuel was 11. His Chicano background invites a macho image that says, "I take care of and handle everything," including alcohol and pills—which he did not handle. He is single and has used alcohol and pills since he was a teenager.

Ruth is a 41-year-old Caucasian who was repeatedly sexually abused by her stepfather when she was a teenager. She married at 18, had two children, and was divorced at 23. She has worked as a bookkeeper for a construction company for the past 10 years. She has had several short, fruitless liaisons with men. She has been an alcohol abuser since her teenage years. She got drunk, took some sleeping pills, and turned on the gas in her apartment. The paramedics brought her to St. Polycarp.

Learning Relationship Skills

Relationship skills occupy center stage in the first few meetings of a group. As Brill (1981, p. 129) indicates, during the initial phases of a group, the group leader should provide support and structure, setting the stage for group members to develop trust and cohesiveness. Videotaping is important to this endeavor. The use of videotaping is a powerful tool for assessment, feedback, and therapeutic purposes, catching in pictures and words the dysfunctional defense systems the clients build for themselves (Brill, 1981; Hay & Nathan, 1982; Sobell & Sobell, 1978).

During session 2 with his group, Gordon's poor relationship skills are evident. Despite Gordon's stated desire and willingness to interact positively with other clients and to work on his own addiction in the group, this initial dialogue shows typical difficulties during early developmental phases of the group. Gordon's long history of denial and lack of communication of feelings, trust, and personal needs carries over into the early group sessions.

Gordon: Nothing against the rest of you here, but I really don't understand the reason for putting me in here with such heavy abusers.

Ray: You don't see yourself fitting in?

Liz: Yeah, Gordon, you think your boozing's different from ours? Looks to me like you're Mr. High and Mighty and we're a bunch of gutter bums.

Alice: Afraid we've got your number? Still denying what you are. Boy, have you got something to learn.

Carolyn: What I see happening here is basically a lack of trust in this group. That's not only an important issue for here but for outside as well. What I want to do is turn on the video and go back over the introductions and the individual goals you'd all set for yourself that we did in our first session. They may help us all begin to see this group as a unified whole with common needs.

Accepting Responsibility

Clients learn to retake control over their lives, but this is not always easily done. Listen to Gordon as he confronts responsibility during session 3.

Gordon: What gripes me is they treat you like kids around here. Do this, go here, learn that!

Alice: Do you know why we're supposed to do that? It's because we need to know those things if we're going to be any good when we finish our treatment.

Gordon: That's fine, but I'm an adult and I can read this on my own.

Liz: Have you? And if you did, could you get anything out of it?

Gordon: I don't know who you are to talk about responsibility. They nailed you for raiding the pharmacy cabinet, didn't they?

Carolyn: When you unload on Liz, that's a neat way of getting the load off your back. If you could make us as angry at you as you feel toward everybody else, then you'd be justified in telling us all to buzz off.

Gordon: She asked for it. We're talking about all the Mickey Mouse stuff like cleaning up your room and so forth. If that's helping me with my drinking problem, I'll kiss your foot.

Manuel (Gordon's roommate): Maybe if you'd paid more attention to the Mickey Mouse stuff and not the booze you wouldn't be here now. Every morning I got to say something about living in a pigsty. If you were that sloppy, I'm surprised you still got that big bucks job.

Gordon: Oh! Now it's my work. I'll have you know I carried my load at work, and I sure as hell don't see what making my bed's got to do with getting back on track.

Ray: When the others say those things to you, it's hard to believe you aren't responsible. Hence, you react angrily to them. Although you were highly responsible and capable in the past, it's tough and hurts to be confronted with the fact that you're having trouble keeping up now.

Gordon: That's not right, I . . .

Ruth: Then what is right, Gordon? Sure, it's not fun. It's not supposed to be a vacation. You've got as many days here as is needed, and no more, to prove that you can be responsible. You haven't been responsible for a long time, is what the others are saying, and now you pull the same thing with us.

Gordon: What do you want from me? You all sound just like my wife.

Ray: It's the same old tune you're hearing from them, and it makes you angry when you have to take on responsibility, so you'll show them.

Manuel: If he can't even get his bed made, he's not showing me much.

Gordon: I'll show you all!

Carolyn: It's not a question of showing them anything. It's a question, I think, of having the courage to show yourself.

Gordon: I don't know. It scares the hell out of me. I'm not sure what I can do anymore.

Ray: When you say it that way, I think we all understand. It's not just the simple things like making a bed or reading the assignment. It's the scary feeling of doing something you haven't done for a long time and wondering whether you'll fail again.

If Gordon can find enough fault with the treatment center, the staff, or their practices, and get them to respond in the same manner, he will be "justified" in his stance and also justified in returning to alcohol. This rebellious attitude is met by the therapist with empathy and some interpretation. Confrontation would be inappropriate and would place the locus of control too far outside the client—it would put control of his sobriety into the hands of someone else (Wallace, 1978, p. 38). When he answers the other group members in caustic ways, the workers respond empathically to the people attacked, and when Gordon is attacked, the workers respond in supportive ways to him, casting hypotheses about how he feels now and how it may generalize to others who have attacked him (Ohlsen, 1970, pp. 116–129). By not reinforcing such dependent behavior but reinforcing Gordon when he takes responsibility on his own shoulders, the workers provide a model for reassuming independence (Blume, 1978, p. 71).

Alice: (*Weeping.*) I know it sounds silly, but that damn wood sculpture I've been working on in art therapy is terrible. I can't get it right. It's just like everything else in my life.

Gordon: Ah, look, Alice. I used to do that as a hobby. If you wouldn't mind, I could maybe give you a hand. I know how frustrating it can be.

Manuel: Hey, man! That's the first time you ever said you'd do anything for anybody. You feelin' OK?

Gordon: It's no big deal.

Ray: Yet I think Manuel's got a point. It's good to see you care about Alice. Offering to help her says you're taking on responsibility for someone else, something you haven't been able to do in a long time. Now if we can just get you to make Manuel's bed. (*General laughter, Gordon included.*)

Getting Past Denial

In adults a rigid, nonmodifiable, and repeated use of denial is a defense that is usually associated with psychotic disorders and addiction. As long as it is intact, the client cannot feel concern with doing anything constructive about his or her illness (Maxwell, 1986, p. 176). The most difficult task of the worker is to lessen the denial and encourage increased self-awareness and disclosure while at the same time keeping anxiety at minimal levels (Wallace, 1978, p. 32).

In the treatment of alcoholism, two levels of denial exist. The first is the denial of the presence and magnitude of a drinking problem (Blume, 1978, pp. 68–69). Continued denial specifically associated with drinking is a poor prognosis, and the chemical dependent who continues to use denial is not likely to stay sober. The second level is denial of long-standing life problems. Although it may sound antithetical to recovery, denial of serious life problems other than drinking is an appropriate defense mechanism early on in treatment. This is so because those are the stressors that probably triggered drug use in the first place. To break down defenses in these areas would put more stress on the system, increase anxiety, and set the client up for failure (Chalmers & Wallace, 1978, p. 262).

Confrontation

When heavy denial and its defensive consorts are encountered, confrontation is probably the most potent and dangerous weapon the worker has (Lawson et al., 1984, p. 125). The use of confrontation as a therapeutic technique needs to be carefully considered. Putting a resisting and denying client on the "hot seat" is a questionable practice for a variety of reasons. First, other clients may viciously attack the client and in the process force compliance or make a scapegoat of the client. Second, focusing only on the one client may permit other members in the group to become less involved (Ohlsen, 1970, pp. 127, 168).

The purpose of confrontation is not to vent personal frustration, impose belief systems contrary to those of the client, or act in punitive ways (Lawson et al., 1984, p. 101). Critical in the confrontation is the worker's emotional astuteness and competence in determining the correct moment to confront (Perez, 1985, p. 164).

A principal characteristic of confrontation is its challenge. The challenge is embedded in a question so that an immediate feeling response is evoked. A second characteristic of confrontation is that it is direct and action oriented. The client is constantly placed in new roles and situations calling for a response. Explored in a sensitive, perceptive manner, these new roles and situations enable a client to be aware of discrepancies between behaviors and intentions, feelings and messages, and insights and actions (Dinkmeyer, Pew, & Dinkmeyer, 1979, p. 110). Confrontive statements can be hooked to reflective and interpretive statements. They also are generally connected with an owning statement, one that says clearly that "I, the counselor, own this." If the client denies the statement, then the confrontation is redirected: "OK, if that's not you, then what is you?" Confrontations are generally made in the form of a demand and are linked to alternatives. Confrontation catches a client in a contradiction and asks the client why he or she behaves in such a contradictory manner. Used judiciously and altered to fit the dilemma, confrontation can be extremely helpful in jarring clients out of old response patterns (Shulman, 1973, p. 198). There are five major areas of confrontation:

1. *Experiential:* a response to any discrepancy perceived by the worker
2. *Strength:* focused on the client's resources, especially if the client does not recognize them
3. *Weakness:* focused on the client's liabilities or pathology
4. *Didactic:* clarification of misinformation or lack of information
5. *Encouragement to action:* pressing the client to act on his or her world in a constructive manner and discouraging a passive attitude toward life.

Experiential, strength, didactic, and encouragement should be used most frequently, with much less reliance on exploiting the client's weaknesses (Lawson et al., 1984, p. 103).

Confrontation is always used in relation to behaviors and never used to attack a client's personhood. Many confrontations will be paradoxical, will be enlarged to farcical dimensions, and will have humor attached so that the client may clearly see the ridiculousness of the behavior called into question. For example, during session 5 with his group, Gordon is confronted by both workers and group members as a way of cracking his denial.

Gordon: It's easy for you to say I shouldn't go drinking with the guys after work. You just can't do that and stay on the inside track.

Carolyn: (*Catching the discrepancy.*) So if you don't do what they want, you're out. Yet the very act of continuing to drink has almost put you out. Do you see the discrepancy there?

Gordon: Yes, but I've got to be a team player. Can't let those young sharks get ahead.

Manuel: (*Calling the question.*) Ahead of what?

Carolyn: (*Creating an exaggerated image.*) Picture this, Gordon. You're a little minnow swimming around in a martini glass with all these big hungry fish circling you, but you're so goofy from that vodka ocean that you swim right into their jaws. How does that fit?

Gordon: (*Chuckles.*) OK. I'll accept that. If only there was some way to get out of that double bind.

Ray: (*Proposing action.*) What would happen if you did exactly the opposite of what you've been doing? That is, just turn that martini lunch down. Become one of the sober sharks instead of the drunken minnows? How could you do that?

Gordon: I don't know. (*Lamely.*) Then I wouldn't be a regular guy.

Ruth: (*Drawing the paradox.*) Yeah. You've been a regular guy, all right. That's with a three-martini lunch. Why don't you put a half-dozen down? Then you'd be Superman. I thought I was Superwoman when I did that crap, and you see me now.

Gordon: (*Sullenly.*) Now, wait a second! I didn't mean that. (*Turns to Carolyn.*) That's not true. How can she say that? We're supposed to be helping each other. How can you let her attack me?

Carolyn: (*Redirecting.*) Then what did you mean? (*Placing a demand with a reflection.*) I understand how that hurts, but I also believe that when you try to get me to support you and imply that I'm a lousy counselor if I don't, I'd just be playing into that game of "poor me." What will you do instead? (*Proposing alternatives.*) You have some choices. You can sit and sulk, you can be dependent and ask me to take your part, or you can use your considerable strength and make a clear assertive statement back. Which will it be?

Alice: (*Creating an image.*) See how you get yourself? You want to be so darn independent, yet you continuously say, "Come and hold me, look what a poor child am I." I get this picture of a big baby in a crib and it's full of empty bourbon bottles and you nestled in there.

Gordon: By God, that isn't true. I'm not a baby. Life's been a bitch.

Carolyn: (*Commiserating overbearingly.*) Yep! Life's that way. It's rotten, cruel and unusual punishment. Wouldn't it be wonderful to make everybody responsible for your drinking put on hair shirts and roll around in cinders? That would pay them back for all the harm they've done to you.

Gordon: People just don't understand me, and that includes all of you. I'm gonna leave this stinkin' place.

Carolyn: (*Avoiding a trap.*) I'd not like to see that happen, but what they're doing is confronting your own ways of fooling yourself and attempting to get you to see the strengths you've got. If I get them off your back, you don't have to be responsible. If I don't, you leave and I'm at fault. Either way you'd have an excuse for continuing to blame somebody else. (*Attributing the projection.*) It seems as if you'd like me to get into the same kinds of double binds you put yourself in. (*Owning.*) So if you believe I'm not much of a counselor because of that, it's certainly your privilege.

Gordon: (*Rocks back in chair.*) I do that? Damn! I guess maybe I do.

Some of the responses may seem to put Gordon on the hot seat, but the other members are willing to own that they too have been where Gordon is now. The confrontations are exhortations to action. The group is pushing Gordon to make changes in his life, particularly in regard to the way he denies and defends his drinking behavior.

Limit Testing

Dependability and consistency apply to the enforcement of rules of the program and are critical to getting better. Clients often test the limits to determine consistency in the therapist's treatment approach by missing appointments, disobeying treatment rules, and taking drugs (Doweiko, 1996, p. 360). Stability and consistency in what is expected from the chemical dependent are the hallmarks of good treatment. As a result, deviancy from the ground rules should be immediately confronted by the crisis worker.

Gordon: Sorry I'm late, I was talking with Ruth and forgot the time.

Carolyn: I may sound really picky here, but that's an excuse for not taking care of business. I wonder how many times you've used that before to not be on time and excuse your drinking.

Gordon: (*Sarcastically.*) Yeah, I stopped and got a martini at the nurse's station.

Carolyn: What you did was take a little step toward excusing your behavior, and that little minidecision can lead to bigger, bad decisions when you get out of here. I want you to recognize and be aware of those little decisions and where they can lead.

Treatment Secrets

Chemical dependents sometimes attempt to co-opt the treatment by telling "secrets" to staff members—usually to a neophyte. The chemical dependent confesses a rules infraction to the staff member but asks the staff person not to tell the other staff members. If the client can get the staff member to go along, the chemical dependent can later blackmail the staff member by threatening to tell his or her supervisors.

Gordon: (*Calls Sheila, a counseling intern, to the side after the group outpatient meeting.*) Errh, ahh, I need to talk to you. . . . I think I can trust you . . . ahh . . . with something I don't want Carolyn to know 'cause she'd chew my ass. Well . . . one of my friends came by and while we were talking in the car he pulled out a beer from a cooler . . . and well doggone it . . . I had one . . . only one . . . I feel bad about it and just had to tell somebody. But please don't tell her.

Sheila: (*In a kind, but assertive voice.*) I'm glad you told me about what you did, Gordon. I want to now encourage you to go to Carolyn and tell her and also tell the group at our next meeting. I don't keep secrets about drug use. If I did, I'd be no different from all the other people who have enabled your drinking. So you decide. Do you tell her now, or do I bring it up in the team meeting?

Besides immediately confronting the "secret," Doweiko (1996, p. 360) suggests that the staffer immediately write down what the client told him or her about the "secret" and refer it to the treatment team.

Disrupting Irrational Mental Sets

According to Ellis (1987), it is not an event itself but our belief about that event that causes us to feel and act in certain irrational ways. By starting to think "insane" thoughts about what people or events "should," "ought," "must" do or be to make it a perfect world, chemical dependents become victims of their irrational thoughts about the events. By putting such irrational statements up in the billboard of their minds, chemical dependents can easily fall back into hurt, rejected feelings and can manifest these feelings in behavior designed to pay back the people or events that intrude into their self-centered universe. It is extremely important to catch chemical dependents as they begin to build these billboards, because this kind of thinking is what starts a chain of events that can ultimately build up to another drinking episode. The key to stopping this "insane" thinking is teaching the person to recognize the cues that appear anteced- ent to the negative feelings and subsequent bad behavioral outcomes. Once these cues are picked up, then new, rational statements can be manufactured to replace the old, de- bilitating ones that underlie beliefs.

For example, in Gordon's treatment, a videotape of session 6 was used as the focus for group therapy in session 7. Session 6 had examined the events and behaviors that brought each client to St. Polycarp. The group viewed excerpts of session 6 that were selected by the group leaders to vividly re-create and model each individual's unique addictive situation and to stimulate and uncover each member's defense mechanisms. Clients first portrayed themselves; then members exchanged roles and attempted to model what the other's defenses appeared to be.

Manuel: Man, those were tough. Liz played me to a T! I also thought Alice really hit Gordon's nail on the head, too!

Ray: How he first rationalizes, and then when things really get hot, regresses.

Gordon: Before I saw that videotape I would never have believed it! But there I was. Rationalizing my drinking by telling myself I was "sick" when I couldn't make it to work because I was hung over or still smashed. Boy, was that sad! It made me sick to watch that. What a jerk!

Ruth: What about that preadolescent stuff, "I'll take my ball and go home," see how Liz did that with the doctor routine. It was just like yesterday with the family therapy. I didn't know whether that was your mother or wife, the way you were manipulating her and sulking like a kid who didn't get any candy.

Gordon: (*Angrily.*) What do you mean, acting like a kid? Why don't we take a look at how you act around that teenager of yours?

Liz: Look at what you just did, Gordon. You're regressing right now!

Alice: That videotape didn't lie. Don't you see how you get into that?

Carolyn: Remember the work we did on cueing in our verbal and nonverbal behavior the other day. Notice what feelings you get when your defense mechanisms kick in and what thoughts go through your head to get that going. (*Gordon looks at video- tape again.*)

Gordon: (*Sheepishly.*) Maybe I *was* acting like a kid. Maybe I wasn't connecting that stuff you call cueing to my real life.

Carolyn: Right here we have a good example of how you might begin to use that cueing. When Ruth confronted you just a minute ago, what messages went through your mind to cause you to react angrily and then attack her—rather than looking at yourself?

Gordon: The first thing that flashed through was "You're just like my wife." She's always implying I'm not capable of acting like an adult. She makes me crazy when she does that.

Carolyn: Using Gordon as an example, what cues did we teach you all to recognize, and what did we learn to do to counteract our irrational thinking as well as our behavior?

Ruth: First off, Gordon needs to recognize that as one of those stop signs you were talking about. Anytime that he relates to the old ways he behaved toward Amy and hears, "I'm not good enough," he needs to see that as a warning sign that he's kicking in a lot of that old dependent put-down crap.

Manuel: He also could change "she" to "I" 'cause it's really him and his beliefs about what she said. He allows that to happen.

Alice: He could make an assertive statement out of it, like, "I understand how you might feel that way, but right now I'm feeling like I'm behaving pretty straight with you and it hurts me that you'd feel I haven't changed."

Cueing provides Gordon with psychological stop signs. These are not easy to see, especially when, in the heat of the moment, it is all too easy to revert to years' worth of programmed thinking. Cueing is like any other new skill and will take much practice and feedback before the client is able to "rewire" his or her thinking.

Carolyn: I want you all to list out your cues for those predicaments that make you crazy, angry, depressed, and so on in your logs. Then let's work on building new belief statements. Monitor yourself as we work together and see if you can catch yourself before others do. If you feel a bit odd when you put those new statements in and say them, then you're on the right track.

If clients cannot catch the insane messages they send themselves, then other physiological or affective responses may work as cues. Sweating hands, a lump in the throat, and a palpitating heart may be good physical cues. The flush of anger, the chagrin of embarrassment, and the gloom of despair may be good affective cues.

Overcoming Environmental Cues That Lead to Drinking

Subtly but surely, settings and the events that occur within them provide powerful cues to respond in particular ways. Returning to a world that is filled with potent environmental cues to drink or take drugs strains the recovering addict's newfound coping skills to the limit and can create another crisis point (Sobell & Sobell, 1978).

Putting chemical dependents in role plays and imaginal sets in groups helps them recognize and manipulate environments that powerfully reinforce their chemical dependency. By learning how to use cognitive restructuring (McMullin & Giles, 1981), imaging (Neisser, 1976), coping thoughts (Cormier & Hackney, 1987), emotive imagery and covert modeling (Cormier & Cormier, 1985), and stress inoculation (Meichenbaum, 1985), clients are able to armor themselves against the negative setting events that they will inevitably encounter.

In session 10 of Gordon's treatment group, the group constructs and role-plays a setting event that portrays Gordon getting into his car after a very stressful day at work, which has been interrupted by phone calls from home saying that Mark has been suspended from school because he was found with a marijuana cigarette in his possession. Gordon watches as Manuel plays the part.

Manuel: (*As Gordon, talking to himself as he guns the car out of the company lot.*) Jesus Christ! Everything was supposed to be better. If this is better, screw it! Work sucks! The president is on my back again. Produce! Produce! Produce! That's all I hear. And now Mark! I suppose that's my fault too. Amy sure laid that one on me while going nuts over the phone. That's what I got to look forward to when I hit the door. Hey, there's the Olde English Inn coming up over the hill. My favorite watering hole. Man, do they make a mean Manhattan in there. I'll bet some of the old crowd's still there too, and Roxie, my favorite bartender. They sure never gave me any flak. It's happy hour too! Two for the price of one. To hell with it. I'll just have one and go. It'll take the edge off before I hit the door and have to deal with Amy and Mark. (*Manuel turns the car into the inn parking lot.*)

Ray: OK! The world isn't perfect, and you're going to run into problems like that, feel those lousy emotions, and those tempting places like the Olde English Inn are going to be there just waiting for a day like that. What are you going to do, Gordon?

Gordon: All right. Let me put my plan into action. My positive self-statements will be "I don't care how rough it's been at work, I did a helluva job today. The boss always gripes like that around the end of the month, so don't take it personally." My stress inoculates will be a number of things. First, I'll put Mozart on the tape deck, that's calming and reminds me of being on the banks of Lake Zurich just watching the sailboats glide by. Behaviorally, I can practice my breathing skills, just taking deep, easy breaths, and letting all that stress flow right out my nose. While I'm doing that, I can see my jogging shoes and sweats waiting for me by the back door at home. I can replace my negative thoughts about home by saying, "I would have come in and blustered and stormed around and grilled Mark, generally raised hell and then sulked. That didn't do a damn bit of good except get me stressed out even more. I know I can think clearer and more rationally after I've worked out. I can feel the sweat pouring out of my body, cleaning it out. That'll feel good." Now here comes the inn over the hill. I'm starting to think how easy it'd be to just turn in there. I can feel my hands getting sweaty, and my throat's dry. I put my thought stopping into gear, "STOP THAT! Switch. Think what your sagging, pulpy body was after you got through with a bout in there, turkey! You couldn't stumble to the john without gasping for air. God, were you ever a sorry sucker." To cue myself on how good I now feel, I'll flex my leg and feel that hard thigh muscle, a great tactile cue to remind me how far I've come, and I'm not giving that up. Reviewing my self-talk, I can say, "Yeah, Roxie and the inn were a great place to get quietly smashed, but that was then. Looking at the place in broad daylight, it's shopworn, and I've got real oak in my study instead of that fiberboard, ersatz stuff in there. Ha! I'll bet the boys look a little shopworn too after today. Further, I never really liked that sweet smell of a Manhattan, always covered it with a cigarette. I don't want that crap. It's a bitch about Mark, but I don't need to catastrophize over it. I can handle that, and I'll take the time to handle it. My family's the most important thing in the world to me, and I'm not just paying lip service to it, I'm living it! Press the accelerator down and go on by with no regrets."

By taping and practicing these new mental images over and over with the assistance of the workers and the group, Gordon learns how to use a wide variety of positive coping mechanisms to get by this potentially dangerous environmental set (Ahsen, 1993). This is not a one-shot exercise. It will take Gordon a great deal of practice to reprogram himself to ignore those old cues that set him up to drink.

Treating the Family

The attitudes, structure, and function of the family system have been shown to be perhaps the most important variables in the outcome of treatment. If the system changes from enabling to more adaptive behavior, it may sustain improvement and change in the alcoholic (Kaufman & Pattison, 1982a, p. 669). However, this is easier said than done because, paradoxically, if the alcoholic makes a commitment to stop drinking, the maladaptive family may become threatened enough to try to reinstitute the perceived homeostasis of alcoholism. In the case of Gordon, the treatment strongly focused on support, encouragement, education, and treatment of family members who had become worn down by the incessant task of coping with the chemical dependency (Knack & Murray, 1996). Each member needed supportive counseling to reframe and cognitively restructure Gordon's and their own relationships, communication style, and the seriousness of both Gordon's and the family's long-term task and commitment to succeed in attaining the family's renewal. Such supportive counseling required all members, including Gordon, to view the situation as far more than Gordon's simply stopping drinking. The family counseling used the drinking cessation only as a starting point to confront the fundamental problems driving the dependency, and each member of the family was seen as having a key role in solving the problems afflicting each other and in building a strong, healthy, and supportive family system.

Family therapy generates the climate to proactively and intentionally work on the many specific problems and gripes each member may have. It also provides a supportive and safe place to tackle such big family issues as the need to change lifestyle, individual members' perfectionism, power imbalances in the family, rivalries, and various ways members jockey for leadership. Many families are not consciously aware of the influence these dynamic factors play in the family. They may not be aware that, through cooperative learning such as the family counseling group, these factors can be handled in balanced, constructive, positive, and even comfortable ways.

Even if both codependents and dependent agree to change, there should not be explicit or implicit assumptions that family ties will be fully reconstituted. Although long-term nurturing of all system members is ideal, such positive interactions will not happen overnight. Each individual member first has to become intimate with him- or herself before trying to do so with the alcoholic. Any attempts to reassume responsibility for the alcoholic, no matter how well intended, have a high probability of enabling and promoting a relapse (Maxwell, 1986, p. 209). Avoidance of enabling behavior and assumption of responsibility are difficult, as Gordon's first family therapy session shows.

Family Therapy Session. The primary task of the worker in the family is to detect and penetrate the defense systems the family has set up to keep things stable. Almost without exception, the alcoholic family members will have real trouble expressing feelings and communicating with one another (Maxwell, 1986, pp. 205–206). By keeping a low profile in the beginning, the worker lets the pathology of the family emerge (Parker, 1986). As Carolyn sits quietly, Gordon, Amy, Lisa, and Mark exchange stilted pleasantries and defensive comments, punctuated by long, awkward silences. As soon as the worker obtains an adequate assessment of the family's dynamic interaction, she becomes involved.

Amy: Now, I don't want you to worry about anything. I talked to your boss, and he assured me the company is behind you 100 percent.

Gordon: That's great!

Carolyn: Amy, I'd like you to notice what you just did. You decided to take care of Gordon. What about your own feelings about carrying the load?

Amy: I just didn't want him to worry about his job. I know how much he's put into it.

Carolyn: Yes, but what about your feelings?

Amy: It just seems to me that Gordon should concentrate his efforts on getting better, don't you think?

Carolyn: Do you see what you're doing? I've asked you twice to speak to your feelings. Yet each time, you take responsibility for Gordon. You talk about him and not yourself. You pose a question that asks for my agreement. And you shift to events rather than dealing with your feelings. How does that strike you, Gordon?

Gordon: Er, I don't know. I guess Amy ought to express how she feels.

Carolyn: How do you feel?

Gordon: I think we probably don't do enough talking about our feelings.

Carolyn: That's right, but how do you feel?

This short exchange graphically demonstrates the tremendous difficulty the two adults have in expressing feelings to one another. They adroitly shift off this topic in a variety of ways. One very subtle way to avoid direct confrontation about feelings is to send a messenger. Of course, the messenger has to be very careful how the news is delivered; otherwise, he or she may get psychologically murdered in completing the task.

Amy: Lisa, tell your father what Grandpa and Grandma had to say.

Lisa: Ah, they said they were real sorry they didn't get to see you, and hoped you get well. They'd have really liked to stay and come here today, but Grandpa had to get back to Chicago for a meeting.

Carolyn: I wonder why you asked Lisa to tell Gordon that. My guess is that's a touchy subject about his parents leaving. Does your mom often ask you to do that?

Lisa: You bet! You do that all the time, Mom. Whenever you've got something you think'll cause a ruckus, you always send me to tell Dad 'cause you think he'll take it from me. Then I'm the bad guy. I hate it!

Carolyn: So you see, there's another way of getting around dealing with feelings. Send somebody else and let them deal with it, because feelings are risky, scary, and hard to handle.

Amy: Lisa has always been the apple of her dad's eye. She's always had a way with him.

Carolyn: Excuse me for picking on you right now, Amy, but what were you just doing?

Amy: I was talking about Lisa and her relationship with her dad.

Carolyn: That's right! You were talking *about* her, not *to* her. What would happen if you said that straight out? You might risk getting a feeling response back.

Lisa: Mom, you wouldn't like that. You always tell me to bear up when I try to talk to you about my feelings, and that goes for you, too, Dad!

Carolyn: Great, Lisa! Lisa's raised some pretty hot issues. Any feelings about them?

Gordon: (*Looking at Carolyn.*) I guess I just didn't realize I wasn't being the father I could be to her. I didn't realize I was doing that. I'm sorry.

Carolyn: Gordon, do you want me to be your messenger to Lisa?

Gordon: No!

Carolyn: Then don't tell me, but tell her that.

Amy: Well, I just know Mark doesn't feel that way. He's kept a stiff upper lip through all this, kept up his grades and done everything around the house, plus made his own spending money mowing yards.

Carolyn: Amy, it is interesting that you find it difficult to feel for yourself, yet can tell others how they feel and even answer for them. What I'd like to do now is give each one of you an assignment for next time that specifically gets at what problems I see with communication in this group. Mark, since you didn't say anything today, I want you to write a letter to each member in the family telling each how you feel about him or her. Lisa, I'd like you to wear a big paper heart next time, and every time somebody doesn't respond directly to you or speak to their feelings, I'd like you to tear a piece of your heart off. Amy, in the codependency group I want you to solicit direct, feeling responses from people. I'll give you the questions to ask. Gordon, I want you to write down some of the feelings you had in here today into a script, and then take it back to the group and we'll role-play it on the videotape.

The major task is to teach all the family members to express their feelings in an open and honest way. Debilitating communication patterns are pointed out over and over to all family members who engage in disruptive communications. It is noteworthy that no one mentions Gordon's drinking. This conspiracy of silence still continues even after Gordon is in a chemical treatment unit and the whole family is in therapy for the problem. As Parker (1986) says, "There's a big, pet, pink elephant [alcoholism] sitting there in the middle of the family, but everybody circles around it as if it didn't even exist, and it just keeps getting bigger and bigger and taking up more space." This problem will need to be reflected by the worker, for the sooner the alcoholism is brought into the open, the quicker the family can start building a new communication system.

Another issue is Mark, who has remained silent throughout the session. Invariably there is someone who can be extremely helpful in changing the system (Kaufman & Pattison, 1982b, p. 1031). Mark may have a great deal to do with changing the family network. Lisa is also a potent member of this system. The worker early on acknowledges her strength and reinforces her for clear, directional feeling responses—a rarity in this family. Finally, to facilitate communication, tasks may be assigned with the session as homework.

Comprehensive Family Treatment. Schaef (1986) criticized typical family therapy as focusing exclusively on the chemical dependent and the enabling behavior of family members while excluding consideration of their own problems. Unwittingly, this treatment approach replicates the sick chemically dependent family with most attention focused on the substance abuser, next on the spouse, and finally on the children. Schaef extends this criticism to Al-Anon, where much of the focus is on how to live with an alcoholic rather than understanding and dealing with codependency (pp. 5–6).

There are three major advantages to family therapy if it is conducted with a view to helping the whole family. First, the family can confront the chemical dependent's addiction and can support his or her attempt to move into recovery. Second, the family learns how substance abuse is related to other patterns of family life, such as roles, rules, and patterns of communication, and may become aware of how they play a part in keeping others in the system in thrall to it (Cable, Noel, & Swanson, 1986, pp. 73–74). Third, and perhaps most important, the children can be educated as to the part they play in the dysfunctional system (Liepman et al., 1986, pp. 56–57).

Therapy for the Children.   Whenever therapeutic assistance is sought or recommended for the family, it should not be surprising if children are resistant. They will feel it is the chemically dependent parent who needs help, not them. The therapist's legitimate and sincere explanation is that although this is the chemical dependent's problem, it is also a family problem and the children in particular deserve special attention (Black, 1981, p. 102). Cable and associates (1986, p. 69) have listed nine common treatment goals for children who experience crisis because of parental chemical dependency:

1. Assessing the children's situations and needs
2. Providing support for the children
3. Providing accurate, nonjudgmental information about alcoholism
4. Correcting the children's inaccurate perceptions that they are the cause or reason for their parent's drinking
5. Helping the children focus on their own behavior by giving them a sense of control and the perception of being able to make responsible choices; and, if necessary, helping them to learn how to have fun
6. Helping the children learn how to cope with real situations that may arise because of the parent's alcohol abuse—for example, if the parent passes out
7. Reducing the children's isolation and helping them to share their dilemma with other children in similar situations
8. Reducing the children's risk of developing substance abuse or alternately treating the children's substance abuse
9. Enlisting the family and/or other support system to reinforce the children's gains

For children going through the crisis of a family member's addiction or recovery, Alateen, family therapy, or specialized counseling groups for codependent children are critical treatment components. Children learn in these groups about the disease concept so they can stop feeling guilt over the alcoholic behavior of their parents, realize which of their family rules and roles are healthy and unhealthy, understand they are not alone in their misery, and discover that there are alternate ways to cope with their problems other than the maladaptive ones taught by their families (Liepman et al., 1986, pp. 56–57). *The bottom line is that the emotional issues of all children raised in chemically dependent homes need to be addressed because all children are affected.*

Radical Attempts to Restore the Old Family System.   As the masking behaviors that support the codependency are stripped away, it may be expected that more and more radical attempts will be made to restore the old system. In Gordon's case, a very traumatic experience from a multiple-family session that occurred the day before session 17 illustrates this dramatically. Ten minutes before the end of the multiple-family session, Amy announced that she was so distraught she was thinking of suicide. This threw things into an uproar and necessitated an individual suicide intervention with Amy that lasted two hours after the group session. Gordon, who had been attempting to deal with some of his feelings with Amy, was paralyzed and shocked into submission. This therapeutic material was immediately brought back to the group.

To help Gordon deal with this ploy, an "alter ego" exercise was videotaped. An alter ego routine is done by having members of this group stand behind each seated role player and verbally state the potent (but unspoken) self-thoughts and self-talk that they perceive to be going on inside the role player's head.

Carolyn: (*Role-playing Amy.*) Gordon, I understand you wanted to talk to me about what happened in the family session yesterday.

Ruth: (*Taking the role of Amy's alter ego, standing behind Carolyn, with her hands resting gently on Carolyn's shoulders.*) I don't like this one little bit. But I really got him, the bastard.

Gordon: (*Avoiding eye contact and stammering.*) Yes . . . I was disturbed about the way you brought up the suicide stuff . . . without me knowing about it.

Ray: (*Taking the role of alter ego of Gordon, standing directly behind Gordon, with his hands resting gently on Gordon's shoulders.*) This is scary as hell! I'd like to kill her myself. I'm struggling like crazy to stay straight and she pulls that number. I want to tell her what I really feel about that. But I can't. Why am I feeling so paralyzed?

Carolyn: (*Role-modeling Amy.*) Dear, I really didn't mean it the way it looked, it just came out. I couldn't help it. They said to get our feelings out. This whole mess is . . . I just want you to get well and for us to be just like we used to be . . . right after we were married.

Ruth: (*As alter ego of Amy.*) I've got to cover this up, put it back on him. Let him wallow in it and see what he's done to me. It's payback time.

Gordon: (*Looking Carolyn straight in the eyes.*) Look, I feel lousy about what I've done in the past. But there's nothing I can do about it now. When you pull that kind of stunt, it's just the past all over again. It hurts like hell when you do that. What I'm concerned about is right now. I'm scared to death I'm not gonna cut this, and I need you to understand that. I don't believe I'll break, whatever happens. You don't have to act helpless or self-destructive to keep me in line or earn my love. You've got that already and you'll have more of it, the better both of us get. By the way, you still haven't talked about how you feel.

Group: (*Cheers.*) All right, Gordon! Way to go!

Ray: (*As alter ego of Gordon.*) Holy cow! I don't believe I did that. I spilled the beans, told her how I felt. I thought I'd throw up, I was so scared, but I didn't. Maybe I *have* got what it takes to get out of this. I really feel *good!* (*Breaks from role.*) How did that go, Gordon?

Gordon: (*Smiling from ear to ear.*) That's the first time in years, maybe ever, I said stuff like that. And you alter egos are right. I do feel good. If that had happened before I came here, it'd be a sure bet I'd have started drinking.

Ray: Could you now do that with Amy?

Gordon: It'd still be scary, but yes. I think, no, I *feel* like I can.

By bouncing submerged feelings off Gordon, the alter egos attempt to make crystal clear what the hidden messages are that drive the codependent and dependent. Given the opportunity to bring these agendas into the open, dependents and codependents can construct self-enhancing, positive, feeling-based, coping statements that untangle the snares and traps they set for one another. Many chemical dependents lack the skills to assert themselves, and there is evidence that assertiveness training is an important piece in the ability of chemical dependents to rehabilitate themselves (Holder et al., 1991; Lewis, Dana, & Blevins, 1988).

Aftercare

At St. Polycarp, the aftercare program requires that the client attend meetings following dismissal from inpatient treatment. Gordon will inevitably encounter several crisis points. To address the issues of codependency and enabling activities, workers try to ensure that all significant family members also participate (McCrory, 1987). The objectives of aftercare are (1) to provide ongoing education and information needed to maintain sobriety; (2) to create an environment in which natural and healthy patterns of social influence reinforce positive behaviors and self-esteem; (3) to establish an ongoing group of caring, accepting, empathic, genuine, trusting individuals who serve as an extended family, among whom the individual can always feel safe and understood; and (4) to serve as the first line of safety any time a crisis occurs.

Gordon's aftercare will extend for a minimum six months on a regular basis. During that time he will have weekly meetings with Carolyn in regard to how well he is following and meeting his aftercare objectives and goals in regard to his work, his family, his physical health, and his mental health.

Cognitive-Behavioral Boosters.   Gordon will continuously practice the cognitive behavioral techniques he has learned through a self-help method called Rational Recovery (Schmidt, 1996), a variation of Rational Emotive Behavior Therapy (Ellis et al., 1988). In particular, Gordon will constantly monitor his addictive voice, the one that tells him there "Should, must be perfect solutions, at work and at home, and if there aren't it is terrible and catastrophic and the only solution is to get drunk." He will immediately recognize that voice when it starts talking to him and will have a variety of positive counterinjunctions he and Carolyn have created to stop it dead in its tracks.

Pharmacology.   Until recently the only drug that had any effect on stopping an alcoholic from drinking was disulfiram (Antabuse). This drug causes a violent physical reaction to occur if the abuser ingests alcohol. However, it is a dangerous drug that can cause severe side effects and even be lethal if not monitored, so it is generally no longer recommended (Schuckit, 1995, pp. 316–317). There now appear to be at least two opioid antagonists that seem to hold some promise in stopping alcohol craving. Those drugs are naltrexone and acamprosate (Besson et al. 1998; Garbutt et al. 1999; Gatch & Lal, 1998; Litten & Allen, 1998; Mann, 1996). Naltrexone is available in the United States but acamprosate is not (at this writing). Whether an aftercare drug regimen is indicated is the decision of the physician on the treatment team, but besides antidrinking drugs Gordon may well also be prescribed an antidepressant, given the long-standing depression he has had.

Euphoria.   The aftercare safety line may need to extend to one of the most difficult crises the drug dependent faces—the euphoria that often accompanies recovery and the distrust and cynicism of family members—in the new and strange home that no longer has the pink elephant of drug addiction sitting in the living room. Maxwell (1986, p. 229) refers to recovery euphoria as a reaction formation. Gordon used euphoria as a highly sophisticated defense to replace the immature defenses that he had used during his active chemical dependency. Almost immediately after he left inpatient treatment, Gordon changed to a rabid proselyte. He made AA and being the completely responsible parent and husband his whole life. Although he was overbearing, his family was so afraid that confronting his behavior would send him back to drinking that they walked on eggshells. In fact, when such reaction formations occur, family members may resent the dependent's sober behavior so much that they secretly wish he or she would return to drinking.

Carolyn: Gordon, a moment ago you described how frustrated you have been because Mark clams up and withdraws from you, and you also spoke to the fact that now Lisa seems to be even more resentful of you than when you were drinking. Notice how Mark is slumped back in his chair and Lisa is sitting with arms and legs crossed as you discuss how exasperated you are.

Gordon: I can't understand it. Dinner is supposed to be our time together. Right after I got out of inpatient treatment, we were really communicating. But that's all changed lately. They've started shutting me out again. I love them, and I want what's best for them. I just want to make it up to them for being the lousy dad and husband I was for so long.

Carolyn: Mark, what are your feelings as your dad is relating his frustration?

Mark: (*Shedding tears.*) I'm mad at him . . . because nothing I say is right and everything I do is either wrong or not good enough.

Lisa: Yeah. I wish sometimes you were drinking again. At least then you left us alone.

Amy: Gordon, the kids are finally saying what we've all been feeling at home. Your personality is so overpowering since you quit drinking that none of us can come up to your standards. And AA, as good as it is, has become the center of our universe. We're worn out. We just need a normal life. We don't need you as Superman.

Gordon: I don't know what to say. I just wanted to make things up to you. I don't know what to do!

Carolyn: This whole thing you're experiencing is not uncommon. As problematic as it is, it's a good sign and sort of a stage of development on the road to recovery. Understand it for that, and we can work on it just like we have the other hot spots that have come up.

Such euphoric responses should be carefully monitored in aftercare settings because they may literally drive significant others to return to enabling behavior.

AA's Role in Aftercare.   Gordon will also have as a goal a minimum of three AA meetings a week. Zealous immersion in programs such as AA is also fraught with peril. For some people, organizations such as AA no longer fulfill a support function but rather become a platform for airing the recovering chemical dependent's self-indulgence. The premise is that the recovering alcoholic now knows all the answers and will gladly tell them to anyone who will listen. On the first sign that others may not share the recovering chemical dependent's viewpoints, the person may fall from these dizzying heights, become depressed and angry, and have a relapse. Gogek (1994) proposes that this depression is characteristic of the "dry drunk" who substitutes something else for drinking and then gets depressed about still suffering from the same symptoms.

Having said that, the very last thing Gordon needs to do is stop going to AA. AA meetings provide a format for alcoholics to socialize and stay away from the isolation that can set a recovering alcoholic up to drink. AA also helps their members to understand that their problems are not unique and allows people to be accepted and restore their self-esteem. Finally, it offers predictability and consistency, which has pretty much gone from the alcoholic's life (Doweiko, 1999, pp. 480–481).

Role Changes. One of the major difficulties in aftercare is getting the family to continue therapy. The family is so euphoric over the cessation of drug use that they believe everything else will go back to "normal" because the worst is behind them. They also believe that only the drug abuse and its immediate effects impacted them, and now that it has ceased, they will no longer feel any adverse effects (Black, 1981, pp. 99–101). Recovering parents may find that children resent their attempts to reclaim the parental roles they have abdicated. To expect the responsible child to just "mess around and play" is likely to cause all kinds of rebellious behavior in that child (McGowan, 1991).

These children will have trouble playing dolls and superheroes when they have had to take care of mother and help get her dressed or remove a smoldering cigarette from the hand of a passed-out father. They also may find it difficult to cry, laugh, cease being fearful, or get angry. Fearfulness needs to be validated as all right. Children need to know that becoming angry will not lose their parents' love or drive them back into substance abuse. They also need to have their anger acknowledged as appropriate and not discounted—particularly by the parent in recovery (Black, 1981, p. 82).

To summarize the major task of aftercare, if the chemical dependent, aside from performing his or her jobs inside and outside the home, is concentrating almost solely on maintaining chemical freedom, he or she is doing about all that needs to be done. If codependents, aside from jobs inside and outside the home, are focusing on themselves rather than on the dependent, then they are doing all that needs to be done (Maxwell, 1986, p. 234).

Gordon: (In family therapy session, six months after inpatient treatment.) One thing strikes me now. I guess I went 180 degrees in the other direction. I was as rigid in my abstinence as I was in my drinking, I was so damned afraid that I'd fall off the wagon. The truth is I was still scared to death and so was everybody else. I sure keep going to the AA meetings and I'm ready to help anyone else, but I don't have to stand out on a street corner looking for drunks. I'll probably always need a support group, and while that bugs me at times, I know there are things that bug everybody else, and that's OK. I guess I'd rate myself as an average father and husband. We still have problems, and I guess that doesn't make me much different from any other guy. And the best part about that is it feels just fine.

Relapse

Relapse is a critical issue for the family and the recovering dependent that is likely to take on crisis proportions sometime during recovery. Percentages of people who relapse have been calculated to be as high as 37 percent in the first year (George, 1990) to 90 percent over time (Svanum & McAdoo, 1989).

The first 90 days following discharge from treatment are a period of special vulnerability. A number of issues need to be monitored very carefully by the worker during this critical time period. Stress, negative emotional states, interpersonal pressure, euphoria, social and environmental drug-related cues, and use of other substances are traps that can cause the chemical dependent to relapse (DeJong, 1994). Denzin (1987) proposes that relapse is a complex social act that occurs in four phases: (1) permissive thinking, such as not going to an AA meeting; (2) use of a drug, such as just one snort at a social occasion; (3) serious use, such as getting high or drunk; and (4) seeking help. Marlatt and Gordon (1985) discuss relapse as issuing out of a series of minidecisions that form a chain of high-risk cognitions and behaviors that allow relapse to occur and are most likely when the individual is in a negative emotional or physical state or under social pressure. According to Chiauzzi (1990), there are four elements common to relapse:

1. *Long-standing personality traits* such as narcissism or dependency resurface. The chemical dependent either can't admit weakness or attempts to please others and starts to drink again.

2. *Symptom substitution* is another danger signal for relapse. Symptom substitution can range from obsessive work habits to immediately falling in love to binge eating. Symptom substitution is the hallmark of the "dry drunk," the person who is still practicing the addictive behavior except that alcohol happens not to be part of the current behavioral repertoire.

3. *Tunnel vision* of the recovery process is also designed to get the recovering chemical dependent set up to drink again. Religiously going to AA meetings is only one part of the overall personality and behavioral change the recovering dependent will have to make to stay sober. Without working on the global issues that led to the addiction in the first place, the chemical dependent will slowly drift back into addiction.

4. *Warning signals* begin flashing wherein recovering dependents start to rationalize thoughts, feelings, and behaviors that set them up to drink again. Examples are going back to the neighborhood bar to "just watch the football game with my buddies," or continuing to buy lottery tickets at the liquor store

Schuckit (1984) suggests that fewer than 2 percent of those individuals with drinking problems can safely return to social drinking, although undoubtedly 100 percent of alcoholics either believe or wish they could (Doweiko, 1990, p. 250). For any alcoholic who suggests a return to social drinking to a crisis worker, it should be quickly pointed out that the odds are from 50 to 100 to 1 against his or her being able to handle it and that is clearly the "stinkin' thinkin'" that helped get the alcoholic in trouble in the first place. From our own experience in working with the chemically dependent, we believe that Schuckit's statistics are very optimistic.

INTERVENTION WITH THE ACOA

To illustrate the steps of intervention with ACOAs, let us move forward two years after Gordon's hospitalization and look at his daughter Lisa, who has just walked into a counselor's office at the university counseling center.

Assessment

Lisa's intake questionnaire indicated low grades, poor relationships with males, depression, and low self-concept. Subsequent follow-up testing indicated moderate depression, borderline drug abuse, and an extremely low self-concept on both intra- and interpersonal dimensions. Lisa's initial appearance is of a willowy ash blonde who is pretty, dressed immaculately in the current "in" clothes. As she meets the counselor, she is smiling, gregarious, and forthright, which is in stark and puzzling contrast to her self-report and her test scores. The counselor is Dr. Maxine Robertson, an expert in addictions, who has been assigned the case based on Lisa's borderline MacAndrew Alcoholism Scale and her self-report of drug abuse and overdose. Lisa comes straight to the point.

Lisa: I'm scared to death. I don't know what's happening to me. When I came to State I was determined not to make the same mistake I made at Tech. I almost flunked out of there. I did real well here the first semester. Good grades and worked 20 hours a week and was in the Young Democrats and real active in a sorority and a good social life. But now it's all falling apart, and I feel terrible and look even worse and then there was the other night.

Dr. Max: This is a tough question right off the bat, but it's made out of concern. Were you feeling bad enough to kill yourself?

Lisa: (*Emphatically.*) No way. I'm down in the dumps, but not that down.

Although it may seem tedious to say so again, by this point in your reading, we never take overdoses or any other "accidents" for granted. The human services worker *must* check out the possibility of suicide. Once she is assured that it was an accident, she moves forward.

Dr. Max: Tell me about the drugs that you put down on your intake sheet.

Lisa: I don't know what came over me. I mean, I drink some beer and wine, and I've smoked a little pot, but I took some speed because I needed to study all night, and then I drank some, and got into a terrible fight with Ron, my boyfriend, and I guess I got pretty weird, and then I passed out, and the next thing I knew they had me over at McKinley Hospital waking me up. It was really scary, and the residence hall director was worried after she brought me back and suggested I come over here. My parents don't know anything about this, and I don't want them to know. It's too much like what happened to Dad and I don't want Mom to worry. (*Her veneer and composure breaks, and she starts to sob vigorously.*) God! I'm such a mess. I'm ugly, stupid, can't get it together. What's the use?

At the least, Lisa is currently a polydrug experimenter, which does not bode well for possible addictive behavior. She also provides the worker significant information when she links her behavior to her father's. The worker makes an open-ended lead to allow Lisa to illuminate the source of her affect.

Dr. Max: (*Hands Lisa a tissue.*) Is the sobbing about feeling guilty about letting your parents down, or anger at yourself, or sorrow for your father's problems, or what? I'm not real clear.

Lisa: (*Sniffling.*) I . . . don't know. All of that and more. I mean, I love my dad and mom, but I hated the drinking and now here I am. Worse—the kinds of guys I go out with, like Robbie. God! He's in engineering just like Dad. He's like all the rest of the guys

I've gone out with except smarter, maybe. Real macho types, actually big babies. I attract them like a magnet, and I always fall for the jerk. Seems like all I ever do is take care of them. Jesus! I even wash his clothes and iron them. Then when I want some help from him, no dice. He'd left after we had that fight and went drinking. He didn't even know I'd been in the hospital. Then I wind up apologizing for the fight, but he decided to break up anyway. I can really pick 'em, can't I?

A clear pattern of an oldest child taking on heroic dimensions is starting to emerge, along with a placating component that nonassertively apologizes for someone else's bad behavior. Although ACOAs don't have some special biorhythms that send electromagnetic waves out to other addictive personalities, long and well-developed personality patterns fit like virus proteins into cell walls. The worker reflects on Lisa's merrygo-round of poor male relationships.

Dr. Max: So there seems to be a pattern of relationships where you give a lot and don't get much back, and it kinda reminds you of how things were at home? You seem pretty angry about that pattern.

Lisa: I guess, I dunno. I mean, I don't have the foggiest notion about what a regular family's like unless you call Dad throwing up every morning and Mom holding his head in the sink and calling into work for him, and him falling into the Christmas tree and knocking it over on Christmas Eve *normal*. Yeah, I am sorry for that all right. I don't know why Mom didn't divorce him. Yet here I am just spinning my wheels and not doing anything, like Mom. Yeah, you could say I'm angry—at me, though, for being so dumb.

What Lisa says is true of her knowledge of relationships. To her, the male relationships she has had, although one-sided and not fulfilling, follow the blueprint of what she saw at home. She has little idea about what relationships look like that are not dependent and enabling. She also brings up a well-learned message ("I'm dumb and incompetent") from her past as a discount. The worker response to the discount is a first step in extinguishing Lisa's negative perception of herself.

Dr. Max: The fact is you are doing something. You came here of your own free will. Nobody put a gun to your head.

Lisa: It wasn't easy. I just feel so bad about myself. I had to do something.

The worker continues her exploration of Lisa's father. Although this may seem to be an invitation for the client to externalize and regress to the past, the therapist is trying to build a connecting link in a dynamic way between past and present behavior.

Dr. Max: Tell me about what happened to your dad.

Lisa: Well, uh, like he has a drinking problem and wound up in like the hospital, but I mean I'm not like him. He got blasted for long stretches and stayed that way. Almost caused a divorce a couple of years back, but he's OK now.

As the counselor gently explores Lisa's use of alcohol and other drugs, the dynamics of her family of origin, and her current functioning in school, a clear picture emerges of a young woman who has served both as hero and scapegoat in her family, with some placating thrown in for good measure.

Her relationships with her boyfriends have the earmarks of a reenactment of her family of origin. Her contemporary use of alcohol and drugs puts her on the edge of abuse. In her own way, she has bottomed out. Her trip to the hospital has jarred her into an awareness that she has more than boyfriend and self-image problems. Her life is in crisis, and although she appears to own some of her feelings in an open and honest way, denial is a major component of her defense system. She has gotten out of control, and for the hero, that is a worst-case scenario.

Education

Given what the counselor now knows, she decides to intervene.

Dr. Max: I'd like for us to work together on some of those problems, particularly your self-concept. I'd like to give you a book to read between now and next week. It's called *Choicemaking* by Sharon Wegscheider-Cruse, and it has some stuff in it that will be helpful to you.

Lisa: What's it about?

Dr. Max: It's about families and particularly children who grew up in alcoholic families—

Lisa: HOLD ON! I'm not an alkie like my old man.

Dr. Max: Lisa, I want to be straight with you. No, you're not chemically dependent yet, but you're headed there. Look at the signs—a blackout, no parties or dates without booze, ready availability through friends who smoke marijuana and can get ups and downs easily. You took a test that puts you right on the line. (*Shows Lisa her MacAndrew score.*) Furthermore, both your past experiences and present ones are telling me you may have walked out of that alcoholic family, but it hasn't left you yet. (*Briefly explains the hero and scapegoat roles.*) Finally, as much as you may hate to hear it, the research says you're a high risk coming out of an alcoholic family, and your recent behavior suggests that you are even more at risk. I'm guessing that a lot of what you did in therapy focused on your dad getting better and not quite so much on you.

The primary thrust of therapy for the ACOA is to provide education. Information about *whats* and *whys* is extremely important to ACOAs who have little idea that the alcoholic family of origin could still be exerting such a profound influence on them.

Lisa: Well kinda, like they did do some stuff with Mark and me, but they didn't say any of the stuff you just told me. It's scary . . . and I guess I probably don't really want to hear about it . . . denial, huh? Yeah, I know that word big time. OK! I'll read the book.

Dr. Max: I am also wondering if you'd be willing to think about joining a group here along with individual counseling.

Lisa: I don't think I want to talk about this to anyone. I went through Alateen for a year. I hated that. They made us go through that for Dad's drinking problem and his rotten behavior to us, like we were responsible for his being a jerk or we needed sympathy.

Dr. Max: This is not an Alateen or Alanon group. This is a standard counseling group. Students like yourself with all kinds of problems. We cover a lot of different issues, and a number of yours would fit nicely. You said you were a risk taker—what do you have to lose?

Lisa: Well, OK, I guess it won't kill me.

The Counseling Group

Lisa's movement out of codependency will not occur just by reading her way out of it and talking to a therapist about codependency dynamics. A group of her college peers will be a safe proving ground for her personal development. Besides providing a sounding board and support system for one another, such counseling groups can help develop what Wegscheider-Cruse (1985, p. 133) calls a sense of responsibility and separateness. By developing her own individuality through sharing and receiving feedback from the group, Lisa's self-worth will grow. The group will also help her come to grips with lousy relationships and provide her with ideas on how to inoculate herself against dependency-eliciting males in particular.

The group will also provide her with the support she needs as she commits to giving herself choices for the future instead of living bound to the past. She will have to surrender her need to be protective and controlling. She'll also have to give up enabling or denying, not regret the past, fear less, and give up guilt and inadequacy (Wegscheider-Cruse, 1985, p. 146). The group will provide the emotional support she needs to move toward being neither codependent nor contradependent, but interdependent (Hogg & Frank, 1992).

Extracting a Commitment to Abstain

Dr. Max: I want you to commit to one more thing. I want you not to drink for one week. You said you were sick of the way you were operating, so for one week, I'd like you to take it a day at a time. I know you don't care much for the AA stuff, but I'd like your word and commitment on that.

Lisa: Well, my social life is down the tubes, and I could use the homework time. You'd trust me to do that on my word alone?

Dr. Max: Should I not? Is that impossible for you right now?

Lisa: Oh, no. I can do it, and I appreciate you for trusting me. It's just that I can't trust people very much.

Lisa's compliance is typical of a responsible and placating ACOA. Her inability to trust may mean a number of perceptual checks with the therapist, and perhaps the acting-out side of her will test some of the limits to which she so compliantly agrees. The therapist is aware of all this as she extracts the commitment to abstain. The therapist also knows that attempting to extract a promise to go to an AA meeting would probably push Lisa away from counseling. However, a responsible ACOA who gives her word will usually stick by it even though it may be difficult. In the not-too-distant future, the therapist will start to encourage Lisa to become more assertive, not only with others but with the therapist as well. For the present, though, Lisa needs information, emotional support, and to not use drugs, and those are the three critical ingredients of an initial crisis intervention with the ACOA.

Pitfalls

Finally, Wegscheider-Cruse (1985) proposes that the recovery process for the codependent, like for the chemical dependent, is continuous and believes that there are certain pitfalls that the recovering codependent must constantly guard against. She lists the following:

1. *Defiance.* Even though one may intellectually accept the diagnosis of co-dependency, anger about the injustices done may poison any growth.
2. *Secret recovery.* Suffering is not noble, and as the individual moves into recovery, successes toward individuation should not be kept a secret; otherwise, the old belief systems will not be expunged.
3. *Emotional binges.* During the process of replacing emotional numbness with emotional catharsis, the codependent who has not had any experience with handling emotions may become fixed on a continuous discharge of emotions, to the exclusion of making any effective behavioral changes.
4. *Avoiding change.* Recognizing and feeling the need to change occurs on cognitive and affective levels. Making the change calls for action behavior. It is scary to do this and easy to rationalize why action doesn't need to be taken right now.
5. *Living by mottoes and frameworks.* If the codependent does not play an active role in recovery but is instead a passive receptacle, all the therapy, literature, and workshops will do little good (pp. 152–154). The danger signs that indicate the codependent is dropping back into old familiar habits include fatigue, workaholism, dishonesty, self-pity, frustration, impatience, relaxing the recovery program, setting unreachable goals, forgetting gratitude, and self-righteousness (p. 155). Keeping constant perceptual checks with and listening to trusted others is important as a safeguard against the denial that is always too readily available to the codependent.

SUMMARY

The crisis of addiction is unique among all crisis categories. It is full of complexities, controversies, and contradictions. The prognosis for cure is poor because the condition is beset with multiple transcrisis points. A person may appear to be cured, only to relapse later into a drug episode more severe than before.

We have summarized several models of addiction, which attribute the problem to inherited, environmental, social, biological, chemical, or psychological causative factors. In terms of dynamics, it seems that there are many types and degrees of addiction. The most prevalent and puzzling dynamic revolves around the concept of psychological denial. The chemical dependent tends to deny adamantly that there is addiction and to deny that any problem exists related to the addictive behavior. The treatment and rehabilitation of clients are enormously complicated when significant others such as family, friends, and even bosses reinforce the narcissistic and sociopathic behavior of the chemical dependent by enabling the dependency.

The stabilization of an addictive crisis is difficult in that it usually requires, first, that the dependent become aware that he or she needs help, and second, that the person have some motivation to seek help. To that end, reasoning with the dependent about the problem is generally useless. Most often, direct confrontation and the generation of a crisis of significant proportions by some significant other such as an employer or spouse are the only ways to propel a drug abuser to treatment.

Clearly, addicted people need a multimodal approach to get through the crisis. Competent medical supervision and counseling are needed from the detoxification phase through aftercare. Group counseling is a primary operating mode because peers who are themselves recovering addicts are highly effective in breaking down denial systems of fellow chemical dependents. Extensive use is made of family, friends, employers, and support groups such as Alcoholics Anonymous, to supplement what professional caregivers can do for clients.

Adult children of alcoholics (ACOAs) have emerged as a treatment group during the 1980s. As with Al-Anon and Alateen, ACOA support groups have sprung up across the country. As with many components of drug addiction and treatment, conflicting views and controversy surround ACOAs. Whether problems ACOAs experience stem from identifiable maladaptive personality constructs as a result of having lived in alcoholic families or whether their substance-abusing parents are excuses for current maladaptive functioning is part of a continuing debate.

CLASSROOM EXERCISES

I. Addictive Behaviors

All of us have addictions, whether they be drinking alcohol, eating chocolate, gambling on blackjack, buying plaid sport coats, overspending on credit cards, or reading the sports page at breakfast. Anything that we start out wanting and not necessarily needing but end up either psychologically or physically craving may be considered addicting. Such addictive behaviors may be as simple as not being able to pass the candy bar machine to attending every University of Memphis basketball game—no matter what!

With the class divided into pairs, each person discusses a behavior around which the person seems to plan his or her life (at least in small part). Each student will isolate one such behavior and then commit to refraining from that behavior for one day. Keep a one-day journal listing your thoughts, feelings, and behaviors as you sweat out the day in abstinence. At the next class meeting, report on the difficulties you faced in forgoing your addiction for a day. This exercise should give people a small bit of empathy for the person who has a serious chemical dependency.

II. Denial

Once you have discussed in class what addictive behavior (in exercise I) does to you, separate again into pairs. One person takes the part of the interventionist and the other that of the client. Role-play for about 10 minutes. The client will engage in denial that the addiction is a problem, using any of the defense mechanisms described in this chapter. The interventionist's task is to crack the denial system of the client by using the confrontational skills listed in the chapter. Audiotape the role play and then reverse roles. Each member will listen to and critique the role play in regard to both denial and confrontation of the denial. Return to the large group, and discuss what each member learned from the experience. Questions may include the following:

1. How difficult was it for the worker to confront the client?
2. What kinds of feelings did both client and worker have as they carried the role play forward?
3. Did the worker confront the specific addicting behavior, the defense used to shield it from awareness, or the total personhood of the client?
4. Did the worker feel insecure or threatened while attempting the confrontation?
5. Did the client feel threatened, or was he or she able easily to fend off the worker's attempts to break down the denial?

RESOURCES

A host of web sites deal with drug addiction in general and alcoholism in particular. The sites have everything from directories of AA programs and inpatient treatment facilities to chat rooms and research bases. Use the search words "drug abuse" or "alcoholism."

REFERENCES

Adler, A. (1956). *The individual psychology of Alfred Adler: A systematic presentation in selections from his writing.* Ed. H. L. Ansbacher & R. R. Ansbacher. New York: Harper & Row.

Ahsen, A. (1993). Imagery treatment of alcoholism and drug abuse: A new methodology for treatment and research. *Journal of Mental Imagery, 17,* 1–60.

American Medical Association. (1956). Hospitalization of patients with alcoholism. *Journal of the American Medical Association, 162,* 750.

American Medical Association. (1993). *Factors contributing to the health care cost problem.* Chicago: Author.

American Psychiatric Association. (1994). *Diagnostic and statistical manual of mental disorders* (4th ed.). Washington, DC: Author.

Ames, G. M. (1985). American beliefs about alcoholism: Historical perspectives on the medical-moral controversy. In L. A. Bennett & G. M. Ames (Eds.), *The American experience with alcohol: Contrasting cultural perspectives* (pp. 23–40). New York: Plenum.

Angell, M., & Kassifer, J. P. (1994). Alcohol and other drugs—Toward a more rational and consistent policy. *New England Journal of Medicine, 331,* 537–539.

Anthony, J. C., Warner, L. A., & Kessler, R. C., (1997). In G. A. Marlatt & G. R. VandenBos (Eds.), *Addictive behaviors: Readings on etiology, prevention, and treatment* (pp. 3–40). Washington, DC: American Psychological Association.

Asbury, H. (1950). *The great illusion: An informal history of prohibition.* Garden City, NY: Doubleday.

Backover, A. (1991, May). Native Americans: Alcoholism, FAS puts a race at risk. *AACD Guidepost, 33,* 1, 3.

Barry, H. (1974). Psychological factors in alcoholism. In B. Kissin & H. Begleiter (Eds.), *The biology of alcoholism: Clinical pa-*

thology (Vol. 3, pp. 53–108). New York: Plenum.

Beasley, J. D. (1987). *Wrong diagnosis, wrong treatment: The plight of the alcoholic in America.* New York: Creative Infomatics.

Beck, A. T., Wright, F. D., Newman, C. F., & Liese, B. S. (1993). *Cognitive therapy of substance abuse.* New York: Guilford Press.

Besson, J., Aeby, F., Kasas, A., Lehert, P., & Potgeiter, A. (1998). *Alcoholism: Clinical and Experimental Research, 22*(3), 573–579.

Beutler, L. E., Patterson, K. M., Jacob, T., & Shoham, V. (1993). Matching treatment to alcoholism subtypes. *Psychotherapy, 30,* 463–472.

Bissell, L. (1982). Recovered alcoholic counselors. In E. M. Pattison & E. Kaufman (Eds.), *Encyclopedic handbook of alcoholism* (pp. 810–820). New York: Gardner Press.

Black, C. (1981). *It will never happen to me.* Denver, CO: M.A.C.

Blondell, R. D., Frierson, R. L., & Lippmann, S. B. (1996). Alcoholism. *Postgraduate Medicine,100,* 69–72.

Blum, K., Noble, E. Sheridan, P, Montgomery, A., Ritchie, T., Jagadeeswaran, P., Nogani, H., Briggs, A., & Cohn, J. (1990). Allellic association of human dopamine D2 receptor gene in alcoholism. *Journal of the American Medical Association, 263*(15), 2055–2060.

Blume, S. B. (1973). Iatrogenic alcoholism. *Quarterly Journal of Studies on Alcohol, 34,* 1348–1352.

Blume, S. B. (1978). Group psychotherapy in the treatment of alcoholism. In S. Zimberg, J. Wallace, & S. B. Blume (Eds.), *Practical approaches to alcoholism psychotherapy* (pp. 63–76). New York: Plenum.

Brabant, S., & Martof, M. (1993). Childhood experiences and complicated grief: A study of adult children of alcoholics. *In-*

ternational Journal of the Addictions, 28, 1111–1125.

Brill, L. (1981). *The clinical treatment of substance abusers.* New York: Free Press.

Brown, V. B., Ridgely, M. S., Pepper, B., Levine, I. S., & Ryglewicz, H. (1989). The dual crisis: Mental illness and substance abuse. *American Psychologist, 44,* 565–569.

Brownlee, S., Roberts, S., Cooper, M., Goode, E., Hetter, K., & Wright, A. (1994). Should cigarettes be outlawed? *U.S. News and World Report, 116*(15), 32–36, 38.

Bugliosi, V. (1996). *The Pheonix solution.* Beverly Hills, CA: Dove.

Cable, L. C., Noel, N. E., & Swanson, S. C. (1986). Clinical intervention with children of alcohol abusers. In D. C. Lewis & C. N. Williams (Eds.), *Providing care for children of alcoholics: Clinical and research perspectives* (pp. 65–80). Pompano Beach, FL: Health Communications.

Cadoret, R. J., & Gaith, A. (1978). Inheritance of alcoholism in adoptees. *British Journal of Psychiatry, 132,* 252–258.

Capps, S. C., Searight, H. R., Russo, J., & Temple, L. E. (1993). The Family of Origin Scale: Discriminant validity with adult children of alcoholics. *American Journal of Family Therapy, 21,* 274–277.

Carey, K. B. (1989). Emerging treatment guidelines for mentally ill chemical abusers. *Hospital and Community Psychiatry, 40,* 341–342, 349.

Carson, A. T., & Baker, R. C. (1994). Psychological correlates of codependency in women. *International Journal of the Addictions, 29,* 395–407.

Chalmers, D. K., & Wallace, J. (1978). Evaluation of patient progress. In S. Zimberg, J. Wallace, & S. B. Blume (Eds.), *Practical approaches to alcoholism psychotherapy* (pp. 255–279). New York: Plenum.

Chiauzzi, E. (1990). Breaking the patterns that lead to relapse. *Psychology Today, 23*(12), 18–19.

Chrisman, N. J. (1985). Alcoholism: Illness or disease. In L. A. Bennett & G. M. Ames (Eds.), *The American experience with alcohol: Contrasting cultural perspectives* (pp. 7–22). New York: Plenum.

Collette, L. (1990). After the anger, what then? *The Family Therapy Networker, 14,* 22–31.

Collier, A. (1989). To deal and die in LA. *Ebony, 44*(10), 106–108.

Cormier, L. S., & Hackney, H. (1987). *The professional counselor: A process guide to helping.* Upper Saddle River, NJ: Prentice Hall.

Cormier, W. H., & Cormier, L. S. (1985). *Interviewing strategies for helpers: Fundamental skills and cognitive behavioral interventions* (2nd ed.). Pacific Grove, CA: Brooks/Cole.

Cormier, W. H., & Cormier, L. S. (1991). *Interviewing strategies for helpers: Fundamental skills and cognitive behavioral interventions* (3rd ed.). Pacific Grove, CA: Brooks/Cole.

Cornish, J. W., McNicholas, L. F., & O'Brien, C.P. (1995). Treatment of substance related disorder. In A. F. Schatzberg & C. B. Nemeroff (Eds.), *Textbook of psychopharmacology.* Washington, DC: American Psychiatric Association.

Costello, R. M. (1982). Evaluation of alcoholism treatment programs. In E. M. Pattison & E. Kaufman (Eds.), *Encyclopedic handbook of alcoholism* (pp. 1179–1210). New York: Gardner Press.

Cotton, N. S. (1979). The familial incidence of alcoholism. *Journal of Studies on Alcohol, 40,* 89–115.

Cowan, G., & Warren, L. M. (1994). Codependency and gender stereotyped traits. *Sex Roles, 30,* 631–645.

D'Andrea, L. M., Fisher, G. L., & Harrison, T. C. (1994). Cluster analysis of adult children of alcoholics. *International Journal of the Addictions, 29,* 565–582.

DeJong, W. (1994). Relapse prevention: An emerging technology for promoting long-term abstinence. *International Journal of the Addictions, 29,* 681–785.

De Leon, G. (1989). Psychopathology and substance abuse: What is being learned from research in therapeutic communities. *Journal of Psychoactive Drugs, 21,* 177–188.

Denzin, N. K. (1987). *The recovering alcoholic.* Newbury Park, CA: Sage.

DiClemente, C. C., Carroll, K. M., Connors, G. J., & Kadden, R. M. (1994). Process assessment in treatment matching research. *Journal of Studies on Alcohol, 12* (December supplement), 156–162.

Dinkmeyer, D. C., & Muro, J. (1979). *Group counseling: Theory and practice.* Itasca, IL: F. E. Peacock.

Dinkmeyer, D. C., Pew, W. L., & Dinkmeyer, D. C., Jr. (1979). *Adlerian counseling and psychotherapy.* Pacific Grove, CA: Brooks/Cole.

Dodd, D. T., & Roberts, R. L. (1994). Differences among adult COAs and adult non-COAs on levels of self-esteem, depression, and anxiety. *Journal of Addictions and Offender Counseling, 14,* 49–56.

Donovan, D. M., Kadden, R. M., DiClemente, C. C., & Carroll, K. M. (1994). Issues in the selection and development of therapies in alcoholism treatment matching research. *Journal of Studies on Alcohol, 12* (December supplement), 138–148.

Donovan, D. M., & Mattson, M. E. (1994). Alcoholism treatment matching research: Methodological and clinical approaches. *Journal of Studies on Alcohol, 12* (December supplement), 5–14.

Doweiko, H. E. (1990). *Concepts of chemical dependency.* Pacific Grove, CA: Brooks/Cole.

Doweiko, H. E. (1996). *Concepts of chemical dependency* (3rd ed.). Pacific Grove, CA: Brooks/Cole.

Doweiko, H. E. (1999). *Concepts of chemical dependency* (4th ed.). Pacific Grove, CA: Brooks/Cole.

Drug Abuse Warning Network (DAWN). (1983). Data from the Drug Abuse Warning Network statistical series, Quarterly Report, Provisional Data Series G, No. 12 (July–September). Rockville, MD: National Institute on Drug Abuse.

Dupont, R. L. (1984). *Getting tough on gateway drugs.* Washington, DC: American Psychiatric Press.

Edwards, G. T. (1985). Appalachia: The effects of cultural values on the consumption of alcohol. In L. A. Bennett & G. M. Ames (Eds.), *The American experience with alcohol* (pp. 131–146). New York: Plenum.

Ellis, A. (1987, January). *Employee assistance training workshop: A rational-emotive approach.* New York: Institute for Rational-Emotive Therapy.

Ellis, A., McInerney, J. F., DiGiuseppe, R., & Yeager, R. J. (1988). *Rational emotive therapy with alcoholics and substance abusers.* New York: Pergamon.

Emonson, D., & Vanderbeek, R. (1995). The use of amphetamines in the U.S. Air Force tactical operations during Desert Shield and Storm. *Aviation, Space, and Environmental Medicine, 66*(3), 260–263.

Fischer, J. L., Spann, L., & Crawford, D. W. (1991). Measuring codependency. *Alcoholism Treatment Quarterly, 8,* 87–100.

Fisher, G. L., Jenkins, S. J., Harrison, T. C., & Jesch, K. (1993). Personality characteristics of adult children of alcoholics, other adults from dysfunctional families, and adults from nondysfunctional families. *International Journal of the Addictions, 28,* 477–485.

Ford, B. (1987). *Betty: A glad awakening.* New York: Doubleday.

Frances, R. J. (1988). Update on alcohol and drug disorder treatment. *Journal of Clinical Psychiatry, 49,* 13–17.

Garbutt, J., West, S., Carey, T. Lohr, K., & Crews, F. (1999). Pharmacological treatment of alcohol dependence: A review of the evidence. *Journal of the American Medical Association, 281*(14), 1318–1325.

Gatch, M., & Lal, H. (1998). Pharmacological treatment of alcoholism. *Progress in Neuro Psychopharmacology and Biological Psychiatry, 22*(6), 917–944.

Gelles, R. J., & Straus, M. A. (1988). *Intimate violence: The definitive study of the causes and consequences of abuse in the American family.* New York: Simon & Schuster.

George, R. L. (1990). *Counseling the chemically dependent: Theory and practice.* Upper Saddle River, NJ: Prentice Hall.

George, R. L., & Dustin, D. (1988). *Group counseling: Theory and practice.* Upper Saddle River, NJ: Prentice Hall.

Giunta, C. T., & Compas, B. E. (1994). Adult children of alcoholics: Are they unique? *Journal of Studies on Alcohol, 55,* 600–606.

Gogek, E. B. (1994). The dry drunk syndrome: Subtype of depression? *American Journal of Psychiatry, 151,* 947–948.

Goode, E. (1984). *Drugs in American society.* New York: Knopf.

Goodwin, D. W. (1979). Alcoholism and heredity. Archives of General Psychiatry, 36, 57–61.

Gorski, T. T. (1994, March–April). A suggestion for conceptualizing dual diagnosis: A systematic analysis to help cut confusion and mismanagement. *Behavioral Health Management,* pp. 50–53.

Graham, D. (Speaker). (1986). *Denial, dependency, and codependency in drug treat-*

ment programs (Cassette Recording No. 8–1). Memphis: Department of Counseling and Personnel Services, Memphis State University.

Graubart, A. V. (1991, April). *The two faces of Eve/Ed: Dual diagnosis (Alcoholism/substance abuse and psychiatric disorders).* Paper presented at Crisis Convening XV, Chicago.

Greene, R. L. (1980). *The MMPI: An interpretative manual.* New York: Grune & Stratton.

Group for the Advancement of Psychiatry. (1990). Substance abuse disorders: A psychiatric priority. *American Journal of Psychiatry, 148,* 1291–1300.

Guffey, D. G. (1992). Ritalin: What educators and parents should know. *Journal of Instructional Psychology, 19,* 167–169.

Haaken, J. (1993). From Al-Anon to ACOA: Codependence and the reconstruction of caregiving. *Signs, 18,* 321–345.

Hall, C. W., Bolen, L. M., & Webster, R. E. (1994). Adjustment issues with adult children of alcoholics. *Journal of Clinical Psychology, 50,* 786–792.

Hamburg, B. A., Kraemer, H. C., & Jahnke, W. (1975). A hierarchy of drug use in adolescence: Behavioral and attitudinal correlates of substantive drug use. *American Journal of Psychiatry, 132,* 1155–1163.

Hands, M., & Dear, G. (1994). Codependency: A critical review. *Drug and Alcohol Review, 13,* 437–445.

Hannah, F. (Speaker). (1996). *Models for understanding and treating chemical dependency* (Cassette Recording No. 8-02-16-96-B). Memphis, TN: Memphis City Schools Mental Health Center/University of Memphis Department of Counseling, Educational Psychology and Research.

Hardwick, C. J., Hansen, N. D., & Bairnsfather, L. (1995). Are adult children of alcoholics unique? A study of object relations and reality testing. *International Journal of the Addictions, 30,* 525–539.

Harvey, J. M., Boswell, D. L., & Romans, J. S. (1995). The relationship of self-perception and stress in adult children of alcoholics and their peers. *Journal of Drug Education, 29,* 23–29.

Hawkins, C. A., & Hawkins, R. C. (1995). Development and validation of an Adult Children of Alcoholics Tool. *Research on Social Work Practice, 5,* 317–339.

Hay, W. M., & Nathan, P. E. (Eds.). (1982). *Clinical case studies in the behavioral treatment of alcoholism.* New York: Plenum.

Heath, D. B. (1978). The sociocultural and model of alcohol use: Problems and prospects. *Journal of Operation Psychiatry, 9,* 56–66.

Heath, D. B. (1985). American experience with alcohol: Commonalities and contrasts. In L. A. Bennett & G. M. Ames (Eds.), *The American experience with alcohol: Contrasting cultural experiences* (pp. 461–480). New York: Plenum.

Hibbard, S. (1993). Adult children of alcoholics: Narcissism, shame, and the differential effects of paternal and maternal alcoholism. *Psychiatry Interpersonal and Biological Processes, 56,* 153–162.

Hinkin, C. H., & Kahn, M. W. (1995). Psychological symptomatology in spouses and adult children of alcoholics: An examination of the hypothesized personality characteristics of codependency. *International Journal of the Addictions, 30,* 843–861.

Hoffman, H. (1970). Depression and defensiveness in self-descriptive moods of alcoholics. *Psychological Reports, 26,* 23–26.

Hogg, J. A., & Frank, M. L. (1992). Toward an interpersonal model of codependence and contradependence. *Journal of Counseling and Development, 70,* 371–375.

Holder, H., Longabraugh, R., Miller, W., & Rubonis, A. (1991). The cost effectiveness of treatment for alcoholism: A first approximation. *Journal of Studies on Alcohol, 52,* 517–540.

Huberty, J. D., & Brandon, J. C. (1982). Nonmedical alcohol detoxification. In E. M. Pattison & E. Kaufman (Eds.), *Encyclopedic handbook of alcoholism* (pp. 1076–1085). New York: Gardner Press.

Hughes, R. (1993). Bitch, bitch, bitch . . . *Psychology Today, 26*(5), pp. 28–30.

Inclan, J., & Hernandez, M. (1992). Cross-cultural perspectives and codependence: The case of poor Hispanics. *American Journal of Orthopsychiatry, 62,* 245–255.

Isenhart, C. & Silversmith, D. (1997). MMPI-2 response styles: Generalization to alcohol assessment. In G. A. Marlatt & G. R. VandenBos (Eds.), *Addictive behaviors: Readings on etiology, prevention, and treatment* (pp. 340–354). Washington, DC: American Psychological Association.

Jellinek, E. M. (1946). Phases in the drinking history of alcoholics. *Quarterly Journal of Studies on Alcohol, 7,* 1–88.

Jellinek, E. M. (1952). Phases of alcohol addiction. *Quarterly Journal of Studies on Alcohol, 13,* 673–684.

Jellinek, A. M. (1960). *The disease concept of alcoholism.* New Haven, CT: Hillhouse Press.

Jenkins, S. J., Fisher, G. L., & Harrison, T. C. (1993). Adult children of dysfunctional families: Childhood roles. *Journal of Mental Health Counseling, 15,* 310–319.

Jessor, R., Chase, J. D., & Donovan, J. E. (1980). Psychosocial correlates of marijuana use and problem drinking in a national sample of adolescents. *American Journal of Public Health, 70,* 604–613.

Jessor, R., & Jessor, S. L. (1977). *Problem behavior and psychosocial development: A longitudinal study of youth.* New York: Academic Press.

Johnson Institute. (1972). *Alcoholism: A treatable disease.* Minneapolis, MN: Author.

Johnson, V. E. (1980). *I'll quit tomorrow.* Minneapolis, MN: Johnson Institute.

Johnson, V. E. (1986). *Intervention: A professional guide.* Minneapolis, MN: Johnson Institute.

Kaminer, W. (1992). *I'm dysfunctional, you're dysfunctional.* New York: Addison-Wesley.

Kandel, D. B., Yamaguchi, K., & Chen, K. (1992). Stages of progression in drug involvement from adolescence to adulthood: Further evidence for the gateway theory. *Journal of Studies on Alcohol, 53,* 447–458.

Kaplan, H. I., & Sadock, B. J. (1990). *Pocket handbook of clinical psychiatry.* Baltimore, MD: Williams & Wilkins.

Kaplan, H. I., Sadock, B. J., & Grebb, J. A. (1994). *Synopsis of psychiatry* (7th ed.). Baltimore, MD: Williams & Wilkins.

Kashubeck, S. (1994). Adult children of alcoholics and psychological distress. *Journal of Counseling and Development, 72,* 538–543.

Katz, S., & Liu, A. (1991). *The codependency conspiracy.* New York: Warner Books.

Kaufman, E., & Pattison, E. M. (1982a). The family and alcoholism. In E. M. Pattison & E. Kaufman (Eds.), *Encyclopedic handbook of alcoholism* (pp. 662–672). New York: Gardner Press.

Kaufman, E., & Pattison, E. M. (1982b). The family and network therapy in alcoholism. In E. M. Pattison & E. Kaufman (Eds.), *Encyclopedic handbook of alcoholism* (pp. 1022–1032). New York: Gardner Press.

Kearney, R. J. (1996). *Within the wall of denial: Conquering addictive behaviors.* New York: Norton.

Kerr, A. S., & Hill, E. W. (1992). An exploratory study comparing ACOAs to non-ACOAs on current family relationships. *Alcoholism Treatment Quarterly, 9,* 23–38.

Kershaw-Bellemare, R., & Mosak, H. H. (1993). Adult children of alcoholics: An Adlerian perspective. *Journal of Alcohol and Drug Education, 38,* 105–119.

Kivlahan, D. R., Heiman, J. R., Wright, R. C., Mundt, J. W., & Shupe, J. A. (1991). Treatment cost and rehospitalization rate in schizophrenic outpatients with a history of substance abuse. *Hospital and Community Psychiatry, 41,* 609–614.

Knack, M. A., & Murray, R. (Speakers). (1996). *Chemical dependency treatment issues* (Cassette Recording No. 8-02-08-96-A). Memphis, TN: Memphis Veterans Administration Medical Center/University of Memphis Department of Counseling, Educational Psychology and Research.

Knox, W. J. (1976). Objective psychological measurement and alcoholism: Review of the literature, 1971–72. *Psychological Reports, 38,* 1023–1050 (Monograph Suppl. 1-V38).

Knox, W. J. (1980). Objective psychological measurement and alcoholism: Survey of the literature, 1974. *Psychological Reports, 47,* 51–68 (Monograph Suppl. 1-V47).

Kotz, M., & Covington, E. (1995). Alcoholism. In R. E. Rakel (Ed.), *Conn's current therapy.* Philadelphia, PA: Saunders.

Kranzler, H., & Anton, R. (1994). Implications of recent neuropharmacologic research for understanding the etiology and development of alcoholism. *Journal of Consulting and Clinical Psychology, 62,* 1116–1126.

Kristianson, P. A. (1970). A comparison study of two alcoholic groups and control group. *British Journal of Medical Psychology, 43,* 161–175.

Larsen, E. (1983). *Basics of codependency.* (Audiotape). Brooklyn Park, MN: E. Larsen Enterprises.

Lawson, G. W., Ellis, D. C., & Rivers, P. C. (Eds.). (1984). *Essentials of chemical dependency counseling.* Rockville, MD: Aspen Systems Corp.

Lease, S. H., & Yanico, B. J. (1995). Evidence of validity for the Children of Alcoholics Screening test. *Measurement and Evaluation in Counseling and Development, 27,* 200–210.

Levine, H. (1984). The alcohol problem in America: From temperance to alcoholism. *British Journal of Addiction, 79,* 109–119.

Lewis, J. A., Dana, R., & Blevins, G. (1988). *Substance abuse counseling.* Pacific Grove, CA: Brooks/Cole.

Lieber, C. S. (1995). Medical disorders of alcoholism. *New England Journal of Medicine, 333,* 1058–1065.

Liepman, M., White, W. T., & Nirenberg, T. D. (1986). Children in alcoholic families. In D. C. Lewis & C. N. Williams (Eds.), *Providing care for children of alcoholics: Clinical and research perspectives* (pp. 39–64). Pompano Beach, FL: Health Communications.

Litten, R., & Allen, J. (1998). Advances in medications for alcohol treatment. *Psychopharmacology, 139* (1–2), 20–33.

Longabaugh, R., Wirtz, P. W., DiClemente, C. C., & Litt, M. (1994). Issues in the development of client-treatment matching hypotheses. *Journal of Studies on Alcohol, 12,* 46–59.

Longabaugh, R., Wirtz, P.W., Beattie, M., Noel, N., & Stout, R. (1997). Matching treatment focus to patient social investment and support: Eighteen month follow-up results. In G. Marlatt & G. VandenBos (Eds.), *Addictive behaviors: Readings on etiology, prevention, and treatment* (pp. 602–628). Washington, DC: American Psychological Association.

Lukoff, I. F. (1980). Toward a sociology of drug use. In D. J. Lettieri, M. Sayers, & H. W. Pearson (Eds.), *Theories on drug abuse: Selected contemporary perspectives* (NIDA Research Monograph No. 30). Rockville, MD: National Institute on Drug Abuse.

Lyon, D., & Greenberg, J. (1991). Evidence of codependency in women with an alcoholic parent: Helping out Mr. Wrong. *Journal of Personality and Social Psychology, 61,* 435–439.

Lyon, M. A., & Seefeldt, R. W. (1995). Failure to validate personality characteristics of adult children of alcoholics: A replication and extension. *Alcoholism Treatment Quarterly, 12,* 69–85.

MacAndrew, C., & Edgerton, R. B. (1969). *Drunken comportment.* Chicago: Aldine.

MacDonald, J. (1961). *The murderer and his victim.* Springfield, IL: Charles C Thomas.

Mann, K. (1996). The pharmacological treatment of alcohol dependence: Needs and possibilities. *Alcohol and Alcoholism, 31*(1), 55–58.

Marlatt, G. A. (1997). Introduction. In G. A. Marlatt & G. R. VandenBos (Eds.), *Addictive behaviors: Readings on etiology, prevention, and treatment* (pp. xi–xxv). Washington, DC: American Psychological Association.

Marlatt, G. A., & Gordon, J. R. (Eds.). (1985). *Relapse prevention.* New York: Guilford Press.

Martin, J. T. (1995). Intimacy, loneliness and openness to feeling in adult children of alcoholics. *Health and Social Work, 20,* 52–59.

Mathew, R. D., Wilson, W. H., Blazer, D. G., & George, L. K. (1993). Psychiatric disorders in adult children of alcoholics: Data from the epidemiologic catchment area project. *American Journal of Psychiatry, 150,* 793–800.

Mattson, M. E., & Donovan, D. M. (1994). Clinical applications: The transition from research to practice. *Journal of Studies on Alcohol, 12* (December supplement), 163–166.

Maxwell, R. (1986). *Breakthrough: What to do when alcoholism or chemical dependency hits close to home.* New York: Ballantine.

McCrady, B. S. (1982). Marital dysfunction: Alcoholism and marriage. In E. M. Pattison & E. Kaufman (Eds.), *Encyclopedic handbook of alcoholism* (pp. 673–685). New York: Gardner Press.

McCrory, J. (Speaker). (1987). *Aftercare and co-dependency in drug treatment programs* (Cassette Recording No. 8-4). Memphis: Department of Counseling and Personnel Services, Memphis State University.

McDermott, P., Alterman, A., Brown, L., Zaballero, A., Snider, E., & McKay, J. (1997). Construct refinement and confirmation of the Addiction Severity Index. In G. A. Marlatt & G. R. VandenBos (Eds.), *Addictive behaviors: Readings on etiology, prevention, and treatment* (pp. 323–339). Washington, DC: American Psychological Association.

McGinnis, J. M., & Foege, W. H. (1993). Actual causes of death in the United States. *Journal of the American Medical Association, 270,* 2207–2212.

McGowan, S. (1991, October). Effects of parental alcoholism. *AACD Guidepost,* pp. 1, 8, 10.

McKay, J. R., & Maistro, S. A. (1993). An overview and critique of advances in the treatment of alcohol use disorders. *Drugs and Society, 8,* 1–29.

McLellan, A. T., Grissom, G., Zanis, D., & Randall, M. (1997). Problem-service matching in addiction treatment: A prospective study in four program. *Archives of General Psychiatry, 54*(8), 730–735.

McMullin, R. E., & Giles, T. R. (1981). *Cognitive behavior therapy: A restructuring approach.* New York: Grune & Stratton.

Meichenbaum, D. (1985). *Stress-inoculation training.* New York: Pergamon Press.

Mendelson, J. H., & Mello, N. K. (Eds.). (1979). *The diagnosis and treatment of alcoholism.* New York: McGraw-Hill.

Miller, G. (1983). *SASSI: Substance Abuse Subtle Screening Inventory.* Bloomington, IN: SASSI Institute.

Miller, W. R., Genefield, G., & Tonigan, J. S. (1993). Enhancing motivation for change in problem drinking: A controlled comparison of two therapist styles. *Journal of Consulting and Clinical Psychology, 61,* 455–462.

Miller, W. R. & Tonigan, J. S. (1997). Assessing drinkers' motivation for change: The Stage of Change Readiness and Treatment Eagerness Scale (SOCRATES). In G. A. Marlatt, & G. R. VandenBos (Eds.), *Addictive behaviors: Readings on etiology, prevention, and treatment* (pp. 355–369). Washington, DC: American Psychological Association.

Myer, R. A., Peterson, S. E., & Stoffel-Rosales, M. (1991). Co-dependency: An examination of underlying assumptions. *Journal of Mental Health Counseling, 13,* 449–458.

Nash, J., & Park, A. (1997). Addicted. *Time, 149*(18), 68–76.

National Foundation for Brain Research. (1992). *The cost of disorders of the brain.* Washington, DC: Author.

National Institute on Alcohol Abuse and Alcoholism, Project Match Research Group. (1998). Matching alcoholism treatments to client heterogeneity: Treatment main effects and matching effects on drinking during treatment. *Journal of Studies in Alcohol, 59*(6), 631–639.

Neff, J. A. (1994). Adult children of alcoholic or mentally ill parents: Alcohol consumption and psychological distress in a tri-ethnic community study. *Addictive Behaviors, 19,* 185–197.

Neisser, U. (1976). *Cognition and reality: Principles and implications of cognitive psychology.* San Francisco: W. H. Freeman.

Noble, E., Blum, K., Ritchie, T., Montgomery, A, & Sheridan, P. (1991). Allelic association of the D2 dopamine receptor gene with receptor-binding characteristics in alcoholism. *Archives of General Psychiatry, 48,* 648–654.

Nielsen, B., Nielsen, A., & Wraae, O. (1998). Patient-treatment matching improves compliance of alcoholics in outpatient treatment. *Journal of Nervous and mental Disease, 186*(12), 752–760.

O'Brien, P. E., & Gaborit, M. (1992). Co-dependency: A disorder separate from chemical dependency. *Journal of Clinical Psychology, 48,* 129–136.

Oetting, E. R., & Beauvais, F. (1986). Peer cluster theory: Drugs and the adolescent. *Journal of Counseling and Development, 65,* 17–22.

Ohlsen, M. (1970). *Group counseling.* New York: Holt, Rinehart & Winston.

Ornstein, P. (1976). The Alcadd Test as a predictor of post-hospital drinking behavior. *Psychological Reports, 43,* 611–617.

Parker, C. (Speaker). (1986). *Alcoholic inpatient treatment* (Cassette Recording No. 8-2). Memphis: Department of Counseling and Personnel Services, Memphis State University.

Pattison, E. M., & Kaufman, E. (Eds.). (1982a). *Encyclopedic handbook of alcoholism.* New York: Gardner Press.

Pattison, E. M., & Kaufman, E. (1982b). The alcoholism syndrome: Definitions and models. In E. M. Pattison & E. Kaufman (Eds.), *Encyclopedic handbook of alcoholism* (pp. 3–30). New York: Gardner Press.

Peele, S. (1986). The "cure" for adolescent drug abuse: Worse than the problem? *Journal of Counseling and Development, 65,* 23–24.

Perez, J. F. (1985). *Counseling the alcoholic.* Muncie, IN: Accelerated Development.

Pernanen, K. (1976). The biology of alcoholism. In B. Kissin & H. Begleiter (Eds.), *Social aspects of alcoholism* (Vol. 4, pp. 42–57). New York: Plenum.

Polcin, D. L. (1992). A comprehensive model for adolescent chemical dependency treatment. *Journal of Counseling and Development, 70,* 376–382.

Poley, W., Lea, G., & Vibe, G. (1979). *Alcoholism: A treatment manual.* New York: Gardner Press.

Potter-Efron, P. S., & Potter-Efron, R. T. (1991). Anger as a treatment concern with alcoholics and affected family members. *Alcoholism Treatment Quarterly, 8,* 31–46.

Project Match Research Group. (1998). Matching patients with alcohol disorders to treatments: Clinical implications from Project MATCH. *Journal of Mental Health, 7*(6), 589–602.

Rodney, H. E. (1994). What differentiates ACOAs and non-ACOAs on a Black college campus? *Journal of American College Health, 43,* 57–63.

Safer, D. J. (1994). The impact of recent lawsuits on methylphenidate sales. *Clinical Pediatrics, 33,* 166–168.

Saitz, R., Mulvey, P., Plough, A., & Samet, J. (1997). Physician unawareness of serious substance abuse. *American Journal of Drug and Alcohol Abuse, 23*(3), 342–354.

Schaef, A. W. (1986). *Co-dependence misunderstood—mistreated.* San Francisco: Harper & Row.

Schafer, C. (1989, March). Many adults face memories of alcoholic home. *AACD Guidepost,* pp. 1, 8, 25.

Schmidt, E. (1996). Rational recovery: Finding an alternative for addiction treatment. *Alcoholism Treatment Quarterly, 14*(4), 47–57.

Schuckit, M. A. (1984). *Drug and alcohol abuse: A clinical guide to diagnosis and treatment* (2nd ed.). New York: Plenum Press.

Schuckit, M. A. (1986). Primary men alcoholics with histories of suicide attempts. *Journal of Studies on Alcohol, 47,* 78–81.

Schuckit, M. A. (1995). *Drug and alcohol abuse: A clinical guide to diagnosis and treatment* (4th ed.). New York: Plenum Press.

Schuckit, M. A., & Rayses, V. (1979). Ethanol ingestion: Differences in blood acetaldehyde concentrations in relatives of alcoholics and controls. *Science, 203,* 54–55.

Selwyn, P. A. (1993). Illicit drug use revisited: What a long strange trip it's been. *Annals of Internal Medicine, 119,* 1044–1046.

Senchak, M., Leonard, K., Greene, B., & Carroll, A. (1995). Comparisons of adult children of alcoholics, divorced, and control parents in four outcome domains. *Psychology of Addictive Behaviors, 9*(3), 147–156.

Shafer, H. J. (1986). Conceptual crises and the addictions: A philosophy of science perspective. *Journal of Substance Abuse Treatment, 3,* 285–296.

Shearer, R. J. (1968). *Manual of alcoholism of the American Medical Association.* Washington, DC: American Medical Association.

Sher, K. J., Walitzer, K. S., Wood, P. K., & Brent, E. E. (1991). Characteristics of children of alcoholics: Putative risk factors, substance abuse, and psychopathology. *Journal of Abnormal Psychology, 100,* 427–448.

Sheridan, M. J. (1995). A psychometric assessment of the Children of Alcoholics Screening Test (CAST). *Journal of Studies on Alcohol, 56,* 156–160.

Sheridan, M. J., & Green, R. G. (1993). Family dynamics and individual characteristics of adult children of alcoholics: An empirical analysis. *Journal of Social Service Research, 17,* 73–97.

Shulman, B. (1973). *Contributions to individual psychology: Selected papers of Bernard Shulman.* Chicago: Alfred Adler Institute.

Shupe, L. (1953). Alcohol and crime. *Journal of Criminal Law and Criminal Political Science, 44,* 661–664.

Smith, J. W. (1982). Treatment of alcoholism in aversion conditioning hospitals. In

E. M. Pattison & E. Kaufman (Eds.), *Encyclopedic handbook of alcoholism* (pp. 874–884). New York: Gardner Press.

Sobell, M. B., & Sobell, L. C. (1978). *Behavioral treatment of alcohol problems: Individualized therapy and controlled drinking.* New York: Plenum Press.

Soyka, M. (1999). Efficacy of outpatient alcoholism treatment. *Addiction, 94*(1), 48–50.

Spiegel, D., Hadley, P. A., & Hadley, R. G. (1970). Personality test patterns of rehabilitation center alcoholics, psychiatric inpatients, and normals. *Journal of Clinical Psychology, 26,* 366–371.

Spotts, J. V., & Shontz, F. C. (1980). A life theme of chronic drug abuse. In D. J. Lettieri, M. Sayers, & H. W. Pearson (Eds.), *Theories on drug abuse: Selected contemporary perspectives* (NIDA Research Monograph No. 30, pp. 59–70). Rockville, MD: National Institute on Drug Abuse.

Stuckey, R. F., & Harrison, J. S. (1982). The alcoholism rehabilitation center. In E. M. Pattison & E. Kaufman (Eds.), *Encyclopedic handbook of alcoholism* (pp. 865–873). New York: Gardner Press.

Svanum, S., & McAdoo, W. B. (1989). Predicting rapid relapse following treatment for chemical dependence: A matched subject design. *Journal of Consulting and Clinical Psychology, 34,* 1027–1030.

Trice, H. M., & Beyer, J. M. (1982). Job-based alcoholism programs: Motivating problem drinkers to rehabilitation. In E. M. Pattison & E. Kaufman (Eds.), *Encyclopedic handbook of alcoholism* (pp. 954–978). New York: Gardner Press.

Trois, F. P. (1995). An examination of Cermak's conceptualization of codependency as personality disorder. *Alcoholism Treatment Quarterly, 12,* 1–15.

Turbo, R. (1989). Drying out is just a start: Alcoholism. *Medical World News, 30,* 56–63.

Tweed, S. H., & Ryff, C. D. (1991). Adult children of alcoholics: Profiles of wellness amidst distress. *The Journal of Studies on Alcohol, 52,* 133–141.

Uhle, S. M. (1994). Codependence: Contextual variables in the language of social pathology. *Issues in Mental Health Nursing, 15,* 307–313.

U.S. Bureau of the Census. (1995). *Statistical abstract of the United States: 1995* (115th ed.). Washington, DC: U.S. Department of Commerce.

Vaillant, G. E. (1983). *The natural history of alcoholism: Causes, patterns, and paths to recovery.* Cambridge, MA: Harvard University Press.

Vaillant, G. E., & Milofsky, E. (1982). The etiology of alcoholism: A prospective viewpoint. *American Psychologist, 37,* 494–503.

Walfish, S., Stenmark, D. E., Shealy, S. E., & Krone, A. M. (1992). MMPI profiles of women in codependency treatment. *Journal of Personality Assessment, 58,* 211–214.

Wallace, J. (1978). Critical issues in alcoholism therapy. In S. Zimberg, J. Wallace, & S. B. Blume (Eds.), *Practical approaches to alcoholism psychotherapy* (pp. 31–46). New York: Plenum.

Wegscheider-Cruse, S. (1984). Codependency: The therapeutic void. In *Codependency: An emerging issue* (pp. 1–19). Pompano Beach, FL: Health Communications.

Wegscheider-Cruse, S. (1985). *Choice-making for codependents, adult children, and spirituality seekers.* Pompano Beach, FL: Health Communications.

Wegscheider-Cruse, S. (1989). *Another chance: Hope and health for the alcoholic family* (2nd ed.). Palo Alto, CA: Science and Behavior Books.

Weisner, C., Greenfield, T., & Room, R. (1995). Trends in treatment of alcohol problems in the U.S. general population, 1979 through 1990. *American Journal of Public Health, 85,* 55–60.

Wills, T. A., & Shiffman, S. (1985). Coping and substance abuse: A conceptual framework. In S. Shiffman & T. A. Wills (Eds.), *Coping and substance abuse* (pp. 3–24). Orlando, FL: Academic Press.

Witkin, G., & Griffin, J. (1994). The new opium wars. *U.S. News and World Report, 117*(114), 39–44.

Woititz, J. G. (1983). *Adult children of alcoholics.* Pompano Beach, FL: Health Communications.

Wolin, S. J., & Wolin, S. (1995). Resilience among youth growing up in substance abusing families. *Pediatric Clinics of North America, 42,* 415–429.

World Health Organization (WHO). (1952). Expert committee on mental health, alcoholism subcommittee. Second report. (World Health Organization Technical

Service Report No. 18). In H. Milt (Ed.), *Basic handbook on alcoholism.* Fairhaven, NJ: Scientific Aids Publication.

Wright, P. H., & Wright, K. D. (1990). Measuring codependents' close relationships: A preliminary study. *Journal of Substance Abuse, 2,* 335–344.

Zimberg, S. (1982). Psychotherapy in the treatment of alcoholism. In E. M. Pattison & E. Kaufman (Eds.), *Encyclopedic handbook of alcoholism* (pp. 999–1010). New York: Gardner Press.

Zwerling, I. (1959). Psychiatric findings in an interdisciplinary study of 46 alcoholic patients. *Quarterly Journal of Studies on Alcohol, 20,* 543–554.

CHAPTER NINE

Personal Loss:
Bereavement and Grief

A family of four (mother, father, daughter, and son) were enjoying a relaxing weekend at a beautiful beach. In an instant, their lives were shattered forever. The daughter, age 20, a college junior, and the son, age 18, a college freshman, were both killed while riding a wave runner just a few yards from where the parents were watching from the beach. A speedboat collided with the wave runner, slicing it in two. This life-shattering event happened the very day the revision to this chapter was finished. Losses akin to this story abound in our society. Every day, somewhere, unfortunate people suffer devastating events that test and challenge the deepest core of their being. Real-life tragedy such as this one makes it unnecessary for us to invent scenarios to illustrate the innumerable crises we address throughout this book. All the examples cited in this text are rooted in the lives of real people, to whom we dedicate this chapter and to whom our hearts, thoughts, prayers, empathy, and concern are extended. A special note of sympathy goes out to the two bereaved parents just mentioned in their sorrow, bereavement, and loss. We trust that this chapter offers some assistance, encouragement, and hope for the multitude of survivors of the many types of loss we describe herein as well as for the crisis workers, families, and friends who offer for them comfort and support during their special time of grief and need.

Indeed, to be human in the world as we know it is to experience loss. Some major losses precipitate emotional trauma in people, which result in crisis. Examples are the death of loved ones, the breakup of a close relationship, separation, and divorce. Other losses are relatively minor. Yet minor losses may also extract an emotional toll that the individual can ill afford to pay. Although not as catastrophic as death, job loss, bankruptcy, a forced move to a different residence, chronic illness (loss of health), having to change to a different school, and loss of one's home or possessions from flood, fire, or robbery can have many or all of the ramifications of loss of a loved one (Colgrove, Bloomfield, & McWilliams, 1991, p. 2; Schliebner & Peregoy, 1994).

Recovery from major losses, such as the death of a child, parent, or spouse, may require several years, and the traumatic event may have a profoundly lasting effect on the remainder of one's life (Costa & Holliday, 1994; Finkbeiner, 1998; McCown & Davies, 1995). Similarly, reconciling oneself to minor losses, such as job loss or sudden attainment of success (loss of striving) that impacts the person less than a death, is also distressing, and may precipitate periods of rather intense grief (Colgrove et al., 1991, p. 8). During normal growth and development, people may experience many minor losses and a few major ones. According to Attig (1996, pp. 128–162) and Freeman (1978, p. 16), the inevitable coping with numerous losses that people must learn to accept plays an important role in their emotional development and in regaining "themselves" and their personal integrity.

Although people can never "recover" from major losses, such as the death of a family member or close friend, it is important to deal with losses over time in a manner that enables everyone, children as well as adults, to reformulate the personal meaning of life, prevent lasting distress, and preserve personal, psychological, and spiritual integrity (Costa & Holliday, 1994; Edgar & Howard-Hamilton, 1994; Holcomb, Neimeyer, & Moore, 1993; Kandt, 1994; Smith, 1995; Stepnick & Perry, 1992). In that regard, it is our perception that in the areas of death and major losses *a significant proportion of people (in all societies, including ours), perhaps a majority, find faith to be their most important resource for coping, recovery, and growth.* Crisis workers must be comfortable in allowing grieving clients to find healing in their faith and spirituality. This stand does not, of course, mean that crisis workers should inject or impose their own religious beliefs on their grieving clients.

The objective of this chapter is to provide a general survey of ways in which crisis workers may help clients understand and cope with losses. The concepts and skills described in the six-step model in Chapter 2 undergird the helping strategies we recommend for workers to use in helping people experiencing a crisis of personal loss. Crisis workers may prepare themselves to assist grieving clients by remembering that *all* crises can eventually be reformulated within a context of growth (Schneider, 1984, pp. 207–227). The phrase "reformulated within a context of growth" refers to the healthy resolution of grief by bereaved individuals—attaining the ability to abstract meaning from a previously totally destructive event and emerging with greater strength, self-trust, and sense of freedom than they had before (p. 208).

The ultimate growth toward coping with loss occurs when the griever comes to grips with his or her own mortality (Rando, 1984, pp. 2–7). The final loss—death—is the conclusive stage in our development (Schoenberg, 1980, pp. 24–28). All living things go through stages of birth, growth, and death. All human losses—great or small—are increments in the journey through life. As Leo Buscaglia (1982) so dramatically put it in *The Fall of Freddie the Leaf,* "No matter how big or small, how weak or strong. We first do our job. We experience the sun and the moon, the wind and the rain. We learn to dance and to laugh. Then we die" (p. 16). Never forgetting the loss of a loved one, still, the healthy progression through grief toward healing arrives when, during what McKenna (1999) identifies as the final (*refocus*) stage of grief, the survivor finds that out of the loss may spring new dreams and opportunities.

Loss can be great or small, but it is always personal. Coping with loss—overcoming, healing, and recovering—is also personal. Crisis workers and counselors have many ways of helping people in grief (Attig, 1996; Dershimer, 1990; Lane & Dickey, 1988). But because no one else can overcome grief, heal, or recover for a person, the development of strategies for helping an individual cope with loss is perhaps the most difficult and emotionally draining intervention area crisis workers encounter. Crisis workers should come to terms with their own mortality and be currently past their own periods of grief before entering into the role of caregiver to clients suffering from debilitating losses (Rando, 1984, pp. 430–444).

DYNAMICS OF BEREAVEMENT

The manner in which humans grieve differs from culture to culture and from time to time. Social influences, within each culture, appear to be one of the catalysts that impel changes in the patterns of bereavement that people develop. Crisis workers who encounter clients experiencing bereavement and grief may find the following discussion of cultural dynamics and sociocultural mores both helpful and interesting.

Cultural Dynamics

Each culture develops its own beliefs, mores, norms, standards, and attitudes toward death (Dutro, 1994; Joffrion & Douglas, 1994). Groups from differing backgrounds within a particular culture may have vastly divergent attitudes and perceptions about death (Dutro, 1994). Rando (1984) stated that "for all societies there seem to be three general patterns of response: *death accepting, death defying,* or *death denying*" (p. 51, italics added). Joffrion and Douglas (1994) characterized modern Western society as a death-defying culture.

Kübler-Ross (1975) writes that our culture seems to believe that "death has become a dreaded and unspeakable issue to be avoided by every means possible" and that it may be "that death reminds us of our human vulnerability in spite of our technological advances" (p. 5). Becker (1973) documents how the fear or denial of death in the United States constitutes a fundamental factor in human behavior. His contention is that much of what people do in terms of cultural and scientific advancement is designed to avoid facing the finality of death. Becker further asserts that human beings have an innate fear of death, which leads them to try to transcend death through erecting hero systems and symbols. These systems and symbols may be observed in many shapes and forms—from monuments to presidential libraries, to tombstones, to this book! They may be manifested even in the choice of one's profession. Kübler-Ross (1981) reports that there have been studies indicating that doctors tend to "choose medicine as a career because of an inordinate fear of death. And medicine is dedicated to defeating death" (p. 128).

Sociocultural Mores

Schoenberg (1980) describes how societal mores and attitudes toward life, death, and dying in the United States have changed over the years. As the country shifted from a rural to an urban orientation and lifestyle, there has been a shift from a death-defying culture to a death-denying culture (pp. 51–56). Whereas farm families (children and adults alike) usually came in contact with birth, life, and death of animals as well as of people, city dwellers rarely encountered dead animals or dead people. People in rural communities cared for their own dying relatives and friends. They prepared the corpses for burial and dug the graves by hand. They laid out the bodies of the dead in the parlor and commemorated the lives of the departed; then they buried them in the family or community cemetery. That is quite a contrast to the way dying, death, grieving in public, and funerals are carried out in most communities in the United States (Crase, 1994; Joffrion & Douglas, 1994; Schoenberg, 1980).

The social organization of bereavement as well as the social reaction to the loss of the loved ones has changed partly because of shifts in age-specific mortality patterns

(Osterweis, Solomon, & Green, 1984). In former times, adult life expectancy was short and infant mortality was high. Epidemics and famines frequently wiped out large numbers of people. Communities were small and close-knit. Death was taken personally by everyone in the community and mourning rituals were communitywide events (pp. 199–200).

In modern times, the bereavement process has tended to become standardized by laws, regulations, and the development of specialists who carry out the laws and regulations. Death usually occurs in a hospital or nursing home. Frequently the deceased is an older person who has been out of the mainstream of community activity for a number of years; as a result, the deceased people are not as widely known as they were in their younger years. Mourning has tended to move out of the home and into funeral parlors and hospital chapels. Laws affecting the role of funeral directors and the policies of employers have influenced the ways society mourns. Workplaces have established rules governing the time employees can take off from work following the death of a close family member or loved one. Many institutional constraints on behavior have tended to impose social uniformity on the previously diverse patterns of grief and bereavement. Grief that follows a death has become institutionalized (Osterweis et al., 1984, pp. 201–202), but such institutionalization is not necessarily negative. For example, some funeral homes offer professional grief counseling programs for their clientele and communities (Riordan & Allen, 1989).

The sociocultural changes that occurred between the 1930s and 2000 brought about important changes in reliance on such helpers as physicians, nurses, psychologists, social workers, counselors, rehabilitation specialists, hospice workers, and caregivers for AIDS patients and other survivors of loss (Dershimer, 1990, pp. 14-36; Huber, 1993; Schneider, 1984, p. ix). Changes in divorce rates, career development, aging patterns, birth control and child-rearing practices, marriage stability, population mobility, the AIDS epidemic, medical and nutritional improvements, and information dissemination have greatly affected people's lives—including the way society views and deals with stress, loss, and grief.

CONCEPTUAL APPROACHES TO BEREAVEMENT

There are a variety of models ranging from psychodynamic to cognitive-behavioral approaches that deal with grief (Osterweis et al., 1984; Raphael, 1983). Of the 19 different conceptual models of response to bereavement we have studied, we will summarize two well-known models that aptly fit under a "crisis" category and one emerging model (Dutro, 1994) that counterpoints the other two. The first is the Kübler-Ross (1969) model, which is probably the most popular and widely known model. The second is the Schneider (1984) model, which is the most comprehensive model we have seen.

The Kübler-Ross Model:
The Dying Patient's Stages of Grief

In her five-stage model, Elisabeth Kübler-Ross (1969) outlines the human reactions or responses that people experience as they attempt to cope with their own imminent deaths. Her concepts have also been applied to the process of grief and bereavement following most personal losses. The model is a general conceptual framework that does not purport to be applicable in every detail to every patient. It was developed for the purpose of providing ways for dying patients to teach caregivers and families how patients feel and what they need.

Stage 1: Denial and Isolation.   The typical response to the first awareness of one's own terminal condition may be something like "No, it cannot be me. There must be a mistake. This is simply not true." Kübler-Ross (1969) regards initial denial as a healthy way of coping with the painful and uncomfortable news. She states that "denial functions as a buffer after unexpected shocking news, allows the patient to collect himself and, with time, mobilize other, less radical, defenses" (p. 35). During this stage the patient may generate a temporary protective denial system and isolate himself or herself from information or persons that might confirm the terminal condition. Or the patient may become energetic in garnering proof and support from others that death is not going to occur.

Stage 2: Anger.   The second stage is characterized by a "why me?" pattern. People in this stage cannot continue the myth of denial, so they may exhibit hostility, rage, envy, and resentment in addition to anger. Kübler-Ross reports that families and staffs find it quite difficult to deal with people during the anger stage (p. 44). The patient's anger is a normal adaptation. It is a desperate attempt to gain attention, to demand respect and understanding, and to establish some small measure of control. The patient's anger should not be taken personally by staff or family members. Such expressions of anger and hostility toward other people, the world, or God appear to be typical ways that patients use to try to cry out for love and acceptance.

Stage 3: Bargaining.   During the third stage, patients bargain with physicians or bargain with God for an extension of life, one more chance, or time to do one more thing. This is another period of self-delusion, hoping to be rewarded for promises of good behavior or good deeds. It is a normal attempt to postpone death. Rather than brushing aside the patient's bargaining, the sensitive caregiver should listen to the concerns that underlie the behavior. The patient may need to deal with guilt or other hidden emotions.

Stage 4: Depression.   Whenever the medical condition, the physical proof, bodily appearance, and evidence of the senses force the patient personally to admit that the prognosis is, indeed, terminal, a sense of loss ensues. Most patients are confronted with many losses as a result of impending death: career, money, loved ones, and possessions, in addition to life itself. It is normal for depression to set in. Kübler-Ross (1969) identifies two kinds of depression in the terminally ill: (1) reactive depression and (2) preparatory depression (p. 76). The first is a reaction to the irrevocable loss; the second is an inner emotional preparation to give up everything. Patients in preparatory depression should be responded to with love, caring, and empathy, using few or no words. Attempts by caregivers to cheer the patient up will only interfere with the person's preparatory grieving.

Stage 5: Acceptance.   Patients who have traveled through the previous four stages may reach the point at which they are tired, weak, finished with their mourning, recon-

ciled to their loss, and accepting of their situation. This stage is characterized by a quiet, peaceful resignation. It is not a happy stage. It is a time in which patients draw into themselves. It is a time when patients do not need conversation or large crowds. Family members and caregivers should show love and support by simply being present, sitting in silence, holding the patient's hand, or calmly responding to the patient's needs or requests. Patients in the fifth stage should be provided with treatment to make their lives as pain free and comfortable as possible.

Corr (1993) illuminated Kübler-Ross's stages by suggesting that we should also learn that (1) the living who are coping with dying are still alive and have unfinished needs they desire to address; (2) we cannot help dying people and their loved ones unless we actively listen and become sensitive to their deep concerns and issues; and (3) we need to learn from those who are dying and coping with dying in order to know ourselves better—that is, to draw on the experiences and lessons of those who are dying for our own benefit and instruction.

The Schneider Model: The Transformational Stages of Grief

John Schneider (1984) developed a comprehensive eight-stage model, which he calls "The Process of Grieving." It is a holistic, growth-promoting model designed to nurture as much personal growth as possible within a context of stress, loss, and grief. The Schneider model of grief integrates people's physical, cognitive, emotional, behavioral, and spiritual responses to loss. Schneider's concept of loss includes "internal events, systems of belief, and the processes of growth and aging as well as the easily recognized losses, such as death and divorce" (p. x).

Stage 1: The Initial Awareness of Loss.   The initial impact of a loss is generally a significant stressor causing a threat to the body's sense of homeostasis (Schneider, 1984, p. 104). The holistic dimensions of this initial awareness stage typically include physical, behavioral, emotional, cognitive, and spiritual dimensions. Shock, confusion, numbness, detachment, disbelief, and disorientation are only a few of a variety of behaviors, emotions, or feelings that the individual may experience as a normal adaptive response to the realization that a significant loss has occurred.

Stage 2: Attempts at Limiting Awareness by Holding On.   Holding on means concentrating one's thoughts and emotional energy, for a period of time, on whatever positive aspects of the loss one can recognize and making use of whatever inner resources or hopes one has to immediately stave off immobility and disequilibrium. Holding-on strategies are normal processes that the individual adopts in order to try to use coping behaviors that have worked in the past to cope with loss, frustration, stress, and conflict. This stage has the effect of providing time to put the present loss into perspective, renew energies, and limit feelings of helplessness and despair (Schneider, 1984, pp. 120–122). Some of the behaviors, emotions, and feelings accompanying holding on are muscular tension, sleep disturbance, independence, replacement search, belief in internal control, yearning, ruminations, euphoria, bargaining, and guilt.

Stage 3: Attempts at Limiting Awareness by Letting Go.   Letting go is described by Schneider (1984) as recognizing one's personal limits with regard to the loss and turning loose "unrealistic goals, unwarranted assumptions, and unnecessary illusions. This stage enables people to separate themselves from dependency or attachment to the lost person or object, paving the way for future adaptive behaviors and attitudes" (pp. 137–138). A few of the characteristic behaviors, emotions, and feelings that may occur during letting go are depression, rejection, disgust, anxiety, shame, pessimism, self-destructive ideation, cynicism, forgetting, and hedonism. During Stage 3, people may decide to give up their formerly held ideals, beliefs, and values.

Stage 4: Awareness of the Extent of the Loss.   Schneider (1984) describes the awareness stage as the one most readily recognized as mourning—the most painful, lonely, helpless, and hopeless phase through which the loss sufferer goes (pp. 161–162). The individual may experience a flooding of consciousness, feelings of deprivation, and extreme grief and may feel defenseless in coping with the reality of the loss. A few of the typical behaviors, emotions, and feelings observed in sufferers are exhaustion, pain, silence, aloneness, preoccupation, sadness, loneliness, helplessness, hopelessness, absence of future time, existential loss, emptiness, and weakness.

Stage 5: Gaining Perspective on the Loss.   The normal function of the perspective-gaining stage is described by Schneider (1984) as reaching a point of accepting that what is done is done and providing the bereaved people with a time to make peace with their past. This gaining of perspective may take two forms: "(1) discovering the balance of the positive and negative aspects of the loss, including how the bereaved has grown as well as what is permanently gone; and (2) gaining perspective on both the extent and the limits of responsibility for the loss, the bereaved's own and that of others" (p. 190). A few of the typical behaviors, emotions, and feelings that people experience during the stage of gaining perspective are patience, solitude, acceptance, forgiveness, openness, reminiscence, healing, and peace.

Stage 6: Resolving the Loss.   Schneider (1984) states that "grief has been resolved when the bereaved can see and pursue activities unconnected with the loss without it being a reaction against (letting go) or identifying with (holding on) the lost person or object" (p. 205). Stage 6 is a time of "self-forgiveness, restitution, commitment, accepting responsibility for actions and beliefs, finishing business, and saying good-bye" (p. 206). Some characteristic behaviors, emotions, and feelings of Stage 6 are self-care, relinquishing, forgiveness of self and others, determination, and peacefulness.

Stage 7: Reformulating Loss in a Context of Growth.   Schneider (1984) views the reformulation of loss as an outgrowth of resolving grief. When grief is faced and experienced through to resolution, it may provide the motivational impetus for personal growth by reminding people of their "strengths and limits, mortality, and the finiteness of the time they have" (p. 226). The reformulation stage of grief focuses on "(1) discovering potential rather than limits; (2) seeing problems as challenges; (3) being curious again; and (4) seeking a balance between the different aspects of self" (p. 226). Some of the observed behaviors, feelings, and emotions accompanying Stage 7 are enhanced sensory awareness, assertion, spontaneity, patience, integrity/balance/centeredness, recognition of illusions, curiosity, and increased tolerance for pain.

Stage 8: Transforming Loss into New Levels of Attachment.   The stage of transformation is an integration of the physical, emotional, cognitive, behavioral, and spiritual aspects of the person—as an integral part of the process of reformulation to higher levels of understanding and acceptance of the loss. Transformation does not end the cycles of loss and grief; but the process makes it possible for people to approach life "with greater openness and the willingness to surrender more readily the necessity of structure in life" and release energies that create new strength (Schneider, 1984, p. 248). It is perhaps ironic that out of life's greatest loss may emerge a reformulation and transformation that produce a greater capacity for growth than before. The transformational stage is accompanied by such behavioral, feeling, or emotional dimensions as awareness of interrelationships, unconditional love, creativity, wholeness, deep empathy, end of searching, and commitment.

A Counterpoint to Traditional Models: The Dutro Model

Dutro (1994) has described how, in the 1990s, our concepts of grief and loss became more dynamic, moving from the medical or pathology theories to more interactive models. Dutro's comprehensive and dynamic model views grief and loss from the perspective that each individual experiences loss according to psychophysiological, affective, and cognitive-behavioral factors, such as the mode of death, relationship of the deceased, prior losses experienced, and dominant subcultural norms. These factors figure into the dynamic structural model of grief that, according to Dutro, are in sync with sociocultural life in the twenty-first century. His research of the current literature refutes many ideas about grief that have been associated with older theories. Some examples are that (1) the common assumptions concerning "stages" of grief are not supported, (2) placing time limitations on grief is inappropriate, and (3) viewing the withholding or suppression of sadness in response to bereavement as pathological is an error. Instead, grief is seen as a multidimensional, interactive, individual experience for every bereaved person, based on a complex set of interwoven variables (p. 2).

TYPES OF LOSS

People may encounter many different types of loss that produce stress, trauma, and/or grief. We have identified several types that crisis workers may encounter. It is not our purpose to provide crisis intervention techniques for dealing with every specific type of loss. What we want to show here is that loss covers a broad scope and that certain fundamental helping skills and strategies apply in a generic way to helping individuals who are suffering from loss.

Death of a Spouse

The death of a spouse is one of the most emotionally stressful and disruptive events in life (Couric, 1999; Cramer, Keitel, & Zevon, 1990; Leahy, 1993). There are more women survivors (widows) than men (widowers), and the bereaved spouse typically faces a number of problems and stages of bereavement alone (Kübler-Ross, 1969). In addition to the immediate shock and stress, many survivors face serious personal, emotional, economic, social, career, family, and community problems (Johnson, 1977; Osterweis et al., 1984, pp. 71–75; Rando, 1984, pp. 144–149).

Death of a Child

The death of a child is a major life crisis for parents (Edelstein, 1984; Finkbeiner, 1998; Hansen & Frantz, 1984, pp. 11–26; Kübler-Ross, 1983; Kushner, 1983; Rando, 1986; Romanoff, 1993; Wass & Corr, 1985).

Differing Effects.   Every parent is unique in terms of needs, history, personality, coping style, relationship to others, social concerns, family situation, and sense of meaning regarding the death of the child (Braun & Berg, 1994; Finkbeiner, 1998; Romanoff, 1993). Therefore, every parent suffers the loss of a child somewhat differently. The death of a child is traumatic for parents, whether it occurs as stillbirth or sudden infant death syndrome (SIDS) or follows accident or illness in adolescence or young adulthood (Osterweis et al., 1984, pp. 75–79). It is equally traumatic for aged parents to lose their children who may be middle aged or older. Regardless of the ages of parents or children, the death of a child is always a major loss.

Meanings of the Loss to a Parent.   Finkbeiner (1998, pp. xxi, 37, 44, 54), after several years of grief and healing, shared her deep personal meanings regarding the loss of her only child, an 18-year-old son who was killed in a train accident.

> I learned two things about the long-term effects of losing a child. One is that a child's death is disorienting. The human mind is wired to find patterns and attach meanings, to associate things that are alike, to generalize from one example to another, in short, to make sense of things. Your mind could no more consciously stop this than your heart could consciously stop beating. But children's deaths make no sense, have no precedents, are part of no pattern; their deaths are unnatural and wrong. So parents fight against their wiring, change their perspectives, and adjust to a reality that makes little sense.
>
> The other thing I learned is that letting go of a child is impossible. One of my earliest and most persistent reactions to T.C.'s death was surprise. I had no idea whatever how much he had meant to me. All I knew was that I hadn't wanted to think about it. Our children are in our blood; the bond with them doesn't seem to break, and the parents find subtle and apparently unconscious ways of preserving that bond.

Bereavement Following a Suicide

Social Influence.   Death as a result of suicide is accompanied by numerous negative cultural messages and meanings felt by families and friends. Bereaved loved ones often blame themselves for the suicide and, more than in any other form of loss, they tend to perceive that they are being neglected by others (Thompson & Range, 1992). Therefore the loss of a loved one by suicide is doubly stressful (Edelstein, 1984, p. 21; Rando, 1984, p. 150). Grieving loved ones left behind by a suicide may refer to themselves as "victims" because, in addition to the emotional stress of the death itself, the survivors must also deal with burdens such as social stigma, guilt, blame, a search for the cause or meaning, unfinished business, and perceived rejection wrought by the suicide (Rando, 1984, pp. 151–152).

Emotional Toll.   The "real victim" of suicide is said to be not the body in the coffin but the family and other loved ones (Hansen & Frantz, 1984, p. 36). Osterweis and associates (1984) report that survivors of the death of a loved one by suicide are thought to be more vulnerable to physical and mental health problems than are grievers from other causes of death (p. 87).

The nature and intensity of the survivor's bereavement depend on various factors, such as the survivor's cultural values, survivor's relationship with the deceased, age and physical condition of the deceased, the nature of the suicide, and the survivor's personality characteristics, mental health, and bonding with the deceased (Attig, 1996, pp. 163–191; Osterweis et al., 1984, p. 88).

Supports.   Bereavement support groups have been recommended to help people cope with loss following the suicide of a family member or friend (Hopmeyer & Werk, 1994). The gender of the deceased (who completed the suicide) may make a difference in how the bereaved person responds in support groups. Before the suicide, women who contemplate killing themselves often experience feelings of hostility and physical violence within themselves, are prone to react to a loss in a relationship or to internal emotional factors, and are more likely to seek counseling than are men. Men who complete suicide are more likely to act in response to external, impersonal events such as loss of employment, income, or health (Canetto, 1994). People in grief support groups who are coping with the loss of a loved one by suicide may need help in understanding these different internal and external forces that drove the individual to self-destruction.

Bereavement in Childhood

Children who experience the death of a parent or sibling may show overt signs of bereavement, but sometimes their grief may be covert, leading caregivers to assume that the children are not affected by the loss. Norris-Shortle, Young, and Williams (1993) have documented the fact that *young children do grieve.* Overt signs, such as aggression, disobedience, irritability, showing off to gain attention, eating changes or difficulties, and nightmares can be readily observed by caregivers (McCown & Davies, 1995). Covert signs of bereavement may include depression, guilt, lethargy, and internalized confusion (Bowes, Fristad, Weller, & Weller, 1992). Tamm and Granqvist (1995) studied the meanings of bereaved children's drawings. The children were asked to draw their impressions of the word *death* and give a verbal commentary on what they had drawn. The qualitative assessment of drawings and commentaries indicated that biological death concepts dominated the younger age groups and that metaphysical death concepts were predominant in the older age group. Boys had more violent death concepts than did girls, and boys personified death more often. Girls depicted death in more feeling and emotional terms than did boys.

Age Differences and Grief.   Studies by Gudas (1990) suggest that signs and symptoms of behavioral and psychological difficulty occur differently between bereaved preschool and school-age children. Older children, with concepts of permanence of death and personalization of their own mortality, experience more anxiety, depression, and somatic symptoms than do younger children (p. 7). But younger children also experience profound reactions to loss and may display feelings of sadness, anger, crying spells, feelings of remorse and guilt, somatization, and separation anxiety (pp. 1–2).

When death is involved in the crisis, Bertoia and Allan (1988) propose that crisis workers need to encourage communication with open-ended and reflective statements that demonstrate concern and a willingness to listen. Depending on the age of children and their cognitive development, compared to adult thinking, their understanding about death may be very different and unsettling. From a Piagetian standpoint, the preoperational child's egocentric view of death may be laced with magical thinking and fantasy with no clear view as to death's finality. Children at the concrete-operational stage may be more specific in understanding death, whereas children at the formal operational stage can understand the finality and irreversibility of death (Matter & Matter, 1982).

Differences Between Grieving Children and Adults.   An essential dynamic in understanding childhood grief is that the emotions and reactions of children differ from those of adults because of developmental considerations (Bertoia & Allan, 1988; Osterweis et al., 1984, pp. 100–101). Children's cognitive, affective, and behavioral responses must be approached not in terms of adult perspectives but in terms of each child's understanding and developmental stage (Rando, 1984, pp. 157–162). Children are especially vulnerable during periods of major loss because their inexperience and their undeveloped personalities can easily lead to confusion and misinterpretation of events and lack of grieving (Schoenberg, 1980, p. 200). Such childhood misinterpretation can lead to the development of pathological disorders in adulthood (Bertoia & Allan, 1988, p. 33). Because children's personalities are growing and absorbing social stimuli at a very rapid and concentrated rate, care must be taken to provide reassurance and support during family bereavement (Schonfeld, 1989). They may ask the same questions over and over about the loss, not so much for the factual information but for reassurance that the adult view is consistent, that the story has not changed, and that the grieving adults and children are safe. Children need to hear, over and over again, the simple, truthful, reassuring words of adults who are relatively secure and who show genuine concern for the children's feelings (Osterweis et al., 1984, p. 100).

Honesty.   Some people believe that children should be shielded and protected from exposure to death and loss. The research suggests, however, that bereaved children will make healthier adjustments to loss if they are informed about the loss truthfully and actively (Osterweis et al., 1984, pp. 99–127; Rando, 1984, p. 155; Schoenberg, 1980, pp. 151–154). Even though children during the bereavement process may exhibit behavioral responses that adults may interpret as "not caring" or "not understanding," children should be permitted to proceed with mourning at a level and pace appropriate to their development.

Bereavement in Adolescence

Kandt (1994) cited research indicating that 90 percent of junior and senior high school students have experienced a loss associated with death. Almost half have experienced the death of a friend, and one out of five have witnessed a death. Adolescents today are encountering death and loss more frequently than ever before, and this presents a challenge to both adolescents and their caregivers. Other crises such as destabilized families and parents' job loss create in adolescents feelings of pessimism, futurelessness, confusion, depression, and isolation (Schliebner & Peregoy, 1994).

Value of Connectedness.   Hansen and Frantz (1984, pp. 36–47, 62–72) describe adolescents who are in bereavement as needing to be included (involved) in the family's grief, while at the same time needing periods of privacy. Often the adolescent may feel excluded, for example, at the sudden death of a grandparent. Other bereaved family members may erroneously assume that the adolescent's perceptions of events are the same as those of the adults. At such times adolescents may not know how to behave because they do not have a sufficient understanding of death, of the circumstances of the death, or of the appropriate mourning role. Adolescents may feel a deep sense of pain, fear, guilt, helplessness, and grief, yet they may not know how to express or feel comfortable in expressing these emotions. Adolescents in grief need to be given understanding, information, and private time. They need opportunities to be included in discussions, planning, mourning, and funeral and commemorative activities (pp. 62–67).

Prolonged Grief Time Needed.   Guerriero-Austrom and Fleming (1990), researching the effects of sibling bereavement on adolescents, found that physical and emotional symptoms fluctuate over time, showing the most severity at 6 to 12 months following the sibling death and emerging again at 18 to 24 months. Females exhibited more death anxiety and health-related problems than did males. Adolescent grief reactions were documented as long as three years following the death of the sibling but were not necessarily debilitating or pathological, suggesting that counseling immediately following loss, although appropriate, may not be enough. Teenagers may benefit from counseling as long as three years following the sibling death. The research clearly indicates that one cannot put a time limit on the grief process (p. 11).

Grief and Mourning After Adolescent Suicide.   Kirk (1993, pp. 112–115) found that suicide of adolescents and other youth represents a type of death that severely complicates survivors' mourning and adjustment. He cited the following reasons:

The adolescent suicide is generally unexpected.

The death of a young person is harder to accept than that of an older person who has lived a full life.

To many people, suicide is incomprehensible and perhaps even morally wrong.

The suicide completer's family and friends are left with guilt, anger, and a sense of unfinished business with the deceased, which mourners must work through.

There is less social support for a suicide completer's family than there may be for other bereaved families because people tend to unjustly ascribe blame to the family.

Kirk also stated that when a suicide occurs in a school setting, grief reaction is often further complicated by the group response of classmates and school personnel. Educators, school crisis response teams, parents, and others involved in designing prevention, intervention, and postvention procedures should be sensitive to the unique grief factors just mentioned.

Separation and Divorce

Almost 50 percent of all marriages end in divorce (U.S. Bureau of the Census, 1995), and this breakup in marriages is an epidemic that is ripping the United States apart (Pauley, 1986). It is devastating to adults and children alike. The crisis of separation and divorce often places children in untenable positions, causing them to feel confused, insecure, fearful, trapped, angry, unloved, and guilty. Bruce and Kim (1992) found that major depression is prevalent among both men and women experiencing marital disruption. Even though both spouses are considered at high risk for depression, they found that the risk is greater for men. According to Johnson (1977), the most common experience that marriage partners have regarding separation is intense and disturbing fear and emotional turmoil. Almost all separations produce negative feelings and outcomes that were not anticipated by either party. Separation is almost always experienced as a loss. Even when the separation is desired and sought, it precipitates a sense of frustration, failure, loss, and mourning. Johnson (1977) says that facing and mourning the loss, rather than denying it, can be both healing and constructive (p. 55).

Vulnerability.   Schneider (1984) reports that people suffering from loss due to divorce or widowhood "show significant and consistently higher vulnerability to almost every major physical and mental disorder, particularly to heart disease" (p. 19). The phenomenon of separation and divorce is a widespread and complex contributor to loss in today's world. Colgrove and associates (1991) advise that surviving and healing, following such loss, begins by recognizing and facing the loss immediately and doing the mourning now (pp. 1–2).

Death of a Pet

The human–animal bond is now recognized as an integral part of pet owners' lives, and it is important for us to recognize and validate the grief pet owners experience when beloved companion animals die (Downs & Walters, 1986; Kay et al., 1984; Lagoni, Butler, & Hetts, 1994; Nieburg & Fischer, 1982). Weisman (1990–1991) and Reitmeyer (2000) compared bereavement following the death of a companion animal to the experience of the loss of another human. Downs and Walters (1986) reported that more and more people seem to be forming bonds of affection and attachment with their pets. When pets die or suffer terminal illness and have to be "put to sleep," the owners may suffer grief, guilt, and other emotional reactions similar to those experienced at the death of human family members. Even when the death of a pet does not constitute a devastating event, it is nonetheless an emotionally sobering time (Bahrick & Sharkin, 1990). Walters and Downs (1997) described an innovative and successful approach to helping people cope with the loss of a pet: providing veterinarians' training in pet loss counseling for bereaved pet owners. Since veterinarians are frequently at the scene of dying pets, they are in a position to help when it is most needed and most of them are already empathic toward the owner and the advent of pet loss. The death of a pet may provide a naturally occurring opportunity for adults in the family to introduce children to the concept and experience of death and dying (Koocher, 1975; Nieburg & Fischer, 1982; Schoenberg, 1980, pp. 203–204). Recently pet loss counseling has become widespread in the United States from coast to coast. It is estimated that in the United States there are 57 million dogs and 62 million cats accounted for (to say nothing of so many other pets, such as horses, snakes, gerbils, and so on). Large numbers of people are bonded with or attached to their pets in some way. When the inevitable demise of pets occur, grief will naturally ensue. Reitmeyer (2000) reveals that many pet loss counselors are now needed and are being specially trained to meet the public demands. The primary concern of pet loss counselors is to relieve the pain, grief, suffering, guilt, and depression that owners usually experience as a result of the loss of their pets. The ideal pet loss counselor is characterized as one who recognizes the human/animal bond and is skilled in the field of bereavement and grief (Reitmeyer, 2000, pp. 26–27).

Bereavement in Elderly People

Demographic data indicate that the elderly population, ages 65 and older, is growing at an increasing rate. It is predicted that by 2030 there will be about 70 million older adults, more than double the number in 1997, and that number will represent 20 percent of the U.S. population (Schwiebert, Myers, & Dice, 2000, p. 123). Crase (1994) reported that 75 percent of all deaths occur in the over-65 group, an indication that personal loss looms heavily among this group.

How Age Compounds.   From a developmental standpoint, bereavement among elderly people is compounded by decreases in sensory acuity, general decline in health, and reduced mobility. Having a lower income and fewer support people available to them than in their younger years also represent changes that may affect them. Elderly people generally experience more losses than do their younger counterparts: loss of relatives and friends; loss of job, status, and money; loss of bodily functions and abilities; and loss of independence and self-respect (Freeman, 1978, p. 116). The most profound and devastating loss older people may encounter is the loss of a spouse (Schoenberg, 1980, pp. 211–214). It is not known whether age, as such, affects the cognitive and behavioral aspects of adult bereavement. It does appear that advancing age tends to correlate with a decrease in coping strategies. But it is not known whether this decrease is related to one's greater awareness of impending death, decrease in physical stamina and function, or other factors (Schoenberg, 1980, pp. 221–223).

Schoenberg (1980, p. 230) summarizes four conclusions that may be drawn from the literature on bereavement and age:

1. Elderly people present more somatic problems than psychological problems.
2. There is no indication that the intensity of grief varies significantly with age.
3. A small amount of evidence suggests that grief among older people may be more prolonged than among younger people.
4. Elderly people tend to be lonelier and to have far longer periods of loneliness than do their younger counterparts.

The research of Rappaport, Fossler, Bross, and Gilden (1993) tends to support Schoenberg's conclusions. Crase (1994) found that the many ways the older generation deals with loss fall into the following three broad categories.

1. One group totally ignores the inevitability of death and makes no preparation for it. People—especially men—in this category engage in little or no open discussion of death. By ignoring death issues, these elderly individuals attempt to avoid negative feelings, using denial as a defense mechanism. They are vulnerable to being unprepared when struck by disabling disease, crisis, or disaster.
2. A second group thinks about death and dying excessively and makes unusual preparations for death's inevitability. These individuals go overboard in making meticulous (even minute) plans for every detail of their decline, death, and funeral.

3. A third group demonstrates a healthy balance between totally ignoring their own death issues and going overboard. They are attuned to the developmental implications of total loss, making appropriate plans and decisions, and going on with their normal lives.

Unique Opportunities.   The realization of disease, suffering, and eventual loss of life should foster the motivation to prepare for our death with intelligent preparation, just as we would prepare for any of life's major stages or events (Kaplan & Gallagher-Thompson, 1995). Our birth and our death are one-time significant events in our lives. Crase (1994) observes that if we ignore any of our major life events, we cheat ourselves out of an opportunity to experience the essence of being totally human. Also, Austad (1992) found that elderly clients often have an enormous amount of knowledge, experience, history, wisdom, and advice to offer younger people and that, when given the opportunity to share their rich past, the self-esteem of elderly people is thereby enhanced.

AIDS: A Modern Dilemma

Since the 1980s, the acquired immune deficiency syndrome (AIDS) and the human immunodeficiency virus (HIV) that precedes and accompanies AIDS have victimized increasing numbers of people. Dworkin and Pincu (1993) and Cho and Cassidy (1994) remind us that the AIDS crisis requires human services workers who have special knowledge, training, and attitudes to deal effectively with AIDS/HIV-positive clients.

HIV/AIDS Crisis Worker Suggestions.   K. D. Fisher (personal communication, February 6, 1996) provided some insights and implications regarding the essential personal qualities that an effective worker with AIDS/HIV-positive people should possess:

1. Workers should be able to continuously monitor and assess their own attitudes, needs, and feelings regarding their own mortality. This means they must be able to become aware of and evaluate their repeated experiences with their clients' loss, bereavement, and declining health and functioning and to objectively but empathically judge what it means for a client to receive a diagnosis of being HIV positive. Do the workers view a diagnosis of being HIV positive as a death sentence? Or do they perceive that the client faces an entirely new adjustment in life—that the client must now endure and experience about a 40-year loss of life in approximately 4 years? The latter is a more realistic view of what an HIV-positive client faces. Therefore, workers should seek to help HIV-positive clients attain and maintain some regular and ongoing positive qualities in their lives.

2. Workers with HIV-positive clients should recognize and be respectful of clients' constant feeling and experiencing of loss and their grief over continuously losing friends—yet refrain from attempting to "fix" or rob clients of their autonomy and self-esteem. Somehow clients must learn, as much as possible, to take care of their own healing and quality of life.

3. Workers and case managers should receive training in the laws, guidelines, and referral resources for medical, social, financial, spiritual, and personal needs.

4. Workers should be trained and skilled in dealing with unusual issues of HIV-positive clients such as (a) alcohol and drug use by clients; (b) special problems

faced by minority HIV-positive clients; (c) clients' sexual promiscuity and the need to assume responsibility for avoiding reinfection and the spread of HIV; and (d) challenging clients to learn about and face the ethical, moral, cultural, and philosophical issues that impact HIV-positive clients.

5. Workers and case managers should take special steps to develop burnout prevention, such as do something regularly to get their minds and bodies away from the constant loss that workers themselves may feel. It is recommended that caregivers take a proactive and preventive stance to regularly acquire for themselves some different experiences. Examples of such experiences might include (a) attending workshops to counteract the bad news one receives following a diagnosis of being HIV positive; (b) planning and carrying out physically renewing and healing activities that include being in nature and doing things that are enjoyable and invigorating; and (c) engaging in esthetic experiences such as art, music, movies, travel, reading, and associating with people not involved in HIV/AIDS work. Worker peer supports are needed to examine, evaluate, and, in a peer group, talk about the very issues listed here: what it is like to have many clients waste away and inevitably die; how to deal with the workers' own loss, anguish, and depression; and how to enhance one's own moral, spiritual, emotional, and professional healing and well-being. These burnout prevention strategies are necessary, because it is vitally important for workers to be models of balance—emotionally, spiritually, financially, socially, and holistically—while working with HIV-positive clients. If workers cannot attain some burnout immunity, their tenure as effective workers with HIV-positive clients is likely to be short, ineffective, and disappointing.

We know of no other crisis work that is more important, challenging, or needed than that done with the AIDS/HIV-positive clientele that is growing throughout the world. The special knowledge, training, and attitudes of workers who counsel and help people in this underserved population deserve special consideration and commendation (Alyson, 1990; Douce, 1993).

INTERVENTION STRATEGIES

We introduce this section on intervention by providing information on clues for identifying grief reaction, applied stages of grief, and suggestions for dealing with the crisis worker's own grief. The bulk of this section, however, focuses on the particular types of grief we have identified earlier in this chapter. A case example and intervention techniques for each type of grief are presented. Use of the Triage Assessment System is illustrated only for the first case, death of a spouse. Even though we have omitted written mention of triage assessment in the other cases, it is just as applicable to them.

Clues for Identifying Grief Reaction

Worden (1991) has constructed clues for identifying complicated grief reaction that may prove useful to crisis workers in cases where there are survivors of loss who are in serious denial. Two examples might be a parent who has experienced the loss of a child and refuses to face the fact that the child is gone or a spouse or partner whose mate has either died or left for good and the survivor carries on as if the partner has simply stepped out to the corner grocery and will shortly return. Survivors who have not initiated or finished grieving for their lost ones are vulnerable to suffering from residual trauma, transcrisis, or impaired functioning. Worden's (1991, pp. 75–77) list of clues may help crisis workers to identify and offer help to people who manifest such severe denial or other debilitating reactions.

Twelve Specific Clues for Identifying Complicated Grief Reaction. Crisis workers and other caregivers should take note of and attend to clients when

> The person cannot speak of the deceased without experiencing intense and fresh grief.
> Some relatively minor event triggers an intense grief reaction.
> The survivor cannot remove material possessions or belongings of the deceased.
> Loss themes continually come up during interviews.
> The griever manifests the same physical symptoms as those of the deceased.
> The individual exhibits radical changes in life style following the death or excludes family, friends, activities, or visitation of places associated with the deceased.
> The person experiences a long history of depression following loss, often earmarked by persistent guilt and lowered self-esteem.
> A compulsion to imitate the dead person is prevalent.
> Self-destructive impulses or suicidal ideation is in evidence.
> Unaccountable sadness at certain times of the year are manifested.
> The person has phobias about illness or death.
> There is definite avoidance of death-related rituals or activities.

Workers are reminded that relatively few grievers may display clues such as those on the list. The value of Worden's clues to the crisis worker lies in the fact that such grievers are encountered more often than one might think, and that workers need to be prepared, and not show surprise, when faced with such behavior in grievers whom they counsel (Worden, 1991, pp. 65–78).

Listening to Grievers: A Worker Imperative. Intervention strategies for helping people who are suffering major losses may include, at one time or another, all the known systems of counseling and other techniques of assisting. The concepts and skills that are basic for these strategies are those discussed in Chapter 2. Both long- and short-term grief work are applicable strategies. Grief work may be enhanced through interdisciplinary teamwork, but empathic listening to the bereaved and their families appears to be the single most useful skill or strategy available to crisis workers (Rando, 1984). Studies by Balk (1990) confirm the value of empathic listening. He found that bereaved college students identify "attentive listening and presence" as being the most helpful to grievers and "avoidance" as being the least helpful. Hughes (1988) believes that the grieving client's expectations are crucial in facilitating the healing process. Hughes stated that the therapist's expectations are "always communicated (directly or subtly) to the client, and that clients heal when they are 'informed' by the therapist that they are never helpless victims but instead are powerful and capable of healing themselves" (p. 77). McKenna (1999) incorporates attentive listening and presence as essential elements in her six stages of applied work with grievers.

Applied Stages of Survivor Grief:
An Operational Concept

McKenna (1999) has developed an operational model or "style" that is characteristic of how crisis counselors might work with clients experiencing loss. She describes six applied or hands-on stages that grief counselors can employ as they work with people who are experiencing acute grief and bereavement.

Stage 1: Shock, Sadness, Anxiety, and Isolation.   Particularly in the early days following loss, it is of vital importance to enlist help for daily tasks, such as child care or elder care, which suddenly become so difficult or even impossible for the person suffering loss to accomplish. During stage 1, crisis workers typically encourage the bereaved to connect with family and friends for support as they undergo the shock.

Stage 2: Sadness.   After the shock come the tears of intense sadness. This stage is characterized by a dramatic spate of emotional release. Bereaved individuals often manifest grief through an outpouring of crying that for them is rarely, if ever, more intensely felt.

Stage 3: Loneliness.   Following sadness is extreme loneliness. Such aloneness can be manifested physically through unusual nervousness, sleeplessness, or loss of appetite. In this stage, crisis workers advise the bereaved person to avail themselves of as much rest and relaxation as they can, drink plenty of fluids, and do some kind of physical activity each day.

Stage 4: Anger and Guilt.   Following loneliness, things usually change pretty rapidly for most bereaved individuals. They find themselves at loose ends and unable to focus on their normal tasks at home and at work. Frustration with this impasse frequently ushers in strong feelings of anger and/or guilt. Because anger and guilt robs one of power, crisis workers advise the bereaved to focus on positive, healthy, and good thoughts and feelings as much as possible to help them regain control and reframe the loss in a more positive direction.

Stage 5: Depression.   Inevitably the bereaved conclude that their lost loved one is not coming back and, as a result, they frequently become depressed. This is the stage that crisis intervention can be of optimum help. Empathic helpers who spend time with the bereaved, listen to their story of the loss, don't rush them, and manifest genuine caring for them are of enormous comfort and help to clients who have suffered loss.

Stage 6: Refocus on the Future.   At some dramatic period near the end of stage 5, survivors usually begin to experience moments of joy. Those moments are the precursors of the final stage of grief: refocus on the future. Out of the experience of losing the loved one and then evolving back through the six stages to a semblance of precrisis equilibrium, the bereaved are usually able to discover new dreams and opportunities. At this point many survivors undertake new initiatives with vigor, enthusiasm, and renewed hope. The establishment of the Mothers Against Drunk Driving (MADD) program was a prime example of such postgrief energy being refocused and reframed to transform one's grief into something positive, lasting, and good.

The Crisis Worker's Own Grief

Before workers engage in grief work with others, they must first take care of themselves. That means becoming proactive in maintaining their own vitality. Failure to do so can result in the phenomenon known as *vicarious traumatization.*

Proactive Reasons Why Caregiver Vitality Comes First.   Schneider (1984) reminds us that "it is not possible to be a facilitator of the growth aspects of bereavement if the helper is not also experiencing growth in relation to personal losses" (p. 270). The knowledge and perspective gained from one's own growth following grief should serve as a quiet reservoir of strength for workers. But the worker's own grief experience should not be projected or imposed on clients. Both Rando (1984) and Schoenberg (1980) challenge caregivers to come to grips with their own personal and professional attitudes toward death, grief, and bereavement before venturing into helping relationships with clients who are in grief. According to Rando (1984), there are several reasons why caregivers should ensure that their own grief and attitudes about grief are not allowed to intrude on their strength and vitality for helping others (pp. 430–435).

1. *Emotional investment in the client.* A certain degree of emotional investment in clients is normal and needed. Overinvestment in those whom they help may require crisis workers to expend an inordinate amount of energy on their own grief responses in cases of dying and bereaved clients.

2. *Bereavement overload.* If the worker forms close bonds with several clients, the emotional load may involve too many risks and grief responses on the part of the worker. A series of client losses may cause the worker to experience bereavement overload or burnout. Workers can deal with their own bereavement overload provided that they are aware of it while it is happening to them and that they act on their internal signals to get help and/or take steps to effect their own renewal before several client losses get them down.

3. *Countertransference.* Sometimes crisis workers engaged in grief work with others find that such work awakens their own feelings, thoughts, memories, and fantasies about losses in their own lives. Workers who experience such countertransference will be severely impaired in helping others. To deal with countertransference, caregivers who regularly work with loss-related clients should be involved in peer supervision, case staffing, psychological autopsies, and debriefing groups for reducing emotional overload caused by constant involvement with client grief.

4. *Emotional replenishment.* Caregivers in the area of grief and bereavement work must take special care to minister to their own emotional needs. Caregivers need support systems to provide for their physical, emotional, and psychological wellness; they themselves need to have regular access to empathic listeners for the purpose of sharing their own feelings; and they need the reinforcement from others that they, the caregivers, are valued. The knowledge that they are helping clients is not enough in itself. Emotional replenishment involves both taking care of oneself internally and having environmental supports from significant others—a supervisor, friends, family, colleagues—and meaningful physical and emotional activities.

5. *Facing one's own mortality.* Work with clients who are dying and/or grieving brings risks of many stressors. One of the important aspects of such work is that it may arouse existential anxiety over one's own death. Support groups, supervision, in-service training, and reading are suggested coping mechanisms. Spiritual growth activities are worthwhile alternatives for many caregivers.

6. *Sense of power.* Caregivers, like all other people, need a sense of power or control. Working with clients in dying, grief, and bereavement may cause workers to identify vicariously with the losses of their clients. Such identification may result in a sense of loss of power or control on the part of workers. Strategies for preventing feelings of loss of power are essentially the same as those recommended for dealing with countertransference.

7. *Tendency to rescue.* It is essential that workers relinquish the rescue fantasy, especially when dealing with grief and bereavement, because rescuing someone who has experienced or is about to suffer loss is to deny the inevitability of the loss.

Vicarious Traumatization.   Crisis workers who regularly work with clients who are suffering from the types of loss we deal with in this chapter are themselves vulnerable to *vicarious traumatizaton* (Saakvitne & Pearlman, 1996). The continuous work with others' grief calls for being empathic, sensitive, supportive, caring, and sharing in their experiences of loss, sorrow, and bereavement. Such intensive work lends itself to actually substituting others' emotions for one's own. When workers absorb into themselves the life events or feelings of others, they have themselves indulged in experiencing their inner world *vicariously.* People can vicariously experience joy and ecstasy as well as pain and grief. When workers come to "own" another person's grief, pain, or tragedy, they are leaving themselves open to vicarious traumatization (see Chapter 13 on burnout). The seven proactive points just noted are good starting points for worker vigilance in preventing vicarious trauma in themselves, and we suggest that the reader visit the burnout chapter for further coping strategies.

Death of a Spouse

Stuart Wynn, a 44-year-old machinist, his wife Kate, a 42-year-old bookkeeper, and their daughter, Anne, an 18-year-old high school senior, were a stable, middle-class family living in a quiet neighborhood in a large city. On her way to work one morning aboard a city bus, Kate Wynn suffered a severe stroke and was taken by ambulance to a hospital emergency room. A neighbor who was also aboard the bus Kate was riding phoned Stuart at work, and Stuart rushed to the hospital. Kate was placed in an intensive care unit but never regained consciousness after the stroke. She lived only 24 hours, leaving Stuart and Anne stunned and in a state of grief. As far as Stuart knew, Kate had been in good health and had had no medical history to indicate that she might have a health problem.

The case of Stuart is an example of immediate short-term crisis intervention. The first intervention session was a very brief meeting that included only the crisis worker and Stuart. The second meeting, approximately 20 minutes later, was also a short-term intervention session that featured a meeting between Stuart and his daughter and a multidisciplinary team consisting of the crisis worker, the attending physician, a psychiatric nurse, and the hospital chaplain. These initial short-term sessions were aimed at providing

1. Empathic understanding and acknowledgment of the special problems related to Kate's sudden death
2. Assurance to Stuart and Anne that all appropriate emergency medical measures had been attempted in efforts to save Kate
3. Emotional support for both Stuart and Anne by the worker and by the other members of the multidisciplinary team
4. Time alone with Kate's body prior to its being picked up for autopsy
5. Referral resources that Stuart needed immediately to make arrangements for the funeral, notification of kin, and other matters
6. Information about autopsy rights and procedures, in case Stuart requested it (which he did)
7. Contact with the family minister, at Stuart's request

On the Triage Assessment Form, the worker mentally computed Stuart's profile: affective, 5 (emotionally shocked but substantially under control); behavioral, 8 (minimally able to perform tasks relevant to his wife's death); cognitive, 3 (thought processes affected by the crisis but under volitional control and congruent with reality); total, 16 (moderate impairment). The crisis worker proceeded to work in a collaborative mode with Stuart. If the total on the triage assessment had been in the 20s, the worker would have intervened far more directively. Despite the sudden death of his spouse, at that moment Stuart was maintaining psychological equilibrium; only later would the impact of the loss catch up with him and would he experience severe affective, behavioral, and cognitive impairment. But for the moment he could cope, even though the help of crisis intervention was needed and welcomed.

The following intervention strategies were provided and issues explored with Stuart during the days immediately following Kate's burial.

1. *Individual counseling and intervention.* Issues of loneliness and bereavement related to Kate's absence. Implications for regaining equilibrium and going on with his life. Emotional supports for Anne. Identification of functions and roles in the family that were previously carried out by Kate and that must be reevaluated or reassigned. Review of either Kübler-Ross's or Schneider's stages of grief and assurance that Stuart would, in time, reformulate the loss. Grief work regarding the new identity without Kate. It was now "I, Stuart," instead of "us, Stuart and Kate." Identifying and dealing with Stuart's areas of vulnerability created by Kate's death. Assessment of ways to remember and use the positive strengths of Kate's life in a healthy and growth-promoting way for both himself and Anne.
2. *Spouse-Survivor Support Group Work.* Assessment of overall implications of Stuart's widowhood, such as loss of social connections. Group-generated alternatives available to Stuart and others who had recently experienced the death of a spouse. Suggestions and guidance from the support group on Stuart's responses and single-parenting role with regard to his daughter, Anne. Referral to other groups, organizations, and institutions offering assistance and support ap-

propriate for Stuart's particular situation. Group focus on ways to cope with the loneliness and other emotions brought on by the absence of one's spouse.

During the first contact with Stuart at the hospital, on the afternoon of Kate's sudden death, the crisis worker met individually with Stuart. The following segment illustrates a part of the first intervention session with Stuart.

CW: (*Holding Stuart's hand.*) Stuart, I realize your wife's death has been sudden and overwhelming to you. I want you to know that I am here to help you with whatever you need done. (*Silence. Still holding Stuart's hand.*) I'll be with you and assist you in whatever way I can. (*Silence. Still holding Stuart's hand.*)

The crisis worker's assessment is that Stuart's emotional status is one of shock, denial, or disbelief.

Stuart: This is so unreal! I just can't believe she's gone. It's such a sudden blow to me. Right now my main thought is Anne—our daughter. She just got here. I guess right now what I want is to make sure she's OK. I want to find out if she wants to see her mother before they take her away from the hospital.

CW: So you're needing to talk with Anne—and it's pretty urgent that you see her right away. Let's see if we can find her. (*A few moments go by.*)

Stuart: (*Accompanied by Anne.*) We want to be with Kate—to be alone with her some before they take her away. Can you arrange for us to do that?

CW: Yes, we'll arrange for that right now.

Stuart: One other thing. I'm afraid we're going to be in a pretty heavy way after we've seen her. Could you arrange for us to sit in the chapel a while after we get back? And is there a chaplain around who could be with us for a few moments?

CW: I'll phone Chaplain Myer again. He's aware of Kate's death, and he said he'd be available anytime, if you want him. I'll go with you and leave you alone with Kate's body and then, when you're ready, I'll go with you to the chapel.

The work with Stuart was immediate and intense. During the first hour, provisions were made for a brief individual session with Stuart, private time for Stuart and Anne in the hospital chapel, and a multidisciplinary team session with Stuart and Anne. Definite plans for follow-up work were established for helping Stuart and Anne during the following days and weeks. The crisis worker's immediate concern was to deal with Stuart's initial phase of grief, which corresponded with Kübler-Ross's (1969) first stage of denial, isolation, shock, and disbelief. The worker's primary goal was to help Stuart, an hour at a time or a day at a time, deal with the loss of Kate.

The worker kept in mind that as time evolved, the emergent stages of anger, bargaining, depression, and acceptance would need to be faced. But for the moment, the short-term intervention focused on Stuart's need to deal with his first stage of grief. The worker was also sensitive to allowing Stuart to become aware of his own loss. The worker never tried to or considered trying to manage, defer, speed up, or otherwise intrude on Stuart's grief process. Short-term grief work, in Stuart's case, was more a supportive way of being than overtly doing. Initial grief work is as much attitude on the part of caregivers as it is behavior.

Some two weeks later, after initially taking the death in stride, Stuart was hit with the full impact of Kate's loss. The daughter, Anne, was similarly impacted and stressed.

Stuart's grief and his feeling of helplessness regarding emotional support for his daughter accompanied a rapid escalation of his observed affective (8), behavioral (7), cognitive (8), and total (23) triage assessment scores. This later assessment prompted an immediate referral of Stuart to a long-term therapist for grief work. Such a rapid escalation is a frequent occurrence among clients who have experienced the loss of a loved one. Crisis workers should be alert to such a possibility following any crisis involving sudden loss.

Death of a Child

Brad Drake, age 34, a rural postal carrier, and his wife Helen, age 30, had twin sons, Herbert and Hubert, age 6. Late one afternoon, while Brad was doing the chores at the barn behind their house and Helen was preparing supper, Hubert tried to cross the highway in front of their house and was struck by an automobile. The parents rushed Hubert to the hospital 22 miles away, but the child was pronounced dead on arrival. The death of Hubert left them feeling a deep sense of grief, hurt, bewilderment, guilt, powerlessness, psychological immobility and vulnerability, and searching for answers and meaning.

Approximately two weeks following Hubert's burial, Brad and Helen together sought counseling. The crisis worker saw them together immediately following the intake interview. The worker decided that crisis intervention could provide three interrelated but equally important things for Brad and Helen: (1) facilitate the release of their grief energy, (2) reassure them that their feelings were normal, and (3) put them into communication with other grieving parents. These goals of intervention, described by Hansen and Frantz (1984, pp. 21–22), formed the basis for starting grief work with Brad and Helen Drake. The intervention strategies with the Drakes provided

1. Empathic understanding and acknowledgment of Brad and Helen's grief related to Hubert's sudden death
2. An opportunity for both parents to talk about their grief, about Hubert, about Hubert's accidental death, about the good times and feelings Hubert had brought into their lives, and about their feelings since Hubert's death
3. A chance to shed tears, which both Brad and Helen did
4. Exploration of previously unidentified and unspoken anger and guilt
5. Assessment of the family's needs related to grief work and tentative plans for continuing the work begun during the initial session

The case of Brad and Helen is an example of long-term intervention. The following strategies were provided and issues explored with Brad and Helen during the days and weeks following Hubert's burial.

1. *Couple counseling and intervention.* The impact of the death on the twin brother, Herbert, and appropriate parental handling of Herbert. Continuation of grief work through talk, tears, expressions of guilt and anger, reminiscence and commemoration of Hubert's life, redirection of energies toward the family and creative work together, and a regular exercise program. Reassurance of Brad and Helen that they were not going crazy. Affirmation that they were the best parents they could be; that their parenting should not be blamed for the accident. Assessment of family problems and potentials. Assessment of marital rela-

tionship following the death of Hubert and exploration of ways to cope with the effects of the bereavement on the marriage. Reassurance of Brad and Helen that the grief and pain will continue for a long time and that this is normal; that they'll always have memories of the loss; that they will, in time, let go of the pattern of holding onto their grief and move on; that there is no set timetable for them to finish their grieving.

2. *Parent–survivor and support group work.* Involvement of Brad and Helen in a group whose common focus is the loss of a child. Group-supported talk, reminiscence, sharing, grief, tears. Making contact with other bereaved parents for mutual support by phone in addition to group meetings. Bringing parents together so that the newly bereaved can be helped by parents who are further advanced in the grieving process than Brad and Helen.

3. *Reading and media helps.* Provision of books, other reading material, films, and other audiovisual material about bereavement in children and youth, as well as in parents. (The book *After the Death of a Child: Living with Loss Through the Years,* by Ann K. Finkbeiner, 1998, is among the best books we know. The booklet *Death Education: A Concern for the Living,* by Gibson, Roberts, and Buttery, 1982, is also a good source.) Putting the parents in touch with intervention supports such as parental self-help bereavement groups (Bordow, 1982; Dickens, 1985; Schiff, 1977).

The first crisis intervention session with Brad and Helen was on a rather emotionally low key, compared with later sessions, because both parents were still in a stage of denial and isolation. The crisis worker noted that they exhibited signs of being physically and emotionally drained; they vacillated between moping and benign circumspection but showed no indication of movement to the later stages of anger, bargaining, or depression. The crisis worker's goal was not to facilitate their advancement to a later stage of grief; rather, the aim was to understand their current inner concerns and to provide them with opportunities to identify and express their immediate and deep feelings openly.

CW: I sense that you are both feeling drainage of your emotional energy—like you're stuck there and cannot seem to move on.

Brad: Yes, stuck is the word. But I need this time. I don't want to rush or be rushed. (*Silence.*) I guess we're in an unknown and uncharted territory.

CW: It is very important not to hurry yourself or to be hurried.

Helen: We've just about stopped talking about it. We've become two lonely recluses in the same house. That worries me.

CW: Helen, what would you like to be doing right now, instead of being stuck and isolated?

Helen: I'd like to be more open. I'd like to know what's going on with Brad, and I'd like to be able to share feelings—even though they may be sad.

The worker was attempting to respond in a way that would give both parents the autonomy to experience their current state of bereavement and, at the same time, encourage them to open up and provide mutual support. Open communication was viewed as important in terms of their grief as well as their relationship. The worker was successful in helping both of them share their concerns, which, in turn, enabled them to move on to other issues of importance to them.

Brad: We just don't know where to turn. We take our religion seriously, and we've talked to our minister. That doesn't seem to help us. I keep on asking, "Why, why, why?"

Helen: We know the story of Job and such as that. We know tragedy strikes anywhere and anybody. Still, we don't know—we can't see—that a God of love or a God of justice can condone or permit the life of a good and innocent child like that to be snuffed out. I'm amazed at myself for talking like that. But my words are nothing compared to my thinking since this happened. I'm thinking I may be going insane or something.

CW: Helen, you're not going insane. You're responding in a way that makes perfect sense to me. You have both lost the most important and precious gift a mother and father can lose. It is natural and normal for you to experience unusual feelings and grief. You're doing a very good thing by talking openly about your thoughts and feelings. That's why I'm glad you came and reached out to me today. Nobody can erase your hurt or bring your son back, but I will help as best I can.

Later in the same session, the crisis worker facilitated their release of grief energy and suggested that they contact a local, ongoing support group.

Brad: I'm glad we came today. We would like to come in again. The group of parents you spoke about is a good idea. I think we need that now, and we are going to need it more.

Helen: We didn't know about Compassionate Friends. I'll call them this afternoon. It's good to know that such a group exists. It sounds like a wonderful thing.

CW: I think you will both be glad you discovered Compassionate Friends. I'm truly glad you came, and I'll look forward to seeing you again. Here's my card, in case you want to call me. And don't forget your books.

Helen: Thank you, so much. It sounds like the books you recommended will be especially helpful for us.

The worker gave them Staudacher's (1987) paperback book *Beyond Grief* and Kushner's (1983) paperback *When Bad Things Happen to Good People.* The two books together represent comprehensive guidelines for surviving the death of a loved one. They are appropriate for both the bereaved and the helping professional because both volumes are readable, objective, positive, comforting, and professionally written. The crisis worker was employing a strategy of *bibliotherapy* (Ellis & Abrahms, 1978, p. 123), which is an effective way of providing information, reinforcement, and support through reading and other media that pertain to specific client concerns.

The fact that Brad and Helen returned for follow-up grief work, made a commitment to become involved in a support group, and accepted relevant reading material indicated to the worker that the objectives for intervention were being attained. The worker continued to meet with Brad and Helen while they were also attending the parent support group.

Brad and Helen's loss represents one unique case. Rando (1986) points out that each case involving the death of a child is different and that various types of bereavement experiences require different intervention strategies. Not all parents would respond as did Brad and Helen. Resources such as Rando's (1986) *Parental Loss of a Child* can greatly enhance the crisis worker's understanding and competency in helping parents who are devastated by the loss of a child.

Bereavement Following a Suicide

Leah Nichols, 54-year-old manager of a branch bank, returned home from work Friday evening and discovered her 24-year-old son, Ronnie, dead from a gunshot wound. Ronnie had left a suicide note where he had apparently killed himself in his bedroom. Leah's husband, a college professor, had been dead (of heart failure) about a year, and she and Ronnie had lived in the family home. Ronnie's other siblings, Brenda, age 31, Richard, age 27, and Larry, age 22, were married and living in cities scattered about the region. Ronnie had been a warm, friendly, loving, and lovable person who had never married or dated much. He was very sensitive and was given to mood swings from deep depression to euphoria. He had expressed suicidal ideations since his primary school years and had been under psychiatric care since his adolescent years. But in recent months he had appeared to be gaining in maturity and had gotten off his medication. Ronnie was employed at a local bookstore, where he was regarded as friendly and dependable. Everyone who knew him liked him. Leah's grief was heavy and painful, but she felt she should set a controlled and circumspect image for the other three siblings and other friends and relatives.

The following intervention strategies were provided and issues explored with the Nichols family during the days and weeks immediately following Ronnie's suicide.

1. *Individual counseling and intervention.* Assessment of the impact of Leah's having lost her husband to heart failure and a son to suicide in such a brief time frame. Opportunities for Leah to release her grief energy. Assessment of Leah's medical and psychological vulnerability. Brief therapy for siblings when appropriate and needed.

2. *Family systems therapy.* Facilitation of the family's release of grief energy. Focus on the value and impact of Ronnie's life as well as his death. Exploration of and dealing with residual guilt among family members. Group search for meaning and understanding of Ronnie's suicide. Assessment and addressing of anger, blame, rejection, unfinished business, and stigma encountered by family members. Facilitation of family decisions and actions to commemorate Ronnie's life. Helping family members become reconciled to the fact that Ronnie chose death and helping family members reformulate his death within a context of their own growth.

Individual crisis counseling following Ronnie's suicide was provided for Leah. The individual follow-up grief work with her dealt with a good many issues that are common in suicide work: denial, guilt, bargaining, and depression. The issue of Leah's martyrdom came out during an individual session approximately three weeks following Ronnie's funeral.

Leah: My kids think I'm holding back. They say I'm too stoic, too unaffected, or too aloof. They think my lack of showing emotions is not normal—not healthy.

CW: What do you think?

Leah: I don't know. I guess I believe somebody has to keep the lid on—keep a steady head during all this. I haven't wanted to trouble any of them with my problems. Their daddy's death, then Ronnie's. They've had enough without me dumping my grief on them.

CW: What are you saying, at a deep level, below the surface, right now?

Leah: I guess I am saying I'm hurting and that I have a need to weep, to feel the impact of the loss of Ronnie, too. I guess my actions have looked pretty cold and strange to them. I guess I've been trying to protect them—to keep them from hurting.

CW: What will it do for you to keep them from hurting?

Leah: Make me a martyr, I guess. I don't know what else it could be.

The crisis worker was not attempting to steer Leah to any particular conclusion. Rather, the questioning strategy, a combination of techniques from reality therapy, rational-emotive behavior therapy, and Gestalt therapy, was used to help Leah gain conscious contact with her own inner world. This crisis intervention technique would be ineffective if the worker were trying to analyze or identify pathology in Leah's behavior. Diagnosing, prescribing a cure, and managing Leah's recovery for her would have also been inappropriate.

Leah: I really had no notion I was playing the martyr when I came in here today. The kids could see something I couldn't see. I'm too close to it, I guess.

CW: What do you want to see happen now?

Leah: I want to get rid of it. I don't need it. The kids don't need it. I want to put it behind me.

CW: How are you going to put it behind you?

The worker continued to use reality therapy techniques (Glasser, 1965) to ascribe autonomy and responsibility to Leah. Leah's stability and mobility were assessed to be excellent. She had the power and the motivation to take the lead, on her own, and to exercise independent judgment and choices. Individual counseling with clients following a suicide may make use of any therapeutic modality that is appropriate for the client.

Group work was also used in the case of Leah. At approximately the same time as the individual session with Leah, the manager of the bookstore where Ronnie had worked requested a session between the crisis worker and the entire bookstore staff. The manager said that the employees were having a hard time becoming reconciled to Ronnie's suicide. One group session was conducted. Every employee of the bookstore attended and participated in the group session. The crisis worker facilitated the crisis group work by using the following format, with the employees sitting in a circle in the conference room.

1. The worker made a brief introduction, outlining the purposes and structure of the meeting.
2. Starting with the bookstore manager, each participant was given an opportunity to verbalize how he or she wished to remember Ronnie and to identify his most positive attribute.
3. During the second round, each employee was given an opportunity to take care of unfinished business with Ronnie and to verbally say goodbye to Ronnie.
4. The crisis worker summarized the content and feelings that the group had expressed. Then the crisis worker ended the session by (a) affirming the legitimate grief expressed by the group, (b) absolving the group of guilt and responsibility for Ronnie's death, (c) honoring the attributes and memory of Ronnie's life by a period of silent meditation, asking all people present to imagine themselves saying goodbye and letting go of Ronnie, and (d) giving permission for each person to end the stage of acute grief at the conclusion of the meeting.

The crisis worker used a format that is useful in many crisis group settings—especially in a group whose concern is loss and grief. A variation of this group technique would be appropriate with a variety of groups representing a family, a fraternal group, the employees in a workplace, a school group, or a church group (any group dealing with a loss-related crisis).

What the worker did with the bookstore staff, in relation to Ronnie's suicide, was to tap into the power and cohesiveness of the group to nurture group restoration of the equilibrium of individual members. The worker's assessment was that the group norm was stuck in a stage of denial, isolation, and guilt. The group session was a powerful one. Although it appeared to the crisis worker that each member was ready to let go of Ronnie and move on toward positive growth, the worker invited members to come in for individual follow-up. In this case, none was requested.

Bereavement in Childhood

Elmer and Irene Kirk, ages 36 and 38 respectively, were spending all the time, energy, and money they could in their attempts to cope with the terminal illness of their son, Charles, 5 years old. After a year of being in and out of the children's research hospital, Charles sensed that he did not have long to live, but Elmer and Irene were attempting to make Charles's remaining days as happy and meaningful as Charles's physical condition would permit. Their only other child, Corine, age 8, felt sad, bewildered, lonely, and neglected.

The whole family was consumed with grief the day Charles died. In addition to grief, Corine suffered from guilt. She felt guilty because she had dared to wish within herself for several months that Charles's illness would just end and get it over. Somehow Corine believed that her wish had contributed to the death of her brother. She also felt guilty because she was alive and didn't deserve to live as much as Charles.

The following intervention strategies were provided and issues explored with the Kirk family during the days and weeks immediately prior to and following Charles's death.

1. *Individual counseling and intervention.* Assessment of Corine's concept of death. Recognition that Corine will react to the loss in her own way and that Corine and her parents may receive a great deal of valuable help from Corine's school counselor (Bertoia & Allan, 1988). Ensuring that Corine has opportunities to participate actively and learn the medical facts relating to Charles's terminal illness in a truthful and realistic manner. Use of child-centered counseling approaches in helping Corine deal with and refute her guilt feelings related to her brother's death: child-centered approaches to include the use of puppets, art work, sand play, and psychodrama. Assessment of the impact of Charles's death on both parents and Corine. Including Corine in the funeral plans and commemorative activities. Providing opportunities for each family member to release grief energy. Assessment of the impact of Charles's illness and death on the marriage and provision of individual therapy for Elmer and Irene as needed.
2. *Family systems therapy.* Assessment of the family's stress level and coping resources. Provision of opportunities for the family together to explore the important issues related to Charles's death: the meaning, the good times and memories,

guilt, blame, anger, rejection, and unfinished business. Focus on Corine: ensuring that she knows that she is loved and that the time and energy that Elmer and Irene have devoted to Charles in no way diminished their love and devotion to Corine. Discussion of feelings openly and honestly, keeping in mind the developmental capacity of Corine. Ensuring that all family members have permission to mourn openly. Assuming that Charles's death will have a lasting impact on Corine and will be manifested through her play, her fantasy life, and her relationship to both Elmer and Irene.

Using puppets in crisis counseling with Corine, the worker was able to help Corine dispute her irrational and magical belief that her covert wish had caused her brother's death. During two previous sessions with the crisis worker, Corine had developed a great deal of trust in the worker and considerable facility and ease in using the raggedy puppets. At the third session, there were five puppets: Raggedy Ann, Raggedy Billy (Raggedy Ann's dying brother), Raggedy Mom, Raggedy Dad, and Raggedy Doctor.

CW: (*Holding Raggedy Billy and Raggedy Mom—Raggedy Billy speaking.*) Mommy, Mommy, Ann said I'm dying because she had bad thoughts—she wished I would die, so you and Daddy could leave the hospital and come back home.

CW: (*Holding Raggedy Billy and Raggedy Mom—Raggedy Mom speaking.*) Oh, Billy! Wishing someone is dead can *never, never* make it happen! Your sister Ann has a perfect right to wish for this hurting and sickness to end. She is so lonesome for Mommy and Daddy and for you, too. It's normal for her to wish this sickness were ending. But Ann should never feel bad or guilty just because she wished something. Remember, *wishing* doesn't make it happen!

CW: (*Holding Raggedy Billy and Raggedy Mom—Raggedy Billy speaking.*) Mommy, I wish I could see my sister Ann. I'd like to tell her it's OK.

CW: (*Holding Raggedy Billy and Raggedy Mom—Raggedy Mom speaking.*) Oh, Billy, my dear son! (*Smack—Raggedy Mom kisses Raggedy Billy.*) I love you and I love Ann. Here comes your sister now. Why don't you talk to her? She's in the hospital to visit you.

CW: (*Holding Raggedy Billy and Raggedy Mom—turning toward Corine, Raggedy Billy speaking.*) Hi, sister Ann. I'm glad you came to the hospital to see me. I wanted to tell you how much I love you and how much I will miss you when I die. I want you to know that you should not worry about the wishes and thoughts you had. My disease is making me die. Your thoughts cannot make me or anyone else die. I want you to know it's all right. I love you, Mom loves you, and Daddy loves you. We will always love you.

Corine: (*Holding Raggedy Ann and Raggedy Dad—Raggedy Ann speaking.*) I'm sorry. I wish you wouldn't die. I'm very, very sorry. I hope you don't die.

CW: (*Holding Raggedy Billy and Raggedy Mom—Raggedy Mom speaking.*) Oh, Ann, we all hope he doesn't die. But I'm afraid he will. Then we will all be sad together. We will miss him. But we will have to learn to live without Billy when he's gone. We will still love him. But we will have each other and love each other. We will never blame you or ourselves for his death. His death will be caused by his sickness, not by your thoughts or wishes nor by my thoughts or wishes.

The segment is an example of puppet dialogue in child-centered crisis counseling. The crisis worker was using a variety of theoretical approaches: rational-emotive behavior, behavioral, and Gestalt therapies. Although the segment cannot reveal all the preparatory work and dialogue that preceded and followed this brief encounter, it provides some idea of how versatile and effective puppetry can be. The crisis worker was focusing on only one dimension of bereavement during childhood—Corine's guilt feelings. But there are few, if any, dimensions of childhood bereavement that cannot be effectively dealt with through play media.

Corine's grief work could have been processed with equal effectiveness by a crisis worker skilled in using art work, sand play, or psychodrama. Any concern or issue related to childhood grief can be approached through child-centered methods. What we want to emphasize is that intervention with children must be handled differently from adult intervention and that it is absolutely necessary for crisis workers who help children to be highly trained and knowledgeable in child-centered counseling techniques.

Bereavement in Adolescence

An accident following the prom in early May resulted in the deaths of four Cedar Grove High School students: Phil, age 16, the driver of the car; Jerry, age 17; Lucille, age 16; and Velma, age 17. The whole school and the entire community were distraught with grief and sadness. The families were in a state of shocked bereavement. A group of seven classmates at school, representing the four youngsters' closest friends, appeared to be stuck in their grief. Even after the commemoration program in the auditorium was concluded, the group did not feel they could resume their school activities or daily lives without further grief work. Shirley, Lee, Peggy, and Bryan, all 17, and Eddie, Sheila, and Cynthia, all 16, requested the help of the school counselor in reaching some understanding and resolution of their feelings of anguish and grief.

The following intervention strategies were provided and issues explored with the adolescents by the school counselor during the days and weeks immediately following the burial of the four teenagers killed in the automobile accident after the prom.

1. *Individual counseling and intervention.* Assessment of individual stress levels. Providing individuals a safe place to release stress energy. Helping adolescents feel comfortable in expressing how they feel. Providing death education for adolescents.

2. *Group grief work.* Providing an atmosphere for the seven adolescents as a group to deal with the deaths of their four classmates in particular and with the area of death and dying in general. Providing for group sessions and projects that commemorate the deceased classmates. Group exploration of unfinished business through written or role-playing exercises. Provision for students to deal with the deaths outside the group within the school environment through peer support groups. Gray (1988) reported that bereaved teens in support groups found peers to be "most helpful," compared to other school-related workers, and that bereaved adolescents did not want to be singled out or treated in special ways (pp. 187–188).

In cases of sudden death, grief, and bereavement among adolescents, a great deal of shock, vulnerability, remorse, and other emotions quickly emerge. Because most adolescents lack experience dealing with the death of their peers and because social influence is powerful and pervasive in a setting such as a high school, the use of adolescent group grief work is an ideal strategy for controlling distortions and rumors and for helping young people release grief energy and begin to resolve their feelings of loss.

The Cedar Grove High School counselor was attentive to the feelings of fear, shock, powerlessness, and emptiness that many students manifested. The counselor believed that a group would be an appropriate setting for the students to share their feelings of grief and vulnerability. The group grief work was also perceived to be an appropriate activity in which the school could nurture learning and provide appropriate modeling for handling real-life bereavement and commemoration. The counselor, meeting with the group in the group guidance room, served as the crisis worker. She met with several grief work groups during the days immediately following the deaths of the four students. Each group, although different in composition, shared a common theme of needing to deal with the deaths of their classmates. The counselor set the tone by introducing the topic and encouraging members to share their emotional responses to the loss. Later during the session, after the release of students' grief energy, the counselor began to use structured techniques to help them sharpen their memories and focus on reality.

CW: I really appreciate all the expressions of your feelings you've given so freely. Before the session begins today, I asked Peggy to go by the yearbook office and pick up a copy of this year's *Wildcat.* I also asked her to pick up some leftover photographs that the yearbook staff did not use. Peggy, would you like to share some of them with the group?

Peggy: I put filing cards in the pages of the annual that I thought we'd like to look at. Oh, and I've got some great shots of Lucille, Jerry, and Velma. I only found one of Phil, and that was in a group. But Phil's class picture is in there (pointing toward the yearbook), and all four of them look so real and alive and so happy in the activities section.

The students in the group showed a great deal of interest and released a great amount of stress energy while examining the photographs of the deceased students. Later in the session, the group discussed death in general, the impact of death on the living, and their own deaths. The counselor was able to use another technique that is sometimes effective in group grief work: the epitaph exercise. Each group member was given four index cards and was instructed: "If you were given the responsibility for writing the epitaphs for Phil, Jerry, Lucille, and Velma, write down the exact words on the cards that would appear on their gravestones." The group shared their epitaphs and discussed them.

Eddie: I thought Cynthia's was really good when she wrote—about Jerry—"Here lies the Will Rogers of Cedar Grove," because he really did like everybody. (*Students nod in agreement.*)

Shirley: I *almost* cried when I wrote Velma's, and then I *did* when Sheila read Velma's. I just felt like I couldn't stand it. It's so true. I'm really going to miss that girl. (*Students nod in agreement. Long period of silence; thoughtful look on all faces.*)

CW: I think what we've done is to write down, in the briefest form, what we want to remember most about each of our beloved classmates.

Before the session ended, the counselor led the group in identifying the positive contributions that each of the deceased students had made and in verbalizing their goodbyes to each of their departed classmates. The counselor was attempting to use the power and social influence of the group setting to enhance the emotional impact on each member and to prepare each member to say goodbye, let go of the deceased, and begin to get ready to go on living.

Separation and Divorce

When Don Nakamura, age 32, an automobile salesman, came home and announced to Hattie, age 30, that he wanted a divorce, it shattered Hattie's world. The marriage had been going downhill for a long time, and during the preceding months Don had been staying out nights. Nevertheless, Hattie, a licensed practical nurse, wanted to patch things up and to have a child. But Don was adamant, and Hattie finally reluctantly admitted that the marriage was over. She was still distraught, with feelings of grief, guilt, worthlessness, and failure. Hattie felt her life was meaningless. She didn't want to face life alone; she was stuck in grief and felt that she was doomed to live the remainder of her life unfulfilled, without a husband or a child, because no decent man would ever want her. She felt like a complete failure and blamed herself for not succeeding in the marriage. Hattie found herself frozen in a state of grief, remorse, guilt, depression, and self-pity.

The following intervention strategies were provided and issues explored with Hattie during the days and weeks immediately following Don's announcement to her that he wanted a divorce.

1. *Individual counseling and intervention.* Assessment of Hattie's lethality level. Assessment of her coping skills and resources. Provision of a safe atmosphere for her to talk it out and cry. Assessment of available support people. Consideration of her feelings of worthlessness, fear, failure, guilt, anger, depression, self-pity, and unfulfillment. Use of rational-emotive behavior therapy, reality therapy, and cognitive-behavioral modalities to help Hattie identify and successfully refute her negative and self-defeating beliefs and self-statements. Reprogramming her internal sentences and developing positive action steps that she can own, practice, and carry out independently of a helping person.

2. *Support group work.* Identification of divorce self-help groups for Hattie to use as supports. Assessment of her social needs on a time continuum from the present forward for several years. Use of the self-help group to assist her in making realistic plans for her personal and social adjustment to her new situation.

3. *Referral resources.* Assessment of Hattie's need for legal, vocational, and financial assistance. If necessary, identification of specific referral people for her to contact immediately. (While interviewing her, careful assessment of statements reflecting her present autonomy and ability to attain her goals. For example, dependence on her husband's attorney, banker, or accountant may not serve her best interests. Many newly estranged wives find that they need a different attorney, banker, and accountant from the ones used by their spouses. They also find that they need to find employment or training to enable them to become economically self-sufficient. Often this is a sudden and difficult switch. Therefore, the worker must be sensitive, supportive, realistic, and assertive, because Hattie is so vulnerable during this phase of her separation.)

The abrupt termination of relationships by separation is frequently accompanied by emotional responses that are as traumatic as after the death of a loved one. People who experience the loss of separation may exhibit shock, disbelief, denial, anger, withdrawal, guilt, and depression. Each person responds in unique ways. Some will cry for several days. Some will verbally ventilate for days on end—to anyone who will listen. Some will go into a state of withdrawal, described by one person like this: "When he came in and told me he was leaving, packed his clothes, and left, I got in the bed and didn't move. I intended to stay there until I died."

The loss by separation may be the result of severance of a marriage, a heterosexual, gay, or lesbian love relationship, a business partnership, or any other close personal attachment. Helping people overcome the emotional and behavioral results of the loss of a relationship requires crisis intervention skills similar to those needed in other types of grief and bereavement.

In Hattie's case, the client presented herself for crisis intervention several days after she had stayed in bed with the intention of crying and grieving herself to death. Hattie truly wanted to die after Don told her he was permanently leaving. At first her denial was so profound that she thought to herself, "This can never be. I will never be a divorcée. My parents must never know. My friends must never find out." Hattie did not talk to anyone about Don's leaving for several days. There was denial: "He really isn't leaving for good. He will be back. We will work things out." There was guilt: "What did I do to cause this? I must have been a terrible wife. I shouldn't have been so blind to his needs. If I just died in an accident, he could go on and marry the other woman and no one would ever have to know." There was anger: "I've got a good mind to find her and pay her back for all the misery she's caused me."

Hattie experienced several stages of grief before she brought herself to the point of presenting her problem to the crisis worker.

CW: Well, Hattie, what brings you to see me today?

Hattie: My whole life is a wreck. It's really a mess. The main thing is that my marriage is breaking up. Well, I guess it has broken up. My husband's gone. Been gone over a week. I guess you could say that the marriage is down the tubes.

CW: You're feeling rather hopeless about the marriage. What has happened today, in relation to your marriage breakup, to impel you to come in right now?

Hattie: Well, I was tired of lying around feeling sorry for myself—thinking about killing myself or harming my husband's girlfriend. My intuition told me that neither one of those acts would solve anything, so I've come in here looking for better answers.

CW: Hattie, I'm really glad you decided to come today. What I want to find out first is whether you are in danger of suicide now. Are you still strongly contemplating suicide? Do you have a means at hand to do it? And how close are you to suicide now?

The crisis worker's first concern was Hattie's immediate safety. It appeared from her verbal and nonverbal cues that she was hopeful and stable enough to have some mobility. The fact that she came to present her problem was another positive factor. Then, when Hattie told the worker that she didn't have a definite plan or a definite means to kill herself, the worker proceeded with other steps in the crisis interview. At one point, Hattie appeared to be in a stage of "holding on," which Schneider (1984) described as having elements of anger, bargaining, and denial.

Hattie: I just can't believe this is happening to me. My whole world has caved in on me. This is simply horrible. I just can't stand it. I just don't know what I'm going to do without him.

CW: You're truly feeling terrible about the breakup of your marriage. But what I believe you're meaning is that this situation is causing you a great deal of hurt and causing you to make some major shifts in your life. But it seems to me you enormously complicate matters when you convince yourself, inside your head, that this is the most terrible catastrophe that could possibly happen to you. *Telling yourself* that you can't stand it and *believing* that it's horrible and that you're terrible seem to be an exaggeration that is getting in the way. That is different from telling yourself that it is very bad, and you hate it, but that you didn't cause it and that this isn't the end of the world—even though it may make your life very difficult for a while. You see where your catastrophizing, exaggerating, and awfulizing color your thinking and get in the way of your clearly and objectively assessing not only what has happened but also what your real options are, don't you?

Hattie: Well, yes. Since you put it that way, I guess I have come down harder on myself and on the problem than is necessary. I know it isn't really horrible, but I feel, at the time, that it's horrible and awful.

CW: Then your *believing* it's horrible and awful is the real culprit, isn't it? There is a difference between your beliefs and how things really are.

Hattie: You're right! It helps just to look at it differently, even though it doesn't solve my big mess.

CW: You're right. It doesn't solve it. But we can objectively examine it and together begin to figure out options you can choose if we know on the front end, even though you're grieving over your hurt, that we are not dealing with a world-shattering catastrophe.

The crisis worker was intervening by using elements of Rational Emotive Behavior Therapy (REBT) described in Ellis and Grieger (1977). The worker was attempting to dispute the client's irrational beliefs about the separation and help her begin to direct her emotional energy toward the real issues. Hattie was an intelligent person who quickly responded to the rational ideas presented. But, as is typical in such cases dealing with the emotional state during loss, the worker knew that repetition, practice, support, and encouragement would need to be provided. A person in Hattie's state must have far more than just a one-shot session using REBT to get her beyond her crisis and back to a state of equilibrium.

In addition to using REBT as a crisis intervention strategy, the crisis worker also used a self-managed behavioral technique (Williams & Long, 1983) to help Hattie expend her grief energy over a period of several weeks. What Hattie did was to make a series of audiotapes—alone, at home—in a sequential and systematic manner. The purposes for making the tapes were (1) to serve as a mechanism for self-catharsis, (2) to present to the crisis worker her full story, (3) to clarify, in her own mind, the stages of grief she was going through, and (4) to document her progress on a set of cassette tapes that might be provided for other women in similar cases of loss. Hattie worked regularly and diligently on the self-taped sessions. The cassettes were quite useful to the crisis worker. But the main value of the behavioral plan was providing Hattie the purpose and the experience of doing it. She described in detail both her feelings and her actions throughout several stages: shock and disbelief, denial, anger, withdrawal, guilt, depression, searching, and resolution.

Hattie made eight cassette tapes. She reported that the most valuable and helpful aspect of the sound-taping activity was that of listening to her own tapes, which she found herself doing over and over. Hattie kept the cassettes with the stated intention of continuing to listen to them. But she later reported that after her crisis subsided, she didn't need to listen to them any more.

Death of a Pet

The Thompsons—Hollis, age 36, Faye, age 33, and their adopted daughter, Dawn, age 4—were grieving over the death of Tinfoil, their aged terrier. Tinfoil had been like a member of the family. He had been a faithful companion to the Thompsons since they were newlyweds; he had been the affectionate and protective playmate of Dawn from the day the Thompsons got her through the adoption agency. Lately he had developed severe health problems, and the veterinarian had finally told the Thompsons that Tinfoil's medical condition made it necessary to terminate his life.

The following intervention strategies were provided and issues were explored with the Thompson family during the days and weeks immediately following the death of their pet.

1. *Individual counseling and intervention.* Assessment of the levels of grief, guilt, and stress in each—Hollis, Faye, and Dawn. Assessment of Dawn's understanding of the death of the pet. Provision of a period to grieve and release grief energy. Follow-up play therapy and ceremonial events as outlets for Dawn (Schoenberg, 1980, pp. 203–204) and display of meaningful objects that link Dawn to her deceased pet (Lagoni et al., 1994, p. 265).
2. *Group work.* Providing an opportunity for the family to talk about Tinfoil's death in a realistic, factual, and honest manner. Using the pet's death to help Dawn to begin to develop her concept of death, free of misinformation. Providing opportunities and activities for the family to commemorate the pet's life and to reformulate the death within a context of growth.

Schoenberg (1980) suggested that families use ceremonial events to help deal with their grief following the death of a pet (pp. 203–204). The Thompsons used a ceremonial event of pet burial to help open up opportunities for discussion, sharing of feelings, and explaining death to their daughter.

Faye: We had a small funeral in the back yard. I helped Dawn invite a few of her close friends to the funeral, and our next-door neighbors mailed us a sympathy card. Hollis and Dawn dug Tinfoil's grave, and we had a simple but beautiful graveside service. There were flowers and friends, and we paid tribute and said goodbye to him. It was a good thing for our family and for the friends who came. The funeral and our family discussions provided a good background later on for Dawn's play therapy. We even had another small ceremony when we put Tinfoil's collar on the bulletin board in Dawn's room. We're still grieving somewhat over his death, but it has been a learning experience for all of us, and I think Dawn will have a more realistic and healthy view of death, loss, and grief as a result of these activities.

Such experiences as those described by Faye are undoubtedly "learning experiences" for adults as well as children. There are many other strategies that can be used to help people who have lost a pet. For instance, where children are involved, puppets, art work, sand play, photographs of the pet, and modeling clay are only a few of the play therapy techniques that might be used to stimulate discussion. Also, variations on ceremonial events can be developed to fit the needs of each specific situation involving loss of a pet. The strategies used in dealing with the loss of pets are aimed at the same goals as those used in any human loss: helping the grievers wind down their various stages of grief in healthy and growth-promoting ways. It is recommended that people who work with clients who have lost pets read from sources such as *The Human–Animal Bond and Grief* (Lagoni et al., 1994) and *Pet Loss and Human Bereavement* (Kay et al., 1984).

Bereavement in Elderly People

Rosa and Robert Kizer, ages 82 and 85 respectively, had been living in a nursing home for four years. Robert had been there more than a year when Rosa had to join him. Their three living children resided in other states and were busy with their own families, so Rosa placed Robert in the nursing home when he was 80 and she was no longer able to care for him because he required 24-hour nursing care. Robert's physical condition continued to deteriorate during his stay at the nursing home until he could not speak or move his body. He could turn his head a little and nod or shake his head for yes and no, and could swallow some liquid foods—but his eating had to be managed skillfully to avoid choking him. By this time Rosa was no longer housed in Robert's room because of the specialized care he required. Rosa was quite mobile physically, but her memory lapses kept her from assuming any role in caring for Robert. Rosa was in the dining room eating breakfast when one of the medical staff members came and requested that she come to Robert's room because they couldn't rouse him. When Rosa arrived at the room, a staff physician met her and informed her that Robert had apparently died in his sleep.

The following intervention strategies were provided and issues explored with Rosa during the days and weeks immediately following Robert's death.

1. *Individual counseling and intervention.* Assessing Rosa's level of grief and coping ability. Providing opportunities for Rosa to release her grief energy. Assessing Rosa's physical and mental capacities to cope. Assessing her children's ability to help. Examination of her economic, medical, legal needs. Using therapeutic strategies such as person-centered therapy, reminiscence techniques, and validation therapy to help Rosa feel calm and secure, and to remember vividly that she is a worthwhile person and that she and Robert have had worthwhile lives.
2. *Group work.* Groups within the nursing home. Support groups.
3. *Referrals.* Medical; religious; organizations; legal assistance. Rosa's church; her children; senior citizens' agencies.

Rosa Kizer continued to live in the nursing home following Robert's death. Her grief was alleviated by several factors: she was physically mobile, she had lots of friends in the nursing home and in the community, she was an outgoing person with an optimistic outlook on life, and she was visited regularly for several weeks by a crisis worker who used reminiscence and validation therapy techniques (American Association of Retired People, 1986). Even with the positive factors she had going for her, Rosa experienced periods of denial, isolation, loneliness, fear, anger, bargaining, and depression. The crisis worker's goal was to help Rosa through the various stages of grief, to achieve a satisfactory degree of reconciliation with and acceptance of Robert's death, and to begin to establish her postcrisis life as a worthwhile person.

Rosa: A lot of times I just mope around. Some of the time I get to feeling sorry for myself. Then sometimes I forget and find myself walking down to Robert's room before I remember that he isn't there any more. My life seems so meaningless without him.

CW: (*Holding Rosa's hand and gently caressing the top of her hand and forearm.*) You're really missing him, and you're also having trouble remembering. What would you like to recall most?

Rosa: Oh, I'd like to recall the times when all of us were at home and healthy. When the kids were home. But that seems so far away in the past.

CW: Rosa, I'd like to know what it means to you to vividly remember the good times in your life—like when your family was together.

The crisis worker was relaxed, talking in a soft and caring tone, and gently caressing Rosa. The worker had taken special care to arrive at Rosa's room at the exact appointment time (many older clients are very sensitive about people promising to come and see them, then arriving late). In facilitating Rosa's reminiscing, the worker was careful not to appear pressed for time or anxious to leave and go on to the next patient. (The "hurried and harried" behavior of caregivers gets on the nerves of many elderly clients and causes them to lose confidence in the caregiver.) The worker was careful to nurture Rosa's trust, which is absolutely necessary for helping people through validation therapy or reminiscence techniques.

Rosa: We lived out on the mountain then. Goodness gracious me, we had such a good time! All of us working hard then, but we played hard and enjoyed life too. (*Long pause. Rosa is smiling.*)

CW: Take just as long as you wish to think about life out on that mountain—just as vividly and clearly as you can get it in your mind. Just relax and take as long as you wish. Just take your memories back there and get hold of those good feelings you have about those good times.

Rosa: (*Long pause.*) Yes, yes! What a beautiful place and a beautiful time in life. We lived on the ridge overlooking a deep, green valley. Had such beautiful children. Grew about everything we ate. Yes, those were the times that warm one's heart. That was a glorious time. A sight for sore eyes! (*Long pause.*)

CW: It sounds wonderful! It sounds like it warms your heart right now, just remembering it clearly and telling me about it so clearly.

The crisis worker's objective was to get Rosa in touch with her vivid memories of real occurrences in her past, which she could recall, identify with, describe, and feel

worthwhile about. The worker also wanted to feel and show genuine respect for and interest in Rosa's memories and descriptions. Such genuineness on the part of an interested listener is a good catalyst for sharing and validating one's own past. The worker assured Rosa that he appreciated the shared journey into her past and that he respected her for it and wanted to continue to do more on the next visit. Rosa was also encouraged, through cognitive-behavior techniques (Cormier & Cormier, 1998; Meichenbaum, 1985) to think about the past between visits and to be prepared to bring other important and memorable events into open expression. The worker reminded Rosa that she had the power, in her mind, to imagine and to go back and experience many healthy and happy times, and then to return in her mind to her room and feel a real sense of pride in her own private history of accomplishments.

The techniques for working with the elderly do not have to be highly formal, structured, or complicated. All intervention should be done by workers who live and model relationship skills (Cormier & Hackney, 1987; Egan, 1982) such as empathy, genuineness, acceptance, respect, warmth, and sincere caring in a relaxed and non-hurried way.

Loss Related to HIV Infection and AIDS Disease

Crisis workers are likely to encounter clients whose presenting problems include dealing with the phenomenon of HIV infection or disease. The six steps of crisis intervention and the triage assessment system presented in Chapter 2 are appropriate for use in assessing and helping HIV-positive/AIDS clients. However, the worker must be prepared to consider additional dimensions such as stigma, personal rejection, prejudice, religious rejection, political apathy, cultural discrimination, legal oppression, fear of contagion, guilt, shame, and loss of self-esteem. According to Miller (1990, pp. 189–195), people living with acute HIV- or AIDS-related problems may present serious psychological symptoms such as shock and denial, anxiety, depression, and other emotional trauma.

Clinical Characteristics.   Shelby (1995) noted that emotional trauma commences when the client first receives notification of seropositivity. Typically expected clinical reactions include disorganization of self, particularly in the initial weeks after notification of results, episodic periods of anxiety, depression, demoralization, psychosomatic symptoms, low self-esteem, exacerbation of premorbid relational conflicts, and social withdrawal in the months following discovery. Stine (1996, p. 355) addresses the emotional effects this way: "More than any other disease, AIDS is about human interactions. HIV is transmitted during the most intimate moments. Diagnosis results in immediate and powerful emotional responses, often long before physical symptoms occur." Even though important advances are being made in medical research and treatment of HIV-positive/AIDS patients, medical care and emotional and practical supports are the chief weapons available to fight against HIV/AIDS.

Multiple Symptoms and Risks.   The HIV-infected person may experience any number of severe physical and emotional manifestations such as nausea, panic attacks, diarrhea, dizziness, skin rashes, lethargy, tremor, visual disturbances, sweating, depression, and sleeplessness. It is difficult to distinguish whether and to what extent these symptoms are related to the HIV infection itself or to its cognitive effects on clients (Miller, 1990, p. 190). However, HIV/AIDS clients, as opposed to many other crisis clients, have a good many reasons for developing anxieties. Their short-term and long-term medical prognosis may be grim. HIV/AIDS clients are particularly at risk of infection as well as being subject to the burden of stigma, marginalization, and social, occupational, domestic, and sexual hostility. They face potential abandonment, isolation, and physical pain. There are many more real problematic burdens in the lives of the HIV-infected than the noninfected encounter.

HIV-infected people may feel it is impossible for them to alter their circumstances. It is difficult for them to maximize their future health, and they have little control over helping loved ones and family members to cope. Adequate medical, dental, and welfare assistance may be very difficult to obtain. They may face negative social pressures and ostracism because they have been identified as homosexual, or drug users, or prostitutes, or unfaithful. The HIV-infected person may also suffer from lack of privacy and confidentiality, feel the loss of dignity with increasing physical dependency, experience sexual unacceptability, and lose physical and financial independence. All these factors militate against clients' coping mechanisms and may lead to what Miller (1990, p. 191) terms functional and social retreat and withdrawal as a direct response.

Formidable Hurdles.   Kübler-Ross (1987), Miller (1990), Ostrow (1990), and others have documented a variety of difficult psychological as well as physical obstacles that people with HIV face. They may view their entire physical being as transformed and obsessively search for new bodily evidence of the disease progression, they may relentlessly pursue fads related to health and diet regimens, and they may become preoccupied with illness, death, and avoidance of new infections. They may exhibit severe shock, denial, helplessness, self-blame, false hope of a cure, anger, frustration, guilt, and suicidal ideation. Crisis workers facing people living with HIV must be aware of these special factors and characteristics as they assess and engage in crisis intervention work.

Sources of Help.   Crisis intervention with HIV-infected clients must start with sensitive and empathic listening. We recommend using the six-step method of relating to clients. Because clients may be experiencing an enormous array of situational, medical, and environmental problems, workers must be diligent in defining the total scope of problems, ensuring physical and psychological safety, and providing emotional supports. Crisis workers usually find that there is very little they can do *for* clients. But in many communities, especially urban and suburban settings, there are a good many resources and alternatives to be used *with* them. Therein lies the necessity of knowing which resources and services are available at any given time and locale.

Sources of Hope.   Borden (1991), Klein (1998), Maslanka (1993), Shelby (1995), Squire (1993), and Stine (1996) have demonstrated that, even though HIV/AIDS clients face formidable and daunting obstacles, counseling and crisis intervention can help them improve the quality of their lives. Borden (1991) and Shelby (1995) describe how object relations–oriented therapy helps clients cope with both their disease and their sense of loss of self.

Growth.   Borden (1991, p. 179), commenting on object relations therapy with HIV/ AIDS male clients, found that many of them were able to find hope in the face of adversity. (Object relations therapy, derived from Freudian psychology, holds that the term *object* refers to a person or a thing, external to the client, toward which the client forms a powerful intrapsychic bond, attachment, alliance, or relationship. Borden's clients may have built on such intrapsychic attachment, bonding, or alliances to generate, within themselves, the confidence and motivation needed to restore their coping skills). Borden observed that tremendous psychological growth can emerge from a previous state of devastation. Borden (p. 445) stated that

> The experience appears to have led to increased reflection, reappraisal of priorities, and consolidation of self and identity for a number of men. In some instances persons revised their outlook and found more meaningful ways of living in view of actual circumstances and realistic prospects. That the men believed they had experienced enduring change since discovery of HIV seropositivity is itself an indication of psychological growth in the face of misfortune and adversity.

Difficulties.   Working with women in People Living with Aids (PLWA) group therapy, Maslanka (1993) and Squire (1993) related the difficulties and drawbacks they encountered. Maslanka (1993, p. 113) quoted Tunnell (1989, p. 9) regarding such difficulties, stating that "conducting an AIDS group dramatically demonstrates our own inadequacies, ineffectiveness, powerlessness, and helplessness—feelings that are rarely as powerful as in other psychotherapy groups." Such stresses can often lead to loss of emotional objectivity on the part of the crisis worker or counselor and consequent drop in the quality and effectiveness of staff and volunteers. The problem in working with women who are HIV positive and PLWAs is that most crisis workers are volunteers who have had little knowledge or training with HIV-positive people or with women of different color or cultures (Maslanka, 1993, pp. 113–114).

Both Squire and Maslanka assert that special training and indoctrination is needed for crisis workers who would work with women living with AIDS or HIV. Such work requires unique skills in understanding, communicating, empathizing, and advocacy with this particular clientele, because many of these women have special issues—related to pregnancy, childbearing, child care, single parenting, insurance and medical needs, legal difficulties, threats of career loss, and homelessness—that many men do not face. Crisis workers and other caregivers who work with women with AIDS or HIV must possess competencies in counseling with both women and PLWAs. In addition, crisis workers need special supervised training in assisting women of color who also have AIDS or HIV (Maslanka, 1993, pp. 110–115; Squire, 1993, pp. 1–12).

Bereavement in HIV-Infected Clients

Ansel's lover of six years died of AIDS 18 months ago. Last week Ansel lost his job as a bank teller and desperately needs a job. He suspects that the people at the bank found out that he, Ansel, tested HIV positive last May. Normally, Ansel is an intelligent, enthusiastic, energetic, outgoing, friendly, and positive individual. He is an exceptionally competent employee whom the bank was grooming for management work. Now he presents himself as unsure of himself, depressed, angry, nervous, and anxious.

Ansel: On top of everything else, I have never come out to my parents. I wouldn't mind telling my mom, but I would have real trouble revealing to my dad that I'm gay. I also worry that telling him that I've tested positive will be too much for his heart, because he's had two bypasses already. I may have to find a cheaper place to live, too. I have too many things to deal with right now.

CW: Ansel, I'm really glad you came in here today. I can see that you are feeling really depressed today. Are you to the point of thinking about killing yourself?

The first thing the crisis worker does is to explore Ansel's lethality level. The crisis worker has the benefit of a brief intake statement and is prepared to explore the most pressing client concerns. But ensuring Ansel's safety takes first priority. Ansel's verbal and nonverbal responses and the worker's rapid assessment of his cognitive, affective, and behavioral functioning on the triage form (affective, 3; behavioral, 6; cognitive, 3; total 12) give the worker the green light to proceed with further exploration of the problem with Ansel. Even so, the crisis worker is sensitive to any changes that might signal a sudden elevation of his cognitive, affective, or behavioral assessment scores.

CW: I'm happy to know that you're safe for now. Ansel, what do we most need to work on right now?

Ansel: I just don't see how I can handle everything, how I can make plans, so much is happening.

CW: You're overwhelmed with all the issues you are facing, and you're needing some help, understanding, and supports right now.

Ansel: It's been hard enough since my lover died. I still miss him terribly, and now I've lost my job—I have to tell my parents I'm gay—God! Gay and HIV-positive, too!

CW: Ansel, I want you to know that I'm very sorry that you have lost your lover. You've suffered tremendous loss. The loss of your lover and now your job. I also sense your difficult struggle as you seek to tell your parents. I want to work with you and help you find some ways to deal with all these difficult and important things you are facing.

The crisis worker acknowledges the continued losses Ansel has faced as well as the problem of revealing to his parents his HIV status and the difficulty he will face in the future. Concomitantly, the crisis worker begins to think about what concrete actions Ansel will need to take immediately: employment counseling, support groups in order to help Ansel regain a sense of control over his life, and medical services. The research of Williams and Stafford (1991) indicates that a fundamental form of intervention with partners and adult family members is the use of peer groups to break down the prevalent feelings of isolation, enhance sharing of personal grief, and to promote healing (pp. 425–426). Additional interventions found to be appropriate are providing adequate and accurate information to dispel anxiety about contagion issues, providing counseling in either group, family, or individual formats, and grief and bereavement work. Grief work was found to be "most effective in a group setting where, due to disparity of psychological adjustment levels, new members could gain hope for eventual healing of acute grief from grievers further along in the process" (p. 426).

Ansel was referred to an existing group at the Aid to AIDS Center that could provide the help he needed in an environment of warmth, acceptance, professional competence, and healing. The crisis worker followed up by contacting the center director to ensure that Ansel obtained the services he needed.

SUMMARY

The major components of the dynamic stages of death, dying, grief, and bereavement are depicted in models developed by Kübler-Ross (1969) and Schneider (1984). There are several types or categories of loss, and a variety of strategies that crisis workers can use in counseling and intervention with examples of each type or category. Crisis workers must come to grips with their own mortality, be prepared to respect the privacy, individuality, and autonomy of the bereaved, and avoid the imposition of their own values on the people they seek to help. The particular culture where people live plays a major role in the manner in which they respond to loss. Modes of handling bereavement and grief are expressed in ways that meet the needs of each individual, family, and local society as well as the sociocultural norms at large.

Several different types of loss typify the kinds of human events or tragedies that might bring crisis workers into contact with persons experiencing grief. Examples of such events depicted are (1) the death of a spouse or significant other, (2) the death of a child, (3) bereavement following a suicide, (4) bereavement in childhood, (5) bereavement in adolescence, (6) separation and divorce, (7) the death of a pet, (8) bereavement in elderly people, and (9) the trauma associated with HIV disease and AIDS. Intervention strategies, techniques, and skills that crisis workers need for helping people in the above categories of grief are described along with methods that crisis workers can use to take care of their own bereavement, grief, and vitality. Crisis workers who do not take care of themselves emotionally, physically, and spiritually become vulnerable to the dilemma and possibly the severe distress of *vicarious traumatization.* Worker vigilance is recommended to prevent trauma associated with the emotional bonding that sometimes becomes attached to the tragedies, bereavement, and grief of clients.

Every human being will, at one time or another, suffer personal loss. During our lives most of us will encounter numerous people who are experiencing bereavement or grief as a result of some personal loss. What may be clearly perceived as a personal loss ranges from a devastating occurrence, such as the death of a spouse or a child, to what many people might view as a minor loss. In any event, it is an important loss if the individual perceives it as such, and workers must treat each client's loss with empathy, caring, and sensitivity.

People in helping roles are encouraged to use their personal assets, listening competencies, compassion, faith and spiritual assets, and skill at making referrals to assist the bereaved in coping, as best they can, with their own unique losses. Although the bereaved can never forget the loss and return to a state of complete precrisis equilibrium, they can be helped to reformulate their loss within a context of growth and hope.

CLASSROOM EXERCISES

I. Simulated Counseling with Prepared Cases

To gain experience and practice in dealing with various bereavement situations, the class will work in small groups. Each group is assigned a different type of bereavement, selected from the following list:

  Case of the Wynn family (death of a spouse)
  Case of the Drake family (death of a child)

Case of the Nichols family (bereavement of a family following suicide)
Case of the Kirk family (bereavement in childhood)
Case of Cedar Grove High School (bereavement in adolescence)
Case of Hattie (separation and divorce)
Case of the Thompson family (death of a pet)
Case of Rosa (bereavement in the elderly)
Case of Ansel (bereavement following discovery of HIV+)

Through role taking of bereaved clients in the various cases, students will spontaneously generate dialogue and crisis intervention techniques in each group.

Each group will select one or more clients from their assigned case. Group members will take the roles of the client(s), the crisis worker(s), and observer(s)/evaluator(s). A specified time limit will be given for the crisis intervention sessions, to be conducted simultaneously within each group. The crisis intervention session will begin as soon as the clients have had time to review the data of their case. While the crisis workers process the case with the clients, the observers/recorders will make a tape recording of the session, take notes, and be prepared to report on the effectiveness of the crisis intervention and to make suggestions for improvement.

Whenever the crisis intervention sessions have been completed, observers/recorders will make their reports to members of their particular groups. The exercise will be completed by providing time in each group for a summarizing discussion.

II. Simulated Counseling with Class-Developed Scenarios

Replicate the preceding exercise, except give each group the task of generating a realistic bereavement situation for the role-taking exercise instead of using one of the nine cases described in the chapter. Group members can draw on their own knowledge and experience for creating realistic scenarios. All groups should be cautioned to (1) refrain from using recognizable people, places, or situations and (2) maintain confidentiality by refraining from mentioning the scenarios outside the classroom, even though only parts of real situations may have been simulated. The facilitator or instructor should monitor the group simulations to provide supportive counseling, after the activities have been completed, to any individual who identifies with the scenario so completely that a state of personal crisis is induced—a situation that is rare, but possible.

At the conclusion of the exercise, individual role players will be instructed to verbally disassociate themselves from the roles they enacted during the simulation. The disassociation is done within each small group.

RESOURCES

We offer here a list of several representative resources that pertain to different categories of loss: death, dying, bereavement, and grief associated with this chapter. Most of the organizations and societies listed have branches in large cities. Local library information centers and crisis intervention agencies have information about how to reach these resources. The *Encyclopedia of Associations* (Maurer & Sheets, 1999) contains a comprehensive annotated listing of similar organizations.

Death of a Child
Compassionate Friends
P.O. Box 3696
Oak Brook, IL 60522-3696
Phone: (360) 990-0010 Fax: (360) 990-0246
e-mail: TCF_National@prodigy.com
Web site: http://www.compassionatefriends.org
Self-help organization open to provide support to parents who have experienced the death of a child of any age from any cause. Objectives are to promote and aid parents in the positive resolution of grief and to foster physical and emotional health of bereaved parents and siblings. Provides "telephone friends" who may be called, identifies sharing groups that meet monthly, and disseminates information concerning the grieving process.

Euthanasia
Choice in Dying—The National Council for the Right to Die (CID)
200 Varick Street, 10th Floor
New York, NY 10014-4810
Phone: (212) 366-5540
Toll free: (800) 989-WILL
Fax: (212) 366-5337
e-mail: CID@cgiuces.org
Web site: http://www.choices.org
Seeks to serve the needs of dying patients and their families. Advocates for the rights of patients to participate fully in decisions about the medical treatment at the end of their lives. Provides state-specific advance directive documents, including living wills and durable powers of attorney for health care for directing end of life health care. Offers free public and professional education and counseling about preparation and use of advance directives. Sponsors specialized educational programs. Maintains speaker's bureau. Sponsors a wide scope of interdisciplinary programs.

Hemlock Society USA (HSUSA)
P.O. Box 101810
Denver, CO 80150
Phone: (303) 639-1202
Toll free: (800) 247-7421
Fax: (303) 639-1224
e-mail: hemlock@privatei.com
Web site: http://www.hemlock.org/hemlock
Maximizes options for dignified death, including voluntary physical aid in dying for mentally competent terminally ill adults who request it, within the context of legal safeguards. Through educational research and legislation, serves as the voice of a national grass roots movement, providing material and information to the public, the media, health care professionals, and legislators. A patient advocacy program promotes the importance of living wills, powers of attorney, and advance health care directives. Supports the option of active voluntary euthanasia for the advanced terminally ill and the seriously incurably ill. Seeks to promote a climate of public opinion tolerant of the terminally ill individual's right to end his or her own life in a planned manner and to improve existing laws on assisted suicide. Does not encourage suicide for any primary

reason other than terminal illness; approves suicide prevention work; believes that the final decision to terminate one's own life should be one's own. Approves suicide prevention and does not advocate self-deliverance for any reason other than terminal illness under legal and ethical protocols.

Care of Terminally Ill
Hospice Association of America (HAA)
228 7th Street, S.E.
Washington, DC 20003
Phone: (202) 546-4759 or (202) 547-7424
Fax: (202) 547-3540
e-mail: djh@nahc.org
Web site: http://www.nahc.org
Promotes concept of hospice, a philosophy of health care expressed through the provision of a variety of medical and nonmedical services to terminally ill patients and their families. Offers technical assistance, educational programs, publications, and representation of industry issues to state and federal governments. Maintains speaker's bureau. Compiles statistical data. Provides referral services and consultations for Medicare reimbursement problems.

AIDS Information
CDC National AIDS Clearinghouse (NAC)
P.O. Box 6003
Rockville, MD 20849-6003
FAX: (301)519-6616
Phone (toll free): (800) 458-5231
e-mail: aidsinfo@cdcnac.org
Web site: http://www.cdcnpin.org
A service of the Centers for Disease Control (CDC). Collects, analyzes, and disseminates information on HIV/AIDS, primarily for health care professionals, educators, social service workers, attorneys, employers and human resource professionals, state HIV/AIDS programs, community organizations, and service associations. Responds to the information needs of health professionals. Referral service and AIDS Clinical Trials Information Services.

Sudden Infant Death Syndrome
SIDS Alliance—National Sudden Infant Death Syndrome Foundation (NSIDSF)
10500 Little Patuxent Parkway, No. 420
Columbia, MD 20144
Phone: (410) 964-8000
Toll free: (800) 221-SIDS (24 hours a day)
Fax: (410) 964-8009
Provides information and referral services to concerned citizens, health professionals, and parents who have lost a child to sudden infant death syndrome (SIDS), a condition commonly known as "crib death" that accounts for 6000 to 7000 infant and child deaths in the United States annually. Assists bereaved parents who have lost a child to SIDS; works with families and professionals in caring for infants at risk due to cardiac and respiratory problems. Supports research and seeks to make the public aware of SIDS and related issues.

Grief

Third Age Home Page

http://www.thirdage.com/features/family/alone/

The Internet offers many sources of support for people who are mourning the loss of a loved one. Hundreds, perhaps thousands, of messages of empathy, sympathy, support, and hope are accessible on the Internet each day among members of several online support groups for the bereaved. People who are suffering from any number of types of loss addressed in this chapter may find some degree of comfort and solace and perhaps find ways to take the first step toward healing in their journey through the throes of grief and bereavement that we all must inevitably pass. The Third Age Home Page is only one example of such information and support one may find on the Internet.

REFERENCES

Alyson, S. (Ed.). (1990). *You can do something about AIDS* (2nd ed.). Boston: The Stop AIDS Project.

American Association of Retired People (AARP). (1986, September). Reminiscence: Thanks for the memory. *AARP News Bulletin*, p. 2.

Attig, T. (1996). *How we grieve: Relearning the world.* New York: Oxford University Press.

Austad, D. S. (1992). The wisdom of group: A psychotherapeutic model for elderly persons. *Psychological Reports, 70,* 356–358.

Bahrick, A. S., & Sharkin, B. S. (1990). Pet loss: Implications for counselors. *Journal of Counseling and Development, 68,* 306–308.

Balk, D. E. (1990, August). *The many faces of bereavement on the college campus.* Paper presented at the annual meeting of the American Psychological Association, Boston.

Becker, E. (1973). *The denial of death.* New York: Free Press.

Bertoia, J., & Allan, J. (1988). School management of the bereaved child. *Elementary School Guidance & Counseling, 23,* 30–38.

Borden, B. (1991, September). Beneficial outcomes in adjustment to HIV seropositivity. *Social Service Review, 65*(3), 434–449.

Bordow, J. (1982). *The ultimate loss: Coping with the death of a child.* New York: Beaufort Books.

Bowes, J., Fristad, M., Weller, E., & Weller, R. (1992). Depression in recently bereaved prepubertal children. *American Journal of Psychiatry, 48,* 1536–1540.

Braun, M. J., & Berg, D. H. (1994). Meaning reconstruction in the experience of parental bereavement. *Death Studies, 18,* 105–129.

Bruce, M. L., & Kim, K. M. (1992). Differences in the effects of divorce on major depression in men and women. *American Journal of Psychiatry, 149,* 914–917.

Buscaglia, L. (1982). *The fall of Freddie the leaf: A story of life for all ages.* New York: Holt, Rinehart & Winston.

Canetto, S. S. (1994). Gender issues in the treatment of suicide individuals. *Death Studies, 18,* 513–523.

Cho, C., & Cassidy, D. F. (1994). Parallel processes for workers and their clients in chronic bereavement resulting from HIV. *Death Studies, 18,* 273–292.

Colgrove, M., Bloomfield, H. H., & McWilliams, P. (1991). *How to survive the loss of a love.* Los Angeles, CA: Prelude Press.

Cormier, L. S., & Hackney, H. (1987). *The professional counselor: A process guide to helping.* Upper Saddle River, NJ: Prentice Hall.

Cormier, S., & Cormier, B. (1998). *Interviewing strategies for helpers: Fundamental skills and cognitive behavioral interventions* (4th ed.). Pacific Grove, CA: Brooks/Cole.

Corr, C. A. (1993). Coping with dying: Lessons that we should and should not learn from the work of Elisabeth Kübler-Ross. *Death Studies, 17,* 69–83.

Costa, L., & Holliday, D. (1994). Helping children cope with the death of a parent. *Elementary School Guidance & Counseling, 28,* 206–213.

Couric, K. (1999, October 4). Step by step.

(People Online; AOL Feature, "Starting Over," on the Internet. [The Katie Couric Story of Losing Her Husband to Cancer]).

Cramer, S. H., Keitel, M. A., & Zevon, M. A. (1990). Spouses of cancer patients: A review of the literature. *Journal of Counseling and Development, 69,* 163–166.

Crase, D. (1994). Important consumer issues surrounding death. *Thanatos, 19*(1), 22–26.

Dershimer, R. A. (1990). *Counseling the bereaved.* New York: Pergamon Press.

Dickens, M. (1985). *Miracles of courage: How families meet the challenge of a child's critical illness.* New York: Dodd, Mead.

Douce, L. A. (1993). AIDS and HIV: Hopes and challenges for the 1990s. *Journal of Counseling and Development, 71,* 259–260.

Downs, H., & Walters, B. (1986, May 15). *20/20 News Magazine* (television program). ABC Television Network.

Dutro, K. R. (1994, April). *A dynamic, structural model of grief.* Paper presented at the Eighteenth Annual Convening of Crisis Intervention Personnel, Chicago.

Dworkin, S. H., & Pincu, L. (1993). Counseling in the era of AIDS. *Journal of Counseling and Development, 71,* 275–281.

Edelstein, L. (1984). *Maternal bereavement: Coping with the unexpected death of a child.* New York: Praeger.

Edgar, L. V., & Howard-Hamilton, M. (1994). Noncrisis death education in the elementary school. *Elementary School Guidance & Counseling, 29,* 38–46.

Egan, G. (1982). *The skilled helper: Model, skills, and methods for effective helping* (2nd ed.). Pacific Grove, CA: Brooks/Cole.

Ellis, A., & Abrahms, E. (1978). *Brief psychotherapy in medical and health practice.* New York: Springer.

Ellis, A., & Grieger, R. (1977). *Handbook of rational-emotive therapy.* New York: Springer.

Finkbeiner, A. K. (1998). *After the death of a child: Living with loss through the years.* Baltimore, MD: The Johns Hopkins University Press.

Freeman, L. (1978). *The sorrow and the fury: Overcoming hurt and loss from childhood to old age.* Upper Saddle River, NJ: Prentice Hall.

Gibson, A. B., Roberts, P. C., & Buttery, T. J. (1982). *Death education: A concern for the living* (Fastback No. 173). Blooming-ton, IN: Phi Delta Kappa Educational Foundation.

Glasser, W. (1965). *Reality therapy.* New York: Harper & Row.

Gray, R. E. (1988). The role of school counselors with bereaved teenagers: With and without peer support groups. *The School Counselor, 35,* 185–192.

Gudas, L. (1990, August). *Children's reactions to bereavement: A developmental perspective.* Paper presented at the annual meeting of the American Psychological Association, Boston.

Guerriero-Austrom, M. G., & Fleming, S. J. (1990, August). *Effects of sibling death on adolescents' physical and emotional well-being: A longitudinal study.* Paper presented at the annual meeting of the American Psychological Association, Boston.

Hansen, J. C., & Frantz, T. T. (Eds.). (1984). *Death and grief in the family.* Rockville, MD: Aspen Systems.

Holcomb, L. E., Neimeyer, R. A., & Moore, M. K. (1993). Personal meanings of death: A content analysis of free-response narratives. *Death Studies, 17,* 225–232.

Hopmeyer, E., & Werk, A. (1994). A comparative study of family bereavement groups. *Death Studies, 18,* 243–256.

Huber, J. T. (1993). Death and AIDS: A review of the medico-legal literature. *Death Studies, 17,* 225–232.

Hughes, R. B. (1988). Grief counseling: Facilitating the healing process. *Journal of Counseling and Development, 67,* 77.

Joffrion, L. P., & Douglas, D. (1994). Grief resolution: Facilitating self-transcendence in the bereaved. *Journal of Psychosocial Nursing and Mental Health Services, 32*(3), 13–19.

Johnson, S. M. (1977). *First person singular: Living the good life alone.* Philadelphia: Lippincott.

Kandt, V. E. (1994). Adolescent bereavement: Turning a fragile time into acceptance and peace. *The School Counselor, 41,* 203–211.

Kaplan, C. P., & Gallagher-Thompson, D. (1995). Treatment of clinical depression in caregivers of spouses with dementia. *Journal of Cognitive Psychotherapy, 9,* 35–44.

Kay, W. J., Neiburg, H. A., Kutscher, A. H., Grey, R. M., & Fudin, C. E. (Eds.). (1984). *Pet loss and human bereavement.* Ames: Iowa State University Press.

Kirk, W. G. (1993). *Adolescent suicide: A school-based approach to assessment and intervention*. Champaign, IL: Research Press.

Klein, S. J. (1998). *Heavenly hurts: Surviving AIDS related deaths and loss*. Amityville, NY: Baywood.

Koocher, G. (1975). Why isn't the gerbil moving? Discussing death in the classroom. *Children Today, 4,* 18–36.

Kübler-Ross, E. (1969). *On death and dying*. New York: Macmillan.

Kübler-Ross, E. (1975). *Death: The final stage of growth*. Upper Saddle River, NJ: Prentice Hall.

Kübler-Ross, E. (1981). *Living with death and dying*. New York: Macmillan.

Kübler-Ross, E. (1983). *On children and death*. New York: Macmillan.

Kübler-Ross, E. (1987). *AIDS: The ultimate challenge*. New York: Macmillan.

Kushner, H. S. (1983). *When bad things happen to good people*. New York: Avon.

Lagoni, L., Butler, C., & Hetts, S. (1994). *The human-animal bond and grief*. Philadelphia, PA: Saunders.

Lane, K. E., & Dickey, T. (1988). New students and grief. *The School Counselor, 35,* 359–362.

Leahy, M. J. (1993). A comparison of depression in women bereaved of a spouse, child, or parent. *Omega: Journal of Death and Dying, 26*(3), 207–215.

Maslanka, H. (1993). Women volunteers at GMHC (Gay Men's Health Crisis Center, New York City). In C. Squire (Ed.), *Women and AIDS: Psychological perspectives* (pp. 110–125). Newbury Park, CA: Sage.

Matter, D., & Matter, R. (1982). Developmental sequences in children's understanding of death with implications for counselors. *Elementary School Guidance and Counseling, 17,* 112–118.

Maurer, C. M., & Sheets, T. E. (Eds.). (1999). *Encyclopedia of associations* (34th ed.) (Vol. 1, Parts 1, 2, and 3). Farmington Hills, MI: Gale Research.

McCown, D. E., & Davies, B. (1995). Patterns of grief in young children following the death of a sibling. *Death Studies, 19,* 41–53.

McKenna, S. (1999, September 28). Stages of grieving. (Third Age Home Page on the Internet at http://www.thirdage.com/features/family/alone/). In Finding Support Online, by Sharon McKenna.

Meichenbaum, D. (1985, May). Cognitive behavior modification: Perspectives, techniques, and applications. Two-day workshop, St. Louis, MO, presented by Evaluation Research Associates (Syracuse, NY).

Miller, D. (1990). Diagnosis and treatment of acute psychological problems related to HIV infection and disease. In D. G. Ostrow (Ed.), *Behavioral aspects of AIDS* (pp. 187–206). New York: Plenum Medical.

Nieburg, H. A., & Fischer, A. (1982). *Pet loss: A thoughtful guide for adults and children*. New York: Harper & Row.

Norris-Shortle, C., Young, P. A., & Williams, M. A. (1993). Understanding death and grief for children three and younger. *Social Work, 38,* 736–741.

Osterweis, M., Solomon, F., & Green, M. (Eds.). (1984). *Bereavement: Reactions, consequences, and care*. Washington, DC: National Academy Press.

Ostrow, D. G. (Ed.). (1990). *Behavioral aspects of AIDS*. New York: Plenum Medical.

Pauley, J. (1986, June 3). *Divorce is changing America* ("White Paper" documentary). National Broadcasting Company (NBC) News.

Rando, T. A. (1984). *Grief, dying, and death: Clinical interventions for caregivers*. Champaign, IL: Research Press.

Rando, T. A. (Ed.). (1986). *Parental loss of a child*. Champaign, IL: Research Press.

Raphael, B. (1983). *The anatomy of bereavement*. New York: Harper & Row/Basic Books.

Rappaport, H., Fossler, R. J., Bross, L. S., & Gilden, D. (1993). Future time, death anxiety, and life purpose among older adults. *Death Studies, 17,* 369–379.

Reitmeyer, R. (2000, March). Dog gone? From cats to snakes, counselors help heal human hearts following a pet loss. *Counseling Today, 42*(9), 1, 26–27.

Riordan, R. J., & Allen, L. (1989). Grief counseling: A funeral home-based model. *Journal of Counseling and Development, 67,* 424–425.

Romanoff, B. (1993). When a child dies: Special consideration for providing mental health counseling for bereaved parents. *Journal of Mental Health Counseling, 15,* 384–393.

Saakvitne, K. W., & Pearlman, L. A. (1996). *Transforming the pain: A workbook on* vicarious traumatization. New York: Norton.

Schiff, H. S. (1977). *The bereaved parent.* New York: Crown.

Schliebner, C. T., & Peregoy, J. J. (1994). Unemployment effects on the family and the child: Interventions for counselors. *Journal of Counseling and Development, 72,* 368–372.

Schneider, J. (1984). *Stress, loss, and grief: Understanding their origins and growth potential.* Baltimore: University Park Press.

Schoenberg, B. M. (Ed.). (1980). *Bereavement counseling: A multidisciplinary handbook.* Westport: CT: Greenwood Press.

Schonfeld, D. J. (1989). Crisis intervention for bereavement support: A model of intervention in the children's school. *Clinical Pediatrics, 28,* 27–33.

Schwiebert, V. L., Myers, J. E., & Dice, C. (2000). Ethical guidelines for counselors working with older adults. *Journal of Counseling & Development, 78,* 123–129.

Shelby, R. D. (1995). *People with HIV and those who help them: Challenges, integration, intervention.* Binghamton, NY: Hayworth Press.

Smith, E. D. (1995). Addressing the psychospiritual distress of death as reality: A transpersonal approach. *Social Work: Journal of the National Association of Social Workers, 40,* 402–413.

Squire, C. (Ed.). (1993). *Women and AIDS: Psychological perspectives.* Newbury Park, CA: Sage.

Staudacher, C. (1987). *Beyond grief: A guide for recovering from the death of a loved one.* Oakland, CA: New Harbinger.

Stepnick, A., & Perry, T. (1992). Preventing spiritual distress in the dying client. *Journal of Psychosocial Nursing, 30,* 17–20.

Stine, G. J. (1996). *Acquired immune deficiency syndrome: Biological, medical, social, and legal issues* (2nd ed.). Upper Saddle River, NJ: Prentice Hall.

Tamm, M. E., & Granqvist, A. (1995). The meaning of death for children and adolescents: A phenomenographic study of drawings. *Death Studies, 19,* 203–222.

Thompson, K. E., & Range, L. M. (1992). Bereavement following suicide and other deaths: Why support systems fail. *Omega: The Journal of Death and Dying, 26,* 61–70.

Tunnell, G. (1989, August). *Complications in working with AIDS patients in group psychotherapy.* Paper presented at the ninety-seventh Annual Convention of the American Psychological Association, New Orleans.

U.S. Bureau of the Census. (1995). *Statistical abstract of the United States 1995.* Washington, DC: Department of Commerce.

Walters, B., & Downs, H. (1997, November 13). *20/20 Thursday: News Magazine* (television program). ABC Television Network.

Wass, H., & Corr, C. A. (1985). *Childhood and death.* New York: Harper & Row.

Weisman, A. D. (1990–1991). Bereavement and companion animals. *Omega: Journal of Death and Dying, 22,* 241–248.

Williams, R. J., & Stafford, W. B. (1991). Silent casualties: Partners, families, and spouses of persons with AIDS. *Journal of Counseling and Development, 69,* 423–427.

Williams, R. L., & Long, J. D. (1983). *Toward a self-managed life style* (3rd ed.). Boston: Houghton Mifflin.

Worden, J. W. (1991). *Grief counseling and grief therapy: A handbook for the mental health practitioner* (2nd ed.). New York: Springer.

Crisis in the
Human Services Workplace

Part Three deals with helping the crisis worker cope with crises that might occur in the human services workplace.

The world in which we live and crisis workers function is becoming increasingly dangerous and violent for clients as well as for human services professionals. Chapter 10, on violent behavior in institutions, provides information and techniques to help workers better understand and deal with both the volatile environment and the dilemmas of clients who strive to cope within that environment.

Chapter 11 is a new chapter about crises in schools. This chapter covers potentially dangerous and lethal situations involving gangs, estranged violent individuals, and suicide. It also deals with developing crisis intervention plans and crisis response teams to deal with traumatic events that affect the school.

Hostage taking is another phenomenon of the contemporary human services setting that has become increasingly prevalent. Chapter 12, on hostage negotiation, discusses concepts and strategies that could save the lives of both crisis workers and/or their clients, although we hope that the reader's only such encounter will be restricted to these pages.

Chapter 13 deals with human services worker burnout. Our philosophy is that preventing worker burnout should be a way of life for both individuals and agencies; that continuous learning or training is a preferred means of acquiring and maintaining helpful attitudes, skills, and competencies; and that individual crisis workers can control their own personal and professional development, thereby enhancing their personal functioning as well as their value to society. Chapter 13, on human services workers in crisis, is written on the assumption that workers and institutions can avoid burnout by attending to their own physical, psychological, and emotional wellness. Individuals not only can prevent burnout but also can choose to positively and constructively nurture their own lifestyles, physical stamina, mental health, and personal vibrancy.

Violent Behavior in Institutions

The average number of people murdered per year in the workplace from 1992 to 1996 in the United States was 1023, and they were not all killed at the post office! The average number of assaults per year during that time frame in teaching, medical, and mental health occupations (the occupations that many readers of this book are most likely to enter or be in) was 351,847. For mental health workers in particular, the average number of assaults was 79.5 per 1000 workers. To put those statistics in terms that tell you how dangerous the mental health services can be, you would be just as likely to be assaulted if you worked at a gas station (79.1/1000) and less likely to be assaulted if you worked in a convenience/liquor store (68.4/1000). Besides law enforcement and corrections occupations, only bartending is more likely to get you assaulted (91.3/1000) (U.S. Bureau of Justice, 1998)! A best estimate is that the chances for human services workers being assaulted during their lifetime on the job is approximately 50 percent (Turns & Blumenreich, 1993, p. 5).

It should be readily apparent from those sobering statistics that disgruntled stock brokerage clients are not the only ones who exact revenge on their service providers! The point of citing these statistics is that the subject concerns you—not just somebody who works down the hall from you. For anyone who has ever seen a client wildly out of control and who has been injured or scared senseless in trying to contain that violence, one time is once too many (Lanza, 1985). In summary, the foregoing statistics should tell you one thing: Although you may believe that you are some combination of Jane Adams, Carl Rogers, and Mother Teresa ministering charitably and caringly to the disenfranchised and outcast, your clients may have a different idea! Why is this so?

PRECIPITATING FACTORS

A variety of hazards now put human services professionals more at risk of being victims of violent behavior than they have been in the past. Probably the most noteworthy trend has been the increase in the number of substance abuse clients (Blumenreich, 1993b, pp. 23–24; Turns & Blumenreich, 1993, p. 7).

Since the "least restrictive environment" movement and subsequent deinstitutionalization of patients in the 1970s, day care centers, halfway houses, and shelters have filled the gap left when the warehousing facilities of state mental institutions were emptied. Lack of facilities for transients, shortage of staff, and inability to monitor medication closely have created a fertile breeding ground for clients to regress to their previous pathological states (Reid, 1986).

Furthermore, with increased societal and judicial awareness of the part that mental illness plays in crime, a number of people who would formerly have been incarcerated are now remanded to mental health facilities. Also, because of prison overcrowding, potentially violent people are released on early parole. Farmed out to halfway houses that are also understaffed, and assigned to parole officers who have tremendous caseloads, parolees do not always get the follow-up and supervision they need. Thus, human services workers are now being asked to deal with a wider variety of ex-felons than before (Hartel, 1993; Walker & Seifert, 1994).

Although many school buildings have become almost prisonlike as a result of efforts to keep from becoming battlegrounds for gangs, they are not unlike other providers of human services. Gang violence can be found in settings ranging from emergency rooms to juvenile detention facilities. Gang members' extreme violence either as a rite of passage into the gang or in retaliation for offenses against them is without fear or remorse regarding any person, at any time, or at any place (Kinney, 1995, pp. 168–169).

The increase in the number of elderly people now institutionalized in nursing homes and hospitals has created a whole new population of potentially violent individuals. Casually dismissed as infirm and incapable of rendering harm to anyone, geriatric patients commit a disproportionate percentage of violent behavior against human services workers (Petrie, 1984, p. 107).

INSTITUTIONAL CULPABILITY

By their very nature, most care providers are readily accessible to clientele and have minimal security checks. Therefore, they are also easy prey to anyone who walks in off the street with intentions other than seeking services (Turner, 1984, pp. v–vi). Furthermore, security training and implementing security devices cost time and money. Administrators trained solely in handling financial, logistical, and personnel functions of institutions with the responsibility of maintaining adequate patient care are unaware of what it takes to provide an adequately secure environment for their staff (Dyer, Murrell, & Wright, 1984). Physical features of mental health facilities built to deemphasize security and confinement as a reaction to the "snake pit" mental hospitals of old have paradoxically put the human services workers at greater risk (Turns, 1993). Emotionally "cold and uncaring" settings, unclear staff roles, poorly structured activities, downsizing of staff, and unpredictable schedules all are stress elevators for the potentially violent client (Blumenreich, 1993a, pp. 38–39).

Because of the negative publicity that accrues from violent incidents, institutions are loath to admit that they occur (Lanza, 1985), and it appears that such episodes go largely unreported (California Occupational Safety and Health Administration, 1998, p. 3; Hartel, 1993). Understaffing, overwork, poor physical environment, poorly educated nonprofessional staff, high staff turnover, absenteeism, on-the-job accidents, poor or incomplete communication between administration and staff, and lack of unifying treatment philosophy allow frustration to build within the staff and disrupt the treatment routine. As the staff transfer their frustration to the clients, the clients in turn become more threatened and start testing the limits of what will be tolerated. When staff attempt to impose behavioral limits under these erratic conditions, the outcome is often violent behavior by clients (Blair, 1991; Jensen & Absher, 1994; Piercy, 1984, pp. 141–142).

Finally, secondary victimization occurs when, after an injury by an assaultive client, there is the underlying belief that "It wasn't handled right by the worker" (Turns, 1993, p. 131). Thus, not only does the human services worker suffer physical assault and all the psychological ramifications that go with it, but he or she also becomes a scapegoat for an administration unable to handle the increased violence.

STAFF CULPABILITY

Staff members are also culpable. A prevailing philosophy is that because human services workers are caring, well-intentioned people, recipients of their services will act in reciprocal ways toward them (Turner, 1984, p. vii). The ostrichlike assumption that "it can't happen to me, and besides, there are so few violent incidents that I really don't need to be concerned" is fallacious (Dyer et al., 1984, p. 1). Madden, Lion, and Penna (1976) interviewed psychiatrists who had been assaulted and found that more than half could have predicted the assault if they had not been in denial and thought themselves immune from the threat.

From the client's viewpoint, becoming violent is invariably seen as a consequence of being provoked by the worker (Rada, 1981). Paradoxically, most staff members have little idea what they or the institution do that is provocative. For many clients, treatment may be perceived as coercive, threatening, or frightening. When a client feels little control over treatment conducted by an authoritarian staff, the client may feel the only option is to aggressively act out (Blair, 1991). Furthermore, if the staff treatment philosophy includes limit setting such as use of restraints, seclusion, medication, locked units, and assaults as "part of the territory," then a self-fulfilling prophecy is likely to develop, with violent acting out as the norm and the only way to get attention. Conversely, staff's failure to set limits in a positive, firm, fair, and empathic manner where choices are clearly outlined is likely to result in limit testing that leads to violence. Particularly when client routine, status, or self-esteem is disrupted by dictatorially taking away food and drink, recreational time, cigarettes, furloughs, or other privileges without defining how those might be lost, giving any reason why they are lost, or explaining how they can be regained, those actions increase the potential for violence toward the limit setter (Blair & New, 1991).

LEGAL LIABILITY

Although health care providers may be the victims of assaults, they may also become legally liable for their actions, no matter how well intended those actions may be (Monahan, 1984). Such liability extends to the institutions and directors of those institutions, who may fall under a heading of "vicarious" civil and criminal liability (Dyer et al., 1984, p. 23). As paradoxical as it may seem, assaultive clients have held institutions and employees liable for failure of "duty of care owed" to those selfsame clients (Belak & Busse, 1993, pp. 137–143). Numerous successful lawsuits also have been brought against health care providers for failure to properly diagnose, treat, and control violent clients or protect third parties from assaultive behavior (Felthous, 1987).

Workplace violence has become so serious that the Centers for Disease Control has declared workplace violence as a national health problem (National Institute for Occupational Safety and Health, 1992) and the federal Occupational Safety and Health

Administration (OSHA) has come to the conclusion that workplace violence can no longer be tolerated (California Occupational Health and Safety Administration, 1998, p. 5). OSHA has recently started issuing citations for employers who fail to adequately protect their employees from violence in the workplace.

Communication and consultation about potentially violent clients is extremely important. One of the better predictors of who will and will not be at risk to become violent is the pooled clinical judgment of human services workers who have come into contact with the client (Durivage, 1989; Werner, Rose, Murdach, & Yesavage, 1989). One of the primary reasons that cases have been decided in favor of the plaintiff involves the failure of one clinician to communicate with another clinician that a client has a history of violence and might present a future danger (Beck, 1988; Belak & Busse, 1993, p. 147). From that standpoint, the institution and worker who wish to avoid a court appearance would do well to flag records of violent acts or ideation and relay that information to other members of the treatment team for feedback and possible action (Blair, 1991; Martin, Francisco, Nichol, & Schweiger, 1991).

DYNAMICS OF VIOLENCE IN HUMAN SERVICES SETTINGS

The dynamics of violence in human services settings is complex. It not only involves the clients themselves, but also the human services workers and the institution.

Assessment

In 1974, the American Psychiatric Association conducted a study on the psychiatric profession's ability to predict violence. The conclusion was that such predictions were unreliable and lacked validity (American Psychiatric Association, 1974). This conclusion has been confirmed by other studies and reviews (Kirk, 1989; Monahan, 1988; Mulvey & Lidz, 1984; Palmstierna & Wistedt, 1990). Even the highly esteemed MMPI has problems in reliably predicting violence (Sloore, 1988).

The current status of prediction and the "real world" of mental health care provision lead us to believe that the ability to predict who will and who will not become violent at what times and under what conditions has not been clearly established. Predictions are especially likely to be wrong when crisis workers have little background information on clients and may not have time to make more than an "eyeball" assessment of the situation before they have to act. Yet data do exist to present general profiles of clients who are more likely than others to become violent given the right constellation of conditions. Keeping in mind the foregoing qualifiers—"general profiles" and "right conditions," the following bases for profiling violence are "best bet" predictors.

Bases for Violence

There are biological, psychological, and social bases for violence. Biologically, low intelligence, hormonal imbalances, organic brain disorders, neurological and systemic changes of a psychiatric nature, disease, chemicals, or traumatic head injury may lead to more violence-prone behavior (Hamstra, 1986; Heilbrun, 1990; Heilbrun & Heilbrun,

1989). Psychologically, specific situational problems, certain functional psychoses, and character disorders are predisposing to violence (Greenfield, McNeil, & Binder, 1989; Heilbrun, 1990; Heilbrun & Heilbrun, 1989; Klassen & O'Connor, 1988). Socially, modeling the behavioral norms of family, peers, and the milieu within which one lives can exacerbate violent tendencies (Nisbett, 1993; Tardiff, 1984a, p. 45; Wood & Khuri, 1984, p. 60). Finally, specific on-site physical environmental stressors such as heat, crowding, noise, conflict, and poor communication are triggers that can cause violence (Jensen & Absher, 1994). When all these ingredients are mixed together, the results start to resemble the kinds of people and environments with which the crisis worker is likely to come in contact (Tardiff, 1984a, p. 45).

Age.   Males between the ages of 15 and 30 tend to be the most violent subgroup (Blumenreich, 1993a, p. 36; Fareta, 1981; Kroll & Mackenzie, 1983; Shah, Fineberg, & James, 1991). Next come elderly clients, who are disproportionately represented in the population that may become violent (Petrie, 1984, p. 107). Crisis workers tend to dismiss this group as being harmless. In a study of 200 cases of assault at the Cincinnati Veterans Administration Medical Center, Jones (1985) discovered that 58.5 percent of the assaults took place in the geriatric facility. This statistic is noteworthy because the institution also had a large psychotic and substance-abusing population.

Substance Abuse.   Simonds and Kashani (1980) found high positive relationships between crimes committed against people and the use of amphetamines, phencyclidine (PCP), barbiturates, cocaine, and Valium. Rada (1981) found that toxic reactions to illicit drugs such as PCP, LSD, barbiturates, amphetamines, and cocaine are common causes of violence in the emergency room.

Whereas barbiturates are commonly understood to depress the central nervous system, on occasion barbiturates may have an excitatory effect. Anyone coming off sedatives or depressants may be as disposed as or even more disposed to violent acting out than those who take stimulants. One of the most popular prescribed and abused drugs, Valium, is a classic example. Effects of withdrawal from Valium may result in irritability and opposition to the health care setting and workers within that setting (Piercy, 1984, pp. 131–132). The popularized versions of withdrawal from heroin as depicted by the media and press are close to reality. Particularly when addicts are suffering withdrawal, they are highly likely to perpetrate violence to secure the drug or the means to obtain it (Piercy, 1984, p. 135).

Cocaine is clearly associated with violence (Blumenreich, 1993b, p. 24). Any clients known to have a cocaine addiction should be considered dangerous, particularly if they are being brought in for treatment while actively using. Amphetamine abusers may overreact to mild and minor stimulations in their environment and at their worst become indistinguishable from paranoids or acute paranoid schizophrenics (Piercy, 1984, p. 132). Amphetamine abusers make up a large portion of the clientele who find their way into groups we run in the penal setting, and they have almost always been incarcerated because of violent crimes.

Alcohol has been associated with more than half of reported cases of violence in emergency rooms and one-fourth of reported cases in psychiatric institutions (Bach y Rita, Lion, & Climent, 1971). In the withdrawal stage, the individual may behave violently either because of being denied alcohol or, less commonly, because of hallucinosis, which causes the individual to fear imagined harm. The potential for violence is further increased when individuals who have a history of psychosis engage in alcohol or drug use (Klassen & O'Connor, 1988; Yesavage & Zarcone, 1983).

Predisposing History of Violence.   A history of serious violence, including homicide, sexual attacks, assault, or threat of assault with a deadly weapon is one of the best predictors of future violence (California Occupational Health and Safety Administration, 1998, p. 3; Fareta, 1981; Monahan, 1981). Any background material that includes contact with the criminal justice system for aggravated felonies, weapons possession, threats against prospective victims, or a history of assaultive behavior while hospitalized should automatically put the human services worker on notice to be extremely cautious with the client (Blumenreich, 1993a, p. 37; Klassen & O'Connor, 1988).

Of all the predisposing clues for violent behavior, probably there are none better than being brought to a facility for violent behavior as a part of emotional disturbance or mental illness. McNeil, Binder, and Greenfield (1988) found that recent violent acts in the community are highly associated with violent acts in the first 72 hours of inpatient care.

Psychological Disturbance.   A variety of mental disorders fall within the category of psychological disturbance: the antisocial personality type, who has a history of violent behavior, emotional callousness, impulsivity, and manipulative behavior; the borderline personality, who floats in and out of reality, lacks adequate ego strength to control intense emotional drives, and repeatedly exhibits emotional outbursts; the paranoid, who is on guard against and constantly anticipating external threat and is willing and able to take action against that threat; the manic, who has elevated moods, hyperactivity, and excessive involvement in activities that may have painful consequences; the explosive personality, who has sudden escalating periods of anger; the schizophrenic who is actively hallucinating, excited, and has bizarre or grandiose delusions; the panic attack victim who is apprehensive, fearful, dissociative and has extreme flight-or-fight reactions; and the depressed suicidal ideator who is hopeless, agitated, and acting out suicidal plans (Blumenrich, 1993b, pp. 21–22; Greenfield et al., 1989; Heilbrun, 1990; Heilbrun & Heilbrun, 1989; Jensen & Absher, 1994; Klassen & O'Connor, 1988; Murdach, 1993).

Social Stressors.   Loss of a job or job stress, breakup in a relationship, a past history of physical or sexual abuse, and financial reversals are a few of the social stressors that cause acute frustration and rage in an out-of-control social environment that leads to violence (Blumenreich, 1993a, p. 370).

Family History.   A recent or past history of violence within the family is often carried into other environments. An early childhood characterized by an unstable and violent home is an excellent model for future violence (Wood & Khuri, 1984, pp. 65–66). A history of social isolation or lack of family and environmental support also may heighten potential for violence (Heilbrun & Heilbrun, 1989). One of the better ways to determine a client's level of dangerousness is to ask a family member or peer, out of earshot of the client, how violent the client has been (Kurlowicz, 1990).

Time.   Time in relation to the person's admission and tenure in the facility is critical. Admission on Friday or Saturday night during "party hours" significantly increases the potential for violence. The evening hours in geriatric and mental hospitals, with the onset of darkness, change of shift, and decrease in staff, often lead to client disorientation and states of confusion. The effects of this time period have become so notorious that they have been labeled the *sundown syndrome* (Piercy, 1984, p. 139). Mealtime, toileting, and bathing are also prime times for violent outbursts (Jones, 1985). Patients in both general and forensic psychiatric hospitals are more likely to be violent immediately after admission to the hospital (McNeil et al., 1991). For most patients committed involuntarily, the possibility of assault is significantly increased during the first 10 to 20 days after admission, and for paranoids it remains high during their first 45 days (Rofman, Askinazi, & Fant, 1980).

Presence of Interactive Participants.   Violent behavior may be contingent on those who bring the person to the institution. Family members or friends who bring patients in for treatment often interact in a volatile manner with admitting staff, particularly if the staff are seen as abrasive and callous (Ruben, Wolkon, & Yamamoto, 1980) and treat either the patient or support persons in a curt or uncaring manner (Wood & Khuri, 1984, p. 58). Arguments that may be occurring between the client and support persons are easily transferred to staff. Furthermore, when admonitions by distraught or intoxicated supporters to "fix" the client are not given immediate attention, they or the client may express grievances against the institution and staff by acting out. Any client who is accompanied to the institution by a police officer should be viewed as potentially violent (Kurlowicz, 1990; McNeil et al., 1991; Piercy, 1984, pp. 140–141).

Motoric Cues.   Close observation by the human services worker of physical cues will often give clues to emergent states predisposing to physical violence (Kurlowicz, 1990; Petrie, 1984, p. 115). Early warning signs include tense muscles; bulging, darting eye movements; staring or completely avoiding eye contact; closed, defensive body posture; twitching muscles, fingers, and eyelids; body tremors; and disheveled appearance (Tardiff, 1989, p. 98; Wood & Khuri, 1984, p. 77). If the client is pacing back and forth, alternately approaching and then retreating from the worker, this may be a sign that the individual is gathering courage for an assault (Dang, 1990). The agitated client may have an expanded sense of personal space up to 8 feet in radius, instead of 3 to 4 feet, and may be extremely sensitive to any intrusion into that space (Moran, 1984, pp. 244–246).

A number of verbal cues are precursors to violent action by the client. Heightened voice pitch, volume, and rapidity of speech may occur, particularly if the client has been using amphetamines. Profanity and threats that are directed at the world in general, significant others, or the worker. Confused speech content can reflect confused thought and psychotic breaks. Finally, there is a high correlation between threats of violence and acting on those threats. The more specific the threat is as to the person, method, and time, the more seriously the threat should be taken (Blumenreich, 1993a, p. 37; Tardiff, 1989, p. 99).

Multiple Indicators.   The more the foregoing indicators are combined, the higher the potential for violence becomes (Klassen & O'Connor, 1988). Tardiff (1989) indicated that if possible, the human services worker should attempt to assess all these factors; and if they are present, the worker should clearly note the potential for violence on an intake form (p. 97). Tardiff further proposes that whether or not this information is available, one of the better verbal assessment techniques is to ask, "Have you ever lost your temper [in a violent manner]?" If the answer is "Yes!" the worker should proceed to ask how, when, and where this happened, and then perform an assessment much like that for suicide (p. 98). If any of the foregoing factors are apparent or are stated by the client, no matter how calm the client may appear to be, then a triage assessment of 10 on the interpersonal behavioral dimension should be made, the client's record should be flagged, and caution should be used in regard to the potential of the client to harm self or others.

Does this mean you should not go into the human services business and go into something less stressful, like hauling explosives? We would propose not, because about 85–90 percent of violence is preventable (Mack et al., 1988), and the rest of this chapter will attempt to demonstrate how that percentage can be achieved.

INTERVENTION STRATEGIES

Because the institution itself plays such a large part in the who, what, why, how, and when of treatment, it may be viewed as an equal and contributing partner in resolving problems with clients disposed to becoming physically and verbally assaultive. No two institutions are alike with respect to a number of variables that affect what the institution can do about the problem of violence. Yet when confronting clients who may be distraught, angry, fearful, and experiencing disequilibrium, all institutions have a common core of problems. Given the financial, legal, treatment, organizational, and philosophical limits idiosyncratic to each setting, the following intervention strategies should be viewed as a best "general" approach.

Security Analysis and Planning

No antiviolence program can be accomplished without the commitment and involvement of top management such that everybody in the institution or agency understands that preventing violence is an absolute top priority (Barret, Riggar, & Flowers, 1997; California Occupational Health and Safety Administration, 1998, p. 6). One of the first steps in preventing violence is understanding what precautions the institution has taken to ensure safety of clients and staff. The institution should have a zero tolerance policy for violence for both clients and providers. It should assign clear responsibility to all staff members so that they know what is expected of them, along with adequate resources to carry out those responsibilities and make them accountable for doing so. It should develop a safety committee that evaluates all reports and records assaults and incidents of aggression and takes action on the committee reports in a timely manner (California Occupational Health and Safety Administration, 1998, p. 7).

Certain precautions can be taken to ensure that workers are not put at extreme risk by their clientele. First and foremost, management should conduct a security management analysis with experts in the security field (Ishimoto, 1984, p. 211; Kinney, 1995, pp. 47–50). Kinney (1995) urges that management recognize that the people with the most knowledge are the frontline workers who deal with the institution's clientele on a day-in, day-out basis, even though management may not want to hear from these workers for fear of what they might say. There should be channels for employees to bring their concerns to management and receive feedback without fear of reprisal or censure. Employees follow a procedure that provides reporting of *all* incidents, with or without injury. Employees participate in a safety and health committee that receives information and reports on security problems, makes facility inspections, analyzes reports, and makes recommendations for corrections. Employees participate in case conference meetings that identify potentially violent clients and discuss safe ways of handling difficult clients. Employees participate in security response teams that are trained to recognize escalating behavior and handle assaultive clients (California Occupational Health and Safety Administration, 1998, p. 7).

Any adequate security analysis must take these workers' responses into consideration. The following questions are representative of what Ishimoto (1984, pp. 211–216) and Kinney (1995, pp. 47–58) believe a security management analysis should entail in prevention, detection, response, and security education:

1. What are the institution's goals, functions, operations, organizational structure, and responsibilities?
2. Who is in charge of what security provisions?
3. What image considerations limit the amount of security used?
4. What balance needs to be maintained between staff security and providing human services?
5. What is the geographical, environmental, and socioeconomic setting in which services are rendered?
6. What kinds of clientele make use of the facilities, and what risk do they pose to others?
7. What kinds of provisions have already been made for staff, clients, visitors, and neighborhood security?
8. What kinds of training have staff received for emergencies?
9. What screening devices are available to monitor clientele, and are they reliable and valid?
10. What screening devices are used for personnel selection, and are they reliable and valid?
11. What physical security is available in the form of barriers, lighting, locks, and dispensing of keys?
12. What security personnel will be needed? Where and when?
13. Are there emergency contingency plans for a variety of problems, and do staff members know what is expected of them under varying circumstances?
14. How secure do you feel in this work setting?
15. Have you experienced verbal abuse? If so, how much? From whom?
16. Have you experienced physical violence? If so, from whom? How serious was it? Did it require medical treatment?
17. Does the organization have a clear statement against violence? Is it known by the clientele?
18. Does the organization have a protocol for dealing with violent situations?
19. Who is in charge of responding to threats or physical violence?
20. How well does your security plan fit OSHA requirements?
21. Overall, what do you think of the security and management's attempt to provide for your safety?

All staff should have input into these questions, and a comprehensive security plan should be worked out and disseminated (California Occupational Health and Safety Administration, 1998, p. 8). Such a plan should be comprehensive and simple, detailing who is responsible for what under which conditions. The plan should cover the entire domain of the institution, starting with the parking lot, moving through the front door to admissions, and proceeding through the building to encompass day treatment facilities, staff offices, food services, pharmaceutical dispensaries, and client rooms (Ishimoto, 1984, pp. 209–223). Although the administration may view the initial costs in time and money for this service as burdensome, net cost will be minimal if this action avoids just one lawsuit by a client or staff member (Moran, 1984, p. 249). If such a survey is not taken, not only does the facility risk outbreaks of violence but also the staff will perceive management as not being greatly concerned about what happens to them (Lewellyn, 1985).

Once the results of the survey are compiled, the organization should institute planning. Although consultants with different areas of expertise in violence containment may be helpful, planning should start by forming a threat team composed of a cross section of the staff and by naming a violence prevention coordinator. The duties of this team and coordinator will be to (1) outline the scope and activities of a threat management policy; (2) have a clear and publicized statement against violence, even if the statement simply says, "This organization will not tolerate violence and aggression either from within or from outside this organization"; (3) identify a location and person for reporting threats; (4) determine when threats are serious enough to convene the team; (5) set training for total staff; and (6) establish a protocol for violence reduction that addresses unacceptable types of behavior as well as appropriate sanctions for that behavior" (Kinney, 1995, pp. 73–80; Nicoletti & Spooner, 1996).

Training

Planning is of little consequence if no training follows. Staff who have been trained in the methods, techniques, and procedures to follow have increased confidence in their ability to deescalate violence and have significantly reduced assaultive behavior (Turnbull, Aitken, Black, & Patterson, 1990). Training should include both knowledge and skill building and should be ongoing, with immediate training for new members of the treatment team and continuing education for veterans (Dyer et al., 1984, pp. 12–15; Turnbull et al., 1990). It should begin with the crisis intervention skills listed in Chapter 2 and additionally cover legal aspects, theories of aggression, reporting and recording of incidents, assessment of contextual and environmental variables, verbal defusing techniques, triggers of aggression, self-defense and restraint techniques, behavioral observation, consultation, follow-up staffing procedures, and debriefing (Blair, 1991; Kinney, 1995; Murray & Snyder, 1991; Turnbull et al., 1990). A critical component of training is not just talking about problems but gaining practice in solving them. There is no better way of doing this than in role-play situations, which can be videotaped for analysis and feedback by instructors and peers (Forster, 1994; Turnbull et al., 1990).

Adequate training should endow the crisis worker with the ability to make certain assumptions and take certain precautions when dealing with potentially violent clients (Turnbull et al., 1990; Zold & Schilt, 1984, pp. 98–99):

1. Assume the need to set limits and provide clear instructions with options that define what positive and negative consequences will occur

2. Assume the client feels a number of debilitating emotions such as fear, depression, anxiety, helplessness, anger, rejection, and hopelessness and demonstrate concern by encouraging verbal ventilation through *how* and *when* questions, showing empathic concern by restatement and reflection of the client's feelings, and reinforcing appropriate behavior and communication of feelings

3. Assume frustration of normal activity and boredom when the client is in residence, and provide activities to keep the client fruitfully busy

4. Assume a threat to the client's self-esteem, independence, and self-control and provide choices and opportunities to help in carrying out medical and psychological activities

5. Assume tension and arousal and provide a calm and relaxing atmosphere, particularly in high-tension periods, by manipulating environmental variables and using a cooperative "we" approach

6. Assume confusion and provide a careful explanation of all procedures to be employed, being particularly sure that all staff are operating from the same frame of reference

7. Assume responsibility and provide for one primary staff member to act as chief caretaker and advocate of each client

8. Assume disconnectedness and rootlessness if the client is to be institutionalized for any length of time and provide familiarity and psychologically calming anchors associated with pleasant memories

While providing support through the preceding proactive behaviors, the wise human services worker should observe a number of precautionary measures (Blair, 1991; Forster, 1994; Greenstone & Leviton, 1993; Moran, 1984, p. 244; Piercy, 1984, p. 143; Turnbull et al., 1990; Wood & Khuri, 1984, p. 69):

1. Don't deny the possibility of violence when early signs of agitation are first noticed in the client.

2. Don't dismiss warnings from records, family and peers, authorities, or fellow workers that the client is violent.

3. Don't become isolated with potentially violent clients unless you have made sure that enough security precautions have been taken to prevent or limit a violent outburst.

4. Don't engage in certain behaviors that may be interpreted as aggressive, such as moving too close, staring directly into the client's eyes for extended periods of time, pointing fingers, or displaying facial expressions and body movements that would appear threatening.

5. Don't allow a number of the institution's workers to interact simultaneously with the client in confusing multiple dialogues.

6. Don't make promises that cannot be kept.

7. Don't allow feelings of fear, anger, or hostility to interfere with self-control and professional understanding of the client's circumstances.

8. Don't argue, give orders, or disagree when not absolutely necessary.

9. Don't be placating by giving in and agreeing to all the real and imagined ills the client is suffering at the hands of the institution.

10. Don't become condescending by using childish responses that are cynical, satirical, or otherwise designed to denigrate the client.

11. Don't let self-talk about your own importance be acted out in an officious and "know-it-all" manner.
12. Don't raise your voice, put a sharp edge on responses, or use threats to gain compliance.
13. Conversely, don't mumble, speak hesitantly, or use a tone of voice so low that the client has trouble understanding what you are saying.
14. Don't argue over small points, given strong opposition from the client.
15. Don't attempt to reason with any client who is under the influence of a mind-altering substance.
16. Don't attempt to gain compliance based on the assumption that the client is as reasonable about things as you are.
17. Don't keep the client waiting or leave a potentially violent client alone with freedom to move about.
18. Don't allow a crowd to congregate as spectators to an altercation.
19. Don't use *why* and *what* questions that put the client on the defensive.
20. Don't allow the client to get between you and an exit.
21. Don't dismiss increasingly vociferous client demands as merely attention-seeking, petulant, or narcissistic behavior.
22. Don't enter a room ahead of unknown clients. Stay behind and visually "frisk" them as you go into the room.
23. Don't remain after hours with a potentially violent client unless proper security is available.
24. Don't fail to make contingency plans for violent incidents. Take your personal safety seriously by playing "what if this happens" scenarios in your mind and with others.
25. Most important, *don't attempt to be a hero.*

In the rapidly changing world of mental health, much crisis intervention now occurs on site (see Chapter 14, "Off the Couch and into the Streets"). Although outreach and "mobile go-out" teams give the crisis interventionist far more mobility and rapid response capability, on-site intervention also has the potential to put crisis workers in extreme danger as they operate in violent neighborhoods and households. Incorporating the foregoing warnings given for in-house operation, the following injunctions generated by Greenstone and Leviton (1993, pp. 31–33) and ourselves should be added to the repertoire of the crisis worker who operates outside the walls of the institution:

1. If at all possible, go with a partner or at least have a cellular phone or other means of communication to get help in a hurry.
2. Let someone else in the office know where you are going and when you will be back.
3. Check out your surroundings. Although time is of the essence in most crisis intervention, move into the situation slowly and carefully, and be fully aware of what is going on in the environment around you.
4. Plan what you are going to do before you go. If at all possible, our Crisis Intervention Team officers for the Memphis Police Department rendezvous and plan who is going to do what before they enter a hazardous situation. You should do the same.
5. Don't park directly in front of the place where the crisis is occurring. Park just beyond the area, and check it out as you drive by. If you have to leave in a hurry,

this position allows you to leave without crossing the line of sight of a person who may be able to harm you.

6. Before knocking on a door or entering a building, listen carefully for a few seconds for clues as to what may be going on inside.

7. Never stand directly in front of a door. Knock and, as the police do, stand aside so you are not assaulted or shot through the door.

8. Consider what you are wearing from a safety viewpoint. A tie or a choke chain may make you look more professional, but it can also get you strangled. High heels are elegant, but you can't run in them. Loose fitting, mobile, and non-flashy clothing is the watchword.

9. Once the door is open, immediately scan the room to determine who is in it and where they are. Compare this visual data to information you may have received previously on the situation. Don't take anyone for granted, particularly elderly people who may look harmless. Ask if there are other people in the house and who and where they are.

10. Monitor the verbal and nonverbal behavior of all the people in the room. What are they doing and what must you do to stabilize the situation?

11. Enter the room only a short distance so that you can first assess what's going on and can get out quickly if you have to.

12. Don't let a crowd of bystanders gather or let neighbors "drop in" to see what's going on. Politely ask them to leave. If they won't leave or refuse to disperse, get out or get the police!

13. Take control as quickly as possible. Separate disputants and have them sit down. Stay calm, and in a clear voice introduce yourself and make assertive statements about what you want them to do: "I'm Jackie Winter from the mobile crisis intervention team, and this is my partner, Rico Minelli. I need for both of you to take a deep breath, let it out, and then sit down. We want to hear both sides of what's happening, so I'll start with Mrs. Rodriguez and Rico will talk to you, Mr. Rodriguez. OK!" If that doesn't work, get their attention by making a tangential request: "Stop that! I need to use the telephone to call in." If all else fails, a police whistle gets everybody's attention.

14. Sit in a chair where you can observe what's going on. Seat yourself so you're leaning forward and can easily get out of the chair quickly! If you sense that the situation is deteriorating, leave. *Don't be a hero!*

These injunctions are not a recipe for avoiding violent confrontations, but they are general working procedures that will help the human services worker move adroitly with the client through the intervention stages.

Precautions in Dealing with the Physical Setting

Safety precautions should be taken that deal with the physical settings of the institution in which staff members are most likely to become involved in potentially violent situations with clients. Two critical areas important to all crisis workers are the admissions area and the worker's office.

The reception or waiting-room area should offer a television set, reading material, and accessibility to snack areas. Availability of entertainment and food and drink gives clients and visitors an opportunity to engage in a pleasurable activity that can offset the hostile feelings that may be engendered by the problems they are facing and can defuse the stressful situation of admission (Wood & Khuri, 1984, pp. 79–80). One admonition is necessary with regard to food and drink: Clients who are extremely rebellious about entering the institution may attempt to choke themselves on foodstuffs or even swallow pull tabs from metal cans. The admissions staff should carefully monitor clients if they are allowed to eat or drink (McCown, 1986).

The admissions area should be clean and well kept, with furniture, carpet, and wall coverings well maintained. First impressions are lasting. If the client's first impression of a facility is that staff have little regard or respect for the facility, the client will have little reason to respect what goes on there either (Marohn, 1982). No sharp, movable objects, including furniture, should be available as potential weapons (McCown, 1986).

The area should be set up so that it is a choke point. Only one way into the rest of the facility should be available from the admissions area (Annis, McClaren, & Baker, 1984, p. 30). Depending on how much security is needed, the reception area may have electronically locked doors that separate it from the rest of the facility, sign-in sheets, identity check procedures, curved mirrors, and metal detectors (California Occupational Health and Safety Administration, 1998, p. 10; Jones, 1984).

The admissions worker will make the first contact with the client and will engage the person during one of the most potentially violent moments the institution is likely to encounter. The admissions worker should be highly skilled in crisis intervention techniques and should have one primary job—*staying with and attending to the client being admitted!* Under no circumstances should a secretary, receptionist, or any other support person who is not professionally well versed in crisis intervention or who has other tasks to perform, such as typing letters or answering the telephone, be delegated to handle this important assignment. The admissions worker does not leave the client until all admitting procedures have been accomplished and the client is safely settled (McCown, 1986).

The admissions worker should never be left in a position of isolation from the rest of the staff (Turnbull et al., 1990). Security support equipment such as a body alarm (a button-activated device that when triggered will automatically send an alarm and position fix to security), an automatic dialer preset to in-house security and 911, convex mirrors to monitor the whole waiting area, panic buttons, closed-circuit television monitoring equipment, button locks on elevators, and a metal detector at the entrance should be available (Doms, 1984, pp. 225–229; Jones, 1984; McCown, 1986; Wood & Khuri, 1984, pp. 79–80).

Personal work environments should also be safe. Desks should be set up so that they allow for separation of client and worker, even though communicating across a desk is not the most desirable counseling setup. Space should be arranged to permit both the worker and the client clear access to the door and to allow the worker to leave the room without having to confront the client or cross the client's personal space. No potential weapons such as paperweights, letter openers, and sharpened pencils should be openly displayed or within easy reach of the client. The same personal warning devices and procedures recommended for the reception area should also be in place in workers' offices. The receptionist or others in the building need to be able to warn the worker if danger is imminent, and vice versa. The furniture should be solid and difficult to move, particularly chairs and tables. There should be a common code word that is understood to mean a summons for immediate help. A panic button and a telephone that the worker can use to get in touch with the outside world should be available. These last two points are particularly critical because of the typical isolation of the human services worker with a client in a therapeutic setting (Jensen & Absher, 1994; Tardiff, 1984a, p. 50).

Although institutional precautions may cause human services workers some embarrassment and chagrin, workers should not disregard them. Our own work in penal institutions is a good example of what we are talking about. The corrections facility we work in mandates that counselors wear a body alarm at all times, that a co-counselor be present in all groups, and that a guard be posted at all times within easy access of the group room. Occasionally group members may make snide remarks about these precautions. The worker may easily respond by stating, "I don't much like it either, but you guys know the rules," and injecting a little humor: "It's probably because they're afraid we might beat up on group members and want to protect you guys."

Stages of Intervention

Management of potentially violent situations should proceed in a sequential manner, based on a nine-stage model developed by Piercy (1984, pp. 147–148). The stages are (1) education, (2) avoidance of conflict, (3) appeasement, (4) deflection, (5) time out, (6) show of force, (7) seclusion, (8) restraints, and (9) sedation. The cardinal rule for all of these stages, as stated by Larry Chavez (1999)—a noted authority on violence prevention in the workplace—is "Never, ever deprive another human being of personal dignity, respect, or hope nor allow anyone else under your control to do so." For each of these stages, personal responsibility is paramount. Furthermore, whether by circumstance or design, the first person who comes in contact with the problem is the most likely to be the agitated client's focus of attention (Moran, 1984, pp. 233–234).

Stages 1 through 5 all rely heavily on talking instead of acting, in accordance with one of the primary goals of crisis intervention with violence-prone individuals: getting them to talk out rather than act out. This approach may seem obvious, but it is difficult to achieve. The agitated client clearly has a limited ability to talk and think through problems, as opposed to acting on them and giving little thought to the consequences (Tardiff, 1984a, p. 52).

As we move through the nine stages, we will follow Jason, a 15-year-old white male client, and Carol, a therapist who by most standards is an old pro. She has been at Seashore Village, an adolescent treatment facility, for four years. Jason is new to the business of institutions. He is not new to being angry, which he is right now as he sits with a deputy sheriff in the reception area waiting for Carol to come through the door. Jason's teen years have been filled with petty larceny, truancy, alcohol and drug use, and parents who have gotten him out of one scrape after another. His latest escapade of stealing a car landed him in front of a juvenile court, and he was sent to Seashore as an alternative to the state juvenile correction system. His father, fed up with Jason's behavior and over the objections of Jason's mother, has pushed for this placement. Jason feels betrayed and is extremely angry at his father for doing so.

Seashore itself is representative of a broad sample of institutions. It is neither the best nor the worst in terms of clients, staff, resources, and security measures. We are endeavoring to paint as representative a picture as possible, asking you to withhold judgments about the efficacy and appropriateness of these strategies in every institution. Our hope is that the procedures used in the case of Jason will make you think carefully about your own present or future role in an institution, compare the ideas proposed here with the requirements imposed on you, analyze the procedures used, and thoughtfully compare these techniques and the real world within which you operate.

Jason: (*Thinking to himself, hands sweating, slight tremors racing through his body.*) Man, this place is scaring the hell out of me. How'd I ever get in this fix? What are they gonna do to me? I'll be at the mercy of the rest of the crazies in here. I'll really go nuts if I stay here. I gotta get out of this place if it's the last thing I ever do.

Jason is extremely angry and anxious about what will happen to him, frustrated that he has lost control of his life and that what he has considered to be normal activity is going to be severely curtailed. He also feels extremely vulnerable, confused, bewildered, and alone. Jason's feelings are typical of those of a client who is being introduced to a long-term treatment facility for the first time (Blair, 1991; Zold & Schilt, 1984, p. 96).

As soon as Jason enters Seashore, admissions immediately calls the adolescent unit. At that time Carol comes quickly to the reception area and meets Jason. She immediately makes a fast visual assessment of Jason's verbal and nonverbal behavior as she enters the room and monitors Jason closely to see what his reaction to her initial query will be.

Carol: (*Thinking to herself.*) What's going on with this kid? Any signs he is agitated? Yes! He's pacing around, eyes darting to and fro, keeps cracking his knuckles, looking at the door and the cop. He'll run if he gets the chance! Muttering to himself. Who brought him in? Nobody else here but that cop over there. He keeps watching him. Must be an adjudication. If a cop brought him here, be careful.

Carol picks up the file the deputy has brought, quickly looks it over, and finds the boy's name and rap sheet. A fast review tells her that Jason has been in a series of escalating scrapes with the law, that his parents are fed up with his behavior and feel he's out of control, and that he has been involved in fights when his explosive personality got out of control. Carol then talks briefly with the deputy and finds out what kind of a trip Jason had from the juvenile detention center.

Carol: (*Thinking to herself.*) OK! Check him out and see how stabilized he is and let him find out what's going to happen to him.

Stage 1: Education.   Clients need to be educated about what is happening to them and why and how it is happening through reasoning and reassurance. One way of doing this is to assume the role of the client's advocate (Pisarick, 1981). Owning statements that indicate concern over the client's welfare are a good opening gambit. It must be assumed that in this new, strange, and alien environment the primary feeling of the client will be fear and anger (Rada, 1981). Open-ended questions and reflection of the client's feelings are crucial to conveying that the client's feelings count for something and are being taken into consideration (Turnbull et al., 1990).

Carol: Hi! My name's Carol, and you must be Jason. I'm the person who'll be working with you.

Jason: (*Gives a menacing look.*) Yeah! So what? (*Points to officer.*) The cop got me in here but I ain't gonna go any farther.

Carol: I understand how you feel. Most people who come here feel about the same way. Seems like everybody's against you, telling you what to do. I'd be angry too! I want you to know, though, that here at Seashore you're going to have some options about what happens.

Jason: Screw your options. I ain't stayin' here. (*Makes a menacing move toward Carol.*)

Carol: (*Senses move and moves back and a little to Jason's left, giving him some increased space.*) One of your immediate options is that I'd like you to come with me and meet some of the other kids here and have them tell you what's going on and see if what they have to say fits with what you're about. On the other hand, the court sent you here, and if you don't like the first option and want to fight it out, you could be carried back to the unit and we can wait until you've got yourself together. I understand you're angry, and I'd be angry too, but I'd like to know if you feel that fighting or running is gonna make it better for you and improve your situation rather than checking things out. So you've got a choice. I think you might be interested in meeting some of the other kids, but you'll have to show me you can handle that, starting right now.

In this initial meeting, the worker uses the technique of providing options (Turnbull et al., 1990). This opening statement includes acknowledging the client's feelings but also conveys expectations that the client can control himself. By doing so, Carol sets the tone for what the behavioral expectations are in a clear and caring, yet firm way (Steveson, 1991). She is letting the client have some semblance of control of the situation but is also clearly outlining what the consequences of his choices are. As soon as possible, she is going to model option therapy (McCown, 1986). Option therapy, in simple terms, says, "You always have a choice. You need to start deciding as soon as possible who's going to have control over those choices, you or us."

Jason: Well . . . all right . . . lady, I'll give it a look-see, but I ain't promisin' nothin' after that.

Carol: I don't expect any more than that at the moment. What I want most for you is to see what's going on here and what some of the other kids think about what we do before you make any kind of promises. We don't lie and we don't make promises we can't keep.

The worker has to make a quick judgment about how directive or nondirective to be. She is directive only to the extent of setting boundaries equivalent to how out of control the client is. Her other mission is to establish rapport and credibility with the client. She does this by accepting and acknowledging the client where he is and in turn stating the same from the institution's perspective. She offers no platitudes or false promises (Turnbull et al., 1990). Her technique of letting the client talk to other people on the unit is designed to let the client hear and see with his own ears and eyes what is going on without feeling he is getting a lot of propaganda. However, she will not provide a format for him to act out, and if in her judgment Jason is not controlled enough to make a tour with her, she will summon assistance and Jason will be escorted to an observation room (McCown, 1986).

Carol: We have a lot of activities, so if you don't clearly understand what's happening or you want to know some more about it, just ask. Your schedule is as follows:

7:00–8:00	Stretch period, clean up room, lavatory, breakfast
8:00–8:15	Community meeting, announcements
8:15–12:00	School
12:00–12:45	Lunch
12:45–2:00	School
2:00–3:00	Group problem solving
3:00–4:00	Individual counseling
4:00–5:00	Quiet time in room
5:00–5:45	Dinner
5:45–7:00	Special groups: assertiveness training, social skills, group counseling, family therapy, Alcoholics Anonymous, art therapy, and so on
7:00–8:00	Group recreation in gym
8:00–9:00	Free time, for recreation, phone calls, and such (privileges depend on level achieved)
9:00–9:30	Shower, clean-up, bedtime (bedtime extended to 10:00 or 10:30, depending on level achieved)

Very little free time is available. For most people who enter a facility such as Seashore, a major problem has been too much free time and the inability to handle it well. Structuring the environment brings some badly needed discipline back into their lives. Particularly for adolescents, burning up energy in constructive ways is of paramount importance. Furthermore, too much free time is a fertile breeding ground for acting out behavior (Jensen & Absher, 1994).

Seashore is also on a behavior management program that makes use of levels. Jason starts at entry level. Depending on how Jason operates in his environment, he will go up or down on the level system and will concomitantly receive more or fewer privileges. At an entry level, he will have few privileges—early bedtime, no passes—and will be under fairly close supervision. By conducting himself in a responsible manner, he may increase his level designation and gain access to a broader array of recreational activities, later bedtime, ground privileges, and weekend passes. The system is explained to Jason in a careful and clear manner, with emphasis on the fact that whether or not he moves to higher levels is his responsibility.

Educating a client about what is to happen medically and psychologically needs to be done slowly, methodically, and in nontechnical terms with numerous perceptual checks. Keeping explanations simple and helping the client gain understanding ameliorates the situation, whereas complexity only increases the chance for violent behavior to occur (Jensen & Absher, 1994; Moran, 1984, p. 234).

Jason: (Somewhat belligerently.) Like, what's this group meeting?

Carol: The group meets every day. We do two things there. First, putting this many kids together means that problems are going to arise. Within the limits of the institution, we decide on a group basis how these problems will be handled. It's a one-person–one-vote program, and that includes the staff. The group decides how to tackle a community problem and then collectively makes a commitment to do something about it. Second, when problems between people arise, we all put our heads together and see how those problems can be solved. You don't necessarily have to accept an idea, but you must listen to what's being said.

Jason: I don't think I got anything to say to these nerds.

Carol: Maybe you don't. However, a lot of kids here do. You're not going to be here forever. Therefore, we look pretty hard at what's going on with you right now as you
deal with other people here, how that behavior may or may not cause you problems,
and what's down the road for you if you do decide to change some things in your
life and what's likely if you don't. We don't ask you to love everybody here, but we
do ask you to respect what they're trying to do, just as we ask them to respect you.

The human services worker's responses are from Glasser's reality therapy (1965, 1969)
and focus on the issues of becoming involved, looking at alternatives, making value
judgments, accepting no excuses, and assuming responsibility and consequences for
one's actions. In this manner Carol goes over the entire schedule with Jason. While she
explains the content of the program, she also makes sure to assess and reflect the emotional content of Jason's responses, again and again reinforcing the idea of options, responsibilities, and commitments.

Stage 2: Avoidance of Conflict.   Conflict and confrontation are avoided whenever
possible. Matching threat for threat is likely to obtain for the human services worker
exactly the opposite of control and containment of the situation (Dubin, 1981). Workers who delight in continuously pushing and escalating issues are not practicing good
therapeutic intervention techniques and are clearly asking for trouble (Blair, 1991).
    One week has elapsed since Jason's admission.

Jason: (*Standing in the hallway, shouting, shaking, and trembling, face flushed.*) If you
think you or anybody else can make me stay in my room or in this place, you're
crazier than I am. I just wanted a drink of water and Mr. Richardson started yelling
at me that it was past quiet time. Just try stopping me and see what happens.
Carol: (*Quietly and calmly.*) Jason, if you'll calm down, I'll bring you a cup of water.
Please go in your room. You can have your drink, and we can talk about it.

If the client is fast approaching a point of no return, let him or her ventilate feelings. Although shouting, cursing, and yelling are not pleasant, they are better than hand-to-hand
combat (McCown, 1986; Vinick, 1986). The worker should attempt to remove the agitated client from the vicinity of other residents who may aggravate the situation
(Chavez, 1999; Turnbull et al., 1990). This is best done by immediately asking the client to go to an area that is away from the other residents (McCown, 1986). If the client
retains some semblance of control, the client's own room may be an appropriate place.
If the client is fast losing control and cannot calm down, a better choice is a room devoid of stimuli. Such a place should be specifically prepared and reserved for this sort
of occurrence. Once the client has relaxed to some degree, then the human services
worker can establish the cause and degree of agitation by determining what occurred
and then pointing out consequences (Vinick, 1986).

Carol: What are you angry about?
Jason: (*Still standing in the hallway, quite agitated.*) He was treating me just like my
old man, just making me feel like a baby.
Carol: And what were you doing?
Jason: Hey, I was just going to get a drink of water. I still had two minutes until quiet
time. He made me so mad I wanted to pick up a chair and bust him. I still feel like
going after that jerk.

Carol: What will that accomplish?

Jason: It'll show him he can't push me around like my old man does.

Carol: If you do that, it'll just confirm that you need to be here. That you can't control yourself. Is that what you want?

Jason: Maybe I just don't care.

Carol does not display anger or fear, even though the situation is potentially volatile. She speaks in a calm controlled voice, lower and slower than Jason. She is setting the example and controlling the dialogue (Chavez, 1999). For those clients who do not respond to verbal attempts to defuse the situation, the next step for the human services worker is to give assurance that violent behavior by anybody, including both staff and clients, is unacceptable and then to indicate what the person's choices and consequences will become if the behavior persists (Kinney, 1995, p. 49; Wood & Khuri, 1984, pp. 67–68).

Carol: You can choose to pick up a chair, Jason, but that'll mean a number of things will happen. First, nobody is allowed to hit anybody else here, and that goes for both staff and kids. We won't permit anybody to do that because we don't want to see anybody hurt here. If it comes to that, we won't hurt you, but we will restrain you, something I'd not like to see happen. Second, if you choose to do that, no one else will get to hear your side of it and we won't have a chance to work your problem out with Mr. Richardson. Another choice would be to go back to your room and then ask for a drink. If you do that, I will get Mr. Richardson and we'll all sit down and work this through. Would you be willing to do that?

Carol is absolutely truthful with what will happen to the client. At this stage, loss of credibility would be catastrophic (Chavez, 1999). Clients should be confronted with their inappropriate behavior, but in a caring, supportive, and problem-solving way that is not tinged with sarcasm or challenge. If the situation is deteriorating so rapidly that the worker no longer feels that communication can be maintained, it may be fruitful to have someone else enter the scene whom the client will perceive as a neutral party (Lakeside Hospital, 1988). This tactic is risky and involves a judgment call on the worker's part. Allowing clients to be rewarded for acting out by getting other people to come to the scene may reinforce inappropriate behavior and lead clients to believe that they and not the institution control the situation.

Jason: It ain't just Richardson, this whole place sucks. They won't let me do nothin'. And you don't understand either. Chaplain Gentry's the only guy who I can really talk to.

Carol: I understand that you're really disappointed and mad that you couldn't get a drink. I also know you're pretty angry at me and everybody else right now and about the last thing you want to do is go peacefully back to your room. I know that you and Chaplain Gentry are pretty close. Would you be willing to go to your room and wait quietly while I get him?

If the client does not choose this option then the worker will have to move the client to a safe place, which will be a time-out room. A show of force may be necessary to send a clear message: "If you can't handle yourself, we will."

Carol: Jason, I want you to go down to observation for 15 minutes and think this out. (*Speaking to technicians.*) Bob and Jerry, will you see that Jason gets to observation? In 15 minutes I'll be down to see if you're ready to talk this through.

Stage 3: Appeasement.   Stages 3 and 4 are probably most appropriate in emergency situations in which the worker has little basis to judge the client's aggressiveness and violence and is unable to obtain immediate assistance. Appeasement is not applicable in a number of settings under ordinary circumstances, and if Jason had reached the point of being removed to involuntary time out, appeasement or deflection of feelings (Stage 4) would be highly inappropriate and run counter to good therapeutic practice.

However, we believe it is better in all situations to err on the side of humility than to project a "tough guy" image, regardless of the client's verbal barbs, threats, and exhortations. This recommendation does not mean that the human services worker should become a doormat to be walked all over by the client. It does mean that by operating in an empathic mode we can see just how frightening and alarming the situation is to the client. Alternately, any attempts by the workers to counter threat with threat in an emergency situation are likely to confirm the client's suspicions that bad things are going to happen.

Appeasement can be attempted if the client's demands are simple and reasonable, even if those demands are made in a bellicose manner. Early on it is better to grant demands and to defer until later worry about what "lessons" need to be taught (Piercy, 1984, p. 148). This approach may be difficult for some human services workers to accept, because it is based on the idea that there is no winner or loser in a potentially violent confrontation between an agitated client and the institution (Moran, 1984, p. 234).

Jason: (*Barges into the human services worker's office, fists clenched, and starts shouting in an agitated, high-pitched voice.*) Listen, big shot! I wanted to mail this letter to my girl, she doesn't know what's happened to me, and that jerk Richardson won't give me a stamp. I could bust all yer heads!

Carol: (*In a calm, collected voice.*) He's going by the rules, but I understand your concern. Please sit down at the table here and I'll see what can be done about getting a stamp.

The human services worker meets this demand because it is easily done and does not seriously conflict with institutional rules. She is also alone with an extremely agitated client who may or may not act out. There may be a discussion afterward with the other worker who gave the original order, but there needs to be a clear understanding among all workers that in emergencies, judgment calls may bend the rules a bit or countermand orders of others.

Stage 4: Deflection.   Deflection of angry feelings is attempted by shifting to other, less threatening topics. This may be done in a variety of ways. Asking the client to take a physically less threatening position shifts the focus away from agitated motor activity to problem solving (Wood & Khuri, 1984, p. 68).

Carol: (*Repeating her statement patiently, firmly, and respectfully.*) Jason, I understand how important it is for you to be able to write to your girlfriend. Please sit down. Then I'll get you a stamp and see if we can iron out this problem.

The human services worker literally and figuratively gets the client off his feet and in a less threatening operating mode (Epstein & Carter, 1988). The worker is also quietly but firmly setting limits by asking the client to sit. Because agitated people seldom listen closely to requests for compliance, Carol acknowledges Jason's feeling state and then uses the broken record routine (Canter & Canter, 1982) of repeating her request. She is also employing another behavior management technique. By making a reward contingent on a compliant behavior, Carol is using "Grandma's law" (Becker, 1971). "Grandma's law" basically states, "First you eat your spinach, and then you get your ice cream."

By using problem-solving techniques, no matter how small the real or imagined injustice is, the human services worker conveys to the client an interest in the client as an individual and not just as another name in the institutional computer (Wood & Khuri, 1984, p. 71). Parceling out the problems into workable pieces, the worker removes them from the realm of the enormous and makes them solvable.

Jason: I can't get nothin' done here. Everything's screwed up. School, home, people, the food, my freedom. It's a concentration camp.

Carol: OK. There seem to be at least three things that are really bugging you right now. Not being able to get a pass yet, the way your dad got angry in family therapy, and your problem with the math assignment yesterday. Together, I can see how it'd become overwhelming. Let's take them one at a time and see what can be done about each. Let me take some notes so I can keep all this straight. (*Jason goes into a long-winded explanation while Carol listens and takes notes.*)

Until absolutely sure what the problem is, the human services worker should never make promises about what can or cannot be done when attempting to calm an agitated client (Wood & Khuri, 1984, p. 71). By allowing Jason to ventilate and by taking notes, Carol affirms that what he has to say is important and plays up rather than down the client's concerns (Chavez, 1999).

Carol: I know that weekend pass is really important. You'd get to see your girlfriend, and you feel like you really deserve it. I'd like to see what could be done, but I can't give you a guarantee. A pass is based on good behavior and your level status. If you feel like you've gotten jerked around, griping about it won't help much. Very specifically, write down why you think you deserve the pass. I'll take it to the staffing this afternoon.

Having the client write down problems also defuses angry feelings and acting out. In many instances, the client may just be testing limits. Testing limits is a given with a client such as Jason, and the human services worker can be expected to be tested over and over again (Poliks, 1999). To write down clearly and logically what the problem is calls for time and effort, which very few clients will invest if the problem is not important (Epstein & Carter, 1988). Writing down the particulars of the problem is also cathartic for clients, allowing them to gain some emotional distance from it and view the situation in a more objective light (McCown, 1986).

When other, more overt ploys are ineffective, the client may use manipulation and threat to obtain demands.

Jason: If you don't get that pass for me, you ain't much of a counselor and they'll be real sorry they didn't give it to me.

Carol: When you try and lay that guilt trip on me and make threats about what you'll do if you don't get your way, that's a pretty good indication that the staff's judgment was right and makes it even more difficult to act as your advocate. It's not so much any of the demands that you want, but more like pushing the limits to see how far you can get by manipulating and threatening me.

The response the human services worker makes is one from Adlerian psychotherapy called "avoiding the tar baby" (Dinkmeyer, Pew, & Dinkmeyer, 1979, p. 118). By responding directly to the client, the human services worker does not allow herself to be caught up in the manipulative trap the client lays for her. Although the response is confrontive, it is exceedingly effective with manipulative individuals because it deflects them from their game plan and causes them to consider the consequences of their actions (Wood & Khuri, 1984, p. 71).

When clients become agitated, despite the normal busy day and physical activity that help to burn up energy, deflecting anger through physical activity can be helpful. Clients can take out their frustrations through activities that range from pounding on a heavy bag (Vinick, 1986) to tearing up telephone directories (McCown, 1986). At the same time, the human services worker can reinforce the client for acting in more appropriate ways (Jensen & Absher, 1994). Although teaching anger management skills may be more effective in the long run (LeCroy, 1988), appropriate and safe physical exertion to burn up angry feelings is an effective short-term solution.

Jason: (*Tearing up the Yellow Pages.*) Umphf! I . . . get so mad . . . I . . . Arggh! I . . . wish this phone book was that no-good SOB's face.

Carol: But in fact you haven't torn anybody's face off. You've made a good choice. Much better than when you were going around clobbering people. You don't have to pay any consequences at all for tearing up the phone book. You get it out of your system and get back in control.

Jason: (*Continues ventilating, until finally he runs out of energy and lets arms hang limply at his side.*)

Carol: (*Continues to reinforce Jason for acting appropriately and within limits.*) Look at what you could have done. You could have swung a chair at Mr. Richardson, which would have got you into hot water. The very kinds of thing that got you here in the first place. But you didn't do that. What you did was perfectly acceptable and within the limits here.

Stage 5: Time Out.   When clients cannot contend with the emotion of the moment, they are asked to go to a reduced-stimulus environment, to be alone and think things out. A clear assessment of how agitated the client is needs to be made at this point. Is the client able and willing to leave a high-stimulus situation for a few minutes to rest and think things over? If the client is not overly reactive, then the worker may ask the client to take a minimal time out in living quarters.

Jason: I don't want to sit, talk, or be reasonable. I want this scumbag place to do something!

Carol: Right now I can see there's no way this is going to get solved. You can go to your room and think things over. Go for 15 minutes. If you can come back and show me you're in control, that's it, no reduction in level, no write-ups, and it's forgotten.

If a threat is made directly to the human services worker, other staff, or clients, the policy should be mandatory time out with a clear and strong statement of reason (Vinick, 1986).

Carol: I've tried to work this through with you and you clearly don't want to hear it. When you continue to make threats, you're saying to me you're not willing to abide by the rules and are choosing to have rules enforced. I want you to go to the observation room for 30 minutes right now. At the end of that time I'll be around to see you. If you don't feel like talking, you don't have to, but you can go back in the room for another 30 minutes. You can continue to do that until you're willing to talk to me about how you think you've been treated unfairly.

The human services worker states these conditions in a matter-of-fact manner and does not press the issue (Vinick, 1986). If the client is so agitated as to be beyond the grasp of reality and is unwilling to be compliant to the human services worker's request, then the worker needs help to contain the situation.

Stage 6: Show of Force. If the client is unable to proceed to time out or is otherwise noncompliant or acting out, then a show of force is needed (Piercy, 1984, p. 148). If the client is already agitated enough to warn the human services workers that help may be warranted, the interview should be carried out in an open hallway or large meeting room where the participants are in plain view of other staff members and the client can be restrained easily (Viner, 1982). The show of force indicates that any display of violence or threat of violence will not be tolerated and often helps disorganized clients regain control of themselves (Wood & Khuri, 1984, p. 68). If this stage is reached, the potential for violence is high and the worker should not attempt to deal with the client alone. Either by paging help through an emergency code or by having assistance readily available, the worker needs to be able to summon enough help to demonstrate that compliance is now required (Lakeside Hospital, 1988).

The problem is that not all individuals give indications that they are about to become violent. Therefore, there are times when, through no fault of the worker, potentially violent situations occur when the worker is alone and not immediately able to call for assistance. The following procedures may keep the worker out of harm's way (Chavez, 1999; Epstein & Carter, 1988; Lakeside Hospital, 1988; Moran, 1984, pp. 238–248; Morrison, 1993, pp. 79–100; Turnbull et al., 1990).

1. *Stay calm and relaxed.* Tensing of muscles and agitated movement only fuel the situation and cause the client to expect that something bad (for the client) is about to happen. Relaxation techniques such as simple deep breathing are extremely helpful, allowing one to stay loose, anticipate client responses, and move quickly.
2. *Practice positive self-talk.* Even in the worst situations, running positive "billboards" through the mind's eye will help keep control of the situation.
3. *Do not stare at the client.* Keep casual eye contact because the eyes of the individual will typically move to where a blow might be struck. Focus on an imaginary spot on the client's upper chest, about where the first button on a shirt would be, occasionally glancing at the eyes and other parts of the individual's body. Keeping focus on the centerline of the client's body will also let the human services worker avoid being faked out by extremity movements.
4. *Stay an arm's length away.* Make a judgment about how long the client's arms are, and stay an arm's length and a bit more away.

5. *Stay to weak side.* Know which of the client's hands is dominant and stay to the client's weak side. Chances are 9 out of 10 the client will be right-handed. In an aggressive stance, a person invariably places the foot of the weak side forward. If the worker keeps to the weak side of the assailant, any blow the client aims is likely to have less power and be a glancing one.

6. *Keep arms at sides.* Folded arms are bad for two reasons. They imply hostility or authority, and they put the worker at a distinct disadvantage because of the time it takes to unfold them and defend oneself.

7. *Assume a defensive posture.* Stand with feet slightly spread, face to face with the client but tending a bit to the client's weak side. Move the dominant leg slightly to the rear with the knee locked. Move the other leg slightly forward of the body and bent slightly at the knee. This position will allow the worker the best chance to stay upright, and staying upright is the best safeguard against being hurt.

8. *Avoid cornering.* Cornering occurs in three ways. When the client is placed in an angle formed by two walls or other objects, with the human services worker directly in front of the client, the only way out is through the worker. Exit cornering occurs when the client cannot get out of a room without first crossing the worker's personal space. Contact cornering occurs when the worker attempts to subdue a client by physical means. The client has two choices: either to submit or to resist. The premise in avoiding cornering is that even an agitated individual will seek to disengage if given the opportunity to do so without losing face. Although we would advise the worker to have a basic understanding of self-defense, we believe that under none but the most extreme circumstances should a worker ever attempt bodily restraint of a client. The risk of physical injury is far too great, and the client's trust in the worker will be destroyed.

9. *Avoid ordering.* When a client is threatening violence, attempting to order or command a client to do something is likely to aggravate the situation further. Staying with the basic empathic listening and responding skills used throughout this book is far more likely to lead to satisfactory results.

10. *Do perceptual checks.* Ask for the client's help. If current verbal responses are merely agitating the situation, ask the client what solutions or techniques might calm things down.

11. *Admit mistakes.* If you've made an error in judgment, admit it and make an apology. If things have gone this far, do not be afraid to lose face.

12. *Do nothing.* If doing something will make matters worse, do nothing. If the client is determined to leave and help is not immediately available, let the client go. *Never* attempt to touch a client under these circumstances without first indicating what you are about to do and getting the client's agreement to do so.

13. *Give validation.* In a sincere and empathic manner, acknowledge that the person has a good reason for feeling that way and let him or her leave.

All human services providers and especially crisis workers should undergo training in simple self-defense and take-down procedures (Blair, 1991; Morrison, 1993, pp. 79–100; Turnbull et al., 1990). Neglecting to learn how to deal with a noncompliant teenager whom one of our co-workers thought could be manhandled cost the worker a broken rib. Following the incident, all human services personnel in the facility underwent training in physical self-defense and containment procedures. Numerous subsequent incidents were handled effectively without injury to either the clients or the staff.

Numerous facilities provide such training for little or no charge. Local YMCAs or YWCAs and college continuing education courses may offer such instruction, or the local high school wrestling coach may even be prevailed on. Instruction should be a priority of the institution, and *all* personnel should receive training.

Stage 7: Seclusion.   Seclusion may be generally differentiated from time out by its length, its setting, and its involuntary nature. Seclusion is a severe type of limit setting for the client in a safe and secure environment where the client can reorganize thinking, feeling, and behavior (Mattson & Sacks, 1978). There are a number of reasons for seclusion: (1) the client is agitated, hyperactive, verbally threatening, or damaging property; (2) the client is impulsive or intrusive and does not respond to limit setting; (3) the client is making suicidal gestures and is unable or unwilling to make a verbal contract about controlling behavior; (4) to protect the client from possible harm by others (Baradell, 1985; Lewis, 1993, p. 105).

Negative emotions such as anger, guilt, confusion, helplessness, and loss of control are typical client responses to seclusion (Outlaw & Lowery, 1992). Given these negative feelings, it is more than likely that the client may not willingly go to seclusion.

In the confrontation with Jason, a response team has been called and is ready to take Jason to seclusion. Carol has slowly and carefully removed her jewelry to avoid cutting anyone in case she becomes involved.

Carol: I'd really like you to go on your own down to time out. It's up to you. You can go on your own right now, or the technicians will take you to seclusion.

Even at this late hour, the worker is still attempting to allow Jason to exercise options and make choices (Baradell, 1985).

Jason: I ain't gonna go nowhere 'ceptin' outta here.

Carol backs away and the response team moves in. On a predetermined signal by the leader, they quickly take Jason down. One member holds his head, and the other four carry him to seclusion.

Once placed in seclusion, the client is oriented to what is going to occur, and a staff member is assigned to monitor the client. Checks are made at 15-, 30-, or 60-minute intervals, depending on the client's mental status. Copies of nursing and general care orders are given to both staff and the client. Seclusion has a low level of sensory input—no radio or television, no visitors—and emphasis is on biological needs. "Low level" does not mean that the client is sensorily deprived; it is important to prevent feelings of abandonment. The client is shown acceptance by the human services worker and reassured that seclusion is necessary and temporary and that the client can return to normal routine when behavior calms down (Baradell, 1985).

Carol: I'm sorry you chose to go to seclusion, Jason. You decided to exercise that option, but when you can agree to not make threats, control your behavior to the point you can talk this through, and make a written contract as to what you will do, you can come back out.

In an acute stage of agitation such as Jason has just experienced, it is no longer appropriate to explore conflicts or feelings (Ruesch, 1973). Carol's communication with the client is brief, direct, concrete, but kind. Given the client's sensory overload, sleep is an excellent therapeutic modality, and the client should be allowed to use it (Baradell, 1985).

Seclusion or extended time out also has an effect on other members of the community (Jones, 1985). Other residents will demonstrate a variety of feelings, ranging from concern to fear. It is important that residents' questions be answered as fully as possible and that plans are made that incorporate their help in expediting the client's return to the community. It is worthwhile to convene a community meeting specifically for dealing with the concerns of the other residents. Many times the group can act as a therapeutic agent, encouraging members to discuss how they can help the client by reinforcing or ignoring particular behaviors that caused the problem in the first place.

One negative footnote is appropriate here: A few clients may use seclusion as a way of achieving notoriety and a macho image (Gutheil, 1978). If such a hidden agenda is suspected, the human services worker should thoroughly discuss this problem with the other residents and obtain their help in being nonresponsive to the client's "tough" behavior.

Stage 8: Restraints.   If the client is acting out and will not go to seclusion, restraints will have to be used. Restraints are controversial, and their use is closely regulated in both a legal and an ethical sense. Restraints are employed when it is evident that the client may be harmful to self or others (Stilling, 1992; Tardiff, 1984a, p. 48). First, a response team trained to apply restraints should be formed and be on call at all times (Wood & Khuri, 1984, p. 81). If the client is to be restrained, then adequate staff should be available, consisting of at least one person for each limb and another person who serves as leader, for a total of five members. Written guidelines and constant rehearsal of procedures with observation and critique should be used to keep the team's skills well honed (Tardiff, 1984b). Seclusion and restraints should *never* be used as a way of controlling clients, making life "easier" for the custodians, or as punishment. These are truly last-resort measures, because their use can cause a host of other problems for the client (Morrison, 1993, p. 105).

If at all possible, the crisis worker should not be involved in the episode, because involvement may erect barriers to future therapeutic endeavors. Once the decision to restrain the client has been made, the team should move fast and no further attempts at communication should be made. At a predetermined signal, each staff member seizes and controls one extremity. With a backward motion, the client is brought gently to the ground. The leader controls the client's head to prevent biting; and without choking, hitting, or verbal abuse, the client is carried face down with four-point restraints to a room where five-point restraints may be applied and the client's condition monitored (Dang, 1990; Tardiff, 1984a, p. 47).

Restraints are most often employed in psychiatric facilities and are used in conjunction with a request from the nursing staff and backed by a doctor's order. When a client is placed in restraints, whether two-, four-, or five-point, close observation is absolutely necessary. Under no circumstances should clients be restrained without such guidelines and available professional medical staff.

Stage 9: Sedation.   If all else fails, the client needs to be sedated. The problem now becomes clearly medical, and until the medical staff believes that medication is no longer necessary, there is little the human services worker can do.

If sedation is needed with Jason, it does not mean the end of Jason's story. Stage 9 is essentially a complete time out for both Jason and the staff. For Jason, it will allow the sensory overload he is experiencing to diminish and return to normal limits. It will give the staff members time to reorganize their thoughts on how best to deal with this highly agitated adolescent. When Jason comes out of sedation, the staff will start down the treatment road with him again and will have developed a new plan to deal with this angry young man.

THE VIOLENT GERIATRIC CLIENT

Although medical science has been able to prolong the lives of Americans, treatment for neuropsychiatric disorders concomitant with increased longevity remains beyond the reach of medical science at present. Accompanying the neuropsychiatric problems of the geriatric client are reduced judgment and increased impulsivity, limited mobility, drug dependency, multiple personal loss, financial problems, and limited social supports, which all potentially contribute to violent behavior (Mentes & Ferrario, 1989; Petrie, 1984, p. 107). The assumption that elderly clients are passive recipients of care is misguided. Study after study indicates this clientele to be at risk for behaving violently (Daugherty et al., 1992; Mentes & Ferrario, 1989; Ochitill & Kreiger, 1982; Petrie, Lawson, & Hollender, 1982).

The case of Cliff demonstrates how the agitated and mildly disoriented elderly client can be stabilized without medication. Reality orientation (Taulbee & Folsom, 1966; Osborn, 1991), reminiscence (Butler, 1963), and remotivation (Garber, 1965) techniques are workable options for the mildly disoriented elderly client. The case of Grace shows how validation therapy (Feil, 1982) may be used with the severely disoriented elderly. These cases illustrate that psychologically infirm elderly clients need not always spend this final stage of their lives in chemically induced compliance.

Mild Disorientation: The Case of Cliff

Cliff Hastings has lived a full and eventful life, but now, at the age of 74, he is a resident of a skilled nursing care facility. He was a strapping man who had worked all over the world on big construction projects until he was 72 years of age. He invented many engineering techniques in steamfitting and chilled water cooling systems. He lost his wife to cancer 10 years ago but submerged himself in his work and lived a highly productive life as a widower. He has had excellent relationships with his two children, Jan and Robert. Although they and their families live geographically distant from Cliff, they love their father very much and are very concerned about him.

At age 73, Cliff got up one morning, prepared to go to work, and fell flat on his face with a stroke. Although he recovered to the extent that he was able to shuffle around the house, lung complications set in. He was diagnosed as having emphysema and went on oxygen. Six months later, he was no longer able to take care of himself physically, was starting to have memory lapses, and was moved to Hursthaven Nursing Home by his children.

At Hursthaven, he has become progressively more confused about people, places, and times, and when asked to do something has been either rebellious or passively resistant. A crisis was precipitated when he knocked over an oxygen bottle in the middle of the night because the "Arabs were after him" and broke the nose of a male attendant who tried to calm him down as he attempted to struggle out of his bed. Cliff is about to meet Marilyn, a gerontological counselor. She has just been retained by Hursthaven to deal with crisis situations such as Cliff's.

Assessment.   Marilyn has thoroughly reviewed Cliff's chart and has discussed his case with the medical and primary care staff. Many of the primary care staff members maintain that Cliff is noncompliant, badly disoriented, and dangerous, and they would like to keep him heavily sedated. Cliff's stroke, his unplanned aggressive outburst, his hostile and uncooperative behavior, his fear of the medical equipment, and his depression, plus the fact that his outburst was at night, all support the staff's contention that little but chemical restraints is left for Cliff. Marilyn decides to conduct her own assessment by interviewing Cliff. The worker has three purposes in mind: (1) to determine the client's degree of disorientation and agitation; (2) to use her therapeutic skills to reduce his disruptive behavior and help him return to a state of equilibrium with as little reliance on medication as possible; and (3) to help Cliff use whatever resources he has to live this final stage of his life as fully as he is able.

Marilyn: Hello, I'm Marilyn. I don't believe I've met you. You seem pretty angry about something.

Cliff: (*Suspiciously.*) Who the hell are you?

Marilyn: I'm new here, part of the staff, and I'm getting around meeting all the residents. Sorry you're so angry. What can I do to help?

Cliff: I'm Cliff Hastings, and I'm mad as hell. Look at what those SOBs have done to me. I pay $4000 a month for this place to strap me down. I'll kill the bastards if I get a chance. Can you get me out of here?

Marilyn: (*Speaking in a strong but soft and empathic voice, while pulling up a chair and sitting down directly in his line of sight.*) No! I can't right now. I guess I'd be mad too if I were strapped in like that. Do you know where you are?

Cliff: I'm in Hell, and these people are all devils.

Marilyn: It may feel like that right now, but this is Hursthaven Nursing Home. Do you know that?

Cliff: Too damn well.

Marilyn: Do you know what day it is?

Cliff: Who cares? They're all the same in here.

The worker assesses Cliff's degree of contact with reality by determining how well oriented he is to person, place, and time. Although the client does not give specific, concrete responses, his retorts indicate that he is fairly well in touch with reality, given his present agitated state.

Marilyn: I'm sorry you're feeling so angry. Can I get you a drink of water?

Eliciting Trust.   Offering clients food or drink tends to defuse the situation and make them more accepting of initiating overtures the worker may tender (Wood & Khuri,

1984, p. 67). The worker also sits down by Cliff and meets him at eye level. She places herself on his physical level and in his direct line of sight. Standing over a client who is confused tends to distort the caregiver's image in grotesque ways and may be very threatening (Wolanin & Phillips, 1981, p. 106).

Cliff: (*Takes a sip of water from cup Marilyn offers.*) Yeah, that's the least somebody around this place could do for the money I pay to be doped up and trussed up like a pig.

Marilyn: How do you feel?

Cliff: How the hell do you think I feel, young lady?

Marilyn: I guess I'd not only feel like a pig all trussed up, but mad as a wildcat in a gunnysack. How did this happen?

The crisis worker matches the vernacular of the client and interjects a bit of humor (Tomine, 1986). The worker is interested in knowing what happened, but her major concern is to continue posing open-ended questions to assess how much in touch with reality Cliff is and to let him know she is interested in and concerned about him. The worker manages to gain a working rapport with the client and explores last night's incident.

Marilyn: So what happened last night that got you in that fix?

Cliff: The Arab, he was after me. He was gonna strangle me, but nobody believes me. (*Points to attendant.*) That guy said it was one of the guys that work here at night. Said I busted his nose. Well, it was the Arabs.

Marilyn: Why do you think it was the Arabs?

Reality Orientation.   The worker is taking a first step in attempting to relieve Cliff's confusion by using reality orientation (Taulbee & Folsom, 1966). Reality orientation focuses on anchoring clients to who they are, where they are, and why they are there. When a client's response or behavior is out of touch with reality, the worker asks the client a *why* question, in an approach contrary to that of most therapeutic interventions (Taulbee, 1978, p. 207). Marilyn does this because she is trying to find out the reason for the behavior. Once the worker knows that, she can start to reorient the client.

Cliff: I spent a lot of time in Arabia, you know. Worked in construction. Put up a lot of refrigeration plants and steam systems. Hard to believe you'd need steam in that hothouse. Sometimes I wish I was back in Arabia. But that doesn't mean any damn Arab can come in here in the middle of the night and kill me. I had plenty of close scrapes back there, and they didn't get me and they won't get me here.

Marilyn: (*Genuinely interested.*) Hey! That sounds pretty exciting. I've hardly been out of the Midwest. I'll bet you've seen some pretty hair-raising things, and I can guess how you might think somebody was an Arab, being in a strange place like this.

Cliff rambles on for quite a while about his experiences there, with Marilyn listening and responding using person-centered techniques of attending, affirming, restating for clarification, reflecting feelings, and asking open-ended questions.

Pacing.   Cliff's response about working in Arabia gives the worker a clue about the image he saw attacking him in the night. However, she does not try to change his mind about what happened. The worker keeps pace with Cliff. She lets him tell his story without hurrying or trying to persuade him that he was mistaken last night. Patience is of maximum benefit in gaining the trust she will need if she is to accomplish anything with the client (Taulbee, 1978, p. 210). This approach is in direct contrast to that of most of the staff members in the facility, who are pressed to get tasks accomplished in a specified time. Indeed, trying to gain compliance by coercing the client to meet institutional needs is likely to engender more agitated behavior.

Reminiscence Therapy.   The worker's approach in urging Cliff to talk about his past is contradictory to most standard operating procedures and generally accepted counseling techniques. Most therapeutic systems try very hard to keep clients in present time and view trips to the past as counterproductive to changing real-time problems. However, allowing geriatric clients to ruminate about past experiences can be therapeutically effective (Ebersole, 1978a, p. 145). Reminiscence therapy (Butler, 1963; Osborn, 1991) is a nonthreatening experience that allows older clients to reflect on their lives and restore credibility to them (Miller, 1986). It also offers the opportunity for physical contact and validation for what the elderly have done with their lives (Baker, 1985). Memory dysfunction and personality disorganization are central to Cliff's current crisis and confusion. Reminiscence helps in personality reorganization and increases self-confidence because it draws on aspects of long-term memory that have been imprinted and can be recalled easily (Singer, Tracz, & Dworkin, 1991). Reminiscence can be therapeutic and healing for the client; it is a simple, enjoyable sharing of anecdotes that allows the worker to form a close affiliation with the client (Ebersole, 1978a, p. 145). Over the long term, using reminiscence can allow the following positive outcomes to occur (McMahon & Rhudick, 1964, pp. 292–298; Singer et al., 1991):

1. maintaining self-esteem in the face of declining physical capacities
2. coping with grief and depression resulting from personal losses
3. contributing significantly to a society of which the elderly client is still a member
4. retaining a sense of identity in an increasingly estranged environment
5. decreasing social and emotional isolation by involvement with others
6. decreasing depression and loneliness through social interaction
7. developing a renewed social network
8. renewing social skills.

Cliff: Yeah . . . (*Voice trails off.*) . . . I used to be hot stuff . . . but I'm not so hot now. Hell, half the time I don't even know who, what, or where I am.

Marilyn: (*Touches client's arm lightly with her hand.*) It sounds like that's pretty scary, having run things most of your life and now things are out of control.

Cliff: I hate to admit it, but that's right. Now I got to have help getting to the john! How'd you like that? It embarrasses the hell out of me. They treat me like a 2-year-old.

Marilyn: So being embarrassed and not being treated like a man is one of the worst parts of being here. I wonder what we might do to change that?

Anchoring.   The worker uses a reflective statement of feeling to integrate the client's past with his present. By bringing up past incidents and hooking them to the present, the worker attempts to reinforce and help the client reassert his competence. She also uses touch to anchor Cliff psychologically to someone in the institution (Wolanin & Phillips, 1981, pp. 105–106). Prior to the assault, a kind but sterile atmosphere had existed for Cliff at Hursthaven. Like most human beings, he has not responded well to living in an emotional vacuum. Since the attack, the atmosphere between Cliff and the staff has become adversarial in nature. Marilyn needs to change Cliff's view of the staff as being against him and the staff's view that Cliff is to be avoided.

Staff members who have hands-on contact with Cliff on a regular basis need to be given training in the approaches Marilyn is using. Ideally, nurses and nurse assistants would be given training on the order of what Mentes and Ferrario (1989) propose in their program Calming Aggressive Reactions in the Elderly (CARE). CARE trains nursing home staff to get to know the resident personally, think about violence prevention, and use proactive and protective intervention before the client becomes agitated. Training components of the program consist of learning about the nature of aggression in elderly clients, risk factors for violence, violence prevention approaches, calming techniques, protective procedures, and case reviews.

Staffing and case review are particularly important for coordinating the different staff members who will deal with Cliff in a 24-hour period. Jensen and Absher (1994) developed a flowchart for planning intervention when behavior becomes violent with the mentally ill. This comprehensive flowchart baselines behavior, constructs a functional analysis of the client's social and physical environment, carefully reviews the client's physical and cognitive impairment, and then holds a staffing with the primary caregivers to determine what changes or interventions in the client's comprehensive care need to be made. The plan is then implemented and monitored on a continuous basis to determine whether change has occurred. If positive change has not occurred, the staff meets again and a new plan is developed.

All staff members who come in contact with Cliff during the course of the day will introduce themselves, call Cliff by name, state the date, give a short preview of the next few hours' activities, and also explain any procedures, medical or otherwise, that they are carrying out. By consistently orienting the client, the staff takes a first step in treating confusion (Taulbee, 1978, p. 209).

The worker also picks up on Cliff's fear of losing control. Being wildly out of control is completely out of character for clients like Cliff, who are frightened at the prospect of losing their minds. Even more fears are generated when elderly clients sense someone is afraid of them or avoiding them because of fear of violence (Lion & Pasternak, 1973).

The crisis worker engages in a number of activities in this dialogue. The most important is that she has made a small but significant change in the interactional system that currently exists between Cliff and the staff by representing herself as an empathic, caring spokesperson for the institution and as an advocate for the client (Fisch, Weakland, & Segal, 1983). Second, she reflects Cliff's anger, fear, and loss of control. She acknowledges and validates his experiences, but she is not just mouthing platitudes. She knows that the more he lacks current orientation, the more the staff will tend to avoid him. The more he is avoided, the less contact he has with people, and the more out of touch and disoriented he is likely to become (Petrie, 1984, pp. 114–115). The cycle can become deeper and deeper if uninterrupted and may cause even more disorientation and aggressive acts in the future (Miller, 1986).

Distinguishing Between Illusions and Hallucinations.   Marilyn understands that what agitated Cliff was probably not a hallucination, as the staff thinks, but more than likely an illusion. While piecing together the tale of the night before, she determines that one of the Sisters of Charity who works at the nursing home made rounds about the time Cliff became agitated. The sister's veil may have made her look like an Arab in the dim light. Thus, what Cliff saw was probably an illusion based in fact, not fiction. By proposing an explanation of the event, she allows Cliff to understand that he was not delusional but was misperceiving reality. The two problems are very different, and the difference is of great significance in calming the client. Although this conclusion may sound very pat, such happenings are all too common among mildly confused and disoriented clients. Very definite, concrete stimuli often create illusions that disrupt peace of mind for geriatric clients, leaving them to doubt their own perceptions. It is extremely important for the worker to relate such a hypothesis to mildly confused clients such as Cliff who are very much concerned about keeping in touch with reality (Wolanin & Phillips, 1981, p. 107).

Marilyn: (*Relates her hypothesis to the client.*) So I believe that you weren't really crazy last night, but actually saw Sister Lucy making rounds. If you think about it, it makes sense.

Cliff: I don't know. I still really believe there was an Arab in here.

Marilyn: From all you've told me about your experiences there, I can understand that. But I also know that when you're zonked out in a strange place with the medical equipment around and strangers passing to and fro, suddenly waking up and seeing things differently is not uncommon and doesn't mean you're nuts. I'll bet if you think about it, it has happened before. I know it has happened to me. There's a big difference between misunderstanding what you see and seeing something that isn't there.

Sundown Syndrome.   Because the event happened in the early evening, the sundown syndrome must be considered. Events that accompany the end of the day in an institution are strange and unsettling to residents who have been used to a regimen of activities based on their own time and the security of their own home. Unmet toilet needs, absence of a snack, staff members' attitudes, different noises, decreased light, effects of sedatives, and presence of fewer personnel all add up to fear and strangeness without the support of another human being. These conditions can lead the client to act out (Blair & New, 1991; Stilling, 1992; Wolanin & Phillips, 1981, p. 107). Given the need to further assure Cliff about the reality of the situation, Marilyn relates the problems that occur with the approach of evening in the institution and makes some suggestions about how things might be changed to make this time less threatening.

Marilyn: So a lot of times when evening comes at Hursthaven things can get exciting for the reasons I mentioned. If you could make things here a bit more like home, what would they be?

Cliff: Well, I used to put my earphones on and listen to some country music and have a beer before I hit the hay. I don't know much else, just watch TV and stuff. No special furniture or anything. I lived in apartments and hotels most of my life.

Marilyn: I notice that there's not much of you in this room. It looks like a hospital room instead of Cliff's room. You mentioned a lot of items you collected over the years and picture albums of all your travels. Where are they?

Cliff: Oh, my kids just stored them away.

Marilyn: I'd like to see if we couldn't get some of those in here, dress the place up a bit so when people come by they'd know it was Cliff Hastings, world-class engineer, who lives here.

Security Blankets.   The worker is proposing that articles familiar to Cliff be brought into the room for two reasons. First, creating a familiar environment may go a long way toward creating a basis in reality for the fact that this is now Cliff's home and reconciling him to this stage in his life (Petrie, 1984, p. 116). Second, suddenly awakening in a medical environment with a variety of strange machines and tubes running in and out of one's body is extremely threatening because such foreign objects alter a person's body images and surroundings in a very negative way (Wolanin & Phillips, 1981, p. 106). Having familiar objects immediately visible can help the client reorient without becoming agitated in the process. Marilyn will check with administrative staff to see whether Cliff's stereo equipment can be brought into his room. The worker will also check with medical staff to see whether a bottle of beer in the evening will confound his medication. If possible, providing these amenities will further approximate the client's routine at home and provide orientation and security (Miller, 1986).

Remotivation.   Finally, the worker will attempt to involve Cliff in the activities of the institution. It is important to involve clients interpersonally and have them become physically and psychologically active in their environment. For people like Cliff who have been highly active throughout their lives, it is critical to fill idle time in meaningful ways to keep such clients from drifting into depression (Donahue, 1965). This does not mean forcing and cajoling clients into doing something contrary to what interests them. Playing bingo might be fun for many people, but forcing a person to engage in such an activity is inappropriate (Miller, 1986). After listening to Cliff, the worker makes a proposal designed to reinvolve him with other humans.

Marilyn: I'd like you to consider a proposition I have to make. Hursthaven has an alliance with St. Peter's Orphanage. None of those kids have anybody to care about them. I have a couple of boys in mind that I think you could do some good with. You've got some great stories that they'd love and probably some wisdom that could be helpful to those guys. They just mainly need a man to talk to, and I wonder if you'd be willing to help out.

The worker's agenda is twofold. She is truthful in what she tells Cliff. She also knows that the two boys will have a positive effect on Cliff in turn. Aged people seem particularly interested in sharing their experiences with the young (Ebersole, 1978b, p. 241). Cliff's candidness, wisdom, and trove of stories are likely to have a positive effect on two boys who are as anchorless as Cliff. He will have to get involved in the planning that the residents of Hursthaven carry out in coordinating activities with St. Peter's. Involvement with other members of the community, heretofore nil, will gently push him back into the mainstream, reinforce his dignity, and provide him with interaction that he will find meaningful and enjoyable. Engaging in this activity will give the client a stake in the community and will, Marilyn hopes, focus his psychic energy on something besides his own outcast state (Miller, 1986).

The worker is engaging in a variation of remotivation therapy at this point. Remotivation therapy is a group technique used to stimulate and revitalize people who are no longer interested in the present or the future (Dennis, 1978, p. 219). It is based on a combination of reminiscence and reality orientation. Remotivation attempts to persuade the client that he is accepted by others as an individual who has unique and important traits that make him distinguishable from everyone else (Garber, 1965). Reminiscing about one's experiences with the concrete world and identifying and asserting one's experiences through interactions with others often lead to strengthening the concept of reality. Being encouraged to describe oneself concretely as a person with roles and specific social functions and speaking accurately about past and present experiences gives a person strength (Dennis, 1978, p. 220).

Here, Marilyn's hypothesis is that Cliff will work better with young boys because he has been a mentor to numerous young engineers over his lifetime. Many other elderly clients can profit from reminiscence groups that are composed of their peers (Singer et al., 1991). These groups enable elderly clients to share their experiences with one another, come to terms with their past experiences, and use them for more meaningful living in the present. Such groups can do much to negate the loneliness, helplessness, and hopelessness that often pervade elderly clients' lives and that in turn lead to further physical and mental deterioration and result in crisis situations such as Cliff's.

Severe Disorientation: The Case of Grace

Whereas Cliff is only mildly confused and fairly coherent as he ruminates about his past, many geriatric clients the worker encounters have lost touch with reality. Verbalization of past events becomes commingled with fantasy. The standard regimen for working with geriatric clients has been to attempt to reality-orient them to the present. Such an approach becomes problematic for moderately confused clients and profoundly so for those who have almost entirely retreated from the reality of the present. Attempts to orient moderately to severely confused very old clients to person, place, and time are generally futile. For many of these clients, nothing could be less worthwhile, for there is clearly not much in the present worth remembering (Miller, 1986).

Seizing on this notion, Naomi Feil developed validation therapy (Feil, 1982). Her thesis is to acknowledge the feelings of the person, no matter how irrational they may seem to be. By dignifying feelings, the worker validates the person. To deny the feelings of the client is to deny past existence and thus deny the personhood of the individual. Feil also believes that validating early memories enables clients to resolve the past and justify their role in old age. Positive outcomes from using the approach are restoring self-worth, reducing stress, justifying life, resolving unfinished conflicts, and establishing a better and more secure feeling for the client (Feil, 1982, p. 1). The worker continuously validates the client as a first step in restoring self-worth and affirming that at least one person is interested and concerned enough to listen to what the client's life has been. Anyone overhearing a dialogue between a worker and a client who has severely regressed into an irrational past would probably wonder at first whether the worker had also become senile. For validation therapy to be effective, the worker must have some creative insight into the verbal meanderings and repetitive behaviors of the client (Miller, 1986). Listen to Marilyn as she attempts to convince an 83-year-old woman to go to dinner.

Grace is standing in the hallway refusing to be moved. She is engaging in a rocking motion with her arms and softly humming to herself. Staff's efforts to get her to go to dinner have been fruitless, and she is becoming increasingly agitated as a number of staff members are attempting to orient her and get her to comply with their requests. Marilyn enters this scene and asks the rest of the staff to leave them.

Grace: There, there! Don't you cry.

Marilyn: I see you're really concerned about your baby.

Grace: Yes, I've been up all night with Ellen. She must have colic, but I can't seem to get her to settle down. I need to get Dr. Heinz, he's our family doctor, but I don't have anyone to drive me to town.

Marilyn: It really worries you that Ellen doesn't seem to be getting any better. You must be awfully tired and hungry!

Grace: Even though Ellen's cranky, she's no bother, she's really a beautiful baby. It's just that her father isn't around much, he works on the railroad and I could use some help sometimes.

Marilyn: You must love her very much. Maybe we could go down to dinner together, and you could tell me some more about her.

Grace: She's got to have quiet to get to sleep. It's too noisy there.

Marilyn: It's important to you that she gets to sleep. Perhaps we could have dinner served in your room. It'd be quiet there.

Grace: Well, I suppose, if you'd really like to.

In this short exchange the worker demonstrates two critical components of validation therapy. The client may well have lost the ability to comprehend and reason with any degree of complexity. By keeping communication short and simple, the worker avoids losing the client in a variety of ideas that may rapidly become overwhelming. The worker also responds directly and continuously to Grace's feelings, validating to her that the symbolic act she is engaging in is highly important (Miller, 1986).

Although the purpose of validation therapy is not to manipulate the client, the worker's approach is far better than forcibly taking the client to the dining room, where she will probably be so distraught over having to neglect her baby that she will not eat anyway. Whether Grace has ever had a baby named Ellen, or whether she is trying to resolve some shortcoming she has long felt in regard to mothering, is of little concern in the present moment. What is of concern is that the worker treat the situation as if it were real and of importance to the client and acknowledge the client's scattered thoughts and feelings in a congruent, empathic manner. Validation therapy is not intended to return the client to reality. However, for the human services worker who has to intervene in a crisis situation with the severely disoriented elderly, it does have the potential to calm them down, avoid situations conducive to acting out, and provide an effective therapeutic technique in an area where few have been found (Miller, 1986). Even though Grace appears to be a pathetic, senile, frail, and confused woman who is easily handled by the crisis worker, don't be misled. The very person Grace represents, who if thwarted and frustrated, is the reason that assaults against geriatric workers who discount the Graces are so high.

FOLLOW-UP WITH STAFF VICTIMS

Staff who are victims of violent attacks by clients may have emotional responses that include hypervigilance, startle responses, intrusive thoughts, unresolved anger and poorer overall mental health and anger control (Lenehan & Turner, 1984, p. 256; Wykes & Whittington, 1998). They may look much like the victims of PTSD (California Occupational Health and Safety Administration, 1998, p. 17; Murray & Snyder, 1991). Lanza (1984) found that nurses who had experienced such attacks had negative emotional, cognitive, and behavioral reactions up to a year afterward. It is extremely important to work through the aftermath of violent behavior suffered by staff, for two reasons: first, so that the victim does not become debilitated personally and professionally by the incident, and second, because other members of the staff will perceive that the institution takes such events very seriously and is concerned for their safety as well.

After an attack, staff members initially may ascribe blame to the victim to ease their own fear and trepidation about the possibility that it could happen to them. Under no circumstances should this be allowed to happen. Sympathy and support for the victim are vital. Pity, condescension, or subtle implications about provoking the assault should be avoided. Institutional support groups for victims of violence should be available (Stortch, 1991), and staff should be prepared to give immediate help with problem solving and decision making, such as determining injuries, providing medical transportation, staying with the victim, providing moral support, and helping with medical, legal, and police reports (Lenehan & Turner, 1984, pp. 255–256). Unit staff should also receive counseling to prevent "a blame the victim attitude" from developing (California Occupational Health and Safety Administration, 1998, p. 17).

As soon as the victim is able, a psychological autopsy should be performed on the incident. A psychological autopsy examines in detail the situation that led to the violent episode. (See Chapter 5, on lethal behavior, for a complete description of this procedure.) All staff members who are involved with the client attend the autopsy. It dissects what the staff and the client did behaviorally before, during, and after the incident. Further attention is given to the environmental setting to determine whether it played a role in instigating the aggressive behavior. Hopefully, the autopsy will provide clues as to the *whys, hows,* and *whats* of the incident so it does not recur. The victim's opinions should be solicited and should be used as expert testimony. Staff gather to discuss what happened, work through feelings about the event, and generate options for preventing a recurrence. By reviewing the traumatic experience, the victim is also able to deal with feelings of loss of security and control (Lenehan & Turner, 1984, pp. 254–259).

Critical incident stress debriefing (CISD) should be conducted simultaneously with the psychological autopsy in helping the assaulted human services worker attain precrisis equilibrium and homeostasis (California Occupational Health and Safety Administration, 1998, p. 17; Kinney, 1995; Mitchell & Everly, 1995; Spitzer & Burke, 1993; Spitzer & Neely, 1992; Vandenberg, 1992). CISD seeks to alleviate the acute stress crisis workers experience when they are traumatized by an event such as a physical assault on them, and generally CISD should occur within 24 hours of the event. Because CISD has a wide range of applicability both for human services workers and their clientele, we will explore this procedure extensively in Chapters 12 ("Hostage Crises") and 14 ("Off the Couch and into the Streets").

In the past, mental health institutions have left worker recovery from a client assault pretty much to chance, with a "Suck it up, it's part of the job!" approach. Dr. James Cavanaugh of the Isaac Ray Center for Rush-Presbyterian-St. Luke's, a pioneer in development of CISD, cites compelling evidence demonstrating that immediate posttrauma care can be very effective in helping both individuals and organizations become stabilized after a crisis (Kinney, 1995, p. 188).

SUMMARY

Violence in the human services setting has increased exponentially in the past two decades. Increased abuse of drugs, closing down of the large state mental hospitals, gang violence, increased adjudication of felons to mental health facilities, and increases in the geriatric population have been major contributors to this phenomenon. The problem pervades all parts of human services. Both service providers and their staffs have largely looked the other way, and when violence against staff has occurred, it has been seen as going with the territory, or the victim has been blamed for being stupid and careless.

Human services statistics indicate a strong likelihood that sometime during the worker's career he or she will become a victim of violence. Techniques ranging from option therapy to validation therapy are intended not only to help the client stabilize, but also to prevent the human services worker from being the object of an assault.

CLASSROOM EXERCISES

I. Dealing with Verbal Abuse

Divide the group into dyads. One person in each pair assumes the role of the human services worker, and the other person assumes the role of an agitated, verbally abusive client. The human services worker's job is to get the client under control. Because the dialogue will probably become rather loud, house the dyads in separate offices or rooms if possible.

The client will take a standing position, and the human services worker will remain seated (all the better to intimidate the worker!). Another chair should be available for the client, but in the beginning the client must not sit down. The client may threaten, be noncompliant, yell, berate, gripe, or say terrible things about the worker. However, when asked a question, the client must respond to the content being asked. Also, when the worker makes a reflective statement, the client must respond by indicating the feeling state felt.

The worker may use any of the techniques discussed in this chapter or, for that matter, anything else that comes to mind. The mission for this exercise is to get the client to sit down. Continue the exercise for 5 to 10 minutes, with tape recorder on. At the end of the time, switch roles. Whenever dyad partners have concluded their experiences of enactment of both worker and client roles, make sure that both people verbally disassociate themselves from the roles to one another. At the end of both sessions, come back together as a group. Discuss the following questions.

1. How did you feel as the worker?
2. Were you able to stay relaxed and keep your wits about you?

3. How did you do that without becoming agitated yourself?
4. How did you attempt to gain compliance from the client?
5. What techniques worked and what didn't?

II. Staffing and Plotting a Strategy

Select some of the tapes made in the previous exercise. In groups of four or five, listen to the tapes and brainstorm what might be a more effective approach. Solicit the client for feedback on which seem to be the most effective ideas and why.

III. Using Validation Therapy with a Disoriented Client

Working in dyads, one member assumes the role of a disoriented client who would like to talk about a past event that is of great importance. To make this event realistic, clients should think back to an important moment in their childhood and attempt to report that moment as if it were present time. The workers will use validation therapy and pace with their clients as if the memories were real, alive, important, and very much here-and-now. Workers should attempt to have their clients comply with a task, but this purpose is secondary to responding empathically to the feelings and content of the memory. After the dialogue has continued for approximately five minutes, stop and switch roles. After another five minutes, again stop and rejoin the group. Discuss the following questions:

1. As the worker, how did you feel as you paced with the client?
2. How frustrated, if at all, did you become?
3. What did you do to stay at an empathic level with the client?
4. How compliant was the client to any requests you made?
5. As the client, how did you feel about the worker's attempts to listen and understand what you were saying?
6. How did you feel and what did you do when the worker attempted to gain compliance with the requested task?

RESOURCES

The California Occupational Health and Safety Administration has a web site that gives detailed information on planning for violent behavior in a variety of different settings. Its web site is http://www.dir.ca.gov/DOSH/dosh_publications/hcworker.html.

REFERENCES

American Psychiatric Association. (1974). *Clinical aspects of the violent individual.* Washington, DC: American Psychiatric Association Press.

Annis, L. V., McClaren, H. A., & Baker, C. A. (1984). Who kills us? In J. T. Turner (Ed.), *Violence in the medical care setting: A survival guide* (pp. 19–31). Rockville, MD: Aspen Systems.

Bach y Rita, G., Lion, J. R., & Climent, C. E. (1971). Episodic dyscontrol: A study of 630 violent patients. *American Journal of Psychiatry, 128,* 1473–1478.

Baker, N. J. (1985). Reminiscing in group therapy for self-worth. *Journal of Gerontological Nursing, 11,* 21–24.

Baradell, J. G. (1985, February). Humanistic care of the patient in seclusion. *Journal of Psychosocial Nursing and Mental Health Services, 23,* 9–14.

Barret, K. E., Riggar, T. F., & Flowers, C. R. (1997). Violence in the workplace. Preparing for the age of rage. *Journal of Rehabilitation Administration, 21*(3), 171–188.

Beck, J. C. (1988). The therapist's legal duty when the patient may be violent. *Psychiatric Clinics of North America, 11,* 665–679.

Becker, W. C. (1971). *Parents are teachers.* Champaign, IL: Research Press.

Belak, A. G., & Busse, D. (1993). Legal issues. In P. E. Blumenreich & S. Lewis (Eds.), *Managing the violent patient: A clinician's guide* (pp. 137–149). New York: Brunner-Mazel.

Blair, D. T. (1991). Assaultive behavior: Does provocation begin in the front office? *Journal of Psychosocial Nursing and Mental Health Services, 29,* 21–24.

Blair, D. T., & New, S. A. (1991). Assaultive behavior: Know the risks. *Journal of Psychosocial Nursing and Mental Health Services, 29,* 25–29.

Blumenreich, P. E. (1993a). Assessment. In P. E. Blumenreich & S. Lewis (Eds.), *Managing the violent patient: A clinician's guide* (pp. 35–40). New York: Brunner/Mazel.

Blumenreich, P. E. (1993b). Etiology. In P. E. Blumenreich & S. Lewis (Eds.), *Managing the violent patient: A clinician's guide* (pp. 21–33). New York: Brunner/Mazel.

Butler, R. (1963). The life review: An interpretation of reminiscence in the aged. *Psychiatry, 26,* 65–76.

California Occupational Health and Safety Administration (1998). *Guidelines of security and safety of health care and community service workers.* Sacramento, CA: Author.

Canter, L., & Canter, E. (1982). *Assertive discipline for parents.* Santa Monica, CA: Canter Associates.

Chavez, L. (1999). *Workplace violence awareness for managers and supervisors.* Internet course. http://members.aol.com/hrtrainer/defuse.html

Dang, S. (1990). When the patient is out of control. *RN, 59,* 57–58.

Daugherty, L. M., Bolger, J. P., Preston, D. G., Jones, S. S., & Paynes, H. C. (1992). Effects of exposure to aggressive behavior on job satisfaction of healthcare staff. *Journal of Applied Gerontology, 11,* 160–172.

Dennis, H. (1978). Remotivation therapy groups. In I. M. Burnside (Ed.), *Working*

with the elderly: Group process and techniques (pp. 219–235). North Scituate, MA: Duxbury Press.

Dinkmeyer, D. C., Pew, W. L., & Dinkmeyer, D. C., Jr. (1979). *Adlerian counseling and psychotherapy.* Pacific Grove, CA: Brooks/Cole.

Doms, R. W. (1984). Personal distress devices for health care personnel. In J. T. Turner (Ed.), *Violence in the medical care setting: A survival guide* (pp. 225–229). Rockville, MD: Aspen Systems.

Donahue, H. H. (1965). Expanding the program. *Hospital and Community Psychiatry, 17,* 117–118.

Dubin, W. R. (1981). Evaluating and managing the violent patient. *Annals of Emergency Medicine, 10,* 481–484.

Durivage, A. (1989). Assaultive behavior: Before it happens. *Canadian Journal of Psychiatry, 34,* 393–397.

Dyer, W. O., Murrell, D. S., & Wright, D. (1984). Training for hospital security: An alternative to training negligence suits. In J. T. Turner (Ed.), *Violence in the medical care setting: A survival guide* (pp. 1–18). Rockville, MD: Aspen Systems.

Ebersole, P. P. (1978a). A theoretical approach to the use of reminiscence. In I. M. Burnside (Ed.), *Working with the elderly: Group process and techniques* (pp. 139–154). North Scituate, MA: Duxbury Press.

Ebersole, P. P. (1978b). Establishing reminiscence groups. In I. M. Burnside (Ed.), *Working with the elderly: Group process and techniques* (pp. 236–254). North Scituate, MA: Duxbury Press.

Epstein, M., & Carter, L. (1988). *Training manual for Headquarters staff.* Lawrence, KS: Headquarters.

Fareta, G. (1981). A profile of aggression from adolescence to adulthood: An 18-year follow-up of psychiatrically disturbed and violent adolescents. *American Journal of Orthopsychiatry, 51,* 439–453.

Feil, N. (1982). *Validation: The Feil method.* Cleveland, OH: Edward Feil Productions.

Felthous, A. R. (1987). Liability of treaters for injuries to others: Erosion of three immunities. *Bulletin of the American Academy of Psychiatry and the Law, 15,* 115–125.

Fisch, R., Weakland, J. H., & Segal, L. (1983). *The tactics of change.* San Francisco: Jossey-Bass.

Forster, J. (1994). The psychiatric emergency: Heading off trouble. *Patient Care, 28,* 130.

Garber, R. S. (1965). A psychiatrist's view of remotivation. *Mental Hospitals, 16,* 219–221.

Glasser, W. (1965). Reality therapy. New York: Harper & Row.

Glasser, W. (1969). Schools without failure. New York: Harper & Row.

Greenfield, T. K., McNeil, D. E., & Binder, R. L. (1989). Violent behavior and length of psychiatric hospitalization. *Hospital and Community Psychiatry, 40,* 809–814.

Greenstone, J. L., & Leviton, S. C. (1993). *Elements of crisis intervention.* Pacific Grove, CA: Brooks/Cole.

Gutheil, T. G. (1978). Observation on the theoretical basis for seclusion of the psychiatric inpatient. *American Journal of Psychiatry, 135,* 325–328.

Hamstra, B. (1986). Neurobiological substrates of violence: An overview for forensic clinicians. *Journal of Psychiatry and Law, 14,* 349–374.

Hartel, J. A. (1993). The prosecution of assaultive clients. *Perspectives in Psychiatric Care, 29,* 7–14.

Heilbrun, A. B. (1990). The measurement of criminal dangerousness as a personality construct: Further validation of a research index. *Journal of Personality Assessment, 54,* 141–148.

Heilbrun, A. B., & Heilbrun, M. R. (1989). Dangerousness and legal insanity. *Journal of Psychiatry and Law, 17,* 39–53.

Ishimoto, W. (1984). Security management for health care administrators. In J. T. Turner (Ed.), *Violence in the medical care setting: A survival guide* (pp. 209–223). Rockville, MD: Aspen Systems.

Jensen, D., & Absher, J. (1994, April). *Assaultive behavior, the crisis is over: Preventing another crisis.* Paper presented at the Eighteenth Annual Convening of Crisis Intervention Personnel, Chicago.

Jones, J. (Speaker). (1984). *Counseling in correctional settings* (Cassette Recording No. 25-6611). Memphis: Memphis State University, Department of Counseling and Personnel Services.

Jones, M. K. (1985, June). Patient violence: Report of 200 incidents. *Journal of Psychosocial Nursing and Mental Health, 23,* 12–17.

Kinney, J. A. (1995). *Violence at Work.* Upper Saddle River, NJ: Prentice Hall.

Kirk, A. (1989). The prediction of violent behavior during short-term civil commitment. *Bulletin of the American Academy of Psychiatry and the Law, 17,* 345–353.

Klassen, D., & O'Connor, W. A. (1988). A prospective study of predictors of violence in adult male mental health admissions. *Law and Human Behavior, 12,* 143–158.

Kroll, J., & Mackenzie, T. B. (1983). When psychiatrists are liable: Risk management and violent patients. *Hospital and Community Psychiatry, 34,* 29–37.

Kurlowicz, L. H. (1990). Violence in the emergency department. *American Journal of Nursing, 90,* 35–40.

Lakeside Hospital. (1988). *Verbal techniques for de-escalating violent behavior.* Memphis, TN: Author.

Lanza, M. L. (1984). A follow-up study of nurses' reactions to physical assault. *Hospital and Community Psychiatry, 35,* 492–494.

Lanza, M. L. (1985, June). How nurses react to patient assault. *Journal of Psychosocial Nursing and Mental Health, 23,* 6–11.

LeCroy, C. W. (1988). Anger management or anger expression: Which is most effective? *Residential Treatment for Children and Youth, 5,* 29–39.

Lenehan, G. P., & Turner, J. T. (1984). Treatment of staff victims of violence. In J. T. Turner (Ed.), *Violence in the medical care setting: A survival guide* (pp. 251–260). Rockville, MD: Aspen Systems.

Lewellyn, A. (Speaker). (1985). Counseling emotionally disturbed high school students: The Mattoon, Illinois, TLC program (Cassette Recording No. 12-6611). Memphis: Memphis State University, Department of Counseling and Personnel Services.

Lewis, S. (1993). Restrain and seclusion. In P. E. Blumenreich & S. Lewis (Eds.), *Managing the violent patient: A clinician's guide* (pp. 101–109). New York: Brunner-Mazel.

Lion, J. R., & Pasternak, S. A. (1973). Countertransference reactions to violent patients. *American Journal of Psychiatry, 130,* 207–210.

Mack, D. A., Shannon, C., Quick, J. D., & Quick, J. C. (1988). Stress and the preventative management of workplace violence. In R. W. Griffin & A. O'Leary-Kelly (Eds.), Dysfunctional behavior in organizations: Violent and deviant behavior. *Monographs in organizational behavior and industrial relations, 23,* Parts A & B (pp. 119–141). Stamford, CT: Jai Press.

Madden, D. J., Lion, J. R., & Penna, M. W. (1976). Assaults on psychiatrists by patients. *American Journal of Psychiatry, 133,* 422–425.

Marohn, R. C. (1982). Adolescent violence: Causes and treatment. *Journal of the American Academy of Child Psychiatry, 21,* 354–360.

Martin, L., Francisco, E., Nichol, C., & Schweiger, J. L. (1991). A hospital-wide approach to crisis control: One inner-city hospital's experience. *Journal of Emergency Nursing, 17,* 395–401.

Mattson, M. R., & Sacks, M. H. (1978). Seclusion: Uses and implications. *American Journal of Psychiatry, 135,* 1210–1212.

McCown, C. (Speaker). (1986). Counseling in an adolescent psychiatric treatment facility (Cassette Recording No. 7). Memphis, TN: Memphis State University, Department of Counseling and Personnel Services.

McMahon, A., & Rhudick, P. (1964). Reminiscing: Adaptional significance in the aged. *Archives of General Psychiatry, 10,* 292–298.

McNeil, D. E., Binder, M. R., & Greenfield, T. L. (1988). Predictors of violence in civilly committed acute psychiatric patients. *American Journal of Psychiatry, 8,* 965–970.

McNeil, D. E., Hatcher, C., Zeiner, H., Wolfe, H. L., & Myers, R. S. (1991). Characteristics of persons referred by police to the psychiatric emergency room. *Hospital and Community Psychiatry, 42,* 425–427.

Mentes, J. C., & Ferrario, J. (1989). Calming aggressive reactions: A prevention program. *Journal of Gerontological Nursing, 15,* 22–27.

Miller, M. (Speaker). (1986). Counseling geriatric clients (Cassette Recording No. 14). Memphis, TN: Memphis State University, Department of Counseling and Personnel Services.

Mitchell, J. T., & Everly, G. S., Jr. (1995). *Critical incidents stress debriefing: The basic course workbook.* Ellicott City, MD: International Critical Incidents Stress Foundation.

Monahan, J. (1981). *The clinical prediction of violent behavior.* Rockville, MD: National Institute of Mental Health.

Monahan, J. (1984). The prediction of violent behavior: Toward a second generation of theory and policy. *American Journal of Psychiatry, 141,* 10–15.

Monahan, J. (1988). Risk assessment of violence among the mentally disordered: Generating useful knowledge. *International Journal of Law and Psychiatry, 11,* 249–257.

Moran, J. F. (1984). Teaching the management of violent behavior to nursing staff: A health care model. In J. T. Turner (Ed.), *Violence in the medical care setting: A survival guide* (pp. 231–250). Rockville, MD: Aspen Systems.

Morrison, J. M. (1993). Physical techniques. In P. E. Blumenreich and S. Lewis (Eds.), *Managing the violent patient: A clinician's guide* (pp. 79–100). New York: Brunner-Mazel.

Mulvey, E. P., & Lidz, C. W. (1984). Clinical considerations on the prediction of dangerous mental patients. *Clinical Psychology Review, 4,* 379–401.

Murdach, A. D. (1993). Working with potentially assaultive clients. *Health and Social Work, 18,* 307–312.

Murray, G., & Snyder, J. C. (1991). When staff are assaulted. *Journal of Psychosocial Nursing, 29,* 24–29.

National Institute for Occupational Safety and Health. (1992, October). *Epidemiology of workplace violence.* Atlanta: Centers for Disease Control.

Nicoletti, J., & Spooner, K. (1996). Violence in the workplace: Response and intervention strategies. In G. R. VandenBos & E. Q. Bulatao (Eds.), *Violence on the job: Identifying risks and developing solutions* (pp. 267–282). Washington, DC: American Psychological Association.

Nisbett, R. E. (1993). Violence and U.S. regional culture. *American Psychologist, 48,* 441–449.

Ochitill, H. N., & Kreiger, M. (1982). Violent behavior among hospitalized medical and surgical patients. *Southern Medical Journal, 75,* 151–155.

Osborn, C. L. (1991). Reminiscence: When the past eases the present. *Journal of Gerontological Nursing, 15,* 6–11.

Outlaw, F. H., & Lowery, B. J. (1992). Seclusion: The nursing challenge. *Journal of Psychosocial Nursing, 30,* 13–17.

Palmstierna, T., & Wistedt, B. (1990). Risk factors for aggressive behaviour are of limited value in predicting the violent behaviour of acute involuntarily admitted patients. *Acta Psychiatrica Scandinavica, 81,* 152–155.

Petrie, W. M. (1984). Violence: The geriatric patient. In J. T. Turner (Ed.), *Violence in the medical care setting: A survival guide* (pp. 107–122). Rockville, MD: Aspen Systems.

Petrie, W. M., Lawson, E. C., & Hollender, M. H. (1982). Violence in geriatric patients. *Journal of the American Medical Association, 248,* 443–444.

Piercy, D. (1984). Violence: The drug and alcohol patient. In J. T. Turner (Ed.), *Violence in the medical care setting: A survival guide* (pp. 123–152). Rockville, MD: Aspen Systems.

Pisarick, G. (1981, September). The violent patient. *Nursing,* pp. 63–65.

Poliks, O. (1999, April). *The noble victim: survival self-care and spirituality.* Paper presented at the Twenty-Third Annual Convening of Crisis Intervention Personnel, Chicago.

Rada, R. T. (1981). The violent patient: Rapid assessment and management. *Psychosomatics, 22,* 101–109.

Reid, B. (Speaker). (1986). Counseling in halfway houses. (Cassette recording No. 9). Memphis, TN: Memphis State University, Department of Counseling and Personnel Services.

Rofman, E. S., Askinazi, C., & Fant, E. (1980). The prediction of dangerous behavior in emergency civil commitment. *American Journal of Psychiatry, 137,* 1061–1064.

Ruben, I., Wolkon, G., & Yamamoto, J. (1980). Physical attacks on psychiatric residents by patients. *Journal of Nervous and Mental Disease, 168,* 243–245.

Ruesch, J. (1973). *Therapeutic communication.* New York: Norton.

Shah, A. K., Fineberg, N. A., & James, D. V. (1991). Violence among psychiatric inpatients. *Acta Psychiatrica Scandinavica, 84,* 305–309.

Simonds, J. F., & Kashani, J. (1980). Specific drug use and violence in delinquent boys. *American Journal of Drug and Alcohol Abuse, 7,* 305–322.

Singer, V. I., Tracz, S. M., & Dworkin, S. H. (1991). Reminiscence group therapy: A treatment modality for older adults. *Journal for Specialists in Group Work 16,* 167–171.

Sloore, H. (1988). Use of the MMPI in the prediction of dangerous behavior. *Acta Psychiatrica Belgica, 88,* 42–51.

Spitzer, W. J., & Burke, L. (1993). A critical incident stress debriefing program for hospital based health care personnel. *Health and Social Work, 18,* 149–156.

Spitzer, W. J., & Neely, K. (1992). The role of hospital-based social work in developing a statewide intervention system for first-responders delivering emergency services. *Social Work in Health Care, 18,* 39–58.

Steveson, S. (1991). Heading off violence with verbal de-escalation. *Journal of Psychosocial Nursing, 29,* 7–10.

Stilling, L. (1992). The pros and cons of physical restraints and behavior controls. *Journal of Psychosocial Nursing, 30,* 18–20.

Stortch, D. D. (1991). Starting an in-hospital support group for victims of violence in the psychiatric hospital. *Psychiatric Hospital, 22,* 5–9.

Tardiff, K. (1984a). Violence: The psychiatric patient. In J. T. Turner (Ed.), *Violence in the medical care setting: A survival guide* (pp. 33–55). Rockville, MD: Aspen Systems.

Tardiff, K. (1984b). *The psychiatric uses of seclusion and restraint.* Washington, DC: American Psychiatric Association Press.

Tardiff, K. (1989). *Assessment and management of violent patients.* Washington, DC: American Psychiatric Association Press.

Taulbee, L. R. (1978). Reality orientation: A therapeutic group activity for elderly persons. In I. M. Burnside (Ed.), *Working with the elderly: Group process and techniques* (pp. 206–218). North Scituate, MA: Duxbury Press.

Taulbee, L. R., & Folsom, J. C. (1966). Reality orientation for geriatric patients. *Hospital and Community Psychiatry, 17,* 133–135.

Tomine, S. (1986). Private practice in gerontological counseling. *Journal of Counseling and Development, 68,* 406–409.

Turnbull, J., Aitken, I., Black, L., & Patterson, B. (1990, June). Turn it around: Short-term management for aggression and anger. *Journal of Psychosocial Nursing and Mental Health Services, 28,* 7–13.

Turner, J. (Ed.). (1984). *Violence in the medical care setting: A survival guide.* Rockville, MD: Aspen Systems.

Turns, D. M. (1993). Institutional response to violent incidents. In P. E. Blumenreich &

S. Lewis (Eds.), *Managing the violent patient: A clinician's guide* (pp. 131–135). New York: Brunner-Mazel.

Turns, D. M., & Blumenreich, P. E. (1993). Epidemiology. In P. E. Blumenreich & S. Lewis (Eds.), *Managing the violent patient: A clinician's guide* (pp. 5–20). New York: Brunner-Mazel.

U.S. Bureau of Justice. (1998). *Data from the National Crime Victimization Survey 1992–1996.* Washington, DC: Author.

Vandenberg, N. (1992). Using critical incidents and debriefing to mediate organizational crisis, change, and loss. *Employee Assistance Quarterly, 8,* 35–55.

Viner, J. (1982). Toward more skillful handling of acutely psychotic patients. Part I: Evaluation. *Emergency Room Report, 3,* 125–130.

Vinick, B. (Speaker). (1986). Counseling in a state mental hospital. (Cassette Recording No. 13). Memphis, TN: Memphis State University, Department of Counseling and Personnel Services.

Walker, Z., & Seifert, R. (1994). Violent incidents in a psychiatric intensive care unit. *British Journal of Psychiatry, 164,* 826–828.

Werner, P. D., Rose, T. L., Murdach, A. D., & Yesavage, J. A. (1989). Social workers' decision making about the violent client. *Social Work Research and Abstracts, 25,* 17–20.

Wolanin, M. O., & Phillips, L. R. (1981). *Confusion: Prevention and care.* St. Louis, MO: Mosby.

Wood, K. A., & Khuri, R. (1984). Violence: The emergency room patient. In J. T. Turner (Ed.), *Violence in the medical care setting: A survival guide* (pp. 57–84). Rockville, MD: Aspen Systems.

Wykes, T., & Whittington, R. (1998). Prevalence and predictors of early traumatic stress reactions in assaulted psychiatric nurses. *Journal of Forensic Psychiatry, 9*(3), 643–658.

Yesavage, J. A., & Zarcone, V. (1983). History of drug abuse and dangerous behavior in inpatient schizophrenics. *Journal of Clinical Psychiatry, 44,* 259–261.

Zold, A. C., & Schilt, S. C. (1984). Violence: The child and the adolescent patient. In J. T. Turner (Ed.), *Violence in the medical care setting: A survival guide* (pp. 85–106). Rockville, MD: Aspen Systems.

Crises in Schools

THE NEW-MILLENNIUM, VIOLENCE-PROOF SCHOOL BUILDING

Welcome to the violence-proof (pretty much) school building of the new millennium. We will not be spending any money on landscaping, because people can hide behind shrubbery and we want every square inch of the exterior in plain view of security vehicles that we are going to have patrolling the perimeter on a 24-hour basis, seven days a week. We really don't want taggers making their artistic statement on the school or common everyday juvenile delinquents vandalizing it, so we are going to have the whole facade flood lit and we are going to have at least a 10-foot-tall cyclone security fence around the grounds. We will certainly want a vehicle path around the perimeter so that security vehicles or police cars can easily keep surveillance on the building.

We prefer that all students come to school in buses equipped with video monitors and two-way radios. If there is to be a student parking lot, then it too is going to be enclosed by a cyclone fence at least 10-feet high and it absolutely will have razor wire on top of it. It will be gated, so all the students will need passes and hanger tags to get in. Here our preference is to have a security guard checking all students and parents who come into the lot. We will also have concrete median dividers angled such that there could be no straight on assault by individuals intent on drive-by shootings. We will have one entrance into the school where all students would go through a metal detector. See-through backpacks would be run through an X-ray machine. School uniforms would be mandatory. On the subject of uniforms, you can probably have your choice of school colors as long as those colors are not used by any known gangs operating in your school. Certainly all students must have holographic ID cards attached to their uniforms, as must the faculty. All faculty are equipped with panic alarms and have mobile phones on their person with preset dialing to security. Kevlar bullet-proof vests in the school colors are issued to all staff.

The building itself has almost no windows; a few very small windows are made of bullet-proof glass. Walls are double-brick thick (the newer munitions can fairly easily penetrate a one-brick thickness). There is a central monitoring station capable of visual, auditory, and motion surveillance of the total school building—both inside and out. All classrooms have timed electronic locks on them that can only be operated through a computer program or overridden from the central monitoring location. Hallways also have locked electronic doors at strategic locations for crowd control and isolation of intruders.

The real savings is in building architecture. First, we are downsizing the gymnasium. We won't need bleachers, because crowds are hazardous to the school's health. Any pep assemblies, sporting events, plays or Christmas pageants can be piped back into classrooms via TV monitors. Athletic events can be played on isolated fields, and spectators can watch via community cable television. As a result, we do not need showers or locker areas. Second, we also cut the width of hallways because there are no lockers in this school, they being too conducive to hiding contraband. There is no need for a cafeteria. Lunches can either be microwaved in classrooms or hotpacked from a central food preparation facility. Cafeterias are places where student congregate. Congregation of students sets a dangerous precedent, so cafeterias and gymnasiums really do need to go the way of the little red schoolhouse. There are no faculty bathrooms. Student bathrooms are dangerous and must be policed, so while faculty are relieving themselves they can also watch students.

Finally, the administrative area has become a command and control center that is target hardened and has maximum security measures for its protection as the nerve center of the school. Because most interaction by students and teachers is by video, there is little if any need for student or teacher access to this area. Therefore, only staff who need access to this area have electronic card keys. The central staff is a little different from what now normally exists. Besides the administrative staff and secretaries and support personnel such as crisis workers, there is a police ready room for the four school police officers especially trained in dealing with school violence. A central communications staff is in charge of all electronic surveillance and media.

The principal in this school plays a somewhat secondary role. The coadministrator is chief of security. She or he is most likely a criminal justice major, has experience in law enforcement, and understands computer and security systems inside and out. In any emergency she or he will be the primary decision-making authority. This will happen because the principal will not begin to have the necessary expertise to coordinate security, any more than he or she would have the ability to operate a nuclear power plant!

If you are having trouble picturing exactly what this school will look like when completed, a reasonable facsimile would be any correctional facility built in the last 10 years. So! You are appalled at the idea of a school that is in effect a penitentiary. Although we have not seen a school with every one of the attributes in the safe school just described, we *have* seen each component we have previously mentioned in at least one school building in our travels around the United States and many experts in school safety have recommended the foregoing features (Astor, 1999; Blauvelt, 1998; Brock, Sandoval, & Lewis, 1996; National School Safety Center, 1990; Poland, 1994, 1999; Stephens, 1994).

Our somewhat tongue-in-cheek school building may seem patently ludicrous in Cook, Minnesota; Bangor, Maine; or Hayti, Missouri. But to say that such a school building as we have planned for you will never be built would be the equivalent of living in Antarctica for the past 10 years to be so unaware of school violence in this country. The violence that has arisen in schools is why many of these building modifications are being deemed necessary by more and more school districts, and that is what this chapter is about.

School systems are generally able to deal with developmental crises, because they are squarely in the middle of one of the greatest developmental crisis of all, growing up! What they have not been prepared to deal with are situational crises that arise unexpectedly and violently. Why is this so?

First, it has simply not been deemed cost expedient to provide all the material and human support needed to do so (Pitcher & Poland, 1992). Our new-millennium school building is not a cheap ticket, and the support personnel to staff it will not be cheap either! Although schools have long been prepared for disasters such as tornadoes and fires, the fact is that preparing for these kinds of disasters is relatively simple. The situational crisis that involves violence perpetrated on students or teachers by others is not.

Another problem that assails schools is public scrutiny and the fact that they will be in the limelight when a crisis of lethality occurs in the school. It is not enough that schools must be prepared to deal with the direct effects of a crisis such as a suicide or homicide. School staff must be prepared for a variety of ripple effects. How to deal with huge numbers of other students affected by the crisis? How to deal with critical and concerned parents? How to keep the school safe without trampling on the rights of individuals who may be under suspicion or alleged to have committed violent acts? How to deal with the media who may descend vulturelike on the school in the event of a crisis? In short, few if any institutions have as many issues to deal with when subjected to a crisis as a school district does.

Why have schools become spawning grounds for violent behavior? Poor parenting practice, an ineffective welfare system, marginalization of minorities and other disenfranchised students, availability of high-powered, automatic weapons, racism, gang growth, violence in homes, bullying, lack of male role models, hate crimes, and drug involvement are but a few of the ills that spill over into schools (Blauvelt, 1998; Collier, 1999; Goldstein, 1991; Goldstein & Kodluboy, 1998; Grossman, 1995; Hazler, 1996; Poland, 1994; Soriano, Soriano, & Jimenez, 1994). Perhaps the most chilling reasons, though, are proposed by David Grossman in his book, *On Killing* (1995, pp. 302–305). He proposes that there are three learning theories at work: Classical conditioning works where one sits comfortably in front of a movie or television screen watching mayhem and carnage while eating popcorn and drinking a soda. Operant conditioning works at video arcades, which provide immediate feedback and rewards for killing and maiming. Social learning whereby a whole new series of role models such as Freddie Kruger, do not end up saving the girl and kissing the horse, but slash the girl's throat and the horse's too. Even the movie and television heroes are anti-heroes and operate outside the law because the justice system is seen as weak and powerless.

Grossman wages an eloquent argument in his book about the historical resistance of the military to fire weapons and kill at close range because of the inherent revulsion at killing one's own species. However, with behavioral conditioning and desensitizing exercises that are closely parallel to the foregoing civilian examples, the military has increased its fire rate and killing capacity exponentially. The major difference is, that someone in authority provides social sanctions that prohibits indiscriminate killing in the military. It is hard to believe those same social sanctions are being instituted by the operator of a video arcade, the manager of a movie house, or, in fact, parents who let their children watch the gratuitous violence and disrespect for morality, justice, authority, religion, or any thing else for that matter, in shows such as *South Park*. It doesn't take a great deal of imagination after reading Grossman's book to understand why Westside Middle School in Jonesboro, Arkansas, and Columbine High School in Littleton, Colorado, become killing fields and any number of drive-by shootings occur at any number of other schools occur across the United States.

This chapter, then, is about the crisis of violence and lethality in schools—both self-inflicted and perpetrated on others. We will deal with three representative examples of lethality in schools: gang violence, the estranged violent student, and suicidal children. These are the archetypal examples of potentially lethal situations that the crisis worker is likely to encounter. Finally, this chapter will also provide the basic elements of what a school crisis plan should entail as a best bet of prevention and postvention when a crisis occurs.

GANGS

As of 1995, estimates of gangs and gang members ranged between 9,000 to 23,000 gangs and 400,000 to 650,00 members in the United States (Klein, 1995). The reason these estimates vary so much is the variety of definitions given to "gangs." Certainly, Spanky and "Our Gang" could hardly be confused with street gangs such as the Crips or the Bloods. However, even within well-established megagangs such as the Latin Kings and the Vicelords, the goals, organizational structure, and makeup differ dramatically. In short, there is no one generic "gang" and thus numbers fluctuate given whose definition we choose to use. Jurisdictions reporting gangs leaped from less than 100 in the 1970s to between 800 and 1100 in 1995 (Klein, 1995; Miller, 1975, 1982; Needle & Stapleton, 1982; Spergel, 1989; U.S. Office of Juvenile Justice and Delinquency Prevention, 1995).

Most major cities have reached the saturation point in gang development. Therefore, for megagangs to continue to develop and prosper they must migrate out to the suburbs and the rural areas of the country. There are few, if any idyllic, pastoral settings such as Andy Griffith's *Mayberry RFD* that do not directly or indirectly feel the impact of gangs. Gangs come to or *originate* in suburbs and rural areas because they can, and they come for different reasons. To suppose that all gangs who see suburbia or rural towns as a place to take root and grow are in the drug business and want to get Opie from *Mayberry RFD* addicted to heroin is a stereotype that is not true. Therefore, in our discussion of gangs as they relate to crises in schools, we are speaking to *all geographic locales*, to *all socioeconomic environments,* and to *all ethnicities* (Klein, 1995; Goldstein & Kodluboy, 1998; U.S. Office of Juvenile Justice and Delinquency Prevention, 1995).

Types of Gangs

There are basically five types of gangs that human services workers in school districts are likely to encounter.

Homegrown Copycats/Wannabes.   There is more than enough media representation of gang members to let every student in the United States who has access to cable TV, movies, magazines, music, and the Internet to set up a stereotypical Vicelords, Gangster Disciples, Crips, or Latin Kings-type gang (Goldstein & Kodluboy, 1998, p. 5; U.S. Office of Juvenile Justice and Delinquency Prevention, 1995). No original gangstas (already experienced gang members) need come to town to start this gang. "Wannabe" status may make them more dangerous in their attempts to prove how tough and cool they are. Generally they are short-lived. Makeup is composed of any ethnic group resident in the population.

Homegrown Survivalist, Aryan Nation, Neo-Nazi, Extreme Rightwingers. These gangs are based on political/religious philosophies inculcated by adults and in response to the perceived "browning" of America and the supposed threat that entails. They are often supported both financially and/or morally as "youth corps" by both local and national organizations. Members are typically related to or are friends of adults that espouse such views. They may be transitory or stable in terms of membership depending on adult support available. They specifically target ethnic/racial minority groups for violence. They are almost always Caucasian and "Christian" (Goldstein, 1991, p. 24; Goldstein & Kodluboy, 1998, p. 7; U.S. Office of Juvenile Justice and Delinquency Prevention, 1995).

Transients from Megagangs.   Offshoots of megagangs are started by gang members moved to supposedly "safe" rural havens by parents seeking to escape the problems of big-city crime or feeling extreme pressure from law enforcement agencies in their city of origin (Goldstein & Kodluboy, 1998, p. 7; U.S. Office of Juvenile Justice and Delinquency Prevention, 1995). Their children are already members of the gangs they try to escape. These transported gang members start their own gangs. Indian reservations receiving families out of big cities are a prime example of this transient population. Once rooted, these gangs may be difficult to eradicate because of criminal enterprise, turf control, and alliances with megagangs. Racial/ethnic makeup may be mixed but is typically ethnic or race based.

Megagangs Opening New Territory.   Increased competition in large metropolitan areas forces gangs to seek new territory to sell their wares (mainly drugs). Interstate arteries and towns adjacent to them are primary targets because of ease of access (Goldstein, 1991, pp. 20–21; Goldstein & Kodluboy, 1998, p. 7). This is the most formidable type of gang organization. It has older adults who are functioning members who may derive their livelihood from its criminal enterprise. It has a clear hierarchy of members, sophisticated organizational plan and operating rules, large numbers, recruitment programs, financial backing, and the will to be very violent in pursuit of its interests. Racial/ethnic makeup of these gangs is predominately African American or Hispanic in the Midwest, but may be a variety of nationalities on the East or West Coasts. This is the stereotypical street gang of the media (U.S. Office of Juvenile Justice and Delinquency Prevention, 1995).

Smorgasbord Home Boys.   Some small gangs are started for a variety of reasons ranging from instrumental criminal behavior such as theft to expressive behavior such as hate crimes. The organizing themes of these gangs range from skinhead Neo-Nazism to demonology and devil worship to auto theft. This gang type generally is transitory and short-lived, with small numbers of members. Depending on the type, it may avoid violence if theft is its major activity to being extremely violent and sadistic if it is into racism or satanism. It is mostly Caucasian in makeup (Goldstein, 1991, pp. 20–24; Goldstein & Kodluboy, 1998, p. 7; U.S. Office of Juvenile Justice and Delinquency Prevention, 1995).

Emergence of Suburban and Rural Gangs

Why have gangs or the threat of gang formation become problematic for suburban and rural areas? A variety of trends have emerged and are occurring as we move into the twenty-first century that make gang formation a probability in *Mayberry RFD*.

Changing Demographics.   The development of diverse, multicultural communities in the United States will proceed at an accelerated rate in the twenty-first century, particularly in historically white farming communities in the Midwest (Goldstein & Kodluboy, 1998, pp. 63–91).

Electronic Media.   Cable television, the Internet, and other electronic information systems makes the most pristine and rustic rural area part of the global community. Glorification of violence and gangs through electronic media sends children who feel powerless against the world, messages about how they can be powerful (Goldstein & Kodluboy, 1998, p. 7). According to our own organized crime task force in Memphis, major gangs have established their own web sites (W. Crews, personal communication, October 23, 1998). Chat rooms, web sites, and email will provide gangs plenty of opportunity to talk to Opie. If Opie is feeling alone and powerless out on Rural Route Three, he is likely to talk back.

Dysfunctional Families.   One-parent poverty-line families, drug and alcohol addiction, two wage-earner parents (both of which work two jobs), child abuse, battering, vicious custody battles, and all the other ills that assail dysfunctional families are as characteristic of suburban and rural families as they are of urban ones. Gang leaders are highly sensitive to these parent-less, throwaway kids, and like Fagan in *Oliver Twist,* recruit them. The gang becomes a surrogate family (Grossman, 1995, pp. 303–305).

Desensitization to Violence.   There is a mountain of evidence to suggest that watching gratuitous violence with few or no consequences to the victimizer desensitizes the viewer and allows the individual the freedom to act violently (Comstock, 1983; Grossman, 1995; Huesmann & Miller, 1994; National Coalition on Television Violence, 1994).

We have become so inured to drive-by shootings and other gang-initiated violence in the big cities that we give little consideration to them. Besides, they don't affect us because they're in big cities. We are shocked by the unfathomable shootings in Paducah, Pearl, Jonesboro, Stockton, Springfield, and Littleton because of their senselessness and that they happened in hometown America. Those are the places we live, and they are supposed to be the places we are safe. The bottom line, though, is that whether children are killed in schoolyard sniper attacks such as Jonesboro or drive-by shootings in east Los Angeles, they are just as dead, and their survivors suffer equally.

Increased Lethality.   The homicide rate for juveniles has leveled off after a steady climb over the last three decades. However, there should be little consolation in that statistic. In the last three decades, the rise of violent crime has been somewhere on the order of 600 to over 1000 percent, depending on how one looks at the statistics and whose statistics are used. One in approximately every three murders is now committed by an adolescent or preadolescent. Murder of adolescents is now second only to automobiles in the cause of death. Girls are becoming more involved as participants of violence, and their means of attack are becoming more lethal. Teenagers in the United States are at an absolute minimum four times as likely to be murdered as are their counterparts in 21 other industrialized countries (Center for Prevention of Handgun Violence, 1990; Goldstein, 1991; Goldstein & Kodluboy, 1998; U.S. Office of Juvenile Justice and Delinquency Prevention, 1994). The statistics go on and on, but suffice it to say that big cities no longer have a corner on violence and big city schools no longer have a corner on it either.

What the Problems Are in School Systems

Size of System.   The neglect of urban schools, the rapid growth of suburbia, and the consolidation of small rural schools has resulted in larger, more diffuse student populations. Although such consolidation allows financial savings and broader academic offerings, it reduces direct student contact with administrators, human service workers, and teachers. Participation in and integration in school life is less likely because large geographical areas and logistics make getting to and from school activities more difficult. There are only so many positions on the basketball, debate, or chess teams, and marginalized students have less opportunity to be woven into the fabric of the larger attendance center (Goldstein & Kodluboy, 1998, pp. 21–22).

Lack of Proactive Intervention.   Gangs and violence grow in a vacuum. A school building where teachers and administrators avoid congregation points, neglect monitoring of "unowned" areas such as the parking lot, bathrooms, and hallways, ignore student complaints about threatening or harassing behavior, dismiss rumors about planned violence or weapons brought onto the grounds, excuse violent behavior of "good kids," and see intervention as "not my job" is asking for trouble (Astor, 1999; Dykeman, 1999; Remboldt, 1994). Schools and teachers that have high expectations, care about and are involved with all their students in inclusive ways, enforce rules and procedures, keep buildings and rooms clean and neat, and believe it's everyone's job to do so, reduce violence (Stephens, 1994, 1997).

Vertical Integration of Programs.   Consistency in and coordination in matriculating students through transition from elementary to middle to high school keeps students from being "dropped through the cracks." Systems who operate elementary, middle, and senior high schools that are isolated programmatically from one another run major risks of losing students not just academically, but socially as well. The total philosophy of the system, starting in kindergarten and working up through high school should be a "Not if, but when you graduate" approach that is constantly reinforced at every grade level. Failure to do so, particularly with academic and social outliers, says the school doesn't care about them. They are likely to find some other group that will (Allen, 1996; Felner, Brand, Adan, & Mulhall, 1993).

School Governance.   A head-in-the-sand policy on gangs is a worst scenario approach. Fairness and consistency with open communication between stakeholders is essential. In "good" schools, communication not only flows outward from the administration but also inward to them. There is shared decision making, with administrators listening closely to their constituencies and heeding what they have to say. There are fair rules and clear sanctions that are mutually decided on. Conversely, the extremes on either side of this "fair but firm" administrative approach, authoritarianism and permissivism, are fertile conditions for development of gangs and other forms of violence (Goldstein & Kodluboy, 1998, p. 22; Stephens, 1994, 1997).

Diversity.   Refusal to recognize that school populations are changing in regard to ethnicity or race and a "business"-as-usual approach or denial and marginalizing of ethnically distinct students makes them attractive for gang membership. Suburban and rural school districts that are experiencing shifts in ethnicity or racial makeup must institute multiculturally sensitive programs that integrate minority students into the full fabric of the school (Feshbach & Feshbach, 1998; Gilbert, 1995; Goldstein & Kodluboy, 1998, p. 23; Soriano, Soriano, & Jimenez, 1994).

Safety.   Safety goes beyond high-tech security devices (Blauvelt, 1998; Brock, Sandoval, & Lewis, 1996; Goldstein & Kodluboy, 1998, pp. 24–25). School safety is not only a sense of physical well-being but also a sense of *psychological* well-being. Cooperatively developed mission statements, shared decisions about school policies, building upkeep and removal of graffiti, gang prevention and awareness programs, and zero tolerance of bullying, harassment, and gang recruitment all make a statement that this is "Our turf, not yours!"

Parent Participation in Schools.   Parent participation goes beyond PTA—it targets specific needs assessments of parental concern and cooperatively seeks to do something about those concerns. Heavy parental involvement in the school and support of its mission severely hampers gang formation (Haynes, 1996; Loeber et al., 1998; Stephens, 1994, 1997).

Gang Intervention/Prevention Programs

Historical Interventions.   A brief history of approaches to gang intervention indicates three distinct approaches and their historical time line (Goldstein & Kodluboy, 1998, pp. 10–13).

1950–1965. Youth outreach/detached worker approach. Youth workers go out into the neighborhood rather than requiring kids to come to them. Workers serve as prosocial role models/mentors and build rapport with clients. A very popular approach, but results were poor because not much outreach and actual contact with street gangs actually occurred.

1965–1975. Opportunities provision. This approach was based on the notion that certain needs met by gangs such as friendship, self-esteem, identity, and excitement could be met through prosocial activities sponsored by schools and agencies—with a great deal of infusion of federal money. This social infusion approach lost popularity when federal money dried up.

1975 to present. A "Get tough" approach. Shift from provision of opportunities to withdrawal of them. Main gang contacts and intervention are now handed over to the police due to increased gang violence and public demand for control.

The New Millennium: A Combinatorial Approach. Contemporary thinking suggests that each of these former models has equal parts to contribute (Goldstein & Kodluboy, 1998). Any gang intervention program should stand on its own and be accountable. It should be able to target specific problems, have measurable outcomes and stand external review such as the SARA program described in this section. We believe none of the following concepts and approaches, if used alone, will do much to reduce gangs and their violence. Intervention in gangs must not be left up to the crisis worker. A comprehensive approach features many components and requires the energies of a number of people and the financial and emotional resolve of people, institutions, and the community to commit for the long haul.

Counseling. Counseling, in the sense of having a continuing person-centered dialogue a la Carl Rogers with a gang member, is one of the least effective intervention strategies (Lipsey, 1992). Counseling that targets behavior and consequences of actions is more likely to be successful (Loeber et al., 1998).

Guidance Programs. Passive, lecture-based guidance programs that target fear arousal, moral appeal, and self-esteem building have not proven to be highly effective (Gottfredson, Gottfredson, & Skroban, 1998; Goldstein & Kodluboy, 1998, p. 118). Active guidance programs that provide direct student involvement through modeling, role play, and behavioral rehearsal in areas such as anger management, bullying, conflict resolution, and peer mediation are more helpful in tackling gang issues (DuRant et al., 1996; Embry et al., 1996; Feindler & Scalley, 1998; Godttfredson, Gottfredson, & Skroban, 1998; Hausman, Pierce, & Briggs, 1996; Hazler, 1996; Larson, 1994; Lupton-Smith et al., 1996). To be effective, these programs must not be one-shot sessions but should have continuous behavioral rehearsal and feedback sessions built into them. They must also have clear, easily implemented practices and be intense and long enough with follow-up sessions to reinforce and change some very resistant behaviors (Gottfredson et al., 1998; Zins, Travis, Brown, & Knighton, 1994).

Peer Counseling. One of the very *worst* approaches is to use peer crisis workers who are gang members, or for the crisis worker to attempt to run homogeneous counseling groups composed entirely of gang members (Goldstein & Kodluboy, 1998, pp. 107–110). The gang members will take over the group. However, there is some evidence that heterogeneous counseling groups where diversity in choosing students from a representative cross-section of the ethnic and social economic strata of the school is helpful in helping gang members look at alternative solutions and develop new behaviors. There is also some evidence that a peer counseling/leader program that provides mentoring, tutoring, and support functions keep at-risk and marginalized students out of trouble and in school (Allen, 1996; Cohen, Kulik, & Kulik, 1982; Fatum & Hoyle, 1996; Scruggs, Mastropieri, & Richter, 1985).

After-School and Community Outreach Programs. As Goldstein and Kodluboy (1998, p. 126) state, "Playing on a basketball team means you are not stealing a car while you're at the game, but it does not prevent you from stealing a car before or after the game." Research indicates that besides having recreational value, such after-school programs are not highly effective in delinquency reduction. However, programs such as the Boys and Girls Clubs of America that have comprehensive programs that integrate recreation with academic and social skill building, and career and personal counseling, do have high potential for stopping delinquency and reducing gang activity (Sherman et al., 1997).

Coordination with Other Agencies.   School systems cannot go it alone. They must be interconnected with other agencies. Turf guarding and territorialism are counterproductive. Gangs are everybody's problem. Specifically, that means that somebody in the school system has to be designated to take the lead in coordinating efforts between school system and agencies and *given the released time to do so*. Such linkages are also not done on a one-shot basis but are continuous. Absolutely essential to such agency interlinks is the court system with its concomitant links to the probation, parole, and correctional systems. These linkages should be ongoing, and continuous meetings with specific, concrete, measurable target-specific agendas should be held that bring cooperative agencies together (Bureau of Justice Assistance, 1991; Loeber et al., 1998; Zins et al., 1994).

The Police.   An absolutely central player in the inclusion of agencies to aid and abet schools in gang abatement is the police. At its most basic level, the sight of a police car in a school parking lot or an officer eating lunch in a school tends to put a damper on the enthusiasm of gang members. But police in the schools can do much more than that (Blauvelt, 1998; Goldstein & Kodluboy, 1998, pp. 141–142).

Coordination of intelligence between police department and the school, conjoint work with crisis workers in gang prevention programs, and role modeling and mentoring are proactive and integrate police officers into the fabric of the school (Goldstein 1991, p. 43; Goldstein & Kodluboy, 1998; Janokowski, 1998). In rural areas such endeavors are more difficult because they may typically fall on a sheriff's office that has far-flung geography to cover and is invariably stretched thin as to its staff and resources. The advantage of a sheriff's department as a primary liaison is its ability to know what's going on in that large geographic area and pass that information along to the school and other concerned agencies (Allen, 1998).

City and County Government.   Backing by city and county governments means putting in place ordinances that say this community has zero tolerance policies. A good deal of research indicates that tolerance of misdemeanor-type behavior, allowing garbage to collect, failure to condemn or clean up abandoned property, and tolerance of graffiti (and not just identifiable gang graffiti) all say that no one cares much about what happens to this community. These are open invitations for increases in seriousness and amount of criminal behavior and are clear signs to gangs that they have open turf on which to operate (Bureau of Justice Assistance, 1991, p. 7; Goldstein, 1991, pp. 181–188).

A Comprehensive Gang Prevention and Intervention Model Named SARA

The critical ingredients in making the SARA model (scanning, analysis, response, assessment) (Eck & Spelman, 1987) work can be summed up in two words, *sweat* and *cooperation*. This model is not a panacea for gangs or any of the other ills that afflict a school building, school system, or community. Success of the SARA model is not measured in one 4-hour workshop on gangs or a one-day DARE program for the whole school system. The SARA model means pooling resources of a variety of constituencies within a community and making a decision that they are going to be involved for the long haul. In essence, the SARA program boils down to a lot of people who might not normally be thought of as significant players in the life of a school, becoming involved with it in a very big way.

"Lots of people" means that parents, service clubs, businesses, churches, the judicial system, and other community agencies and organizations are major stakeholders in the problem of dealing with gangs. "Lots of people" also means that school districts have designated members of the system that come together with all the other stakeholders and trade information and cooperatively help institute change across the whole community and not just the school.

As noted, the SARA model is an acronym for (S) Scanning, (A) Analysis, (R) Response, and (A) Assessment.

Scanning.   The initial stage of scanning involves identifying problems and bringing them to the attention of the group. Citizen complaints, census data, police reports, police intelligence and service calls, public health information, usage of parks and recreation facilities, media coverage, and school and community surveys are examples of the data collection necessary to scan the environment for gang activity (Bureau of Justice Assistance, 1991, p. 17).

A problem is a group of harmful incidents occurring in a community that are similar in one or more ways and of concern to the public. To analyze that problem, a clear problem statement is developed: (Victims) are (harmed) by the (behaviors) of (offenders) at or in (places) at (times). An example might be: "Seventh-grade girls are strong armed for lunch money in the Graves Middle School south hall restroom by the Rosebud girls' gang during fourth period." This clear behavioral statement allows consensus on the problem being addressed and provides direction for a plan of action (Bureau of Justice Assistance, 1991, p. 18).

Analysis.   Analysis is critical because of the information it provides to put the problem in concrete, measurable terms about the actors, incidents, and reactions. The actors are the offenders, victims, and third parties. Some of the questions that an analysis asks are: What is the age, dress, sex, race, signs, and other common features of offenders? What are the benefits gained from the offenders' behaviors? How do they get to the problem area? Where do they go after they leave it? Questions about the victims include, What is their age, sex, race, appearance, size, dress and other shared features? What acts are victims involved in prior to the harmful activity? How do victims get to the problem location? Third parties are important to the problem because their action or inaction may contribute to the problem. Third parties may be divided into controllers who try to prevent offenders from committing crimes, guardians who try to prevent harm to potential victims, and managers who oversee places where problems occur. All these actors need to be identified and analyzed in regard to the part they play in the problem (Bureau of Justice Assistance, 1991, pp. 19–20).

Incidents should be considered in their social and environmental context, the sequence of actions leading up to and including the incidents, and the results of the actions taken by the offenders and victims. Typical questions include, What harm is occurring? How is it carried out? Where and what times of day does it occur? What policies or practices encourage its occurrence? What are the environmental conditions at the location? Are there secondary effects because of the problem (Bureau of Justice Assistance, 1991, p. 21)?

A problem causes some kind of reaction to occur from the government, school system, media, or public. Public perception of a problem's seriousness often affects the response. Questions to be asked are, What are the reactions of the people in the immediate area? What publicity occurred because of the problem? How seriously is this regarded by different institutions and the public in general? Information needs to be targeted specifically to the problem to be tackled (Bureau of Justice Assistance, 1991, p. 22). A major failure in attempting to solve gang-related problems is caused by launching a global attack on it because of pressure from stakeholders to "solve the gang problem." SARA works best by seeking "little victories." That is, attempting to wipe the Rosebud girls' gang from the school and neighborhood may be commendable, but it is probably fruitless. Keeping the Rosebuds out of the seventh-grade girls' bathroom is not.

Response.   The response stage has three objectives: Developing options based on the information gathered, selecting a response, and implementing it. Developing options is based on focusing in on the problem. Options should concentrate on the small number of offenders who are involved in the majority of problems, the controllers, guardians, or managers who can stop or facilitate it, and the victims who suffer from it. What other agencies and institutions will need to be included? What interlinks and coordination are needed between these other agencies and institutions? Do services need to be changed or added? How can the community be mobilized? How can existing forms of social control be used? How does authority need to be expanded? What physical alterations in the environment need to occur (Bureau of Justice Assistance, 1991, pp. 25–26)?

Selecting a response calls for taking into account community values and the values of individuals directly affected by the problem. Questions to consider are, What are the people and financial resources needed? How likely is the response to reduce the problem? Implementing the response requires listing the tasks required to carry it out, selecting a coordinator to see that it happens, setting timelines to accomplish the tasks, developing a written action plan, and designing an assessment of the response to know whether it is working (Bureau of Justice Assistance, 1991, p. 27).

Assessment.   Assessment is used to gauge the effectiveness of the response, change it, improve the analysis, or redefine the problem. Assessment should focus on the problem statement rather than the response. The assessment should reflect in what manner the problem was affected. If 13 incident reports are filed by seventh-grade girls on strong-arm tactics used in the south hall restroom at Graves Middle School by the Rosebuds in a two-week time period, then that baseline incident frequency should be reduced by the action taken. Assessment might not only count the reduction of incidents, but might also survey the seventh-grade girls as to the degree of fear reduction they have experienced and their willingness to use the restroom. Assessment does not always mean "number crunching." Photographs that show how the physical environment has changed and survey results that indicate students feel more secure are just as important as indicating that the problem has been reduced by so many percentage points (Bureau of Justice Assistance, 1991, p. 29).

Implementing the SARA model costs time, effort, and money. Not implementing the plan will cost the community who lets gangs gain a foothold far more. It will cost in terms of poor school performance for students who go to school in fear everyday. It will cost in terms of teacher stress and burnout. It will cost money, a lot of money, for all the security needed. It will invariably cost in physical injuries and lives lost. But ultimately it will cost something more precious than any of the foregoing. It will cost a school and a community its freedom.

THE ESTRANGED VIOLENT JUVENILE OFFENDER

The U.S. Department of Education (Dwyer, Osher, & Warger, 1998) has recently released an excellent booklet that deals with safe schools in a general way. The booklet specifically mentions the school counselor as one of the lead professionals in helping prevent violence but says little about the specifics of the counselor's role, or any other human services worker's role, for that matter. Although gang violence is a major component of violence perpetrated by and among school-age children and is a major contributor to violence perpetrated by what Loeber and associates (1998) call the serious violent juvenile offender (SVJO), recent school shootings and subsequent homicides and injuries have been perpetrated by juveniles who do not typically fall into the "gang" SVJO category. The purpose of this section is to examine these different, potentially violent juveniles in regard to their psychological profile, screening mechanisms to detect them, and counseling methods to uncover their violent thoughts before those thoughts turn into action.

We choose to categorize these individuals as "estranged" violent juvenile offenders (EVJOs). Although we do not arbitrarily exclude the potential for females to be included in this group, the preponderance of offenders will be male. As a result, we use the male gender only to describe the potential offender. We use the term "estranged" because these juveniles typically are separated from their peers in distinctive ways and harbor a great deal of enmity toward their peers or the school system. In contrast to a gang culture, where violence is generated in order to bind its members together in perpetuation of the gang's growth and stature, the EVJO is typically a loner who has no allegiances unless to a very few others who are also experiencing the same estrangement.

EVJOs can be partitioned into two major categories, those who are mentally ill and those who are not. Although it could be argued that anyone who would shoot a number of his fellow students is "crazy," that does not necessarily make them mentally ill by the American Psychiatric Association's (1994) *DSM-IV* classification system. Therefore, it is also important to discriminate between EVJOs who are and are not mentally ill because of differences in profiles, screening, and intervention.

A Profile Comparison of Traits and Characteristics of SVJOs and EVJOs

The following traits and characteristics have been compiled from a number of published sources and interviews with human services workers who deal with both the SVJO and EVJO (Batsch & Knoff, 1994; Busch et al., 1990; Carney, Hazler, Higgins, & Danser, 1999; Corder et al., 1976; Cunningham & Davis, 1999; Duncan & Duncan, 1971; Dwyer, Osher, & Warger, 1998; Galatzen-Levy, 1993; Hardwick & Rowton-Lee,

1996; James & Dorner, 1999; Lemp, 1990; Levis, 1992; Loeber, 1990; Marohn, Locke, Rosenthal, & Curtis, 1982; Myers & Mutch, 1992; National School Safety Center, 1998; Sage & Dietz, 1994; Sloan, 1988; Webster & Wilson, 1994; Zagar et al., 1990).

Abusive Childhood.   Sexual, psychological, and physical abuse in childhood are fertile fields in which the SVJO and EVJO take root and grow. Exposure to violent role models at home, maternal or paternal deprivation, inconsistent and punitive discipline, and rejection are characteristics of both. For the EVJO who does have a positive and supportive family, his sense of integration into the family likely will be weak and alienated. Such alienation may be particularly true for the mentally ill EVJO who has an extremely supportive family situation and has received a great deal of nurturing and care. The parents of the EVJO may be in a great deal of denial about the potential for violence in their son.

Academic Problems.   The SVJO will probably have a history of school problems that includes truancy, poor grades, discipline problems, and trouble with teachers. A combination of ADHD and conduct disorder is a high predictor of future violent behavior for the SVJO. In contrast, the EVJO will likely be passively compliant to school and may even do well academically. Unless some traumatic incident causes him to act out, he may well go unnoticed, or even be respected by his teachers. Both may have mild to severe language disorders that, when they are placed under stress, will cause them to be more likely to act than talk. The mentally ill EVJO will be likely to experience many academic problems because of his difficulty in maintaining contact with the reality and demands of the classroom.

Anger/Low Frustration Tolerance.   Both types react to stress in self-defeating ways. The SVJO is likely to have a "short fuse" and immediately aggress in a stressful situation, whereas the EVJO typically will flee the situation or act in a more passive way. The low frustration tolerance of the SVJO is much more immediate and seen in highly observable ways. In contrast, the EVJO may have less observable behavioral manifestations because his anger is turned inward and sublimated. He erroneously may be seen to have a high frustration tolerance. In contrast, the mentally ill EVJO may have a very low frustration tolerance because of his tenuous grip on reality.

Altered States of Consciousness.   Even if psychoactive substances are not ingested, their cognitive processes lead both the SVJO and the EVJO to limited reality testing. Typical reports after a violent incident include derealization, decompensation, and depersonalization. Statements such as "I was just seeing red and sort of blanking out" or "It's like I wasn't there, sorta watching a videotape so it was like me but really not me" are characteristic of both the SVJO and the EVJO. The mentally ill EVJO may operate in a continued state of altered consciousness if not controlled by medication and have minimum contact with the reality of the situation.

Bully/Bullied.   The SVJO is the stereotypical bully. A bully at school, he is most probably a victim at home. The EVJO is the stereotypical bullied child. He may fall into two categories, the passive victim and the aggressive victim. The aggressive victim may be hot tempered and attempt to retaliate when attacked. Paradoxically, the aggressive victim may also be seen as a bully. Whereas the passive bullied child is depicted as lonely and socially isolated at school, the aggressive victim is one of the most disliked and notorious members of his peer group. Although the passive bullied child may be much slower to act than his aggressive counterpart, both may bring weapons to school to counterbalance their perceived inferiority to their tormentors.

Chemical and Substance Abuse.   Both types may alter consciousness by using psychoactive substances and freeing themselves of psychological restraints to commit violent acts. A variety of drugs can accelerate the SVJO into violent mood swings and exacerbate a potentially violent personality. For the EVJO, use of drugs may allow him the freedom to externalize his anger. With the mentally ill EVJO, discontinued use of prescribed psychotropic medication, combined with using illicit drugs, has a high likelihood of precipitating a violent episode.

Criminal Behavior.   Contrary to the gang member who probably has a long history of contacts with the police and juvenile authorities, the EVJO most likely does not. The EVJO is as likely to be seen as a good and compliant student by his teachers as he is not. Comments from his neighbors are typically "He's a real quiet, polite boy." He may have excellent church attendance, belong to the Boy Scouts, and belong to other socially appropriate organizations. If the EVJO has any contacts with the police, it will most likely be of a petty, misdemeanor nature and involve passive acts against objects rather than aggressive acts against people. If the EVJO is mentally ill, he may have had contacts with the authorities through domestic disturbance or "mentally ill" calls.

Delayed Cognitive and Affective Development.   Because many of both violent offender types have not reached Piaget's formal cognitive operational or even concrete stage, their thinking may be nonlinear. For prepubescent offenders, their notion of the finality of death or the realness and pain of bodily injury may be very much like a game of cops and robbers where they are shot and killed over and over in the course of an afternoon. They may not relate their violent actions to any negative emotional outcomes, both for their victims and themselves.

Emotional Lability/Depression.   Whereas the SVJO demonstrates a quick temper, "short fuse," and rapid mood swings, the EVJO typically may be characterized by depressive characteristics where anger is turned inward. The EVJO may be serious to the point of sullenness, and see little humor in his world, particularly if he has been the object of derisive humor by his peers or significant others in his life. The severely depressed EVJO may see the endpoint of retaliation against his tormentors as also the endpoint for himself and may see suicide as a viable option after he has exacted revenge. The mentally ill EVJO may have bizarre thoughts and emotions with correlative mood swings that range from rage to fear. He also may have suicidal ideation depending on his emotional state.

External Locus of Control.   Fate, God, "The Man" and other external entities play a large part in the behavior of the SVJO and the EVJO. The SVJO may view himself as both the victimizer as a way of gaining power, and the victim because of his circumstances. The EVJO clearly assumes a victim status. Both place blame on others for their outcast state. The EVJO's external locus is tied to a low self-concept that is constantly reaffirmed as being inadequate by the world around him.

History and Threats of Violence.   One of the best predictors of violence is past violence. Particularly when threats of violence are coupled with a past history of violence, the probability of violence increases. Whereas the SVJO will more likely be clear, immediate, and direct with his threats, the EVJO's threats are likely to be more implied, conditional, and veiled for a longer period of time. The mentally ill EVJO may make threats that commingle reality with fantasy such that specific individuals may be symbolized as "monsters" or other objects that are threatening to him.

Hypersensitivity.   Both the SVJO and EVJO are hypersensitive to criticism and real or perceived slights and threats. They will both be suspicious, fearful, distrustful, and paranoid in their worldview. Whereas the SVJO will be more overt in his manifestation of these characteristics through name calling, swearing and angry outbursts, the EVJO will be more passive. Both are overly sensitive to what they believe others think, feel, and act toward them. The mentally ill EVJO will be exponentially more hypersensitive to imagined threats to his well-being and angrily react to them.

Impulsivity.   The SVJO is quick to act and wants immediate gratification. He has little consideration for the consequences of his immediate actions, lacks insight, has poor judgment, and has little understanding of how his belief system filters actions and resulting consequences. He habitually makes violent threats when angry. In contrast, the EVJO may be slow to act. He may be hypersensitive as a result of past negative experiences that have been socially and emotionally punitive. His belief system will turn to a "them against me" view that continues to build until his frustration spills out and he aggresses against his real or imagined tormentors. The mentally ill EVJO may fall along a continuum of high to low impulsivity depending on the disorder from which he suffers.

Loner Status.   The SVJO may be ostentatious and gregarious in his social relations as a means of gaining status. A social assessment of the EVJO would depict him as being a social isolate from his peers. If asked by his classmates, the EVJO might be characterized by terms such as "Geek," "Goth," "nerd," "freak," "different," "weird," and other terms that clearly set him apart from the social mainstream. His attempts to form relationships with the opposite sex will generally be clumsy and fraught with failure. Females who attempt to be kind to him may well have their kindness misinterpreted, and when the EVJO makes abortive attempts to move beyond "kindness" in the relationship and his romantic overtures are rejected, the isolation he feels is further compounded. Because of his bizarre behavior, the mentally ill EVJO will be extremely socially isolated from his peers and be labeled as "nuts," "mental," or "crazy."

Mental Illness.   Hospitalization for mental illness alone is not an indicator of potential violence. However, when hospitalization of the mentally ill SVJO or EVJO is preceded by a history of violent offenses it is an indicator. Violence potential is further exacerbated when psychotropic medication is stopped because of its side affects, the inability to obtain it, or inadequate supervision in administering it.

Odd/Bizarre Beliefs.   Odd or bizarre beliefs fall into two categories. Schizophrenic-type mental illnesses and personality disorders certainly are defined by odd and bizarre beliefs and behavior that would characterize the mentally ill EVJO. The second category of odd and bizarre behavior more closely typifies the EVJO without mental illness. These thoughts and behaviors may range from interests in demonology, magical thinking, and satanic cults, to extremely rigid political and religious views that promote violent solutions to society's problems. Joining splinter groups that advocate such views is a way of achieving the affiliation, status, and power that the EVJO craves.

Pathology and Deviance.   A psychological smorgasbord of problems may reside with both types of juvenile offenders. Fire setting, cruelty to animals, defacing and destroying property, temper tantrums, running away from home, and oppositional defiance to authority are some examples. When these behaviors have a long history, they are probably more characteristic of the SVJO. When they seem to occur spontaneously with no prior history, or are kept under wraps by parents concerned about the social stigma attached to these behaviors and who are in denial, they more aptly characterize the EVJO.

Physical Problems.   Particularly for the EVJO, physical problems that range from stuttering to severe acne to delayed physical development may contribute to a poor body image and feelings of inferiority. Internal head injuries, congenital brain damage and a variety of neurological problems may contribute to the potential for violence in the mentally ill EVJO.

Preoccupation with Violent Themes.   Both the SVJO and the EVJO may become fixated on movies, books, television shows, videos, and music that glamorize violence. Interest in violent pornography, weapons collections, sadomasochistic paraphernalia, and instruments of torture allow the powerless EVJO, in particular, to fantasize dominance over his persecutors.

Weapons.   Both the SVJO and the EVJO may have an undue fascination with and knowledge of weapons. The SVJO may commonly carry or have access to a weapon for both "protection" or "revenge" against other gang members. When the EVJO carries a weapon to school, he is most likely getting ready to act out against his tormentors. The mentally ill EVJO may be much like the SVJO in carrying weapons for both protection and revenge against his imagined enemies.

In summarizing these characteristics of the potentially violent juvenile, we would emphatically echo the U.S. Department of Education's *Early Warning, Timely Response: A Guide to Safe Schools* (Dwyer et al., 1998, p. 3) warning that it is important to avoid inappropriate labeling, stereotyping, or stigmatizing individuals based on the foregoing categories. None of the categories by themselves or in combination can absolutely predict who will become violent and who will not. However, if the child fits into multiple categories, the crisis worker should be aware that the *potential* for violence increases and that this is an extremely troubled individual.

Screening the EVJO

The problem with profiling the estranged violent juvenile offender who is not mentally ill is that any staff member in a school could probably identify at least 20 percent of the male population who might fit the foregoing profile and have many of the characteristics detailed in the foregoing section. How then can this population be screened for those students who might have such characteristics and, more importantly, the intent to carry out a violent act?

Writings and Drawings.   The writings and drawings of EVJOs are often an open pathway into their troubled minds. In cases of potential violent behavior, art work may make the point more vividly than a verbal description. Graphic themes of violence that pervade the writing and the drawings of EVJOs are a tipoff to a student who may be contemplating violent action against school staff or fellow students. These hard-copy emotional messages should be taken very seriously when previous incidents of violent behavior have occurred and should not be discounted when such graphic displays of violent ideation are issuing from the "quiet kid" who has no history of disruption in the school. School crisis workers need to apprise teachers of these indicators of predispositions to violence, and such student-generated work should be passed to the crisis worker (Duncan & Duncan, 1971; Hammond & Gantt, 1998; James & Dorner, 1999).

Peer Referral.   There are very, very few instances when the EVJO does not give some warning of his intentions to harm himself or others. Invariably, in psychological postmortems of situations that resulted in injury or death due to violence by an EVJO, students had heard statements or seen notes from the student indicating his intent to do harm but had generally dismissed them as just "talk" (Hardwick & Rowton-Lee, 1996; James & Dorner, 1999).

However, the problem with peer referral is twofold. First, other students are afraid of and repelled by the notion of "narking" or "snitching" on another student. This reticence to inform on another is particularly true when the student in question may be so threatening that other students fear for their own safety or dismiss the threat of a student they have known for years and in their opinion is absolutely harmless. Students need to feel safe in providing information about a potentially dangerous situation (Dwyer et al., 1998, p. 4).

We believe one of the best ways to screen for potentially violent students is through a peer referral and notification system. The keys to a functional peer referral and notification system are programs run by peers and coordinated by school crisis workers (Allen, 1996). Conflict resolution, peer mediation, peer leadership, and peer counseling are all programs that allow students to legitimately notify faculty of potentially violent students without becoming informers. Whatever type of peer program is offered should not be operated from the standpoint that its only purpose is to "catch bad kids." The primary purpose of peer programs should be to help other students resolve conflicts, mediate disputes, and provide support, help, and referral for common maturational problems associated with adolescence. However, when in the course of providing such peer helping services, peer helpers gain information about fellow students in crisis who may commit violent acts, then it is clearly appropriate for them to apprise the crisis worker of the information they have received (James & Dorner, 1999).

Peer helpers need to be carefully trained, monitored, and supervised by crisis workers lest they exceed their limits (Allen 1996). Peer helpers should be selected from a broad cross-section of the school population (Day-Vines et al., 1996). It has been our experience that students who represent all spectrums of the student population are much more effective in reaching their peers and being accepted by them. That does not mean that we have lowered expectations of peer helpers either academically or morally. The best peer helpers have been able to demonstrate a willingness to work with and help all of their fellow students. Their very diversity allows the program to reach a broader constellation of students than it otherwise might (Allen, 1996).

Interviewing the Potential EVJO

When interviewing the potential EVJO, we believe the first three steps of the six-step crisis intervention/prevention model are particularly critical in preventing the EVJO from committing a violent act.

Problem Definition.   The school crisis worker who interviews a potential EVJO initially needs to proceed with basic listening and responding skills that deeply reflect the student's feelings and allow him to ventilate his angry feelings. It should be understood that other negative emotions are undergirding and supporting the anger the student feels. Suspicion, betrayal, embarrassment, grief, anxiety, inadequacy, threat, insecurity, and frustration are but a few of the negative feelings that may be pushing the student toward violence.

Case of John.   John is a 14-year-old high school freshman who was referred to the school counselor by a teacher who had screened out John's theme after she had been through a workshop on profiling potentially violent students. The counselor has read the theme, which is filled with angry and violent threats about a group of girls who have been teasing John.

CW: John, I've read your theme Mrs. Smith sent to me. You seem really angry. Would you like to tell me about what's making you so angry right now?

John: I'm sick of the Tri-beta club. Particularly the girls. They ask me to do stuff, and I do it, but then they make fun of me.

CW: Sounds like you're not only angry but hurt too. How do they hurt you?

These feelings and their antecedent causes need to be fully explored by the crisis worker to make a clear determination of what is going on and with whom it is occurring. Exploration is important for two reasons. First, by allowing the student to ventilate, the crisis worker does much towards defusing the potentially violent situation and can start to help the student develop alternate coping and problem-solving strategies. We want to establish an open and trusting relationship with this troubled student. Clearly hearing the student and affirming him through summary clarification and restatement of the content of his problem and reflection of his feelings goes a long way toward doing that.

John: Yeah. I want to be friends, but I don't think they really want me for a friend. When they need somebody to build a float or put up posters I'm just fine. But when I asked Sally Johnson if she wanted to go get a coke after the float was done, she laughed at me, said I was a loser, and then told the other girls and they laughed too. I hate them!

CW: So they really put you down and embarrassed you when you did everything they wanted you to do.

Second, by adequately exploring the affective, behavioral, and cognitive dimensions of the student's problem, the crisis worker may gain valuable information about the "who," "what," "where," "when," and "how" of the student's purposed course of action. We stay away from "why" questions because of their interrogative nature. These students are already defensive, and we wish to do nothing that will alienate them further from the crisis worker.

CW: John, It sounds like you'd really like to get back at them for the way they've treated you. How might you do that?

Ensuring Safety.   Assessment of lethality is primary in any crisis intervention. Contrary to exploring issues by using open-ended questions, we subsequently assess the potential for suicidal or homicidal behavior by asking specific, close-ended questions that are designed to get direct answers to the student's potential for lethality. The questions we ask could come straight from a detective's homicide manual and fall within the following areas:

1. Is there a motive?
2. Is there opportunity?
3. What is the method or plan?
4. What are the means?

We find that most people in psychological crisis who have suicidal or homicidal ideation will talk about what they are going to do, and talking about their plan does not, contrary to popular myth, make them more likely to carry out their plan. Even though they may believe they have exhausted all their possibilities besides taking lethal action, we believe that their willingness to talk about their thoughts and contemplated actions is a positive sign and an indication that at least some part of them believes there is an alternative left. We believe the potential EVJO, in particular, fits this pattern because of his anger and his need to ventilate it. If questions are asked in an empathic, nonjudgmental way, we believe he will be willing to talk about the four points listed above.

As we cover motive, opportunity, method, and means, our threat assessment goes up as each becomes more concrete. The motive of the EVJO is often unclear and muddled, and therefore may be dismissed as inconsequential. It would be a mistake to dismiss such ideation, because it is not just the motive itself, but the intensity and the lability with which it is discussed that is important. The more emotive the EVJO is about the injustices done him, the more he clarifies and elaborates on his plan and the opportunity to carry it out, and the more lethal his means, the higher the threat assessment.

It should be abundantly clear that if the potential EVJO has access to firearms and knows how to use them, the threat becomes critical and there is increased risk for violence (Dwyer, Osher, & Warger, 1998, p. 10). Thus the crisis worker should not hesitate to ask the student what he knows about firearms and if he has access to them. If

the crisis worker does not know about types and use of firearms, a police officer should be consulted.

Scenario 1

John: I wish they were all dead, it'd serve them right!

CW: So if they were dead it'd pay them back for what they've done to you. How might that happen?

John: Well, I don't know for sure. I'd wish they'd get some incurable disease and really suffer a lot.

CW: So you'd like to see them hurt as much as they've hurt you. How might that happen?

John: Yeah. Well, I dunno know for sure. Maybe they'd get that ebola virus or food poisoning from the cafeteria.

Here, the student's wish for the death of his tormentors is couched in fantasy with no clear means or method for carrying out his plan. This fantasized revenge would not carry a high lethality level, but would certainly indicate that this student is in need of support and continued work with the crisis worker.

Scenario 2

John: I wish they were dead, it'd serve them right.

CW: So if they were dead, it'd pay them back for what they've done to you. How might that happen?

John: It'd be easy. I'd wait for them after school. When they go out to work on the homecoming float at the bus barn, I'd be behind the incinerator. I could shoot them real easy.

CW: John, do you know how to use a gun?

John: Sure. My dad's got a 9mm pistol. He showed me how to use it. He says I'm pretty good with it.

CW: Can you get your dad's gun?

John: Well, he's got it locked up in the gun safe, but I know the combination.

CW: John, when are you planning on doing this?

John: I don't know, but if they make fun of me one more time, soon.

In this second scenario, the student's motive, method, opportunity and access to lethal means are much clearer and well defined. Such a response would indicate a much higher threat level and would call for clear and immediate action on the part of the crisis worker.

Provide Support.　In any case where a student's lethality level is high, we need to provide clear owning statements about what we will need to do to keep the client and others he may intend to harm safe. Parents must be informed and a clear line of communication needs to be established with the school administration, law enforcement, and other agencies that may become involved (Dwyer et al., 1998, p. 11).

CW: *(Responding to scenario 2.)* John, what you have said really concerns me. It sounds like you've really worked this out, and if you carry this out, I'm afraid for you and the other students. I understand you're really angry and hurt by what they've done to you, but I don't want to see you get hurt anymore, either by the other students in what they say and do to you or by the police. I don't want you to shoot anybody, and I don't want the police to shoot you. I need to get some help for you right now, and I need to be sure you're safe. I want you to stay with me until I can make sure you are safe. I need to talk to your parents because I'm sure they would be concerned for you. I also need to talk to the principal to make sure that she understands what's going on so she can make sure that you stay safe. I understand that you might be upset with me for doing this, but I'm really concerned about you right now, John. I understand that right now you think this is the only solution you've got, but I believe there are other ways to handle this and I want you to understand that I'll help you to figure some of those out. I'll stay with you and work with you until we do get things worked out and you are safe.

Many clients will not be happy when they are informed about what is going to happen to them. One of the best responses the crisis worker can make when this happens is to use a combination of what we call "I understand" statements and the "broken record" technique, which continuously and repeatedly acknowledges the client's unhappiness about our decision, but also reaffirms our concern and caring for him.

Acting

How the crisis worker acts depends on a continuous assessment of the student. If the crisis worker determines that the student is indeed a threat, then the crisis worker's response should be to make an immediate referral and notify parents, administrators, and, if necessary, law enforcement personnel. If the crisis worker determines that the student's lethality level is not high, then the crisis worker can move forward in the model to examining alternatives, making plans, and obtaining a commitment to work on positive actions that will help him become less alienated and angry. An investigation might indicate that the behavior was merely a "throwaway" statement that had no meaning other than ordinary misguided playfulness or a momentary pique of anger. Even then, it would be a proper educative and counseling activity to teach the student not to play this game. However, in today's school environment, in any instance where threats are made against others, those threats should not automatically be discounted. Thus the crisis worker needs to keep a record of the encounter, and follow-up with the student should occur to ensure that those threats do not escalate into action (Crawford, 1998).

A primary consideration in "acting" is what to do if the student is carrying a weapon. If the crisis worker feels the relationship is positive enough with the student, and the student indicates that he has a weapon on his person, then the crisis worker may ask for it for safekeeping. In exchanging a weapon, it should always be handed over butt first, or if a knife, haft first. If the crisis worker is unsure of the student's intent or if the student is resistant, the crisis worker should *immediately seek help and get out of the room*. If the student indicates he has a weapon in his locker or some other hiding place, the crisis worker should have another person go with him or her to the hiding place. *In no instance should the crisis worker attempt to be a hero and forcibly attempt to take a weapon away from a student* (Crews, 1998). There is no formula we know of for determining whether to go ahead and attempt to get the weapon away from the student or leave the premises and get help. We believe the best rule to follow is what the crisis worker believes will be the safest course of action for both the crisis worker and the student.

SCHOOL-BASED SUICIDE PREVENTION AND INTERVENTION

A study by the Centers for Disease Control (1991) indicates that 11.3 per every 100,000 high school students commit suicide annually. If that figure is extrapolated to a 2000-student high school in the United States, that means on an average, that school will experience a suicide every five years (Davis & Sandoval, 1991). The Centers for Disease Control survey (1991) found that among high school students, 8 percent had already attempted suicide, 16 percent had made a plan to commit suicide, and 27 percent had seriously contemplated it.

From these figures it would seem apparent that crisis response programs in schools should incorporate suicide prevention, intervention, and postvention components that are comprehensive and systematic (Berman & Jobes, 1994; Kernberg, 1994; Komar, 1994; Malley et al., 1994; Webb & Griffiths, 1998–1999). If a school system does not have a written formal policy, the board and the community should require that suicide prevention/intervention/postvention procedures be developed and implemented (Malley et al., 1994, p. 135). Malley and associates (1994, p. 131) recommend that school-based child and adolescent suicide prevention/intervention/postvention include

1. A written, formal suicide policy statement
2. Written procedures to address and ensure the safety of at-risk students
3. Faculty and staff in-service orientation and training in warning signs and referral of at-risk students
4. Identification of mental health professionals on site or readily available
5. Prevention materials for distribution to students, parents, and the community and for classroom discussion
6. Procedures for psychological screening, identification, and counseling of at-risk students
7. Postvention responses and strategies that occur following any completed suicide
8. Written criteria for crisis workers to assess lethality of a potential suicide student
9. Written policies on how the school-based child and adolescent suicide prevention/intervention/postvention program is evaluated

Do suicide prevention programs work? Zenere and Lazarus (1997) studied a comprehensive suicide prevention and intervention program in a large, urban, multicultural diverse school district. Students were tracked over a five-year period. What they found was that although suicidal ideation remained stable, the rate of attempts and completions was dramatically reduced. This study echoes our own experience. Although prevention programs may not be able to stop a student from thinking about committing suicide, an effective program can stop the act!

Myths of Child Suicide

Greene (1994) lists a number of myths about childhood suicide:

1. *"Children under the age of 6 do not commit suicide."* On the contrary, too frequently, children in the age range of 5 to 14 have completed suicide.

2. *"Suicide in the latency years is extremely rare."* Over the last decade, the child suicide rate has increased.

3. *"Psychodynamically and developmentally, true depression is not possible in childhood."* This outmoded myth has been proved untrue by recent findings in developmental psychology.

4. *"A child cannot understand the finality of death."* The issue is not whether this statement is true or false; the fact is that children do attempt and complete suicide.

5. *"Children are cognitively and physically incapable of implementing a suicide plan successfully."* The increasing number of childhood suicides is prima facie evidence of the error of this myth.

6. *"Children who have sudden and radical shifts in characteristic behaviors or moods such as apathy, withdrawal, isolation, irritability, and anxiety, or changed social, sleeping, eating, school, or work habits are not indicators of suicidal behavior. These children are only in the process of change and development and they will grow out of it."* To the contrary, all these characteristics have been associated with suicidal behavior in children and adolescents.

7. *"Children who display sudden and radical shifts in personal appearance, clothing, and hygiene are merely characteristic of children who want to be distinct from adults and their peers."* A sudden change in grooming habits, such as cutting long, beautiful hair, starting to wear "gothic" clothes after being a "preppy," or becoming disheveled, untidy, and sloppy after being a "neatnik" could indicate that the child has reached a state of hopelessness, doesn't care anymore, and is not going to be around much longer. Such a shift may not be a sign of youthful rebellion, but one of suicidal ideation.

Child and Adolescent Cases of Suicidal Ideation

Here are some strategies and suggestions (Fujimira, Weis, & Cochran, 1985) for anyone (crisis worker or layperson) who comes into contact with a child or adolescent suspected of being suicidal:

1. Trust your suspicions that the young person may be self-destructive.

2. Tell the person you're worried about him or her, then listen to the person.

3. Ask direct questions, including whether the youngster is thinking about suicide and, if so, has a plan.

4. Don't act shocked at what the youngster tells you. Don't debate whether suicide is right or wrong, or counsel the person yourself if you're not qualified. Don't promise to keep the youngster's intentions a secret.

5. Don't leave the youngster alone if you think the risk of suicide is immediate.

6. If necessary, get help from a competent counselor, therapist, or other responsible adult.

7. Ensure that the youngster is safe and that the appropriate adults responsible for the youngster are notified and become actively involved with the youngster.

8. Assure the youngster that something is being done, that the youngster's suicidal urges are not being discounted, and that, in time, the emergency will most likely pass.

9. Apprise the youngster that survival is a step-by-step, day-to-day process; that help is at hand; and that calling for help in a direct manner is necessary whenever the suicidal urge gets strong.
10. Assume an active and authoritarian role as needed to protect the child at risk.
11. After the youngster has apparently resolved the high-risk crisis, monitor progress very closely. Many persons have been known to suddenly commit suicide after they seemed to be renewed and strong.

The following scenarios incorporate many of the suggestions just given.

Billy, Age 11. In a group counseling session, children ages 9 to 12 (including Billy) were engaged in relaxation training, emotive imagery, and self-esteem building. The children were taking turns disclosing a positive image each was experiencing. Billy had been rather quiet and complacent in previous counseling sessions.

Billy: I see myself beside the highway. There's a big 18-wheeler—going fast. I'm feeling like I'm gonna die. I want to die. I see myself jumping in front of it.

CW: Billy, it frightens me terribly to hear you say that! Could you and I talk about that after the others leave? And Billy, I want you to know that I'm glad you didn't keep that image a secret from us. I'm sure we all want to help you stay alive and to learn how to be safe.

The crisis worker was shaken and surprised at Billy's sudden, unexpected description of his images. The worker assessed the suicide risk to be high because of the content and the context of the disclosure (the group activity had been clearly structured to facilitate sharing only positive, growth-promoting images, which other members of the group had done). Billy's nonverbal body posture and profoundly serious facial expression communicated that he was not fooling. The crisis worker did not deny, refute, or admonish Billy. Recognizing that Billy was taking a great risk by disclosing his death wish, the worker responded by assuring Billy that he had received the message as sent and conveying to members of the group the worker's willingness to attend to and answer Billy's cry for help.

Lester, Age 14. Lester was an intelligent youngster who made good grades in school and had a reputation for being quiet, cooperative, and well behaved. Following his parents' bitter divorce, while living with his mother and a younger sister and brother, Lester began to get into trouble in school because of his overt acting out and belligerent behavior. He lost interest in his studies and school activities, and his grades began to tumble. He became rebellious with his mother, and his appetite decreased to the degree that he just picked at his food. He became very withdrawn—seldom leaving his room—in contrast to his previous behavior of being actively engaged in outside activities whenever possible.

Lester's mother and the school counselor decided to place him in a student support group consisting of male and female middle school students, all of whom were experiencing severe difficulty following the separation and/or divorce of their parents. At the conclusion of one of the group sessions, Lester asked to speak with the crisis worker.

CW: Lester, sounds like something happened in the group today that got pretty close to you.

Lester: (*Hesitant; looking down; nervous.*) I . . . I've been feeling weird lately. Strange. Like I'm somewhere else.

CW: You mean like you're outside your own body observing yourself?

Lester: Yeah. Even at night. I don't understand it. I've even thought I might be going crazy.

CW: (*Closely observing Lester's body language.*) Lester, it sounds like this is so serious you may have even been wishing you were dead.

Lester: Yeah. I've been scared. I've just thought about how it would be to just go to sleep and not wake up.

CW: Have you thought about making that happen? Killing yourself, so that you'd never wake up?

Lester: Thought about it, yeah. Thought about it more lately.

The crisis worker had sensed prior to the interview that Lester might be suicidal. At least five indicators on the risk assessment checklist pointed to the conclusion that Lester was at a high risk level: his changing family life, his changing behavior and attitudes, his body language, his eating habits, his social habits, and his grades—any one of these alone would have been an important lethality signal (Curran, 1987, pp. 111–118).

Jennifer, Age 17.   Jennifer was terrified. Although she had suffered from depression, loneliness, and low self-esteem for several years, she had managed to have a satisfactory social life, maintain average grades in school, and regain her equilibrium following each depressive episode. Several stressors during the past year had combined to complicate and disrupt her life. Her parents' separation and divorce were unexpected and bitter. Her maternal grandmother, to whom she had been very close, died from rapidly progressing intestinal cancer. Jennifer was living with her mother and two younger sisters. The mother began dating a single man and permitted him to move in with them. Jennifer changed schools during the middle of the year when her parents' original home was sold. Because of her lack of social adjustment and academic achievement in the new school, Jennifer was placed in a support group at the school and was also seen regularly by an individual counselor.

Following a weekend episode of trauma over the suicide of a friend who attended another school, Jennifer showed signs of being upset, severely depressed, exhausted, and withdrawn. The crisis worker had been notified that Jennifer had missed school on Friday to attend her friend's funeral. Being wary of *contagion suicide,* sometimes called *copycat suicide,* the crisis worker knew that Jennifer's risk level was probably elevated because of her trauma over her friend's suicide, in addition to her already stressful family situation.

CW: Jennifer, it frightens me to see you this way. What's happening to cause you so much pain right now?

The crisis worker could see the physical and emotional devastation Jennifer was feeling. It was important to communicate to Jennifer the worker's affective concern and to provide a direct and open opportunity for Jennifer to feel safe and to respond (Patros & Shamoo, 1989, pp. 126–128).

Jennifer: (*After a long pause, in a very low, subdued voice.*) I . . . I've never been this scared before in my life. (*Pause.*) All weekend I've been at the end of my rope. I've just thought, There's no use going on anymore. And ever since last Friday at Etta's funeral, I've wondered if it wouldn't be better if I just went like she did. They said such nice things about her. She and I were so close. It was so sad but so comforting to hear all the wonderful things they said about her.

CW: Well, Jennifer, I'm glad you're here now. I can sense that the eulogy about Etta greatly affected you. What frightens me right now is what you just said, that it would be better if you joined her. Does this mean that you're planning to kill yourself over this?

The crisis worker's questioning was aimed at swiftly making an assessment of Jennifer's lethality and quickly heading off the idea of contagion suicide. The answer to such a question drastically impacts and changes what the crisis worker does. Even though Jennifer's destabilized family situation would have been signal enough to inquire into any suicidal thoughts and plans she might have, the hint of contagion suicide served as a red flag, alerting the crisis worker to be assertive and direct in asking the suicide question.

Crisis workers and other adults who work with suicidal youngsters must pay careful attention to clues that indicate suicidal ideation is present. Hunt, Osten, and Teague (1991, pp. 20–21) found that classroom teachers who are sensitive to the emotional changes in and have a close relationship with youth can be primary identification, support, and referral sources for youth who are suicidal. Lester's science teacher, Mr. Birch, overheard Lester talking to another classmate about giving him his "boombox" and some compact discs. Lester had also taken a pair of scissors and cut his long hair down to a chopped cut. He had gotten in a shouting match with a girl in class and almost come to blows with her before the teacher intervened. These behaviors were clearly uncharacteristic of Lester. He also knew from a staffing with Lester's teachers that Lester had thoughts of killing himself. The teacher had a list of warning signs he had received at an in-service training on suicide. After he became suspicious of Lester's behavior, he looked over the warning signs and made an immediate referral for Lester to the crisis worker. The crisis worker called Lester's mother, who confirmed Mr. Birch's suspicions. The assistant principal also indicated Lester had two disciplinary referrals for fighting after school in the last two weeks.

CW: (*Three months after the initial intervention.*) Lester, I asked for this conference because I'm worried about you again. I thought you were doing great! But now, frankly, I'm scared to death for you. Mr. Birch and your mom are worried too and asked me to see you.

Lester: Oh, I'm OK. Things are going great.

CW: (*In a calm, soft, caring, empathic voice—not a lecturing or agitated tone.*) They may seem OK to you, but what concerns me right now is what you've been doing lately. Your mother is very upset and puzzled because you've given your CD player to a friend, and the principal is livid because you've picked two fights on the way home from school this week. I've noticed that the last two days in the hallways and cafeteria you've been like an entirely different person. If these things say what they appear to say, I don't think I can leave here today until I can be sure you're safe. I don't want to wake up in the morning and hear that you're dead!

Lester: It's really not anything you should feel worried about. I'm OK, really I am.

CW: (*Soft, empathic vocal tone continued.*) Fine, then you can help me feel OK by discussing with me what's going on. I just want you to know that the clues I'm picking up spell danger, and that I'm as concerned for you as I've ever been. And I need to know that you're safe, even though you say you're OK. I really care about you.

The crisis worker was confrontive and persistent even though it would have been desirable and comforting to believe that Lester was OK. As it turned out, Lester was indeed on the threshold of suicide again. The important thing was that the worker interpreted Lester's unusual actions as clues that called for help—whether the client overtly called for help or not.

Many of the suicide intervention techniques that are found in Chapter 5, "Crises of Lethality," fit equally well for children and adolescents. What is particularly helpful for them is decreasing their feelings of isolation and marginalization. Including suicidal children and adolescents in support groups and other activities that make them feel valued and contributing members to their school and peer group are an important part of moving them away from suicidal thinking and behaving. Berman and Jobes (1994) found that suicidal adolescents particularly need empathic therapeutic alliances to help them feel affirmed, valued, and understood.

Suicide of Impulsivity. One particular type of suicidal ideation is particularly characteristic of children and adolescents, and on the face of it, seems absolutely "crazy." Yet as in all suicides, a suicide of impulsivity makes perfect sense to the individual contemplating it. Even though they have reached the formal operational stage of cognitive development, most teenagers believe they are immortal and really don't personalize the finality and irreversibility of their own death. When children and adolescents are enraged at some perceived injustice, one way to get back at their alleged persecutors is to plan to kill themselves. They believe they will die as martyrs and everybody will feel guilty and sorry for the terrible injustices they have done to them. In a fit of pique, they are sometimes able to do just what they intended.

The following aversive use of emotive imagery (Cormier & Cormier, 1998, pp. 317–341; Lazarus, 1977) is designed to be shocking and confront the client with his or her irrational thinking about what the true consequences of a suicide are. By flooding the client with vivid pictures of death and decay and counterpointing them with the rest of his or her family living, growing, and changing, it is designed to show the client that his or her "payback" will be short lived. It is constructed to help the client reframe his or her thinking about what the real consequences of suicide are and is used as a vehicle to offer the client ways to adapt and change his or her lifestyle to a more positive approach that has options other than an impulsive suicide attempt.

A few words of caution in using this technique. This type of aversive imagery should only be used when the crisis worker is sure that suicidal ideation and attempts are impulsive, angry acts intended to pay back others or get attention without consideration of what the finality of death is all about. It should never be used with a clinically depressed client who may well see the peace and quiet and "dust to dust" images as a highly desirable option. When used with minors, this technique should be very carefully explained to parents so that they fully understand what is going to happen and why it is going to be used. Consent forms that spell out what the treatment regimen will be should be signed by both parents. If you are getting the idea that this is a radical procedure, you are right. Be forewarned! What you are about to read may be very unsettling.

Ivana, Age 14.   Ivana is a pretty, popular, and petulant 14-year-old freshman cheer-leader. She has an older sister, Charlotte, 18, and a brother, Bill, who is 16. The opera-tive term to describe her would be "spoiled." She was referred to the crisis worker after a teacher found her attempting to slice her wrists in the ninth-grade girls restroom. Ivana was not hurt too badly and received first aid at the local emergency room. Her aborted attempt caused quite a stir, and everybody in the school is talking about her. She seems to like the attention and in an angry tirade with her parents told them she hated them and was sorry she was alive. Her parents were shocked to think their won-derful daughter would even think of suicide, much less attempt it. Her reasons for at-tempting the suicide were twofold. She was mad at her boyfriend for not doing what she wanted to do on their last date, and she was mad at her parents for not permitting her to go on an unchaperoned weekend trip with some male and female college cheer-leaders. After a consultation with her parents, the crisis worker explained the following technique to them and why it would be used. They signed a consent agreement, and the crisis worker went to work with Ivana.

CW: Would you like to tell me what caused you to consider killing yourself?

Ivana: (*Quickly angry and defiantly gesturing in a loud, demanding voice.*) I'll tell you why for sure. It's, like, my rotten parents and my rotten boyfriend, you know. Like really! They never let me do anything, and it's always what he wants to do, not what I want to do, you know. I'll just kill myself. Then they'll all be, like, sorry. Like really sad and sorry. It'll serve them right, you know. And I'll do it too. Next time I'll get some pills or turn the gas on in the kitchen or whatever. Like, you know, that would be awesome. Do it at home. Then they'd find me themselves, like, really. That would really, like, hurt them bad, you know! And the other girls in this school, like, in my crowd, suck, really. They never do what I want, you know. And the school sucks to, like, really sucks, man. I hate this place, really!

After listening to this defiant and impulsive adolescent's diatribe against her parents her boyfriend, the school, her friends, and the world in general, the crisis worker decides that the impulsive and angry teenager she has in front of her needs a dose of reality in regard to what death is. Her assessment is that this young woman's threats and gestures are more theatrical and attention seeking than intentional. However, the possibility that she might accidentally kill herself is real, and no threat should ever be dismissed as in-consequential. As a result, the crisis worker will use guided imagery to aversively give her as graphic a picture as possible about what killing herself will really mean.

CW: (*Controlling her distaste for Ivana's petulant behavior and responding emphati-cally.*) I understand how mad and disappointed you are that everybody seems to be against you. So I wonder if you'd like to picture what killing yourself would really mean to all these people, particularly your family. Would you like an idea of how they would pay for that the rest of their lives?

Ivana: You bet, like really, that'd be cool.

CW: Ivana, I want you to close your eyes and picture the following scenes in your mind. Picture yourself now dead. (*Ivana has a little difficulty in complying. The crisis worker in a methodical, soft, soothing voice offers a few words of guidance and reassurance and coaches her in relaxing. Ivana is able to close her eyes and image the scene.*) You are in the funeral home, there are lots of beautiful flowers around you, the room is full of your friends. Your family is in the front row. They are all red-eyed and teary. Your favorite music is being played. You are in a beautiful rosewood and silver casket in your beautiful pink dress. You look just like Sleeping Beauty. You are so lovely. As you look at the scene, it is just so perfect. Your boyfriend is almost in pieces, he is feeling so bad. They all feel so bad and guilty that they didn't do what you wanted. *(A flicker of a sly smile crosses Ivana's face as she contemplates the scene.)* Now the pastor gives the eulogy and everyone files by the casket and your beautiful body to say goodbye. Your family is last, and they are crying. It serves them right for how badly they treated you. After the room empties the funeral home director comes over and shuts the lid on the casket and screws the clamps down. Now it is absolutely dark and absolutely quiet. You feel your body being lifted up, and then suddenly you feel a slight bump. Then you feel yourself moving. You are in the hearse headed for the cemetery. After about fifteen minutes you feel the hearse stop. You then feel yourself being lifted up and then abruptly put down. You hear some muffled sounds and then it is absolutely quiet and absolutely dark. Suddenly you feel a short drop, and then you start to hear muffled thuds. You have been put in the grave and they are now burying you. It is absolutely dark and absolutely quiet and that is because you are DEAD!

Now, Ivana, I want you to erase that scene from your mind and move forward a year. You're looking in at your family's house. Your picture is up on the mantle. It's the anniversary of your death. Your mom has been teary-eyed all day, and it's a somber family that sits down to dinner. But after dinner, your brother Bill has a ball game and your sister Charlotte has a recital, so the family is off and running. Now erase that scene. Picture this in your mind. You are in your casket, it is absolutely dark and absolutely quiet. Water has started to leak through the vault and your pink dress is starting to mildew. The coffin worms have found their way to your body and thousands of them are wiggling and crawling throughout your body as they feast on your decaying flesh. The elasticity on your skin has shrunk back against your bones as the worms eat the flesh away from your once beautiful body. You have in fact really started to be nothing but skin and bones because you are DEAD!

Now erase that scene and move forward five years. It is the anniversary of your suicide. Look in on your home. There is your picture on the mantle, but there are other new pictures there too. There is a picture of your brother in the baseball uniform of State University. There's your sister—in a wedding dress—with a really great-looking guy you don't know. Your dad sits at the table and looks at your picture and wonders aloud what you might have become if you had lived. He sets your picture back on the mantle and goes back to reading his paper. Your mother is getting a package ready. It looks like a care package for your brother she's going to send to State U. You'd always wanted to go there. Now erase that scene from your mind. Picture the cemetery and go down into your grave. Your rosewood casket is starting to rot through, and what the worms didn't get, the water and bacteria will. Your pink dress is in tatters, with large blotches of mildew all over it. Your skin has pulled tight around your bones and is like parchment. You can see patches of your skull where the skin has peeled away and bones are starting to stick through your skin. Your eyes have sunken in and the eyelids are just covering your sockets. There is no flesh left since the worms have long finished their job. It is absolutely dark and absolutely quiet because you are DEAD!

Ivana: (*Twisting uncomfortably in her chair with a grimace on her face.*) I . . . I don't think I want to do anymore of this.

CW: One more time and we are finished. It is now 10 years after the anniversary of your suicide. Picture your house in your mind. There are new pictures on the mantle. It's your brother and he's in a military uniform, standing beside an airplane. He must be a pilot. Wow! And there's your sister, but there are also pictures of three cute children there. They must be hers. Your picture is now in the back, covered with dust and the varnish on the frame starting to peel. Of course, it has not changed. It never will. As your gaze moves through the house you see your mother and father packing. They are talking. What's this! They're taking all of your old school stuff and clothes, teddy bears, and games, and there's your cheerleader uniform. They're packing it in boxes. They're GOING TO GIVE IT TO GOOD-WILL. As they talk your mother goes over your stuff lovingly, as she packs it up. But your parents are planning on moving to a retirement community so they really don't have room for all the stuff in the attic. All that ever was of you that could have enjoyed life is now reduced to one dusty picture on the back of the mantel and memories, because you chose death instead of life by committing suicide.

Now go back to the cemetery. Your beautiful rosewood casket is decayed and riddled from termites. It has collapsed in on what is left of your body. There are a few scraps of bones left, but the gophers are chewing those up for the minerals. Your teeth and fillings are still attached to your skull, but barely. Earth and water have leaked into the vault and now what is mostly left is mud, which of course is what it should be since your body has gone back to the earth. It is absolutely dark and absolutely quiet, because you are DEAD. You can open your eyes up when you want.

Ivana: (*Agitated, shaking, and sweating.*) That was, like, really terrible! How could you do that? You're supposed to help people.

CW: Do what? Is that not what you wanted, to kill yourself? To show your parents and everybody else. I gave you a picture of what it is like to live and move on with your life or be dead and not. What did you expect?

Ivana: That's not what I meant at all. That's gruesome. I don't want to be like that.

CW: Ivana, I nor your parents nor anyone else want that for you. But you need to understand that death is final and irreversible. You cannot come back from it like Sleeping Beauty. I think we can do some things that will help you get a more positive outlook about why life is worth living. But you must choose. Nobody else can do that for you. I think you really do want to live and have a great life, but if you continue to act on your anger by attempting suicide, you may well succeed. Then that is the true picture of what your life (or death) will be. It's like Charles Dickens, *A Christmas Carol* and Scrooge. You have the power to change that if you want.

Ivana: Well, maybe I would like to talk to you some about some stuff, like, maybe I do get a little pushy and demanding, but sometimes I just don't know what to do and get really frustrated and angry and then get my feelings hurt and I just want to lash back, like, you know?

CW: Fine. I'd be glad to talk with you about that, and I believe we can plan some things that will deal with some of those angry hurt feelings. Do we have a deal? If so, I'd like your handshake on it, and also your promise that you're not going to try committing suicide while we do this.

Ivana: OK, I can shake on that, but I don't think I want to go through one of those image things again, you know.

CW: I know, and it's a deal.

Finally, use of this intrusive, aversive technique should be closely monitored in aftercare so that the client is not traumatized by it to the extent that we now have replaced a suicide of impulse with PTSD. Even though Ivana seems to have gotten a wakeup call, the crisis worker still institutes an antisuicide agreement as part of a transcrisis treatment plan. Until Ivana has a good deal more control over her impulsive behavior, the crisis worker, her parents, and teachers will need to be vigilant about knee-jerk reactions about killing herself. Teaching Ivana behavioral alternatives to her angry, petulant outbursts as a reaction to her insecurity about her typical adolescent identity crisis and ego involvement is a high priority. Group work with peers who give her honest feedback about her selfish behaviors and what that does to destroy relationships will help her to learn more equitable and amicable behavior towards her peers. Working with her parents to provide logical and natural consequences of behavior without feeling guilty that they may be driving her to suicide is also a vital piece of a comprehensive aftercare treatment that will decrease her impulsivity and make her suicide proof.

Clustering of Suicides: Contagion

Cluster or contagion suicides occur when more than one suicide attempt or completion happens within a proximate geographical area giving the appearance that these events are related (Kirk, 1993, p. 15; Webb & Griffiths, 1998–1999, pp. B43–48). There is some evidence that publicity about child and adolescent suicide completions and media programs depicting factual or fictional suicides have been associated with suicide attempts and completion in geographical areas reached by the publicity (Kalafat, 1990, p. 364). Kirk (1993, pp. 15–16) likens such clustering to the infectious disease concept; that is, when a pathogen is introduced into a vulnerable population, the probability of infection is spontaneously increased. Similarly, when an adolescent suicide occurs and is reported sensationally or the deceased's death is somehow glorified, other adolescents who may already be in a state of despair, helplessness, or hopelessness may be influenced toward terminating their lives or see it as an excellent way to get a great deal of attention. Shaffer, Vieland, and Garland (1990) reported that among adolescent suicide attempters, "talking about suicide in the classroom makes some kids more likely to try to kill themselves" (pp. 3153–3155). Thus, "postvention" classroom programs designed for suicide education and prevention may be appropriate for the majority of adolescents who are not currently at risk, but may not be appropriate for the at-risk population.

Publicity and Contagion.   Kirk (1993, p. 17), in his investigation about media effects on adolescent suicide, makes several interesting observations: (1) the more sensational the reporting of the suicide, the greater was the increase in suicides within the reporting area; (2) there was a significant increase in auto accidents involving teenagers following media reports of youth suicides; and (3) there was an increase in adolescent suicides following certain made-for-television motion pictures that focused on episodes showing suicides in the lives of troubled and suicidal adolescents.

The concept of contagion suicide is controversial. Skeptics and critics claim that there is little scientific proof of clustering and copycatting because it is difficult to prove that one suicide attempt or completion directly causes another. But according to

Kirk (1993, pp. 16–17) there is too much evidence of recent contagion suicides in the United states to ignore or dismiss claims of clustering. We agree with his conclusions and believe it is extremely important for crisis response teams (CRTs) that go into a school after a suicide to know this phenomenon has a possibility of being activated if postvention is not handled correctly

Imperatives for CRTs in Suicides.   School CRTs must be knowledgeable about suicide postvention so that clustering does not occur. Crises of suicide are different from other crises because of the self-instigating behavior that goes with them and because so many different emotional evaluations are placed on suicide. If CRT members do not know about the dynamics of suicidal behavior, they need to get outside consultive help that does, and they need to have it available immediately. The worst possible scenario is an insecure CRT that does not want to "look bad" because it needs outside help to handle the crisis. In our own experience we have witnessed a CRT that did not know what it was doing and wound up with three more completed suicides and two attempts on its hands in the space of two months in the same high school!

A suicide absolutely must not be glorified or made heroic. However, that doesn't mean that feelings are ignored or questions concerning the deceased are not answered as truthfully and honestly as possible. Empathic understanding of concerns of other students or faculty is of primary importance and no questions or comments should be summarily dismissed. We have witnessed one instance where the faculty of a school assembled after school to engage in a debriefing with the CRT of the district, and who had all sorts of questions and emotions to deal with concerning the suicide of a fellow teacher the previous night. They were told, and we quote, "If you are having problems with your fellow teacher's death, we suggest you call your behavioral health service provider and talk with them." Whereon the CRT leader dismissed the group and the CRT left the principal and school counselor to deal with over 50 enraged and frustrated faculty members.

As in any crisis, being at the school of the completed suicide as soon as possible after notification is critical to planning, making assessments about the emotional state of faculty and students, quelling rumors, assessing for other possible suicides, and depropagandizing and deglorifying the suicide by debriefing faculty and students. It is fruitless and damaging for the CRT to come straggling in late in the afternoon or the next day. Such dilatory behavior lets rumor and chaos run wild, and makes a statement that there is not a great deal of concern about the health and well-being of the school.

Probably one of the toughest jobs of a CRT and the school administration is not allowing parents, students, or various other interest groups in the community to take over and honor the suicide by a commemorative service or other memorial at or by the school. We cannot overemphasize that the school administration and the CRT should be the ones that make decisions about the response to be made to school tragedies where suicides and homicides occur.

LEGAL AND ETHICAL ISSUES OF POTENTIALLY VIOLENT BEHAVIOR

Confidentiality and Duty to Warn.   Although the overriding ethical consideration of any counseling session is confidentiality, we have now ventured into *Tarasoff* legal territory (*Tarasoff* v. *Board of Regents of the University of California,* 1976). The primary legal concern related to providing services for students prior to, during, or after a crisis is negligence. Although we are speaking of intent to harm others here, negligence can occur in any crisis situation, and the school district would be well advised to make a written policy statement that details its procedures for all crisis situations as an initial step in avoiding liable suits (Brock et al., 1996, p. 42).

A decision must be made about duty to warn. This is not a simple decision, particularly when we are dealing with juveniles, and can create a difficult dilemma for a crisis worker. The dilemma has to be weighed between two alternatives that may be unattractive. The first is that by informing the student's parents and bringing authorities into the case, we run the risk of compromising our credibility with the student population and making the parents extremely angry because they will believe the school has labeled their son or daughter as "a homicidal maniac" or "suicidal nut case" to the whole community. Informing the cheerleaders' parents that John is out to "get" them, as he indicated in the first scenario for John is unwarranted, because it is not based on clear intent, method, or any other substantiating evidence other than his vague, fantasized notions of revenge. It would probably cause a panic and might well invite a lawsuit. We do not wish to take any action that would have the effect of labeling the student as violence prone or use other negative terms that might cause embarrassment to the child or the child's family without substantiating evidence. However, even in his vague threats in the first scenario, John's parents should be brought in and told about his problems in an empathic, nonaccusatory, problem-solving manner. The question is not, Should the parents be called? because that is a given, but rather what to say to parents and how to elicit a supportive reaction from them (Poland, 1989). Although Poland speaks specifically to suicidal ideation, we see no reason that what he says should not apply to homicidal ideation as well.

On the other side of the issue, if the crisis worker does not warn others, he or she puts at risk the lives of the student and others who may be in harm's way, and may suffer civil liability as a result. In cases of suicide and homicide, growing case law indicates that school systems are liable if they do not have plans in place to prevent acts of lethality from happening. The issue is not whether the school might have caused it, but whether they attempted to prevent it (Poland, 1994). The second scenario where John details the intent, the method, and the means is reason to label the act as lethal and warn both the parents of the child and the parents of the intended victims.

Although most state statutes do not give clear guidance on this point, it is likely that existing law will support any warning that is based on specific behavior indicating an obvious and unequivocal danger. Such obvious and unequivocal danger is best determined by focusing on the specific behaviors themselves. Although it may be easy for complaining parents to dispute the meaning of a particular behavior, it is more difficult to deny the fact of the behavior itself. The *in loco parentis* status of the schools (being in the position of a parent to the child in the absence of the parent) is reason enough to take action, if based on such concrete behaviors, a reasonable suspicion, and follows the school district's plan as to what to do about a possible lethal act (Crawford, 1998; James, 1994). Thus, any school safety issue is tied to the concept of reasonableness, the intent of educators to promote a safe learning environment, and is based on what the educator knows or objectively suspects about a student (James, 1994).

Keeping Records.   We believe that taking clear and precise notes is of the utmost importance in substantiating our duty to warn. These notes should include date, time, parties involved, specific behaviors observed, statements made, and procedures followed. Mere intuition or "gut feelings" are not sufficient to explain why a particular intervention was made. It is necessary to articulate and record the behaviors, subtle that they may have been, that led to the intervention (Crawford, 1998).

Consultation. We believe it is also of critical importance that the crisis worker immediately consult with another trusted professional in the field, receive validation that his or her analysis of the situation is correct, and keep clear and concise notes about who, when, and why the crisis worker sought consultation. School officials have been very cautious about transmittal of data to other individuals or institutions because of the Family Educational Rights and Privacy Act regulations (James, 1997). However, when the student demonstrates the kinds of behaviors that may have lethal intent, or the crisis worker has reasonable suspicion to believe those behaviors are lethal, then there should be little question about sharing data and information. To do otherwise would be unethical and may invite a lawsuit.

Regrettably, as opposed to the mandatory reporting of child abuse, most states do not as yet have legislation that would make it mandatory to report threatening student behavior and indemnify the crisis worker from being liable for a good-faith report (Crawford, 1998). However, the ethical standards of most human services professions promote consultation with trusted other professionals as a reasonable endeavor in providing a good standard of care. Given agreement between professionals, it would seem reasonable to assume that any reports that were supported by others in the field would go a long way toward insulating crisis workers or school systems from legal liability.

Consistency of Intervention. Inconsistent actions invite complaints of bad faith or individual prejudice; consistent actions indicate that the interventions are based on behaviors and not on the attributes of any one individual. When exceptions occur they should be explainable as mere mistakes or lapses of judgment rather than decisions to intervene differently from time to time in a capricious manner. It is only partly in jest that we say that it is better to be consistently wrong than inconsistently right. That is why establishing a set safety plan and applying its procedures universally is legally critical (Crawford, 1998).

PLANNING FOR A CRISIS

A crisis plan for a school system is not done overnight. It takes a great deal of planning and commitment by the school district and the staff (Brock et al., 1996; Luna & Hoffman, 1999; Petersen, 1999; Petersen & Straub, 1992; Rubin, 1999; Steele & Couillard, 1994; Stephens, 1994, 1997). Crisis plans are both generic and idiosyncratic. Crisis plans of other schools and consultants can be extremely helpful in making a skeletal outline for what needs to be covered in containing a crisis. No matter whether the crisis occurs in Brooklyn, New York, or Brooklyn, Mississippi, many of the same needs and responses generic to all crises of lethality will be applicable to each. However, each school district and each school building has its own peculiarities in regard to its physical plant, its staffing, its student population, and its community makeup. Each of these variables play a critical part in how specific planning for a crisis will be conducted. To think that a crisis plan for the Los Angeles school district can be taken wholesale and applied to Waterloo, Iowa, would be misguided, to say the least. A crisis response in a school needs a delivery system. The chief components of any service delivery system are the written policy of what to do when a crisis occurs, the physical resources to carry out the policy, and the trained personnel to implement the service (Nelson & Slaikeu, 1990, p. 339).

The Crisis Response Planning Committee

Initial planning should use a crisis response planning committee (Brock et al., 1996; Petersen, 1999; Petersen & Straub, 1992; Poland, 1999; Rubin, 1999; Steele & Couillard, 1994; Stephens, 1994, 1997). A decision needs to be made on the size of the committee. If it's too large, it becomes unwieldy. If it's too small, it's not viable enough to meet a large crisis. The ideal is probably a two-tiered team if the district is large enough to support it. The first-tier team is a district-wide effort that deals with the big picture of crises. This team should be composed of a wide variety of individuals that represent a cross-section of social services and government institutions that will have to respond to the crisis. The second tier is a building response team that is familiar with its physical plant and its constituency. These individuals represent the teaching staff and administration, the parents, and most importantly the support staff (failure to include the custodian might mean that nobody knows how to shut off the gas or electricity in the building) (Brock et al., 1996, p. 31). One of the critical ingredients is coordination between these two tiers. If these two levels are at cross-purposes with one another, not only will they hinder crisis resolution, but they can make it worse.

A needs assessment should be conducted to determine what the school staff needs in the way of training and, even more importantly, whether the constituency believes in and is willing to support it (Davis & Salasin, 1975; Stephens, 1994). Although we might suppose that there would be very few opposed to implementing a full-scale crisis prevention and intervention program in a school given the current publicity about school violence, that may not necessarily be true when the reality of passing a bond issue, providing released time for staff, or upsetting ease of access to school buildings comes into being. Therefore, fully apprising the community and determining their resistance or acceptance is critical to implementing an effective plan (Davis & Salasin, 1975).

A clear system for dealing with potentially violent behavior should be established long before the intervention. There should be attention to a quality assurance plan that provides that all personnel are clear as to what is going to happen, when it is going to happen, who is going to be responsible for each component, how a report is made, who is to make the report, and subsequent follow-up action. Such planning should include all the school staff and administration. Furthermore, because such interventions will undoubtedly involve law enforcement and perhaps other mental health agencies, they too, should be involved in planning for violence intervention and know what part they are to play in it (Blauvelt, 1998; Brock et al., 1996, pp. 33–37; Stephens, 1994).

We have seen a number of voluminous crisis plans developed by school systems that are quite impressive. They are gathering dust on the principal's bookshelf! Any crisis plan should be usable, and it should be simple enough that everybody knows their role in implementing it (Blauvelt, 1998; Goldstein & Kodluboy, 1998, pp. 170–171). From that standpoint, whereas no school district goes without a tornado, earthquake, or fire drill on a regular basis, very few schools have drills regarding armed intruders or other kinds of crises. In fact, if staff is not trained to implement the plan, and if a school crisis plan is not practiced, evaluated, critiqued, reviewed, and updated on a regular basis (Brock et al., 1996, pp. 243–248; Poland, 1999, p. 4), we believe it is useless!

The Crisis Response Team (CRT)

Consider this statement by an "expert volunteer" after a recent mass shooting in a school building as he "counseled" a group of extremely distraught parents. "I'm not from around here, so this doesn't really concern me, but I'm here to help. Who wants to start talking about their problems?" Volunteers who show up on the day of the crisis should politely but firmly be kept away (Poland, 1994). The sad truth of a disaster such as the shooting at Jonesboro's West Side School is that people with good and not-so-good intentions will flock to the scene of a disaster and offer their services "to help," and that "help" may do far more harm than good.

However, when a crisis is of such magnitude that local staff are overwhelmed or emotionally devastated because of personal involvement, then outside help should be summoned. Outside help should be planned for a long time before the crisis occurs. In small, rural school districts where the labor power and expertise for the following positions are beyond capabilities of the district, it is absolutely mandatory that linkages be established between districts and support personnel. It is even more important for these small districts that they have close linkages between county-wide, state, and federal disaster management teams.

If the crisis can be handled with help from within the district, the community generally will be better served because those people will be familiar with the setting and their clientele and the district will know what level of expertise these people have (Brock et al., 1996, p. 61; Rubin, 1999). Not everyone is cut out to do crisis intervention work. Just because a person is a counselor, social worker, a school psychologist, or a caring teacher or administrator does not automatically make her or him the best person to be involved with the team. Careful consideration should be given to team composition, and people who feel that they might not be capable of handling a severe crisis should not be discriminated against because they are truthful about their trepidation. The following roles comprise what we believe would be a competent CRT. There should be redundancy in these roles (Brock et al., 1996, pp. 74–75): If the crisis response coordinator is a principal who is being held hostage or the intervention coordinator is a school counselor who is injured in an explosion, there needs to be someone else familiar enough with that role to take over.

Poland (1999, p. 4) speaks to three waves in the aftermath of a disaster. The first wave is the medical personnel and police. The second wave is the media. The third wave is the parents. Therefore, it is not just the victims and survivors that a school must be concerned with, but a host of other problems as well. Therefore, a CRT will need to have a number of other people on it who may not have any expertise at all in crisis intervention, but do have the expertise to allow the CRT to handle the crisis effectively.

Crisis Response Coordinator. This person should be someone with decision making capacity. Most likely a school administrator who is knowledgeable about the school district and staff. He or she is highly knowledgeable about the crisis plan and has good communication links within and outside the system. This person is in charge of coordinating, implementing, and evaluating crisis response plans (Brock et al., 1996, pp. 67–68; Rubin, 1999). This is a different role from that of the person who would actually coordinate the intervention.

Crisis Intervention Coordinator. This person is responsible for implementing and carrying out the crisis plan. The person who is the intervention coordinator should have a thorough understanding of crisis intervention techniques and strategies. He or she should have a clear understanding of the objectives and methods of the crisis intervention plan and should be able to deal with a multiplicity of crises that range from individual suicides to natural and human-made disasters. This person also needs to be a good administrator and delegator who can coordinate a number of activities and people under very stressful and chaotic conditions (Brock et al., 1996, pp. 68–69; Petersen, 1999). It should be readily apparent that time should be allocated for the crisis intervention coordinator to plan and coordinate for crisis events, and not just have these "added on" as a supplementary task.

Media Liaison. It is one thing to deal with the local news crew that the CRT leaders may have developed close personal relationships with over the course of time. It is quite another thing to deal with national news media. Imagine yourself as a school counselor in Anytown Middle School who has been designated as the CRT coordinator. An assault at 8:30 A.M. by a paranoid schizophrenic leaves six children and two teachers dead, the school principal seriously wounded, and nine other children in the hospital with severe gunshot injuries. A panic ensues as frantic parents come to the school to get their children, you are attempting to get information out about who is hurt and dead, trying to coordinate psychological triage of survivors who witnessed the carnage, giving information to law enforcement personnel who are looking for the still-at-large perpetrator, attempting to reunite distraught students with equally distraught parents, plus a myriad of other tasks when at 10 A.M. the first national news helicopter lands on the football field, and is quickly followed at around noon by a convoy of national news trucks with satellite uplink capability. There are a horde of reporters attempting to interview anybody they can get their hands on. They are particularly interested in getting any school personnel to comment on who is responsible, why it happened, why the school didn't do something about this to stop it before it happened, what the school is now doing, who the dead and survivors are, and how you personally feel about this, among other intrusive and invasive questions that they are clamoring for answers.

It should become very clear from the foregoing scenario that dealing with the media is a major responsibility and should be the sole responsibility of one person especially designated and trained for the job. Such a person should be able to keep relationships with the media positive, but should also be able to effectively control them by determining what and how information should be shared with them through well-thought-out and -prepared statements (Brock et al., 1996, pp. 69–70). One of the worst scenarios in a school crisis is to allow anybody and everybody to talk to the media. The repercussions from the innuendo, rumor, half-truths, and incomplete data can be extremely severe for survivors and further exacerbate the psychological trauma.

Security Liaison. The security liaison should have close links with local law enforcement agencies and would coordinate responses to single events such as a bus wreck or recurring events such as gang-initiated drive-by shootings. One of the major preventive tasks of the safety liaison is training staff in implementing safety procedures across a wide array of potential crisis scenarios (Brock et al., 1996, p. 71).

Community/Medical Liaison.   The medical liaison will have established close links between the local emergency, fire, medical, and mental health system and the school. A critical component in her or his role and function is planning for medical triage of victims of a school crisis and communicating to parents and staff the medical conditions of those involved in the crisis (Brock et al., 1996, pp. 71–72; Rubin, 1999). If there is a local emergency management agency, the liaison should have a seat on its board so that he or she knows who to contact and what kinds of resources are available in a disaster.

Parent Liaison.   The parent liaison's job is dealing with parents, period, paragraph! Keeping parents calm, providing them with information, and furnishing them support is critical in containment of a crisis. Where there is a part of the community that is not fluent in English, provisions for translators will have to be made as well as with all written information that goes out to parents. Because parents may need the services of other components of the team, this school official must have a good working knowledge of each member's role (Rubin, 1999).

Crisis Interveners.   Whereas direct service crisis interventionists most likely come from the ranks of school counselors, psychologists, social workers and nurses, it is important to obtain interventionists who are directly linked to children. Thus, it is helpful to have teachers who have direct contact with a broad sample of students who might be affected. In an elementary school at least one primary and intermediate teacher should be on the team, and in middle and senior high schools teachers that represent many different subject matter areas or curriculum tracks should be part of the team (Brock et al., 1996, p. 72). The school and district unit should be capable of handling a small crisis such as the suicide of a teacher or a gang shooting. In a large crisis such as a bus–train wreck, backup workers from the local mental health system should be available, and in a very large crisis such as the Columbine shooting, the crisis interventionists would be an even larger integrated team of school, local, state, and national teams of interventionists. Incorporating students into the team is a good idea. They can act as messengers, help identify which students are missing, provide information about the status of other students, and function as peer counselors (Rubin, 1999).

Resource Person.   This member will need to know where a variety of available supplies are and how to get them from point A to point B in a hurry. Depending on the size and type of the crisis, the resource person may need to know how to obtain everything from pencils and paper to a backup diesel generator. This is not a menial job. If the material supplies are not available, including provision of food and drink when a crisis is going full tilt, then everything grinds to a halt (Rubin, 1999).

IMPLEMENTING THE CRISIS PLAN

The following minimum requirements are critical to a school crisis plan (Brock et al., 1996, pp. 75–76; Petersen & Straus, 1992; Rubin, 1999; Steele & Couillard, 1994).

Physical Requirements

Counseling Locations.   As many locations as possible need to be identified for crisis counseling offices. Crisis counseling will involve a wide variety of activities that will require different accommodations. Auditorium-sized rooms will be needed to handle large groups of people for briefings of factual information about the crisis as it unfolds and psychoeducational information about what people can expect and need to do in the aftermath of the crisis. Classrooms will need to be designated to administer psychological first aid. Offices will be needed to perform psychological triage and provide individual counseling. If school is in session, a great deal of rescheduling and shuffling of rooms and assignments is going to be necessary and should be planned for ahead of time or alternate buildings such as churches will need to be used.

Operations/Communications Center.   In a very large crisis, a room that will become the nerve center for a crisis needs to be identified and equipped. Additional phone lines, supplies and furniture for additional staff, computers with Internet capability, emergency equipment such as portable phones, citizen band and police band radios, and portable generators are necessary for the operations center to function. It will become the key component to an efficient crisis operation. It will be in charge of monitoring procedures to determine what staff is available, procedures for getting written messages to staff, screening outsiders, and disseminating and coordinating media releases and crisis intervention procedures.

Break Room.   A place that is private and will allow workers time to relax, eat, and rest. It may also double as a debriefing room for CRT members and other crisis personnel.

Information Center.   A room large enough to handle a number of media personnel. It should be equipped with a sound system and other visual media equipment. It may also double as an information dissemination or briefing room for parents.

First-Aid Room.   Stocked with first-aid supplies for minor physical problems.

Logistics

On-Site Communications.   Message boards, computers linked to central files, dedicated telephone lines, citizen and police band radios, and walkie-talkies should be accessible. Because telephone lines may be jammed or otherwise inoperable, a central message board should be available for announcements, bulletins, student lists, and other personal information. If possible, dedicated phone lines with the numbers known only to officials and staff responsible for handling the crisis should be available. Because there may be little or no communication on-site, walkie-talkies are vital.

Establishing a Phone Tree Among All Staff.   In any size crisis, a redundant phone tree is absolutely imperative. All staff members of a school building need to be informed of a crisis event as soon as there is knowledge of it. The phone tree is critical so that all staff members can begin to operate in a crisis mode and assume preplanned positions and duties. Messages about the crisis should be written down by each person on the tree. Relying on memory and verbal transmission will guarantee that facts will get commingled with fiction. One of the worst mistakes that can be made is for staff not to be aware of what is happening and go blundering into an ongoing crisis. We have experienced such lack of communication firsthand, and it is, to say the least, a nightmare.

Procedural Checklist.   Although it may seem time wasteful to go through a procedural checklist when a crisis is in full swing, not to do so in a chaotic situation is asking for trouble. It is too easy to overlook a critical component of the intervention plan and assume it has been taken care of by somebody else.

Building Plans.   Building plans are vital to emergency personnel and police. Blueprints of every building in the district should be quickly available. Someone with knowledge of the building should be available to interpret the plans to emergency personnel.

Provisions.   Because crisis personnel may be involved for extended periods of time, food and drink should be provided or be delivered on-site.

Responding to the Crisis

The following points, in linear order, indicate what needs to occur in a crisis response (Brock et al., 1996, pp. 80–104; Petersen, 1999; Petersen & Straub, 1992; Poland, 1999; Rubin, 1999).

Getting the Facts.   The ability to quash the rumor mill that invariably starts up in a crisis is critical to calming fears and anxiety of the public, and also providing valid information to crisis workers on who and how many students were affected, what level of response will be required, what information needs to be disseminated, and to whom it will be given. Facts need to be checked and rechecked. Getting a team member to the scene of a crisis to make a factual report is critical. Distraught parents and hysterical children make for extremely unreliable sources of information. Especially in the case of a suicide, getting verification from the medical examiner is a must.

Impact Assessment.   As soon as the facts are known, a CRT meeting should be held and an assessment should be made on the impact the crisis will have on the school. Considerations in assessing the impact are popularity of the victim, degree of exposure by staff and students, history and recency of similar crises, resources currently available, and timing (a crisis during vacation is likely to be less traumatic than one during school time). At that time a decision will have to made as to the degree of mobilization of internal staff and what, if any, outside assistance will be needed.

Triage Assessment.   Once the facts are determined and the possible impact of the crisis event is gauged, a triage assessment needs to be conducted to determine those individuals most affected by the crisis. The CRT needs to compile a list of those that may be directly and indirectly affected and determine who is most in need of acute intervention and those who may need less immediate, intensive attention. Once this list is compiled, interviews and paper-and-pencil tests such as those described in the chapter on

PTSD may be used to further divide individuals into primary- and tertiary-care groups. It should not be assumed that just relatives, survivors, witnesses to the event, and close friends within the school will be the only people needing immediate and intensive attention. Siblings and close friends in other schools may be just as traumatized, and efforts should be made to assess these individuals as well. Individuals who are known to be at high risk due to other factors and those students whose reaction is out of proportion to their involvement should also be considered as high risk. Parents and teachers need to be given checklists and warning signs that will let them know whether their children are starting to develop the symptoms of acute or posttraumatic stress disorder and referral sheets and phone numbers that will enable them to refer those students who may have been missed by the CRT. Embedded within these referrals should be questions on lethality. Any student who is expressing thoughts about harming him- or herself or others should immediately be assessed at high risk and in need of immediate crisis intervention.

Psychological First Aid.   Psychological first aid (Aguileria, 1997; Slaikeu, 1990, pp. 105–129) is a first order response that deals with all of the affected individuals no matter what their degree of involvement. The components of psychological first aid are making psychological contact, exploring dimensions of the problem, examining possible solutions, gaining assistance in taking action, and follow-up services. The objective of psychological first aid is intended as a method to provide support, furnish a platform to be heard and valued, dispel rumors, allow catharsis and ventilation of emotions, reactivate problem-solving abilities, reducing potential lethality, and restore general stability to the school. It is probably most easily done in classroom meetings with teachers who are trained and supported by the CRT. Such classroom meetings are an excellent vehicle for providing factual information about the event, giving students information about the psychological effects they may incur, and dealing with personal issues and problems they may have as they come to grips with, and attempt to resolve the crisis.

The NOVA Model.   For older students, the NOVA group crisis intervention model may be used (National Organization for Victim Assistance, 1997). This model operates along the lines of the Critical Incidents Stress Debriefing (CISD) program of Mitchell and Everly (1995). However, it is not as tightly structured as CISD and the facilitator is a great deal more interactive with participants. These groups are usually no more than two hours in length.

The session has a brief introduction detailing safety and security for the participants. Time is then spent on reviewing physical sensory perceptions, emotional reactions of shock and disbelief, and giving opportunity for ventilation and validation of these reactions. Typical questions posed are "Where were they when it happened? Who were they with? What did they see, hear, smell, taste or touch at the time? What did they do? How did they react?" Time is then taken to review the emotional turmoil that has been experienced and to allow ventilation and validation of these feelings. Questions are asked in regard to the aftermath of the event. "What are some of the memories that stand out in your mind? What has happened in the last 48 hours? What do you remember seeing or hearing during that time? How have you reacted?" The facilitator validates the thoughts and feelings of the group members. No judgments are made as to right or wrong. Where applicable, the facilitator draws comparisons between members to create a common bond and normalize thoughts and feeling that go with the abnormal event (National Organization for Victim Assistance, 1997, pp. 8–10).

Questions are then posed to elicit expectations about the future, what coping strategies can be used, and help predict and prepare the group for what may happen over the near future. "After all that you've been through, what do you think will happen at school in the next few days and weeks? Do you think your family has been or will be affected? How do you believe you might deal with the problems and issues that have been raised?" As the members identify positive coping strategies they are reinforced and given alternative strategies if they are generating negative coping methods. Referrals for more in-depth help are suggested. These components are then followed by a summary recapitulation to validate what has been said and reaffirm the validity of the participants' experiences. A postgroup session of about 30 minutes is used to pass out handouts, answer individual questions, and say goodbye (National Organization for Victim Assistance, 1997, pp. 9–10).

We do not recommend conducting a large assembly of all the school to do this. Although a large assembly may be deemed as efficient and expedient, it does not begin to address the many personal questions and issues that students may have. Psychological first aid is a two-way street, and to be effective, should allow an interchange of information between staff and students. In and of itself, psychological first aid may be an excellent way of determining who may be in need of more in-depth crisis intervention by observing reactions of students as they talk about the crisis. This admonition is particularly important in the case of suicide where other students may have "caught" the contagion and need to be identified.

Crisis Intervention.   Any student who is assessed as needing more than psychological first aid should be given a complete screening interview (Aronin & Ransdell, 1994). That interview should consider what the student's exposure and recollection of the events are, whether the event is persistently reexperienced, whether there are attempts to avoid reminders of the event, increased levels of physical and mental arousal, feelings of survivors guilt, failure of previous coping skills to ameliorate problems, somatic complaints, self-destructive or impulsive behaviors, and pre-and postevent comparisons on effectiveness of daily functioning. In short, the screening interview should look at the diagnostic criteria set forth by the *DSM-IV* (American Psychiatric Association, 1994) for the onset of traumatic stress disorder.

We believe it is important to take the time necessary to completely discuss the crisis, and that attempts to immediately reintroduce the academic regimen should be held in abeyance until this task can be completed. Although getting back to the standard hum-drum schedule of school is important in normalizing the situation, very few students are going to be academically able to do so if they are struggling with attempts to resolve the crisis. Classroom meetings can help students move from reaction to proaction. That is, students can move from talking about the event to planning how they can take action to solve the residual effects of the event. By moving to a proactive stance, students can begin to obtain a feeling of empowerment and reinstitute control in their lives. They can also gain closure on the event by cooperatively planning memorials and memorial services (note the previously mentioned exception of suicide memorialization in this chapter).

The worker should be especially watchful for client reports that perserverate on special details, worst moments, and violence or physical mutilation. These will be extremely potent points in the crisis and need to be thoroughly worked through and controlled (Pynoos & Eth, 1986, p. 309). If there are perpetrators involved in the crisis, one of the greatest fears of children is that the perpetrators "will get them." Whether these perpetrators are caught and punished or are still at large makes little difference. The worker needs to take time to clarify what happened to the perpetrators or what is being done to catch them. Feeling of self-blame for not having done enough and an inability to take action, desires to retaliate and punish the perpetrators, and fear that they will be revictimized need to be explored and worked through (Brock et al., 1996, p. 168).

Briefing, Debriefing, Demobilizing. Each morning of the aftermath of the crisis, a morning briefing and planning session needs to be held to obtain updated information review responsibilities, assign tasks, and plan interventions. Here we are speaking of debriefing in a more logistical rather than a therapeutic sense such as a one-time Critical Incident Stress Debriefing (CISD). At the end of each day, actions need to be reviewed, weaknesses and strengths need to be examined, and reviews of referred students, staff, and parents need to made. Plans are then made for the next day and what staff and resources will be needed to accomplish the goals. The nightly debriefing gives the CRT a chance to exchange information, obtain reassurance, and ventilate feelings (Berman & Jobes, 1991; Davidson, 1989; Rubin, 1999).

Demobilizing occurs when the crisis is finished. It allows the CRT to integrate the experience into their lives and go back to their regular jobs. An overall evaluation is conducted by the crisis response coordinator with the CRT. The crisis intervention coordinator writes an after-action report that describes the crisis event, the interventions conducted, an evaluation of the effectiveness of the intervention, and recommendations for future events. As such it provides the CRT with a potent learning tool. Furthermore, if questions are raised in the future about what was done or not done, this report documents what happened (Brock et al., 1996, p. 100).

BEREAVEMENT IN SCHOOLS

The sudden death of a student, teacher, or principal may precipitate a bereavement crisis for an entire school or school community. A CRT approach to dealing with such crises (Allan & Anderson, 1986; Bertoia & Allan, 1988; Hunt, 1987; Pelej, 1987; Sorensen, 1989; Stevenson, 1986) would promptly take several initiatives to help students, faculty, and others who support and supplement bereavement procedures in the chapter on loss.

Individually or in groups, team members may focus on the grief of a specific grade level, provide group discussion for particular subgroups, temporarily relieve bereaved teachers of classroom responsibilities, staff mini-counseling centers, or work with parents. The CRT provides the appropriate responses needed to nurture the healing process and foster a postvention return to as near normalcy as possible (Sorensen, 1989).

Assessing students' needs prior to returning to school may help lessen anxiety. A home visit or a phone call that empathically responds to the student's progress can be made. Questions such as "How are you feeling about coming back to school? What is the most difficult thing for you about returning? Is there something you would like me to do to help you? Are you worried about what other students will think?" All these questions are designed to allow the student to talk about his or her fears and trepidations and allow the CRT member to help him or her start to feel less anxious. After the student has been back to school a few days, the crisis worker may discuss with the child how she or he is doing with questions such as "Now that you are back at school, what has been the hardest thing for you? What has been on your mind the most? How has the death affected you at school?" These questions allow the worker to determine how well the child is making the transition back into school (Rubin, 1999).

Kandt (1994, p. 207) suggests that school human services personnel working with grieving adolescents should (1) educate themselves about the grief process; (2) give permission to grieve; (3) allow time to grieve; (4) listen, listen, listen; (5) understand that reminiscing is essential; (6) give support for a variety of feelings; (7) know they can't "fix" the pain; (8) draw the adolescent out, keep in touch, and don't abandon him or her; (9) design a support group; and (10) let them know that they are not alone.

Swihart, Silliman, and McNeil (1992) illuminated the role of high school counselors, administrators, teachers, and parents in responding to the death of a teenager. Students listed the following issues that caregivers should be sensitive to:

1. Many students were affected by the loss, even students who were not close to the deceased; therefore, they were reminded of their own mortality.
2. Teachers should not expect peak performance from students who are still too numb the first week following the death.
3. Teachers should be allowed to express their own grief to students who are willing to simply listen.
4. Students should be allowed to grieve in different ways—some in groups, some in their individual ways.
5. After-school activities should be provided for students to work off their grief by expending physical energy.
6. Students should be brought together in commemorative activities so that students who were not very close to the deceased one are not excluded.
7. Students should be permitted to discuss grief issues; denial of the opportunity to openly discuss their thoughts and feelings may cut the teenagers off from an open forum of support.
8. School administrators should be cognizant of the deceased student's role in the school; if the deceased was in a leadership role, the school will need to have administrative leadership in filling the role vacated by the deceased.
9. The school should be prepared to respond to the loss for a considerable length of time.

In contrast, the following points are recommended when the death of a student or teacher is due to a suicide (American Association of Suicidology, 1991):

1. Don't dismiss school or encourage funeral attendance during school hours.
2. Don't hold a large-scale memorial to the deceased.
3. Do provide individual and group counseling.
4. Verify the facts and do treat the death as a suicide.
5. Do emphasize that no one is to blame for the suicide.
6. Do emphasize that help is available and that suicide is preventable and everyone has a role to play in prevention

A common theme that pervaded the Swihart, Silliman, and McNeil (1992) study was that the crisis intervention program of the school should be conducted by human services workers who are fully engaged with and sensitive to the feelings of students and who can communicate with students using skills such as genuineness, acceptance, empathic listening, and respect. So given all the other techniques and theories that may be employed in a school crisis, probably the very best technique is the staple of any good therapeutic relationship, being there with the client.

TRANSCRISIS INTERVENTION

For those children who are in need of assistance beyond psychological first aid, transcrisis intervention uses many of the approaches detailed in the chapters on PTSD and sexual assault. Use of drawings, modeling clay, and other manipulative play materials are particularly helpful in empowering children to take control of a situation that may seem beyond their ability to do so. Initially, the child should be allowed to use the materials to construct whatever he or she desires. The crisis interventionist uses this time to build trust and rapport. Invariably the crisis will be manifested in the play of the child and will provide clues to the source of the child's anxiety and means of coping (Pynoos & Eth, 1986, p. 307). At some time during the process, a child who has been numbing and repressing the crisis event is going to have an emotional release that may be shocking and unsettling to the crisis worker (Pynoos & Eth, 1986, p. 308). At this point in time, the worker must be calm, cool, and collected and be able to psychologically and physically comfort the child.

The use of guided imagery and the employment of superheroes as helpers in those images (Lazarus, 1977), conscious dreaming to help stop recurring nightmares (Garfield, 1984), and relaxation and desensitization techniques to teach anxiety control (Thompson & Rudolph, 1992, p. 173) are all potent ways in helping children empower themselves and take control back over their feelings, thoughts, and behaviors.

The Case of Josh.   Josh is a 7-year-old second-grader who has just recovered from a bite from a brown recluse spider (one of the most poisonous spiders in North America). Bitten in the leg, the necrosis that developed caused surgeons to have to do reconstructive surgery. Josh now walks with a cane and a limp. He is embarrassed by his disability and feels his classmates are making fun of him behind his back. For a time, it was feared that Josh might lose his leg. What has compounded the problem is that recently thousands of brown recluses were discovered in the steam tunnels of Josh's school. This discovery set off a panic, because the children had seen what happened to Josh and had also viewed news items on television about the brown recluses' movement into their geographic area. Although the school district immediately hired exterminators to rid the school of the spiders, the children's fears were not allayed. Josh is now hypervigilant in regard to any insects, is afraid to sleep in his own bed, has developed school phobia, and shrieks and screams in terror at going to school. He has recurrent nightmares about hoards of huge, hairy spiders covering his body. He is very sure he is going to die from a spider bite. His academic achievement has fallen, and he is in danger of failing second grade. His parents have talked to him about switching schools, but he is sure that all schools now contain brown recluses. Most of his conversation is centered on insects. He avoids outdoor activities for fear of getting bitten. The duration of his symptoms is now into its sixth week. After an interview with the school psychologist, Josh is given a diagnosis of acute traumatic stress disorder.

Because many other of the schoolchildren are manifesting symptoms of traumatic stress due to the brown recluse infestation, the CRT has a meeting and determines that intervention is necessary both with the student population as a whole and Josh individually. Josh's parents are called, and they agree to individual intervention. The team's media person prepares a number of press releases and goes on radio and television news shows to explain what is being done to control the situation. Bulletins are also sent home to all parents.

The medical liaison has classroom meetings with every homeroom in the school. She provides detailed information about what brown recluse bites look like, what medical care needs to be given, and answers the questions of the students in a truthful, no-nonsense manner. Another classroom meeting is held with the high school biology teacher who shows the students what the spiders look like, tells them about its habits, and also indicates to them that although the brown recluse is poisonous, it is a very shy spider that tries to avoid contact with people. Question-and-answer sessions follow, and students get a good idea of what they need to do both at school and home to avoid being bitten. Parents are invited to a special parent–teacher meeting where all the CRT staff are there to provide information about helping children cope with the sudden siege of arachnophobia (fear of spiders and similar creatures). After completing the psychological first aid program, the CRT staff poll the teachers, who indicate the students seem to have conquered their fears of spiders. But Josh has not!

The crisis worker goes to Josh's home and, after making Josh's acquaintance, sets up the following exercise:

CW: I want you to draw me the feeling of what "scared" looks like, Josh.

Josh: (Takes markers and poster board and draws a picture of a very large tarantula-like spider with huge dripping fangs about to pounce on a small boy cowering in a corner. While drawing, Josh gives the crisis worker a blow-by-blow gruesome description of what the spider is going to do the little boy.)

CW: Boy! that's scary all right. I wonder what we could do to make that big nasty spider run away and hide?

Josh: I dunno. Nothin', I think.

CW: Well, that is pretty tough with a spider that big, but you know, I've got an idea. It takes a spider to catch a spider. And I've got just the guy to do it. *(Pulls out a Spiderman comic book.)* Have you ever read a Spiderman comic? He is some kind of waycool.

Josh: (Eyes light up and takes the comic book and starts looking at it.) Yeah, and I've seen him on TV. He is cool!

CW: So let's get him to help us. Takes a Spiderman to catch a spider right?

Josh: Well, I guess that's right.

CW: All right! Let's jump Spiderman off the comic book and onto your poster board. Can you draw him on there and tell me what's happening?

Josh: Well, OK. *(Draws Spiderman casting a big net over the spider.)* Spiderman throws this big net over him, see, and the spider doesn't like it. But the more it struggles, the more it gets tangled up. Ha! Ha! Caught in a spider net. That's cool! He can't get out, but he's still there though, I don't like him right there.

CW: OK! How could we get rid of him?

Josh: Well we could take him to the bugman, and let him douse him with bug juice.

CW: Fine. Go ahead and do that. (*Gives Josh another piece of poster board.*)

Josh: (*Continues to draw Spiderman pulling the spider over to an exterminator who looks very much like Josh.*)

CW: Now what?

Josh: I'm gonna douse him good.

CW: Good! Do that! What does that spider look like now?

Josh: He's gonna shrivel up and blow away. (*Continues to draw the spider all shriveled up, with he and Spiderman triumphantly holding the spider up as a trophy.*)

Over the course of the next several sessions, the crisis worker continues to use modeling clay and drawing to give Josh and Spiderman increasing control over his environment. The crisis worker uses the superhero to help empower this frightened and traumatized little boy. The crisis worker now moves further to help Josh regain control over more of his environment by taking him outside to the backyard. Although Josh is somewhat timid about going outside, he goes with the crisis worker, one hand clutching the worker's hand and the other clutching a Spiderman figurine.

CW: Boy! We're outside here, how do you feel?

Josh: Yeah, I think the backyard is where I got bit.

CW: And you're back out here, that's pretty courageous, almost like Spiderman.

Josh: Well, it's OK 'cause Spiderman's here with me . . . and well . . . you too.

CW: Josh, I wonder if Spiderman could help us with those nightmares too. What I'd like you to do is just sort of have a daydream, you know like let your mind wander like there was sort of nothing to do and you were just kind of relaxing, and just shut your eyes and instead of having a nightmare, just imagine yourself and Spiderman. Just you and Spiderman out on patrol, saving the world from those huge spiders. Can you picture yourself and Spiderman like that? Now just lay back and listen to me and just let yourself relax. (*The crisis worker deeply relaxes Josh and then helps him create an image of him and Spiderman.*)

The crisis worker uses a combination of relaxation training and guided imagery to decrease Josh's anxiety and help him build a mental image of he and his powerful friend taking control of the night-time environment.

Josh: (*With his eyes closed.*) Yeah, me and Spiderman are scaling up a tall building, looking for big old hairy spiders. (*Josh goes on to explain how they are out on patrol catching all kinds of spiders. The crisis worker helps keep Josh on track, and when he gets stuck trying to catch a really huge, fast, fluorescent, chartreuse spider, the crisis worker gives him a can of superstrong glue and Josh and Spiderman spread it out and get the spider stuck in it.*)

CW: Good. Now what I want you to do is get that image real clear in your mind. You and Spiderman giving each other high-fives for catching that really monstrous spider. If you start to have that same old nightmare tonight I want you to change that nightmare, and do just what you and Spiderman did. That's what I want you to dream. I'll bet you can do that! (*Gives and returns a high-five from Josh.*)

The power of suggestion and use of guided imagery to enable a child to change his dreams may seem farfetched, but it must be remembered that children work out their problems through fantasy and play. By continuously reinforcing Josh for getting back in control of his environment through the help of the superhero, he can start to feel safe not only in his backyard, but also in his sleep.

Finally, to expedite Josh's return to school, the crisis worker sets up a classroom meeting with his classmates. Josh tells his classmates about his real spider bite and all the things that happened to him in the hospital. The rest of the children are very curious about all this and ask him many questions. Josh has been embarrassed about his scar and his limp, but now he's in the limelight and eagerly starts to tell them what went on while he was in the hospital and doesn't hesitate to tell them some of the more gruesome details with accompanying "Ohs," "Ahs," and "Ughs" from the class. He also shows them the pictures he drew and tells them, with the help of the crisis worker, how he's "Not afraid of any darned old spiders anymore." An examination of Josh's drawings indicate just how potent serial drawing can be (Gumaer, 1984). Over a series of sessions, the spiders get smaller and smaller and Josh and Spiderman get bigger and bigger until the spider is in realistic proportion to Josh in the drawings, no more than a spot on the poster board. In the course of eight weeks, Josh was able to return to school, his nightmares of spiders went away, and he was able to resume the life of a normal 7-year-old boy.

SUMMARY

The rise of school violence perpetrated by the estranged violent student has caused a great deal of public concern and received widespread media coverage because of its perceived senselessness and its occurrence in communities that previously thought they were immune from such horrific events. Although the focus has been on the tragedy of estranged students who act out their frustration and anger in lethal ways, the growth and spread of gang-initiated violence in urban, suburban, and rural communities far outnumbers the tragedies the estranged juvenile has perpetrated.

Homicides are not the only lethal malady to afflict schools and cause crises. The suicide rate has risen to epidemic proportions among children and adolescents. Along with other natural and human-caused disasters, school personnel face a wide variety of crises that reach far beyond the normal developmental issues and crises of childhood and adolescence. Schools have been called upon to develop wide-ranging prevention strategies for profiling, screening, and preventing acts of violence both to oneself and to others. Contemporary crisis strategies in schools deal not only with prevention, but with intervention and postvention as well. Crisis workers interact with students, faculty, and parents who have been associated with, witnessed, or suffered from traumatic events originating within the school or with students.

Although no known intervention plan will guarantee that tragedies will not take place, there are approaches that hold promise of discouraging and counteracting the violence perpetrated by gangs and currently assailing school buildings. These approaches call for everyone—community service organizations, child welfare agencies, mental health facilities, local, state, and national governments, the courts, law enforcement agencies, and all of the staff in schools—to work cooperatively in developing and implementing crisis intervention plans. Most importantly, no school moving into the new millennium should be without a crisis plan and a well-trained crisis response team.

CLASSROOM EXERCISES

Exercise 1

Divide the class into groups of six. Designate each person as a member of a SARA team. There is a police officer, a school counselor, a social worker from the local mental health clinic, an assistant principal, an assistant district attorney, and a school board member who runs an auto repair service. Using the SARA model have them construct a brief written plan about how they'll scan, analyze, respond, and assess the scenario. Allow about 20 minutes for this exercise; after the teams are finished have them discuss how they will deal with each of the components of SARA.

Scenario. Everybody is in an uproar at Hometown High School. Somebody did a job with spray cans on the high school. The graffiti looks suspiciously like something you saw at a recent drive-in conference on gangs. Other teachers in the lounge mention the fact that this stuff has also been showing up on buildings around town. While this discussion is going on, the librarian says that she picked up some hard copy dropped beside one of the computers that looks like it might be about some outfit that labels itself Growth and Development and its contents seem to be directed toward some kid with the computer screen name "Deaddog." The contents seem to have something to do with how one goes about establishing a "Growth and Development" chapter in Hometown (hint: the Gangster Disciples use this name to camouflage their movements by using words that start with "G" and "D") and talks about something called "tagging." The school board has called a special meeting to talk about this problem. You remember that a new kid has come to town from Detroit. He also seems to be wearing his clothes a certain way and constantly has on colors that you vaguely remember the speaker at that gang conference talked about. The new kid has generated quite a following. He seems to have a lot of money, a "kul" car, and a number of kids that are not going to be National Merit Scholar semifinalists are hangin' with him.

Exercise 2

Form into groups of five to construct a crisis response team. There will be a coordinator, a media person, a medical liaison, a security liaison, and the lead interventionist. Choose one of the scenarios. In 10 minutes, no more—you are under pressure here— have a plan you can release to the media (the class) who will ask you tough, on-the-scene reporter questions. After you are done, have the class give you feedback on whether they believe you kept the scenario contained.

Scenario. This kind of disaster happened a hundred years ago. It can't happen now, but it did. It appears that the old boiler in Lincoln elementary school blew up. When it went, the principal, Dr. Priest, and his office, Mrs. Ethington's third-grade class, and Miss Nishimura's' second-grade class went with it. Mr. Sayger's sixth-grade class and kids who were in the library with Mrs. Lease fell through the second floor when it caved in. You get an emergency phone call from the superintendent to leave your job and bring the district CRT together. The Lincoln CRT essentially no longer exists. You arrive on the scene minutes after the first firetrucks, ambulances, and rescue vehicles make the scene of a school that essentially has been blown in half. You hear moans coming from the rubble, and dazed survivors wandering about. Many children are in shock, and others are screaming hysterically. You overhear a fireman say that there are many dead, many wounded, many buried, and many burned. He can barely control himself and says he's never seen anything like this, not in 25 years as a firefighter and not in Vietnam. This is clearly a major disaster.

RESOURCES

There are many resources to help institute a crisis plan and a crisis response team in a school district. Two excellent videotapes for planning for disasters in schools are The Federal Emergency Management Agency's *Children and Trauma: The School's Response* (1992) and the National School Safety Center's *School Crisis: Under Control* (1991). NSSC's web site is www.nsscl.org/home.htm. Two excellent books for dealing with crises in schools are *Preparing for Crisis in the Schools* (Brock et al., 1996) from Clinical Psychology Publishing Company, 4 Conant Square, Brandon, VT 05733, and *Coping with Crisis: Lessons Learned* (Poland & McCormick, 1999) from Sopris West, 4093 Specialty Place, Longmont, CO 80504. The complete SARA model for gang intervention may be obtained from the U.S. Department of Justice Response Center by calling 1-800-421-6770, or contacting the Department of Justice home page at http://www.ncjrs.org or writing to the U.S. Department of Justice Response Center at 1100 Vermont Ave. NW, Washington, DC.

REFERENCES

Aguileria, D. C. (1997). *Crisis intervention: Theory and methodology* (8th ed.). St. Louis, MO: Mosby.

Allan, J., & Anderson, E. (1986). Children and crisis: A classroom guidance approach. *Elementary School Guidance & Counseling, 21,* 143–149.

Allen, S. (1996, November). *The rural school counselor.* Paper presented at the Tennessee Counseling Association Convention, Memphis.

Allen, S. (1998). *Peer leader violence prevention for Douglas County* (videotape). Memphis, TN: Department of Counseling, Educational Psychology, and Research. University of Memphis.

American Association of Suicidology. (1991). *Postvention guidelines for the schools.* Denver, CO: Author.

American Psychiatric Association. (1994). *Diagnostic and statistical manual of mental disorders* (4th ed.). Washington, DC: Author.

Aronin, L., & Ransdell, J. (1994). *A handbook for crisis intervention.* Reseda, CA: Los Angeles Unified School District.

Astor, R. (1999). Unknown places and times. *American Educational Research Journal, 36,* 3–42.

Batsch, G. M., & Knoff, H. M. (1994). Bullies and their victims: Understanding a pervasive problem in the schools. *School Psychology Review, 23*(2), 165–174.

Berman, A. L., & Jobes, D. A. (1991). *Adolescent suicide: Assessment and intervention.* Washington, DC: American Psychological Association.

Berman, A. L., & Jobes, D. A. (1994). Treatment of the suicidal adolescent. (Special Issue: Suicide assessment and intervention). *Death Studies, 18,* 375–389.

Bertoia, J., & Allan, J. (1988). School management of the bereaved child. *Elementary School Guidance and Counseling, 23,* 30–38.

Blauvelt, P. D. (1998). *Blauvelt . . . on making our schools safe* (2nd rev.). College Park, MD: National Alliance for Safe Schools.

Brock, S. E., Sandoval, J., & Lewis, S. (1996). *Preparing for crisis in the schools.* Brandon, VT: Clinical Psychology Publishing.

Bureau of Justice Assistance. (1991). *Addressing community gang problems: A model for problem solving.* Washington, DC: Author.

Busch, K. G., Zagar, R. , Hughes, J. R., Arbit, J., & Bussell, R. E. (1990). Adolescents who kill. *Journal of Clinical Psychology, 46*(4), 472–485.

Carney, J., Hazler, R., Higgins, J., & Danser, S. (1999, April). *Peer-on-peer violence.* Poster session at the American Counseling Association World Conference, San Diego.

Centers for Disease Control. (1991). *Attempted suicide among high school students—United States 1990.* Atlanta, GA: U.S. Department of Health and Human Services, Public Health Service.

Center for the Prevention of Handgun Violence. (1990). *Caught in the crossfire: A report on gun violence in our nations' schools.* Washington, DC: Author.

Cohen, P. A., Kulik, J. A., & Kulik, C. C. (1982). Educational outcomes of tutoring. A meta-analysis of findings. *American Educational Research Journal, 19,* 237–248.

Collier, C. (1999). *School violence: Facts, causes and recommendations.* Poster session presented at the American Counseling Association World Conference, San Diego.

Comstock, G. (1983). Media influences on aggression. In Center for Research on Aggression (Ed.), *Prevention and control of aggression* (pp. 25–38). New York: Pergamon.

Corder, B. F., Ball, B. C., Haizlip, T. M., Rollins, R., & Beaumont, R. (1976). Adolescent paracide: A comparison with other adolescent murder. *American Journal of Psychiatry, 133*(8), 957–961.

Cormier, S., & Cormier, B. (1998). *Interviewing strategies for helpers: Fundamental skills and cognitive behavioral interventions* (4th ed.). Pacific Grove, CA: Brooks/Cole.

Crawford, R. (1998, October). *Legal consideration for dealing with the potentially violent student.* Paper presented at the Memphis City School—Memphis Police Department Anti-violence Conference, Memphis.

Crews, W. (1998). *Memphis Police Department Procedures Manual for School Police Officers.* Memphis, TN: Memphis Police Department.

Cunningham, N. J., & Davis, B. (1999, April). *A study of middle school bullying using a framework for violence prevention.* Poster session at the American Counseling Association World Conference, San Diego.

Curran, D. K. (1987). Adolescent suicidal behavior. New York: Hemisphere Publishing.

Davis, H. T., & Salasin, S. E. (1975). The utilization of evaluation. In E. L. Struening & M. Guttentag (Eds.), *Handbook of evaluation research* (Vol. 1, pp. 621–666). Beverly Hills, CA: Sage.

Davis, J, M., & Sandoval, J. (1991). *Suicidal youth: School based intervention and prevention.* San Francisco: Jossey-Bass.

Davidson, L. E. (1989). Suicide clusters and youth. In C. R. Pfeffer (Ed.), *Suicide among youth: Perspective on risk and prevention* (pp. 83–99). Washington, DC: American Psychiatric Association.

Day-Vines, N., Day-Hairston, B. O., Carruthers, W. L., Wall, J. A., & Lupton-Smith, H. (1996). Conflict resolution: The value of diversity in the recruitment, selection, and training of peer mediators. *The School Counselor, 43,* 393–410.

Duncan, J. W., & Duncan, G. M. (1971). Murder in the family: A study of some homicidal adolescents. *American Journal of Psychiatry, 127*(11), 74–78.

DuRant, R. H., Treiber, F., Getts, A., McCloud, K., Linder, C. W., & Woods, E. R. (1996). Comparison of two violence prevention curricula for middle school adolescents. *Journal of Adolescent Health, 19,* 111–117.

Dwyer, K. Osher, D., & Warger, C. (1998). Early warning, timely response: A guide to safe schools. Washington, DC: U.S. Department of Education.

Dykeman, C. (1999, June). Preventing school-based violence: Practical steps for school counselors. Paper presented at the American School Counselor Association convention, Phoenix, AZ.

Eck, J. E., & Spelman. (1987). Problem-solving: Problem oriented policing in Newport News. Washington, DC: Police Executive Research forum.

Embry, D. L., Flannery, D. J., Vazsonyi, A. T., Powell, K. B., & Atha, H. (1996). Peacebuilders: A theoretically driven, school-based model for early violence prevention. *American Journal of Preventive Medicine, 12*(5), 91–100.

Fatum, W. R., & Hoyle, J. C. (1996). Is it violence? School violence from the student perspective: trends and interventions. *The School Counselor, 44*(1), 28–34.

Federal Emergency Management Agency. (1992). *Children and trauma: The school's response* (videotape). Washington, DC: Author.

Feindler, E. L., & Scalley, M. (1998). Adolescent anger management for violence reduction. In K. C. Stoiber & T. R. Kratochwill (Eds.), *Handbook of group intervention for children and families* (pp. 100–119). Boston: Allyn and Bacon.

Felner, R., Brand, S., Adan, A. M., & Mulhall, P. F. (1993). Restructuring the ecology of the school as an approach to prevention during school transitions: Longitudinal followups and extensions of the School Transitional Environment Project (STEP). *Prevention in Human Services, 10*(2), 103–136.

Feshbach, N. D., & Feshbach, S. (1998). Aggression in the schools: Toward reducing ethnic conflict and enhancing ethnic understanding. In *Violence against children in the family and the community* (pp. 269–286). Washington, DC: American Psychological Association.

Fujimura, L. E., Weis, D. M., & Cochran, J. R. (1985). Suicide: Dynamics an implications for counseling. *Journal of Counseling and Development, 63,* 612–615.

Galatzen-Levy, A. (1993). Adolescent violence and the adolescent self. *Adolescent Psychiatry, 19,* 418–441.

Garfield, P. (1984). *Your child's dreams.* New York: Ballantine Books.

Gilbert, S. E. (1995). Violence in schools: Why—and what can we do about it? *Journal of Health Care for the Poor & Underserved, 6*(2), 205–208.

Goldstein, A. P. (1991). *Delinquent gangs: A psychological perspective.* Champaign, IL: Research Press.

Goldstein, A. P., & Kodluboy, D. W. (1998). *Gangs in schools: Signs, symbols, and solutions.* Champaign, IL: Research Press.

Gottfredson, D. C., Gottfredson, G. D., & Skroban, S. (1998). Can prevention work where it is needed most? *Evaluation Review, 22*(3), 315–340.

Greene, D. B. (1994). Childhood suicide and myths surrounding it, *Social Work, 39,* 230–233.

Grossman, D. (1995). *On killing: The psychological cost of learning to kill in war and society.* Boston: Little, Brown.

Gumaer, J. (1984). *Counseling and therapy for children.* New York: Free Press.

Hammond, L. C., & Gantt, L. (1998). Using art in counseling: Ethical considerations. *Journal of Counseling and Development, 76,* 271–275.

Hardwick, P. J., & Rowton-Lee, M. A. (1996). Adolescent homicide: Towards assessment of risk. *Journal of Adolescence, 19*(3), 263–276.

Hausman, A., Pierce, G., & Briggs, L. (1996). School based violence prevention education. *Journal of Adolescent Health, 19*(2), 104–110.

Haynes, N. M. (1996). Creating safe and caring school communities: Comer School Development Program schools. *Journal of Negro Education, 65*(3), 308–314.

Hazler, R. J. (1996). *Breaking the cycle of violence: Interventions for bullying and victimization.* Washington, DC: Accelerated Development.

Huesmann, L. R., & Miller, L. S. (1994). Long term effect or repeated exposure to media violence in childhood. In L. R. Huesmann (Ed.), *Aggressive behavior: Current perspectives* (pp. 146–167). New York: Plenum.

Hunt, C. (1987). How your school can live through the tragedy of teen suicides. *American School Board Journal, 174,* 34–37.

Hunt, R. D., Osten, C., & Teague, S. (1991). Youth suicide: teachers should know . . . *Tennessee Teacher, 91,* 16-21, 29.

James, B. (1994). School violence and the law: The search for suitable tools. *School Psychology Review, 23*(2), 190–203.

James, B. (1997). FERPA and school violence: The silence that kills. In A. P. Goldstein & J. C. Conoley (Eds.), *School violence prevention: A practical handbook* (pp. 460–489). New York: Guilford Press.

James, R., & Dorner, K. (1999, June). *Profiling, screening, and counseling the estranged juvenile violent offender.* Paper presented at the American School Counselor Association convention, Phoenix, AZ.

Janokowski, R. (1998, October). *Using the SARA model for violence reduction in the schools.* Paper presented at Memphis City Schools-Memphis Police Department Anti-violence Conference, Memphis.

Kalafat, J. (1990). Adolescent suicide and the implications for school response programs. *The School Counselor, 37,* 359–369.

Kandt, V. E. (1994). Adolescent bereavement: Turning a fragile time into acceptance and peace. *The School Counselor, 41,* 203–211.

Kernberg, P. F. (1994). Psychological interventions for the suicidal adolescent. *American Journal of Psychotherapy, 48,* 52–63.

Kirk, W. (1993). *Adolescent suicide: A school-based approach to assessment and intervention.* Champaign, IL: Research Press.

Klein, M. W. (1995). *The American street gang.* New York: Oxford University Press.

Komar, A. A. (1994). Adolescent school crises: Structures, issues, and techniques for postventions. *International Journal of Adolescence and Youth, 5*(1–2), 35–46.

Larson, J. (1994). Violence prevention in the schools. A review of selected programs and procedures. *School Psychology Review, 23*(2), 151–164.

Lazarus, A. (1977). *In the mind's eye: The powers of imagery for personal enrichment.* New York: Guilford Press.

Lemp, R. C. (1990). To the diagnostic of "incomprehensible " offenses of adolescents and juveniles. *Acta Paedopsychiatrica, 53,* 173–175.

Levis, D. O. (1992). From abuse to violence: Psychophysiological consequences of maltreatment. *Journal of American Academy Child and Adolescent Psychiatry, 142*(10), 1161–1166.

Lipsey, M. W. (1992). Juvenile delinquency treatment: A meta-analytic inquiry into the variability of effects. In T. D. Cook (Ed., *Meta-analysis for explanation* (pp. 67–89). Beverly Hills, CA: Sage.

Loeber, R. (1990). Development and risk factors of juvenile antisocial behavior and delinquency. *Clinical Psychology Review, 10,* 1–41.

Loeber, R., Farrington, D. P., Rumsey, C. A., & Allen-Hagen, B. (1998, May). Serious and violent juvenile offenders. *Juvenile Justice Bulletin.* Washington, DC: U.S. Department of Justice.

Luna, J. T., & Hoffman, R. M. (1999, June). *The counselor as catalyst: Forming partnerships for school violence reduction.* Paper presented at the American School Counselor convention, Phoenix, AZ.

Lupton-Smith, H., Carruthers, W. L., Flythe, R., Goette, E., & Modest, K. H. (1996). Conflict resolution as peer mediation: Programs for elementary, middle, and high school students. *The School Counselor, 43,* 375–391.

Malley, P. B., Kush, F., & Bogo, R. J. (1994). School based adolescent suicide prevention and intervention programs. *The School Counselor, 42*(2), 1301–1336.

Marohn, R., Locke, E., Rosenthal, R., & Curtis, G. (1982). Juvenile delinquents and violent deaths. *Adolescent Psychiatry, 10,* 147–170.

Miller, W. B. (1975). *Violence by youth gangs and youth groups as a crime problem in major American cities.* Washington, DC: National Institute for Juvenile Justice and Delinquency Prevention.

Miller, W. B. (1982). Crime by youth gangs and groups in the United States. Washington, DC: National Institute for Juvenile Justice and Delinquency Prevention.

Mitchell, J. T., & Everly, G. S., Jr. (1995). *Advanced critical incidents stress debriefing.* Ellicott City, MD: International Critical Incidents Stress Foundation.

Myers, W. C., & Mutch, P. J. (1992). Language disorders in disruptive behavior disordered homicidal youth. *Journal of Forensic Sciences, 37*(3), 919–992.

National Coalition on Television Violence. (1994, July–September). School Violence. *NCTV News,* p. 2.

National Organization for Victim Assistance. (1997). *Community crisis response team training manual* (2nd ed.). Washington, DC: Author.

National School Safety Center. (1990). *School safety check book.* Malibu, CA: Pepperdine University Press.

National School Safety Center. (1991). *School crisis: Under control* (videotape). Westlake Village, CA: Author.

National School Safety Center. (1998). *Checklist of characteristics of youth who have caused school associated violent deaths.* Westlake Village, CA: Author.

Needle, J. A., & Stapleton, W. V. (1982). *Police handling of youth gangs.* Washington, DC: National Juvenile Justice Assessment Center.

Nelson, E. R., & Slaikeu, K. A. (1990). Crisis intervention in schools. In K. A. Slaikeu (Ed.), *Crisis intervention: A handbook for research and practice* (2nd ed.), (pp. 329–347). Boston: Allyn and Bacon.

Patros, P. G., & Shamoo, T. K. (1989). *Depression and suicide in children and adolescents: Prevention, intervention, and postvention.* Boston: Allyn and Bacon.

Pelej, J. (1987, April). Help your school survive a suicide. *Executive Educator,* pp. 26–31.

Petersen, S. (1999, April). *School crisis planning.* Workshop at the American Counseling Association World Conference, San Diego.

Petersen, S., & Straub, R. L. (1992). *School crisis survival guide: Management techniques and materials for counselor and administrators.* West Nyack, NY: Center for Applied Research in Education.

Pitcher, G. D., & Poland, S. (1992). *Crisis intervention in the schools.* New York: Guilford Press.

Poland, S. (1989). *Suicide intervention in the schools.* New York: Guilford Press.

Poland, S. (1994). The role of school crisis intervention team to prevent and reduce school violence and trauma. *School Psychology Review, 239*(2), 175–189.

Poland, S. (1999). *School crisis & youth violence: Lessons learned.* Houston, TX: Cypress-Fairbanks Independent School district, Department of Psychological Services.

Poland, S., & McCormick, J. S. (1999). *Coping with crisis: Lessons learned.* Longmont, CO: Sopris West.

Pynoos, R. S., & Eth, S. (1986). Witness to violence: The child interview. *Journal of the American Academy of Child Psychiatry, 25*(3), 306–319.

Remboldt, C. (1994). *Violence in schools: The enabling factor.* Minneapolis: Johnson Institute.

Rubin, R. (1999, June). *Crisis intervention.* Paper presented at the American School Counselor Association convention, Phoenix, AZ.

Sage, R., & Dietz, W. (1994). Television viewing and violence in children: The pediatrician's agent for change. *Paediatrics, 94*(4), 600–607.

Scruggs, T. E., Mastropieri, M. A, & Richter, L. (1985). Peer tutoring with behaviorally disordered students: Social and academic benefits. *Behavioral Disorders, 10,* 283–294.

Shaffer, D., Vieland, V., & Garland, A. (1990). Adolescent suicide attempters: Response to suicide-prevention programs. *Journal of the American Medical Association, 264,* 3151–3155.

Sherman, L. W., Gottfredson, D., MacKenzie, D., Eck, J., Reuter, P., & Bushway, S. (1997*). Preventing crime: What works, what doesn't, what's promising.* (Report to the United States Congress). Baltimore: University of Maryland, Department of Criminology and Criminal Justice, Office of Justice Program.

Slaikeu, K. A. (1990). *Crisis intervention: A handbook for practice and research* (2nd ed.). Boston: Allyn and Bacon.

Sloan, J. H. (1988). Handgun regulations, crime, assaults and homicide. *New England Journal of Medicine, 319,* 1256–1262.

Sorensen, J. R. (1989). Responding to student or teacher death: Preplanning crisis intervention. *Journal of Counseling and Development, 67,* 426–427.

Soriano, M., Soriano, F., & Jimenez, E. (1994). School violence among culturally diverse populations: Sociocultural and institutional considerations. *School Psychology Review, 23*(2), 216–235.

Spergel, I. A. (1989). *Survey of youth gang problems and programs in 45 cities and 6 states.* Washington, DC: Office of Juvenile Justice and Delinquency.

Steele, W., & Couillard, J. (1994). *Violence prevention/intervention: Readiness for schools.* Grosse Point Woods, MI: The Institute for Trauma and Loss in Children.

Stephens, R. D. (1994). Planning for safer and better schools: School violence prevention and intervention strategies. *School Psychology Review, 23*(2), 204–215.

Stephens, R. D. (1997). National trends in school violence: Statistics and prevention strategies. In A. P. Goldstein & J. C. Conoley (Eds.), *School violence prevention: A practical handbook* (pp. 72–90). New York: Guilford Press.

Stevenson, R. (1986). *How to handle death in the schools. Tips for Principals.* Reston, VA: National Association of Secondary School Principals.

Swihart, J., Silliman, B., & McNeil, J. (1992). Death of a student: Implications for secondary school counselors. *The School Counselor, 40,* 55–58.

Tarasoff v. *Board of Regents of the University of California,* 551 P.2d 334 (1976).

Thompson, C. L., & Rudolph, L. B. (1992). *Counseling children.* Pacific Grove, CA: Brooks/Cole.

U.S. Office of Juvenile Justice and Delinquency Prevention. (1994). *Juvenile crime, 1988–1992.* Washington, DC: Author.

U.S. Office of Juvenile Justice and Delinquency Prevention. (1995). *A comprehensive response to America's youth gang problem.* Washington, DC: Author.

Webb, S. B., & Griffiths, F. (1998–1999). *Young people at risk of suicide:* Part A, *School facilitators' handbook*; Part B,

Supplementary resources. New Zealand: College of Education, Massey University.

Webster, D. W., & Wilson, M. (1994). Gun violence, angry youth and the pediatrician's role in primary prevention. *Paediatrics, 94*(4), 617–622.

Zagar, R., Arbit, J., Sylvies, R., Busch, K., & Hughes, J. (1990). Homicidal adolescent: A replication. *Psychological Reports, 67,* 1235–1242.

Zenere, F. J., & Lazarus, P. J. (1997). The decline of youth suicidal behavior in an urban, multicultural public school system following the introduction of a suicide prevention and intervention program. *Suicide and Life Threatening Behavior, 27*(4), 387–403.

Zins, J. E., Travis, L., Brown M., & Knighton, A. (1994). Schools and the prevention of interpersonal violence: Mobilizing and coordinating community resources. *Special Services in the Schools, 8*(2), 1–19.

CHAPTER TWELVE

Hostage Crises

We include a chapter on hostages in this book for several reasons. We hope that the majority of the people reading this book will never become involved in a hostage situation. However, given Kinney's (1995) research on the tremendous increase of violence in the workplace, we also believe that in a randomly cruel universe, some of you are going to be subjected to the terror of a hostage situation, or you are going to be in a position where you may fall into the role of de facto negotiator until help arrives.

The second reason to include this chapter is that because violence is rising in the workplace and acts of hostage taking occur there, it is likely that crisis interventionists will be involved in debriefing the hostages (McWhirter & Linzer, 1994).

The third reason is that crisis intervention is the core of hostage negotiation. Donohue, Ramesh, and Borchgrevink (1991) call hostage negotiation "crisis bargaining," which they define as negotiation aimed at coercing another person to comply with some course of action. All the elements of a crisis are present: disequilibrium and stress, dysfunctional behavior, poor cognition, heightened emotionality, and the traumatic wake that occurs after the resolution of the event are all part and parcel of a hostage situation. Further complicating matters, while the event itself is occurring the interventionist is dealing with the victimizer, not the victims themselves. We know of no other crisis situation where an intervener will need to be so skillful in handling a variety of difficult problems in rapidly changing circumstances under such dangerous conditions.

The fourth reason is that the psychological dynamics of those who survive being held hostage are not unlike those of victims of battering, coerced prostitutes, and abused children and can give you a perspective on what it means to go through those traumas essentially as a hostage (Herman, 1995, p. 92).

Finally, over 95 percent of hostage situations are resolved peacefully without shots being fired, and this is due to the purposeful use of crisis intervention theory and techniques (Strentz, 1995, p. 134).

The chilling accounts of hostage takings that occur a continent away from us, or in social institutions such as penitentiaries that are psychologically a continent away, make sensational headlines. Most of us assume that being taken hostage would happen to "the other guy" but not to us. Yet if you are a school counselor, a mental health worker, or a medical staff member at a world-famous hospital such as St. Jude's Children's Research Hospital in Memphis, Tennessee, you might be "the other guy." About 52 percent of all hostage takings are instigated by mentally ill or emotionally disturbed individuals (Blau, 1994, p. 257). This statistic should indicate that human services providers are not insulated from the potential for being taken hostage. Of those, most can be categorized as having paranoid schizophrenia, extreme depression, inadequate personality disorder, or antisocial personality disorder (Strentz, 1995, p. 133). In other words, these people typically will have very high triage assessment scores when in crisis and their lethality level will be commensurately high as well.

To bring the issue "up close and personal," the human services worker is likely to meet people who have had their lives radically altered in what they may feel are very negative ways by human services agencies. The rise of the American health care system as a bureaucratic institution has led people to feel uncared for and ignored in times of emotional stress, particularly when they do not seem to have the ability to find coping mechanisms or resources on their own (Turner, 1984, p. 177). Just as hostage taking is a political act for terrorists too weak to cause revolution, it is, in the health care setting, a feeling act from people too weak to change what they believe to be grave injustices perpetrated on them by that system (Turner, 1984, p. 172).

DYNAMICS OF HOSTAGE TAKING

First, hostage takers should be viewed as people who have reached an acute level of frustration. Second, the taking of hostages should be viewed as an attempt at problem solving. Third, hostage takers in most cases see hostages as mere pawns in a larger game and use them as bargaining chips throughout the negotiation process. Finally, the taking of hostages is an attention-seeking behavior to attract an audience, for without an audience the hostage taking is meaningless (Schlossberg, 1980, pp. 113–114).

Dynamically, two general classifications of behavior may be observed in hostage takers: *instrumental* behavior and *expressive* behavior. Instrumental behavior has some recognizable goal the perpetrator seeks to have fulfilled. Those engaging in expressive behavior seek to display their power. Understanding the dynamics of the hostage taker is extremely important, because it is expressive (emotion based) as opposed to instrumental (material gain) that the human service worker is most likely to encounter. Hostage-taking acts that are more likely to result in injuries or fatalities are expressive in nature (Lipsedge & Littlewood, 1997).

Of the two, expressive acts are the more difficult to understand, for such action appears to the casual observer to be senseless. There would seem to be no way that the perpetrators can gain anything except their own or others' destruction (Miron & Goldstein, 1978, p. 10). However, as an expressive gesture, such action is extremely powerful and indicates to the world at large that the perpetrators are able for a short while to take matters and destiny into their own hands. These dynamics combine variously to generate a number of types of hostage takers that the human services worker is likely to encounter.

Types of Hostage Takers

If the negotiator can ferret out characteristics and identify the particular type of hostage taker being dealt with, then a valid triage assessment can be made and appropriate psychological and behavioral responses constructed. In general, with criminal types who are engaging in instrumental behavior, a rational, problem-solving approach that seeks a compromise in concrete terms is proposed. With psychotic or other emotionally disturbed nes who are engaging in expressive behavior, emphasis is on affective techniques that seek to promote affiliation and interdependence between the negotiator and the hostage taker (Donohue & Roberto, 1993). With terrorists who are "emotionally rational," a mix of the two basic techniques is probably best suited (Miron & Goldstein, 1978, pp. 96–97). We have omitted instrumental and instrumental/expressive hostage takers such as bank robbers and political terrorists from our discussion because of the unlikelihood of the worker's encountering these types. However, the true expressive types that the worker is likely to encounter are legion and are frequent recipients of human services.

The Mentally Disturbed

Mentally disturbed hostage takers suffer from various kinds of psychological maladies. A mentally disturbed person may or may not be in touch with reality. This individual will likely be a loner, acting in obedience to some intensely personal, often obscure impulse (Cooper, 1981, p. 57). This person may believe that taking hostages will carry out some sacred mission or prove that he or she can do something important (Fuselier, 1981a).

The ideal relationship with the mentally disturbed hostage taker is one in which affiliation and interdependence are high, because those factors lead to mutual trust. It is crucial that the negotiator attempt to establish a trusting relationship early on because research has found that once the tone of the relationship is established (high or low), it tends to stay that way for the duration of the negotiation. When negotiators establish low affiliation, the content of the perpetrator's messages is much more negative and therefore more dangerous (Donohue & Roberto, 1993).

Negotiators also need to establish a continuous state of interdependence between themselves and perpetrators, which is not easy given that perpetrators often undergo mercurial behavioral, cognitive, and affective shifts. Indeed, it may be tempting for negotiators to try to get their mentally disturbed hostage takers to start thinking more realistically about their problems by getting them to withdraw from the situation or nail down their goals to achieve crisis resolution. However, negotiators need to reject this need for closure and focus on directing and controlling affiliation so that positive affect and mutual liking for one another is developed. In so doing, negotiators can keep the perpetrator talking, gather intelligence, improve leverage, and move to more normative bargaining issues (Donohue & Roberto, 1993). There are four major diagnostic categories of mentally disturbed hostage takers that the negotiator is likely to encounter.

The Paranoid Schizophrenic Personality. Paranoid schizophrenics are out of touch with reality. They are easily recognized by their false system of beliefs and especially by their hallucinations or delusions. They often take hostages in order to carry out what they believe is a "master plan" or to obey "orders from some special person or deity" (Fuselier, 1981a). Paranoid schizophrenics are conflicted and have difficulty coping with even minimally stressful situations. They operate out of logic-tight mental compartments that may be extremely bizarre such as demanding the removal of all white people from the planet within 24 hours (Strentz, 1995, p. 142). This combination of frustration and conflict produces a tremendous amount of anxiety. Excessive anxiety tends to make such people extremely sensitive and volatile, particularly when they are off their medication and their hallucinations and delusions are very active.

Real time may be sped up or slowed down for the paranoid schizophrenic. Dissociation from reality is a hallmark of this type, and the negotiator must try to keep the dialogue at an even pace and keep the individual calm enough to stay in touch with the reality of the moment. Good negotiating strategy calls for reducing anxiety and at the same time attempting to create a problem-solving atmosphere (Maher, 1977, pp. 64–65). The best approach is to accept the paranoid schizophrenic's statements as true, although the negotiator should not agree with them. The negotiator should not try to convince the person that he or she is wrong (Fuselier, 1981a). Empathic understanding of the beliefs of the paranoid and reflection of the disturbed individual's feelings are appropriate responses.

HT (hostage taker): The radio messages keep coming, even though I've told these people to shut their radios off. They're driving me crazy!

Neg (negotiator): It must be really exasperating that they won't do what you tell them, particularly when all you want is peace and quiet.

The Depressive Personality. Hostage takers who are depressed seem incapacitated mentally and may not make clear demands (Strentz, 1995, p. 142). They are very confused, and identify themselves by their inability to make a firm decision. They may be characterized by having slow, subdued speech, a negative outlook on life, and demands intermingled with references to death. Their hostages are frequently persons known to them. Depressed people are very unpredictable and are extremely dangerous. Often they are suicidal and may take a hostage to force the police to shoot them (Strentz, 1984, p. 185).

In depressive cases, a problem-solving approach would most likely be futile. With the depressive, the negotiator must be firm and manipulative. Providing clear instructions (Slatkin, 1996) targeted at the depressive's indecision may cause mobility to occur.

HT: I just don't know what to do, it's just a mess.

Neg: The mess will just get worse if you keep putting yourself deeper in this hole. Send the children out, and we'll talk about you and the mess you're in.

If the individual is suicidal, the negotiator needs to extract a commitment, no matter how tenuous, to keep the person from acting out a threat, and if possible change the subject to get the person's mind off the actions he or she is about to take. In the following dialogue, the negotiator attempts to shift the hostage taker's focus away from suicidal ideation and onto more effective communication. Negotiations in this case involve applying in a very paced way the intervention procedures described in the chapter on suicide.

HT: I wonder if you'd see that the picture albums get to the kids?

Neg: I'd be willing to help in any way I can, but I want you to agree to not do anything until we get all these other issues settled.

One indication that the hostage taker may be suicidal is the use of hostages to conduct the negotiations. Although getting information from the hostages is a plus, the refusal of the hostage taker to personally negotiate is a bad sign and has a high possibility of ending in violence (Strentz, 1995, p. 142).

Hostage: This is Molly Higgins, I'm a secretary here. He says he doesn't want to talk, that I'm to do his talking.

Neg: Thanks for getting on the line, Molly. If you could tell me who else is there and how they are, I'd appreciate it, if it's OK with Jeb. But I really need to talk to Jeb. So would you tell him to get back on the line so I can tell him that.

The Inadequate Personality. The inadequate personality usually displays a good deal of narcissistic, attention-seeking behavior. Often this person has attempted a crime and has been caught in the process. Because the hostage-taking incident may be the high point of the person's life, the inadequate personality tends to stretch the situation for all it is worth. Identified by key phrases such as "I'll show them who's boss" and "Now they'll see what I can do," this hostage taker basks in the limelight of the situation. Such pronouncements are indicative of a low self-image. Therefore, the motivation for taking hostages may be to prove that the inadequate type can succeed at something. Yet in the same instance, inadequate types may appear contrite and apologetic for their behavior. Initially, the inadequate personality type may state demands with considerable conviction and then turn around and provide the negotiator with several options (Strentz, 1984, p. 185). Negotiators need to be aware of and seize those options.

The primary strategy of the negotiator is to present problem-solving alternatives so that the hostage taker will not feel that he or she has "failed again." Playing up to this hostage taker's ego and helping the person find a face-saving alternative is an excellent tactic. Inadequate personalities have a need to prove themselves to some "significant" others. The "I'll show them" statements indicate this need, and they may murder the hostages if their egos are not handled with extreme care.

HT: I want a personal interview with the news director of Channel 3 right now. I've got some things I want to say. You do that and I'll let them go.

Neg: I understand how important it is to you to get on television. You let those people go now, and I'll see that you get on the 10 o'clock news.

Reinforcement (Slatkin, 1996) also boosts the inadequate personality's image and sets the stage for compliance.

Neg: So you made it through Parchman Prison for seven years. It takes a smart guy to do that. My bet is you'll be just as smart here and make the exchange for the food.

The Antisocial Personality. The antisocial personality repeatedly comes into conflict with society and is incapable of having significant loyalty to individuals, groups, or social values. Antisocial types tend to blame others and offer rationalizations for their behavior (American Psychiatric Association, 1994). The antisocial type is likely to dehumanize the hostages and should be considered extremely dangerous to them because the person will manifest little feeling for their well-being. Although antisocial personalities have not internalized moral values, they do understand their effect on others and are therefore potent adversaries. While antisocials lack emotional depth, they may display a wide range of skillful emotional overlays in place of true emotional responses (Lanceley, 1981, pp. 31–32).

The only concern of these hostage takers is for themselves. Therefore, the negotiator should be aware that this type has no compunction about doing anything to anybody. If at any point this hostage taker decides that hostages are a burden, they will be killed.

HT: Don't give me that crap about "more time." You get that car in here or I start doing some fun things to this little 6-year-old, and her mommy gets to watch.

Neg: I know you're mad about the car, but you know I gotta go through procedures. I understand you could work the kid over, but I wonder if you've thought about the good that'll do you in the long run. It's your hide you're dealing with, too! So let's work on that side of it.

The profound egocentricity of the antisocial type requires constant stimulation. Again, reinforcement (Slatkin, 1996), along with confrontation about negative consequences can induce the antisocial type to become more reasonable. A primary objective in the negotiation process is to keep the holder's attention and avoid having him or her turn attention to the hostages as a source of stimulus.

Neg: You're the man here. You're the one calling the shots. We both know that chance brought the security cop back and except for that you'd be outta here. I gotta hand it to you, it was a great plan. So use your smarts here too. You and I can work a deal.

This person is not only streetwise but also policewise, so trickery is not a good idea. Also, the negotiator should avoid references to jail or hospitalization, because antisocial types are likely to become highly agitated if they believe they are going to lose their freedom or it is insinuated that they are crazy.

The Estranged Person.   Invariably the estranged hostage taker will know the hostage, who will probably be a spouse, a lover, or his or her children. The estranged hostage taker is experiencing a breakdown in his or her interpersonal relationships. These breakdowns lead to domestic quarrels and, in turn, the escalating nature of the quarrels and the feared loss of the significant other lead the estranged person to take the hostage. (Alcohol often provides the liquid courage necessary to carry out the taking.) The estranged hostage taker seeks to coerce the maintenance of the relationship through force. The most distinctive feature of this kind of hostage taking is its intensely personal nature and the unique purpose of the hostage taker in attempting continued domination over the significant other (Cooper, 1981, pp. 27–28).

As in any other domestic dispute, the negotiator should be extremely careful of this volatile situation and use empathic listening and responding skills to their fullest. Empathic responding (Slatkin, 1996) that reflects the hurt and despair of the estranged person's feelings demonstrates concern and caring.

Neg: Things really seem to have come unraveled even after you tried your damnedest. It really hurts that she doesn't appreciate what you've done for the family.

Self-disclosure of like problems (Slatkin, 1996) may be a way of creating a bond with the estranged person who is looking for a sympathetic shoulder to cry on.

Neg: I haven't had it as bad as you, but I sure do know about working two jobs to make ends meet and then coming home to a cold shoulder, a cold dinner, and a cold bed. So I do know how it feels.

With this type, the negotiator must contend with the highly personal nature of the hostage taking and the continued denial of reality. Intrinsic to intervention is the negotiator's ability to keep denial from turning into despair. The key to resolution is that the estranged hostage taker needs to be shown a graceful way out (Cooper, 1981, p. 28).

HT: It's not my fault. I've done everything she asked, and then she still jilted me. If I can't have her, nobody will.

Neg: She really hurt you, then. I can start to see why you feel you had to do this. I'm wondering, though, if she can't see now just how strongly you feel. Perhaps you've made your point to her. You certainly have to me!

The Institutionalized Individual.   Institutionalized hostage takers are inmates who have a grievance, usually about conditions within the system in which they are confined. The only other reason for taking hostages is to obtain a passport to freedom. Hostage takings of this sort are usually deemed instrumental acts planned to produce concrete changes in the institution (Maher, 1977, p. 65). However, an institutional hostage situation invariably also involves expressive elements, and there may be more than one spokesperson among the perpetrators. Therefore, it is extremely important for the negotiator to initiate a dialogue that seeks an empathic understanding of the hostage takers, balanced with focusing on their demands. Because such individuals are very wise in the ways of institutional and law enforcement policy, the negotiator needs to be very careful about attempting to manipulate or trick the perpetrators.

HT: Go to hell! We want to see the warden, and we want these 25 demands met, and they ain't negotiable!
Neg: I understand you're pissed that he wouldn't listen to you. I'll certainly convey your message to him, but before I do I want to know that the hostages are all right.
HT: Kiss off! You ain't gettin' nuthin'.
Neg: Look! You know how the game goes. You want something, they want something. So let's get going and see if we can't get what you want.

The Wronged Person.   The wronged hostage taker is dissatisfied or aggrieved by the system at large or a particular bureaucracy. Wronged individuals may be identified by the "crosses" they bear and the paranoia associated with their beliefs. These hostage takers feel so grossly discriminated against by the "establishment" that they seek to remake society to their own satisfaction (Cooper, 1981, p. 10).

Aggrieved or wronged individuals are high on the list of potential candidates with whom the human services worker may become involved—if not as a negotiator, then as being taken hostage. Aggrieved people feel that no one in a position of responsibility will willingly redress the terrible wrongs that have been done to them. After exhausting a variety of acceptable options within the system and still receiving no redress, such people may do something dramatic (Turner, 1984, p. 178).

The wronged individual needs a chance to ventilate his or her feelings to an empathic and sympathetic listener. Summary restatement and reflection (Slatkin, 1996) allow the negotiator to convey to the wronged individual how deeply understood he or she is, that for once, somebody in authority is listening.

HT: The doctors, nurses, the administrators, the psychologists, the social workers, they're all at fault. She wouldn't have died if they'd done their job. Everybody thinks this is such a hot-shot hospital. It's really Murder Incorporated, and people need to know the truth. They killed my wife. She was everything to me. I'm lost without her.
Neg: So what you're saying is that the hospital up and down the line couldn't have screwed things up worse. And in screwing them up they lost your wife. She was the center of your world, and now your world is gone. It really sounds as if the hurt

and anger goes bone deep, and the frustration you've felt make this the only way you can get some respect and command their attention.

Associated with this type of hostage taking is the high priority attached to publicity, because the hostage taker is usually motivated to make the public aware of the wrongs imposed by the particular authorities in question. Proper involvement of the media can enhance the opportunity for the releasing the hostages, if the hostage taker perceives that a wrong can be made right by a public airing (Gladis, 1979).

Neg: I realize what a terrible shock her death was, and how you trusted all those people. Yet you believe they let you down and should be exposed for the incompetent blunders they've made. Would you be willing to make a deal? If I can set it up so you can read that statement you've prepared about the hospital, will you let those people out?

The Religious Fanatic.   Religious fanatics have the same inflexible and uncompromising attitude in their beliefs that political terrorists do. But unlike political terrorists, religious fanatics do not usually take hostages for offensive purposes. Rather, they see hostages as sacrificial lambs who must be made to pay for the "sins" of the unrepentant. The taking of the American embassy in Iran in 1979 is a classic example of this situation. The hostage takers are unwilling to talk with those who are in a position to negotiate because the hostage takers are not in the business of negotiation. What they are in the business of is atonement. Therefore, their demands are such that they are invariably impossible to meet—at least for a considerable time into the future.

Because religious zealots do not consider themselves accountable to anyone except their own deity, negotiations with them are very difficult and invariably call for outside help by someone whose nationality, religion, or some other attribute does not cast them in the "devil" category (Maher, 1977, p. viii). Hostages are subject to the religious and moral whims of such fanatics and may expect a long, arduous, and dangerous experience. Thus the religious fanatic who is a hostage taker poses a particular problem to the negotiation process, because such an individual must either die for the cause or relinquish it (Cooper, 1981, p. 45). In nearly every case of hostage taking by a religious fanatic, some sort of face-saving gesture is required to resolve the situation (Cooper, 1976, p. 104).

HT: This is God's will. If I let you pack me off to jail like a common thief, no one will believe in our holy cause.

Neg: What if we consider setting a low bond, maybe even self-recognizance? That way you wouldn't have to go to jail, and both your honor and your cause would be untarnished.

Stages and Dynamics of a Hostage Situation

Throughout the entire hostage episode, emotions of both parties move on a curve that oscillates between desperation and euphoria. As the episode is protracted, the cycle tends to dampen and retreat from both emotional extremes (Schreiber, 1978, p. 50). It is within this context that the following stages should be examined. There are four stages to a hostage situation: alarm, crisis, accommodation, and resolution (Strentz, 1984, pp. 189–194; 1995, pp. 137–146).

Alarm.   The alarm stage is the most traumatic and dangerous and typically lasts about an hour. Whatever the type of hostage takers, in this first stage their emotions are running exceedingly high, their reason may be diminished, and they may be extremely aggressive in their reaction to any perceived threat. To force their will on the hostages, the hostage takers' general belief is that hostages must be terrorized into submission. Therefore, hostage takers may be inclined to harass, abuse, or even kill anyone who seems to be interfering with their attempts to consolidate their position (Strentz, 1984, p. 190).

For the unprepared individual who suddenly becomes a hostage, the alarm stage is traumatic in every aspect. A previously tranquil situation now becomes a life-and-death one that pivots every minute. For the victim, defenseless and confused, the nightmarish experience takes on an unreal aspect. Many begin to deny the reality of the situation, particularly when people from whom they expect help seem to be doing nothing.

The hostage taker becomes the most important person in the life of the victim, and over time his or her actions shape the victim's psychology. The accounts of battered women, abused children, and coerced prostitutes bear an uncanny resemblance to those of hostages, concentration camp survivors, and political prisoners (Herman, 1995, p. 92). From that standpoint, the behavioral dynamics during and after their escape or release for these groups tend to run parallel.

Effective coping at this early stage means immediately putting into place a strong will to survive and not succumbing to panic. It is at this stage that most injuries occur (Strentz, 1995, p. 137). Any sign of panic may cause the perpetrators to overreact to a highly charged situation and may dramatically diminish the chances of survival (Strentz, 1984, p. 196).

Crisis.   The crisis stage marks the beginning of reason for the hostage takers. However, there is still a great deal of unpredictability and danger as they try to consolidate their position. Initial attempts at negotiation at this stage may be marked by outrageous demands and emotional diatribes by the hostage holders. Because they fear assault by the authorities, hostage takers may move hostages to a more secure area or enlist their cooperation in making the area they are in more secure (Strentz, 1984, p. 191). The hostage taker is put at center stage and is tasked with decision making. Although this may seem surprising, there are two reasons why this is done. First, the act of making constant decisions in a stressful situation is extremely fatiguing and wears the hostage taker down. Second, the hostage taker's need for an audience gives him or her a chance to be put in the limelight and focuses attention on the taker and not the hostages (Strentz, 1995, pp. 139–140).

For the hostage, the crisis stage is the most critical because it sets the tone for the remainder of the situation. Hostage–captor interaction at this stage can either enhance or reduce hostages' chances of survival. Although denial by hostages may still be in place as a defense mechanism, the decision to face reality and engage in normal behavior generally provides some emotional relief and mental escape (Strentz, 1984, p. 203). Hostages who are in positions of responsibility must be very careful not to intimidate their captors. If their captors feel inferior, they may see defiance as the hostage's attempt to humiliate them. In particular, verbal humiliation precipitates violence (p. 203).

Fear is also increased by unpredictable outbursts of violence and by inconsistent enforcement of numerous trivial demands and petty rules. But violence is not the only way the hostage taker gains control over a hostage. The capricious granting of small indulgences may undermine the victim's psychological resistance far more effectively than unremitting deprivation and fear (Herman, 1995, pp. 92–93). There is little difference in these dynamics between the hostage taker and a pimp who controls his prostitutes.

In addition to inducing terror, the perpetrator seeks to destroy the victim's sense of autonomy. Deprivation of food, sleep, shelter, exercise, personal hygiene, or privacy are common practices (Herman, 1995, pp. 92–93). These same deprivation tactics are certainly understood and employed by batterers and child abusers.

At this stage, hostages may start to experience three problems: isolation, claustrophobia, and/or the loss of a sense of time. People who are isolated have to come to grips with the fact that the only human contacts they have may be extremely hostile toward them. Claustrophobia can take its toll even if the individual is not isolated and confined to a small cell. And losing a sense of time becomes a very important problem. By this stage, captors have usually removed personal items, including watches, from the hostages. Sense of time becomes very important to someone held captive who is hoping for rescue. Asking for such small favors as information about time or date puts hostages completely at the mercy of their captors. Hostage takers use such requests to good advantage in earning compliance from their captives (Herman, 1995, p. 93; Strentz, 1984, p. 197). The message is "We can do with you what we want. There is no hope other than what we give you!"

Accommodation.   The accommodation stage is the longest and most tranquil. Constantly assessing the mental status of the hostage taker clarifies his or her personality and typology (Strentz, 1995, p. 143). For the hostage, the accommodation stage is marked by time dragging by. Boredom, punctuated only by moments of terror, is the hallmark of this stage. The crests and troughs of emotions that have occurred until this point are likely to induce fatigue in both hostage and hostage taker.

With increased control by their captors, hostages suffer from a constriction of initiative and planning. The hostage no longer thinks of how to escape but rather of how to stay alive. With prolonged captivity, constriction becomes habitual. Thus chronically traumatized people are often characterized as passive or helpless, which certainly lends credence to Walker's (1984) theory of learned helplessness in battered women who are held captive by their abusive mates (Herman, 1995, p. 93). If this stage becomes protracted, then there is a likelihood that the Stockholm syndrome, named after an aborted bank holdup in Sweden during which one of the hostages fell in love with her captor, will come into operation (Strentz, 1984, p. 198).

The Stockholm syndrome is possible if three conditions are met: extended period of time, not being isolated from one's captor, and positive contact between captor and captives (Fuselier, 1981b). The phenomenon comprises the three following elements (Strentz, 1984, p. 198):

1. Positive feelings are generated toward the hostage taker by the hostages.
2. Negative feelings are generated toward the authorities by the hostages.
3. Positive feelings are generated toward the hostages by their captors.

Whether the victim is part of a religious cult, a child who has been physically abused by a parent, a political terrorist's hostage, or a customer caught in a bank holdup, the potential for such traumatic bonding is strikingly similar.

Evidence seems to support the idea that the Stockholm syndrome is not a well-gauged ploy by the hostage to ensure survival. The phenomenon is probably an automatic, unconscious emotional response to the trauma of being taken hostage (Strentz, 1979, p. 2). It seems that as people are thrown together, both captor and captive start to respond to one another on more personal terms. If this occurs, it becomes very hard to regard one another as faceless entities to be despised and used. Familiarity with each other provides a fertile ground for identification with the other's problems, hopes, fears, and outlook on life. If such positive identification by a hostage is reciprocated by the holder, the hostage's chances of survival increase considerably (Ochberg, 1977). During this stage, it is not uncommon for hostages to believe that the authorities are the chief cause of the problem and that if the authorities would only go home the siege would end (Strentz, 1984, p. 200).

Auerbach, Kiesler, Strentz, and Schmidt (1994) used simulated hostage role plays and determined that captives who found their captors most aversive were those who perceived the "terrorists" as most dominant and least friendly. Those "hostages" who had received training in emotion- versus problem-focused coping perceived their "captors" as less threatening and were perceived by the "terrorists" in the same way.

The hostage can make use of this phenomenon. In as genuine a way as possible, the hostage should seek to build a positive relationship with his or her captors. The easiest way to do this is to be as real a person as possible by attempting to share the more personal aspects of one's life and to elicit the same from the holders. If hostages make attempts to gain familiarity with the hostage takers, they would probably be wise to avoid political discussions with them, because such discussions accentuate differences between captor and captive (Miron & Goldstein, 1978, p. 92).

A captive who is a well-integrated individual may boost hostage morale by exploiting perceived weaknesses in the captors, although this ploy is extremely dangerous if it backfires. The approach takes strength of character and is not generally recommended unless captives are isolated for a long period of time with only their own resources on which to fall back. In a protracted situation, hostages must take care of their physical needs. Eating and exercising are musts. Hostages should take whatever food is offered. Even if it is possible to do only flexibility exercises, hostages should do them regularly (Strentz, 1984, p. 204).

Resolution. In the resolution stage, the hostage takers have become fatigued as the long hours or days take their toll. The high expectations that they held early become dashed as they find they have lost most of the bargaining chips. Whether there is a positive or negative resolution to the situation now depends on the ability of the negotiator to skillfully bring closure to the situation (Strentz, 1984, p. 193).

In particular, it is important to understand the difference between the behavior of a hostage taker who is planning to surrender and one who is planning to commit suicide (see the chapter on suicide for clues indicating that the hostage taker is also suicidal). Inadequate personality types are a high risk for suicide. They may see surrender as just another in a long list of failures, whereas suicide may seem a positive solution. The problem with suicide is that the hostage taker may not have enough courage to accomplish the act on his or her own. To force the issue, the hostage taker may engage the police by failing to heed their instructions, firing at them, or firing at a hostage (Strentz, 1984, pp. 193–194). If the hostage taker gives any clues at all during this final stage, the negotiator should be prepared to move immediately into a suicide prevention mode. Whatever the type, and however long and arduous the incident, the trained negotiator takes a purposeful and dignified approach to the perpetrator's surrender.

INTERVENTION STRATEGIES

Because hostage takings epitomize crisis conditions, the hostage negotiator is very much like an eclectic counselor who must have a variety of techniques to fit different and constantly changing situations. The only difference is that the negotiator is dealing with a victimizer rather than the victim, and the main object of the negotiator's attention is invariably holding a weapon.

The six-step crisis intervention model provides the nucleus of the concepts and skills negotiators need to successfully intervene in hostage crises. Assessing the motives and emotional status of the hostage taker is an extremely important and delicate task, because people's lives are generally at stake. Negotiators must be competent in listening and relationship skills because the hostage taker cannot be tested or evaluated in any normal way during the period of the emergency.

Triage assessment is especially difficult in these circumstances. Often the negotiator has no way of knowing, other than by information that can be obtained verbally, what might be motivating the captor to take such extreme measures. Even then, the negotiator may have to make a determination based only on a verbal assessment taken over the telephone. A compounding problem is that the negotiator must determine a great deal of personal information beyond the current mental status of the perpetrator, including the expertise to carry out threats. At best, much of this information will be obtained from secondhand sources such as friends or relatives, who may provide a very biased picture of the captor. Worse, this entire scenario may take place with a great deal of noise, confusion, and a crowd and the media present. Understanding and assessing the degree of mobility/immobility the hostage taker feels is of particular importance, because the negotiator needs to decide how directive, collaborative, or nondirective to be. Examining alternatives available is critical to the outcome of the negotiation. The negotiator will want to get the hostage taker to consider options other than killing the hostages.

The following intervention procedures are universally recognized by hostage negotiation teams and can be considered constants in the negotiating process. Yet each hostage situation is unique, and resolution cannot be reduced to any formula that works for all cases. Therefore, the successful negotiator, like other crisis interventionists, is creative but follows a standard procedure, takes risks but proceeds with caution, has empathy but believes in justice, and has patience but moves decisively.

Communication Techniques

Throughout the negotiations, the basic listening and responding skills critical to any crisis situation are employed. First and foremost is the primary step of problem definition. Very clear problem definition is crucial to learning what the motives and concerns of the hostage taker are. Use of active listening through clarification and paraphrasing of content, reflection of feelings and summary restatement, and open ended questions and leads are important in letting the hostage taker ventilate feelings (Slatkin, 1996). This process also allows assessment of the emotional state and mental condition of the hostage taker (Strentz, 1995, p. 136).

The focus is on the person who most wants and needs to be the center of attention—the hostage taker. The hostage taker is encouraged to tell his or her story in as much detail as he or she needs to do (Strentz, 1995, p. 138). Owning or "I" statements of self-disclosure, immediacy and reinforcement (Slatkin, 1996) are used to make a bond between the hostage taker and the negotiator. In all hostage situations, the initial operating mode between the hostage taker and the negotiator is one of collaboration, wherein the negotiator appears to act as the bargaining agent between the hostage taker and the authorities. Although the hostages themselves want immediate resolution of the crisis, it is crucial to stretch the time out, wearing down the hostage taker to a point of fatigue (Strentz, 1995, p. 140). As a result, the standard refrain of the negotiator is "I'm concerned about your problems, and I want you to know I'm going to take all the time that's necessary to understand your concerns." Therefore, letting the hostage taker ventilate for as long as he or she wants may be considered a positive outcome because of time consumed.

Action responses (Slatkin, 1996) such as asking closed questions, confronting, interpreting, and giving information and instructions are used throughout the process in ensuring safety, establishing a support system, examining alternatives, generating a plan for resolution of the event and extracting a commitment from the hostage taker. Toward the end of the hostage situation, the negotiator will most likely move from a collaborative to a more directive operating mode. Directive statements that are designed to elicit commitment and move the hostage taker toward giving up, but also allow him or her to appear in control and save face, are used extensively.

Containing the Scene

As in all other law enforcement operations, safety is the foremost consideration. In a hostage situation, inner and outer perimeters are secured around the hostage scene and a command post is established in the inner perimeter. SWAT (special weapons and tactics) teams and other emergency units are put in place. Situation boards (Duffy, 1997) will be set up that list all the critical components in the hostage taking, such as perpetrator profile; number, type, and names of hostages; weapons and expertise of use; issues to avoid; actions taken or not taken; diagrams of the site; plans of delivery; and so on. Although it may appear to the hostages that the authorities are confused and disorganized and are letting their lives run out through the sands of an hourglass, that is not the case at all. Containing and stabilizing the scene prevents the scope of the event from expanding (Schlossberg, 1980).

Gathering Information

The most important information the negotiator needs to know, as quickly as possible, is who the hostage taker is, to obtain a profile. Who are his or her close friends, family, relatives? What kind of criminal record? Is there a psychiatric record? Is he or she currently obtaining professional help? Is the professional available? What kinds of specialized skills does the hostage taker have? What does the person know about weapons, explosives, electronics? Can the person fly, drive, operate special equipment? Does the hostage taker belong to a religious order? a sect? a gang? What are the individual's deviations? sexual preferences? Does the person use drugs, alcohol? What are his or her immediate problems—money? love life? parole problems? addiction? All these pieces make up the puzzle of who the hostage taker is and will perhaps give the negotiator a clue to a positive solution (Miron & Goldstein, 1978, pp. 92–93).

The next piece of information to be determined is just who the hostages are. Are there really hostages? If so, how many, how old, and what sex are they? What is their current emotional state? Are they intelligent? Do they have potential for aggression? Does anybody need medical assistance or have special requirements? Are they related to their captor or complete strangers (Miron & Goldstein, 1978, p. 93)?

The last piece of initial information needed concerns the hostage site itself. What are safe observation positions? What are the safest approach and escape routes? Are there telephones or other means of communication present? What amount of space, number of rooms, obstacles, ventilation, and so on, compose the site? What is the access to food, water, toilet facilities? Depending on the situation, collecting this information may be accomplished quickly or take an extended period of time, but gaining this information is critical to prevent injury or loss of life.

Stabilizing the Situation

The initial tasks of the negotiator are to contain and stabilize the situation (Miron & Goldstein, 1978, p. 95). These initial minutes are the most critical for the hostages, and what the negotiating team does now will determine whether the situation is safely resolved (Turner, 1984, pp. 179–180). The negotiator's first goals are to calm the perpetrator and build rapport with him or her (Miron & Goldstein, 1978, p. 95). A low-key counseling approach that emphasizes reflective listening skills, letting the hostage taker know that the negotiator understands how strongly he or she feels, is an excellent opening strategy (Donohue & Roberto, 1993).

Neg: From what you're saying, you really feel angry at them. I understand how frustrated you are at the housing authority folks. It's as if they haven't heard a thing you've been saying.

It is important that the negotiator stay calm, especially during these opening gambits (Schreiber, 1978, p. 103). By tone of voice, choice of words, facial expression, and gestures, the negotiator models a calmness that will, one hopes, transfer itself to the hostage taker. Reassurance is part of the attempt to keep the situation tranquil (Miron & Goldstein, 1978, p. 97).

Neg: (*Sits down, takes off coat, pulls out a stick of gum, but not in the same room or within reach of the hostage taker.*) It doesn't seem like we're going anyplace for a while, so just take your time and tell me what it is you want. I'm sure we can reach a mutually agreeable solution.

The negotiator needs to allow the hostage taker the opportunity to ventilate feelings (Miron & Goldstein, 1978, p. 98). Ventilating provides a number of positive outcomes. The perpetrator's continued talking permits the negotiator to identify the person's mental state and personal problems and to assess the general atmosphere of the situation (Maher, 1977, p. 36). It is also very difficult for the hostage taker to re-

main emotionally charged and at the same time present lengthy discourses and answer questions about his or her problems to the negotiator (Miron & Goldstein, 1978, p. 98). One of the best ways to keep the perpetrator engaged is to ask open-ended questions.

Neg: I'm not sure I understand what you're really peeved about. How would you like them to set up the tenant grievance procedure with the housing authority? What would you see your role as being in that?

At the same time, the negotiator must be careful not to intrude into the hostage taker's psychological space (Maher, 1977, p. 36). Interpretive statements about the causal dynamics that motivate the hostage taker may generate hostility and increased agitation. To suggest that some personal inadequacy is at the root of the hostage taker's problem is unwise. The following type of statement is *not* suggested.

Neg: So it's really going way back to those inadequate feelings you had as a child. Your mother and father always put you down, so now you're really trying to show them how potent you are, when in fact you really know that it isn't so.

Under no circumstances should the negotiator try to provoke the hostage taker. Arguing, demeaning remarks; outright rejection of demands; and sudden surprises have no place in the dialogue. Any signs of increased agitation or aggression in the hostage taker should be monitored carefully. Disjointed and speeded-up speech, flared nostrils, flushed checks, restlessness, pounding or shaking of fists, and so on, are all indicators that the negotiator needs to cool the situation down. One of the best ways to accomplish this is to distract the hostage taker by asking questions totally irrelevant to the situation or suggesting something contrary to what the perpetrator thinks the authorities might want (Miron & Goldstein, 1978, pp. 98–99).

Neg: You said you were interested in pro basketball and the Knicks in particular. Think they've got a chance against the Celtics tonight?

. . .

Neg: Well, if you think we're all infidel, godless swine, I guess that's your right. If you feel like you've got to let people know about your feelings, then maybe you ought to go on the radio. (*The negotiator and the media have previously worked out the conditions under which this would happen.*)

By trying to see the problem through the hostage taker's eyes, the negotiator tries to build rapport with the perpetrator. Using owning or "I" statements is one way the negotiator can establish a relationship with the hostage taker. Genuine and noncontrived self-disclosure about the negotiator's own life as it seems to apply to the conversation is a useful way of establishing the relationship and instigating reciprocal disclosure on the part of the hostage taker (Maher, 1977, p. 41).

Neg: I can sure understand that. I put in long hours, do good work, and still catch hell from the boss even though somebody else screwed up the job. It sure seems like the department isn't very damn grateful for all the effort I put out. Is that about the way you feel about your job?

Pacing the dialogue in a slow and purposeful manner is a key component in the negotiations and works in favor of the authorities. Although hostages may become depressed and question the handling of the situation as time drags by, delay is to their benefit. By not rushing, the negotiator allows the relationship to develop. Also, time wears down the hostage taker's resources faster than it does those of the authorities. Lack of sleep, hunger, thirst, and unrelenting tension focus the hostage taker on the calm reasonableness of the negotiator and aid and abet the problem-solving process (Maher, 1977, p. 13; Miron & Goldstein, 1978, p. 99).

Neg: (*Eleven hours into negotiations.*) Man! I'm getting tired. Gonna get a cup of coffee and pump some caffeine in my body. How about taking a break off the heavy stuff and just talk some basketball for a while? Maybe if you want some coffee we could talk about that. (*The coffee will have some strings attached.*)

Finally, a good negotiator, like a good therapist, is excellent at restating the hostage taker's ideas back to him. This technique serves to clarify both to the hostage taker and to the negotiator what is really being said. It also builds rapport with the hostage taker because he or she is assured of being listened to very carefully. The hostage taker's words mean something and count for something with the negotiator (Miron & Goldstein, 1978, p. 102).

Neg: OK! Let me see if I understand you correctly. You want to read your manifesto over the radio, but you're worried that they'll ask you some questions you don't want to answer right now. You're also concerned that they'll try to keep your attention diverted so we can pull something on you. Is that about it?

Persuading the Hostage Taker to Give Up

The ultimate mission of the negotiator is to persuade the hostage taker to give up without harming anyone. There are a number of guidelines to which the negotiator should adhere in accomplishing this task. Persuasion should start with agreement with some of the perpetrator's ideas. Agreement in principle tends to soften the hostage taker's resistance to later negotiations (Miron & Goldstein, 1978, p. 103).

Neg: I agree with you. The scandalous conditions in public housing need to be aired, and you've done your research well.

The negotiator should start by negotiating smaller issues first, such as foodstuffs, medicine, cigarettes, and ways of communicating (Miron & Goldstein, 1978, p. 103). However, the negotiator should make it clear from the start that the hostage taker gets nothing without giving something in return (Maher, 1977, p. 13).

Neg: I'll see about getting the lights turned back on, but I want some indication that the people are all right.

The less attention paid to the hostages in the dialogue, the better. Continuous reference to hostages may exaggerate the hostage taker's sense of importance, turn his or her attention obsessively to them, and steer the dialogue away from resolution (Maher, 1977, p. 12).

Neg: Yes. I understand you'll start shooting one every 30 minutes if we don't comply with your demands, but what I'm not clear about is how you particularly want the transportation provided.

There is one exception to this rule, and that is an attempt by the negotiator to foster the Stockholm syndrome. Any action the negotiator can instigate to emphasize the human qualities of the hostages to the hostage taker should be considered. Most people have difficulty inflicting pain on another unless the victim remains dehumanized (Strentz, 1979, p. 10). Thus, flag words such "hostage" should never be used (Fuselier, 1981b). The negotiator should attempt to make the captives appear as human as possible.

Neg: I wonder if you could check on Mr. Smith and see how he's feeling. We understand from his wife that he has a heart problem. Also as a good-faith gesture, we'd like you to let Mrs. Jones speak to her children. They don't have a father, and they're pretty scared.

If at all possible, the negotiator should try to convince the hostage takers that their hostages are actually useless (Schreiber, 1978, p. 111). At points like this, closed questions are better than open-ended ones because they force yes-or-no answers and do not allow for a lot of philosophizing or emotional diatribe (Miron & Goldstein, 1978, p. 101).

Neg: How in the world are you going to make your escape with all those people, anyway? Seems to me like the old folks and kids are just going to slow you down. Do you agree?

At some point in the negotiations there comes a time when the most powerful argument can be made to the most telling effect (Schreiber, 1978, p. 112). When that time comes, the negotiator must clearly and with conviction not only state what the facts are, but also give his or her conclusions (Miron & Goldstein, 1978, p. 103). Some things absolutely cannot be negotiated: firearms, exchange of hostages, and, most generally, drugs (Maher, 1977, p. 67). If drugs are part of the negotiation package, the effects should carefully be evaluated by a physician before they are ever made a bargaining tool (Maher, 1977, p. 39).

Neg: As a total package you've got to realize that it's unacceptable. The guns are not acceptable, for instance. Think about it! The rest of the package is a good one and we can make a deal on it.

Under most circumstances, friends, relatives, family, clergy, and other associates should not be brought to the scene. This is particularly true if the hostage taker asks for them, because he or she may want to kill them. If people such as these could help, the perpetrator would probably not be in this situation in the first place. If bringing such people to the scene becomes an absolute must, then the negotiator also needs to know clearly what their feelings are and needs to be close enough that he or she can hear what's going on (Maher, 1977, pp. 14–15, 67).

Neg: If we brought your wife down here, how could she help?

The negotiator should argue both sides of any point. By presenting both sides, the negotiator is more likely to be taken seriously by the perpetrator. Furthermore, the negotiator should argue against one or more unimportant aspects of the authorities' position as a way of showing how fair and open-minded the negotiator is (Miron & Goldstein, 1978, p. 104).

Neg: I can understand why you don't like having the area outside the building dark. I know it makes you nervous when you can't see what's going on. However, think about it from our side. The cops are just as nervous as you. What's to keep you from taking a shot at them if they're silhouetted? By the way, that letter you quoted to me that you want to read to the housing authority sounds pretty good. I can't see why the mayor is taking such a hard line in not letting you read it to the media.

A combination of delaying compliance, minimizing counterarguments, and promoting active listening with the perpetrator are excellent techniques when negotiations get down to the finish. In delaying compliance, the negotiator proposes that the perpetrator not make up his or her mind immediately, think it over, and see whether he or she will not see it the negotiator's way at some future point. Immediately, the negotiator should follow up by offering weakened counterarguments to the proposition. Such counterarguments compromise and weaken the captor's own arguments. Finally, passive listening does little for the problem-solving process. Active listening should be used. The perpetrator should be asked to think about his or her position and what the consequences might be (Miron & Goldstein, 1978, pp. 103–104).

Neg: You've heard what the offer is. I know it's not everything you wanted. I know that reading that letter to the media is nonnegotiable, but what if I could get them to guarantee it right after you give up? The TV crews are all here, and I don't think the city administration could get away with just hustling you off. I believe I could get authorization for you to do that. Think about it for a while. There's no rush.

Although it may seem irrational to do so, the negotiator should agree reluctantly with demands that may in reality benefit the authorities' position because these points may then be used to garner further concessions down the road (Miron & Goldstein, 1978, p. 106).

Neg: OK. If you really want a car instead of a bus, we'll see what we can do, but I don't think my boss is gonna like it. (*The situation is beneficial because fewer hostages have the possibility of being moved.*)

The negotiator should refrain from making suggestions unless absolutely necessary. This tactic keeps the hostage taker in a decision-making process (Fuselier, 1981b). The perpetrator is then the one who has to make movement. Offering suggestions may also speed up time factors, which may not be advantageous to the negotiator (Miron & Goldstein, 1978, pp. 106–107).

Neg: You're the guy who's in control. You'll have to decide what to come back with. I'm just the go-between.

Two positions the negotiator must take that may seem in opposition to the goal are keeping the hostage taker's hopes alive and realizing that the hostage taker may have to be allowed to escape. The perpetrator must feel, up until the time that all hostages are released, that he or she has not undertaken the seizure in vain and that there is some hope of escape. One way of sustaining this assurance is by continuously reinforcing the hostage taker every time he or she gives in on a point (Miron & Goldstein, 1978, pp. 105–107).

Neg: Personally, I really respect you for letting the old people and children go. I know that wasn't easy, but you did get agreement on your transfer conditions to the airport.

. . .

Neg: All right! We're agreed. The Barangan government has agreed to give you asylum and has provided the plane to take you to their country. As soon as you step inside the Baranga National Airliner, the last hostage at the foot of the ladder walks away. You clearly understand that if anything bad happens to that last hostage, that airliner, no matter who's on it, does not leave the airport.

Negotiating in a Hostage Situation: The Case of James

The scene is the diagnostic unit of a large penitentiary. Ricardo Cuervo, a psychologist, has just stepped out of his office. He almost runs into an officer escorting an inmate to some part of the unit. The inmate asks him in a rather abrasive manner, "Who are you?" Ricardo responds civilly, "Do you need to see me?" The response of the inmate is curt: "No! I ain't crazy!" Ricardo reenters his office and thinks, "Something is wrong with that picture!" Stepping back out into the hall, Ricardo sees what was bothering him. First, the officer and inmate are still standing outside his door. There is no reason for the officer and the inmate to be together in the educational unit. Second, the inmate is a half-step in back of the officer and pressing against his back.

The officer's face looks like he has seen a ghost, and he shouts, "Do what he says, he's got a shank!" (A shank is a prison-manufactured knife.) Ricardo does not know it yet, but he is about to become a hostage.

The inmate immediately says in a low, menacing voice, "Do what I say, or he gets it right now!"

As Ricardo moves down the hall in front of the two, another psychologist happens along and becomes part of the procession. Before they are halfway down the hall, another corrections officer and a secretary are commandeered by the inmate. The inmate casts back and forth, looking for a sanctuary, and finally hustles his entourage into a small office of the secretary to the director of social services. The office is approximately 8 feet by 12 feet and has a doorway leading to the director's office. The office secretary, Sandra, is at once seized by the inmate, and the director, alarmed at what he sees taking place out of the corner of his vision, opens the adjoining office door. He is promptly taken captive by the inmate, who now threatens to kill the secretary if anyone does anything. Seven people are now the hostages of James Worthington, a convicted murderer of a clerk in a convenience store holdup.

Worthington, with a firm grip on Sandra and the shank pressed below her rib cage, is at the side of the outer door, with a peripheral view of the hallway. Two others, the original corrections officer and Delphinia, another secretary, are in front of Sandra's desk, situated three or four feet from the door to the hallway. The rest of the hostages, including Cuervo, are behind the desk, sandwiched between it and some file cabinets, away from the door to the director's office. This is the setting as the hostage situation, which is to last three hours, begins.

Ricardo: What do you want?

James: (*Very aggressive, labile, agitated, with eyes glazed and bulging and rigid posture.*) You shut the hell up. I know I'm gonna die today. This is it!

Sandra: (*Screaming.*) Don't hurt me! I'm afraid! Please put the knife away.

Officer: (*Arms waving in a random way.*) Yeah, what do you want?

James: (*Becomes violently agitated and yanks the woman tighter to him and screams.*) Shut up, goddamnit! I'm goin' out today, and I'll take every one of you with me. You think I give a shit about you?

At this point a crowd and a lot of confusion invade the hallway. It is apparent that a riot alarm has been set off. A number of custodial officers attempt to get in the doorway.

James: (*Shouting at the top of his lungs.*) Tell those bastards not to come in here or the woman dies, NOW!
Chorus from hostages: Stay out! He's got a knife! He means business! He'll kill her!
James: (*Screaming, with menacing gestures.*) I'll stick her, I mean it.

In these early moments of the alarm stage, the hostages make a big mistake by pushing the panic button. The screaming of the secretary and motor movements of the officer are highly agitating to the hostage holder. The attempts by the psychologist to find out what the problem is are miscalculated. The hostage taker is engaging in expressive behavior, and the instrumental responses of the psychologist and the officer merely agitate James. Compounding James's agitation is the confusion in the hallway. The situation out there is far from contained. A custody captain comes to the door and tries to persuade James to throw out the knife.

James: I can't take it anymore—I've had enough of this bullshit!
Captain: (*In a commanding voice.*) Don't hurt anyone.
James: If I'm gonna die, I might as well take as many of these mothers with me as I can.
Captain: (*In a more subdued voice.*) Tell me what the problem is, let's see if we can resolve it.

The captain's initial assessment is by the book. He responds in an instrumental way to the hostage taker by trying to find out what his goal is. However, whatever has happened to James, it is plain that this is the wrong approach at this moment. Dr. Harold Deacon, director of psychology, is now on the scene outside the doorway. Although not trained as a hostage negotiator, Dr. Deacon offers his services to the captain.

Captain: Doc Deacon is out here and would like to talk to you.
James: I told you, I ain't nuts. I don't wanta talk to no shrink.

Deacon makes a quick assessment of the hostage holder's behavior and responds in an expressive mode. James's vehemence about his mental status tells Dr. Deacon that he is going to have to be very careful.

Deacon: Sounds as if you're pretty angry and nobody's listening to you.
James: That ain't the half of it, Doc.

James's response gives Deacon two clues. First, James responds by acknowledging Deacon's reflective statement. The acknowledgment indicates that the hostage holder has a lot of angry feelings that need ventilating. Second, "the half of it" indicates that the holder does have some kind of agenda, but that there is more of an affective than cognitive basis to it at the moment. The dialogue continues for a few minutes as the holder angrily ventilates, and Deacon responds in a deeply empathic manner. Finally, Deacon takes a risk, one that probably would be seen as tactically unsound in most hostage situations.

Deacon: I'm really having trouble hearing from out here in the hallway. I wonder if I might step into the room?

James: No!
Deacon: I understand how you feel, but I really am having a hard time hearing.
James: Well, OK! But I'm not coming out.

As Deacon enters the room, the original corrections officer taken by James, arms waving wildly, bolts out the door. James is unable to stop the officer because of his hold on Sandra. He immediately flies into a rage.

James: Comes back here, you sonofabitch. You tricked me, Doc. Now I'm gonna cut her good.

This foolish, panic-stricken move by the officer is exceedingly dangerous. Although he makes good his escape, he immediately jeopardizes the other hostages. The hostage holder, fearing he may lose control of the rest of the hostages, will invariably feel he has to reassert his power over them in very aggressive ways. Deacon will have to respond quickly with a statement designed to restore some equilibrium to the situation.

Deacon: Hold it! That was stupid. But I'm here now. You've got me, the director of psychology. Frankly, I'm a helluva lot more valuable than he is. So relax. You've come out ahead in the deal.
James: (*Still highly agitated.*) OK! OK! I got you, it's cool. That jerk was driving me nuts anyways, wavin' his arms around like some freak.

In one respect, the officer's escape helps the situation. His uncontrolled behavior heightened the hostage taker's tension. The officer's inability to get control of himself put the hostages in harm's way, given the high degree of emotional strain that James is experiencing. The officer's departure allows James to divert his attention from controlling the hostages to concentrating on what Deacon is saying.

Generally, going into the room would be unwise because it gives up another person to the situation. However, Deacon's assessment is that as James continues to ventilate, his voice has toned down and he is not swearing as much. Furthermore, Deacon wants to be able to see clearly the hostage holder's nonverbal behavior and measure it against verbal behavior presented. Deacon is having a hard time hearing, and although he uses the fact as a ploy to get into the room, it is something the hostage taker can accept as reasonable.

Deacon: (*About 30 minutes into the situation.*) Something's really hurting. I wonder if you could help me understand why you're so angry.
James: (*Slowly, but with increasing speed and vitriol, opens up.*) They wouldn't let me go to my grandfather's funeral. Gave me some jive talk that he wasn't on no relative list in my jacket. The social worker never even come back and give me an explanation after I asked him. No respect, man! None at all! Then last week, Furdy, down in metal shop, says I got me an attitude, says he's gonna lay me up for six months without pay. Sent my ass up to the PCC [Prison Classification Committee], which lays a lot of shuck on me—six months with no pay. Man! How they expect me not to have an attitude, the time hard enough without that? Those be unjust, unrighteous people, man! They don't listen to nothin'. I may be a con, but I deserve some respect, and they really piss me off, man! Well, look at me and them now. I got seven hostages. Who's got the respect now? They damn sure gonna kill me when this is done so I might as well take as many with me as I can. Particularly

that sucker over there. (*Points to the director of social services.*) He sat there this morning on the PCC and didn't say jack, didn't listen to a word I said. (*Turns menacingly to director of social services.*)

Deacon: (*Seeks to get James's focus of attention off the hostage and back to his feelings about the problem.*) It doesn't have to be that way. (*Rapidly but clearly restates the hostage taker's problems and feelings about the administration's response to them.*)

Deacon's restatement seeks to affirm and clarify for James that at least someone in the administration is now listening to him. He also seeks to affirm that James is still in good shape, that nothing irreparable has happened. It is extremely important that James understands he still has options at this point and that doing harm to the director will severely limit those options for him. The key feeling seems to be loss of respect. Deacon's assessment is that James is not overly angry with what happened as much as with how it happened. The information confirms for Deacon the negotiation approach he has taken with James and gives the psychologist information on areas he will need to pursue.

What Deacon hypothesizes from James's diatribe is that he feels both wronged and inadequate. Deacon needs to reinforce at any opportunity the respect James feels he has lost. He can also use this information to set up a problem-solving situation based on restoration of James's lost self-esteem to resolve the situation. Furthermore, Deacon obtains two pieces of concrete information, the grandfather's death and the confinement to his cell with no work, pay, or privileges, that make James feel he has been unjustly dealt with by the authorities. The combined weight of these two problems, plus James's impulsivity, has pushed him over the edge.

Deacon has another piece of information, which is alarming. The hostage taker has an axe to grind with one of the hostages, the director of social services. For the moment, all Deacon can do is hope to take attention and heat away from the director by refocusing attention to the problem. Deacon also understands from James's rapid mood swings and emotional outbursts that James is on the borderline of having a psychotic breakdown. Those swings need to be contained and stabilized. By this time a professional negotiator has arrived in the hallway outside the office.

James: I don't want to talk to anybody here. (*To Cuervo.*) You, get me the governor on the phone. Or the commissioner of corrections.

Cuervo: I'd be glad to try, but I don't know the number.

James: (*Shouts out the door.*) Hey, I wanta talk to the governor or the commissioner. Somebody get 'em on the line.

Neg: (*Outside the room.*) They're not available. Tell me what you want and deal with me. Let's see what we can work out.

James: Screw you, I want the governor.

Although the negotiator is technically right in keeping the negotiations contained, his response creates a problem. Deacon has effectively taken over the negotiation role in the eyes of the hostage taker. For better or worse, Deacon is the controlling factor, and the professional negotiator is now relegated to a backup role. Deacon immediately picks up on this and regains control.

Deacon: James, it seems like what we have going can be solved between us. Whatever needs to be done, I'll see that it gets done.

James: You'll just say I'm crazy. Think I'm crazy?

Deacon: No, I don't think you're crazy. I believe you're under a lot of stress and feel
like no one would listen to you to the point that you had to do something that
would get some attention. I can't imagine anyone not being under a lot of stress
given all that's happened to you and what's going on right now. I'd be willing to go
up before a judge or the institutional administration and go to bat for you, but you
have to give up your weapon and walk out if you want that from me.

Cuervo: Dr. Deacon's right. Anybody would feel the stress, I know I do.

James: You shut up! The doc's doin' the talkin'.

Even though Cuervo is also a psychologist, his reinforcement of Deacon does not
help the situation. James sees Cuervo and the others as only one thing, bargaining tools.
Cuervo and the other hostages would best be advised to be quiet and unobtrusive in the
situation.

Meanwhile, Deacon has used James's question about being crazy as a wedge. He
goes on to give James a plausible, rational reason that speaks directly to James's
wounded pride. He is giving James a way out with some honor attached to it and in the
bargain is saying that James has an ally. He is also saying that part of the bargain will
be no violence. What's more, he is shifting attention away from the hostages to James's
own well-being. Notice that no time limit is put on dropping the weapon, but Deacon
states this as a logical prerequisite to the things that need to happen for James. It is now
about one hour into the situation. Although James is still making some erratic emotional swings, he is much calmer than before.

In general, the crisis stage has passed and the accommodation stage has com-
menced. Deacon has seated himself on the edge of the desk, rolled up his shirtsleeves,
loosened his tie, and put his hands in his pockets. At this point a subtle change occurs
in James. He pulls a six-page letter from a back pocket and asks Deacon to look
it over.

Deacon: I'm frankly amazed. This is a precise, articulate, well-written letter that
clearly spells out specifics of your complaints. You've obviously thought this out
carefully. It surely isn't the typical jailhouse crap I see. This is good information to
support your case.

James: (Flicker of a smile, head up.) You really think so, Doc? Would you read it out
loud to those guys out there?

Deacon has won a major victory here. The letter from James is well written, and
Deacon can legitimately state that. By reinforcing James, he allows the hostage taker to
regain some of his lost self-esteem. Deacon reads the letter, and it is decided that a copy
of the letter should be made to give to the administration and the commission. James
has calmed down quite a bit.

The one major expressive problem still centers on the director of social services,
who continuously receives threatening and vicious statements from James. It seems that
the director is the focal point for all of James's frustrations. Deacon decides that there
must be a resolution to this problem before anything else can be accomplished.

James: Heeey, Mr. Dye-rec-tore! How you feel now, baby? You ain't so noncommitted
now, are you, sucker? How'd you like to get your big fat ego punctured with this?
(Waves knife around.)

Deacon: Well, my guess is that you're scaring the hell out of him, and if that's your intention you're doing a fine job.

James: Hey, Doc, I just want to make him feel like I did when he was sittin' up there
this mornin' playin' God with me.

Deacon: What you're saying is, he made you lose your self-respect and you hurt because of that. Why don't you ask him how he feels now?

He interprets what James's feelings are and attributes the causality of those feelings directly to the hostage. What the hostage says will determine a lot about how the
hostage taker reacts. However, Deacon knows the capabilities of the director of social
services and believes the bet is a good one.

Director of social services: James, I don't know what else to say but that I'm sorry you
feel like I wasn't paying attention to you this morning. I sure wish you'd had the
letter and read it, because that would have made a difference. I don't know if you
believe I'm sincere or not, but I feel bad about it, particularly since some of these
people might get hurt for something I did.

Deacon: James, he said that pretty straight. How do you feel about that?

James: (*Visibly calmer.*) Yeah, man, well, we all make mistakes and yours was a big
one.

Director of social services: Well, I'd say you're right.

James: How do I know I'll be safe if I let these people go?

It is now more than two hours into the situation. This is the first time that James
has talked about letting people go and voiced a concern for his own well-being. It is a
crucial point in the situation that must not be missed. If Deacon can capitalize on it, the
resolution stage is at hand.

Deacon: What's of most concern to you?

James: That I stay alive. I want to be transported to another institution. I don't want
any of the guards to get up my backside here. I also want some guarantees that I
don't get worked over.

Deacon: I can't guarantee any of that, but let's pass it on to the captain. None of it
sounds unreasonable. I can understand your concerns.

Deacon makes no promises, but he owns his feelings about James's position and
further increases the bond between himself and the hostage taker. A good deal of negotiation now takes place about the possibility of a transfer, statements to the press, some
new demands, how the transfer will take place, recriminations, how the hostages will be
released, and a variety of other subjects. The exchanges proceed with Deacon serving
as the conduit between James and the captain and professional negotiator.

Captain: We can do that. I got the OK from the commissioner. We could move you to
Starkton.

James: How do I know I can trust you?

Captain: James, you and I have had dealings before, right, man? Did I ever run a game
on you? Tell you I could do something and didn't? If I could do it, it got done. Isn't
that right?

James: Doc, what do you think about that? Is he runnin' a game on me?

Deacon: I believe him, but how's that square with you? Is he right?

James: I guess that's right. But what about all those other dudes?

Deacon: Look, I'll be willing to walk out of here with you and ride over to Starkton and see you get settled in over there. With me around there's no way that any of the officers would risk working you over.

James: OK. Let's work out the details.

When James checks the situation out with Deacon, it is a good indication that a bond of trust between the two has been established. Deacon serves as James's perceptual check throughout the negotiations but is careful to allow James to continue to feel that he is the person with ultimate responsibility. Final details are worked out between the captain, Deacon, and James. The women are let go first. The captain and negotiator come into the room and the other men are ushered out. James is given some paper and a pencil to write down some more statements he has to make to the media. To get the paper and pencil, he relinquishes the knife. Once his statement is finished, James is transported to another institution, with Deacon going along to be sure he is safe.

In this hostage situation, although it took place in a penitentiary, James typifies the kind of emotionally overwrought person with whom human services workers are likely to come in contact in the course of their work. Even though Deacon had no formal training in hostage negotiation, he was able to use his considerable therapeutic and crisis intervention skills to resolve the situation. We are categorically in favor of using trained negotiators, but a professional negotiator may not always be available. The skills that human services workers such as Deacon bring to the situation may be the best and most expert available. At such times, like it or not, the human services worker becomes a negotiator.

The Crisis Worker as Consultant

Because negotiation strategies are based on psychological principles, it would seem natural to employ social workers, counselors, psychologists, and psychiatrists, as negotiators. Still, this is a controversial issue. A number of arguments militate against using mental health professionals as negotiators. First and foremost, hostage negotiations are law enforcement operations and therefore should be dealt with in terms of immediate resolution of conflict rather than in terms of therapy. Second, the use of mental health professionals supplants the use of a negotiating team approach, particularly if decisive physical action needs to be taken. Third, a mental health professional may not be nearly as capable as a person who has been trained to understand the hostage taker. Fourth, identification of the negotiator as a mental health professional may make hostage takers extremely agitated if they conclude that the authorities believe them to be mentally deranged (Maher, 1977, p. 9).

Yet a mental health professional, by virtue of training and personality characteristics, fits many of the criteria Miron and Goldstein (1978, pp. 93–94, 137–166) propose for selection of a negotiator. The resolution of this dilemma has been to make a psychologist a member of the negotiating team in a consultative capacity (Maher, 1977, p. 9). As a consultant, the psychologist serves as a resource person, advisor to the negotiator, intelligence gatherer, debriefer of victims and witnesses, and post hoc evaluator of the total response effort (Hatcher, Mohandie, Turner, & Gelles, 1998; Powitzky, 1979). According to Butler, Leitenberg, and Fuselier (1993), the psychologist—particularly as a consultant to the negotiator—should

1. Constantly assess the mental state of the hostage taker, as well as that of the negotiator.
2. Not become directly involved in the negotiations, thereby remaining as objective as possible.
3. Recommend techniques, approaches, or responses that will help resolve the situation. Indeed, police departments that do use mental health professionals as consultants have more hostage situations end by negotiated surrender, as opposed to a tactical team assault.

If You Are Put in the Role of Negotiator

Often, in the mental health business, and particularly in crisis intervention, we are cast into roles that we may not be expert in or necessarily want to assume. However, at the time, we are the proverbial Dutch boy holding his finger in the dike until help arrives. If you happen to be first on the scene of a hostage situation, these 14 points, abridged from Blau (1994, p. 253), are good guidelines to follow.

1. Ensure your own safety; don't be a hero. Stay out of reach or gunshot range of the hostage taker.
2. Avoid soliciting demands the negotiator can't or won't keep.
3. Don't bargain or make concessions the negotiator can't or won't keep.
4. Listen for clues regarding the perpetrator's emotional state and remember them so you can pass that information to the negotiator.
5. Don't offer anything to the perpetrator of a material nature. "Anything" ranges from a glass of water to the gold at Ft. Knox.
6. You probably can promise that the police won't rush in and storm the building; the last thing they want are dead police officers or dead hostages.
7. Minimize the seriousness of the perpetrator's crime. Things are never as bad as they seem, and any crime can be plea-bargained.
8. Don't refer to anybody as "hostage." Ask about the "people," not the "hostages."
9. Don't try to trick the hostage taker or be dishonest. That subterfuge is sure to be found out and will make the negotiator's job that much harder.
10. Never say absolutely no or yes to a demand. Hedge and be cautious.
11. Don't be creative in making suggestions or putting thoughts in the perpetrator's mind.
12. If the perpetrator seems suicidal, ask about it and adopt a suicide prevention mode.
13. No relatives, friends, bosses, or anybody else needs to be brought to the scene unless the negotiator decides to do so later. If they are already at the scene, it is probably best to get them away from it.
14. Don't offer to exchange yourself, as Deacon did. You are not a hero for doing so.

IF YOU ARE HELD HOSTAGE

Frank Bolz (1987), former chief hostage negotiator for the New York City Police Department, outlined the following basic ways to protect yourself if you are held hostage (pp. 13–23, 66–71).

1. *Don't be a hero.* Accept the situation and be prepared to wait. This may be a challenge for human services workers who are used to being in control. For example, a counselor we knew at a college counseling center tried to take action on behalf of another counselor who was being threatened by a gun-carrying female client, and ended up being shot and killed. The counselor had never seen the woman before and had no idea of her potential for violence. Instead of keeping a low profile, attempting to minimally assess the woman's agitated state, practicing any of the calming techniques in this chapter, or merely waiting for police to arrive, the counselor attempted to physically contain the woman. He attempted to make a heroic rescue and died trying. The chances of your being able to react faster than a captor can bring a weapon to bear are practically nonexistent. Underestimating the physical ability of a captor who is excited and "pumped up" with adrenaline is exceedingly foolish, no matter how much stronger or more agile you may believe yourself to be.

2. *Follow instructions.* Particularly in the first minutes after being taken hostage, it is extremely important to follow instructions. Hostage takers are highly agitated in the initial moments of a hostage taking. Any resistance or hesitation in following directions is likely to indicate to the hostage takers that they must show they are in command of the situation. A clear way of demonstrating that they are now the ones in power is to physically hurt somebody.

3. *Don't speak unless spoken to.* Although the human services worker may make good use of verbal skills when the perpetrator initiates a dialogue, any attempts by the worker to take the lead in a conversation may result in the hostage taker feeling a loss of control.

4. *Don't make suggestions.* Any notion about being "helpful" is likely only to antagonize the captors. Only the authorities have the power to solve the problem. It is their job; they know what they are doing, so let them do it.

5. *Try to rest and eat.* Although it may seem impossible at the time, conserving energy is important. No one can foretell how long the situation may go on. The rollercoaster ride of emotions inherent in the situation is extremely energy draining. Being fully alert and acting in a capable manner requires having the psychic and physical energy to do so, and that requires rest and nourishment.

6. *Carefully weigh escape options.* Any attempt to escape should be weighed very, very carefully against the chances of being caught or provoking harm to other hostages. The odds must be highly in your favor and then weighed against whether you have the wits, physical capability, and energy to escape.

7. *Request aid if needed.* Once the initial takeover is complete and the situation is clearly under the hostage taker's control it may be appropriate to ask for assistance, such as for medication. Do this directly and quietly to the hostage taker. Do not dwell on this issue, because constant queries may bring unwanted attention to you.

8. *Be observant.* If you are released and others are still held hostage, you may be an invaluable source of information to the authorities. The number of perpetrators, their appearance, what their routine is, what other hostages are in the area, and so on are in are all important pieces of information that the authorities can use. Furthermore, being observant enables you to keep mentally busy, avoid panic, and adapt to conditions that may change rapidly.

9. *Do not be argumentive.* Argumentiveness is likely to make you stand out and focus attention on you. As such, you may be perceived by your captors as a threat and be

treated accordingly. Philosophical, political, religious, or any other emotionally loaded topics should be met with simple agreement and validation of the captor's beliefs.

10. *Be patient.* It may appear that nothing is happening to relieve the situation. Remember that time is on the side of the authorities and you.

11. *Avoid standing out.* Besides avoiding verbally standing out, get rid of any identifying information that would make you seem like a threat, an important person, or an object of hatred.

12. *Treat captors with deference and respect.* One way of establishing the Stockholm syndrome is maintaining eye contact, not assuming a physically aggressive stance, speaking politely when spoken to, and gently establishing a personal relationship with the hostage taker. Remember that no matter how bizarre and ludicrous they may seem, the captors are operating out of an instrumental and/or expressive mode that makes absolute sense to them at the time.

13. *Don't slight the seriousness of the situation by attempting to inject humor into it.* Making humorous remarks about the dilemma may cause the captors to perceive that they are not being taken seriously.

14. *Be careful of trickery.* Attempting to gain an advantage by resorting to tricks or subterfuge is extremely risky. If the captors find out you are attempting to deceive them, they may use you as a punitive example to other hostages.

15. *Do not embarrass your captors.* Many hostage takers will not have the mental capabilities or the verbal abilities of the human services worker. By engaging in mental or verbal one-upmanship, you run the risk of embarrassing your captors and making them feel foolish.

16. *When rescue comes, follow the rescuers' directions precisely.* Rescuers may not know who captors and hostages are. Staying flat on the ground with hands and arms covering your head lets the rescuers know you are not a threat to them. Many times during a hostage rescue, there will be a lot of noise and confusion, which is purposively designed by the rescuers. Temper the urge to stand up and run with the realization that by so doing you will put yourself in harm's way.

INTERVENTION AFTER RELEASE

For a variety of reasons, a postcrisis may occur after the hostage situation is resolved. There is often a sense that the perpetrator is still present even after liberation. The enforced relationship becomes part of their inner life and continues to engross their attention after release. Released hostages continue to track their captors and fear them even if they are safely behind bars or otherwise far removed from them (Herman, 1995, p. 94).

If the Stockholm syndrome was generated, the hostages may hate their rescuers and bitterly protest their captors' treatment. If hostages were killed or injured, there may be unresolved grief resolution. Reestablishing relationships with family and friends that existed prior to captivity may be problematic. Survivors of a hostage situation need to have their sense of power and control returned to them to reduce their sense of isolation and helplessness from being dominated by their captors. Physical rest and proper nourishment, isolation from the media, social support, judicious use of psychotropic medication, and debriefing are all critical to a return to normalcy (Allodi, 1994; McDuff, 1992; McWhirter & Lindzer, 1994).

Survivors of a hostage situation indicate that a variety of physical and psychological problems, ranging from paranoia about repeat occurrences and survival guilt to posttrauma anxiety attacks, may appear a long time after the incident. Thus survivors need to be aware that resolving the situation may not necessarily mean the end of their problems associated with being taken hostage (Strentz, 1984, p. 201). The potential for acute stress disorder (American Psychiatric Association, 1994, pp. 429–430) in survivors of a hostage incident is high (Bisson, Searle, & Srinivasan, 1998; Cremniter, Crocq, Louville, & Batista, 1997; Vila, Porche, & Mouren-Simeoni, 1998).

Acute Stress Disorder.   Acute stress disorder (ASD) is the much younger sibling of its nasty psychological big brother, PTSD. ASD has been classified as a stand-alone disorder for the first time in the *DSM-IV* (American Psychiatric Association, 1994). Its clinical symptoms look very much like those of PTSD; the major difference is that the disturbance lasts for a minimum of two days and occurs within four weeks of the traumatic event (American Psychiatric Association, 1994, p. 430). ASD certainly is problematic in its own right. However, if individuals are unable to resolve the psychological disturbances that invariably go with traumatic events, they become candidates for PTSD (Classen, Koopman, Hales, & Spiegel, 1998; Harvey & Bryant, 1998). Although no one can predict who will or will not become a candidate for ASD or PTSD, quick, proactive crisis intervention with individuals who are experiencing acute stress is an excellent vaccination against the virulence of PTSD. Therefore, it is of utmost importance that all individuals who have experienced a traumatic event be given the opportunity to get immediate psychological support as soon after the event as is humanly possible.

As a result, two important follow-up activities can do much to help the hostage survivor regain psychological equilibrium quickly. Those are the postincident interview by the police (Strentz, 1995, p. 145) and critical incidents stress debriefing (Mitchell, 1983).

Postincident Interview.   The postincident interview aids both law enforcement and the hostages. It occurs as soon after resolution of the incident as possible before memories fade or are contaminated by the media. Law enforcement officials are eager to know what happened so that they may incorporate their findings into knowledge on how to contain future events and use the information in any legal proceedings against the hostage taker. Time is of no consequence, and the interviews continue until all participants are satisfied it is over (Strentz, 1995, p. 145).

For the hostages, having the undivided attention of law enforcement is an excellent ventilation source. They are also telling their story to someone whom they believe can redress the suffering perpetrated on them and can get even in some small way (Strentz, 1995, pp. 145–146).

Critical Incident Stress Debriefing (CISD).   CISD was developed by Jeffrey Mitchell, a firefighter and paramedic in Baltimore County, Maryland, as a result of his own responses to the traumatic incidents he continuously witnessed. Originally designed to deal only with emergency workers, it now finds use with a variety of people who have suffered trauma (Morrissey, 1994).

CISD teams are typically composed of two members who must hold a minimum of a master's degree in the mental health professions and who have undergone training and received certification in CISD. Debriefing is designed to mitigate the psychological impact of a traumatic event, restore homeostasis and equilibrium, prevent PTSD from developing, and identify people who will need professional mental health follow-up (Mitchell & Everly, 1995a, p. 270).

Informal Defusing.   Informal defusing is a first-order intervention following traumatic incidents and is typically performed by CISD-trained on-site personnel. This three-stage intervention is a shortened version of a full-scale debriefing and usually takes about one hour. First, team members introduce themselves, and then explain the process and delineate expectations. Second, the traumatic experience is explored via participants' disclosure of facts, cognitive and emotional reactions, and finally symptoms of distress related to the traumatic event. Third, participants are given information to normalize the dissonant cognitions of the event and educate them with regard to stress, stress management, and trauma (Mitchell & Everly, 1995a, p. 275).

Formal Debriefing.   The formal debriefing process has seven stages and typically takes place within 24 hours after a traumatic event. It is generally two to three hours long. It is a combination of psychological and educational elements formatted in a structured group setting, and it involves personnel who have been directly affected by a traumatic event. Debriefing helps make the transition from processing facts about the event to emotional responses to the event and, finally, back to cognitive information about reactions and coping with traumatic experiences. It is not psychotherapy, but rather a controlled meeting that allows participants to discuss their emotions and thoughts about the event in a nonthreatening environment (Mitchell & Everly, 1995b). The seven stages are described as follows:

1. *Introduction.* The introduction is crucial to setting the tone of the debriefing. Besides introducing team members and explaining the process and guidelines for the CISD, the introduction also seeks to lower resistance and motivate the participants by discussing sensitive issues such as confidentiality (Mitchell & Everly, 1995a, p. 271).
2. *Fact finding.* Facts are initially discussed because they are easiest to deal with and are typical of what may be discussed with emergency workers after a traumatic event. The leaders typically start by making statements such as "We only have a sketch of what happened. We'd like you to fill us in on what happened. So we can get an overall picture, we'd like everyone, no matter what part you played, to give us your perspective of it. If you don't feel ready to do that, that's OK too, just shake your head and we'll move past you. We need to know who you are, what your involvement was, and what happened from your point of view." Order doesn't matter; the episode will sort itself through the facilitative ability of the CISD leaders (Mitchell & Everly, 1995a, p. 272).
3. *Thoughts.* The CISD leaders ask the participants about their initial or most poignant thoughts about what happened. Moving from facts to thoughts starts to personalize the event and allows emotions to surface. As participants voice their thoughts, the leaders should elicit those emotions that come naturally with their thinking about the situation and that allow for movement into the next phase, reaction (Mitchell & Everly, 1995a, p. 272).
4. *Reaction.* This phase is the most emotionally powerful for participants. Questions that elicit responses are variations on a theme of "What about the situation

was most bothersome to you? If you could change one part of it, what would it be?" Leaders will act more as passive facilitators at this point, as participants spontaneously speak to their affective responses to the event (Mitchell & Everly, 1995a, pp. 272–273).

5. *Symptoms.* The symptom phase is used to shift the group back to more cognitive material. The discussion deals with what went on both during and after the event. The leaders ask the group to describe their experience in terms of affective, behavioral, cognitive, or physical experiences they had. To get the group going, the leaders may give examples such as "My whole body was shaking for five minutes after the firing quit; I was under control, but I kept thinking I can't stand another minute of this; I wanted to say something, but my tongue was tied; I'm scared to death, but I know I have to go back into that building so my feet move me there somehow" (Mitchell & Everly, 1995a, p. 273).

6. *Teaching.* Leaders may point out that what the participants have talked about fits precisely into the symptoms of acute stress. The leaders let the participants know that these are normal, typical reactions, that they are not losing their minds or otherwise somehow not equal to the task. The participants are also instructed in how to recognize and understand symptoms that might not have surfaced yet. Participants are also given information in stress management techniques. This phase moves the participants even further away from the emotional content they have worked through in the reaction phase (Mitchell & Everly, 1995a, p. 274).

7. *Reentry.* The reentry phase is a final opportunity to summarize and bring closure to all the issues that have been discussed. The CISD team's job at this time is to answer questions, provide reassurance, reflect any agendas they believe have not been brought out, dispense handouts, and provide referral sources for extended psychological work (Mitchell & Everly, 1995a, p. 274).

In summary, the CISD derives its effectiveness from early intervention, the opportunity to experience catharsis in safety, the opportunity to verbalize the trauma, a definite behavioral structure, group and peer support, and a provision for follow-up if needed (Mitchell & Everly, 1995b, p. 41).

Crisis Intervention with Hostage Survivors

Employee assistance programs (EAPs) are in a unique position to provide services in the aftermath of a traumatic event because of their close working relationship with organizations and their individual employees (Hosie, West, & Mackey, 1993). The following incident is abstracted from McWhirter and Linzer's (1994) report of a crisis intervention after a bank holdup, in which bank employees were held hostage, one hostage was subsequently wounded, and the hostage taker was killed by the FBI. This represents a typical comprehensive critical incident stress management process. Depending on what the length and severity of the crisis is, critical incident stress debriefing may not be enough, and additional components of crisis intervention are warranted, particularly when social and environmental reordering are necessary (Mayer, 1999).

The incident occurred on a Friday, and a crisis team from the bank's EAP was immediately called. After postincident interviews by police, former hostages were given the telephone number for around-the-clock access to the crisis incident stress management

(CISM) team. Employees repeatedly used this access until the first CISD session on Monday morning. Over the weekend, bank officials and crisis team members planned a course of action that included the following.

1. The bank was closed for a week, employees were given paid vacation, and the bank was redecorated.
2. On Monday, a mandatory all-day debriefing for all employees was scheduled at a hotel.
3. On Wednesday, a voluntary 3-hour support group session was held for any employee who wanted to attend.
4. On Friday morning, all employees met at the bank for a reentry orientation with the CISM team.
5. On Friday afternoon, employees met with law enforcement officials to ask questions, raise concerns, and receive feedback from officials regarding their performance while hostages.
6. On the following Monday, CISM team members returned to the bank when it reopened and remained there throughout the day.
7. An 8-week follow-up session was held at the bank.
8. Unlimited individual counseling was provided through the EAP.
9. Ongoing consultation with management was conducted by the CISM team leader.

Initial Debriefing. The bank employees' initial debriefing dealt with psychoeducation about stress responses and processing of the event itself. Employees were given information on the wide range of affective, cognitive, and behavioral reactions to a traumatic event and were assured of the absolute normalcy of the reactions they were experiencing. The employees were taught guided relaxation exercises to reduce stress and were given handouts on information about trauma survivors and support functions for family members (McWhirter & Linzer, 1994).

The informational component of involving an immediate and understanding support system is critically important at this juncture. Observers who have never experienced prolonged terror and who have no understanding of coercive methods of control often assume that they would show greater psychological resistance than the victim in similar circumstances. The survivors' difficulties are all too easily attributed to underlying character problems, even when the trauma is known (Herman, 1995, p. 97), and a "blame the victim" attitude may start to occur within the support system at a time when the survivor needs the most support.

For the bank employees, the fact-thought-feeling model developed by Mitchell (1983) was used to process the event. First, each group member shared his or her view of the facts of the incident. This fact finding allowed the members to fill in voids in their understanding of the event and why things happened as they did. Next, employees processed their cognitions during the event. Their thoughts had ranged from the mundane ("What'll I fix for dinner if I'm late?") to self-reproach ("I shouldn't be so scared") to bravery ("I ought to do something") to the ridiculous ("This must be some sick joke"). Processing these thoughts allowed employees to understand that they had all experienced a wide range of thoughts during the event and that they were not crazy for having done so. Employees then processed the event from an affective basis and addressed the wide range of negative emotions they felt at different stages of the event, from terror and anger to apathy and guilt. As is typical in the aftermath of a hostage event, guilt feelings predominated and centered on feeling guilty about not doing something, feeling guilty about somebody else being hurt when they were not, feeling guilty about relief at being freed when others were not, and feeling guilty that the robber had been killed. This initial CISD progression from facts to thoughts to feelings allowed the group to safely move deeper into self-disclosure and quickly generated group cohesiveness and trust for the process (McWhirter & Linzer, 1994).

After the large-group session, employees were separated into two smaller groups: employees released early in the siege and those held until the gunman was killed. Those employees who had been released had specific issues about a co-worker being wounded in the shootout, and they had difficulty believing that the gunman was actually dead. Employees held throughout the ordeal had qualitatively and quantitatively different stressors because they had been witness to all the events, including having a gun pointed at them, seeing a fellow employee marched around the bank with a gun at her neck, seeing her wounded, and watching the gunman be killed. These small groups were employee focused and thus allowed everyone to speak to their own evolving issues, rather than following a prescribed model. Finally, individual sessions were also made available for employees who had experienced previous traumatic events and needed assurance that flashing back to remembrances of those past traumas was a normal reaction (McWhirter & Linzer, 1994).

Subsequent Intervention Procedures. On the fifth day after the event, a voluntary group support session was held. Employees were given additional psychoeducational information and the opportunity to process additional thoughts and feelings about the event, including fears about returning to the bank on Friday morning and returning to work on Monday. A week after the event, employees returned to the redecorated bank and were met in the parking lot and given a guided tour through the bank by the CISM team. As employees moved through the bank, the CISM team helped them work through feelings by talking them through their panic while using progressive muscle relaxation techniques. A meeting with law enforcement officials helped ease questions about why the authorities had seemed to be doing nothing. The employees were also given a great deal of positive feedback by law enforcement officials on their cool demeanor and appropriate responses during the siege (McWhirter & Linzer, 1994).

On the following Monday, 10 days after the incident, the bank was reopened with the crisis team on the premises, either to consult individually with employees as the need arose or to merely be present as a comforting resource. As is typical following such a trauma, employees closely monitored every person who walked into the bank, experienced a great deal of silent panic over customers whom they could not clearly hear or see, and were unsettled by repeated intrusive and invasive questioning by curious customers. CISM team members helped employees handle each of these situations when requested (McWhirter & Linzer, 1994).

Finally, an eight-week follow-up found that while there were still some startle responses to loud customers and some anger at customers who made jokes or asked personal questions about the robbery, the employees were tired of thinking about the event and were ready to put it behind them. They reported that although the event had changed their lives forever, they were ready to move forward (McWhirter & Linzer,

1994). Those who requested it were provided individual counseling on the order of what we described in the chapters on PTSD and sexual assault. As may be seen from this scenario, a comprehensive triage assessment of the group members indicated a graded crisis intervention approach was needed. That approach ranged from simple postincident interviews and CISD sessions for everybody to specific crisis intervention techniques that included individual therapy (Mayer, 1999).

SUMMARY

With wide-ranging access to the media as a format to air a variety of grievances, hostage taking has increased tremendously since 1970. A great deal of publicity surrounds terrorist hostage takings, but the human services worker is more likely to become involved with a variety of hostage-taker types who have little to do with worldwide political agendas.

Although hostage taking is certainly a crisis-oriented problem, it is unlike other crisis situations in that it is invariably a law enforcement operation and one that deals much more closely with the victimizer than with the victim.

Hostage takers come in a variety of types. Understanding which type the hostage negotiator is dealing with is of critical importance because subsequent negotiating strategies will differ by type. In general, all hostage takers are engaged in either instrumental or expressive behavior or some combination of the two. Instrumental hostage takers are after a very clear, concrete goal. Expressive hostage takers are pursuing power.

A variety of negotiating techniques are available. These techniques range from the typical active listening and responding skills that most other crisis interventionists would commonly use to some very sophisticated and, perhaps, somewhat devious methods. In all hostage situations, time is clearly on the side of the negotiators. Therefore, it is imperative that hostage negotiators proceed slowly and with patience.

For hostages, it is clear that keeping a low profile and staying psychologically and physically alert are the best initial moves in the early stages of this crisis situation. If the situation becomes extended, hostages may attempt, in careful and congruent ways, to convey personal aspects of their lives to their captors and attempt to generate the Stockholm syndrome. Becoming a person rather than a bargaining chip in the eyes of one's holders makes it very difficult for them to dehumanize the hostage to the point that he or she can be easily killed. Resolution for the hostage does not necessarily occur when the perpetrators are taken into custody and the hostages are freed; acute and posttrauma stress associated with this crisis may call for extended psychological intervention.

C L A S S R O O M   E X E R C I S E S

There Are Hostages in the Social Work Department!

Simulated Negotiations with Mr. X

The setting is a university building. The only information available is that there is a man with a gun who has locked himself in a suite of offices on the second floor of the five-floor building. The Social Work Department is on that floor. Gunshots were heard in the department office. Eyewitnesses who have escaped from the scene describe a man as dressed in casual clothes, polite but very firm in giving directions and commands. It appears someone has been shot. Campus security has sealed off the second floor, but there are still people on the floors above. There are hostages in the second-floor area, but nobody knows just exactly how many staff and students were there when the takeover occurred. Neither does anyone know for sure whether any hostages have been hurt, even though several shots were fired and there was a lot of shouting in the initial minutes of the takeover. The police have contained the scene and have the telephone number of the second floor. An action news team from Channel 5 has just arrived, and a fairly large crowd is beginning to gather. As the principal negotiator, you have just arrived on the scene.

You will need two rooms for this activity and a telephone connection between the two. Audiotape and/or videotape recorders should be available in each room. Roles to be played are those of a hostage taker, four hostages, and two negotiators. The rest of the class, half in each of the two rooms, will be responsible for taking observational notes during the process. One way of handling observation is to assign certain members to monitor each of the actors in the role play.

Mr. X, the hostage taker, will have to decide which of the types, as outlined in this chapter, he will portray. He is not to tell anybody his type. Participants will have to decide, on the basis of the hostage taker's actions as the drama unfolds, what his type is. The main objective of the hostage taker should be to get what he wants from the situation. What he wants, of course, depends on what his type is, and it is one of the missions of the negotiation team to find that out.

The hostages themselves should be portrayed as people in the crisis stage of the hostage situation. Things are starting to settle down, but there is still a lot of confusion. Hostages are advised to act on their own resources, using whatever skills and knowledge they have available. They must follow, to the best of their ability, the directives of the hostage taker. The one thing they cannot do is escape. The main objective of the hostages is to stay alive.

The negotiators are to act in coordination with one another, but only one negotiator is allowed to speak on the telephone at any time. The instructor may wish to rotate available class members in the role of negotiators. The negotiators are on their own resources, but have the opportunity to consult with one another. The ultimate objective of the exercise is to get everyone, including the hostage taker, out safely.

Although it is impossible to draw out the exercise to the duration of a typical hostage situation, we recommend taking at least 30 minutes for the exercise. On completion of the exercise all role players will be called on to verbally disassociate themselves from the parts they played. They will do this in front of the entire class. Questions to be discussed by the class following the activity are

1. What type would you say the hostage taker was?
2. How did he demonstrate that?
3. How do you think the negotiators handled the situation?
4. What negotiating techniques did they use?
5. Can you specifically identify some of them?
6. At what points were the negotiators able to get the hostage taker to give in on some of his demands?

7. At what points did the negotiators have problems?
8. What were those problems?
9. What might the negotiators have done differently when they encountered problems?
10. How did the hostages feel as they went through the experience?
11. How did they feel toward their captor?
12. How did they feel toward their rescuers?
13. How did they feel about their fellow hostages?
14. How did they feel about themselves after the siege was over?

Debriefing the Hostages

Using steps 2 through 5 in the critical incident stress debriefing procedure (Mitchell & Everly, 1995b) have the hostages debrief. You may use the role-play content generated in the preceding exercise or use this one:

> A description of the aftermath of the scenario indicated that the estranged boyfriend of the social work department secretary came into the department office and shot her three times, killing her. The scene is of the secretary slumped over her computer terminal with blood all over the monitor, her desk, and puddling on the floor. The boyfriend has thrown desk and chairs up against the only entrance and has herded the hostages into a far corner of the office away from the door. He has closed all the window shades. He vacillates from sobbing and weeping over his lost love to angry, irrational outbursts that everybody is going to die in here today. The police have cut the electricity, so it is dark and hot. He has taken another secretary, two students, the department chair, and a professor hostage. Subsequent attempts to talk him out resulted in an escalation of suicidal behavior. After two hours of negotiations, the subject turned the gun on himself and committed suicide by shooting himself in the mouth, taking most of the back of his head off and blowing brain matter and blood and bone onto the wall. The hostages were all witness to this.

Choose two members of the class to be the debriefers. Have the hostage survivors each identify themselves, and then proceed to go through the steps indicated. Remember! This is not a therapy session, so move through the steps in a methodical, workmanlike way and don't get sidetracked. This exercise should take about 20–30 minutes. After you are done, have participants de-role and process the debriefing with these questions:

1. How did it feel to be a member of the group?
2. Even though this was a role play, was there relief in talking it through?
3. What steps seemed most poignant?
4. Did it feel like the steps moved you deeper into more feeling-based responses and then lightened up to more cognitive-based responses?

RESOURCE

For those who are interested in hostage negotiation, the Texas Association for Hostage Negotiators at http://www.tahn.org/ has a web site that offers the latest in hostage negotiation information. There is a membership fee.

REFERENCES

American Psychiatric Association. (1994). *Diagnostic and statistical manual of mental disorders* (4th ed.). Washington, DC: Author.

Allodi, F. A. (1994). Posttraumatic stress disorder in hostages and victims of torture. *Psychiatric Clinics of North America, 17,* 279–288.

Auerbach, S. M., Kiesler, D. J., Strentz, T., & Schmidt, J. A. (1994). Interpersonal impacts and adjustment to the stress of simulated captivity: An empirical test of the Stockholm syndrome. *Journal of Social and Clinical Psychology, 13,* 207–221.

Blau, T. H. (1994). *Psychological services for law enforcement.* New York: Wiley.

Bolz, F. A. (1987). *How to be a hostage and live.* Secaucus, NJ: Lyle Stuart.

Bisson, J., Searle, M., & Srinivasan, M. (1998). Follow-up study of British military hostages and their families held in Kuwait during the Gulf War. *British Journal of Medical Psychology, 71*(3), 247–252.

Butler, W. M., Leitenberg, H., & Fuselier, G. D. (1993). The use of mental health professional consultants to police hostage negotiation teams. *Behavioral Sciences and the Law, 11,* 213–221.

Classen, C., Koopman, C., Hales, R., & Spiegel, D. (1998). Acute stress disorder as a predictor of posttraumatic stress symptoms. *American Journal of Psychiatry, 155*(35), 620–624.

Cooper, A. (1976). Panelist's report. In R. D. Crelinsten, D. Laberge-Altmejd, & D. Szabo (Eds.), *Hostage-taking: Problems of prevention and control* (pp. 101–107). Montreal, Canada: Universite de Montreal.

Cooper, H. (1981). *The hostage-takers.* Boulder, CO: Paladin Press.

Cremniter, D., Crocq, L., Louville, P., & Batista, G. (1997). Posttraumatic reactions of hostages after an aircraft hijacking. *Journal of Nervous and Mental Disease, 185*(5), 344–346.

Donohue, W. A., Ramesh, C., & Borchgrevink, C. (1991). Crisis bargaining: Tracking relational paradox in hostage negotiation. *International Journal of Conflict Management, 2,* 257–274.

Donohue, W. A., & Roberto, A. J. (1993). Relational development as negotiated order in hostage negotiation. *Human Communications Research, 20,* 175–198.

Duffy, J. E. (1997). Situation boards for police negotiations in hostage situations. *FBI Law Enforcement Bulletin, 66*(6), 12–15.

Fuselier, G. N. (1981a). A practical overview of hostage negotiations. *FBI Law Enforcement Bulletin, 50* (Pt. 1), 2–6.

Fuselier, G. N. (1981b). A practical overview of hostage negotiations. *FBI Law Enforcement Bulletin, 50* (Pt. 2), 10–15.

Gladis, S. D. (1979). The hostage terrorist situation and the media. *FBI Law Enforcement Bulletin, 48,* 10–15.

Harvey, A., & Bryant, R. (1998). The relationship between acute stress disorder and posttraumatic stress disorder: A prospective evaluation of motor vehicle accident survivors. *Journal of Consulting and Clinical Psychology, 66*(3), 507–512.

Hatcher, C., Mohandie, K., Turner, J., & Gelles, M. (1998). The role of the psychologist in crisis/hostage negotiations. *Behavioral Sciences and the Law, 16*(4), 455–472.

Herman, J. L. (1995). Complex PTSD: A syndrome in survivors of prolonged and repeated trauma. In G. S. Everly, Jr., & J. M. Lating (Eds.), *Psychotraumatology: Key papers and core concepts in posttraumatic stress* (pp. 87–100). New York: Plenum.

Hosie, T. W., West, J. D., & Mackey, J. A. (1993). Employment and roles of counselors in employee assistance programs. *Journal of Counseling and Development, 71,* 355–359.

Kinney, J. A. (1995). *Violence at work.* Upper Saddle River, NJ: Prentice Hall.

Lanceley, F. J. (1981). The antisocial personality as a hostage taker. *Journal of Police Science and Administration, 9,* 28–34.

Lipsedge, M., & Littlewood, R. (1997). Psychopathology and its publice sources: From a provisional typology to a dramaturgy of domestic seiges. *Anthroplogy and Medicine, 4*(1), 25–43.

Maher, G. F. (1977). *Hostage: A police approach to a contemporary crisis.* Springfield, IL: Charles C Thomas.

Mayer, D. (1999, April). *Trauma response planning : An integral part of critical incident stress management.* Paper presented at the Twenty-Third Annual Convening of Crisis Intervention Personnel, Chicago.

McDuff, D. R. (1992). Social issues in the management of released hostages. *Hospital and Community Psychiatry, 43,* 825–828.

McWhirter, E. H., & Linzer, M. (1994). The provision of critical incidents services by EAPs: A case study. *Journal of Mental Health Counseling, 16,* 403–414.

Miron, M. S., & Goldstein, A. P. (1978). *Hostage.* Kalamazoo, MI: Behaviordelia.

Mitchell, J. T. (1983). When disaster strikes: The critical incident stress debriefing process. *Journal of Emergency Medical Services, 8,* 36–39.

Mitchell, J. T., & Everly, G. S., Jr. (1995a). Critical incidents stress debriefing (CISD) and the prevention of work-related traumatic stress among high risk occupational groups. In G. S. Everly, Jr., & J. M. Lating (Eds.), *Psychotraumatology: Key papers and core concepts in post-traumatic stress* (pp. 267–280). New York: Plenum.

Mitchell, J. T., & Everly, G. S. Jr. (1995b). *Critical incidents stress debriefing: The basic course workbook.* Ellicott City, MD: International Critical Incidents Stress Foundation.

Morrissey, M. (1994, December). Counselors "helping the helpers" from becoming casualties. *Counseling Today, 37*(1), 6–7,12.

Ochberg, F. M. (1977). The victims of terrorism: Psychiatric considerations. *Terrorism, 1,* 147–168.

Powitzky, R. J. (1979). The use and misuse of psychologists in a hostage situation. *The Police Chief, 46,* 30–33.

Schlossberg, G. (1980). Values and organization on hostage and crisis negotiation teams. *Annals of the New York Academy of Sciences, 347,* 113–116.

Schreiber, J. (1978). *The ultimate weapon: Terrorists and world order.* New York: Morrow.

Slatkin, A. (1996). Enhanced hostage negotiation: Therapeutic communication. *FBI Law Enforcement Bulletin, 65*(5), 1–6.

Strentz, T. (1979, April). The Stockholm syndrome: Law enforcement policy and ego defenses of the hostage. *Law Enforcement Bulletin,* p. 1–11.

Strentz, T. (1984). Hostage survival guidelines. In J. Turner (Ed.), *Violence in the medical care setting: A survival guide* (pp. 183–208). Rockville, MD: Aspen Systems.

Strentz, T. (1995). Strategies for victims of hostage situations. In A. R. Roberts (ed.), *Crisis intervention and time limited cognitive treatment* (pp. 127–147). Newbury Park, CA: Sage.

Turner, J. (1984). Hostage incidents in health care settings. In J. Turner (Ed.), *Violence in the medical care setting: A survival guide* (pp. 171–181). Rockville, MD: Aspen Systems.

Vila, G., Porche, L., & Mouren-Simeoni, M. (1998). Étude longitudinale prospective de la pathologie psychotraumatique après une prise d'otages dans une école. *Annales Medico Psychologiques, 156*(1), 14–20.

Walker, L. (1984). *The battered woman syndrome.* New York: Springer.

CHAPTER THIRTEEN

Human Services Workers in Crisis: Burnout

Respond to the following questions with a yes or no.

1. Have you left parties early because the occasion offered you no opportunity to counsel?
2. Do you continue to counsel even though it interferes with your earning a living?
3. Do you sometimes have the "shakes" in the morning and find that this unpleasantness is relieved by counseling a little?
4. Do you repeat everything you hear? I mean, do you repeat or paraphrase everything you hear?

These questions are part of Adams's (1989) humorous, satirical test of counseling addiction. Yet the questions may not be too far off target when viewed in terms of another severe problem that strikes many professionals in the human services business—burnout! Burnout, though, is far from humorous. Burnout is not just some pop psychology term designed to elicit sympathetic responses from one's co-workers or spouse. It is a complex individual-societal phenomenon that affects the welfare of not only millions of human services workers but also tens of millions of those workers' clients (Farber, 1983, pp. vii, 1). Put in economic terms, billions of dollars are lost each year because of workers in all fields who can no longer function adequately in their jobs. Signs and symptoms of burnout include turnover, absenteeism, lowered productivity, and psychological problems (Golembiewski, Munzenrider, & Stevenson, 1986; Riggar, 1985). Yet if burnout has been discussed in all occupations, why should it be endemic to the helping professions?

HELPING PROFESSIONALS: PRIME CANDIDATES

The bulk of writing and research that has been done on burnout has come from the helping professions. The very nature of the job is to be intensely involved with people, and generally these are people who are not at the highest levels of self-actualized behavior (Maslach, 1982b, pp. 32–33). Burnout tends to afflict people who enter their professions highly motivated and idealistic and who expect their work to give their life a sense of meaning (Pines & Aronson, 1988, p. 11). When many of the clients get worse instead of better despite all of the worker's skill and effort, burnout becomes a high probability for these idealistic people. Compounding the harsh realities of historically low success rates, the human services business is becoming tougher. Human services workers are likely to intervene with people with severe psychological and physical traumatic problems connected with sexual and physical assault, murder, Alzheimer's, and AIDS. These traumatic problems call for tremendous amounts of the worker's energy, resilience, and hardiness. When handled day in and day out, the severity of these problems and their duration can wear down the optimism and motivation of any worker (McRaith, 1991).

AIDS counselors are an outstanding example of what we are talking about. They must deal with concerns about safe working practices, fear of infection, intensity of counselor/client/significant other relationships over long periods of physical decline to death, the broad range of services needed, transcrisis events involving a variety of issues, increasing numbers of clients, lack of support by other organizations, and shunning by many health care providers (D'Andrea, 1995; Marino, 1995; Miller, 1995; Oktay, 1992).

The foregoing problems are at the core of the helping professions, making them not just some of the most challenging but also some of the most stress-prone occupations. Thus, human services professionals must be able to tolerate a variety of complex problems that are generally couched in ambiguity, deal with conflict from both clients and institutions, and somehow meet a myriad of demands from the ecological framework in which they operate (Paine, 1982, p. 21).

For the crisis worker, this is true many times over. Crisis center work settings are notorious for long and erratic hours, short pay, poorly functioning clients, immediate deadlines, a lack of control over when clients will arrive or phone, few second chances, repeat callers with chronic problems, hostile and emotionally "raw" clients, and interagency red tape. These are only a few of the stressors that assault crisis workers, making them prime candidates for burnout (Distler, 1990). When the crisis worker is exposed to a high incidence of trauma for extended periods of time, phrases such as "compassion fatigue" (Figley, 1995) and "vicarious traumatization" (McCann & Pearlman, 1990; Pearlman & Mac Ian, 1995; Pearlman & Saakvitne, 1995a, 1995b) have found their way into the literature to describe what happens when workers are faced over and over with unspeakable trauma.

However, a question arises about whether burnout is really dynamically identifiable. Paine (1982, p. 11) and Maslach (1982b, p. 29) report that critics propose that burnout is "part of the job," so if a human services professional "can't stand the heat then he or she ought to get out of the kitchen," because there "always has been stress on this job and always will be." Such cursory dismissal of burnout does not consider the major personal, social, and organizational costs that accrue when job stress turns into crisis (Paine, 1982, p. 11). Burnout is connected to loss of job productivity, impairment of inter- and intrapersonal relationships, and a variety of health problems (Golembiewski & Munzenrider, 1993; Golembiewski, Munzenrider, Scherb, & Billingsley, 1992; Golembiewski et al., 1986). Burnout is not just part of the territory; it has major ramifications for both individuals and institutions (Maslach, 1982b, p. 39). It is a very real problem, with chronic occupational stress as the primary cause (Paine, 1982, p. 16; Tubesing & Tubesing, 1982, p. 156).

DEFINING BURNOUT

A historical definition of burnout places it as a child of the 1970s. The term comes from the psychiatric concept of patients who were burned out physically, emotionally, spiritually, interpersonally, and behaviorally to the point of exhaustion (Paine, 1982, p. 16).

It was first coined as a workplace term by Herbert Freudenberger, to describe young, idealistic volunteers who were working with him in alternative health care settings and who started to look and act worse than many of their clients (Freudenberger, 1974, 1975). Yet defining burnout adequately is not simple.

A very broad definition depicts burnout as an internal psychological experience involving feelings, attitudes, motives, and expectations (Maslach, 1982b, p. 29). Being burned out means that the total psychic energy of the person has been consumed in trying to fuel the fires of existence. This energy crisis occurs because the psychic demand exceeds the supply (Tubesing & Tubesing, 1982, p. 156). It is experienced as a state of physical, mental, and emotional exhaustion caused by long-term involvement in emotionally demanding situations. It is accompanied by an array of symptoms including physical depletion, feelings of helplessness and hopelessness, disillusionment, negative self-concept, and negative attitudes toward work, people, and life itself. It represents a breaking point beyond which the ability to cope with the environment is severely hampered (Pines & Aronson, 1988, pp. 9–10).

DYNAMICS OF BURNOUT

Burnout is not generally perceived as a crisis event, because its onset is slow and insidious. There is no one point or incident that is readily identifiable as the instigating trauma. Rather, it is a slow and steady erosion of the spirit and energy as a result of the daily struggles and chronic stress typical of everyday life and work (Pines & Aronson, 1988, p. 11). Because of the difficulty in identifying burnout, it becomes much easier to chalk it up as a character deficit. A crisis appears only when people are so defeated and exhausted by the environment that they take extraordinary means to find relief, such as quitting a job or occupational field, developing a serious psychosomatic disease, becoming a substance abuser, or attempting suicide. What is even more problematic is that recovery from burnout is not always linear and tends toward chaos and crisis as the individual tries to come to grips with core issues of vocation, personality, and relationships (Kesler, 1990). As a result, the precipitating crisis of job burnout may move toward a more global, existential crisis wherein the person is in a state of crisis over living.

Occupationally, burnout occurs when past and present problems from the job continuously pile up. The problems may come from a variety of sources: demanding and overbearing bosses, unending blizzards of paperwork, jack-of-all-trades-and-master-of-none job descriptions, tidal waves of clients, catastrophic dilemmas far beyond the expertise of the worker, ironclad and unbending institutional rules and procedures, communication problems, and 16-hour workdays. The problems may vary in degree and kind, but the result is a continuous and grinding interface between the person and the work environment (Pines & Aronson, 1988, pp. 43–44; Riggar, 1985, p. xvi). From the worker's standpoint, no short-term or long-term relief is forthcoming.

The body's nonspecific response to any demand is stress. Humans need some stress for optimal performance. However, there comes a point of maximal return for each person. That point is a function of genetic, biological, behavioral, and acquired physiological factors. Beyond that point, stress is harmful (Selye, 1974).

There are two types of stressors. *Psychosocial stressors* become stressors by virtue of the cognitive interpretation assigned to a stimulus (Ellis, 1973; Meichenbaum, 1977). *Biogenic stressors* possess some electrical or biochemical property that is capable of initiating a stress response. Coffee, amphetamines, exercise, and electrical shock produce stress regardless of one's cognitive interpretation of them. By far, though, the greater part of stress in a person's life is self-initiated and self-propagated (Everly, 1989, p. 7).

Environmental events may either "cause" the activation of the stress response or, more often, set the stage for it through cognitive-affective processing (Everly, 1989, p. 45). The actual stress response itself involves enervation of neurological, neuroendocrine, and endocrine systems either singularly or in tandem with one another, which in turn activates various physiological mechanisms directed toward numerous target organs (p. 47). In Selye's (1956) general adaption syndrome, overstimulation and excessive wear of target organs leads to stress-related dysfunction and disease. If the stressor is persistent and there is a chronic drain on adaptive energy, eventual exhaustion of the target organ will occur. The end result physiologically may be as dramatic as a heart attack or as common as a headache.

Stress occurs when there is a substantial imbalance (perceived or real) between environmental demands and the individual's response capability. Burnout occurs when the stress becomes unmediated and the person has no support systems or other buffers to ease the unrelenting pressure (Farber, 1983, p. 14). The outcome is a person affected in every dimension of life by unlimited combinations of symptoms. Such a description very adequately meets the crisis conditions of being in a state of disequilibrium and paralysis.

CORNERSTONES OF BURNOUT

Let us now look at three human services professionals who are experientially and professionally different, but by almost any definition are in the process of burning out.

Elaine. Elaine is a telephone counselor at the local rape crisis center. She has been a volunteer at the center for eight months and has been one of the best crisis workers ever employed there: smart, vivacious, cheery, and full of boundless zeal and energy. Lately, Elaine has become exceedingly curt and short-tempered with her clients and fellow volunteers, to the point that all her co-workers give her a wide berth. They are frankly fed up with her complaints about work, clients, and life in general. Elaine responds by blaming them for being uncommitted and redoubles her efforts to be the greatest crisis worker in the universe.

Mr. Templeton. Mr. Templeton has worked as a school counselor at Central Junior High School for two years. In that time he has instituted some sweeping changes in a guidance program that was, before he came, notorious for running attendance checks and not much more. Mr. Templeton's counseling approach changed all that. Formerly, the last place that students would have gone for help with personal problems would have been the counseling office. By getting out and explaining what his job was all about to students, faculty, parent groups, civic organizations, and anybody else who would listen, and indeed, making good on his promises, Mr. Templeton has turned the guidance office into something akin to a land office during the California gold rush. His principal would now fight a circular saw to keep Mr. Templeton around. What the principal does not know is that Mr. Templeton has fantasies about sending the entire ninth grade to an Outward Bound camp in the Sahara Desert.

He has not had a new idea about how to improve the counseling program in six months and is wondering if maybe that stockbroker's job that he so capriciously turned down last year was not such a bad idea after all. As he considers all this, he wistfully looks at his wristwatch, then at the ninth-grader sitting across from him, and wonders whether she is in his office because of grade problems or a problem at home. She has been talking for 30 minutes, and he cannot remember two sentences she has said.

Josh. Josh is a social worker at an outpatient clinic for a community mental health center. He has worked there for five years. His patient load resembles something on the order of bus traffic to Mecca. He has just received a memorandum from the director further increasing his caseload by 20 percent, along with a rather curt directive to move on some of those old cases and get them off the clinic rolls. Josh is sitting in his friendly local tavern quietly getting drunk and wondering how he is going to put 20 people out on the street with no support. He is also mulling over what response he will make to his wife, who just this morning asked for a separation. Among the complaints she voiced, his job was prominent: the lousy pay for somebody with a master's degree, the long hours with no compensatory time, the emergencies in the middle of the night, and particularly forgetting he is the father of their two children and a husband to her. Josh stares across the bar and orders another drink. While waiting for his order, he swallows an antacid tablet for the dull, burning pain slowly working its way outward from the pit of his stomach.

What do these three human services professionals have in common? They are alike in that they are all empathic, sensitive, humane, idealistic, and people oriented and have been highly committed and dedicated to their profession. However, like most other human services workers prone to burnout, they also tend to be overly anxious, obsessional, enthusiastic, a bit neurotic, extraverted, conscientious, and susceptible to identifying with their clients (Farber, 1983, p. 4; Piedmont, 1993). For each of them, one or more of the following foundation blocks of burnout have been laid (Farber, 1983, p. 6; Lee & Ashforth, 1993; Powell, 1994; Sek-yum, 1993; Turnipseed, 1994):

1. *Role ambiguity.* They lack clarity concerning rights, responsibilities, methods, goals, status, and accountability to themselves or their institutions.
2. *Role conflict.* Demands placed on them are incompatible, inappropriate, and inconsistent with values and ethics.
3. *Role overload.* The quantity and quality of demands placed on them have become too great.
4. *Inconsequentiality.* They have a feeling that no matter how hard they work, the outcome means little in terms of recognition, accomplishment, appreciation, or success.
5. *Isolation.* They have little social support either in the institution or outside of it.
6. *Autonomy.* Their ability to make decisions as to what they will do and how they will deal with their clients is co-opted by the bureaucracy of their place of employment.

These foundation stones are not thrown down haphazardly. They are built up slowly but surely over time through a variety of dynamics.

RESEARCH ON BURNOUT DYNAMICS

The following points have been supported to varying degrees by research on burnout (Carroll & White, 1982; Golembiewski & Munzenrider, 1993; Golembiewski et al., 1992; Golembiewski et al., 1986; Grouse, 1984; Hoeksma, Guy, Brown, & Brady,

1993; Koeske, Kirk, & Koeske, 1993; Lee & Ashforth, 1993; Maslach, 1982a; Piedmont, 1993; Pines & Aronson, 1988; Powell, 1994; Sek-yum, 1993; Turnipseed, 1994).

1. All stressors can help lead to burnout.
2. Burnout is psychobiological.
3. Environmental factors other than work can be contributors.
4. A lack of effective interpersonal relationships exists.
5. Signs of burnout will occur, but recognition of them depends on the observer's astuteness.
6. Symptoms sometimes appear quickly, but most usually occur over time.
7. Burnout is process oriented rather than event oriented.
8. Burnout varies in severity from mild energy loss to death.
9. Burnout also varies in duration.
10. Burnout and resulting crisis can occur more than once.
11. Awareness varies from complete denial to full consciousness of the problem.
12. Burnout is infectious in that it puts additional stress on other workers.
13. Burnout is greatest for young workers and least for older workers.
14. Minorities tend to be less susceptible to burnout than whites.
15. Men and women are fairly similar with their experience of burnout.
16. Those who are single experience the most burnout, whereas those with families experience the least.
17. Restorative and preventive measures have to be individually tailored because of the idiosyncratic nature of burnout.
18. Burnout has progressive phases that can be identified by varying degrees of depersonalization, personal accomplishment (or lack thereof), and emotional exhaustion the individual exhibits.
19. Burnout is not a disease, and the medical model is not an appropriate analytical model.
20. Burnout should not be confused with malingering.
21. Progressive deterioration in physical and mental health occurs as burnout increases.
22. Job autonomy and social support buffers are critical to preventing, containing, and reducing burnout.
23. Making time for leisure and using it wisely are as important as any job variable.
24. Burnout can lead to personal and professional growth as well as to despair and trauma.

MYTHS THAT ENGENDER BURNOUT

Candidates for burnout believe a number of myths about themselves and how they must operate in their environment (Everly, 1989; Friedman & Rosenman, 1974; Kesler, 1990; Maslach, 1982a; Pines & Aronson, 1988; Rodesch, 1994). They tend to distort the reality of the situation in typical Type A personality patterns (Friedman & Rosenman, 1974) such that they compose a variety of irrational statements about themselves and their work. These statements are modeled after Albert Ellis's (Patterson, 1980, pp. 68–70) insane thoughts people say to themselves about their predicaments:

1. "My job is my life." This means long hours, no leisure time, and difficulty delegating authority. Anxiety, defensiveness, anger, and frustration are the result when things do not go perfectly.
2. "I must be totally competent, knowledgeable, and able to help everyone." Unrealistic expectations of performance, a need to prove oneself, lack of confidence, and overriding guilt occur when one is not perfect.
3. "To accomplish my job and maintain my own sense of self-worth, I must be liked and approved of by everyone with whom I work." Thus, such workers cannot assert themselves, set limits, say no, disagree with others, or give negative feedback. Therefore, they get manipulated by others in the work setting—including clients. Self-doubt, passive hostility, insecurity, and subsequent depression are the reward.
4. "Other people are hardheaded and difficult to deal with, do not understand the real value of my work, and should be more supportive." Stereotyping and generalizing about specific problems and people occur and lack of creativity, wasted energy, and decreased motivation result. The person has a defeatist attitude and a passive acceptance of the status quo.
5. "Any negative feedback indicates there is something wrong with what I do." The person cannot evaluate his or her work realistically and make constructive changes. There is a great deal of anger with critics, which may manifest itself in either passive or aggressive hostility, depending on the person toward whom the anger is directed. Frustration and immobilization are the outcomes.
6. "Because of past blunders and failures by others, things will not work the way they must." Old programs are not carried to fruition, nor are new ones created. Stagnation and decay in the work setting are the result.
7. "Things have to work out the way I want." The person's behavior is thus characterized by working extra hours, checking up on staff members' work, and shows inability to compromise or delegate, overattention to detail, repetition of tasks, impatience with others, and an authoritarian style.
8. "I must be omniscient and infallible." The person can never be wrong. The very act of doing therapy with humans in all their infinite ways of behaving means fallibility for the worker, particularly when the client is in crisis. These dynamics provide a wide array of symptoms.

SYMPTOMS OF BURNOUT

Burnout is a multidimensional phenomenon, consisting of behavioral, physical, interpersonal, and attitudinal components. We have gleaned the symptoms of burnout from a variety of sources and present them in Table 13.1 for ready reference. Undoubtedly the list is not all-encompassing. Certainly not all human services workers in crisis manifest all the symptoms listed. Yet for the watchful observer, many will become noticeable, particularly if one looks back in time and notes any pronounced changes in the worker.

LEVELS OF BURNOUT

Burnout can be categorized as occurring at one of three levels: trait, state, and activity (Forney, Wallace-Schutzman, & Wiggers, 1982). At a trait level, it is all-pervasive, encompassing every facet of the worker's life. The worker is completely nonfunctional in

TABLE 13.1 Symptoms of Burnout

Behavioral	Physical	Interpersonal	Attitudinal
Reduced quantity or efficiency of work	Chronic fatigue and exhaustion	Withdrawal from family	Depression
Use and abuse of alcohol and illicit drugs	Lower resistance	Compulsion to do all and be all at home	Feeling of emptiness, meaninglessness
Increase in absenteeism	Maladies occurring at organ weak points: ulcers, migraines, gastrointestinal upset, facial tics, etc.	No mature inter-actions—keeping hidden agendas	Ranging from omnipotence to incompetence
Increase in risk taking	Colds and viral infections	Keeping everyone subservient	Cynicism
Increase in medication	Poor coordination	Feeling drawn to people who are less secure	Paranoia
Clock watching	Insomnia, nightmares, excessive sleeping		Compulsiveness and obsessiveness
Complaining	Muscular tension	Reduction of significant others to status of clients	Callousness
Changing or quitting the job	Addiction to alcohol and/or drugs	Breaking up of long-lasting relationships	Guilt
Inability to cope with minor problems	Increased use of tobacco and caffeine	Becoming therapeuti-cally minded and overreacting to comments of friends	Boredom
Lack of creativity	Over- and undereating		Helplessness
Loss of enjoyment	Hyperactivity	No separation of professional and social life	Terrifying and paralyzing feelings and thoughts
Loss of control	Sudden weight gain or loss	Allowing clients to abuse privacy of home by calls or visits at any time	Stereotyping
Tardiness	Flare-ups in preexist-ing medical condi-tions: high blood pressure, ulcers, asthma, diabetes, etc.		Depersonalizing
Dread of work		No opportunity for or enjoyment in just being one's self	Pessimism
Vacillation between extremes of over-involvement and detachment	Injury from high-risk behavior	Loneliness, trust issues	Air of righteousness
Mechanistic responding	Missed menstrual cycle	Loss of authenticity	Grandiosity
Accident proneness	Increased pre-menstrual tension	Loss of ability to relate to friends, family, or to clients	Sick humor, particu-larly aimed at clients
Change in or cessation of religious affiliation	Injury from accident	Avoidance of close interpersonal contact	Distrust of manage-ment, supervisors, and peers
Errors in setting therapeutic boundaries	Increased vigilance and safety issues for self and loved ones	Switch from open and accepting to closed and denying	Hypercritical attitude toward institution and co-workers
Errors in judgment and strategy in and outside therapy		Inability to cope with minor interpersonal problems	Hopelessness
PTSD-like symptoms of intrusive thoughts, numbing of affect, and hypervigilance		Isolation from or overbonding with staff	Entrapment in job and relations
Suicide attempts		Increased expression of anger and mistrust	Free-floating feelings of inadequacy, inferi-ority, and incompe-tence and guilt
Homicide attempts			Self-criticism and perfectionism
			Rapid mood swings
			Loss of faith, meaning, purpose
			Change in religious beliefs
			Sense of grounding, inner balance lost
			Increased sense of vulnerability to world at-large

regard to person, place, and time. The trait level of burnout is extremely serious and calls for immediate intervention in the worker's life.

At a state level, burnout may be periodic or situational. A classic example is what occurs during the period of full moon at a crisis line center. At such times it seems as if every crisis-prone person in town takes a signal from a lunar clock to go berserk. Although problematic, such crisis situations are relieved when the moon wanes, and the crisis line worker returns to some semblance of normalcy. However, over the long term, such state events contribute mightily to anticipatory anxiety, which if not dealt with can precipitate total burnout.

Finally, burnout may be activity based. Any activity that is performed over and over at an intense level, as in encounter group counseling of substance abusers or serving as a chaplain to the grief-stricken in a trauma center, will invariably wear the armor off the most emotionally bullet-proof crisis worker. A simple way of decreasing chances of burnout when the stressor is activity based is to change the routine. However, such change is not always easily accomplished or even recognized as needed.

STAGES OF BURNOUT

Another way of characterizing the road to burnout is by stages. Edelwich and Brodsky (1982, pp. 135–136) delineated four stages through which the typical candidate for burnout goes.

Stage 1: Enthusiasm. The worker enters the job with high hopes and unrealistic expectations. If such idealism is not tempered by orientation and training programs that define what the worker can reasonably expect to accomplish, such a rose-colored view of human services work will inevitably lead to the stage of stagnation.

Stage 2: Stagnation. Stagnation occurs when the worker starts to feel that personal, financial, and career needs are not being met. Awareness may come from seeing people perceived as less able moving up the career ladder faster, pressures from home to meet increased financial obligations, and lack of personal intrinsic reinforcement for doing the job well. Astute management policy will head off stagnation by providing a variety of incentives that clearly say to the worker, "You're doing a good job here, and we appreciate it." If intrinsic and extrinsic reinforcement does not occur, the worker will move into the next stage, frustration.

Stage 3: Frustration. Frustration clearly indicates that the worker is in trouble. The worker starts questioning the effectiveness, value, and impact of his or her efforts in the face of ever-mounting obstacles. Because the effects of burnout are highly contagious in the organizational setting, one person's frustration is likely to have a domino effect on others. One appropriate way of meeting frustration is to confront the problem head on by arranging workshops or support groups to increase awareness of the burnout syndrome, and generate problem solving as a group to bring about changes within both the institution and the individual. Catching the problem at this stage may well lead back to a more tempered stage of enthusiasm. If the problem is not resolved, then the final stage, apathy, is reached.

Stage 4: Apathy. Apathy is burnout. It is a chronic indifference to the situation and defies most efforts at intervention. Apathy is truly a crisis stage: The person is in a state of disequilibrium and immobility. Further compounding this stage are denial and little objective understanding of what is occurring. At this point psychotherapy is almost mandatory if reversal is to take place.

WORKER–CLIENT RELATIONSHIPS AND BURNOUT

As crisis intervention has spread to more and more areas of psychological trauma, interest in what happens to the workers who deal with these clients has led to the concept of secondary stress disorder or what McCann and Pearlman (1990) call *vicarious traumatization* and Figley (1995) calls *compassion fatigue.* These are the very real, concrete negative effects that occur when human service workers have prolonged exposure to traumatized clients who are in crisis. Research does indicate that crisis workers experience more negative effects from their work than other types of human services workers (Arvay & Uhlemann, 1996; Blanchard & Jones, 1997; Charney & Pearlman, 1998; Johnson & Hunter, 1997). Why is this so?

Because trauma work and crisis intervention is so potentially addictive and at the same time, so potentially destructive! Much like police officers, paramedics, and other emergency workers, the "rush" that occurs from being in the middle of traumatic events and the "adrenaline high" that accompanies successful crisis intervention with some of the most difficult and intense problems the human services worker is likely to face makes the work highly addictive. Yet the constant exposure to the "highs" that come with dealing with traumatic events also means that the crisis worker is exposed to a constant barrage of some of the most graphic and horrible physical and psychological ramifications that nature or humankind can visit on people. Two psychological concepts are hallmarks of dealing with crisis clients, and, if not understood and dealt with, have the potential to infect the crisis worker and lead to burnout. Those two concepts are countertransference and vicarious traumatization/compassion fatigue.

Countertransference

Whenever therapy becomes intense as in crisis work, the potential for countertransference to occur rises dramatically. Countertransference is the attributing to the client, by the crisis worker, of traits and behaviors of past and present significant others or events in the crisis worker's own life. Countertransference responses may be positive or negative, spoken or unspoken, conscious or unconscious. They may include physical, psychological, social, gender, racial, moral, spiritual, cultural, or ecological factors that have impacted the worker through past experiences and are manifested in the "here and now" of therapy by the client. At times, emotional aspects of the client may agitate feelings, thoughts, and behaviors that are deeply buried within the worker's own personality. When confronted with their own shortcomings, fears, faults, prejudices, and stereotypes as mirrored by the client, human services workers may begin behaving in inappropriate ways. Workers may act in ways designed to meet their own needs and not the clients'. The result is that clients are made to fit neatly into the workers' preconceived patterns for the way things "ought to be" and not necessarily in reference to the client but how they "ought to be" for the crisis worker (Freudenberger, 1977).

The general axiom of psychoanalytic therapy is that countertransference needs to be guarded against and the therapist's refusal to recognize it and deal with it can, at the least, inhibit the therapist's effectiveness, and at the most, be destructive to the relationship. If the phenomenon of countertransference is not recognized and dealt with in positive ways, the human services worker ends up feeling guilty about having negative feelings toward the client and is not even sure why those feelings are occurring. Such feelings are antithetical to what the worker has been taught and believes and can significantly compound the occupational stresses that lead to burnout.

However, Pearlman and Saakvitne (1995a, pp. 22–24) propose that if crisis workers are to deal successfully and understand the pain of their clients in deeply empathic ways, then countertransference is inevitable and necessary. Particularly emotion-laden issues such as physical and sexual abuse of children, terminal illnesses, and chronic suicidal ideation are prime examples of content that may be exceedingly stressful to the worker because of strong feelings and experiences the worker may have about the problem (Daley, 1979; Fox & Cooper, 1998; Pearlman & Saakvitne, 1995a).

Vicarious Traumatization/Compassion Fatigue

Vicarious traumatization and compassion fatigue are different than the phenomenon of countertransference. They occur as a result of an accumulation of experiences across therapies and clients and are felt far beyond the transference–countertransference issues of a specific client–therapist relationship. Whereas countertransference is temporary, vicarious traumatization and compassion fatigue permanently change the psychological constructs of workers who engage in intense and long-term trauma and are an inevitable occupational hazard of trauma work (Saakvitne & Pearlman, 1996, p. 31). The end result of vicarious traumatization and compassion fatigue are their generalizing effects on countertransference issues. As vicarious traumatization is multiplied and generalized over clients, countertransference reactions become stronger through the human service worker acting them out against the client or submerging them even deeper from awareness (Saakvitne & Pearlman, 1996, p. 48). We believe that for human services workers in general, and crisis workers in particular, vicarious traumatization and compassion fatigue are major mediating factors that lead to burnout.

Maslach (1982b, pp. 36–37) stated that the only human services workers who burn out are the ones who are on fire. For such workers, Saakvitne and Pearlman (1996, pp. 26, 49) and Figley (1995) believe that the deep empathy needed to deal with such heart-wrenching situations that often accompany crises makes the worker vulnerable to intense and overwhelming feelings and profound disruptions in their beliefs, and assaults the very core of the worker's hope and idealism. Over time, such assaults lead to compassion fatigue (Figley, 1995) wherein the crisis worker's energy is literally wrung out by the incidence and amplitude of dealing with the horrific problems that trauma clients face.

Between a very real dedicatory ethic and at times an insatiable need to assist everyone with any type of problem, the idealistic human services worker sees his or her job as a calling. In an imperfect world, such an idealistic outlook can lead to overinvolvement and identification with the client—often to the worker's detriment (Koeske & Kelly, 1995). As the human services worker becomes more deeply enmeshed in the helping relationship, the worker's strong need to be accepted and liked makes it harder and harder to say no to the client's demands. At this point, the worker has started to take on responsibility for the client. The worker's overinvolvement with the client may be manifested in a variety of ways. Extending the session beyond its usual time limit, taking and responding to phone calls at home at all hours of the night, experiencing hurt feelings over client failures, attempting dramatic cures on impossible cases, becoming panic stricken when well-laid plans go awry, refusing to withdraw from the case when it is clearly beyond the worker's purview, becoming angry or bored with clients, discounting the client's problems, becoming frustrated over lack of progress and losing one's sense of humor over the human dilemma are some of the many indicators that the worker is not paying attention to his or her own needs or, frankly, to the client's (Van Auken, 1979). The foregoing are all indicators that unresolved countertransference and vicarious trauma/compassion fatigue issues are flourishing.

Under these circumstances, the helping relationship quickly comes to be seen by the worker as a chore, and the client may regress and act out as a way of announcing the client's awareness of the worker's apathetic attitude. As this psychological vortex continues and the worker becomes even more overwrought and discouraged, termination of the therapeutic relationship by the client is the likely result (Watkins, 1983). Such negative reinforcement does little to mollify the worker's already bruised ego and leads further to a downward spiral into burnout. Whether exposure to these occupational hazards has negative or positive outcomes depends a great deal on how both the individual worker and human services institutions deal with them in proactive ways (Deiter & Pearlman, 1998; Figley, 1995; Pearlman & Saakvitne, 1995a; Saakvitne & Pearlman, 1996).

THE CULPABILITY OF ORGANIZATIONS

Much of the responsibility for burnout rests with the employing agency and its inability to either recognize or do anything about organizational problems that lead to burnout (Everly, 1989, pp. 295–297; Pines & Aronson, 1988, pp. 97–111; Shinn & Mørch, 1983, p. 238). Savicki and Cooley (1987) compared degree of burnout with work environment and found that those workers who scored highest on burnout indexes felt that they had little impact on procedural and policy issues, lacked autonomy within the guidelines of the job structure, were unclear about agency objectives, had a high intensity of work assignments over extended periods of time, were highly restricted in how they could deal with clients, and felt generally unappreciated by their co-workers or supervisors. Above all, the organization's inability to clearly define job roles and functions causes role conflict and role ambiguity, and these are two of the best predictors of the workplace's contribution to burnout (Barber & Iwai, 1996). These findings should not be construed as representing "gripes" of the respondents. Numerous other studies (Burke & Greenglass, 1995; Duquette, Kerouac, Sandhu, & Beaudet, 1994; Jayaratne, Vinokur-Kaplan, & Chess, 1995; Lee & Ashforth, 1993; Sek-yum, 1993; Turnipseed, 1994) have substantiated findings that agencies that do not take pains to communicate clearly with and support their staff have high burnout rates.

One of the most critical support mechanisms for crisis workers is easy access to consultation and supervision. We contend that crisis intervention should never be done in isolation, and the case example we present in this chapter is an excellent example of why that is so. Yet, as Pearlman and Saakvitne (1995a, p. 359) report, unsupervised trauma therapy seems all too common. Pearlman and Mac Ian (1995) found that less than two-thirds of trauma therapists they interviewed reported getting any kind of supervision, although more than 80 percent who did receive supervision and consultation found it helpful.

In contrast, those agencies that do allow input into the mission of the organization, are flexible in providing instrumental and emotional support to workers, generate support groups, provide consultation, have job clarity, promote managers with social leadership styles, retain realistic expectations for the progress of their clients and furnish supervision to help workers solve problems associated with the high stress of their jobs report workers with lower indexes of burnout (Everly, 1989, pp. 299–309; Melchior, van den Berg, Halfens, & Abu-Saad, 1997; Pines & Aronson, 1988, pp. 107–111; Savicki & Cooley, 1987).

SELF-RECOGNITION OF BURNOUT

Whatever the degree of burnout, human services workers and their organizations have a notorious blind spot. What they can detect in others and change by therapeutic intervention, they are generally unaware of in themselves. Furthermore, they have extreme difficulty maintaining both the personal and professional objectivity to self-diagnose burnout or foster the discipline and devote the energy to integrate effective intervention strategies into their own lives (Spicuzza & Devoe, 1982). If they finally are confronted with the fact that something is terribly wrong in their professional lives, their initial maladaptive response is likely to be "What's wrong with me?" rather than "What can I do to change the situation?" If they are able to move to the second question, their typical operating mode is not to change the situation but rather to increase the amount of effort and subsequently increase the original problem (Pines & Aronson, 1988, pp. 5–9).

What is problematic about burnout is that its symptoms and causes are neither universal nor specific in nature (Forney et al., 1982). Recognizing burnout is not always easy. In a medical analogy, its presenting symptoms might look like anything from typhoid fever to a broken leg.

Nevertheless, whereas no formula can be applied to diagnose its onset or to treat it, the affliction need not be terminal (Forney et al., 1982). Indeed, given the variety of symptoms and dynamics presented, both preventive and curative measures can be taken. Before we delve into intervention, we want to be very clear that we agree with Watkins (1983) that no one—and we would go a step further and state that *absolutely no one*—who practices in the human services professions is immune to burnout. It is a dangerous malady that in its extremes can be vocationally or even physically lethal if not dealt with in assertive ways.

Furthermore, it has been our experience that human services workers, like some of you who are reading this passage and are saying, "It'll never happen to me," are invariably the kinds of fellow professionals we end up treating; or, in the absence of treatment, become those who can no longer stand to ply the trade and quit; or, at the extreme, become substance abusers or suicidal. In these circumstances, the outcomes range from bad to worse: bad for the profession and worse for you, the professional.

INTERVENTION STRATEGIES

Emphasis in applying the six-step method will usually focus on the directive end of the continuum because of the depth of the crisis and the client, a "I know more than you do and I'm not nuts" fellow worker. The crisis interventionist who helps a burned-out human services worker typically must proceed in a very directive manner while confronting the client's irrational beliefs, proposing definite alternatives, and getting the client to commit to specific action steps that will get the person out of the state of immobility. Put in simple terms, fellow human services workers are some of the most stubborn and denial-prone clients there are when they have reached the later stages of burnout.

Intervention for the human services worker suffering from burnout may best be considered in three distinct dimensions: intervention through training, intervention with the organization, and intervention with the individual. Triage assessment of the level of burnout is important in determining the type of intervention to be used. At a trait level, individual therapeutic intervention will clearly be warranted. At a state or activity level, training or organizational intervention may be sufficient. When the organization itself becomes a client, triage assessment would clearly include the administering of both burnout and work setting instruments to all members of the organization and following up that administration with individual interviews.

Assessment

Two types of instruments are important in determining burnout. The first type has to do with determining the degree of burnout in the individual. The Maslach Burnout Inventory (Maslach & Jackson, 1981a) is a valid cross-oocupational and cross-cultural (Gorter, Albrecht, Hoostraten, & Eijkman, 1999) instrument that measures three symptom patterns associated with burnout. The Emotional Exhaustion scale assesses feelings of being emotionally worn out by work. The Personal Accomplishment scale measures feelings of competence and achievement with work. The Depersonalization scale measures unfeeling and impersonal responses toward clients. The scales can also be combined to produce a total frequency and intensity score for burnout.

Golembiewski and associates (1986) used the Maslach Burnout Inventory's three domains to develop a progressive phase model of burnout. In their model, depersonalization is seen as the least potent and initial burnout phase. It must occur prior to any substantial reductions in feelings of personal accomplishment, which they see as a secondary response and more potent level of burnout. Emotional exhaustion, the third and most potent indicator of burnout (Lee & Ashforth, 1996; Wright & Bonett, 1997), would follow heightening of the prior two stages. On the basis of high or low scores from the three Maslach scales, individuals can be placed in eight progressively higher categories of burnout. Whereas in Phase I, all three scales would be low, at Phase VIII all would be high (Golembiewski et al., 1986, p. 23).

The second type of instrument measures the work setting. Typical of this type of assessment device is the Work Environment Scale (Moos, 1981), which measures ten different dimensions of an organizational component named "social climate." Scales range across job commitment, support from co-workers and management, independence in decision making, efficient and planful approaches to tasks, performance pressure, role clarity, degree of control by management, variety and change in job, and physical comfort. Taken together, these two types of instruments provide a way of examining the degree of burnout in relation to environmental factors within the organization, yield a fairly comprehensive picture of how burned out the worker is, and indicate the degree of intervention necessary (Savicki & Cooley, 1987).

Intervention Through Training

Today's students in the human services badly need to know how to work their way through and around the paper blizzard that managed care, third-party insurance, and government compliance regulations have created that effectively hamstring the worker's autonomy. Nothing is more frustrating and causes workers to become burned out more quickly than loss of control over decision making for clients (Arches, 1991). Operating effectively within the bureaucracy and being able to do so as stress free as possible should be one of the top priorities of training programs (Pines & Aronson, 1988, p. 194; Sowa, May, & Niles, 1994).

Early in a human services worker's training, and on an ongoing basis when in practice, emphasis needs to be placed on correcting worker attitudes that lead to over-involvement (Koeske & Kelly, 1995). Although Saakvitne and Pearlman (1996, pp. 25–26) argue that the deep empathy needed for trauma work inevitably begets counter-transference and vicarious traumatization, at least a part of training should focus on increasing therapeutic detachment and moderating idealism (Warnath & Shelton, 1976). Beginning human services practitioners need to have their rose-colored glasses gently removed so they can see that their good intentions are doing neither themselves nor their clients much good (Pines & Aronson, 1988, p. 194). Most particularly, students need to examine their limited insight into their own unresolved issues and conflicts and how those interact with those of their clients, particularly when they are dealing with the often horrific material that is a hallmark of crisis intervention and trauma work (Watkins, 1983, Pearlman & Saakvitne, 1995a, pp. 359–380).

Not all students in the human services field are psychologically equipped to go into crisis work. Although this work is absolutely some of the most gratifying and reinforcing there is in the human service field, it is also some of the most gut-wrenching and heart-breaking. Students who are not exposed to realistic field experiences and good supervision may go blindly into one of the most stressful occupational fields we know.

Intervention with the Organization

Much of the literature shows burnout to be situation based (Barber & Iwai, 1996; Kesler, 1990; Melchior et al., 1997). Thus, the organization can also be considered as client. When an organization is in danger of burnout, all those who work in the organization who should be involved in restructuring working conditions. Indeed, one of the major criticisms of burnout intervention has been the lack of change in the total system (Carroll & White, 1982, p. 56). What makes the major difference between obtaining peak performance from workers as opposed to having them burn out is whether the work environment is supportive or stressful (Pines & Aronson, 1988, p. 48). Lack of positive reinforcement by the institution is not at all uncommon and fits neatly into an aversive management policy: "There is no such thing as burnout, only staff who don't work and have malicious motives toward the organization." As staff become increasingly burned out, they tend to fulfill management's negative predictions about them (Carroll & White, 1982, pp. 53–54). Although much is mentioned in the burnout literature about eradicating the negative aspects of the work environment, research indicates that a lack of positive features is significantly correlated with burnout independent of the presence of negative work features (Pines & Aronson, 1988, p. 48).

Human services organizations are notorious for having to live continuously on the edge of financial exigency. Lack of physical, human, and financial resources militates against comprehensive service provision and long-term planning. Organizations that face crises such as funding and human resource cutbacks often cope with problems by unwittingly adapting crisis characteristics and operating in a state of disequilibrium and immobility. Just letting the crisis "run its course" is no more appropriate for organizations than for individuals in crisis (Devine, 1984).

Therefore, from an ecological standpoint, the organization needs to move away from piecemeal interventions and apply techniques that have general inputs to the total organization rather than just inputs focused on individuals (Paine, 1982, p. 25). Ideally, interventions should be multifaceted and take into consideration both individual and environmental issues in a balanced and sensitive fashion (Carroll & White, 1982, p. 53).

When the total organization is burned out, Freudenberger (1975) suggests shutting it down for a period of time. Short of closing down, which is probably a pragmatic impossibility, the organization has a number of options. As a start, the administration can take the time to articulate clearly the organization's mission. Cherniss and Krantz (1983) found that organizations that have a clear ideology of purpose have reduced burnout in staff because they minimize ambiguity and doubt about what kind of action is to be taken. Time should be devoted both to establishing positive co-worker and supervisory relationships and to reducing the rules, regulations, and paper work that line staff face as they attempt to provide service to their clients (Savicki & Cooley, 1987). Improving job design, flexible hours, continuous supervision and training, intrinsic and extrinsic reinforcement, and emotional support are a few of many changes that will go a long way toward reducing burnout (Shinn & Mørch, 1983, p. 238). The organization needs to establish, as a high priority, understanding and dealing with the vicarious traumatization that workers invariably experience as they do crisis intervention (Saakvitne & Pearlman, 1996, p. 21).

Most attempts to deal with the organization by people who are burned out are typified by passively hostile actions that include physical, emotional, and mental withdrawal from problems the organization faces (Pines & Aronson, 1988, pp. 91–93). However, effective organizational change rarely is generated solely by the administration. To effect change in the organization, each individual must recognize that there is an institutional problem and be responsible for doing something about it. Beginning to take responsibility for effecting change in a difficult situation is therapeutic in and of itself simply because it reduces the debilitating effects of the feeling of helplessness. Yet workers who believe that everything about an organization is wrong and should be changed are the most likely to be burnouts. Some aspects of the bureaucracy cannot be changed short of destroying it. Thus workers need to develop the ability to distinguish between those aspects of the organization that can be changed and those that cannot (Pines & Aronson, 1988, p. 29).

Social Support Systems.   Social support systems are critical to avoiding burnout, whether at home or in the workplace (Brown & O'Brien, 1998; Distler, 1990; Greenglass, Fiksenbaum, & Burke, 1996; Kesler, 1990; Pines & Aronson, 1988). Support systems act as buffers for the individual and help maintain psychological and physical well-being over time (Pines, 1983, p. 157). However, in the human services business, chaotic work schedules militate heavily against strong social ties (Farber, 1983, pp. 16–17) and allow workers little time to enjoy positive interaction with one another, because the focus is constantly on trying to solve client problems (Maslach, 1978).

In that regard, Golembiewski and associates (1986) propose that both instrumental support to achieve an end, such as material assistance, and expressive support to provide a sense of belonging and caring are needed (p. 52). They found that employee concern and commitment to the job, peer friendliness and support for one another, and management's support and encouragement of employees all characterized low- as opposed to high-burnout groups (p. 189).

Social support systems have six basic functions: listening, technical support, technical challenge, emotional support, emotional challenge, and sharing social reality (Pines, 1983).

1. *Listening.* Periodically, all workers need someone to listen actively to them in an empathic manner without giving advice or making judgments (p. 158).
2. *Technical support.* When confronted with complex client problems, all workers need someone who can affirm confidence in their endeavors. Such a person must have the expertise to understand the complexities of the job and be able to give the worker honest feedback (p. 158).
3. *Technical challenge.* If workers are not intellectually challenged, they will stagnate. Intellectual contact with significant others stretches the worker in a positive way. Such challenges can come only from people who do not intend to humiliate or gain an advantage and who have professional expertise equivalent to that of the worker (p. 158).
4. *Emotional support.* Workers need someone to be on their side in difficult situations, even if the significant others do not necessarily agree totally with the workers. Professional expertise is not necessary for this function (pp. 158–159).
5. *Emotional challenge.* It is comforting for workers to believe that they have explored all avenues in attempting to resolve their problems. Support persons serve a valuable function when they question such assumptions and confront the worker's excuses. This function should be used sparingly; otherwise it may be construed as nagging (p. 159).
6. *Sharing social reality.* When workers become unsure of the reliability of their own perceptions about the reality of the situation, they need external validation. This function is especially important when workers feel that they are losing the ability to evaluate what is happening with their clients and with the organization (p. 159).

Although Maslach and Jackson (1981b) found that the support system of spouses makes married workers less prone to burnout than their unmarried colleagues, it is impossible for one's spouse or close friend to fulfill all these tasks (Pines, 1983, p. 172). Clearly, the worker needs to have functioning support systems at the job site. How, then, might this occur if it does not happen spontaneously?

Support Groups. Within the organizational structure, time should be set aside for formal, structured support groups. Structurally, a support group resembles a problem-solving discussion group. The goal of such a group is to build a sense of competence and help workers feel that they can deal with the stresses they encounter in their work situation. A support group is a safe place for workers to disagree and challenge feelings of helplessness. The group serves as a cathartic agent for releasing pent-up emotions related to the job. Once catharsis occurs, members can realistically examine feelings associated with job stressors. By providing feedback, the support group validates for members that they are not alone in their feelings and reassures them that they are not abnormal in their response to the situation (Sculley, 1983, pp. 188–191). The group should also fulfill the six basic functions suggested by Pines (1983).

To do this effectively, a support group not only needs the support of the administration but also must have a consultant/facilitator who is sensitive to the issues involved and can walk a tight-wire between allowing the group to vent feelings and keeping the group in a problem-solving mode. The consultant/facilitator also needs to be in a position to provide the administration with information from the group that will allow for effective organizational change without becoming a "snitch" in the process (Sculley, 1983, pp. 193–194).

Workshops on Burnout.   For a deeper level of intervention, we would propose institution of workshops that deal with burnout of the organization, with everybody in attendance, particularly administrative heads. The involvement of administration is critical at this juncture. If workers do not have confidence that organizational leadership is concerned, and if they believe that no lines of communication to their administrative supervisors are open, then little change is likely to result (Berkeley Planning Associates, 1977). Attendance of supervisors is crucial to ensure that everyone understands the sources of stress that occur in the work setting, because the factors that cause burnout in administrators are very different from those for direct service staff (Savicki & Cooley, 1987). The line staff may have some reticence to speak openly and honestly about their concerns when administrators are present. Carefully laid ground rules by the outside consultant that include the administrator leading off with his or her concerns, no recrimination statements, and speaking to institutional behaviors rather than staff or administrators' personalities goes a long way in freeing up communication and problem solving.

A comprehensive workshop should be designed to explore the individual symptoms of burnout, analyze personal, professional, and organizational sources of burnout, and culminate by forming personal contracts designed to counteract on-the-job disillusionment and stress (Baron & Cohen, 1982). We also believe that specific components of the workshop should be designed to address vicarious traumatization. Spicuzza and Devoe (1982) proposed a mutual aid group that would concentrate on cognitive strategies such as participant presentations, guest lectures, films, and reading assignments on causes of burnout, holistic health, alienation, isolation, organizational principles, and the art of effective management. Therefore, we suggest that Baron and Cohen's (1982) initiating procedures be followed and combined with the following three-stage paradigm proposed by Spicuzza and Devoe (1982).

Stage 1. All participants complete the Maslach Burnout Scale (Maslach & Jackson, 1981a) and then score themselves. Working along the lines of Saakvitne and Pearlman's (1996) vicarious traumatization workbook, *Transforming the Pain,* workers should assess themselves on the nature of their work, their clientele, workplace, and the social-cultural context of their setting. They should also conduct a self-assessment in regard to their identity and beliefs, their inner sense of balance, their basic psychological needs, and changes in sensory images such as intrusive images, numbing, and hypervigilance—the hallmarks of PTSD (pp. 53–59).

To ascertain the organization's degree of culpability in causing burnout, the Work Environment Scale (Moos, 1981) should also be administered. Participants are then asked to write down what personal contributions they have made to burnout in themselves and others in the organization. These comments are collected anonymously and recorded on newsprint. The total group then processes these ideas with a view toward problem resolution. Processing of myths about how human services workers must be omniscient and omnipotent demonstrate clearly how such myths can exert stress on the individual. Finally, organizational and environmental factors that make for a positive or negative work setting need to be carefully examined.

Stage 2. At this point group members should feel safe enough to share some of their more deeply felt personal inadequacies in regard to their daily functioning. Relationships with clients, loss of empathy, guilt over therapeutic failures, absenteeism, drug and alcohol abuse, and family problems due to job stress are but a few of the many problems that may surface. Confidentiality and a no-recrimination clause are mandatory if the group is to make progress at this stage. It is extremely important that administrators understand and abide by these ground rules. As the group works its way through personal, professional, and organizational problems, members should gain increased understanding of themselves and their own situation within the organization. Members find they are not alone as others speak to the same kinds of problems.

Stage 3. The group members are asked to write down and discuss the positive aspects of their work setting. By doing this, they gain a positive outlook, and the workshop does not degenerate into a gripe session. The third stage is behaviorally oriented; that is, members are asked to concentrate on development of skills and behavioral plans to disrupt the burnout syndrome. Members should be asked to complete Saakvitne and Pearlman's (1996, pp. 63–66) checklist on self-care and determine where new goals for self-care should be implemented that will provide nurture and escape for them. Lots of social reinforcement should be provided by the leader and other group members for individuals as they plan new and more effective coping behaviors. Typically, relaxation and assertiveness training, realistic goal planning, more effective time management, systematic reinforcement schedules, restructured organizational policies, role clarity, safer and better workspace, clearer channels of communication, job changes, time sharing, and alternative compensation procedures for case overloads and long hours are some of the contractual agreements that may come out of the program. Whatever agreements are reached, whether for the organization or for the individual, they should be put down on paper in contractual, performance terms. Regular follow-up on the progress of both organizational and individual performance contracts is vital if the procedure is to have lasting effects.

Finally, for those members suffering from vicarious traumatization, compassion fatigue, and the latter stages of burnout, referring them for personal counseling should be done with the understanding that these outcomes are indeed occupational hazards no different from carpal tunnel syndrome for keyboard operators or arthritis for concrete finishers. In that regard, organizations must be careful to not secondarily victimize such people as being of weak character or lacking in the "right stuff."

Experience has taught us that such programs should be set up for approximately three half-day sessions and should be spread out over a period of three weeks. Adhering to this schedule gives participants time to digest material presented and also sustains interest for the return sessions. At the completion of the workshop, it may be suggested that support groups be formed to continue the work started.

In a time of tight institutional finances, a question arises as to whether paying for burnout consultation and psychoeducational workshops on burnout is worthwhile. Golembiewski and Munzenrider (1987) argue that because of the high cost of burnout to the institution, it must devote financial resources to such activities. Indeed, such programs do seem to effectively reduce vocational and interpersonal stress, depersonalization, and emotional exhaustion and improving a sense of personal accomplishment (Kagen, Kagen, & Watts, 1995).

The Individual and the Organization.   Vocationally, there are four major maladaptive responses to the onset of burnout. As the level of burnout increases, so does escape avoidance behavior (Thornton, 1992). Workers may attempt horizontal job mobility. They continuously look for the "right" boss or organization when it is the job they are in that is causing their unhappiness. Others tire of the constant interaction with clients and decide to move vertically up the job ladder into administrative positions. What they fail to realize is that their cynical and jaundiced view of the system will not be left behind but will be carried with them into a whole new set of stresses. It is an understatement to say that these people do not make very good bosses. There are also people who become what Pines and Aronson (1988, p. 18) call "deadwood." These people have long ago decided that their best bet is to not "rock the boat" so they can make it to retirement. When asked to do something, they politely indicate they are too busy, or agree with every idea put forth but venture none of their own, or contribute only what is minimally necessary to escape notice or censure. Finally, some people quit their job and the vocation, and in some instances this may be the wisest choice of all.

At the stage of frustration, choices may seem to be limited to job change or job stagnation, but the individual does have other options. First, clearly defining one's role within the organization is a high priority (Kesler, 1990). The worker should conduct a job analysis and determine which tasks are necessary, which are self-imposed, and which contribute to role overload (Pines & Aronson, 1988, p. 109). Through assertive negotiation with the administration, the worker needs to define a reasonable work level and clearly apprise clients of the limits of service in regard to time as well as the amount and kind of service to be provided. Although service to client needs to be a high priority, other tasks should be clearly prioritized. If chores that do not have a high priority cannot be delegated, then serious consideration should be given to dropping them (Poliks, 1991).

Second, coping strategies are tied up in beliefs about the job (Bernstein, 1989). Regaining control of what is perceived to be an out-of-control situation is critical to avoiding burnout. Changing one's view of a setback from a catastrophe to a challenging problem to be solved is typical of those individuals who develop what Bernstein (1989) calls "stress hardiness" and is a critical cognitive component in avoiding burnout (Kesler, 1990). Keeping a log of daily stresses encountered, what, if any, behavioral and cognitive strategies were used, and how successful they were can provide an accurate behavioral record for monitoring and reinforcing successful coping behaviors (Pines & Aronson, 1988, p. 149).

Finally, if it is apparent that the organization is so entrenched and regressive that little change in policies and programs can be effected, it is probably time to look for greener occupational pastures. It would behoove a worker who is in the frustration stage to consider what a near-future job change entails and start planning for it before reaching the apathy stage. Knowing company severance policies and state unemployment benefits, updating a resume, saving money, and commencing a job search are examples of prudent measures workers may take before they are so mentally, physically, and emotionally exhausted that there is little energy left for a major shift in one's life.

PRIVATE PRACTITIONERS AND BURNOUT

The occupational dream of many of our students is to start their own private practice. They fantasize that they could do the kind of therapy they wanted with the clients they selected, be rid of overbearing supervisors and be their own boss, not be bothered with bureaucratic hassles and avalanches of paper work, could set their own hours, and make lots of money! Yet the private practitioner has the potential for even greater problems.

There are a variety of reasons for this state of affairs. First, so little is said about burnout that practitioners often attribute their experience to personal inadequacy (Maslach, 1982b, p. 37). Type A professionals typically see themselves as sociable, talented, responsive, performance driven, and high achievers. Such people are not likely to feel secure enough to own or even recognize that there are too many things going on in their lives and that they are not being handled well. Given a Type A personality, practitioners tend to invest a great deal of time in the job as a means of finding a sense of fulfillment and identity. Competition and achievement serve as guiding values that correlate highly with the need to be seen as worthy and capable (Everly, 1989, p. 105; Huebner & Mills, 1994; Pines & Aronson, 1988, pp. 6–9).

Although the aloneness that pervades a private practice is not the same as the isolation that agency workers sometimes impose on themselves when placed in high-stress situations, it can be more complete. Fenced off from other professionals by ethical and ecological boundaries, the private practitioner has few others with whom to discuss client problems. More important, there are few other individuals with whom they can discuss their own personal problems.

Private practice is clearly a business. As such, it promotes the continuing fear that there will be no clients or that there will never be enough no matter how successfully the business is going (Mitchell, 1977, pp. 145–146). Every client termination raises questions: "Will there be someone to take her place?" "Will he pass the word along that I did him some good?" The private practitioner who is moving toward crisis invariably answers these questions negatively and redoubles his or her efforts to increase client loads and effect cures.

Starting and maintaining a private practice also calls for maintaining a public presence. Whether such a presence involves making speeches to the Rotary Club on stress and the businessperson, consultation with the oncology staff on death and dying at the local hospital, or giving a workshop on discipline for Parents Without Partners, the continuous pressure of needing to be seen as active, abreast of current developments, and visible are part of the sales program that must constantly be maintained and upgraded.

Although the private practitioner is his or her own boss, being an independent businessperson also means being completely responsible for maintaining the practice. Long hours and difficult work periods are the rule rather than the exception. Because most clients work regular hours, private practitioners devote many evenings and weekends to their work. Usually there is no one to pick up caseloads, so vacations or even short respites are few and far between. Certainly not all private practitioners suffer from burnout. However, when burnout does occur with human services workers who are in private practice, it is accelerated by the foregoing problems and issues.

Intervention with the Individual

Direct action, in which the worker tries to master the environmental stressors, and palliative action, in which the worker tries to reduce disturbances when unable to manage the environment, are the two positive ways to cope with stress (Pines & Aronson, 1988, p. 144). Direct action is applied externally to the situational stressor in the environment, whereas palliative action is applied internally to one's cognitions and emotions about the stressor. Social support groups, workshops, assertiveness training, flex time, taking time off, salary increase, and role shifts are all examples of direct action. Meditation, relaxation techniques, biofeedback, physical exercise with no ego involvement, adopting positive cognitions, engaging in leisure time pursuits, adopting better eating habits, reducing addictive substance intake, and adding more humor and joy to one's life are all palliative "decompensation activities" that allow the worker to put stressors aside (Hoeksma et al., 1993; Melamed, Meir, & Samson, 1995; Pines & Aronson, 1988, p. 152; Poliks, 1991; Saakvitne & Pearlman, 1996, pp. 78–87; Stark, 1994).

Whereas workers who are at the frustration stage may well be helped by being involved in self-initiated directive and palliative actions, those at the more serious stage of apathy will not (Edelwich & Brodsky, 1982, p. 137). In such cases, individual counseling is more appropriate (Baron & Cohen, 1982). Kesler (1990) proposed using Arnold Lazarus's (1976) BASIC ID (behavior, affect, sensation, imagery, cognition, interpersonal relationships, and drugs/biology) paradigm as a treatment approach to burnout. To this formulation Kesler adds an S for setting. Given the interactive effects of burnout across multiple facets of the individual, the BASIC IDS approach seems valid for attacking burnout in a comprehensive way.

The following case illustrates the crisis worker using combinations of direct and palliative actions in an abbreviated BASIC IDS approach. It should be clearly understood that neither symptoms nor intervention procedures are all-inclusive. For example, Tubesing and Tubesing (1982, p. 161) listed 36 possible intervention strategies that cover physical, intellectual, social, emotional, spiritual, and environmental components of burnout, and those are not comprehensive by any means. The case presented is that of a professional with many years of experience and a doctorate, but neophytes should understand that Dr. Jane Lee is genotypical of any human services worker. Her case clearly points out that no worker is immune to burnout, no matter how much experience or expertise that worker may have.

Dr. Jane Lee is a striking, raven-haired 43-year-old woman with aquiline features, a low, melodious voice, aquamarine eyes that twinkle, and a smile that could serve as a toothpaste commercial. She is extremely witty and incisive of intellect, is widely read, and can talk as easily with truck drivers as she can with lawyers. At any social function people gravitate toward her. She seems to have been born with the natural empathy and easy familiarity that many people consciously work their whole life for, yet never quite obtain. Divorced for 10 years, Jane has raised her only son while carrying on an exceedingly successful professional life.

Jane has a thriving practice in marriage and family therapy. She has a heavy client load and is clearing approximately $90,000 a year. She is seen by her peers as extremely capable, and her clients speak highly of her. Jane has been in private practice for eight years. Prior to entering private practice she worked in a community mental health facility. She was so skillful at therapy there that she rose to the directorship of the clinical program.

Jane graduated from a major university with a doctorate in counseling psychology and completed her internship in a VA hospital. She then successfully completed an American Association of Marriage and Family Therapists internship at a private clinic. She has written and published many articles on therapy for anorexics and the families of individuals suffering from catastrophic illnesses. She has also given many in-service programs and presentations at national human services conferences.

By any stretch of the imagination, Jane appears to be a highly competent, successful therapist and an exceptionally endowed woman overall. Her ability and demeanor have made her a role model that many in her community aspire to emulate. As Jane sits down with the crisis worker, she is seriously considering driving her new Pontiac Booneville into a bridge abutment.

Jane: I came here today because of what you said to me the other night when we were having a drink. You pretty much have me pegged. I'm burned out even more than what you think, more than what I like to admit. Today I had a decision to make, whether to kill myself or come here. I came here but I'm not sure it's the right decision. If I killed myself, it seems like it would just be over and done with. I've taken care of everything concerning Bobby, my son. He's practically through with college, and even though we're very close, I really think it'd be better for him if I were gone. He wouldn't have to put up with my lousy behavior, and believe me, it's lousy right now. There's enough insurance to get him finished up in school, and he could sell the house. He's the only one that really matters besides my clients, and right now I'm not doing worth a damn with them. I'm probably hurting more than I help, and I'm just not up to it anymore, so much pain and so damn little I can do about it. The only thing I can think about now when I go into a cancer ward is how bad the patients smell. Whoever said, "You don't have to smell them, all you gotta do is help them!" sure wasn't in this end of the business. I'm also starting to behave like those screwed-up anorexics I work with, too. It's starting to seem pretty reasonable to me that they aren't eating. Why the hell should they? Why the hell should *I*? Just sort of fade away and look thin while you're doing it. At least I'd make a great-looking corpse. Anyway, the main reason I came over today was to see if you'd be willing to take my clients. I've thought this over and you've got what it takes. I think you could help them, and if you agree, I'll start talking to them about coming over to your practice.

CW: What you just said scares the living hell out of me. There's a part of me that wants to run right out of here because what you're saying is really hitting home with the way I feel at times. There's another part of me that wants to tie you up in log chains until you come to your senses. Finally, there's another part of me that cares for you so much that I'm angry that you've let yourself get into this predicament. Most of all, though, I'm glad I made that reflection the other night and it finally sank in. I've seen you going downhill for quite a while now. My guess is that you didn't even know it was happening or just laid another piece of armor plate over yourself and said something like "I've got to gut this through" or some of that other irrational garbage I hear you unload on yourself. First of all, I won't even consider what you said about the clients until we agree on one thing, and that is, you don't do any harm to yourself until we talk this through. So I want an agreement both as your therapist and as your friend that we shake on that before anything else happens. I won't take no for an answer. If that's not acceptable, we'll negotiate it. No matter what, we're now in this together.

The crisis worker is in a difficult position as the client's friend, fellow professional, and now as a therapist dealing with another human being in crisis. Although there are ethical issues in treating a friend and a colleague, when a client is in crisis and lethality is involved, the primary concern is keeping the client safe and returning the individual to a state of equilibrium. The nuances of this dilemma can be argued after the fact, but right now the crisis worker needs to act. Particularly in small towns where there are essentially no other professionals with the necessary expertise to provide immediate assistance, the appropriate ethical response would be to provide the best level of care as quickly as possible. In that regard, it is most likely that the crisis worker will have some personal or professional relationship with the client.

Because the crisis worker knows the client, she feels free to make some initial owning statements that let the client know exactly how she feels about the situation without becoming sympathetic in the bargain, which she could easily do because she has felt much the same way at prior times in her professional life (countertransference).

The crisis worker also makes an initial assessment of the lethality level of the client. Her reflective statement to the client a few evenings earlier was not made for idle conversation. The crisis worker has seen a slow but steady change coming over Jane in the last three months, and as she thinks about it, she sees that it was coming a good while before that. Jane has been keeping a stiff upper lip, but there have been indicators that all has not been well lately. She has been rather cynical about clients, as evidenced by her comment about how they smell. She has been suffering a variety of physical maladies that have ranged from unending colds to some severe gastrointestinal problems ominous enough to indicate that surgery might be needed in the near future.

As the crisis worker continues to assess the situation, she further realizes that Jane has truncated relationships with most of her acquaintances and has done this lately with the crisis worker on at least two occasions. Their relationship has been characterized by an easy rivalry, good comradeship, and just generally a lot of good times together without ever engaging in one-upmanship. Lately, though, the crisis worker has had the feeling that Jane has treated her more as a client than as a friend and has attributed some deeper psychological meaning to even the most innocent conversation.

Behaviorally, Jane is in serious trouble. Her performance of daily tasks has become seriously compromised. Her uncharacteristic behavior coupled with her suicidal thoughts places her at a triage level of 7 to 8 on behavior. The only positive behavior she is currently exhibiting is seeking out her colleague. Even though she says she is doing that only to transfer clients, dynamically she is making a clear call for help.

The rather detached, mechanistic way that Jane has reported all this and her blank, hollow look are completely at odds with Jane's usual sparkle, which has been absent the past few months. Performing a quick synthesis of all this background data, what Jane is saying, and the depressed way she is looking and behaving, the crisis worker makes the assessment that Jane is not kidding about killing herself and that the threat must be taken seriously. The crisis worker immediately goes into a suicide prevention mode and institutes a verbal contract with Jane not to kill herself. Even though Jane is a practicing therapist, she is no different from any other client in this regard.

Besides the threat of suicide, a triage assessment of Jane by a worker unfamiliar with burnout might cursorily dismiss her problem as typical whining about one's work. However, the difficult clients she deals with, the amount of time that she has done so, the isolation she has imposed on herself, and the absence of social support systems in her work and at home all lead to a hypothesis of vicarious trauma/compassion fatigue that is rippling out into every component of her life. Triage assessment for affect is 7 to 8. Although her outward demeanor is calm and collected, her affective responses are uncharacteristically angry and hostile for someone in the helping professions. Jane is using considerable effort to control her feelings. Coupled with the emotional exhaustion that is the most salient factor of burnout, she is close to being acutely depressed. This should come as no surprise, because depression and burnout often go hand in hand (Glass, McKnight, & Valdimarsdottir, 1993; McKnight & Glass, 1995).

Cognitively, Jane is operating at a triage level of 6 to 7. Although Jane is thinking in a linear manner, her logic is twisted and her belief system is severely compromised by obsessional self-doubt. She is manifesting a great deal of Ellis's (1973) "musturbatory" thinking and demonstrating another hallmark of burnout: a severe decline in her belief in her personal competence, along with depersonalization of her clients. Her complaints go beyond her job and indicate problems with social relationships, physical health, personal integrity, professional identity, belief system, and her total environment. Jane's total triage assessment scale score of 20 to 23 places her in the moderate to marked impairment range. She is currently functioning between the frustration and apathy stage of burnout and is at a trait level where burnout has become pervasive across her environments. Without intervention, she is likely to move quickly into severe and lethal impairment.

Jane has done one thing right. She has gone to a significant other and is using that trusted other to self-disclose in a very intimate way some of her most troubled feelings (Maslach, 1976; Watkins, 1983). Because Jane's problems have spread out across her environment, the crisis worker will do exploratory counseling across BASIC IDS components with the idea that no component of Jane's life is immune to the burnout currently assailing her.

Jane: All right, I can agree to a no-suicide contract. I know that's part of the procedure. Hell! I guess I knew you'd do that when I came in here. Maybe I'm only kidding myself about all this anyway, just a bit of the blues, feeling sorry for myself and all that crap.

CW: I'm glad you came here, for whatever reason, and I'm also glad you agree to our contract even though you know it's part of the program. I also don't believe that about having the blues, either. I think it's much more than that. I believe right now you're hurting quite a bit. But first I'd like to hear what you think and feel is going on in your life right now.

While the crisis worker is acknowledging her regard for Jane, she is also doing quite a bit more. First, she has decided to take a pretty directive stance with Jane for the time being. The worker balances between making emotional challenges to the client and listening closely and accurately to Jane's problems. She also knows Jane is extremely astute at the business they are engaged in, as evidenced by her comment about the contract. She is not going to let Jane play the game ahead of her. Her analysis is that Jane is out of control right now. The crisis worker is therefore going to take control of the situation and will not sit back in a passive mode.

Jane: I don't know. I've dealt with all kinds of problems in my life, and right now there's nothing I can really put my finger on. In comparison to what is going on now, I can tell you that going through the divorce with Jeff, taking off on my own to finish up the doctorate, and fighting my way up the ladder in the agency and then finally making a decision to go out on my own while raising Bobby make what's happening to me now seem like peanuts.

CW: Right! Those were really tough times, and you went through those like Super-woman. But that was then, and we're right here, right now, and from the looks of it you don't much feel like you're Superwoman, and what's happening in your life surely isn't peanuts, or we wouldn't be having this talk right now. So what do you feel like right now?

The crisis worker acknowledges how tough the client has been, but will not let her get stuck in the past. The crisis worker wants to find out what is happening right now. What is more important about this now than it was a year ago? Furthermore, the crisis worker will not let the client discount the problem. It is interesting that if Jane were the counselor here, she would probably ferret out what she has just done—retreating into the past—in a second. The difference is that Jane has really become a client, and she is as blind to the way she talks, thinks, and behaves as any other client. Jane's being a therapist gives her no edge in dealing with her own problems. In fact, her own expertise may militate heavily against her (Kesler, 1990).

Jane: All I can tell you is I'm washed out. Like I get dates and appointments all mixed up. Last week topped that all off. I saw 44 clients last week. I think I got about a dozen appointments mixed up. My appointment book was really screwed up. It was a madhouse, and some of the people got agitated. Nothing like that ever happened before.

CW: Never?

Jane: Well, to a far lesser extent. I've been strung out before, but I could always get it straightened out.

CW: How?

Jane: About every three months things would start to get out of hand. I'd just sit back and say, "Janie, old girl, you've got to get out of here for a while." I'd just hop in the car and take off for a weekend in Chicago. Check into a hotel, take in a show, and eat some really special meals, and use about half the hotel's hot water washing the clients off of me. Seems like that would clear the cobwebs out of my head.

CW: When was the last time you did that?

Jane: (*Wistfully.*) About nine months ago.

CW: Why so long?

Jane: Well, I bought that new office and went in and remodeled the whole thing. I cut the contractor a deal. If I could work on it too, he'd reduce the price.

CW: So being the omnipotent individual you are, you threw out at least one thing that keeps you on an even keel. In fact, rather than getting away from the office, you've been spending almost all your time there. Let's see, we've got a couple of charac-

ters running around inside of Jane—Dr. Jane, healer to the world, and Jane the carpenter. Wonder who else is inside there?

The crisis worker is looking for a link between the past and the present. If Jane had some coping mechanisms in the past, what were they? She is specifically looking for coping mechanisms in the past that can be linked to the present and what is happening in the present to keep those coping mechanisms from being put into place. She is also beginning to build a character repertoire with Jane in the hope that Jane can start to see all the various aspects of herself that are now motivating her to do some of the things she does (Butts, 1996). To set the stage for the client's regaining control of her life, the crisis worker proposes a positive character in Jane.

CW: I also heard a character that I'd call Janice. A person who knows when her stress bucket is full, and is practical and smart enough to get away from the crap that goes on at that office. Where have you stuck her?

Jane: Back up on the shelf with Janie?

CW: Who's Janie?

Jane: She's the gal who's a little crazy. Who can joke with her clients and get up in the middle of the night and go out and start seeding her lawn and sing Chuck Berry songs while she's doing it. (*Embarrassed.*) There's just no time for them right now. It's not just the new office, but I also needed another car, and since Bobby has changed schools there were a lot of added expenses in that. So I really needed to devote my time to building my caseload up. If I can get through the next two years, I can breathe easier.

CW: Well, I'm sure glad to hear you're planning on being around for the next two years, anyway. But that's not the question now, is it, because right now it sounds to me as if you're wrung out. You don't have any more energy to give, and you've set up on the wall a couple of people who are pretty important in recharging your batteries. Do you see how important they are and what it's cost you to do that?

The crisis worker is not yet making direct suggestions as to what Jane needs to do; however, she is hoping to raise Jane's consciousness to the fact that she has unconsciously changed her operating method. The crisis worker attempts to get her to recognize this by describing what these very positive characters have done for her. By doing so, the crisis worker is attempting to reintroduce some very healthy defense mechanisms that have previously helped Jane cope well with the stressful life she leads.

Jane: I guess so, but I don't know how to get out of it.

CW: What will happen if you don't work on the office this next weekend?

Jane: The new plumbing isn't in. Clients wouldn't be able to use the bathroom. I'd also feel guilty for not working on it.

CW: (*Laughing.*) Well, the first part of that problem is pretty easily handled. Call the Porta-Potty people. I can imagine a sign that says "The crap stops here" hanging from the door as clients walk in. (*Jane starts to smile and giggle for the first time since walking in the door.*) The other part of that is, who's the character laying a guilt trip on you? Tell me some more about her.

The crisis worker takes a little bit of a well-gauged risk here by injecting some humor into the situation. She does this because humor has been important in Jane's life, is helpful to her in coping, and turns her away from some of the cynicism she feels toward her clients and starts to allow her to laugh at herself a little. The ability to laugh at one's own foibles and some of the bizarre and ridiculously funny things that happen in our clients' lives cannot be overemphasized (Pines & Aronson, 1988, p. 154). Van Auken (1979) extols the judicious use of humor even in the most pathetic of situations. Getting a smile or a laugh from clients is a direct intrusion into the depressive thought processes and behaviors in which they are mired.

The crisis worker also starts to hammer a bit on Jane's guilt. Generally the crisis worker sees guilt as a pretty useless emotion, consumptive of energy that could be used in other, more positive ways. Guilt is invariably an emotion of the past, and whatever was done can never again be retrieved. It is one thing to learn from one's past mistakes and quite another to carry past, unfinished business into the present, particularly when one is feeling guilty about not measuring up.

Jane: That's Mother Superior. I get all kinds of lectures from her. (*Bitterly.*) She's just like Sister Angeline at St. Mary's, where I went to school. "Say your Hail Marys and Our Fathers, get your homework done. God doesn't like a shirker, watch how you dress." Jesus, I hated that!

CW: You hate it, but it sure sounds like you're living it. Small wonder you're feeling so lousy.

The crisis worker starts hooking up feelings with thoughts and actions. The response the crisis worker gets indicates that the burnout has spread out into the client's family life.

Jane: You know, I think that's maybe why Bobby and I are having problems right now. I really sound and act like a Mother Superior to him. My Lord! He's 21 years old, and I've started treating him like he was a 6-year-old. He's about like some of those clients I have to lead around by the nose.

CW: Did you hear what you just said? "He's about like some of those clients I lead around." First of all, I didn't know that was the business you were in. Sounds like Jane the handywoman. Fix 'em up the way you do your office. Second, I wonder how many people outside the office you've decided to fix up and look out for. I have to tell you that's one of the kinds of feelings I've had around you lately.

With this information, the client gives the crisis worker a chance to plunge into some core issues that have definable behavioral outcomes. By stating how she deals with Bobby, Jane is manifesting another of the typical signs of burnout: trying to treat significant others in her life as if they were in the therapeutic situation (Van Auken, 1979). Her relationship with Bobby is extremely important because one way of decreasing burnout is to have a satisfying family life, especially with one's children (Forney et al., 1982). Worse yet is that she has become autocratic in the therapeutic situation, so it is not surprising that a major component of her life that has been highly reinforcing to her is no longer so, and, in fact, has taken on some very negative connotations. The crisis worker lays that squarely on her. She is mixing up her characters and has replaced Dr. Jane with Jane the handywoman. This state of events is not so surprising since both characters are working in the same office. Jane needs a break in her day-to-day activities and needs to get away from the office to do it (Forney et al., 1982). Finally, the crisis worker relates and owns her own experience of having been treated the same way by Jane. She tries to make Jane aware that, like rings on a pond, the ripple effect from her burnout goes far beyond her immediate line of sight (Kesler, 1990).

CW: Indeed, I wonder about your relationships other than those with Bobby, myself, and your clients. Anyone else you're trying to control right now?

Jane: (*Frostily.*) If you mean men, absolutely no. When I get home at night, I'm so bushed all I want to do is fall asleep, but then all those clients go tumbling around in my head, and I start thinking about car payments, mortgage payments, how to straighten things out with Bobby, and I wind up getting about two or three hours of sleep a night.

CW: So right now you're so exhausted that you'd just rather be alone.

Jane: That's right, but I feel like I ought to be out mingling with people. I'm so damned isolated anyway.

CW: OK! I can understand that, and I'd agree with you, but let's look at right now. Seems as if you really need some time to just curl up in the fetal position, turn the electric blanket up to nine, and get your batteries recharged. Could you just go home and go to bed, put the answering service on until Monday, and not get up for the whole weekend?

Jane: I suppose.

CW: No supposes. If you don't want to do that, we'll look at something else. But right now you look like *The Grapes of Wrath* and just seem to really need to rest before you think about doing anything else. Are you willing to call the contractor up and tell him you won't be there Saturday and Sunday without feeling guilty about it?

Jane: I could use the rest. All right! I'll give it this weekend.

CW: Fine. But there's one more thing. If you really get to feeling blue, plug the phone in and call me at home. I also want a report next week, so what time do you want to come in?

Jane: Sounds like I'm a client.

CW: Sounds like you're right. (*Laughs.*)

The crisis worker is basically assisting Jane to make a simple commitment to do one thing—get some rest. A critical component in treating burnout is revitalization (Tubesing & Tubesing, 1982, p. 160). Jane is physically fatigued, and the first order of business is to get her physical batteries recharged. A number of other options are available at this juncture, but the crisis worker follows Tubesing and Strosahl's (1976) advice to let the client make the choice of what treatment is appropriate. Keying on the client's own words about needing sleep, the crisis worker follows up and gains commitment to a specific behavior that the client will engage in over the short term. This is not a dramatic first step, but considering the least dramatic steps first is probably the way to go (Van Auken, 1979). The most important objective of this initial encounter is finding some short-term intervention techniques the client is able and willing to use (Freudenberger & Robbins, 1979).

A particular behavior the crisis worker touches on is the use of the telephone. Private practitioners are notorious for taking phone calls from clients at all hours of the night and on weekends. Van Auken (1979) urges human services workers not to let clients run or, for that matter, ruin their personal lives. The crisis worker makes sure that Jane follows this dictum. Finally, the worker provides emotional support, but once Jane is able to ventilate her feelings, the worker moves into a problem-solving mode.

(Next week.)

Jane: I'll have to admit I do feel better. Couldn't sleep at all Friday night, but I got ten
hours in Saturday. I can't believe it! I woke up and I was all curled up in the fetal
position. The clients looked somewhat better this week. I can't say it was wonderful, but at least I wasn't an ogre to them. I guess what bothers me most about that
is that I've lost all my creativity.

CW: OK! Let's talk about that a bit. You haven't been paying very much attention to
the right side of your brain, so what do you expect? What could you do creatively
that isn't client involved that'd get the right side of your head going again?

Jane: I've got a couple of articles I've been putting off—how about that?

CW: Got anything to do with clients?

Jane: Yes.

CW: Is that going to help you out?

Jane: I don't guess so, the same old stuff, only I'm writing about it.

CW: What else, then?

Forney and associates (1982) propose that a variety of professional activities may
be an excellent coping mechanism; nevertheless, the crisis worker confronts Jane about
this suggested alternative. The crisis worker is fairly sure that the client's stress bucket
is full to the brim professionally. Jane needs to become less, not more, involved in her
professional life.

Jane: Well, there is something else. I bought this sailboat for Bobby and me. The Coast
Guard Auxiliary is putting on a sailing class. It would sure surprise Bobby if the
next time he came home I could handle that Y flyer.

CW: Is that something you want to do? Would like to do, not need to do it?

Jane: Yes!

CW: And not pile it on top of everything else. Really reserve some time for yourself to
enjoy it.

Jane: You sure drive a hard bargain, but I can do it.

This is a wedge in the behavioral repertoire of the client that the crisis worker has
been looking to find. Writer after writer in the burnout literature has promoted the use of
leisure, particularly physical exercise, as a way of breaking up the dogmatic, work-brittle
behavior of just going through the motions that often characterizes the burned-out human
services worker (Hoeksma et al., 1993; Melamed et al., 1995; Savicki & Cooley, 1982).
By proposing for the client a combination of leisure, physical exercise, and quality time
with her son, the crisis worker has neatly integrated a number of positive interventions.
The crisis worker now takes on the main issue of the client's private practice.

CW: Fine. Let's talk about your practice for a while.

Jane: You know as well as I do about that. Sure, I've got a great caseload now. But
who knows, it might dry up next week, and then where would I be?

CW: Has it ever dried up? Even in the last recession?

Jane: No, it hasn't, but I keep expecting the worst.

CW: You've been in private practice eight years now, right? Has it ever been such that
you didn't have enough clients to keep the wolves away from your door?

Jane: No. I guess there's something else. I feel a little foolish saying this, but it's almost like if I don't live up to my reputation and take on those really tough cases, I

start feeling like I'm not the queen of the mountain. I mean in the past, I've been real proud of that, but now I don't seem to feel anything but that there's an albatross around my neck.

CW: Sounds like Superwoman again. I frankly admire you for dealing with those terminals' families, and you're right! Not many could do that. But if there's no intrinsic payoff, why are you fooling yourself into thinking you can heal the whole world? See the trap you've put yourself into?

Jane: Well, no! I guess I don't.

CW: OK! I want to try something. Maybe you've used it on some of your clients before. It's a game of "Who Told You?" I want you to move over to my chair and ask that empty chair, which will represent Jane, some questions. I'm going to stand aside and process as we go along, but it'll mostly be up to you. I want you to use all your insight as a therapist and really bore in and go to work on Jane's fictional goals, those crazy things she tells herself that have no counterpart in reality.

Jane as CW: (*Shifts chairs and gets a glitter in her eyes.*) OK, toots! Who told you you had to be Superwoman?

CW: Now shift back.

Jane: Nobody really, I've just got a lot of responsibilities.

Jane as CW: Responsibilities, my foot! You've been going up that success ladder so fast you've scorched the rungs. Always got to show them. Be number one. My God! You little twerp. You're 43 years old, and you still think you're back on the VA ward. Got to show them you're better than any man. Volunteer for the worst cases. Scared to death you won't succeed. And when you did, you were scared you wouldn't succeed the second time. Who told you that?

Jane: Nobody! It was reality. I had to be better than the men there.

Jane as CW: That was 20 years ago, nerd! The only men you deal with now are your clients. And that's another thing, is that why you're so damned afraid of going out with any other man? And don't give me that stuff about getting burned again, you know why that divorce happened, and it sure doesn't have anything to do with having good social relationships now.

Jane: It's just that with the financial obligations for Bobby, I really don't have the time.

Jane as CW: (*Really angry and shouting.*) I won't have that! How long will you be responsible for him? He's 21 years old. Who supported you when you were 21? I'll tell you who. You did! You just use that as an excuse. Just like you use all those clients as an excuse. You don't fool me, you little martyr. Oh, sure! You get those strokes. (*Dripping sarcasm.*) Just like Annette here said, "I really admire you, Jane." You go around fooling everybody, but worst of all you fool yourself. Look at you. Sitting here the pathetic little wretch. You don't fool me. You're not little Miss Goody Two-Shoes. Behind all that depression is a really angry, bitter bitch who's always going around being everybody's servant. So just who told you you had to be that?

Jane: (*Breaks and sobs. The CW goes to Jane, gathers her into her arms, and hugs her for dear life. Five minutes elapse.*) Good Lord! I didn't realize that was all in there. I really got on a roll.

CW: Neither did I, but I figured if anybody could get it out, you could. What have you got out of that?

Jane: Besides spilling my guts, which I haven't done in 25 years, I see now how I got into this. I really set myself up.

CW: What do you want to do?

Jane: Well, I'm not going to kill myself literally or figuratively. I've got some living to do, and although I'm not going to quit the practice, there sure are going to be some limits put on it.

The "Who Told You?" technique is a combination of Adlerian, rational-emotive behavior, and Gestalt therapy that is extremely powerful. Given a person with the kind of insight Jane has, it often has dramatic results in pointing out the way clients delude themselves. By using Jane as her own therapist, the crisis worker provides no one for the client to rationalize to, attack, manipulate, or otherwise attempt to fool but herself. For a person with Jane's abilities and insight, that seldom happens for very long. Underneath most depression lies anger. If that anger can be mobilized, then the client has taken a major step toward getting back into control of the situation. By putting Jane in a position to view her behavior from outside herself and also giving her a stimulus to attack her irrational ideas by the "Who Told You?" technique, the crisis worker provides an arena in which Jane can combat the apathy she is experiencing.

Such a dramatic shift to being mobile is uncommon among the general populace and in Jane's case is a condensed version of what may generally happen. The crisis worker often must provide the stimulus statements that are the core of clients' irrational ideas because of clients' poor cognition of their own negative self-talk. However, in dealing with highly trained professionals, it is not uncommon for such rapid shifts to occur. Given the initial stimulus, they may pick up on the technique and provide their own dialogue with little or no help from the crisis worker. When emotional catharsis occurs, the crisis worker then takes a nondirective stance and serves as little more than a sounding board as their fellow professionals put reasonable parameters back into their lives. At that point, human services workers as clients tend to be able to make good decisions quickly about the behavioral, emotional, and cognitive aspects of their lives. Indeed, if burnout syndrome is successfully overcome, it is not unreasonable to expect that human services workers will come back to their profession with hardier personalities, stronger commitments to self and profession, better self-temperance, a greater sense of meaningfulness, and increased vigor toward their environment (Kobasa, 1979). Furthermore, new coping styles that include greater self-awareness, increased self-insight, and a more direct approach to problem solving are likely to result for those who successfully navigate these treacherous waters (Cooley & Keesey, 1981). Finally, it is our own observation that human services professionals who have successfully conquered burnout respond not only to their work but also to their daily living with calmer and wiser choices, behaviors, and work style.

In this vignette the crisis worker uses the BASIC IDS model to deal with multiple, overlapping issues in the client's life (Kesler, 1990). Jane's workload affects her relationship with her family and friends. Her role as mother affects her image of herself. Her image of herself affects her beliefs about her abilities as therapist and mother and finally affects her coping behaviors across the board. The crisis worker links all of these dimensions into a unified whole because each modality interacts with other modalities and should not be treated in isolation (Cormier & Cormier, 1985, p. 153). Jane's sailing expeditions not only will provide her with fun, relaxation, and togetherness with her son, but also are as necessary to her therapeutic functioning as her doctoral training. Achieving balance among the various parts of her life and compartmentalizing them to the extent that they do not start to run into or over one another allows Dr. Jane Lee to be fully functioning in all of them and at the same time limits the stresses inherent in each (Pines & Aronson, 1988, p. 152).

SUMMARY

Burnout is not simply a sympathy-eliciting term to use when one has had a hard day at the office. It is a very real malady that strikes people and can have extremely severe consequences. It is prevalent in the human services professions because of the kinds of clients, environments, working conditions, and resultant stresses that are operational there. Because of the intense and stressful nature of crisis intervention, a major contributor to burnout is constant exposure to clients who have had horrific experiences. Prolonged exposure can induce what is variously called *vicarious traumatization, compassion fatigue,* or *secondary traumatization* in the crisis worker. No one particular individual is more prone to experience burnout than another. However, by their very nature, most human services workers tend to be highly committed to their profession, and such commitment is a necessary precursor to burnout. Private practitioners may experience burnout even more severely than their counterparts in organizations because of their professional isolation. All human services workers, public or private, tend to be unable to identify the problem when it is their own. No one is immune to its effects.

Burnout moves through stages of enthusiasm, stagnation, frustration, and apathy. In its end stage, burnout is a crisis situation. The crisis takes many forms. It can be manifested behaviorally, physically, interpersonally, and attitudinally. It pervades the professional's life and can have effects on clients, co-workers, family, friends, and the organization itself.

Recognition of the beginning symptoms of burnout can alleviate its personal and organizational ramifications. Raising consciousness levels in regard to the dynamics of burnout in training programs and conducting on-the-job workshops are important ways of halting and ameliorating its effects. Support groups within the organization that provide instrumental and emotional resources to victims are important. In the past, burnout has been regarded as a malady that resides only within the individual. That view is archaic. Burnout should also be viewed in a systems perspective and as an organizational problem.

Intervention may occur on both an organizational and an individual level. At its end stage, burnout is a crisis situation that calls for immediate, direct, and reality-oriented therapeutic intervention. Given corrective remediation, victims of burnout can return to the job and again become productive.

CLASSROOM EXERCISES

Exerise 1: What Leads to Burnout?

Think of an organization you have worked for. If you have not yet worked in the human services field, any organization will do, even a fast food or convenience store. Take a piece of paper and jot down some responses to the following questions. Write your responses not as gripes, but as specific behaviors and identifiable concrete problems that occurred there. As an example, instead of writing "The shift supervisor was a louse!"

write "The shift supervisor never gave specific instructions on clean-up procedures as to who was to do what, when. As a result, there was a lot of confusion, and we often flunked health inspection." Write these down as quickly as you can. Now think about and respond to the following questions.

1. What observable stress did you see in fellow workers because of a problem?
2. What stress responses did you have, behaviorally, cognitively, and affectively?
3. What do you think would have happened if management would have brought in an outside consultant to deal with the workers and the organization?
4. What stumbling blocks might there have been?
5. Picture yourself as the outside consultant. How might you have handled these issues?

Come back together as a class and write some of these examples on the chalk board. Discuss any organizationally based commonalities you can see in a wide range of different job settings that can all lead to burnout.

Exercise 2: Simulated Intervention in Pairs

The group is divided into dyads: crisis worker and burned-out human services worker. Using the "Who Told You?" technique, the human services worker starts a monologue about his or her gripes, complaints, frustrations, perceived shortcomings with clients, bureaucratic problems, and so on. (If participants do not currently hold a human services job, they can role-play one of the examples from the beginning of this chapter.) As the burned-out worker unfolds verbally, the crisis worker will use a combination of active listening skills and the "Who told you?" technique. (Hint: you must be confrontive here, empathic but confrontive. The default question is always "Who told you?" If the client says, "I told myself that!" then dig further and define those characters that are surely running around in the client's head just like those of Dr. Jane.) The idea is to confront the shoulds, oughts, and musts that propagandize clients into believing that they need to continue unproductive and debilitating ways of thinking and behaving. The exercise should be continued for about 10 minutes, and then the roles should be reversed. After the exercise is completed, all members rejoin the group and process the experience. Special emphasis should be given to comparing the irrational ideas brought out by each participant. The leader may want to list and tally each irrational idea so that all participants can start to experience the commonality of ways in which they delude and fool themselves into making these irrational beliefs a dysfunctional part of their lives.

RESOURCES

There are many providers of stress management and burnout workshop services that can be accessed through professional journals or the net. We make no recommendation in regard to those, because of their commercial nature. However, we do believe that Karen Saakvitne and Laurie Pearlman's workshop material on vicarious traumatization is worthwhile. For more information on resources they have, the address is

Trauma Stress Institute, Center for Adult & Adolescent Psychiatry
22 Morgan Farms Drive
South Windsor, CT 06074

REFERENCES

Adams, K. O. (1989). Have you been counseling too hard and too long? *The School Counselor, 36,* 165–166.

Arches, J. (1991). Social structure, burnout, and job satisfaction, *Social Work, 36,* 202–206.

Arvay, M. J., & Uhlemann, M. R. (1996). Counselor stress in the field of trauma: A preliminary study. *Canadian Journal of Counselling, 30*(3), 193–210.

Barber, C., & Iwai, M. (1996). Role conflict and role ambiguity as predictors of burnout among staff caring for elderly dementia patients. *Journal of Gerontological Social Work, 26*(1–2), 101–116.

Baron, A., Jr., & Cohen, R. B. (1982). Helping telephone counselors cope with burnout: A consciousness-raising workshop. *Personnel and Guidance Journal, 60,* 508–510.

Berkeley Planning Associates. (1977). *Evaluation of child abuse and neglect demonstration projects, 1974–1977: Vol. IX. Project management and worker burnout.* Washington, DC: U.S. Department of Commerce.

Bernstein, A. J. (1989). *Dinosaur brains.* New York: Wiley.

Blanchard, E. A., & Jones, M. (1997). Care of clinicians doing trauma work. In M. Harris & C. L. Landis (Eds.), *Sexual abuse in the lives of women diagnosed with serious mental illness: New direction in therapuetic interventions,* Vol. 2 (pp. 303–319). India: Harwood Academic.

Brown, C., & O'Brien, K. (1998). Understanding stress and burnout in shelter workers. *Professional Psychology Research and Practice, 29*(4), 383–385.

Burke, R. J., & Greenglass, E. R. (1995). A longitudinal examination of the Cherniss model of psychological burnout. *Social Science and Medicine, 40,* 1357–1363.

Butts, S. (Speaker). (1996). Therapeutic techniques, marriage and family therapy (Cassette Recording No. 7640-96). Memphis: Department of Counseling, Educational Psychology and Research, University of Memphis.

Carroll, J. F. X., & White, W. L. (1982). Theory building: Integrating individual and environmental factors within an ecological framework. In W. S. Paine (Ed.), *Job stress and burnout* (pp. 41–60). Newbury Park, CA: Sage.

Charney, A. M., & Pearlman, L. A. (1998). The ecstasy and the agony: The impact of disaster and trauma work on the self of the clinician. In P. M. Kleespies (Ed.), *Emergencies in mental health practice: Evaluation and management* (pp. 418–435). New York: The Guilford Press.

Cherniss, C., & Krantz, D. L. (1983). The ideological community as an antidote to burnout in the human services. In B. A. Farber (Ed.), *Stress and burnout in the human service professions* (pp. 198–212). New York: Pergamon Press.

Cooley, E. J., & Keesey, J. C. (1981). Relationship between life change and illness in coping versus sensitive persons. *Psychological Reports, 48,* 711–714.

Cormier, W. H., & Cormier, L. S. (1985). *Interviewing strategies for helpers: Fundamental skills and cognitive behavioral interventions* (2nd ed.). Pacific Grove, CA: Brooks/Cole.

Daley, M. R. (1979). Burnout—Smoldering problem in protective services. *Social Work, 58,* 375–379.

D'Andrea, M. (1995, March). Caring for the caregivers in Denver: A special event for AIDS counselors. *Counseling Today, 37*(9), 24–27.

Deiter, P. J., & Pearlman, L. A. (1998). Responding to self-injurious behavior. In P. M. Kleespies (Ed.), *Emergencies in mental health practice: Evaluation and management* (pp. 235–257). New York: The Guilford Press.

Devine, I. (1984). Organizational crisis and individual response: New trends for human service professionals (Special issue: Education and training in Canadian human services). *Canadian Journal of Community Mental Health, 3,* 63–72.

Distler, B. J. (1990). *Reducing the potential for burnout.* Paper presented at Fourteenth Annual Convening of Crisis Intervention Personnel, Chicago.

Duquette, A., Kerouac, S., Sandhu, B. K., & Beaudet, L. (1994). *Issues in Mental Health Nursing, 15,* 337–358.

Edelwich, J., & Brodsky, A. (1982). Training guidelines: Linking the workshop experience to needs on and off the job. In W. S. Paine (Ed.), *Job stress and burnout* (pp. 133–154). Newbury Park, CA: Sage.

Ellis, A. (1973). *Humanistic psychology: The*

rational-emotive approach. New York: Julian.

Everly, G. S., Jr. (1989). *A clinical guide to the treatment of the human stress response.* New York: Plenum.

Farber, B. A. (Ed.). (1983). *Stress and burnout in the human service professions.* New York: Pergamon Press.

Figley, C. R. (Ed.). (1995). *Compassion fatigue: Coping with secondary traumatic stress disorder in those who treat the traumatized.* New York: Brunner-Mazel.

Forney, D. S., Wallace-Schutzman, F., & Wiggers, T. T. (1982). Burnout among career development professionals: Preliminary findings and implications. *Personnel and Guidance Journal, 60,* 435–439.

Fox, R., & Cooper, M. (1998). The effects of suicide on the private practitioner: A professional and personal perspective. *Clinical Social Work Journal, 26*(2), 143–157.

Freudenberger, H. J. (1974). Staff burn-out. *Journal of Social Issues, 30,* 159–165.

Freudenberger, H. J. (1975). The staff burnout syndrome in alternative institutions. *Psychotherapy: Theory, research, and practice, 12,* 73–82.

Freudenberger, H. J. (1977). Burn-out: Occupational hazard of child care workers. *Child Care Quarterly, 6,* 90–99.

Freudenberger, H. J., & Robbins, A. (1979). The hazards of being a psychoanalyst. *Psychoanalytic Review, 66,* 275–296.

Friedman, M., & Rosenman, R. (1974). Type A behavior and your heart. Greenwich, CT: Fawcett.

Glass, D. C., McKnight, D. J., & Valdimarsdottir, H. (1993). Depression, burnout, and perceptions of control in hospital nurses. *Journal of Clinical and Consulting Psychology, 61,* 147–155.

Golembiewski, R. T., & Munzenrider, R. F. (1987). Social support and burnout covariants of physical symptoms: Where to put marginal dollars? *Organizational Development Journal, 5,* 92–96.

Golembiewski, R. T., & Munzenrider, R. F. (1993). Health related covariants of phases of burnout. *Organizational Development Journal, 11,* 1–12.

Golembiewski, R. T., Munzenrider, R. F., Scherb, K., & Billingsley, W. (1992). Burnout and "psychiatric" cases. Early evidence of an association. *Anxiety, Stress and Coping: An International Journal, 5,* 69–78.

Golembiewski, R. T., Munzenrider, R. F., & Stevenson, J. G. (1986). *Stress in organizations: Toward a phase model of burnout.* New York: Praeger.

Gorter, R., Albrecht, G., Hoostraten, J., & Eijkman, M. (1999). Factor validity of the Maslach Burnout Inventory—Dutch version (MBI-NL) among dentists. *Journal of Organizational Behavior, 20*(2), 209–217.

Greenglass, E., Fiksenbaum, L., & Burke, R. (1996). Components of social support, buffering effects and burnout: Implications for psychological functioning. *Anxiety, Stress, and Coping, 9*(3), 185–197.

Grouse, A. S. (1984). The effects of organizational stress on inpatient psychiatric medication patterns. *American Journal of Psychiatry, 141,* 878–881.

Hoeksma, J. H., Guy, J. D., Brown, C. K., & Brady, J. L. (1993). The relationship between psychotherapist burnout and satisfaction with leisure activities. *Psychotherapy in Private Practice, 12,* 51–57.

Huebner, E. S., & Mills, L. B. (1994). Burnout in school psychology: The contribution of personality characteristics and role expectations. *Special Services in the Schools, 8,* 53–67.

Jayaratne, S., Vinokur-Kaplan, D., & Chess, W. A. (1995). The importance of personal control: A comparison of social workers in private practice and public agency settings. *Journal of Applied Social Sciences, 19,* 47–59.

Johnson, C. N. E., & Hunter, M. (1997). Vicarious traumatization in counsellors working in the New South Wales Sexual Assault Service: An exploratory study. *Work and Stress 11*(4), 319–328.

Kagen, H. K., Kagen, N. L., & Watts, M. G. (1995). Stress reduction in the workplace: The effectiveness of psycho-educational programs. *Journal of Counseling Psychology, 42,* 71–78.

Kesler, K. D. (1990). Burnout: A multimodal approach to assessment and resolution. *Elementary School Guidance & Counseling, 24,* 303–311.

Kobasa, S. (1979). Stressful life events, personality, and health: An inquiry into hardiness. *Journal of Personality and Social Psychology, 37,* 1–11.

Koeske, G. F., & Kelly, T. (1995). The impact of overinvolvement on burnout and job satisfaction. *American Journal of Orthopsychiatry, 65,* 282–292.

Koeske, G. F., Kirk, S. A., & Koeske, R. D. (1993). Coping with job stress: Which strategies work best? *Journal of Occupational and Organizational Psychology, 66,* 319–335.

Lazarus, A. A. (1976). *Multimodal behavior therapy.* New York: Springer.

Lee, R. T., & Ashforth, B. E. (1993). A longitudinal study of burnout among supervisors and managers: Comparisons between the Leiter and Maslach and Golembiewski models. *Organizational Behavior and Human Decision Processes, 54,* 369–398.

Lee, R. T., & Ashforth, B. E. (1996). A meta-analytic examination of the correlates of the three dimensions of job burnout. *Journal of Applied Psychology, 81*(2), 123–133.

Marino, T. W. (1995, March). Caring for the caregivers in Denver: A special event for AIDS counselors. *Counseling Today, 37*(9), 26–27.

Maslach, C. (1976). Burned-out. *Human Behavior, 5,* 16–22.

Maslach, C. (1978). The client role in staff burn-out. *Journal of Social Issues, 34,* 111–124.

Maslach, C. (1982a). *Burnout—The cost of caring.* Upper Saddle River, NJ: Prentice Hall.

Maslach, C. (1982b). Understanding burnout: Definitional issues in analyzing a complex phenomenon. In W. S. Paine (Ed.), *Job stress and burnout* (pp. 29–40). Newbury Park, CA: Sage.

Maslach, C., & Jackson, S. E. (1981a). *The Maslach Burnout Inventory.* Palo Alto, CA: Consulting Psychologists Press.

Maslach, C., & Jackson, S. E. (1981b). The measurement of experienced burnout. *Journal of Occupational Behavior, 2,* 99–113.

McCann, I. L., & Pearlman, L. A. (1990). Vicarious traumatization: A framework for understanding the psychological effects of working with victims. *Journal of Traumatic Stress, 3*(1), 131–149.

McKnight, D. J., & Glass, D. C. (1995). Perceptions of control, burnout, and depressive symptomatology: A replication and extension. *Journal of Consulting and Clinical Psychology, 63,* 490–494.

McRaith, C. F. (1991, April). *Coping with society's secret: Social support, job stress, and burnout among therapists treating victims of sexual abuse.* Paper presented at the Fifteenth Annual Convening of Crisis Intervention Personnel, Chicago.

Meichenbaum, D. (1977). *Cognitive-behavior modification.* New York: Plenum.

Melamed, S., Meir, E. I., & Samson, A. (1995). The benefits of personality-leisure congruence: Evidence and implications. *Journal of Leisure Research, 27,* 25–40.

Melchior, M., van der Berg, A., Halfens, R., & Abu-Saad, H. (1997). Burnout and the work environment of nurses in psychiatric long-stay care settings. *Social Psychiatry and Psychiatric Epidemiology, 32*(3), 158–164.

Miller, D. (1995). Stress and burnout among health care staff working with people affected by HIV. *British Journal of Guidance and Counselling, 23,* 19–31.

Mitchell, M. D. (1977). Consultant burnout. In J. W. Pfeiffer & J. E. Jones (Eds.), *The 1977 annual handbook for group facilitators* (pp. 143–146). La Jolla, CA: University Associates.

Moos, R. H. (1981). *Work Environment Scale manual.* Palo Alto, CA: Consulting Psychologists Press.

Oktay, J. S. (1992). Burnout in hospital social workers who work with AIDS patients. *Social Work, 37,* 432–437.

Paine, W. S. (1982). Overview of burnout stress syndromes and the 1980's. In W. S. Paine (Ed.), *Job stress and burnout* (pp. 11–25). Newbury Park, CA: Sage.

Patterson, C. H. (1980). *Theories of counseling and psychotherapy* (3rd ed.). New York: Harper & Row.

Pearlman, L. A., & Mac Ian, P. S. (1995). Vicarious traumatization: An empirical study of the effects of trauma work on trauma therapists. *Professional Psychology, 26*(6), 558–565.

Pearlman, L. A., & Saakvitne, K. W. (1995a). *Trauma and the therapist.* New York: Norton.

Pearlman, L. A., & Saakvitne, K. W. (1995b). Treating therapists with vicarious traumatization and secondary traumatic stress disorders. In C. R. Figley (Ed.), *Compassion fatigue: Coping with secondary traumatic stress disorder in those who treat the traumatized* (pp. 150–177). New York: Brunner-Mazel.

Piedmont, R. L. (1993). A longitudinal analysis of burnout in the health care setting: The role of personal dispositions. *Journal of Personality Assessment, 61,* 457–473.

Pines, A. M. (1983). On burnout and the buffering effects of social support. In B. A. Farber (Ed.), *Stress and burnout in the human service professions* (pp. 155–173). New York: Pergamon Press.

Pines, A., & Aronson, E. (1988). *Career burnout: Causes and cures.* New York: Free Press.

Poliks, O. (1991, June). *Helping the helpers: Stress management and burnout prevention for schools.* Paper presented at the American School Counselor Association Conference, Des Moines, IA.

Powell, W. E. (1994). The relationship between feelings of alienation and burnout in social work. *Families in Society, 75,* 229–235.

Riggar, T. F. (1985). *Stress burnout: An annotated bibliography.* Carbondale: Southern Illinois University Press.

Rodesch, C. K. (1994, April). *Keeping the counselor sane.* Paper presented at the Eighteenth Annual Convening of Crisis Intervention Personnel, Chicago.

Saakvitne, K. W., & Pearlman, L. A. (1996). *Transforming the pain: A workbook on vicarious traumatization.* New York: Norton.

Savicki, V., & Cooley, E. J. (1982). Implications of burnout research and theory for counselor education. *Personnel and Guidance Journal, 60,* 415–419.

Savicki, V., & Cooley, E. J. (1987). The relationship of work environment and client contact to burnout in mental health professionals. *Journal of Counseling and Development, 65,* 249–252.

Sculley, R. (1983). The work-setting support group: A means of preventing burnout. In B. A. Farber (Ed.), *Stress and burnout in the human service professions* (pp. 198–212). New York: Pergamon Press.

Sek-yum, S. N. (1993). Occupational stress and burnout among outreaching social workers in Hong Kong. *International Social Work, 36,* 101–117.

Selye, H. (1956). *The stress of life.* New York: McGraw-Hill.

Selye, H. (1974). *Stress without distress.* Philadelphia: Lippincott.

Shinn, M., & Mørch, H. (1983). A tripartite model of coping with burnout. In B. A.

Farber (Ed.), *Stress and burnout in the human service professions* (pp. 227–239). New York: Pergamon Press.

Sowa, C. J., May, K. M., & Niles, S. G. (1994). Occupational stress within the counseling profession: Implications for counselor training. *Counselor Education and Supervision, 34,* 19–29.

Spicuzza, F. J., & Devoe, M. W. (1982). Burnout in the helping professions: Mutual aid as self-help. *Personnel and Guidance Journal, 61,* 95–98.

Stark, E. (1994). Stress! It's all relative...and relatively easy to manage. In R. Yarian (Ed.), *Health 94/95* (15th ed.) (pp. 62–65). Guilford, CT: Dushkin.

Thornton, P. T. (1992). The relation of coping, appraisal, and burnout in mental health workers. *Journal of Psychology, 126,* 261–271.

Tubesing, D. A., & Strosahl, S. G. (1976). *Wholistic health centers: Survey research report.* Hinsdale, IL: Society for Wholistic Medicine.

Tubesing, N. L., & Tubesing, D. A. (1982). The treatment of choice: Selecting stress skills to suit the individual and the situation. In W. S. Paine (Ed.), *Job stress and burnout* (pp. 155–172). Newbury Park, CA: Sage.

Turnipseed, D. L. (1994). An analysis of the influence of work environment variables and moderators on the burnout syndrome. *Journal of Applied Social Psychology, 24,* 782–800.

Van Auken, S. (1979). Youth counselor burnout. *Personnel and Guidance Journal, 58,* 143–144.

Warnath, C. F., & Shelton, J. L. (1976). The ultimate disappointment: The burned-out counselor. *Personnel and Guidance Journal, 55,* 172–175.

Watkins, C. E. (1983). Burnout in counseling practice: Some potential professional and personal hazards of becoming a counselor. *Personnel and Guidance Journal, 61,* 304–308.

Wright, T., & Bonett, D. (1997). The contribution of burnout to work performance. *Journal of Organizational Behavior, 18*(5), 491–499.

PART FOUR

New Directions

The objectives of the final chapter of this book are (1) to highlight the evolution and importance of crisis intervention as a potent, innovative, and maturing subspecialty of psychotherapy, and (2) to empower crisis workers to progress toward more proactive, preventive, and creative initiatives than they have ordinarily taken in the past. We hope that the perspectives in "Off the Couch and into the Streets" will enhance the reader's vision of the future as well as personal and professional growth. Probably at no time in history has society had a greater need for competent, proactive crisis workers.

CHAPTER FOURTEEN

Off the Couch and into the Streets

Two recent and significant developments in the helping and human services professions define and give impetus to the emergent directions of the crisis intervention movement. First and foremost, crisis intervention has evolved into a major human services subspecialty (James & Gilliland, 1991). Second, it has become widely apparent that a reactive approach to crisis intervention is not enough; proactive and preventive models of systemwide crisis intervention need to be developed and implemented. The latter recognition, simply put, means that crisis work need not be only the purview of the mental health professional. These two developments, within the context of an increasingly complex society, provide the setting for this chapter.

THE EVOLUTION OF THE CRISIS INTERVENTION SUBSPECIALTY

Crisis intervention has evolved from being a grassroots movement implemented by volunteers into a professional subspecialty with institutional support. Let us trace the process by which any particular type of crisis is first addressed by volunteers and later by professionals in institutions.

The need for crisis intervention services is at first unrecognized by the public and by existing institutions until such time as a critical mass of victims comes together to exert enough legal, political, or economic pressure to cause the particular crisis category, malady, or social problem to become formalized. Until that time, it remains informal, nonprofessional, and unsubsidized. The problem is responded to or handled mainly through ad hoc informal means by former victims, current victims, friends, or significant others who are affected by the problem. Examples are Mothers Against Drunk Driving (MADD) to try to reduce the number of young people killed by drunk drivers, the veterans groups organized to respond to the PTSD epidemic among military veterans following the Vietnam War, and the Aid to End AIDS Committee to prevent the spread of AIDS and enhance the quality of life of HIV-infected people.

The Grassroots Movement

Initiators of crisis intervention services are generally concerned with one particular crisis category that personally affects them in some way. Typically, the crisis gets out of hand enough to cause noticeable problems before remedial responses are initiated. At first, the initiators are mavericks who are starting a victims' revolt. The revolt is against an entrenched status quo or power structure that shows little awareness of or responsiveness to the problem. The victims' revolt somehow manages to get an infant crisis agency started despite the benign neglect and reluctance of mainstream society. The infant agency is initially funded by private donations. The services are provided by ad hoc workers who are quite informally organized. The crisis agency gains access to public funding only after the agency has attained validation and some recognition by a substantial portion of the power structure. If, after a time, the infant crisis agency does not attain credibility sufficient to garner substantial private support or a modicum of public support, the agency begins to falter and eventually folds and ceases to operate.

Initially, community leaders may deny that the crisis exists, minimize its seriousness, or express doubt whether it may represent a recurring problem. But whenever the crisis persists, they finally come to realize that someone must become proactive— someone must exert the leadership, energy, time, resources, and resolve to confront the crisis problem. Thus the formation of an agency is sanctioned or even encouraged. If the infant agency born from the need to contain the crisis succeeds and is publicly recognized as fulfilling a need, the quest to expand and mature begins.

The Importance of Volunteerism

Volunteer workers perform all kinds of service in most crisis agencies—from menial chores to answering the phone to front-line crisis intervention with clients. Many established agencies owe their initial successful debuts to groups of dependable, committed, and loyal volunteers.

Public Validation.   A stable cadre of volunteers can help an agency attain credibility, provide needed services to clients, and strengthen the financial condition by carrying out fund drives and locating financial assistance. Volunteerism is often the key to getting the infant crisis agency rolling. It is the grassroots influence that often captures the attention of the media, impels people to join as volunteers, and causes a greater number of clients and victims to seek the services of the agency. As the services increase and become publicized, political entities take note of the crisis problem and the services being rendered.

As mainstream institutions, such as governmental structures, become aware of the problem and as volunteer centers reach the saturation point where needs are obviously going unmet, some governmental or institutional funding is provided. Typically, as the numbers and needs of the clientele increase, the agency reaches the point where compassion and volunteerism alone cannot handle all of the complex personal, social, economic, public relations, psychological, and political problems that assail it.

Volunteers as Front-Line Workers.   The use of trained volunteers as crisis workers has been a recognized component of many crisis centers and agencies for years (Clark & McKiernan, 1981; Roberts, 1991, p. 29; Slaikeu & Leff-Simon, 1990, p. 321). Probably the greatest number of front-line volunteers are used in staffing 24-hour suicide hotlines in major cities. Such hotlines require an enormous number of crisis workers because the crisis service never ceases—it must be provided seven days a week, 52 weeks a year. Roberts (1991, p. 29) reported that more than three-quarters of all crisis centers in the United States indicate that they rely on volunteer crisis workers and that such volunteers outnumber professional staff by more than six to one. Although volunteers cannot replace professionals, highly selective screening procedures and effective preservice and in-service training programs usually make the volunteer cadre in crisis centers the mainstay of services by hotlines in this country.

The Need for Trained Professional Consultants

As a crisis intervention center becomes saturated with numbers of clients and complex issues arise that are beyond the scope of the volunteers to handle, the need for professional assistance and/or formalized learning emerges. Also, the heavy demands of the client population impel the agency to create preservice and inservice training, using professional consultants to improve the knowledge and skills of the volunteers. Thus, training programs become systematically organized.

After the agency has established a formalized relationship with professionals to train the volunteers and act as volunteer backup consultants, the director can become more selective in screening, interviewing, and placing volunteers. Pairing newly acquired volunteers with experienced volunteers for apprenticeship periods tends to stabilize the volunteer workforce. The agency begins to mature.

The Quest for Maturity and Power

It is essential that the agency in its developmental stages validate itself within the professional community. Some ways to do this are (1) ensuring that professionals in the human services/mental health field are represented on the agency's board of directors; (2) using professionals in the human services/mental health fields to facilitate both preservice and inservice training of volunteers; (3) legitimizing the mission and purpose of the agency, thereby helping the agency to garner support from charitable and governmental organizations; (4) providing a critical mass of people for the agency's own fund-raising efforts; (5) gaining access to the political power structure; and (6) publicizing the role and successes of the agency.

As crisis agencies mature, they often gain proficiency in lobbying, building good public relations, being politically active, utilizing the legislative process, gaining corporate backing, publishing newsletters, compiling lists for solicitation of funds, and getting leading power structure people involved. Fund raising becomes bigger and bigger business. If the agency is very successful, it may receive steady funding from a variety of sources—from local and state government, corporations, foundations, and charitable organizations such as the United Way.

Institutionalization. As crisis agencies become well known and as their clientele are drawn from a wider scope of the community (to the point that the work cannot be handled by the communication system of grapevine, word of mouth, notepad, and e-mail), the agency sees that if it is to continue to grow and serve its clients, it must institutionalize. The seeds of bureaucracy are thus born. To manage all the vital functions, the agency must centralize and formalize most aspects of the center operation. It takes on a formal board of directors, establishes rigorous auditing and recordkeeping functions, and requires more money, paid staff, and staff support.

As crisis agencies become crisis organizations, they gain more power, prestige, and notoriety. They tend to attract the attention of the human services professions because they offer fertile fields for funded research, placement of practicum and internship students, and employment of graduates. Sometimes established and emerging agencies become involved in professional turf battles. Different agencies may serve the same client population and compete for volunteers and funding. Agencies may become defunct because of inadequate funding, inept leadership, lack of public interest, or overpowering competition from rival organizations. Crisis agencies sometimes attain eminent success, to the point that it becomes a vested interest of the human services professions to formalize the competencies of the personnel of such successful agencies through certification, licensure, and accreditation. The successful agencies may also tend to compete for resources and gain recognition through affiliating with national or regional agency networks and through linkages with national professional organizations and accrediting bodies.

Professionalization.   Some agencies attain exemplary status through being recognized regionally or nationally as ranking among the top service providers in specific crisis categories. As a specialty evolves, it develops its own empirical base, professional research, and writings. For example, for crisis intervention we have publications such as *Crisis Intervention, Journal of Interpersonal Violence, Victimology, Violence and Victims, Journal of Family Violence, Death Studies, Journal of Traumatic Stress, Suicide and Life Threatening Behavior, Child Abuse and Neglect, Journal of Child Sexual Abuse, Aggression and Violent Behavior,* and *Violence Against Women.* A further manifestation of the professionalization of crisis intervention as a subspecialty is its textbooks. Such textbooks evolve in two ways:

1. Field-based experiential activities are written into narrative form and distributed through printed handouts to groups such as volunteer orientation, workshop seminars, and in-service training classes. The handouts are later edited and bound into either monographs or training manuals. Finally, the training manuals or monographs are carefully revised and rewritten to form field-validated publications for wider dissemination and greater appeal to people who want a straightforward, applied textbook.
2. Empirical research reports are collected, edited, and combined in theory and research-based texts. These books are valued by people who prefer materials based on proven scientific principles.

A particular book may follow either format or it may be a combination of the two. Crisis textbooks have tended to combine theory and practice in a unified whole as the need to train crisis workers has emerged. Formalized training in crisis intervention has necessitated the integration of theory and practice (Aguilera & Messick, 1982; Brock, Sandoval, & Lewis, 1996; Gilliland & James, 1997; Roberts, 1991; Slaikeu, 1990). As formal textbooks have become available, crisis agencies have tended to assimilate the text material into their training programs. Such assimilation has had the effect of further formalizing crisis intervention as a subspecialty among the psychological and human services professions.

Specialty areas may also attain a distinct level of recognition through building a base of national or regional affiliates, such as is evidenced through suicide hotlines, AA, spouse abuse centers, AIDS hotlines and assistance centers, and victim assistance programs. Local, state, regional, and national conferences are organized to provide for exchange of ideas and problem-solving strategies. These conferences range from specialty areas that bring together some of the greatest research minds in the field—such as the First Annual Conference on Trauma, Loss, and Dissociation in 1995—to "in the trenches" conferences such as the Annual Convening of Crisis Intervention Personnel, which provides practical, hands-on programs for crisis interventionists. The emergence of hundreds of crisis-oriented organizations in the 1970s, 1980s, and 1990s (Maurer & Sheets, 1999) and the realization of the role that immediate intervention plays in alleviating traumatic stress (Mitchell & Everly, 1995b) attest to the dramatic transformation and national acceptance of crisis intervention as a pervasive subspecialty. Attaining maturity and professionalization have become goals of many crisis agencies and professionals in the field.

The Societal Impetus for Crisis Intervention

Why, from the 1970s to the present, has the crisis intervention movement experienced such extraordinary growth? Probably no one factor alone can explain why. The stresses, strains, and unprecedented changes that tear at the fabric of society itself may account for some of the growth: lack of personal fulfillment, poverty, homelessness, the population explosion among the underclasses, increased experimentation with and use of drugs, alcoholism, the emergence of HIV infection and AIDS disease, Vietnam, the immediacy and power of the visual media to stir people's emotions and demand for action, the development and use of birth control pills by the middle and upper class, the feminist movement, the environmental movement, increased mobility of people, technological advances, and a rise in crime and terrorism are examples of possible catalysts. The demand arose for crisis agencies, journals, textbooks, courses, training, conferences, conventions, and such because people everywhere felt a need to respond to the kinds of dilemmas individuals face every day—in their communities, families, workplaces, schools, and in the streets.

Job-Related Impetus for Crisis Intervention

Researchers have found that stress in the workplace has reached a critical point (McGuire, 1999). In March 1999, psychologists who were studying the effects and risks of stress in modern America held a conference entitled "Work, Stress, and Health '99" in Baltimore, Maryland. An encapsulation of their pooled research findings indicated that the overall workforce was more at risk than ever for psychological, physical, and behavioral health problems. Two sources of the increase in stress were cited as the increasing workload and longer working hours, shouldered by men and women, caused by economic policies that encourage downsizing and wage inequality. Another source of stress was found to be fear of job loss, even among employees who felt they were performing well or very well on their jobs. It was reported that not long ago employees and researchers calmly discussed "work overload." Then, recently, the more serious term "time poverty" was brought into discussion. Now, the critical concept of "time famine" is being used to describe higher levels of employee stress that lead to increased job loss and absences due to stress-related illness.

The McGuire report (1999) cited data indicating that the stressors were not so serious for the people in the best-paid 30 percent of the workforce. But the 40 percent at the bottom were reported to be worse off than in 1970, and the middle 30 percent were neither sustaining their income nor their standard of living. Research studies of the bottom 40 percent of workers found that increases in poverty, inequality, and unemployment were linked with rising rates of mortality, suicide, homicide, assault, and rape. These important psychological reports clearly point toward an increased impetus for crisis intervention as well as the critical need to find long-term solutions to problems that generate stress in the workplace.

PROACTIVE AND PREVENTIVE MODELS OF CRISIS INTERVENTION

Crisis intervention organizations of all kinds tend to evolve pragmatically. They may spring from governmental research grants. They may develop from independently generated successful projects that gain local attention and later take on a national posture. The *Encyclopedia of Associations* (Maurer & Sheets, 1999), a comprehensive compilation and annotated description of organizations and agencies, offers some proof of the spectacular growth of crisis-oriented organizations during the 1970s, 1980s, and 1990s. Few crisis categories or situations have been omitted from some sort of widespread attention and organized response. Most of the organizations purport to deal with the specific targeted crisis category not only in reactive modes but also in proactive and preventive modes.

Crisis Intervention in the Real World

Although crisis intervention theories and agencies applying those theories are barely two generations old, the spectacular growth and development since the 1950s has placed them virtually in the mainstream of mental health and human services (Blinder, 1991). No longer is crisis intervention considered the informal grassroots purview of paraprofessionals and volunteers. Rather, the theories, methodologies, and strategies of crisis intervention have come to be viewed as legitimate in both society and the mental health world (In Touch Hotline Counseling Center, 1991). People in general have become more positive in their acceptance of outreach strategies. There is less blaming of the victim. It has become accepted that dealing early on with a crisis is cost effective (Roberts, 1991).

There are valid reasons for the widespread acceptance of crisis intervention as a therapeutic specialty. People in human services and political leadership positions have discovered that when they either ignore crisis situations or leave solutions entirely to the experts who have little political clout, lasting solutions elude them and the leaders themselves are blamed and held publicly responsible. Reactive responding has not worked very well. Leaders have discovered that endemic crisis problems will not easily go away; that reaction or no action may result in the problems' becoming pandemic or out of control. In a sense then, political expediency has dictated not only the widespread acceptance of effective crisis intervention strategies but also that crisis intervention become proactive and preventive on the local, national, and international levels. Many recent examples of providing global outreach crisis services come to mind, such as the American Counseling Association sponsoring teams of counselors to help war victims in Bosnia (Hayes, 1999). Counselors who traveled to Bosnia reported that the people in that war-torn region were in need of everything from career counseling to help in coping with loss of loved ones and survivor's guilt.

Indeed, the proactive and preventive concept has evolved all the way from the local to the national and international levels. The Violence and Traumatic Stress Branch of the National Institute of Mental Health (NIMH, 1990) was created for the purpose of supporting research projects on the mental health sequelae resulting from exposure to traumatic life crises and catastrophic events. These experiences include interpersonal and mass violence, war, physical and sexual abuse, natural disaster, technological (human-made) hazards, accidents, forced relocation, and other individual and collective traumatic situations.

The NIMH role and function illustrate the use of governmental influence and resources to develop proactive and preventive strategies on both national and local scale. Piggybacked onto the NIMH model is the American National Red Cross Disaster Services plan. This plan was developed in 1989 with the realization that disaster victims needed mental health services as much as they needed food, shelter, and clothing. The American Red Cross Disaster Mental Health Service team is composed of volunteer mental health workers who are trained through a Red Cross Disaster Mental Health Services course. Professional organizations such as the American Counseling Association and the American Psychological Association have formed joint agreements with the Red Cross to train their members (Morrissey, 1994). If you are interested in such training, information can be obtained from your local Red Cross chapter.

Cost and Managed Care Considerations

The concept of "managed care" (Blinder, 1991) has emerged to bring balance, efficiency, and maximization of benefit use to consumers of insured health care services. Crisis intervention is well suited to the managed care environment because of its rapid assessment, intervention and stabilization, facilitation of supports and resources, teaching of coping skills, formulation of prevention plans, and provision for enhanced insight and expedient return of clients to the community. Another important role of crisis intervention as a part of the managed care concept is the networking and referral function between case managers and others who are responsible for consumer health care. Such networking and use of crisis skills for enhanced communication and intervention often facilitate overcoming difficulties and red tape among family members, mental health facilities, hospitals, individual practitioners, employee assistance programs (EAPs), and third-party insurance payers. The outlook for the continued growth and importance of crisis intervention skills and services is positive indeed, given the proven philosophy and methodology of crisis intervention and its immediacy, proximity, expectancy, visibility, and positive viability in the streets and neighborhoods where crises occur (In Touch Hotline Counseling Center, 1991; Roberts, 1991). Most important, crisis intervention contains the soaring cost of mental health care and is therefore promoted by insurance carriers and businesses (Boyack & Bucknum, 1991; Lambert, 1995).

Collaborating/Networking

Successful crisis agency leaders understand the value of cooperation. Crisis intervention cannot be owned by any one organization, therapeutic modality, or discipline. In any city or community, what we call collaborating, networking, alliance building, systematizing, or the pooling of efforts works very well. Regardless of how efficiently local mental health agencies, police departments, local governments, health care systems, and other entities by themselves are run, collective efforts save time and money and make life easier for individual public servants. Effective collaborating/networking reaches not only different levels (local to national) but also different degrees of power, authority, and financial resources. Sometimes pressure politics, public relations, and public image building affect the course and extent of collaboration. For example, the plight of the Vietnam veterans suffering from PTSD was largely ignored until the problem spilled out of the streets and into the seats of power and authority—from personal crisis to politics. Whenever the PTSD problem began to impact members of Congress, the power of the federal government and the resources of the Veterans Administration were brought to bear not only to create a network of veterans centers throughout the country but also to slash bureaucratic red tape to ensure that services to Vietnam veterans were taken to the streets where PTSD sufferers were living rather than require veterans to report to regular VA hospitals.

Prevention Programs

Roberts (1991) identified three types of contemporary prevention strategies used by professionals in the fields of public health, social work, and mental health (p. 146): primary, secondary, and tertiary prevention.

Primary Prevention.   Primary prevention involves the intentional and proactive planning of strategies and activities to keep specific crises from developing in the first place. Examples of primary prevention are (1) parenting education programs to prevent child neglect/abuse, (2) HIV/AIDS education programs to prevent the spread of the AIDS virus, (3) educational programs on college campuses to prevent date rape, and (4) educational programs for teenage males and females regarding the consequences of adolescent pregnancies.

Secondary Prevention.   Secondary prevention strategies are designed to intervene in a particular crisis category early enough to contain and/or ameliorate the problem. Examples of secondary prevention are (1) providing counseling programs in Family Link/Runaway Houses to help families and teenage runners to control the behavior of running away; (2) establishing counseling services designed to stop battering behavior in households; and (3) designing and implementing victim assistance programs to ensure that the rights of victims (of crime or stark misfortune) are protected and honored.

Tertiary Prevention.   Tertiary prevention entails the comprehensive use of crisis intervention strategies to contain and control the spread of the crisis. An example is the provision of a telephone hotline for suicidal people and mounting a public information program sufficiently strong so that virtually every suicidal person in the catchment area will call the hotline as an alternative to a suicide attempt.

EMERGING TRENDS IN CRISIS INTERVENTION

We have devoted several chapters in this book to specific crisis categories such as suicide, battering, sexual assault, hostage taking, and violent behavior in institutions. The crises that emerge from the streets call for crisis workers to respond not only reactively and with immediacy and presence, but also with proactivity and intentional planning for future directions. Thus, several types of programs of contemporary concern to crisis workers are

1. Crisis stabilization units
2. Outreach programs and crisis response teams
3. Psychiatric emergency services
4. Debriefing procedures
5. Electronic outreach services
6. Programs to enable law enforcement officers' response to mentally ill and other people in crisis

Crisis Stabilization Programs

Crisis stabilization programs range from inpatient facilities such as the Crisis Stabilization Unit detailed in Chapter 3 that provided for short-term maximum safety and control to a variety of programs that exert less control over the safety needs of clients.

Crisis intervention managers in many communities have begun to organize systematic programs and initiatives to respond to crises and even to prevent crises from getting out of control. Crisis stabilization units, involving multidisciplinary talents from a broad community catchment area, are one vehicle that has been successful in providing alternatives to long-term hospitalization for people in crisis (Wilson, 1991). An alternative crisis stabilization program for some patients suffering from chronic emotional problems who formerly were hospitalized has been described by Leaman (1987). In that program, eligible patients spend an average of five days with a licensed foster care family in the family's home. Family members receive training and some cost reimbursement as foster care providers.

Halfway houses have also been used extensively as a short-term alternative to hospitalization for acutely disturbed chronic patients (Weisman, 1985). Such use of halfway houses combines crisis intervention techniques with techniques developed in halfway houses to enhance independent functioning and to counteract regressive, dependent behavior. Highly structured activities and expectations of appropriate behavior enable most patients to leave the halfway house within nine days and begin outpatient and day treatment programs.

Britton and Mattson-Melcher (1985) described a crisis stabilization program administered by a crisis intervention center in which chronically mentally ill people are provided short-term housing, in lieu of hospitalization, with carefully selected families. Coordination of services, screening of home providers, assessment of needs, and referrals to the community are some components of the program.

Outreach Programs and Crisis Response Teams

A variety of reasons may make transporting crisis workers to the site of the event more efficient than bringing the survivors to the workers. Logistical problems, financial efficiency, the critical nature of care, safety needs, speed of response, and efficacy of treatment are all part of the move to make crisis intervention teams mobile. Because of these positive factors, many communities have now developed crisis intervention teams that will travel to the scene (Reding & Raphelson, 1995). Some teams are local in origin to serve individual incidents, and some may be part of a national emergency relief effort when disasters assail large numbers of people.

Rapid Response Teams.   The Oklahoma City Federal Building bombing touched a nerve in the nation. The massive amounts of media coverage of that traumatic experience and the disaster relief that followed in its wake brought graphic attention to how disasters are handled, including the work of immediate follow-up rapid response teams. These teams did not just spring up full grown. Rather, throughout the late 1980s and 1990s, rapid response teams were developed to handle numerous tragedies and disasters, including hurricanes (Shelby & Tredinnick, 1995), serial murders (Wakelee-Lynch, 1990), plane crashes (Modrak, 1992; Shafer, 1989a), bank robberies and hijackings (Brom & Kleber, 1989), campus shootings (Guerra, 1999; Guerra & Schmitt, 1999; Schmitt, 1999; Sleek, 1998), and a host of other unexpected human-made and natural disasters. The specific purpose of these teams is to make contact with individuals while they are still in the acute stress stage and, through counseling and debriefing procedures, return them to homeostasis and equilibrium.

The Integrated Agencies Approach.   At the local level each agency has its own particular strengths and weaknesses. Because of the many agencies that need to be brought to bear in many crisis situations, close interrelationships between agencies are critical. The alliance for intervening in domestic violence in our own city of Memphis is an excellent example of an integrated agency approach. Because of the success of the Memphis Police Department's Family Trouble Center (reported later in this chapter), it became apparent that the center alone would not be able to handle the growing number of victims and perpetrators being channeled into it. As a result, a domestic violence coordinating committee composed of a variety of social service agencies, mental health clinics, private practitioners, the court system, the state's attorney's office, probation and parole offices, and the police department cooperatively worked out agreements with one another to horizontally integrate their organizations into a unified family intervention system. This committee is responsible for overseeing and providing quality assurance for domestic violence intervention in both the city and county. Each player in this integrated system knows what the other is doing and does not duplicate efforts. This integrated system is much more capable of providing systematic evaluation, individually tailored treatment plans, and assuring follow-up and compliance. Furthermore, where formerly a number of recipients of service might have slipped through institutional cracks, those cracks have now been seamed over through the coordinating efforts of these agencies. Because crises are often complex and call for systematic intervention, we absolutely see an integrated agency approach as the wave of the future and as mandatory if complex crises are to be dealt with effectively and efficiently.

National Crisis Response Teams.   The rapid crisis response team movement received impetus and support on a national level with the establishment of the National Crisis Response Project by the National Organization for Victim Assistance (NOVA) in the late 1980s (Young, 1991). The National Crisis Response Project set up national crisis response teams (NCRTs) to assist communities following communitywide crises or disasters. The main objective of an NCRT in dealing with local community disaster is to form local crisis response teams that are in a position to deal with the community's grief reactions, stress effects, and posttraumatic stress disorder resultant from the disaster. According to Young (1991), the "project is based on the premise that disasters can cause individual and communitywide crisis reactions and that immediate intervention can provide communities with tools that are useful in mitigating long-term distress" (pp. 83–84).

NCRTs are dispatched on request of leaders in the affected community. "When a disaster occurs, NOVA is placed in contact with the community in one of two ways: either the community calls NOVA, or NOVA, on hearing of the tragedy, calls the community and offers assistance" (Young, 1991, p. 95). Three types of disaster service are available: (1) providing written material giving details of how to deal with the aftermath of disaster; (2) providing telephone consultation to leading caregivers in the area affected; and (3) sending in a trained team of volunteer crisis workers to assist the community.

Federal Emergency Management Agency (FEMA).   Sometimes more than one agency of the federal government coordinates the work of crisis response teams. Several instances of events during modern times that triggered such a coordinated effort were the earthquakes in both the Los Angeles and San Francisco areas of the West Coast and Hurricanes Hugo, Andrew, and Floyd that brought devastation and flooding to large parts of the southeastern United States. The response teams were sent in by the National Institute of Mental Health (NIMH) and sponsored and funded by FEMA. In all such national disasters, FEMA and NIMH provided the widely affected areas with instruction, consultation, and expertise in developing local and regional support systems to cope with the enormous aftermath of these natural disasters (Shafer, 1989b). Teams of counselors, crisis workers, and other caregivers intervened with a wide range of populations and age groups (from children through senior citizens). Special emphasis was placed on enabling clients to cope with their psychological trauma, with two important objectives in mind: to ensure their immediate safety and to help people of all ages in both regions prepare themselves to face the future as free as possible from posttraumatic stress disorder.

Constructing an Outreach Team.   Depending on the nature of the crisis and the ecological setting, outreach teams generally have a diverse occupational range: from psychiatric nurses, paramedics, emergency workers, and psychiatrists to social workers, volunteers, rehabilitation counselors, police officers, and psychologists. These outreach teams are characterized by their multidisciplinary team approach, strong social and community networks, user participation in policy and service delivery, and egalitarianism in the workplace (Gulati & Guest, 1990).

Members of integrative-collaborative teams have a distinctive operational setup and are characteristic of many geographical areas where financial and human resources are not sufficient to form freestanding, specialized crisis units. They are not an ad hoc group collected after a crisis, but rather are trained prior to the crisis. Each member has different skills that, combined, allow the team to respond to a variety of crisis situations. They operate much as a volunteer fire department does. Members typically have primary jobs in other settings, but when a crisis call comes in on a hotline, they immediately leave their regular job, form a crisis team, and go to the crisis site. They are identifiable within the community as the crisis response team and are a cost-efficient and effective way to provide generic crisis intervention (Silver & Goldstein, 1992).

Multicultural Issues in Outreach

Understanding the cultural milieu in which he or she operates is of critical importance to the crisis worker who performs outreach services. Cultural differences, the ways that environmental factors impact clients, and negative images portrayed through the mass media are particularly problematic when the worker is transported to and works on the "turf" of the client and has little time to become attuned to the cultural and ecological framework within which the client operates (Arredondo & D'Andrea, 1999). We are not just talking about "foreigners" either. Midwestern farmers faced with rebuilding after a disastrous flood, or transient street people in dire need of social and mental health services, may have views about what constitutes helpful intervention that are very different from the crisis worker's. These people may take umbrage at the crisis worker's attempts to intrude into their world (Hopper, Johnston, & Brinkhoff, 1988; Kiselica, 1998; Sue, 1999).

Geographic Locale as a Cultural Barrier.   Lenihan and Kirk (1999) have developed a rural community-level crisis intervention plan for very small towns and rural areas that lack the typical crisis infrastructure and support systems available to even medium-sized communities. Many small communities and isolated rural areas have crises assail them, yet they are not large enough to call for state or federal responses. People in these small communities and rural areas may also be very suspicious of outsiders attempting to "tell them what to do." Yet collective fear, rumor, parochialism, and inaccessibility to services can keep the community traumatized. Lenihan and Kirk propose that intervention strategies must absolutely address the cultural issues that will exist between outside service providers and recipients of service before any meaningful work can be done. They advocate an immediate assessment of the traumatic event's effect not only on individuals, but also on the culture as well. In a sense, they are "triaging" the whole community. They propose that no outside crisis response team can do an adequate job if it first does not seek out, identify, and consult with a broad cross-section of community leaders about how and with whom crisis intervention should proceed. Particularly important is ascertaining what the community's belief systems are and if there are subcultures within the system that may have different responses from those of the community at large.

Any crisis response must be integrated into the community leadership and organizations such as social clubs, churches, civic groups, and fraternal organizations. Providing sensitive consultative help for community leaders without "ramming it down their throats" is imperative. The same is true of using basic listening skills in hearing what the community has to say, instead of a "bull-in-a-China-shop," officious, expert, "We know what's best for you!" approach. Evaluating and finding the natural leaders of the community and teaming up with them is important in forming workable alliances and providing the citizens an anchor of familiarity, security, and control at the scene. Any action plans should be developed cooperatively and should be concrete, doable, and manageable, considering the available community financial and human resources. In short, outside interventionists in such communities do best when they function as guides and helpers who operate along a continuum of directive to nondirective intervention. That is, the interventionist should be only as directive as the degree to which their client (the community) is immobilized.

An ecological model posits that the efficacy of trauma-focused interventions depends on the degree to which they enhance the person–community relationship and achieve a fit within individually varied recovery and cultural contexts (Harvey, 1996). If you view the ecology of such rural communities as having a great deal of resiliency, self-reliance, and belief in the community as the primary source of support, then you should also get a vivid picture of how delicately you intrude on such a community.

Language as a Cultural Barrier.   Although it is difficult enough in crisis to work with people from the same generic cultural background and who speak English as a first language, the manifestation and communication of first-generation Americans' or immigrants' personal problems may be very different from what the crisis worker is used to handling. As a result, assessment and intervention become more complex and difficult. Confidentiality issues are also problematic. People in the United States with "green cards" or student visas run the risk of having information about their mental health status given to government agencies, who may then make negative evaluations about their immigrant status. This issue is further compounded by language problems that make communication of clients' needs and crisis workers' attempts to communicate their services subject to misinterpretation. Particularly for foreign college students, having to leave school because of "mental problems" may cause tremendous loss of face in their families and in their home countries. If not handled in a sensitive manner, the worker's attempts to provide help may exacerbate rather than mollify the crisis (Oropeza, Clark, Fitzgibbon, & Baron, 1991; Sue, 1999).

Divergent Beliefs as Cultural Barriers.   Shelby and Tredinnick (1995) spent considerable space reporting on the cultural differences they encountered doing disaster relief work in the aftermath of Hurricane Andrew. The large Caribbean and Latin American populations they dealt with had punitive religious interpretations of the disaster and punitive child-rearing practices, particularly when put under stress, that were very different from what the crisis workers had previously encountered in their work. The workers had to be very sensitive in not challenging these deeply held beliefs, instead allowing survivors to process feelings of guilt and responsibility in line with their religious interpretation of the event. Furthermore, educating parents with ethnically different views of child rearing about the ways children generically respond after a trauma, along with the normal developmental issues they face, may indeed be a tall order given the brevity of crisis intervention. Such interventions, although needed, may be something the crisis worker wishes to consider carefully. Shelby and Tredinnick also found that African-American and Hispanic populations tended to rely on extended support systems much more heavily than did Caucasians. Therefore, the workers' efforts needed to focus more on systemic approaches that dealt with extended family networks as opposed to individuals. In summary, although crisis work is never easy, cultural insensitivity may make it even more difficult.

Occupation as a Cultural Barrier.   The ecological model may also be applied to the "culture" of particular occupations. Police work is an excellent example. Although police officers and deputies in rural and small community sheriff's law enforcement patrols might be thought of as psychologically at risk due solely to the high stress and potentially lethal situations they face, that is far from true. Any crisis worker who proceeded to deal with a police officer or deputy based on the erroneous notion that high stress caused by exposure to lethal situations was the sole factor contributing to a crisis would be very mistaken. Police officers and deputies constitute a distinct occupational culture and closed ecosystem because of their authority roles, their segregation from the rest of society, irregular work schedules, the reactive nature of their job, the constant exposure to the negative side of life, the constant emotional control they must maintain, and the definitive manner in which they must judge right and wrong. A major issue that bedevils law enforcement officers is their married life. They have one of the highest divorce rates of any occupation. They do not usually talk about their jobs or their feelings, because they sense their spouses are uncomfortable hearing about such matters. Their job stress occurs because of "burst stress." That is, they may go from a long period of tedium and boredom to an immediate high-adrenaline moment. Over the long run, that psychological roller-coaster ride is extremely stress producing. Furthermore, because law enforcement officers see the failure of the mental health system every day in the United States, the are likely to have a very jaundiced view of the mental health profession as a whole (Hayes, 1999). It is not because of thrill seeking that we trainers of the Memphis Police Department Crisis Intervention Team (CIT) ride patrol shifts with CIT officers. Although those rides provide us with valuable on-the-scene experience, they also help us appreciate what the ecosystem is within which the officer operates. The alliance with CIT officers that emerges from riding the Saturday night shifts with them helps break down occupational barriers, and establishes our own "bona fides" as "culturally aware" of what the officers are going through. No amount of reading or expertise that we know of compensates for not knowing and being sensitized to this cultural milieu.

Going to the Crisis Populations.   Pritchard, Brownstein, and Johnan (1989) have described a creative, youth-oriented outreach program that is a good example of taking crisis services to youth who would not likely come to a center or seek out services. Booths in shopping malls were set up to present vignettes to at-risk youth as a strategy to provide crisis information to youth on critical topics such as AIDS and teenage runaways.

University campuses are well suited to the process of taking crisis intervention services to the geographical locale of prospective clientele. White and Rubenstein (1984) assessed a unique program conducted by the Cornell University Psychological Services Center and local radio stations that broadcast hourly announcements targeted toward high-risk suicidal undergraduate students. Research on the effects of the program showed a significant increase in high-risk clients presenting for counseling services. Another example of college and university campus outreach, aimed at curbing campus violence, was sponsored by the American College Personnel Association (ACPA) (McGowan, 1992). That program targeted both the crisis problem and the population through setting up an outreach task force on campus violence to seek to improve institutional policy, organize and conduct workshops to educate administrators about ways to reduce violence on campuses, and develop a 102-page manual for dealing with violence in the university setting (pp. 9–10).

Intrater (1991) reported on outreach programs instituted to take services to three different youthful populations: (1) runaways, (2) "throwaways," and (3) pregnant teens and adolescent parents. From the Neon Street Center for Homeless Youth in Illinois, outreach services addressed a myriad of homeless youth needs such as obtaining food, housing, health care, education, and employment as well as alleviation of crises related to prostitution, sexual identity, substance abuse, HIV infection, teen pregnancy, and gang solicitation.

In Memphis, the police department's Family Trouble Center has equipped a motor home to respond to domestic disturbance calls. Crisis workers operate the vehicle during the night shift and respond to police calls for immediate assistance in containing out-of-control domestic disturbances. Crisis workers coordinate their activities with police officers, can be at the scene within ten minutes, and usually have the situation in control within thirty minutes (B. A. Winter, 1996, personal communication).

PSYCHIATRIC EMERGENCY SERVICES

The rise of psychiatric emergency services (PESs) over recent decades has begun to fill a definite void in the delivery of emergency crisis intervention. PESs are treatment facilities established for the express purpose of providing either emergency psychiatric outpatient or short-term psychiatric inpatient evaluation, emergency care, referral, and aftercare as alternatives to long-term hospitalization or makeshift psychiatric care in emergency rooms of general hospitals (Bassuk & Cote, 1983; Dubin & Fink, 1986). Not only have the numbers of PESs greatly increased and provided crisis intervention services in urban areas (McDermott & Gordon, 1984; Wellin, Slesinger, & Hollister, 1987), but also emergency services in rural areas have been enhanced as well (Bassuk & Cote, 1983; McDermott & Gordon, 1984). PESs have proved effective in serving the crisis intervention needs of the elderly (Dubin & Fink, 1986) and adolescents (Piersma & Van-Wingen, 1988) as well as the general population.

Psychiatric emergency services also go to the streets. Chiu and Primeau (1991) and Marcos, Cohen, Nardacci, and Brittain (1990) described mobile teams in New York City that deal with the homeless or families that cannot otherwise avail themselves of mental health services. Psychiatrists, nurses, and social workers compose the mobile team. The psychiatrists make diagnoses and write orders for medication and hospitalization. Nurses administer and track medication. Social workers provide support services. The teams treat a variety of problems that range from schizophrenia to severe mental retardation.

Many community mental health centers have established service components that amount to PESs. For example, we know of one mental health center that houses and operates an externally funded victim assistance program. Another center has developed a comprehensive program of services for the homeless in an inner city. Still another center has set up a program for emergency vocational counseling for people in the community who suddenly lose their jobs due to plant closings. The growth and proliferation of PESs have followed the trend, started a couple of decades ago, to greatly reduce the inpatient population in mental health facilities. Although many users of PESs are probably former long-term inpatients, many other people who need temporary psychiatric care receive quality emergency services that would otherwise be provided during hospitalization (Dubin & Fink, 1986).

THE ECOSYSTEM APPROACH

A rising number of innovative approaches are being developed to take crisis intervention onto the streets of communities across the country. But perhaps more important has been the ecosystem approach taken by national agencies in on-site delivery of mental health services at major disasters and the coordination of these services with other relief efforts. Because of past criticism of how both charitable and federal agencies have handled major disasters, a great deal of work has been done by those agencies to better coordinate their efforts in providing comprehensive disaster relief that cuts across the total environment of the survivors. Mental health support does little good when people don't have a roof over their heads because it has been blown away in a hurricane. However, it also does little good for survivors to obtain housing but be so traumatized and depressed from the disaster that they cannot begin to retain control over their lives. The following reports depict what happens when large-scale disasters tear up the total environmental systems of survivors and represent what we believe is an ecosystem approach to crisis intervention.

The 1998 TWA Flight 800, en route to Paris, crashed in 120 feet of water off the coast of Long Island, New York, taking the lives of all the men, women, and children aboard the huge jet plane. News coverage was swift and enormous. The nation was in grief. A study of U.S. Navy occupational divers (Leffler & Dembert, 1998) involved in the recovery of wreckage and passenger remains found that divers who recovered bodies after the disaster experienced exposure to remains, especially those of children, to be more stressful than safety hazards. Professional caregivers provided immediate grief counseling and crisis intervention services for the families of the deceased. The U.S. government, state and local governments, TWA, law enforcement departments, professional associations (such as the American Counseling Association and the American Psychological Association), the American Red Cross, and a number of other organizations provided and sponsored a wide array of crisis intervention services for families, friends, and co-workers of people who were lost in the flight. Massive debriefings were conducted to assist victims' families, friends, and co-workers as well as law enforcement personnel, TWA employees, caregivers, and rescue workers on Long Island near the scene of the crash.

Modrak (1992) reported on the deployment of rapid response teams to the scenes of two separate tragedies. The first was the April 4, 1991, plane crash near Philadelphia. A plane carrying Pennsylvania Senator John Heinz collided with a helicopter, resulting in the crash of fiery sections of the plane and helicopter onto the Merion Elementary School grounds. The senator and others on both aircraft and two first-grade girls at the school were killed; three other children and two adults were wounded. A rapid response team composed of counselors, psychologists, and psychiatrists provided individual and group counseling, handed out referrals as appropriate, set up a crisis hotline, and formed a drop-in crisis center. The crisis services proved to be in constant demand as the team helped the multiple victims generated by the plane collision and crash at the school.

Another tragedy reported by Modrak (1992) occurred on November 1, 1991, at the University of Iowa. The whole campus as well as the community was affected by an angry graduate student's shooting and killing five people and critically injuring another before fatally shooting himself. A crisis response team was organized by the University of Iowa Counseling Center. First priority was given to counseling eyewitnesses. Then team members worked with individuals and groups identified as needing crisis intervention. University classes were canceled, a memorial service was televised for the student body and the community, needs assessments and appropriate referrals were made, open meetings of mourning were conducted during three consecutive mornings, and group sessions were held in every room of the student union in the afternoons.

Volunteers from the American Red Cross Disaster Mental Health Services Team provided support to survivors of Hurricane Andrew, which struck south Florida in 1992 and left 200,000 people homeless (Shelby & Tredinnick, 1995), and Hurricane Floyd, which caused devastating flooding in the Eastern regions of the Carolinas and Virginia in September of 1999, leaving hundreds of thousands of people homeless. These disaster workers went immediately to the scene and provided crisis counseling to people as they stood in line waiting to obtain disaster relief. They helped adult survivors obtain basic human needs such as food, clothing, and shelter while at the same time working with survivors' emotions of mourning, anxiety, numbness, sadness, anger, and the sudden sense of loss of control and worry about even having a roof over their heads. Crisis workers also dealt with children who experienced not only loss of their homes but also the loss of security and the shattering of the illusion that their parents could provide for them. Positive reframing of terrifying thoughts about the hurricanes, flooding, or having children draw pictures of the storm and then destroy the pictures while yelling at them, using puppetry to reenact the event and then rebuild control, giving positive reinforcement for coping, and giving reassurances of safety were examples of techniques used to help the children regain control of their lives.

Immediately after the Oklahoma City Federal Building bombing, on April 19, 1995, an American Counseling Association team of Oklahoma school counselors and an art teacher wrote and illustrated *The Terrible, Scary Explosion.* This book, modeled after one written for children after Hurricane Hugo in South Carolina, was in the hands of Oklahoma City schoolchildren by April 25. The purpose of the book was to help children of all ages process the whole incident and provide a tool to help adults help children (Morrissey, 1995).

DEBRIEFING THE CRISIS WORKER

The debriefing process is indispensable in assisting crisis workers themselves to regain a state of emotional, cognitive, and behavioral equilibrium following their intensive intervention work in the aftermath of a chaotic crisis. The detailed procedures that follow are provided because it is essential for crisis workers to know how to debrief disaster survivors as well as to understand the value of being debriefed themselves. The techniques and perspectives we offer may even enable the crisis worker to debrief the debriefers.

Crisis Workers at the Disaster.   Crisis workers have a wide range of duties after a disaster. Foremost is simply being available for survivors to talk with and listen to their experiences and empathize and process with them as they attempt to make sense of it. Workers may help survivors locate significant others, helping relatives with identification of victims, and making arrangements for the deceased. They may provide information on the affective, behavioral, cognitive, interpersonal, and physiological response to traumatic events. They may help relatives through the grieving process, promote social support systems for survivors, and devise a plan of action to mobilize the survivors' resources. They may make appropriate referrals and provide follow-up services. They may also provide debriefing to other emergency service workers (Walker, 1990).

The Need for Debriefing.   Throughout this book we have often depicted crisis intervention as complex and chaotic. In the aftermath of natural disaster, mechanical or human-caused accidents (for example, airliner crashes), or mass murders, the confused and chaotic disorder can be so disorienting that, for crisis workers, there are no scripts and little time for reflection, planning, or rehearsal.

It is not surprising that crisis workers themselves tend to suffer psychological problems from the same trauma they are trying to alleviate in others. Thus what the crisis worker sees, hears, smells, and touches may also rattle long-buried skeletons in the worker's own emotional closet. This phenomenon is known as vicarious traumatization (Saakvitne & Pearlman, 1996) wherein the worker unwittingly absorbs and internalizes the very trauma that the client manifests (see Chapter 13 for more on this phenomenon). Finally, compounding it all, mental health crisis workers may be called on to debrief other emergency personnel who have been up to their arms in blood, gore, wreckage, and tragedy. It is important, then, that crisis workers themselves go through debriefing and that certain precautions are taken to arm them against the multiple stressors they will face when doing disaster work (Armstrong, O'Callahan, & Marmar, 1991).

Precautions.   First of all, crisis work of this kind is done in teams. Whether at the scene with a number of specialists or in an after-action debriefing, workers do not act in isolation from one another. Using the buddy system allows workers to rotate with difficult clients, ventilate to one another, check out perceptions, watch each other for signs of fatigue, and give each other a break (Hayes, Goodwin, & Miars, 1990; Mitchell & Everly, 1995b; Talbot, Manton, & Dunn, 1995, p. 286; Walker, 1990).

Second, crisis workers in a disaster need to take time off to sleep and decompress. An eight-hour shift is a long time under disaster conditions (Hayes et al., 1990). Crisis workers need to be rotated off of high-stress jobs such as body identification and survivor notification on a regular basis and be given less stressful duties (Walker, 1990). They also need time off between crises to rest and recuperate physically and psychologically (Talbot et al., 1995, p. 293).

Third, crisis workers should not debrief each other (Spitzer & Neely, 1992; Talbot et al., 1995, p. 286). Another team of crisis workers who have not been at the scene should be brought in to lead debriefing. In this manner, the leaders cannot be construed as engaging in recriminations, second-guessing, or accusations about who did or didn't do what.

Fourth, the debriefing is held away from the crisis scene if possible (Talbot et al., 1995, p. 286). Physically moving from the scene allows the crisis workers to move away psychologically.

Fifth, the organizational context within which the group operates is taken into consideration because it too plays a part in how the group is affected (Talbot et al., 1995, p. 286). The way the organization—and this includes even charitable organizations such as the Red Cross—runs its disaster relief program is critically important to how the individual handles stress at the disaster site.

Sixth, the crisis workers need to be in excellent physical and mental health themselves. From both a physical and mental standpoint, they will be stretched to the limit. Diving into the wake of a traumatic event is no place for someone who is out of shape either physically or mentally (Walker, 1990). But no matter how good the shape a crisis worker is in, no one is immune from the cumulative and acute onset of stress (see Chapter 13, on burnout). Therefore, a standing rule of thumb for all emergency workers and crisis workers should be a debriefing after the event, whether they believe they need it or not and no matter what their protests, excuses, or reasons might be for not going through it. Debriefing should be the natural and final act of the emergency and crisis workers' job and should be no less expected than that of a fighter pilot after a combat mission.

Dynamics of Debriefing.   The debriefers of crisis workers are dealing with a matrix of issues: the crisis event and its victims, the response to that event by the crisis workers, the individual crisis worker's personal and professional response to the survivors, and the dynamics of the group as it goes through the debriefing process (Talbot et al., 1995, p. 286).

From a professional standpoint, each crisis worker needs to understand and evaluate the usefulness of his or her interventions, explore alternatives, and plan future courses of action. Individual crisis workers also need to look at how they operate as a member of the group. Group dynamics and cohesiveness impart a powerful influence on each worker, so the group as client may need to be examined. Such dynamics may, in fact, parallel the dynamics of the victim group and are referred to as *parallel processing* (Talbot et al., 1995, p. 291).

On a personal basis, the debriefers need to explore with workers their own personal issues that may intrude into their crisis intervention work. Particularly, parallel processing and countertransference issues need to be examined. As opposed to the CISD approach of Mitchell and Everly (1995b), which does not delve into personal dynamics of emergency workers, Talbot and associates (1995) believe that psychological understanding and integration are exceedingly important to crisis workers, because this is the stuff they are made of and how they operate. The personal history of the individuals in the group and of the group itself may also be of importance. Past baggage of the group, or the individual workers' issues with the group, may carry over into the present, and everyone needs to acknowledge that baggage and be helped to set it down and leave it.

Confidentiality.   A continuing issue in debriefings centers on ethical concerns about acts of commission or omission, issues of responsibility or integrity, and even larger questions concerning life-and-death decisions (Walker, 1990). In that regard, all debriefings of emergency workers or mental health workers should be absolutely confidential, and that fact should be stated and enforced from the beginning (Mitchell & Everly, 1995a).

Understanding.   One of the main tasks of the debriefer is to make psychological sense of what is going on and to help the crisis workers gain that knowledge. Thus debriefers should be well grounded in group dynamics, group functioning, and group counseling skills. Finally, and most importantly, the debriefer needs to summarize, and allow people to verbalize, what they have learned from the crisis and the debriefing, in order to minimize workers' vulnerability to the phenomenon of vicarious traumatization (Saakvitne & Pearlman, 1996)—referred to in the "Need for Debriefing" section earlier. Crisis workers need to have a sense of mastery over what they have done as well as to feel positive about themselves as they take their leave of the traumatic event and the debriefing (Talbot et al., 1995, p. 296).

In summary, the combined processes that Mitchell and Everly (1995a) and Talbot and associates (1995) described derive their effectiveness from:

1. An early intervention before the trauma is concretized and becomes a disease reservoir
2. An opportunity for catharsis by ventilating emotions in a safe surrounding with a structured environment and a knowledgeable and trusted facilitator
3. An opportunity to verbalize the traumatic event and the part played by reconstructing it, making sense of it, and integrating it into awareness
4. The provision of structure through the debriefing procedure of a definite beginning and a definite end that provides a clear, linear sequence of events that leads to closure, as opposed to the chaos so recently encountered
5. The dispelling of myths that one must be able to "handle" all things and that emotions are liabilities
6. Peer support from others who belong to the same "club"
7. Provision of follow-up if the traumatic stress and the symptoms are not expunged
8. Education about the effects of stress and the concept that it is a naturally occurring process and not a "weakness"
9. Dynamic understanding of both past and present motivators and causative factors that actuate specific responses in each individual
10. A knowledge that such debriefings allow individuals not only to survive stress in their jobs but to do them better

Electronic Outreach Services

The advent of the electronic revolution is undoubtedly only now in its infancy. From the telephone to the most sophisticated web site, the electronic technologies are substantive tools in crisis work. It seems safe to predict that the future use of electronic outreach services will undergo enormous changes and exponential use compared to the current status.

Emergency Telephone Crisis Services.   Slaikeu (1990, pp. 105–141) refers to emergency telephone help as "first-order intervention" or "psychological first aid." Indeed, the telephone is the most prevalent medium for the initial contact in most crisis service delivery. Even the vast outreach networks such as the services provided by NOVA, described earlier, depend heavily on the telephone as the basic mode of communication.

Chapter 3 dealt at length with handling calls on community crisis hotlines. However, two other types of hotlines are worthy of mention that are quite different from the standard community crisis hotline. First is the time-limited hotline. A time-limited hotline is one that is put into operation for a specified period of time and is typically used to deal with a specific problem or to engage a special client population, such as immediately before a potential disaster or after a disaster happens. It may provide brief, supportive therapy or serve as an information or referral source. As the mass media produce more documentaries directed toward social problems and issues, human services agencies become increasingly motivated to establish a public forum and provide critical information through such hotlines (Loring & Wimberly, 1993).

Second is a specialized national hotline. A specialized hotline deals with a specific topic, such as troubled youths. A national toll-free number is available for callers. Although brief, supportive therapy may occur on such hotlines, generally the major purpose is to provide information about the geographical location nearest the caller where help can be obtained. These lines are heavily used and cut across all geographical areas, cultural groups, and socioeconomic classes. As an example, The Boys Town national hotline received 63,000 calls from troubled children in a nine-month period (Teare et al., 1995). The two national runaway hotlines not only spend time talking to runaways about their problems, but also encourage them to get off the mean streets and into the nearest runaway shelter. These two runaway hotline numbers may be helpful: Covenant House Nineline, 1-800-999-9999; National Runaway Switchboard, 1-800-621-4000.

The Internet and Web Sites.   Since the advent of the establishment of the Internet and web sites, there has never been any doubt that there would be counseling services on the "Net." If counseling occurs, then what about crisis intervention on the Net? In fact, that is already being done (Ruiz & Lipford-Sanders, 1999). The relevant questions, then, are "How can we ethically and effectively do crisis intervention on the Internet?" or "What crisis intervention services can be ethically and effectively provided on the Internet?" (Ruiz & Lipford-Sanders, 1999, p. 12). Web sites that provide opportunities for Net "surfers" to seek emergency help or advice, counseling, or psychological help continue to grow exponentially. Hotlines for crisis intervention are increasing in number. The Samaritans in Cheltenham, England, provide an excellent example of a Net address that offers help to suicidal individuals and other people in crisis. This group has been in the business of helping people for more than 40 years via letter, telephone, and in-person visits. E-mail sent to the Samaritans remains anonymous if the sender desires. Trained volunteers read and reply to e-mail once a day, every day of the year. Their address is jo@samaritans.org.

Dozens of hotlines for almost every conceivable crisis or counseling category are springing up all over the country. Examples are the Suicide Information and Education Centre (www.sieca.ca) and the online counseling services at CounselingNet (www.counselingnet.com). Ruiz and Lipford-Sanders (1999, p. 12) found that in September 1999 a keyword search on Alta Vista yielded 901,250 sites for counseling, 125,274 sites for support groups, 11,061 sites for career counseling, and 3,056 sites for professional mental health counseling. Undoubtedly, this is just the beginning.

Clearly, the Internet, web sites, e-mail, and other technological and online electronic advances have the potential to provide a great deal of help to people who are geographically or psychologically isolated from specialized crisis services or are suffering physical or mental disabilities that do not permit them to travel to those services (Gilliland & James, 1998, pp. 404–420). However, two major problems cloud this new electronic horizon. One of the major issues is confidentiality. Even though web sites may guarantee anonymity, once a message goes into the airwaves we know of no absolute guarantee that it cannot be pulled out of the ether by people or agencies you might not be too thrilled to have read your thoughts. Actually, almost all are guaranteed to be pulled out by the federal security canvassing service.

Another problem is that it is one thing to chat with another person half a world away but it is quite another to have people doing therapy or interventions about whose credentials you know nothing more than what they tell you. Sad to say, the field is ripe for electronic charlatans. Myer (1999) reported on his review of Internet sites that purport to provide "crisis counseling" that not only are some of the fees exorbitantly high, but their promotional advertisements also indicate that a person who chose some of these services might be putting themselves at risk for even more traumatization through secondary victimization at the hands of some very incompetent "service providers." Clearly, although this venue holds much promise, it is a "buyer beware" undertaking.

Many city and county libraries provide an information service, such as the LINC (Library Information Center) phone line, for public information and referral. LINC phone lines are often accessible via the Internet, and they typically provide a wide range of telephone listings for all sorts of public needs, including all the emergency and crisis services in the local area.

POLICE AND CRISIS INTERVENTION

The role of the police is rapidly changing and expanding. In most communities, police departments are being tasked with more and more responsibilities that are in addition to the purview of traditional law enforcement. Increasingly, crisis work is one of those responsibilities, and, in that regard, many police departments are providing exemplary public service.

Changing Role of the Police.   Front-line police work is rapidly being altered. Whereas a few years ago patrol officers concerned themselves mainly with *instrumental* crimes such as theft, robbery, and assault, today they also deal with a multitude of *expressive* kinds of crime, where individuals pose a serious threat to themselves or others because of their own anger, fear, vulnerability, depression, or lack of emotional control. It has been estimated that in recent years police officers typically have spent 80 to 90 percent of their working time on order maintenance, many involving crisis intervention (Luckett & Slaikeu, 1990, p. 228). Many of the calls officers respond to involve domestic disturbance or domestic violence, rated by police as having a higher degree of physical danger than any other calls they receive (Baumann et al., 1987). An increasing number of domestic disturbance calls involve police officers responding to a scene and having to confront a presumably mentally ill person or persons (Gillig et al., 1990, p. 663). Even though police departments do not relish diverting much of their time away from providing for the public safety and enforcing the law, they have found themselves more and more in a modality of law enforcement/crisis intervention (Fein & Knaut, 1986; Gillig et al., 1990; Luckett & Slaikeu, 1990; Scales, 1991; Winter, 1991).

Police and the Mentally Ill/Mentally Disturbed

Gillig and associates (1990) studied a sample of 309 police officers in Cincinnati and Hamilton County, Ohio, and found that during a one-month period, almost 60 percent of the officers had responded to at least one call where a presumably mentally ill person had to be confronted. Almost half of the officers had responded to more than one such call during the one-month period. According to Luckett and Slaikeu (1990), those figures are fairly standard throughout the country. The changing role of the police patrol officer to include all kinds of crisis calls means that the responding officer can never be sure of the situation he or she may encounter. This modern dilemma puts a heavy responsibility on the shoulders of law enforcement officers and, although many dislike spending their time on crises of a social service nature, they are accepting encounters with the mentally ill as an appropriate aspect of modern police work. They are also requesting more information, training, and collaboration with mental health and crisis intervention agencies (Gillig et al., 1990; Luckett & Slaikeu, 1990; Winter, 1991). The foregoing has highlighted a need to develop training models that include police crisis intervention (Luckett & Slaikeu, 1990, pp. 231–242).

Because police workers are being confronted with an upsurge in the number of dispatch calls to the scene of expressive activity (by out-of-control individuals), the Memphis Police Department developed and implemented two innovative and formidable programs that address the dangers to both police officers and the public: the Crisis Intervention Team (CIT) (James, 1990, 1994; James, Crews, & Gilliland, 1995) and the Family Trouble Center (FTC) (Scales, 1991; Winter, 1991). The CIT program uses experienced police officers, trained in crisis intervention by experts in counseling and mental health, to intervene in on-the-spot crises to contain and control the situation before an act of violence occurs. The FTC program targets family violence situations by providing counseling and referral services to both battered people and batterers who are identified in daily police reports.

The Crisis Intervention Team (CIT) Program

Because budget constraints, economic factors, and social problems have generated enormous numbers of homeless people, dumped onto the streets mental patients who formerly would have been hospitalized as inpatients, and increased drug use and abuse, many more mentally disturbed people now come into contact with the general public than ever before. Consequently, the Memphis city government, the mental health community, and the police department realized that incidents of police involvement with the mentally ill had resulted in the mentally ill themselves being vulnerable to serious harm and the increased possibility of police officers, untrained in dealing with the mentally ill, getting seriously injured or even killed. Why can't mental health workers take care of the enormous numbers of emotionally out-of-control people on the streets? Because it is a physical and fiscal impossibility to put enough mental health workers into the streets to monitor and serve the needs of these out-of-control people and to do so in accordance with the "least restrictive environment" movement in a democratic society. Spearheaded by the local affiliate of the Alliance for the Mentally Ill, the police department, the mental health community, the city government, and the counselor education and social work departments of two local universities formed a unique and creative alliance for the purpose of developing and implementing proactive and preventive methods of containing emotionally explosive situations in the streets that frequently led to violence. That encapsulates the founding of the CIT program (James, 1994, p. 187).

Because the police were the first and often the only responsible officials on the scene of an out-of-control situation, calling in outside consultants proved unworkable. Therefore, the unique and cohesive alliance of several important community groups determined that highly trained and motivated police officers were the logical personnel to form a front-line defense against the crisis of dangerously expressive, out-of-control persons in the streets. The massive alliance effort resulted in the CIT program's becoming an example of how a successful program can work to accomplish the objectives of public safety and welfare, economic feasibility, and police accountability (James et al., 1995, pp. 140–144).

To comprehend what a difficult and delicate task it has been to bring to fruition a successful and workable CIT program, one must understand how the alliance network functions. The network consists of the Memphis city government and the Memphis Police Department (hereafter just referred to as the police); the Alliance for the Mentally Ill; five of the six local community mental health centers; the emergency room components of public hospitals; academic educators from the Department of Counseling, Educational Psychology and Research from the University of Memphis and the School of Social Work from the University of Tennessee; the YWCA Abused Women's Services; the Sexual Assault Resource Center; and several private practice psychologists (hereafter referred to as the mental health community). The power, force, and success of the alliance derive from the process and fundamental working relationship that the police and mental health community have used to both form and maintain the CIT program. The alliance was formed because both the police and the mental health community realized that the problem of crisis in the streets was too severe for either to handle alone and that working together would make life much easier and safer for both as well as providing improved and safer service for clients and the community (James et al., 1995, pp. 136–137).

The alliance conducted a great many collaborative, systematic, and democratic meetings over a period of several months to hammer out a workable CIT blueprint. As a result of these meetings, key individuals from all segments of both police and community mental health developed effective working relationships with one another and learned a great deal about each other's problems, competencies, rules, and boundaries. Police were brought into mental health facilities for orientation into the world of mental health. Mental health personnel were brought into the police academy and accompanied police on patrols to learn about the problems, procedures, competencies, roles, and boundaries that law enforcement officers face in their everyday work. Then formal training was developed to ensure that not only the CIT officer selectees but also all supervisory-level police personnel understood the problems, objectives, and operational procedures of the CIT program (James, 1994, p. 187; James et al., 1995, pp. 137–138).

The development and training phases provided some essential attitudinal and professional understanding between the police and the mental health community. As a result, CIT officers and their superiors know precisely what training and consultation resources the mental health community can provide. And the mental health professionals know what competencies and resources the police in general and the CIT officers in particular have to offer. Concomitantly, both sides develop mutual respect, understanding, trust, and cooperation. A CIT officer intervening with a distraught mental patient will likely listen empathically to the patient's feelings and concerns, be familiar with the mental health services available (will possibly know the patient's caseworker personally), and will, within the boundaries of professional ethics, communicate to the patient an understanding of the short-term needs of that person as well as a desire to provide for the immediate safety and referral requirements to contain and stabilize the patient's current crisis. The mental health center caseworker will also understand and have confidence in the CIT officer's ability to be a stabilizing and safety influence on the patient and will, if needed, likely call on the CIT officer for emergency assistance with a particular client. The mental health caseworker may collaborate with the CIT officer in obtaining anecdotal information needed to enhance the patient's treatment plan and prevent the recurrence of that particular patient's crisis in the streets (James, 1994, p. 191).

Based on the trust and confidence built through the powerful and cohesive alliance just described, the police department opted to select experienced police patrol officers to receive training and then serve in the dual role of police officers and crisis intervention team specialists. Volunteers for the program had to have good records as officers, pass personality tests for maturity and mental stability, and be recommended, interviewed, screened, and selected to receive CIT training. The police department committed itself to putting trained CIT officers on duty in every precinct in the city, 24 hours every day. All upper-echelon supervisory officers received formal orientation about the role and function of CIT officers, so that whenever any call involving a suspected mentally disturbed person anywhere in the city is received, the CIT officer is the designated responsible law enforcement official at the scene—regardless of the rank—and all other officers at the scene serve as backups to the CIT officer who handles the case (James, 1994, p. 194; James et al., 1995, p. 145).

CIT Training Using Mental Health Experts and Providers.   An integral part of the CIT program is the special preservice training provided for the officers. The importance of effective training by competent, committed, motivated professionals cannot be overemphasized. We have found that the most effective trainers are flexible, innovative, enthusiastic, personable, and expert in their disciplines. We also insist that they ride with experienced CIT officers on a Friday or Saturday evening shift prior to the scheduled training of each new group of CIT officer selectees. The training is also greatly enhanced if the trainer can skillfully integrate the conceptual with the experiential. Realistic role play, video technology, playback, and discussion are essential. Most mental health workers cannot effectively facilitate role-play exercises or use video technology in such training unless they are very conversant with the problems CIT officers face. Another fundamental element of the training is the use of experienced CIT officers as training assistants. These assistants bring many valuable firsthand experiences into the learning environment that heighten interest, enhance motivation, and provide realism (James, 1994, p. 187).

The following topics are addressed by the CIT training:

1. Diagnostic and clinical issues related to the concept of danger in the mentally ill
2. Posttraumatic stress disorder
3. Treatment strategies and mental health resources
4. Patient rights and legal aspects of crisis intervention
5. Suicide intervention
6. Alcohol and drug behavior in dual-diagnosed patients
7. Psychotropic medications and their side effects
8. Verbal defusing and deescalating techniques
9. Controlling aggressive behavior in the mentally ill
10. Fishbowl discussion on site with mentally ill patients on patient perceptions of the police

These fishbowl discussions are unique and powerful sessions for CIT trainees. During the training component when trainees are actually brought into mental health facilities for orientation, discussion groups provide opportunities for trainees to meet in a circle with selected mental health patients. A mental health professional, who also serves as an instructor in the CIT training program, sits in the center of the circle with the patients. They are surrounded by CIT trainees. The professional engages in interviews and dialogue with the mental health patients, in the "fishbowl," so to speak. CIT trainees observe and hear what the mental patients have to say about their own personal needs and about their prior interactions, experiences, and perceptions of the police. After the "fishbowl" interview and dialogue, trainees who had been observing the professional/patient dialogue have an opportunity to ask questions and interact directly with the patients. The fishbowl discussion has been described by CIT trainees as a profoundly motivational and essential part of their learning, orientation, and training.

The foregoing techniques use a lecture-modeling-practice format. Veteran CIT officers and mental health professionals work closely together to provide the foregoing training. A great deal of role-play and discussion of intervention techniques is used during the 40-hour training session. Officer candidates are videotaped in role-play situations using scenarios from actual CIT cases. CIT officers play the role of patients as officer candidates attempt to deescalate their out-of-control behavior. CIT officers and trainers then critique and process candidates' performance (James et al., 1995, pp. 146–147).

By 1999 the Memphis Police Department had trained 549 CIT officers with more than 180 officers currently operating 24 hours each day in precincts in every part of the city; and a good many former CIT officers had been promoted to positions of leadership and responsibility in other key areas such as in the detective bureau. Active CIT officers respond to approximately 500 mental patient emergencies each month. When they are not involved in crisis intervention calls, the CIT officers perform regular patrol duties. The approach to using these trained officers can be classified as the specialist-generalist model in that they serve in a dual role as CIT specialists and regular patrol officers. When a mental disturbance call is received, a CIT officer is immediately dispatched to the scene.

In its first 16 months of operation in 1987–1988, MPD CIT officers responded to 5831 mental disturbance calls and transported 3424 cases to mental health facilities without any patient fatalities. In the latest 16 months, these figures have increased to 7330 calls and 4490 transports. Both calls and transports have increased significantly without a single fatality to a recipient of service by CIT officers. Although no figures exist to determine how many patients have been injured during this time period while being taken into protective custody, statistics indicate that injuries to officers have been reduced significantly. Furthermore, barricade situations have also been reduced significantly. The advent of the CIT program has almost put the MPD hostage negotiation team out of business because CIT officers arriving on the scene are able to defuse and control the situation before the hostage team arrives (James, 1994, pp. 189–190).

The Family Trouble Center (FTC) Program

An alliance process, quite similar to that described in the development of the CIT program, was used in developing and implementing the FTC in Memphis. Two distinct populations were targeted for proactive and preventive intervention by the FTC. These were battered persons and batterers themselves. The FTC concept evolved out of the need of the police department and the mental health community to effectively reduce the level of battering and other forms of household violence and to reduce the number of repeat dispatches to the same addresses. For instance, computer printouts revealed that during a one-year period the police were dispatched up to 28 times to one particular household due to violence or threats of violence such as beatings. Both the police and the mental health community recognized the need for proactive and preventive strategies because of safety and efficiency considerations (Scales, 1991; Winter, 1991).

Several months of intensive collaborative planning by essentially the same police and mental health workers (alliance) who founded the CIT program laid the groundwork for the FTC. Three additional groups involved were the leadership of the Memphis Housing Authority, the Family Service of Memphis, and the judicial branches of both city and county governments. Also, the mayor's office provided a great deal of leadership and support for forming the FTC. The city government provided the physical facilities and the alliance sought and obtained two privately funded grants to enhance the initial start-up. The grants paid for an FTC director and for secretarial assistance.

In evolving the basic FTC operational blueprint, the collaborative alliance conducted needs assessments, planning sessions, and team-building sessions over a period of almost a year. During that blueprint-building period, a training program was developed and implemented for all the major players in the alliance; in other words, the planners first obtained training themselves. Then police patrol personnel as well as police supervisory and management personnel were trained in the FTC concept. Finally, volunteer crisis workers were trained. When the center opened, it was a full-blown proactive crisis intervention/prevention agency with several unique features:

1. A cadre of highly trained volunteers, mostly graduate students in counseling and social work
2. An attractive and functional physical facility in a strategic location
3. A police force whose front-line patrol personnel understood the FTC concept and whose police procedures included systematic reporting and referral of all household violence or threats of violence
4. A consistent and supportive judiciary that understood the FTC concept and was committed to ordering batterers to either serve jail time or receive treatment in the FTC's anger management clinic
5. A comprehensive counseling and referral clinic for battered persons
6. Complete computerized printouts of all daily domestic disturbance dispatches (whereon FTC counselors follow up on every instance of reported battering of any kind)
7. A comprehensive preservice and in-service training program for all volunteer counselors and anger management group facilitators
8. Expert volunteer consultants, trainers, and anger management group leaders from the mental health community
9. An effective network for collaboration and public and community relations
10. A child care center to attend to children of battered parents who come to the FTC for counseling/referral services

After six years of service, the FTC has counseled 5701 victims of battering. It has conducted 152 anger management groups and has graduated 2121 batterers through that program. Its recidivism rate for batterers who are rearrested is estimated to be 20 percent.

The FTC is a unique, creative, and comprehensive example of what a proactive and futuristic community crisis response center can be. Its development and implementation did not come easy. But the basic concepts of both the FTC and the CIT programs are not beyond the grasp of any community to organize and put into place. We include the following section to serve as a perspective, from our vantage point of heavy involvement in the development and implementation, on both the CIT and the FTC programs.

COMMUNITY DEVELOPMENT OF PROACTIVE-PREVENTIVE CRISIS INTERVENTION SERVICES

Probably every community has the resources, personnel, and expertise to develop and provide proactive-preventive crisis intervention services. The foregoing brief description of both the CIT and FTC programs provides an appropriate occasion for setting forth what we feel are some important considerations for communities or groups that are interested in initiating similar programs.

The Importance of Multidisciplinary Thinking

Crisis intervention programs should be planned and implemented by persons from different disciplines, perspectives, and cultural and training backgrounds. From the initial idea to the operational program, teamwork, cooperation, coordination, and collaboration are essential. There are many reasons to insist that crisis intervention programs of the future be based on multidisciplinary thinking. Such a process

1. Enables cross-fertilization of ideas from many different conceptual and experiential points of view
2. Includes patient advocate groups (such as the Alliance for the Mentally Ill in the Memphis programs) not only to serve as advocates but also to lobby, agitate, bring urgency for change to the forefront, and serve as a catalyst to bring different people/disciplines together
3. Achieves collective power and clout
4. Enables collaboration/cooperation among different people/disciplines that probably would not come together otherwise
5. Minimizes turf battles/competition and vested interest (the volatile streets belong to no one professional group in particular, with the exception of the police)
6. Ensures a multicultural mix in thinking about, planning, formulating, and implementing the program.

The Need for Innovative Alliances

The involvement of the Alliance for the Mentally Ill (AMI) of Memphis is an example of both appropriate use of the multidisciplinary approach and a pure form of proactive-preventive crisis intervention. The targeted crises were immediate, volatile, and located in every area of the city, and no segment of the community, except the police, had access to the crisis territory—the streets. Neither the police nor the mental health community alone had the means to cope with the crises. Such a milieu presented a prime opportunity to bring together all the components extant to solve the problem and to do so without the usual impediments of competition, jealousy, throat-cutting tactics, battles over turf, and other antagonistic factors. Also, an entity such as AMI was an ideal group to build cohesion and teamwork. Who could say no to that group when they were asking for reasonable and needed action to reduce the dangers to everyone? Who could possibly say no to strategies that would result in reducing expressive crimes and even murder, stabilizing and containing out-of-control people and violence that affects everyone? The truth is that when AMI obtained a firm commitment from a few key players in the police department and the mental health community, the remaining individuals and groups fell into line because it was clear that AMI was headed in the right direction. The result was the formation of an all-out community effort, relatively free of jealousies, blaming others, and credit or glory seeking. There was even pervasive excitement and relief that affirmative, nonpartisan, proactive steps were being taken to benefit the whole community and that the volatile streets would not be left to the police alone. The community alliance took the purest form of what crisis intervention can become—the bringing together of representatives of all mental health components to figure out ways to train and use police, paramedics, and others who are most likely to come into contact with distraught, out-of-control people.

A Blueprint for the Future

Clearly, the goal is not for police, paramedics, and other similar workers to become psychologists, psychiatrists, counselors, or social workers. Rather, the goal is to give those workers enough basic knowledge and skills to contain and stabilize out-of-control situations in the streets until enough equilibrium can be restored, specialized help or referral provided, or the person can be transported to a place of safety and assistance. Through built-in referral and consultation mechanisms, mental health personnel support, supplement, and function where the police leave off. Individual members of the police–mental health community alliance can do those jobs for which they are best suited and trained. The rich multidisciplinary and proactive-preventive approach we have described is radically different from traditional reactive crisis work. This approach is applicable to many community crisis situations. Perhaps it is a blueprint for the future of crisis intervention—for new directions. We view it as encouragement for people in communities to believe "We've got people and situations like that. We can build teamwork and alliances like that. We have the expertise, resolve, motivation, and leadership to do that. We can form an effective and cohesive community action team." The important factor to take into account is that no one group or entity can or should do it alone.

The community alliance approach is quite a contrast to the national crisis response teams we have described elsewhere in this chapter. What we are talking about here is deriving the ideas, resources, and delivery of crisis intervention services from the community rather than depending on external expertise, even though expertise from without may at times be necessary and accepted. The community action concept also provides for the local community to assess its own needs, develop its own blueprint, formulate its own unique alliances, and use its own expert personnel to take proactive-preventive action steps in a systematic, measured, cost-effective, and autonomous fashion. We believe that any community, large or small, can create its own proactive-preventive crisis intervention teams using its own talents, leadership, and resources; and that such a procedure is cost-effective. We might note that almost all the Memphis model components we have described were implemented at low or no cost. All the mental health personnel contributed their time. The police department used its regularly budgeted resources to meet its CIT and FTC commitments without asking for any increase, even though it did obtain start-up funding for the FTC through a couple of privately financed grants. Otherwise, the total cost of both the CIT and FTC programs was formulated and met without any additional public funding.

LAST WORDS

If we have sounded enthusiastic and idealistic in our reporting on the proactive-preventive model of crisis intervention, it is because we are. We have been privileged to be totally immersed in every phase of the Memphis models—the CIT and the FTC programs. We have observed firsthand how effective highly trained police (CIT) officers can be under the most trying circumstances in the streets of Memphis. We have witnessed how effective our graduate student volunteers and practicum students can be in dealing with and counseling the most severely beaten clients and in learning and using group techniques to teach hostile and defensive batterers to control and manage their anger. We have ourselves participated in the hands-on crisis work. We have been involved in the conceptualizing, planning, training, and implementing of all phases of both the CIT and the FTC programs. These experiences have given us confidence that crisis intervention can and indeed should move off the couch and into the streets! We are quite sure that effective crisis intervention is more than reactive responding; that the new directions for crisis work clearly point toward systematic, collaborative, proactive, and preventive strategies involving highly skilled and motivated crisis workers from a wide variety of disciplines, competencies, and experiences. In summary, crisis work is tough, demanding, and sometimes scary, but it is also fun, rewarding, and, when done right, is one of the greatest natural highs a person can get!

SUMMARY

Although historically crisis intervention has been largely limited to a reactive function of the human services professions, two newly emergent directions redefine that function. First, crisis intervention has evolved from a grassroots movement driven mainly by volunteers into a formidable professional subspecialty. Second, it has further advanced into the realm of proactive and preventive interventions while concomitantly responding to a continuously expanding number of different crisis categories. The impetus for these new directions, initiated by actions of people at the grassroots level, has spread from volunteers to professional human services specialists and to institutions.

Crisis intervention has taken on a proactive stance that includes outreach initiatives at both local and national levels. The philosophy of taking intervention services to the people in the streets or in the region has been widely accepted. The concept of networking and sharing ideas, strategies, and resources among diverse agencies has become common practice. Crisis interventionists have become more and more proactive and preventive in their training and their work. Public and private sources of support have come to recognize the wisdom and the economic benefits of prevention.

We have described representative and innovative strategies and specific examples of taking crisis intervention directly to the populations and locations where crises occur. Some of these were crisis stabilization programs, crisis response outreach teams, telephone interventions, a crisis intervention team approach to crises encountered by police officers, and a family trouble center for intervention with both victims of battering and batterers themselves. These programs are only a small sampling of the emerging world of crisis intervention that includes crisis workers in the modern complex arena of rapid response to human disasters and dilemmas as well as in the business of both ameliorating the effects of and preventing crises from occurring.

RESOURCES

The first two listings shown here are governmental entities that provide an enormous amount of effort and resources pertaining to the subject of this chapter. They are the Federal Emergency Management Agency (FEMA) and the National Institute of Mental Health (NIMH) (*U.S. Government Manual*, 1998–1999, pp. 290, 541–543). In addition, two emergency response organizations, one crisis specialization service, and one annual crisis convention are included. Information pertaining to most service agencies and organizations can be obtained from *The Encyclopedia of Associations* (34th edition), edited by Maurer and Sheets (1999). Brief descriptions are herewith provided for all six of the resources just named.

Governmental
Federal Emergency Management Agency (FEMA)
500 C Street SW
Washington, DC 20472
FEMA is the central agency within the federal government for emergency planning, preparedness, response, and recovery. The agency works closely with state and local governments to fund emergency programs, offer technical assistance, guidance, and training for dealing with emergencies and disasters. It deploys federal resources in times of catastrophic disaster, and coordinates activities to ensure that a broad-based program is available to protect life and property and provide recovery assistance after a disaster. FEMA is a large umbrella agency that oversees many different federal emergency programs and carries out the major part of its responsibilities through 10 regional offices located in major cities throughout the United States.

National Institute of Mental Health (NIMH)
Phone: (301) 443-6480
Web site: http://www.nimh.nih.gov/
The NIMH supports and conducts fundamental research in neuroscience, genetics, molecular biology, and behavior as the foundation for an extensive clinical research portfolio that seeks to expand and refine treatments available for illnesses such as schizophrenia, depressive disorders, severe anxiety, childhood mental disorders (including autism and attention-deficit/hyperactivity disorder), and other mental disorders that occur across the life span. NIMH supports research on treatment outcomes in actual practice settings and seeks to establish sound scientific bases for the prevention of mental illness. It distributes educational and informational materials about mental disorders and related science to public and scientific audiences.

Emergency Response Organizations
National Coordinating Council on Emergency Management (NCCEM)
111 Park Place
Falls Church, VA 22046-4513

Phone: (703) 538-1795
Fax: (703) 241-5603
E-mail: nccem@aol.com
Web site: http://www.nccem.org
Plans and prepares for emergency and civil defense on city and county levels. Serves as liaison among units of local government, state, and Federal emergency and civil defense agencies. Provides for exchange of information. Seeks to develop comprehensive, workable, and all-hazard emergency programs through coordinated action. Conducts research and educational programs and maintains a speakers' bureau.

Disaster Emergency Response Association (DERA)
P.O. Box 280795
Denver, CO 80228-0795
Phone: (303) 809-4412
E-mail: dera@disasters.org
Web site: http://www.disasters.org
Works in the field of disaster preparedness, including professional disaster researchers, response and recovery specialists, trainers, and project managers. Assists communities, businesses, and industries in preparing for emergencies. Conducts risk management assessments and training and provides disaster relief.

Crisis Intervention Specialization
American Academy of Crisis Interveners (AACI)
215 Breckenridge Lane, Suite 102
Louisville, KY 40207
Phone: (502) 896-0200
Fax: (502) 896-0200
Serves as catalyst for professionals from the fields of mental health, law enforcement, education, religion, counseling, and medicine whose work brings them in direct contact with behavioral and psychological crises and emergencies. Provides forums for professionals from many disciplines to interact, enhance knowledge/skills, share research ideas. Sponsors training institutes; maintains speakers' bureau. Provides instructors in all areas of crisis intervention.

Crisis Convention
Annual Convening of Crisis Intervention Personnel (Crisis Convening)
Crisis Convening is a conference held in Chicago each April that we highly recommend for all human services workers interested in crisis work. This small, intimate conference brings together crisis workers from all over the United States to give practice-based papers, network, and relax for three days. The web site for Crisis Convening is: http://www.uic.edu/orgs/convening. You will find materials, proceedings from previous Convenings, and the Call for Papers and advance programs and registration materials for the next Convening Conference at the site. The Convening web site also maintains an e-mail news list for people interested in crisis work. It can be used to post announcements, conferences, and organizational needs, or just to "chat" with others who have an interest in crisis intervention. To become a member of the list, send an e-mail message addressed to LISTSERV@LISTSERV.UIC.EDU. Your message should read SUBSCRIBE CONVENING (your e-mail address)(your full name).

REFERENCES

American Psychiatric Association. (1994). *Diagnostic and statistical manual of mental disorders* (4th ed.). Washington, DC: Author.

Aguilera, D. C., & Messick, J. M. (1982). *Crisis intervention: Theory and methodology* (4th ed.). St. Louis: Mosby.

Armstrong, K., O'Callahan, W., & Marmar, C. R. (1991). Debriefing Red Cross disaster personnel: The Multiple Stressor Debriefing Model. *Journal of Traumatic Stress, 4,* 581–593.

Arredondo, P., & D'Andrea, M. (1999, June). Media portrayals of multiculturalism and diversity. *Counseling Today, 41,* 23–25.

Bassuk, E. L., & Cote, W. (1983). A network approach to rural psychiatric emergency training. *Hospital and Community Psychiatry, 34,* 233–238.

Baumann, D. J., et al. (1987). Citizen participation in police crisis intervention activities. *American Journal of Community Psychology, 15,* 459–471.

Blinder, A. (1991, April). *Crisis intervention in the world of managed care—Legitimacy at last.* Paper presented at the Fifteenth Annual Convening of Crisis Intervention Personnel, Chicago.

Boyack, V., & Bucknum, A. E. (1991). The quick response team: A pilot project. *Social Work in Health Care, 16,* 55–68.

Britton, J. G., & Mattson-Melcher, D. M. (1985). The crisis home: Sheltering patients in emotional crisis. *Journal of Psychosocial Nursing and Mental Health Services, 23,* 18–23.

Brock, S. E., Sandoval, J., & Lewis, S. (1996). *Preparing for crises in the schools: A manual for building school crisis response teams.* Brandon, VT: Clinical Psychology Publishing.

Brom, D., & Kleber, R. J. (1989). Prevention of post-traumatic stress disorders. *Journal of Traumatic Stress, 2,* 335–351.

Chiu, T. L., & Primeau, C. (1991). A psychiatric mobile crisis unit in New York City: Description and assessment, with implications for mental health care in the 1990s. *International Journal of Social Psychiatry, 37,* 251–258.

Clark, S. C., & McKiernan, W. (1981). Contacts with a Canadian "street level" drug and crisis centre, 1975–1978. *Bulletin on Narcotics, 33,* 23–31.

Dubin, W. R., & Fink, P. J. (1986). The psychiatric short procedure unit: A cost-saving innovation. *Hospital and Community Psychiatry, 37,* 227–229.

Fein, E., & Knaut, S. A. (1986). Crisis intervention and support: Working with the police. *Social Casework, 67,* 276–282.

Gillig, P. M., Dumaine, M., Stammer, J. W., Hillard, J. R., & Grubb, P. (1990). What do police officers really want from the mental health system? *Hospital and Community Psychiatry, 41,* 663–665.

Gilliland, B. E., & James, R. K. (1997). *Crisis intervention strategies* (3rd ed.). Pacific Grove, CA: Brooks/Cole.

Gilliland, B. E., & James, R. K. (1998). *Theories and strategies in counseling and psychotherapy* (4th ed.). Boston: Allyn & Bacon.

Guerra, P. (1999, May). Counselors help victims of school shooting. *Counseling Today, 41,* 12–14.

Guerra, P., & Schmitt, S. M. (1999, June). Reactions to Littleton shooting. *Counseling Today, 41,* 26–27.

Gulati, P., & Guest, G. (1990). The community-centered model: A garden-variety approach or a radical transformation of community practice? *Social Work, 35,* 63–68.

Harvey, M. R. (1996). An ecological view of psychological trauma and trauma recovery. *Journal of Traumatic Stress, 9*(1), 3–23.

Hayes, L. T. (1999, May). Breaking the blue wall of silence: Counseling police officers. *Counseling Today, 41*(11), pp. 1, 6.

Hayes, G., Goodwin, T., & Miars, B. (1990). After disaster: A crisis support team at work. *American Journal of Nursing, 2,* 61–64.

Hayes, L. L. (1999, June). Counselor helps out war victims in Bosnia. *Counseling Today, 41,* 22.

Hopper, M. J., Johnston, J., & Brinkhoff, J. (1988). Creating a career hotline for rural residents. *Journal of Counseling and Development, 66,* 340–341.

In Touch Hotline Counseling Center. (1991). *Proceedings of the Fifteenth Annual Convening of Crisis Intervention Personnel.* Chicago: University of Illinois at Chicago.

Intrater, L. C. (1991, April). *Working with homeless throwaway youth in crisis.* Paper presented at the Fifteenth Annual

Convening of Crisis Intervention Personnel, Chicago.

James, R. K. (1990, April). *Training Memphis police officers for crisis intervention with the mentally disturbed.* Paper presented at the Fourteenth Annual Convening of Crisis Intervention Personnel, Chicago.

James, R. K. (1994). Dial 911: Commentary. In P. Backlar (Ed.), *The family face of schizophrenia* (pp. 182–200). New York: Putnam's.

James, R. K., Crews, W., & Gilliland, B. E. (1995). Program consultation with a police department. In A. M. Dougherty (Ed.), *Case studies in human services consultation* (pp. 133–154). Pacific Grove, CA: Brooks/Cole.

James, R. K., & Gilliland, B. E. (1991, April). *Future directions of crisis intervention.* Paper presented at the Fifteenth Annual Convening of Crisis Intervention Personnel, Chicago.

Kiselica, M. S. (1998). Preparing Anglos for the challenges and joys of multiculturalism. *The Counseling Psychologist, 26,* 5–21.

Lambert, M. (1995). Psychiatric crisis intervention in the general emergency service of a veteran's hospital. *Psychiatric Services, 46,* 283–284.

Leaman, K. (1987). A hospital alternative for patients in crisis. *Hospital and Community Psychiatry, 38,* 1221–1223.

Leffler, C. T., & Dembert, M. L. (1998). Post-traumatic stress symptoms among U. S. Navy divers recovering TWA Flight 800. *Journal of Nervous & Mental Disease, 186,* 574–577.

Lenihan, G. O., & Kirk, W. G. (1999, April). *Rural community level crisis intervention.* Paper presented at the Twenty-Third Annual Convening of Crisis Intervention Personnel, Chicago.

Loring, M. F., & Wimberly, E. F. (1993). The time-limited hotline. *Social Work, 38,* 344–346.

Luckett, J. B., & Slaikeu, K. A. (1990). Crisis intervention by police. In K. A. Slaikeu (Ed.), *Crisis intervention: A handbook for practice and research* (2nd ed.) (pp. 227–242). Boston: Allyn and Bacon.

Marcos, L. R., Cohen, N. L., Nardacci, D., & Brittain, J. (1990). Psychiatry takes to the streets: The New York City initiative for the homeless mentally ill. *American Journal of Psychiatry, 147,* 1557–1561.

Maurer, C. M., & Sheets, T. E. (Eds.). (1999). *Encyclopedia of associations* (34th ed.) (Vol. I, Part 1, Part 2, and Part 3). Farmington Hills, MI: Gale Research.

McDermott, P. M., & Gordon, C. I. (1984). The emergency psychiatric service system. *Crisis Intervention, 13,* 55–60.

McGowan, S. (1992, January). ACPA holds campus violence workshop. *Guidepost,* pp. 9–10.

McGuire, P. A. (1999, May). Worker stress, health reaching critical point. *APA Monitor, 30,* 1, 27.

Mitchell, J. T., & Everly, G. S., Jr. (1995a). *Advanced critical incidents stress debriefing.* Ellicott City, MD: International Critical Incidents Stress Foundation.

Mitchell, J. T., & Everly, G. S., Jr. (1995b). Critical incidents stress debriefing (CISD) and the prevention of work-related traumatic stress among high risk occupational groups. In G. S. Everly, Jr., & J. T. Lating (Eds.), *Psychotraumatology* (pp. 267–280). New York: Plenum Press.

Modrak, R. (1992, January). Mass shootings and airplane crashes: Counselors respond to the changing face of community crisis. *Guidepost,* p. 4.

Morrissey, M. (1994, June). ACA, Red Cross to work together to help disaster victims. *Guidepost, 36,* pp. 1, 6.

Morrissey M. (1995, June). Members write children's book to help youngsters cope with Oklahoma City tragedy. *Counseling Today, 37*(12), p. 20.

Myer, R. A. (1999, April). *Crisis intervention using the Internet.* Paper presented at the Twenty-Third Annual Convening of Crisis Intervention Personnel, Chicago.

National Institute of Mental Health. (NIMH). (1990, September). *Rapid assessment post-impact of disaster (RAPID)* (Program Announcement PA-91-04). Rockville, MD: Department of Health and Human Services, Public Health Service, Alcohol, Drug Abuse, and Mental Health Administration.

Oropeza, B. A., Clark, F., Fitzgibbon, M., & Baron, A. (1991). Managing mental health crises of foreign college students. *Journal of Counseling and Development, 69,* 280–283.

Piersma, H. L., & Van-Wingen, S. (1988). A hospital-based crisis service for adolescents: A program description. *Adolescence, 23,* 491–500.

Pritchard, L., Brownstein, J., & Johnan, M. (1989). The youth booth in the mall: Reaching youth in the 80's. *Prevention in Human Services, 6,* 87–92.

Reding, G. R., & Raphelson, M. (1995). Around-the-clock mobile psychiatric crisis intervention: Another effective alternative to psychiatric hospitalization. *Community Mental Health Journal, 31,* 179–187.

Roberts, A. R. (Ed.). (1991). *Contemporary perspectives on crisis intervention and prevention.* Upper Saddle River, NJ: Prentice Hall.

Ruiz, N. J., & Lipford-Sanders, J. A. (1999, October). Online counseling: Further considerations. *Counseling Today, 42*(4), 12, 33.

Saakvitne, K. W., & Pearlman, L. A. (1996). *Transforming the pain: A workbook on vicarious traumatization.* New York: Norton.

Scales, P. K. (1991, April). *The Family Trouble Center: A domestic violence intervention project.* Paper presented at the Fifteenth Annual Convening of Crisis Intervention Personnel, Chicago, IL.

Schmitt, S. M. (1999, June). Crisis response plans reviewed following school shootings. *Counseling Today, 41,* 28–29.

Shafer, C. (1989a, September). Counselors offer crisis intervention at Iowa crash site. *Guidepost,* pp. 1, 3, 6.

Shafer, C. (1989b, December). Recent disasters trigger NIMH response. *Guidepost,* pp. 1, 5.

Shelby, J. S., & Tredinnick, M. G. (1995). Crisis intervention with survivors of natural disaster: Lessons from Hurricane Andrew. *Journal of Counseling and Development, 73,* 491–497.

Silver, T., & Goldstein, H. (1992). A collaborative model of a county intervention team: The Lake County experience. *Community Mental Health Journal, 28,* 249–253.

Slaikeu, K. A. (Ed). (1990). *Crisis intervention: A handbook for practice and research* (2nd ed.). Boston: Allyn and Bacon.

Slaikeu, K. A., & Leff-Simon, S. I. (1990). In K. A. Slaikeu (Ed.), *Crisis intervention: A handbook for practice and research* (2nd ed.) (pp. 319–328). Boston: Allyn and Bacon.

Sleek, S. (1998, August). Experts scrambling on school shootings: School violence in rural areas could worsen. *APA Monitor, 29,* 1, 35–36.

Spitzer, W. J., & Neely, K. (1992). Critical incident stress: The role of hospital-based social work in developing a statewide intervention system for first responders delivering emergency services. *Social Work in Health Care, 18,* 39–58.

Sue, D. W. (1999, August). *Multicultural competencies in the profession of psychology.* Symposium address delivered at the 107th Annual Convention of the American Psychological Association, Boston, MA.

Talbot, A., Manton, M., & Dunn, P. J. (1995). Debriefing the debriefers: An intervention strategy to assist psychologists after a crisis. In G. S. Everly, Jr., & J. M. Lating (Eds.), *Psychotraumatology* (pp. 281–298). New York: Plenum Press.

Teare, J., Garrett, C., Coughlin, D., Shanahan, D., & Daly, D. (1995). America's children in crisis: Adolescents' request for support from a national telephone hotline. *Journal of Applied Developmental Psychology, 16,* 21–33.

The United States Government Manual. (1998–1999). National Archives and Records Administration, Office of the Federal Register. Washington, DC 20402-9328: Superintendent of Documents, U.S. Government Printing Office.

Wakelee-Lynch, J. (1990, October). Florida crisis elicits aid from college officials and counselors. *Guidepost,* pp. 1, 3.

Walker, G. (1990). Crisis-care in critical incident debriefing. *Death Studies, 14,* 121–133.

Weisman, G. K. (1985). Crisis-oriented residential treatment as an alternative to hospitalization. *Hospital and Community Psychiatry, 36,* 1302–1305.

Wellin, E., Slesinger, D. P., & Hollister, C. D. (1987). Psychiatric emergency services: Evolution, adaptation, and proliferation. *Social Science and Medicine, 24,* 475–482.

White, W. C., & Rubenstein, A. S. (1984). Crisis intervention on campus. *Crisis Intervention, 13,* 42–54.

Wilson, J. M. (1991, April). *Crisis stabilization: An alternative to hospitalization.* Paper presented at the Fifteenth Annual Convening of Crisis Intervention Personnel, Chicago.

Winter, B. A. (1991, April). *The Family Trouble Center: A pilot program for do-*

mestic violence. Paper presented at the Fifteenth Annual Convening of Crisis Intervention Personnel, Chicago, IL.

Young, M. A. (1991). Crisis intervention and the aftermath of disaster. In A. R. Roberts (Ed.), *Contemporary perspectives on crisis intervention* (pp. 83–103). Upper Saddle River, NJ: Prentice Hall.